PRENTICE HALL

BIOLOGY
THE STUDY OF LIFE
SEVENTH EDITION

William D. Schraer
Formerly, Chairperson
Science Department
Middletown High School
Middletown, NY

Herbert J. Stoltze
Professor Emeritus of Biology
Northeastern Illinois University
Chicago, IL

PRENTICE HALL
Upper Saddle River, New Jersey
Needham, Massachusetts
Glenview, Illinois

PRENTICE HALL

BIOLOGY
THE STUDY OF LIFE

Components

Student Edition
Annotated Teacher's Edition
Teaching Resources
Laboratory Manual and
   Annotated Teacher's Edition
Computer Test Bank With
   Dial-A-Test™
Study Guide and
   Annotated Teacher's Edition
Biotechnology Workbook and
   Solutions Manual

Science Fair Manual
Biology Transparencies
Biology Posters
Product Testing Activities
1001 Ideas for Science Projects
New York Public Library Science Desk Reference
BioVue Videodiscs, and Videotapes
BioVue Plus CD-ROMs
Biology Media Guide

The photograph on the cover shows a female Alaskan brown bear and her cub. Brown bears are the largest bears. They are more than 2.7 meters long and may have a mass of 750 kilograms.

Credits begin on page 943.

Prentice
Hall

ISBN 0-13-435086-3
11 12 13 14 15 16 17   10 09 08 07 06 05

Staff Credits

Advertising and Promotion: Judy Goldstein, Carol Leslie, Rip Odell, Rob Richman, Ann Shea
Business Office: Emily Heins
Design: Laura Jane Bird, Jim O'Shea, AnnMarie Roselli, Gerry Schrenk
Electronic Services: Gregory Myers, Cleasta Wilburn, Lorena Cerisano
Manufacturing and Inventory Planning: Katherine Clarke
Market Research: Eileen Friend, Christopher Brown
Media Resources: Martha Conway, Libby Forsyth, Melissa Shustyk
National Science Consultants: Charles Balko, Jeannie Dennard, Kathleen French, Brenda Underwood
Pre-Press Production: Kathryn Dix, Paula Massenaro
Production: Christina Burghard, Annette Simmons
Science Department: Director: Julie Levin Alexander
  Editorial: Laura Baselice, Joseph Berman, Christine Caputo, Maureen Grassi, Rekha Sheorey, Lorraine Smith-Phelan
  Marketing: Arthur Germano, Kathleen Ventura, Jane Walker Neff, Victoria Willows
Technology Development: Matthew Hart

Acknowledgments Many people contributed their ideas and services in the preparation of the current and past editions of *Biology: The Study of Life*. Their contributions are gratefully acknowledged.

Reviewers

Donald W. Deters (Respiration)
Department of Biological Science
Bowling Green State University
Bowling Green, OH

Gary B. Ellis (Vertebrates)
Office of Technology Assessment
600 Pennsylvania Avenue, S.E.
Washington, DC

Kenneth Miller (Photosynthesis)
Biology Department
Brown University
Providence, RI

M.V. Parthasarathy
(Plant Structure and Function)
Biology Department
Cornell University
Ithaca, NY

Irwin Rubenstein (Cell Biology)
Department of Genetics
*   and Cell Biology*
University of Minnesota
Minneapolis, MN

Charles F. Stevens
(Nervous and Endocrine Systems)
Section of Molecular
*   Neurobiology*
Yale University Medical School
New Haven, CT

Daryl Sweeney (Invertebrates)
Department of Biology
University of Illinois
Champaign-Urbana, IL

Marjorie B. Zucker
(Circulatory Systems)
Pathology Department
New York University School
*   of Medicine*
New York, NY

Other Contributors

Cathy Banks
Wheeler High School
Marietta, GA

Diane G. Bemis
Watertown High School
Watertown, MA

Cathy Bennett
Dunbar High School
Dunbar, WV

Carol J. Bershad
formerly, Learning for Life
Boston, MA

Warren Bjork
Glenbrook South High School
Glenview, IL

Paula Borinsky
Science Teaching Center
University of Maryland
College Park, MD

Carole Brenkacz
West Seneca East
Senior High School
West Seneca, NY

Lornie D. Bullerwell
Dedham High School
Dedham, MA

Barbara A. Cauchon
Brookline High School
Brookline, MA

Brenda L. Dorsey
York Community High School
Elmhurst, IL

Sarah Carolyn Dolde Duff
Baltimore City Public Schools
Baltimore, MD

Michael J. Flanagan
Dedham High School
Dedham, MA

Karen L. Fout
Fenwick High School
Tiffin, OH

Anne R. Fraulo
Career High School
New Haven, CT

Richard L. Gaume
Plain Local Schools
Canton, OH

Norm Grimes
Columbian High School
Tiffin, OH

Deborah S. Haber
formerly, Watertown High School
Watertown, MA

Emiel Hamberlin
Du Sable High School
Chicago, IL

Sister M. Francis Hopcus
Pomona Catholic High School
Pomona, CA

Mic Jaeger
East Union High School
Manteca, CA

Nevin Longenecker
John Adams High School
South Bend, IN

Rose H. Moskowitz
Director of Curricular Services
Orange/Ulster BOCES
Goshen, NY

Ernest Nichol
Newton North High School
Newton, MA

Susan Offner
Milton High School
Milton, MA

Susan Stone Plati
Brookline High School
Brookline, MA

Harold Pratt
Jefferson County Schools
Lakewood, CO

Henry Rosenbaum
Fasman Yeshiva High School
Skokie, IL

Deborah A. Sandall
Pennichuck Junior High School
Nashua, NH

Hazel M. Schroder
Shrewsbury High School
Shrewsbury, MA

Helen Louis Shafer
Science and Technology
*   Magnet School*
Dallas, TX

Raymond D. Spencer
Somerville High School
Somerville, MA

Harlow B. Swartout
Woodstock High School
Woodstock, IL

Devin Thornburg, Ph.D
Associate Professor of Educational
*   Psychology*
Adelphi University, Garden City, NY

Robert C. Wallace
formerly, Reavis High School
Burbank, IL

Fredrick J. Watson
Silver Lake Regional High School
Pembroke, MA

Harold A. Wiper
Newton North High School
Newton, MA

Melanie Wojtulewicz
Whitney M. Young
*   Magnet High School*
Chicago, IL

Russell G. Wright
Montgomery County
*   Public Schools*
Rockville, MD

Michael A. Zunno
West Hempstead High School
West Hempstead, NY

Contents

Features

Key Concepts at a Glance

Oryx on the Namib Dunes, Namibia.

The Littlest Bits of Life

1. Working in a group, have each member visit at least one station. After observing each slide, each group member should make a sketch and take notes about what he or she observes at the station.

2. Each member should review their sketches and notes and look for common characteristics of all cells.

3. Then each member should develop a list of what he or she thinks are the common characteristics of all cells.

4. Discuss the lists with other group members. What characteristics do all cells have in common? What are some of the differences among the cells?

The Nature of Life

Guide for Reading

Previewing the Chapter

The bleak surface of Mars does not seem very hospitable to life. Billions of years ago, Mars may have been more earth-like, with rivers, lakes, and perhaps even oceans. Unlike Mars, life on earth is everywhere, in incredibly diverse and fascinating forms. But what is life? What are the characteristics that define life? What are the functions of each of the life processes?

Key Words

growth, homeostasis, metabolism, nutrition, organism, reproduction, respiration, transport

Key Concepts

- **Identify** the nine characteristics of living things.
- **Describe** the functions of each of the life processes.
- **Define** homeostasis.
- **Observe** a living thing and **identify** its characteristics. (Laboratory Investigation)

1-1 Understanding Life

Section Objectives:

- *Define* the terms *biology* and *organism*.
- *List* nine general characteristics that distinguish living things from nonliving things.

Life on Mars?

In 1984, a small rock about the size of a potato was found by a team of scientists in Antarctica. But this was no ordinary rock. Dubbed ALH84001, it was eventually identified as a meteorite (a meteor that strikes the earth's surface) that had originated on the planet Mars! Scientists determined that an asteroid impact had probably blasted ALH84001 into space millions of years ago. But this was not the only surprise that awaited the scientists that were studying meteorite ALH84001.

As scientists from the National Aeronautics and Space Administration (NASA) and Stanford University began to examine ALH84001 more closely, they made an amazing discovery. Using a powerful scanning electron microscope, they were able to identify what might be the microfossils, or the tiny remains, of bacterialike living things deep within the metorite. Was this evidence of "life on Mars"?

▲ **Figure 1–1**

Meteorite ALH84001. This 4.5 billion-year-old rock is believed to have once been a part of Mars.

◀ Mars—the Red Planet.

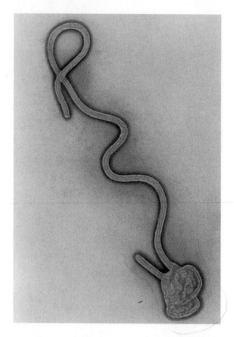

▲ **Figure 1–2**

Living or Nonliving? Viruses, such as this Ebola virus, contain some, but not all, of the characteristics of living things. (Magnification: 29 000 X)

Mars has always held a strange fascination for humans. Beginning with the *Viking* landings in 1976 through the Mars *Pathfinder* landing in 1997, scientists have searched Mars for evidence of life. Although there does not appear to be life on Mars today, the discovery of ALH84001 may indicate that primitive life once existed on Mars.

Life on Earth

Scientists are still divided over the question of whether living things ever existed on Mars. But there is no question that the earth is home to an astounding diversity of living things. The study of these living things is called **biology.** Although biologists have been studying living things on earth for hundreds of years, some basic questions still remain. For example, what does it mean to be alive? Although biologists have not been able to agree on a simple definition of life, they have agreed on what the "signs of life" are. Taken together, these signs of life, or characteristics, can become a working definition of life—on earth or on Mars.

Characteristics of Living Things

Living things, or **organisms,** have the following characteristics:

■ Living things are highly organized and contain many complex chemical substances. ■ Living things are made up of one or more cells. ■ Living things use energy. ■ Living things have a definite form and a limited size. ■ Living things have a limited life span. ■ Living things grow. ■ Living things respond to changes in the environment. ■ Living things are able to reproduce. ■ Groups of living things change over time.

Nonliving things may exhibit one or more of these characteristics, but never all of them. In some borderline cases, such as viruses, it may not be clear whether a thing is living or nonliving. Are the Mars fossils the remains of living or nonliving things? Only time, and more research, will tell.

1-1 **Section Review**

1. Define the term *biology.*
2. What is another name for a living thing?
3. Name three characteristics of living things.

Critical Thinking

4. Look back over the list of the characteristics of living things. Which characteristics are found only in living things? Which are found in both living and nonliving things? (Classifying)

1-2 Life Processes

Section Objectives:

- *Name* and *define* eight general processes by which the life of an organism is maintained.
- *Define* the terms *homeostasis* and *metabolism.*

Homeostasis

Living things carry out many different kinds of processes. Some of these processes, such as growth, reproduction, and the use of energy, already have been discussed as basic characteristics of life. These, of course, are not the only processes carried out by living things. Biologists have identified a number of other general processes that relate to the functioning of living things. Many of these life processes are necessary for maintaining a fairly constant environment within an organism in spite of its constantly changing external environment. The condition of a constant internal environment is known as **homeostasis** (hoh mee oh STAY sis).

Nutrition

Every organism takes materials from its external environment and changes them into forms it can use. This is called **nutrition. Nutrients** (NOO tree unts) are the substances that an organism needs for energy, growth, repair, or maintenance.

There are only two basic types of nutrition. In one type, the organism can produce complex nutrients from simple substances found in the environment. All green plants and some bacteria and other one-celled organisms are able to make their own nutrients in this way.

In the second type, organisms that cannot make their own nutrients obtain them ready-made from the environment. Animals, for example, get their nutrients by eating other organisms in their environment.

The taking in of food from the environment is known as **ingestion.** Usually, the nutrients in food are not in forms that an organism can use directly. They are too complex chemically, and the organism must break them into simpler forms. The breakdown of complex food materials into simpler forms that an organism can use is called **digestion.**

Transport

The process by which substances enter and leave cells and become distributed within the cells is known as **transport.** In the smallest and simplest organisms, materials are exchanged directly with the external environment.

In larger, multicellular organisms, however, most cells are not in direct contact with the external environment. In many animals,

▲ **Figure 1–3**

Nutrition. All living things must take in energy, such as food, from the environment in order to live.

for example, a *circulatory system* transports materials to, and wastes away from, the cells of the organism. The fluid, or blood, of the circulatory system is kept in motion, distributing these materials among the cells of the organism. In plants, specialized conducting structures transport substances from the roots and leaves to all parts of the plant.

Respiration

All life processes require a constant supply of energy. Organisms obtain their energy by releasing the chemical energy stored in nutrients. The process of releasing chemical energy is known as **respiration** (res puh RAY shun).

Respiration involves a complex series of chemical reactions. In one type of respiration, sugar or another food substance is broken down to produce water and carbon dioxide. This process requires oxygen from the air and is known as *aerobic respiration*. Some organisms break down food without using oxygen. This is called *anaerobic respiration.*

Synthesis

Organisms are able to combine simple substances chemically to form more complex substances. This process is called **synthesis** (SIN thuh sis). Usually, in animals, the substances used in synthesis are the products of digestion.

Synthesis produces materials that can become part of the structure of an organism. In this way, the organism can repair or replace worn-out parts. These materials also allow the organism to grow. The incorporation of materials into the organism's body is called assimilation (uh sim uh LAY shun).

Growth

The process by which living organisms increase in size is called **growth.** It is one result of the assimilation of nutrients. In one-celled organisms, growth is simply an increase in the size of the cell. In organisms made up of many cells, growth is usually the result of an increase in both the number and the size of cells. Growth in multicellular organisms is accompanied by *cellular specialization*. This process involves different cells becoming specialized for different functions. In animals, growth usually follows a particular pattern and ends after a certain period of time. Some plants, however, continue growing indefinitely.

Excretion

Every organism produces waste substances that it cannot use and that may be harmful if accumulated in the body. These wastes are the products of many of the chemical reactions that occur within cells. The removal of these wastes from the organism's body is called **excretion.**

▲ **Figure 1–4**

Growth. All living things, such as these emperor penguins, grow and develop.

Regulation

All the activities that help to maintain an organism's homeostasis make up the process of **regulation.** In animals, the nervous system and endocrine (EN duh krin) system are involved in the process of regulation. The nervous system carries messages in the form of nerve impulses throughout the body through a network of specialized cells. The endocrine system is made up of a number of organs that release chemicals, called *hormones,* into the bloodstream. Hormones act as chemical messengers. Both nerve impulses and hormones can bring about changes in the organism in response to changes in either the internal or the external environment.

Plants do not have nervous systems, but they do have parts that produce hormones. These hormones allow a plant to respond to various changes in its environment.

Reproduction

Reproduction is the process by which living things produce new organisms of their own kind. Reproduction is not necessary for the continued life of a single organism. However, it is necessary for the continued existence of that kind of organism.

There are two types of reproduction—**asexual** (ay SEK shuh wul) **reproduction** and **sexual reproduction.** In asexual reproduction, a single individual produces offspring that are identical to that parent. In sexual reproduction, there are two parents, and the offspring are not identical to either parent.

Metabolism

All the chemical reactions occurring within the cells of an organism are called its **metabolism** (muh TAB uh liz um). Metabolism includes processes that build complex substances from simpler ones and processes that break down complex substances into simpler ones. Metabolism also involves the continuous release and use of energy. Many biologists consider metabolic activity to be the single most important characteristic of life.

1-2 **Section Review**

1. What life process involves obtaining material and changing it into useful forms?
2. What life process releases chemical energy from nutrients?
3. What is homeostasis?

Critical Thinking

4. How is the transport system in your community (roads, sidewalks, etc.) similar to the transport system in your body? How do these systems differ? (*Comparing and Contrasting*)

▲ **Figure 1–5**

Adaptations. In order to maintain homeostasis, all living things, including these Saguaro cacti, must adapt to their environment.

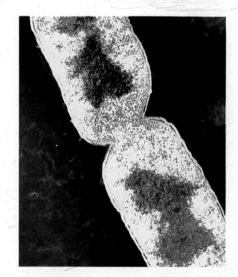

▲ **Figure 1–6**

Reproduction. The bacterium, *Escherichia coli,* reproduces by one method of asexual reproduction—binary fission. (Magnification: 17 650 X)

Laboratory
Investigation

Looking Closely at Living Things

As you know, living things come in a variety of sizes, forms, shapes, and colors. Yet, all living things share certain characteristics. You can discover some of these characteristics just by carefully observing a living thing.

Problem

What are the characteristics of life? **Observe** a living organism to discover possible answers.

Materials (per group)

- a live organism
- hand lens
- metric ruler
- laboratory balance
- penlight or flashlight
- white and dark paper

Procedure

1. Obtain a live organism from your teacher. Be sure to follow any special precautions that your teacher gives you for handling the organism.

2. Observe the organism for 5 minutes, using your senses of sight, smell, and hearing. Record your observations in a data table similar to the one shown.

3. On a sheet of paper, sketch the organism. Indicate its color, shape, and size, as well as any other characteristics that you observe. Label any parts that you can identify.

4. Observe the organism through the hand lens. Sketch any interesting features that you see.

5. Use a metric ruler to measure the length, width, and height of the organism. In addition, measure any noticeable projections on the organism. Record all measurements.

6. If the organism can be placed on a balance, find and record the organism's mass.

7. Use a penlight or flashlight to shine a beam of light on the organism, and observe its response. Record your observations.

8. Use a sheet of dark paper to shade the organism from the light, and observe its response. Record your observations.

Observations

Share your observations with your classmates, who studied different organisms. How are the organisms different? How are they similar?

Analysis and Conclusions

1. Which characteristics of life did you observe in the organism you studied?

2. For the characteristics of life that you did not observe in the organism, discuss whether or not you believe the organism has them. Use your observations as evidence for your answer.

3. Are you convinced that the organism you studied is alive? Explain your answer.

4. Among the organisms your class studied, was there a common color, shape, mass, or other physical characteristic? Discuss the significance of your answer.

Extensions

Design an experiment to show how your organism is affected by temperature or some other factor. Be sure your experiment does not harm your organism.

Data Table	
Organism's name	
Color	
Shape	
Measurements	
Mass	
Response to light	

Chapter 1 Review

Study Outline

1-1 Understanding Life

▸ Biology is the study of living things.

▸ All living things share certain characteristics that distinguish them from nonliving things. All living things are highly organized and contain many complex chemical substances; are made up of one or more cells; use energy; have a definite form and a limited size; have a limited life span; grow; respond to changes in the environment; are able to reproduce; and change over time.

▸ Some things, such as viruses, are difficult to classify as either living or nonliving.

1-2 Life Processes

▸ The function of many life processes is to maintain homeostasis, a constant internal environment.

▸ All living things carry on certain life processes that are characteristic of life. These processes include nutrition, transport, respiration, synthesis, growth, excretion, regulation, and reproduction.

▸ Metabolism includes all the chemical reactions occurring within the cells of an organism.

Chapter Assessment

Multiple Choice

Choose the letter of the answer that best completes each statement or answers the question.

1. Which term refers to all the chemical activities required to sustain life? (a) homeostasis (b) metabolism (c) excretion (d) synthesis

2. The process by which animals take in materials to be used for nourishment is called (a) digestion. (b) ingestion. (c) egestion. (d) transport.

3. Simple substances are combined chemically to form more complex substances by the process of (a) ingestion. (b) digestion. (c) assimilation. (d) synthesis.

4. Which life function includes the absorption and circulation of essential substances throughout an organism? (a) transport (b) excretion (c) ingestion (d) nutrition

5. The energy-releasing process in all plant and animal cells is called (a) secretion. (b) photosynthesis. (c) respiration. (d) circulation.

6. The process by which an organism maintains homeostasis in a constantly changing environment is (a) reproduction. (b) growth. (c) regulation. (d) synthesis.

7. The process by which a sugar or other food substance is broken down into carbon dioxide and water in the presence of oxygen is called (a) aerobic respiration. (b) anaerobic respiration. (c) nutrition. (d) assimilation.

8. Substances that organisms obtain from the environment and use for energy, growth, repair, or maintenance are called (a) cells. (b) seeds. (c) nutrients. (d) hormones.

9. The process of cellular specialization is the (a) specialization of cells for specific functions. (b) regulation of a constant internal environment. (c) incorporation of new materials into an organism. (d) reproduction between identical parents.

10. Growth, reproduction, and nutrition are all examples of (a) organisms. (b) life processes. (c) organ systems. (d) cells.

Content Review

Answer each of the following in complete sentences.

11. List the nine characteristics of living things.

12. How does nutrition in green plants differ from nutrition in animals?

13. Explain the relationship between the processes of ingestion and digestion.

14. In animals, what materials are used in synthesis?

15. How does growth occur in large multicellular organisms?

16. How does the excretory system help to maintain homeostasis in the body?

17. Describe the difference in function between the nervous system and the endocrine system.

18. Compare the appearance of a parent with its offspring produced by asexual reproduction.

19. Describe the two opposing processes that occur in metabolism.

20. Explain how nutrients are related to respiration.

Graphic Organizing

For information on graphic organizers, see Appendix G at the back of this text.

21. **Word Map** Copy the incomplete word map for metabolism onto a sheet of paper. Then complete it, using the word map for biology as a model.

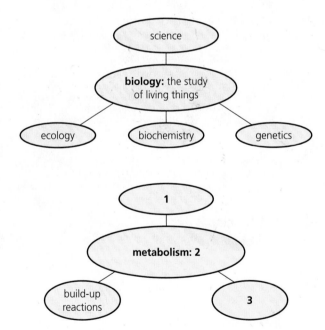

Critical Thinking and Problem Solving

Discuss each of the following in a brief paragraph.

22. **Comparing** List four ways in which an automobile is similar to a living thing. List four ways in which an automobile is different than a living thing.

23. **Classifying** Would you classify a virus as living or nonliving? Explain the reasons for your answer.

24. **Relating** A "computer virus" is a program that can reproduce itself inside a computer. In time, it can grow and evolve. Is a computer virus alive? Why or why not?

25. **Experimenting** Design an experiment to determine if seeds that have been stored for many years are viable.

26. **Predicting** Baby chickens require a constant source of food. As chicks grow, more energy is needed for daily activities. The following table gives the grams of food eaten by a chick over a five-day period.

Number of Days	Food Eaten (grams)
0	0.0
1	1.0
2	3.2
3	6.5
4	10.6
5	15.4

On a separate sheet of paper, construct a line graph using this data. Based on your graph, predict the amount of grain that will be eaten by the chick on the sixth and seventh day.

Discovery Learning Activity

Testing a Hypothesis

1. Suppose that a deadly disease is being spread through the water supply in your area.

2. Formulate a hypothesis that explains how the disease is being spread.

3. Describe a controlled experiment that could be used to test your hypothesis.

Biology as a Science

Previewing the Chapter

Dangling precariously from a branch high above the forest floor, a biologist studies a rain forest tree—up close and personal! The science of biology can take on a variety of forms, from studying trees in the rain forest of Costa Rica to using a microscope to observe microorganisms. As technology improves, so do the tools that biologists can use to study the living world. What are some of these tools? How do they make scientific observations more accurate? What methods do scientists use to study the natural world?

Key Words

control, hypothesis, magnification, resolution, scientific method, theory, variable

Key Concepts

- **List** the steps of the scientific method.
- **Describe** some of the tools used by biologists.
- **Interpret** the results from a controlled experiment. (Laboratory Investigation)

2-1 The Nature of Science

Section Objectives:

- *List* the essential steps of a scientific investigation.
- *Explain* what is meant by a controlled experiment.
- *Define* the terms *hypothesis, theory,* and *scientific law.*
- *List* the basic units of measurement in the metric system.

The Scientific Method

Broadly speaking, science is an attempt to understand the world we live in. By this, we mean that science goes beyond the simple observation and description of objects and events. It tries to find general principles to explain why things are as they are and why things happen the way they do.

There are so many different kinds of phenomena to be explained that scientists have had to become specialists—physicists, chemists, astronomers, earth scientists, biologists, and so on. Within each of these fields, there are numerous subdivisions. Even so, scientists in all fields approach their problems in the same way. When a scientist announces a finding or proposes a new idea, other scientists may repeat the work or test its conclusions. This universal approach to scientific problems is called the **scientific method.** Its main features are the same in all areas of science.

▲ **Figure 2–1**
Observation in Science. Biologists often observe organisms in controlled environments and in nature as part of their research.

◀ A biologist studying trees in a Costa Rican rain forest.

▲ **Figure 2–2**

Scientific Investigation. Careful observations of phenomena in nature and in the laboratory help scientists define a specific problem for investigation.

Defining the Problem   The scientific method begins when a person asks a question about a particular phenomenon or set of facts he or she has observed. See Figure 2–2. For example, a scientist interested in seed germination might ask, "Do the seeds of a particular plant species need light to germinate?" The subject may be one about which little is known, or it may be a well-understood one. In either case, by asking a question, the scientist consciously defines a specific problem for investigation.

The question is usually followed by a thorough search for information about the topic. Most of the information is derived from the data of experiments performed by other scientists and reported in scientific journals. By becoming familiar with existing knowledge, the scientist can avoid duplicating work already done and can plan the best approach to the problem.

Formulating a Hypothesis   In analyzing a problem, the scientist may find a specific pattern of events or some definite relationship between certain factors. However, by themselves, these observations do not explain anything. What a scientist really wants to know is what causes the pattern. It is here that reasoning, guesswork, and inspiration enter. At this stage in the scientific method, the scientist usually formulates a **hypothesis,** a possible explanation for an observed set of facts. This is a critical step in the scientific method.

Testing the Hypothesis—Experimentation   A hypothesis may offer a possible explanation for everything that is known about a problem. Until it is tested, however, it remains only a hypothesis—a logical guess. A hypothesis cannot be tested by carrying out the same types of experiments that established the pattern or relationship. That would only verify the known pattern rather than provide the explanation. A good hypothesis will predict other kinds of patterns or interactions that have not yet been observed. Thus, the scientist must test a hypothesis by designing experiments that will either verify or disprove the predictions of the hypothesis. A hypothesis is accepted as probably correct if all

Figure 2–4
Common Metric System Prefixes. ▶

Common SI Prefixes		
Prefix	**Meaning**	
mega-	1 000 000	(1 million)
kilo-	1 000	(1 thousand)
deci-	0.10	(one-tenth)
centi-	0.01	(one-hundredth)
milli-	0.001	(one-thousandth)
micro-	0.000 001	(one-millionth)
nano-	0.000 000 001	(one-billionth)

basic unit of length is the meter (m); the unit of mass is the gram (g); the unit of volume is the liter (L); the unit of time is the second (s); and the unit of temperature is either the Celsius degree or the Kelvin. In the system of measurement commonly used in the United States, units of different size have different names. For example, inches, feet, yards, and miles are all units of length. For a particular measurement, we choose the unit that is most convenient. Thus, we express the size of a sheet of paper in inches; the dimensions of a room in feet; and the distance between cities in miles. In the SI system, a simpler method is used to make units of convenient size. A prefix is attached to the basic unit name to make it larger or smaller. The most commonly used prefixes are defined in Figure 2–4. A complete listing of SI units appears in Appendix E at the back of this text. Some familiar examples of the use of SI units are shown in Figure 2–5.

The biologist needs to use small units of measurements because of the small size of the structures in living cells. Many of these structures are no more than a few millionths of a meter (micrometers) in length or diameter. Since so many measurements in biology are in this range, biologists often use the term *micron* in place of micrometer. One micron (symbol, μ) is the same as one micrometer, or one-millionth of a meter. It is also equal to one-thousandth of a millimeter (0.001 mm).

Figure 2–5
SI Units. SI units are used worldwide for all types of measurements. ▶

---

its predicted effects are observed and if these effects are repeatable. A hypothesis can never be completely proved. However, at any time it may be disproved by a single experiment! (Of course, that experiment, like all experiments, must be repeated and checked to make sure its results are correct.)

The design of an experiment is critical to its success. In an experiment, the scientist sets up a situation in which a particular observation can be made. The scientist makes changes in the situation and observes the results or response.

In biology, research often involves the use of **controlled experiments.** In a controlled experiment, two identical experiments are set up. Controlled experiments allow researchers to isolate and test the effects of a single factor, called a **variable.** The variable may be any factor, such as temperature or light intensity. In the other setup, no factor is changed. If any difference occurs in the results or response of the two setups, it can be assumed to be caused by the changed factor. The setup in which no change was made, serves as a reference and is called the **control.** See the controlled experiment setup in Figure 2–3.

Observing and Measuring   Since the goal of science is to explain what is observed, every investigation must include observations. In the early history of science, observations were often

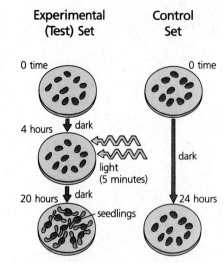

Experimental (Test) Set — Control Set

Seeds on moist filter paper in the dark for 4 hours, followed by 5 minutes light, followed by 20 hours dark at 25° C.

Seeds on moist filter paper in the dark for 24 hours at 25° C.

▲ **Figure 2–3**
A Controlled Experiment.

MiniLab

Skill: Designing an Experiment

A Moldy Question

Procedure

1. Mold will grow on bread that is exposed to air at room temperature. Design an experiment to test the effects of water and sunlight on the growth of bread mold. You may use up to four slices of bread and any materials available in your classroom.

2. With your teacher's approval, perform the experiment you designed. **CAUTION:** *If you have any allergies to molds, do not perform the experiment.*

Problem

Why does bread turn moldy? **Design an experiment** to help answer this question.

Analyze and Conclude

1. What were the variables in your experiment?

2. What were the controls in your experiment?

3. Could factors other than water and sunlight have influenced the results? Explain your answer.

4. What conclusions can you draw from this experiment? Explain your answer.

imprecise. One thing might be described as larger than another, or an event might be described as more likely to happen at warm temperatures than at cold temperatures. Today, we know that generalizations are not very useful. The heart of modern science is accurate measurement and the statement of results in numerical, or quantitative, form. To obtain precise, quantitative results, scientists use many special tools and instruments. You will learn about some of these tools and instruments in the next section.

Analyzing and Drawing Conclusions   Once obtained, the data from an experiment need to be analyzed. Analysis can reveal patterns or relationships that are not apparent from unanalyzed, or raw, data. Analysis allows a scientist to interpret results and to draw conclusions. Ultimately, experimental data can provide evidence to support, modify, or reject a hypothesis or to formulate a new hypothesis.

Reporting Observations   For progress to occur in any field of science, there must be no secrecy. The materials and procedures used in all investigations, as well as all observations and results, must be recorded accurately and reported in detail. If an experiment cannot be repeated by other investigators, the results of the original investigation cannot be considered valid.

MiniLab

Skill: Hypothesizing

The Mystery Box

Procedure

1. Obtain a mystery box from your instructor. The box contains a unique arrangement of partitions and one or more marbles.

2. Tilt, turn, and tap the box to move the marbles inside. The sounds and sensations provide clues to the arrangement of partitions inside the box.

3. On a sheet of paper, sketch your hypothesis of how the partitions are arranged inside the mystery box.

Problem

What is inside the mystery box?
Formulate a hypothesis.

Analyze and Conclude

1. How certain can you be of your hypothesis? Explain your answer.

2. Without opening the mystery box, what further tests might you perform to verify your hypothesis?

3. Open the mystery box. How accurate was your hypothesis?

When a research project has been completed, the investigator may publish a paper describing the project in a scientific journal. These journals are usually publications of scientific societies that specialize in a particular branch of science. The journals serve as sources of information on recent developments in various scientific fields. Before a research paper is accepted for publication, it is reviewed by several scientists. The reviewers are usually scientists working in an area the same as, or related to, that of the research paper. Reviewers look to see that correct scientific methodology has been used, that results are reported clearly, and that conclusions are supported by the experimental data. If they find deficiencies, their criticisms and suggestions are passed on to the original scientist. The scientist can then perform additional experiments, analysis, and/or interpretation of data to correct and improve the paper before it is resubmitted. In this way, the quality of science that is reported is maintained at a high level.

Can You Explain This

"I have this *theory* that red u forms will result in more wins."

"The cell *theory* states that t cell is the basic unit of all livi things."

Note the use of the term t ory in the statements above.

■ *Is there any difference betwe the two uses of the term? Expl Which is the meaning used by entists? Explain.*

Theories and Laws

As hypotheses are tested through experimentation, new and better hypotheses are proposed. In fact, scientists are constantly trying to refine hypotheses, or to have them describe nature more accurately. While hypotheses are important, each one is usually an idea limited to observations in a particular investigation. Explanations that apply to a broad range of phenomena and that are supported by experimental evidence are called **theories.** Theories are harder to establish than hypotheses. The germ theory of disease, developed from the work of Louis Pasteur, is an example of a well-tested theory. According to this theory, diseases are the effects of microscopic organisms living and reproducing inside the body of the diseased individual. The germ theory led to methods of treating and preventing many human diseases. The theory does have limits, however, because many diseases, such as arthritis, diabetes, and heart disease, are not caused by germs.

A theory attempts to explain everything about a phenomenon, including its cause. A **scientific law,** on the other hand, is a statement that describes some aspect of a phenomenon that is always true. A law does not explain how or why something occurs as it does, only that it occurs. Scientists can state a law only after they have observed that a particular event or relationship always exists under a given set of circumstances. The law of gravity, for example, states that any two objects attract each other. This law is based on thousands of observations. There are also scientific laws in biology. In Unit 5, you will learn about the laws of genetics.

Scientific Measurement

In scientific investigations, measurements need to be expressed in units of a standardized system that everyone understands. The International System of Units, abbreviated as **SI,** is the system used by scientists. Many SI units are units of the *metric system.* In SI, the

In this text, when a number has more than four digits, a space rather than a comma will be used to mark off groups of three digits. For example, 5976 remains as 5976 but 85,463 becomes 85 463. Also, 0.1523 remains as 0.1523 but 0.52186 becomes 0.52 186.

2-1 Section Review

1. Name the principal steps in the scientific method.
2. Define the term *hypothesis.*
3. List the basic units of measurement in the metric system.

Critical Thinking

4. Suppose you were given seed packages for two varieties of radishes. How would you determine experimentally the variety that had the better rate of germination? (*Problem Solving*)

2-2 Tools of the Biologist

Section Objectives:

- *State* why instruments are necessary for scientific research.
- *Name* and *state* the functions of the parts of a compound microscope.
- *Distinguish* between magnification and resolution in a microscope.
- *Describe* the steps in preparing a specimen for examination with a compound microscope.

Observation and measurement are the backbone of scientific investigation. The observations that can be made by the unaided senses are limited. Therefore, every branch of science makes use of instruments that increase the range and accuracy of the human senses. Even in daily life we use instruments to help our senses. Eyeglasses are an obvious example. But we also use thermometers, measuring cups, scales, and rulers. We seldom think of these things as scientific instruments, but that is what they are. In this section of the text, we will describe a few of the important instruments that are used in biological research.

The Light Microscope

A **light microscope,** or optical microscope, is any device that uses light to produce an enlarged view of an object. What we see when we use a microscope to examine an object is called an *image.* The ratio of the image size to the object size is the **magnification,** or magnifying power, of the instrument. Light microscopes depend on the fact that light rays change direction when they pass from one transparent medium to another. Optical microscopes contain lenses, pieces of glass with curved surfaces. The lenses cause light rays from an object to bend in such a way as to produce an enlarged image.

The Simple Microscope The **simple microscope** is what we know as a magnifying glass, such as the one shown in Figure 2–6. It consists of a single lens. Lenses of this type were used as early as the tenth century. They are still used by biologists to identify specimens in the field and to make quick observations that do not require the high magnifications of a laboratory instrument.

The Compound Microscope A **compound microscope,** like the one in Figure 2–7, uses two lenses. One lens produces an enlarged image that is further magnified by the second lens. A compound microscope has an optical system, a mechanical system, and a light system. See Figure 2–8. Its use has led to dramatic advances in nearly all fields of science.

Lenses make up the **optical system** of the compound microscope. The two lenses of the optical system are the *objective* and the *ocular* (AHK yuh ler), or eyepiece. In modern microscopes, the objective and the ocular each consist of several lenses combined to give the desired optical properties. As far as the operation of the instrument is concerned, each set of lenses acts as a single lens.

A compound microscope usually has two or more objectives of different magnifying powers. A *low-power objective* is used to locate the region of the specimen to be examined. A *high-power objective* is moved into position if further magnification is wanted. The ocular can be removed and replaced by a lens of different power.

The **mechanical system** is made up of the structural parts that hold the specimen and lenses and permit focusing of the image.

The *base* is the structure on which the microscope stands. Most of the other mechanical parts are attached to the *arm.* The *stage,* which is a platform coming out from the arm, has a round opening over which the specimen is placed. The specimen is usually mounted on a glass or plastic slide for observation. Two *clips* attached to the stage hold the slide in place. Attached to the top of the arm is the cylindrical *body tube,* which holds the lenses. The eyepiece is at the top of the body tube. At the bottom of the body tube is a revolving *nosepiece,* which holds the objective lenses. The objectives are changed by turning the nosepiece.

To focus the microscope, two adjustment knobs are used. The large knob is the *coarse adjustment,* which is used for approximate focusing of the low-power objective. The smaller knob is the *fine adjustment,* which is used for final focusing of the low-power objective and for all focusing of the high-power objective. Both knobs vary the distance between the objective and the specimen by moving either the body tube or the stage. The specimen is in focus when the image appears sharp. When the high-power objective is in position, it lies close to the slide on which the specimen is mounted. For this reason, only the fine adjustment knob should be used in focusing the high-power objective.

▲ **Figure 2–6**
A Simple Microscope. A magnifying glass is also known as a simple microscope.

Figure 2–7
The Modern Compound Light Microscope. Work in numerous fields of science and technology is dependent on the use of the light microscope. ▼

Math, Science, and Technology

Through the Looking Glass

Problem

The microscope ranks as one of the most important tools of science. It reveals an entire world of organisms too small to be seen by the unaided human eye. The human eye cannot see objects smaller than 100 micrometers (μm) in diameter.

The simplest light microscope is the magnifying glass, which is capable of magnifying objects 10 to 20 times. A magnifying glass, or hand lens, cannot be used to magnify an object any further because the image becomes fuzzy. Greater magnification is achieved by using a compound light microscope. Some advanced compound microscopes have more powerful lenses for greater magnification, thus enabling scientists to see objects as small as 0.5 μm in diameter. Electron microscopes, on the other hand, permit scientists to see objects as small as 0.2 nanometers (nm).

Because magnification causes us to lose the idea of the actual size of an object, size must be measured indirectly. That is, size must be compared with the size of something that is already known. The diameter of the microscope field as seen through the ocular is a convenient standard to use. The low-power field diameter of most compound microscopes used in schools is approximately 1500 μm (1.5 mm; 1 mm = 1000 μm).

Task

You have been asked by a local natural history museum to teach a group of visiting fifth-grade students how a compound microscope works. In order to do this task, you must complete each of the following:

1. Calculate the diameter, area, and volume of several different types of spherical cells as seen under the high-power magnification of a compound microscope used in school labs. Use the following formulas: radius = 1/2d; area of a circle = πr^2; volume of a sphere = 4/3 πr^3.

2. Find the high-power field diameter using the following formula:

$$\frac{\text{low-power field diameter} \times \text{low-power magnification}}{\text{high-power magnification}}$$

Calculate the diameter of one cell under low power, by dividing the low-power field diameter by the number of cells that fit across the diameter of the low-power field. Calculate the diameter of the same cell under high power, by dividing the high-power field diameter by the number of cells that fit across the diameter of the high-power field.

3. Obtain directions on how to construct a compound microscope. Using these directions and the diagram, construct a compound microscope that will magnify the letters on the page of a newspaper.

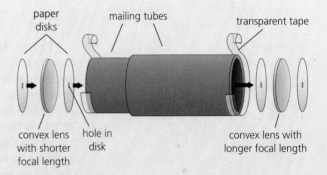

paper disks   mailing tubes   transparent tape

convex lens with shorter focal length   hole in disk   convex lens with longer focal length

4. Determine the approximate magnifying power of the microscope that you constructed and make a sketch of what you saw under your compound microscope.

5. Explain how a compound microscope works and how it is useful to biologists using information you have found in the library and on the Internet.

6. Keep a journal of what you did to teach the fifth graders about the compound microscope. Include all the information, ideas, and drawings that you have gathered from your research. Your journal should be well organized and easy to understand.

Solution

Use the diagram and the directions to build your own microscope.

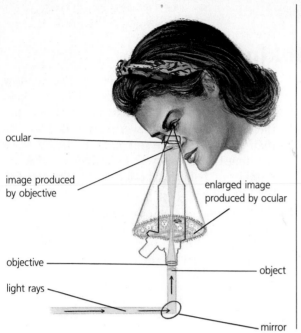

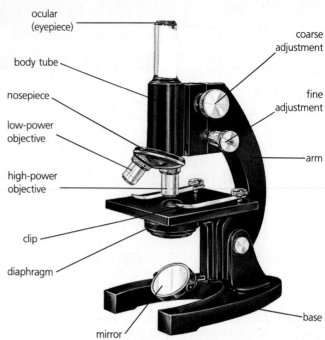

▲ **Figure 2–8**

A Compound Microscope. The objective produces an enlarged image of the specimen. When this image is viewed through the ocular, a still larger image of the specimen is seen.

In its simplest form, the **light system** consists of a mirror and a diaphragm. The *mirror,* which is under the opening in the stage, can be adjusted to direct light up through the specimen into the objective. In some microscopes, light is supplied directly by a *substage illuminator,* which is a small electric light. The amount of light reaching the objective is regulated by the *diaphragm* (DY uh fram), which is mounted below the stage. Some microscopes have *condensers* located in or below the stage. Condensers are lenses that concentrate the light on the specimen.

Magnification **Magnification** refers to the enlargement of an image. The extent to which a microscope magnifies images is known as its magnifying power. It is expressed as a number followed by a multiplication sign, such as 100 ×. The magnifying power refers to enlargement in one direction. For example, the image of a line 1 millimeter long will appear to be 100 millimeters long when viewed through a microscope with a magnifying power of 100 ×.

In a compound microscope, the total magnification can be found by multiplying the magnifying power of the objective by the magnifying power of the ocular. In most student microscopes, the power of the high-power objective is 43 × and the power of the ocular is 10 ×. With the high-power objective in use, the total magnifying power of the microscope is 43 × 10, or 430 ×. This means that the distance between two points in the image is 430 times greater than it is in the actual object.

Resolution Although a microscope enlarges images, it does not add detail to objects. The details are always there. A microscope spreads the details apart so the human eye can make them out. To the unaided eye, two tiny spots close together appear as one. They are not seen as separate spots. Under the microscope, these two spots appear farther apart, which allows us to see them separately.

The ability of a microscope to show two points that are close together as separate images is called **resolution** (rez uh LOO shun), or resolving power. Resolution is another term for the sharpness of an image. It does no good to increase the magnifying power of a microscope if its resolving power is not also increased. If only the magnification is increased, the image becomes larger, but you cannot make out any more detail. Small blurred spots simply become large blurred spots.

Up to a point, the resolving power of a microscope depends on the precision and quality of the lenses. However, there is a limit to the resolving power of any optical lens system. Because of the properties of light, a light microscope cannot distinguish two points that are less than 0.2 micrometers apart. This property of light limits what can be discovered about the structure of cells through the optical microscope. This limit remained until the development of the electron microscope, which does not depend on light. The electron microscope will be described later in this chapter.

Preparation of Specimens To observe a specimen under the compound microscope, the specimen must be thin enough for light to pass through it. This is the case for all *microorganisms*— organisms too small to be seen clearly with the naked eye. Most other organisms or biological materials, however, are too thick. For this reason, they must be fixed, embedded, and sliced into thin sections. *Fixation* is done by cutting the material into small pieces and allowing it to soak in a fixative, such as formalin. The fixed material is then *embedded* in liquid wax or plastic, which is allowed to harden. The wax or plastic holds the material in place so that it can be sliced or *sectioned.* The instrument used for slicing thin sections is called a *microtome,* which is shown in Figure 2–9.

The thin sections are then attached to a glass slide and stained. Without staining, few structural details can be observed with the compound microscope since cells are transparent. However, as Figure 2–10 illustrates, by using one or more colored stains, which

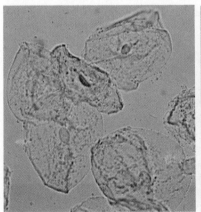

◀ **Figure 2–10**

Staining. Unstained (left) and stained (right) preparations of human cheek cells are seen through a light microscope.

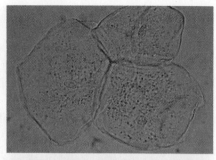

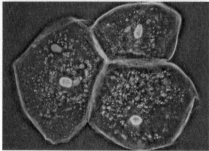

▲ **Figure 2–11**
Phase-Contrast Microscopy. Human cheek cells as seen through an ordinary light microscope (top) and through a phase-contrast microscope (bottom). (Magnification 396 ×)

Figure 2–12
A Transmission Electron Microscope and Micrograph. With the transmission electron microscope, scientists can study cell structure at extremely high magnifications. Nerve cell mitochondria magnified 124 800 times are shown in the electron micrograph on the right. ▼

are absorbed only by certain structures in the section, the details can be seen. There are some stains, called *vital stains,* that can be used with living tissues. Although they are taken in by the tissue, they do not kill it, and the structural details can be seen with the microscope.

The Phase-Contrast Microscope A **phase-contrast microscope** is a special type of compound microscope that allows the details within living specimens to be seen without staining. This microscope enhances the differences that occur in light as it passes through different regions of a cell. As a result, structures in living cells that cannot be seen with the ordinary compound microscope are made visible. See Figure 2–11.

The Stereomicroscope The type of light microscope used in studying the external, or surface, structure of specimens is the **stereomicroscope.** A stereomicroscope has an ocular and objective for each eye and a low magnifying power, usually from 6 × to 50 ×. These characteristics provide a more three-dimensional image of the specimen. In addition, the image produced by a stereomicroscope is not reversed as it is with a compound microscope. For this reason, procedures, such as dissections that require magnification, are performed using stereomicroscopes.

The Electron Microscope

Magnification and resolution beyond the limits of the light microscope were not available until the development of electron microscopes in the 1930s. The **transmission electron microscope** can magnify images more than 250 000 times. It uses electron beams, rather than light, and electromagnetic lenses, rather than glass lenses. The electron beam is directed through a vacuum chamber that contains a series of electromagnets. The electromagnets serve as lenses to focus the electron beam. When the electrons hit the specimen, some pass through, some are absorbed, and some are scattered. Those that are transmitted through the specimen are focused on a viewing screen similar to a television screen. Denser portions of the specimen absorb more electrons than less dense portions and thus appear darker on the viewing screen. Electron microscopes also contain cameras to photograph the image of the specimen. See Figure 2–12.

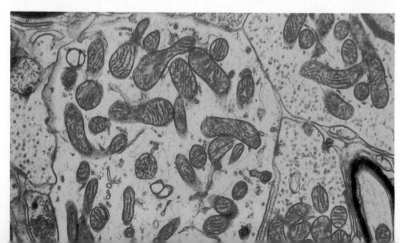

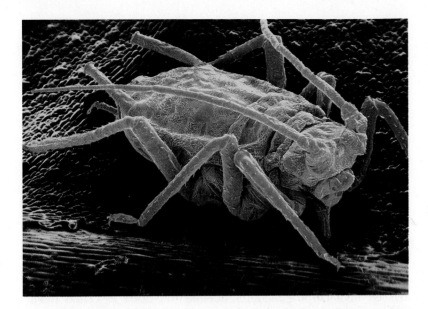

◀ **Figure 2–13**
Scanning Electron Micrograph. The scanning electron microscope allows the viewing of whole organisms. It produces a three-dimensional image, such as this one of a peach aphid on a leaf. (Magnification 68 ×)

Specimens that are going to be viewed in an electron microscope first must be dried, embedded in plastic, and sliced into thin sections no more than one micron in thickness. After this has been done, the sections are mounted on fine grids and stained with a metal to increase contrast.

The **scanning electron microscope** operates in a somewhat different way. It uses an electron beam that has been focused to a fine point. The beam is passed back and forth over the surface of the specimen. Electrons reflected or ejected from the specimen's surface are collected and used to produce an image of great depth. See Figure 2–13. The magnification of the scanning electron microscope is not as great as that of the transmission electron microscope. However, it can reveal fine details of the surface structure of whole specimens. There are many scanning electron microscope photographs in this text.

Laboratory Techniques

A number of important techniques are used routinely in day-to-day biological research. Many of these techniques are improved or refined continually as new and better instruments and other materials become available.

Centrifugation   Materials of different densities suspended in a liquid can be separated from each other by the process of **centrifugation** (sen truh fyoo GAY shun). The material that is to be separated is suspended in liquid in a test tube that is put into a centrifuge. The centrifuge spins the tube around. The heaviest particles in the liquid settle to the bottom the fastest. The next heaviest form a layer on top of the heaviest, and so on. The lightest layer is left on top. Each layer, or fraction, then can be removed from the tube.

The *ultracentrifuge* is much more powerful than a regular centrifuge. It spins at rates from 40 000 to 100 000 revolutions per minute. It can be used to separate very light particles, including various parts of the cell, from one another.

Microdissection In **microdissection** (my kroh dis EK shun), tiny instruments are used to perform various operations on living cells. This work must be done under a microscope. First, a *micromanipulator* (my croh muh NIP yuh lay ter) is attached to the microscope stage. This apparatus controls the tools used in microdissection. Among the tools that can be used with a micromanipulator are *microelectrodes,* which are used to measure or produce electrical currents in the cell; *microknives,* or *microneedles,* which are used to remove cell structures; and *micropipettes* (my croh py PETS), which are used to introduce materials into, or remove materials from, the cell.

Tissue Culture The technique of maintaining living cells or tissues in a culture medium outside the body is called **tissue culture.** Cells from living organisms are placed in culture tubes and bathed in fluid containing all necessary nutrients, oxygen, and other factors. Cells grown in tissue cultures are used in many types of biological and medical research.

Chromatography Any technique that separates different substances from each other on the basis of their chemical or physical properties is known as **chromatography** (kroh muh TAHG ruh fee). In chromatography, the mixture to be separated is placed on a solid material to which it adheres. A solvent then is introduced. Those substances that adhere loosely to the material will be carried away first in the solvent. Those substances that adhere more tightly will be carried away last. In this way, the different substances in the mixture separate. If the test substances are colored, they will form colored bands or spots, as shown in Figure 2–14. If they are colorless, they can react with chemicals that give them a color. The rate at which a given substance moves in a given solvent is a characteristic of that substance. By comparing the distance that the test substances have moved with the pattern of known substances, the test substances can be identified.

Figure 2–14
Chromatography. Each band of color in this paper chromatogram indicates the presence of a separate substance. ▼

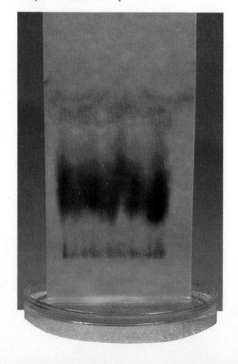

Electrophoresis The technique for separating substances made up of particles that have an electrical charge is called **electrophoresis** (ih lek truh fuh REE sis). An electric current is run through a solution containing a variety of dissolved substances. Since different substances move at different rates in the electrical field, the substances that make up the mixture are separated. Again, the rate at which each substance moves is a characteristic of that substance.

Spectrophotometry Sometimes, a scientist can determine what a substance is and how much is present in a sample by knowing the kind and amount of light absorbed by the sample. This method of using light to analyze samples is called **spectrophotometry** (spek truh fuh TAH muh tree). Measurements of this type are made with an instrument called a *spectrophotometer.*

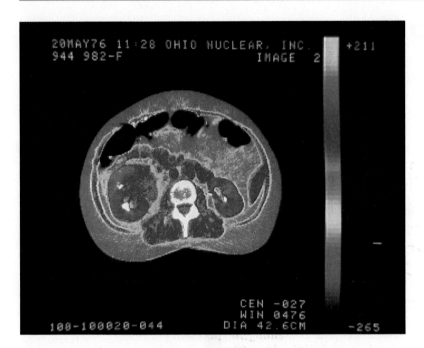

◀ **Figure 2–15**

Computerized Axial Tomography. CAT scans, such as this one showing a cross-sectional view through the trunk of a body, are important in medical diagnosis and treatment.

Computers   Computers have become increasingly important in all areas of biological study. Computers are used to collect, store, and analyze data. In these uses alone, computers have greatly increased the progress of science. To gain an understanding of complex biological processes, scientists are using computers to simulate processes. Our understanding of the complex relationships between organisms and their environments has been advanced as a result of computer analysis and simulation. Images produced by various types of microscopes can be enhanced by computers to show details otherwise not visible. In medicine, sophisticated diagnostic methods depend upon computers. Magnetic resonance imaging (MRI), computerized axial tomography (CAT), and sonography, for example, are three different methods that use computers to generate images of body tissues. See Figure 2–15. In these and countless other ways, computers are increasing our knowledge and improving our lives.

2-2 Section Review

1. How do instruments improve observations?
2. List the systems of a compound microscope.
3. Explain the difference between magnification and resolution.

Critical Thinking

4. Suppose you wanted to study a living microorganism and record its feeding behavior. Which type of microscope, light or electron, would you use to carry out this study? Explain your answer. (*Judging Usefulness*)

Laboratory
Investigation

Interpreting a Controlled Experiment

Controlled experiments allow researchers to isolate and test the effects of a single variable. Carefully planned controlled experiments produce data that relate directly to the hypothesis being tested. In this investigation, you will perform a controlled experiment and interpret the results.

Problem

What effect does the amount of water given to seeds have on the rate of seed germination? **Interpret** the results of a controlled experiment to answer the question.

Materials (per group)

▶ 200 mustard seeds

▶ 3 Petri dishes with covers

▶ 2 50-mL beakers

▶ graduated cylinder

▶ glass-marking pencil

Procedure

1. Formulate a hypothesis about the effect that varying amounts of water might have on mustard seed germination.

2. Place 50 mustard seeds in each of two Petri dishes.

3. Using the graduated cylinder, pour 5 mL of water into one Petri dish. Then pour 30 mL of water into the other Petri dish. Cover each Petri dish. Use the glass-marking pencil to indicate the volume of water in each.

4. Set both Petri dishes aside for 48 hours. After 48 hours, count the number of seeds in each Petri dish that have begun to germinate. Record your observations in a data table similar to the one shown.

5. Place 50 mustard seeds in each of the two beakers.

6. Using the graduated cylinder, pour 5 mL of water into one beaker and 30 mL of water into the other. Cover each beaker with the top or bottom of the remaining Petri dish. Then, using the glass-marking pencil, indicate on the cover the volume of water in each beaker.

7. Set the beakers aside for 48 hours. After 48 hours, count the number of seeds in each beaker that have begun to germinate. Record your observations in the data table.

Observations

Data Table		
	Volume of Water	
Type of Container	**5 mL**	**30 mL**
Petri dish		
Beaker		

1. Did the mustard seeds float in any of the containers? If so, were these seeds more likely to germinate?

2. In which container did the germinated seeds have the longest roots?

Analysis and Conclusions

1. How did the number of germinated seeds in the Petri dishes compare to the number of germinated seeds in the beakers?

2. Did the amount of water in the Petri dishes appear to affect the number of germinated seeds? Did these results confirm your original hypothesis?

3. Did the amount of water in the beakers appear to affect the number of germinated seeds? Did these results confirm your original hypothesis?

4. Sometimes the results of different parts of an experiment provide different interpretations. When this occurs, scientists often look to see if a hidden variable, which might affect the overall results of an investigation, was introduced. What hidden variable might account for the results you observed in the Petri dishes and in the beakers? (*Hint:* Other than water, what substance may have played a role in your experiment?)

Extensions

Design an experiment to determine whether light or temperature has an effect on the number of mustard seeds that germinate. Avoid the presence of any hidden variables in your experiment.

Chapter 2 Review

Study Outline

2-1 The Nature of Science

▶ Scientists use the scientific method to find answers to questions and to solve problems. The scientific method consists of a series of logical steps aimed at establishing facts about some object, event, or process.

▶ Through observation and review of the literature, a scientist may find a problem of interest. He or she then formulates a hypothesis that may solve or explain the problem. Then, the scientists tests the hypothesis, often by means of a controlled experiment.

▶ An accepted hypothesis is subject to verification and further refinement based on the results of new experiments.

▶ Theories are explanations that are based on well-established evidence, usually from many sources.

▶ Experimental observation frequently includes measurement using the International System of Units (SI). Some SI units are the meter, gram, liter, second, and Celsius degree.

2-2 Tools of the Biologist

▶ Instruments increase the range and accuracy of human senses. Instruments commonly used by biologists include the simple and compound microscopes, the stereomicroscope, and the electron microscope.

▶ To be useful, a microscope must provide both magnification and resolution. Magnification refers to enlargement of an image. Resolution refers to sharpness of an image.

▶ Special techniques used in biological research include centrifugation, microdissection, tissue culture, chromatography, electrophoresis, and spectrophotometry.

▶ Computers are used to collect, analyze, and store data, to carry out simulations of various processes, and to generate and enhance images from a variety of instruments.

Chapter Assessment

Multiple Choice

Choose the letter of the answer that best completes each statement or answers the question.

1. A possible explanation for an observed set of facts is called a (a) variable. (b) control. (c) hypothesis. (d) theory.

2. The ability of a microscope to show two points close together as separate images is called (a) magnification. (b) mechanical system. (c) resolution. (d) microdissection.

3. An explanation that applies to a broad range of phenomena and that is based on well-established evidence is known as a (a) control. (b) variable. (c) hypothesis. (d) theory.

4. A type of microscope that does not use light is the (a) stereomicroscope. (b) phase-contrast microscope. (c) scanning electron microscope. (d) compound microscope.

5. In a controlled experiment, the factor that changes is known as the (a) variable. (b) hypothesis. (c) control. (d) theory.

6. Which of the following is not a unit of measurement in the metric system? (a) meter (b) liter (c) inch (d) gram

7. How many millimeters are in 9 meters? (a) 0.9 (b) 90 (c) 900 (d) 9000

8. The coarse adjustment knob is used to (a) regulate light. (b) concentrate light on the specimen. (c) focus with the low-power objective. (d) focus with the high-power objective.

9. The total magnification of a compound microscope is 45 X. If the ocular power is 15 X, then the objective power is (a) 30 X. (b) 3 X. (c) 10 X. (d) 1 X.

10. The technique for separating substances made up of particles that have an electrical charge is (a) centrifugation. (b) chromatography. (c) electrophoresis. (d) spectrophotometry.

Content Review

Answer each of the following in complete sentences.

11. Explain the function of a control in a scientific experiment.

12. Why are scientific papers reviewed by other scientists before they are published?

13. Why would the size of an elephant be expressed in meters but that of a bacterium in microns?

14. How is the total magnification of a compound microscope calculated?

15. Explain the steps necessary in preparing materials to be viewed with the light microscope.

16. What are vital stains, and why are they used?

17. Describe how a transmission electron microscope produces the image of a specimen.

18. Explain the technique of centrifugation.

19. Explain the principles behind chromatography.

20. How is spectrophotometry useful to a scientist?

Graphic Organizing

For information on graphic organizers, see Appendix G at the back of this text.

21. **Flow Chart** Copy the flow chart below onto a separate sheet of paper. Complete the chart by filling in the missing steps of the scientific method.

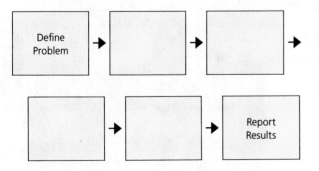

Critical Thinking and Problem Solving

Discuss each of the following in a brief paragraph.

22. **Drawing conclusions** Can hypotheses and theories change? Explain your answer.

23. **Comparing** How are the compound microscope and the electron microscope alike? How are they different?

24. **Predicting** Suppose you centrifuged a test tube containing particles of five different densities. What would you expect to see in the test tube?

25. **Interpreting** A water plant placed in a bright light gives off bubbles of oxygen. In the lab, it was noticed that if the light was placed at different distances from the plant in the aquarium, the rate of bubbling varied. The data are shown in the table below.

Distance From Light (cm)	O_2 Bubbles/Minute
10	40
20	20
30	10
40	5

On a separate sheet of paper, plot the data on a line graph. What is the variable in this investigation? Draw a conclusion from the data. Predict the amount of oxygen that will be released at 50 and at 60 cm.

26. **Hypothesizing** A biologist studying life in a lake noticed that from day to day the depth at which single-celled, green organisms lived varied greatly. These organisms were as much as 1.5 m below the surface of the water on sunny days but were only 15 cm below on cloudy days. Propose a hypothesis to explain these findings. Design an experiment to test the hypothesis.

Discovery Learning Activity

A Property of Water

1. Fill a pitcher or large beaker with water.

2. Place a glass or small beaker on a plate or saucer and fill it to the brim with water. Stop adding water when the glass or beaker is just about to overflow.

3. Add salt to the glass of water, teaspoon by teaspoon. Record how many teaspoons of salt the water can hold before it overflows the glass. How do you think the water can hold the salt without overflowing?

Basic Chemistry

Chapter 3

············· **Guide** *for Reading* ·············

Previewing the Chapter

If you live in certain parts of the country, you are probably familiar with the spectacular changes that autumn brings to the forest. As the days grow shorter and cooler, the green leaves of summer gradually give way to the brilliant reds, yellows, and golds of autumn. What causes these colorful changes? How does chemistry affect the biology of green plants? Why is it important for you to understand some basic chemistry before beginning your study of biology?

Key Words

acid, atom, base, compound, covalent bond, element, ionic bond, solution

Key Concepts

- **Describe** how an atom's structure determines its chemical properties.
- **Compare** the properties of acids and bases.
- **Classify** common substances as either acidic, basic, or neutral. (Laboratory Investigation)

3-1 Atomic Theory of Matter

Section Objectives:

- *Define* the terms *element, compound, atomic number, mass number,* and *isotope.*
- *Describe* the structure of an atom and the arrangement of electrons around the nucleus.
- *Explain* how radioisotopes are used in biological and chemical research.

Atoms, Elements, and Compounds

In this century, people have made great progress in understanding the processes of life. Because these processes are chemical, the biology student needs to know some basic chemistry. Living systems, from the smallest organism to a forest filled with living things, are made of the same basic building blocks as are nonliving systems. These substances react according to the same laws of chemistry that other substances obey. In this chapter and the next, you will study the chemistry that will enable you to understand the basic processes of life.

As you can see just by looking around you, the world is made up of many different substances. Hundreds of thousands of different substances are known. Hundreds of thousands of others probably exist. The study of chemistry tells us that all of these different kinds of matter

▲ **Figure 3–1**
Chemistry and Matter. All things, whether living or nonliving, are made up of the same basic chemical building blocks.

◄ Red maple trees in autumn.

▲ **Figure 3–2**
Elements and compounds. Glass (top) can look very much like diamond (bottom). However, diamond is a crystalline form of the element carbon. Glass is a mixture of compounds.

are made of atoms combined in various ways. **Atoms** are the basic building blocks of matter. They cannot be subdivided any further by any ordinary chemical means. You will learn more about the structure of atoms later in this chapter.

In spite of the large number of different substances, there are only about 100 kinds of atoms. Some substances are made of only one kind of atom. These substances are called **elements.** Iron, for example, is an element. All iron consists entirely of iron atoms. Oxygen is an element made entirely of oxygen atoms. Because there are 112 different kinds of atoms, there are 112 different elements.

Most substances are **compounds.** In a compound, two or more kinds of atoms are combined in definite proportions. For example, water is a compound made of hydrogen atoms and oxygen atoms in the proportion of 2 to 1. This means that there are always 2 hydrogen atoms for each oxygen atom.

Just looking at substances like the ones in Figure 3–2 will not tell you whether they are elements (made of a single kind of atom) or compounds (made of two or more kinds of atoms). For example, both oxygen and carbon dioxide are gases, but oxygen is an element and carbon dioxide is a compound. For this reason, scientists use chemical means to decide whether a substance is an element or a compound. Compounds can be separated into the elements that make them up. Carbon dioxide can be separated into carbon and oxygen. Carbon and oxygen cannot be separated into anything else. Elements, unlike compounds, cannot be broken down into simpler substances by ordinary means.

Chemists have given names and symbols to all the elements. The symbols are a kind of shorthand for showing the makeup of compounds and for showing what happens during chemical reactions. Figure 3–3 lists the names and symbols of some elements that are important in living things. You will find it useful to learn these symbols. Most of the symbols are abbreviations or the initials of the name of the element in English. The other symbols come from the Latin names of the elements. These are elements that were known to scientists hundreds of years ago, when Latin was used for most scholarly writing. Although the name of an element is not capitalized, the first letter of the symbol is capitalized.

Structure of Atoms

The idea that matter is made of atoms is very old. It goes back at least 2500 years to the philosophers of ancient Greece. Early scientists believed that an atom was an extremely small particle that could not be changed in any way. Research in the twentieth century has shown that atoms are not hard, solid balls. Instead, atoms consist of still smaller particles. Each atom has a small central part called the **nucleus.** The nucleus of every atom contains particles called **protons** (PROH tahnz) and **neutrons** (NOO trahnz). Protons and neutrons have about the same mass, or quantity of matter. Protons have one unit of positive electric charge, while

Elements of Importance in Biology		
Name of Element	Symbol	Atomic Number
hydrogen	H	1
carbon	C	6
nitrogen	N	7
oxygen	O	8
sodium (*natrium*)	Na	11
magnesium	Mg	12
phosphorus	P	15
sulfur	S	16
chlorine	Cl	17
potassium (*kalium*)	K	19
calcium	Ca	20
iron (*ferrum*)	Fe	26

◀ **Figure 3–3**

Elements of Importance in Biology. The Latin name is given when the symbol is derived from it.

neutrons are neutral. That is, they have no electric charge. The nucleus of the atom is stable. That is, it does not change under normal circumstances. In the space outside the nucleus, there are other particles, called **electrons** (ih LEK trahnz). Electrons have one unit of negative electric charge. They also have much less mass than protons or neutrons.

The Nucleus   The number of protons in the nucleus determines the atomic number of an element. The **atomic number** also tells you how many units of positive charge are in the nucleus. Each element has a different atomic number which is used to identify it. For example, a single atom of hydrogen has 1 proton in its nucleus. Therefore, the atomic number of hydrogen is 1. The nucleus of an oxygen atom has 8 protons. Therefore, the atomic number of oxygen is 8. See Figure 3–4.

Figure 3–4

Diagrams of some atoms. The atomic number of an atom equals the number of protons in the nucleus. It also equals the number of electrons surrounding the nucleus. ▼

Hydrogen (H)
atomic number: 1

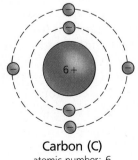

Carbon (C)
atomic number: 6

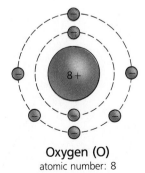

Oxygen (O)
atomic number: 8

⊖ = electron   + = proton   (Neutrons in nucleus are not shown.)

Figure 3–5

Elements with Filled Outer Energy Levels. ▼

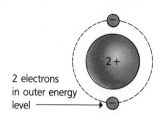

2 electrons in outer energy level

Helium (He)

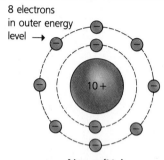

8 electrons in outer energy level →

Neon (Ne)

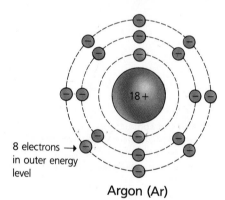

8 electrons → in outer energy level

Argon (Ar)

Most of an atom's mass lies in its nucleus. This is because protons and neutrons have about 2000 times the mass of electrons. If you think of each proton and each neutron as having one unit of mass, then the mass of the entire atom is equal, roughly, to the sum of its protons and neutrons. This sum is called the **mass number.** For example, hydrogen has 1 proton and 0 neutrons in its nucleus. Therefore, the mass number of hydrogen is 1, the sum of the proton and neutron. Oxygen has a mass number of 16 because it has 8 protons and 8 neutrons in its nucleus.

Electrons Normally, atoms have the same number of electrons as protons. For example, the hydrogen atom has 1 electron and 1 proton. The oxygen atom has 8 electrons and 8 protons. In each atom, the total positive charge of the protons is balanced by the equal number of negative charges of its electrons. Therefore, under normal circumstances, an atom is electrically neutral. The electrons in an atom determine the atom's chemical properties. The electrons are arranged in levels, known as energy levels. Each energy level is at a different distance from the nucleus. Based on modern atomic theory, there are rules for determining how electrons are arranged in an atom. While you do not need to know all of this theory, you do need to know that the first energy level can hold only 2 electrons. Once it has 2 electrons, it is said to be filled. An atom with more than 2 electrons has some of its electrons occupying other energy levels. In all of these atoms, the outside level can hold only 8 electrons.

A filled outer energy level is a stable electron arrangement. Elements that have filled outer levels are chemically inactive. Except for a few special cases, they do not form compounds with other elements. These elements are all gases under ordinary conditions. Examples are helium, neon, and argon. The structures of these atoms are shown in Figure 3–5.

If the outside level of an atom has fewer than 8 electrons, it is unfilled. Atoms with unfilled outer energy levels can form compounds with other elements. When the atoms combine to form compounds, their outside electrons are rearranged to give each atom a filled outer level. The ways in which this can happen are described in Section 3-2.

To visualize atomic structure, imagine having a special camera that is able to take pictures of a single atom. The photograph would not look like a miniature solar system as envisioned by Ernest Rutherford in the early 1900s because electrons do not move in a specific path around the nucleus. Instead, they move in a region determined by their energy at approximately the speed of light. The electrons move so fast that each energy level resembles a cloud composed of numerous individual dots. The individual

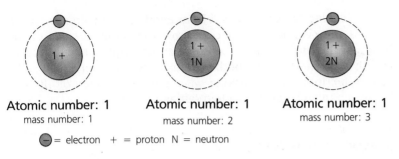

Atomic number: 1
mass number: 1

Atomic number: 1
mass number: 2

Atomic number: 1
mass number: 3

⊖ = electron + = proton N = neutron

▲ **Figure 3–6**
Isotopes of Hydrogen. The number of protons in the nucleus is the same for all isotopes of the same element. Only the number of neutrons in the nucleus is different for each isotope.

dots represent the position of electrons at a given moment. The more dots in the cloud, the more likely an electron would be found in that location.

Isotopes

The atoms of an element may have different numbers of neutrons. For example, most hydrogen atoms have no neutrons. The nucleus is simply a single proton. However, as shown in Figure 3–6, there are hydrogen atoms with 1 neutron in the nucleus and others with 2 neutrons. Although these atoms are not exactly alike, they behave the same chemically because they all have only 1 electron. Therefore, these three kinds of atoms are considered atoms of the element hydrogen. Varieties of an element that differ only in the number of neutrons in their atomic nuclei are called **isotopes** (I suh tohps).

All elements have isotopes. Isotopes of the same element have the same atomic number but different mass numbers since the mass is the total of protons and neutrons. See Figure 3–7. For example, the three common isotopes of oxygen have mass numbers of 16, 17, and 18.

Figure 3–7

Isotopes of Oxygen. The mass number of each isotope of an element is different. The atomic number remains the same. ▼

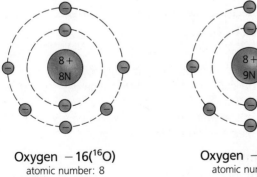

Oxygen − 16(^{16}O)
atomic number: 8
mass number: 16

Oxygen − 17(^{17}O)
atomic number: 8
mass number: 17

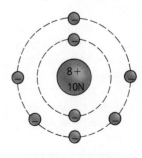

Oxygen − 18(^{18}O)
atomic number: 8
mass number: 18

To distinguish one isotope from another, a number is placed next to the chemical symbol to show the mass number of the isotope. The number is written as a superscript, a small number usually written to the left of the chemical symbol. For example, ^{18}O stands for the oxygen isotope with a mass number of 18. The isotope ^{18}O also could be spelled out as oxygen-18.

Radioactive Isotopes

The nuclei of many isotopes are unstable. An unstable nucleus emits, or gives off, charged particles and radiation at times that cannot be predicted. This causes the number of protons or neutrons in the nucleus to change. During emission, the atom changes to another isotope, usually an isotope of a different element. The process is called **radioactivity** (ray dee oh ak TIV uh tee). It was discovered in 1896 during experiments with minerals containing the element uranium.

Radioactivity is a nuclear process, not a chemical process. That is, it changes the nuclear structure, not the electron structure of the atom. It is mentioned here because radioactivity is an important means of studying biological processes. Instruments sensitive to radiation can detect and measure the radioactivity given off by radioactive isotopes, or **radioisotopes** (ray dee oh I suh tohps). Thus, radioisotopes can be used to detect abnormalities in the size, shape, or function of organs. See Figure 3–8. Sometimes, radioisotopes are used in the treatment of certain cancers. They can also be used to study chemical reactions in living things. The atoms of the radioisotope act as *tracers,* or tagged atoms. As they move from one compound to another, they can be detected and followed. Thus, the detailed chemical steps of a process can be determined.

Isotopes do not need to be radioactive to act as tracers. An instrument called a *mass spectrometer* (spek TRAHM uh ter) can detect the different mass numbers of isotopes. Oxygen-18, a stable isotope, has been used in this way to study the process of photosynthesis.

3-1 Section Review

1. How is an element different from a compound?
2. Which atomic particles have electric charges? What are these charges?
3. Define the terms *atomic number* and *mass number*.
4. How are the electrons arranged in an atom?

Critical Thinking

5. Explain the relationship between the nucleus of an atom and its electrons, protons, and neutrons. (*Relating Parts and Wholes*)

3-2 Chemical Bonding and Chemical Reactions

Section Objectives:

- *Explain* the formation of covalent and ionic bonds.
- *Define* the following terms and give examples of each: *molecule, diatomic molecule, ion, chemical formula,* and *structural formula*.
- *Describe* the changes that can occur when a chemical reaction takes place.
- *Determine* whether or not a chemical equation is balanced and label the reactants and the products.

How do chemists know that two substances react with each other to form a compound? Only observing the substances in the laboratory will answer this question. A change in temperature, a change in color, and the formation of a gas are some of the signs that a reaction has taken place. When a reaction does take place, it can take a great deal of work to determine just what substance or substances have been formed.

Covalent Bonds

Water is a compound of the elements hydrogen and oxygen. Each particle of water has 2 atoms of hydrogen and 1 atom of oxygen. A particle of this kind, in which two or more atoms are combined and act as a single particle, is called a **molecule** (MAHL ih kyool). Let us see how a molecule of water is formed.

The structures of a hydrogen atom and an oxygen atom are shown in Figure 3–9. The hydrogen atom has only 1 electron. This electron occupies the first energy level. As you have read, this level can hold 2 electrons. One more electron can be added to the level to fill it. The oxygen atom has 8 electrons. Two of its electrons are in

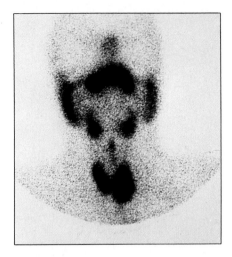

▲ **Figure 3–8**
Use of Radioactive Iodine to Diagnose Thyroid Disorders. Iodine is absorbed by the cells of the thyroid gland. This nuclear scan shows iodine concentrated in an enlarged thyroid gland (below the neck).

Figure 3–9
Covalent Bonding in Water. The hydrogen atom needs one electron to fill its outer energy level. The oxygen atom needs two electrons to fill its outer energy level. By sharing two pairs of electrons, the outer levels of the three atoms in the water molecule (H_2O) are filled. Each pair of shared electrons forms one single covalent bond. ▼

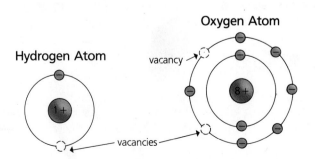

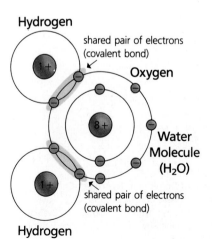

the first energy level, which, therefore, is filled. The other 6 electrons are in the second level. This level, which is the outer energy level, can hold 8 electrons. Two more electrons can be added to fill it.

In Figure 3–9, there is also a diagram of a water molecule, which shows 2 hydrogen atoms combined with 1 oxygen atom. Each hydrogen atom is sharing its electron with the oxygen atom. At the same time, the oxygen atom is sharing one of its electrons with each hydrogen atom. In this arrangement, the outer levels of all three atoms are filled. That is, the first energy level of each hydrogen atom is now filled with 2 electrons. At the same time, the second energy level of the oxygen atom is filled with 8 electrons.

The sharing of a pair of electrons by two atoms creates a force of attraction that holds the atoms together. This force of attraction is called a **chemical bond.** When a chemical bond is formed by the sharing of electrons, it is called a **covalent** (koh VAY lent) **bond.** In 1 molecule of water, there are two covalent bonds holding the molecule together.

Figure 3–10 shows the electron structure of chlorine. The outer energy level of a chlorine atom has 7 electrons. The chlorine atom needs only 1 more electron to fill its outer level. It can fill this level by sharing a pair of electrons with a hydrogen atom. When this happens, a molecule of the compound hydrogen chloride is formed. This molecule is held together by a covalent bond between the chlorine atom and the hydrogen atom.

A few elements have atoms that react with atoms of the same element to make two-atom molecules. For example, a hydrogen atom will react with another hydrogen atom to form a molecule made up of 2 hydrogen atoms. This type of two-atom molecule is called a **diatomic** (dy uh TAHM ik) **molecule.** Most elements that form diatomic molecules are gases under ordinary conditions. These elements are hydrogen, oxygen, nitrogen, chlorine, and fluorine. See Figure 3–11.

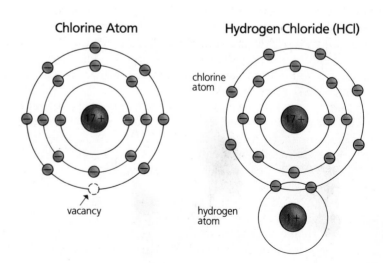

Figure 3–10

Covalent Bonding in Hydrogen Chloride.
Chlorine needs one electron to fill its outer energy level. In hydrogen chloride, a covalent bond is formed by the sharing of one pair of electrons. ▶

Chlorine Molecule (Cl₂)

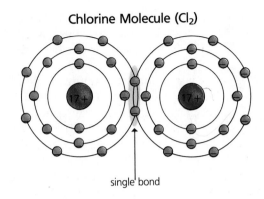

single bond

Oxygen Molecule (O₂)   Hydrogen Molecule (H₂)

double bond →   single bond →

◄   **Figure 3–11**
Diatomic Molecules of Some Gases. In a diatomic molecule of hydrogen or chlorine, two atoms form one covalent bond. In diatomic molecules of oxygen, atoms form two covalent bonds (a double bond).

Ionic Bonds

Figure 3–12 shows the electron structures of a sodium atom and a chlorine atom before bonding. The outer energy level of a sodium atom has only 1 electron. To fill this level, 7 more electrons would be needed. Could a sodium atom fill its outside energy level by combining with a chlorine atom? No, there is no way for this to happen. Electrons are usually shared in pairs, 1 electron from each atom. The sodium atom has only 1 outside electron to share and, therefore, could share in only one pair.

However, the sodium atom can transfer its outer electron to a chlorine atom. This transfer will fill the outer energy level of the chlorine atom. At the same time, the sodium atom, having lost its outer electron, will be left with a new outer energy level of 8 electrons. Thus, the new outer level of the sodium atom will also be filled.

After the chlorine atom has received an electron from the sodium atom, the chlorine atom has 17 protons and 18 electrons. Thus, it has an excess negative charge of 1 unit. An atom that has an excess charge is called an **ion** (I ahn). When the chlorine atom has

Figure 3–12

Ionic Bonding in Sodium Chloride. After sodium gives one outer electron to chlorine, each atom becomes an ion with a filled outer energy level. The sodium ion has a single positive charge. The chloride ion has a single negative charge. An ionic bond is formed between them. ▶

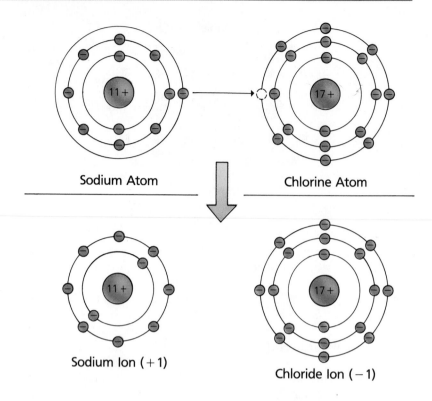

Sodium Atom   Chlorine Atom

Sodium Ion (+1)

Chloride Ion (−1)

become an ion, it has a negative charge of 1 unit. It is then called a chloride ion and is represented by the symbol Cl^-. Look again at Figure 3–12.

When a sodium atom gives up an electron, it is left with 11 protons and only 10 electrons. Therefore, it has an excess positive charge of 1 unit. The sodium atom has become a sodium ion, written as Na^+.

According to the laws of electric charge, particles with opposite charges attract each other. When a sodium atom loses an electron to a chlorine atom, the two ions that form are attracted to each other. The force of attraction between two ions is called an **ionic** (i AHN ik) **bond.** The compound of sodium and chlorine, called sodium chloride, consists of sodium and chloride ions held together by ionic bonds. Notice that the sodium and chloride ions do not form molecules. See Figure 3–13. Molecules are formed only when atoms share electrons and form covalent bonds. In sodium chloride, the ions remain separate. Each sodium ion is attracted to several chloride ions around it. Each chloride ion is attracted to several sodium ions around it. Materials with this type of structure are called crystals. No distinct molecules are present in crystals.

Chemical Formulas

Every compound consists of atoms combined in definite proportions. In water, for example, the proportion is 2 hydrogen atoms to 1 oxygen atom. In sodium chloride, the proportion is 1 sodium atom to 1 chlorine atom. This information about a compound can be

Structure of Sodium Chloride. Ionic compounds do not form molecules. Each ion in the crystal structure is attracted to several oppositely charged ions around it. This results in the cubic shape of sodium chloride crystals.

given in a **chemical formula.** In a chemical formula, each element is represented by its chemical symbol. The proportions in which the atoms combine are shown by subscripts. Subscripts are small numbers written after the symbol and slightly below the line. The subscript 1 is not written in the formula, but it is understood to be there when no other subscript is shown. For example, the chemical formula for water is H_2O, and the formula for sodium chloride is NaCl.

A **structural formula** is a kind of chemical formula. It shows not only the number and kind of atoms in a molecule but also how the atoms are bonded to one another. In a structural formula, each pair of shared electrons—that is, each covalent bond—is shown by a short line joining the atoms that are connected by the bond. The structural formulas of benzene and glucose are shown in Figure 3–14. Glucose is one of the sugars made by plants. It is the chief source of energy for living things.

Note that the formula of glucose has several OH symbols. The covalent bond between the O and the H has been omitted. This is often done to simplify structural formulas that contain certain common groups of atoms.

Water (H_2O)

Acetylene (C_2H_2)

Benzene (C_6H_6)

Glucose ($C_6H_{12}O_6$)

◀ **Figure 3–14**
Structural Formulas. Structural formulas can be written only for molecular compounds. Note that every carbon atom has four bonds, every oxygen atom has two bonds, and every hydrogen atom has one bond.

▲ **Figure 3–15**

A Familiar Chemical Reaction. Whenever chemical bonds are broken or formed, energy is involved. Some chemical reactions absorb energy. Others, like the burning of wood, release energy.

Chemical Reactions

Every compound is a combination of the atoms of certain elements bonded to one another in definite proportions and patterns. Chemical bonds can be broken, and atoms can form new bonds in new combinations. When this happens, different substances are formed. Whenever different substances are formed, we say that a chemical change, or **chemical reaction,** has taken place. See Figure 3–15. The substances that were present before the reaction started are called **reactants** (ree AK tunts). The new substances produced by the reaction are called **products.**

A chemical equation can be written to represent the changes in a chemical reaction. A chemical equation is a short way of explaining a chemical reaction. For example, consider the reaction that occurs when water is formed from hydrogen and oxygen. The equation for this reaction could be written as:

$$\text{hydrogen} + \text{oxygen} \longrightarrow \text{water}$$

or

$$H_2 + O_2 \longrightarrow H_2O$$

The reactants appear to the left of the arrow. The products always appear on the right.

There is, however, something wrong with this equation. Look carefully at Figure 3–16a. There are 2 oxygen atoms on the left side of the equation but only 1 oxygen atom on the right side of the equation. This violates the **law of conservation of mass,** which states that mass can be neither created nor destroyed. Because atoms have mass, they are not created or destroyed in chemical reactions. They are merely rearranged. Thus, there should be equal numbers of each kind of atom on the left and right sides of a chemical equation. An equation written this way is called a *balanced equation.* The balanced equation for the reaction of hydrogen with oxygen is:

$$2H_2 + O_2 \longrightarrow 2H_2O$$

This equation states that 2 molecules of hydrogen combine with 1 molecule of oxygen to form 2 molecules of water. You can confirm that this equation is balanced if you count the atoms in Figure 3–16b. There are 4 hydrogen atoms and 2 oxygen atoms on each side of the equation.

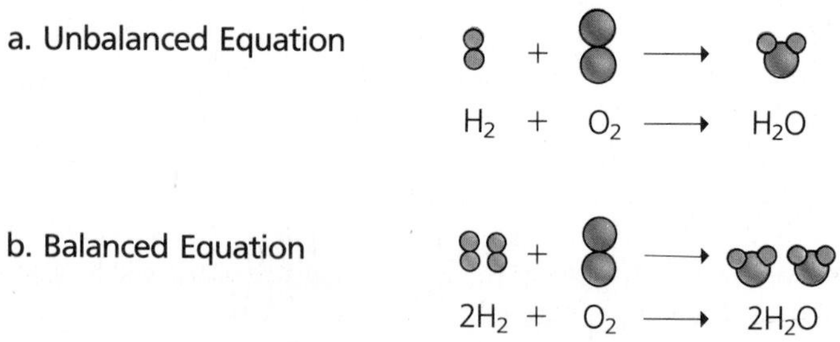

Figure 3–16

Unbalanced and Balanced Equations. Note that in the balanced equation there are equal numbers of hydrogen and oxygen atoms on each side of the equation. ▶

a. Unbalanced Equation

$$H_2 + O_2 \longrightarrow H_2O$$

b. Balanced Equation

$$2H_2 + O_2 \longrightarrow 2H_2O$$

Chemical equations are almost always written in balanced form. Here is the balanced equation for the breakdown of glucose.

$$\underset{\text{glucose}}{C_6H_{12}O_6} + \underset{\text{oxygen}}{6O_2} \longrightarrow \underset{\substack{\text{carbon}\\\text{dioxide}}}{6CO_2} + \underset{\text{water}}{6H_2O}$$

This reaction provides most of the energy for living organisms.

3-2 Section Review

1. Name two types of chemical bonds. Which type of chemical bond forms molecules?
2. Describe the two ways that an ion can be formed.
3. On which side of a chemical equation do the products appear?
4. Explain why the equation for the breakdown of glucose is a balanced equation.

Critical Thinking

5. As you know, there are no molecules in ionic compounds. What, then, does the formula for an ionic compound such as $MgCl_2$ represent? (*Relating Parts and Wholes*)

3-3 Mixtures

Section Objectives

- *Define* the following terms and give an example of each: *mixture, solvent,* and *solute.*
- *Explain* the difference between solutions, suspensions, and colloidal dispersions.

In every compound, the atoms or ions are joined by chemical bonds. The atoms or ions are present in fixed proportions and in a definite arrangement in space. It is possible, however, for many substances to be physically mixed without forming new chemical bonds. The result is called a **mixture.** The substances in a mixture may be present in any proportions. In fact, the proportions can change as one substance is added to or removed from the mixture. No matter what their proportions, however, the different substances in the mixture retain their usual properties.

For example, consider a mixture of table salt (sodium chloride) and iron filings. If this mixture is placed in water, the salt will dissolve, as it normally does. The iron filings will remain undissolved. On the other hand, a magnet will attract the iron filings in the mixture and leave the salt behind. See Figure 3–17.

The substances in a mixture may be spread evenly throughout the mixture. Such a mixture is said to be *homogeneous* (hoh muh JEE nee us). Air, for example, is a homogeneous mixture of several different gases. The gases in air include nitrogen, oxygen, carbon dioxide, water vapor, and a few others.

Figure 3–17

A Mixture. In a mixture of salt and iron filings, each substance retains its own properties. A magnet can remove the iron filings from the dry mixture, leaving the salt behind. ▼

Solutions

Although any homogeneous mixture can be called a **solution,** the term is usually used for mixtures that are liquid. The liquid substance that makes up the bulk of the solution is called the **solvent.** The other substances, which are dissolved in the solvent, are called **solutes** (SAHL yoots). Solutes may be solids, liquids, or gases before they are dissolved in the solvent. The most common solutions have water as the solvent.

When a molecular substance dissolves in a liquid, the substance separates into its individual molecules. The solute is spread through the solvent in the form of separate molecules. For example, when sugar dissolves in water, the molecules of sugar spread throughout the water. When an ionic substance dissolves, the compound breaks into its ions. Thus, when sodium chloride dissolves in water, it breaks into sodium and chloride ions. See Figure 3–18. This process is called *dissociation* (dis soh see AY shun). It can be shown by the following equation:

$$NaCl \longrightarrow Na^+ + Cl^-$$

You will learn in later chapters that many important processes in living cells and tissues depend upon the presence of dissolved ions.

Suspensions

There are many substances that do not dissolve noticeably in water. For example, sand is insoluble in water. If you put sand in a pail of water and shake the water, the sand will form a cloudy mixture with the water. If you let this mixture stand, tiny particles of sand will slowly settle to the bottom of the pail. A mixture that separates on standing is called a **suspension** (suh SPEN shun).

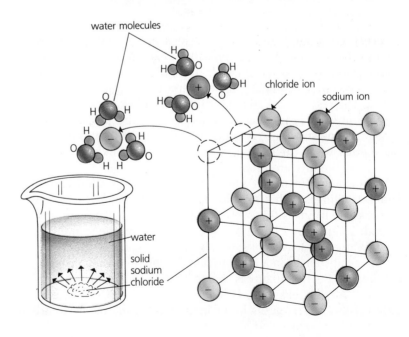

Figure 3–18

Dissociation of an Ionic Compound. When sodium chloride is dissolved in water, the structure of the salt breaks down. The compound separates into its individual ions, which become surrounded by water molecules. A solution of sodium chloride is formed. ▶

◀ **Figure 3–19**
Colloidal Dispersions and Solutions. Note the cloudiness of the colloidal dispersion of clay particles in water on the left. The solution on the right is completely transparent.

Colloidal Dispersions

In a true solution, the particles of the solute are either molecules or ions. They remain spread throughout the solvent indefinitely. In a suspension, the particles are large enough to give the liquid a cloudy appearance, and the force of gravity gradually causes them to settle out of the solvent. There is still another type of mixture known as a **colloidal dispersion** (kuh LOYD ul dis PER zhun). In a colloidal dispersion, the particles are larger than molecules or ions but too small to settle out.

The medium in which a colloidal dispersion forms does not need to be a liquid. It can be a gas or even a solid. The dispersed substance also may be a solid, liquid, or gas. Smoke, for example, is a colloidal dispersion of carbon particles in air. Milk and mayonnaise are colloidal dispersions of several liquids. Whipped cream is a colloidal dispersion of a gas (air) in a liquid.

Solutions, suspensions, and colloidal dispersions are all present in living cells and tissues. All of the activities of life depend upon the special properties that each one of these three different types of mixtures possesses.

3-3 Section Review

1. What is a mixture?
2. What are substances that dissolve in a solvent called?
3. What happens to particles in a suspension?

Critical Thinking

4. How large are the particles in a colloidal dispersion compared to the particles found in a solution and to the particles found in a suspension? (*Ordering*)

Science, Technology and Society

Issue: Acid Rain

Many scientists blame acid rain for the destruction of pine forests and lakes in the eastern United States. Studies also link acid rain to the corrosion of buildings and statues and to possible harmful effects on human health. These scientists believe that industry and automobile emissions are responsible for the acid rain problem. They fear that the environmental damage soon may be irreversible. To control acid rain, they claim, strict regulations must be imposed, especially on industrial emissions.

Opponents of regulation argue that the causes of acid rain are not yet understood. They point to studies showing that natural processes, not acid rain, are to blame for the damage. Other studies have concluded that motor vehicle emissions are the major source of acid rain. Thus, this group argues, industry controls will not cure the problem. Instead, controls will reduce the industries' efficiency and waste the public's money.

■ *Should we regulate industries to control acid rain? Why or why not?*

3-4 Acids, Bases, and Salts

Section Objectives:

■ *Define* and *compare* acids and bases and give examples of each.
■ *Describe* what happens in a neutralization reaction.
■ *Explain* the meaning of the pH scale and what is indicated by pH values of 1, 7, and 14.
■ *Explain* how pH indicators are used.

There are many compounds that form ions when they are dissolved in water. Two important groups of these compounds are the acids and the bases. How are these produced?

Acids and Bases

An **acid** is any compound that produces hydrogen ions in solution. All acids consist of molecules that contain hydrogen covalently bonded to another atom or group of atoms. When these molecules are dissolved in water, the hydrogen breaks loose as a hydrogen ion, H^+. The rest of the molecule forms a negative ion.

Hydrochloric acid, HCl, is one example of an acid that is important to life activities. When not mixed with water, hydrochloric acid is a gas made of HCl molecules. However, when it is dissolved in water, it separates into H^+ and Cl^- ions:

$$HCl \longrightarrow H^+ + Cl^-$$

Another example of an important acid is acid rain. Acid rain occurs when fossil fuels are burned, which releases oxides of sulfur and nitrogen into the air. These compounds then form acids when they dissolve in rain.

A compound that produces *hydroxide* (hy DRAHK syd) *ions* (OH^-) when dissolved in water is called a **base.** In the dry state, many bases are ionic compounds. Sodium hydroxide (NaOH) is one example. This is a solid compound made of sodium and hydroxide ions. When it is dissolved in water, it separates into its ions:

$$NaOH \longrightarrow Na^+ + OH^-$$

Neutralization

When solutions of an acid and a base are mixed, a reaction takes place. The hydrogen ions from the acid combine with the hydroxide ions from the base to form molecules of water:

$$H^+ + OH^- \longrightarrow HOH \text{ (or } H_2O)$$

If the quantities of acid and base are right, all the H^+ ions and the OH^- ions will combine, and there will be no excess of either one in the solution. The solution will be neither an acid nor a base. When

◀ **Figure 3–20**
Effects of Acid Rain. The damage to this leaf was caused by acid rain.

this occurs, the solution is said to be neutral. The process of reacting an acid and a base to produce a neutral solution is called **neutralization** (noo truh luh ZAY shun).

Acids and bases are both caustic. That is, in concentrated solutions, they can damage both living tissue and nonliving material. The best first-aid treatment for an acid or base spill is to flush the spill with water and consult a doctor. When an acid or base is accidentally spilled on nonliving matter, it can be neutralized. An acid can be neutralized with a base. A base can be neutralized with an acid.

Salts

When an acid and a base react, their hydrogen and hydroxide combine to form water molecules. This reaction removes these two ions from the solution. That is, they are no longer present as separate ions. However, the negative ions of the acid and the positive ions of the base are still present. For example, when hydrochloric acid reacts with sodium hydroxide, sodium and chloride ions remain in the solution. In other words, the neutralization reaction produces a solution of sodium and chloride ions.

$$HCl + NaOH \longrightarrow Na^+ + Cl^- + HOH$$

Solid sodium chloride can be obtained from the solution by evaporating the water.

The ionic compound produced by the neutralization reaction between an acid and a base is called a **salt.** Sodium chloride, or table salt, is actually only one of many different salts that can be formed by a neutralization reaction. Most of the substances in food that are called minerals are salts. Salts provide many essential ions for body processes.

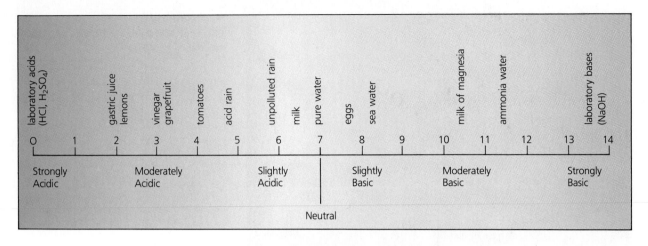

▲ **Figure 3–21**

The pH Scale. Each change of 1 unit on this scale is a change of 10 times in the hydrogen ion concentration. For example, a solution with a pH of 4 has 10 times as many hydrogen ions as a solution with a pH of 5.

Figure 3–22

Indicators. Phenolphthalein is an indicator that changes from colorless to red in moderately basic solutions. ▼

The pH Scale

We have said that water is the molecular compound, H_2O. However, at any given moment a small fraction of the molecules in water are broken into hydrogen and hydroxide ions:

$$H_2O \longrightarrow H^+ + OH^-$$

Since each water molecule produces 1 hydrogen ion and 1 hydroxide ion, there will be equal numbers of these ions in pure water. Water is therefore neutral because it has no excess of either H^+ or OH^- ions.

When an acid is dissolved in water, the concentration of H^+ ions increases. This means that in acid solutions, the H^+ concentration is greater than it is in pure water.

When a base is dissolved in water, the concentration of OH^- ions increases. These excess OH^- ions will react with the H^+ ions already present in the water. In doing so, they form additional molecules of water. This, in turn, reduces the concentration of H^+ ions. As a result, the H^+ concentration in basic solutions is less than it is in water.

The H^+ concentration is indicated by a unit of measure called **pH.** The pH scale has been set up in such a way that high concentrations of H^+ (acid solutions) have low values of pH. See Figure 3–21. Low concentrations of H^+ (basic solutions) have high pH values. The pH scale runs from 0 (highly acidic) to 14 (highly basic). A neutral solution has a pH of 7. This is the pH of pure water.

Whether a solution is acidic or basic can be shown by indicators. An **indicator** is a substance that changes color when the pH goes above or below a certain value. *Litmus* (LIT mus) *paper,* for example, turns red when the pH is moderately acidic (below 5); it turns blue when the pH is slightly basic (above 8). *Methyl orange* changes from yellow to red in moderately acidic solutions (pH below 3). *Phenolphthalein* (feen ul THAL leen) changes from colorless to red in moderately basic solutions (pH above 10). See Figure 3–22.

◀ **Figure 3–23**
Soil Chemistry. Soil can be acidic, neutral, or basic. Most plants grow best in soil that has a pH between 6 and 7. However, some plants, such as blueberries, flourish in acidic soil that has a pH of about 5.

Indicators can show whether a solution is acid or basic. They do not, however, tell the actual value of the pH. There are special indicator papers that can be used to find pH more closely. This is done by wetting the paper with the solution and comparing the color of the indicator paper with a chart. These papers will determine pH within a few tenths of a unit. More accurate measurements can be made with pH meters. These work by measuring the electrical properties of the solution.

If you are a gardener, you probably know that the pH of the soil must be right for the plants you want to grow in your garden. See Figure 3–23. The pH levels of body tissues are also important for the body's activities. For example, the contents of the stomach must be slightly acid for digestion to take place normally. Keeping the pH at the correct levels in different parts of the body is a part of homeostasis.

3-4 Section Review

1. When acids are dissolved in water, what positive ion is produced in excess?
2. When bases are dissolved in water, an excess of which negative ion is produced?
3. What substances are formed from the reaction of an acid and a base?
4. What would be the pH of a neutral solution? An acid solution? A basic solution?

Critical Thinking

5. You are given a solution with a pH of 9. Predict the color produced after adding some of this solution to litmus paper. To phenolphthalein? To methyl orange? (*Predicting*)

Laboratory
Investigation

An Investigation of pH

You can determine whether a solution is acidic, basic, or neutral by using an indicator. An indicator is a substance that changes color when the pH goes above or below a certain value. In this investigation, you will use pH indicators to measure the pH of various substances. From this information, you will classify each substance as acidic, basic, or neutral.

Problem

How can you **classify** common substances as acidic, basic, or neutral?

Materials (per group)

- white vinegar
- fresh milk
- boiled water
- lemon juice
- apple juice
- cola
- ammonia
- bleach
- shampoo
- litmus paper
- wide-range pH paper
- distilled water
- test tubes
- medicine droppers
- graduated cylinder
- paper towel
- stirring rod

Procedure

1. Tear off nine 1-cm strips of litmus paper. Space the strips evenly along the length of a paper towel.

2. Place a single drop of each substance on a strip of litmus paper. Record whether the substance is acidic, basic, or neutral in a data table similar to Data Table 1.
   CAUTION: *Do not mix ammonia and bleach.*

3. Test the same substances again using wide-range pH paper. Determine the pH of each substance by matching the color of the test paper with the reference color chart. Record the pH in Data Table 1.

4. Pour 1 mL of ammonia into a test tube. Using wide-range pH paper, find the pH. Record the pH in a data table similar to Data Table 2. Add vinegar, one drop at a time. After each drop, mix well, test the pH, and record it. Stop when the pH reaches 7.

5. Label two clean test tubes A and B. Pour 2 mL of milk into each test tube. Add six drops of distilled water, one drop at a time, to test tube A. After each drop, mix well and record any change. Using vinegar, repeat the procedure with test tube B.

Observations

Data Table 1		
Substance	**Litmus Paper (acidic, basic, or neutral)**	**pH Paper (pH)**
White vinegar		
Fresh milk		
Boiled water		
Lemon juice		
Apple juice		
Cola		
Ammonia		
Bleach		
Shampoo		

Data Table 2	
Drops of Vinegar	**pH of Ammonia**
0	
1	

1. Which of the nine substances you tested are acidic? Which are basic?

2. Which of the substances are neutral?

Analysis and Conclusions

1. Did the results using wide-range pH paper agree with the results using litmus paper? What additional information did the wide-range pH paper provide?

2. What happened to the pH of the ammonia as acid was added to it? Explain the results in terms of the chemical reaction that occurred.

3. Predict what would happen to the pH of the ammonia-vinegar solution if you continued to add acid to the test tube.

4. In step 5, what problem was being investigated? What was the variable? What served as the control? What can you conclude from the results?

5. In living things, pH is maintained within a narrow range. Based on your results, why is this an important aspect of homeostasis?

Extensions

Using the same procedure as in the laboratory investigation, determine the pH of various sources of water and rainwater. Explain the differences and similarities that you find.

Chapter ③ Review

Study Outline

3-1 Atomic Theory of Matter

▶ Matter is divided into elements and compounds.

▶ The nucleus of the atom contains neutrons, which have no charge, and protons, which are positively charged. Electrons, found outside the nucleus, are negatively charged.

▶ The atomic number is the number of protons in the nucleus. The mass number equals the sum of an atom's protons and neutrons.

▶ Electrons are found outside of the nucleus in clouds of different energy levels.

▶ Isotopes are varieties of the same element that have the same number of protons but different numbers of neutrons.

▶ Radioisotopes have unstable nuclei that emit charged particles and radiation.

3-2 Chemical Bonding and Chemical Reactions

▶ An atom can form a chemical bond if its outermost energy level is unfilled. There are two types of chemical bonds—ionic bonds and covalent bonds.

▶ Diatomic molecules form when a covalent bond joins two atoms of the same element.

▶ In a chemical formula for a compound, each element is represented by its chemical symbol. The subscripts in the formula give the proportions of each element.

▶ A chemical equation represents the results of a chemical reaction. In a chemical reaction, matter is neither created nor destroyed.

3-3 Mixtures

▶ Mixtures contain substances that are physically mixed but are not chemically bonded to each other.

▶ There are three types of mixtures: solutions, suspensions, and colloidal dispersions.

3-4 Acids, Bases, and Salts

▶ Acids release excess hydrogen ions (H^+) in solutions. Bases release excess hydroxide ions (OH^-) when dissolved in water. A neutralization reaction results when an acid and a base react together to form a salt and water.

▶ The hydrogen ion concentration of a solution is measured in units on the pH scale. Acids have a pH less than 7; bases have a pH greater than 7.

Chapter Assessment

Multiple Choice

Choose the letter of the answer that best completes each statement or answers the question.

1. Unstable isotopes that emit charged particles are known as (a) compounds. (b) diatomic molecules. (c) ions. (d) radioactive.

2. A pH greater than 7 represents a(n) (a) element. (b) base. (c) acid. (d) salt.

3. Varieties of an element that differ only in the number of neutrons are (a) neutrons. (b) ions. (c) molecules. (d) isotopes.

4. When a chlorine atom gains an electron, it becomes (a) an ion. (b) diatomic. (c) a molecule. (d) an isotope.

5. A mixture in which particles settle to the bottom is called a (a) colloidal dispersion. (b) suspension. (c) solution. (d) solute.

6. Excess hydrogen ions are produced in solution by (a) acids. (b) bases. (c) salts. (d) mixtures.

7. In a neutral atom, the number of protons in the nucleus equals the number of (a) electrons. (b) ions. (c) neutrons. (d) molecules.

8. A covalent bond is formed as the result of the (a) transfer of electrons. (b) transfer of protons. (c) sharing of an electron pair. (d) sharing of a proton pair.

9. In chemical reactions, atoms are (a) created. (b) destroyed. (c) rearranged. (d) neutralized.

10. In the chemical reaction in which hydrogen and oxygen combine to form water, hydrogen is a(n) (a) product. (b) reactant. (c) salt. (d) isotope.

Content Review

Answer each of the following in complete sentences.

11. How can you determine chemically whether a substance is an element or a compound?

12. Explain why electrons determine an atom's chemical properties.

13. What is the pH scale?

14. What changes occur to a radioactive isotope?

15. Describe a covalent bond.

16. Explain what happens when an ionic bond forms between magnesium (atomic number: 12) and oxygen (atomic number: 8).

17. What happens when a molecular substance dissolves in a liquid?

18. What happens when an ionic compound dissolves in a liquid?

19. How does a colloid dispersion differ from a suspension?

20. What color is litmus paper if the pH is above 8? What color will it turn if the pH is below 5?

Graphic Organizing

For information on graphic organizers, see Appendix G at the back of this text.

21. **Scale** Copy the scale below onto a separate sheet of paper. Add the following elements to the scale (the mass number is indicated by the superscript): carbon (^{12}C), nitrogen (^{14}N), sodium (^{23}Na), phosphorus (^{31}P), sulfur (^{32}S), chlorine (^{35}Cl), and potassium (^{39}K).

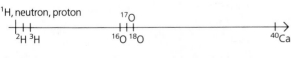

Low Mass Number   High Mass Number

Critical Thinking and Problem Solving

Discuss each of the following in a brief paragraph.

22. **Comparing** How are the atoms of different elements alike? How do they differ?

23. **Classifying** Acids produce excess H^+ ions in water. Bases, on the other hand, produce excess OH^- ions in solution. Which of the following are likely to be acids? Which are probably bases? HBr, LiOH, HCl, HNO_3, H_2SO_4, NH_4OH, NaOH, $Zn(OH)_2$.

24. **Predicting** Suppose a person's stomach wall were irritated by an oversecretion of stomach acid. What would happen to the pH in the stomach if the person drank milk of magnesia (a basic solution)? Explain your answer.

25. **Experimenting** Using radioisotopes to monitor the flow of water, design a controlled experiment to test the following hypothesis: The flow of water in plants is faster in narrower branches than in thicker branches. What should be the variable in your experiment? What response should be measured? What factors should be held constant?

26. **Interpreting** To study the structure of atoms, Ernest Rutherford did the experiment shown in the diagram below. He bombarded a thin sheet of metal foil with tiny, subatomic particles. He found that most of the particles passed through the metal foil without seeming to have any effect on it. However, a few of the particles bounced back. What did his results tell him about the structure of the atom?

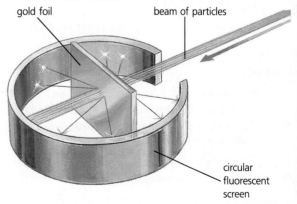

55

Discovery Learning Activity

Enzyme Action

1. Working in a group, count out 200 wooden toothpicks.

2. Designate one member of your group to act as a timer. When the "timer" says go, the rest of the group should begin to break all of the toothpicks in half. When all the toothpicks are broken, the "timer" will stop the clock.

3. Record how long it took the group to break all of the toothpicks. Report the time to the rest of the class.

4. Graph the class data, with the number of students in a given group on the X axis and the time it took to break the toothpicks on the Y axis.

Chemical Compounds of Life

Chapter 4

·············· Guide for Reading ··············

Previewing the Chapter

What does the photograph on the opposite page look like to you? To some people it might resemble an abstract painting or a stained-glass window. Actually, it is a highly magnified photograph of crystals of the hormone progesterone, a lipid. What exactly is a lipid? Why is this particular lipid—progesterone—important to the life processes of living things? What are some other biologically important compounds found in living things?

Key Words

amino acid, carbohydrate, catalyst, coenzyme, DNA, enzyme, lipid, nucleic acid, protein, RNA

Key Concepts

- **Describe** the importance of water to living things.
- **Identify** the compounds that make up living things.
- **Describe** the importance of enzymes.
- **Draw a conclusion** about the effects of enzymes by performing a controlled experiment. (Laboratory Investigation)

4-1 Biologically Important Compounds

Section Objectives:

- *Compare* organic and inorganic compounds.
- *Define* the terms *polar molecule, cohesion,* and *adhesion.*
- *Explain* why organic compounds are usually larger and more complex than inorganic compounds.
- *Name* the four major types of organic compounds found in living cells.

Organic and Inorganic Compounds

Every chemical compound is either an organic compound or an inorganic compound. All **organic compounds** contain the element carbon. Most organic compounds occur naturally only in living organisms or in their products, although many of them can be produced in chemistry laboratories. In addition to carbon, most organic compounds contain hydrogen, and many contain either oxygen or nitrogen, or both. Less frequently, the elements phosphorus, sulfur, iron, calcium, sodium, chlorine, magnesium, and potassium are found in organic compounds. Thus, of the 92 elements found in nature, only a few appear in organic compounds.

▲ **Figure 4–1**

Crystals of Sulfur. Of the more than 90 elements found in nature, only a few, such as sulfur, appear in organic compounds.

◀ These progesterone crystals have been magnified 20 X.

Every compound that is not an organic compound is an **inorganic compound.** Usually, inorganic compounds do not contain carbon. Carbon dioxide (CO_2) and other carbonate compounds like calcium carbonate ($CaCO_3$) are exceptions. Living organisms contain inorganic compounds as well as organic compounds. Water, carbon dioxide, various salts, and inorganic bases and acids are some of the inorganic compounds that are commonly found in living things.

At one time, people believed that there was something special about the chemistry of life. Many chemists were sure that the substances found in living things could not be made in a laboratory. Today, we know that all the chemical changes in living cells can be explained by the same principles that apply to chemistry in a test tube. The only difference is that most of the compounds in living cells are enormously complex. The reactions among these compounds are also complicated.

Water—An Important Inorganic Compound

Of all the inorganic compounds found in living things, water is the most important. All living organisms need water to survive, and most organisms contain water. About 65 percent of your body weight is water. People have been known to survive for weeks without food but only a few days without water. Water is essential because many biological processes can take place only in water solutions. The properties of water, which are discussed below, will help you to understand the way living things function.

Cohesion   As you read in Chapter 3, the oxygen atom in a water molecule shares a pair of electrons with each of the hydrogen atoms. But, as you can see from Figure 4–2, the electrons are not shared equally. Because oxygen has a stronger attraction for electrons than hydrogen does, the electrons are held closer to the oxygen atom. As a result, the oxygen end of a water molecule has a partial negative charge. The hydrogen end has a partial positive charge.

A molecule with regions of partial negative and partial positive charges is called a **polar molecule.** Because opposite charges attract each other, the negative end of one polar molecule will be attracted to the positive end of another polar molecule. This force of attraction between molecules of the same substance is called **cohesion** (koh HEE zhun).

It is the cohesion between water molecules that holds a drop of water together. Cohesion also explains why water can store heat better than most other liquids. When water is heated, the water molecules move faster and faster as the temperature rises. But, the molecules can move faster only if the cohesion that holds the molecules together is overcome. Therefore, some of the heat that is applied to the water will raise the temperature, but much of the heat must be used to overcome the cohesion. As a result, water is able to

▲ **Figure 4–2**
Water—A Polar Molecule. The oxygen end of the water molecule has a partial negative charge. The hydrogen end of the molecule has a positive charge.

absorb a great deal of heat without undergoing an abrupt change in temperature. This ability to store heat protects organisms from damaging changes in temperature. For example, if you become overheated, your body responds to this situation by producing sweat. As the sweat evaporates, the water in it absorbs heat from your body. Thus, the evaporation of sweat cools you by removing heat from your body.

Adhesion   The attraction between the molecules of one substance and the molecules of another substance is called **adhesion** (ad HEE zhun). Water adheres well to many substances because of its polar molecules. Adhesion makes water one of the best solvents. Water can dissolve most polar substances because the adhesion between the water molecules and the polar solute molecules is greater than the cohesion among the solute molecules. For example, HCl (a polar molecule) dissolves easily in water, but O_2 (a nonpolar molecule) does not. Water also can dissolve most ionic compounds.

The adhesion between water molecules and glass molecules is particularly strong. If you were to put two dry, glass slides together and then dip their ends into water, the water would be drawn up between the two slides. See Figure 4–3. This action is called **capillary action,** or **capillarity.**

Adhesion and cohesion both play important roles in the transport of water in plants. These forces help water to rise up through the roots into the plant. You will be reading more about this process in Chapter 19.

▲ **Figure 4–3**
Capillary Action. Water rises between the glass slides because of the adhesion between water and glass.

Structure and Types of Organic Compounds

The big difference between organic compounds and inorganic compounds lies in the greater size and complexity of many organic molecules. Organic molecules are often larger and more complex than inorganic molecules. This is because of the electron structure of the carbon atoms they contain.

A carbon atom has 6 electrons. As you can see in Figure 4–4, 2 of these electrons occupy the first energy level, which leaves 4 electrons for the second level. This means that the carbon atom can fill its outer energy level by forming 4 covalent bonds with other atoms. One electron in each bond comes from the carbon atom. The other electron comes from another atom bonded to the carbon. The atoms bonded to a carbon atom can be other carbon atoms. These atoms may be bonded into long chains. A long chain may have other groups of chains of atoms branching from it. Carbon atoms may also be bonded into rings with side branches or bonded with other rings. The possible size and variety of these arrangements is unlimited.

In many cases, the bond that is formed by the carbon atoms present in organic compounds is a double bond. That is, there are two bonds between the same pair of atoms. In a few cases, a pair of

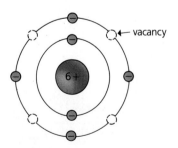

▲ **Figure 4–4**
Structure of the Carbon Atom. The four vacancies in the outer energy level allow a carbon atom to form four covalent bonds. This special characteristic accounts for the great variety of organic compounds.

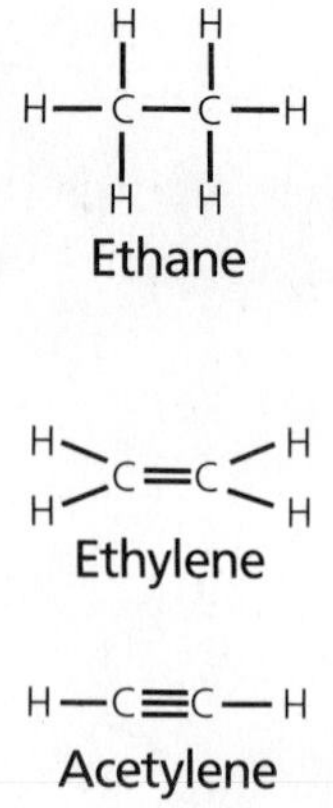

Ethane

Ethylene

Acetylene

▲ **Figure 4–5**

Bonds Between Carbon Atoms. Carbon atoms can form single bonds (top), double bonds (middle), or triple bonds (bottom).

carbon atoms may be joined by a triple bond. Figure 4–5 provides several simple examples of possible single, double, and triple carbon-to-carbon bonds.

Although there are many organic compounds, they can be classified into a fairly small number of types. Four types of organic compounds will be discussed in this chapter—carbohydrates, lipids, nucleic acids, and proteins.

4-1 Section Review

1. In what ways is an organic compound different from an inorganic compound?
2. What four elements are most often found in organic compounds?
3. Which end of the water molecule is positively charged? Which end is negatively charged?
4. How many covalent bonds can a carbon atom form?

Critical Thinking

5. Compare the following compounds and classify them into three groups: organic, inorganic, not sure. Explain all "not sure" answers. (*Classifying*)

C_2H_6 NaOH C_2H_5OH Fe_2O_3 HCl   CO $C_{18}H_{36}O_2$

4-2 Carbohydrates and Lipids

Section Objectives:

- *Describe* the basic chemical makeup of carbohydrates.
- *Explain* the relationship between dehydration synthesis and hydrolysis.
- *Describe* how a fat is formed by dehydration synthesis.
- *Explain* the relationship between saturated fats, cholesterol, and circulatory disorders.

Carbohydrates

Carbohydrates (kar boh HY drayts) are compounds of carbon, hydrogen, and oxygen. Carbohydrates have the same ratio of hydrogen to oxygen as water has (2 atoms of hydrogen for every 1 atom of oxygen). The simplest carbohydrates are the simple sugars, or **monosaccharides** (mahn uh SAK uh ryds). The most common monosaccharides have the chemical formula, $C_6H_{12}O_6$. However, these atoms can be arranged in several different structures, each corresponding to a different sugar. Figure 4–6 shows the structural formulas of three simple sugars. Simple sugars with 5 carbons ($C_5H_{10}O_5$) and 4 carbons ($C_4H_8O_4$) also exist. The chemical names of the sugars always end in *-ose*.

The sugars are important because they contain large amounts of energy. This energy can be released in the presence of oxygen by breaking the sugars down to carbon dioxide and water. Nearly all organisms use glucose as a source of energy.

Dehydration Synthesis   Sugar molecules can be bonded together by a process called **dehydration synthesis** (dee hy DRAY shun SIN thuh sis). *Synthesis* means "putting together" and *dehydration* means "removing water." Thus, dehydration synthesis means "putting together by removing water." When sugar molecules are bonded together, the bond forms where an OH group is present in each molecule. At this point, 1 OH combines with the H from the other OH, forming a molecule of water. The 2 molecules are then joined through the remaining O. See Figure 4–7. In living cells, dehydration synthesis is brought about by the action of *enzymes,* which are discussed on page 68. It is an important process in making the many complex organic compounds that an organism needs.

The molecule formed by joining two simple sugars is called a double sugar, or **disaccharide** (dy SAK uh ryd). The disaccharide formed by the dehydration synthesis shown in Figure 4–7 is maltose. When several simple sugars are joined by dehydration synthesis, they form **polysaccharides** (pahl ee SAK uh ryds), or long chains of repeating sugar units. Large molecules consisting of chains of repeating units are called **polymers** (PAHL uh merz). The polysaccharides are sugar polymers. The largest polysaccharides may contain hundreds or thousands of sugar units.

Organisms store excess sugar in the form of polysaccharides. In plants, this form of stored sugar is called **starch.** Starch is found in seeds and in roots and stems specialized for food storage. In humans, surplus sugar is stored in the liver as the polysaccharide *glycogen* (GLY kuh jen), sometimes called "animal starch." Other types of polysaccharides form the tough structural parts of organisms. For example, *cellulose* (SEL yuh lohs) is a polysaccharide found in plants. *Chitin* (KYT un) is a polysaccharide that makes up the shells of insects.

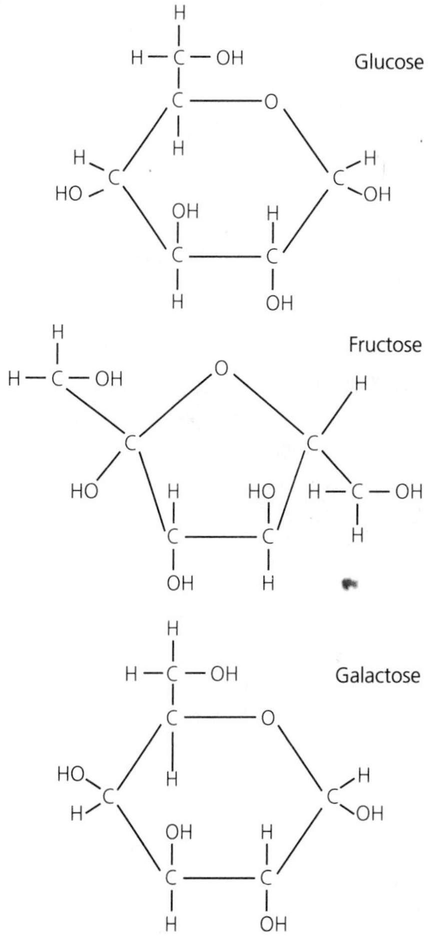

▲ **Figure 4–6**
Structure of Three Simple Sugars. Glucose, fructose, and galactose have the same chemical formula ($C_6H_{12}O_6$), but their atoms are arranged differently.

Figure 4–7
Dehydration Synthesis. In dehydration synthesis, two simple molecules bond together to form a more complex molecule. In this process, one or more molecules of water are released. ▼

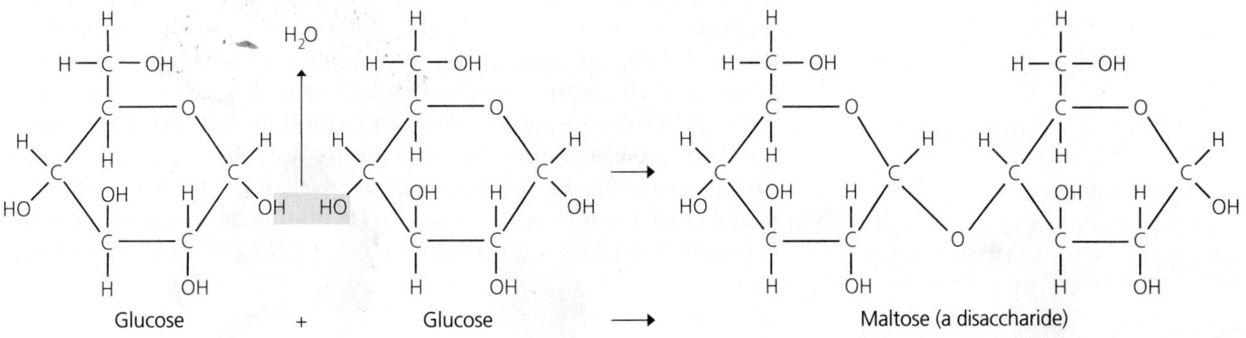

Glucose   +   Glucose   ⟶   Maltose (a disaccharide)

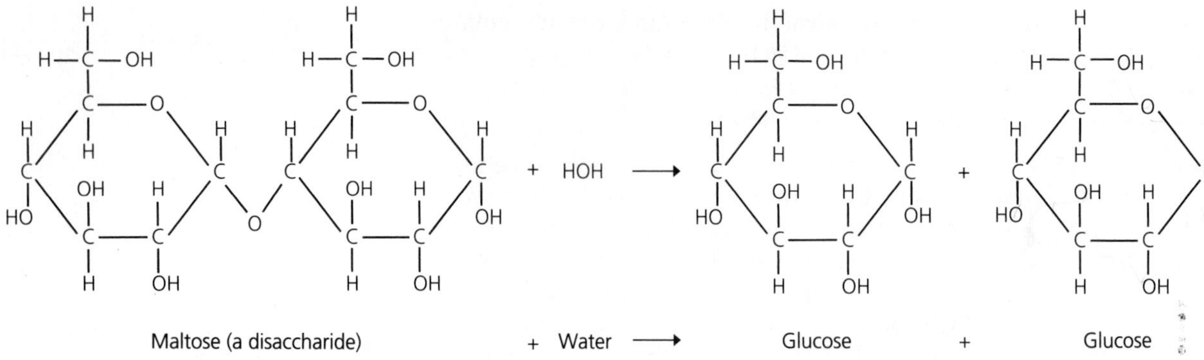

Maltose (a disaccharide) + Water ⟶ Glucose + Glucose

▲ **Figure 4–8**

Hydrolysis. A complex molecule can be broken down into simpler molecules by the addition of a water molecule. Hydrolysis is the most common process used by organisms to change organic compounds into usable forms.

Hydrolysis Disaccharides and polysaccharides may be broken apart by a process called **hydrolysis** (hy DRAHL uh sis). As Figure 4–8 shows, in this type of reaction, a water molecule reacts with a chain of sugar molecules to produce two simpler sugars. When hydrolysis occurs, a bond between two simple sugars is broken, and the original OH groups are restored. Hydrolysis can be repeated on long chains until an entire polysaccharide has been split into its simple sugars. In living organisms, the process of hydrolysis, like dehydration synthesis, is brought about by the action of different enzymes.

Lipids

Lipids (LIP idz) include the substances commonly called fats, oils, and waxes. Like carbohydrates, lipids are made of carbon, hydrogen, and oxygen. However, there is less oxygen in lipids than in carbohydrates. Lipids are a part of cell structures and serve as a reserve energy supply in an organism. Lipids furnish about twice as much energy as the same amount of carbohydrates.

Fats and oils are chemically similar. Unlike fats, however, oils remain liquid at room temperature. Plants store oils in seeds. Some familiar oils are peanut oil, corn oil, and castor oil. Mammals store fat under the skin. There, it cushions the body and helps to stop heat loss. Although fats in animals are storage products, they are not stored for long. Instead, they are constantly broken down and replaced. Investigations have shown that mice, for example, replace about one-half of their stored fat each week.

The Formation of Lipids Waxes are lipids formed by the combination of fatty acids with compounds that are similar to glycerol. Fats and oils, on the other hand, are formed when fatty acids combine with glycerol. Glycerol is a simple 3-carbon chain with an OH group bonded to each carbon. A **fatty acid** molecule has two parts: a chain of carbon atoms to which hydrogen atoms are bonded and a **carboxyl** (kar BAHK sul) **group.** The carboxyl group consists of 1 carbon atom that is bonded to 1 oxygen atom by a double bond and to an OH group. Figure 4–9 shows a typical fatty acid.

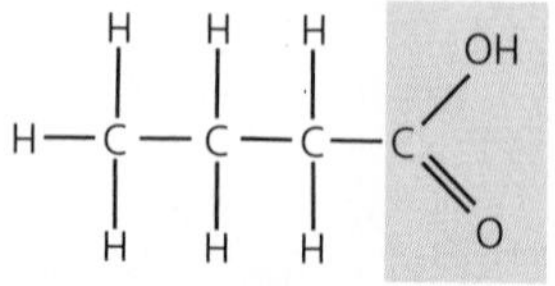

▲ **Figure 4–9**

Structure of a Fatty Acid. A fatty acid consists of a chain of carbon and hydrogen atoms with a carboxyl group at one end.

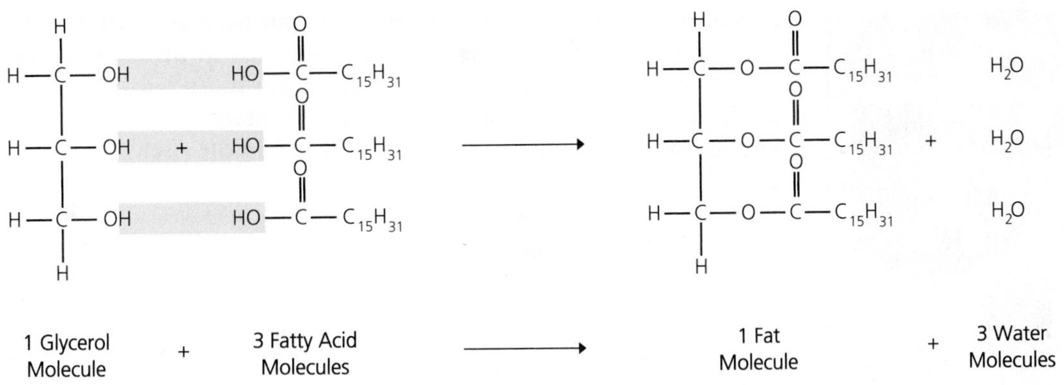

$$1 \text{ Glycerol Molecule} + 3 \text{ Fatty Acid Molecules} \longrightarrow 1 \text{ Fat Molecule} + 3 \text{ Water Molecules}$$

▲ **Figure 4–10**

Synthesis of a Fat. A molecule of fat is formed by the dehydration synthesis of three fatty acid molecules and one glycerol molecule.

As you can see in Figure 4–10, the dehydration synthesis of 3 fatty acid molecules and 1 glycerol molecule produces 1 molecule of fat or oil. When glycerol reacts with the 3 fatty acids, each fatty acid becomes attached to the glycerol molecule at one of the OH groups. In this dehydration synthesis, 3 molecules of water are released for each molecule of fat or oil that is formed.

Saturated and Unsaturated Fats   When all the carbon-to-carbon bonds in a fatty acid are single bonds, the acid is said to be saturated. Fats that are formed from fatty acids with single carbon-to-carbon bonds are called **saturated** (SATCH uh rayt ed) **fats.** In **unsaturated fats,** one or more pairs of carbon atoms in the fatty acid molecules are joined together by a double bond or even a triple bond. A fat that has chains with more than one double or triple bond is called *polyunsaturated*. A typical unsaturated fatty acid is shown in Figure 4–11.

In a saturated fatty acid, each carbon atom along the chain is bonded to 2 hydrogen atoms. (The carbon at the start of the chain is bonded to 3 hydrogens.) An unsaturated acid of the same length will have fewer hydrogen atoms. Unsaturated fats can be changed to saturated fats by adding hydrogen to them. This process is called *hydrogenation* (hy drahj uh NAY shun). Many processed foods contain partially hydrogenated fats.

There is an easy way to tell what kind of fats you are eating. Unsaturated fats tend to be oils; that is, they are liquid at room temperature. Saturated fats usually are solid.

There is evidence that saturated fats, such as those found in animal products like butter and meat, tend to increase the amount of cholesterol produced in the body. **Cholesterol** (kuh LES tuh rohl) is an essential compound, found in most animal tissues. However, it also plays an important part in the buildup of deposits that harden

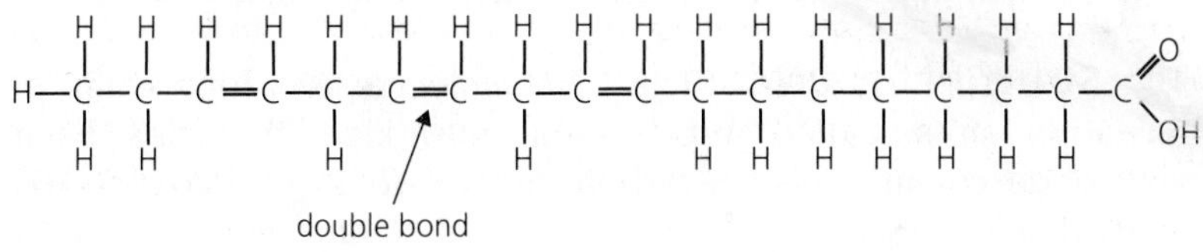

double bond

◀ **Figure 4–11**

Structure of an Unsaturated Fatty Acid. An unsaturated fatty acid contains at least one double or triple carbon-carbon bond.

Biology and You

Q: I am a healthy, active teenager who is not overweight. Several times a week, my friends and I stop by a fast-food restaurant for hamburgers, fries, and shakes. My parents say that this is not good for me. Is it doing me any harm?

A: It may be. Fast-food meals are usually low in certain vitamins and minerals and high in fat, salt, and calories.

Diets high in fat and salt have been linked to heart disease and certain cancers in later years. Fried foods are especially high in cholesterol. Extra cholesterol can collect in your bloodstream and can eventually block the arteries to your heart, causing major heart problems. Because cholesterol starts to build up early in life, you need to limit your cholesterol intake even as a teenager.

Regarding calories, a typical fast-food meal (cheeseburger, fries, and a shake) provides as many as 1000 calories. Eating these meals can result in a gradual weight gain. Once growth has stopped and a taste for these foods has formed, the extra pounds are difficult to lose.

■ **List some ways that people can eat more nutritiously when eating at fast-food restaurants.**

and narrow the arteries. This condition can lead to heart attacks and strokes. Unsaturated fats, like those found in plant products, tend to decrease blood cholesterol levels. For these reasons, many medical authorities recommend a reduced intake of saturated fats and an increased intake of unsaturated fats in the diet.

4-2 Section Review

1. What is a monosaccharide, and how can two monosaccharides combine to form a larger molecule?
2. How are the complex sugar molecules broken apart?
3. What substances are commonly called lipids?
4. How is a fat formed from glycerol and a fatty acid?

Critical Thinking

5. Use what you know about carbohydrates and lipids to group the following compounds: (*Classifying*)

$$C_{12}H_{24}O_2 \quad C_6H_{12}O_6 \quad C_{10}H_{18}O_2 \quad C_{12}H_{22}O_{11}$$

4-3 Nucleic Acids and Proteins

Section Objectives:

- *Describe* where the two types of nucleic acids are found and give the functions of these acids.
- *Compare* the structures of DNA and RNA.
- *Illustrate* the general molecular structure of an amino acid.
- *Describe* a peptide bond and explain the difference between a polypeptide and a protein.

Nucleic Acids

Nucleic (noo KLAY ik) **acids** are compounds that contain phosphorous and nitrogen in addition to carbon, hydrogen, and oxygen. There are two kinds of nucleic acids. One is called **DNA**—*deoxyribonucleic* (dee AHK see ry boh noo KLAY ik) *acid.* The other is called **RNA**—*ribonucleic* (ry boh noo KLAY ik) *acid.* These substances were first found in the part of the cell called the nucleus. DNA is the hereditary material that is passed on from one generation to the next during reproduction. As you will learn in Chapter 26, working with RNA, DNA directs and controls the development and activities of all the cells in an organism.

The Structure of DNA   The DNA molecule is a long chain of repeating units, called **nucleotides** (NOO klee uh tyds). Each nucleotide consists of a 5-carbon sugar (*ribose* or *deoxyribose*) bonded to a *phosphate* group (PO_4) and a *nitrogenous base*. A nitrogenous base is an organic base that contains nitrogen. There are only four nitrogenous bases in a DNA molecule. They are *adenine* (AD uh neen), *thymine* (THY meen), *cytosine* (SYT uh seen), and *guanine* (GWAH neen). In any particular pair of bases, an adenine is always bonded to a thymine. A cytosine is always bonded to a guanine. These four bases can be attached in any sequence along the length of the molecule.

As you can see in Figure 4–12a, the shape of the DNA molecule resembles the shape of a ladder—two sides connected to each other by rungs. Each side of the molecule is a chain of nucleotides. The bases act like the rungs of the ladder, bonding together the nucleotides on each side. Notice that each "rung" consists of two, and only two, bases. In human cells, a single DNA molecule may have as many as 3 billion pairs of these bases. As you will learn in Chapter 26, the sequence of bases acts as a code that determines what proteins will be made in the cell. In turn, the proteins determine the nature and activities of the cell.

The entire DNA molecule is coiled into the form called a double helix (HEE liks). See Figure 4–12b. The double helix is coiled upon itself many times. A human DNA molecule would be about four centimeters long if it were stretched out in a straight line. Repeated coilings enable it to fit into tiny structures in the cell.

The Structure of RNA   Although an RNA molecule is similar in chemical composition to DNA, it has certain differences. The RNA molecule consists of only one chain, or strand, of bases. The sugar in RNA is ribose, not deoxyribose. The base thymine is replaced by *uracil* (YOOR uh sil). RNA is involved in protein synthesis.

a.

b.

Double Helix

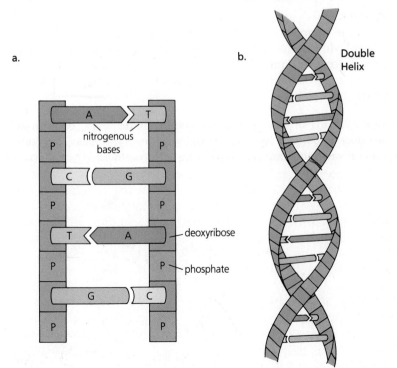

nitrogenous bases

deoxyribose

phosphate

◄ **Figure 4–12**

DNA Molecule. The nitrogenous bases in DNA bond together, adenine (A) with thymine (T) and cytosine (C) with guanine (G). The side chains are formed of alternating deoxyribose and phosphate groups (P). The entire molecule is coiled in a shape called a double helix.

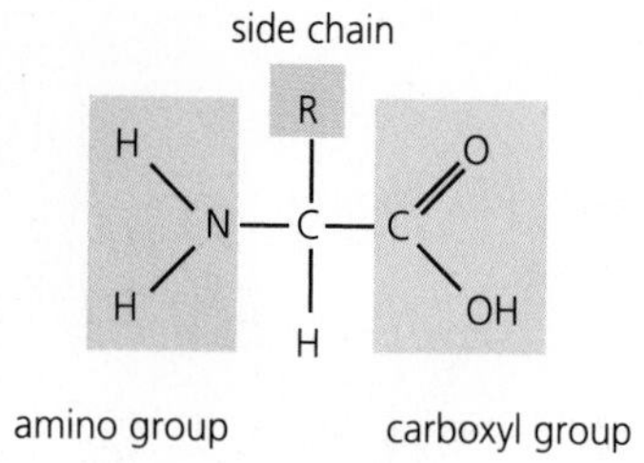

side chain

amino group   carboxyl group

▲ **Figure 4–13**

Structure of an Amino Acid. The side chains of the 20 amino acids give each its special chemical properties.

Proteins

Proteins (PROH teenz) are compounds that contain nitrogen as well as carbon, hydrogen, and oxygen. Some proteins also contain sulfur and phosphorus. The number of possible proteins is virtually unlimited. Proteins have an astonishing range of properties. The reasons for this variety will become clear when you look at the way in which proteins are formed.

Proteins make life possible in its present degree of complexity. You can begin to understand the importance of proteins when you realize that they are found throughout living organisms. There are proteins in the structural parts of cells and body tissues, such as cartilage, bones, and muscles. There are proteins in hormones, the chemical messengers that regulate body functions in plants and animals. There also are proteins in antibodies, the substances that protect animals against disease organisms. Even enzymes, which allow complex chemical reactions to take place are proteins.

To understand how proteins do all this and much more, you need to understand their chemical makeup and structure.

Amino Acids   **Amino** (uh MEE noh) **acids** are the structural units of proteins. As you can see in Figure 4–13, an amino acid is a simple compound. It consists of a central carbon atom to which are bonded

- 1 carboxyl group (COOH)
- 1 **amino group** (NH_2)
- 1 hydrogen atom
- 1 side chain, symbolized by the letter R, which is different in each amino acid.

In the simplest amino acid, glycine, the side chain is just another H. In alanine, it is a CH_3 group. While other side chains may be more complex, none of the amino acid molecules is especially large. There are 20 different amino acids that are commonly found as parts of proteins.

The Peptide Bond   As you can see in Figure 4–14, two amino acids may be bonded together by dehydration synthesis. The bond forms between the amino group of one amino acid and the carboxyl

Figure 4–14

Formation of a Peptide Bond. In this dehydration synthesis reaction, a peptide bond forms between two amino acids. The resulting molecule is a dipeptide. ▼

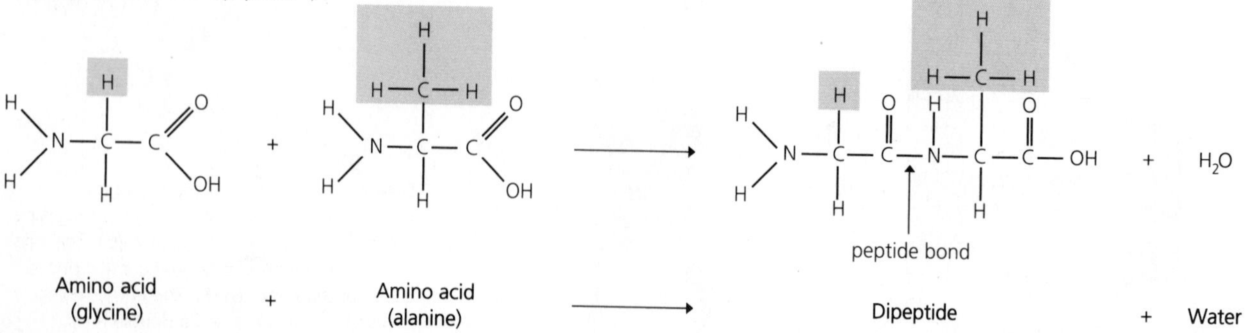

Amino acid
(glycine)   +   Amino acid
(alanine)   ⟶   Dipeptide   +   Water

peptide bond

group of the other, with the resulting loss of 1 water molecule. The bond between two amino acids is called a **peptide** (PEP tyd) **bond.** The resulting molecule is called a **dipeptide.** (dy PEP tyd).

Amino acids can be added to either end of a dipeptide by dehydration synthesis. In this way, a long chain of amino acids can be formed. This type of a chain is called a **polypeptide.** All proteins are made of one or more polypeptides bonded together.

The Structure of Proteins   Amino acids can be linked together in any sequence and in chains of varying length. Each different sequence makes a different protein. Furthermore, the chains can fold and twist in space. Typical shapes of protein molecules are coils or helixes, pleated sheets, and globules. Often, neighboring sections of a folded chain become bonded to each other by what are called *cross-links.* It is the variations in the shapes and formations of cross-links that make possible the enormous variety of proteins.

All protein molecules contain many atoms and amino acid units. The smallest protein molecules have about 50 amino acids, or about 1000 atoms. The largest have over 100 000 amino acids and millions of atoms.

Determining the order of the amino acids in a particular protein is obviously a difficult task. The first protein structure to be determined was that of *insulin,* a hormone that controls blood-glucose levels. This was done by Frederick Sanger at Cambridge University, England, in 1954. Sanger later received the Nobel Prize for his work.

Today, the molecular structures of several hundred proteins have been worked out by painstaking methods. These methods include breaking the molecule into smaller and smaller pieces and identifying the amino acid at the end of each broken section. Machines are now being built that will analyze a protein and print out its amino acid sequence.

4-3 Section Review

1. Name the two types of nucleic acids.
2. Which nucleic acid occurs as a double helix?
3. List the elements found in both proteins and nucleic acids. What additional element is found in proteins?
4. What groups are found in each amino acid?

Critical Thinking

5. A molecule has been isolated from an animal's muscle cells. The molecule has over 1000 atoms and contains the elements carbon, hydrogen, nitrogen, oxygen, and phosphorus. What kind of molecule is it likely to be? Explain. (*Reasoning Categorically*)

Science, Technology and Society

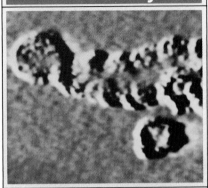

Technology: Scanning Tunneling Microscope

A new device, called a scanning tunneling microscope (STM) can make high-magnification images of objects too small to be examined by an electron microscope. The objects an STM examines are molecules. The pictures it creates appear on a computer screen.

The key to the STM is a tiny probe with a slight electrical charge. The probe is positioned about .001 microns above the surface of a molecule. As the probe moves above the molecule's surface, electrons on the surface cross the gap between the surface and the probe tip. The number of electrons that "tunnel" through the gap depends on the gap's size. Because the molecule's surface is irregular, the probe moves up and down to keep the size of the gap constant. A computer translates the probe's movements into a map of the molecule's surface profile.

The resolution of the STM is so good that scientists can now view DNA (see photo), look at enzymes, or watch polymers form.

■ *Why would the ability to view an enzyme's structure be useful?*

4-4 Enzymes

Section Objectives:

- *Explain* the functions of enzymes in living cells.
- *Describe* the lock-and-key model and the induced-fit model of enzyme action.
- *Explain* the effects of temperature, pH, and enzyme and substrate concentrations on enzyme action.
- *Define* the term *coenzyme*.

The Importance of Enzymes

Enzymes (EN zymz) are protein substances that are necessary for most of the chemical reactions that occur in living cells. There is a major difference between chemical reactions in nonliving things and the reactions in living things. Consider, for example, the burning of gasoline in an automobile engine. The gasoline vapor is admitted to the engine cylinder. It is ignited by a spark. The vapor burns in a fraction of a second. In fact, the burning is so rapid that it produces a small explosion, which helps to drive the engine.

The chemical reactions of life are different. Although we sometimes say that glucose is "burned" to release energy in the cell, the "burning" occurs in dozens of small steps. In some of these steps, a small part of a molecule is removed. In others, a small group of atoms is added. In still others, atoms are rearranged within the molecule. These steps must occur with great precision and in the right order. They also must occur at ordinary temperatures inside the cell and must not give off large amounts of heat. Otherwise, the cell will be destroyed.

Enzymes make this possible in the living cell. For each step of a reaction, there is a particular enzyme at work. Enzymes enter into a chemical reaction only temporarily. Enzymes are not changed by the reaction. They are used again and again for the same chemical step with other molecules. A substance that brings about a reaction without being changed itself is called a **catalyst** (KAT uh list). Enzymes are organic catalysts.

The substance that an enzyme acts upon is called its **substrate** (SUB strayt). The names of enzymes usually end with the suffix -*ase*. The rest of the name is often derived from the name of the substrate. For example, the enzyme that splits maltose into 2 glucose molecules is called *maltase*. Enzymes that break down proteins are called *proteases* (PROH tee ay zez). Enzymes that break down lipids are called *lipases* (LY pay zez).

All enzymes in a living organism are made by the cells of the organism. Most of these enzymes are used within the cell in which they are made. However, some enzymes are passed out of the cell to catalyze reactions outside the cell. All the digestive enzymes that are produced in the human digestive tract are of this type. For example, pepsin is an enzyme made inside the cells of glands in the stomach wall. It leaves the cells and mixes with food in the stomach. Here, pepsin breaks down proteins in the food into simpler molecules.

How Enzymes Work

The ability of enzymes to act as catalysts depends on their shape. Somewhere on the surface of each enzyme there is a region called the **active site.** The substrate molecules fit the shape of the active site. See Figure 4–15a. When the substrate molecule comes in contact with the active site of the enzyme, it forms a temporary union with the enzyme. This is called an *enzyme-substrate complex.* During this time, the enzyme may break bonds within the substrate molecule. The substrate is thus separated into 2 smaller molecules.

An enzyme may also cause 2 molecules to join. In this case, there are two substrates. Each fits into the active site in such a way that they are brought into close contact. This enables bonds to form between the two substrate molecules.

There is a theory to explain how the enzyme and substrate fit together at an active site. It is called the *lock-and-key model.* Just as the notched surface of a key can open only one lock, the shape of the active site of an enzyme only fits certain substrates. Thus, each enzyme can catalyze a reaction only of those substrates.

Recently, another theory has been proposed to explain how some enzymes work. It is called the *induced-fit model.* In this model, the enzyme is not a rigid shape. Instead, the enzyme changes shape slightly as the substrate enters the active site. Once it has changed shape, the enzyme fits snugly around the substrate, as shown in Figure 4–15b. This induced fit is similar to the way a hand grasps a baseball. As the enzyme embraces the substrate, it can weaken the chemical bonds in the substrate, helping the reaction to proceed. In the induced-fit model, as in the lock-and-key model, each enzyme catalyzes a reaction only with certain substrates.

Figure 4–15

Two Models of Enzyme Action. a. In the lock-and-key model, the substrate fits exactly into the active site on the enzyme. **b.** In the induced fit model, the enzyme changes shape slightly to "grasp" the substrate at the active site. ▼

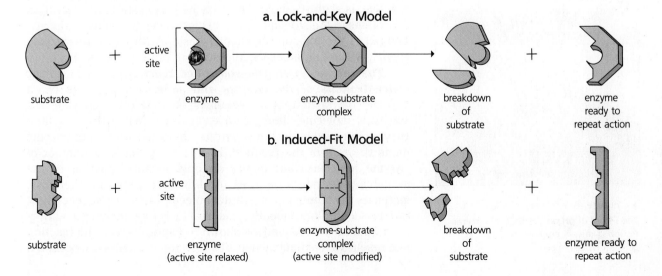

a. Lock-and-Key Model

substrate   +   active site   enzyme → enzyme-substrate complex → breakdown of substrate   +   enzyme ready to repeat action

b. Induced-Fit Model

substrate   +   active site   enzyme (active site relaxed) → enzyme-substrate complex (active site modified) → breakdown of substrate   +   enzyme ready to repeat action

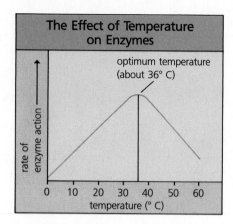

The Effect of Temperature on Enzymes

optimum temperature (about 36° C)

rate of enzyme action

temperature (° C)

▲ **Figure 4–16**

The Effect of Temperature on the Rate of Enzyme Action. Most enzymes work best at normal cell temperatures.

Factors Affecting Enzyme Action

Experiments have shown that many factors can affect the action of enzymes in living cells. These factors, outlined below, affect only the rate of a catalyzed reaction. The products formed by the reaction do not change.

Small amounts of an enzyme can cause the reaction of large quantities of substrate. The time needed for an enzyme-substrate complex to form and a reaction to occur is very short. A single enzyme molecule can catalyze thousands of substrate reactions each second. Thus, only small amounts of any enzyme need to be present in a cell at any given time.

Enzymes enable cell reactions to take place at normal temperatures. Many chemical reactions that take place slowly at ordinary temperatures can be speeded up by raising temperatures. However, high temperatures can kill living cells. Enzymes speed up reactions in the cell without requiring high temperatures.

Enzymes work best at certain temperatures. Enzyme action depends on the random motion of molecules because this motion brings the substrates into contact with the enzymes. The motion increases as the temperature rises. If the temperature is low, the rate at which enzyme-substrate complexes form will be low, and the effect of the enzyme will be reduced. See Figure 4–16. At higher temperatures, the enzyme becomes more effective, because complexes are forming at a faster rate. At still higher temperatures, however, the enzyme itself starts to break down. This process is called *denaturation.* When the shape of the enzyme molecule changes, its active site no longer fits the substrate molecule, and it loses its effectiveness. There is a particular temperature—the optimum temperature—at which an enzyme is most effective. Optimum temperatures for enzymes in living cells are usually close to the normal cell temperature.

Each enzyme works best at a certain pH. The effectiveness of an enzyme depends on the pH of the surrounding medium. See Figure 4–17. The pH of the contents of the human stomach, for example, is slightly acidic. The enzyme *pepsin* starts the digestion of proteins in the stomach. Pepsin is most effective at this pH level. The pH in the intestine is slightly basic. At this pH, the enzyme *trypsin,* which continues the digestion of proteins, works best.

The rate of an enzyme-controlled reaction depends on the concentrations of the enzyme and substrate. The rate of an enzyme-controlled reaction depends on how often enzyme and substrate molecules bump into each other. When there is little enzyme but a great deal of substrate, the concentration of enzyme limits the rate of the reaction. In this case, the total number of enzyme molecules are acting on only a small fraction of the available substrate molecules. Adding more enzyme, therefore, increases the number of substrate molecules that can be reacting at any moment. Consequently, the reaction rate increases until a maximum rate is reached, as shown in Figure 4–18a. The reaction rate reaches a maximum when all substrate molecules are occupied

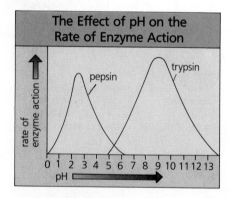

The Effect of pH on the Rate of Enzyme Action

trypsin

pepsin

rate of enzyme action

0 1 2 3 4 5 6 7 8 9 10 11 12 13
pH

▲ **Figure 4–17**

The Effect of pH on the Rate of Enzyme Action. Different enzymes work best at different ranges of pH.

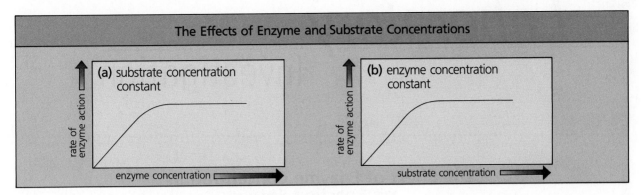

The Effects of Enzyme and Substrate Concentrations

(a) substrate concentration constant

rate of enzyme action

enzyme concentration

(b) enzyme concentration constant

rate of enzyme action

substrate concentration

▲ **Figure 4–18**
The Effects of Enzyme and Substrate Concentration on the Rate of Enzyme Action.

continuously. After this point, adding more enzyme will not increase the rate of reaction.

Similarly, when there is less substrate than enzyme, the amount of substrate limits the reaction rate. That is, there are not enough substrate molecules to occupy all the enzyme molecules all the time. Thus, adding more substrate allows all the enzyme molecules to function simultaneously. Therefore, the reaction rate increases until a maximum rate is reached, as shown in Figure 4–18b. This rate is reached because all the enzyme molecules are occupied. Adding more substrate will have no effect.

The concentrations of enzyme or substrate determine reaction rates as long as both are freely accessible to each other. However, enzyme and substrate may not be accessible to each other when, for example, a membrane or other structure separates them. In this case, the rate at which the substrate crosses the membrane or other barrier limits the rate of the reaction.

Some enzymes need substances called coenzymes in order to function. **Coenzymes** (koh EN zymz) are organic substances but not proteins. A coenzyme allows an enzyme to perform its catalytic function. Some coenzymes are built into the structure of an enzyme. Others are separate molecules. During the formation of the enzyme-substrate complex, the coenzyme is changed in a way that helps the reaction. After the reaction, the coenzyme is restored to its original form. It is now known that some vitamins are coenzymes or are made into coenzymes in the cell.

4-4 Section Review

1. What are enzymes?
2. Describe two models of enzyme action.
3. What factors affect the action of enzymes?

Critical Thinking

4. As you know, enzymes are not changed in chemical reactions. If enzymes were changed or were used up by reactions, how would this affect the rate of catalyzed reactions? (*Predicting*)

Laboratory
Investigation

The Effect of Enzyme Concentration on Reaction Rate

The enzyme catalase speeds up the breakdown of hydrogen peroxide (H_2O_2) into water (H_2O) and oxygen gas (O_2). The reaction is described by the following equation:

$$2\ H_2O_2 \longrightarrow 2\ H_2O + O_2$$

Problem

How does the concentration of an enzyme affect the rate of a reaction? Perform a controlled experiment to **draw a conclusion** about the function of enzymes.

Materials (per group)

- potato extract solution
- 1% hydrogen peroxide (H_2O_2) solution
- 8 50-mL beakers
- distilled water
- filter paper disks
- forceps
- paper towels
- glass-marking pencil
- clock with second hand

Procedure

1. Catalase is found in potato extract. Using five of the 50-mL beakers, prepare the five solutions of potato extract that are described in the table shown. Label each beaker with a glass-marking pencil to indicate the percentage of potato extract in the solution.

Solution	Potato Extract	Distilled Water
0% potato extract	0 mL	20 mL
25% potato extract	5 mL	15 mL
50% potato extract	10 mL	10 mL
75% potato extract	15 mL	5 mL
100% potato extract	20 mL	0 mL

2. Label each of the remaining three beakers H_2O_2. Pour 25 mL of the 1% hydrogen peroxide solution into each beaker.

3. Using the forceps, dip a filter paper disk into the beaker labeled 0% potato extract. Keep the disk in the solution for 4 seconds, then remove it.

4. Place the disk on a paper towel for 4 seconds to remove any access liquid.

5. Using the forceps, transfer the filter paper disk to the bottom of one of the beakers labeled H_2O_2. The enzyme in the potato extract catalyzes the formation of bubbles of oxygen gas, which causes the disk to rise to the surface.

6. Release the filter paper disk. Have one person in your group measure how long it takes for the bubbles to carry the disk to the top of the beaker. Record the time in a data table similar to the one shown.

7. Repeat step 6 two more times, using the other two beakers labeled H_2O_2.

8. Repeat steps 3 to 7 for each of the four remaining potato extract solutions.

9. Calculate the average rising time for each of the potato extract solutions. Record this information in your data table.

Observations

Construct a graph that plots the concentration of potato extract (on the X axis) versus the average rising time (on the Y axis).

Analysis and Conclusions

1. Suppose you dipped a filter paper disk in a 30% potato extract solution. Using the graph, predict how long it would take this disk to rise to the top of a beaker of H_2O_2.

2. How does the concentration of the enzyme affect the rate of the breakdown of hydrogen peroxide? Use the results of this experiment to justify your answer.

Extensions

Design an experiment to show how the concentration of hydrogen peroxide affects the rate of its breakdown.

Data Table				
Beaker	Rising Time Trial 1	Rising Time Trial 2	Rising Time Trial 3	Rising Time Average
0% potato extract				
25% potato extract				
50% potato extract				
75% potato extract				
100% potato extract				

Chapter ④ Review......................................

Study Outline

4-1 Biologically Important Compounds

▶ All organic compounds contain carbon, whereas inorganic compounds do not.

▶ Water's unique properties help account for the functioning of living things.

▶ Organic compounds are often large and complex because of the chemical nature of the carbon atom.

4-2 Carbohydrates and Lipids

▶ Carbohydrates are compounds containing carbon, hydrogen, and oxygen. The simplest carbohydrates are the simple sugars or monosaccharides.

▶ Lipids are composed of carbon, hydrogen, and oxygen and include fats, oils, and waxes. Fats and oils are formed by combination of fatty acids and glycerol.

4-3 Nucleic Acids and Proteins

▶ Nucleic acids contain carbon, hydrogen, oxygen, phosphorus, and nitrogen. The two kinds of nucleic acids are DNA and RNA.

▶ DNA contains hereditary information. Each DNA molecule contains two strands made up of many repeating nucleotide units. Each nucleotide consists of a nitrogenous base, a 5-carbon sugar, and a phosphate. The molecule has the shape of a long double helix.

▶ RNA molecules are similar to DNA but have only a single strand. RNA plays an important role in protein synthesis.

▶ Proteins are composed of amino acid molecules containing the elements carbon, hydrogen, oxygen, and nitrogen. Amino acids are linked by peptide bonds.

4-4 Enzymes

▶ Enzymes are proteins that act as catalysts for biochemical reactions that occur in the living cell.

▶ Each enzyme reacts with a specific substance called a substrate. The enzyme may break bonds within substrate molecules.

▶ The two theories of enzyme action are the lock-and-key model and the induced-fit model.

▶ Reaction rates depend on the temperature, the pH, and the concentration of enzyme and substrate. Enzymes sometimes work in conjunction with coenzymes.

Chapter Assessment

Multiple Choice

Choose the letter of the answer that best completes each statement or answers the question.

1. A type of reaction in which a bond is formed between sugar molecules is called (a) hydrolysis. (b) dehydration synthesis. (c) cohesion. (d) adhesion.

2. The active site of an enzyme will fit only a specific (a) catalyst. (b) lipid. (c) substrate. (d) cholesterol.

3. One type of carbohydrate is a(n) (a) dipeptide. (b) polypeptide. (c) amino acid. (d) polysaccharide.

4. Which type of reaction occurs when a water molecule reacts with a chain of sugar molecules to produce two simpler sugars? (a) hydrolysis (b) dehydration synthesis (c) adhesion (d) cohesion

5. Which chemical group is found in all fatty acids? (a) amino (b) carboxyl (c) peptide (d) starch

6. Proteins are composed of (a) monosaccharides. (b) fatty acids. (c) lipids. (d) amino acids.

7. DNA and RNA are examples of (a) nucleotides. (b) nucleic acids. (c) carbohydrates. (d) proteins.

8. The force of attraction between molecules of the same substance is called (a) dehydration synthesis. (b) hydrolysis. (c) adhesion. (d) cohesion.

9. Which of the following are not lipids? (a) fats (b) waxes (c) oils (d) enzymes

10. Which molecule is shaped like a double helix? (a) fat (b) glucose (c) DNA (d) protein

Content Review

Answer each of the following in complete sentences.

11. How do cohesion and adhesion differ?

12. Describe capillary action.

13. In what form does the human body store excess sugar? In what form do plants store excess sugar?

14. List several functions of lipids in living things.

15. Explain the difference between saturated and unsaturated fats.

16. Describe the general structures of DNA and RNA.

17. Explain the lock-and-key model of enzyme action.

18. Describe how enzyme action is affected by temperature, pH, enzyme concentration, and substrate concentration.

19. What is a coenzyme and what is its function?

20. Describe the formation of a peptide bond.

Graphic Organizing

For information on graphic organizers, see Appendix G at the back of this text.

21. **Compare/Contrast Matrix** Use the matrix below to compare the structure and functions of carbohydrates and proteins. Copy the matrix onto a separate sheet of paper and complete it.

Characteristic	Carbohydrates	Proteins
building blocks	?	?
functions in organisms	?	?
examples	?	?

Critical Thinking and Problem Solving

Discuss each of the following in a brief paragraph.

22. **Classifying** Classify the following substances as a carbohydrate, lipid, protein, or nucleic acid: maltose, chlorophyll, DNA, vegetable oil, fructose, RNA, wax, glycogen, insulin, and albumin.

23. **Comparing** Compare the dehydration synthesis of starch with the hydrolysis of glycogen.

24. **Predicting** What might happen to a cell whose DNA is destroyed? What might happen to a cell whose DNA is changed?

25. **Comparing** In what respects is the fitting of a lock and key similar to the fitting of an enzyme and substrate? In what respects are the two processes different?

26. **Interpreting** Amylase is an enzyme that converts starch, by hydrolysis, into sugars. An experiment was performed to determine how rapidly amylase works at different temperatures. The data from this experiment are listed in the table below.

Temperature (°C)	Rate of Starch Conversion (grams/minute)
0	0.0
10	0.4
20	0.6
30	0.8
40	1.0
50	0.4
60	0.2
70	0.0

a. Identify the variable in this experiment. What response is being measured?

b. Graph the data in the table.

c. Draw a conclusion about the effect of temperature on the rate of activity of amylase.

d. According to the data, at what temperature does amylase function most efficiently? (This value is called the optimum temperature of the enzyme.)

27. **Experimenting** If you were to study the enzyme amylase more carefully, you would find that its actual optimum temperature is 37°C. Design an experiment that would confirm this.

28. **Classifying** Two substances are found in the leaves of a desert plant. A biochemist analyzed the substances and determined that molecules in Substance 1 were made up of 12 atoms of carbon, 22 atoms of hydrogen, and 11 atoms of oxygen. Molecules in Substance 2 were made up of 2 atoms of carbon, 5 atoms of hydrogen, 1 atom of oxygen, and 1 atom of nitrogen. Identify the class to which each compound belongs.

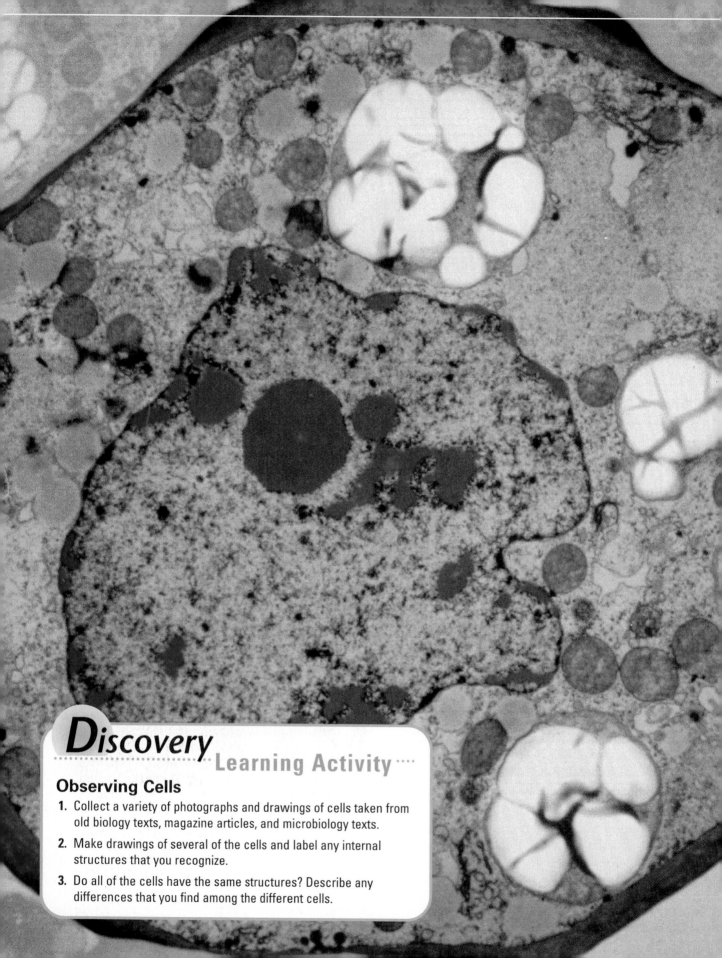

Discovery
Learning Activity

Observing Cells

1. Collect a variety of photographs and drawings of cells taken from old biology texts, magazine articles, and microbiology texts.

2. Make drawings of several of the cells and label any internal structures that you recognize.

3. Do all of the cells have the same structures? Describe any differences that you find among the different cells.

The Cell

Previewing the Chapter

The magnified photograph of a plant cell captures an image of the cell frozen in time. Such an image reveals in exquisite detail the structure that underlies its functions. In life, the collective and cooperative activities of millions of cells maintain the life of the plant. What are some of the structures and functions of plant cells? How are plant cells different from animal cells? How do cells work together in many-celled living things?

Key Words

cell, diffusion, eukaryote, organ, organelle, osmosis, prokaryote, tissue

Key Concepts

- **Identify** the basic structures of a cell.
- **Describe** how selective permeability is involved in cellular homeostasis.
- **List** the different levels of organization in living things.
- **Compare** the characteristics of plant cells and animal cells. (Laboratory Investigation)

5-1 What Is a Cell?

Section Objectives:

- *Describe* the contributions of Robert Hooke, Anton van Leeuwenhoek, Robert Brown, Matthias Schleiden, Theodor Schwann, and Rudolf Virchow to the development of the cell theory.
- *State* the cell theory.
- *Compare* prokaryotic cells and eukaryotic cells.

The Cell Theory

As you may recall from Chapter 1, all living things are made up of small individual units that usually cannot be seen with the naked eye. These units are called **cells.** Some organisms consist of one cell; others are made up of many cells. Regardless of whether the organism is one-celled or many-celled, its life processes are carried on by its cells.

It was not until the mid-1600s that microscopes were used to study biological materials. In England, a scientist named Robert Hooke examined thin slices of cork and other plant tissues with a compound microscope. He found that these substances were made

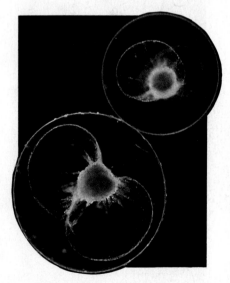

▲ **Figure 5–1**

Cellular Reproduction. This single-celled organism is dividing to produce two new cells.

◀ An electron micrograph of a plant cell. (Magnification 1945 X)

of boxlike structures that he called *cells.* What Hooke saw were the walls of dead cells. He never studied living materials in which the contents of cells could be seen.

At the time that Hooke was making and using compound microscopes, Anton van Leeuwenhoek (LAY ven huke) in Holland was making single-lens microscopes of amazing power. Looking at drops of pond water with these microscopes, Leeuwenhoek saw living things that no one had ever seen before. We know now that many of these living things were one-celled organisms. Leeuwenhoek also observed and described human blood cells. In 1683, he described what must have been bacteria—the smallest kinds of cells. Leeuwenhoek, however, did not know that he was seeing single cells, and he drew no conclusions about the cellular nature of organisms.

It was not until the early 1800s that the cellular nature of biological materials began to receive attention. In 1824, Henry Dutrochet (doo troh SHAY) of France proposed that all living things were made of cells. In 1831, Robert Brown noticed that the small, dense, round body that had been observed in cells by other users of microscopes also appeared in all plant cells. He called this structure the *nucleus* (NOO klee us). However, the role of the nucleus in cell function was not known at this time.

In 1838, Matthias Schleiden (SHLY den) developed the theory that all plants were made of cells. In the following year, Theodor Schwann (shvahn) proposed that all animals were made of cells. In that same year, Johannes Purkinje (per KIN jee) used the term *protoplasm* to refer to the jellylike material that fills the cell. The last part of the cell theory was expressed by Rudolf Virchow (VIHR koh) in 1855, when he stated that all cells arise only from preexisting cells.

In 1861, Max Schultze (shults) defined protoplasm as "the physical basis of life." He proposed that this material was found in the cells of all types of organisms. At about the same time, Felix Dujardin (doo zhar DAHN) recognized the existence of one-celled organisms.

By the end of the 1800s, biologists had discovered many of the structures that lie within the cell. They were also able to describe the events of cell division in which one cell divides to form two cells.

The ideas that make up the cell theory are:

- All organisms are made of one or more cells and the products of those cells. An organism may be a single cell, such as a bacterium, or many cells organized to function together, as in an animal or plant. In many-celled organisms, there may be intercellular material made by the cells.

- All cells carry on life activities. The life activities of a many-celled organism are the combined result of the activities of its individual cells.

- New cells arise only from other living cells by the process of cell division.

Figure 5–2

A Single-Lens Microscope. Van Leeuwenhoek's single-lens microscope (shown approximately actual size at top) could magnify single-celled organisms like those below about 200 times. ▼

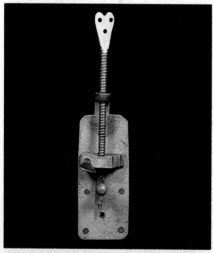

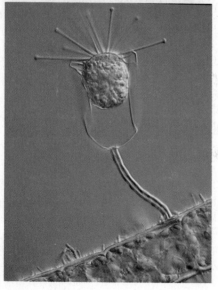

The Two Basic Cell Types

New and better instruments, such as the electron microscope, have allowed scientists to probe into the structure of living things in increasing detail. In doing so, biologists have discovered that there are two basic kinds of cells: prokaryotic (proh kar ee AHT ik) and eukaryotic (yoo kar ee AHT ik). These two types of cells have marked structural differences.

Prokaryotic cells, which are shown in Figure 5–3a, lack any internal membrane-bound structures. In other words, within a prokaryotic cell, membranes do not separate different areas of the cell from each other. Prokaryotic cells make up the smallest single-celled organisms, bacteria. Although membranes are present in some bacteria, these membranes are in contact with the rest of the cell's contents.

In contrast to prokaryotic cells, **eukaryotic cells** are present in all living things except bacteria. Eukaryotic cells have many kinds of internal membrane-bound structures. See Figure 5–3b. The most important of these is the **nucleus,** the structure in which the cell's hereditary material (DNA) is located. In fact, the term *eukaryotic* means "true nucleus." *Prokaryotic* means "without nucleus." Compared to prokaryotic cells, eukaryotic cells are much more compartmentalized. You will learn more about the nucleus and the other membrane-bound structures that are present in eukaryotic cells in the following sections.

Apart from their structural differences, prokaryotic and eukaryotic cells are fundamentally alike. Both types of cells, for example, are surrounded by a membrane that helps to keep their internal environment constant and different from their external environment. Both kinds of cells carry out the same life processes, using the same kinds of organic compounds—carbohydrates, fats, proteins, and nucleic acids—and the same kind of metabolic machinery.

Cell Size

The diameters of prokaryotic cells can range between 1 and 10 micrometers. Eukaryotic cells are, on the average, about 10 times larger, with diameters that can range between 10 and 100 micrometers. There are, however, exceptions to these various sizes. A chicken egg cell, for example, may be as large as 6 centimeters across, and some nerve cells, although thin, reach a total length of close to 1 meter.

The small size of cells has to do with the necessity of getting materials into and out of the cell at rates that will meet the cell's needs. Nutrients must be able to get into a cell at rates that will meet the cell's needs for nutrients. Similarly, wastes must be able to move out of a cell rapidly, so that they do not build up to harmful levels. What limits the rate of exchange of materials between the contents of a cell and its surroundings is the cell's surface area-to-volume ratio.

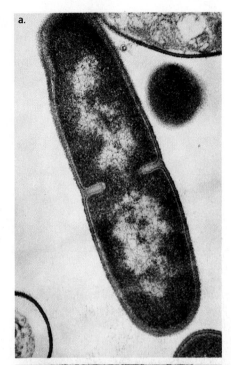

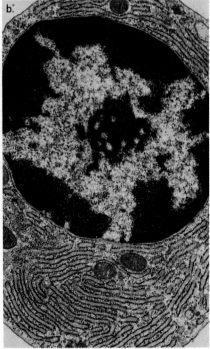

▲ **Figure 5–3**

Prokaryotic and Eukaryotic Cells. A prokaryotic cell (top) lacks a nucleus or any kind of membrane-bound organelles. In contrast, the eukaryotic cell (bottom) contains both a nucleus and many membrane-bound organelles.

Surface Area and Volume Relationships			
	1 cm 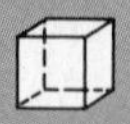 ↕ ⬜	2 cm 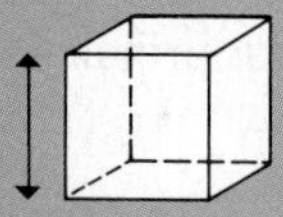 ↕ ⬜	3 cm 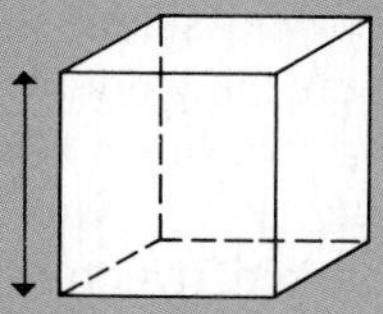 ↕ ⬜
Length of Side (cm)	1	2	3
Total Surface Area (cm²)	(1 x 1 x 6) = 6	(2 x 2 x 6) = 24	(3 x 3 x 6) = 54
Total Volume (cm³)	(1 x 1 x 1) = 1	(2 x 2 x 2) = 8	(3 x 3 x 3) = 27
Surface Area-to-Volume Ratio	6/1 = 6	24/8 = 3	54/27 = 2

▲ **Figure 5–4**

Surface Area and Volume Relationships.
The ratio of surface area to volume
decreases as cell size increases.

To understand why this is so, consider that a cell is the approximate shape of a cube or a sphere. Substances move into and out of the cell by passing through the cell membrane that covers the entire surface of the cell. The more surface area there is for a given amount of cell volume (that is, the larger the surface area-to-volume ratio), the more materials a cell can exchange with its environment in a given amount of time. For small cells, the surface area-to-volume ratio is high. This means all parts of the cell are close to the external environment. As cell size increases, however, the ratio of surface area to volume becomes smaller, and many parts of the cell are farther from the environment. This is because volume increases proportionately more than surface area for any increases in the size of an object like a cube or sphere. As you can see in Figure 5–4, if the sides of a cube are doubled, the surface area increases fourfold, but the volume increases eightfold. Similarly, if the cube dimensions are increased by a factor of 3, the surface area increases 9 times, while the volume increases 27 times. Thus, as the surface area-to-volume ratios indicate, there is proportionately less surface area per cell volume in a large cell than in a smaller cell of the same shape. Surface area-to-volume relationships, therefore, place a limit on cell size.

5-1 Section Review

1. What instrument led to the discovery of cells?
2. How many cells make up an organism?
3. How do new cells arise?

Critical Thinking

4. List three similarities and three differences between eukaryotic and prokaryotic cells. (*Comparing and Contrasting*)

Math, Science, and Technology

$A = \pi r^2$

$V = l \times w \times h$

An Isolation Chamber for Martian Soil

Problem

Sometime in the future, NASA may send out a robotic interplanetary probe that will scoop up some soil from the surface of Mars, place it in a cylindrical canister, take off from Mars, and return to earth with its alien cargo. After returning to earth, the Martian soil will be tested for any signs of life. To make sure that no microscopic organisms from earth get inside the canister and contaminate the soil, the cylindrical canister must be stored in an isolation chamber. Another reason for storing the soil in an isolation chamber is to prevent any microscopic Martian organisms—if they are present—from escaping into the earth's environment.

Task

You are a member of an engineering team that has been asked by NASA to help design an isolation chamber that will enclose the cylindrical canister.

In order to perform this task, you must complete each of the following:

1. Calculate the volume of the cylindrical canister, which is 28 cm long and has a diameter of 28 cm. (Volume = $\pi r^2 h$)

2. Determine the volume of the isolation chamber that has the following dimensions: 30 cm long, 30 cm wide, and 30 cm deep. Are there any other shapes that are equally suitable for an isolation chamber?

3. Design and make a detailed scale drawing of the isolation chamber in which the cylindrical canister would fit. Use the scale 5 mm = 1 cm. Make sure your drawing contains a seal to prevent contamination or loss of contents.

4. Research the types of material that you could use in constructing the isolation chamber that would satisfy its requirements.

5. Research and collect information about the Martian surface and its atmosphere.

6. Use a design brief that includes the hypothesis, materials, procedure, data, observations, and conclusions for your design of the isolation chamber.

7. Keep a journal containing all the information you collected and drawings of your design.

Solution

Prepare a presentation for the project engineers at NASA describing your team's solution to the design problem. Explain your team's approach to the problem, the sources of information used, and what was learned through your research design. The presentation should include details of the design including drawings, list of materials needed, assumptions made by the team, and the supporting information used in the design. In addition, include any information that will persuade NASA to use your design for the isolation chamber.

28 cm

28 cm

5-2 Cell Structure

Section Objectives:

- *Describe* the structure and functions of the following cell parts: *cell wall, cell membrane,* and *cytoplasm.*
- *Describe* the structure and functions of the following cell organelles: *nucleus, endoplasmic reticulum, ribosomes, Golgi bodies, lysosomes, mitochondria, microtubules, microfilaments, centrioles, cilia, flagella, vacuoles,* and *plastids.*
- *Compare* and *contrast* the structures of an animal cell and a plant cell.

Eukaryotic cells have many specialized internal structures, called **organelles.** Some organelles are enclosed in their own membrane while other organelles are not. Figure 5–5 shows the organelles of animal and plant cells. In reality, most plant and animal cells are specialized for specific functions and, therefore, do not appear the same as these idealized drawings. Referring to these two illustrations, however, will help as you read descriptions of the various organelles.

Cell Walls

The cells of most bacteria, various other microorganisms, and all plants are enclosed by a rigid **cell wall,** which lies just outside the cell membrane. The cell wall gives the cell its shape and provides protection for the cell. In plants, this wall is composed largely of *cellulose* (SEL yuh lohs). In other organisms, it may contain other compounds. The cell wall has many small openings that allow materials to pass to and from the cell membrane. Thin strands of cytoplasm sometimes extend through the walls of neighboring cells, which allow materials to pass directly from one cell to another. Animal cells do not have a cell wall.

The Cell Membrane

The **cell membrane,** or *plasma* (PLAZ muh) *membrane,* separates the cell from its surrounding environment. The membrane controls the movement of materials into and out of the cell, which makes it possible for the cell contents to be chemically different from the environment. The membrane keeps the internal conditions of the cell constant. It maintains homeostasis.

Structure of the Cell Membrane The cell membrane is a two-layered structure that is composed of lipids, proteins, and carbohydrates. The two layers are made of lipids with proteins embedded in them like mosaic tiles. Some of the proteins are on the outer surface of the membrane, some are on the inner surface, and some are thought to extend through the membrane. Carbohydrates, which are linked chemically to some membrane proteins or lipids, branch from the external surface of the membrane. Evidence

Animal Cell

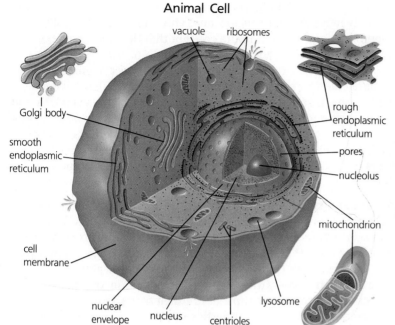

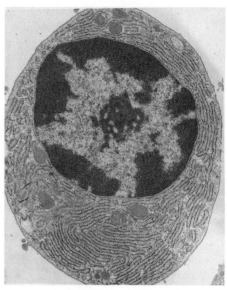

Plant Cell

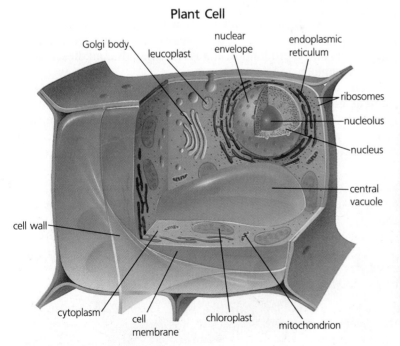

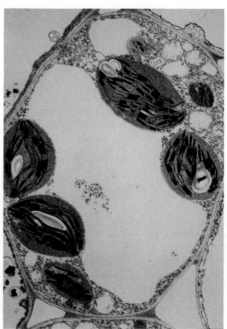

▲ **Figure 5–5**

Generalized Structure of Animal and Plant Cells. Animal and plant cells are eukaryotic in structure with many membrane-bound organelles. Plant cells differ from animal cells in having a cell wall, a large central vacuole, and plastids.

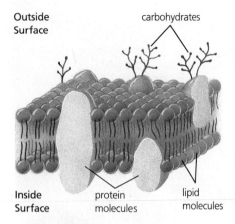

Outside Surface

carbohydrates

Inside Surface

protein molecules

lipid molecules

▲ **Figure 5–6**
Fluid-Mosaic Model of Cell Membrane.
According to the fluid-mosaic model of the cell membrane, proteins are embedded in, but still able to move along, the lipid layer, which is in a fluid state.

indicates that the lipid and protein molecules of the membrane actually move along the membrane. This "fluid" property of the cell membrane has resulted in the concept that the membrane behaves like a fluid mosaic structure. See Figure 5–6.

The proteins of the cell membrane serve a number of functions. Some are *transport proteins.* They control the movement of substances through the membrane. Some act as *receptors,* that is, binding sites for specific messenger molecules that signal the cell to begin or to stop some metabolic activity. Other membrane proteins act as enzymes. Still others help bind the membrane to neighboring cells or to structural elements in the *cytoplasm* (SYT uh plaz um) of the cell.

Permeability of the Cell Membrane   The cell membrane is **selectively permeable.** That is, some substances can pass through it freely. Other substances can pass through only to some slight extent or only at certain times. Still other substances cannot pass through it at all. Through its selective permeability, the cell membrane regulates the chemical composition of the cell. The selectively permeable nature of the membrane is the result of the chemical and electrical properties of the membrane's molecules. The passage of materials through cell membranes is discussed in detail later in this chapter.

The Nucleus

The cell **nucleus** (plural, nuclei), shown in Figure 5–7, is a round, membrane-bound structure that serves as the control center for cell metabolism and reproduction. If it is removed, the cell dies. It is the largest organelle.

The membrane that surrounds the nucleus is called the **nuclear envelope.** It is actually a double membrane—two membranes lying close to each other. Like the cell membrane, it is selectively permeable. The inner and outer membranes of the nuclear envelope fuse at certain points, forming well-defined pores.

Figure 5–7
The Cell Nucleus. A double-membrane nuclear envelope with pores surrounds the nucleus, seen in this electron micrograph. The round, darkly stained structure within the nucleus is the nucleolus. ▼

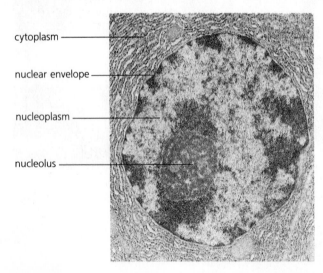

cytoplasm

nuclear envelope

nucleoplasm

nucleolus

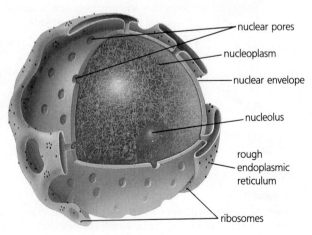

nuclear pores

nucleoplasm

nuclear envelope

nucleolus

rough endoplasmic reticulum

ribosomes

The pores control the passage of certain substances into and out of the nucleus. The selective permeability of the nuclear membrane allows the contents of the nucleus, the *nucleoplasm,* to remain chemically different from the rest of the cell.

Within the nucleus are one or more **nucleoli** (noo KLEE uh ly) (singular, nucleolus). These are dense, granular bodies that disappear at the beginning of cell division and reappear at the end. They are made up of DNA, RNA, and protein. Nucleoli are the sites of production of ribosomes.

Much of the nucleoplasm consists of chromatin. *Chromatin* (KROH muh tin) is DNA bound to various proteins. Chromatin in the form of long, thin threads makes up the structures called *chromosomes* (KROH muh sohmz). During cell division, the chromosomes shorten by coiling and become thick enough to be clearly visible when they are stained. The DNA in the chromosomes is the hereditary material of the cell.

The Cytoplasm

The watery material lying within the cell between the cell membrane and the nucleus is the **cytoplasm.** Many of the substances involved in cell metabolism are dissolved in the cytoplasm. In fact, many of the chemical reactions of cell metabolism take place in the cytoplasm. The cytoplasm also contains a variety of organelles that have specific functions in cell metabolism.

Endoplasmic Reticulum   The **endoplasmic reticulum** (en duh PLAZ mik rih TIK yuh lum) is a system of fluid-filled canals, or channels, enclosed by membranes. As shown in Figure 5–8, these canals usually form a continuous network throughout the cytoplasm. The canals of the endoplasmic reticulum serve as paths for the transport of materials through the cell. In addition, the membranes of the network provide a large surface area on which many biochemical reactions may occur. The endoplasmic reticulum also divides the cell into compartments, making it possible for a number of different reactions to go on at the same time.

The membranes of the endoplasmic reticulum are similar in structure to the cell membrane. In places, the membranes of the endoplasmic reticulum are joined to the outer membrane of the nuclear envelope. In electron micrographs, endoplasmic reticulum has either a rough or smooth appearance. In *rough endoplasmic reticulum*, the outer surfaces of the membranes are lined with tiny particles called *ribosomes* (RY buh sohmz). The ribosomes give the membrane a granular appearance. On *smooth endoplasmic reticulum*, there are no ribosomes.

Ribosomes   Small particles, called **ribosomes,** are sites of protein synthesis in the cell. They are found lining the membranes of the endoplasmic reticulum and in the cytoplasm. In cells that synthesize proteins to be released from the cell, the ribosomes are usually attached to the outer membrane surface of the endoplasmic reticulum. The proteins pass through these membranes into the

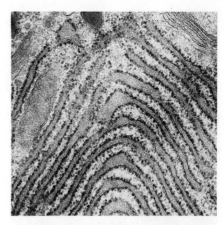

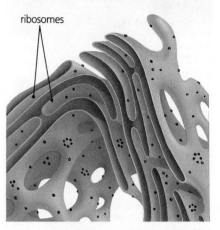

ribosomes

▲ **Figure 5–8**

Rough Endoplasmic Reticulum. The outer surfaces of the endoplasmic reticulum, shown in this electron micrograph (top), are covered with ribosomes, giving them a rough appearance. The endoplasmic reticulum serves as a system of channels through which proteins may be transported within the cell. It also divides the cell into many compartments.

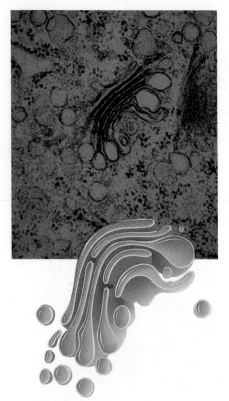

▲ **Figure 5–9**

Golgi Bodies. A Golgi body, shown here in cross section, is made up of stacks of flattened membrane sacs. Golgi bodies aid in the preparation and storage of molecules to be secreted by the cell.

canals, which carry the proteins to the cell membrane and out of the cell. Proteins that are to be used within the cell are synthesized on ribosomes that are free in the cytoplasm. These proteins are usually enzymes that function in the cell's cytoplasm.

Golgi Bodies   Stacks of flattened membrane sacs make up the organelles called **Golgi** (GOHL jee) **bodies.** See Figure 5–9. Golgi bodies serve as processing, packaging, and storage centers for the products released from the cell. Animal cells usually have only one Golgi body, which frequently is located near the nucleus. Plant cells may have several hundred Golgi bodies.

Golgi bodies and the endoplasmic reticulum work together to modify proteins and transport them to different parts of the cell. Proteins synthesized on the ribosomes pass through the canals of the endoplasmic reticulum. At the end, the protein is pinched off forming a vesicle that then moves into the Golgi bodies. Here special enzymes attach carbohydrates or lipids to the protein. The modified proteins migrate to the cell surface, where their membranes fuse with the cell membrane. The materials are then released outside the cell. Some products are delivered to other parts of the cell to form cell structures or to be stored for release at a later time. In plant cells, the Golgi bodies are thought to be involved in assembling materials for the cell wall.

Lysosomes   Small, saclike structures surrounded by a single membrane and containing strong digestive, or hydrolytic, enzymes are **lysosomes** (LY suh sohmz). Lysosomes are thought to be produced by the Golgi bodies. Lysosomes are found in most animal cells and in some plant cells. In one-celled organisms, lysosomes are involved in the digestion of food within the cell. In multicellular organisms, lysosomes serve several different functions. They break down worn-out cell organelles. In some animals, they are part of the body's defense against disease. White blood cells, which ingest disease-causing bacteria, contain lysosomes that break down the bacteria. Lysosomes are also involved in certain developmental processes. For example, as a frog develops from a tadpole to a mature frog, it loses its tail. Lysosomes are involved in the digestion and absorption of the tail.

Mitochondria   Round or slipper-shaped organelles that release the energy in food molecules for use by the cell are called **mitochondria** (myt uh KAHN dree uh) (singular, mitochondrion). As shown in Figure 5–10, mitochondria are surrounded by a double membrane. The inner membrane is highly folded, forming *cristae* (KRIS tee) that extend into the middle of mitochondrion. The cristae of the mitochondria provide a large surface area on which many biochemical reactions occur. Cells that require large amounts of energy, such as muscle cells, contain large numbers of mitochondria. Because most of the energy needed by cells is released in the mitochondria, this organelle is often called "the powerhouse of the cell." The process by which the energy of food is released in the mitochondria and elsewhere in the cell is called *cellular respiration.*

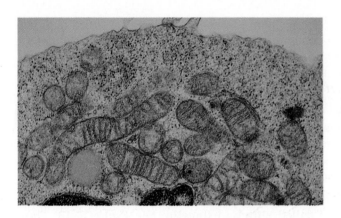

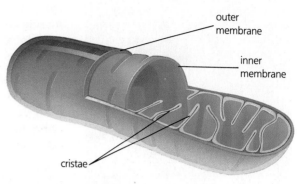

outer
membrane

inner
membrane

cristae

A cell may contain from 300 to 800 mitochondria, depending on its activity. Within the cell, the mitochondria are usually in motion, moving individually or in groups. They may also be found at specific locations within the cell. For example, in muscle cells, the mitochondria are found along the protein fibers that cause the muscle cell to contract. Mitochondria contain their own DNA and are capable of duplicating themselves.

Microtubules   Long, hollow, cylindrical structures found in the cytoplasm are **microtubules** (my kroh TOOB yoolz). As shown in Figure 5–11, they serve as a sort of "skeleton" for the cell, giving it shape. Microtubules are found in *centrioles* (SEN tree ohlz), *cilia* (SIL ee uh), and *flagella* (fluh JEL uh)—organelles discussed later in this section. They may also be involved in movement of the chromosomes during cell division. Microtubules are composed of a protein called *tubulin* (TOOB yuh lin). The molecules of this protein consist of two subunits that stack alternately in a helix. This gives the microtubule its form.

Microfilaments   Long, solid, threadlike strands found in some cells are called **microfilaments** (my kroh FIL uh ments). Most are composed of the protein *actin* (AK tin) and are associated with cell movement. Microfilaments are thought to have the capacity to contract and to be involved in the movement of cytoplasm within

▲ **Figure 5–10**
Mitochondria. Mitochondria, seen here in longitudinal and cross sections, carry out many of the reactions of cellular respiration. (Magnification 144 000 X)

Figure 5–11
Microtubules. The system of microtubules present throughout the cytoplasm is evident in this photomicrograph (left) of a specially prepared cell. (Magnification 2695 X) Cross sectional views of the microtubules within a flagellum can be seen in the electron micrograph (right). ▼

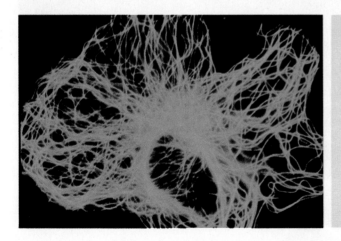

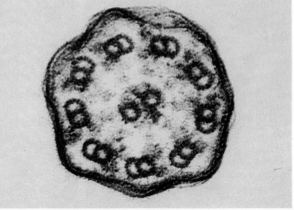

▲ **Figure 5–12**
Centrioles. An animal cell has a pair of centrioles near the nucleus. Each centriole consists of a ring of nine sets of three microtubules.

the cell, a phenomenon known as *cyclosis* (sy KLOH sis), or cytoplasmic streaming. Actin microfilaments are also found in muscle cells and are involved in muscle contraction. Some microfilaments are not made of actin and may serve as supporting structures for the cell.

Centrioles Near the nucleus in animal cells is a pair of cylindrical **centrioles** that lie at right angles to each other. See Figure 5–12. Each centriole consists of a ring of nine groups of three microtubules. Centrioles are involved in cell division in animal cells. They are also found in the moving cells of algae, fungi, and plants.

Cilia and Flagella Hairlike organelles with the capacity for movement are called **cilia** and **flagella.** See Figure 5–13. They extend from the surface of many different types of cells. Their structure is identical, except that flagella are longer than cilia. There are usually only a few flagella on a cell, but cilia may cover the entire cell surface. In one-celled organisms, cilia and flagella are involved in cell movement. In larger, many-celled animals, cilia serve to move substances over the surface of the cells.

Cilia and flagella arise from structures called *basal bodies*. The structure of a basal body is similar to that of a centriole. The cilia and flagella are slightly different in structure from the basal body. They have a ring of nine pairs of microtubules and, in the center of the ring, another pair of microtubules.

Vacuoles **Vacuoles** (VAK yoo wohlz) are fluid-filled organelles enclosed by a membrane. The vacuoles found in plant cells are filled with a fluid called *cell sap.* In most mature plant cells, a single, large vacuole occupies most of the interior of the cell. In various microorganisms and simple animals, food is digested in special *food vacuoles* within the cells. Many of these organisms also have *contractile vacuoles* in which excess water from the cell collects. The water is periodically pumped out from the cell directly into the environment. Vacuoles may also serve as storage sites for certain cell products.

Figure 5–13
Cilia. The respiratory cilia (left) line the human trachea. An electron micrograph shows a row of cilia in cross section (right). Each cilium is made up of one central pair of microtubules surrounded by nine other pairs. (Magnification 192 500 X) ▼

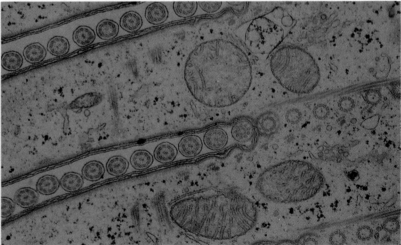

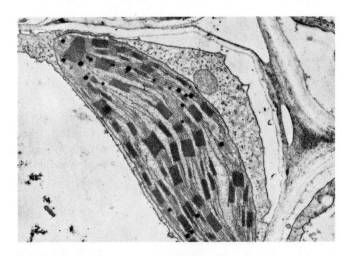

photosynthetic membranes

stroma

grana

double membrane

▲   **Figure 5–14**
The Chloroplast. The internal membranes of chloroplasts contain the photosynthetic pigments. These stacks of photosynthetic membranes are called grana. (Magnification 25 450 X)

Plastids   Membrane-enclosed organelles that are found only in the cells of photosynthetic, eukaryotic organisms are called **plastids.** Plastids are not present in the cells of animals or fungi. Like mitochondria, plastids are bounded by a double membrane and have systems of membranes within the organelle. There are two types of plastids. **Leucoplasts** (LOO kuh plasts) are colorless plastids in which starch or other plant nutrients are stored. **Chromoplasts** (KROH muh plasts) contain the pigments that give certain colors to fruits, flowers, and leaves. The most important type of chromoplasts are **chloroplasts** (KLOR uh plasts), which contain the green pigment *chlorophyll* (KLOR uh fil). The chloroplasts are the site of *photosynthesis,* the food-making process that uses light energy.

As shown in Figure 5–14, the inside of the chloroplast contains a system of photosynthetic membranes. These membranes are often arranged in the form of stacks, called *grana* (GRAH nuh). The pigments involved in photosynthesis are located in these membranes. The protein-containing material that fills the rest of the chloroplast is called the *stroma* (STROH muh). Chloroplasts, like mitochondria, contain their own DNA and have the ability to duplicate themselves.

Origins of the Eukaryotic Cell

The structural differences between eukaryotic and prokaryotic cells are so great that biologists have wondered how these two kinds of cells are related. The answer is not certain, but based on the evidence they have collected, biologists have developed a theory to explain the connection. According to this theory, known as the *endosymbiotic theory,* eukaryotic cells are the result of **endosymbiosis**—the condition in which one organism lives inside the cell of another organism to the benefit of both. Mitochondria and chloroplasts, for example, are thought to have evolved from bacteria that were engulfed by, and then lived within, other, larger cells. The bacteria that evolved into mitochondria were probably oxygen-consuming bacteria that supplied their host cells with energy, as mitochondria now do. The bacteria that evolved into chloroplasts may have been photosynthetic bacteria similar to today's blue-green bacteria.

There is strong evidence to support the endosymbiotic theory. Mitochondria and chloroplasts contain their own DNA and can reproduce themselves as can bacteria. They are about the same size as bacteria, and they have the same metabolic machinery, including ribosomes, on which they make some of their own proteins. In addition, endosymbiosis involving eukaryotic and prokaryotic organisms is known to occur in many modern organisms. This and other evidence has led many biologists to conclude that mitochondria and chloroplasts, and perhaps other organelles, are bacteria or other prokaryotic forms in disguise.

5-2 Section Review

1. What is the function of the cell membrane?
2. Where in the cell is the hereditary material located?
3. Name the function of mitochondria.
4. What organelle is the site of protein synthesis?

Critical Thinking

5. Suppose that a great improvement is made in the magnifying power and resolution of microscopes. What effect might this have on our understanding of the cell? (*Predicting*)

5-3 Maintaining a Constant Cell Environment

Section Objectives:

- *Relate* the structure of the cell membrane to the role of the cell membrane in maintaining homeostasis.
- *Describe* the roles of diffusion, facilitated diffusion, and osmosis in the passage of materials into and out of cells.
- *Explain* what is meant by *selective permeability, concentration gradient, turgor pressure,* and *plasmolysis.*
- *Compare* passive transport with active transport.

As you know, the internal environment of a cell remains relatively constant at all times. This condition, known as homeostasis, means that factors such as pH and the concentrations of all cell substances are held constant over the life of a cell. Cellular homeostasis occurs even though the external environment may be different from the conditions in the cell. If homeostasis is disrupted, a cell will die. The ability of cells to establish and maintain homeostasis is the result of the special properties of the cell membrane. These special properties are the subject of this section.

Selective Permeability of the Cell Membrane

Certain types of substances pass through cell membranes more easily than others. For example, lipid molecules and molecules that dissolve in lipids, such as alcohol, ether, and chloroform, pass through cell membranes easily. Small molecules, such as water, glucose, amino acids, carbon dioxide, and oxygen, also can pass through cell membranes easily. Large molecules, such as starch and proteins, cannot. Electrically neutral molecules enter and leave cells more easily than electrically charged ions. In addition, the permeability of cell membranes to certain substances varies from one type of cell to another. Even in the same cell, the permeability may vary from one moment to another. Thus, a given substance may pass freely through the cell membranes of one type of cell but not another, or it may pass through a cell membrane at one time but be held back at another.

Some of the mechanisms by which substances move through cell membranes will be explained later in the chapter. Before reading about these mechanisms, however, it is necessary to understand how molecules move from place to place and what determines the direction of their movement.

Diffusion

Molecules of gases and liquids are in constant motion. They move in straight lines in all directions until they run into other molecules or into the walls of their container. Collisions send them off in new directions so that their paths zigzag. As a result of this motion, the molecules of a substance tend to spread from a region in which they are more concentrated to regions in which they are less concentrated. For example, if instant coffee granules are placed at the bottom of a glass of water, a concentrated solution of coffee will first form near the bottom. See Figure 5–15. However, gradually, the coffee molecules will spread upward through the liquid. Similarly, if a perfume bottle is opened in one corner of a room, molecules of perfume will evaporate into the air near the bottle. At first, the odor will be noticeable only in the vicinity of the bottle. Eventually, the

Figure 5–15
Diffusion. (A) Instant coffee will, at first, be concentrated at the bottom of a glass of water. (B) With time, the coffee diffuses into other regions of the glass. (C) Eventually, the coffee becomes evenly distributed throughout the water. ▼

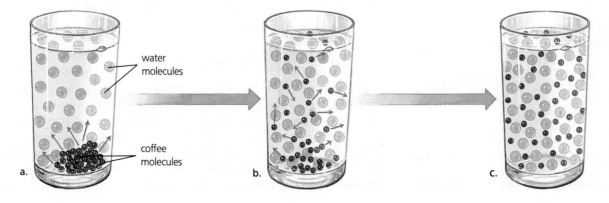

water
molecules

coffee
molecules

a.   b.   c.

odor will spread to all parts of the room. Both of these examples illustrate the process of diffusion. **Diffusion** is the movement of molecules or particles from an area of high concentration to an area of lower concentration. Diffusion occurs because molecules are in constant motion.

The difference in concentration between a region of high concentration and a region of lower concentration is called the **concentration gradient.** Diffusion occurs only if there is a concentration gradient. As a result of diffusion, the molecules become evenly distributed throughout the available space. Once they are evenly distributed, no further change in concentration occurs. The molecules are still in motion, but over any time period, as many molecules move out of a given area as move into the area. Such a situation is called an *equilibrium* (ee kwuh LIB ree um). In the example with instant coffee in water, equilibrium is reached when every drop of water in the glass contains the same amount of coffee.

Diffusion is important in the movement of molecules into and out of cells. Depending on the concentration gradient, certain materials will either enter or leave cells by diffusion. You can understand the importance of diffusion when you consider the role of diffusion in a cell using oxygen and producing carbon dioxide during gas exchange.

Oxygen and carbon dioxide will be in solution inside the cell and in the liquid medium surrounding the cell membrane. As the cell uses the oxygen dissolved in its cytoplasm, the concentration of oxygen inside the cell will decrease. At first, the concentration outside the cell will not change. Therefore, a concentration gradient toward the inside of the cell will develop across the cell membrane. As a result, oxygen will diffuse into the cell.

The opposite situation will develop over carbon dioxide. As the cell produces carbon dioxide, its concentration inside the cell increases, while its concentration outside remains the same. Therefore, a concentration gradient for carbon dioxide develops across the cell membrane toward the outside of the cell. Carbon dioxide diffuses out of the cell. If the concentration gradients of oxygen and carbon dioxide were reversed, then oxygen would leave the cell and carbon dioxide would enter. Thus, the process of diffusion plays an important role in the entry and exit of molecules in living cells. It should be noted that many different substances may be diffusing through the cell membrane at the same time without affecting each other's rate of diffusion.

Facilitated Diffusion

Some substances diffuse across cell membranes more rapidly than you might expect from the chemical properties of these substances. This type of transport, called **facilitated diffusion,** occurs because of specialized transport proteins in the cell membrane. Each type of transport protein is specific to the substance that it carries, just as an enzyme is specific for its substrate. Unlike enzymes, however, a transport protein does not cause a chemical reaction. Rather, it

Can You Explain This?

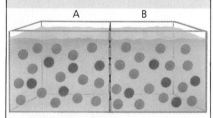

molecules of iodine   molecules of water

Suppose an apparatus is set up as shown above. Two chambers of a container are separated by a membrane permeable to both water and iodine. Chamber A contains a solution of water and iodine. Chamber B contains pure water.

■ *Describe the movement of molecules through the membrane. What will happen to the molecules of iodine in Chamber A? What will happen to the molecules of water in Chamber A? What will happen to the molecules of water in Chamber B?*

Shown below are the two liquids in a state of equilibrium.

A   B

■ *What will happen to the molecules of water and iodine after equilibrium has been reached?*

The concentration of sodium, on the other hand, is lower inside the cell than it is outside. The cell uses active transport to maintain these differences in concentration. In certain seaweeds, minerals such as potassium and iodine build up in concentrations that are 1000 times the concentrations found in ocean water. In the human kidney, active transport is involved in concentrating wastes in urine.

There are two processes by which active transport can occur. In one process, a substance is moved across a membrane molecule by molecule. In this case, each molecule that is transported must first bind to a transport protein on one side of a membrane and then be released by the same protein on the other side of the membrane. As with facilitated diffusion, the transport protein is specific for each kind of transported substance. Unlike facilitated transport, however, the process requires the expenditure of cellular energy in the form of *ATP.* You will learn about ATP in the discussion found in Chapter 6.

The other kind of active transport involves membrane vesicles. Materials that enter a cell by this method become enclosed within an inpocketing of the cell membrane, shown in Figure 5–19. The outer surface of the membrane closes over, pinching off the pouch, which becomes a sac, or vesicle, within the cell. Inside the cell, the contents of the vesicle are released. This process of transporting material into a cell by means of a vesicle is known as **endocytosis.** When small amounts of liquid are taken into the cell in this way, the process is called **pinocytosis.** Another form of endocytosis, called **phagocytosis,** occurs when solid particles are ingested into a cell. In this case, part of the cell surrounds a particle. The cell membrane fuses, sealing the particle within its own vesicle, or food vacuole. Enzymes then digest the particle.

The movement of materials out of the cell by the reverse of endocytosis is called **exocytosis.** In this case, a vacuole carrying materials within the cell fuses to the inside surface of the cell membrane. The contents of the vacuole then are released to the outside of the cell membrane.

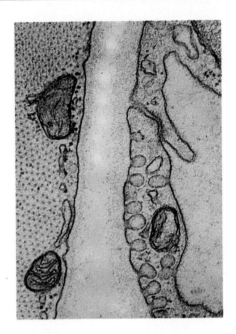

▲ **Figure 5–19**

Pinocytosis. In pinocytosis, inpocketings of the cell membrane close over small particles or liquid droplets, forming small vacuoles in the cytoplasm.

5-3 Section Review

1. Define the terms *diffusion* and *osmosis*.
2. What is meant by the term *facilitated diffusion?*
3. What is a hypertonic solution?
4. Name two kinds of active transport.

Critical Thinking

5. A person is more likely to recover from a near drowning in sea water than in fresh water. How would osmosis account for this? (*Identifying Causes*)

5-4 Organization of Cells in Living Things

Section Objectives:

- *Describe* and *compare* the different levels of organization and specialization that exist in unicellular, colonial, and multicellular organisms.

A cell may exist alone, or it may be part of a larger organism made up of many cells. A cell that exists independently is regarded as a one-celled, or unicellular, *organism.* Many-celled, or multicellular, organisms may be made up of hundreds, thousands, millions, or billions of cells.

Unicellular and Colonial Organisms

Unicellular organisms are able to carry on all the life processes. They synthesize and obtain nutrients, break them down for energy, synthesize new materials, reproduce, and perform all the other activities that living things do. Unicellular organisms include bacteria, protozoa, many algae, and some fungi. These organisms vary in size and in the complexity of their structure.

The simplest level of multicellular organization occurs in *colonial organisms.* A colonial organism, also called a *colony,* is an organism of a few to many cells that are loosely attached to each other and that show little or no specialization among themselves. In some colonies, the cells are all alike, and each cell carries on all the life processes. These colonies are like a group of unicellular organisms that are stuck together. Any one of the cells has the capacity to reproduce and form a new colony.

In more complex colonies, the cells show some specialization. That is, the cells forming the colony vary in their structure and function. For example, *Volvox,* an alga, shown in Figure 5–20, forms spherical colonies that can include many thousands of cells. However, only about 20 of these cells in one part of the colony are capable of reproducing and forming new colonies. In another part of the colony are smaller cells containing large, light-sensitive organelles. These cells control the positioning and movement of the colony in the water. The cells of a *Volvox* colony are connected by thin strands of cytoplasm.

Multicellular Organisms

True multicellular organisms can consist of hundreds to billions of cells of many different types. In multicellular organisms, the cells are specialized. They cannot function as independent, single-celled organisms, each performing all life functions. Instead, in multicellular organisms, each cell carries out only some of its own life

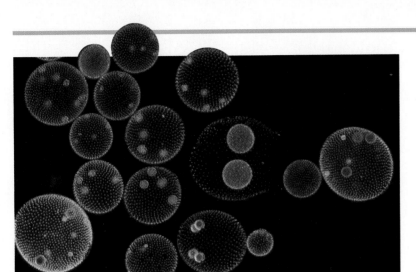

Volvox **Colonies.** Each sphere in this light micrograph is a colony of *Volvox* made up of thousands of cells. The flagella of all the cells beat in sequence, causing the colony to rotate through the water.

processes, while accomplishing the specific whole-organism functions for which it is specialized. Each type of cell depends on all the other types of cells. These complex relationships require many levels of multicellular organization and interaction.

Tissues   In multicellular organisms, a group of cells that are structurally similar and perform the same function forms a **tissue.** Each cell in a tissue carries on many life processes at the same time. Each cell also carries on some special processes that are related to the specific function of the tissue. In plants, for example, there are tissues that transport water and nutrients throughout the plant, tissues that cover and protect the parts of the plant, tissues that carry on photosynthesis, and so on. The structures and functions of plant tissues are discussed in detail in Chapter 18. Complex multicellular animals contain a greater variety of tissues than plants, and many of these tissues are more highly specialized than plant tissues.

Figure 5–21 lists the main types of tissues found in animals. Most animal tissues are a form of either *epithelial tissue* or *connective tissue.* Muscle, nerve, and blood are highly specialized tissues that do not belong to either of these groups.

Tissues that cover body surfaces and line body cavities and organs are **epithelial tissues.** They also form glands, structures made of a few to many cells that produce and release one or more substances. As you can see in Figure 5–22, epithelial tissues are generally in the form of sheets of closely packed cells. The simplest epithelial tissues consist of sheets only one cell layer thick. More complex forms consist of several cell layers.

Tissues that support other body tissues and bind tissues and organs together are called **connective tissues.** They give the body form. Unlike the cells of epithelial tissues, the cells of connective tissues are widely separated. The space between them is filled with various types of substances. In bone, for example, the bone-producing cells secrete the hard, bony material that fills the spaces between the cells. In tendons, which connect muscles to bones, dense bundles of tough elastic fibers lie between cells.

Tissues that are specialized for contraction, or shortening, are **muscle tissues.** There are three types of muscle tissues. *Cardiac muscle* tissue is found only in the heart. *Skeletal muscle* tissue makes up the muscles that are attached to the bones of the skeleton. Movement of these muscles is under voluntary control by the animal. *Smooth muscle* tissue is found in various organs of the body, such as the stomach, intestine, and blood vessels. Contraction of smooth muscles is involuntary and automatic. Skeletal and smooth muscles are discussed in Chapter 13, blood is discussed in Chapter 10, and nervous tissue is discussed in Chapter 14.

Organs and Organ Systems   A group of tissues that work together to perform a specific function forms an **organ.** The stomach, which has nerves, muscles, and blood vessels, is an organ.

Figure 5–21
Types of Animal Tissues. ▼

Types of Animal Tissues

Type of Tissue	Structure	Functions	Location
Epithelium (epithelial tissue)	cells arranged in sheets one or more cell layers in thickness	protection (outer layer of skin); absorption (inner lining of intestine); secretion (glands)	lines cavities; covers surfaces; forms glands
Connective tissue	cells and fibers embedded in an extra-cellular "ground substance," or matrix	support of other tissues and binding of organs; connects or binds tissues and organs together	throughout body
Adipose tissue	specialized ovoid fat cells in connective tissue fibers	stores fat	throughout body; found in large numbers in some areas
Bone and cartilage	cells and fibers embedded in an extracellular formless "ground substance," or matrix	make up the skeleton giving the body support and form, and, with muscles, allowing for movement	*bone:* in skeleton; *cartilage:* in skeleton, trachea, outer ear, nose, and discs of spinal column
Blood	specialized liquid tissue	transport of nutrients, wastes, oxygen, and carbon dioxide throughout body	within vessels of the circulatory system
Nerve tissue	specialized cells, called neurons, that are bound together by connective tissue to form nerves	conduction of impulses	brain and spinal cord; nerves and sense receptors throughout body
Muscle tissue	individual cells or fused cells bound together by connective tissue to form bundles or sheets	*skeletal muscle:* voluntary movement of body parts; *smooth muscle:* involuntary movement of internal organs; *cardiac muscle:* makes up heart and generates heart beat stimulus	skeletal muscles; internal organs; heart

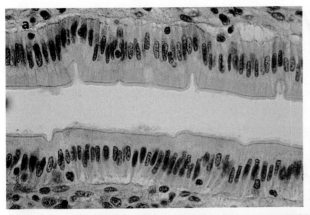
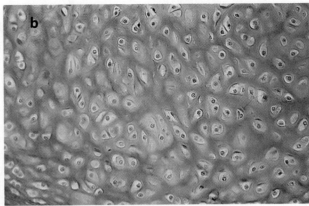
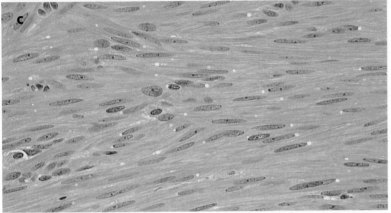

▲ **Figure 5–22**

Animal Tissues. (a) Epithelial cells cover surfaces and line cavities. (b) Connective tissues support and bind together other body tissues. Cartilage, one type of connective tissue, is firm and flexible. (c) Muscle tissue is made up of cells that are able to contract. Smooth muscle cells are long and spindle shaped.

A group of organs that work together to perform a specific function forms an **organ system.** An example of an organ system is the digestive system, which includes the mouth, esophagus, stomach, intestines, pancreas, liver, and so forth.

Although the parts of a multicellular organism can be described in terms of separate cells, tissues, organs, and organ systems, all these parts must function together for the organism to carry on its life processes.

5-4 Section Review

1. What is a colonial organism?
2. List the levels of organization, simple to complex, in multicellular organisms.
3. Describe the locations of epithelial tissue.
4. Define an organ system and give an example.

Critical Thinking

5. Why do you think the cells of all multicellular organisms are specialized? (*Reasoning Conditionally*)

Laboratory Investigation

Inside Plant and Animal Cells

Ever since the first microscopes were invented, biologists have been studying the structure of all living cells. In this investigation, you will compare the structures of plant and animal cells.

Problem

How do the structures of plant and animal cells **compare**?

Materials (per group)

- scalpel
- tweezers
- onion
- medicine dropper
- microscope slide
- coverslip
- iodine solution
- paper towel
- prepared slide of human cheek cells
- microscope

Procedure

1. Using tweezers, peel the thin, transparent skin from the inner surface of an onion, as shown.

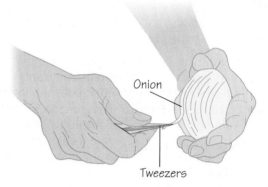

2. With a scalpel, cut a small piece of the skin from the section that was removed from the onion. **CAUTION:** *Be careful when using a scalpel or other sharp instrument.* Place the small piece of onion skin on a clean microscope slide.

3. Add a drop of water to the piece of onion skin and cover with a coverslip.

4. Using the medicine dropper, place a drop of iodine solution at one end of the coverslip. Holding a piece of paper towel near the opposite edge, draw the iodine solution underneath the coverslip.

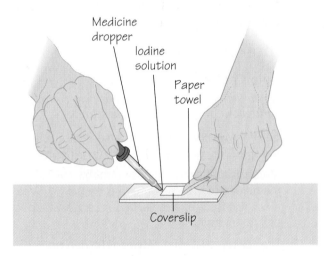

5. Examine the onion skin slide under the low-power objective of the microscope. Sketch and label what you observe.

6. Repeat step 5 using the high-power objective.

7. Repeat steps 5 and 6 using the prepared slide of the human cheek cells.

Observations

1. What is the shape of the onion skin cells? The shape of the human cheek cells?

2. Describe the general structures of the onion cells and the cheek cells.

Analysis and Conclusions

1. How are plant and animals similar in structure? How are they different?

2. What was the purpose of adding the iodine solution to the onion cells?

3. In onion plants, the liquid outside the cells is significantly less concentrated than the liquid inside the cells. This concentration difference creates high osmotic pressure. Describe how onion cells respond to osmotic pressure.

4. Of the cell structures presented in this chapter, which did you not see in either the cheek cell or the onion cell? Discuss the reasons why you did not see these structures.

5. Based on your observations, draw and label a generalized structure of a plant cell and an animal cell.

Extensions

Remove the skin from tomatoes or leeks. Prepare wet-mount slides of the skin. How do these cells compare with the onion cells? With human cheek cells?

Chapter 5 Review

Study Outline

5-1 What Is a Cell?

▶ All living things are made up of one or more cells that carry on life-sustaining metabolic processes.

▶ There are two types of cells—prokaryotic, without membrane-bound organelles, and eukaryotic, with a membrane-bound nucleus and other distinct organelles.

▶ A cell exchanges materials with its environment across its surface. As a cell grows, its surface enlarges less than its volume, thus limiting cell size.

5-2 Cell Structure

▶ Every cell has a selectively permeable cell membrane. A cell wall surrounds the cell membrane in plants and in some microorganisms.

▶ Plant and animal cells have specialized structures, called organelles, in the cytoplasm. One organelle—the nucleus—contains the cell's hereditary material and controls cell metabolism and reproduction.

▶ Other cellular organelles are specialized for different functions, such as protein synthesis. Unlike animal cells, plant cells have organelles called plastids that have several functions including the use of light energy for making food.

5-3 Maintaining a Constant Cell Environment

▶ Cellular homeostasis is maintained by the cell membrane, which controls movement of substances into and out of the cell.

▶ Some substances pass through the cell membrane by diffusion, moving from higher to lower concentration. Water enters or leaves the cell by osmosis, the diffusion of water through a selectively permeable membrane.

▶ Diffusion, facilitated diffusion, and osmosis are types of passive transport, requiring no cell energy. Active transport requires energy to move substances into or out of the cell.

5-4 Organization of Cells in Living Things

▶ A one-celled organism carries on all the life processes within itself. In multicellular organisms, all cells are specialized to perform specific functions for the entire organism.

▶ Cells of similar structure and function form a tissue. Tissues working together form an organ; organs that function together, in turn, form an organ system.

Chapter Assessment

Multiple Choice

Choose the letter of the answer that best completes each statement or answers the question.

1. Cell energy is needed in (a) osmosis. (b) active transport. (c) passive transport. (d) diffusion.

2. Materials that cannot diffuse through the cell membrane may be brought into the cell by (a) exocytosis. (b) plasmolysis. (c) endosymbiosis. (d) endocytosis.

3. The cell material lying between the nucleus and cell membrane is called the (a) cytoplasm. (b) protoplasm. (c) centriole. (d) chloroplast.

4. Because bacteria lack a nuclear membrane, they are classified as (a) prokaryotic cells. (b) eukaryotic cells. (c) leucoplasts. (d) nucleoli.

5. A type of tissue that lines body cavities and covers body surfaces is (a) connective tissue. (b) muscle tissue. (c) epithelial tissue. (d) endothelial tissue.

6. Mitochondria, ribosomes, and vacuoles are examples of (a) tissues. (b) organs. (c) cells. (d) organelles.

7. Which of the following are prokaryotic? (a) ameba (b) fungi (c) bacteria (d) humans

8. As the surface area of a cell increases in size, the volume of the cell (a) increases relatively more than the surface area. (b) increases about the same as the surface area. (c) decreases. (d) does not change.

9. Cells that use a great amount of energy usually contain numerous (a) lysosomes. (b) vacuoles. (c) ribosomes. (d) mitochondria.

10. Robert Hooke was the first scientist to use the term (a) cell. (b) nucleus. (c) microscope. (d) cytoplasm.

Content Review

Answer each of the following in complete sentences.

11. State the three main points of the cell theory.

12. List four functions of the proteins that are present in the cell membrane.

13. Explain the difference between the nucleus and the nucleolus.

14. Is the structure of endoplasmic reticulum uniform throughout the cell? Explain your answer.

15. Where are ribosomes found in cells, and what is their function?

16. Describe the structure and function of micro-tubules.

17. Which structures are found in plant cells but not animal cells?

18. How does diffusion differ from facilitated diffusion?

19. Why is active transport important to a cell?

20. What is the difference between a tissue, an organ, and an organ system?

Graphic Organizing

For information on graphic organizers, see Appendix G at the back of this text.

21. **Line Graph** Copy the incomplete graph in the next column onto a separate sheet of paper. Refer to Figure 5–4 and add data points for cubes with sides of 2 and 3 cm. Then, compute the surface area-to-volume ratios for cubes with sides of 4 and 5 cm. Complete the graph. What conclusion can you draw from the graph?

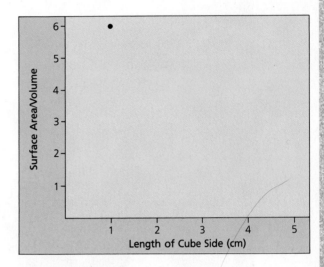

Critical Thinking and Problem Solving

Discuss each of the following in a brief paragraph.

22. **Inferring** Leeuwenhoek's microscope revealed one-celled living things he called "animalcules." Yet, he never identified cells as the smallest units of living things. Why not?

23. **Predicting** If the cell membrane were completely permeable, how would this affect the cell?

24. **Comparing** How does a one-celled organism differ from the single cell of a multicellular organism?

25. **Relating** A living cell has been compared to a factory. Explain which cell part matches each of the following: factory manager, power plant, assembly line, storage and shipping center, liquid storage tank, and security guard.

26. **Interpreting** When living yeast cells were placed in congo red dye and examined under the microscope, the yeast cells remained colorless. However, when placed in methylene blue, they became blue. Later, dead yeast cells were placed in congo red dye. These cells turned red. Explain these three observations.

Discovery
Learning Activity

Sun Power

1. Examine several of the instruments that your teacher has provided.

2. Write a paragraph explaining how you think these instruments are powered.

Cellular Respiration

Previewing the Chapter

Using her well-trained and powerful leg muscles, a basketball player jumps and shoots for the basket. Another equally well-trained player attempts to block her shot. How do the basketball players get the energy they need to perform well in such a fast-paced game? Where do you get the energy to get you through a busy day at school? How do all living things—animals, plants, bacteria—obtain the energy they need to live?

Key Words

ATP, cellular respiration, chemiosmosis, electron transport chain, fermentation, glycolysis, Krebs cycle

Key Concepts

- **Describe** how living things get the energy they need to carry out life functions.
- **Compare** aerobic respiration and anaerobic respiration.
- **Predict** which sugar will produce the fastest respiration in yeast. (Laboratory Investigation)

6-1 Energy for Life

Section Objectives:

- *Explain* why energy is important for living things.
- *Describe* the role of ATP in energy transfer.
- *Compare* oxidation and reduction and explain why one cannot take place without the other.
- *Discuss* the function of electron carriers in cellular respiration.

The Uses of Energy

Energy is the ability to do work. Just open any newspaper and you are sure to find articles about energy—energy needs, energy policies, and sources of energy. Some of the energy that fuels the world is gotten from falling water used by hydroelectric power plants. Some comes from nuclear energy. Still more comes directly from solar radiation.

Most of our energy, however, comes from the burning of fuels such as oil, gas, and coal. Burning a fuel releases energy in the form of heat and light. The heat can be used to run engines and electric generators, which turn the heat energy into other forms of energy. The burning of fuel is a chemical process. Carbon and hydrogen in the fuel combine with oxygen from the air to form carbon dioxide and water. The fuels contain stored chemical energy. The stored chemical energy is released mostly as heat during the chemical changes of burning.

▲ **Figure 6–1**
Energy for Life. Like all organisms, this hummingbird must use energy to carry out its daily activities.

Biology and You

Q: Is "carbo-loading" a good way for athletes to improve their performance in endurance events?

A: Athletes are always looking for ways to improve their game. One technique is carbohydrate (carbo) loading, eating foods high in carbohydrates before athletic events. Some athletes feast on spaghetti and other complex carbohydrates the night before a race. They hope to store extra carbohydrates in their muscles and liver. The stored carbohydrates may act as reserve energy, thus delaying exhaustion during the event.

Reports show that carbo-loading may be effective only for the highly conditioned athlete who has trained for a long event, such as a marathon. Although it may increase the amount of stored carbohydrates, carbo-loading does not increase speed or power.

For the casual athlete, carbo-loading probably will not increase energy and may cause water retention and discomfort. These effects may make an athlete feel stiff and bloated. The best plan is to eat a balanced diet, rich in complex carbohydrates, on a regular basis.

■ *Write a sample menu that you would suggest to the head of an athletic training camp.*

Just as machines need energy to run, all living things need energy to carry on their life activities. Some of this energy is needed for physical or mechanical work. A flying bird needs energy just as an airplane does. A beaver building a dam or a worm burrowing in the soil needs energy just as earth-moving equipment does. Even tree frogs singing on a spring evening need energy just as a radio does. Most of the movements of living things require energy. Energy is also needed for less obvious purposes. Making complex compounds from simpler ones and transferring some materials across cell membranes require energy. In fact, cells need a continuous supply of energy to stay alive.

Energy from Food

Living things rely on the chemical energy stored in their food. Carbohydrates are the foods most commonly broken down for energy. In most cases, this energy is released by chemical changes that resemble burning. However, when organisms break down food, only part of the energy is released as heat. This heat maintains your body temperature. The rest of the energy is stored in chemical form. Living things can only use chemical energy to carry out their life functions. They cannot use heat energy to do work. It is not surprising, therefore, that the breakdown of food, and the resulting release of energy, takes place without a direct reaction between carbohydrate and oxygen. Instead, the breakdown takes place in many small chemical steps that are linked to the formation of new, high-energy compounds.

The release of the energy stored in food goes on inside the cells of both autotrophs and heterotrophs. Organisms as diverse as plants, animals, and microorganisms show remarkable similarities in the way they obtain energy from food. This energy-releasing process is called **cellular respiration.** In this chapter, you will learn how cells obtain from food the energy they need to carry out life functions.

ATP and ADP

The energy released during cellular respiration is not used directly. It is first "packaged" in the molecules of certain compounds. One such compound is called *adenosine triphosphate* (uh DEN uh seen try FAHS fayt), which is abbreviated as **ATP.** Figure 6–2 shows the structure of an ATP molecule. The main part of the molecule is made up of 1 molecule of adenine joined to 1 molecule of ribose. As you learned in Chapter 4, adenine is one of the nitrogenous bases found in DNA and RNA. Ribose is the 5-carbon sugar found in RNA. The combination of these two molecules is called *adenosine.* There are three phosphate groups bonded end-to-end to the adenosine in ATP. Phosphate groups are also part of the structure of DNA and RNA. Notice how the cell uses the same molecular units for different purposes. There are many examples of such multiple uses of chemical groups in the chemistry of life.

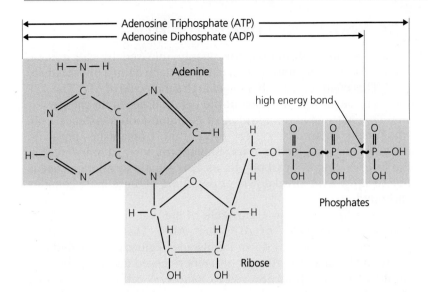

◄ **Figure 6–2**

Structure of ATP and ADP. When the third phosphate group is removed from ATP, chemical energy is released. The remaining molecule, ADP, has only two phosphate groups. ADP has less energy than ATP.

For energy storage, the bond linking the last phosphate group to the molecule is the important part of the ATP molecule. The bond is shown as a wavy line. This symbol means that the bond contains a large amount of energy. It is called a *high-energy bond.* When the third phosphate in ATP is removed and bonded to another compound, it transfers energy to the other compound. This transfer of energy is called *phosphorylation* (fahs for uh LAY shun). Phosphorylation is a common way for chemical energy to be transferred in living cells. See Figure 6–3.

When the third phosphate is removed from ATP, the remaining molecule is called *adenosine diphosphate,* or **ADP.** ADP has less energy than ATP. Although ADP's second phosphate is attached by a high-energy bond, this bond is used less often as a source of energy. Look again at Figure 6–2 to compare ATP with ADP.

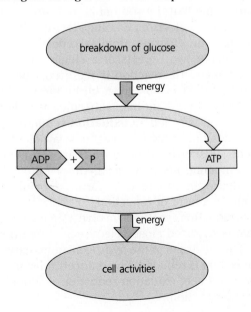

◄ **Figure 6–3**

The Energy Cycle in the Cell. ATP supplies the cell with the energy needed for cell activities. As glucose is broken down, the energy released is used to attach a third phosphate group to ADP, forming ATP. When the third phosphate group is detached from the ATP, the energy released is used for cell activities. The low-energy ADP is returned for reuse. The energy from a single glucose molecule can form 36 molecules of ATP.

The Source of Energy for ATP

During cellular respiration, the energy released by the gradual breakdown of food molecules is used to attach a third phosphate to ADP. This changes the ADP molecule to a molecule of ATP. The ATP then can be used in any part of the cell that needs its energy.

The sugar glucose is the most common food substance from which cells obtain energy. The food of most organisms, however, does not contain glucose in its simple form. Instead, it is found in the form of complex carbohydrates. The simple form of glucose is obtained from the breakdown, or digestion, of these more complex carbohydrates.

From the energy in 1 molecule of glucose, a cell can make a number of molecules of ATP from ADP. That is, the energy produced from breaking down 1 molecule of glucose is divided into many small units. If all this energy were released in a single burst, it would be too much for the cell to handle. A cell cannot use that much energy all at once. However, the amount of energy held in a single molecule of ATP is just about right for the average cellular reaction that requires energy. Thus, the packaging of energy in ATP is convenient and efficient for the needs of the cell.

Oxidation-Reduction Reactions

There are several steps by which the energy in glucose is used to produce ATP. The idea of chemical oxidation and reduction can help you understand these steps. The term **oxidation** (ox sih DAY shun) refers to any chemical change in which an atom or a molecule loses electrons. For example, when sodium combines with chlorine, the sodium atom loses an electron (see Chapter 3, section 3–2). This is an example of oxidation. We say that the sodium atom is oxidized.

At the same time that the sodium atom loses an electron, the chlorine atom gains an electron. Gaining electrons is called **reduction.** We say that the chlorine atom is reduced. Oxidation and reduction are simply two aspects of a single chemical reaction. When one substance in a reaction is oxidized, another must be reduced. That is, the electrons given up by the substance that is oxidized are taken up by another substance that is reduced. A reaction of this kind is called an **oxidation-reduction reaction.**

In some oxidation-reduction reactions, an electron is transferred from one substance to another as part of a hydrogen atom. That is, one compound may transfer hydrogen atoms to another. The loss of hydrogen atoms is a form of oxidation. Gaining hydrogen atoms is a form of reduction.

Oxidation-reduction reactions involve a transfer of energy. The substance that is oxidized (loses electrons or hydrogen) usually loses energy. The electrons or the hydrogen atoms carry the energy to the substance that is reduced. The reduced substance thus gains energy. As you will see, oxidation-reduction reactions play a key role in cellular respiration.

Electron Acceptors

In cellular respiration, after complex carbohydrates have been broken down to obtain glucose, the glucose itself is broken down in a series of chemical steps. A sequence of chemical reactions that leads to a particular result in a living cell is called a *biochemical pathway*. At several points along the biochemical pathway of cellular respiration, a compound is oxidized by giving up hydrogen atoms, more accurately, their high-energy electrons. As you have read, for oxidation to occur, some other compound must accept the hydrogen atoms or electrons and thus be reduced. Each of these oxidation-reduction steps involves a transfer of electrons.

One of the molecules that acts as an electron carrier is NAD^+ (*nicotinamide adenine dinucleotide*). Another is FAD (*flavine adenine dinucleotide*). Each of these molecules can accept a pair of high-energy electrons and a proton (H^+), thus undergoing a reduction reaction:

$$NAD^+ + 2e^- + 2\ H^+ \longrightarrow NADH$$
$$FAD + 2e^- + 2\ H^+ \longrightarrow FADH_2$$

As the electrons are transferred to NAD^+ or FAD, these molecules gain energy because they are carrying high-energy electrons. This energy gain is temporary. In another series of reactions, the electron carriers give up electrons and return to their oxidized form. At the same time, the extra energy the electron carriers were carrying can be used to form ATP from ADP. Electrons are passed along in this manner until the last step in the pathway. At that point, either oxygen or another substance acts as the final acceptor of the electrons. In later sections of this chapter, we will examine some of the details of this process.

6-1 Section Review

1. How many phosphate groups are there in a molecule of ATP?
2. How many phosphate groups are there in a molecule of ADP?
3. What is the main source of the energy that is released during cellular respiration?
4. What is an oxidation-reduction reaction?
5. What is the function of the electron carriers NAD^+ and FAD?

Critical Thinking

6. ATP is often termed the "currency" of the cell. In what ways is the function of ATP in the cell similar to the function of money in society? (*Reasoning by Analogy*)

6-2 Anaerobic Respiration

Section Objectives:

- *Distinguish* between aerobic respiration and anaerobic respiration in organisms.
- *Describe* the overall scheme of glycolysis.
- *Explain* the process of fermentation.

Types of Respiration

In most organisms, respiration is carried on in the presence of free oxygen, or O_2. Free oxygen is oxygen that is not combined with another element. Free oxygen is obtained from the air or from the water in which it is dissolved. Respiration requiring free oxygen is known as **aerobic respiration.** In aerobic respiration, glucose is completely oxidized to carbon dioxide and water. Complete oxidation allows the maximum amount of energy to be removed from the glucose.

A number of organisms, including yeast and many forms of bacteria, carry on cellular respiration without oxygen. This is called **anaerobic respiration.** In anaerobic respiration, the cell receives little of the chemical energy in the glucose.

The first steps of both aerobic and anaerobic respiration are the same. For this reason, you will first study the chemical pathway that includes the steps common to both forms of respiration.

Splitting of Glucose (Glycolysis)

The first steps in respiration take place in the cytoplasm of the cell. The process begins with phosphorylation reactions. In these reactions, two phosphate groups are bonded to a glucose molecule. These steps need energy. The energy and the phosphate groups are gotten from the breakdown of 2 ATP molecules to ADP. The energized glucose molecule then goes through a series of chemical reactions. These reactions split the glucose molecule into 2 molecules of a 3-carbon compound, *PGAL* (*phosphoglyceraldehyde*). PGAL is then oxidized by the loss of two pairs of electrons and changes to another 3-carbon compound called *pyruvic* (py ROO vik) *acid.* The oxidation of PGAL gives off energy. Some of this energy is used directly to form 2 ATP molecules. At the same time, the two pairs of electrons are accepted by the electron carrier NAD^+, forming NADH. The process of breaking down the glucose molecule into 2 3-carbon pyruvic acid molecules is called **glycolysis** (gly KAHL uh sis). Figure 6–4 shows this process.

For each pyruvic acid molecule produced by glycolysis, 2 ATP molecules are formed. Since the splitting of 1 glucose molecule produces 2 pyruvic acid molecules, a total of 4 ATP molecules are formed per glucose molecule. Remember, however, that 2 ATP molecules were used to energize the glucose molecule. The net

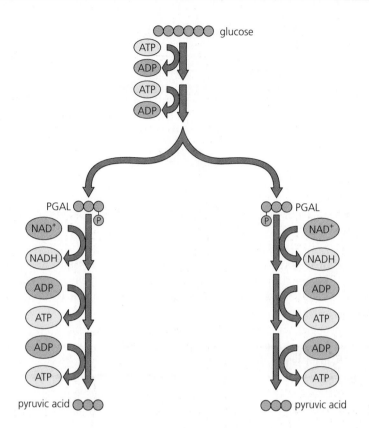

◀ **Figure 6–4**
Glycolysis. The first stage of both aerobic and anaerobic respiration is glycolysis, which takes place in the cytoplasm of the cell. In glycolysis, 1 molecule of glucose is split into 2 molecules of pyruvic acid, a 3-carbon compound. Two ATP molecules are used up in the reaction, and 4 ATP molecules are made. Thus, glycolysis produces 2 molecules of ATP for every 1 molecule of glucose. In addition, 2 molecules of NADH are formed.

energy output of glycolysis, then, is 2 ATP molecules for each molecule of glucose, plus the energy in 2 NADH. The energy carried by 2 NADH may be used to form more ATP at a later stage but only if oxygen is present.

Fermentation

In anaerobic respiration, all of the energy obtained by the cell comes from the process of glycolysis. Several different chemical changes may follow glycolysis, but no additional ATP is produced. The kind of change that follows glycolysis depends on the particular organism. In all cases, however, the pyruvic acid molecules act as acceptors. They accept the electrons from NADH, and form NAD$^+$. The NAD$^+$ molecules are then available to be used again in the next round of glycolysis.

In anaerobic respiration, after glycolysis has occurred, the pyruvic acid is changed to other compounds. In yeast cells, it is converted to ethyl alcohol and carbon dioxide. See Figure 6–5a. In certain bacteria, the end product is lactic acid. See Figure 6–5b.

When glycolysis is followed by the conversion of pyruvic acid to some end product with no further release of energy, it is called **fermentation** (fer men TAY shun). There are several industrial processes that make use of natural fermentation. One of the most

Figure 6–5

Fermentation. In the absence of oxygen, pyruvic acid generated by glycolysis accepts electrons from NADH. Lactic acid or ethyl alcohol and carbon dioxide form, and NAD$^+$ is regenerated. ▶

(a)

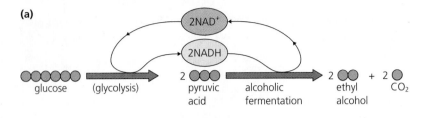

(b)

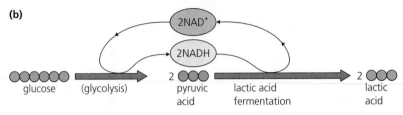

familiar processes is yeast fermentation, which is used in making bread. The carbon dioxide produced by the yeast causes the bread to "rise." The manufacture of ethyl alcohol for beverages is another well-known example.

6-2 Section Review

1. What does aerobic respiration require that is not required by anaerobic respiration?
2. How many ATP molecules must be used to activate one glucose molecule for glycolysis?
3. Name the product of fermentation that is important in making bread.

Critical Thinking

4. Why might winemakers try to minimize the amount of air available to yeast during fermentation? (*Identifying Reasons*)

6-3 Aerobic Respiration

Section Objectives:

- *Describe* the function of the Krebs cycle.
- *Explain* where and how the electron transport chain operates in an organism's body.
- *Compare* the efficiency of aerobic and anaerobic respiration.
- *Relate* muscle fatigue to oxygen debt.

The Importance of Oxygen

In anaerobic respiration, the only energy-yielding process is the formation of pyruvic acid. The end products of fermentation, ethyl alcohol or lactic acid, have almost as much energy as the glucose from which they are made. In contrast, a cell that uses oxygen for respiration can remove much more energy from glucose. It can do this because, after a series of reactions, oxygen will accept the electrons removed by oxidation during aerobic respiration.

Pyruvic Acid Breakdown

Aerobic respiration begins with glycolysis—the same step as in anaerobic respiration. In anaerobic respiration, you will recall, pyruvic acid accepts a pair of electrons from NADH. No further energy is released. In aerobic respiration, however, the pyruvic acid undergoes a further breakdown and energy release. Some energy is also obtained from the NADH formed during glycolysis.

The remaining steps of aerobic respiration take place inside the mitochondria of the cell. The pyruvic acid produced by glycolysis enters the mitochondrion. As you read in Chapter 5, a mitochondrion has a double membrane. The inner membrane is deeply folded. This gives it a large surface area. Most of the enzymes, electron carriers, and other special molecules needed for aerobic respiration are located inside or on the surface of this inner membrane. It is the presence of these molecules within or on the membrane that makes aerobic respiration possible.

Inside the mitochondrion, the pyruvic acid breaks down into carbon dioxide, NADH, and a 2-carbon compound, which combines with a coenzyme, called coenzyme A (CoA), to form **acetyl CoA.** The acetyl CoA molecule enters into the next stage of aerobic respiration.

Krebs Cycle

The series of chemical reactions that begin with the acetyl CoA formed from pyruvic acid is called the **Krebs cycle.** See Figure 6–7. The Krebs cycle is named for its discoverer, Sir Hans Krebs of Oxford University in England. Krebs found that the series of reactions has the form of a repeating cycle. Certain organic acid molecules that are part of the cycle are used over and over again. During the cycle, they are changed to other compounds. Then, before the cycle begins again, they change back to their original form.

Each "turn" of the Krebs cycle requires 1 molecule of acetyl CoA. Each turn yields 2 molecules of carbon dioxide, 3 molecules of NADH, and 1 molecule of FADH$_2$, which provide 4 pairs of electrons. Almost all the chemical energy removed from the pyruvic acid is carried by these electrons. Only 1 ATP molecule is produced by each turn of the Krebs cycle.

Electron Transport Chain

So far you have learned that in aerobic respiration, each time 1 molecule of glucose is split into 2 molecules of pyruvic acid, 2 ATP molecules are produced. An additional ATP molecule is produced by each turn of the Krebs cycle (2 ATP molecules for each glucose molecule). This is a total of 4 ATP molecules per glucose molecule. All the remaining energy released by the breakdown of glucose is carried by the electrons in NADH and FADH$_2$.

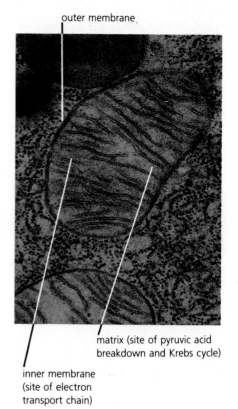

outer membrane

matrix (site of pyruvic acid breakdown and Krebs cycle)

inner membrane (site of electron transport chain)

▲   **Figure 6–6**

A Mitochondrion. The mitochondrion has a double membrane. The inner membrane contains the enzymes and coenzymes that make up the electron transport chain. The area enclosed by the inner membrane is the matrix. Within the matrix, pyruvic acid breakdown and the Krebs cycle take place. The inner membrane has protein pumps that push protons (H$^+$) produced by the breakdown of pyruvic acid and the Krebs cycle out of the matrix into the outer space where they accumulate. As the concentration of protons increases in the outer space, some pass back across the membrane through special channels producing energy. The energy converts ADP to ATP. (Magnification 52 400 X)

Figure 6–7

Pyruvic Acid Breakdown and the Krebs Cycle. Pyruvic acid from glycolysis reacts to form acetyl CoA, which then enters the Krebs cycle. For every turn of the cycle, 2 molecules of CO_2, 3 molecules of NADH, 1 molecule of $FADH_2$, and 1 ATP molecule are produced. ▶

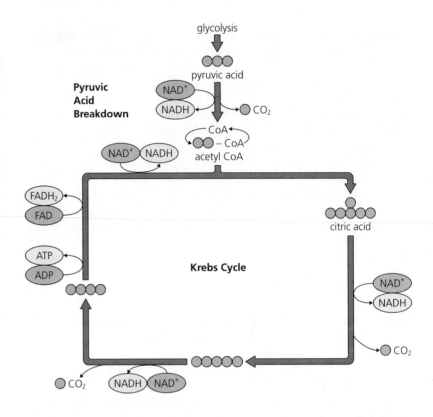

There are 12 pairs of these electrons—1 pair from glycolysis, 1 pair from pyruvic acid breakdown, and 4 pair from the Krebs cycle. The energy still contained in these electrons is used to form additional ATP. These energy-releasing reactions are carried out by the **electron transport chain,** a highly organized system of enzymes and coenzymes located in the inner mitochondrial membrane. In the electron transport chain, a series of oxidation-reduction reactions take place. Electrons are carried into the chain by NADH and $FADH_2$. The electrons are then passed along from one compound to another. See Figure 6–8. At various places along the chain, the electrons give up some energy that is used to pump protons (H^+) across the mitochondrial membrane. After the proton pumping has gone on for a while, it produces a gradient of charge across the membrane. In other words, the concentration of H^+ in the space outside the inner membrane increases, providing the energy needed to convert ADP to ATP. Much of the ATP made by aerobic respiration is produced by this process called **chemiosmosis.**

The final step in this process involves free oxygen, which acts as the final electron acceptor. One oxygen atom combines with each pair of H^+ and a pair of electrons to form water.

Water may be used by the cell, or it may be excreted as a waste product. Altogether, in most cells 32 ATP molecules are produced by the electron transport chain for each molecule of glucose. This is in addition to the 2 ATP molecules that come directly from glycolysis and the 2 ATP molecules that come from the

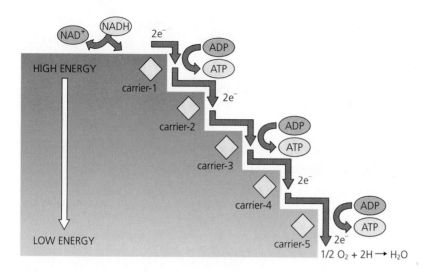

Figure 6–8
The Electron Transport Chain. The electron transport chain is a series of electron carriers on the inner membrane of the mitochondrion. NADH and $FADH_2$ deliver electrons to the electron transport chain. As the electrons pass from one electron carrier to the next, they release energy, and ATP is formed. At the end, the electrons, hydrogen ions, and free oxygen combine to form water molecules.

Krebs cycle. Therefore, aerobic respiration can produce a total of 36 ATP molecules from each molecule of glucose.

Net Reactions of Aerobic Respiration

The net result of all the steps of aerobic respiration is usually summarized in the following chemical equation:

$$C_6H_{12}O_6 + 6\ O_2 \longrightarrow 6\ CO_2 + 6\ H_2O + \text{Energy (36 ATP)}$$

This equation is somewhat oversimplified. Water is needed as a raw material for the Krebs cycle. Looking back at Figure 6–7, you can see three places where a molecule of water enters the cycle. Since the Krebs cycle runs twice for each glucose molecule, 6 molecules of water are needed for each glucose molecule that is broken down. This water should be shown as a raw material in the equation. Therefore, the equation should be written as follows:

$$C_6H_{12}O_6 + 6\ H_2O + 6\ O_2 \longrightarrow 6\ CO_2 + 12\ H_2O + \text{Energy (36 ATP)}$$

Efficiency of Cellular Respiration

Figure 6–9 summarizes all of the biochemical pathways involved in cellular respiration. In anaerobic respiration, you may recall, glycolysis produces a net yield of 2 ATP molecules per molecule of glucose. This type of respiration is fairly inefficient. It leaves most of the potential energy of the glucose in the end products of fermentation. Anaerobic respiration, however, does meet the energy needs of many simple organisms, such as yeast and bacteria.

Aerobic respiration yields almost 20 times as much energy per molecule of glucose as fermentation does. It is, moreover, an efficient process. About 45% of the total energy obtainable from the oxidation of glucose is stored as ATP molecules after aerobic

Figure 6–9

Cellular Respiration—A Summary. During glycolysis, glucose is broken down to pyruvic acid, producing 2 molecules of ATP. In anaerobic respiration, pyruvic acid is further broken down, but no more ATP is produced. In aerobic respiration, the Krebs cycle and the electron transport chain yield 34 ATP (for a total of 36 molecules of ATP). ▶

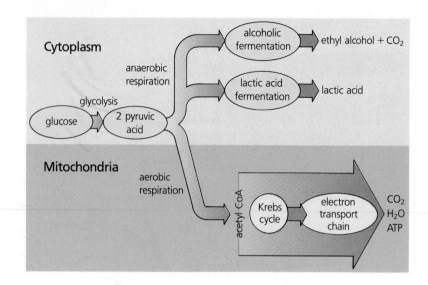

respiration. By comparison, an automobile engine converts only about 25% of the chemical energy of its fuel to useful work.

Muscle Fatigue and Oxygen Debt

Some organisms that have the capacity for aerobic respiration can function by anaerobic respiration alone when free oxygen is not available. Yeast cells, for example, use aerobic respiration when oxygen is present, but they can live and grow by anaerobic respiration in the absence of oxygen. Muscle cells in humans and other animals normally rely on aerobic respiration to meet their energy needs. They can, however, function for a short time without oxygen by using the energy obtained from glycolysis alone.

During periods of prolonged physical activity, the muscle cells may use oxygen faster than it can be supplied. When the oxygen supply becomes too low, the electron transport chain cannot work. This forces the Krebs cycle to stop.

When the Krebs cycle stops, the muscle cells continue to release energy by glycolysis. Pyruvic acid becomes the acceptor for electrons and is converted to lactic acid. The buildup of lactic acid in the muscle cells produces feelings of fatigue and gradually reduces the ability of the cells to do their normal work.

When lactic acid builds up, the cells need a period of rest or reduced activity to recover to a normal condition. During this time, fresh supplies of oxygen allow the lactic acid to be oxidized back to pyruvic acid, and the accumulated hydrogen is passed down through the electron transport chain. The amount of oxygen needed to get rid of the lactic acid is called oxygen debt.

Respiration of Fats and Proteins

This discussion of aerobic respiration has focused on the breakdown of glucose to supply energy for the cell. Cells that carry on

Figure 6–10

Energy. Heavy exercise can cause a buildup of lactic acid in muscle cells, leading to muscle fatigue. ▼

aerobic respiration can also extract energy from other types of food substances, such as fats and proteins. These substances are broken down and converted into compounds that can enter the respiratory pathway at some intermediate point in the glucose breakdown pathway. Figure 6–11 shows where these compounds enter into the pathway.

When fats are used as a source of energy, twice as much ATP is produced as when glucose is used. This is why a diet high in fat can lead to weight gain. You must be twice as active to burn a gram of fat as you must be to burn a gram of carbohydrate. A gram of protein, on the other hand, yields about the same amount of energy as a gram of carbohydrate. However, proteins are not a preferred source of energy for the cell.

The Evolution of Cellular Respiration

The environment of early earth contained little or no oxygen. Life forms that evolved were primitive cells much like the prokaryotic cells we find today. Their internal structure contained few, if any, organelles, certainly nothing as complex as mitochondria or chloroplasts.

Biologists believe glycolysis, the breakdown of glucose, was the first biochemical process to evolve. It uses no oxygen, occurs in the cytoplasm, and is not associated with any organelle. The reactions were well-suited to early prokaryotic cells on a primitive planet. Every living organism can carry out glycolysis, but most have developed efficient biochemical pathways that can extract more energy from glucose molecules.

How did the more efficient pathways evolve? It is believed that respiration became more efficient through evolution. Evolution is a step-by-step process building upon its earlier successes. Cellular respiration evolved as one series of reactions added to another.

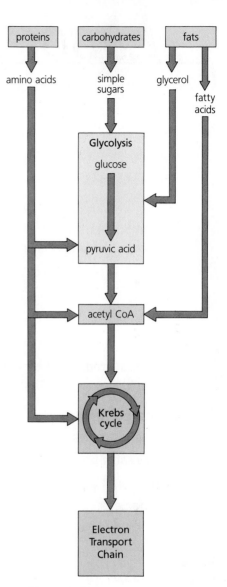

▲ **Figure 6–11**

The Role of Proteins and Fats in Respiration. Proteins, fats, and carbohydrates can be used as fuel for respiration. Once the molecules are broken down, they enter the respiratory pathway at various points.

6-3 Section Review

1. What is the function of oxygen in aerobic respiration?
2. What is the Krebs cycle?
3. Which system of enzymes and coenzymes uses the energy from NADH and $FADH_2$ to form ATP?
4. What are the three end products of aerobic respiration?
5. During strenuous exercise, what substance becomes an end product of respiration in muscle cells?

Critical Thinking

6. Imagine a hot potato being passed down a line, from one person to another. In what ways can this be thought of as similar to aerobic respiration? How does it differ? (*Comparing*)

Laboratory
Investigation

Fermentation of Yeast

Yeast are single-celled organisms that use sugar as a food source. In this investigation, you will observe the substances produced by yeast cells from the breakdown of food molecules.

Problem

How can you **predict** which kind of sugar produces the most rapid respiration in yeast cells?

Materials (per group)

▶ 5 large test tubes

▶ 5 disposable plastic pipettes

▶ weight to fit on pipette stem

▶ thermometer

▶ yeast solutions
  yeast-sucrose
  yeast-glucose
  yeast-lactose
  yeast-molasses
  yeast-water

▶ glass-marking pencil

▶ watch with second hand or timer

Procedure

1. Label the test tubes from 1 to 5.

2. Fill the bulb section of a pipette with the yeast-sucrose solution. To fill the pipettes, pull up as much liquid as possible into the stem by squeezing the bulb and then slowly releasing it. Turn the pipette upside down and tap the pipette to move the liquid into the bulb. Keep the pipette upside down.

3. Attach a weight to the pipette stem just above the bulb and place the pipette (still upside down) into test tube 1, which is three-quarters full with warm water (about 37°C). The pipette should be completely covered by the water and have about 2 to 3 cm of water above the tip.

4. You should observe tiny bubbles being released from the tip of the pipette. Count the number of bubbles released over a period of 10 minutes and record your results.

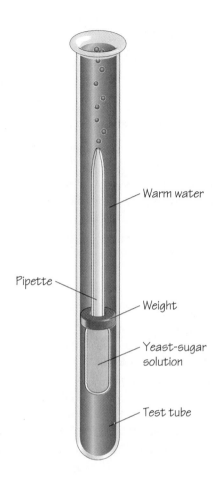

Warm water

Pipette

Weight

Yeast-sugar
solution

Test tube

Observations

1. What differences do you note in the number of bubbles that you see?

2. How did your data compare with the class average?

Analysis and Conclusions

1. What was the purpose of the yeast-and-water solution?

2. What is the name of the gas that is inside the bubbles released from the solutions? Can you design a test to identify this gas?

3. Explain how the counting of the gas bubbles is a way of measuring fermentation.

4. Which sugar was the best food source for yeast? Give evidence to support your answer.

5. How does the molasses differ from the other sugars that you used?

Extensions

Design an experiment to determine the effect of different temperatures on fermentation in yeast.

5. Repeat steps 2 to 4 for each of the remaining solutions. Record your observations for each.

6. Collect data from the class and calculate the average number of bubbles produced by each solution. Construct a graph of your data and the class average.

Chapter 6 Review

Study Outline

6-1 Energy for Life

▶ All living things obtain energy for their life processes through cellular respiration.

▶ Cellular respiration consists of the step-by-step breakdown of a nutrient, most commonly glucose, to release its energy in order to produce ATP.

▶ Energy for cell function is stored in the high-energy compound ATP.

▶ In the breakdown of glucose, energy is transferred from substance to substance in a series of oxidation-reduction reactions that are controlled by enzymes. Molecules such as NAD^+ and FAD act as electron carriers.

6-2 Anaerobic Respiration

▶ Both aerobic and anaerobic respiration begin with glycolysis. Each glucose molecule is broken apart into 2 pyruvic acid molecules, with a net gain of 2 ATP molecules.

▶ In anaerobic respiration, glycolysis is followed by further chemical reactions in which pyruvic acid is converted either to lactic acid or to ethyl alcohol and carbon dioxide. This process is called fermentation.

6-3 Aerobic Respiration

▶ In aerobic respiration, pyruvic acid is broken down after glycolysis to yield additional energy. These steps take place within the mitochondria and in the presence of oxygen.

▶ Acetyl CoA enters the Krebs cycle, which yields 2 molecules of carbon dioxide, 4 pairs of electrons, and 1 ATP per "turn." There are two "turns" of the cycle per glucose molecule.

▶ The electrons enter the electron transport chain, where they are carried along by electron carriers. As the electrons are transferred, energy is released. Thirty-two ATP molecules are formed.

▶ Fats and proteins may also be used as a source of energy, entering the respiratory pathway at intermediate points.

Chapter Assessment

Multiple Choice

Choose the letter of the answer that best completes each statement or answers the question.

1. The cell's main energy-storing compound is (a) FADH. (b) NAD^+. (c) ATP. (d) AMP

2. Pyruvic acid is a product of (a) respiration. (b) photosynthesis. (c) fermentation. (d) glycolysis.

3. During vigorous activity, muscle cells produce (a) alcohol. (b) lactic acid. (c) glucose. (d) starch.

4. During respiration, the final acceptor of electrons in the electron transport chain is (a) oxygen. (b) carbon dioxide. (c) water. (d) ATP.

5. Carbon is released from the Krebs cycle in the form of (a) glucose. (b) carbon dioxide. (d) citric acid. (d) water.

6. The movement of hydrogen ions across a membrane to generate energy to form ATP is called (a) chemiosmosis. (b) photosynthesis. (c) respiration. (d) fermentation.

7. An end product formed during fermentation in yeast is (a) FAD. (b) hydrogen. (c) water. (d) alcohol.

8. Electron transport occurs in the (a) mitochondria. (b) nucleus. (c) ribosomes. (d) cell membrane.

9. The end products of aerobic respiration are (a) carbon dioxide and water. (b) glucose and water. (c) glucose and oxygen. (d) carbon dioxide and oxygen.

10. Anaerobic respiration (a) only occurs in bacteria. (b) requires oxygen. (c) begins with glycolysis. (d) yields no ATP.

Content Review

Answer each of the following in complete sentences.

11. Why must all living things carry on cellular respiration?

12. Why are oxidation-reduction reactions always coupled?

13. State two differences between anaerobic respiration and aerobic respiration.

14. After glycolysis, what happens to pyruvic acid if no oxygen is present?

15. In anaerobic respiration, what is the net gain in ATP from one glucose molecule?

16. Where do the following processes take place in the cell: glycolysis, Krebs cycle, electron transport chain?

17. What is the chief function of the Krebs cycle?

18. In anaerobic respiration, what happens to most of the energy stored in glucose?

19. What happens to most of the energy stored in glucose in aerobic respiration?

20. Explain what happens in muscle cells to form lactic acid.

Graphic Organizing

For information on graphic organizers, see Appendix G at the back of this text.

21. **Compare/Contrast Matrix** Use the matrix shown to compare aerobic respiration and anaerobic respiration. Copy the matrix onto a separate sheet of paper and complete it.

Characteristic	Aerobic Respiration	Anaerobic Respiration
starting material	?	?
pathways involved	?	?
final hydrogen acceptor	?	?
end products	?	?
energy produced	?	?

Critical Thinking and Problem Solving

Discuss each of the following in a brief paragraph.

22. **Predicting** What would happen if the energy in glucose were released all at once instead of in a series of small steps?

23. **Drawing conclusions** Do you think yeast cells would grow more rapidly when carrying out fermentation or aerobic respiration? Support your answer.

24. **Relating** Why are oxidation-reduction reactions important to the cell?

25. **Inferring** Victims of a heart attack often have small amounts of lactic acid in the blood leaving the heart. What does this suggest about a possible factor in heart attacks?

26. **Relating** Compounds that participate in energy changes in living cells have been compared to "charged batteries" and "uncharged batteries." Which cell compound would the charged battery represent? Which compound would the uncharged battery represent? How does the uncharged battery become charged again?

27. **Drawing conclusions** A student had a packet of seeds several years old. To avoid planting seeds that might not grow, he first tested them as shown below. In jar A he placed 10 bean seeds that had been soaked in water overnight. In jar B he placed the indicator bromthymol blue, which turns yellow-green when mixed with carbon dioxide. By the next day, the bromthymol blue was a strong yellow-green color. The student decided to plant the seeds. Why did the student conclude that the seeds were alive? What control should he have set up to verify the cause of the color change?

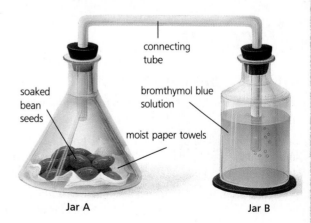

Jar A   Jar B

Discovery
Learning Activity

Sorting the Animals

1. Working in a group, make a list of 20 to 30 different kinds of animals.

2. Sort the animals into different categories (for example, cats, bears, canines, etc.) based on their apparent similarities and differences, listing each category and its animals in a chart.

3. Choose one category and use a field guide to verify the group's decisions, noting any errors or questionable classifications on the chart.

4. Revise the group's chart as needed and produce a final version.

Classification of Living Things

Guide for Reading

Previewing the Chapter

Like small armored tanks, two rhinoceros beetles confront each other on a tree branch. How do you think the rhinoceros beetle got its name? Biologists estimate that there are millions of different kinds of beetles. How do biologists manage to distinguish one kind of beetle from another? How are biologists able to classify living things? What are the characteristics of the six kingdoms of living things?

Key Words

binomial nomenclature, genus, kingdom, species, taxonomy

Key Concepts

- **Explain** the importance of classification systems.
- **Classify** living things into six kingdoms.
- **Classify** organisms into their specific kingdom (Laboratory Investigation)

7-1 Classification

Section Objectives:

- *Describe* the naming system used in modern biology.
- *Explain* how the theory of evolution has affected taxonomy.
- *Describe* the types of evidence now used to determine relationships between groups of organisms.

Classification Systems

About 1.5 million different kinds of living things are known today, and each year thousands more are identified. Some experts believe there are as many as 10 million different organisms. They vary in form and size from microscopic bacteria to giant redwood trees.

To deal with this huge number of organisms, biologists name and group, or classify, the organisms according to an established international system. This makes it easier for scientists to discuss the types and characteristics of living things. The branch of biology that deals with the classification and naming of living things is known as **taxonomy** (tak SAHN uh mee).

You face many situations every day in which you need to find objects or information. If the objects or information have been organized—or classified—into groups, you should be able to find what you are looking for without checking every single item in a large group. To

▲ **Figure 2–1**

Observation in Science. Biologists often observe organisms in controlled environments and in nature as part of their research.

◀ Rhinoceros beetles.

Figure 7–2

Classification in a Supermarket. All items in a supermarket are grouped with similar items, in order to make finding the items easier. ▶

help you understand what is involved in classification, consider the arrangement of goods in a supermarket.

A large supermarket, like the one shown in Figure 7–2, carries 7000 to 10 000 items. If these items were placed on the shelves randomly, shopping for the week's groceries might take an entire day or even longer. However, the basis for any classification system is the grouping of things according to similarities. You can find the items you need fairly quickly because related items are arranged in groups. First, items are grouped into broad categories—frozen foods, meat, produce, cleaning supplies, paper goods, and dairy products. Each of these departments is subdivided into a series of smaller, related categories. For example, the frozen food department has separate sections for vegetables, juices, cakes, fish, TV dinners, and ice cream. Each of these sections is further subdivided. The ice cream section is divided into half-gallons, quarts, pints, and cups. Within each size range, the ice cream may be grouped by flavor or brand name.

Once you are familiar with the organization of the supermarket, it is easy to find an item. If the market manager gets a new kind of frozen cake, it is a simple matter to place it with the other frozen cakes. In a similar manner, the classification system used in modern biology allows biologists to identify an organism and place it in the correct group with related organisms.

Early Classification Schemes

In early attempts at classification, living things were separated into two major groups—the plant kingdom and the animal kingdom. These two groups were then subdivided in various ways. In early historical documents, for example, plants were divided into grasses, herbs, and trees, while animals were classified as fish, creeping creatures, fowl, beasts, and cattle.

In the fourth century B.C., the Greek philosopher Aristotle made a study of animals; another philosopher, Theophrastus, studied plants. Aristotle grouped animals according to the kind of environment in which they lived. Thus, there were air-dwellers, land-dwellers, and water-dwellers. Theophrastus grouped plants according to stem structure. Thus, there were herbs (soft stems), shrubs (several woody stems), and trees (a single woody stem). Using these crude subdivisions, Aristotle and Theophrastus classified more than 500 kinds of plants and 500 kinds of animals.

The classification systems of Aristotle and Theophrastus worked well for the small number of organisms that were familiar to the people of Europe and the Mediterranean region at the time. However, during the 1400s and 1500s, European explorers returned home from their travels with many new types of organisms. The development of the microscope in the 1600s also led to the discovery of many microorganisms not previously known to exist. As the number of known organisms increased, the need for a more effective classification system became clear.

The next major advance in classification was made in the mid-1600s by the English naturalist John Ray. In his travels through England and Europe, Ray identified and classified more than 18 000 different types of plants. He also classified the members of several different animal groups. Ray was the first to use the term *species* (SPEE sheez) for each different kind of organism. Ray defined a species as a group of organisms that were structurally similar and that passed these similarities to their offspring. Closely related species were included in a broader group called a **genus** (JEE nus) (plural, genera). See Figure 7–4. Related genera were arranged in still broader groups.

The Swedish botanist Carolus Linnaeus (luh NEE us), considered the founder of modern taxonomy, improved upon the work of earlier taxonomists. Linnaeus established methods for classifying and naming organisms that are still used. In his system, plants and animals were arranged in such a way that they could be identified easily. Like Ray, Linnaeus used structural similarities as a basis for his classification system.

Figure 7–3
An Early Classification System. Aristotle grouped organisms as air-dwellers, land-dwellers, and water-dwellers. ▼

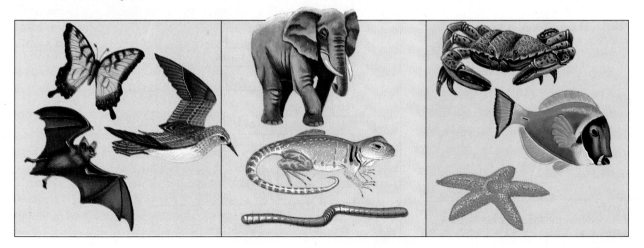

▲ **Figure 7–4**
Species of Cats. The tiger (top), lion (middle), and jaguar (bottom) all belong to the same genus, *Panthera*.

Classification Categories

Since the time of Linnaeus, taxonomists have added several categories to the classification system. The broadest category is the *kingdom*. The narrowest category is the species. In classifying living things, biologists generally use the following categories: **kingdom, phylum** (FY lum) (plural, phyla), **class, order, family, genus,** and **species.** In plant taxonomy, the term *division* is used in place of phylum.

As shown in Figure 7–4, related species are grouped in a *genus;* related genera are grouped in a *family;* related families are grouped in an *order;* related orders are grouped in a *class;* related classes are grouped in a *phylum;* and related phyla are grouped in a *kingdom.* Each species—that is, each type of organism—belongs to one kingdom, one phylum, one class, one order, one family, and one genus. Figure 7–6 shows the complete classification for several different species.

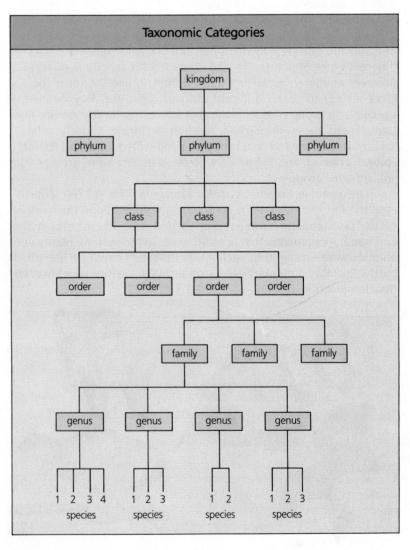

Figure 7–5
Categories in the Modern Classification System. ▶

Classification of Some Familiar Organisms				
Category	**Human**	**Chimpanzee**	**Housefly**	**Dandelion**
Kingdom	Animalia	Animalia	Animalia	Plantae
Phylum	Chordata	Chordata	Arthropoda	Tracheophyta
Class	Mammalia	Mammalia	Insecta	Angiospermae
Order	Primates	Primates	Diptera	Asterales
Family	Hominidae	Pongidae	Muscidae	Asteraceae
Genus	*Homo*	*Pan*	*Musca*	*Taraxacum*
Species	*Homo sapiens*	*Pan troglodytes*	*Musca domestica*	*Taraxacum officinale*

▲ **Figure 7–6**
Classification of Some Familiar Organisms.

Naming Organisms

A system for naming things is called **nomenclature** (NOH men klay chur). Before Linnaeus, each species was identified by its genus name followed by a string of Latin words that described the species. In some cases, 8 or 10 words followed the genus name. As you can imagine, using such long descriptions as a way of naming organisms was inefficient and inconvenient. In his descriptions of organisms, Linnaeus named each species with a genus name followed by a single descriptive word. Both words were in Latin, which was the language scholars used. Within each genus, no two species could be described by the same word.

This two-word system of identifying each kind of organism, which is still used, is known as **binomial** (by NOH mee ul) ("two names") **nomenclature.** It is equivalent to the system of using two names to identify a person—a family name and a given (or first) name. The genus name is like a person's family (or last) name, while the specific name is like a person's first name.

In modern biology, each kind of organism has a two-word Latin name—its scientific name. The first word is its genus name, the second identifies the species within the genus. Both names together make up the species name. The Latin terms are not chosen randomly. Usually, they point out some aspect of the organism, such as where it lives, its size, or one of its features. For example, *Hystrix indica* is the Indian porcupine and *Carnegiea gigantea* is the giant saguaro cactus. A fragrant species of water lily is *Nymphaea ordorata.*

It is common to abbreviate a genus name with its first letter. This usually is done when the names of species within the same genus appear over and over in a written document. For example, in a scientific article about oak trees, genus *Quercus*, species names such as *Quercus rubra* and *Quercus alba,* would appear as *Q. rubra* and *Q. alba.*

Most large plants and animals also have common names. However, common names are often confusing and inexact. A starfish, for example, is not a fish. Also, one species may have several different common names. The blue jay, *Cyanocitta christata,* is also known as the blue coat, the corn thief, and the nest robber. In other cases, the same common name is used for two or more different species. More than a dozen different species of plants are commonly known as raspberries. Finally, common names vary from language to language. An English "dog" is a Spanish "perro" and a Japanese "inu." However, the scientific name for dog, *Canis familiaris,* is understood by biologists everywhere.

Modern Taxonomy

Until the mid-1800s, most scientists viewed each species as constant and unchanging. Every species was thought to be independent and unrelated to other species, no matter how many characteristics they had in common. The groupings in which taxonomists placed organisms merely indicated different degrees of similarity in structure or appearance.

This view of the biological world as static began to change as evidence grew that species gradually change, or evolve, over time. According to this theory of gradual change, which is known as the **theory of evolution,** new species arise, or evolve, over long periods of time from preexisting species. As new species evolve, older species may become extinct. Unit 6 discusses the mechanisms that most scientists believe are involved in evolution.

Today, the definition of a species has been further refined. Now, a **species** is a natural group, or *population,* of similar organisms that interbreed in nature. If the members of a species become separated into groups that breed independently for long periods of time, each group will evolve differently. Their evolution will depend on the opportunities and demands of the particular environment. Eventually, the separated groups may become so different that they must be classified as different species.

The theory of evolution serves as the basis of modern taxonomy. The number and kinds of similarities between different species are used to estimate the hereditary relationship between species. Species sharing many of the same characteristics are believed to share a common ancestral species. Many scientists believe that the more similarities between organisms in any two groups, the more recently in evolutionary history the species evolved from a common ancestor. Similarly, the fewer shared characteristics, the further back in evolutionary time the species evolved. This kind of information often is represented in the form of a branched diagram called a *phylogenetic tree.* **Phylogeny** is the evolutionary history of a species or a group of organisms. A phylogenetic tree indicates when related groups of organisms have evolved from common ancestors and, in some cases, how much they have diverged from each other. Figure 7–7 is an example of a phylogenetic tree.

But what information about an organism do taxonomists use when they classify? Taxonomists use structural, biochemical, cytological, embryological, behavioral, and fossil information. Usually, the more kinds of information used, the more likely the classification will reflect true evolutionary relationships.

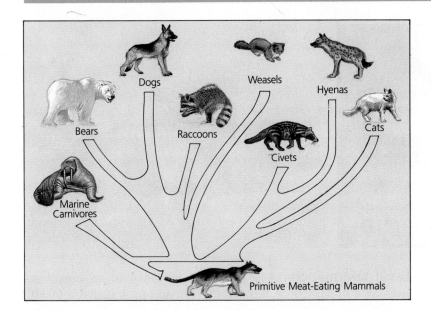

Structural Information Structural similarities, such as those in skeletal structure or leaf anatomy, are the primary basis for grouping organisms. There are instances, however, in which additional information may be needed to make a classification judgment. Furthermore, it is always desirable to pair structural information with other kinds of available information.

Biochemical Information Today, taxonomists frequently use biochemical data when classifying organisms. Information about the DNA, RNA, and proteins of different species can be compared to establish relationships. This kind of information was used recently to show that the giant panda of Asia probably is closely related to bears.

Cytological Information Details about the cellular structure of organisms can also offer clues to evolutionary relationships. Many single-celled organisms, for example, have been classified on the basis of their similarities in cellular structure, which can be seen with the electron microscope. Another source of cytological information that taxonomists have used is information on numbers of chromosomes in a species. Many plant species have been classified, in part, according to their chromosome numbers.

Embryological Information The term *embryo* refers to any multicellular organism in its early stages of development. While the adult forms of different animal species may look very different, the embryos can look very similar. Taxonomists use embryological data to establish taxonomic relationships that otherwise might be overlooked.

Behavioral Information Sometimes, behavior may be the only basis for distinguishing one species from another. For example, some species of crickets can be distinguished only on the basis of their mating calls.

▲ **Figure 7–8**

Modern and Fossil Fish. A modern-day fish (left) shows striking similarity to the fossil of an ancient fish (right).

Fossil Information Any preserved evidence of an organism, such as a bone, footprint, or body impression, is called a **fossil.** Fossils are useful in establishing likely relationships between modern-day species and species that lived thousands or even millions of years ago.

Taxonomy in Perspective

Although taxonomy has come a long way since Aristotle, not all classification problems have been solved. In fact, taxonomists constantly reexamine and refine previous classifications. A good part of taxonomy is subjective. While taxonomists follow general, established principles, their decisions are judgment calls that often vary from one taxonomist to another. Taxonomists may disagree over whether a species belongs in one genus or another or whether several species should be considered one species. Add to this process the task of classifying and naming newly discovered organisms and you realize taxonomy is a dynamic and important field of biology.

7-1 Section Review

1. Describe the system of binomial nomenclature used by biologists.
2. How has the theory of evolution affected the science of taxonomy?
3. What is the modern definition of a species?
4. What kinds of information are used by taxonomists to determine relationships between groups of organisms?

Critical Thinking

5. Explain the relationship between a class and an order. (*Relating Parts and Wholes*)

7-2 Major Taxonomic Groups

Section Objectives:

- *List* the six kingdoms and describe the characteristics of each.
- *Explain* the advantages of the six-kingdom system.

Early Classification Systems

In all early classification schemes, living things were divided into two kingdoms—plants and animals. Trees, grass, and flowers are plants, while frogs, fishes, insects, birds, and cats are animals. However, some organisms have both plant and animal characteristics. The unicellular organism, *euglena* (yoo GLEEN uh), for example, carries on photosynthesis like a plant, yet moves like an animal.

To solve the problem of classifying organisms that are not obviously animals or plants, taxonomists have added new kingdoms to the classification system. For years, biologists used a five-kingdom system of classification—Monera, Protista, Fungi, Plantae, and Animalia.

Today, because recent molecular studies using DNA and protein analysis has enabled biologists to better understand evolutionary relationships, most taxonomists use a six-kingdom system of classification. These scientists recognize that bacteria must be placed into two separate kingdoms—Archaebacteria (ahr kee bak TEER ee uh) and Eubacteria (yoo bak TEER ee uh)—because they are so different from one another. The six-kingdom system of classification—Archaebacteria, Eubacteria, Protista, Fungi, Plantae, and Animalia—is used in this textbook. The general characteristics of the six kingdoms are described briefly in Figure 7–9.

Figure 7–9

The Six Kingdoms. All living things can be classified into one of the six kingdoms. ▼

Kingdom	Archaebacteria	Eubacteria	Protista	Fungi	Plantae	Animalia
Cell type	prokaryotic	prokaryotic	eukaryotic	eukaryotic	eukaryotic	eukaryotic
Cell structures	have cell walls that lack peptidoglycan	have cell walls made up of peptidoglycan	have a nucleus, mitochondria, some have chloroplasts	have a nucleus, mitochondria; cell wall of chitin	have a nucleus, mitochondria, chloroplasts; cell wall of cellulose	have a nucleus, mitochondria; no cell wall
Body form	unicellular	unicellular	mostly unicellular, some multicellular	some unicellular, most multicellular	multicellular	multicellular
Nutrition	autotrophic or heterotrophic	autotrophic or heterotrophic	autotrophic or heterotrophic	heterotrophic (absorption)	autotrophic	heterotrophic
Examples	methanogens, halophiles	*Rhizobium, Bacillus*	amebae, paramecia	yeasts, molds, mushrooms	mosses, ferns, flowering plants, seaweeds	sponges, worms, snails, insects, mammals

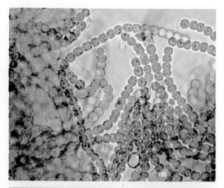

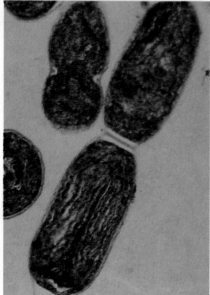

Prokaryotic Kingdoms

The group of bacteria that makes up the kingdom **Archaebacteria** live in extremely hostile environments—volcanic hot springs, salt lakes or seas, and black organic mud at the bottom of marshes and swamps. Many can grow only in oxygen-free environments. These bacteria are unicellular, prokaryotic cells—cells that lack an organized nucleus with a nuclear membrane. Archaebacteria also have cell walls that lack the carbohydrate peptidoglycan. In this group of bacteria are the methane-producing methanogens, the salt-loving halophiles, and the bacteria that live in hot, acidic environments—the thermoacidophiles.

Most bacteria are members of the kingdom **Eubacteria.** These bacteria are mostly unicellular, although some form chains or colonies of cells. Eubacteria are prokaryotic, and have peptidoglycan cell walls. Most eubacteria are heterotrophic. Included in this group of bacteria are the disease-producing bacteria and the cyanobacteria.

Kingdom Protista

Members of the kingdom **Protista** (proh TIST ah) are mostly unicellular, although there are colonial and simple, multicellular forms. The cells of *protists* are eukaryotic. That is, like the cells of multicellular organisms, each contains a membrane-bound nucleus and other organelles. Some protists are motile and feed upon bacteria and bits of organic matter. These animal-like protists are called *protozoa.* Other protists carry out photosynthesis. These plantlike protists are members of a group of organisms called algae.

▲ **Figure 7–10**

Examples From the Kingdom Eubacteria.
A colonial blue-green bacterium (top) and a blue-green bacterium at higher magnification. Note the lack of a membrane-bound nucleus. (Bottom magnification 99 900 X)

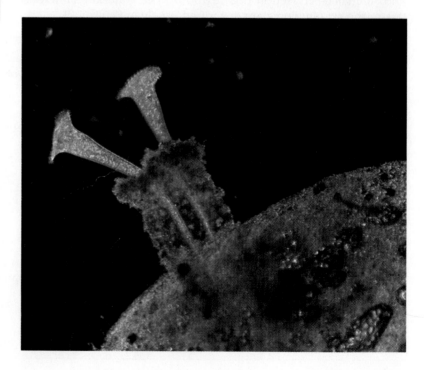

Figure 7–11

An Example from the Kingdom Protista.
This colonial species of *Stentor* is a type of protozoan. (Magnification 52X) ▶

Algae is the term used for all eukaryotic, unicellular and simple multicellular, organisms that carry out photosynthesis and live in water. The different groups of algae are not thought to be directly related to each other.

Kingdom Fungi

The kingdom **Fungi** (FUN jy) includes molds, yeasts, mushrooms, rusts, and smuts. *Fungi* (singular, fungus) live either as parasites on other living things or as decomposers of dead matter. Some fungi are unicellular, but most are multicellular. Fungi are eukaryotic. That is, they have cell organelles and distinct nuclei surrounded by nuclear membranes. Although fungi have cell walls, the walls are chemically different from those of other organisms. In the past, members of the kingdom Fungi were placed in the plant kingdom because they resemble plants more than animals. See Figure 7–12. The differences between fungi and plants are so great, however, that biologists have placed fungi in their own kingdom. Unlike plants, fungi contain no chlorophyll and cannot synthesize food. Instead, they secrete enzymes that digest food material outside the organism. The fungi then absorb the nutrients.

▲ **Figure 7–12**
An Example from the Kingdom Fungi. Mushrooms, like the poisonous one shown here, are just one of many types of fungi.

Kingdom Plantae

The *plants,* members of the kingdom **Plantae** (PLAN tee), include mosses, liverworts, ferns, and seed plants. See Figure 7–13. The cells of plants have cell walls. Members of the plant kingdom show a true tissue and organ organization. Plants cannot move from place to place on their own. Nearly all plants carry on photosynthesis and most live on land. Within plant cells, chlorophyll is found in chloroplasts.

Kingdom Animalia

There are more species in kingdom **Animalia** (an uh MAL ee ah) than in any other kingdom. Members of the animal kingdom are multicellular and usually show an organ and organ system level of organization. During some part of their life cycle, most animals can move from place to place on their own. Since animals cannot carry on photosynthesis, they must obtain food from their environment. Most animals actively search for food, relying upon highly specialized sensory systems, brains, and nerve-muscle systems to do so. These same systems permit other complex types of behavior. Animals such as sponges, worms, and insects have no backbone and are called *invertebrates.* Animals with backbones, such as fish, snakes, and humans, are called *vertebrates.* Sexual reproduction is more common in animals than asexual reproduction. In some species, there is specialized courtship behavior, and there may be extensive parental care of the young.

A more complete list of all the taxonomic groups is found in Appendix F at the back of this book.

▲ **Figure 7–13**
Examples from the Plant and Animal Kingdoms. The leaf is part of a plant, while the lizard is a member of the animal kingdom.

The Taxonomic Key

What questions would you ask if you were playing a game in which you had to identify a famous person of whom another player was thinking? You might begin by asking: Is the person male or female? If female, is she American, or non-American? If non-American, is she European or non-European? By continuing with questions that became more and more specific, you may be able to identify the person.

Biologists use a similar procedure to identify an organism. The procedure they use is a series of instructions called a taxonomic key. A **taxonomic key** is a tool used to identify organisms already classified by taxonomists. Most keys are dichotomous. That is, they consist of a series of paired statements that describe alternative possible characteristics of the organism. These paired statements usually describe the presence or absence of certain characteristics or structures that are easily seen. For example, an animal may or may not have a spinal column. If it has a spinal column, it may or may not have gills. If gills are absent, its body may or may not be covered with scales, and so on. Each set of choices must be arranged in such a way that each step produces a smaller grouping. Figure 7–14 shows a sample taxonomic key that is used for identifying vertebrates.

MiniLab

Skill: Classifying

A Taxing Situation

Problem

What rules do you use to **classify** common objects?

Procedure

1. Working in a group, think of a characteristic that will divide the following materials into two groups: plain straight pins, straight pins with colored plastic tops, safety pins of different sizes, buttons, a zipper, steel nails of various sizes, steel screws of various sizes, brass nails of various sizes, brass screws of various sizes, galvanized nails of various sizes, and galvanized screws of various sizes.

2. Divide each of the two groups into two smaller groups.

3. Further divide each smaller group into subgroups.

4. Continue this process until there is only one object in each group.

Analyze and Conclude

1. What characteristics do all of these objects have in common? In what ways are they different?

2. How many groups does your classification system have?

3. On what basis did you choose to place each object?

Key for Identifying Vertebrates	
1	1A. spinal column present . . . go to 2. 1B. spinal column absent . . . Invertebrate.
2	2A. fins and gills present . . . Fish. 2B. fins and gills absent . . . go to 3.
3	3A. scales present . . . Reptile. 3B. scales absent . . . go to 4.
4	4A. feathers present . . . Bird. 4B. feathers absent . . . go to 5.
5	5A. hair or fur present . . . Mammal. 5B. hair or fur absent . . . Amphibian.

◀ **Figure 7–14**
A Sample Taxonomic Key For Identifying Vertebrates.

Representative Organisms

As you learned in Chapter 1, all living things carry on certain processes such as nutrition, respiration, transport, excretion, and regulation. Size greatly influences how an organism performs these processes. The cells of single-celled and small multicellular organisms are in close contact with the external environment. Because they are small, they can carry on their life processes in a simple fashion. However, as animals become larger, most of their cells are not in contact with the environment. In these animals, the life functions are carried out by groups of organs arranged in systems.

In Unit 2, you will study how certain organisms solve the problems of life. Since you cannot consider every organism, you will study six representative organisms in order of increasing complexity. Two of these organisms, the ameba and the paramecium, are unicellular and are classified as protists. The others are animals: the hydra, the earthworm, the grasshopper, and the human. All these organisms are **heterotrophs** (HET uh ruh trohfs) —organisms that obtain their food from the environment. In contrast, plants and certain other organisms make their own food. These organisms are called **autotrophs.**

Ameba and Paramecium   The ameba and paramecium are common inhabitants of ponds and streams. As protists, they carry out their life processes within a single cell. Although they are small, they can be seen without a microscope. Under the microscope, the ameba, shown in Figure 7–15, appears as a transparent mass that constantly changes shape. It has cytoplasm with a cell membrane and a nucleus. It creeps along through the flowing of cytoplasm into temporary structures called *pseudopods,* or false feet.

The paramecium, shown in Figure 7–16, is easy to recognize because of its slipperlike shape. It contains two nuclei. The larger macronucleus controls general cell activities. The smaller micronucleus is involved in reproduction. A stiffened cell membrane with

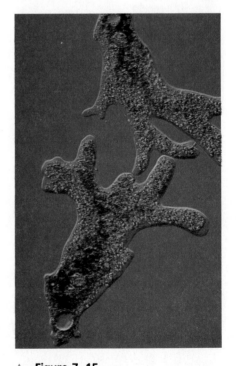

▲ **Figure 7–15**
Ameba. The ameba is just one of many types of protozoan. Organelles and other particles are evident in the cytoplasm of these ameba. (Magnification 108X)

Figure 7–16

Paramecium. The paramecium is another type of protozoan. The cilia that cover the surface of a paramecium can be seen along the edge of this specimen. (Magnification 325X) ▶

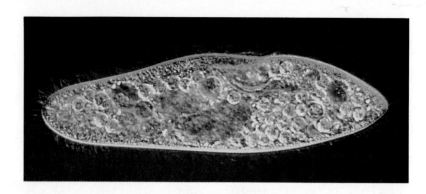

numerous, hairlike cilia surrounds the paramecium. The cilia allow the paramecium to swim. On one side of the paramecium is a depression, known as the oral groove, that leads into a tubular gullet. Both the oral groove and the gullet are involved in nutrition.

Hydra   The hydra, shown in Figure 7–17, belongs to the phylum **Cnidaria.** In its structure and function, the hydra is a simple animal. It is about 5 mm long and lives in fresh water. Usually it attaches itself to an underwater plant or some other solid object. The hydra has a tubelike body with only one opening, a mouth. The mouth, which leads into an internal cavity, is surrounded by tentacles. The body wall is made of only two cell layers.

Earthworm   The earthworm, shown in Figure 7–18, belongs to the phylum **Annelida.** Its long, round body is composed of many segments. The earthworm has a well-developed digestive system, a circulatory system, excretory organs, and a well-defined nervous system.

Grasshopper   The grasshopper, shown in Figure 7–19, belongs to the class *Insecta* of the phylum **Arthropoda.** The grasshopper has a well-developed digestive system, a circulatory system, a respiratory system, excretory organs, and a nervous system.

Human   Humans belong to the class *Mammalia* of the subphylum *Vertebrata* of the phylum **Chordata.** Mammals nourish their young with milk. Their bodies are covered with hair or fur. Many have well-developed brains.

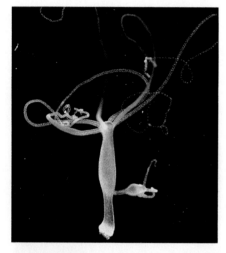

▲   **Figure 7–17**

Hydra. The hydra represents a simple, multicellular organism. This hydra is reproducing by budding a new hydra.

Figure 7–18

Earthworm. Earthworms have a more complex body organization than hydra. ▶

Grasshopper. The grasshopper shows a level of complexity in its body structure that is greater than that in the earthworm.

Evolution: A Unifying Theme

As you have read, the modern taxonomy system attempts to classify organisms into groups that reflect their hereditary and, therefore, evolutionary relationships. To classify an organism, taxonomists must gather whatever is known about the organism's structure, chemistry, embryological development, and behavior and try to reconstruct, based on the modern theory of evolution, a reasonable picture of the organism and its relationship to other organisms.

When scientists observe striking similarities between some species, they are led to conclude that similar species have evolved from a common ancestor. Scientists may note, for example, that while a bird's wing and a seal's flippers look very different and have very different functions, their internal structure as well as their embryological development is quite similar. Using these similarities as clues to a common ancestor, scientists have some basis for classifying the bird and the seal.

As a unifying theme in biology, evolution explains why there is such a diversity of life on earth today as well as how various groups of organisms are related. It also explains how the organisms of today are related to organisms of the past.

7-2 Section Review

1. List the six kingdoms.
2. In what fundamental way are the members of the Archaebacteria and Eubacteria different from organisms in the other kingdoms?
3. What are protozoa?
4. To what phylum and class do humans belong?

Critical Thinking

5. Why do scientists prefer the six-kingdom system of classification over a three- or four-kingdom system? (*Identifying Reasons*)

Laboratory
Investigation

Classifying Organisms

Organisms from all six kingdoms of living things can be found in most areas on the Earth. In this investigation, you will classify organisms found near your home or school.

Problem

Classify organisms into their specific kingdom.

Materials (per group)

- microscope
- medicine droppers
- microscope slides
- coverslips
- forceps
- Petri dish and cover
- bread
- sour milk, sauerkraut, or yogurt
- pond water
- small plants
- worms and insects in soil

Procedure

1. In a data table similar to the one shown, list the general characteristics of each kingdom in its appropriate place. Note: Because it is difficult to observe the differences in the characteristics of Archaebacteria and Eubacteria, they have been grouped together under Bacteria.

2. Use a medicine dropper to put a drop of liquid from sauerkraut, yogurt, or sour milk on a microscope slide. Cover the drop with a coverslip. Examine your specimen under the high-power objective of the microscope. On a separate sheet of paper, draw what you observe. Label the drawing with the kingdom of the organism and record the name of the organism in the appropriate place in the data table.

3. Use a clean medicine dropper to place a drop of pond water on a second microscope slide. Put a coverslip over the drop. Observe the pond water under the microscope. Draw the organisms you observe. Label the drawings with the kingdoms of the organisms and record the names of the organisms in the appropriate place in the data table.

4. Obtain a moistened piece of bread that has been sitting in an open Petri dish for one week. Use forceps to remove some of the "fuzzy" material that has grown on the bread. Place this material on a clean microscope slide. Add a drop of tap water and cover the drop with a coverslip. Examine this slide with the low-power objective. Draw what you observe. Record the name of the organism in the appropriate place in the data table.

5. Examine several small plants, leaves, or flowers. Record the names of the organisms in the appropriate place in the data table.

6. Look for worms, grubs, and pill bugs in the soil. Find some insects on plants in areas near your home or school. Record the names of the organisms in the appropriate place in the data table.

Observations

1. For organisms in which kingdoms did you require a microscope for observation?

2. What similarities and differences did you observe among organisms from different kingdoms?

3. For which kingdom was it easiest to find a variety of organisms? Most difficult?

Analysis and Conclusions

1. What difficulties did you encounter in classifying organisms?

2. Although you were not able to observe the differences between members of the kingdoms Archaebacteria and Eubacteria, can you think of a way in which you would be able to distinguish one from another?

Extensions

Repeat the investigation using specimens obtained from a different ecosystem, such as a beach or lake. Compare the organisms you find in this ecosystem with those you examined in the investigation.

Kingdom	Characteristics	Organisms
Bacteria (Archaebacteria and Eubacteria)		
Protista		
Fungi		
Plantae		
Animalia		

Chapter 7 Review

Study Outline

7-1 Classification

▶ All living things are classified according to an established, international classification system.

▶ Linnaeus classified organisms with a genus name followed by a specific name. This system of binomial nomenclature is still in use.

▶ Each species belongs to one genus, one family, one order, one class, one phylum, and one kingdom. Related species are grouped in a genus, related genera in a family, and so forth.

▶ The theory of evolution is the basis of the modern taxonomy system in which species are defined in terms of interbreeding populations.

▶ In addition to structural similarities, taxonomists base their classifications on evolutionary relationships.

7-2 Major Taxonomic Groups

▶ All organisms are classified into one of the six kingdoms—Archaebacteria, Eubacteria, Protista, Fungi, Plantae, and Animalia.

▶ The Archaebacteria and Eubacteria are the prokaryotic organisms—the bacteria.

▶ Protists are simple eukaryotic organisms such as the protozoa and algae.

▶ Fungi include molds, yeasts, and mushrooms.

▶ The plant kingdom includes the mosses, ferns, and seed plants.

▶ The animal kingdom is divided into vertebrates—animals with backbones—and invertebrates—animals without backbones.

Chapter Assessment

Multiple Choice

Choose the letter of the answer that best completes each statement or answers the question.

1. Scientific classification is based primarily on (a) utility. (b) size. (c) evolutionary relationships. (d) habitat.

2. In the six-kingdom system of classification, methanogens are classified as (a) Eubacteria. (b) Fungi. (c) Archaebacteria. (d) Protista.

3. Prokaryotes are different from the other kingdoms in that they (a) have flagella. (b) are green. (c) do not carry on photosynthesis. (d) lack a nucleus and most organelles.

4. The two classification groups used in binomial nomenclature are (a) kingdom and phylum. (b) class and order. (c) family and genus. (d) genus and species.

5. The system of taxonomy used today was developed by (a) Hooke. (b) Linnaeus. (c) Aristotle. (d) Schwann.

6. Related phyla are grouped into a (a) family. (b) genus. (c) species. (d) kingdom.

7. The hydra is classified as a (a) protist. (b) animal. (c) Eubacteria. (d) fungi.

8. The ability to interbreed is characteristic of all organisms in the same (a) phylum. (b) order. (c) family. (d) species.

9. Which are in the same kingdom? (a) protozoans and bacteria (b) green algae and fungi (c) grasshopper and protozoans (d) algae and protozoans

10. Animalia is a (a) kingdom. (b) phylum. (c) genus. (d) class.

Content Review

Answer each of the following in complete sentences.

11. Why is binomial nomenclature useful to biologists?

12. Why have modern taxonomists added new kingdoms to their classification schemes?

13. Describe the basic characteristics of the protist kingdom.

14. How do fungi digest their food?

15. Describe the basic characteristics of plants.

16. Describe the basic characteristics of animals.

17. What is the major difference between vertebrates and invertebrates?

18. How do plants and animals differ?

19. Describe what a taxonomic key is, and explain how it is used.

20. How does evolution act as a unifying theme in biology?

Graphic Organizing

For information on graphic organizers, see Appendix G at the back of this text.

21. Concept Map Copy the incomplete concept map that is shown below onto a separate sheet of paper. Then, fill in the missing terms. You may add additional concepts and relationships.

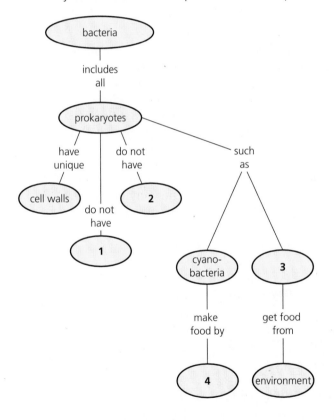

Critical Thinking and Problem Solving

Discuss each of the following in a brief paragraph.

22. Sequencing Place the following groups of classification in order, from the largest to the smallest: class, family, genus, kingdom, phylum, and species.

23. Inferring Why is it useful for a biologist to be able to place an unidentified organism in its proper group with related organisms?

24. Drawing conclusions Two organisms can interbreed if they belong to the same species. Saint Bernards and Great Danes belong to the species, which is known as *Canis familiaris*. What can you conclude about Saint Bernards and Great Danes? What factors could make this conclusion incorrect?

25. Drawing conclusions Suppose that you are given a jar containing hundreds of various organisms. After examining a dozen randomly picked specimens, you discover that each of the dozen belongs to the class Insecta. Make a generalization about the entire group of organisms in the jar. What could make this generalization invalid? What steps could you take to increase your confidence in your generalization?

26. Calculating You are a taxonomist interested in estimating how many new species of orchids exist in a tropical rain forest of 22 square kilometers. You randomly select five sites, each 0.1 square kilometer in area, and count the number of new species at each site. Once you identify a new species, it is no longer considered new. Based on the data in the table below, calculate the average number of new species of orchids present in a 0.1 square kilometer area. Then, when you have found the average, estimate how many new species of orchids are present in the forest.

Rain Forest Samples	
Site	**Number of New Species of Orchids**
A	3
B	2
C	0
D	8
E	1

Performance-Based Assessment

The Wall

Background

To a marathon runner, the 42-kilometer race can be neatly broken into two parts. Many long-distance runners have no trouble surviving the first 28 kilometers. At about 29 kilometers, however, many runners experience a point of complete exhaustion, which they refer to as "the wall." When they hit the wall, even determined runners fade, some begin to walk, and others are unable to complete the race. What happens to a runner physically when she or he hits the wall?

The wall seems to correspond to the point at which the body's glycogen reserves are depleted. This usually occurs after two or three hours of slow running. When the glycogen reserve is depleted, the runner's body must switch to fat reserves as a source of energy. The transition appears to be stressful to runners. At this point, the blood sugar level drops and the marathon runner may experience psychological depression. Many athletic coaches believe that the wall can be overcome by a rigorous training regimen. Part of the regimen, in addition to physical exercise, is a carefully planned diet.

Problem

You and your team of cell biologists have been asked to advise trainers at an Olympic training camp on the effectiveness of diet in helping runners prepare for long-distance races. The head coach believes that the wall can be overcome by eating large amounts of carbohydrates over a period of several days preceding a race. The excess carbohydrates, it is believed, will be stored as glycogen, which may help the runner break through the 29-kilometer barrier.

Data Table 1

Diet	Nutrient	Day 1	Day 2	Day 3	Day 4
1	Refined sugar	10%	15%	20%	25%
	Complex carbohydrates	48%	48%	48%	48%
	Protein	0%	0%	0%	0%
2	Refined sugar	10%	10%	10%	10%
	Complex carbohydrates	55%	60%	65%	70%
	Protein	0%	0%	0%	0%
3	Refined sugar	15%	20%	25%	30%
	Complex carbohydrates	55%	60%	65%	70%
	Protein	0%	0%	0%	0%
4	Refined sugar	10%	10%	10%	10%
	Complex carbohydrates	48%	48%	48%	48%
	Protein	12%	12%	12%	12%

Task

Choose one of the following tasks.

1. Your team will test the coach's hypothesis by using four different diets containing different percentages of nutrients. See Data Table 1. Each of four runners will test one of the diets for four days in a row. Runner 1 will test Diet 1, Runner 2 will test Diet 2, and so forth.

   On each of the four days of testing, the runners ran the equivalent of a 42-kilometer race. Data Table 2 shows the results for each runner.

Data Table 2

Runner	Day	Pace (km/hr)	Distance (km)
1	1	8	8
	2	5	16
	3	4	24
	4	0	28
2	1	8	8
	2	5	24
	3	5	32
	4	5	42
3	1	8	16
	2	3	24
	3	3	32
	4	1	42
4	1	8	8
	2	6	16
	3	2	24
	4	0	32

Graph the results shown in Data Table 2 to help you analyze the results of the experiment.

Answer these questions.

- What effect does diet have on a runner's performance?
- Does the body metabolize different nutrients differently?
- Did the results of the experiment support the coach's hypothesis?
- What was the purpose of Diet 4 in terms of research design?

  Include an analysis of the four diets and any additional information from research on the Internet and from other sources.

2. Several coaches at the camp want the athletes to drink a commercial preparation of glucose and glucose polymers every 15 minutes during long-distance events. This protocol is untested. Your team is asked to develop a research design for testing the effects of this drink on the endurance of the runners. The team will have to answer the question, What happens to the body when a large quantity of glucose is added to the diet? How will you design an experiment to test the effects of the glucose drink on the runners' performance? Describe your research design for testing the commercial drink and the possible effects on the body.

3. Many self-proclaimed nutritionists promote a wide variety of diets and food supplements to improve athletic performance. Often their claims are unsubstantiated. Do manufacturers and vendors have an ethical and moral responsibility to consider the well-being of potential users when selling such products? If you were a vendor, how would you approach the issue of food supplements? Prepare a presentation combining graphs, charts, and other visuals with a written report. Address your presentation to high school athletic coaches.

Kingfisher hunting fish.

Discovery Learning Activity

Field Work

1. Select an area, such as a park, backyard, or corner of the school grounds, where you can observe the animals found in the area for one hour.

2. On a separate sheet of paper, describe the area you have chosen and the weather. Include the time of day of your observations.

3. List all the animals that you observed, including those on the ground, in trees and shrubs, and in the air.

4. Describe the physical characteristics of the animals, as well as their behaviors and interactions with other animals. Make sketches of the animals in their environment.

5. Compare your observations with those of your classmates. Make a class list of animals found in your area.

6. Working in groups, classify the animals on your class list. Compare your group's classification system with those from other groups.

Discovery
Learning Activity

How Do Arthropods Eat?

1. Observe the various arthropods. **CAUTION:** *Do not touch the arthropods.*

2. Using field guides and other sources, research the type of food each animal eats. Then choose the type of food, from those your teacher has provided, that the arthropods would most likely eat.

3. Describe how each arthropod consumes the food.

Nutrition

···················· *Guide for Reading* ····················

Previewing the Chapter

Lured by the promise of a meal, a hummingbird uses its delicate beak to gently suck nectar from a flower. The nectar contains the nutrients the hummingbird needs to survive. All animals need food to provide the energy to carry out their life processes. How do different animals obtain the food they need to survive? How is food broken down to provide usable nutrients? How do you know if your diet contains enough of the proper kinds of nutrients?

Key Words

absorption, alimentary canal, digestion, extracellular digestion, intestine, intracellular digestion, nutrient, nutrition, stomach

Key Concepts

- **Compare** nutrition in simple organisms with nutrition in more complex organisms.
- **Describe** how food is digested and absorbed by the human digestive system.
- **Design an experiment** to determine the effect of air exposure on the vitamin C content of foods. (Laboratory Investigation)

8-1 The Process of Nutrition

Section Objectives:

- *Compare* autotrophs and heterotrophs.
- *Define* the term *calorie* and explain how the energy content of food is measured.
- *Describe* the functions of the six basic types of nutrients found in the human diet.

Nutrients

Living organisms need food. All food contains **nutrients.** Nutrients are substances that provide the energy and materials needed for metabolic activities—growth, repair and maintenance of cells, and regulation. **Nutrition** is the process by which organisms get food and break it down so it can be used for metabolism.

Nutrients include proteins, carbohydrates, fats, vitamins, minerals, and water. Inorganic nutrients, such as minerals and water, are simple compounds that must be obtained from the environment. **Minerals** are chemical elements that organisms need for normal functioning. Plants absorb minerals such as iron, calcium, phosphorus, and iodine from the soil. Animals obtain minerals by eating plants or by eating other animals that have eaten plants.

▲ **Figure 8–1**

Nutrition. This hungry meadowlark obtains its nutrients by feeding on caterpillars.

◀ A hummingbird obtains its food (nectar) from a flower.

Organic nutrients include essential organic compounds such as proteins, carbohydrates, fats, and vitamins. You read about the structure and function of these organic compounds in Chapter 4. Recall that **vitamins** are coenzymes or are converted into coenzymes in cells. Many important biological reactions need vitamins.

Organisms get the organic nutrients they need in two basic ways. Some organisms are capable of making, or synthesizing, organic nutrients from simple inorganic substances. Such organisms are **autotrophs** (AWT uh trohfs). Green plants, algae, and various other types of microorganisms are autotrophs. Most autotrophs are photosynthetic—that is, they use energy from sunlight, and carbon dioxide and water from the environment to make their own food. These organisms are called *phototrophs*. However, certain types of bacteria that are autotrophs do not use light as a source of energy. They are chemosynthetic, i.e., they make their own food using the energy from special types of chemical reactions. Such organisms are called *chemotrophs* (KEE muh trohfs). Photosynthesis and chemosynthesis are discussed in Chapter 17.

Organisms that cannot synthesize their own organic nutrients from inorganic compounds are called **heterotrophs** (HET ur ruh trohfs). All animals and certain types of microorganisms are heterotrophs. Such organisms must take in, or ingest, food containing "ready-made" organic nutrients from other plants or animals.

Energy Content of Food

Living organisms need energy to carry on their life processes. This energy is provided in most cases by the chemical breakdown of carbohydrates, fats, and proteins. As explained in the discussion of cellular respiration in Chapter 6, the energy is released in a series of small steps and stored in molecules of ATP for later use.

For any given quantity of food, the total energy released by cellular respiration is the same as would be released by burning the food. The energy content of a food sample is determined by completely burning a sample of the food and measuring the amount of heat given off during burning. The instrument used to measure the energy content of a food sample is a *calorimeter* (kal uh RIM uh ter). See Figure 8–2.

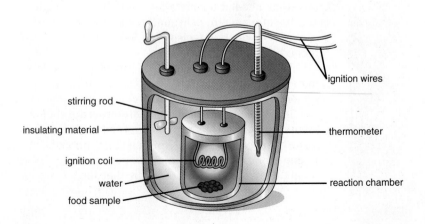

Figure 8–2

Calorimeter. In a calorimeter, a food sample is burned, and the heat produced is measured. The amount of heat produced is equal to the energy content of the food. ▶

ignition wires

stirring rod

insulating material

thermometer

ignition coil

water

reaction chamber

food sample

Although the *joule* (jool) is the unit of energy in the International System of Units, the **calorie** (KAL uh ree) is the unit commonly used in measuring the energy content of food. One calorie equals 4.2 joules. It also is defined as the amount of heat that is needed to raise the temperature of 1 gram of water 1°C. Because the calorie is a very small unit, the preferred unit is the kilocalorie. A kilocalorie is 1000 calories, or 1 Calorie. In tables giving the "calorie" content of foods, the unit of measurement used is actually a kilocalorie (Calorie).

With the use of a calorimeter, it has been determined that the amount of heat given off by 1 gram of carbohydrate or 1 gram of protein is about 4 Calories. One gram of fat on the other hand, releases 9 Calories. Fat contains more than twice as many calories as an equal mass of carbohydrate or protein.

Human Nutritional Needs

Energy from Food   Age, sex, lifestyle, weight, and body condition are factors that affect daily Calorie needs. Usually, younger people need more Calories than older people, males need more Calories than females, and active people need more Calories than inactive people. A person whose diet contains more Calories than are needed gains weight. A person whose diet includes fewer Calories than are needed loses weight. The energy contents of some common foods are shown in Figure 8–3.

Energy Content of Some Common Foods		
Food	**Portion**	**Calories**
apple	1 medium (150g)	70
bacon	2 slices (16g)	100
banana	1 (150g)	85
bread, white	1 slice (23g)	70
candy bar	1 plain (57g)	300
carrot	1 cup (145g)	45
cheese, American	1 oz. (28g)	105
corn	1 cup (256g)	170
cupcake	1 (50g)	185
egg	1 large (50g)	80
frankfurter	1 (51g)	155
ham	3 oz. (85g)	245
hamburger	3 oz. (85g)	245
ice cream	½ cup (74g)	175
milk	1 cup (244g)	150
orange	1 (180g)	60
peas	1 cup (160g)	115
potato	1 medium (130g)	105
tomato	1 medium (150g)	35

◀   **Figure 8–3**

Energy Content of Some Common Foods.
The Calorie content of different foods varies greatly.

Healthy Diets Humans, like any other living organisms, need six basic nutrients. These are proteins, carbohydrates, fats, vitamins, minerals, and water. Sources and functions of these nutrients are given in Figure 8–4.

The nutrients necessary for humans are found in many different kinds of foods. For this reason, nutritionists recommend eating a wide variety of foods. To help people plan their diets, nutritionists have designed the Food Guide Pyramid, which is shown in Figure 8-5. The Food Guide Pyramid is a graph that groups foods according to types and indicates how many servings of each type should be eaten daily.

Figure 8–4
Nutrients Important for Human Metabolism. Each of the six basic nutrients is essential for good health. Too much or too little of any one nutrient can result in poor health. ▼

Nutrients Important for Human Metabolism		
Nutrient	**Dietary Sources**	**Function**
Proteins	Meat, fish, poultry, milk, eggs, nuts, beans	Supply building materials to form new cells for growth; repair and maintain tissue.
Carbohydrates: Sugar	Molasses, jelly & jam, candy, cake, brown and white sugar	Supply energy for body functions. Help the body to use fat, spare protein.
Starch	Pasta, bread, grains, cereal, corn, potatoes, rice, beans	
Fiber	Fruits, vegetables, whole grains	Gives bulk to digestive materials.
Fats	Butter, margarine, bacon, meat, egg yolk, cream, cooking oils	Supply energy. May be stored as fuel for the body. Carry vitamins and flavors.
Vitamins: A	Liver, carrots, spinach, sweet potatoes, whole milk products	Maintains healthy skin, bones, and eyes
B Complex	Pork, liver, legumes, whole grain products, fresh vegetables	Aids in carbohydrate use. Necessary for heart, nervous system and appetite.
C (ascorbic acid)	Citrus fruits, melons, green vegetables, potatoes	Maintains healthy cells and tissues. Helps to maintain healthy blood vessels, heal wounds, and resist infection. Promotes iron absorption.
D	Fortified milk, cod liver oil, eggs	Aids in calcium and phosphorus use.
K	Dark-green leafy vegetables, liver	Aids in blood clotting
Minerals: Calcium	Milk and dairy products, dark-green vegetables, sardines, canned salmon	Aids in bone/tooth formation and blood clotting.
Chlorine	Table salt, meat, milk, eggs	Helps digestion and cellular water balance.
Iodine	Seafood, added to salt	Essential for normal metabolism. Part of the thyroid hormone.
Iron	Liver, red meat, eggs, green leafy vegetables	Prevents anemia. Part of hemoglobin.
Potassium	Orange juice, citrus fruits, bananas, green leafy vegetables	Helps to maintain heartbeat, water balance, and nerve transmission; aids in carbohydrate and protein metabolism.
Water	Milk, fruit, vegetables, beverages	Serves as building material in all cells. Aids digestion, carries nutrients through the body and transports wastes.

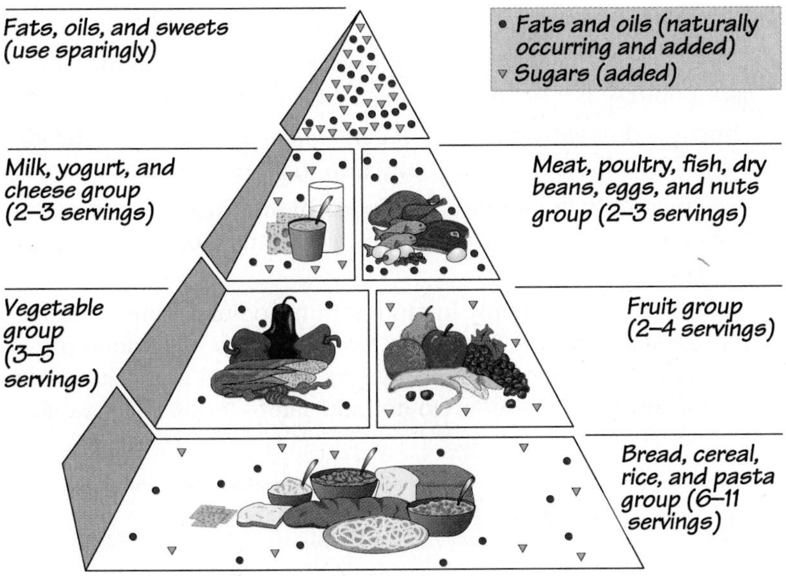

Fats, oils, and sweets
(use sparingly)

- Fats and oils (naturally occurring and added)
- Sugars (added)

Milk, yogurt, and cheese group
(2–3 servings)

Meat, poultry, fish, dry beans, eggs, and nuts group (2–3 servings)

Vegetable group
(3–5 servings)

Fruit group
(2–4 servings)

Bread, cereal, rice, and pasta group (6–11 servings)

◀ **Figure 8–5**

The Food Guide Pyramid. The Food Guide Pyramid should be used as a model for a healthful diet. The largest percentage of your daily food choices should come from foods at the base of the pyramid. Fats, oils, and sweets should be eaten in limited amounts.

There are six different groups of food in the pyramid. These six groups are grain foods; vegetables; fruits; milk products; meat, poultry, fish, eggs, beans, and nuts; and finally fats, oils, and sweets. The structure of the Food Guide Pyramid conveys the idea that the bulk of people's diets should consist of grains, vegetables, and fruits. The width of each level indicates the proportion of food that should be eaten from that level. Thus a healthy diet would contain many more foods from the grains group, which is found in the wide bottom level, than from the fats, oils, and sweets group at the narrow peak of the pyramid.

The Food Guide Pyramid also emphasizes a diet low in fats and sugars. Notice the little triangles and circles scattered throughout the pyramid. The triangles represent sugar, and the circles represent fat. These symbols roughly indicate how much fat and sugar can be found in different levels.

In addition to nutrients, a healthy human diet must contain bulky, indigestible materials called **fiber**. Fiber is made of cellulose and other indigestible materials found in the cell walls of fruits, vegetables, and grains. Fiber stimulates the muscles of the digestive system to keep food moving through it. Eating adequate amounts of fiber also provides other health benefits, such as reducing the risk of colon and rectal cancers.

Many foods have been linked to health problems, such as obesity, heart disease, and cancer. The average American diet is high in sugar, saturated fat, and sodium, which contribute to these health problems. Most Americans can improve their diets by recognizing their nutritional needs, developing a plan for meeting these needs, and making wise food choices. Nutritionists have developed the following guidelines for a healthful diet.

- Eat a variety of foods. To obtain all the different nutrients you need, choose a wide selection of foods.
- Maintain a healthy weight.
- Choose a diet low in fat and cholesterol. Choose lean meats, fish, poultry, and beans instead of fatty meat. Limit fried foods.
- Choose a diet with plenty of vegetables, fruits, and grain products. These foods are especially rich in starch and fiber.
- Use sugar only in moderation. Foods high in sugar are often low in more useful nutrients. Limit your intake of sweet snacks and soft drinks.
- Use salt and sodium only in moderation. Sodium, which is found in table salt and salty foods, has been linked to high blood pressure. Avoid eating too many salty snacks, pickled foods, luncheon meats, and canned soups. Do not add salt to foods at the table.

8-1 Section Review

1. What is nutrition?
2. Name six nutrients required by living organisms.
3. Identify the six food groups in the Food Guide Pyramid.

Critical Thinking

4. Would you say humans are autotrophs or heterotrophs? Why or why not? (*Reasoning Categorically*)

MiniLab

Skill: Observing

Magnetism in Your Cereal?

Procedure

1. In a sealable plastic bag, crush 50 grams of a dry breakfast cereal that contains 100% of the U.S. Required Daily Allowance for iron.

Problem

How can you **observe** the iron in your cereal?

2. Shake all the crushed cereal to one corner of the bag. Pass the magnet under the cereal and observe what happens. Use the magnet to drag any particles that are attracted to it to the empty part of the bag. Remove the magnetized cereal and find its mass.

Analyze and Conclude

1. What evidence do you have that iron was in the cereal?

2. Describe a procedure you could use to compare the amount of iron in the cereal at the top of a cereal box and at the bottom.

8-2 Adaptations for Nutrition and Digestion

Section Objectives:

- *Distinguish* between mechanical breakdown and chemical digestion of food.
- *Contrast* intracellular digestion and extracellular digestion.
- *Compare* digestive processes in protozoa, the hydra, the earthworm, and the grasshopper.

Digestion and Absorption

For a nutrient to be used by the cells of an organism, it must pass through the cell membranes. This process is called **absorption.** The nutrient molecules in food are usually too large to pass through cell membranes. Thus, to be absorbed by the cells, most food molecules must be broken down into smaller, simpler forms. The process by which food molecules are broken down is called **digestion** (dy JES chun).

Digestion is part of the process of nutrition. The term *digestion* usually refers to the chemical breakdown of food substances into simpler compounds. In many organisms, pieces of food are first cut, crushed, or broken into smaller particles without being changed chemically. This results in the mechanical breakdown of the food. Mechanical breakdown increases the surface area of the food particles. Chemical digestion is carried out by digestive enzymes, which act only on the surface of food particles. Thus, mechanical breakdown prepares the food for faster chemical digestion by exposing more food surface to the action of the digestive enzymes. Chemical digestion, like mechanical breakdown, takes place in stages. Large molecules are broken down into smaller molecules. In turn, these are broken down into still simpler forms. The usable, simplest products of digestion are the end products of the process of nutrition.

Nutrition in Protists

Among the protists digestion is *intracellular* (in truh SEL yuh ler)—that is, it happens inside the cell. However, members of this group have different ways of getting food. The ameba and paramecium are protists that live in fresh water and feed on small organisms. Both can move in response to various stimuli. They appear to be attracted to food by chemical stimuli.

Amebas crawl along solid surfaces using projections of the cell called *pseudopods,* or "false feet." The pseudopods move when cytoplasm flows into or out of them. When an ameba comes in contact with a food particle, pseudopods surround the particle. The cell membranes of the pseudopods join so that the particle is taken into the cell but is enclosed within a membrane. Although the food

▲ **Figure 8–6**

Mechanical Breakdown of Food. Giant pandas feed primarily on bamboo. When a giant panda bites and gnaws a bamboo shoot, the mechanical breakdown of food results.

Figure 8–7

Food-Getting in the Ameba. As the ameba senses its food (left), its pseudopods reach out to surround it (center). The engulfed food is enclosed in a food vacuole inside the ameba (right). (Magnification 310 X) ▶

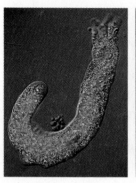

is inside the cell, it is separated from the other cell contents by a membrane. A food vacuole then forms, free to move about within the cell cytoplasm. The food vacuole fuses with a lysosome, and digestive enzymes from the lysosome break down the food in the vacuole into forms usable by the cell. See Figure 8–7. These products of digestion, because they are small particles, can diffuse across the vacuole membrane into the cytoplasm. Indigestible materials remain in the food vacuole. The food vacuole eventually fuses with the cell membrane, and its contents are expelled from the cell.

The paramecium moves by the beating of hairlike cilia that cover the outside of the organism. The movement of the cilia also sweeps food particles down the **oral groove** into the **gullet** (GUHL et). See Figure 8–8. As food collects at the end of the gullet, the cell membrane bulges inward and pinches off, forming a food vacuole. The food vacuole travels through the cytoplasm and fuses with a lysosome, which contains digestive enzymes. Digestion occurs within the vacuole, and the usable products diffuse into the cytoplasm. Indigestible material is discharged from the cell through an opening called the **anal** (AYN ul) **pore.**

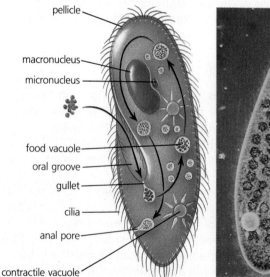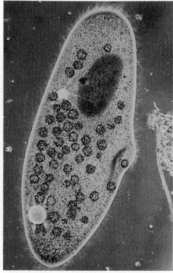

pellicle

macronucleus

micronucleus

food vacuole

oral groove

gullet

cilia

anal pore

contractile vacuole

Figure 8–8

Food-Getting in the Paramecium. Food particles are swept down the oral groove into the gullet by the beating of the cilia. (Magnification 416 X) ▶

Nutrition in the Hydra

The hydra is a relatively simple multicellular animal about five millimeters long from the tip of its tentacles to its base. The body of the hydra is a hollow cylinder made up of two layers of cells. See Figure 8–9. The outer layer is the *ectoderm* (EK tuh derm), and the inner layer is the *endoderm* (EN duh derm). The tentacles, which surround the mouth, contain stinging cells called *cnidoblasts* (NYD uh blasts). Inside each cnidoblast is a capsule called a *nematocyst* (neh MAT uh sist), which contains a coiled, hollow thread.

The hydra captures its food with its tentacles. When a water flea or some other small animal comes in contact with a tentacle, the nematocysts release their long threads. Some of the threads wind around the prey, while others inject a poison that paralyzes the animal. The movement of the tentacles pushes the food through the mouth and into the **gastrovascular cavity,** where digestion begins. See Figure 8–10.

Digestion in hydra is both intracellular and extracellular. *Extracellular digestion* takes place outside the cells. Specialized cells in the endoderm secrete digestive enzymes into the gastrovascular cavity. These enzymes partially break down the food. Nutrients are then absorbed into the cells.

Some endoderm cells have flagella, and the waving of these organelles circulates the food particles through the gastrovascular cavity. *Intracellular digestion* takes place when endoderm cells form pseudopods and engulf the small food particles, thus forming food vacuoles. Digestion is completed by enzymes secreted into the food vacuoles.

Because the hydra is only two cell layers thick, the end products of digestion pass easily from the cells of the endoderm into the cells of the ectoderm by diffusion. Wastes from the ectoderm cells diffuse directly into the surrounding water. Wastes from the endoderm diffuse back into the gastrovascular cavity and are carried out through the mouth by water currents. Because hydras have only one body opening, the mouth is both an entrance for food and an exit for wastes.

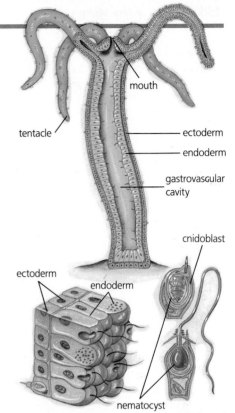

▲ **Figure 8–9**

Structure of Hydra. The hydra's body has two cell layers, the ectoderm and the endoderm. Tentacles containing stinging cells called cnidoblasts surround the mouth.

Figure 8–10

Food-Getting in Hydra. The hydra uses its tentacles to capture a water flea (daphnia) and stuff it into its gastrovascular cavity, where digestion will occur. ▼

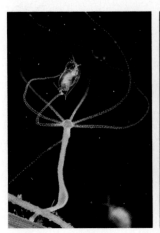

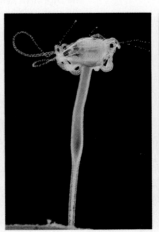
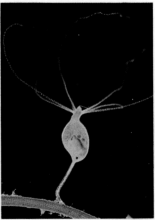

Nutrition in the Earthworm

The earthworm is a complex multicellular animal with a "tube-within-a-tube" body plan. The inner tube is the digestive system, while the outer tube is the body wall. See Figure 8–11. The digestive tube, or **alimentary** (al uh MENT uh ree) **canal,** has two openings—the mouth, through which food enters the body, and the **anus** (AYN us) through which waste matter leaves. Food travels through the digestive system in one direction—from the mouth to the anus. The food is broken down both mechanically and chemically in the digestive tract. Usable nutrients are then absorbed into the body cells.

As earthworms burrow through the ground, they ingest large quantities of soil. They also come to the surface to eat leaf litter and other decaying plant matter. Food is pulled into the mouth by the sucking action of the muscular **pharynx** (FA rinks). The food is then pushed through the digestive tube by waves of muscular contraction. From the pharynx, food passes through the **esophagus** (eh SAHF uh gus) into a round, thin-walled organ called the **crop.** The crop, which functions as a storage chamber, gradually releases food into the **gizzard** (GIZ urd). The gizzard is a thick-walled grinding organ that crushes the food. Mechanical breakdown is accomplished by the muscular movements of the gizzard, which grind the organic material against sand grains from the soil.

From the gizzard, the pastelike food mass passes into the long intestine. The **intestine** is where chemical digestion and absorption take place. The surface area of the intestine is increased by a fold in the wall called the **typhlosole** (TIF luh sohl). Cells lining the intestine secrete enzymes that break down large food molecules into smaller molecules. The products of digestion are absorbed by cells of the intestine and are picked up by the blood. The food molecules are transported in the blood to all parts of the body. Undigested materials and soil from which the food has been removed pass out of the worm through the anus.

Figure 8–11
The Digestive System of the Earthworm. ▼

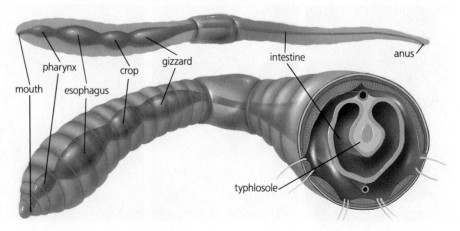

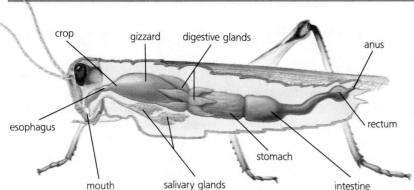

▲ **Figure 8–12**

The Grasshopper. As the grasshopper chews on leaves, digestive enzymes begin the chemical breakdown of food, a process that is completed in the stomach.

Nutrition in the Grasshopper

The grasshopper, like the earthworm, has a tubular digestive system, shown in Figure 8–12. Food is broken down mechanically by the mouthparts, which are well-adapted for chewing leafy vegetation. In the mouth the food is mixed with **saliva** (suh LY vuh) secreted by the **salivary** (SAL uh ver ee) **glands.** Saliva contains enzymes that begin the chemical breakdown of food. The food then passes through the esophagus into the crop, where it is stored temporarily. From the crop the food passes into the muscular gizzard, where it is ground into smaller particles by the action of teethlike plates made of *chitin* (KYT un). From the gizzard, food passes into the **stomach,** where chemical digestion and absorption take place. Digestive enzymes produced by glands just outside the stomach pass into the stomach, where they act on food particles. The products of digestion are absorbed into the bloodstream through the stomach walls and are transported to all the cells of the body. Undigested material passes through the intestine and is stored temporarily in the **rectum** where water is absorbed. The dried wastes are eliminated through the anus.

8-2 Section Review

1. Where does digestion happen in the ameba and paramecium?
2. Name an organism that uses both intracellular and extracellular digestion.
3. In the earthworm, what is the function of the typhlosole?
4. Describe the path food takes in the digestive system of the grasshopper.

Critical Thinking

5. Compare and contrast intracellular and extracellular digestion. (*Comparing and Contrasting*)

8-3 The Human Digestive System

Section Objectives:

- *Describe* the functions of the different parts of the human digestive system—the mouth, esophagus, stomach, small intestine, liver, gallbladder, pancreas, large intestine, rectum, and anus.
- *List* the principle digestive enzymes, where they are produced, the type of food they act upon, and the end products of enzymatic breakdown.

Parts of the Human Digestive System

Figure 8–13

The Human Digestive System. Each organ in the digestive system carries out specific functions. Digestion is aided by accessory digestive glands. These glands secrete digestive enzymes and juices into the digestive tube. ▼

The structure and function of the human digestive system are basically similar to those of the earthworm and the grasshopper. The digestive tube is made up of a series of specialized organs, with different phases of digestion taking place in each organ. See Figure 8–13. Food passes through the digestive tube in the following order: oral cavity (mouth), pharynx (throat), esophagus (gullet),

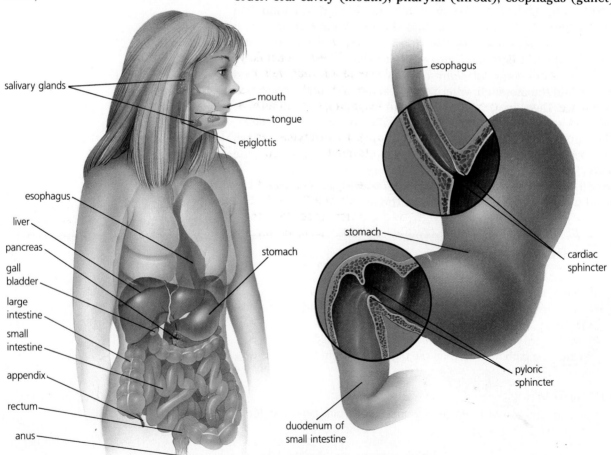

stomach, small intestine, large intestine, rectum, and anus. Several glands secrete digestive enzymes and juices into the digestive tube, where extracellular digestion occurs.

The *digestive glands* are groups of specialized secretory cells that are found in the lining of the alimentary canal or in separate accessory organs. The accessory glands lie outside the digestive tract. Their secretions pass into the digestive tract by way of a tube or duct. Food is never found within the accessory glands, only within the alimentary canal itself. The accessory glands include the salivary glands, the **liver,** and the **pancreas** (PAN kree us). The liver and pancreas have many functions. These organs aid digestion by the secretion of digestive fluids.

Cells in the lining of the walls of the alimentary canal also secrete *mucus* (MYOO kus), which acts as a lubricant for the food mass. It also provides a coating that protects the delicate cells of the digestive tube from the action of acid, digestive enzymes, and abrasive substances in food.

The Mouth and Pharynx

Food enters the body through the mouth, where both mechanical breakdown and chemical digestion occur. Chunks of food are bitten off with the teeth and ground into pieces small enough to swallow. The tongue moves and shapes the food mass in the mouth.

As food is chewed, it is mixed with saliva, which is secreted into the mouth by three pairs of salivary glands. There are actually two types of saliva. One is a thin, watery secretion that wets the food. The other is a thicker, mucous secretion that acts as a lubricant and causes the food particles to stick together to form a food mass, or *bolus* (BOH lus). Saliva also contains a digestive enzyme called **salivary amylase** (AM uh layz). This enzyme breaks down starch, which is a polysaccharide, into maltose, which is a disaccharide.

When the food has been chewed sufficiently, it is pushed by the tongue to the back of the throat, or pharynx. See Figure 8–14. This starts the automatic swallowing reflex, which forces food into the esophagus, the tube leading to the stomach. However, air as

Figure 8–14

Swallowing. The epiglottis prevents food or liquid from entering the air passages during swallowing. ▼

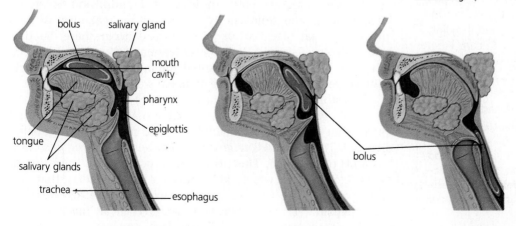

bolus · salivary gland · mouth cavity · pharynx · epiglottis · tongue · salivary glands · trachea · esophagus · bolus

Biology and You

Q: My best friend always thinks about losing weight. She makes herself vomit after eating. Should I be worried about her?

A: Your friend has bulimia, an eating disorder, which is common among young, high-achieving women. Although there are also cases of men with bulimia, about 90 percent are female. Bulimics fear becoming fat, even though most are of average weight or only slightly overweight. They go on eating binges and then purge themselves by vomiting or with laxatives.

Many doctors think that society's overconcern with thinness is a major cause of bulimia. Bulimics often have distorted views of their bodies. They are perfectionists who have trouble feeling good about themselves. No matter how thin they are, it is never thin enough for them.

Bulimia is a psychological and a physical problem. Constant vomiting may damage teeth, gums, stomach, kidneys, and heart. Purging may result in dehydration and vitamin and mineral deficiencies. Your friend should get counseling and medical help immediately.

Look through a teenage magazine for articles and advertisements that emphasize thinness. Write a letter to the editor expressing your views on your findings.

well as food passes through the pharynx. The air must pass through the voice box, or *larynx* (LA rinks), and down the *trachea* (TRAY kee uh) to the lungs. To prevent food and liquids from entering the larynx, it is automatically closed off during swallowing by a flap of tissue called the **epiglottis** (ep uh GLAHT is). At the same time, breathing stops momentarily, and the passageways to the nose, ears, and mouth are blocked. When a person "swallows the wrong way" and food enters the trachea, it is brought back up into the throat by coughing.

The Esophagus

The esophagus is a tube through which food passes from the pharynx to the stomach. Beginning in the esophagus, the movement of food down the digestive tube is aided by alternate waves of relaxation and contraction in the muscular walls of the alimentary canal. This is called **peristalsis** (pehr uh STAHL sis). The muscles in front of the food mass relax, while those behind the food mass contract, pushing the food forward.

Aided by peristaltic contractions, food passes quickly down the esophagus. Where the esophagus opens into the stomach, there is a ring of muscle called a **sphincter** (SFINK ter). The sphincter acts as a valve and controls the passage of food from the esophagus into the stomach. When the wave of peristalsis reaches the sphincter, it relaxes and opens, and the food enters the stomach. The sphincter between the esophagus and the stomach is called the *cardiac sphincter.* During vomiting, a wave of peristalsis passes upward—reverse peristalsis—causing the cardiac sphincter to open, and the contents of the stomach to be "thrown up."

Sometimes, when the cardiac sphincter relaxes, hydrochloric acid (HCl) from the stomach backs up into the esophagus. When the acid comes into contact with the sensitive lining of the lower esophagus, the result is discomfort, commonly known as acid indigestion or "heartburn."

The Stomach

The stomach is a thick-walled, muscular sac that can expand to hold more than two liters of food or liquid. Food is stored temporarily in the stomach. The mechanical breakdown of food and the partial digestion of proteins also occur there. Food is broken down mechanically by contractions of the muscular stomach walls. The food mass is churned and mixed with acidic **gastric juice** secreted by glands in the stomach walls.

The stomach lining contains three types of glands. The *pyloric* (pi LOR ik) *glands* and the *cardiac gastric* (GAS trik) *glands* secrete mucus that covers the stomach lining and protects it from being digested. The *intermediate gastric glands* secrete *gastric juice* that has a pH of 1.5 to 2.5. This pH is due to its high concentration of hydrochloric acid, which kills most of the bacteria that are swallowed in food. Gastric juice also contains the digestive enzyme **pepsin** (PEP sin). Pepsin is secreted in an inactive form called *pepsinogen* (pep SIN uh jen), which is activated after it is mixed with the hydrochloric acid. Pepsin breaks down large protein molecules into shorter chains of amino acids called *polypeptides* (pol ee PEP tydz).

The breakdown of starch by salivary amylase, which begins in the mouth, continues for some time after the food mass reaches the stomach. Gradually, however, the low pH of the acid in the stomach inactivates this enzyme, and starch breakdown stops.

When the stomach is empty, only small amounts of gastric juice are present. When food is eaten, the flow of gastric juice increases. There are three mechanisms involved in stimulating the flow of gastric juice.

1. The thought, sight, smell, or taste of food stimulates the brain to send messages to the gastric glands, causing them to secrete moderate amounts of gastric juice.

2. Food touching the lining of the stomach stimulates the secretion of moderate amounts of gastric juice.

3. When a food mass enters the stomach, it stretches the stomach walls. The stretching of the stomach wall, as well as the presence of proteins, caffeine, alcohol, and certain other substances, stimulates the lining of the stomach to secrete a hormone called *gastrin* (GAS trin) directly into the blood. (A *hormone* is a substance that is secreted directly into the bloodstream and that produces a specific effect on a particular tissue.) Gastrin further stimulates the gastric glands in the stomach to secrete large amounts of gastric juice.

Liquids pass through the stomach in 20 minutes or less. Solids, on the other hand, must first be reduced to a thin, soupy liquid called **chyme** (kyme). The chyme passes in small amounts at a time through the *pyloric sphincter,* the muscle that controls the passage of food from the stomach into the small intestine. The stomach empties from 2 to 6 hours after a meal. Hunger is felt when an empty stomach is churning.

If the thick mucous layer that protects the stomach wall breaks down, a part of the stomach wall may be digested. When this happens, a painful ulcer develops. See Figure 8–15. Ulcers are

Figure 8–15
Stomach Ulcer. A mucous layer protects the sensitive cells of the stomach wall. If this layer is damaged, digestive juices eat away at the cells creating an ulcer. ▼

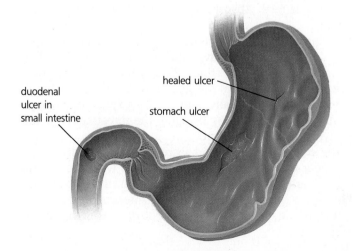

duodenal ulcer in small intestine

healed ulcer

stomach ulcer

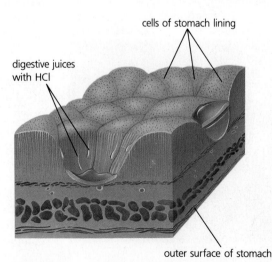

cells of stomach lining

digestive juices with HCl

outer surface of stomach

Figure 8–16

Structure of a Villus. The small intestine wall is covered by fingerlike projections called villi. Within each villus are a network of blood vessels and a lacteal. An electron micrograph shows how the intestinal epithelial cell membrane folds inward, creating microvilli. (Magnification 16 200 X) ▼

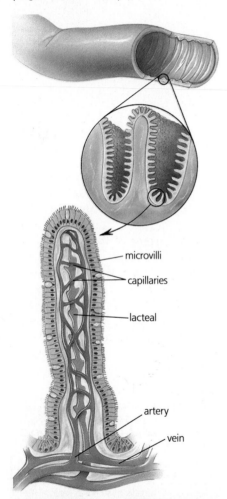

- microvilli
- capillaries
- lacteal
- artery
- vein

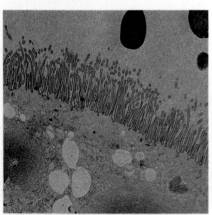

painful because hydrochloric acid comes into contact with the stomach wall. Doctors used to think that stress caused ulcers. Recently, however, it was discovered that most ulcers are caused by a bacterium, *Helicobacter pylori*. By using powerful antibiotics that destroy the bacterium, many ulcers have been cured.

The Small Intestine

The **small intestine** is a coiled tube about 6.5 meters long and about 2.5 centimeters in diameter. The small intestine has three parts. Food leaving the stomach through the pyloric sphincter enters the *duodenum* (doo uh DEE num). This is the shortest section of the small intestine, about 25 centimeters long. The middle section is called the *jejunum* (jeh JOO num). The last section is the *ileum* (ILL ee um).

Most chemical digestion takes place in the small intestine. This also is the site of absorption. After digestion is complete, simple sugars, amino acids, vitamins, minerals, and other substances are absorbed through the wall of the small intestine into the blood vessels of the circulatory system. At the same time, fatty acids and glycerol are absorbed into tiny vessels of the lymphatic system called **lacteals** (LAK tee uls). The lymphatic system is discussed in greater detail in Chapter 9.

The small intestine has a number of structural features that increase its surface area and make it ideally suited for absorption. These features are illustrated in Figure 8–16. First, the small intestine is very long. Second, its lining has many folds. Third, the lining is covered with millions of fingerlike projections, which are called **villi** (VIL ly). Fourth, the epithelial cells that make up the intestinal lining have *brush borders*. In the brush borders, the membranes of cells that face into the intestinal opening have tiny projections called *microvilli* that further increase the surface area of the cells.

Within each villus there is a network of blood capillaries, and in the center is a lacteal. The outer covering of each villus is a layer of epithelial cells with microvilli. During absorption, digested nutrients pass through the epithelial cells and enter either the capillaries or the lacteal. Absorption involves both diffusion and active transport.

When food is present, the small intestine is in constant motion. These peristaltic movements have four main effects: (1) they squeeze chyme through the intestine; (2) they mix the chyme with the digestive enzymes present in the small intestine; (3) they break down food particles mechanically; and (4) they speed up absorption of digestive end products by bringing the intestinal contents into contact with the intestinal wall.

Unlike the stomach with its acid secretions, fluids in the small intestine are generally alkaline. Chyme is mixed with **pancreatic** (pan kree AT ik) **juice** from the pancreas, **bile** from the liver, and **intestinal juice** from glands in the wall of the intestine. These three secretions contain the enzymes and other substances necessary to complete digestion.

Pancreatic Juice   When the acid chyme from the stomach enters the small intestine, it stimulates cells in the intestinal lining to secrete two hormones into the blood. These hormones are *secretin* (sih KREET in) and *cholecystokinin* (koh luh sis tuh KY nin). These hormones stimulate the pancreas to secrete pancreatic juice and pancreatic enzymes, which pass through the *pancreatic duct* into the upper part of the small intestine. Pancreatic juice contains sodium bicarbonate, which neutralizes the acid in the chyme and makes the pH of the contents of the small intestine slightly alkaline (pH 8). The enzymes secreted by the pancreas act on proteins, carbohydrates, fats, and nucleic acids.

The pancreatic enzymes include *amylase,* which hydrolyzes any remaining starch to maltose; *proteases* (PRO tee ay zez) (protein-splitting enzymes), including *trypsin* (TRIP sin) and *chymotrypsin* (ky muh TRIP sin), which continue the breakdown of large protein molecules begun in the stomach; and *lipase,* which breaks down fats.

Bile   The cells of the liver produce bile, which passes through ducts into the **gallbladder,** where it is stored. Bile passes from the gallbladder to the upper part of the small intestine through the *bile duct.* The release of bile from the gallbladder is stimulated by the hormone cholecystokinin, which also acts on the pancreas. Bile contains no enzymes, but it aids in the digestion of fats and oils by breaking them up into tiny droplets. This process, called *emulsification* (ih mul suh fuh KAY shun), increases the surface area for enzyme action. Since bile is alkaline, it aids in neutralizing the acid chyme from the stomach.

Intestinal Juice   The walls of the small intestine contain millions of intestinal glands, which secrete intestinal juice. Intestinal juice contains the enzymes peptidase and maltase that complete the digestion of carbohydrates, fats, and proteins.

In the small intestine, molecules of proteins, carbohydrates, and fats are broken down into the end products of digestion. Proteins are broken down into amino acids, carbohydrates into simple sugars, and fats into fatty acids and glycerol. A summary of the secretions of the human digestive system and their functions is given in Figure 8–17.

The Large Intestine

Undigested and unabsorbed materials pass from the small intestine through a sphincter into the **large intestine.** The large intestine is about 1.5 meters long and 6 centimeters in diameter. No digestion occurs in this portion of the digestive system.

On the lower right side of the abdomen, where the small intestine joins the large intestine, is a small pouch, the **appendix** (uh PEN diks). The appendix plays no part in the functioning of the human digestive system. Occasionally, however, the appendix becomes infected or inflamed, a condition known as **appendicitis** (uh pen duh SY tus). If the condition is not treated, the appendix may burst, spreading the infection.

Science, Technology and Society

Issue: Food Irradiation

Imagine storing food for weeks without spoiling. Food irradiation may make this possible. Food is exposed to the radioactive elements cesium or cobalt. The food absorbs some of the energy without becoming radioactive. Bacteria and insects are destroyed and the ripening process is halted. The Food and Drug Administration (FDA) allows irradiation of pork, wheat, spices, and fruits and vegetables.

People who favor irradiation point to its potential for fighting world hunger. Food might be stored indefinitely. Many diseases caused by bacteria and insects could be eliminated. Chemical pesticides, which are used to kill microorganisms, may not be needed.

People opposed to food irradiation believe that research is incomplete. They are unsure of the dangers associated with it. Some fear that the chemical byproducts may cause cancer. Others note that the process changes the texture and taste of some foods and may decrease nutritive values. These people believe that other safe alternatives should be pursued.

■ *Do you think the FDA should allow food irradiation? Why or why not?*

One of the principal functions of the large intestine is the reabsorption of water from the food mass. During digestion, water is mixed with the food as it moves through the digestive system. Under normal conditions, about three-fourths of the water is reabsorbed. This reabsorption into the capillaries of the large intestine helps the body conserve water. If too little water is absorbed, diarrhea results; if too much water is absorbed, constipation results.

A second function of the large intestine is the absorption of the vitamins that are produced by bacteria that normally live in the large intestine. These vitamins are absorbed with the water from the food mass. Intestinal bacteria live on undigested food material. They produce vitamin K, which is essential for blood clotting, and some of the B vitamins. When large doses of antibiotics are given to overcome an infection, they can destroy the intestinal bacteria, and a vitamin K deficiency may result.

The third function of the large intestine is *elimination*— removal of undigested and indigestible material from the digestive tract. This material consists of cellulose from plant cell walls; large quantities of bacteria, bile, and mucus; and worn-out cells from the digestive tract. As this material travels through the intestine, it

Figure 8–17

Secretions of the Human Digestive System and Their Functions. ▼

Secretions of the Human Digestive System		
Digestive Secretions and Enzymes	**Origin**	**Function**
Saliva	Salivary glands	Wets food. Helps to form food into bolus.
Salivary amylase		Breaks down starch into maltose.
Gastric juice:	Stomach (gastric glands)	
Pepsin		Breaks down proteins into smaller molecules (peptones and proteoses).
Hydrochloric acid		Activates pepsin.
Bile	Liver	Breaks down fat mechanically into small droplets (emulsification).
Pancreatic juice:	Pancreas	
Amylase		Continues the digestion of starch to disaccharides.
Trypsin		Digests peptones and proteoses into peptides.
Lipase		Digests fat droplets into fatty acids and glycerol.
Intestinal juice:	Small intestine (intestinal glands)	
Peptidase		Breaks down peptides into amino acids.
Maltase		Breaks down maltose (a disaccharide) into glucose (a monosaccharide).

becomes **feces** (FEE seez), or stool. Fecal matter is stored in the last part of the large intestine, the rectum, and periodically eliminated, or defecated, through the anus.

8-3 **Section Review**

1. What is the role of each of the digestive glands in the process of digestion?
2. What are the functions of saliva and its enzyme, salivary amylase?
3. Name the process that causes food to move through the digestive tube.
4. List three fluids that mix with food in the small intestine.
5. What are the functions of the large intestine?

Critical Thinking

6. Which of these nutrients need to be digested in order to be absorbed? starch, maltose, amino acids, proteins, fat, glucose, glycerol, peptides (*Classifying*)

MiniLab

Skill: Observing

The Starch Test

Procedure

1. Place pieces of a soda cracker into a test tube.

2. Add five drops of Lugol's solution to the test tube. Lugol's solution is a test for starch. If the solution turns dark blue or black, starch is present.

3. Record your observations.

4. Repeat the procedure using small amounts of peeled potato, white bread, oatmeal, and granulated sugar.

Problem

Which foods contain starch? **Observe** the results of adding Lugol's solution to different foods.

Analyze and Conclude

1. Of the foods you tested, which contain starch?

2. Which foods do not contain starch?

3. Why might this procedure not indicate starch in a dark-colored food, such as a graham cracker?

Laboratory Investigation

Designing an Experiment

Vitamin C in Fruit Juice

Although many vertebrate animals can synthesize their own vitamin C, humans cannot. For this reason, you need to consume foods that will supply you with adequate amounts of this essential nutrient. Vitamin C is found in many vegetables, such as potatoes and broccoli, but orange juice is probably the best source for vitamin C. In this investigation, you will design an experiment to determine the effect exposure to air has on the vitamin C content of selected foods.

Problem

How does exposure to air affect the vitamin C content of certain foods? **Design an experiment** to answer the question.

Suggested Materials

- small beakers
- 100% orange juice, refrigerated
- burette
- indophenol solution
- other kinds of fruit drinks
- glass stirring rod
- funnel

Suggested Procedure

1. Set up your equipment as shown in the diagram.

2. While carefully standing on a chair, pour orange juice into the funnel at the top of the burette. Record the initial level of the juice in milliliters.

3. Pour 10 mL of indophenol indicator solution into a beaker. **CAUTION:** *Be careful using indophenol because it stains. Do not drink any of the substances used in the lab. Wash your hands thoroughly after cleaning up.*

4. Place the beaker below the burette and turn the stop valve to the open position so that only one drop of orange juice falls into the indophenol.

5. As each drop of juice falls into the indophenol, stir the mixture and note the color.

6. Keep adding drops until the blue indicator color becomes colorless when you stir. Turn the burette valve off.

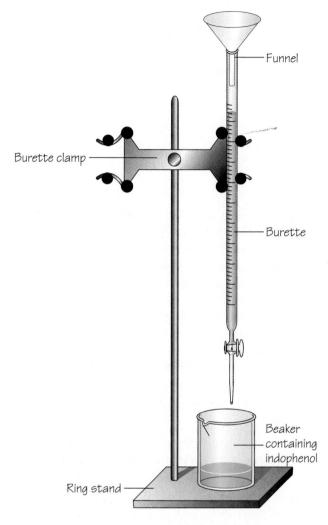

Funnel

Burette clamp

Burette

Beaker
containing
indophenol

Ring stand

7. Read the level of the juice in the burette. Record this measurement.

8. Using the same technique as in steps 1 to 7, design an experiment to determine the effect that exposure to air has on the vitamin C content in orange juice. You may also wish to do a similar experiment with powdered drinks that are fortified with vitamin C.

9. Propose a hypothesis and write up your procedure. Make sure the procedure has only one variable and includes a control.

10. Obtain the approval of your teacher before carrying out your experiment.

Observations

1. How many milliliters of orange juice were needed to change the color of the indophenol?

2. Construct a bar graph to compare the number of milliliters of juice required in each trial of your experiment.

3. How did your data compare with that of other groups?

Analysis and Conclusions

1. What is the relationship between the volume of juice required to reach the end point of the titration and the vitamin C content of the juice?

2. Under what conditions did the orange juice have the highest vitamin C content? The lowest? Did your results support your hypothesis?

3. Do the results of your experiment suggest how to handle foods with vitamin C? Explain your answer.

Extensions

What effect does temperature have on the vitamin C content in orange juice? Design an experiment to answer the question.

Chapter **8** Review

Study Outline

8-1 The Process of Nutrition

▶ Nutrition is the process by which organisms obtain nutrients and use them to carry on their life activities. These nutrients include proteins, carbohydrates, fats, vitamins, minerals, and water.

▶ Autotrophs are capable of making nutrients from simple inorganic substances. Heterotrophs must depend on other living things for food.

▶ Energy to carry on life processes comes from the breakdown of fats, carbohydrates, and proteins. The kilocalorie (Calorie) is commonly used to measure the energy content of foods.

▶ A healthy human diet includes foods from the five food groups in the Food Guide Pyramid as well as a limited amount of fats and oils.

8-2 Adaptations for Nutrition and Digestion

▶ Digestion is the process by which foods are broken down into simpler compounds. Absorption is the movement of digested food molecules across cell membranes and into cells.

▶ In protists, digestion is intracellular, and food particles are digested within food vacuoles. In the hydra, digestion is both extracellular and intracellular. It begins in the gastrovascular cavity and is completed by endoderm cells that engulf food particles.

▶ The digestive systems of the earthworm and grasshopper are tubular. The inner tube, called the alimentary canal, contains the organs of digestion, and the outer tube is the body wall.

8-3 The Human Digestive System

▶ Humans, like earthworms and grasshoppers, have a "tube-within-a-tube" body plan, in which the inner tube is the digestive tract.

▶ The human digestive tract includes the mouth, pharynx, esophagus, stomach, small intestine, large intestine, rectum, and anus. Accessory glands include the salivary glands, the liver, and the pancreas.

Chapter Assessment

Multiple Choice

Choose the letter of the answer that best completes each statement or answers the question.

1. Unlike heterotrophs, autotrophs (a) possess adaptations for locomotion. (b) can convert inorganic molecules into organic nutrients. (c) must obtain organic nutrients from the environment. (d) require energy for digestion.

2. Indigestible material is discharged through the anal pore in which organism? (a) hydra (b) earthworm (c) grasshopper (d) paramecium

3. Which organism has only one body opening, which functions as an entrance for food and an exit for waste? (a) human (b) grasshopper (c) hydra (d) earthworm

4. In the earthworm, mechanical breakdown of food occurs in the (a) crop. (b) esophagus. (c) pharynx. (d) gizzard.

5. An organism with a one-way digestive tube is the (a) paramecium. (b) earthworm. (c) ameba. (d) hydra.

6. In a grasshopper's gizzard, food is (a) chemically digested. (b) stored. (c) mechanically broken down. (d) absorbed into the bloodstream.

7. In humans, an enzyme in saliva begins digestion of (a) protein. (b) nucleic acids. (c) fat. (d) starch.

8. Mucus secreted by the pyloric glands protects the lining of the (a) large intestine. (b) stomach. (c) small intestine. (d) esophagus.

9. Bile is produced by the (a) liver. (b) small intestine. (c) large intestine. (d) stomach.

10. In the human digestive system, chemical digestion does not occur in the (a) stomach. (b) large intestine. (c) small intestine. (d) esophagus.

Content Review

Answer each of the following in complete sentences.

11. How is the energy content of food determined, and in what unit of energy is it expressed?

12. What is the difference between intracellular digestion and extracellular digestion?

13. Describe digestion in the hydra.

14. Trace the path of food through the digestive system of the earthworm.

15. Explain why food and air are not usually mixed during swallowing.

16. How is the passage of food from the esophagus into the stomach controlled?

17. Describe the functions of hydrochloric acid and pepsin in the stomach.

18. What mechanisms stimulate the flow of gastric juice?

19. Describe the structure and function of villi.

20. What are the effects of peristalsis in the small intestine?

Graphic Organizing

For information on graphic organizers, see Appendix G at the back of this text.

21. **Circle Graph** The completed circle graph below shows the percentages of major nutrients in a typical current American diet. To the right is an incomplete graph for a diet recommended by nutritionists. The recommended percentages of these nutrients are refined sugars, 10%; complex carbohydrates and naturally occurring sugars, 48%; proteins, 12%; saturated fats, 10%; and unsaturated fats, 20%. Copy the incomplete graph on the right onto a sheet of paper and complete it.

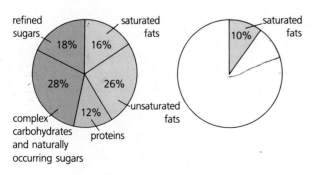

Current Diet   Recommended Diet

22. **Flow Chart** Construct a flow chart tracing the path of food through the organs of the human digestive system.

Critical Thinking and Problem Solving

Discuss each of the following in a brief paragraph.

23. **Comparing** Referring to Figure 8–3, compare the energy content of a medium apple and a slice of white bread; three ounces of hamburger and three ounces of American cheese; a candy bar and two cups of milk. Should calorie comparisons alone be used to make nutritional choices? Explain your answer.

24. **Drawing conclusions** Why are the salivary glands, liver, and pancreas usually considered a part of the digestive system? Why might they not be considered a part of the digestive system in the same way that the esophagus, stomach, or intestines are?

25. **Interpreting** Pancreatic juice contains both sodium bicarbonate and digestive enzymes. It is secreted by the pancreas in response to the specific composition of chyme in the upper portion of the small intestine. The graph below shows data from a study to determine the secretion of the pancreas in response to the presence of three different substances in the small intestine. What does the graph show about the secretion of bicarbonate and enzymes in response to hydrochloric acid, fat, and proteins? How would you interpret these findings?

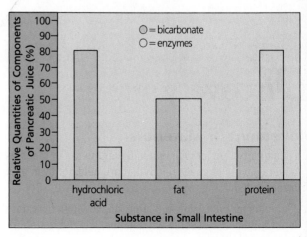

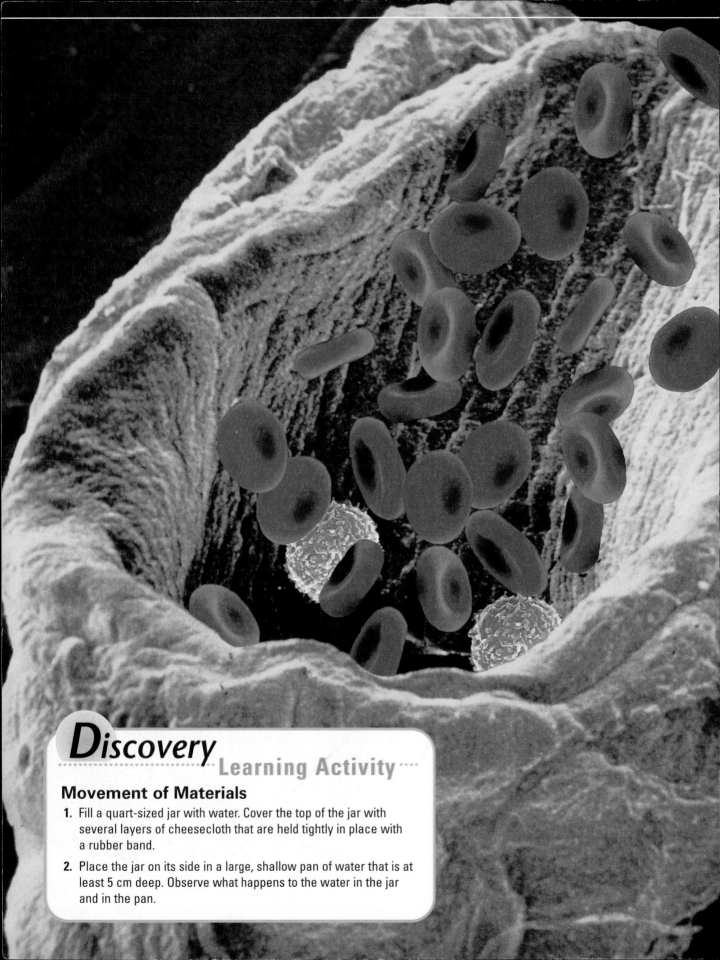

Discovery Learning Activity

Movement of Materials

1. Fill a quart-sized jar with water. Cover the top of the jar with several layers of cheesecloth that are held tightly in place with a rubber band.

2. Place the jar on its side in a large, shallow pan of water that is at least 5 cm deep. Observe what happens to the water in the jar and in the pan.

Transport

Guide for Reading

Previewing the Chapter

Each individual cell exists in a fluid environment. This fluid helps to carry nutrients to the cell and wastes away from the cell. In most animals, a network of blood vessels transports nutrients to every cell in an organism and flushes away wastes. What are the mechanisms through which living things keep individual cells nourished and healthy? How does the heart pump blood to all parts of your body? What are the major circulatory pathways in the human body?

Key Words

arteries, capillaries, circulatory system, heart, lymph, lymphatic system, transport, veins

Key Concepts

- **Compare** methods of transport in protists, hydra, earthworms, and grasshoppers.
- **Describe** how the heart pumps blood to all parts of the human body.
- **Design an experiment** to compare a single-loop circulatory system and a double-loop circulatory system. (Laboratory Investigation)

9-1 Adaptations for Transport

Section Objectives:

- *Explain* the importance of the transport process for both simple and complex organisms.
- *Describe* transport in the ameba, paramecium, and hydra.
- *Compare* the circulatory system of the earthworm with that of the grasshopper.

Transport and Circulation

Transport is the process by which substances move into or out of cells or are distributed within cells. Every cell needs substances from the environment to carry on its life processes. In order to enter the cell, these substances must move across cell membranes. Once they are inside the cell, the substances must be moved to places where they can be used or stored. In simple organisms, the cells are in close contact with their outside environment. However, in large or complex organisms, a **circulatory system** is needed to transport materials to and from all parts of the organism. The circulatory system acts as a link between the cells of a complex organism and its environment. In the following sections, you will learn how transport occurs in four representative organisms.

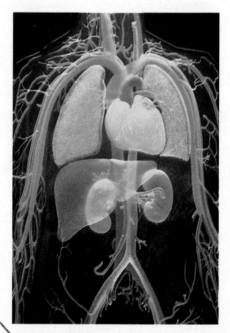

▲ **Figure 9–1**
The Human Circulatory System. The heart, lungs, liver, and kidneys are shown in this model of the human circulatory system.

◀ Red and white blood cells flowing through a vein.

Figure 9–2

Transport in Ameba and Paramecium. Because one-celled animals such as the ameba (left) and paramecium (right) have no circulatory system, the exchange of materials between the cells and the environment occurs by diffusion through the cell membrane. Within the cell, cytoplasmic streaming helps movement of materials. ▶

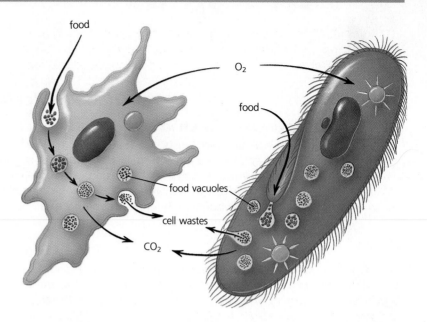

Figure 9–3

Transport in the Hydra. In the hydra, cells of both the ectoderm and the endoderm are in direct contact with the environment. The exchange of materials between the cells and the environment takes place by diffusion through the cell membranes. ▼

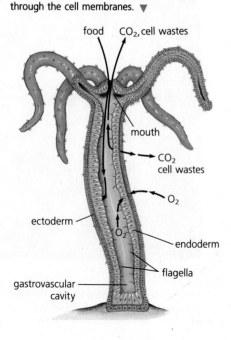

A circulatory system is made up of three parts: (1) a fluid in which materials are transported; (2) a network of tubes or body spaces through which the fluid flows; and (3) a means of driving the fluid through the tubes or spaces. For example, in humans, the most familiar circulatory fluid is the *blood*. The organ that pumps blood through the circulatory system is the **heart.**

Transport in Protists

Protists are usually one-celled animals that have no circulatory systems. Even in colonies, most protist cells are in direct contact with their surroundings. Diffusion and active transport alone are enough to move materials into and out of the cell. Within the cell, the movement of the material is aided by *cyclosis,* the streaming of the cytoplasm.

In the ameba and paramecium, food vacuoles move around in the cytoplasm by cyclosis. See Figure 9–2. As the food is digested, the absorption of nutrients takes place by diffusion or active transport across the food vacuole membrane.

Transport in Hydra

Simple multicellular animals, such as the hydra, can also get along without a circulatory system. The hydra lives in fresh water. As you can see in Figure 9–3, its body is shaped like a hollow sac. The body wall of the hydra is composed of two layers of cells. The outer layer, the ectoderm, is in direct contact with the surrounding water. The inner layer, the endoderm, lines the gastrovascular cavity. The endoderm is also in contact with water because water enters and leaves the gastrovascular cavity through the mouth. Therefore, through diffusion, both cell layers can exchange dissolved oxygen, carbon dioxide, and wastes with their surroundings.

Nutrients from the gastrovascular cavity pass into the cells of the endoderm by both active transport and diffusion. The outer layer of ectodermal cells absorbs nutrients from the endoderm cells by diffusion. Within all cells, nutrients and other substances move around by cyclosis.

The muscular movements of the hydra as it stretches and contracts help to distribute materials within the gastrovascular cavity. This movement carries materials to all the inner cells of the endoderm. It also stops wastes from collecting near the surface of the endoderm. The flagella of endoderm cells also help to move materials. Thus, the gastrovascular cavity serves both to transport and to digest materials in the hydra.

Transport in the Earthworm

The earthworm is much more complex than the hydra. It contains true organs and organ systems. Most of its cells are not in direct contact with its surroundings. It is the circulatory system of the earthworm that makes possible the exchange of materials between its outside environment and its body cells.

Figure 9–4 illustrates the main features of the earthworm's circulatory system. The blood carries dissolved nutrients, gases, wastes, water, and other substances. It is red because it contains the red, iron-containing pigment **hemoglobin** (HEE muh gloh bin). Hemoglobin increases the amount of oxygen the blood can carry. The circulatory system of the earthworm is an example of a **closed circulatory system.** In a closed circulatory system, the blood is always contained within tubes or vessels in the body.

There are two major blood vessels in the earthworm. One is the *dorsal* (DOR sul) *vessel,* which runs along the top of the digestive tract. The other is the *ventral* (VEN trul) *vessel,* which runs below the digestive tract. These two vessels are connected near the head end of the worm by five pairs of blood vessels known as *aortic* (ay ORT ik) *arches,* or "hearts." The beating of these heartlike blood vessels pumps the blood from the dorsal to the ventral vessel.

The ventral vessel divides into many smaller vessels that go to all parts of the body. These small blood vessels gradually branch into still smaller and smaller vessels. The smallest blood vessels of

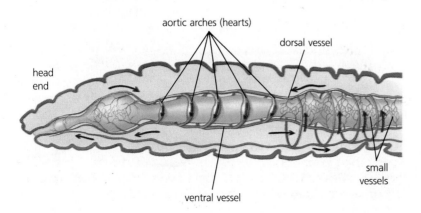

aortic arches (hearts)

dorsal vessel

head end

small vessels

ventral vessel

◀ **Figure 9–4**
Closed Circulatory System of the Earthworm. In the closed circulatory system of the earthworm, five pairs of contracting "hearts" pump blood through a system of vessels.

all are the microscopic **capillaries** (KAP uh ler eez). There are so many capillaries that every cell in the body of an earthworm is near one. The exchange of materials between the blood and the body cells takes place through the walls of the capillaries. Dissolved materials are able to diffuse across the thin walls of capillaries. The capillaries then join to form larger vessels. These larger vessels carry the blood back to the dorsal vessel. The dorsal blood vessel contracts rhythmically. By doing so, it forces the blood back into the aortic arches.

Transport in the Grasshopper

The grasshopper has an **open circulatory system.** In an open circulatory system, the blood is not always enclosed in blood vessels. Instead, it flows directly into body spaces where it bathes the tissues.

The colorless blood of the grasshopper does not contain hemoglobin, and it does not transport oxygen or carbon dioxide. Instead, these respiratory gases are transported through a series of tubes that are separate from the circulatory system. In the grasshopper, the blood serves mainly to transport nutrients and nitrogen-containing wastes.

As you can see in Figure 9–5, the open circulatory system of the grasshopper is quite different from the closed system of the earthworm. Along the back, above the digestive and reproductive systems, is a single vessel, the *aorta* (ay OR tah), and a tubular heart. Contraction of the heart, which is near the rear of the animal, forces the blood forward through the aorta toward the head. In the head, the blood flows out of the aorta. It then trickles through the body spaces and over the body tissues. The exchange of materials between the blood and the body cells takes place while the blood is in the body spaces. The blood is kept moving through the spaces by breathing and other movements of the body. Eventually, the blood circulates back into the heart through valvelike openings in the heart wall.

Figure 9–5

Open Circulatory System of the Grasshopper. In the open circulatory system of the grasshopper, blood pumped by the tubular heart passes through the aorta and into the body spaces, where it bathes the body tissues. ▶

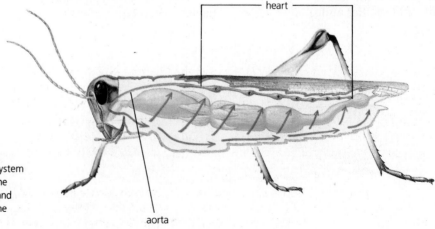

There is an important difference between a closed circulatory system and an open circulatory system. In a closed circulatory system, the blood is under pressure. This pressure, which does not exist in an open circulatory system, causes the blood of an organism to move faster. However, an open circulatory system does move blood fast enough to meet the needs of those organisms that have this type of system.

9-1 Section Review

1. What are the three main parts of a circulatory system?
2. Name the processes that are involved in the transport of materials in protists.
3. How does a closed circulatory system differ from an open circulatory system?
4. What does the blood of a grasshopper transport?

Critical Thinking

5. What type of circulatory system would you expect to find in a bee? Explain your reasoning. (*Reasoning by Analogy*)

9-2 The Human Circulatory System

Section Objectives:

- *Compare* the structure and function of an artery, a vein, and a capillary.
- *Trace* the path of blood through the heart.
- *Explain* the heartbeat cycle and the mechanisms that control the rate and strength of the heartbeat.
- *List* the factors that cause variations in blood pressure.

Blood Vessels

Humans, like other vertebrates, have a closed circulatory system. The system is similar to that of an earthworm but more complex. It includes a single heart and a network of blood vessels. The heart pumps the blood, and the vessels carry the blood to and from all the cells of the body. There are three kinds of blood vessels—arteries, veins, and capillaries. These blood vessels are shown in Figure 9-6.

Arteries   The **arteries** (AR tuh reez) are the blood vessels that carry blood away from the heart to the organs and tissues of the body. The walls of arteries are thick and elastic. They contain

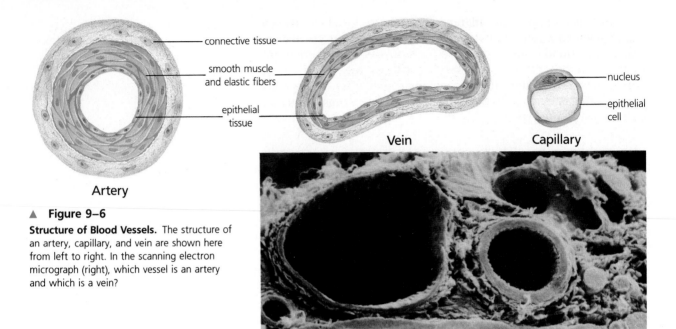

connective tissue

smooth muscle and elastic fibers

epithelial tissue

Artery

Vein

nucleus

epithelial cell

Capillary

▲ **Figure 9–6**

Structure of Blood Vessels. The structure of an artery, capillary, and vein are shown here from left to right. In the scanning electron micrograph (right), which vessel is an artery and which is a vein?

Figure 9–7

Valves in a Vein. Pressure on the veins opens valves and allows blood to flow toward the heart (left). The valves close when the pressure decreases (right), thus preventing a backflow of blood. ▼

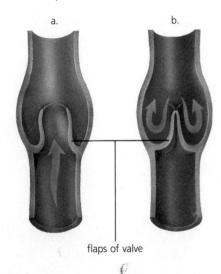

a.   b.

flaps of valve

layers of connective tissue, muscle tissue, and epithelial tissue. As an artery enters a tissue or organ, it divides and subdivides many times to form smaller and smaller arteries. The smallest arteries are called *arterioles* (ar TEER ee olz).

Veins   The **veins** (vaynz) are the blood vessels that return blood from the body tissues to the heart. The smallest veins are called *venules* (VEEN yoolz). The venules join together to form veins, which also merge, forming larger and larger veins. Unlike the artery walls, the walls of veins are thin and only slightly elastic. Inside the veins are flaplike **valves** that allow the blood to flow in only one direction—toward the heart. See Figure 9–7. When the valves do not work properly, blood tends to build up within the vein. The walls of the vein become stretched and lose their elasticity. This condition, called *varicose* (VAR uh kohs) *veins,* sometimes occurs in the veins of the leg.

Capillaries   Arterioles and venules are connected by networks of microscopic capillaries. The walls of the capillaries consist of a single layer of epithelial cells. These vessels are so narrow that red blood cells pass through them in single file. The thin walls of the capillaries allow the exchange of dissolved nutrients, wastes, oxygen, and other substances between the blood and the body cells.

The Heart

The heart acts as a pump. Its regular contractions force the blood through the vessels. This muscular organ is somewhat larger than your fist and can be found slightly to the left of the middle of the chest cavity. It is made mostly of cardiac muscle, which consists of

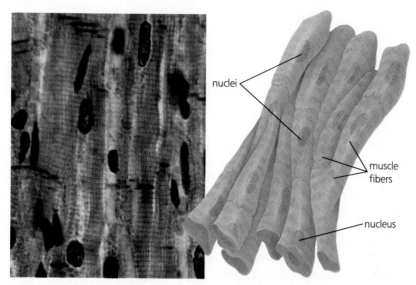

nuclei

muscle fibers

nucleus

◀ **Figure 9–8**
Structure of Cardiac Muscle. The nuclei of muscle cells are visible in this scanning electron micrograph of cardiac muscle tissue (left). (Magnification 648 X) Fibers in cardiac muscle are interconnected (right), which helps to regulate the heartbeat.

individual cells, each with a single nucleus. See Figure 9–8. The cardiac muscle cells form a branching, interlocking network. This allows them to contract with greater force.

A tough membrane, the **pericardium** (per uh KARD ee um), covers the heart and protects it. Inside, the heart is divided into four chambers, as you can see in Figure 9–9. The two upper, thin-walled chambers are the **atria** (AY tree uh), or *auricles* (OR ih kulz). The two lower, thick-walled chambers are the **ventricles** (VEN trih kulz). The right and left sides of the heart are separated by

Figure 9–9

Structure of the Human Heart. The cross section of the heart shows the four chambers, the valves, and the blood vessels that connect with the heart chambers. In the drawing below arrows trace the path of blood through the heart. ▼

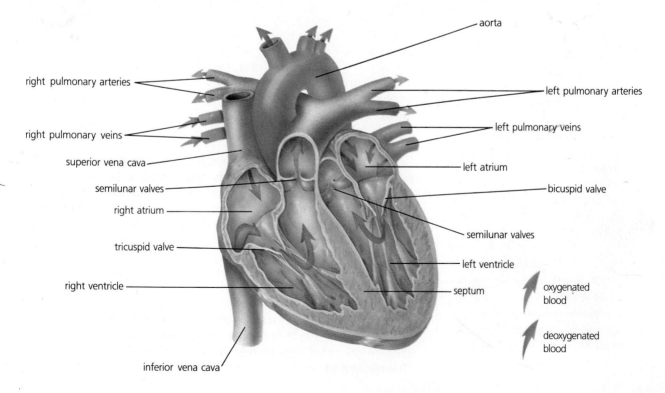

aorta

right pulmonary arteries

left pulmonary arteries

right pulmonary veins

left pulmonary veins

superior vena cava

left atrium

semilunar valves

bicuspid valve

right atrium

semilunar valves

tricuspid valve

left ventricle

right ventricle

septum

oxygenated blood

deoxygenated blood

inferior vena cava

a wall, called the *septum* (SEP tum). The septum prevents the oxygen-poor blood found in the right side of the heart from mixing with the oxygen-rich blood of the left side. Entering from the back are the arteries and veins.

Four flaplike valves control the direction of the blood flow inside the heart. Two of these valves are called the *atrioventricular* (ay tree oh ven TRIK yoo ler), or *A-V, valves.* They allow blood to flow only from the atria into the ventricles. In the right side of the heart, the A-V valve is called the *tricuspid* (try KUS pid) *valve* because it has three flaps. In the left side, it is called the *bicuspid* (by KUS pid), or *mitral* (MY trul), *valve.* The other two valves are called the *semilunar* (sem ee LOON er) *valves.* When open, these valves allow blood to move from the ventricles into the arteries that carry blood away from the heart. When closed, the valves stop blood from flowing back into the ventricles.

Actually, the heart is a double pump. The right side of the heart sends oxygen-poor blood to the lungs. The left side sends oxygen-rich blood to the rest of the body.

The Heartbeat Cycle   The pumping action of the heart has two main periods. During one of these periods, the heart muscle is relaxed. This period of relaxation is called **diastole** (dy AS tuh lee). During the other period, the heart muscle contracts. The period of contraction is called **systole** (SIS tuh lee).

During diastole—the period of relaxation—the A-V valves are open. Blood flows from the atria into the ventricles. By the end of diastole, the ventricles are about 70 percent filled. Systole—the period of contraction—begins with contraction of the atria. The contraction of the atria forces more blood into the ventricles, filling them. The ventricles then contract. The pressure of this contraction closes the A-V valves and opens the semilunar valves. Blood flows out of the right ventricle into the **pulmonary** (PUL muh nair ee) **artery.** This artery divides into two branches, each of which goes to one of the lungs. Blood flows out of the left ventricle into the **aorta,** the largest artery of the body. The aorta branches and divides into many smaller arteries. These carry blood to all the body tissues.

While the ventricles are contracting, the atria relax. This permits blood to flow into the atria from the veins. Blood returning from all the body tissues except the lungs enters the right atrium. Blood returning from the lungs enters the left atrium. When the ventricles relax, a new period of diastole begins, and the cycle repeats.

As the heart valves open and close, they make a "lub-dup" sound. This sound can be heard clearly through a stethoscope. The "lub" sound is produced by the closing of the A-V valves. The "dup" sound is made by the closing of the semilunar valves. If the septum or any of the heart valves are damaged, there will be a leak, or backflow, of blood at certain times during the heartbeat cycle. This produces an abnormal heart sound, commonly known as a "heart murmur."

Control of the Heartbeat   The cardiac muscle that makes up the heart is different from the other muscle tissues of the body. As you have read, cardiac muscle fibers form a network, or lattice. The interlocking arrangement of muscle fibers in the two atria cause the atria to function together as one unit. Similarly, the two ventricles function together as another unit.

Although the nervous system controls the contraction of other types of muscle, cardiac muscle has a built-in ability to contract. Even when it is removed from the body, the heart will keep beating for a while if it is kept in a special solution. Each heart-muscle fiber has its own rate of contraction. However, the heart as a whole must work as a unit. This is made possible by a structure in the heart called the *sinoatrial* (sy no AY tree ul) *node,* or **S-A node,** also known as the pacemaker. The S-A node is a small group of specialized muscle cells in the wall of the right atrium. Contraction of the heart begins when the heart receives electrical impulses from the S-A node. This causes the atria to contract. Almost immediately the impulse reaches the *atrioventricular node,* or **A-V node.** This small bundle of muscle cells is located at the base of the right atrium. The A-V node triggers an impulse that causes the ventricles to contract. See Figure 9–10.

The tiny electrical current produced each time the heart contracts can be recorded on a machine that produces an *electrocardiogram* (eh lek troh KARD ee oh gram), or ECG. Physicians use electrocardiograms to check the health of the heart.

Figure 9–10
Controlling and Recording the Heartbeat. (Left). Electrical impulses from the S-A node cause the atria to contract. These contractions trigger an A-V node impulse, which causes the ventricles to contract. (Right). An electrocardiogram, or ECG, machine records the changing currents produced by contractions of the heart and helps to detect any abnormalities. ▼

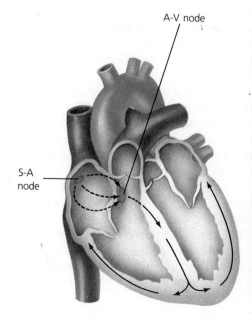
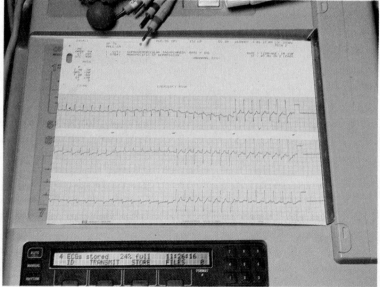

The rate of the heartbeat is regulated by certain nerves that enter the pacemaker. Impulses from the *vagus* (VAY gus) *nerves* slow down the pacemaker. Those from the *cardioaccelerator* (KARD ee oh ak sel uh ray tur) *nerves* speed up the pacemaker. The built-in rhythm of the heart is also affected by changes in body temperature and by certain chemicals circulating in the blood.

Sometimes, the natural pacemaker of the heart fails to work properly, and the rhythm of the heart is disturbed. When this happens, a battery-powered electronic pacemaker can be surgically placed inside a person's body. This artificial pacemaker regulates the heartbeat by delivering an electric shock to the heart at regular intervals.

Blood Pressure and the Flow of Blood

The thick, muscular walls of the arteries are elastic. When the ventricles contract, blood is forced out of them under great pressure into the arteries. Because they are elastic, the arteries are able to expand and to absorb this great pressure. As the ventricles relax, the pressure decreases. The elasticity of the artery walls helps to maintain the pressure between heartbeats. In this way, blood is kept flowing throughout the body continuously. The **pulse** is the expansion (high pressure) and relaxation (lower pressure) that can be felt in an artery each time the left ventricle contracts and relaxes. Both the rate and the force of the heartbeat can be measured by the pulse.

Physicians measure the pressure on the blood in the artery of the upper arm with an instrument called a *sphygmomanometer* (sfig moh muh NAHM uh ter). Pressure is measured in terms of the height of a column of mercury in a tube in this instrument. In an average adult at rest, the pressure during systole is enough to support a column of mercury about 120 millimeters high. During diastole, the pressure drops. The maximum height of the mercury is only about 80 millimeters. Usually, blood pressure is stated in the form of systolic pressure/diastolic pressure. Thus, the normal blood pressure in a resting adult is 120/80. During exercise and times of stress, blood pressure increases.

High blood pressure, or *hypertension* (HY per ten shun), is a medical condition. The blood pressure in people with this condition remains above normal throughout the heartbeat cycle. It is a serious and fairly common health problem. One frequent cause of high blood pressure is *atherosclerosis* (ath uh roh skluh ROH sis), a disease commonly called "hardening of the arteries." In this disease, deposits of cholesterol and other fatty materials collect on the inner walls of the arteries. See Figure 9–11. The arteries become narrower and the walls become more rigid, which causes blood pressure to increase. The condition puts a strain on both the heart and the blood vessels. If untreated, atherosclerosis can lead to heart attacks and strokes. Studies show that the chance of developing atherosclerosis increases with the amount of cholesterol

Figure 9–11

Atherosclerosis. The large deposit of fatty material in this artery has narrowed the space through which blood can flow. ▼

Preventing Heart Disease

- Do not smoke tobacco. The more you smoke, the greater the risk of heart disease.

- If you do smoke, quit. The risks of heart disease are greatly reduced within two years of quitting.

- Monitor your blood pressure. It should be checked regularly by a doctor or nurse.

- Reduce the amount of high-cholesterol foods you eat. Eat less butter, mayonnaise, and fatty meat. Eat more chicken, fish, fresh fruits, and vegetables.

- Cut down on salt. Reducing the amount of salt you eat will help prevent high blood pressure.

- Exercise regularly. Twenty minutes of exercise at least three times a week strengthens the heart and improves blood circulation.

- Avoid obesity. If you are overweight, your heart has to work harder than it should.

- Learn to manage stress. Feelings of stress and anxiety can contribute to heart disease.

◀ **Figure 9–12**
Preventing Heart Disease. Following these tips promotes good health and may prevent serious illness.

in the blood. In turn, the amount of cholesterol in the blood seems to be related to the amount of fat, particularly animal fat, in the diet. Many physicians suggest that the amount of animal and certain other fats in the diet should be kept low for this reason. Figure 9–12 lists other ways to reduce your risk of atherosclerosis and other heart diseases.

As blood flows through the arteries, there is little drop in pressure. However, there is a large drop in pressure when the blood reaches the arterioles. At the capillary ends of the arterioles there are rings of muscle that control the blood flow through the capillaries. The capillaries are the most numerous blood vessels in the body. If all the capillaries were open at the same time, there would not be enough blood in the body to fill them. The opening and closing of the rings of muscle at the capillary ends of the arterioles direct the flow of blood to the parts of the body where it is needed. For example, when an individual runs, the flow of blood into the capillaries of the skeletal muscles is increased. At the same time, the supply of blood to the capillaries of the digestive tract is decreased.

By the time blood reaches the veins, pressure is low. It is too low to return the blood to the heart, especially from the lower parts of the body. Blood flow in the veins is helped by the squeezing action of the skeletal muscles as the body moves. As a contracting muscle presses against a vein, the blood in the vein is forced to move. The blood moves toward the heart since the valves in the veins prevent flow in the opposite direction.

9-2 Section Review

1. Name the three kinds of blood vessels.
2. Describe the structure of the human heart.
3. What structure makes the heart-muscle fibers function as a unit?
4. What is the pulse?

Critical Thinking

5. Where would you expect blood pressure to be higher—in an artery in the arm or in an artery in the leg? Explain. (*Ordering*)

9-3 Pathways of Human Circulation

Section Objectives:

- *Trace* the path of the blood through the pulmonary circulation.
- *Discuss* the exchange of gases that occurs in the lungs.
- *Describe* the path of the blood through the systemic circulation, including the coronary, hepatic-portal, and renal circulations.
- *Identify* the structures of the lymphatic system and explain their functions.

Circulation of Blood

In the second century A.D., a Greek physician proposed that blood flowed back and forth from the heart to the rest of the body through the veins. It was not until 1628 that the correct pathway for blood circulation was identified. William Harvey, an English physician, showed that the heart pumps blood to the organs through arteries and that veins carry blood back to the heart. Harvey thought that connections between the ends of tiny arteries and the ends of tiny veins must exist. However, he could not find these connecting vessels. In 1660, an Italian anatomist showed that capillaries connect arteries to veins. Thus, Harvey's theory of the circulation of the blood was proven correct.

The major arteries and veins of the human circulatory system are shown in Figure 9-13. The circulatory system consists of two major pathways. **Pulmonary circulation**—the first pathway—carries blood between the heart and the lungs. **Systemic** (sys TEM ik) **circulation**—the second pathway—carries blood between the heart and the rest of the body. These two pathways are illustrated in Figure 9-14.

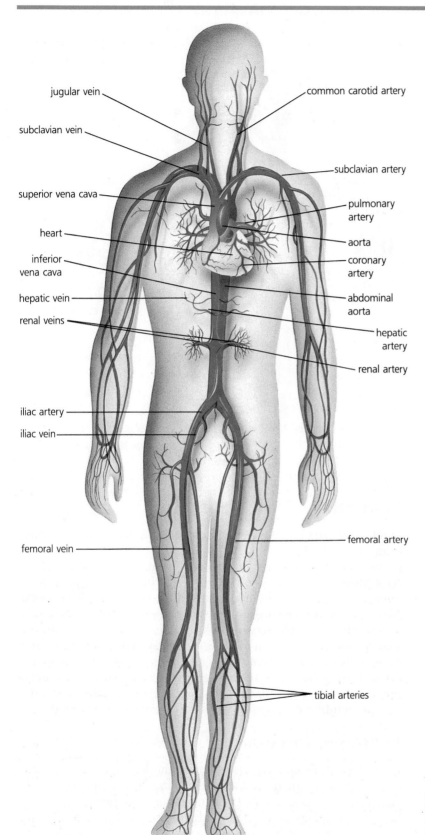

jugular vein

common carotid artery

subclavian vein

subclavian artery

superior vena cava

pulmonary artery

heart

aorta

inferior vena cava

coronary artery

hepatic vein

abdominal aorta

renal veins

hepatic artery

renal artery

iliac artery

iliac vein

femoral artery

femoral vein

tibial arteries

◀ **Figure 9–13**

Major Arteries and Veins of the Human Body. Notice that the names of many veins and arteries provide clues to their location in the body.

Figure 9–14

Pulmonary and Systemic Circulatory Systems. Pulmonary circulation carries blood between the heart and lungs. Systemic circulation carries blood from the heart to the rest of the body. ▶

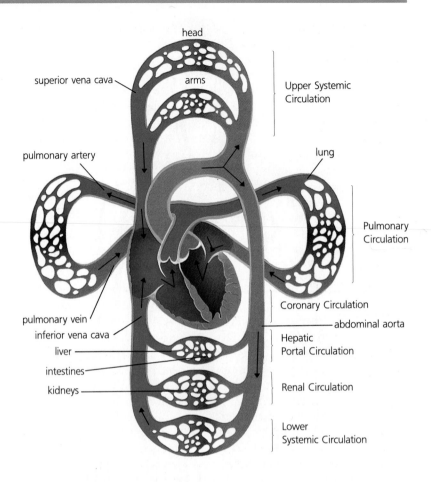

Pulmonary Circulation

Pulmonary circulation adds oxygen and removes carbon dioxide from the blood. Blood returning to the heart from the body tissues is low in oxygen and high in carbon dioxide. This blood enters the right atrium and flows into the right ventricle. The right ventricle pumps it through the pulmonary arteries to the lungs. The pulmonary arteries are the only arteries that carry oxygen-poor blood. All other arteries carry oxygen-rich blood. As the blood travels through the capillaries in the lungs, it gains oxygen and gets rid of carbon dioxide. The pulmonary capillaries merge into pulmonary veins. These veins carry the oxygen-rich blood to the left atrium of the heart. The pulmonary veins are the only veins that carry oxygen-rich blood. All other veins carry oxygen-poor blood.

Systemic Circulation

From the left atrium, the blood enters the left ventricle. Systemic circulation begins in the left ventricle of the heart. The powerful left ventricle has thicker walls than the other chambers of the heart because it pumps blood throughout the body. From the left ventricle, the blood is pumped into the aorta. The aorta branches, forming arteries that serve all parts of the body. The arteries divide and subdivide, forming smaller and smaller vessels. The smaller vessels finally form capillaries. Every cell in the body is near a capillary. The exchange of materials between the blood and the body tissues takes place through the walls of the capillaries. Capillaries merge to form veins. These veins finally return the blood to the heart. The largest veins of the body are the **superior vena cava** (VEE nuh KAY vuh) and the **inferior vena cava.** These large veins empty into the right atrium of the heart. The superior vena cava returns blood from the head, arms, and chest to the heart. The inferior vena cava returns blood from the lower body regions to the heart.

The systemic circulation includes three branches of special importance—the *coronary* (KOR uh ner ee) *circulation,* the *hepatic-portal* (heh PAT ik PORT ul) *circulation,* and the *renal* (REEN ul) *circulation.*

Coronary Circulation   **Coronary circulation** is the branch of the systemic circulation that supplies blood to the muscle of the heart. The right and left coronary arteries branch off the aorta just after the aorta leaves the heart. The coronary arteries run down either side of the heart, with branches entering the heart muscle. Within the heart, the arteries divide, eventually forming capillaries. The veins in the heart muscle drain the blood directly into the chambers of the heart, mostly the right atrium.

The cells of the heart need a constant supply of nutrients and oxygen. When a coronary artery is blocked by a blood clot or fat deposit, a heart attack can occur. Today, surgeons routinely perform coronary bypass surgery in these cases. A vein, usually from the person's leg, or an artificial vessel is used to construct a detour around the blocked artery. See Figure 9–15.

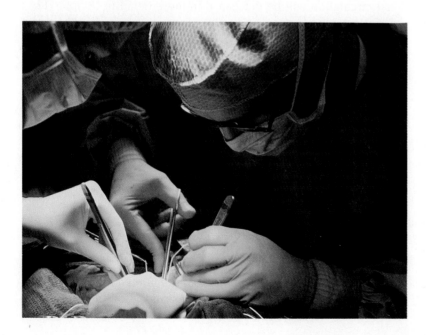

◀ **Figure 9–15**
Coronary Bypass Surgery. To improve the flow of blood to the heart, doctors use a vein (often from the leg) or an artificial vessel to build a detour around a blocked artery.

Hepatic-Portal Circulation Generally, blood travels through only one set of capillaries before it returns to the heart. An exception is the hepatic-portal circulation. The **hepatic-portal circulation** is the branch of systemic circulation that carries blood from the digestive tract to the liver. Blood passing through the capillaries of the digestive tract picks up nutrients. The veins draining these capillaries do not lead directly back to the heart. Instead, they form the *portal vein,* which goes to the liver. Within the liver, the vein divides into smaller veins. These veins divide into vessels similar to capillaries—the *hepatic sinuses.* Fluids, nutrients, and even blood proteins diffuse easily out of the blood and into the spaces between the cells of the liver. Blood in the sinuses of the liver is collected by a number of hepatic veins, which empty into the inferior vena cava.

Hepatic-portal circulation helps to maintain the balance of glucose in the blood. As blood passes through the liver, excess glucose is absorbed by the liver cells. In the liver cells, the glucose is converted to glycogen, which is then stored. If no food has been eaten for a long time, the blood reaching the liver from the digestive tract will be low in glucose. The liver then converts some of its stored glycogen to glucose, which diffuses out of the liver cells and into the blood. Thus, the liver helps to keep the amount of glucose in the blood at a constant level.

Renal Circulation One of the functions of the blood is to carry off some of the wastes of the body tissues. These wastes must be disposed of, or excreted. One waste product is the gas carbon dioxide. It is carried by the pulmonary circulation to the lungs, where it is excreted. Other wastes are removed from the blood and excreted by the kidneys. **Renal circulation** is the branch of the systemic circulation that carries blood to and from the kidneys. Renal circulation will be discussed in more detail in Chapter 12.

Circulation of Lymph

All the cells of the body are bathed in a colorless, watery fluid called the **intercellular** (in ter SEL yoo ler) **fluid,** or *interstitial* (in ter STISH ul) *fluid.* This fluid helps move materials between the capillaries and the body cells. All substances exchanged between blood and body cells diffuse through the intercellular fluid.

The intercellular fluid is formed from the parts of the blood that diffuse out of the capillaries. Intercellular fluid consists of water and salts and proteins and nutrients. Diffusion of intercellular fluid into the body tissues occurs when capillaries merge with arterioles. At the opposite end of the capillaries, close to the venules, most of the intercellular fluid and some of the substances it contains diffuse into the capillaries. However, all the proteins and some fluid remain outside the capillaries.

The excess fluid and proteins from the intercellular spaces are returned to the blood by a system of vessels called the **lymphatic** (lim FAT ik) **system.** See Figure 9-16. Without the lymphatic system,

Figure 9–16

Human Lymphatic System. The lymphatic system collects the excess fluid and proteins from intercellular spaces in the body and returns them to the blood. ▼

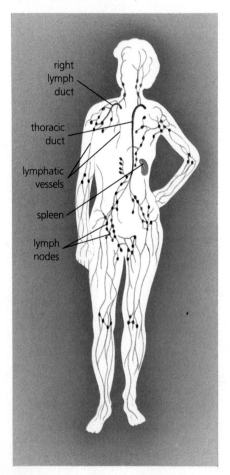

right lymph duct

thoracic duct

lymphatic vessels

spleen

lymph nodes

the constant loss of fluid from the blood eventually would drain the circulatory system. At the same time, body tissues would become flooded and swell. The lymphatic system begins in the body tissues with *lymph capillaries.* Lymph capillaries are microscopic tubes that are closed at one end. The walls of these tubes are only one cell thick. Intercellular fluid and proteins pass readily into the lymphatic capillaries. Once inside the lymphatic system, the fluid is called **lymph.**

The lymphatic capillaries merge to form larger and larger vessels. Like veins, lymphatic vessels have flaplike valves that allow the lymph to flow only in one direction. Muscular activity squeezes the lymph vessels and pushes the lymph along. Eventually, all the lymph from the lower part of the body, the left side of the head and chest, and the left arm flows into the *thoracic* (thuh RAS ik) *duct.* This is the largest lymphatic vessel in the body. Lymph from the thoracic duct is emptied into a large vein at the left side of the neck. All lymph from the right side of the head, the right arm, and the right side of the chest enters the *right lymph duct,* which drains into a large vein on the right side of the neck. In this way, the fluid and proteins lost from the blood in the capillaries are returned to the blood.

At various places along the lymphatic vessels, there are **lymph nodes,** or *lymph glands.* These glands play an important role in the body's defense against disease. See Figure 9–17. They filter foreign matter from the lymph. This prevents cancer cells, bacteria, and other disease-causing organisms from entering the bloodstream. Lymph nodes also produce some types of white blood cells that contain products able to destroy bacteria and other foreign substances. In the area of an infection, the lymph node may become enlarged and sore. These "swollen glands" show that the body is fighting an infection.

Lymphoid tissue like that found in lymph nodes is also found in the *spleen,* an organ near the stomach. In the spleen, the lymphoid tissues filter out bacteria and worn-out red cells from the blood.

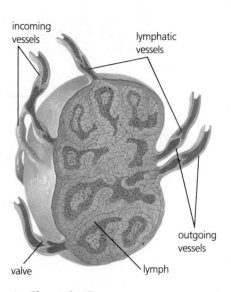

▲ **Figure 9–17**
Structure of a Lymph Node. Foreign matter, including disease-causing organisms, is filtered out of the lymph in the lymph nodes.

9-3 Section Review

1. How do the pulmonary arteries differ from all other arteries in the body?
2. What parts of the body are served by the systemic circulation?
3. What are the three major branches of the systemic circulation?
4. What is the role of the lymphatic system?

Critical Thinking

5. Filaria are parasitic worms that live in and block the lymphatic vessels of the legs. What do you think would be the result of filarial infection? (*Predicting*)

Laboratory
Investigation

Designing an Experiment

Vertebrate Circulatory Systems

The heart is a part of the transport system that pumps blood throughout the body. In this investigation, you will compare a two-chambered, single-loop circulatory system in fishes to a four-chambered, double-loop circulatory system in birds and mammals.

Problem

How do a double-loop circulatory system and a single-loop circulatory system compare? **Design an experiment** to answer the question.

Suggested Materials

- 4 8-oz plastic bottles
- 1 sheet each of red and blue construction paper
- red and blue yarn
- scissors
- scalpel
- clear mailing tape

Suggested Procedure

1. Remove the labels from two of the plastic bottles.

2. Using a scalpel, pierce a hole in one of the bottles where it tapers to form the bottom of the bottle. Place the point of a scissors in the hole and cut around the bottle until the bottom of the bottle is removed. **CAUTION:** *Be careful when using sharp instruments.*

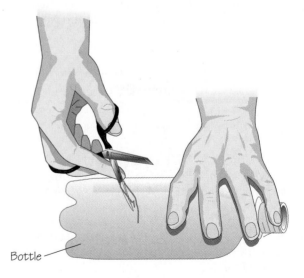

Bottle

3. Cut a sheet of blue construction paper just large enough to fit inside the uncut bottle. You will have to roll the paper tightly so that it can be inserted into the bottle. Remove the cap and insert the rolled paper into the bottle. This bottle represents the atrium filled with oxygen-poor blood.

4. Insert the remainder of the blue construction paper into the top portion of the cut bottle. This represents the ventricle filled with oxygen-poor blood.

5. Insert the bottle representing the atrium into the bottle representing the ventricle. They should fit snugly together. Tape them together if necessary.

6. Remove the bottle cap from the "ventricle" and insert a 15- to 20-cm length of blue yarn into the neck of the bottle. Secure one end of the yarn by placing the bottle cap back on. This piece of yarn represents the blood vessel leading to the gills.

7. Unravel the free end of the blue yarn.

8. Unravel both ends of a 15- to 20-cm length of red yarn.

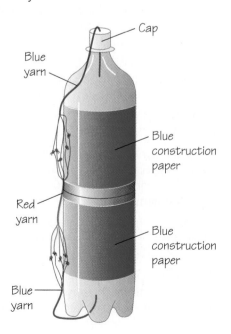

Cap

Blue yarn

Blue construction paper

Red yarn

Blue construction paper

Blue yarn

9. Tie the unraveled free ends of the blue yarn to one of the unraveled free ends of the red yarn to represent a capillary network in the gills.

10. Using another 15- to 20-cm length of blue yarn, unravel one end. Tie these unraveled ends to the remaining unraveled free ends of the red yarn. This will represent a capillary network of the body cells.

11. Tape the remaining free end of the blue yarn to the "atrium." This completes the two-chambered, single-loop model.

12. Using a procedure similar to the one given in steps 1 to 11, construct a model of a four-chambered, double-loop circulatory system.

Observations

1. What modifications did you have to make to your single-loop system in order to construct your double-loop system?

2. In the double-loop system, what does the red construction paper symbolize?

Analysis and Conclusions

1. In the single-loop system, where did the blood go after leaving the ventricle? Where did the blood go after leaving the ventricle in the double-loop system?

2. In the single-loop system, where did the blood go after leaving the atrium? Where did the blood go after leaving the atrium in the double-loop system?

3. Why were the red and blue yarns unraveled and joined?

4. Compare the similarities and differences between the two systems you constructed.

Extensions

Using the same types of materials, design a double-loop circulatory system similar to the one found in amphibians. (*Hint:* These vertebrate hearts have three chambers.)

Chapter **9** Review

Study Outline

9-1 Adaptations for Transport

- ◗ All cells need materials from their environment to sustain their life processes. A circulatory system transports these materials to and from all parts of the organism. The circulatory system also links the organism's cells with its environment.

- ◗ Protists have no circulatory system. Cells are in direct contact with the environment and obtain materials through diffusion and active transport.

- ◗ Simple multicellular organisms, such as the hydra, are also able to obtain materials through diffusion and active transport because their body cells are in direct contact with their environment.

- ◗ The earthworm has a closed circulatory system in which blood is always confined in vessels.

- ◗ The grasshopper has an open circulatory system in which blood flows into open spaces and bathes the tissues.

9-2 The Human Circulatory System

- ◗ Humans have a closed circulatory system made up of a single heart and a network of arteries, veins, and capillaries.

- ◗ Arteries transport blood away from the heart to the organs and tissues of the body. Veins return blood from the body tissues to the heart. Capillaries connect the smallest arteries to the smallest veins. The thin walls of the capillaries allow for the exchange of materials between the blood and the body cells.

- ◗ The heart is divided into four chambers—two atria and two ventricles.

- ◗ High blood pressure is a serious and fairly common medical condition that is often caused by atherosclerosis.

9-3 Pathways of Human Circulation

- ◗ Pulmonary circulation carries blood between the heart and the lungs. Systemic circulation carries blood between the heart and the rest of the body.

- ◗ The lymphatic system returns excess fluid and proteins from the intercellular spaces to the blood.

Chapter Assessment

Multiple Choice

Choose the letter of the answer that best completes each statement or answers the question.

1. In protists, which process serves a function similar to the circulation of blood in humans? (a) movement of the cilia (b) cyclosis (c) intracellular synthesis (d) hydrolysis

2. In the earthworm, (a) blood is pumped through a closed system of vessels. (b) blood diffuses through the moist skin. (c) blood flows out of open vessels into body cavities. (d) blood does not transport much oxygen because it has no hemoglobin.

3. In which organism is the transport of oxygen aided by hemoglobin? (a) grasshopper (b) earthworm (c) hydra (d) ameba

4. An open circulatory system is an adaptation for transport in (a) grasshoppers. (b) hydras. (c) earthworms. (d) humans.

5. If the flow of blood in a vessel is toward the heart, then the vessel is called a(n) (a) ventricle. (b) artery. (c) atrium. (d) vein.

6. In humans, the backward flow of blood in veins is prevented by (a) muscles. (b) heart action. (c) valves. (d) lymph nodes.

7. The number of chambers in the human heart is (a) 1. (b) 2. (c) 3. (d) 4.

8. The movement of blood between the heart and the lungs is called (a) coronary circulation. (b) lymphatic circulation. (c) pulmonary circulation. (d) systemic circulation.

9. Compared to the diastolic blood pressure, the systolic pressure is (a) always lower. (b) always higher. (c) usually the same. (d) at first higher, then lower.

10. Blood flowing to the heart is received by a(n) (a) ventricle. (b) valve. (c) atrium. d) lymph duct.

Content Review

Answer each of the following in complete sentences.

11. How is the body form of the hydra limited by its lack of a circulatory system?

12. Compare transport in protists with transport in hydra

13. What is the function of hemoglobin?

14. Describe blood circulation in the grasshopper.

15. Trace the path of blood through the human heart.

16. How are the aortic arches of the earthworm similar to the human heart?

17. How is the rate of the heartbeat controlled?

18. What happens when arteries lose elasticity?

19. Trace the path of lymph from a lymph capillary until it is returned to the blood.

20. What does swelling of the lymph nodes usually mean?

Graphic Organizing

For information on graphic organizers, see Appendix G at the back of this text.

21. Bar Graph The bar graph has been constructed using data from the table below for death rates from heart disease among American females in one year. Copy the graph onto graph paper. Then, construct a similar bar graph using the data given for males.

| Ages | Deaths per 100 000 | |
	Females	**Males**
15–24	6	10
25–34	19	39
35–44	64	175
45–54	233	574
55–64	700	1575
65–74	1802	3114
75–84	4804	6813
85 and over	12 720	14 407

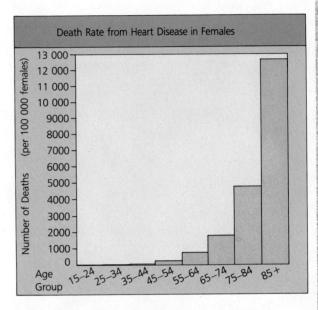

Death Rate from Heart Disease in Females

Critical Thinking and Problem Solving

Discuss each of the following in a brief paragraph.

22. Comparing How are the human circulatory system and lymphatic system alike? How are they different?

23. Inferring If you were a scientist trying to construct artificial arteries for use in surgery, what qualities would you look for in the material to be used?

24. Experimenting Do you think that changes in atmospheric temperature have an effect on the heart rate of a human being? Design an experiment to test whether or not your answer is correct.

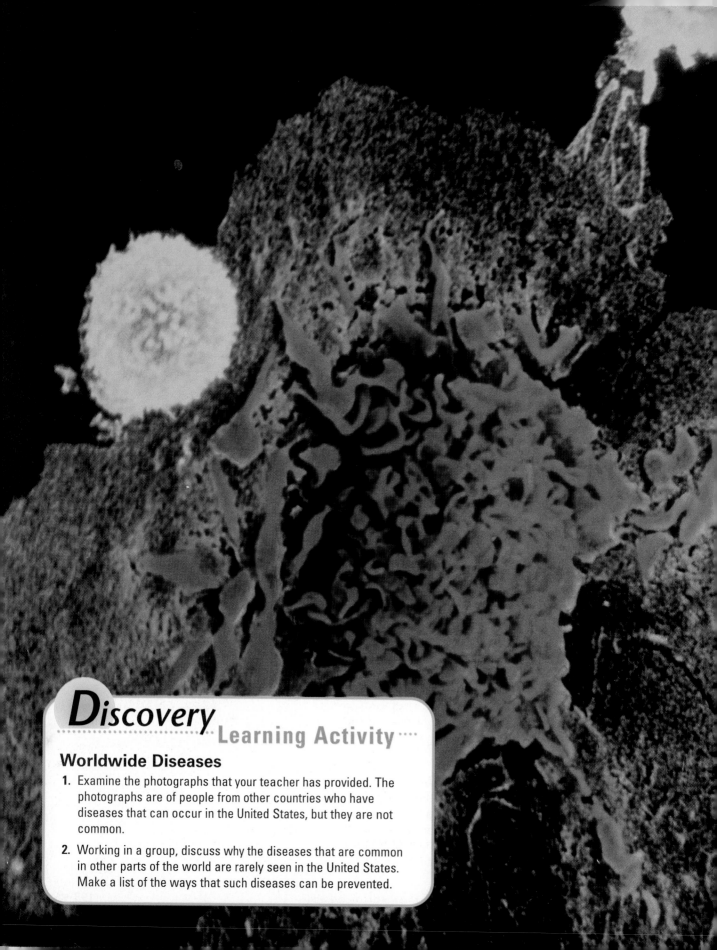

Discovery
Learning Activity

Worldwide Diseases

1. Examine the photographs that your teacher has provided. The photographs are of people from other countries who have diseases that can occur in the United States, but they are not common.

2. Working in a group, discuss why the diseases that are common in other parts of the world are rarely seen in the United States. Make a list of the ways that such diseases can be prevented.

The Blood and Immunity

Guide for Reading

Previewing the Chapter

Through the vast, intricate passageways of the circulatory system, red and white blood cells make their appointed rounds, driven by the forceful contractions of the heart. Red blood cells deliver oxygen and nutrients, and carry away wastes. Vigilant white blood cells search out and destroy any foreign invaders. How is blood able to carry out so many different functions in the body? What are the parts of the immune system? How does the immune system function to protect the body?

Key Words

AIDS, antibodies, antigen, immune response, immunity, platelets, red blood cells, white blood cells

Key Concepts

- **Describe** the functions of blood.
- **Describe** the functions of the immune system.
- **Construct a model** to simulate the spread of an infectious disease in a community. (Laboratory Investigation)

10-1 Blood—A Multipurpose Fluid

Section Objectives:

- *Explain* the functions of blood.
- *Describe* the components of blood.
- *Trace* the sequence of events that results in blood clotting.

Functions of Blood

Blood is a remarkable tissue. It contains both dissolved and suspended materials that travel through the blood vessels to every part of the body. Each one of the many components of blood plays an essential role in the maintenance of homeostasis throughout your body.

Blood is a liquid tissue that has three major functions: transportation, regulation, and protection. In humans and other vertebrates, blood transports materials to and from all the cells of the body. The nutrients and oxygen in blood are supplied to cells at levels that meet the needs of the cells. Wastes, produced by the cells, are carried away in blood to organs where the wastes are removed. Chemical messengers produced and released in one part of the

Figure 10–1

Blood Clotting. Clotting will stop the flow of blood from a wound. Here, protein strands trap platelets, forming a clot.

White blood cells (colored green) attack a tumor (colored red).

body are carried in the blood to other areas where they regulate cell activity. In this way, the activities of different tissues throughout the body are coordinated.

Blood itself acts as a regulator. For example, blood absorbs heat from warm areas of the body and releases heat in cooler areas. Blood also tends to maintain a constant pH and water balance. Some substances dissolved in blood resist changes in pH. Others prevent too much water from leaving the blood and entering body tissues.

Blood also protects the body. It carries specialized cells and chemicals that defend the body against disease-causing organisms. Blood also has the ability to clot, thus protecting the body against blood loss from an injury.

The Components of Blood

As you might expect from reading about its functions, blood is made up of many different parts. The liquid part of blood is called **plasma** (PLAZ muh). Plasma makes up about 55 percent of the total volume of blood. The other 45 percent of the blood is made up of *red blood cells, white blood cells,* and *platelets.* See Figure 10–2. An adult human has between four and six liters of blood in his or her body.

Plasma Plasma is the clear, straw-colored liquid portion of blood. Ninety percent of plasma is water. The remaining 10 percent is made of a variety of substances that are dissolved in the water. These dissolved substances include salts, glucose, amino acids, fatty acids, vitamins, enzymes, hormones, cellular wastes, and proteins.

Three major types of proteins are present in plasma: *albumin* (al BYOO min), *fibrinogen* (fy BRIN uh jen), and *globulins* (GLAHB yoo linz). Each of these proteins has its own function. Albumin, the most abundant of the plasma proteins, keeps water from leaving the blood and entering the surrounding cells by osmosis. See Chapter 5. It does this by helping to maintain the concentration of water in the blood at the same concentration as the water in the body tissues.

Fibrinogen is involved in the clotting of blood. Its role in this process will be discussed later in this chapter. The globulins have several different functions. Some globulins are involved in the transport of proteins and other substances from one part of the body to another. Other globulins, called antibodies (AN tee bod eez), help to fight infection. **Antibodies** are proteins that bind to, and thus help to destroy, foreign substances in the body. These substances include disease-causing organisms.

Red Blood Cells Cells that are red in color and carry oxygen and carbon dioxide are called **red blood cells,** or *erythrocytes* (eh RITH ruh syts). They are present in enormous numbers in the blood. The human body contains 30 trillion red blood cells, or about 5 million

Figure 10–2

Plasma. When whole blood is centrifuged, the red blood cells, white blood cells, and platelets collect at the bottom of the test tube, leaving the clear, straw-colored plasma at the top. ▼

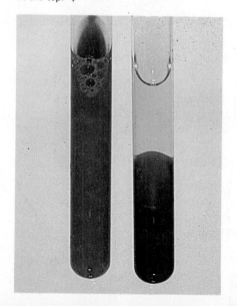

cells per cubic millimeter of blood. Red blood cells transport oxygen from the lungs to the body tissues. They also carry carbon dioxide from the body tissues to the lungs. Red blood cells are disk-shaped but are thinner in the center than around the rim. See Figure 10–3. In humans, mature red blood cells contain no nuclei. Their cytoplasm is filled with an iron-containing protein known as hemoglobin. **Hemoglobin** is the substance that gives blood its red color. In Chapter 11, you will learn how hemoglobin functions in the transport of oxygen and carbon dioxide.

Human red blood cells are made by bone marrow and have an average life span of 120 days. New red blood cells are formed at the same rate that old red cells are destroyed—about 2 million every second. Worn-out red cells are removed from the blood by the liver and spleen and then broken down. The iron from hemoglobin is held by the body and reused.

A condition in which a person has too few red blood cells or an insufficient amount of hemoglobin is called **anemia** (uh NEE mee uh). Either of these conditions lowers the amount of oxygen that can be carried in the blood. Anemia, therefore, results in the cells of the body not receiving enough oxygen. Some forms of anemia can be treated by eating iron-rich foods or by injections of vitamin B12. Sickle-cell anemia, a hereditary disorder, is caused by an abnormal form of hemoglobin rather than a vitamin deficiency.

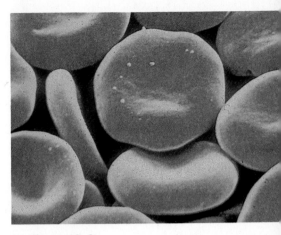

▲ **Figure 10–3**
Red Blood Cells. Red blood cells affect the survival of all the cells in the body because the red blood cells transport oxygen.

White Blood Cells   A variety of colorless blood cells make up the **white blood cells,** or *leukocytes* (LOO kuh syts). White blood cells are the defenders of the body. They protect the body from disease-causing organisms, such as bacteria and viruses. Mature white cells have a nucleus and are larger than red cells. They are less numerous than red blood cells, but their numbers are still impressive—about 60 billion in the adult human body. Bone marrow and lymphatic tissue produce about 1 million white blood cells every second. White blood cells are carried throughout the body in the circulatory system. Moreover, they can move on their own in the same way that ameba move. Using ameboid movement, they can squeeze between the cells of capillary walls and move through the body tissues. When there is an infection in the body, white blood cells collect in the infected area and attack the invading organisms.

As you can see in Figure 10–4, there are five different kinds of white blood cells. Most function in some way to protect the body. Some white cells—*neutrophils* and *monocytes*—are phagocytic. They protect the body by engulfing bacterial invaders, foreign substances, and cancer cells. **Lymphocytes** (LIM fuh syts) are responsible for the production of antibodies and cells that destroy foreign cells and substances.

Normally, there are 7000 to 10 000 white blood cells per cubic millimeter of blood. When there is an infection in the blood, however, the number may increase to 30 000 or more per cubic millimeter. As shown in Figure 10–5, the phagocytic white blood

Figure 10–4

White Blood Cells and Platelets. Note how the five types of white blood cells and the platelets differ in shape, size, and function. ▶

White Blood Cells and Platelets		
Type	**Function**	**Appearance**
neutrophils	phagocytosis of small particles	
monocytes	phagocytosis of large particles	
eosinophils	release clot-digesting enzyme; combat allergy-causing substances	
basophils	release heparin, an anticoagulant, and histamine, a substance causing inflammation	
lymphocytes	involved in immune response	
platelets	involved in blood clotting	

Figure 10–5

A Phagocytic White Blood Cell. At the center of this micrograph is a white blood cell ingesting a chain of bacteria. ▼

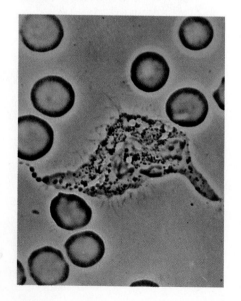

cells eat bacteria. The pus that forms at the site of an infected wound consists, in part, of white cells that have died after eating bacteria.

Cancer of the cells that produce white blood cells is called *leukemia*. Persons with leukemia have abnormally high levels of some types of white blood cells. Fortunately, some forms of leukemia can be controlled by drugs.

Platelets Cell fragments that are involved in blood clotting are called **platelets** (PLAYT lets). Platelets are formed by the pinching off of bits of cytoplasm from large cells within the bone marrow. Although these bits of cytoplasm contain no nuclei, they are surrounded by a membrane. About 300 000 platelets are present in a cubic millimeter of blood. That is a total of about 1.5 trillion platelets in the blood of an adult human. They live for about seven days and are produced at a rate of 200 billion a day.

Blood Clotting

Although cuts and scrapes are common occurrences, bleeding from these injuries seldom becomes life-threatening. The torn blood vessels are quickly patched. The solid mass that plugs the hole in the torn vessel is called a blood clot. This solidification of blood at the site of an injured blood vessel is called **clotting.**

The Clotting Process   When a blood vessel is injured, the platelets in the blood stick to the wall of the damaged vessel and rupture. If the vessel damage is minor, the material from the ruptured platelets seals the leak. If the break is more serious, then the clotting process is triggered. More than 30 different substances are known to be involved in clotting. The major steps in this process are summarized here and in Figure 10–6.

▪ The ruptured platelets and the wall of the injured blood vessel release an enzyme, *thromboplastin* (throm boh PLAS tin).

▪ Thromboplastin initiates a series of enzyme-controlled reactions. The result of these reactions is the conversion of *prothrombin* (proh THROM bin), a plasma protein, into *thrombin*.

▪ Thrombin, an enzyme, converts soluble plasma fibrinogen into insoluble strands of *fibrin*.

▪ Fibrin forms a network of strands that traps red blood cells and platelets to form a clot.

The clot stops the bleeding, contracts, and hardens. In time, the wound is repaired by the growth of cells that replace the cells damaged by the injury. When healing is completed, a plasma enzyme called *plasmin* is activated and dissolves the fibrin clot.

Two factors prevent clots from forming inside uninjured blood vessels. First, the smoothness of the inner wall of the vessels prevents platelets from becoming activated. Second, substances in the blood act as *anticoagulants* (an tee koh AG yuh lunts) and prevent clot formation. One of these anticoagulants, *heparin,* is used as a drug after surgery to prevent clotting.

Figure 10–6
The Process of Blood Clotting. An injured blood vessel triggers a complex chain of reactions known as the clotting process. ▼

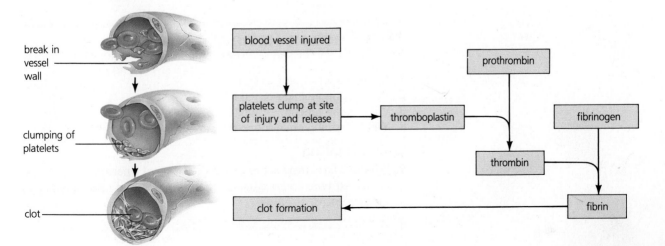

Figure 10-7

Use of Anticoagulants. The patient shown here is receiving an intravenous injection of heparin to prevent postsurgical clotting. ▶

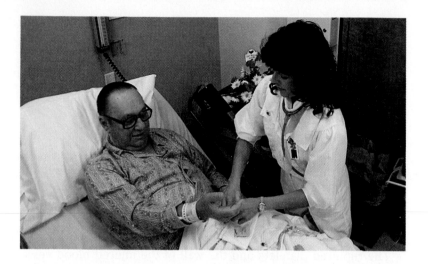

Clotting Problems   Various conditions can cause the clotting system to malfunction. Not enough platelets in the blood or lack of vitamin K in a diet reduces the ability of blood to clot. Vitamin K is needed for the synthesis of prothrombin. Persons with **hemophilia** (hee muh FIL ee uh), a hereditary disease, lack one of the clotting factors. Now, they can receive injections of the missing factor, which is obtained from genetically engineered bacteria.

Not all clotting problems involve a failure to clot. Sometimes, a clot forms within a blood vessel when there is no injury. Clots can even form in one part of the circulatory system and travel through the body. If a clot cuts off or reduces the flow of blood to a whole organ, the effects can be disastrous. A blocked coronary artery, for example, can cause a heart attack. A block in an artery to the brain can cause a stroke. An obstructed artery in the lung can drastically reduce the oxygen supply of the body. Recently, scientists have produced bacteria that can manufacture large amounts of clot-digesting enzyme. If the enzyme is injected within a few hours of a heart attack, it can prevent, or limit, damage to the heart or other vital organs.

10-1 Section Review

1. Name the liquid part of blood.
2. What is the function of red blood cells?
3. What is the function of white blood cells?
4. What plasma protein forms the strands in a blood clot?

Critical Thinking

5. What would you expect to be the condition of a person whose blood contained twice the normal levels of white blood cells? (*Predicting Consequences*)

10-2 The Immune System

Section Objectives:

- *Explain* the three lines of defense existing against disease-causing organisms.
- *Describe* what occurs during an immune response.
- *Compare* a primary immune response to a secondary immune response.
- *Explain* the ABO and Rh blood groups.

The immune system carries out a major part of the protective function of blood. Cells of the immune system are on constant patrol, ready to attack foreign invaders that get past other body defenses. While the immune system is not the only infection-fighting system in the body, it is the most complex.

Defenses Against Infection

Viruses, bacteria, and other microorganisms that cause disease are called **pathogens** (PATH uh jenz). These microorganisms are present everywhere in the environment. In fact, you are exposed to various pathogens every day in the food you eat, the water you drink, and the air you breathe. Fortunately, your body has several effective defenses against pathogens. These defenses are what keep you healthy most of the time.

First-Line Defenses   The body's first line of defense against pathogens involves several kinds of physical and chemical barriers. These include skin, sweat, tears, saliva, membranes lining body passages, mucus, stomach acid, and urine. Unbroken skin and the membranes lining body passages are effective barriers to most pathogens. Sweat, tears, and saliva contain chemicals that kill or inhibit some bacteria. Mucus that covers internal membranes entraps pathogens that are then washed away or destroyed by chemicals. Stomach acid destroys many pathogens that may be present in food.

Second-Line Defenses   If a pathogen gets past the first line of defense and starts an infection, parts of the second line of defense become activated. This results in the **inflammatory response,** a reaction of the body that causes swelling, redness, warmth, and pain in the area of an infection. Cells that are damaged from the infection release certain chemicals. These chemicals increase the flow of blood to the area. The increased blood flow causes puffiness and warmth and attracts phagocytes—neutrophils and macrophages. **Macrophages** (MAC ruh fay jez) are giant white blood cells that can ingest large numbers of bacteria. They develop from monocytes.

As the inflammatory response proceeds, the phagocytes ingest the pathogen and any damaged tissue. Eventually pus, a mixture of phagocytes, dead cells, bacteria, and body fluid, collects in the wound. The pus either drains or is absorbed by the body. Most of the time, the pathogen is destroyed, the inflammation dies down, and the wound heals.

When the pathogen is a virus, the infected cells produce a protein called **interferon** (in tuh FIR ahn). This substance causes nearby uninfected cells to produce enzymes that block the reproduction of the virus. In this way, healthy cells are protected from attack by the virus. As you will read in Chapter 27, through genetic engineering, scientists have produced bacteria that can make large amounts of interferon.

Third-Line Defenses   When the inflammatory response defense is insufficient, the pathogen is targeted for destruction by the body's last line of defense—the immune system. The immune system recognizes, attacks, destroys, and "remembers" each kind of pathogen or foreign substance that enters the body. It does this by producing antibodies and specialized cells that bind to and inactivate pathogens. Unlike the first two lines of defense, the immune system discriminates between different kinds of pathogens. For each kind of pathogen, the immune system produces antibodies or cells that are specific to that pathogen.

The Immune Response

The immune system includes all the parts of the body that are involved in the recognition and destruction of foreign materials. Bone marrow, white blood cells, especially phagocytes and lymphocytes, and various tissues of the lymphatic system, such as the lymph nodes, tonsils, thymus, and spleen, make up the immune system. The immune system provides **immunity** (ih MYOO nuh tee), the ability of the body to fight infection through the production of antibodies or cells that inactivate foreign substances or cells.

The basis of immunity lies in the body's ability to distinguish between its own substances or "itself," and foreign substances, or "nonself." This recognition is based on differences in certain large molecules, such as proteins, between one organism and another. When the body recognizes foreign cells or molecules, it produces antibodies or special cells that bind to the foreign substance and inactivate it. The production of antibodies and specialized cells that bind to and inactivate foreign substances is called the **immune response.**

Antigens   Any substance that can cause an immune response is called an **antigen** (ANT uh jin). Viruses and microorganisms have substances on their outer surfaces that are antigens. Most antigens are proteins, but carbohydrates and nucleic acids also may be antigens. The cells of each human contain a unique combination of proteins that no other human has. As a result, tissue from one person transplanted into another will act as an antigen. An immune response to an antigen acts to destroy the antigen.

Lymphocytes

Lymphocytes are the cells of the immune system that recognize specific antigens and either produce antibodies or kill foreign cells directly. There are two types of lymphocytes: B lymphocytes, or **B cells,** and T lymphocytes, or **T cells.** See Figure 10–8. B cells and T cells are produced in the bone marrow. B cells remain in the marrow and mature there, while T cells mature in the thymus gland. Millions of B and T cells are produced. At maturity, these cells are released and move into the circulatory and lymphatic systems.

B and T cells are capable of recognizing different antigens. In fact, B and T cells develop this ability while they are maturing— before they are ever exposed to any of the millions of antigens in the environment. As a result, each of the millions of individual B and T cells in a person will respond to a different antigen from among the millions of possible antigens.

When an antigen enters your body for the first time, your immune system undergoes a **primary immune response.** During the first 5 days following exposure to the antigen, no measurable amounts of antibodies or specialized immune cells are present. Then, over the next 10 to 15 days, there is a gradual rise in the levels of these products. If the same antigen enters the body another time, a more rapid **secondary immune response** happens. Within 1 to 2 days after infection, high levels of antibodies or specialized immune cells are present in the blood.

Whether primary or secondary, an immune response can involve two categories of reactions. One involves specialized B cells that produce antibodies. The other involves specialized T cells that attack foreign cells directly. The activation of both B and T cells, however, depends on the activities of regular phagocytic white blood cells as they engulf all foreign materials.

B Cells and Antibodies
When a B cell comes in contact with the antigen that it recognizes for the first time, it does not immediately produce antibodies. Instead, the B cell must be stimulated by a helper T cell that recognizes the same antigen. The helper T cell recognizes the antigen only after the antigen has been ingested by a macrophage and has been "displayed" on the macrophage's cell membrane. Following this stimulation, the B cell undergoes cell division, producing plasma cells and memory B cells. Plasma cells make antibody molecules that are released into the blood or lymph and bind to the antigen. The binding of antibodies to an antigen attracts other phagocytes that engulf and then destroy the antigen-antibody complex. When the antigen is a bacterium, an additional system, which is known as the complement system, helps to

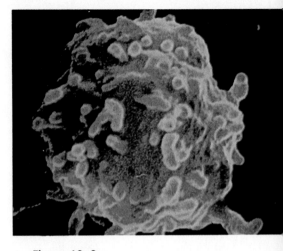

▲ **Figure 10–8**

Lymphocytes. B cells and T cells have specific surface receptors that recognize specific antigens.

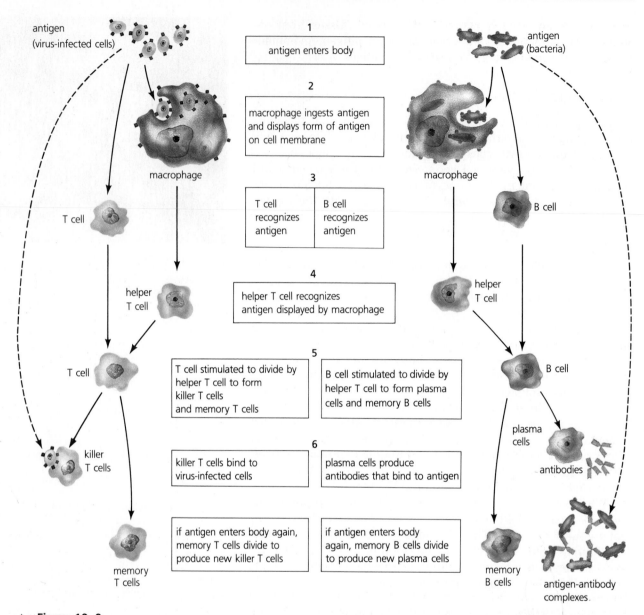

▲ **Figure 10–9**

The Immune Response. Trace the sequence of actions and interactions involved in the immune response.

destroy the bacteria. The **complement system** is a series of enzymes in blood that catalyze reactions that result in the bursting of the bacterial cell.

As the antibodies and phagocytes overcome the infection, other T cells, called suppressor T cells, release substances that slow down and eventually stop the plasma cells from producing antibodies. Thus, the immune response is kept under control. See Figure 10–9.

While plasma cells live for only a few days, the memory cells produced by the stimulated B cell can live for a lifetime. These cells produce a secondary immune response if the same antigen enters the body again. If this happens, the memory cells divide rapidly, forming new plasma cells that produce large quantities of antibodies, which act to destroy the invader. This rapid secondary response explains why the same disease usually does not strike the same person twice.

T Cells and Immunity   When an antigen is a virus-infected cell or a tumor cell, a single T cell, rather than a B cell, recognizes the antigen on the cell surface. In addition, a helper T cell recognizes the antigen when it is displayed by a macrophage and stimulates the T cell into dividing. Cell division in the T cell results in memory T cells and killer T cells, which are also called cytotoxic T cells. Receptors on the surface of the killer T cells are like antibodies and cause the cell to bind to the antigens on the infected cell. Eventually, through enzyme-controlled reactions, the killer T cell causes the infected cell to burst.

As the foreign cells are brought under control, suppressor T cells release substances that shut down the killer T cells. The memory T cells, like the memory B cells, will cause a secondary response if the same antigen appears again.

Types of Immunity

There are two types of immunity: active and passive. In **active immunity,** the body produces its own antibodies or killer T cells to attack a particular antigen. In **passive immunity,** a person is given antibodies obtained from the blood of either another person or an animal. Passive immunity is "borrowed" immunity.

Active immunity may develop as the result of having had a disease. For example, a person who has had chicken pox rarely gets the disease a second time. Memory cells remaining in the body tissues quickly produce antibodies or killer T cells if the chicken pox virus invades the body again.

Thanks to the British physician Edward Jenner, the father of vaccination, active immunity may also develop through the use of a vaccine. See Figure 10–10. A vaccine consists of dead or weakened bacteria or viruses, or modified bacterial poisons. In each case, the organism or poison can still act as an antigen, but because it is weakened or modified, it can no longer cause disease. When the vaccine is injected into the body, the immune system responds to it as it would to the pathogen and produces antibodies or killer T cells. In this way, a person develops an immunity to a disease without actually suffering through it.

In contrast, passive immunity is only temporary. It usually does not last for more than a month because the body destroys the borrowed antibodies. Although it is short-lived, it is fast-acting. One type of passive immunity, called maternal immunity, occurs in infants. Antibodies from the mother enter the baby's blood before birth and provide the infant with passive immunity. Antibodies are also present in the mother's milk. Maternal immunity protects a child against most infectious diseases for the first few months of the child's life.

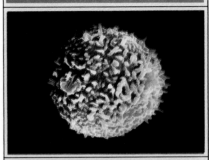

Figure 10–10
The Father of Vaccination. Edward Jenner (1749–1823) developed a vaccine for smallpox. ▶

Blood Groups and Transplants

Antibodies do more than fight infections. On the surface of every human cell are antigens that cause an immune response when recognized as foreign. In this section, you will see how the immune system is involved in blood types, transfusions, and transplants.

ABO Blood Group In the early 1900s, Dr. Karl Landsteiner discovered that there are four major human blood types, or groups. These types, named A, B, AB, and O, make up the **ABO blood group.** A person's blood type depends on the presence or absence of two antigens, called A and B, on the surface of red blood cells. Figure 10–11 shows that individuals with type A blood have A antigens on their red cells. Individuals with B blood have B

Figure 10–11
Major Blood Groups. Human blood types depend on the presence of particular antigens on the surface of red blood cells. ▶

ABO Blood Groups		
Blood Type	**Antigens (on red cells)**	**Antibodies (in plasma)**
A	A	anti-b
B	B	anti-a
AB	A, B	none
O	none	anti-a, anti-b

Math, Science, and Technology

New Ways to Treat AIDS

Problem

The first drugs that were used to treat AIDS were AZT (azidothymidine) and DDI (didanosine). There is now a new class of potent antiviral drugs called protease inhibitors that inhibit viral replication. Unfortunately, all these drugs have side effects and do not cure AIDS.

Task

You are a medical doctor and have been asked by the Federal Centers for Disease Control and Prevention in Atlanta, Georgia, to analyze some data and make a presentation on the advances that have been made in treatment of AIDS.

In order to complete this task, you must provide answers to the following questions:

1. What drugs should be used to treat an HIV infection? How effective are they?
2. What types of technology do drug companies use in the development of these drugs?
3. Why do these drugs eventually become ineffective?
4. Why is it necessary to be retested for AIDS even though one test proved to be negative?
5. Why is it hard to develop a vaccine for AIDS?

Solution

Based on your research and the data provided, prepare your presentation. Include information found in library resource materials, from drug companies, and on the Internet.

Year	Untreated		AZT Treated		Treated With Protease Inhibitor		Treated With AZT and Protease Inhibitor	
	HIV/ mm³ blood	CD4 count/ mm³	HIV/ mm³ blood	CD4 count/ mm³	HIV/ mm³ blood	CD4 count/ mm³	HIV/ mm³ blood	CD4 count/ mm³
0	0	1000	0	1000	0	1000	0	1000
1	1000	500	2000	700	3000	400	1000	500
2	10 000	300	100	400	0	1000	0	1000
3	1000	350	100	400	0	1000	0	1000
4	1000	350	100	400	0	1000	0	1000
5	1000	300	100	400	0	1000	0	1000
6	20 000	200	100	400	0	1000	0	1000
7	100 000	175	10 000	350	*0*	*1000*	*0*	*1000*
8	500 000	150	100 000	250	*0*	*1000*	*0*	*1000*
9	1 000 000	100	300 000	200	*0*	*1000*	*0*	*1000*
10	5 000 000	20	1 000 000	150	*1000*	*500*	*0*	*1000*
11			2 000 000	100	*10 000*	*300*	*0*	*1000*
12			6 000 000	30	*100 000*	*200*	*0*	*1000*
13					*800 000*	*150*	*0*	*1000*
14					*1 000 000*	*100*	*0*	*1000*
15					*5 000 000*	*20*	*?*	*?*

*Represents patients who are treated as soon as HIV is detected. Numbers in italics are computer projections because complete data for new drugs are not available. CD4 counts (helper T cells/mm³) follow the disease's progression. Counts between 1000 and 500 are normal, no symptoms; counts between 500 and 200, indicate the individual's immune system is compromised; counts less than 200, the individual has AIDS. HIV in blood or viral load (viruses/mm³) are also used to follow the disease's progression. Less than 10 000, the patient's status is stable; between 10 000 and 1 000 000 there is a risk of other infections; and above 1 000 000 the patient has AIDS.

antigens on their red cells, and people with type AB blood have A and B antigens on their red cells. People with type O blood have neither A nor B antigens on their red cells.

The ABO system has an odd feature. An individual is born with antibodies against red blood cell antigens that his or her blood does not have. In other words, the plasma of a person contains antibodies that will bind to "foreign" red blood cells. Thus, as shown in Figure 10–11, type A blood contains anti-b antibodies. Type B blood contains anti-a antibodies. Type AB blood does not have either of these antibodies. Type O blood has both anti-a and anti-b antibodies. This kind of information is necessary to give safe blood transfusions.

Rh Factors   The **Rh factors** are another group of antigens found on the surface of red blood cells. They are called Rh factors because they were first found in rhesus monkeys. About 85 percent of the human population have the Rh factors on their red cells and are said to be Rh positive, or Rh+. The remaining 15 percent lack the Rh antigens and are said to be Rh negative, or Rh−. Unlike the ABO system, antibodies to the Rh factors are not produced until the individual is exposed to Rh factors.

The Rh factors may present a problem during pregnancy when the mother is Rh− but the baby has inherited Rh+ factors from its father. During birth, there may be some leak between the circulatory systems of the baby and the mother. Some of the baby's Rh+ red cells enter the mother's blood. Her immune system detects the Rh antigens as foreign and begins to form anti-Rh antibodies. In later pregnancies, anti-Rh antibodies from the mother's blood can enter the new baby's blood. If the baby is Rh+, the anti-Rh antibodies destroy the baby's red blood cells. The Rh problem in pregnancies can be eliminated if the Rh− mother is given an injection of anti-Rh antibodies, called RhoGAM™, during her pregnancy, and again after the birth of each Rh+ child. These antibodies

Figure 10–12

Rh Factors. In order to avoid problems associated with Rh incompatibility, pregnant women provide their physicians with a complete medical history, including blood type. ▶

destroy any Rh antigens on the baby's blood cells that have entered the mother's circulatory system. In this way, the mother's immune system does not produce anti-Rh antibodies, and there is no problem with the next Rh+ baby.

Transfusions   For a blood transfusion to be safe, the person receiving blood, the recipient, must *not* have antibodies that will react with any A, B, or Rh antigens in the donor's blood. Knowing this, it is a simple matter to determine ABO and Rh blood types and match the blood types of the recipient and donor before a transfusion.

Figure 10–13 shows which blood types a recipient can safely receive. People with the same type of blood can donate blood to each other. People who have type O blood are called **universal donors.** Their blood can be given to anyone because type O blood does not contain A or B antigens. A person with type AB blood can receive a transfusion of any type of blood because type AB blood does not have anti-a or anti-b antibodies. People with AB blood are called **universal recipients.** In a transfusion, if the wrong blood groups are mixed, the red blood cells of the donor may clump together and break open because of the antigen-antibody reactions. This antigen-antibody reaction clogs the blood vessels and can cause kidney failure.

In matching blood types for transfusions, the Rh factor also must be determined. An Rh+ individual can receive both Rh+ and Rh− blood, whereas an Rh− individual can receive only Rh− blood. Although there are no ill effects the first time an Rh− person receives Rh+ blood, such a transfusion stimulates the formation of anti-Rh antibodies. If a second transfusion of Rh+ blood is given, an antigen-antibody reaction will cause the donated red blood cells to clump.

In emergency situations, plasma, instead of whole blood, is used for transfusions. The plasma restores blood volume and maintains blood pressure. When plasma is used, since no red blood cells are present, the donor and recipient need not be matched and no blood typing is necessary.

You might wonder why only the antigens and not the antibodies in the donor's blood are considered when matching blood types for transfusions. For example, when type A blood is given to a person with type AB blood, why don't the anti-b antibodies in the donor's blood bind to and clump the recipient's red blood cells? The reason is that the anti-b antibodies are greatly diluted in the much greater volume of the recipient's blood. At such low concentrations, there are too few antibodies to cause clumping.

Transplants   When an organ or tissue, such as a heart, kidney, or skin, is transplanted from one person (the donor) to another (the recipient), the transplant is recognized by the recipient's immune system as foreign. This activates the immune response, and the transplant is destroyed in a process called rejection. The rejection

Matching ABO Blood Types for Transfusions	
Recipient	**Donor**
A	A, O
B	B, O
AB	A, B, O
O	O

▲ **Figure 10–13**

Matching Blood Types for Transfusions. When transfusions are given, the blood types of recipient and donor must be matched for ABO antigens to prevent clumping of red blood cells.

response to a transplant can be lessened if the donor and recipient are closely related. Rejection also may be controlled by suppressing the immune system with drugs, such as cyclosporine, an antibiotic. Unfortunately, when immunity is suppressed, the individual is more susceptible to infection.

10-2 Section Review

1. What are the two types of lymphocytes?
2. Define the term *antigen.*
3. What happens to an antigen-antibody complex?
4. What antibodies are in the plasma of a person with type B blood?

Critical Thinking

5. Compare and contrast the primary and secondary immune responses. (*Comparing and Contrasting*)

10-3 AIDS and Immune System Disorders

Section Objectives:

- *Describe* how AIDS affects the immune system.
- *Explain* how the spread of AIDS can be prevented.
- *Describe* some immune system disorders.

A healthy immune system is central to the health of the whole body. As you would expect, serious conditions result when parts or all of the immune system do not work correctly. The causes of many immune system disorders are not known. One immune system disease—AIDS—has been studied only since the 1980s. Its spread, and the efforts to cure and control it, make one of the most dramatic episodes in modern public health history.

What Is AIDS?

The disease **AIDS—Acquired Immune Deficiency Syndrome**—affects the immune system. *Acquired* means people pick up the disease from other people. *Immune deficiency* means a breakdown of the body's immune system. *Syndrome* means a group of symptoms that indicate disease.

The cause of AIDS is a virus called the **human immunodeficiency virus,** or **HIV.** HIV attacks the helper T cells of the immune system. How viruses reproduce and cause infection will be discussed in Chapter 30.

When HIV enters the body, the immune system recognizes it as an antigen and responds to it as it would to any antigen. However, for reasons that are not understood, the body's defenses are

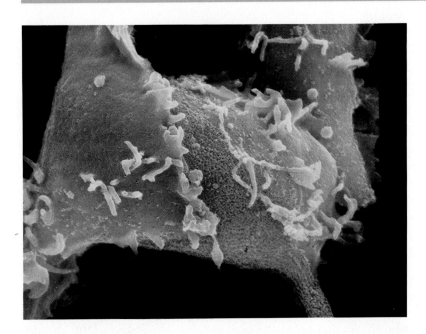

◀   **Figure 10–14**
HIV Attacking a T Cell. HIV, shown
here as small blue particles, invades helper
T cells, destroying them and weakening the
immune system.

unsuccessful. HIV infects the helper T cells and remains within these cells for months or even years without producing any symptoms. When HIV suddenly becomes active, it reproduces, spreads, and destroys the helper T cells. See Figure 10–14. The decrease in helper T cells weakens the immune system. The body cannot fight infections, and the person is diagnosed with AIDS.

The first symptoms of HIV infection are similar to those of a cold. Swollen lymph glands, fever, weakness, and unexplained weight loss are common. Usually, the HIV-infected person goes on to develop other infections, called opportunistic infections, that the weakened immune system cannot overcome. One of these infections is a type of pneumonia caused by the microorganism *Pneumocystis carinii* (noo moh SIS tis kar RIN ee ee). Another is a blood vessel cancer called Kaposi's sarcoma (KAH poh sheez sar KOH muh). These two diseases are the most common causes of death in people with AIDS.

HIV also attacks the nervous system, including the brain. This attack may show up as memory loss, loss of coordination, partial paralysis, or mental disorder.

How Is AIDS Spread?

AIDS is primarily a sexually transmitted disease. This means that HIV is passed from an infected person to an uninfected person during intimate sexual contact that involves the exchange of body fluids, namely semen and vaginal secretions. AIDS also can be transmitted by blood-to-blood contact. In the United States, this mode of transmission occurs most frequently among intravenous drug users who sometimes share needles and syringes. Prior to 1985, some people became infected with HIV when they received HIV-contaminated blood in a transfusion. However, donated blood

Biology and You

Q: What are some of the misunderstandings concerning the transmission of AIDS?

A: There are many misunderstandings concerning the transmission of AIDS and HIV. For example, some people are afraid that they can get AIDS by casual contact with an infected person. This fear is unfounded. You cannot get AIDS from being sneezed on, coughed on, or cried on by an infected person. In addition, you cannot get AIDS from touching or hugging someone who is infected with HIV.

Another misunderstanding is that you can become infected with HIV while donating blood. In fact, there is no risk of infection because hospitals and blood collection centers use sterile equipment, as well as disposable needles.

Remember—the only way HIV is transmitted is through direct contact with an infected person's body fluids. Therefore, by avoiding sexual contact with another person and avoiding intravenous drug use, you can eliminate your risk of HIV infection.

■ *Find two current newspaper articles about AIDS. Prepare a brief oral report in the form of a television news story and present it to the class.*

in the United States now is tested for the presence of HIV. Finally, HIV can be transmitted from an infected pregnant woman to her unborn child before birth.

Prevention and Treatment of AIDS

It is estimated that about 1 million people in the United States are infected with HIV. All of these individuals are capable of spreading the virus. However, the spread of AIDS is preventable. Preventing it is a matter of avoiding those behaviors that put an individual at risk. Because AIDS is sexually transmitted, the only no-risk behavior is sexual abstinence—avoiding intimate sexual contact with another person. According to the United States Surgeon General, the next safest course of action is the use of latex condoms. Condoms will reduce, but unfortunately not eliminate, the risk of infection. Of course, avoiding intravenous drug use prevents transmission of AIDS by blood-to-blood contact.

There is a blood test that detects antibodies to HIV. The test tells whether a person has been exposed to the virus. Anyone who thinks that he or she may have been exposed to HIV should be tested. Although there is a home test for HIV, the most accurate and reliable testing is done at hospitals and clinics.

Currently, there is no cure for AIDS. However, progress has been made in developing some promising drugs that will treat the disease and prolong the life of people infected with HIV.

Immune Disorders

Because the immune system is so complex, it is not surprising that it sometimes fails. A number of common and not-so-common human ailments are the result of immune system disorders.

Allergies A rapid overreaction to an antigen that is not normally harmful is known as an **allergy** (AL ur gee). The wind-carried pollen of some plants causes a common allergy known as hay fever. Dust mites, insect stings, certain foods, and animal "hair" are a few other examples of allergy-causing antigens, or *allergens.* The typical symptoms of an allergy include a runny nose, swollen eyes, sneezing, coughing, and a rash. These symptoms are caused by the release of the substance *histamine* from the body cells at the site of the immune reaction. Histamine induces an inflammatory response, as it does whenever there is an injury or infection. Antihistamines are drugs that are commonly used to counteract the effects of histamine.

Autoimmune Diseases In an **autoimmune disease,** the immune system of an individual fails to recognize some of the person's body cells as "self" and, therefore, produces antibodies against them. In juvenile diabetes, antibodies destroy the insulin-producing cells in the pancreas. When a person has rheumatoid arthritis, an immune reaction causes inflammation and crippling of the joints of the body. In multiple sclerosis, antibodies attack the

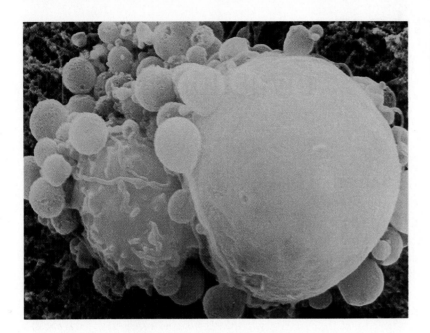

Killer T Cell Attacking a Tumor Cell. The smooth-surfaced tumor cell (on the right) is being attacked by a killer T cell (on the left).

fatty covering of nerve cells. A person with *lupus erythematosus* (uh rith ma TOH sis) forms antibodies to different parts of the body, such as kidneys. Some viral or bacterial infections may trigger autoimmune diseases. For example, rheumatic fever is caused by a bacterium that triggers an immune response against heart and joint tissues.

Cancer is a variety of diseases in which cells of the body multiply without control. Cancer cells probably form in the body continuously. Fortunately, the immune system recognizes abnormal proteins on the surface of cancer cells as antigens. In healthy people, some T cells search the body and destroy the cancer cells. See Figure 10–15. Sometimes, the immune response does not recognize cancer cells as "nonself." Ignored by the immune system, the cancer grows and spreads. That is why the suppression of the immune system, whether by drugs or a pathogen, such as HIV, often results in cancer.

10-3 Section Review

1. What is the pathogen that causes AIDS?
2. How can a person infected with AIDS not show any symptoms of the disease?
3. Name three ways AIDS can be transmitted.
4. What is histamine?

Critical Thinking

5. If a two-year-old child were found to have AIDS, what would be the most likely cause of the infection? (*Identifying Probable Causes*)

Laboratory
Investigation

The Spread of Disease

The way in which a disease spreads through a population demands the careful collection and analysis of data. When an outbreak of a serious infectious disease occurs, scientists must track down the disease and determine its origin. In this investigation, you will simulate the spread of an infectious disease and determine the original carrier of the disease.

Problem

How can you simulate the spread of disease in a community? **Construct a model** for the simulation.

Materials (per group)

- large test tube of stock solution
- clean test tube
- large pipette
- medicine dropper

Procedure

1. Select one stock solution from a numbered set of stock solutions provided by your teacher. Record the number in your data table.

2. Carefully fill the pipette with the stock solution and transfer it to the clean test tube.

3. At your teacher's signal, begin circulating among your classmates until the teacher tells you to stop. Using the medicine dropper, exchange a dropperful of your solution with the person closest to you. Make the exchange by putting a dropperful of the solution from your clean test tube into the clean test tube of the contact. You should also receive a dropperful of the solution from your contact's test tube. Record the name of that person as Contact 1 in a data table similar to Data Table 1.

4. Repeat step 3 and record the name of this person as Contact 2.

5. Repeat step 3 and record the name of this person as Contact 3.

6. Your teacher will now add several drops of an indicator to your test tube to determine whether you have been infected.

7. After performing the indicator test for the presence of infection for all the students in the class, your teacher will record the names and contacts of the infected individuals. Record this information in a data table similar to Data Table 2.

Observations

1. How many individuals were infected by the end of the simulation? How many were not infected?

2. How many infected individuals were there at the end of the first round of contacts?

Analysis and Conclusions

1. Using the class data, eliminate the names of those who were not infected. From this, try to find the original source of the infection by examining the remaining sequence of contacts.

2. Were you able to identify correctly the original carrier of the disease? If not, specify what information or test is required to identify the original source.

3. Make a diagram of the transmission route.

4. Suppose you came into contact with as many people as possible during a specified period of time. What effect would this have on the outcome of this simulation?

Extensions

Research how the bacteria that causes Lyme disease and Legionnaires' disease are transmitted.

Data Table 1			
Your Stock Number	Contact 1	Contact 2	Contact 3

Data Table 2			
Infected Person	Contact 1	Contact 2	Contact 3

Chapter 10 Review

Study Outline

10-1 Blood—A Multipurpose Fluid

▶ Blood is a liquid tissue that transports nutrients and oxygen to all the cells in the body and carries away wastes. It regulates body functions and cell activities by carrying chemical messengers. It protects the body against disease-causing organisms.

▶ Plasma accounts for about 55% of the total volume of blood in the body. The remaining 45% is made up of red blood cells, white blood cells, and platelets.

▶ Red blood cells carry oxygen and carbon dioxide. White blood cells play key roles in the body's natural defense mechanisms against disease-causing bacteria and viruses. Platelets are cell fragments involved in blood clotting.

10-2 The Immune System

▶ The body has three lines of defense against infection: physical barriers, the inflammatory response, and the immune system.

▶ The immune system protects the body by destroying foreign substances that can cause disease. It includes bone marrow, white blood cells, and certain lymphoid tissues, such as the lymph nodes and the spleen.

▶ Antigens are substances that cause an immune response. Lymphocytes, which include T cells and B cells, respond to the presence of antigens either by attacking them directly or by producing antibodies that bind specifically to the antigens.

10-3 AIDS and Immune System Disorders

▶ Acquired Immune Deficiency Syndrome (AIDS) is caused by the human immunodeficiency virus (HIV), which attacks helper T cells.

▶ AIDS can be transmitted by intimate sexual contact involving the exchange of body fluids, by blood-to-blood contact, and by an infected woman to her unborn child.

▶ Allergies, autoimmune diseases, and cancer represent other functional disorders of the immune system.

Chapter Assessment

Multiple Choice

Choose the letter of the answer that best completes each statement or answers the question.

1. Cell fragments necessary in clotting are
   (a) pathogens. (b) platelets. (c) B cells. (d) T cells.

2. A disease spread primarily through sexual contact is
   (a) anemia. (b) AIDS. (c) hemophilia. (d) allergies.

3. Cells that pick up and release oxygen and carbon dioxide as they pass throughout the body are called (a) red blood cells. (b) lymphocytes. (c) white blood cells. (d) macrophages.

4. People with blood type AB are known as
   (a) antibodies. (b) universal recipients. (c) universal donors. (d) pathogens.

5. A condition in which a person has too few red blood cells or an insufficient amount of hemoglobin is called (a) AIDS. (b) hemophilia. (c) anemia. (d) HIV.

6. A substance that is made by cells when they are attacked by viruses and that protects nearby uninfected cells from the virus is (a) plasma. (b) interferon. (c) hemoglobin. (d) Rh factor.

7. Antibodies from the mother's body entering a baby's blood before birth is an example of
   (a) inflammatory response. (b) red blood cells. (c) active immunity. (d) passive immunity.

8. Type O blood may safely be given to people with which types of blood? (a) A and B only (b) O and B only (c) AB and A only (d) A, B, AB, and O

9. Cells in the blood capable of destroying bacteria are called (a) phagocytes. (b) antigens. (c) islets. (d) platelets.

10. A person who has had chicken pox rarely gets it again because of (a) inborn immunity. (b) active immunity. (c) passive immunity. (d) maternal immunity.

Content Review

Answer each of the following in complete sentences.

11. Describe the three functions of blood.

12. Describe the body's three lines of defense against disease.

13. Explain how body cells respond when they are attacked by viruses.

14. What is the basis of immunity?

15. What is ABO blood group?

16. Under what circumstances is the Rh factor a problem during pregnancy?

17. What causes the rejection of organs transplanted from one person to another?

18. Name two ways to avoid or reduce the risk of HIV infection.

19. Explain why antihistamines are used by people who have allergies.

20. Why might the suppression of the immune system result in cancer?

Graphic Organizing

For information on graphic organizers, see Appendix G at the back of this text.

21. **Concept Map** Copy the concept map onto a separate sheet of paper and fill in the missing concepts and linking words.

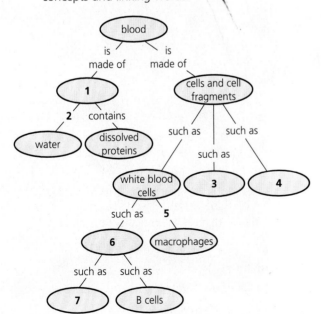

Critical Thinking and Problem Solving

Discuss each of the following in a brief paragraph.

22. **Comparing** Compare the action of phagocytes responding to a bacterial infection with the action of T lymphocytes in the presence of an antigen.

23. **Predicting** Drugs must be given to recipients of organ transplants to lessen the immune system's response to the foreign tissue. Predict how this necessity could affect the way the recipients live their lives.

24. **Drawing conclusions** Person X donated blood to a friend, person Y, who was undergoing surgery. One year later, X needed a transfusion, but the doctor would not allow Y's blood to be used. Suggest some probable reasons for the doctor's decision.

25. **Inferring** Suppose a person's immune response is operating at a below-normal level. Suggest several possible general causes for this deficiency.

26. **Drawing conclusions** Why do you think a person can come down with the common cold over and over again without developing immunity to it?

27. **Calculating** A laboratory technician carried out a differential white blood-cell count on a patient. Of the 200 white blood cells counted, 122 were neutrophils, 61 were lymphocytes, 5 were eosinophils, 1 was a basophil, and 11 were monocytes. Calculate the percentage of white blood cells of each type.

28. **Experimenting** Design an experiment to determine the distribution of the ABO blood types among the students in your school. Indicate how you would present your data.

29. **Calculating** Normally, in humans, there are about 7000 white blood cells and 5 million red blood cells per cubic millimeter of blood. What is the ratio of white cells to red cells?

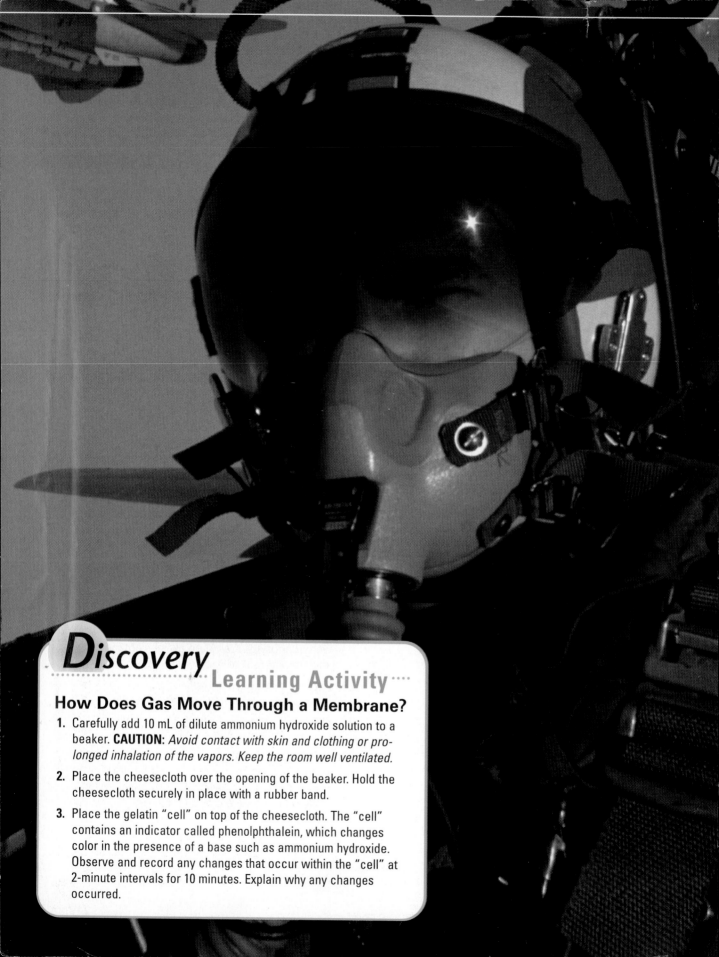

Discovery Learning Activity

How Does Gas Move Through a Membrane?

1. Carefully add 10 mL of dilute ammonium hydroxide solution to a beaker. **CAUTION:** *Avoid contact with skin and clothing or prolonged inhalation of the vapors. Keep the room well ventilated.*

2. Place the cheesecloth over the opening of the beaker. Hold the cheesecloth securely in place with a rubber band.

3. Place the gelatin "cell" on top of the cheesecloth. The "cell" contains an indicator called phenolphthalein, which changes color in the presence of a base such as ammonium hydroxide. Observe and record any changes that occur within the "cell" at 2-minute intervals for 10 minutes. Explain why any changes occurred.

Gas Exchange

Previewing the Chapter

On the surface of the earth, breathing is not usually a problem. After all, there is air all around you. At high altitudes, however, a jet pilot must carry his own air supply with him. To survive, animals must take in oxygen from the air and expel carbon dioxide from their bodies. How do different organisms accomplish this process of gas exchange? Which organs function in gas exchange in humans? Why does smoking cigarettes often lead to breathing disorders?

Key Words

alveoli, bronchi, gas exchange, gills, lungs, tracheal tubes

Key Concepts

- **Compare** methods of gas exchange in simple organisms, earthworms, grasshoppers, and fish.
- **List** the organs used by humans for gas exchange.
- **Construct a model** of the human respiratory system to study the mechanics of breathing. (Laboratory Investigation)

11-1 Adaptations for Gas Exchange

Section Objectives:

- *Describe* the physical methods of gas exchange in protists and in hydra.
- *Explain* why specialized gas exchange systems are necessary in large, multicellular animals.
- *Compare* gas exchange in earthworms, grass-hoppers, and animals with gills.

Gas Exchange and Respiration

As you may recall from previous chapters, most pro-tists and animals need to obtain oxygen from their surroundings and to remove carbon dioxide from their bodies. The oxygen is needed for *aerobic cellular respiration*. As you may remember from Chapter 6, cellular respiration is a chemical process that allows organisms to release energy from substances such as glucose. During aerobic cellular respiration, carbon dioxide is produced. Protist and animal cells must get rid of the excess carbon dioxide that has been pro-duced. **Gas exchange** refers to the physical methods that organisms have for obtaining oxygen from their surroundings and removing excess carbon dioxide.

▲ **Figure 11–1**

Gas Exchange. Like all organisms, this wood bison must exchange oxygen and carbon dioxide with the environment.

◄ Flying at high altitudes requires the aid of an oxygen mask.

Often, biologists use the term *respiration* to describe gas exchange. In this book, however, the term *gas exchange* will be used wherever possible. This will avoid confusion between the process of gas exchange and the energy-releasing process of cellular respiration.

The Respiratory Surface

When oxygen and carbon dioxide are exchanged between an organism and its environment, the gases pass through a boundary surface. The surface through which gas exchange takes place is called the **respiratory surface.** A respiratory surface must have the following characteristics.

- The surface must be thin-walled so that diffusion across it can occur rapidly.

- It must be moist because the oxygen and carbon dioxide must be in solution.

- It must be in contact with a source of oxygen that exists in the surroundings.

- In most multicellular organisms, it must be in contact with the transport system that carries dissolved materials to and from the cells of the organism.

Gas exchange through the respiratory surface takes place by diffusion. The direction of the gas exchange depends on the amounts of the gases on each side of the respiratory surface. For example, when oxygen is used up inside an organism's tissues, more oxygen diffuses into the tissues. When carbon dioxide builds up within tissues, the excess diffuses out of the tissues. The larger the area of the respiratory surface, the greater the amount of gas exchange that can occur during a given time period.

In protists and small multicellular animals, the exchange of gases takes place directly between the cells and the environment. In larger animals, however, the majority of the body cells are not near the outside environment. Therefore, gas exchange cannot take place directly between all the cells and the environment. Furthermore, larger animals often have an outer protective layer, such as scales, feathers, or dry skin, that prevents direct gas exchange through the skin. Therefore, most large, multicellular animals have respiratory surfaces in specialized organs or organ systems.

Gas Exchange in Protists

The exchange of gases with the surroundings is fairly simple in protists. It takes place directly through the body surface—the cell membrane. In the ameba and paramecium, oxygen, which is dissolved in the surrounding water, passes through the cell membrane into the cytoplasm by diffusion. See Figure 11–2. The carbon dioxide formed by cellular respiration diffuses out of the cytoplasm into the surrounding water.

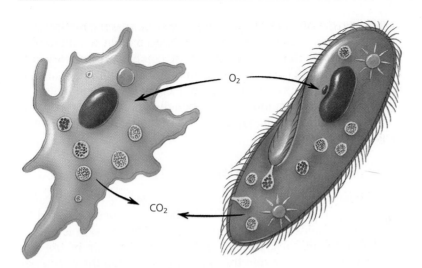

◀ **Figure 11–2**
Gas Exchange in Protists. The exchange of respiratory gases in the ameba (left) and paramecium (right) takes place directly through the cell membrane.

Gas Exchange in Hydra

Hydra are small and simple in structure. As you can see in Figure 11–3, the cells of the two layers that make up a hydra's body are in direct contact with water. Because they are, the exchange of respiratory gases can take place by direct diffusion between the body cells and the environment. There are no special structures for gas exchange.

Gas Exchange in Large, Multicellular Animals

A large, multicellular animal must exchange large amounts of gases across a respiratory surface. Animals that depend on gas dissolved in water have different exchange problems than animals that breathe air. First, the amount of oxygen dissolved in water is usually less than 1 percent. In contrast, oxygen makes up about 21 percent of the air. (The oxygen that is chemically part of the water molecules is, of course, not available for gas exchange. Only the free oxygen dissolved in the water can be used.) Second, oxygen diffuses more slowly in water than in air. Therefore, to obtain enough oxygen, an animal living underwater must constantly move a large amount of water over its respiratory surface.

Since gases must be in solution before they can diffuse across living membranes, air-breathing animals must keep their respiratory surfaces moist. Most air-breathing animals have respiratory systems that extend inside the organism. This protects the respiratory surface and lowers the amount of water lost by evaporation.

Respiratory Pigments

Many multicellular animals have colored substances in their blood. These substances, called **respiratory pigments,** carry oxygen and carbon dioxide between the respiratory surface and the body cells. Respiratory pigments allow the blood to carry more oxygen and

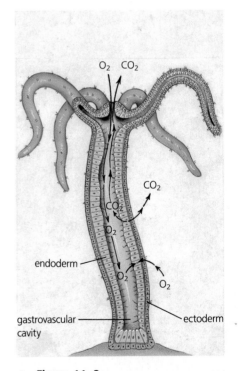

▲ **Figure 11–3**
Gas Exchange in Hydra. The exchange of respiratory gases in the hydra takes place by direct diffusion between the body cells and the environment.

▲ **Figure 11–4**

Gas Exchange in the Earthworm. The moist skin of the earthworm is its respiratory surface. Gases are exchanged with the environment through the skin and are carried to and from the body cells by the blood.

carbon dioxide than plain water can. For example, 100 milliliters of water can carry about 0.2 milliliters of oxygen and 0.3 milliliters of carbon dioxide. Hemoglobin, the most common respiratory pigment in the blood, can carry large amounts of respiratory gases. It allows 100 milliliters of human blood to carry about 20 milliliters of oxygen and 30 to 60 milliliters of carbon dioxide. (These are not the volumes of the gases when in solution but their equivalent volumes as gases in the air.)

Gas Exchange in the Earthworm

In earthworms, which live in moist soil, the skin is the respiratory surface. See Figure 11–4. The skin is thin, and mucus secreted by special cells helps to keep it moist. Just below the skin is a large number of capillaries. Oxygen diffuses from the air in the soil through the moist skin into the capillaries. Blood in the capillaries picks up the oxygen and carries it to the cells of the body. The blood contains hemoglobin, which aids in the transport of oxygen and carbon dioxide. At the body cells, the blood gives up oxygen and picks up carbon dioxide. The blood carries the carbon dioxide to the capillaries in the skin. The carbon dioxide diffuses through the skin into the air.

Damp soil keeps the earthworm's skin moist and helps its respiratory system to work well. If earthworms are exposed to air, their skin soon dries out, and they suffocate. When the weather is dry, they burrow deeper into the soil until they reach a moist area. Rain causes other problems for earthworms. Rain can flood their burrows. Because the water contains too little dissolved oxygen, earthworms have to leave their burrows to avoid drowning.

Gas Exchange in the Grasshopper

In grasshoppers, gas exchange does not depend on the circulatory system. A grasshopper's blood does not carry oxygen or carbon dioxide. Instead, a system of branching air tubes carries air directly to all the cells of the body. See Figure 11-5. These tubes are called **tracheal** (TRAY kee ul) **tubes.** Air enters and leaves the grasshop-

Figure 11–5

Gas Exchange in the Grasshopper. In the grasshopper, air enters and leaves through the spiracles. A branching system of tracheal tubes carries the air to and from the body tissues. ▶

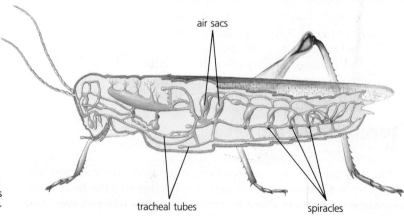

air sacs

tracheal tubes

spiracles

per's body through 10 pairs of openings called **spiracles** (SPEER uh kulz). From each spiracle, the tracheal tubes branch into smaller and smaller tubes. The fluid-filled ends of these microscopic air tubes act as a respiratory surface. They are in direct contact with the body cells. Oxygen in the air diffuses from the tracheal tubes to the body cells. Carbon dioxide diffuses from the body cells into the tracheal tubes.

Air is pumped into and out of the tracheal system by contraction of the grasshopper's muscles. When the area around the tracheal tubes expands, air flows in through the front four pairs of spiracles. Several large, collapsible, balloonlike chambers, called **air sacs,** are connected to the tubes. The air sacs help to pump air in and out of the tracheal system. When the area around the tracheal tubes contracts, the four pairs of spiracles close, and air is pumped out of the tracheal tubes through the six rear pairs of spiracles.

The system of tracheal tubes works well for gas exchange in small animals, such as grasshoppers and other insects. However, in a large animal, it would be impossible to move the needed volume of gases through this type of system.

Gas Exchange Through Gills

The gas-exchange organs of many animals that live in water, including fish, clams, oysters, and lobsters, are called **gills.** Gills are thin layers of tissue that are richly supplied with blood vessels. See Figure 11–6. Gills provide a large surface area for gas exchange. As water passes over them, dissolved oxygen diffuses from the water across the gill tissue and into the blood. The blood carries the oxygen to all parts of the body. Carbon dioxide from the blood diffuses out of the gills and into the water. There must be a constant flow of water over the gills. If the water flow is stopped, the animal will die from too little oxygen. Without water, the gills dry and stick to each other, and gas exchange cannot take place.

▲ **Figure 11–6**
Gills of a Fish. The thin filaments of a gill are richly supplied with blood vessels and provide a large surface area for the exchange of respiratory gases.

11-1 Section Review

1. Which two gases do organisms exchange with their surroundings?
2. What is a respiratory surface?
3. How does gas exchange occur in protists? How does it occur in the earthworm?
4. Name the gas-exchange organs of such water-dwellers as fish, clams, and lobsters. gills

Critical Thinking

5. Suppose that earthworms were short and thick rather than long and thin. Would their current method of gas exchange meet their needs? Why or why not? (*Predicting*)

11-2 The Human Respiratory System

Section Objectives:

- *Identify* the structures of the human respiratory system and state their functions.
- *Describe* the four phases of gas exchange in humans.
- *Explain* how body cells obtain oxygen and get rid of carbon dioxide.
- *Name* five diseases of the human respiratory system.

Structure of the Human Respiratory System

The human respiratory system is made up of the *lungs* and the system of air tubes that carry air to and from the lungs. See Figure 11–7. **Lungs** are the gas exchange organ in air-breathing vertebrates and some other animals. They are made up of many small

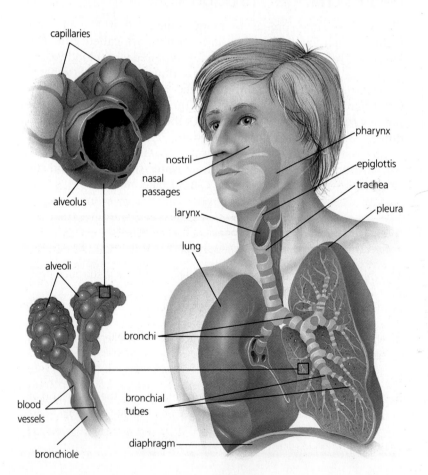

capillaries

pharynx

nostril

epiglottis

nasal passages

trachea

alveolus

pleura

larynx

lung

alveoli

bronchi

blood vessels

bronchial tubes

diaphragm

bronchiole

Figure 11–7

The Human Respiratory System. Air enters the body through the nose and travels down the trachea and bronchi to the bronchioles and alveoli in the lungs. ▶

chambers. Each chamber is surrounded by capillaries. Inside these small chambers is a huge respiratory surface for the diffusion of oxygen into the blood and the diffusion of carbon dioxide out of the blood.

The lungs fill a large part of the chest cavity in humans. They are separated from the abdominal cavity by the **diaphragm** (DY uh fram). The diaphragm is a muscle that forms the floor of the chest cavity. Each lung is completely enclosed by a two-layered membrane, which is called the **pleura** (PLUR uh). One layer of the pleura covers each lung, while the other layer is in contact with the diaphragm and the other organs of the chest cavity. A lubricating fluid between the two layers allows the lungs to move freely in the chest during breathing.

Air passes from the environment to the respiratory surface in the lungs. It goes through the nose, pharynx, larynx, trachea, bronchi, bronchial tubes, bronchioles, and alveoli. These structures are also shown in Figure 11–7.

The Nose   Air normally enters the respiratory system through the *nostrils*. These lead into hollow spaces in the nose called the **nasal passages.** Hairs at the openings of the nostrils stop various foreign particles from entering. The walls of the nasal passages and other air passageways are lined with a mucous membrane. Many of the cells that make up this membrane have cilia. Others secrete mucus, which is a sticky fluid. The mucus and the cilia trap bacteria, dust, and other particles in the air. The mucus also moistens the air. Just below the mucous membrane are a large number of capillaries. As air passes through the nose, it is warmed by the blood in these capillaries. Thus, the nasal passages serve to filter, moisten, and warm the air before it reaches the delicate lining of the lungs. When you breathe through your mouth, you lose these advantages.

Pharynx and Larynx   From the nasal passages, air travels through the **pharynx** (FAR inks), or throat. After leaving the pharynx, air passes into the **larynx** (LAR inks), or voice box. The voice box is made mainly of *cartilage,* which is a flexible connective tissue. The **vocal cords** are two pairs of membranes that are stretched across the inside of the larynx. As air is breathed out, the vocal cords vibrate. By controlling the vibrations of the vocal cords, humans are able to make sounds. To prevent choking during swallowing, food and liquids are blocked from entering the opening of the larynx by the *epiglottis* (ep ih GLOT is).

Trachea   The larynx runs directly into the **trachea** (TRAY kee uh), or windpipe. The trachea is a tube about 12 centimeters long and 2.5 centimeters wide. The trachea is kept open by horseshoe-shaped rings of cartilage embedded in its walls. Like the nasal passages, the trachea is lined with a ciliated mucous membrane. See Figure 11–8. Normally, the cilia move mucus and trapped foreign matter to the pharynx. There, they leave the air passages and are usually swallowed.

▲ **Figure 11–8**
The Lining of the Trachea. The cilia of the cells lining the trachea beat rhythmically, moving mucus and foreign particles toward the pharynx. (Magnification 10 500 X)

Science, Technology and Society

Issue: Passive Smoking

Recent research shows that non-smokers may suffer negative health effects from passive smoking, inhaling the cigarette smoke of others. Some people are calling for a "smoke-free society," in which smoking is prohibited in public places.

Many nonsmokers find it impossible to avoid inhaling other people's cigarette smoke. This passive smoking has been linked to a high rate of lung cancer, bronchitis, and pneumonia. It can also irritate the eyes, nose, and throat. Some people feel that nonsmokers have the right to a healthy environment. Thus, they say, smoking should be banned in public.

Other people claim that research linking passive smoking to cancer and other illnesses is incomplete. They feel that a ban on public smoking would make smokers a persecuted minority. They contend, for example, that smokers might be discriminated against when they apply for jobs. Smoking, they say, is a personal freedom that should be protected.

■ *Do you think smoking should be banned in public places? Why or why not?*

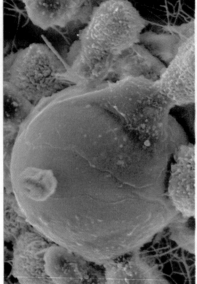

▲ **Figure 11–9**

The Consequences of Smoking. The phagocytic macrophages ingest foreign particles (left). However, when an excess of particles from smoking accumulates, the macrophages become overwhelmed and can no longer prevent damage to the lungs. Compare the nonsmoker's lung (bottom right) with the smoker's lung (top right).

As many people have discovered, the respiratory system cannot handle tobacco smoke. Smoking stops the cilia from moving. Just one cigarette stops their motion for about 20 minutes. Furthermore, tobacco smoke increases the amount of mucus in the air passages. See Figure 11–9. When smokers cough, their bodies are trying to remove the extra mucus.

Bronchi   In the middle of the chest, the trachea divides into two cartilage-ringed tubes called **bronchi** (BRAHN kee). Like the trachea, this part of the respiratory system is lined with ciliated cells. The bronchi enter the lungs and branch in a treelike fashion into smaller tubes called **bronchial** (BRAHN kee ul) **tubes.**

Bronchioles   The bronchial tubes divide and subdivide. As they do so, their walls become thinner with less and less cartilage. Finally, they become a group of tiny tubes called **bronchioles** (BRAHN kee ohlz).

Alveoli   Each bronchiole ends in a tiny air chamber that looks like a cluster of grapes. Each chamber contains several cup-shaped cavities called **alveoli** (al VEE uh ly). The walls of the alveoli, which are only one cell thick, are the respiratory surface. They are thin, moist, and surrounded by a large number of capillaries. It is through these walls that the exchange of oxygen and carbon dioxide between blood and air takes place. It has been estimated that the lungs contain about 300 million alveoli. Their total surface area would be between 80–100 square meters. This would be about 40 times the surface area of the skin.

Smoking makes it hard for oxygen to be taken through the alveoli. When cigarette smoke is inhaled, about one-third of the particles remain in the alveoli. Phagocytic cells called *macrophages* (MAK ruh fay jez) can slowly remove many of the particles. Look again at Figure 11–9. Too many particles from smoking or from other sources of air pollution damage the walls of the alveoli. This causes inelastic, scarlike tissue to form. This reduces the working area of the respiratory surface and leads to a disease called *emphysema* (em fuh ZEE muh).

Gas Exchange in Humans

Gas exchange in humans can be divided into four stages.

- Breathing is the movement of air into and out of the lungs.
- External respiration is the exchange of oxygen and carbon dioxide between the air and the blood in the lungs.
- Internal respiration is the exchange of oxygen and carbon dioxide between the blood in the capillaries and the body cells.
- Oxygen and carbon dioxide transport is the movement between the lungs and other body parts.

These stages of gas exchange are *physical* processes. They should not be confused with the chemical processes that take place within cells during cellular respiration. As you read in Chapter 6, during cellular respiration, nutrients are broken down, and energy is released.

Breathing   Breathing moves air into and out of the lungs. There are two phases of breathing. **Inhalation** (in huh LAY shun) draws air into the lungs. **Exhalation** (eks huh LAY shun) forces air out of the lungs. Since the lungs contain no muscle tissue, they cannot move by themselves. However, they are elastic. During breathing, they are forced to expand or contract as a result of pressure changes caused by the movement of the diaphragm, ribs, and rib muscles, as well as the force of air pressure.

Inhalation is the active phase of breathing. As the ribs are pulled up and out and the diaphragm is pulled downward, the chest cavity becomes larger. See Figure 11–10. As a result, the pressure within the chest cavity is reduced. Air from outside the body rushes down the air passageways into the lungs. This forces the lungs to expand.

Exhalation is the passive phase of breathing. The diaphragm relaxes and moves upward. The rib muscles relax, causing the ribs to drop. This causes the chest cavity to become smaller, and the pressure of the lungs to become greater. Thus, air is squeezed out of the lungs. Normal rates of breathing vary from about 12 to 25 times per minute.

Although people can control their breathing to some extent, it is, for the most part, an involuntary process. It is controlled by the *respiratory center* in the brain. There are also special structures in the aorta and several other larger arteries that can sense the

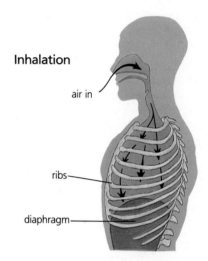

Inhalation

air in

ribs

diaphragm

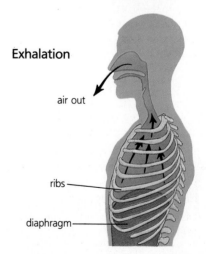

Exhalation

air out

ribs

diaphragm

▲ **Figure 11–10**

Breathing. Pressure changes caused by the movements of the diaphragm, ribs, and rib muscles force air into and out of the lungs.

Figure 11–11

External and Internal Respiration. In human body tissues, all cells exchange gases with the internal environment by diffusion across the moist cell membranes. The gases are transported to and from the lungs by the blood and the circulatory system. Exchange with the external environment occurs by diffusion across moist cell membranes in the alveoli of the lungs. ▶

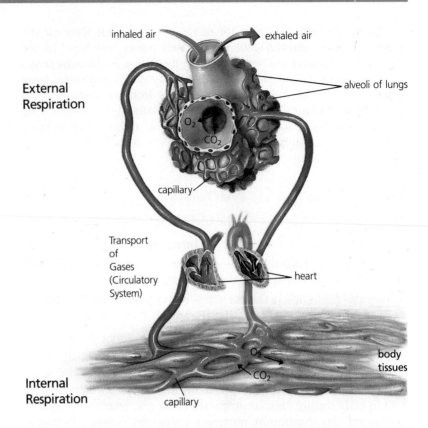

amount of oxygen and carbon dioxide in the blood. These *chemoreceptors* send messages to the respiratory center. When the amount of carbon dioxide in the blood increases, the respiratory center of the brain is stimulated. Nerves from the respiratory center carry impulses to the diaphragm and chest muscles that raise the rate and depth of breathing. This lowers the amount of carbon dioxide and raises the amount of oxygen in the blood.

During heavy exercise, lactic acid is produced by muscle cells. This increases the acidity of the blood and stimulates the respiratory center of the brain. Once the respiratory center is stimulated, the rate of breathing increases.

External and Internal Respiration   External respiration is the exchange of oxygen and carbon dioxide between the air and the blood in the lungs. See Figure 11–11. After inhalation, the amount of oxygen in the alveoli is higher than the amount of oxygen in the blood. Oxygen dissolves into the moist lining of the alveoli and diffuses from the region of higher concentration (the alveoli) to the region of lower concentration (the blood).

As the blood is pumped through the vessels of the body by the heart, oxygen-rich blood from the lungs is carried to the body tissues. Blood that is rich in carbon dioxide from the body tissues is returned to the lungs. In the lungs, then, the amount of carbon dioxide in the blood is higher than it is in the alveoli. Carbon dioxide diffuses out of the blood and into the alveoli—in the opposite direction from oxygen.

Internal respiration is the exchange of oxygen and carbon dioxide between the blood in the capillaries and the body cells. In the capillaries of the body tissues, oxygen diffuses from the blood through the intercellular fluid in the body cells. Carbon dioxide diffuses from the cells through the intercellular fluid into the blood. Each gas diffuses down a concentration gradient. That is, each gas diffuses from a region of higher concentration to a region of lower concentration.

Oxygen Transport   Most oxygen is carried from the lungs to the body tissues by the hemoglobin in the red blood cells. Little of it is dissolved in the plasma. Hemoglobin (abbreviated Hb) is a red, iron-containing protein that combines easily with oxygen. Hemoglobin holds the oxygen loosely.

The amount of oxygen in the surrounding tissues determines whether hemoglobin will combine with oxygen or will release oxygen. In the lungs, where there is a large amount of oxygen, hemoglobin combines with oxygen to form *oxyhemoglobin* (HbO_2). Oxygen-rich blood is a bright red color because of the oxyhemoglobin. When the blood reaches the capillaries of the body tissues, where the amount of oxygen in the surrounding tissues is low, the oxyhemoglobin breaks down into oxygen and hemoglobin. The

MiniLab

Skill: Measuring

A Ballooning Effect

Procedure

CAUTION: *If you have any respiratory or circulatory conditions, do not perform this activity.*

1. Take two normal breaths. On the next breath inhale as much air as you can. Then exhale into an empty round balloon. Try to empty your lungs as much as possible.

2. Hold the balloon closed while your partner uses a string to measure the circumference of the balloon at it widest part. Record the measurement.

3. Repeat steps 1 and 2.

4. Properly dispose of the balloons when you are finished.

Problem

How can you **measure** your lung capacity?

Analyze and Conclude

1. How did your measurements compare? Compare them with those of other members of your class. How did the measurements of males and females compare?

2. Do you think people who exercise regularly would have a larger lung capacity? Explain why or why not.

oxygen diffuses from the blood into the body cells. Once in the cells, the oxygen is used in aerobic respiration. The blood, now low in oxygen, is a dark red or dull purple color.

People who smoke cigarettes have a significantly lower level of oxygen in their blood. This is because cigarette smoke contains the gas *carbon monoxide*. Carbon monoxide has a greater attraction for hemoglobin than does oxygen. This means that, when carbon monoxide is present, it prevents oxygen from joining with hemoglobin. Because their blood contains too little oxygen, smokers often experience a shortness of breath when they are active.

Carbon Dioxide Transport   As you may recall from Chapter 6, cellular respiration produces carbon dioxide. Thus, the amount of carbon dioxide tends to be greater in the body cells than in the capillary blood. Therefore, the carbon dioxide diffuses out of the cells and into the blood. Carbon dioxide is carried by the blood to the lungs in three ways.

Most (about 70 percent) of the carbon dioxide that diffuses into the blood combines with water, forming carbonic acid, H_2CO_3.

$$CO_2 + H_2O \longrightarrow H_2CO_3$$

The H_2CO_3 quickly breaks down into hydrogen ions, H^+, and bicarbonate ions, HCO_3^-.

$$H_2CO_3 \longrightarrow H^+ + HCO_3^-$$

These two reactions take place quickly because of an enzyme in the red blood cells. Therefore, most of the carbon dioxide from the body cells is carried away in the plasma in the form of bicarbonate ions.

Some (about 20 percent) of the carbon dioxide that diffuses into the blood combines with hemoglobin. This carbon dioxide is carried in the red blood cells as carboxyhemoglobin, $HbCO_2$.

$$CO_2 + Hb \longrightarrow HbCO_2$$

A small amount (about 10 percent) of the carbon dioxide that diffuses into the blood is dissolved in the plasma. This carbon dioxide is carried away from the body cells to the lungs in the plasma.

All these reactions are easily reversed. In the lungs, carbon dioxide is released from the blood.

Diseases of the Respiratory System

The following list gives some of the common disorders of the respiratory system.

- *Asthma* (AZ muh) is a severe allergic reaction that causes wheezing, coughing, and breathing difficulties. During an asthma attack, the bronchioles go into spasms, squeezing the air passages.

- *Bronchitis* is a condition in which the linings of the bronchial tubes become irritated and swollen. The passageways to the alveoli may swell and clog with mucus. This often causes severe coughing

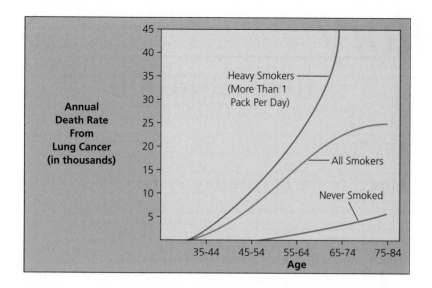

Tobacco Smoking and Lung Cancer Deaths. Lung cancer is the leading cause of cancer-related deaths in both men and women. The major cause of lung cancer in the United States is smoking tobacco.

and makes it hard to breathe. Bronchitis is more common in smokers than in nonsmokers.

- *Emphysema* is a condition in which the lungs lose their elasticity. The walls of the alveoli become damaged, making the respiratory surface smaller. Emphysema causes shortness of breath. Some people with emphysema have difficulty blowing out a match. As you already know, smoking greatly increases a person's chances of getting emphysema. The damage done to the lungs by emphysema cannot be undone. Even if an emphysema victim were to quit smoking, the condition would not improve.

- *Pneumonia* (noo MOH nyuh) is a condition in which the alveoli become filled with fluid. This prevents the exchange of gases in the lungs.

- *Lung cancer* is a disease in which tumors (masses of tissue) form in the lungs as a result of irregular and uncontrolled cell growth. Many studies have shown a relationship between lung cancer and smoking. See Figure 11–12.

11-2 **Section Review**

1. What role do the nasal passages and the diaphragm play in gas exchange?
2. What is the name of the respiratory surface in humans?
3. What are the four phases of gas exchange in humans?
4. Name three respiratory diseases that are more common in cigarette smokers than in nonsmokers.

Critical Thinking

5. People with emphysema often suffer from heart problems as well. Offer an explanation for this finding. (*Identifying Causes*)

Laboratory
Investigation

Constructing a Model of the Respiratory System

The structures of the respiratory system that cause breathing are the rib cage, lungs, and diaphragm. Air is drawn into the lungs and expelled from the lungs because of unequal air pressure. In this investigation, you will construct a model of the human respiratory system to determine how this difference in air pressure makes you breathe.

Problem

How do humans breathe? **Construct a model** of the human respiratory system to study the mechanics of human breathing.

Materials (per group)

▶ #2 one-hole rubber stopper

▶ 200-mL polyethylene bottle

▶ round balloon (large)

▶ round balloon (small)

▶ scissors

Procedure

1. Place a small polyethylene bottle on its side. Press one point of a scissors through the side of the bottle about 1 cm from the bottom.

2. Using the scissors, cut off the bottom of the bottle by cutting all the way around.

3. Stretch a small balloon and blow it up several times to make it pliable.

4. Pull the lip of the small balloon over the bottom of a #2 one-hole rubber stopper.

5. Insert the balloon through the mouth of the polyethylene bottle. Press the stopper tightly into the bottle so it holds the lip of the balloon in place.

6. Stretch a large balloon and blow it up several times to make it pliable.

7. Using the scissors, cut off about 1 cm from the rounded closed end of the large balloon. Tie the other end closed.

8. Stretch the large balloon far enough over the cut end of the polyethylene bottle so it does not slip off. See the accompanying diagram.

9. As you watch the small balloon, pull down on the knot of the large balloon. Then, still watching the small balloon, press up on the large balloon.

Observations

1. What happened to the small balloon when you pulled down on the large balloon?

2. What happened to the small balloon when you pressed up on the large balloon?

Analysis and Conclusions

1. What happened to the volume inside the bottle when the large balloon was moved up and down?

2. What caused the small balloon to expand and contract?

3. How is the model you constructed similar to the human respiratory system?

4. How do humans breathe?

Extensions

Repeat the investigation but this time add 50 mL of water to the bottle before you stretch the large balloon over the bottom of the bottle. (Be sure the large balloon is securely fastened to the bottom of the bottle. What effect does the addition of water have on the model?

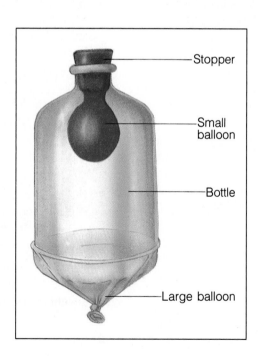

Stopper

Small balloon

Bottle

Large balloon

Chapter **11** Review

Study Outline

11-1 Adaptations for Gas Exchange

▶ Gas exchange takes place by diffusion across a thin, moist respiratory surface. The direction of exchange depends on the amount of the gas on each side of the respiratory surface.

▶ In simple organisms, such as protists and hydra, cells exchange gases directly with the environment through the cell membrane.

▶ In complex, multicellular organisms, complex respiratory and transport systems provide for gas exchange.

▶ In earthworms, gas exchange is not dependent on the circulatory system. Air enters a system of tracheal tubes, which carries oxygen to body cells and carbon dioxide from the body cells.

▶ In fish and many other aquatic animals, the respiratory organs are gills. Respiratory gases are exchanged as water flows over gills.

11-2 The Human Respiratory System

▶ In humans, the respiratory system consists of the lungs and a system of tubes that carry gases to and from the lungs.

▶ Air enters the human respiratory system through the nostrils, which lead into the nasal passages. From the nasal passages, the air travels through the pharynx and larynx and into the trachea. Air continues through the bronchial tubes and into the bronchioles within the lungs.

▶ Within the lungs are tiny, thin-walled alveoli surrounded by capillaries. Gas exchange takes place through the walls of the alveoli and capillaries.

▶ The hemoglobin that is found in the red blood cells carries most oxygen from the lungs to the body tissues. Carbon dioxide diffuses out of the body cells and into the blood. From the blood, carbon dioxide is carried to the lungs.

▶ Cigarette smoking has been linked to respiratory disorders such as bronchitis, emphysema, and lung cancer. Other respiratory disorders include pneumonia and asthma.

Chapter Assessment

Multiple Choice

Choose the letter of the answer that best completes each statement or answers the question.

1. In the hydra, gas exchange occurs by diffusion across the membranes of (a) only the inner layer of cells. (b) only the outer layer of cells. (c) only the cells of the tentacles. (d) all the cells of the organism.

2. Inhaled air is filtered, moistened, and warmed in the (a) nasal passages. (b) air sacs. (c) larynx. (d) tracheal tubes.

3. The two pairs of membranes that are stretched across the inside of thelarynx in humans are called (a) nasal passages. (b) tracheal tubes. (c) vocal cords. (d) bronchioles.

4. In humans, the exchange of respiratory gases between the air and the blood occurs through the walls of the (a) spiracles. (b) larynx. (c) alveoli. (d) trachea.

5. The trachea divides into two cartilage-ringed tubes called (a) pleura. (b) bronchi. (c) bronchioles. (d) alveoli.

6. The gas exchange organs in humans and in some other air-breathing animals are called (a) tracheal tubes. (b) pleura. (c) air sacs. (d) lungs.

7. The phase of breathing during which air is drawn into the lungs is called (a) inhalation. (b) gas exchange. (c) exhalation. (d) diaphragm.

8. In the blood, hemoglobin is one of the (a) air sacs. (b) respiratory pigments. (c) bronchioles. (d) alveoli.

9. Breathing is controlled by the (a) pituitary. (b) thyroid. (c) brain. (d) lungs.

10. Humans breathe more rapidly during exercise than before it because during exercise the blood contains (a) an increased level of oxygen. (b) a decreased number of red blood cells. (c) an increased level of carbon dioxide. (d) a decreased amount of hemoglobin.

Content Review

Answer each of the following in complete sentences.

11. What are the primary characteristics of a respiratory surface?

12. In protists, how is gas exchange with the environment accomplished?

13. How do the cells of hydra obtain oxygen and get rid of carbon dioxide?

14. Why must aquatic animals move large volumes of water over their respiratory surfaces?

15. Why is it important for earthworms to maintain a moist skin surface?

16. How do gills function in gas exchange?

17. What advantages are lost when a person breathes through the mouth instead of the nasal passages?

18. Trace the path of air from the nasal passages to the alveoli.

19. How does smoking affect the air passages?

20. Describe the transport of oxygen in the blood from the lungs to the body cells.

Graphic Organizing

For information on graphic organizers, see Appendix G at the back of this text.

21. Compare/Contrast Matrix Use the matrix below to compare gas exchange in earthworms, grasshoppers, and humans. Copy the matrix onto a separate sheet of paper and complete it.

Characteristic	Earth-worms	Grass-hoppers	Humans
respiratory surface	?	?	?
respiratory pigment	?	?	?
open or closed system?	?	?	?
gas exchange organs	?	?	?

Critical Thinking and Problem Solving

Discuss each of the following in a brief paragraph.

22. Comparing What are three ways in which gas exchange in protists is similar to gas exchange in humans?

23. Sequencing Place the following organs in the order in which air passes through them on the way to the lungs: alveoli, bronchi, bronchioles, larynx, nose, pharynx, and trachea. On what other basis could the same organs be ordered?

24. Comparing How is the blood of humans similar to the blood of grasshoppers? How is it different?

25. Relating In terms of gas exchange, explain why it is not possible to have giant insects, such as the 20-meter-high grasshoppers or 15-meter-long ants, that are seen in old science fiction movies.

26. Interpreting An investigation was carried out to determine what factors cause an increase in the rate of breathing during and after exercise. Individuals' blood and breathing rates were analyzed before and immediately after exercise, with the results shown in the table below. Make a bar graph of the data, and use it to answer the following questions: (a) What is the relationship between exercise and oxygen concentration? Between exercise and carbon dioxide concentration? (b) Why does the lactic acid concentration increase during exercise? (You may wish to refer back to Chapter 6.)

Analysis	Before Exercise	After Exercise
oxygen concentration	15 units/mL	10 units/mL
carbon dioxide concentration	50 units/mL	55 units/mL
lactic acid concentration	10 units/mL	35 units/mL
breathing rate	12 breaths/min	28 breaths/min

Discovery Learning Activity

Filtering a Fluid

1. Place some water in a cup and add a few drops of blue food coloring to the water.

2. Add a pinch of sand to the colored water and stir throughly.

3. Open a coffee filter and place it into an empty cup. Pour the colored water containing the sand through the filter. Observe what happens. Which material passed through the filter? Which did not?

Excretion

············· *Guide for Reading* ·············

Previewing the Chapter

All animals produce various metabolic wastes that must be removed from the body. Animals remove wastes through the process of excretion, which can be accomplished in several ways. Like other seabirds, kittiwakes leave deposits of a milky white paste called guano on their rocky nesting sites. How does the process of excretion differ in various organisms? What role do the liver, the kidneys, the lungs, and the skin play in human excretion?

Key Words

dermis, epidermis, excretion, kidney, Malpighian tubules, nephridia, nephron, urinary bladder

Key Concepts

- **Compare** the methods of excretion in earthworms and grasshoppers.
- **Describe** the roles of the liver, kidneys, lungs, and skin in human excretion.
- **Predict** which areas of the skin have the most sweat glands. (Laboratory Investigation)

12-1 Adaptations for Excretion

Section Objectives:

- *Describe* how excretion helps maintain homeostasis.
- *Explain* how metabolic wastes are removed from protists and hydra.
- *Compare* the excretory structures of the earthworm and grasshopper.

Excretion

As an organism carries out its life processes, waste products build up in the body fluids. If these metabolic wastes are not removed from the body, the organism will die. Therefore, the organism must be able to remove metabolic wastes and other excess substances that build up over time. **Excretion** (ek SKREE shun) is the process by which these wastes and excess substances are removed from the organism. The process of excretion also removes excess heat from the body, thus helping to keep the temperature of the body constant.

In humans and other complex animals, the organs of excretion are the lungs, kidneys, liver, and skin. These organs work with the circulatory, nervous, and endocrine systems to keep the body's internal environment constant. In other words, these organ systems maintain homeostasis.

▲ **Figure 12–1**

Excretion. The skin is just one of the excretory organs of the body.

◄ Black-legged kittiwakes.

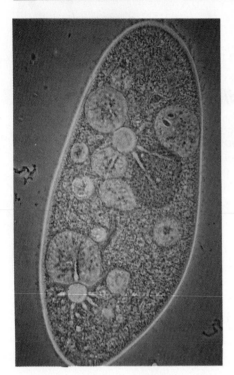

▲　**Figure 12–2**
Expanded Contractile Vacuole in Paramecium. Water balance in the paramecium is maintained by contractile vacuoles. When excess water collects in the vacuoles, the vacuoles expand, as shown here. When the expanded vacuoles are full, they contract, ejecting water from the organism.

Major Metabolic Wastes

The most important of the metabolic wastes are carbon dioxide, water, certain nitrogen compounds, and mineral salts. Carbon dioxide and water are formed during cellular respiration. Dehydration synthesis, described in Chapter 4, also produces water. Nitrogen compounds, such as ammonia, urea, and uric acid, are produced by the breakdown of amino acids. Mineral salts, such as sodium chloride and potassium sulfate, build up during metabolism. All of these wastes are poisonous in high concentrations.

Many people confuse excretion with elimination. Elimination, or *defecation,* is the removal from the digestive tract of unabsorbed and undigested food in the form of *feces.* Since these materials have never entered the body cells, they are not metabolic wastes.

Excretion in Protists

Excretion in protists is a simple process. Wastes diffuse out of the cell through the cell membrane into the surrounding water. Metabolic wastes include carbon dioxide, mineral salts, and ammonia. Ammonia (NH_3) is the chief nitrogenous waste of all microorganisms and many aquatic multicellular animals. Although ammonia is poisonous to cells, it is soluble in water. Thus, ammonia can be excreted as a waste product if there is water to wash it away.

Freshwater protists, such as ameba and paramecium, must use active transport to maintain homeostasis. Water constantly diffuses into the cell by osmosis. Because water is also produced as a byproduct of cellular respiration, excess water must be "pumped out" of the cell against a concentration gradient. The excess water collects in *contractile vacuoles.* From time to time, when it is full, the vacuole contracts, ejecting water from the cell. See Figure 12–2.

Excretion in Hydra

Hydra are small, freshwater organisms. Most of their cells are in contact with their aquatic environment. This allows the metabolic wastes, which include carbon dioxide, ammonia, and mineral salts, to diffuse directly through the cell membrane of each cell into the surrounding water.

Water tends to enter a hydra's cells by osmosis. However, no contractile vacuole has been seen in the cells of the hydra. For this reason, scientists believe that the excess water may be pumped out of the organism through the cell membrane by some other means of active transport.

Excretion in Earthworms

When most of the cells of an animal are not in contact with its surroundings, special excretory organs must remove the metabolic wastes. The excretory organs of the earthworm are the **nephridia**

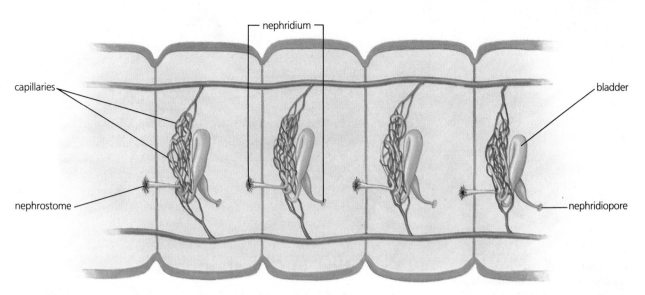

▲ **Figure 12–3**

Excretory System of the Earthworm. A pair of nephridia surrounded by capillaries is found in almost every segment of the earthworm. Fluid from the body cavity enters the nephridium, and useful substances are reabsorbed into the bloodstream. Wastes, in the form of urine, pass through the bladder and leave the body through the nephridiopore.

(nih FRID ee uh). These structures are found in pairs—one on each side—in most segments of the earthworm's body. Each nephridium extends slightly into the neighboring segment. See Figure 12–3.

Some cellular wastes diffuse directly into the fluid in the body cavity of the earthworm. This body fluid enters the nephridium at the *nephrostome* (NIH fruh stom), the funnel-shaped opening of each nephridium. The beating of cilia then moves the fluid through a tubule to the major part of the nephridium in the next segment. Here, the tubule loops several times and widens into a large bladder. The bladder drains to the outside of the body through an external opening called the *nephridiopore* (nih FRID ee oh por).

The coiled loops of the nephridium are surrounded by capillaries. As you read in Chapter 10, the blood carries metabolic wastes. Wastes from the bloodstream pass from the capillaries into the nephridium. At the same time, useful substances, such as glucose and water, pass from the body fluid in the nephridium into the blood. This exchange of wastes and useful substances is found in the excretory systems of most complex animals.

The wastes remaining in the nephridium leave the body through the nephridiopore as a dilute solution called **urine** (YUR en). The urine is made up of water, mineral salts, ammonia, and **urea** (yuh REE uh). Urea is formed from ammonia and carbon dioxide. Like ammonia, urea is soluble in water. However, it is less poisonous to cells than ammonia.

In the earthworm, carbon dioxide is excreted through the moist skin. See Chapter 11.

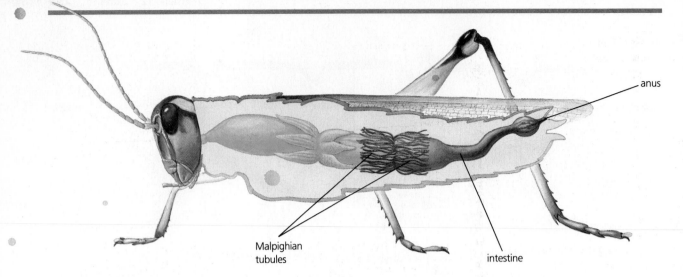

anus

Malpighian
tubules

intestine

▲ **Figure 12–4**

Excretory System of the Grasshopper. The Malpighian tubules of the grasshopper remove wastes from the blood by diffusion and active transport. A dry nitrogenous waste product, uric acid, leaves the body with the feces through the anus.

Excretion in Grasshoppers

The excretory organs of grasshoppers and other insects are the **Malpighian** (mal PIG ee en) **tubules** shown in Figure 12–4. As you read in Chapter 9, insects have open circulatory systems. Thus, the slender excretory tubules are bathed directly by the blood, which moves freely within the body spaces. Wastes and other substances from the blood enter the tubules by diffusion and active transport. From the tubules, these materials pass into the intestine. Water, nutrients, and other useful substances are reabsorbed from the tubules and the digestive tract and are returned to the body fluids. The dry nitrogenous waste product, **uric** (YUR ik) **acid,** passes out of the body with the feces through the anus.

Of all wastes containing nitrogen, uric acid is the least poisonous. In fact, because it does not dissolve much in water, it is almost completely harmless. It is excreted as a solid or semisolid by birds and reptiles, as well as insects. Because so little water leaves the body in the excretion of uric acid, this type of excretion helps to save water in land animals that have a limited water supply.

Carbon dioxide diffuses from the body tissues into the tracheal tubes. From there, it diffuses out of the grasshopper through the spiracles. See Chapter 11.

12-1 Section Review

1. What is excretion?
2. List the major metabolic wastes.
3. Why does excretion in the earthworm require specialized organs?
4. What animals excrete uric acid, and how does it help them?

Critical Thinking
5. Order the following nitrogenous waste products from least to most poisonous: urea, ammonia, uric acid. (*Ordering*)

12-2 The Human Excretory System

Section Objectives:

- *Identify* the principal metabolic wastes of the human body.
- *Describe* the excretory functions of the liver.
- *Draw* and *label* the parts of the human urinary system, and describe the process of urine formation.
- *Explain* the excretory functions of the lungs and skin.

The complex and highly developed excretory system of humans plays a major role in the maintenance of homeostasis. Carbon dioxide, urea, water, and mineral salts are the metabolic wastes of humans. The organs of excretion are the liver, kidneys, lungs, and skin. See Figure 12–5.

The Role of the Liver in Excretion

The role of the liver in digestion was discussed in Chapter 8. As an excretory organ, the liver works in several ways to regulate the makeup of body fluids.

Detoxification   The liver removes harmful substances, such as bacteria, certain drugs, and hormones, from the blood. Within the liver, these substances are changed into inactive or less poisonous forms. Thus, the liver purifies, or *detoxifies,* the blood. The inactive substances formed in the liver are returned to the bloodstream and are finally excreted from the body by the kidneys.

Overloading the liver with harmful materials, such as alcohol, can lead to a disease called *cirrhosis.* In this disease, the liver becomes overgrown with excess tissue. The excess tissue cuts down the blood flow through the liver and limits the amount of purification that it can perform. Eventually, the liver may cease to function altogether, resulting in death. Cirrhosis causes the death of about 13 000 Americans yearly.

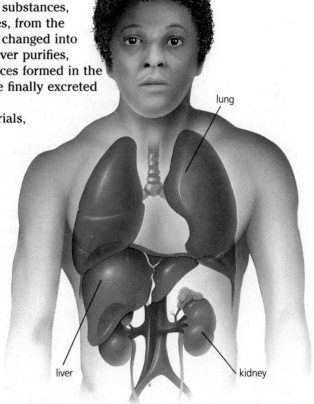

Figure 12–5

Organs of the Human Excretory System. The excretory system prevents the buildup of wastes produced by body cells. The organs of excretion in humans are the liver, kidneys, lungs, and skin. ▶

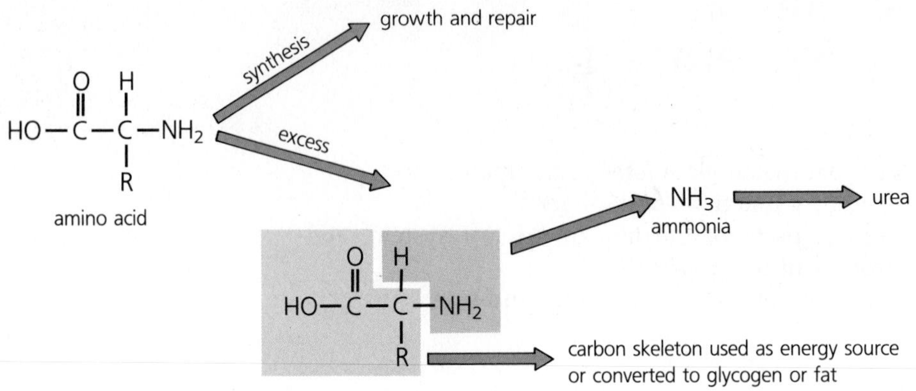

▲ **Figure 12–6**

Excess Amino Acids in the Body. Excess amino acids are broken down in the liver. The amino group is removed and converted to ammonia. The ammonia is quickly converted to urea, which is excreted from the body in urine. The carbon skeleton of the amino acid can be converted to pyruvic acid and used in cellular respiration, or it can be converted to glycogen or fat and stored.

Excretion of Bile   Bile, which is made by the cells of the liver, contains bile salts, cholesterol, and part of the hemoglobin molecule from worn-out red blood cells. Because some of the ingredients of bile are metabolic wastes, bile is considered an excretory product. Bile collects in the gall bladder and passes through the bile duct to the small intestine. There, it helps in the digestion and absorption of fats. In the last part of the small intestine, most of the bile salts are reabsorbed into the blood and returned to the liver. From the liver, they again pass to the small intestine. Thus, bile salts are reused. The rest of the bile passes into the large intestine and leaves the body in the feces. When the bile is not excreted properly, its metabolic wastes are reabsorbed into the blood, resulting in a condition called *jaundice.* Reabsorbed hemoglobin fragments in the bloodstream cause the skin to look yellow.

Formation of Urea   Amino acids are the breakdown products of proteins. Because excess amino acids cannot be stored in the body, they are broken down in the liver. The parts of the amino acids are changed into other substances. From each amino acid, the amino group (NH_2) is changed into ammonia (NH_3). The remainder of the amino acid molecule either is changed into pyruvic acid and used as an energy source in cellular respiration or is changed into glycogen or fat for storage. See Figure 12–6.

Because the ammonia produced from the amino group is very poisonous, it is changed into the less harmful substance urea by a series of enzyme-catalyzed reactions. The urea diffuses from the liver into the bloodstream. The bloodstream then carries the urea to the kidneys. The kidneys filter the urea from the blood, and it is finally excreted from the body in the urine.

The Urinary System

The **urinary** (YUR uh ner ee) **system** is made up of the kidneys, the ureters, the bladder, and the urethra. The two **kidneys** are the organs that produce urine. Urine passes from each kidney through a tube called a **ureter** (YUR et ur) to the **urinary bladder,** where it

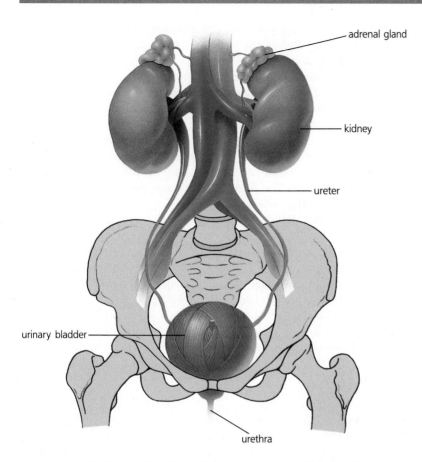

The Human Urinary System. The urinary system consists of the kidneys, ureters, bladder, urethra, and associated blood vessels. The adrenal glands rest on the kidneys but are not part of the excretory system.

is stored. During urination, the stored urine travels from the bladder to the outside of the body through the **urethra** (yuh REE thruh). See Figure 12–7.

The kidneys are bean-shaped organs that are about 10 centimeters long. They lie against the muscles of the back in the abdomen just below the diaphragm. The kidneys are important for two reasons. First, they remove the wastes of cellular metabolism from the blood. Second, they regulate the concentrations of the substances found in the body fluids. If the kidneys cannot perform these two functions, a person will die.

Structure of the Kidneys   The kidney has three parts. The outer part is the *cortex.* The middle part is the *medulla* (meh DUHL uh). The inner region is the *pelvis.* Blood is filtered in the cortex. The medulla is made up of tubes, called *collecting ducts.* The collecting ducts carry the filtered substances, called the *filtrate,* to the pelvis. The pelvis is a cavity connected to the ureter. Urine formed from the filtrate drains from the pelvis into the ureter. The three parts of the kidney are shown in Figure 12–8.

The most important work of the kidneys—the filtering of wastes from the blood—takes place in the **nephrons** (NEF rahnz). Each kidney has about 1.25 million nephrons. A part of each nephron is in the cortex. The remainder of the nephron lies in the medulla. At one end of a nephron, shown in Figure 12–8, is the

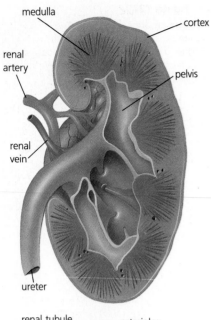

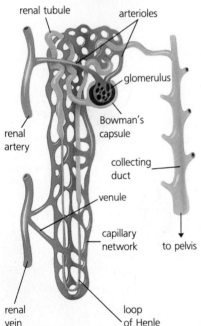

▲ **Figure 12-8**

The Kidney and the Nephron. The cross section of the kidney (top) shows three distinct regions. Blood is filtered in the outermost region, the *cortex*. The filtrate passes through the tubes in the middle region, the *medulla*, and drains into the ureter from the innermost region, the *pelvis*. The nephron (bottom) is the functional unit of the kidney. Each nephron is made of a glomerulus, Bowman's capsule, and renal tubule.

glomerulus (glah MER yuh lus). The glomerulus (plural, *glomeruli*), is a group of capillaries that form a tight ball. The glomerulus is surrounded by a double-walled, cup-shaped structure, which is known as **Bowman's capsule.**

From the blood in the glomerulus, substances are filtered into Bowman's capsule. The filtrate then exits Bowman's capsule through the *renal tubule,* a long tubule that empties into a collecting duct. The middle section of the renal tubule forms a long loop, called the *loop of Henle* (HEN lee), which extends into the medulla. Some reabsorption takes place in the loop of Henle. The collecting duct, which receives the filtrate from many nephrons, leads from the medulla into the pelvis.

Blood enters the kidneys through the **renal arteries** and leaves the kidneys through the **renal veins.** Each nephron has one arteriole that carries blood from the renal artery to the nephron. The arteriole branches to form the capillaries that make up the glomerulus. Before leaving Bowman's capsule, the capillaries join together into a single arteriole. The new arteriole subdivides into a second capillary network that surrounds the renal tubule. The capillaries then merge again, this time to form a venule. This pattern of blood flow around the nephrons is unusual because there are two sets of capillaries, rather than one, between the arteries and veins.

Urine Formation   Urine is made in the nephrons in two stages: filtration and reabsorption. It is important to realize that during the first stage—the filtration stage—both useful substances and wastes are removed from the blood. During the second stage—the reabsorption stage—some of the useful substances reenter the blood to be used by the body.

Filtration   To understand reabsorption, we need to look at filtration in more detail. Filtration takes place in the glomeruli and Bowman's capsules. The blood that enters a glomerulus is under pressure. The pressure forces the filtrate, which includes water, urea, glucose, amino acids, and various salts, through the thin walls of the glomerulus into Bowman's capsule. Blood cells and blood proteins, however, are too large to pass through the walls of the glomerulus. These substances remain in the blood. The filtrate that enters Bowman's capsule is like blood plasma, but it does not contain proteins.

The kidneys form about 180 liters of filtrate in a 24-hour period. However, only about 1 liter to 1.5 liters of urine (only a fraction of the filtrate) are actually produced by the kidneys in 24 hours. If all of the filtrate that is formed were excreted, the body would lose too much water along with important nutrients and salts dissolved in that water.

Reabsorption   After the filtrate has left Bowman's capsule, reabsorption occurs in the renal tubule. It is the process of *reabsorption* that reduces the volume of filtrate and returns various important substances to the blood. Normally, as the filtrate passes through the renal tubules of the nephrons, about 99 percent of the water, all of the glucose and amino acids, and many of the salts are reabsorbed. These substances are reabsorbed into the blood by the capillaries that surround the tubules. The reabsorption of water from the renal tubules is an important means of water conservation in mammals. Since most of the water is reabsorbed, the substances left in the filtrate are highly concentrated.

While water is reabsorbed by osmosis, glucose, amino acids, and salts need active transport to be reabsorbed. ATP, the energy source for active transport, is supplied by the many mitochondria found in the cells of the renal tubule. The tubules are lined with microvilli that greatly increase the surface area through which reabsorption can occur. The large area allows the reabsorption of huge amounts of water and other substances.

Most substances have what is called a *kidney threshold level*. If the concentration of a substance in the blood is greater than a certain level, the excess substance is not reabsorbed. The excess remains in the urine and is excreted from the body. For example, the blood sugar level of a person who has diabetes is so high that not all the glucose in the filtrate can be returned to the blood. As a result, glucose appears in the urine.

After reabsorption, the fluid remaining in the tubules is urine. The urine is made up of water, urea, and various salts. Urine flows from the tubules into the collecting ducts. It passes out of the kidneys through the ureters to the bladder, which is emptied from time to time through the urethra.

Sometimes, substances crystallize out of the urine in the urinary tract or kidney. These crystallized substances are called kidney stones. If the stones are too big to be passed with the urine, they must be surgically removed or shattered into small pieces with sound waves or lasers.

If one kidney stops working, the second kidney can take over its work. If both kidneys fail, however, excess fluid and wastes build up rapidly in the body, which can lead to death. In this case, an artificial kidney machine may be used to filter the blood. This process is known as *dialysis*. See Figure 12–10. The patient is connected to the machine with tubes leading into blood vessels. Blood flows from the body into the dialysis machine, where wastes are filtered out. The filtered blood is then returned to the body. By undergoing several hours of dialysis each week, a person can live for years after kidney failure.

The Lungs

The lungs are considered a part of the excretory system because they rid the body of carbon dioxide and water (in the form of water vapor). Both of these substances are the end products of aerobic cellular respiration. The lungs are discussed in greater detail in Chapter 11.

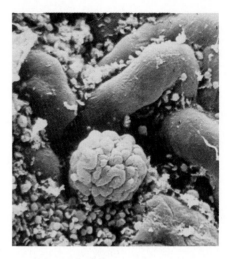

▲   **Figure 12–9**

A Glomerulus. At the center of this scanning electron micrograph is a glomerulus surrounded by renal tubules. The Bowman's capsule of the glomerulus has been removed. (Magnification 921 X)

Figure 12–10

The Kidney Dialysis Machine. This patient is undergoing kidney dialysis. When a person's kidneys do not function properly, a dialysis machine can be used to filter excess fluids and wastes from the blood. ▼

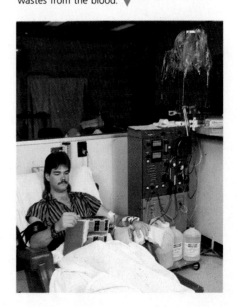

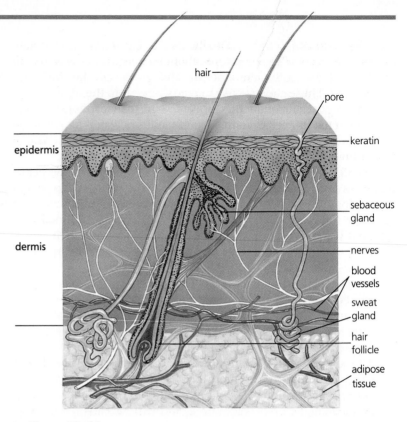

▲ **Figure 12–11**

Structure of the Skin. The epidermis acts as protection for the dermis, which contains blood and lymph vessels, sebaceous glands, sweat glands, nerves, sense receptors, and many hair follicles.

The Skin

The skin, which is made up of many different kinds of tissues, performs a number of functions. One of these functions is the excretion of wastes.

Structure of the Skin As shown in Figure 12–11, the skin has two layers. The outer layer is the *epidermis* (ep uh DER mis) and the inner layer is the dermis.

The **epidermis** is formed of layers of tightly packed epithelial cells. The deepest portion of the epidermis is made up of rapidly dividing cells. As these cells are pushed farther and farther away from the dermis by the new cells that are forming, they receive less nourishment and die. Before dying, they produce large amounts of a tough, waterproofing protein, which is called *keratin* (KER uh tin). The outer part of the epidermis consists of these hardened, dead epithelial cells. This part of the epidermis is always wearing away. As it wears away, it is replaced by new cells from the dividing layer underneath it. The tough, waterproof epidermis acts as protection for the dermis.

The **dermis** lies below the epidermis. It is made up of elastic connective tissue. The dermis is a thick layer that supports the skin and binds it to the muscle and bone lying beneath it. Within the dermis are blood vessels, lymph vessels, nerves, sense receptors, sebaceous glands, sweat glands, and hair follicles. Beneath the dermis is a layer of fat, or *adipose,* tissue. Thin people have little fat in this layer. On the other hand, in overweight people, this adipose layer of tissue is very thick.

The **sebaceous** (sih BAY shus) **glands** produce oily secretions that provide a protective coating to the skin and hair and keep them soft and pliable. **Sweat glands** are made of tiny coiled tubes that open to the surface of the skin through holes called *pores.* Sweat is released through these holes.

Functions of the Skin   The skin keeps microorganisms and other foreign materials from entering the body. Since the outermost layer is waterproof, the skin also keeps the body from drying out. The skin excretes a small amount of urea and salts in sweat, which is 99 percent water. However, the skin's major role in excretion is the removal of excess heat.

When the body becomes too warm, extra heat is lost in two ways. First, the blood vessels in the skin open wider. This increases the blood flow through the skin's capillaries (causing a flushed appearance) and allows more heat to be given off to the air. Second, sweat begins to evaporate. As you read in Chapter 4, energy for the evaporation of sweat comes from body heat. Therefore, the evaporation of sweat cools the body by using, and thus removing, some of its heat.

The skin also helps keep heat in when the body is too cool. Blood vessels in the skin narrow slightly, reducing the supply of blood to the skin capillaries. The body also sweats less. In these ways, less heat is lost from the body. If the body is too cold, it can even produce heat by muscle tension and shivering. These ways by which the body holds a constant temperature are good examples of homeostatic control.

12-2 **Section Review**

1. Name the organs of excretion in humans.
2. Name the parts of the urinary system.
3. Describe the two stages involved in the formation of urine by the nephron.
4. In what way is the nephron's filtrate different from urine?

Critical Thinking

5. Explain the relationship between a renal tubule and Bowman's capsule. (*Relating Parts and Wholes*)

Biology and You

Q: My friends and I enjoy sunbathing during the summer. Is suntanning bad for your skin?

A: Too much sun can permanently damage your skin and lead to skin cancer. The sun emits short, intense waves called ultraviolet (UV) light. It is these waves, and not the sun's heat, that can injure your skin. Ultraviolet light can damage the DNA in your skin cells. This is why suntanning can cause aging skin and may lead to skin cancer.

Some individuals are more prone to skin cancer than others. The lighter your skin, the greater the danger. Yet, even if you are at high risk, you can protect your skin. Use a sunscreen when in the sun, especially in the middle of the day when the sun is most intense. You can also shield your skin from ultraviolet rays by covering up with clothing, a hat, or an umbrella.

Contrary to what some people think, tanning machines are *not* a safe alternative. These machines emit ultraviolet rays. You may be surprised to learn that most of the sun's harmful rays also can reach you through haze and clouds, but they cannot penetrate glass.

■ *Create a public service announcement for television warning teenagers about sunbathing.*

Laboratory
Investigation

Mapping Your Sweat Glands

A solution of iodine reacts with starch by turning a blue-black color. When dried iodine comes in contact with the water given off by sweat glands, it becomes a solution again and will react with the starch in a piece of blotting paper, causing it to turn a blue-black color. In this investigation, you will take advantage of these changes to locate sweat glands in your skin.

Problem

Which areas of your skin have the most sweat glands? **Make a prediction** to answer this question.

Materials (per group)

- 4 squares of blotting paper, 1 cm x 1 cm
- medical adhesive tape
- iodine solution
- cotton swab

Procedure

1. Wash and dry your hands and forearms thoroughly. Roll your sleeves up to above the elbow. Carefully dip the cotton swab into the iodine solution. **CAUTION:** *Be careful when using iodine because it stains clothing.*

2. Find an area in the center of the palm of one of your hands that is free of creases. Using the iodine-soaked cotton swab, paint a 2-cm square on your palm and let it dry.

3. Repeat step 2 on the inside of one of your forearms.

4. Using a pencil, label one of the blotting-paper squares "Palm" and the other one "Forearm." Have your partner tape the blotting-paper square labeled "Palm" over the iodine on your palm and the square labeled "Forearm" over the iodine on your forearm. Allow the blotting paper to remain in place for 20 minutes.

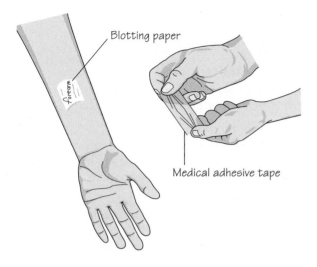

Blotting paper

forearm

Medical adhesive tape

Data Table		
Location of Sweat Glands	Number of Active Sweat Glands	Distribution of Sweat Glands
Middle surface of palm		
Inside of forearm		

5. While you are waiting, write a prediction about whether the palm of your hand or your forearm has more sweat glands. Also predict whether all members of the class will have the same results.

6. After 20 minutes, have your lab partner remove the two paper squares. Count the number of blue-black dots on each one. Each dot indicates the presence of an active sweat gland.

7. Construct a data table similar to the one shown. Record the number of dots on the paper square for your palm. In the space marked "Distribution of Sweat Glands," draw or write a description of the pattern of dots.

Observations

1. What difference did you observe in the number of sweat glands per square centimeter on your palm and forearm?

2. What differences were there in the patterns of sweat glands?

Analysis and Conclusions

1. Which area tested—palm or forearm—had the greater density of active sweat glands?

2. Were your predictions correct? Explain your answer.

3. How did the information in your data table compare with the information your classmates compiled?

4. What conclusion can you draw about the distribution of sweat glands on the skin?

5. Do all sweat glands produce the same amount of sweat? What evidence did you observe to support your answer?

Extensions

Using the same materials, design an experiment to find out whether exercise affects the number of sweat glands that are active at any one time.

Chapter 12 Review

Study Outline

12-1 Adaptations for Excretion

▶ Waste products of the metabolic processes of cells build up in the body fluids. Metabolic wastes include carbon dioxide, water, nitrogen compounds, and mineral salts. These wastes are removed from the organism by the process of excretion.

▶ In simple organisms, wastes diffuse directly from the cells into the environment.

▶ Complex multicellular organisms have specialized excretory organs, such as the nephridia, which are found in earthworms, and the Malpighian tubules, which are found in grasshoppers.

▶ Insects, birds, and reptiles excrete the dry, nitrogenous waste product uric acid.

12-2 The Human Excretory System

▶ In humans, excretion involves the liver, kidneys, lungs, and skin. The functioning of these organs is important in the maintenance of homeostasis.

▶ The liver functions to detoxify harmful substances in the blood and to synthesize and excrete bile. Urea is formed in the liver by the breakdown of amino acids, and it is transported through the bloodstream to the kidneys for excretion.

▶ The urinary system consists of the kidneys, ureters, urinary bladder, and urethra. The kidneys remove metabolic wastes from the blood and regulate the concentrations of substances in the body fluids.

▶ In the kidneys, the nephrons produce urine by the processes of filtration and reabsorption. Urine passes from the kidneys and through the ureters to the bladder and leaves the bladder through the urethra.

▶ During respiration, the lungs remove carbon dioxide and water vapor from the body. The skin excretes small amounts of urea and salt in perspiration, protects the internal tissues of the body, and helps maintain a constant body temperature.

Chapter Assessment

Multiple Choice

Choose the letter of the answer that best completes each statement or answers the question.

1. A major function of the human urinary bladder is (a) transforming urine into a nitrogenous waste. (b) releasing urine directly into the bloodstream. (c) storing urine until it is eliminated. (d) filtering urine out of the blood.

2. Which organism has specialized organs for the excretion of metabolic wastes? (a) yeast (b) ameba (c) earthworm (d) hydra

3. The organs of excretion in humans do not include the (a) skin. (b) liver. (c) kidneys. (d) large intestine.

4. Nitrogen compounds, such as ammonia, urea, and uric acid, are produced by the breakdown of (a) carbohydrates. (b) fats. (c) amino acids. (d) salts.

5. Excretion in hydra occurs by means of (a) contractile vacuoles. (b) nephridia. (c) Malpighian tubules. (d) active transport.

6. Uric acid is the least toxic nitrogenous waste because it (a) is soluble in water. (b) contains little nitrogen. (c) is insoluble in water. (d) breaks down quickly.

7. In the kidneys, the filtering of blood takes place in the (a) cortex. (b) medulla. (c) pelvis. (d) loop of Henle.

8. The functional unit of the human kidney is called (a) nephridium. (b) Malpighian tubule. (c) nephron. (d) urinary bladder.

9. An excretory function performed by the skin is (a) elimination of urea and salt in perspiration. (b) evaporation of carbon dioxide and water. (c) elimination of excess glucose. (d) regulation of body temperature.

10. In addition to water, the principal components of urine are (a) amino acids and fatty acids. (b) urea and salts. (c) ammonia and bile. (d) hydrochloric acid and bases.

Content Review

Answer each of the following in complete sentences.

11. Why must metabolic wastes be removed from an organism?

12. Explain how water balance is maintained in fresh water protists.

13. How is carbon dioxide excreted by the earthworm?

14. What is the relationship between the nephridium and the capillaries of the earthworm?

15. Explain the function of the Malpighian tubules of the grasshopper.

16. What is the role of the human liver in regulating the composition of body fluids?

17. Draw a diagram of the nephron and label the following parts:
(a) glomerulus
(b) Bowman's capsule
(c) renal tubules
(d) loop of Henle
(e) collecting duct.

18. Draw a diagram of the skin and label the following parts:
(a) epidermis
(b) dermis
(c) keratin
(d) sebaceous gland
(e) hair follicle
(f) hair
(g) sweat gland
(h) pore.

19. What are the two main functions of the kidneys?

20. How does the human body eliminate excess heat? How does it conserve heat?

Graphic Organizing

For information on graphic organizers, see Appendix G at the back of this text.

21. Word Map In the next column are two incomplete word maps for the terms kidney and nephron. Copy the word maps onto a separate sheet and complete them.

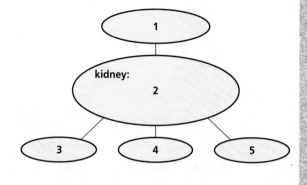

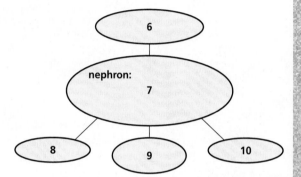

Critical Thinking and Problem Solving

Discuss each of the following in a brief paragraph.

22. Drawing conclusions Suggest a list of foods that a person hiking through the desert might pack in order to minimize the kidneys' job of maintaining homeostasis.

23. Relating An organism with an increased metabolic rate could move faster, obtain more food, and defend its territory more vigorously than one without. Suggest some possible reasons why the organisms excretory requirements would limit how much its metabolic rate could increase.

24. Experimenting Design a controlled experiment to determine the effect of exercise on body temperature. What hypothesis will be tested in your experiment? What variable will you change? What factors will be kept constant? What response will you measure?

Discovery
Learning Activity

Joints and Tools

1. Examine each of the following to determine how its moves: wrench and bolt, joy stick, and hinge.

2. Identify joints in your body that move the same way as each of the tools.

Support and Locomotion

Guide for Reading

Previewing the Chapter

Down under, a kangaroo bounds out of the surf after a refreshing dip. Kangaroos have their own unique method of locomotion. Every animal moves in its own way. Earthworms burrow through soil. Dolphins swim gracefully through the open sea. And humans walk upright on two legs. Why is locomotion essential to many organisms? How do methods of locomotion differ among organisms? How do bones and muscles work together to allow movement in humans?

Key Words

bone, cilia, endoskeleton, exoskeleton, flagella, joint, pseudopod, setae, skeletal muscle

Key Concepts

- **Describe** the different methods of locomotion in simple organisms.
- **Describe** the roles of bones and muscles in human locomotion.
- **Relate** the structures of a chicken wing to their functions. (Laboratory Investigation)

13-1 Adaptations for Locomotion

Section Objectives:

- *List* the advantages of locomotion.
- *Compare* exoskeletons and endoskeletons.
- *Describe* methods of locomotion in the protist, hydra, earthworm, and grasshopper.

The Advantages of Locomotion

Many types of living things are able to move on their own from one place to another. Being able to move oneself from place to place is called *locomotion*. Organisms that are capable of locomotion are said to be *motile* (MOH til). Most animals and many protists are motile. On the other hand, plants are not motile.

Some animals that live in water, such as corals and adult sponges, cannot move from place to place on their own. They live fastened to the ocean floor or to some object. These animals are stationary, or *sessile* (SES il). By moving parts of their bodies, however, they create water currents that allow them to get food and oxygen and to carry out their life processes.

▲ **Figure 13–1**

Locomotion. This bright orange tropical crab scuttles over rocks and sand with its five pairs of walking legs.

▲ **Figure 13–2**
Exoskeleton of a Mollusk. The exoskeleton of a clam is a hard double shell composed of calcium compounds.

Figure 13–3
Exoskeleton of an Arthropod. The exoskeleton of the rock crab is composed of lightweight chitin. It protects the soft body parts and is jointed to allow movement. ▼

Being able to move from place to place offers a number of advantages for an organism.

■ Locomotion makes it easier for organisms to get food. (A cougar may hunt for food over a territory of more than 160 square kilometers.)

■ Locomotion allows organisms to find suitable places to live and to move away from harmful conditions in the environment. (Some kinds of fish swim away from warm, oxygen-poor water toward cooler, oxygen-rich water.)

■ Locomotion allows organisms to escape enemies or to seek shelter. (Rabbits and deer escape from danger by moving quickly.)

■ Locomotion allows organisms to find mates and reproduce. (Male and female salmon swim thousands of kilometers to reach their spawning grounds.)

Living things have many different methods of locomotion. In single-celled organisms, such as protists, *pseudopods* or various cell structures may be used for locomotion. In multicellular animals, locomotion always involves specialized muscle tissue. Whatever the method, the basis for nearly all protist and animal movement is *contractile proteins*—proteins that can change in length.

Muscles and Skeletons

In all but the simplest animals, locomotion uses both muscles and a skeleton to which the muscles are fastened. Muscles can exert force when they *contract,* or shorten. When they contract, they move the parts of the skeleton to which they are fastened.

Most skeletons are made up of hard materials. If the skeleton is outside the body, enclosing the soft parts, it is called an **exoskeleton** (eks oh SKEL uh tun). Some protists and many invertebrates have exoskeletons. For example, clams, oysters, and other mollusks have hard shells made of calcium compounds. See Figure 13–2. The animal lives inside the shell, and its movement is limited. Crabs, spiders, insects, and other arthropods have exoskeletons made of **chitin** (KYT in), which is a tough, but lightweight, carbohydrate material. Exoskeletons serve as the site of attachment for muscles. In arthropods, the exoskeleton is jointed, so that it is flexible and can move in various ways. Exoskeletons protect the soft parts of the body. However, because they are not made of living cells, they cannot grow. For this reason, from time to time, arthropods shed, or *molt,* their exoskeletons and replace them with new, larger ones. See Figure 13–3. During the time between molting and growth of the new exoskeleton, the animal's soft body is unprotected.

In vertebrates, the skeleton is made of *bone* and *cartilage,* two types of connective tissue, and is located within the body walls. This type of skeleton, found inside the body, is called an **endoskeleton** (en doh SKEL uh tun). An endoskeleton does not protect the animal as well as an exoskeleton. However, because bones and cartilage contain living cells and can grow, the skeleton grows larger along with the rest of the animal. Skeletal muscles are fastened to the endoskeleton, making the movement of body parts possible. Endoskeletons are found in fish, amphibians, reptiles, birds, and mammals.

Locomotion in Protists

Among the protists, some forms have no means of locomotion, while others are highly motile. Motile protists usually move by pseudopods, cilia, or flagella.

Pseudopods   **Pseudopods** are temporary projections of the cell surfaces. The organism moves when cytoplasm flows into or out of the pseudopods. This type of locomotion is best known in amebas. It is also found in other organisms as well as in some white blood cells. Locomotion by means of pseudopods is also known as *ameboid movement.*

Studies of the ameba show that the cytoplasm within the organism is in two states. In the central part of the cell, the cytoplasm is more fluid and is called the *endoplasm.* As the ameba moves, the endoplasm flows forward through the center of the pseudopod. See Figure 13–4. At the tip, it spreads out in all directions and changes into a firmer, less fluid state. In this state, the cytoplasm is known as *ectoplasm.* The ectoplasm travels backward along the sides of the cell. Near the "back," it changes back into endoplasm and joins the forward-flowing stream. Energy for movement comes from the breakdown of ATP to ADP.

Cilia and Flagella   Protists having cilia, such as the paramecium, move quickly compared to the ameba. The paramecium is covered with thousands of short, hairlike **cilia,** whose rhythmic, oarlike

Figure 13–4

Ameboid Movement. In ameboid movement, the cell cytoplasm alternates between a more fluid endoplasm and a less fluid ectoplasm. Cytoplasm in the endoplasm flows forward into newly forming pseudopods and then changes to ectoplasm. At the rear of the cell, cytoplasm flows forward as it changes from ectoplasm to endoplasm. In this way, the cell contents move in the direction of the new pseudopods. ▼

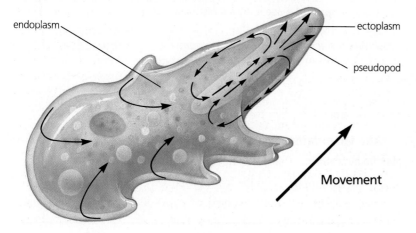

endoplasm — ectoplasm

pseudopod

Movement

Figure 13–5

Locomotion in the Paramecium. The entire outer surface of a paramecium is covered with cilia that beat rhythmically to propel it through the water. The beating of the cilia is coordinated by a network of fibrils. ▶

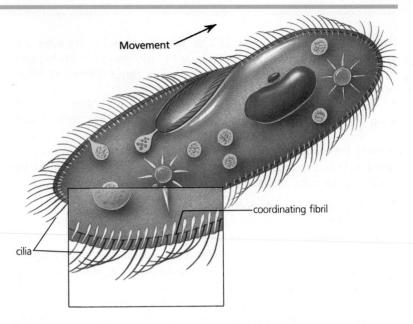

Movement

coordinating fibril

cilia

beating moves the organism through the water. See Figure 13–5. A system of tiny fibers connects the cilia at their bases. These tiny fibers, or fibrils, cause the cilia to beat in the right order.

Flagella are like cilia except that they are longer, and there are usually only one or two per cell. Euglena is a protist that moves by means of one long, thin, flagellum. See Figure 13–6. The whiplike movements of the flagellum pull the euglena through the water.

MiniLab

Skill: Observing

Slimy Movements

Procedure

1. Obtain an earthworm and place it on a moist paper towel.

2. With a hand lens, observe the skin, setae, and segments of the earthworm. **CAUTION:** *Be careful not to harm the earthworm when handling it.* Make a sketch of the earthworm and label its external features.

3. Allow the earthworm to crawl around and observe how it moves.

4. Place the earthworm on a smooth desk top or a glass plate. Allow the earthworm to crawl around and observe how it moves.

Problem

What can you **observe** about an earthworm's movements?

Analyze and Conclude

1. Describe the earthworm's external features.

2. How did the earthworm move on the moist towel? On the smooth surface?

3. What is the role of the earthworm's slimy skin?

Locomotion in the Hydra

The hydra has cells specialized for contraction. Although the hydra tends to stay in one place, contractile fibers allow it to move about in several ways. The presence of mucus-secreting cells and ameboid cells allow it to "glide" along on its base. It can move quickly by somersaulting its base completely over its tentacles. It can also inch along by bending over and fastening its tentacles to an object and then pulling its base closer. The hydra can float upside down in the water by making an air bubble on its base.

Locomotion in the Earthworm

The earthworm uses muscles to burrow through the soil. Within its body wall are two layers of muscles. See Figure 13–7. An outer layer of circular muscles goes around the worm. An inner layer of longitudinal muscles goes along the full length of the body. When the circular muscles contract, the worm becomes longer and thinner. When the longitudinal muscles contract, the body becomes shorter and thicker. Within the earthworm, the body cavity is filled with fluid. When the surrounding muscle layers contract, the fluid stiffens the body of the worm and allows it to push through the soil.

On almost all of the earthworm's segments, there are four pairs of tiny bristles called **setae** (SEE tee). In locomotion, the setae in the rear of the earthworm hook into the ground while the circular muscles contract. This lengthens the body and pushes the worm forward. Then, the setae near the front of the worm anchor into the ground, and the setae in the rear relax. The longitudinal muscles contract, shortening the body and pulling forward the hind end of the worm. The earthworm moves by repeating these movements over and over again.

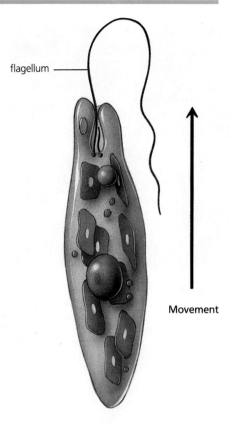

flagellum

Movement

▲   **Figure 13–6**

Locomotion in the Euglena. Movement of the long, whiplike flagellum pulls the organism through the water.

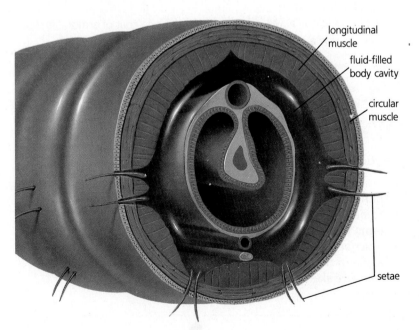

longitudinal muscle

fluid-filled body cavity

circular muscle

setae

◀   **Figure 13–7**

Locomotion in the Earthworm. Both circular and longitudinal muscle layers can be seen in this cross section of an earthworm. When the outer layer of circular muscles contracts, the worm lengthens and becomes thinner. When the inner layer of longitudinal muscles contracts, the worm becomes shorter and thicker.

▲ **Figure 13–8**

A Short-Horned Grasshopper Jumping. The first two pairs of legs of the grasshopper are used for walking. The powerful hind legs are used in jumping. The tough outer wings protect the delicate inner wings that are used for flying.

Locomotion in the Grasshopper

The body of the grasshopper is covered by an exoskeleton of chitin. The exoskeleton is divided into plates separated from each other by flexible joints. This arrangement allows the grasshopper to move freely. Grasshoppers can walk, jump, and fly. See page 721, Figure 33–15.

Like other insects, the body of the grasshopper has three major divisions—the *head, thorax* (THOR aks), and *abdomen* (AB duh men). Fastened to the thorax are three pairs of jointed legs. The first two pairs are used for walking, while the powerful hind pair is used for jumping. A grasshopper can jump more than 20 times its body length. Also fastened to the thorax are two pairs of wings. The outer pair is hard and protects the delicate inner pair, which is used in flying. The powerful muscles used in flight are fastened to the exoskeleton of the thorax. The muscles have no direct connection with the wings but move the wings by changing the shape of the body wall of the thorax.

The muscles of a grasshopper work in pairs. When one muscle of a pair contracts and bends a joint, the other muscle relaxes. When the second muscle contracts, extending the joint, the first muscle relaxes.

13-1 Section Review

1. What is locomotion?
2. What is an exoskeleton? An endoskeleton?
3. Name some means used by protists for locomotion.
4. Name the two layers of muscles used in locomotion in the earthworm.

Critical Thinking

5. An exoskeleton is sometimes referred to as a "coat of armor." In what ways is this a good analogy? (*Reasoning by Analogy*)

13-2 The Human Musculoskeletal System

Section Objectives:

- *Describe* the functions and structure of the bones and cartilage found in the human musculoskeletal system.
- *Name* the major parts of the human skeleton and the types of joints found in it.
- *Describe* the structure of skeletal muscle and explain how voluntary movement is accomplished.
- *Compare* skeletal muscle with smooth muscle.

Bones and Cartilage

Bone is a type of connective tissue that is hard and inflexible. The bones of the human skeletal system serve a number of different purposes.

- They serve as sites of attachment for skeletal muscles, and they serve as levers that make body parts move when these muscles contract.

- They give the body its general shape and support body structures.

- They protect delicate structures, such as the brain, spinal cord, heart, and lungs.

- They serve as storage places for minerals, such as calcium and phosphorus.

- They serve as the places where red blood cells and some white blood cells are produced.

Bone is made up of living bone cells, connective tissue fibers, and inorganic compounds. It is an active tissue. There is a constant destruction of old tissue and laying down of new tissue. A basic part of the structure is **collagen** (KAHL uh jen), a protein material with great strength. When bones are being formed, living cells called *osteoblasts* (AHS tee uh blasts) secrete collagen and certain polysaccharides. The collagen forms fibers that are bound together by the polysaccharides, which act as cement. Bone is formed when calcium and phosphate ions from the body fluids combine, forming calcium phosphate. The calcium phosphate precipitates as crystals within the mass of collagen fibers and cement. The hardness and heaviness of bone are due to the presence of the calcium phosphate. The osteoblasts are trapped in small cavities inside the bone substance to form bone cells called **osteocytes** (AHS tee uh syts).

In the bone, the osteocytes are arranged in a series of smaller and smaller circles with a common center. See Figure 13-9. In the center of each series of circles, there is a cavity called the **Haversian** (huh VER zhun) **canal,** which contains blood vessels and nerves. Tiny canals connect the osteocytes to each other and to the Haversian canal. The blood vessels within the Haversian canals carry oxygen and nutrients to the bone cells and remove wastes. If a bone is broken, the osteocytes become active, producing new bone tissue to heal the wound.

The outside of a bone, except at its ends where it connects to other bones, is covered by a tough membrane called the **periosteum** (pehr ee AHS tee um). The main purpose of the periosteum is to make new bone for growth and repair. The periosteum is also the point at which muscles are fastened to bones. This membrane contains blood vessels and nerves that enter the bone.

There are two types of bony tissue—*compact bone* and *spongy bone.* They are made of the same material, but compact bone is very dense and strong, while spongy bone is more porous. Most bones contain both types of tissue, as shown in Figure 13-9.

Figure 13–9

Internal Structure of Bone. The photo (left) shows a cross section of a human thigh bone. Surrounding the central Haversian canals are concentric circles of cavities in which osteocytes are found. The Haversian canals contain blood vessels and nerve cells and are connected to the osteocytes by tiny canals. The drawing (right) shows the structure of a long bone. ▶

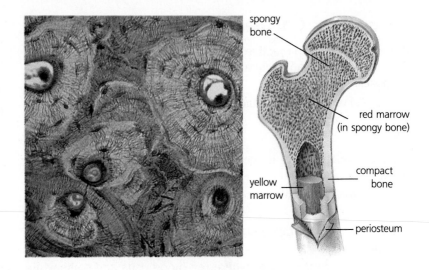

Some of the bones of the body are hollow. There is also a great deal of space in spongy bone. These spaces are filled with a soft tissue called **marrow** (MAR oh). There are two types of marrow—*red marrow* and *yellow marrow*. Red marrow makes red blood cells, platelets, and some types of white blood cells. In adults, red marrow is found in the spongy bone of the vertebrae, ribs, breastbone, cranium, and long bones. Yellow marrow is made of fat cells. In adults, it is found in the hollow center of long bones.

Cartilage (KART il idj), like bone, is a type of connective tissue. While bone is rigid, cartilage bends easily. In the embryo, most of the skeleton is cartilage. As the embryo develops, minerals are laid down, and much of the cartilage slowly changes into bone. This process, called **ossification** (ahs if fih KAY shun), goes on into adulthood. The bones of small children contain more cartilage than the bones of adults. Children's bones are therefore more elastic and not as easily broken. In adults, cartilage is found at the ends of ribs, at joints, and in the nose and outer ear. Cartilage gives support while still allowing some bending motion. It allows the bones to bend more easily at joints and cushions against impact or pressure.

The Human Skeleton

Parts of the Skeleton   The adult human skeleton contains 206 bones. See Figure 13–10. The skeleton has two main parts: the *axial* (AK see ul) *skeleton* and the *appendicular* (ap en DIK yuh ler) *skeleton*.

The **axial skeleton** is made up of the skull, vertebrae, ribs, and breastbone. The upper part of the skull, the **cranium** (KRAY nee um), houses and protects the brain. The rest of the skull is made up of the facial and jaw bones. The **spinal column**, or *backbone*, has 29–33 bones called **vertebrae** (VERT uh bree). Most are separated from each other by disks of cartilage. The disks act as shock absorbers and allow the spine to bend. The ribs are fastened at the back to the upper vertebrae and at the front of the breastbone, or

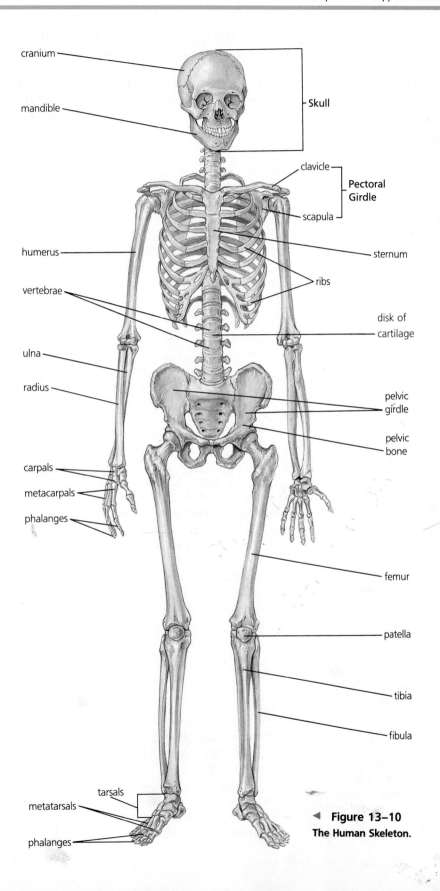

cranium

mandible

Skull

clavicle

Pectoral
Girdle

scapula

humerus

sternum

ribs

vertebrae

disk of
cartilage

ulna

radius

pelvic
girdle

pelvic
bone

carpals

metacarpals

phalanges

femur

patella

tibia

fibula

tarsals

metatarsals

phalanges

◄ **Figure 13–10**
The Human Skeleton.

Science, Technology and Society

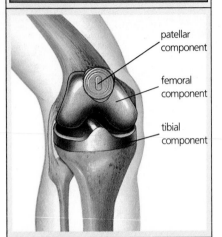

patellar component

femoral component

tibial component

Technology: Artificial Joints

For millions of Americans, everyday movement is difficult. These people suffer from arthritis, a painful inflammation of the joints. Today, the surgical replacement of diseased joints can mean a new freedom from pain for many of these arthritis sufferers.

Over half a million joints are replaced with artificial joints each year. Knees and hips are the most frequently replaced joints. The knee replacement joint is made up of three components (see above). Two curved metal plates are arranged side by side. They rotate in a plastic dish attached to the bone and allow the leg to move. Many artificial joints used today can last as long as 15 years. With the development of new materials, researchers are hopeful that the lifetime of these replacement joints will be extended significantly.

■ *Aside from arthritis sufferers, who else might stand to benefit from developments in artificial joint technology?*

sternum. The space enclosed by the sternum, ribs, and backbone is the *chest cavity.* Within the chest cavity, the heart and lungs are supported and protected by the ribs and sternum.

The **appendicular skeleton** is made up of arm and leg bones and the *pectoral* (PEK tuh rul) *girdle* and the *pelvic girdle.* The shoulder blades (scapula) and collar bones (clavicle) make up the pectoral girdle. It connects the arms to the spine. The pelvic girdle is made up of the hip bones and connects the legs to the spine.

Joints   A point in the skeleton where bones meet is called a **joint.** There are several different types of joints in the body. See Figure 13–11. Joints in which bones are tightly fitted together, as in the cranium, are **immovable joints.** Most joints, however, are movable. **Hinge joints,** such as those at the elbow and knee, permit back-and-forth motion. **Ball-and-socket joints,** such as those at the shoulder and hip, allow movement in all directions. In this type of joint, the ball-shaped end of one bone fits into the cuplike hollow, or socket, of another bone. **Pivot** (PIV it) **joints,** such as those at the base of the skull, allow side-to-side as well as up-and-down movement. **Gliding joints,** such as the wrists or the joints between the vertebrae, allow some bending and twisting movements.

At movable joints, bones are held together by tough, fibrous bands of connective tissue called **ligaments** (LIG uh ments). A fluid, called *synovial* (sih NOH vee ul) *fluid,* is secreted into movable joints. This fluid acts as a lubricant and reduces friction at the joint.

Figure 13–11

Types of Joints. Hinge joints permit back-and-forth motion. Ball-and-socket joints permit a wide range of movement. Gliding joints offer limited flexibility in all directions. The bones of the cranium are joined by immovable joints. Pivot joints allow side-to-side and up-and-down movement. ▼

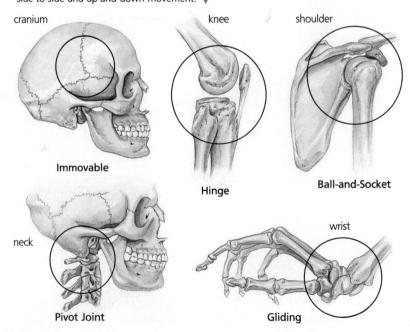

cranium

Immovable

knee

Hinge

shoulder

Ball-and-Socket

neck

Pivot Joint

wrist

Gliding

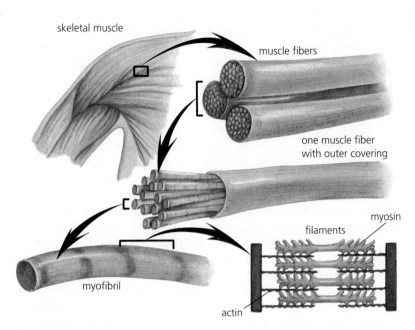

Structure of Skeletal Muscle. A skeletal muscle is composed of a bundle of muscle fibers. Each muscle fiber is made up of a bundle of myofibrils. A myofibril consists of protein filaments arranged in an overlapping pattern.

Skeletal Muscle

Skeletal, or *striated* (STRY ay ted), **muscles** are used in locomotion and all other voluntary movement. They are fastened to the bones of the skeleton. Skeletal muscle tissue is not made up of clearly defined, separate cells. Instead, during development, cells fuse together, forming individual *muscle fibers.* A skeletal muscle is made up of bundles of muscle fibers bound together by connective tissue.

Under a light microscope, the muscle fibers appear striped, or striated. That is, they show alternating bands of light and dark. See Figure 13–12. Electron microscope studies have shown that each fiber is actually a bundle of smaller fibers, called **myofibrils** (my oh FY brilz). Each myofibril is made up of still finer protein filaments, one thick and one thin. The thick filaments are *myosin.* The thin ones are *actin.* The two types of filaments are arranged in an overlapping pattern that makes the whole muscle fiber look striped.

According to the *sliding filament theory* of muscle contraction, the muscle fibers shorten when the actin slides over the myosin. As the overlap increases, the fiber shortens. See Figure 13–13. Cross bridges between actin and myosin allow the fibers to exert a pull. Energy for the sliding of the filaments is supplied by ATP. ATP is produced in the mitochondria of many of the muscle fibers.

Voluntary Movement

All voluntary movement is started and coordinated by impulses from the brain and spinal cord. Voluntary movement includes any action that is under conscious control. For example, picking up a pencil and throwing a baseball are voluntary movements. Voluntary movements require the action of skeletal muscles.

Figure 13–13

Contraction of Skeletal Muscle. According to the sliding filament theory, muscles contract (shorten) when the actin filaments slide over the myosin filaments. ▼

Relaxed Muscle

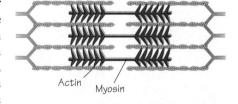

Contracted Muscle

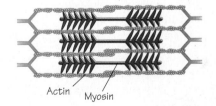

Skeletal muscles are fastened to bones by strong fibers of connective tissue called **tendons.** Tendons are attached to skeletal muscles in such a way that they pull on the bones. The movements of the muscles and joints enable the bones to act as levers. Usually, there are several muscles around each joint that pull in different directions.

Muscles can pull when they contract, but they cannot push when they relax. Therefore, they must always work in *antagonistic* pairs. The two muscles in an antagonistic pair move a bone in opposite directions. The bending and extending of the arm at the elbow show how muscles and bones work together to produce movement. See Figure 13–14. When the *biceps* (BY seps) muscle on the front of the upper arm contracts, the arm bends. Because the biceps muscle bends, or flexes, the joint, it is called a **flexor** (FLEK ser). Whenever the biceps contracts, the *triceps* (TRY seps) muscle in the back of the arm relaxes, making it possible for the arm to bend. When the triceps muscle contracts, the biceps muscle relaxes, and the arm is extended, or straightened. Because the triceps muscle extends the joint, it is called an **extensor** (ek STEN ser). Throughout the body, antagonistic pairs of muscles cause the bones of the skeleton to move.

MiniLab

Skill: Comparing

Whose Side Are You On?

Procedure

1. Stand up and hold a book in your right hand. Your right arm should hang straight down at your side.

2. When your partner says "go," lift the book to shoulder height. Be sure to keep your arm straight and extended out to your side. Then lower it.

3. Repeat step 2 for 30 seconds at which time your partner will say "stop." Record the results.

4. Rest for 1 minute and repeat steps 2 and 3. Record the results.

5. Repeat steps 2 to 4 with your left arm. Record the results.

Problem

How do the actions of the muscles of your left arm **compare** with those of your right arm?

Analyze and Conclude

1. Compare the two performances of your right-arm muscles.

2. Compare the two performances of your left-arm muscles.

3. How did the performance of your right arm compare with that of your left arm?

4. What conclusions can you draw from these results?

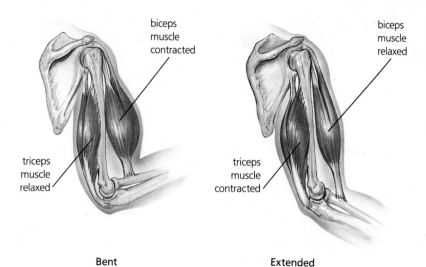

Bent   Extended

◀ **Figure 13–14**
Muscles of the Upper Arm. The biceps and triceps muscles of the upper arm work as an antagonistic pair. When the biceps muscle in the front of the arm contracts (left), the triceps muscle in the back of the arm relaxes and the arm bends. When the triceps muscle contracts (right), the biceps muscle relaxes and the arm straightens.

As long as you are conscious, your skeletal muscles are never completely relaxed. Instead, your brain keeps all your muscles partly contracted. This is called **muscle tone.** Muscle tone keeps the muscles ready for the powerful contractions of movement. It also maintains posture by keeping the muscles of the back and neck partly contracted.

Smooth Muscle

In addition to skeletal muscle, which is under voluntary control, the body also contains muscle that works involuntarily, or without conscious control. This involuntary muscle tissue is called **smooth muscle.** It is found in the walls of the digestive organs, in the walls of arteries and veins, in the diaphragm, and in other internal organs. The cells of smooth muscle are long and overlap to form sheets of muscle rather than bundles of fibers. Smooth muscle does not look striated. See Figure 13–15.

Cardiac muscle is a type of muscle that is found only in the heart. Cardiac muscle was discussed in Chapter 9.

Figure 13–15
Smooth Muscle. This micrograph shows the smooth muscle fibers of the urinary bladder. (Magnification 630 X). ▼

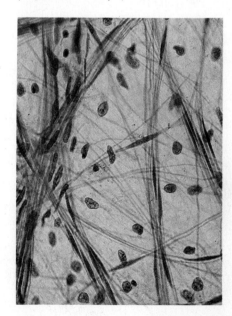

13-2 **Section Review**

1. What is the difference between bone and cartilage?
2. Name the two main parts of the skeleton.
3. What is a joint?
4. What are the three types of muscles in the human body?

Critical Thinking

5. Explain the central role played by actin-myosin cross bridges in muscle contraction. (*Relating Parts and Wholes*)

Laboratory
Investigation

Anatomy of the Chicken Wing

The limbs of vertebrates are complex structures that are adapted for a variety of movements. In this investigation, you will examine the muscles, bones, and joints of a chicken wing to relate these structures to their functions.

Problem

How can you **relate** the structures of a chicken wing to their functions?

Materials (per student)

- ▶ raw chicken wing
- ▶ non-latex gloves
- ▶ dissecting pan
- ▶ scissors
- ▶ forceps

Procedure

1. Put on the non-latex gloves. Examine the external characteristics of the chicken wing. Carefully bend the wing to see how many major sections it has. Draw a diagram of the external structure. Label the upper arm, elbow, lower arm, wrist, and hand.

2. Place the wing in the dissecting pan. With the forceps, grasp the skin and pull the skin away from the underlying muscles. Use the scissors to cut the skin along the entire length of the chicken wing. Be careful not to damage the muscles and other structures. Draw a diagram of the chicken wing with the skin removed. Label the upper arm, elbow, lower arm, wrist, hand, thumb, fingers, and muscles.

3. Examine the muscles. In the upper arm, there are two groups of muscles. Pull on each of these groups of muscles, and observe what happens to the rest of the wing. Repeat this step for the muscles in the lower arm.

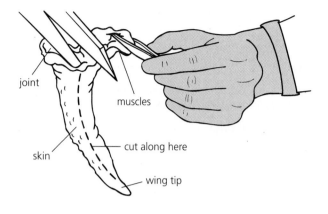

joint

muscles

skin

cut along here

wing tip

4. Locate the tough, shiny, ribbonlike structures at the ends of the muscles. These are called tendons. Notice where the tendons attach the upper and lower arm muscles to the bones. Sketch the tendons in the drawing you made in step 2.

5. Remove the muscles and tendons to expose the bones of the upper and lower arm. Locate the shiny, ribbonlike structures connecting two bones. These are ligaments. Also, locate the shiny, white substance covering the ends of the bones. This is cartilage. Feel its texture. Draw a diagram of the chicken wing with the muscles removed. Label the humerus (upper arm bone), radius (smaller lower arm bone), ulna (larger lower arm bone), ligaments, and cartilage.

6. Examine the elbow joint. Move the arm bones back and forth to observe the motion allowed by this joint.

7. Study a model of the human skeleton or refer to Figure 13–10 on page 261 and Figure 13–11 on page 262. Compare the structure of the human arm with that of the chicken wing.

Observations

1. What happens to the wing when you pull on each of the upper and lower arm muscle groups?

2. Draw the muscles of the wing and indicate those that would need to contract in order to stretch out the wing.

3. Describe the freedom of motion allowed by the elbow joint. How many ligaments hold it in place?

Analysis and Conclusions

1. What similarities can you see between the chicken wing and the human arm?

2. How are the chicken wing and the human arm adapted to serve different functions?

Extensions

Using detailed anatomical drawings of the human muscular system, select specific body movements and identify the muscles that are involved in each movement.

Chapter 13 Review

Study Outline

13-1 Adaptations for Locomotion

▶ Locomotion is the ability to move oneself from place to place. In all but the simplest animals, locomotion involves muscles and a skeleton to which the muscles are attached.

▶ The two types of skeletons are exoskeletons and endoskeletons.

▶ Among protists, locomotion is usually carried out by pseudopods, cilia, or flagella.

▶ The hydra, although often sessile, has specialized contractile cells that make movement possible. Mucus-secreting cells allow it to glide along on its base.

▶ The earthworm uses its longitudinal and circular muscles, its fluid-filled body cavity, and its setae for locomotion.

▶ The grasshopper has a flexible, jointed exoskeleton that enables it to move freely. Three pairs of legs and two pairs of wings allow it to walk, jump, and fly.

13-2 The Human Musculoskeletal System

▶ The human skeleton is made up of bones and cartilage. Bones allow movement, give the body shape and support, protect internal organs, store minerals, and serve as a site of blood cell production.

▶ The axial skeleton includes the skull, vertebrae, ribs, and breastbone. The appendicular skeleton includes the arm and leg bones, as well as the pectoral and pelvic girdles.

▶ A joint is the place in the skeleton where bones meet. Most joints are movable to some extent.

▶ Skeletal muscle is made up of bundles of muscle fibers. Muscle contraction occurs when the fibers shorten. Muscles act in antagonistic pairs, with one muscle contracting and the other relaxing.

▶ Smooth muscle works without conscious control. It is found in the walls of arteries and veins and in some internal organs. It is made up of long, overlapping cells that form sheets of muscle.

Chapter Assessment

Multiple Choice

Choose the letter of the answer that best completes each statement or answers the question.

1. In which organism is locomotion accomplished by the interaction of muscles and chitinous appendages? (a) grasshopper (b) hydra (c) human (d) paramecium

2. Producing blood cells and providing attachment sites for muscles are two functions of (a) skin. (b) cartilage. (c) bones. (d) ligaments.

3. Tendons are best described as (a) tissue that is found between bones and that protects them from damage. (b) fibrous cords that connect muscles to bones. (c) striated tissue that provides a wide range of motion. (d) connective tissue that connects bone to bone and that stretches at the point of attachment.

4. Organisms that lack the ability to move from place to place are referred to as (a) motile. (b) sessile. (c) autotrophic. (d) saprophytic.

5. Exoskeletons cannot grow because (a) they are not made up of living cells. (b) they contain only cartilage. (c) they contain only bone. (d) they contain only chitin.

6. Cilia are structures used for locomotion in (a) protists. (b) earthworms. (c) grasshoppers. (d) hydra.

7. In locomotion in the earthworm, as the rear setae hook into the ground, (a) the front setae also hook into the ground. (b) the longitudinal muscles contract and the body shortens. (c) the circular muscles contract and the body lengthens. (d) the circular muscles contract and the body shortens.

8. Haversian canals contain (a) bone cells. (b) blood vessels and nerves. (c) calcium phosphate crystals. (d) periosteum.

9. Which of the following contains the greatest amount of skeletal muscle tissue? (a) cerebrum (b) small intestine (c) kidney (d) foot

10. The skeletal muscles of the body are normally in a state of partial contraction called (a) flexion. (b) tendonitis. (c) strain. (d) muscle tone.

Content Review

Answer each of the following in complete sentences.

11. Why do organisms with exoskeletons usually molt from time to time?

12. Compare locomotion in paramecia with locomotion in euglena.

13. Identify and give the function of the parts of the grasshopper that are used in locomotion.

14. Describe the role of osteoblasts in human bone formation.

15. What three functions does the periosteum serve?

16. How does the skeleton of a child differ from that of an adult?

17. Name and compare the motion of the four types of moveable joints. Give an example of each.

18. Draw a labeled diagram describing the sliding filament theory of muscle contraction.

19. Briefly describe the muscle movements involved in bending and extending an arm at the elbow.

20. How does the structure of smooth muscle differ from that of striated muscle?

Graphic Organizing

For information on graphic organizers, see Appendix G at the back of this text.

21. **Concept Map** Copy the incomplete concept map below onto a separate sheet of paper. Fill in the missing concepts and the missing linking words.

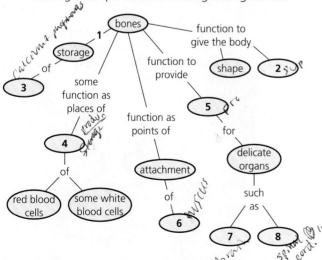

Critical Thinking and Problem Solving

Discuss each of the following in a brief paragraph.

22. **Hypothesizing** Suppose that after adding a chemical compound to a culture of normally fast-swimming paramecia you found the paramecia unable to move. They were in no other way affected. What is the most probable cause of their inability to swim?

23. **Relating** If smooth muscle had to be consciously controlled, as skeletal muscle does, what types of activities would you have to "think" about?

24. **Relating** Aquatic animals need less skeletal support than land animals of similar size. Why do you think this is so?

25. **Experimenting** Design a controlled experiment to determine whether calcium phosphate plays a role in controlling bone strength. (Hint: Calcium phosphate can be dissolved in dilute acid.) What is the variable in your experiment? What factors are kept constant? What response is measured?

26. **Interpreting** A scientist wanted to find out if the distance that teenagers can hike is affected by environmental temperature. The results of an investigation are presented in the graph below. Summarize the relationship shown in the graph. Can you draw any other conclusions from the data? What factors should the scientist have kept constant for the experiment to be valid?

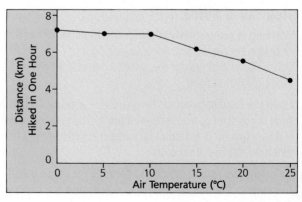

Discovery
Learning Activity

Quick As a Wink

1. Working in groups of three, have one member of each group repeat a simple motion, such as raising one finger at irregular intervals, as a signal for the second member of the group to move his or her foot.

2. Have the third member of the group use a stopwatch to measure how much time passes between the signal and the movement. If the response is too quick to measure, estimate the time; for example, 0.1 or 0.2 seconds.

3. Calculate the rate at which the nervous message traveled from the eyes to the foot, by dividing the distance the message traveled by the time the message took to travel between the two organs.

4. Repeat steps 1 to 3 until each group member's response rate has been calculated. Compare response rates with other groups.

Nervous Regulation

Guide for Reading

Previewing the Chapter

A pair of watchful meerkats alertly scan the horizon near their den. They are prepared to react instantly at the first sign of danger. Such immediate reactions to stimuli are the function of nerve cells in the body. These nerve cells allow an organism to sense and react to its environment. What are these nerve cells, and how do they transmit signals throughout the body? What changes take place as an impulse moves along a nerve?

Key Words

axon, dendrite, impulse, neuron, neurotransmitter, stimulus, synapse, threshold

Key Concepts

- **Describe** how organisms respond to changes in their environment.
- **Describe** a nerve impulse.
- **Design an experiment** to determine the instinctive behavior of a planarian. (Laboratory Investigation)

14-1 The Regulatory Process

Section Objectives:

- *Explain* the functions of a nervous system.
- *Define* stimulus.
- *Describe* the structure and the function of a neuron.
- *Name* the different types of nerves and describe their functions.

Functions of Regulation

An organism's environment is always changing. Some of the changes take place outside the body. These changes may include a change in temperature, the appearance of food, and the appearance of an enemy. Changes also take place within the organism. For example, the amount of a waste product may increase; a disease-causing organism may enter the body; and the supply of a needed substance may decrease.

An organism is always responding to a wide variety of changes that take place both inside and outside its body. In fact, the various life activities of an organism are in themselves examples of complex responses. These responses must be *regulated*. That is, they must be controlled in amount and directed to the right place. They must also be *coordinated*. That is, they must be made to take place in the right order or relationship.

▲ **Figure 14–1**

A Nervous Response. A well-developed nervous system allows this owl chick to respond to a perceived threat by assuming a complex defensive posture.

◀ South African meerkats.

In one-celled organisms and some simple multicellular organisms, regulation and coordination of responses are functions of each cell as a whole. The ability of a cell to respond to its environment is called **irritability.** In more complex multicellular animals, a *nervous system* and an *endocrine system* control the regulation and coordination of responses. In this chapter and in Chapter 15, you will learn how nervous systems work. In Chapter 16, you will read about the human endocrine system.

Mechanisms of Nervous Regulation

A nervous system is a network of specialized cells, known as *nerve cells,* that carry messages, or **impulses,** throughout the organism. Along with the nerve cells, two other types of body structures—receptors and effectors—interact with this network. **Receptors,** or *sense organs,* are specialized structures that are sensitive to certain changes, physical forces, or chemicals both inside and outside the organism. Stimulation of a receptor causes impulses to be carried, or transmitted, over a pathway of nerve cells. These impulses finally reach an **effector,** which is a specialized structure that responds to the commands of the nervous system. For example, in humans, an effector is either a gland or a muscle. If the effector is a gland, it will respond to the impulse by either decreasing or increasing its activity, depending on the nerve pathways the impulse has followed. If the effector is a muscle, a nerve impulse will cause it to contract.

Anything that causes a receptor to start impulses in a nerve pathway is called a **stimulus** (STIM yuh lus). The stimulus causes electrical and chemical changes in the receptor. These changes start the nerve impulses. Thus, there are three basic events in nervous regulation. First, a stimulus activates a receptor. Second, impulses are started in associated nerve pathways. Third, an effector responds to the impulse.

Although these three steps sound simple, a nerve pathway is not a straightforward connection from a particular receptor to a particular effector. In most animals, each nerve pathway crosses and interconnects with many other pathways. Impulses from a single receptor are usually carried to a number of different nerve pathways. Impulses reaching an effector are the result of the combination and interaction of many impulses from many different pathways.

Multicellular animals have several different types of receptors. In general, each type of receptor is sensitive to a different type of stimulus. For example, a particular receptor may respond to a certain stimulus, such as heat. Other receptors may respond to cold, light, sound, pressure, or chemicals. The way in which each receptor works is described in detail in the next chapter.

All but the simplest animals have a **brain,** a specialized group of nerve cells that controls and coordinates the activities of the nervous system. The more complex the organism is, the more complex are the structure and functions of the brain.

Structure of Neurons

The *nerve cell,* or **neuron** (NOO rahn), is the basic structure in the nervous systems of all multicellular animals. Neurons can send both electrical and chemical (electrochemical) impulses. Being able to send impulses is a property of the nerve cell membrane. Nerve impulses do not pass through the cytoplasm of neurons. They are transmitted only along the cell membrane.

A nerve cell usually is made of three basic parts: a cell body, dendrites, and an axon. These are illustrated in Figure 14–2. The **cell body** contains the nucleus and the cell organelles. The metabolic activities that take place in all cells are carried out in the cell body, which also controls the growth of the nerve cell. Materials that are needed for the maintenance of the nerve cell are made in the cell body. They are then moved to other parts of the cell where they are needed.

The **dendrites** (DEN dryts) are short, highly branched fibers that receive impulses. Dendrites generally conduct impulses toward the cell body. In some neurons, the dendrites branch out around the cell body, giving the cell a bushy appearance.

The **axon** (AK sahn) is usually a long, thin fiber that extends from the cell body. Axons usually carry impulses away from the cell body and send them either to other neurons or to effectors. Axons range in length from a part of one centimeter to more than one meter. Sometimes, either the axon or the dendrite of a neuron is called a *nerve fiber.*

Many vertebrate axons are surrounded by cells known as **Schwann** (shwahn) **cells.** On some axons, the Schwann cells produce layers of a white, fatty substance called **myelin** (MY uh lin). The myelin forms a covering around the axon, and axons having such a covering are said to be *myelinated.* At places along a myelinated axon, there are gaps in the myelin that expose the axon membrane to the surrounding medium. These gaps, which are between neighboring Schwann cells, are called the *nodes of Ranvier* (RAHN vee ay). See Figure 14–3.

Figure 14–2
Structure of a Neuron. ▼

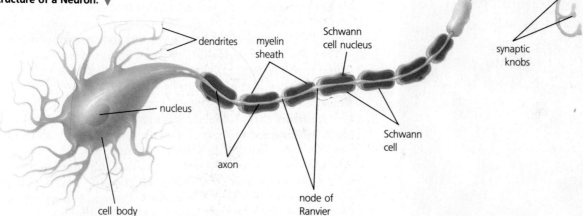

synaptic knobs

terminal branches

dendrites

myelin sheath

Schwann cell nucleus

nucleus

axon

Schwann cell

node of Ranvier

synaptic knobs

cell body

Figure 14–3

Cross Section of a Myelinated Axon. The myelin, which covers the axon, is produced by Schwann cells. ▶

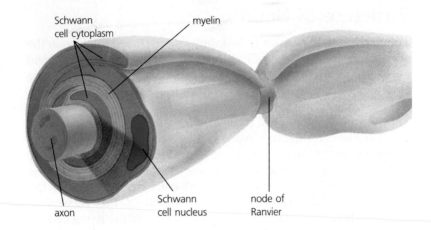

Schwann cell cytoplasm

myelin

axon

Schwann cell nucleus

node of Ranvier

Unlike other cells in the body, the nerve cells of mature animals cannot divide, so neurons cannot be replaced. If, however, the cell body of the neuron is unhurt, damaged axons and dendrites outside the brain and spinal cord can grow back.

The Synapse

The axon of a neuron usually has no branches along its length, but it may have a great many branches at its end. Each of these *terminal branches* almost touches another cell. The place between the terminal branch of a neuron and the membrane of another cell is called a **synapse** (SIN aps). The synapse has a microscopic gap between the end of the terminal branch and the neighboring cell. Impulses are carried across this gap from the axon to the neighboring cell. The structure of a synapse and the way in which impulses are carried across it are described on page 279. Each axon may have one or more synapses with as many as 1000 other neurons. Axons from other neurons may also make contact with these cells. All of these synapses make the interconnections and impulse pathways of a typical nervous system very complex.

Types of Nerves and Neurons

Figure 14–4

Structure of a Nerve. Nerves are made up of bundles of neurons bound together by connective tissue. Note the blood vessels that provide nutrients for the nerve fibers. ▼

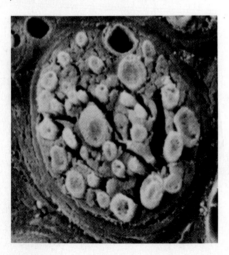

Nerves are bundles of axons or dendrites that are bound together by connective tissues. See Figure 14–4. Nerves are called *sensory nerves* if they carry impulses from receptors to the spinal cord and brain. They are *motor nerves* if they carry impulses from the brain and spinal cord to effectors. They are *mixed nerves* if they are made up of both sensory and motor fibers.

Neurons are usually grouped according to what they do. **Sensory neurons** carry impulses from receptors to the spinal cord and brain. **Motor neurons** carry impulses from the brain and spinal cord to effectors, usually muscles. **Interneurons,** or *associative* (uh SOH shee ay tiv) *neurons,* relay impulses from one neuron to another in the brain and spinal cord. Most of the neurons in the human nervous system are interneurons. Figure 14–5 shows how the structure of each kind of neuron is slightly different.

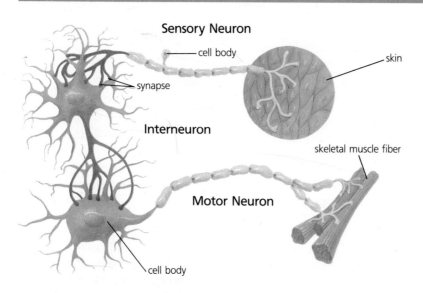

Sensory Neuron
— cell body
synapse
skin
Interneuron
skeletal muscle fiber
Motor Neuron
cell body

◀   **Figure 14–5**

Pathway of Nerve Impulses. Sensory neurons receive stimuli and trigger impulses in other neurons. Motor neurons carry impulses toward effectors, such as skeletal muscle. Interneurons, which are found in the brain and spinal cord, relay impulses from one neuron to another.

14-1 Section Review

1. What are the three types of structures found in a true nervous system?
2. What happens when a receptor is stimulated?
3. List the three parts of a nerve cell.
4. What is a synapse?

Critical Thinking

5. What would happen if the motor neurons in one of your legs stopped functioning? *(Predicting)*

14-2 The Nerve Impulse

Section Objectives:

- *Describe* the electrical state of a resting neuron and the function of the sodium-potassium pump.
- *List* the changes that occur as an impulse travels along an axon.
- *Explain* how the nervous system distinguishes between stimuli of different types and strengths.
- *Identify* the structures of a synapse and describe the transmission of an impulse across a synapse and at a neuromuscular junction.

The Resting Neuron

It is the difference in electrical charge between the outer and inner surfaces of the nerve cell membrane that makes the transmission of a nerve impulse possible. When the neuron is resting (not transmitting an impulse), the outside of the membrane has a net positive charge, and the inside has a net negative charge. See Figure 14–6.

Figure 14–6

Electrical State of a Resting Neuron. As a result of the action of the sodium pump, the outside of the membrane of a resting neuron has a net positive charge, and the inside of the membrane has a net negative charge. ▶

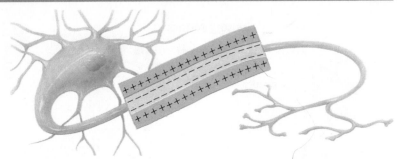

The cell membrane is said to be electrically *polarized* because there is a difference in electrical charge between its outer and inner surfaces. The polarization is caused by different concentrations of certain ions outside and inside the cell. While some of the concentration differences result from the selective permeability of the membrane, most of the differences are the result of the active transport of ions across the membrane. The ions that take part in the polarization of the nerve cell membrane are mainly sodium ions and potassium ions, both of which have a positive electrical charge.

The nerve cell membrane pumps sodium ions out of the cell and potassium ions into the cell by means of active transport. The active transport mechanism that performs this pumping action is called the **sodium-potassium pump.** In its resting state, the nerve cell membrane is freely permeable to potassium ions but not to sodium ions. As a result, the potassium ions pumped into the cell tend to diffuse back out. Because the sodium ions pumped out of the cell cannot diffuse freely through the membrane, the number of them increases outside the cell. As a result, an excess of positive charge (due to sodium ions) builds up outside the membrane. An excess of negative charge is left behind inside the membrane.

The Nerve Impulse

Membrane Changes in the Area of the Impulse   The arrival of an impulse from a neuron or a stimulus from a receptor starts a nerve impulse in the membrane of a neuron. At the place on the neuron where the impulse is started, the permeability of the membrane to sodium ions suddenly increases. Because there are more sodium ions outside the membrane than inside, sodium ions diffuse rapidly to the inside of the membrane. This flow of positive sodium ions reverses the polarization of the membrane. In the area of the impulse, the inside of the nerve cell membrane becomes positively charged; the outside becomes negatively charged. See Figure 14–7.

This reversal of polarity takes place in only a small area of the membrane. However, it results in a flow of electrical current that affects the permeability of neighboring areas of the membrane. Sodium ions rush through these new regions of increased permeability, causing the polarization in these regions to become reversed. In this way, the reversal of polarization travels over the entire length of the nerve cell. The nerve impulse is the reversal of

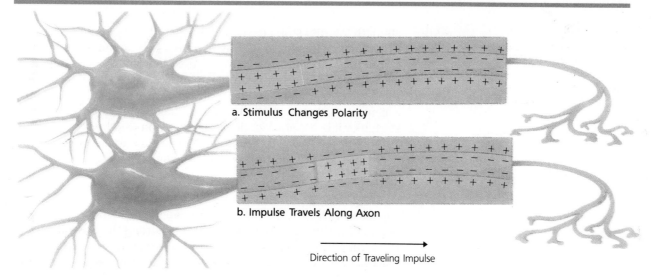

a. Stimulus Changes Polarity

b. Impulse Travels Along Axon

Direction of Traveling Impulse

polarization. The passage of the impulse along an axon is similar to a relay race. Once the impulse moves to the next section of the neuron, the first section returns to its original polarized state.

In the area of the nerve impulse, the high permeability of the cell membrane to sodium ions lasts for only a part of a second. It then returns to normal, which stops the sodium ions from diffusing across the membrane. The diffusion of potassium to the outside of the membrane, together with the action of the sodium pump, restores the normal distribution of ions. Once this happens, the polarity of the membrane is returned to normal, with a positive charge outside and a negative charge inside.

Following the passage of an impulse, there is a brief period during which the nerve cell membrane cannot be stimulated to carry impulses. This time, which lasts only a few thousandths of a second, is called the **refractory period.** When it is over, the membrane is again ready to carry impulses.

Rate of Impulse Conduction
The rate at which impulses travel depends on two factors: the size of the nerve fiber, and whether or not it has a myelin covering. In small fibers without myelin, the nerve impulse travels at a rather slow two meters per second. In large myelinated fibers, it may travel more than 100 meters per second.

Myelinated fibers carry impulses more quickly because the impulse travels in "jumps" from one node of Ranvier, where the axon is bare, to the next. This is called *saltatory* (SAL tuh tor ee) *conduction.* Because myelin prevents the flow of ions, depolarization occurs only at the nodes that are highly sensitive. Less active transport is needed for restoring the normal distribution of ions after the impulse has passed. Thus, saltatory conduction is faster and uses less energy.

Nerve Cell Thresholds
For an impulse to be started in a nerve cell, the stimulus must have a certain minimum strength. Each nerve cell has a minimum level of sensitivity, or **threshold.** If the

▲ **Figure 14–7**

A Nerve Impulse. In the area of an impulse, the nerve cell membrane becomes permeable to sodium ions, which enter the cell. This causes a reversal of the polarity of the membrane. The area of reversed polarity is the nerve impulse, and it travels quickly down the axon membrane.

strength of the stimulus is below that threshold, the stimulus cannot start impulses in the neuron. Any stimulus above the threshold will start impulses in the neuron. All the impulses transmitted by a given neuron are alike. That is, they are all the same "size," and they pass along the neuron at the same rate. Thus, a neuron works on an "all-or-none" basis. Either an impulse is started or it is not started, depending only on whether the stimulus is above or below the threshold level. The situation is like the firing of a gun. The gun does not fire until enough force is exerted on the trigger.

Distinguishing Strength and Type of Stimulus   If all nerve impulses are basically alike, how does an organism know what type of stimulus caused the impulses or how strong the stimulus was? For example, why does touching a hot stove feel different from touching a warm surface? How do you tell the difference between a bright light and a loud sound?

The strength of a stimulus is measured by two effects. First, a stronger stimulus causes more impulses to be transmitted each second. See Figure 14–8. That is, the impulses follow each other more closely. Second, different neurons have different thresholds. Some need a stronger stimulus than others to transmit an impulse. When a stimulus is stronger, both low-threshold and high-threshold neurons will transmit impulses.

Recognition of the *type* of stimulus depends on the particular pathways that carry the nerve impulse. Each type of receptor is sensitive to a certain type of stimulus. For example, light-sensitive receptors in the retina of the eye transmit nerve impulses only when light strikes them. Impulses from the retina travel along the optic nerve to a part of the brain that interprets them as sight. Artificial stimulation of the optic nerve causes a person to "see"

Figure 14–8

Strength of a Stimulus. A strong stimulus (hot object, bottom) triggers more impulses in more neurons than a weak stimulus (warm object, top). These differences enable the brain to determine the strength of the stimulus. ▼

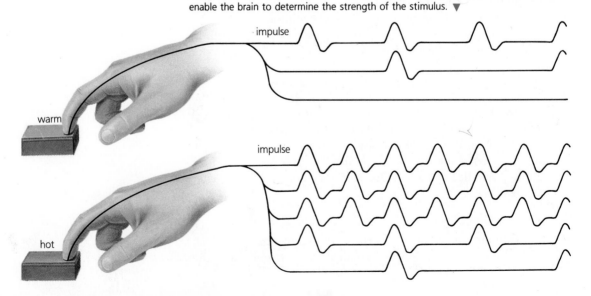

flashes of light. Sound waves, on the other hand, have no effect on the receptors in the eye. Instead, if the sounds are within the range of human hearing, they trigger receptors inside the ear. The impulses then travel to the brain by way of the auditory nerve. When these impulses reach the brain, they are interpreted as sound.

Transmission at the Synapse

As you read earlier, there is a tiny gap, called a synapse, between the end of one neuron and the dendrite or cell body of another cell. The structure of a synapse is shown in Figure 14–9. At the synapse, the axon ends in a *synaptic knob.* When an impulse arrives at the synaptic knob, it must be carried across a narrow space to the membrane of the neighboring cell. This narrow space is sometimes known as a synaptic gap.

The transmission of impulses across the synaptic gap is a chemical process. Within the synaptic knob are many small sacs, *synaptic vesicles,* that contain special chemicals called **neurotransmitters.** Among the most common of these are *acetylcholine* (uh seet uh KOH leen) and *norepinephrine* (NOR ep uh NEF rin). When an impulse reaches the synaptic knob, some of the neurotransmitters are released into the synaptic gap. The neurotransmitter diffuses across the synaptic gap and starts impulses in the neighboring nerve cell by changing the permeability of its membrane. To do this, the neurotransmitters react with special receptor proteins in the membrane of the dendrites.

Note that it is not the nerve impulse that crosses the synaptic gap. Instead, it is a chemical compound—the neurotransmitter— that is sent across the gap. Each impulse that reaches a synapse causes the release of a certain amount of neurotransmitter. When the impulses are arriving quickly (representing a stronger initial stimulus), more neurotransmitter is released into the synaptic gap. This greater amount of neurotransmitter acts as a stronger stimulus on the neighboring neuron, and the neuron then carries more impulses per second. In this way, information about the strength of the original stimulus is passed across the synapse and down the nerve pathway. As soon as the neurotransmitter has done its work, it must be removed from the synaptic gap to clear the way for new signals. This is usually done by enzymes present in the synaptic gap. These enzymes quickly break down the molecules of neurotransmitter after the neuron has responded to them.

Usually, neurotransmitters are released only by the ends of axons, and they exert their effects only at specialized receptor sites. This means that information usually travels in only one direction across synapses. This direction is from axons of one neuron to the dendrites or cell bodies of another. Thus, synapses control the direction in which information flows over nerve pathways.

Different types of neurons release different neurotransmitters. Some neurons release *excitatory neurotransmitters.* These chemicals start impulses in their neighboring neurons. Acetylcholine,

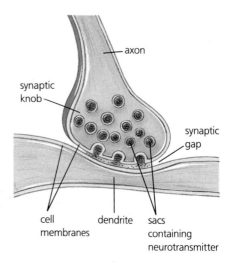

▲ **Figure 14–9**
Structure of the Synapse. When a nerve impulse reaches the synaptic knob, some neurotransmitters are released into the synaptic gap. The neurotransmitters diffuse across the synaptic gap and initiate nerve impulses in the neighboring neuron.

norepinephrine, and the amino acids histamine and glutamic acid are excitatory neurotransmitters. Still other neurons release neurotransmitters that block, or *inhibit,* the start of impulses in neighboring neurons. *Inhibitory neurotransmitters* include serotonin, epinephrine, and the amino acid glycine. Thus, while some synapses transmit impulses from one neuron to the next, other synapses block the transmission of impulses.

As you have learned, the axon of a single neuron may form 1000 or more synapses. These may include many synapses on the same neuron. The dendrites of one neuron may also have synaptic connections with 1000 or more other neurons. Thus, the dendrites of a single neuron receive impulses from many neurons. Some of these impulses may be excitatory, while others may be inhibitory. The cell body totals or averages these impulses. If the overall results are excitatory, impulses are sent down the axon to the next set of synapses. If the results are inhibitory, no impulses are sent. Thus, in a nerve pathway, stimulation of certain neurons results in the inhibition of certain other neurons. A great deal of the complex behavior of an organism results from the great number and variety of synaptic circuits that are formed when neurons are "switched" on and off.

Neuromuscular Junctions

Impulses pass from motor neurons to muscles at special points of contact called **neuromuscular** (noor oh MUS kyoo ler) **junctions.** See Figure 14–10. The axons of motor neurons end in structures called *motor end plates.* Like synaptic knobs, motor end plates contain neurotransmitters. When impulses reach the motor end plates, they cause the release of the chemical transmitter acetylcholine. The acetylcholine diffuses across the gap between the end of the axon and the membrane of the muscle cell. Then, it combines with receptor molecules on the muscle cell membrane. The acetylcholine increases the permeability of the muscle cell membrane to sodium, causing impulses to travel along the muscle cell membrane. These impulses cause the muscle cell to contract. As in the synapses between neurons, enzymes quickly destroy the acetylcholine at the neuromuscular junction.

Drugs and the Synapse

Many poisons and drugs affect the activity of chemical transmitters at synapses. Nerve gas, *curare* (kyoo RAH ree), *botulin* (BAHCH uh lin) *toxin* (a bacterial poison), and some insecticides are poisons that interfere with the functioning of acetylcholine at neuromuscular junctions. These poisons cause muscle paralysis. If the muscles of the respiratory system become paralyzed, death follows.

Drugs that affect the mind and the emotions or alter the activity of body systems also act on synapses. *Stimulants* are drugs that speed up the body's activity. Overuse can cause heart damage and other problems. Among the stimulants, *amphetamines* (am FET uh meenz), or "uppers," produce their effects by binding to certain receptors. This causes short-lived feelings of well-being and excitement, followed by depression. *Caffeine* (kah FEEN), which is found in coffee, tea, and some cola drinks, increases synaptic transmission. This can result in sleeplessness and nervousness.

Depressants are drugs that slow down body activities. *Barbiturates* (bar BICH uh ritz), or "downers," produce a depressant effect by blocking the formation of norepinephrine.

Some of the mind-altering or hallucinatory drugs, such as *LSD* ("acid") and *mescaline* (MES kuh lin), interfere with the effect of serotonin, an inhibitory transmitter.

14-2 **Section Review**

1. What name is given to a neuron that is not sending a nerve impulse?
2. What is the sodium-potassium pump?
3. What crosses the synapse when a nerve impulse is traveling over a pathway of nerve cells?
4. What are neuromuscular junctions?

Critical Thinking

5. What would happen if the enzymes that break down neurotransmitters were not present at a given synapse? *(Predicting)*

14-3 Adaptations for Nervous Regulation

Section Objectives:

- *Describe* the responses of protists to stimuli.
- *Compare* and *contrast* the nervous systems of the hydra, earthworm, and grasshopper.

Regulation in Protists

Although protists do not have true nervous systems, they are able to respond to certain stimuli in a coordinated way. Amebas have no specialized sense receptors, but they can tell the difference between food and nonfood and move away from such things as strong light and harmful chemicals. How these responses are brought about is not yet understood.

Some protists have specialized filaments that work in a manner similar to the neurons of more complex animals. In the paramecium, a system of interconnected fibers, found at the bases of the cilia, controls the cilia's beating. The paramecium can respond to

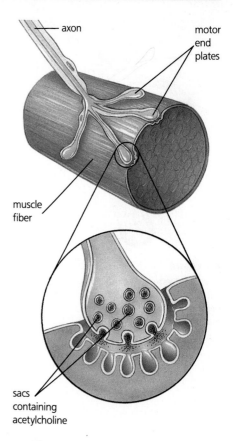

▲ **Figure 14–10**

Structure of the Neuromuscular Junction. When a nerve impulse reaches the motor end plates of a motor neuron, acetylcholine is released. The acetylcholine diffuses across the synaptic gap and initiates impulses that cause the muscle cell to contract.

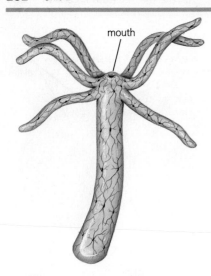

▲ **Figure 14–11**
Nervous System of the Hydra. The nerve net of the hydra allows the muscles of the organism to react to stimuli in a coordinated manner.

various stimuli. It can move toward food or away from strong acids and can change direction to stay away from solid matter in its path. Some protists have organelles that are sensitive to certain stimuli and initiate responses in the organism.

Regulation in Hydra

The nervous system of the hydra is in the form of a **nerve net.** See Figure 14–11. In this system, the nerve cells form an irregular network between the two layers of the body wall. This network connects special receptor cells in the body wall with muscle and gland cells. There is no organized center, such as a brain or nerve cord, to control and coordinate the nerve impulses. Instead, when a stimulus is received by any part of the body, impulses spread slowly from the stimulated area throughout the nerve net. Thus, all the muscle fibers in the organism respond, but the response shows coordination. For example, when a tentacle touches food, the impulses travel slowly through the entire organism. In response, the animal stretches toward the food, and the tentacles work together to capture the food and stuff it into the mouth.

Regulation in the Earthworm

The nervous system of the earthworm is more complex. It includes a **central nervous system** and a **peripheral nervous system.** See Figure 14–12. The central nervous system is made up of a "brain" connected to a pair of solid, ventral nerve cords. The nerve cords enlarge into *ganglia* (GANG lee uh) in each segment. A **ganglion** (GANG lee un) is a group of cell bodies and interneurons that switch, relay, and coordinate nerve impulses. The so-called "brain" is actually a pair of ganglia joined together.

The peripheral nervous system is made of the nerves branching from the central nervous system and passing to all parts of the

Figure 14–12
Nervous System of the Earthworm. The nervous system is made up of a brain and two ventral nerve cords. Sensory and motor nerves branch from the nerve cords. ▼

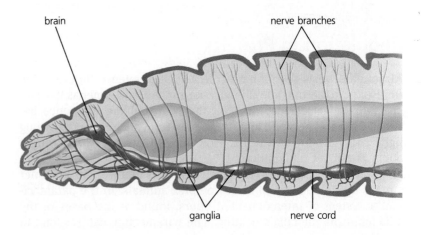

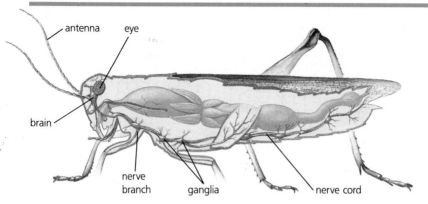

Nervous System of the Grasshopper. The nervous system of the grasshopper includes a brain, a pair of ventral nerve cords, and branching nerves. In addition, the grasshopper has well-developed sense organs.

body. These nerves contain sensory neurons and motor neurons. The sensory neurons carry impulses from receptors in the skin to the nerve cords. The motor neurons carry impulses from the nerve cords to muscles and glands (effectors). The specialized receptors in the skin are sensitive to light, vibrations, chemicals, and heat.

In the earthworm, the nerves of the peripheral nervous system connect receptors and effectors to the central nervous system. Impulses travel over definite pathways in only one direction. The nervous systems of more complex animals are similar to the nervous system of the earthworm.

Regulation of the Grasshopper

The nervous system of the grasshopper is similar to that of the earthworm. See Figure 14–13. It is made up of a brain in the head region; a pair of solid, ventral nerve cords that run the length of the body; and ganglia. Nerves branch from the ganglia to all parts of the body. The sense organs of the grasshopper are more highly developed than those of the earthworm. The grasshopper has eyes, *antennae* (an TEN ee), or "feelers," and taste organs that respond to a variety of stimuli. Grasshoppers are also sensitive to sound. Because the grasshopper has a more highly developed nervous system than the earthworm, it is able to behave in more complex ways.

14-3 **Section Review**

1. Name the types of stimuli to which some protists respond.
2. What type of nervous system does the hydra have?
3. Name the two parts of the nervous system of the earthworm.
4. What specialized sense organs does the grasshopper possess?

Critical Thinking

5. Based on their capacity for nervous regulation, place each of the following organisms in order from most complex to least complex: ameba, earthworm, grasshopper, human, hydra, and paramecium. *(Ordering)*

Laboratory
Investigation

Designing an Experiment

Investigating the Instinctive Behaviors of Planarians

Many animals rely on simple instincts called taxes (singular: taxis). A taxis is a movement either toward or away from a stimulus, such as light, gravity, or chemical changes in the environment. In this investigation, you will explore the taxes of a planarian, a type of free-living flatworm found in ponds and streams.

Problem

How can you determine the taxes of a planarian? **Design an experiment** to answer the question.

Suggested Materials

- glass-marking pencil
- test tube, with cork or stopper
- planarian
- pond water
- test-tube rack
- Petri dish
- forceps
- small piece of liver
- index card
- dilute acetic acid
- salt

Suggested Procedure

1. Using the glass-marking pencil, draw a circle around the test tube at its midpoint. The circle divides the test tube into top and bottom halves.

2. Obtain a planarian from your teacher. Gently transfer the planarian to the test tube. **CAUTION:** *Be careful when handling live animals.* Add pond water as necessary to fill the test tube. Seal the test tube with the stopper or cork.

3. Gently move the test tube back and forth until the planarian is in the center of the test tube.

4. Place the test tube in a test-tube rack. For 3 minutes, measure the amount of time the planarian spends in the top half of the test tube and the amount of time it spends in the bottom half of the test tube.

5. Turn the test tube upside down, then repeat steps 3 and 4.

6. Carefully transfer the planarian and pond water to a Petri dish. Add more pond water, if necessary, to cover the bottom of the dish. Using forceps, place a piece of liver in the Petri dish. Observe the planarian's response.

7. Design an experiment to determine whether the planarian has a taxis for any one of the following stimuli:
   • light
   • change in pH
   • change in salinity
   Make sure your experiment does not harm the planarian in any way. Your experiment should include a control group.

8. With your teacher's permission, perform the experiment you designed.

Observations

1. Compare the time the planarian spent in the top half of the test tube with the time it spent in the bottom half of the test tube.

2. Describe the planarian's response to liver.

3. Describe the planarian's response to the stimulus you tested in your experiment.

Analysis and Conclusions

1. What is a taxis? Why are taxes important to animals with a limited nervous system?

2. Do planarians have a taxis for gravity? Explain your answer.

3. Why was it necessary to turn the test tube upside down in step 5?

4. Can planarians detect food in nearby water, then move toward the food? Or do they encounter food only by chance? Explain your answer.

5. Do planarians have a taxis for the stimulus you tested in your experiment? Use the data you generated to justify your answer.

6. Explain how a planarian's taxes help it to survive in its environment.

Extensions

Try to train a planarian to navigate through a simple maze.

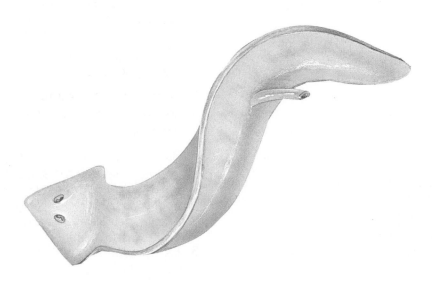

Chapter **14** Review ....

Study Outline

14-1 The Regulatory Process

▶ The nervous system and the endocrine system regulate and coordinate responses to external and internal change.

▶ Neurons are cells specialized for the rapid conduction of impulses. A neuron is usually made up of dendrites, a cell body, and an axon.

▶ Impulses usually travel along the neuron from dendrites to cell body to axon. Impulses are carried across synapses to neighboring cells by chemicals called neurotransmitters.

14-2 The Nerve Impulse

▶ In a resting neuron, the outside of the cell membrane is electrically positive, and the inside is negative. The membrane is polarized because of an unequal distribution of sodium and potassium ions inside and outside the membrane.

▶ When a neuron is stimulated, cell membrane permeability changes at the point of stimulation, reversing its polarity. This change alters the permeability of an adjacent area of the membrane and reverses its polarity. In this way, an impulse is transmitted along the length of the neuron.

▶ The rate at which an impulse travels depends on the size of the nerve fiber and on the presence or absence of a myelin covering.

▶ An impulse is an "all or nothing" response. Any stimulus above a minimum strength, or threshold, will start an impulse in the neuron. Any stimulus below the threshold will not start an impulse.

▶ When impulses reach the end of the axon, neurotransmitters are released into the synaptic gap. These chemical compounds stimulate or inhibit the firing of impulses in the neighboring neuron.

▶ At neuromuscular junctions, the motor end plates of axons release the chemical transmitter acetylcholine, which stimulates the contraction of neighboring muscles fibers.

▶ Drugs, such as stimulants, depressants, LSD, and mescaline, act on synapses and alter body activity.

14-3 Adaptations for Nervous Regulation

▶ Protists do not have true nervous systems, but they can respond to stimuli. In the hydra, a nerve net transmits impulses throughout the organism, producing coordinated responses.

▶ The earthworm has a primitive "brain" and two ventral nerve cords that enlarge into ganglia in each segment. Sensory and motor nerves branch from the "brain" and nerve cords.

▶ The nervous system of the grasshopper is similar to that of the earthworm, but the sense organs are more highly developed in the grasshopper. The grasshopper has eyes, antennae, and taste organs, and is sensitive to sound.

Chapter Assessment

Multiple Choice

Choose the letter of the answer that best completes each statement or answers the question.

1. A change in the external or internal environment of an organism is called a(n) (a) response. (b) synapse. (c) impulse. (d) stimulus.

2. Neurons that carry impulses from the brain and spinal cord to effectors are the (a) interneurons. (b) sensory neurons. (c) nerves. (d) motor neurons.

3. Impulses pass from motor neurons to muscles at special points of contact called (a) synapses. (b) neuromuscular junctions. (c) thresholds. (d) interneurons.

4. All but the simplest animals have a (a) brain. (b) nerve net. (c) cell body. (d) sodium-potassium pump.

5. Each nerve cell has a minimum level of sensitivity or (a) stimulus. (b) threshold. (c) irritability. (d) refractory period.

6. Many vertebrate axons are surrounded by (a) nerves. (b) motor neurons. (c) dendrites. (d) Schwann cells.

7. Throughout the organism, a network of nerve cells carries (a) sensory neurons. (b) effectors. (c) impulses. (d) receptors.

8. The long, thin fiber that extends from the cell body of a neuron is the (a) ganglion. (b) myelin. (c) axon. (d) synapse.

9. The regulatory system of a hydra can be described as a (a) nerve net. (b) fused ganglion. (c) central nervous system. (d) system similar to control in protists.

10. The nervous system of the grasshopper differs from that of the earthworm in that the grasshopper has (a) ventral nerve cords. (b) a brain. (c) ganglia. (d) highly developed sense organs.

Content Review

Answer each of the following in complete sentences.

11. Draw a labeled diagram of a neuron. Then, compare the structure and function of the three basic parts of the neuron.

12. What are the functions of the three types of neurons?

13. How is the difference in electrical charge across the nerve cell membrane maintained?

14. What changes in ion distribution occur in the area of an impulse?

15. Why do myelinated fiber carry impulses faster than those without a myelin covering?

16. Explain the following statement, "A neuron fires on an all-or-nothing basis."

17. How do impulses pass from a motor neuron to a muscle cell?

18. How does the hydra respond when a part of its body receives a stimulus? Describe the structures of the central and peripheral nervous systems of the earthworm.

19. How do the nervous systems of the grasshopper and the earthworm differ? How are they alike?

20. Explain how a nerve impulse crosses a synapse.

Graphic Organizing

For information on graphic organizers, see Appendix G at the back of this text.

21. **Flow Chart** Construct a flow chart that shows the path of a nerve impulse from a stimulated sensory organ to a responding muscle.

Critical Thinking and Problem Solving

Discuss each of the following in a brief paragraph.

22. **Inferring** Suggest some possible causes for a person's inability to move his or her muscles.

23. **Predicting** Imagine that the nerve fibers from pain receptors in your thumb could be exchanged with those in your index finger. If you were to prick your thumb with a needle, where would you feel the pain?

24. **Drawing conclusions** How do you think a painkiller works to stop the sensation of pain?

25. **Inferring** A rare genetic disease in which babies are born with no pain receptors results in their feeling no pain. How would this affect the babies as they grow up? How might it affect the way their parents care for them?

26. **Calculating** In a myelinated nerve fiber, the nerve impulse travels at about 100 meters per second, and in an unmyelinated fiber, at about 2 meters per second. How long would it take for an impulse to travel: (a) 88 centimeters through a myelinated fiber running from the spinal cord to the tip of the toe? (b) 45 centimeters through an unmyelinated fiber running from the base of the brain to the end of the spinal cord?

27. **Experimenting** Design a controlled experiment on how paramecia, hydras, or earthworms respond to stimuli such as light and dark acidic and basic substances, or warmth and cold. Get your teacher's permission before carrying out the experiment.

Discovery
Learning Activity

Vision and Balance

1. Working with a partner, stand on one foot and keep your balance as long as you can for up to 3 minutes. Have your partner record the time.

2. Repeat step 1 with your eyes closed.

3. Switch places with your partner and repeat steps 1 and 2.

4. Compare how long you and your partner kept your balance with your eyes open and with them closed. Compare your results with the rest of the class. What can you conclude about the sense of vision and balance from the class data?

The Human Nervous System

Chapter 15

Previewing the Chapter

Every instant, nerves flash information to your brain. The brain orders subtle adjustments in your muscles. Thoughts and ideas come and go. How does the structure of the human brain make all these activities possible? How does the elaborate system of senses and nerves connect your brain to the rest of your body and to the outside world?

Key Words

autonomic nervous system, cerebellum, cerebrum, medulla oblongata, reflex, somatic nervous system, spinal cord

Key Concepts

- **Compare** the human nervous system with those of other vertebrates.
- **Distinguish** between the somatic and autonomic nervous systems.
- **Identify** the parts of a sheep brain. (Laboratory Investigation)

15-1 The Central Nervous System

Section Objectives:

- *Describe* the functions of the skull, spinal column, meninges, and cerebrospinal fluid.
- *Name* the major parts of the brain.
- *Explain* how momentary memory, short-term memory, and long-term memory differ from one another.

The Role of the Central Nervous System

The human nervous system, similar to the nervous systems of other vertebrates, can be divided into two subsystems. One of these subsystems is the *central nervous system*. The central nervous system is made up of the brain and the spinal cord. The other subsystem is called the *peripheral nervous system*. This system is made up of the vast network of nerves that conducts impulses between the central nervous system and the receptors and effectors of the body.

The central nervous system—the brain and the spinal cord—controls most of the activities of the body. Impulses from sense receptors throughout the body bring a constant flow of information about conditions inside and outside the body. The information is

▲ **Figure Figure 15–1**
Body Control. The nervous system enables fine coordination of body movements, as shown with these ballet dancers.

◄ Terminal branches of a neuron (colored purple) making contact with other cells (colored yellow). (Magnification: 20 000 X)

Figure 15–2

The Brain and the Spinal Column. The spinal cord is protected by the vertebrae of the spinal column (below), and the brain (right) is protected by the cranium. Added protection is provided by the meninges and by the cerebrospinal fluid, which cushions the tissues against shock. ▼

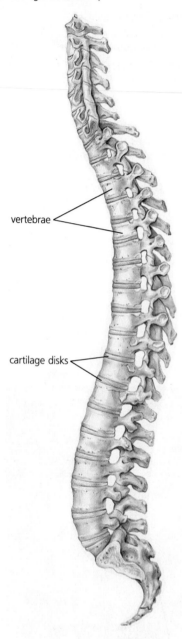

vertebrae

cartilage disks

interpreted, or responded to, by the brain or the spinal cord. Then, impulses that cause appropriate responses are sent out to muscles and glands.

The Skull and Spinal Column

The brain and the spinal cord are protected by bone. See Figure 15–2. The brain is enclosed by the cranium, which is the upper part of the skull. The spinal cord is surrounded by the vertebrae of the spinal column, or backbone. Disks of cartilage between the vertebrae absorb the shocks of running, walking, or jumping. The brain and the spinal cord are also covered and protected by three tough membranes known as the *meninges* (muh NIN jeez). A liquid, the *cerebrospinal* (suh ree broh SPYN ul) *fluid,* fills the space between the inner and middle membranes. This fluid cushions the delicate nervous tissues against shock. A *concussion* occurs when the brain is severely shaken, causing it to bump against the cranium. Inside the brain, four spaces, called *ventricles,* are filled with the cerebrospinal fluid. The ventricles connect with the fluid-filled space between the meninges and with the central canal of the spinal cord, which is also filled with cerebrospinal fluid.

The Brain

The brain is one of the most active organs in the human body. It receives 20 percent of the blood that is pumped from the heart, and it replaces most of its protein every three weeks. The brain is the major user of glucose in the body. Unlike the cells of other tissues, the cells of the brain usually metabolize only glucose for the release of energy.

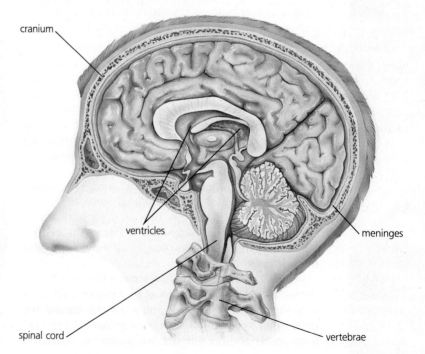

cranium

ventricles

meninges

spinal cord

vertebrae

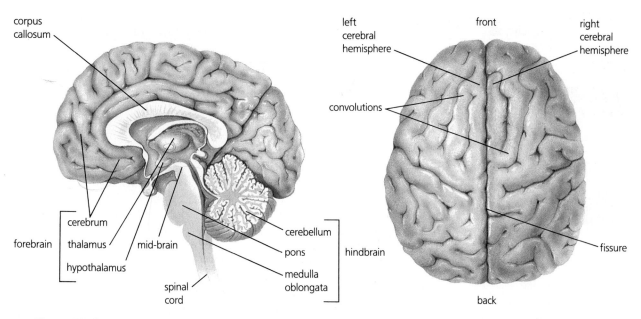

▲ **Figure 15–3**

Structure of the Brain. The major regions of the brain can be seen in the lengthwise section of the brain (left). A top view of the brain (right) shows the division of the cerebrum into two hemispheres.

The major parts of the brain are the *cerebrum* (suh REE brum), *cerebellum* (sehr uh BEL um), and the *medulla oblongata* (muh DUHL uh ahb lon GHAT uh). See Figure 15–3. Other parts of the brain are the thalamus, hypothalamus, and pons. The **thalamus** serves as a relay center between various parts of the brain and the spinal cord. It also receives and changes all sensory impulses, except those involved in smell, before they travel to the cerebral cortex. It may also be involved in feeling pain and keeping a person conscious. The **hypothalamus** helps control body temperature, blood pressure, sleep, and emotions. It also plays a role in the functioning of the endocrine system. See Chapter 16. The **pons** serves as a relay system, linking the spinal cord, medulla oblongata, cerebellum, and cerebrum. The pons, the medulla oblongata, and the midbrain are often called the **brainstem.**

The cerebrum, thalamus, and the hypothalamus make up the *forebrain.* The small *midbrain* connects the forebrain with the hindbrain and is a center for some visual and reflex functions. The *hindbrain* is another name for the brainstem, the cerebellum, the pons, and the medulla oblongata.

The Cerebrum   The **cerebrum** is the largest part of the human brain. It makes up about two-thirds of the entire organ. The greatest difference between the human brain and the brains of other vertebrates is the larger size and greater development of the human cerebrum. The cerebrum is divided in half from front to back by a deep groove, or fissure. This groove separates the cerebrum into the right and left **cerebral hemispheres.** See Figure 15–3. Nerve fibers from each hemisphere pass to the other hemisphere and to

Science, Technology and Society

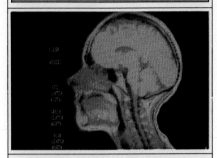

Technology: Magnetic Resonance Imaging

A new tool called Magnetic Resonance Imaging (MRI) allows doctors to "see" inside their patients. It does this by displaying the inside of the body on a computer screen (see photo).

When MRI is used, a patient is placed in the hollow cylinder of a giant electromagnet. The strong magnetic field acts upon the hydrogen atoms in the body, causing them to enter a high energy state. In this state, the atoms are unstable. As the atoms return to a lower energy state, they emit radio waves.

The intensity of the radio waves is in proportion to the concentration of hydrogen atoms present in the area scanned. This concentration differs in different organs and in tumors. A computer maps the intensity differences that correspond to the various organs and to any abnormalities.

MRI enables doctors to "see" vital organs, identify tumors, and spot early signs of disease. Although MRI scans are expensive, they often eliminate the need for exploratory surgery and harmful X rays.

■ *List some potential benefits and drawbacks of MRI.*

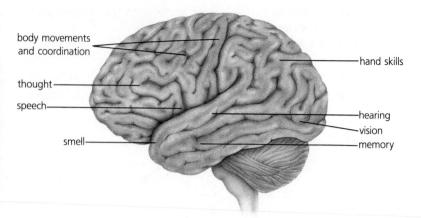

▲ **Figure 15–4**
Motor and Sensory Regions of the Cerebral Cortex.

other parts of the nervous system. These nerve fibers make a bridgelike connection between hemispheres that is called the **corpus callosum** (KOR puhs kuh LOH suhm).

The outermost layer of the cerebrum is the **cerebral cortex,** or *gray matter.* The gray matter is made up of the cell bodies of motor neurons and a huge number of interneurons. These are interconnected by unmyelinated fibers. The outer surface of the cortex has many folds. These folds, or *convolutions* (kahn vuh LOO shunz), greatly increase the surface area of the gray matter.

The cerebral cortex has three major functions—sensory, motor, and associative. Each part of the cortex carries out a particular function. Some functions, however, may be carried out in two or more areas of the cortex as well as in other parts of the brain. Some functions of the various parts are shown in Figure 15–4.

The sensory areas of the cortex receive and interpret impulses from the sense receptors. These receptors include the eyes, ears, taste buds, and nose, as well as the touch, pain, pressure, heat, and cold receptors in the skin and other organs. The motor areas of the cortex start impulses that are responsible for all voluntary movement and for the position of the movable parts of the body. Impulses from the motor cortex may be slightly changed by other parts of the brain. The associative areas of the brain are responsible for memory, learning, and thought.

The two cerebral hemispheres do not usually function in exactly the same way. Instead, some functions are carried out by the left hemisphere and others by the right hemisphere. For example, in many people, the left hemisphere is the center for mathematical thinking. The right hemisphere is often the center for artistic and musical ability.

Beneath the gray matter of the cerebrum is an inner area called the *white matter.* This area is made up of myelinated nerve fibers. One of the bundles, or tracts, of fibers in the white matter is the *corpus callosum.* This connects the right and left hemispheres, so that information can pass between the two halves of the cerebrum.

Other tracts from the white matter connect the cortex to other parts of the nervous system.

Nerve fibers leaving the cerebral hemispheres pass through the brain and spinal cord. At some point along their pathway, these fibers cross over to the opposite side of the brain or spinal cord before going to various parts of the body. Thus, the left cerebral hemisphere controls the right side of the body, and the right hemisphere controls the left side. For this reason, an injury to one side of the cerebrum will affect the other side of the body.

The Cerebellum   The **cerebellum** is found below the rear part of the cerebrum. See Figure 15–5. The cerebellum, like the cerebral cortex, is divided into two hemispheres. It also has gray matter and white matter. The highly folded outer layer of the cerebellum consists of gray matter, while the inner portion is white matter.

The cerebellum controls all voluntary movements and some involuntary movements. Motor impulses from the cerebral cortex are carried by nerve pathways that send some branches directly to the muscles involved and other branches to the cerebellum. The muscles also send impulses over sensory nerve pathways to the cerebellum. These impulses provide information about the muscles' position, rate of contraction, and so on. The cerebellum then sends impulses to the cerebral cortex to correct and coordinate the movement of the muscles. Thus, the cerebral cortex and the cerebellum work together to produce smooth, orderly voluntary movement. With certain involuntary movements, the cerebellum works in the same manner with other parts of the brain. For example, the cerebellum, using information from receptors in the inner ear, maintains balance, or *equilibrium*. It also plays a role in the maintenance of *muscle tone* (keeping the muscles slightly tensed). Damage to the cerebellum results in jerky movements, tremor, or loss of equilibrium. Staggering and other signs of loss of coordination—seen when someone has had too much to drink—are caused by a temporary loss of cerebellar function.

The Medulla Oblongata   As you saw in Figure 15–5, beneath the cerebellum and connected to the spinal cord is the **medulla oblongata.** In this lowest part of the brain, the white matter makes up the outer layer, while the gray matter is the inner layer. The medulla oblongata is made mainly of nerve fibers that connect the spinal cord to other parts of the brain. Nerve centers in the medulla oblongata control many involuntary activities. These include breathing, heartbeat, blood flow, and coughing.

Memory

Most learning depends on being able to store and recall memories of past experiences. Memory is thought to be a function of the cerebral cortex. Although there are several theories about how memory is stored, little is really known about the process. However, scientists now believe that there are three kinds of memory—momentary, short-term, and long-term memory.

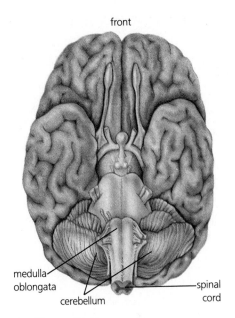

front

medulla oblongata

cerebellum

spinal cord

▲   **Figure 15–5**

The Underside of the Brain. The cerebellum coordinates and controls voluntary movements and some involuntary movements. The medulla controls many involuntary activities, such as breathing, heart beat, and blood flow.

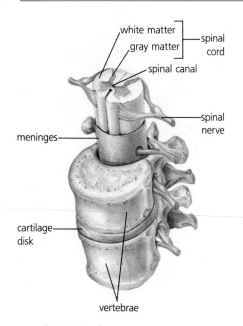

white matter
gray matter
spinal cord
spinal canal
spinal nerve
meninges
cartilage disk
vertebrae

▲ **Figure 15–6**

Structure of the Spinal Cord. Note that the spinal cord is completely surrounded by the bone tissue of the vertebrae. Cartilage disks between most of the vertebrae serve as shock absorbers.

Momentary memory lasts for a few minutes at most. Remembering a phone number only long enough to dial it is an example of momentary memory. *Short-term memory* can be recalled for as long as several hours. Memory lasting weeks or years is *long-term memory.* By some process not yet known, a short-term memory is sometimes changed into a long-term memory. A person can lose momentary and short-term memories and still keep long-term memory. This is sometimes found in older people, who may be unable to remember something that just happened but can recall in detail things that took place many years earlier.

At present no one knows how memories are stored, transferred, or recalled in the human brain. There is some evidence that short-term memory is associated with patterns of impulses circulating repeatedly through particular pathways of neurons. Long-term memory may be the result of permanent changes in particular synapses, or changes within certain neurons.

The Spinal Cord

The **spinal cord,** which is about 45 centimeters long, goes from the base of the brain down through the vertebrae of the spinal column. A cross section of the spinal cord shows an inner H-shaped region of gray matter surrounded by an outer layer of white matter. See Figure 15–6. The gray matter contains many interneurons, as well as the cell bodies of motor neurons. The white matter contains myelinated fibers that carry impulses between all parts of the body and the spinal cord and brain. In the center of the cord is the *spinal canal,* which is filled with cerebrospinal fluid.

The spinal cord is important for two reasons. First, it connects the nerves of the peripheral nervous system with the brain. Impulses reaching the spinal cord from sensory neurons travel up the cord through interneurons to the brain. Impulses from the brain are sent down the spinal cord by interneurons to motor neurons. These impulses travel through peripheral nerves to muscles and glands. Second, the spinal cord controls certain reflexes, which are automatic responses. See page 296.

15-1 **Section Review**

1. What are the two main subdivisions of the human nervous system?
2. List the three major parts of the brain.
3. Identify the three kinds of memory.
4. Give two functions of the spinal cord.

Critical Thinking

5. If someone had an injury that damaged the cerebellum, how would that affect the person's ability to drive a car? *(Relating Parts and Wholes)*

15-2 The Peripheral Nervous System

Section Objectives:

- *Identify* the nerves that make up the peripheral nervous system.
- *Compare* and *contrast* the structures and functions of the somatic and autonomic nervous systems.
- *Name* the two divisions of the autonomic nervous system and state their functions.
- *Distinguish* between a reflex and a voluntary behavior.

Structure of the Peripheral Nervous System

The peripheral nervous system is made up of all the neurons and nerve fibers outside the brain and spinal cord. The neurons of the peripheral nervous system are connected to either the brain or the spinal cord. The neurons are in bundles that form nerves. The nerves connected to the spinal cord are called the **spinal nerves,** while those connected to the brain are called the **cranial** (KRAY nee ul) **nerves.**

There are 31 pairs of spinal nerves. Each pair serves a particular part of the body. Each nerve contains both sensory and motor fibers. See Figure 15–7. The cell bodies of the sensory neurons are found in ganglia outside the spinal cord. The cell bodies of the motor neurons and all of the interneurons are found in the gray matter of the spinal cord. As a spinal nerve gets close to the spinal cord, the sensory and motor fibers separate. The sensory fibers enter the *dorsal root* (toward the back) of the spinal cord, while the motor fibers leave through the *ventral root* (toward the front) of the cord.

There are 12 pairs of cranial nerves. Those serving the eyes, ears, and nose are made up mostly of sensory fibers. The other cranial nerves contain more equal numbers of sensory and motor fibers. Most of the cranial nerves serve the sense organs and other structures of the head.

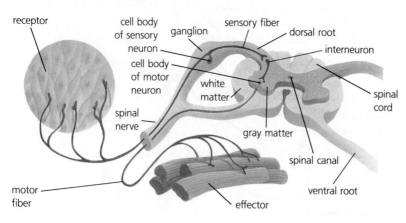

receptor
cell body of sensory neuron
ganglion
sensory fiber
dorsal root
interneuron
cell body of motor neuron
white matter
spinal cord
spinal nerve
gray matter
spinal canal
ventral root
motor fiber
effector

◀ **Figure 15–7**
Structure of a Spinal Nerve. A spinal nerve contains both motor and sensory fibers. Sensory fibers transmit impulses into the dorsal root of the spinal cord, and motor fibers transmit impulses from the ventral root to effectors. Note that the cell bodies of sensory neurons are outside the spinal cord.

The peripheral nervous system is divided into two parts. One part, called the *somatic* (soh MAT ik) *nervous system,* is under voluntary control. The other part, the *autonomic* (awt uh NAHM ik) *nervous system,* usually is not under voluntary control.

The Somatic Nervous System The **somatic nervous system** contains both sensory and motor neurons that connect the central nervous system to skeletal muscles, the skin, and the sense organs. This system is responsible for body movements over which the individual has some conscious awareness or voluntary control.

The Autonomic Nervous System The **autonomic nervous system** is made up of certain motor fibers from the brain and spinal cord that serve the internal organs of the body. Usually, there is no voluntary control over the activities of the autonomic system, which is made up of two divisions, the **parasympathetic** (par uh sim puh THET ik) **nervous system** and the **sympathetic nervous system.** See Figure 15–8. The entire system controls many important functions of the body. These include the rate of heartbeat, blood flow through arteries, breathing movements, movements of the digestive system, and secretions of certain glands.

The autonomic system is made entirely of motor neurons. The same sensory nerves that serve the somatic system provide sensory information for this system. Impulses in the autonomic system

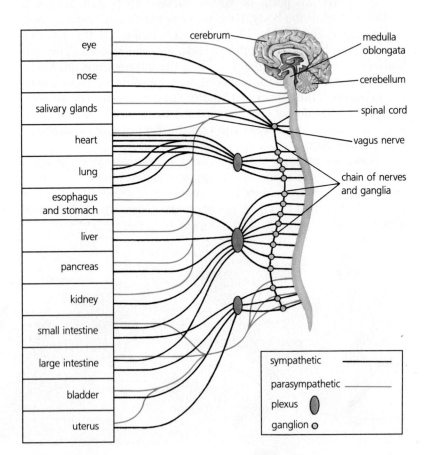

Figure 15–8
Nerve Pathways to the Sympathetic and Parasympathetic Nervous Systems. ▶

start in motor neurons in the brain or spinal cord. However, the axons of these neurons do not go to the organ involved. Instead, each axon synapses with a second motor neuron, which then carries the impulses to the muscle or gland. Some of the cell bodies of these second motor neurons are found in ganglia just outside the brain and spinal cord. The ganglia, which are interconnected by nerves, form two chains alongside the spinal column. Other ganglia are found elsewhere in the body. Some of them form large clusters called *plexuses* (PLEKS us sez).

Organs served by the autonomic nervous system generally contain nerve endings from both the sympathetic and parasympathetic divisions. The effects of these two types of nerve endings are antagonistic, or opposite, because they release different neurotransmitters in the organs. Nerves of the sympathetic system release *norepinephrine,* while those of the parasympathetic system release *acetylcholine.* When the sympathetic system speeds up an activity, the parasympathetic system slows down the same activity. For example, the beating of the heart is speeded up by the accelerator nerves of the sympathetic system and slowed down by the vagus nerves of the parasympathetic system. The antagonistic relationship that exists between the two divisions of the autonomic nervous system helps to control the organs and to maintain the homeostatic balance of the body.

Figure 15–9 lists the actions of the parasympathetic and sympathetic systems on various structures. Generally, the sympathetic system helps the body deal with emergency situations. In many cases, it does so by accelerating body activities. The parasympathetic system promotes normal, relaxed body functioning.

Reflexes

A **reflex** is an involuntary, automatic response to a given stimulus. It makes use of a relatively simple pathway between a receptor, the spinal cord or brain, and an effector. Many normal body functions

Figure 15–9
Functions of the Autonomic Nervous System. ▼

Effects of the Autonomic Nervous System		
Organ	**Sympathetic Division**	**Parasympathetic Division**
heart	speeds up and strengthens beat (stimulates)	slows and weakens beat (inhibits)
digestive tract	slows peristalsis, slows activity (inhibits)	speeds peristalsis increases activity (stimulates)
blood vessels	mostly constricts	mostly dilates
bladder	relaxes	constricts
bronchi	widens passages	constricts passages
eye	makes pupil larger	makes pupil smaller

are controlled by reflexes. These include blinking, sneezing, coughing, breathing movements, heartbeat, and peristalsis. The knee-jerk reflex and the reflex that changes the size of the pupil of the eye in response to light are used by doctors to check the condition of the nervous system. When there is no reflex response or when the response is slow, a disorder of the nervous system may be present.

Reflex Arcs   The pathway over which the nerve impulses travel in a reflex is called a **reflex arc.** The simplest reflex arcs use only two neurons—one sensory and one motor. The pathway of the knee-jerk reflex is of this type. Most reflexes, however, use three or more neurons. Withdrawal reflexes, for example, use a three-neuron reflex arc. See Figure 15–10. As Figure 15–10 shows, pulling your hand back from a hot object is an example of a withdrawal reflex involving three neurons: a sensory neuron, an interneuron, and a motor neuron.

When your hand touches a hot stove, it is pulled back before you feel the sensation of heat or pain. Removing your hand is brought about by a withdrawal reflex. The parts of this reflex arc are as follow.

1. A receptor in the skin is stimulated by the heat.

2. The receptor starts impulses in a sensory neuron, which carries impulses to the spinal cord.

3. Within the spinal cord, the sensory neuron synapses with an interneuron, which synapses with a motor neuron.

4. The motor neuron sends impulses to the effector. In this example, impulses are carried to certain muscles of the arm.

5. The muscles receiving impulses from the motor neuron contract, moving the hand and arm.

The withdrawal reflex takes place without the use of the brain. However, shortly after the hand is withdrawn from the hot object, there may be sensations of heat and pain. These result from impulses that pass up the spinal cord to the brain.

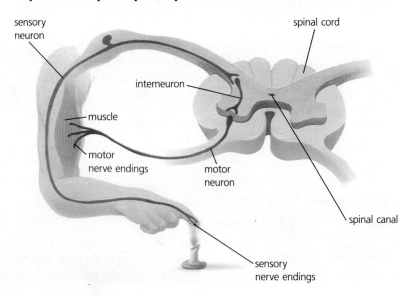

Figure 15–10

A Reflex Arc. The withdrawal reflex involves a sensory neuron, an interneuron, and a motor neuron. ▶

Voluntary Behavior

Unlike reflexes, voluntary behavior is under conscious control. It includes all the physical and mental activities that a person chooses to do, such as writing a story, running a race, or cooking. All voluntary behavior is controlled by the cerebrum and makes use of a combination of memory of past experiences, associations, reasoning, and judgments. This most complex type of behavior is more developed in humans than in other animals.

15-2 **Section Review**

1. What are the names of the nerves of the peripheral nervous system that are connected to the spinal cord and to the brain?
2. Name the two divisions of the peripheral nervous system.
3. Name the two divisions of the autonomic nervous system.
4. Give an example of a reflex and a voluntary behavior.

Critical Thinking

5. Compare and contrast the somatic and autonomic nervous systems. *(Comparing and Contrasting)*

15-3 Sense Receptors

Section Objectives:

- *Name* the parts of the eye and explain how vision works.
- *Indicate* the parts of the ear and explain how the ear functions in hearing and balance.
- *Identify* the sense receptors of the skin.
- *Describe* the structures and functions of taste buds and olfactory cells.

In animals, sense receptors provide information about what is taking place both inside and outside the body. The receptors of the human nervous system range from those in the skin, which are relatively simple structures, to the eye and ear, which are very complex organs.

The Eye

Sight is the most important sense in humans. It gives us more than 80 percent of the information we receive about the outside world.

Structure of the Eye The walls of the human eye are made of three layers. The tough outer layer of the eye is the **sclera** (SKLEHR uh), or the "white" of the eye. It helps to give the eye shape and

Figure 15–11
Structure of the Human Eye. ▶

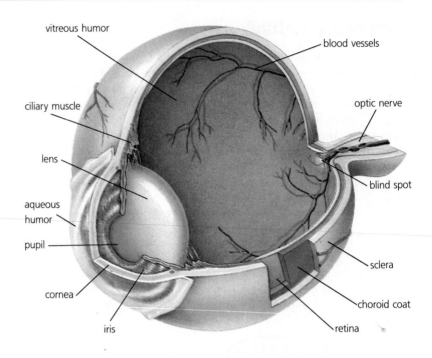

protects the inner parts of the eye. In the front of the eye, the outer layer bulges and becomes the transparent **cornea** (KOR nee uh). See Figure 15–11. Light enters the eye through the cornea.

Just inside the sclera is a dark-brown middle layer, the **choroid** (KOR oyd) **coat.** This layer, which contains many blood vessels, stops the reflection of light within the eye. At the front of the eye, the choroid layer forms the **iris** (I ris), which is the colored part of the eye. In the center of the iris is an opening called the **pupil.** The iris works like the diaphragm of a camera. It has muscles that can make the size of the pupil larger or smaller. In dim light, the pupil becomes larger, or dilates, which allows more light to enter the eye. In bright light, the pupil becomes smaller, or constricts, which lets less light into the eye. The size of the pupil is controlled by the autonomic nervous system.

Behind the iris is the **lens.** The lens focuses the light on the back of the innermost layer, the **retina** (RET in uh), producing an image similar to the image on the film in a camera. *Ciliary* (SIL ee ehr ee) *muscles* attached to the choroid layer hold the lens in place. These muscles also change the shape of the lens. This allows the eye to focus on objects.

The retina contains light receptors. At the rear of the eye, the retina is attached to the **optic** (OP tik) **nerve.** This nerve carries impulses from the light-sensitive cells to the brain.

The eyeball is a hollow sphere that is divided into two cavities. The cavity between the cornea and the lens is filled with a transparent watery fluid called the *aqueous* (AHK wee us) *humor.* The large cavity behind the lens is filled with a colorless, jellylike liquid called the *vitreous* (VIH tree us) *humor.* The vitreous humor gives the eye a firm shape.

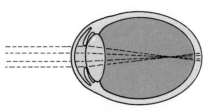

Nearsightedness

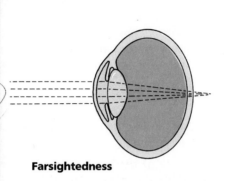

Farsightedness

◀ **Figure 15–12**

Nearsightedness and Farsightedness. In nearsightedness (top), the eyeball is too long. Light rays are brought into focus in front of the retina, causing a person to see near objects clearly and distant objects out of focus. In farsightedness (bottom), the eyeball is too short. Light rays are focused behind the retina, causing a person to see distant objects clearly and near objects out of focus.

Vision   Light entering the eye passes through the cornea, aqueous humor, pupil, lens, and vitreous humor, and forms an image on the retina. People who are **nearsighted** can see objects near to them more clearly than objects far from them. This happens because they have a long-shaped eye. Light rays from far away form an image that is blurred. See Figure 15–12. In **farsighted** people, the eyeball is too short. This causes the lens to focus light from nearby objects at a point beyond the retina. This results in a blurred image of close objects. Both conditions are easily corrected by prescribed eyeglasses or contact lenses.

The retina is made up of several different layers of cells. One inner layer contains light-sensitive cells—the **rods** and the **cones.** See Figure 15–13. Rods are sensitive to weak light but not to color. They allow a person to see in dim light, which is black-and-white vision. Cones are sensitive to color but must have bright light to function. There are three types of cones in the retina. One type is sensitive to red light, one to green light, and one to blue light. The retina contains about 125 million rods and 6.5 million cones.

Both black-and-white and color vision make use of the light-sensitive pigment *retinal* (RET in al), which is made from vitamin A. Retinal combines with proteins within the rods and cones. The

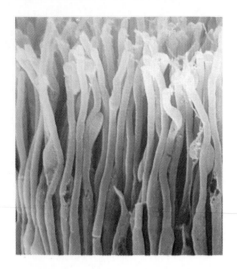

▲ **Figure 15–13**

Rods and Cones. One of the inner layers of the retina is made up of rods and cones, seen in this scanning electron micrograph.

proteins in the rods and in the three types of cones are all different, and each binds with retinal differently. It is the effect of each type of protein on the retinal that allows this pigment to respond to different colors and intensities of light.

When light strikes a rod or cone, it breaks the chemical bond between the retinal and the protein with which it was combined. This starts impulses traveling from that rod or cone. Nerve fibers from the rods and cones join to form the optic nerve, which carries the impulses to the brain. The brain interprets them as vision. The point where the optic nerve leaves the eye contains no rods or cones and is called the *blind spot.*

Too little vitamin A leads to a condition called *night blindness.* Night-blind people have trouble seeing in dim light. In this condition, the amount of retinal in both the rods and cones is decreased, and therefore both the rods and the cones become less sensitive to light. Thus, vision in dim light is affected, but there is enough pigment for vision in bright light.

Color blindness, which is an inability to see certain colors, is a hereditary condition in which the proteins of one or more of the three types of cones do not work properly.

The Ear

The human ear has two sensory functions. One is hearing. The other is helping to keep balance, or equilibrium.

Structure of the Ear   The three parts of the ear are the *outer ear,* the *middle ear,* and the *inner ear.* See Figure 15–14. The outer ear is the part that can be seen. It consists of the *pinna* (PIN uh), a flap of skin supported by cartilage, and a short **auditory** (AW dih tor ee) **canal.** The pinna functions mainly as a collecting funnel for sound

Figure 15–14
Structure of the Human Ear. ▼

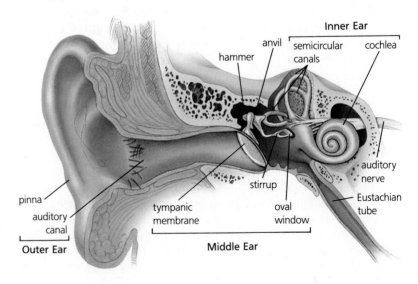

waves. Along the auditory canal are special glands that secrete a waxy material. This wax prevents foreign objects from entering the ear. Stretched across the inner end of the auditory canal is the delicate **tympanic** (tim PAN ik) **membrane,** which is also called the *eardrum*.

The middle ear is an air-filled chamber that begins at the eardrum. It contains three tiny bones—the *hammer* (malleus), the *anvil* (incus), and the *stirrup* (stapes). These bones form a chain across the middle ear that links the eardrum to another membrane, which is known as the **oval window.** The oval window covers the opening of the inner ear. The hammer is attached to the eardrum, the anvil connects the hammer to the stirrup, and the stirrup is connected to the oval window. Going from the middle ear to the throat is the **Eustachian** (yoo STAY shun) **tube.** The function of the Eustachian tube is to make the pressure in the middle ear equal to the pressure of the atmosphere outside the body.

MiniLab

Skill: Observing

A Change in Pitch

Procedure

1. Place five test tubes into a test tube rack.

2. Place 2 cm of water into one of the test tubes. Use a metric ruler to measure the height of the water in the test tube.

3. Repeat step 2 using 4 cm, 6 cm, 8 cm, and 10 cm of water in the four remaining test tubes.

4. Blow air across the top of each test tube. Put the test tubes in order from the lowest pitch to the highest pitch. Observe the order of the test tubes.

5. Close your eyes. Have a partner switch the order of the test tubes.

6. Keeping your eyes closed, try to put the test tubes back in order by the sound of their pitches. Observe the order of the test tubes.

Problem

What can you **observe** about changes in pitch?

Analyze and Conclude

1. Which test tube had the lowest pitch?

2. Which test tube had the highest pitch?

3. How does the height of the water affect the pitch of the sound?

4. Were you able to put the test tubes in order of increasing pitch with your eyes closed?

Science, Technology and Society

Issue: Noise Pollution

Airplanes, cars, construction machinery, and stereos are just a few of the factors that contribute to daily noise. Studies have linked excessive noise with hearing loss and other health effects. This has prompted some people to favor laws that regulate public noise.

People favoring such laws argue that they have the right to a healthful environment. They feel that communities should regulate car and truck noise, radios, and loud parties. They also believe that manufacturers of cars, airplanes, and appliances should be required to produce quieter equipment.

Other people argue that anti-noise laws would be impossible to enforce. They claim that the regulation of noise should be left to individuals. People who work in noisy occupations, for example, can wear protective ear equipment. Homes can be made less noisy by using sound-dampening materials and by lowering the volume of televisions, radios, and stereos. In addition, people can make an effort to avoid loud parties, rock concerts, and other noisy settings.

■ *Do you think public noise should be regulated? Why or why not?*

Infections can travel from the nose and throat through the Eustachian tube to the middle ear causing an ear infection. The symptoms of an ear infection can include an ear ache, the ear feeling warm, and a sensation of fluid in the ear. Doctors usually prescribe antibiotics to help fight an ear infection. Severe ear infections can cause the eardrum to rupture.

The inner ear is made up of the **cochlea** (KAHK lee uh) and the **semicircular canals.** The cochlea is the organ of hearing. It is made of coiled, liquid-filled tubes that are separated from one another by membranes. Lining one of the membranes are specialized hair cells that are sensitive to vibration.

The semicircular canals allow the body to maintain balance. They are made of three, interconnected, loop-shaped tubes at right angles to one another. These canals contain fluid and hairlike projections that detect changes in body position.

Hearing   Sound waves are vibrations in air or some other medium, such as water. Hearing takes place when these vibrations travel to the inner ear, where they start impulses that are carried to the brain by the **auditory nerve.**

Sound waves collected by the outer ear pass down the auditory canal to the eardrum. They cause the eardrum to vibrate. The vibrations are carried across the middle ear by the hammer, anvil, and stirrup. Vibrations of the stirrup cause vibrations in the oval window, which in turn cause the fluid within the cochlea to vibrate. The movement of the fluid causes vibrations in specialized hair cells lining one of the membranes within the cochlea. The vibrations start impulses in nerve endings around the cells. These impulses are carried to the cerebral cortex, where they are interpreted. The number of cells in the cochlea stimulated, and therefore the number of impulses sent to the brain, determines the sound's loudness. The more cells stimulated, the louder the sound.

Balance   Balance, or equilibrium, is a function of both the inner ear and the cerebellum. In the inner ear, the fluid-filled semicircular canals lie at right angles to one another. As the head changes position, the fluid in the canals also changes position, which causes the hairlike projections to move. This in turn stimulates nerve endings, which start impulses traveling through a branch of the auditory nerve to the cerebellum. The cerebellum interprets the direction of movement and sends impulses to the cerebrum. Impulses started by the cerebrum correct the position of the body.

If you spin around for a time, the fluid in the semicircular canals also moves. When you stop suddenly, you feel as though you are still moving. You become dizzy because the fluid in the canals keeps moving and stimulating the nerve endings. In some people, the rhythmic motions of a ship, plane, or car overstimulate the semicircular canals, resulting in motion sickness.

Also in the inner ear are two sacs containing crystals, or stones, that rest on sensory hairs. The pressure of the stones on the sensory hairs provides information on the body's position in relation to the direction of gravitational pull.

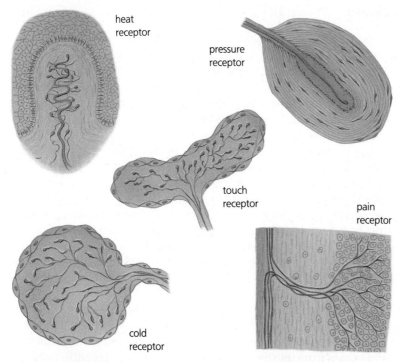

heat
receptor

pressure
receptor

touch
receptor

pain
receptor

cold
receptor

▲ **Figure 15–15**

Sense Receptors of the Human Skin. Much of what we know about our external
environment comes from information that is detected by the sense receptors found in
the skin.

Receptors of the Skin

There are sense receptors in the skin for touch, pressure, heat, cold,
and pain. See Figure 15–15. Each type of receptor differs in
structure from the others and is sensitive to only one kind of
stimulus. When a receptor is stimulated, it produces impulses that
travel over sensory nerve pathways to the brain, where they are
interpreted.

Although all types of receptors are present all over the human
body, the different types are not evenly distributed. For example,
receptors sensitive to touch are farthest apart on the back, much
closer together on the fingertips, and closest together on the tip of
the tongue. The ability to judge the size of an object by the way it
feels is partly determined by the number of touch receptors
stimulated.

Pressure receptors lie deep in the skin. They are stimulated
only when firm pressure is applied to the skin. Heat receptors and
cold receptors respond to the direction of heat flow. The sensation
of warmth is the result of heat flowing into the skin and stimulating
the heat receptors. The sensation of coolness is the result of heat
flowing out of the skin and stimulating the cold receptors. Pain
receptors warn against injury. They respond to all types of massive
stimulation. The sensation of pain is the same no matter what is
causing it.

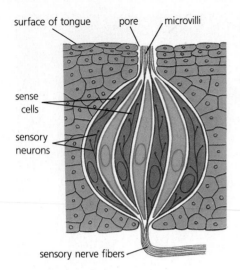

surface of tongue pore microvilli

sense cells

sensory neurons

sensory nerve fibers

▲ **Figure 15–16**
Structure of a Human Taste Bud.

Taste

The surface of the tongue is covered with small projections called *papillae* (puh PIL ee). Within the papillae are the taste receptors, or **taste buds.** Each taste bud is made of a number of sense cells and opens to the surface of the tongue through a pore. See Figure 15–16. Microvilli from the sense cells extend through the pore. Nerve fibers branch among the cells of the taste bud, and each cell is in contact with one or more neurons.

Only substances in solutions can stimulate the taste buds. Many substances dissolve in the saliva in the mouth. Taste buds are sensitive to only four basic tastes—sour, bitter, sweet, and salty. Each taste bud is particularly sensitive to one of these tastes and responds only slightly to the others. The taste buds for each taste tend to be found on specific areas of the tongue. Taste buds for sourness, for example, are found along the sides of the tongue. Taste buds for bitterness are located at the back of the tongue. Taste buds for sweetness and saltiness are on the tip of the tongue. See Figure 15–17.

When taste buds are stimulated, impulses are started by the sensory cells of the structure and carried by sensory pathways to the brain, where they are interpreted. Actually, most of the flavor of food comes from its smell. This is why most food has little taste to a person with a stuffy nose.

Smell

The receptors for smell, the **olfactory** (ol FAK tuh ree) **cells,** are found in the mucous membrane lining the upper nasal cavity. Odor is detected when molecules of a gaseous substance enter the nose, dissolve in the mucus, and stimulate the olfactory receptors. The olfactory cells are specialized nerve cells. See Figure 15–18. When they are stimulated, impulses are carried by the *olfactory nerves* to the brain, where they are interpreted.

Figure 15–17
Location of Taste Buds on a Human Tongue. Licking an ice cream cone makes sense because the taste buds for sweetness are found on the tip of the tongue. ▼

sour   bitter   sweet   salty

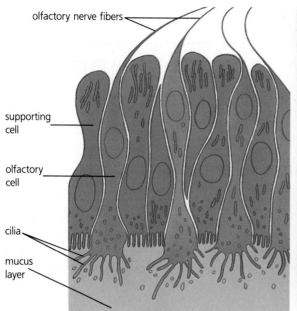

olfactory nerve fibers

supporting cell

olfactory cell

cilia

mucus layer

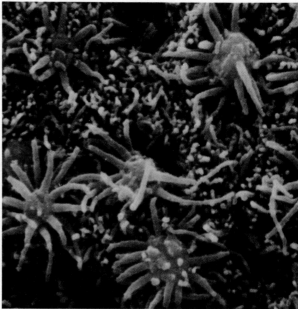

▲ **Figure 15–18**
Structure of Human Olfactory Receptors. Humans smell by using olfactory receptors located in the mucous membrane of the nasal cavity. The receptor cells are neurons. Sensory cilia (right) project from the neuron into the mucous layer.

Unlike taste buds, which respond to only four basic tastes, olfactory cells appear to respond to more than 50 different basic odors. Like the taste buds, each olfactory cell appears to be more sensitive to one basic odor than to all the others. Continuous exposure to a specific odor quickly leads to an inability to detect that odor but does not interfere with the detection of other odors. This is called *adaptation* and is thought to be partly a response of the central nervous system.

Both taste and smell result from the chemical stimulation of receptors. However, olfactory receptors are much more sensitive than the cells of the taste buds. Olfactory receptors are stimulated by much smaller amounts of chemicals, and they are sensitive to many more types of chemicals.

15-3 **Section Review**

1. Which part of the eye regulates the amount of light entering the eye?
2. What are the two kinds of light-sensitive cells found in the retina?
3. Name the three main divisions of the ear and the structure in the ear that is involved in balance or equilibrium.
4. List the five kinds of sense receptors of the skin and the four basic taste receptors found on the human tongue.

Critical Thinking

5. If you had to find an object in a darkened room, which senses would be most useful? Which would be least useful?   (*Ranking*)

Laboratory
Investigation

Identifying the Structures of the Brain

In structure, the brain of a sheep is similar to the brain of a human. Most of the parts are located in identical areas. In this investigation, you will use the sheep brain to illustrate the anatomy of the human brain.

Problem

How can you **identify** the parts of the sheep brain?

Materials (per group)

▶ dissecting pan

▶ scalpel

▶ probe

▶ gloves

▶ sheep brain

Procedure

1. Put on the pair of gloves provided. Place the sheep brain in a dissecting pan so that the raised side (dorsal) is up and the flat side (ventral) is resting on the pan.

2. Notice the large anterior section, the cerebrum. The cerebral cortex has many convolutions, or gyri (singular: gyrus), and grooves, called sulci (singular: sulcus). Each sulcus separates the cerebrum into lobes.

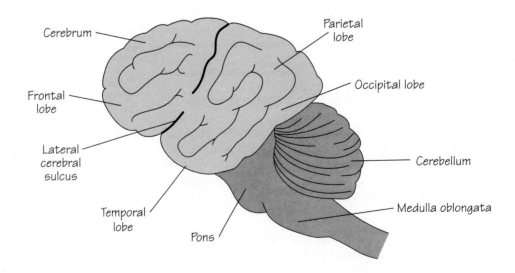

3. Locate the central sulcus that runs downward from the top to the bottom of the cerebrum, midway between the front (anterior) and the back (posterior). In front of the central sulcus, you will find the frontal lobe. Behind the central sulcus is the parietal lobe.

4. Locate the lateral cerebral sulcus, a groove that runs horizontally along the cerebrum, separating the frontal lobe (above) from the temporal lobe (below).

5. Locate the occipital lobe, which is found posterior to the parietal lobe.

6. Posterior to the cerebrum is a smaller lobed structure called the cerebellum. Holding the brain in your hand, gently bend the cerebellum down. Although in the sheep the cerebellum is directly behind the cerebrum, in humans it is positioned similarly to where it is located when you bend the sheep's brain downward.

7. Posterior to the cerebellum, you will find the medulla oblongata, which forms a triangular shape. This part of the brain narrows into and becomes the spinal cord.

8. The midbrain section is more visible on the ventral (underneath) side. Locate the pons—a bridgelike, raised area in the cerebellum region. The pons is in front of the medulla oblongata.

9. With a scalpel, carefully cut the brain in half lengthwise. **CAUTION:** *Be very careful when using a sharp instrument.*

10. Distinguish between the outer gray cortex area of the cerebellum and its inner white matter. The gray matter is slightly darker than the white and not really gray at all.

11. Dispose of the brain as directed by your teacher. Clean your dissecting pan, scalpel, and probe. Remove your gloves and wash your hands thoroughly.

Observations

1. Compare the sheep brain to the human brain.

2. Compare the size of the cerebrum with the other parts of the brain. What significance does the size of the cerebrum have?

3. Describe the location of the "gray" matter and the "white" matter in the brain. Other than by color, how do they differ?

Analysis and Conclusions

1. Were you able to identify the parts of the four lobes of the brain? Why or why not?

2. The hypothalamus is connected to the pituitary gland. What is the relationship between the hypothalamus and the pituitary gland?

3. What is the function of the medulla oblongata? Of the cerebellum?

Extensions

Using reference materials, determine the areas of the cerebral cortex that have been successfully mapped by scientists according to their specific function.

Chapter  Review

Study Outline

15-1 The Central Nervous System

▶ The central nervous system consists of the brain and the spinal cord.

▶ The major parts of the brain are the cerebrum, cerebellum, and medulla oblongata.

▶ The spinal cord connects the nerve network of the peripheral nervous system with the brain. It controls certain reflexes that do not involve the brain.

15-2 The Peripheral Nervous System

▶ The peripheral nervous system contains all the neurons and nerve fibers outside the brain and spinal cord. It is divided into the somatic nervous system, which controls voluntary body movements, and the autonomic nervous system, which controls involuntary body movements.

▶ The autonomic nervous system is divided into two systems—the sympathetic and parasympathetic nervous systems—whose effects are antagonistic.

▶ A reflex is an involuntary, autonomic response to a stimulus. The nerve pathway followed by impulses in a reflex is called a reflex arc.

15-3 Sense Receptors

▶ The eye is made up of three layers—the sclera, the choroid, and the retina. The retina contains light-sensitive cells called rods and cones.

▶ Hearing takes place when sound vibrations travel to the inner ear, where they start impulses that are carried to the brain by the auditory nerve. Balance is a function of the inner ear and the cerebellum.

▶ Sense receptors in the skin are sensitive to touch, pressure, heat, cold, and pain. Each type of receptor is sensitive to only one kind of stimulus.

▶ Taste buds are receptors that are sensitive to taste found within papillae on the surface of the tongue.

▶ Olfactory cells are receptors for smell and are found in the mucous membrane of the nasal cavity.

Chapter Assessment

Multiple Choice

Choose the letter of the answer that best completes each statement or answers the question.

1. A specialized neuron ending that detects changes in pressure in the skin is functioning as a(n) (a) effector. (b) synapse. (c) terminal branch. (d) receptor.

2. Loss of memory as a result of an accident would indicate damage to the (a) spinal cord. (b) cerebellum. (c) cerebrum. (d) medulla.

3. Which portion of the central nervous system coordinates motor activities and aids in maintaining balance? (a) cerebrum (b) medulla (c) cerebellum (d) spinal cord

4. Activities such as coughing, heartbeat, and breathing are controlled by the (a) cerebrum. (b) medulla. (c) cerebellum. (d) thalamus.

5. The cerebral cortex is not involved in (a) sensory functions. (b) motor functions. (c) associative functions. (d) involuntary functions.

6. In the human nervous system, (a) the left cerebral hemisphere controls the right side of the body. (b) the left cerebral hemisphere controls the left side of the body. (c) the gray matter is made up of myelinated fibers. (d) spinal nerves contain only sensory nerve fibers.

7. A reflex arc begins with an impulse through a (a) motor neuron. (b) cranial nerve. (c) sensory neuron. (d) parasympathetic nerve.

8. Remembering a phone number only long enough to dial it is an example of (a) sudden memory. (b) short-term memory. (c) momentary memory. (d) long-term memory.

9. Which eye structure regulates the amount of light that enters the eye? (a) lens (b) pupil (c) retina (d) iris

10. The hammer, anvil, and stirrup are (a) bones of the middle ear. (b) parts of the cochlea. (c) responsible for balance. (d) parts of the eardrum.

Content Review

Answer each of the following in complete sentences.

11. What are the functions of the hypothalamus?

12. Explain three functions of the cerebral cortex.

13. Describe the function of the cerebellum.

14. What involuntary activities does the medulla oblongata control?

15. What body functions does the autonomic nervous system control?

16. How do the parasympathetic and sympathetic nervous systems work together?

17. What is the end result of the reflex arc that is stimulated by touching a hot object?

18. What are the functions of rods and cones?

19. How does the ear help maintain equilibrium?

20. How do the senses of taste and smell work together?

Graphic Organizing

For information on graphic organizers, see Appendix G at the back of this text.

21. Concept Map Copy the incomplete concept map onto a sheet of paper, and fill in the missing concepts and linking words.

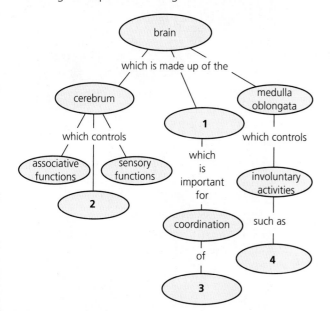

Critical Thinking and Problem Solving

Discuss each of the following in a brief paragraph.

22. Relating How is the arrangement of the semi-circular canals related to their function?

23. Predicting A physician observes that the pupils in a patient's eyes are unable to change size. What effect would this have on light reaching the retina?

24. Interpreting A scientist was asked to develop an eye chart that used symbols of different sizes instead of letters. To standardize the eye chart, she determined the percentage of all the symbols that could be correctly identified at different distances from the chart. The results of the study are shown in the line graph below. Identify the variable in this study and the response that was measured. What is the relationship between the variable in this study and the response that was measured? What is the relationship between the variable and the response?

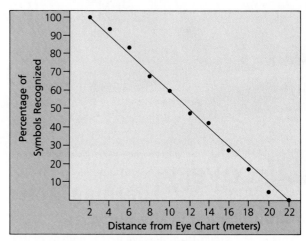

25. Experimenting Design an experiment to determine the role of color in food selection by aquatic turtles. (Hint: Turtles can be fed raw fish.) What hypothesis is being tested in your experiment? Identify the variable being manipulated and the response being measured.

Discovery Learning Activity

Communication in the Body

1. Working in a group, try to achieve a goal such as rearranging furniture in a classroom or books in a bookcase in a specific amount of time.

2. Repeat step 1, but this time each member in the group should work independently and avoid any form of communication with each other.

3. Describe what happened in each situation. Why do you think it is important to work together and communicate information? How is this activity similar to what happens between the nervous system and the endocrine system?

Chemical Regulation

······· *Guide for Reading* ·······

Previewing the Chapter

Fastened securely in place, the people on this roller coaster can enjoy the thrills of the ride in perfect safety. Even so, the high-speed turns, twists, and loops can provoke plenty of screams! What is it that triggers such heart-pounding reactions? What are hormones and how do they control the activity of specific target tissues in the body? What are the functions of the human endocrine glands and their hormones?

Key Words

endocrine system, gland, hormone, hypothalamus, pituitary gland

Key Concepts

- **Explain** how hormones control the activity of particular target tissues.
- **Describe** the functions of the human endocrine glands their hormones.
- **Design an experiment** to observe the effect of epinephrine on *Daphnia*. (Laboratory Investigation)

16-1 Glands and Hormones

Section Objectives:

- *Compare* the operations of the nervous system and the endocrine system.
- *Define* the terms *exocrine gland, endocrine gland,* and *hormone.*
- *Explain* the regulation of hormone secretion through negative feedback.
- *Identify* the two basic mechanisms of hormone action.

Chemical Versus Nervous Regulation

The body systems of animals are never at rest. To maintain *homeostasis,* they constantly make adjustments to changing conditions outside and inside the body. You have already read how the nervous system takes part in this process in complex multicellular animals. In these animals, the nervous system sends electrochemical impulses through nerve fibers. Neurotransmitters bridge the tiny gaps between adjacent neurons. To help maintain homeostasis, the nervous system acts quickly and directs its messages to specific parts of the body.

▲ **Figure 16–1**

Courtship Behavior of Masai Giraffe. Mating behavior is just one of many functions controlled by both chemical and nervous signals

Animals also use another system to maintain homeostasis. Through chemicals released into the bloodstream, the **endocrine system** regulates overall metabolism, homeostasis, growth, and reproduction. The bloodstream carries these chemicals to all the tissues of the body. When the chemicals reach the correct organ, a reaction occurs.

It takes time for chemicals to reach the correct organ through the bloodstream. For this reason, the endocrine system is slower than the nervous system in producing an effect. Its effects also tend to last longer. For the most part, the nervous system allows the body to make rapid responses for short periods of time. The endocrine system produces effects that last for hours, days, or even years. However, these two systems also work together. For example, when you run from danger, the nervous system not only controls your muscles but also stimulates parts of the endocrine system. The endocrine system then stimulates your heartbeat and respiration rate. Together, these two systems provide the energy and oxygen needed to maintain the body's activity.

Glands

Glands are organs made up of *epithelial* cells that specialize in the secretion of substances needed by the organism. Some glands, such as the digestive glands, discharge their secretions into ducts, which then carry the secretions to where they are used. These glands are called **exocrine** (EK suh krin) **glands.** Other glands release their secretions directly into the bloodstream. These glands are called **endocrine glands,** or *ductless glands.* They make up the endocrine system. See Figure 16–2.

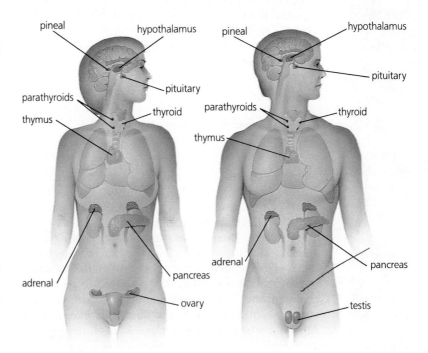

Figure 16–2
Glands of the Human Endocrine System. ▶

The secretions produced by the endocrine glands are called **hormones.** Traveling through the bloodstream, hormones regulate overall metabolism, maintenance of homeostasis, growth, and reproduction as well as other body processes.

Hormones

Although hormones are released into the bloodstream in one part of the body, they do not affect that area. Instead, they exert their effects elsewhere in the body. Because of this, hormones are sometimes called "chemical messengers."

Usually, there are low hormone concentrations in the bloodstream. Each type of hormone is recognized only by specific tissues. The tissue regulated by a given hormone is called the *target tissue.* The hormone may stimulate the target tissue and increase its activities, or it may inhibit the target tissue and decrease its activities. This is done by changing the rates of certain biochemical reactions in the target tissue. A hormone may cause a reaction to start, to speed up, to slow down, or to stop. Unlike enzymes, however, hormones do not act directly on the reacting substances. They appear to act always through some intermediate cellular process. The mechanisms of hormone action will be discussed in detail later in this chapter.

Most hormones fall into two classes. *Protein-type hormones* consist of chains of amino acids or related compounds. These hormones cannot pass through the cell membrane because they cannot dissolve in the lipids that are present in the cell membrane. **Insulin** (IN suh lin) is an example of this type of hormone. *Steroid* (STIHR oyd) *hormones* are lipidlike, carbon-ring compounds that are able to pass through the cell membrane. Steroid hormones are produced in the outer layer of the adrenal gland and in the gonads. Estrogen is an example of a steroid hormone.

Prostaglandins

Prostaglandins (prahs tuh GLAN dinz) are "local hormones" produced by nearly every cell in the body. They are manufactured and released in response to cell injury or other hormones. Prostaglandins influence many metabolic activities, including heartbeat, blood pressure, and the immune response. Scientists are studying prostaglandins and their effects for use in the treatment of asthma and high blood pressure.

The Regulation of Hormone Secretion

Usually, endocrine glands do not secrete their hormones at a constant rate. The rate varies with the needs of the body. A nerve impulse may cause a gland to speed up, slow down, or stop its production of a hormone. However, in most cases, chemical stimuli, including other hormones, regulate the secretions of the endocrine system.

Biology and You

Q: Some athletes in my school use steroids. Is steroid use common among high-school students?

A: Many people were shocked to learn that more than 1 in 15 males in high school admitted to using steroids in a recent survey. When asked why they used steroids, some students mentioned pressure from parents and coaches to excel. Others said they wanted to improve their appearance.

Anabolic steroids, synthetic versions of the male hormone testosterone, increase muscle bulk and strength in both males and females. Most people who take steroids do so without medical supervision and are unaware of their negative side effects.

Side effects of steroid use may range from acne, headaches, and fatigue to more serious problems. These may include sterility, stunted growth, heart problems, aggressive behavior, cancer, and even death. Teenagers risk effects because their growing bodies can be permanently damaged.

■ *Create a poster warning teenagers about steroid use. You may want to use photos from the sports section of the newspaper. Be sure to explain why steroid use is dangerous.*

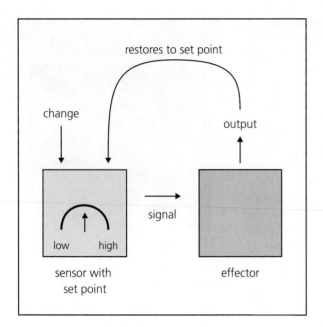

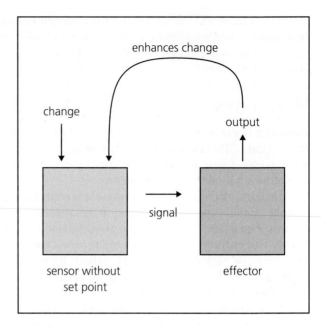

a

b

▲ **Figure 16–3**

Negative and Positive Feedback. Negative feedback controls the temperature in most buildings. For example, when the room cools down below a certain temperature (the change), the change is sensed by a sensor with a specific set point (the thermostat). This sends a signal to the effector (the furnace) to turn on and return the system to the set point. During positive feedback, a change in the system is sensed by a sensor. The sensor sends the signal to the effector. The output of the effector causes an even greater change in the system.

The chemical regulation of glandular secretions is accomplished by *feedback*. A feedback system operates as a cycle in which the last step affects the first step. There are two kinds of feedback systems—negative feedback and positive feedback.

During **negative feedback,** an activity alters a condition in the body, and this triggers a series of events that reverses the altered condition (Figure 16–3a). This feedback is called negative because it opposes the change. Negative feedback tends to keep a variable, such as blood glucose concentration or body temperature, close to some value, called the set point. A familiar example of negative feedback is a thermostat and furnace that keeps a room at a constant temperature. When the temperature falls below the set point, the thermostat turns the furnace on. When the temperature rises above the set point, the thermostat turns the furnace off. Negative feedback requires a set point (thermostat setting), a sensor (thermometer in the thermostat), and an effector (furnace), which accomplishes the change.

Similarly, negative feedback keeps body temperature near 37°C. This set point is established in the hypothalamus, a region of the brain. When your body temperature drops, the hypothalamus stimulates the muscles to shiver, which generates heat and increases body temperature. When normal body temperature is restored, the hypothalamus turns off this temperature control mechanism.

Most glands are regulated by negative feedback because it maintains homeostasis. For example, the secretion of the hormone **thyroxine** (thy RAHK sin) by the thyroid gland is regulated by *thyroid stimulating hormone* (TSH). TSH is produced by the pituitary gland. When the level of thyroxine in the blood is low, the pituitary is stimulated to secrete TSH. In turn, TSH stimulates the thyroid to produce thyroxine. When the thyroxine level reaches a certain point, the secretion of TSH by the pituitary is reduced. The pituitary then stops secreting TSH, and the thyroid stops secreting thyroxine. This is one example of how the secretions of one gland is regulated by the secretions of another. In other cases, endocrine glands are controlled by the levels of simple substances, such as calcium and glucose, in the blood.

In cases of **positive feedback,** a change initiates a response, and that response intensifies the original change (Figure 16–3b). Positive feedback plays an important role in the contractions of the uterus during childbirth. The early contractions of labor push the baby's head against the wall of the uterus. This in turn increases the contractions of the muscles surrounding the uterus. These contractions cause the baby's head to be pushed even harder against the uterine wall, causing even stronger contractions.

The Mechanisms of Hormone Action

Each hormone controls the activity of a particular target tissue. Because hormones are carried in the bloodstream, each target tissue must have a way of recognizing the hormone that is intended for it. There also must be a mechanism through which the hormone can produce its effect within the target cells.

There are two basic mechanisms governing hormone action. One of these mechanisms involves hormones that enter cells and is mainly characteristic of steroid hormones. The other involves hormones that do not enter cells and is characteristic of protein-type hormones.

Steroid Hormones   Steroid hormones are small, lipid-soluble molecules that are able to pass through cell membranes. These hormones enter most of the cells of the body but produce their effects only in the target cells. In the target cells, there are receptor proteins that recognize a particular steroid hormone and react with it, forming a hormone-receptor complex. See Figure 16–4 on the next page. This hormone-receptor complex then enters the nucleus and binds to DNA. The hormone-receptor complex produces its effect by acting on DNA, the genetic material that controls the cell's activities. Because steroid hormones directly affect gene expression, they can produce changes in cellular function.

Figure 16–4

Steroid Hormones. One mechanism of hormone action involves steroid hormones entering target cells and binding to receptors inside the cell. ▶

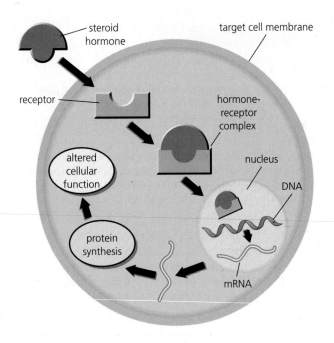

Protein-Type Hormones Protein-type hormones are either amino acids, polypeptides (chains of amino acids), or proteins and usually cannot pass through cell membranes. This type of hormone acts without entering the target cells. It binds to receptor proteins located on the surface of the target cell's cell membrane. See Figure 16–5. When the hormone binds to the cell membrane, it activates an enzyme inside the cell membrane to produce *second*

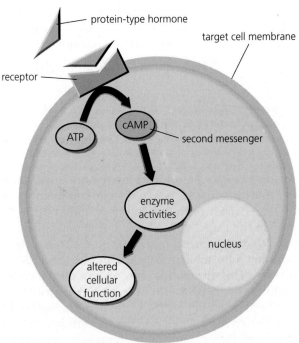

Figure 16–5

Protein-Type Hormones. Another mechanism of hormone action involves protein-type hormones. These hormones do not enter the cell, but bind to receptors on the cell membrane, causing second messenger molecules to be produced. ▶

messenger molecules. (The hormone is the *first messenger.*) These second messenger molecules may be calcium ions (Ca^{2+}) or small molecules such as cyclic adenosine monophosphate (cAMP). The second messengers actually trigger the response that alters cell function.

Cyclic AMP produces different effects in different cells. For example, it can cause thyroid cells to produce thyroxine, adrenal cells to produce cortisol, and kidney tubules to reabsorb water.

16-1 Section Review

1. What two systems regulate and coordinate body functions?
2. Name the two types of glands found in the human body.
3. What are hormones?
4. Name the two basic mechanisms governing hormone action.

Critical Thinking

5. What kind of feedback would occur if an increase in hormone A caused hormone B to increase which then caused hormone A to decrease? Explain. (*Reasoning Conditionally*)

16-2 The Human Endocrine System

Section Objectives:

- *Name* the major endocrine glands of the human body.
- *Describe* the role of the hypothalamus within the endocrine system.
- *List* the hormones released by each endocrine gland and briefly describe their functions.
- *Identify* disorders caused by hypersecretion or hyposecretion of specific hormones.

The Functioning of Endocrine Glands

The human endocrine system consists of a number of endocrine glands that regulate a wide range of activities. The improper functioning of an endocrine gland may result in a disease or disorder of the body. An excess, or **hypersecretion** (hy per suh KREE shun), of a hormone may cause one type of disorder. A deficiency, or **hyposecretion** (hy poh suh KREE shun), of a hormone may cause another type of disorder. See Figure 16–6 for an outline of these disorders. In the following sections, you will read about the human endocrine system in more detail.

Glandular Disorders			
Gland	**Hormone**	**Effects of Oversecretion (Hypersecretion)**	**Effects of Undersecretion (Hyposecretion)**
anterior pituitary	growth hormone	*in childhood* effects include giantism. Individual grows tall but is normally proportioned. Mental development is not affected. *In adulthood* effects include acromegaly. Individual has abnormally large hands and feet and enlarged facial structures. Does not affect mental processes.	*in childhood* effects include dwarfism. Individual is small but is normally proportioned. Adult sexual development often does not occur.
adrenal cortex	aldosterone, cortisol	Cushing's disease. Individual has excess fat deposits in the upper body, a puffy face, excess growth of facial hair, and a high blood glucose level. Decreased immunity to disease also occurs.	Addison's disease. Normal blood glucose level cannot be maintained. Individual becomes sluggish, weak, loses weight, and develops increased skin pigmentation. Tolerance to stress is reduced. Without medication, the disease causes death.
thyroid	thyroxine	hyperthyroidism. Individual is nervous, irritable, loses weight, and cannot sleep. Often, eyes protrude, a condition called exophthalmos. Hyperthyroidism is often accompanied by a goiter, or enlarged thyroid.	*in infancy,* effects include cretinism. Individual is a dwarf whose body parts are out of proportion. Mental retardation occurs. *in adulthood* results include hypothyroidism. Individual is sluggish, gains weight.
pancreas (β cells, islets of Langerhans)	insulin	diabetic shock. The blood glucose level falls dangerously, and convulsions, unconsciousness, and death may occur if untreated.	diabetes. Individual has an abnormally high blood glucose level, becomes dehydrated, loses weight, and cannot resist infections. If untreated, can cause death.
pancreas (α cells, islets of Langerhans)	glucagon	abnormally high blood glucose level. Results are similar to diabetes.	abnormally low blood glucose level also known as hypoglycemia.

▲ **Figure 16–6**   Effects of Oversecretion and Undersecretion of Hormones.

The Pituitary Gland and the Hypothalamus

The **pituitary** (pih TOO uh tehr ee) **gland** is a small gland attached to the brain. See Figure 16–7. Often called the "master gland" of the body, the pituitary controls the activity of a number of other endocrine glands. It consists of an anterior, or front, lobe and a

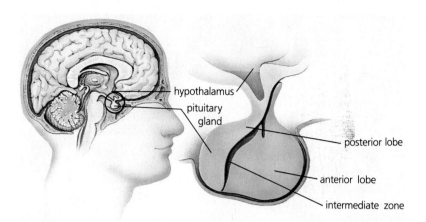

posterior, or back, lobe. Between these two lobes is a small intermediate zone that does not work in humans. In other animals, this area is larger and is an active part of the endocrine system.

The part of the brain that is connected to the pituitary is called the **hypothalamus** (hy poh THAL uh mus). It acts like an endocrine gland and controls the release of hormones from the pituitary. The hypothalamus receives information from the nervous system. This information helps to determine when the hypothalamus should stimulate the pituitary to release a hormone. The hypothalamus is the major link between the body's two regulating systems. It is also influenced by the concentration of various hormones in the blood. Thus, the hypothalamus directs the work of the pituitary.

The Anterior Pituitary
The anterior lobe of the pituitary secretes several different hormones. Many of them help to control the body's metabolism. Hormones produced by the hypothalamus, called *releasing hormones,* or **releasing factors,** control the release of hormones from the anterior lobe. The releasing factors are produced in the ends of specific neurons within the hypothalamus. When they are released by the neurons, the factors are absorbed directly into capillaries that carry them to the anterior pituitary. A specific factor controls the release of each type of hormone from the anterior pituitary. The hormones released by the pituitary stimulate other endocrine glands to secrete their hormones.

The major hormones of the anterior pituitary are as follows:

■ *Thyroid-stimulating hormone,* or TSH, stimulates the production and release of thyroxine by the thyroid gland.

■ *Adrenocorticotropic* (uh DREE noh kort ih koh troh pik) *hormone,* or ACTH, stimulates the production and release of hormones from the cortex layer of the adrenal glands. It is used in the treatment of arthritis, asthma, and allergies.

■ *Growth hormone,* or GH, controls growth. It indirectly affects the growth of bone and cartilage by regulating production of another factor that acts directly on these tissues. GH directly affects protein, carbohydrate, and fat metabolism at a cellular level. See Figure 16–6 for the effects of oversecretion and undersecretion of GH.

Figure 16–8

Human Egg Cell Being Released from Ovary. The release of this egg cell from the ovary is caused by luteinizing hormone. ▶

■ *Follicle-stimulating hormone,* or FSH, stimulates the development of egg cells in the ovaries of females. In males, it controls the production of sperm cells in the testes.

■ *Luteinizing* (LOOT ee in iz ing) *hormone,* or LH, causes the release of egg cells from the ovaries in females. It controls the production of sex hormones in both males and females.

■ *Prolactin* (proh LAK tin) stimulates the secretion of milk by the mammary glands of the female after she gives birth. Otherwise, it is secreted only in small amounts. It is thought that the production of prolactin is normally inhibited by a factor secreted by the hypothalamus. Following childbirth, the secretion of this inhibitory factor is blocked, and prolactin is produced.

The Posterior Pituitary The posterior lobe of the pituitary is directly connected to the hypothalamus. Two tracts of nerve fibers beginning in the hypothalamus have their endings in the posterior pituitary. Two hormones, *oxytocin* (ahk sih TOH sin) and *vasopressin* (vay zoh PRES in), are produced by these nerve cells in the hypothalamus. The hormones then pass down the axons to the posterior lobe of the pituitary for storage and eventual release.

Oxytocin stimulates contractions of the smooth muscles of the uterus during childbirth. Vasopressin, also known as *antidiuretic* (an tee dy uh RET ik) *hormone,* or ADH, controls the reabsorption of water by the nephrons of the kidneys. ADH increases the permeability of the tubules to water, so that water is reabsorbed by osmosis.

The Thyroid Gland

As seen in Figure 16–9, the **thyroid** (THY royd) **gland** is located in the neck just below the larynx and in front of the trachea. This gland secretes the iodine-containing hormone thyroxine, which you read about earlier in this chapter. Thyroxine regulates the rate of metabolism in the body. It increases the rate of protein, carbohy-

Figure 16–9

The Thyroid Gland. The hormones of the thyroid regulate the blood calcium level and the rate of metabolism in the body. ▼

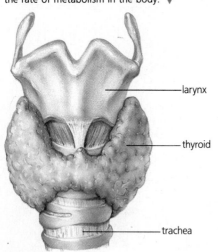

larynx

thyroid

trachea

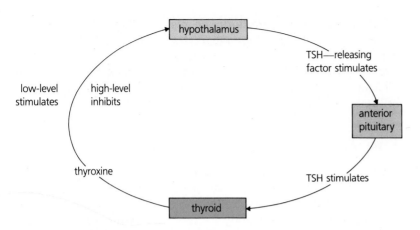

◀ **Figure 16–10**
Regulation of Thyroxine Secretion.

drate, and fat metabolism, and the rate of cellular respiration. This hormone is needed for normal mental and physical development. The thyroid also secretes another hormone, *calcitonin* (kal suh TOH nin), which is involved in the regulation of the blood calcium level.

The interaction of several hormones regulates the secretion of thyroxine. See Figure 16–10. If the concentration of thyroxine in the blood falls below a certain level, the hypothalamus is stimulated to produce TSH-releasing factor. The releasing factor stimulates the anterior pituitary to secrete thyroid-stimulating hormone (TSH). TSH, in turn, stimulates the release of thyroxine by the thyroid. Increasing levels of thyroxine in the blood inhibit the production of releasing factor by the hypothalamus. This inhibits the production of TSH and decreases the stimulation of the thyroid. Thus, by negative feedback, the concentration of thyroxine in the blood controls the system that produces it. Refer to Figure 16–6 for the effects of oversecretion and undersecretion of thyroxine.

The Parathyroid Glands

Four tiny, oval glands called the **parathyroid** (par uh THY royd) **glands** are embedded in the back of the thyroid. See Figure 16–11. They secrete parathyroid hormone, or *parathormone* (par uh THOR mohn). This hormone regulates calcium and phosphate metabolism.

Calcium is necessary for proper growth, the health of bones and teeth, blood clotting, nerve function, and muscle contraction. Phosphate is found in bones and in many important compounds in the body, including ATP, DNA, and RNA.

For the nerves and muscles to function normally, the concentration of calcium ions in the blood must be kept within fairly narrow limits. While some calcium is stored within cells, most of it is stored in bones in the form of calcium phosphate compounds. When the blood calcium level drops even slightly, the parathyroids are stimulated to secrete parathormone. This hormone causes the release of calcium from bone into the plasma. When the blood calcium concentration rises above a certain level, calcium is stored in bones. Excess calcium can be excreted by the kidneys and intestines.

Figure 16–11

The Parathyroid Glands. The four small parathyroid glands embedded in the back of the thyroid produce hormones that regulate calcium and phosphate metabolism in the body. ▼

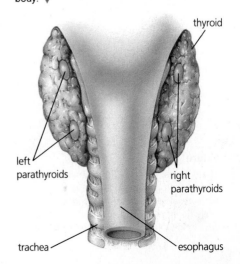

A deficiency of parathormone results in low blood calcium levels. If the level is low enough, the skeletal muscles become hypersensitive and contract violently. This condition is called *tetany* (TET uh nee). Oversecretion of parathormone results in the removal of calcium from bones to the point where they become brittle and break easily.

The Adrenal Glands

Capping the two kidneys are the **adrenal** (uh DREEN ul) **glands.** See Figure 16–12. Each gland consists of an inner layer, called the *medulla,* and an outer layer, called the *cortex.* The hormones of the adrenal gland help the body to deal with stress. The medulla releases hormones that handle sudden stress. Hormones of the cortex help the body deal with long-term stress.

The Adrenal Medulla The tissue of the adrenal medulla is related to nerve tissue. **Epinephrine,** or *adrenalin* (uh DREN uh lin), and **norepinephrine,** or *noradrenalin* (nor uh DREN uh lin), are the two hormones secreted by the adrenal medulla. About 80 percent of the secretion is epinephrine and 20 percent norepinephrine. The nerves in the sympathetic nervous system regulate the secretion of these hormones by the adrenal medulla. The effects of these hormones are the same as those produced by stimulation of the sympathetic nervous system. However, the effects of these hormones last much longer.

Epinephrine and norepinephrine produce what is called the "emergency response," or "fight-or-flight" reaction. They are secreted in response to sudden stresses, such as fear, anger, pain, or physical exertion. Both hormones constrict the blood vessels of the body. Epinephrine increases the rate of metabolism and the release of glucose by the liver. It also increases the rate and strength of the heartbeat, blood pressure, breathing rate, blood clotting rate, and sweating.

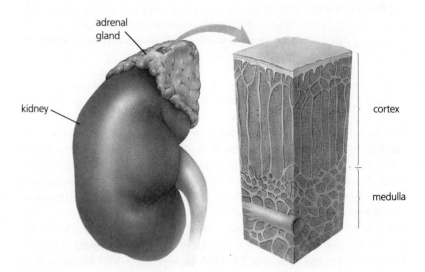

Figure 16–12

The Adrenal Glands. The adrenal glands are located on top of the kidneys. Hormones of the adrenal medulla deal with sudden stress, while hormones of the adrenal cortex deal with long-term stress. ▶

The Adrenal Cortex The hormones of the adrenal cortex are compounds called **corticosteroids** (kort ih koh STIHR oyds). They are all synthesized from cholesterol. The major hormones of the adrenal cortex are cortisol and aldosterone, but more than 30 others are also known.

Cortisol (KORT uh sahl), or *hydrocortisone* (hy druh KORT uh sohn), affects the metabolism of carbohydrates, proteins, and fats. Its major action involves the synthesis of glucose in the liver and other tissues. It is important in regulating the glucose level in the blood.

Cortisone is a compound that is closely related to cortisol. Produced synthetically, cortisone is used as a drug for the treatment of arthritis. It is also used to counteract the symptoms of allergies.

Aldosterone and related hormones maintain the normal mineral balance in the blood. Aldosterone increases both the reabsorption of sodium by the kidney tubules and the excretion of potassium by the kidney tubules. By controlling the concentrations of these ions, aldosterone also controls the volume of the intercellular fluid and the blood.

The adrenal cortex also secretes male and female sex hormones, but the amount of female hormones produced is slight. The male sex hormones may play some role in regulating sexual development in males. See Figure 16–6 for the effects of oversecretion and undersecretion of the hormones of the adrenal cortex.

The Pancreas—Islets of Langerhans

You read about the function of the pancreas in the digestive system in Chapter 8. The pancreas is both an exocrine gland and an endocrine gland. The exocrine portion secretes digestive juices into the pancreatic duct. The endocrine portion consists of small clusters, or islands, of hormone-secreting cells. These cells, called the **islets of Langerhans** (LAHNG er hahnz), are scattered throughout the pancreas. There are two types of cells in the islets—*alpha* (*α*) *cells* and *beta* (*β*) *cells.* Alpha cells secrete the hormone **glucagon** (GLOO kuh gahn). Beta cells secrete the hormone insulin. Both of these hormones function in the control of carbohydrate metabolism.

Insulin Insulin affects glucose metabolism in several ways. It increases the rate at which glucose is moved through cell membranes in most of the tissues of the body. Insulin secretion is controlled by the concentration of glucose in the blood. When the level of glucose in the blood is high after the ingestion of glucose, the beta cells of the pancreas are stimulated to secrete insulin. The insulin promotes the passage of the glucose into the body cells, which lowers the blood glucose level. Within the cells of the liver and skeletal muscle, insulin promotes the change of glucose to glycogen. In fatty tissues, it promotes the change of glucose to fat. It also increases the rate of oxidation of glucose within cells.

Biology and You

Q: When I'm nervous, my hands feel icy. Is this normal?

A: Icy hands, a "knotted" stomach, and a racing heart are all common when you are nervous, angry, or frightened. These emotions cause the release of the hormone epinephrine, which prepares your body for "fight or flight"—that is, to fight against or run away from the threat or challenge.

Extremities, such as hands and feet, feel cold because there is less blood flowing to them. Epinephrine constricts certain blood vessels, pushing blood away from your skin and toward vital organs—your heart, lungs, brain, and muscles. To increase blood flow, your heart beats faster and harder, perhaps making your chest feel tight. Breathing quickens to send more oxygen to your cells.

There are other common feelings associated with fright. Your stomach may feel "knotted" or gassy as epinephrine slows the flow of digestive enzymes. You may feel a "lump" in your throat as your throat muscles contract to open the airway to your lungs.

Write a short story of one page about a person who is nervous or frightened. Include details on how the body reacts and why.

Glucagon   Usually, the effects of glucagon on glucose metabolism are opposite, or antagonistic, to those of insulin. While insulin lowers the blood glucose level, glucagon raises it. When the glucose concentration in the blood falls below a certain level, the alpha cells of the pancreas are stimulated to secrete glucagon. Glucagon promotes the conversion of glycogen to glucose in the liver. This glucose quickly diffuses out of the liver into the bloodstream.

When the supply of liver glycogen is exhausted, glucagon causes the conversion of amino acids and fatty acids to glucose. Thus, when there are not enough carbohydrates for the body, body fat and proteins are broken down to provide glucose to meet energy requirements.

Diabetes   When the islets of Langerhans fail to produce enough insulin, the amount of glucose that can enter the body cells is decreased. As a result, the concentration of glucose in the blood increases, and the excess sugar is excreted in the urine. This condition, called **diabetes** (dy uh BEET eez) **mellitus,** can be inherited. Symptoms of diabetes include loss of weight despite increased appetite, thirst, and general weakness. If untreated, diabetes causes death. Proper diet, the use of oral medication, and/or daily injections of insulin can control the disease. See Figure 16–6 for the effects of oversecretion and undersecretion of the hormones of the islets of Langerhans.

The Gonads

The **gonads** (GOH nadz), or sex glands, are the ovaries of the female and the testes of the male. The *ovaries* (OH vuh reez) produce egg cells and the *testes* (TES teez) produce sperm cells. The gonads also secrete *sex hormones,* which control all aspects of sexual development and reproduction. The role of sex hormones in reproduction is discussed in Chapter 23.

Figure 16–13

A Woman Buying Insulin. Daily injections of insulin allow many people with diabetes to lead normal lives. The amount of insulin administered must be adjusted according to the kinds of foods eaten and the amount of exercise performed. ▶

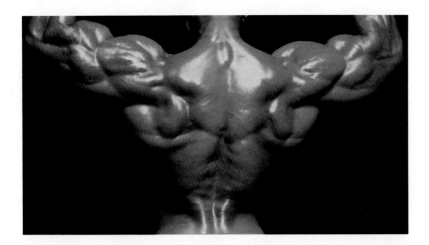

The Ovaries   The ovaries produce two hormones, **estrogen** (ES truh jen) and **progesterone** (proh JES tuh rohn). During development, estrogen stimulates the development of the female reproductive system. Estrogen also promotes the development of female *secondary sex characteristics,* such as broadening of the hips and development of breasts. Estrogen acts with progesterone to regulate the menstrual cycle.

The Testes   The testes secrete male sex hormones called *androgens.* The most important androgen is **testosterone** (tes TAHS tuh rohn). During fetal development, testosterone stimulates development of the male reproductive system. This hormone also promotes development of male *secondary sex characteristics,* such as a deep voice, beard, body hair, and the male body form.

Anabolic steroids are derived from this male hormone. Unfortunately, many athletes use these steroids to build body mass and strength. See Figure 16–14. Steroid use, however, poses serious health risks. Liver and kidney disorders, high blood pressure, and addiction can occur. Women may experience menstrual irregularities and masculinization. In men, aggressive behavior, a decreased sperm count, and impotence often develop. Little is known about long-range side effects. Medical experts believe some of these effects may be irreversible. As a result, anabolic steroids have been banned in many sports to protect the health of athletes.

Other Glands and Hormones

The Thymus   The **thymus** (THY mus) is a gland located in the upper chest near the heart. It is large in infants and children but shrinks after the start of adolescence. Early in life, the thymus helps in the processing of lymphocytes, which are part of the body's defense against infection. See Chapter 10. Current research indicates that the thymus produces a hormone called *thymosin* (THY muh sin) throughout childhood. Thymosin is thought to stimulate development of T lymphocytes, which are important in immunity. The thymus appears to serve no function in adults.

Can You Explain This?

To perform better in competitions, an athlete took anabolic steroids in order to build up muscle mass. Although he developed significant muscle growth, a medical examination revealed that his body was producing less than normal amounts of testosterone.

■ *Propose an explanation for why the athlete's testosterone level was so low.*

▲ **Figure 16–15**
A White Flounder. Flounders are famous for their ability to match the color of their background. This effect is produced by melatonin, which acts on pigment cells of the flounder.

The Pineal Gland The **pineal** (PY nee uhl) **gland** is a pea-sized structure that is attached to the base of the brain. It produces a hormone called *melatonin* (mel uh TOH nin). In flounder and other ectotherms, melatonin acts on the pigment cells. See Figure 16–15. The pineal gland is involved in daily cycles. Normally, melatonin levels rise at night and are lower during the day. International travelers develop jet lag because the body is producing melatonin on the old schedule. After a few days, the pineal gland adjusts its production of melatonin.

The Stomach and Small Intestine Hormones also function in the digestive system. Special cells in the lining of the stomach secrete the hormone *gastrin,* which stimulates the flow of gastric juice. In the lining of the small intestine, there are cells that secrete the hormone *secretin,* which stimulates the flow of pancreatic juice. Secretin was the first hormone to be discovered.

16-2 Section Review

1. Define the terms *hypersecretion* and *hyposecretion*.
2. What are releasing factors?
3. What two hormones are secreted by the thyroid?
4. What causes diabetes?

Critical Thinking

5. What ethical values do you think are violated by the use of anabolic steroids by athletes? (*Making Ethical Judgments*)

Math, Science, and Technology

$A = \pi r^2$

$V = l \times w \times h$

Melatonin—Fact or Hype?

Problem

In the United States, melatonin is classified as a dietary supplement. And as such, it is not under the control of the Food and Drug Administration (an agency of the Department of Health and Human Services) and can be sold in drug stores and health food stores and on television and the Internet. Some physicians and scientists are concerned about the purity of the melatonin that is sold at these places.

Unfortunately, the effects of melatonin in humans and animals are not well understood. Most claims are backed by testimonials of melatonin users and supporters. The supporters of melatonin claim that it induces sleep and can be used as a safe, nonaddictive sleep aid and is safe and can be used for extended periods of time. What is the scientific basis of these claims?

Task

You and your team of scientists have been asked by a consumer group to investigate the sleep-inducing claims for melatonin.

In order to do this task, you must complete each of the following:

1. Research the accuracy of the sleep-inducing claims of melatonin on the Internet and in the library.

2. Interpret the data table below, which shows the results of a sleep study of eight people who had trouble sleeping. They did not know what type of pill they were taking. Each pill was taken for five days.

3. Prepare an oral and written presentation to the consumer group on the sleep-inducing claims of melatonin.

4. Design and prepare a radio announcement for the public reporting on these claims.

5. Keep a journal of all the information and data that you have collected regarding melatonin.

Solution

In your presentation only include information and data from sources that you can verify as being accurate, current, and relevant. Include appropriate tables or graphs, interpretations, recommendations, and conclusions. Explain sources of error in the study and how it could be improved.

Melatonin Sleep Study (hours slept)

	Placebo (sugar pill)					3 mg Melatonin					0.3 mg Melatonin					Time Release 3 mg Melatonin					Average Night Sleep Unaided
	M	T	W	T	F	M	T	W	T	F	M	T	W	T	F	M	T	W	T	F	
1	5.5	6.25	7.25	5.0	6.0	6.0	4.25	5.5	5.25	6.0	4.5	6.75	4.25	5.0	4.5	6.75	7.0	6.25	4.5	5.5	5.0
2	5.5	5.0	7.5	6.25	6.75	7.75	6.25	7.5	6.0	7.5	4.25	6.25	5.25	5.25	6.0	7.25	6.75	5.5	7.5	5.0	6.4
3	6.0	7.5	7.75	6.75	8.0	6.25	8.5	6.0	8.25	8.0	6.0	8.25	7.5	5.25	8.0	8.0	5.75	7.0	8.25	7.0	7.0
4	6.25	6.0	7.0	8.0	7.75	8.5	5.75	7.0	6.75	6.0	5.5	4.0	6.75	8.0	6.75	5.0	7.5	6.0	7.0	5.5	5.2
5	8.0	6.0	6.5	7.5	8.0	6.25	4.5	6.0	4.75	6.0	7.0	8.0	5.75	7.25	8.0	6.25	5.75	8.0	5.0	7.0	6.6
6	8.5	7.0	6.75	9.0	5.75	6.5	8.0	6.0	8.5	6.0	5.0	5.25	6.0	3.75	6.0	7.0	6.5	5.75	8.0	7.75	6.0
7	6.5	4.75	6.75	4.0	7.0	7.0	5.5	7.25	5.25	8.0	6.5	5.0	8.0	6.5	5.0	7.5	8.0	6.75	6.0	5.75	5.8
8	7.0	8.0	6.5	7.0	5.50	6.25	7.0	4.75	4.0	5.0	5.0	6.5	4.75	6.75	6.0	7.25	5.0	6.0	4.75	4.02	6.2

Laboratory
Investigation

Designing an Experiment

Daphnia and Epinephrine

Although hormones are very small molecules that are released in minute amounts, they cause very noticeable effects in an organism. Epinephrine is a hormone that prepares the body to deal with stress. It increases the heart rate and the metabolic rate. In this investigation, you will observe the heart of a small crustacean called *Daphnia*, or water flea, and you will determine the effects epinephrine has on its heart.

Problem

What effects does epinephrine have on a *Daphnia*? **Design an experiment** to answer this question.

Suggested Materials (per group)

- *Daphnia* culture
- 0.01% epinephrine solution
- depression slides
- medicine droppers
- microscope

Suggested Procedure

1. Use the medicine dropper to transfer a single *Daphnia* from the culture to the center of the depression slide. The *Daphnia* will look like a small white dot.

2. Place the slide under the low-power objective of a microscope and observe the *Daphnia*. Locate the heart.

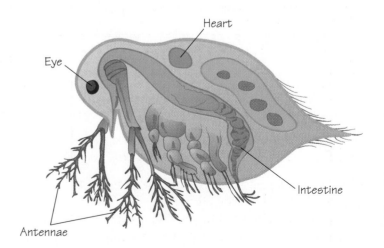

Heart

Eye

Intestine

Antennae

3. Count the number of times the heart beats in one minute. Record this information in a data table similar to Data Table 1.

4. Repeat step 3 two more times. Then average the three measurements. Record your data. Return the *Daphnia* to the culture dish.

5. Using a procedure similar to the one given in steps 1 through 4, determine the effect a 0.01% solution of epinephrine has on the *Daphnia's* heart.

6. Formulate a hypothesis. Make sure that you have your teacher's approval before you perform the experiment.

7. Be sure to return the *Daphnia's* heartbeat to its normal rate. To do so, remove some of the epinephrine solution from the slide with a medicine dropper. Using a clean medicine dropper, replace the volume of the liquid with water from the culture. Continue observing and counting the heart rate every other minute until the heart rate returns to normal.

8. Carry out your experiment and record your data in a data table similar to Data Table 2.

Observations

Data Table 1
Normal Heart Rate
Count 1
Count 2
Count 3
Average

1. Share your observations and measurements with the rest of the class. As a class, find the average number of heartbeats for the *Daphnia* before the epinephrine solution was added and just after it was added.

Data Table 2	
Heart Rate With Epinephrine	
Time (minutes)	**Heart Rate**
1	
3	
5	
7	
9	

2. What was the effect on the heart rate when you added the epinephrine solution?

3. How long did it take the *Daphnia* to return to a normal heart rate?

Analysis and Conclusions

1. Formulate a hypothesis to explain the results of your experiment. Could a different hypothesis also explain the results? Discuss this possibility.

2. How do you think the *Daphnia* adjusted its heart rate to the epinephrine solution?

3. Why might it be a good idea to take an average of the class data in this experiment?

4. Why do you think the *Daphnia* are useful organisms in an experiment such as this? Explain your answer.

Extensions

Design an experiment to determine the effects of various concentrations of epinephrine solution on a *Daphnia*.

Chapter 16 Review

Study Outline

16-1 Glands and Hormones

▶ The endocrine system regulates overall metabolism, homeostasis, growth, and reproduction. It is composed of specialized glands and tissues that secrete hormones.

▶ Hormones, which act as chemical messengers, are released directly into the bloodstream and travel through the body to specific target tissues.

▶ Protein-type hormones consist of chains of amino acids or related compounds. Steroid hormones are lipidlike, carbon-ring compounds that can pass through cell membranes.

▶ The activity of most endocrine glands is controlled by a negative-feedback mechanism, whereby the concentration of a certain substance in the blood stimulates or inhibits gland function.

▶ There are two mechanisms by which a hormone produces its effect within target cells. Steroid hormones directly enter the cell. Protein-type hormones do not enter the cell, but bind to receptors on the cell membrane.

16-2 The Human Endocrine System

▶ The pituitary gland controls a number of other endocrine glands. The hypothalamus connects the pituitary to the brain and controls the release of hormones by the pituitary.

▶ Other endocrine glands include the thyroid gland, the parathyroid gland, the adrenal glands, the islets of Langerhans, ovaries, and the testes.

▶ Other glands in the body that produce hormones include the thymus, the stomach, and the small intestine.

Chapter Assessment

Multiple Choice

Choose the letter of the answer that best completes each statement or answers the question.

1. The adrenal medulla secretes the hormone
(a) thyroxine. (b) estrogen. (c) epinephrine.
(d) testosterone.

2. Glands that discharge their secretions into ducts are called (a) endocrine glands. (b) exocrine glands. (c) prostaglandins. (d) gonads.

3. The most important androgen secreted by the testes is (a) testosterone. (b) estrogen. (c) pro-gesterone. (d) prostaglandin.

4. The thyroid secrets the iodine-containing hormone (a) glucagon. (b) thyroxine. (c) norepinephrine. (d) progesterone.

5. Diabetes mellitus results when insulin is not produced in sufficient quantities by the (a) pituitary gland. (b) parathyroid glands. (c) gonads. (d) islets of Langerhans.

6. The regulatory mechanism that tends to return a hormone level to its normal value is called (a) positive feedback. (b) hypersecretion. (c) hyposecretion. (d) negative feedback.

7. Hormones of the adrenal cortex that include cortisol and aldosterone are called (a) corticosteroids. (b) releasing factors. (c) gonads. (d) prostaglandins.

8. The development of the female reproductive system is stimulated by a hormone produced by the ovaries called (a) glucagon. (b) estrogen. (c) epinephrine. (d) thyroxine.

9. Which gland produces parathormone, which regulates metabolism of calcium? (a) pituitary (b) parathyroid (c) thyroid (d) adrenal

10. Which gland could become enlarged due to a lack of iodine in the diet? (a) pituitary (b) adrenal (c) thyroid (d) islets of Langerhans

Content Review

Answer each of the following in complete sentences.

11. How do exocrine glands and endocrine glands differ?

12. Compare positive feedback with negative feedback.

13. Why is the pituitary called the master gland?

14. How is the release of hormones by the anterior pituitary controlled?

15. Why must blood calcium levels be kept fairly constant?

16. What are the effects of epinephrine and norepinephrine?

17. What is diabetes? How is it caused, and what are its symptoms?

18. What are the risks of anabolic steroid misuse?

19. What are the functions of the hormones thymosin and melatonin?

20. How do the hormones gastrin and secretin function in the digestive system?

Graphic Organizing

For information on graphic organizers, see Appendix G at the back of this text.

21. **Word Map** Construct a word map for the term *endocrine gland.* Include at lease five examples.

22. **Line Graph** Construct a line graph using the data in the chart. The data are from an experiment on two rats in which only rat B received daily injections of growth hormone. Plot body weight (grams) on the vertical axis and time (days) on the horizontal axis. Plot the data for both rats on the same graph, using a different color for each line. What can you conclude about the effect of growth hormone on body weight?

Time	Body Weight (grams)	
(days)	Rat A	Rat B
0	20	20
100	140	230
200	200	310
300	240	370
400	245	440
500	250	460
600	250	500

Critical Thinking and Problem Solving

Discuss each of the following in a brief paragraph.

23. **Comparing** Compare the structure, secretion, and action of hormones with those of enzymes.

24. **Predicting** Predict the effects of permanent damage to the beta cells of the islets of Langerhans.

25. **Communicating** Use an everyday example that is not described in the text to explain the process of negative feedback.

26. **Interpreting** In normal individuals the blood glucose concentration before breakfast is between 80 and 90 mg/100 mL of blood. A blood-sugar level above 110 mg/100 mL of blood is indicative of diabetes. Each of two patients suspected of having diabetes is given a glucose tolerance test, in which ingestion of a glucose solution is followed by the periodic measurement of blood samples of glucose levels. The results of the test are recorded in the table below. Prepare a line graph of the data, identify the normal individual (a) and the diabetic individual (b), and describe what happens to the glucose concentration in each. Using the data in your graph, make a hypothesis regarding insulin secretion in the diabetic person.

Time	Blood Glucose (mg/100 mL)	
(hrs.)	Individual A	Individual B
0	90	150
$\frac{1}{2}$	120	180
1	140	220
$1\frac{1}{2}$	110	250
2	90	240
$2\frac{1}{2}$	85	230
3	90	210
$3\frac{1}{2}$	85	190
4	90	170

27. **Communicating** Construct a simple flow chart to illustrate the stages in the human body's response to sudden stress. Include major chemical pathways, involved organs and body systems, and resulting behaviors.

333

Performance-Based Assessment

Eating Disorders

Background

More than 50 million Americans, including 20% of all teenagers, are considered overweight (10–20% above ideal weight) or obese (20% above ideal weight). Many overweight people, if not most, have tried to lose weight. Most of these efforts are unsuccessful.

Why is it so difficult to lose weight and keep it off? There are many reasons. When a person goes on a diet, the first few pounds disappear easily, but then the body seems to resist losing weight. The body interprets weight loss as starvation and makes certain metabolic changes to retain fat. The body begins to burn fat more slowly and adapts to a lower caloric intake. This is why very few people are able to meet their weight goals. Despite pills and fad diets, 90% of dieters will regain lost weight within a year or two. Although weight is genetically determined, experts believe that long-term weight loss or weight control involves a combination of moderate dieting, moderate exercise, and behavior modification.

For most people, maintaining their ideal weight is not a problem. Others, however, seem to be obsessed with their body image, and this obsession can lead to severe eating disorders. Approximately 1% of adolescent girls develop anorexia nervosa, a dangerous condition in which they can literally starve themselves to death. This disorder involves extreme weight loss—at least 15% below the individual's normal body weight. Many people with this dangerous condition look emaciated but are convinced they are overweight. Sometimes they must be hospitalized to prevent starvation.

Another 2–3% of young women develop bulimia, a destructive pattern of excessive overeating followed by vomiting or other "purging" behaviors to control their weight. People with bulimia consume large amounts of food and then rid their bodies of the excess calories by vomiting. Because individuals with bulimia "binge and purge" in secret, and maintain normal body weight, they can hide their problem. Both anorexia and bulimia also occur in men and older women, but much less frequently than in young woman. Like anorexics, bulimics are often hard-driving perfectionists seeking to gain control of some aspects of their lives. Both bulimia and anorexia can be difficult to treat and often require long-term therapy.

Binge eating disorder (BED), a condition in which the individual periodically eats huge quantities of food, is found in about 2% of the general population. Like bulimia, the disorder is characterized by episodes of uncontrolled eating or bingeing. However, BED differs from bulimia because people with BED do not purge their bodies of excess food. Individuals with BED feel that they lose control of themselves when eating. They eat large quantities of food and do not stop until they are stuffed. Most people with the disorder are obese and have a history of weight fluctuations.

The complex interaction of emotional and physiological problems in eating disorders calls for a comprehensive treatment plan, involving a variety of experts and approaches. Ideally, the treatment team includes a doctor, a nutritionist, and a counselor. Group therapy, in which people share their experiences with others who have similar problems, is very effective.

Problem

You are a licensed therapist specializing in eating disorders and have been asked by the National Institute of Mental Health to address this problem.

Task

Choose one of the following tasks.

1. Submit a written proposal for a public service advertising campaign about eating disorders. Using the chart on this page and research sources, include the answers to the following questions:

- What are the causes of eating disorders?
- How do eating disorders affect the various systems of the body?

- What personality traits, genetic factors, environmental factors, and physiological makeup are common to people with eating disorders?
- How can specific treatments, and support from family and friends, help a person with an eating disorder?
- Why are eating disorders more common in women than in men?
- How can you tell the difference between a thin person and an anorexic person?
- Has our cultural emphasis on thinness helped create eating disorders?
- Where can people find help for eating disorders?

2. Based on your Internet and library research, prepare a series of one-minute television commercials or a series of print advertisements that will appear in popular magazines. Keep a journal of your research.

Some Symptoms of Anorexia and Bulimia	
Mind	**Body**
Obsession or preoccupation with food	Frequent headaches
Low self-esteem, poor self-image	Irregular or slow heart rate
Perfectionism, feelings of guilt	Tingling in extremities
Depression or mood swings	Dizziness, light-headedness
Excuses for not eating regularly	Teeth and gum deterioration
Anxiety or panic attacks	Dry skin, hair loss

Poppies growing on the Kenai Peninsula, Alaska.

Discovery Learning Activity

Plant Parts

1. Working in a group, obtain photographs of plants from your teacher.

2. After examining each photograph, make a labeled drawing of a "generic" plant. In labeling the drawing, use the most general terms you know for the plant parts. Make sure you draw what is both above ground and below ground.

3. Include a brief phrase with each label to describe the function of that part. What is a typical plant? What parts do all plants have?

Discovery Learning Activity

Do Plants Need Light?

1. Working in a group, obtain a potted plant from your teacher.

2. Then cut two pieces of black construction paper large enough to cover one leaf on the plant. Sandwich the leaf between the two pieces of construction paper, making sure that the leaf will not receive any sunlight. Tape the pieces of construction paper together.

3. Place the plant in an area that will receive sufficient sunlight for seven days. After this time, uncover the leaf and observe its color.

Plant Nutrition

········· **Guide for Reading** ·········

Previewing the Chapter

Bright sunlight dapples the leaves of these colorful pink water lilies. Their waxy green leaves float on the surface of the water, capturing some of the sun's energy and absorbing carbon dioxide. Below the water's surface, the lily's roots soak up water and minerals. The sun's energy will transform these raw materials into food for the water lily. What is photosynthesis? How is sunlight used to drive the reactions of photosynthesis?

Key Words

chemosynthesis, chlorophyll, light-independent reactions, grana, light-dependent reactions, photosynthesis, stroma

Key Concepts

- **Describe** the role that light plays in photosynthesis.
- **Compare** the light-dependent reactions and light-independent reactions of photosynthesis.
- **Identify** the photosynthetic pigments in spinach leaves. (Laboratory Investigation)

17-1 Plants and Light

Section Objectives:

- *Describe* the experiments that provided the basic facts about the process of photosynthesis.
- *Explain* what happens when light is absorbed by a pigment.
- *List* some of the characteristics of chlorophyll.
- *Draw* a chloroplast and label its parts.

Historical Background

In the early 1600s, the Flemish physician Jan van Helmont grew a small willow tree in a pot for five years, adding only water to the pot. At the end of the five years, he found that the tree had gained 75 kilograms, but there was no change in the mass of the soil. Van Helmont concluded that the new plant material came directly from water.

In the 1770s, Joseph Priestley, an English chemist, wanted to know what would happen to a plant placed in air "damaged" by a burning candle. It was known that a burning

▲ **Figure 17–1**

Capturing Light Energy. Plants capture energy from the sun and use it to make the high-energy compounds essential for life.

Figure 17–2

Antoine Lavoisier. Through his experiments, Lavoisier showed that burning removes oxygen from the air.

candle placed in a closed container went out and that animals could not live in air in which an object could no longer burn. Priestley found that plants were able to grow well in this "damaged" air. In fact, the plant could restore the ability of the air to support a flame and an animal. This was the first real evidence that plants interact with air in some way.

Within a few years, the French chemist Antoine Lavoisier (lah vwahz ee AY) showed that oxygen is removed from the air during burning. See Figure 17–2. Scientists then realized that animals need oxygen from the air, just as a flame does. When the oxygen in air has been used up, air can no longer support animal life or burning. On the other hand, plants give off oxygen to the air.

Other discoveries about plant growth followed throughout the 1700s. The Dutch physician Jan Ingenhousz (ING en howz) found that plants give oxygen to the air only in sunlight. Jean Senebier, a Swiss clergyman, found that plants take in carbon dioxide during growth in sunlight. By the beginning of the 1800s, scientists had identified the basic requirements for plant growth: carbon dioxide, water, and light.

Photosynthesis

Some organisms, such as green plants, capture the energy of sunlight and transform it into chemical energy. This process of capturing and transforming the energy of sunlight into chemical energy is called **photosynthesis** (foh tuh SIN thuh sis). When green plants carry out photosynthesis, they use carbon dioxide and water to make glucose, and they release oxygen. Most of the oxygen in the atmosphere is thought to be the result of photosynthesis.

As you read in Chapter 8, organisms that are capable of making food from simple inorganic substances are called *autotrophs* (AWT uh trohfs). All green plants, many protists, and some forms of bacteria are autotrophic. *Heterotrophs* (HET uh ruh trohfs) are organisms that cannot make their own food and must depend on other plants and animals as their source of food.

There are two major types of autotrophs. Both types use carbon dioxide as a source of carbon to make food. Those that use light energy to drive the reactions needed to make food are called **photoautotrophs** (foh toh AWT uh trohfs). Normally, these organisms are referred to as photosynthetic organisms. The other, less familiar, types of autotrophs are certain kinds of bacteria. These bacteria oxidize inorganic chemicals for the energy to drive their food-making reactions. These bacteria are called **chemoautotrophs** (keem oh AWT uh trohfs).

Light Energy Sunlight is a form of energy that is known as *radiation*. Radiation travels in waves. The distance between the crest of one wave and the crest of the next wave is the *wavelength* of the light, as shown in Figure 17–3. Sunlight is a mixture of all visible wavelengths. If all wavelengths of light are reflected equally by an object, the object appears white to the human eye. Thus,

Figure 17–3

The Meaning of Wavelength. Light is energy that travels in waves. The distance between the crests of two consecutive waves is the wavelength. ▼

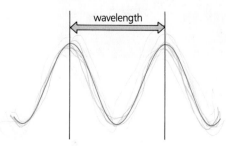

wavelength

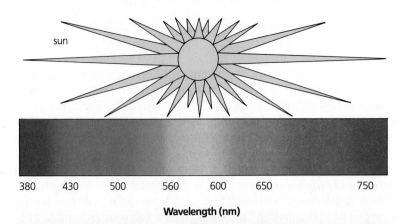

The Visible Light Spectrum. We perceive different wavelengths of light as different colors (top). Shorter wavelengths of light have higher energy than longer wavelengths. White light is made up of all visible wavelengths. When white light is passed through a prism (bottom), the light rays of different wavelengths spread out to form a spectrum. The colors in a spectrum appear in order of wavelength.

sunlight is called "white light." When a beam of white light passes through a prism, the rays of different wavelengths are bent by different amounts. This causes the light to spread out, forming a *spectrum* (SPEK trum) similar to the one in Figure 17–4 (bottom). The colors appear in the order of their wavelengths with the shortest wavelength (violet) at one end and the longest (red) at the opposite end. Figure 17–4 (top) shows the visible light spectrum.

Although light travels in waves, it acts as if it were made up of particles. Each particle of light, which is called a **photon** (FOH tahn), has a fixed amount of energy. The shorter the wavelength of light, the more energy its photons carry.

When light strikes matter, some of the matter's atoms may absorb photons. When the energy of a single photon is transferred to one of the electrons in the atom, it raises the atom's energy. In most cases, the absorbed energy is changed to heat. In photosynthetic organisms, however, the absorbed energy is used to make chemical bond energy.

A substance that absorbs light is called a **pigment**. Wavelengths of light that are not absorbed either pass through the material or are reflected off it. What your eye sees as the color of an object is the color of the reflected light. For example, a red object absorbs all the visible colors of the spectrum except red, which is reflected. The different colors, or wavelengths, of light absorbed by a particular pigment make up its **absorption spectrum.**

Photosynthetic Pigments

The most abundant and important photosynthetic pigments are the **chlorophylls** (KLOR uh fils). In plants, there are two types of chlorophyll—chlorophyll *a* and chlorophyll *b*. Both forms of chlorophyll absorb red and blue light and reflect green light. This is what gives chlorophyll its green color and explains why plants appear green to the unaided human eye. Chlorophyll *a* is the primary photosynthetic pigment. It is involved directly in converting light energy to chemical energy. Chlorophyll *b* and other pigments, known as *carotenes* and *xanthophylls,* absorb light and transfer the energy to chlorophyll *a.* Carotenes, which are orange, and xanthophylls, which are yellow, absorb light in regions of the spectrum different from chlorophyll *a.* Because of this, plants can absorb and use light from a wider region of the spectrum than would be possible if chlorophyll *a* were the only photosynthetic pigment. See Figure 17–5.

Normally, the presence of chlorophyll *a* hides the carotenes and xanthophylls in leaves. Carotenes, xanthophylls, and other pigments can be seen in autumn when chlorophyll starts to break down and the leaves turn color.

MiniLab

Skill: Designing an Experiment

Breaking Out of Prism

Problem

How is white light separated into the colors of the visible spectrum? **Design an experiment** to find out.

Procedure

1. Obtain a sheet of white paper, a flashlight (or a lamp), and a prism.

2. Formulate a hypothesis to explain what will happen to the light when it is passed through a prism.

3. Design an experiment to test your hypothesis.

4. On a separate sheet of paper, write the procedure for your experiment.

5. With your teacher's approval, conduct your experiment.

Analyze and Conclude

1. What was your hypothesis?

2. What happened to the light as it passed through the prism?

3. What do you think the prism does to the wavelengths of light, which enables you to see the different colors?

4. What colors of the visible spectrum did you observe?

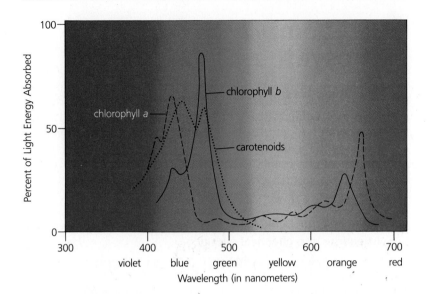

◀ **Figure 17–5**
Absorption Spectrum for Chlorophylls and Carotenes. The peaks on this graph represent wavelengths of high absorption. The chlorophylls absorb light in the red and blue ranges of the spectrum and reflect light in the green-yellow range. Carotenes absorb only in the blue and blue-green ranges.

The Chloroplasts

In green plants, photosynthesis occurs within **chloroplasts** (KLOR uh plasts). As you may recall from Chapter 5, section 5–2, chloroplasts are organelles containing *photosynthetic membranes* in which the photosynthetic pigments are found. The photosynthetic membranes are arranged in the form of flattened sacs called **thylakoids** (THY luh koidz). Stacks of thylakoids are called **grana** (GRAH nuh). The regions between the grana make up the part of the chloroplast known as the **stroma** (STROH muh).

The combination of chlorophyll and photosynthetic membranes is vital for converting light energy to chemical energy. If chlorophyll is removed from photosynthetic membranes and exposed to light, it absorbs the energy in light but immediately loses it as heat and light of a longer wavelength. Only when chlorophyll is combined with the specialized proteins and other substances in photosynthetic membranes can the light energy be captured *and* stored as chemical energy.

17-1 Section Review

1. Name the process used by plants to make food.
2. What substance is restored to air by photosynthesis?
3. Name the pigments found in chloroplasts.
4. What are stacks of thylakoids called?

Critical Thinking

5. Classify the following organisms as autotrophic or heterotrophic: oak tree, mushroom, seaweed, wolf, human, ameba, tomato plant, fish. (*Classifying*)

17-2 Chemistry of Photosynthesis

Section Objectives:

- *Write* the equation for photosynthesis.
- *Explain* what happens during the light-dependent reactions and during the light-independent reactions.
- *Compare* cellular respiration with photosynthesis.

Reactions of Photosynthesis

In green plants, the following equation summarizes the conversion of light energy into chemical energy:

$$6CO_2 + 12H_2O \xrightarrow{\text{light}} C_6H_{12}O_6 + 6O_2 + 6H_2O$$

This equation for photosynthesis represents many separate chemical reactions that occur in chloroplasts in the light. These reactions are classified into two types. Reactions of the first type are called the **light-dependent reactions.** As their name suggests, light-dependent reactions take place only in the presence of light. Light supplies the energy for these reactions. Reactions of the second type are called the **light-independent reactions.** Although these reactions can occur without light, they depend upon the high-energy chemical products made in the light-dependent reactions. Both sets of reactions are part of the process of photosynthesis. In green plants, light-dependent reactions produce high-energy compounds that the light-independent reactions use to make glucose. Figure 17–6 shows how the light-dependent reactions and the light-independent reactions depend on each other.

Figure 17–6

Photosynthesis. The chemical reactions of photosynthesis can be divided into two types—the light-dependent reactions and the light-independent reactions. The light-dependent reactions require sunlight, and take place in the grana of the chloroplast. The light-independent reactions do not require light. These reactions take place in the stroma of the chloroplast. The two sets of reactions work together to convert light energy into the chemical energy of glucose. ▶

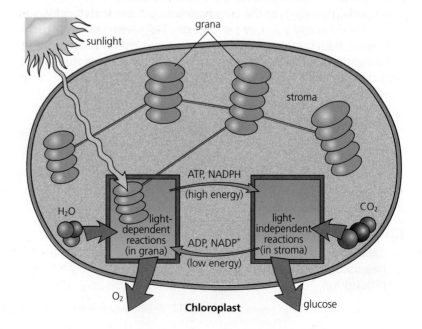

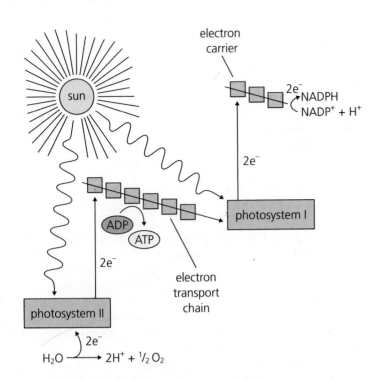

◀ **Figure 17–7**

The Light-Dependent Reactions. Light absorbed by photosystem II raises the electrons to a higher state of energy. The electrons are passed from the electron carrier along an electron transport chain to a lower energy state. In the process, some of their energy is packaged in the form of ATP. Light absorbed by photosystem I boosts the electrons to another electron carrier. These electrons are passed to $NADP^+$ forming NADPH. The electrons removed from photosystem I are replaced by those from photosystem II. The final products of the light-dependent reactions are ATP and NADPH.

Light-Dependent Reactions

Light-dependent reactions begin when the pigments in the photosynthetic membranes of the chloroplasts absorb light. The chlorophyll molecules in these membranes are packaged into two light-absorbing forms, called *photosystem I* and *photosystem II*. Each of these photosystems is made up of several hundred chlorophyll molecules. In the photosynthetic membrane of a single chloroplast, there are millions of these photosystems.

Photosystems I and II are linked together structurally and functionally. As you can see in Figure 17–7, when photosystem II absorbs light, electrons are passed to an electron transport chain. Similar to the electron transport chain used in cellular respiration (see Chapter 6), this chain uses the energy of the electrons to make ATP by pumping hydrogen ions (H^+), released from the splitting of water, into the interior of the grana. Inside the grana, there is a high concentration of hydrogen ions. ATP is formed when the H^+ move from the high concentration back across the grana membrane through special channels. These channels are linked with the ATP-synthesizing enzyme ATPase. This process of making ATP is called *chemiosmosis*. At the end of the chain, the electrons are passed to photosystem I. When photosystem I absorbs light, the high-energy electrons in it are passed to $NADP^+$ (nicotinamide adenine dinucleotide phosphate). The electrons and hydrogen ions combine with $NADP^+$ to form NADPH. $NADP^+$ is similar to the electron carrier NAD^+, which is used in cellular respiration. Photosystem II provides a continuous supply of electrons for the reactions. When it absorbs light and loses electrons, it replaces the lost electrons by removing electrons from water. As a result, oxygen is produced. In light, both photosystems simultaneously absorb light. One photosystem generates ATP, the other, NADPH. These two high-energy products are used to power the remaining reactions of photosynthesis—the light-independent reactions.

Light-Independent Reactions

While the light-dependent reactions are happening in the membranes of the chloroplasts, the light-independent reactions are taking place in the stroma. There, carbon dioxide, which diffuses into stroma from the external environment, is used to form glucose. The incorporation of carbon dioxide into an organic compound during photosynthesis is called *carbon fixation*. Carbon fixation occurs through a series of enzyme-controlled reactions called the *Calvin cycle*. The Calvin cycle is named after its discoverer, an American scientist, Melvin Calvin. Calvin won the Nobel Prize in 1961 for his discovery of this cycle. As you read about the Calvin cycle, refer to Figure 17–8.

The starting and ending compound in the Calvin cycle is a 5-carbon sugar called *ribulose bisphosphate,* or *RuBP.* The cycle begins when carbon dioxide reacts with RuBP. The products of this reaction are two molecules of a 3-carbon compound called

Can You Explain This?

Erica knew that plants release oxygen in the process of photosynthesis. She assumed she could determine the amount of photosynthesis a plant performed by measuring the amount of oxygen released.

On a sunny morning, Erica placed a plant inside a bell jar and measured the amount of oxygen. At the end of the day she measured the oxygen a second time to determine the amount of increase. Erica's teacher pointed out that the increase was not a true measure of the amount of photosynthesis. Her teacher said there was *more* oxygen involved in photosynthesis than was released in the bell jar.

■ *Propose an explanation for what happened to the "missing" oxygen.*

Figure 17–8

The Light-Independent Reactions (Calvin Cycle). In the Calvin cycle, carbon dioxide from the environment reacts with ribulose biphosphate (RuBP) to produce the 3-carbon compound PGA. ATP and NADPH are used to convert PGA to PGAL. Most of the PGAL reacts with ATP to make more RuBP, allowing the cycle to begin again. A small portion of the PGAL is used to produce glucose. ▶

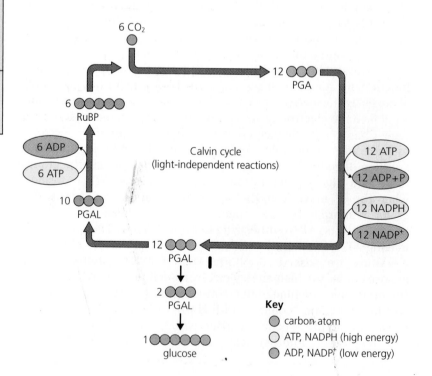

Key
- carbon atom
- ATP, NADPH (high energy)
- ADP, NADP⁺ (low energy)

phosphoglycerate, or *PGA.* The PGA molecules formed in the first reaction are converted to *phosphoglyceraldehyde,* or *PGAL.* NADPH and ATP—which are produced in the light-dependent reactions—provide the energy for this reaction.

As you can see in Figure 17–8, most of the PGAL is used to make more RuBP, so that the cycle can continue. For example, for every 6 molecules of CO_2 that react in the cycle, 12 molecules of PGAL are formed. Ten of these molecules are used to form 6 molecules of RuBP, while 2 PGAL molecules react to form 1 glucose molecule.

Factors Affecting Photosynthesis

Light intensity, temperature, and water and mineral availability are only a few of the factors that affect the rate of photosynthesis. As the intensity of sunlight increases, the rate of photosynthesis increases, but only up to a point. Usually, photosynthesis takes place most rapidly at a specific temperature. At extremes of temperature—below 0°C or above 35°C—the enzymes are damaged, and the rate of photosynthesis is slowed. A shortage of water tends to slow photosynthesis. If the shortage is severe, photosynthesis may stop. Of course, many minerals play a role in photosynthesis. If these minerals are in short supply, photosynthesis, as well as other metabolic processes, is affected.

Photosynthesis and Cellular Respiration

In its effect, photosynthesis is the reverse of cellular respiration. Both processes occur simultaneously in light. Respiration, however, takes place in the cytoplasm and mitochondria. Photosynthesis occurs in the chloroplasts. In respiration, glucose and oxygen are used to produce carbon dioxide and water and to release energy (see Chapter 6). In photosynthesis, carbon dioxide, water, and energy are used to produce glucose and to release oxygen. Thus, photosynthesis captures light energy, storing it as chemical energy, and cellular respiration releases chemical energy. Figure 17–9 compares photosynthesis and cellular respiration.

Photosynthesis and Respiration		
	Photo-synthesis	Respir-ation
Function	energy storage	energy release
Location	chloroplasts	mitochondria
Reactants	CO_2, H_2O	$C_6H_{12}O_6$, O_2
Products	$C_6H_{12}O_6$, O_2	CO_2, H_2O
Equation	$6CO_2 + 12H_2O +$ light energy $\rightarrow$ $C_6H_{12}O_6 + 6O_2 + 6H_2O$	$C_6H_{12}O_6 + 6O_2 + 6H_2O \rightarrow$ $6CO_2 + 12H_2O +$ chemical energy

▲ **Figure 17–9**
Comparison of Photosynthesis and Respiration.

17-2 **Section Review**

1. Write the equation for photosynthesis.
2. Name the two sets of reactions in photosynthesis.
3. What are the end products of the light-dependent reactions?
4. What is another name for the light-independent reactions?
5. Name two factors that affect the rate of photosynthesis.

Critical Thinking

6. Compare photosynthesis with cellular respiration. (*Comparing*)

▲ **Figure 17–10**

Sugar Cane. The C_4 pathway allows such plants as sugar cane and corn to photosynthesize rapidly.

17-3 Special Cases

Section Objectives:

■ *Explain* the adaptive advantages of C_4 photosynthesis.
■ *Compare* photosynthesis in bacteria and plants.

C_4 Plants

Although the process of photosynthesis is the same in all photosynthetic organisms, there are some interesting variations on the process. In addition to the Calvin cycle, some plants have another pathway that improves the efficiency of the Calvin cycle. Moreover, plants are not the only photosynthetic organisms. Many protists and bacteria carry out photosynthesis, and in some forms of bacterial photosynthesis, oxygen is not produced.

Some flowering plants use more than the Calvin cycle to fix CO_2. In these plants, called C_4 plants, CO_2 is first fixed in some of the leaf cells into a 4-carbon compound. This compound is transported into other nearby leaf cells where the Calvin cycle operates. In these cells, the C_4 compound breaks down, releasing the CO_2 previously incorporated into the compound. The released CO_2 enters the Calvin cycle and is made into glucose.

The extra photosynthetic pathway, called the *C_4 pathway*, acts as a CO_2 "pump." That is, it increases the concentration of CO_2 in the cells in which the Calvin cycle operates. This allows C_4 plants to fix CO_2 more rapidly than plants without a C_4 pathway. However, with this extra pathway, C_4 plants need more energy to fix CO_2 than plants with only the Calvin cycle. This is not a problem for C_4 plants because they grow best under conditions of high light intensity where there is more than enough light to generate the extra ATP needed. Sugar cane and corn are examples of C_4 plants.

CAM Plants

Many plants adapted to hot and dry climates prevent water loss by closing their stomates during the day. This prevents water loss, but it also prevents carbon dioxide from entering the leaf. To compensate, these plants take in carbon dioxide during the night when the temperature is lower. The CO_2 is stored temporarily, and converted to glucose when photosynthesis resumes the next day. Because the plants that use this process include members of the family *Crassulaceae*, it is called *crassulacean acid metabolism (CAM)*. CAM plants include many desert cacti.

Food-Making in Bacteria

All of the photosynthetic bacteria have photosynthetic membranes throughout their cytoplasm. The most familiar of these bacteria are the cyanobacteria. Cyanobacteria and another similar group carry out photosynthesis in the same way as plants.

Figure 17–11

A Cyanobacterium. Photosynthetic bacteria do not contain chloroplasts. Instead, photosynthetic membranes are present throughout the cytoplasm. (Magnification 6500 X). ▼

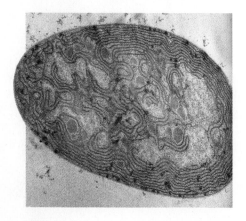

Some types of bacteria carry out **chemosynthesis**—a process in which food is made from carbon dioxide by using the energy of inorganic substances. Similar to photosynthetic organisms, the chemosynthetic bacteria fix carbon dioxide through the reactions of the Calvin cycle. However, the energy needed to make ATP and NADPH comes from the oxidation of inorganic substances, not from the absorption of light.

▲ **Figure 17–12**

Carnivorous Plants. Each leaf of a pitcher plant (left) is made up of a funnel with a pool of water at its base. If an insect falls into the funnel, it drowns in the pool. The insect is digested by enzymes secreted into the water. When an insect lands on the Venus flytrap (right), it is quickly trapped as the modified leaves snap shut. Glands within the trap secrete digestive enzymes, and nutrients are later absorbed by the leaves.

Heterotrophic Plants

Some plants have developed heterotrophic methods of nutrition in addition to, or instead of, photosynthesis. Some of these plants are parasitic. The mistletoe, for example, is a parasite of oaks and other trees. Although mistletoe is photosynthetic, it adds to its nutrition by siphoning sap from the vascular tissue of the host tree. The dodder plant is also parasitic, but it cannot photosynthesize. The roots of the dodder plant grow into the tissues of its host, from which it draws nutrients and water.

Some plants rely on insects to supplement their mineral nutrition. In bogs and marshes, the acidic water slows the rate of decay of dead organisms and limits the amount of nitrogen in the soil. In nitrogen-poor areas such as these, insects provide a source of nitrogen for making plant proteins.

17-3 Section Review

1. What is the C_4 pathway named after?
2. What is chemosynthesis?
3. How do CAM plants adapt for life in hot, dry climates?
4. Name two parasitic plants.

Critical Thinking

5. What would happen to a C_4 plant growing in a shaded area among plants without a C_4 pathway? Explain. (*Predicting*)

Laboratory Investigation

Chromatography of Plant Pigments

A biological process such as photosynthesis involves hundreds of substances. Separating and identifying these substances is one way of analyzing such a process. Chromatography is a method of separating substances from each other. In this activity, you will use paper chromatography to discover the photosynthetic pigments in spinach leaves.

Problem

What are the photosynthetic pigments in spinach leaves? Use paper chromatography to separate and **identify** the leaf pigments.

Materials (per group)

- isopropyl alcohol, 70%
- spinach leaf extract
- #3 filter paper
- scissors
- micropipette
- plastic eyedropper
- pencil
- metric ruler
- large test tube
- test-tube stopper
- test-tube rack
- beaker

Procedure

1. With scissors, cut a strip of filter paper narrow enough to fit inside the test tube without touching its sides. Cut it to be about 2 cm shorter than the test tube. Cut an arrow-shaped point 1.5 cm long, at one end of the strip. This end will be at the bottom of the test tube, as shown in the figure.

alcohol

350

2. Measure 2.5 cm up from the bottom tip of the strip and mark a point with a pencil at the midline of the strip. Do not use ink. Also place a pencil line across the strip about 1 cm below the top edge. See the figure.

3. Place the paper strip on a paper towel. Draw some leaf extract into the micro-pipette. Briefly touch the tip of the pipette to the pencil mark on the strip so a small spot of extract seeps onto the paper. Let the spot dry completely. Repeat this procedure until the spot is dark green.

4. Make a mark 1 cm from the bottom of the test tube and add alcohol with an eyedropper up to the mark. Place the paper strip into the test tube, making sure that the pigment spot is above the solvent. Seal the tube with a stopper.

5. Let the solvent rise until it reaches the mark at the top of the paper. Remove the paper strip and set it on a paper towel to dry.

6. Label a beaker "waste solvent." Pour the solvent remaining in the test tube into the beaker.

7. Observe the spots of color on the chromatogram. Draw a circle around each spot and label its color.

Observations

1. How many different colors were separated on your chromatogram?
2. Describe the various colors in order of their appearance.

Analysis and Conclusions

1. Name the pigment indicated by each color on the chromatogram.

2. Why do you think pencil, not ink, was used to make marks on the chromatogram?

3. Based on your results and the discussion of paper chromatography in Chapter 2, which pigment would you conclude is most soluble in the solvent? (You may wish to refer back to page 26.)

4. In addition to pigments, what other substances may have been separated, but are not visible on your chromatogram?

5. What would you predict about the photosynthesis of a plant whose leaf extract showed three instead of four pigments?

Extensions

Compare the pigments of spinach leaves to those of other types of leaves, such as pea, carnation, or snapdragon. Compare the width of the pigments on the chromatogram as well as the different numbers of pigment colors of each type of leaf.

Chapter 17 Review

Study Outline

17-1 Plants and Light

▶ In photosynthesis, light energy, carbon dioxide, and water are used to make glucose. Oxygen is released into the atmosphere as a byproduct.

▶ Plants contain the pigment chlorophyll that absorbs blue and red light and reflects green light.

▶ Chloroplasts are organelles that contain photosynthetic membranes arranged in sacs called thylakoids. Stacks of thylakoids, called grana, are surrounded by material called stroma.

17-2 Chemistry of Photosynthesis

▶ In the light-dependent reactions of photosynthesis, light energy is absorbed and used to remove electrons from water molecules and produce ATP, NADPH, and oxygen.

▶ ATP and NADPH from the light-dependent reactions drive the light-independent reactions, in which carbon dioxide combines with a 5-carbon sugar, forming two molecules of a 3-carbon compound. This process, called carbon fixation, repeats in a cyclic series of reactions called the Calvin cycle.

17-3 Special Cases

▶ Some flowering plants use a C_4 pathway in addition to the Calvin cycle to speed up the fixation of carbon dioxide.

▶ Cyanobacteria have chlorophyll *a* and carry out photosynthesis in the same way as plants.

▶ Chemosynthetic bacteria make ATP and NADPH from the energy produced by the oxidation of inorganic substances.

Chapter Assessment

Multiple Choice

Choose the letter of the answer that best completes each statement or answers the question.

1. The pigment in green plants, where photosynthesis takes place, is (a) chlorophyll. (b) mitochondrion. (c) grana. (d) stoma.

2. The Calvin cycle is part of (a) the light-dependent reactions. (b) the light-independent reactions. (c) respiration. (d) fermentation.

3. An experiment that showed that part of a growing plant's mass comes from water was performed by (a) Priestley. (b) Ingenhousz. (c) Van Helmont. (d) Calvin.

4. Photosynthesis produces (a) carbon dioxide. (b) water. (c) alcohol. (d) glucose.

5. Which of these is produced by the light-independent reactions? (a) PGAL (b) water (c) oxygen (d) ATP

6. Which of these is not produced in the light-dependent reactions? (a) NADPH (b) ATP (c) glucose (d) oxygen

7. What do the dodder plant and mistletoe plants have in common? (a) They feed on insects. (b) They are autotrophic. (c) They are not capable of photosynthesis. (d) They have developed some heterotrophic characteristics.

8. Leaves appear green because they (a) absorb only green wavelengths of light. (b) reflect green light while absorbing other wavelengths. (c) reradiate green light as well as heat. (d) reflect all wavelengths of light.

9. Which of the following statements about the rate of photosynthesis is correct? (a) It increases as water shortages increase. (b) It is unaffected by the supply of minerals. (c) It is usually highest at a specific temperature. (d) It decreases as the light intensity increases to a certain point and then it may increase.

10. All of the following statements about chloroplasts are correct except (a) Chloroplasts usually are found in the leaves of most plants. (b) The light-dependent reactions usually occur outside of the chloroplast. (c) The Calvin cycle occurs in the stroma. (d) Grana are stacks of thylakoids.

Content Review

Answer each of the following in complete sentences.

11. Explain what happens when a substance absorbs light.

12. When a nonphotosynthetic pigment absorbs light, what normally happens to the absorbed energy?

13. What function do photosynthetic pigments other than chlorophyll serve?

14. Explain the importance of photosynthetic membranes in photosynthesis.

15. Write the balanced chemical equation for the overall reaction of photosynthesis.

16. How do photosystems I and II work together?

17. Explain why the minimum number of carbon dioxide molecules needed to make a molecule of glucose is six.

18. How does the location of the stroma with respect to the thylakoids make for efficient photosynthesis?

19. Explain how temperature, light intensity, and the availability of water and minerals affect the rate of photosynthesis.

20. What are C_4 plants?

Graphic Organizing

For information on graphic organizers, see Appendix G at the back of this text.

21. Compare/Contrast Matrix Construct a compare/contrast matrix to compare photosynthesis and aerobic respiration (see Chapter 6). Use the following characteristics in your comparison: starting reactants; location of process within cell; whether energy-requiring or energy-releasing; end products; and organisms (autotrophs, heterotrophs, or both) that carry out the process.

Critical Thinking and Problem Solving

Discuss each of the following in a brief paragraph.

22. Predicting What do you think would happen to a plant that was placed in an airtight jar by a window? Explain your answer.

23. Inferring Suggest some possible physical characteristics of an environment in which chemosynthetic bacteria would thrive but photosynthetic bacteria would not.

24. Experimenting A student is told that sunlight causes a higher rate of photosynthesis than would an equally bright electric light. Design a controlled experiment that the student could use to test this statement.

25. Interpreting In 1882, an experiment was carried out by T. W. Engelmann in which oxygen-using bacteria and a filamentous strand of a green alga were exposed to light of different colors. As you can see in the graph below, the bacteria clustered in the areas of the alga exposed to violet light and red light. Propose an explanation for these results.

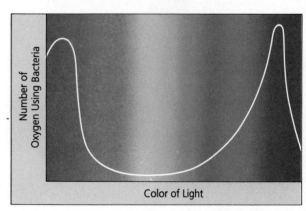

Discovery
Learning Activity

Which Side Are You On?

1. Working in a group, obtain a potted plant from your teacher.

2. Coat half of the plant's leaves on the top surface and the other half on the bottom surface with petroleum jelly.

3. Place the plant in an area that will receive sufficient sunlight for seven days.

4. Examine the plant each day. Based on your results, does carbon dioxide enter the plant through the top or the bottom of the leaves? Compare your plant with the other groups' plants. Did they have similar results?

Plant Structure

Previewing the Chapter

Palm trees sway in the tropical breezes along the Puna Coast of Hawaii. Unlike other trees, the leaves, or fronds, of the palm tree are all clustered at the top of its long, curving stem. As in other plants, tubelike tissues carry food and water throughout the palm tree. At the tips of roots and stem, areas of rapidly dividing cells allow for continued growth. How is the structure of a leaf suited to its function? How do roots and stems develop? What is the difference between herbaceous and woody stems?

Key Words

guard cells, leaf, meristem, mesophyll, phloem, root, stem, xylem

Key Concepts

- **Identify** the different types of plant tissues.
- **Compare** herbaceous and woody stems.
- **Observe** the water-transport tissues in certain types of vegetables. (Laboratory Investigation)

18-1 Plant Tissues

Section Objectives:

- *Name* the organs of a plant and describe their functions.
- *Explain* the functions of meristematic, protective, vascular, and ground tissues.
- *Describe* the structure and function of xylem and phloem.
- *Name* and *describe* the three types of cells that make up ground tissue.

Organization of Tissues

Plants, similar to animals, are made up of tissues that form organs. The organs of a plant are its roots, stems, leaves, and reproductive structures. See Figure 18–2. Unlike animals, however, plants do not have organ systems.

A plant is held in the soil and takes up water and minerals from the soil through its **roots. Stems** hold the leaves and allow them to receive sunlight. They also hold flowers, fruits, and seeds. **Leaves** are where photosynthesis—the process by which plants make food—takes place. *Flowers* and *cones* are reproductive structures. You will read about plant reproduction in Chapter 24.

Plants have fewer types of tissues than animals. Some plant tissues are made of only one type of cell. Others are made of two or more types of cells that work together. Some tissues are found throughout the plant,

▲ **Figure 18–1**

A Flowering Plant. These sunflowers, and all other plants, are made of various cell types organized into tissues.

Figure 18–2

Organs of a Plant. A longitudinal section through the stem tip shows the location of meristematic tissue. The cells of the apical meristem undergo rapid cell division, producing the cells that form new leaves and new stem tissue. The cells of the lateral buds are inactive but, at some future time, may start to divide and become the apical meristems of branches. ▶

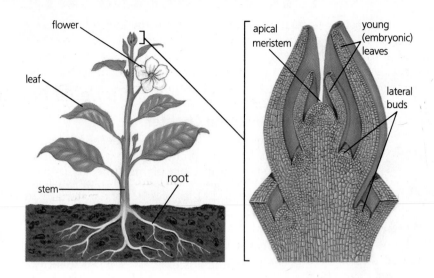

flower

leaf

stem

root

apical meristem

young (embryonic) leaves

lateral buds

while others are found only in specific structures. The main types of tissues are meristematic (mur ah stuh MAT ik), protective, vascular (VAS kyuh luhr), and ground.

Meristematic Tissues

In most animals, cell division takes place throughout the animal's body during periods of growth. In plants, however, cell division takes place in certain regions called **meristems** (MUR ah stehms). **Meristematic tissues** are made of cells that undergo mitosis and cell division frequently. The cells are thin-walled and lack vacuoles and are usually much smaller than mature plant cells. As you can see in Figures 18–2 and 18–10, meristems are present in the growing tips of stems and roots. These places are called apical meristems because they are found at the *apex* of the root or the stem. The cells made by apical meristems become the mature tissues of the plant body. They cause roots and stems to grow longer. However, many woody plants also grow wider. In woody plants, another type of meristem, called a **cambium,** adds tissues that increase the thickness of stems and roots. The **vascular cambium** produces layers of tissues that transport water and nutrients. Another type of cambium, the **cork cambium,** produces a layer of protective tissue called cork.

Protective Tissues

The **epidermis** is the *protective tissue* that forms the outer layer on leaves, green stems, and roots. The epidermal layer is usually one cell thick and its cells fit tightly together. The cells of the epidermis, which covers above-ground parts of a plant, secrete a waxy substance called *cutin* (KYOOT in). Cutin forms a layer over the outer surface of the epidermis. This layer, which is called the **cuticle** (KYOOT ih kul), cuts down on water loss and protects against infection by microorganisms.

Cork is a protective tissue that covers the surface of woody stems and roots. See Figure 18–3. It protects the more delicate inner tissues from mechanical injury. It also waterproofs the outer surface and prevents infection. Cork is produced by the cells of the *cork cambium.* Cork cells live for only a short time. Fully grown cork cells are dead. It is these dead cells with their waxy cell walls that protect the underlying living tissues.

Vascular Tissues

Xylem (ZY lum) and **phloem** (FLOH em) are the **vascular,** or conducting, **tissues** of the plant. Xylem, which is the material you think of as wood, conducts water and minerals from the roots upward through the stems and into the leaves of the plant. It also helps to support the plant and to hold it upright. Phloem conducts food and other dissolved materials in both directions along the length of the plant.

Most of the cells that form mature xylem are dead. They do not have cytoplasm. They form tubes that go from the roots up through the stems and leaves. Xylem is made mainly of two types of cells—*tracheids* (TRAY kee idz) and *vessel elements.* See Figure 18–4. Tracheids contain pits, or depressions, in their cell walls. The pits of neighboring tracheids are lined up, which permits the passage of water and minerals. Vessel elements are cells that form conducting tubes. These cells, which do not have end walls, are placed end to end, forming long, thin, hollow tubes called *vessels.* Xylem also has some living cells that serve as storage cells.

Unlike the tracheids and vessel elements of xylem, most of the cells that make up phloem are alive and contain cytoplasm. The substances transported by phloem are mainly organic compounds dissolved in water. Among these compounds are amino acids, sugars, and other carbohydrates. Food made in the leaves moves through the phloem to other parts of the plant. Unneeded food is

▲ **Figure 18–3**

Cork. The nonliving cork cells protect the internal tissues of woody stems and roots.

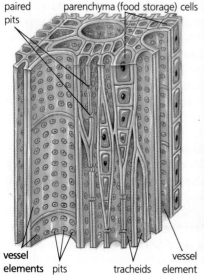

paired pits

parenchyma (food storage) cells

vessel elements pits tracheids vessel element

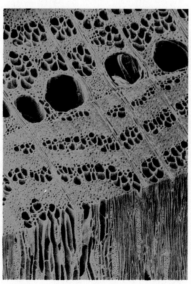

◀ **Figure 18–4**

Structure of Xylem. The water-conducting cells of the xylem are the elongated tracheids and open-ended vessel elements. Vessel elements form conducting tubes, vessels, which are seen in this scanning electron micrograph.

Figure 18–5

Figure 18–5
Structure of Phloem. Dissolved nutrients are transported through the phloem of the plant. Phloem is made up of sieve cells and companion cells. The dark-staining end-walls (sieve plates) of sieve cells are seen in the photograph on the right. ▶

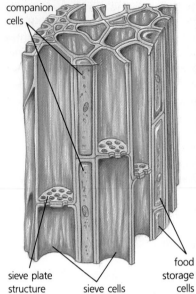
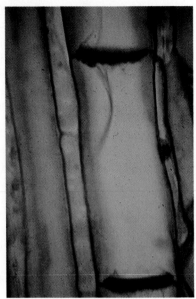

companion cells

sieve plate structure   sieve cells   food storage cells

often carried to the roots where it is stored. In the spring, sap, containing dissolved materials, is moved upward through the phloem.

Phloem is made of two types of cells, *sieve cells* and *companion cells.* See Figure 18–5. A sieve cell contains cytoplasm but does not have a nucleus when it is fully grown. The end walls of sieve cells have many small openings. Sieve cells line up end to end to form tubes, called *sieve tubes,* through which dissolved nutrients are transported. Companion cells are connected to neighboring sieve tubes by thin strands of cytoplasm. These cells, which have nuclei and cytoplasm, are thought to control the transport activities of sieve cells.

Ground Tissues

Tissues used in the production and storage of food and in the support of the plant are called **ground tissues.** The three types of ground tissues are parenchyma (puh REN kuh muh), collenchyma (kuh LEN kuh muh), and sclerenchyma (skluh REN kuh muh). These tissues are shown in Figure 18–6.

Parenchyma is a tissue made of unspecialized cells with thin cell walls. These cells are found in roots, stems, leaves, and fruits. The parenchyma cells in leaves and young stems have chloroplasts and make food by photosynthesis. In roots, fruits, and portions of stems, parenchyma cells are used for food storage.

Collenchyma cells are similar to parenchyma cells, but they are longer and have thick, but flexible, cell walls. They support stems and leaves and other parts of the plant.

Sclerenchyma tissue is made of cells with greatly thickened cell walls that are stiffened with a substance called *lignin.* Lignin is what makes wood rigid. Sclerenchyma tissue is found where support is needed. When fully grown, the cells usually do not have cytoplasm.

Figure 18–6
Ground Tissues. The three types of cells that make up ground tissues are parenchyma cells (top), collenchyma cells (center), and sclerenchyma cells (bottom). ▼

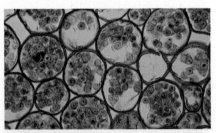
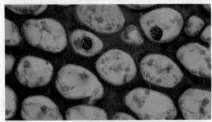
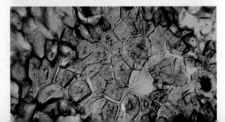

In fact, the cell walls are so thick that the space inside the cell is nearly eliminated. *Fibers* are a type of sclerenchyma cell. They are long cells that have tapered ends. They are often found in xylem and phloem. Fibers are used to make twine, rope, and thread. The term *fiber,* meaning a type of schlerenchyma cell, should not be confused with the term *fiber* when it is used in the dietary sense. Dietary fiber is the indigestible material that is present in all plant cell walls.

18-1 Section Review

1. Name the organs of a plant.
2. What type of tissue produces new plant cells?
3. What two conducting tissues are found in plants?
4. List the ground tissues found in plants.

Critical Thinking

5. If, for some reason, the phloem in the branches of a tree was not able to conduct food, how would the tree be affected? (*Relating Parts and Wholes*)

18-2 Roots

Section Objectives:

- *Explain* the functions of the root.
- *Describe* each of the following: primary root, secondary root, taproot, fibrous root, and adventitious root.
- *Name* the different zones of the root tip, and describe what happens to the cells in each zone.
- *Name* and *describe* the tissues of the root, and explain their arrangement and functions.

Types of Roots

The roots of a plant are usually found underground. As you have read, they hold the plant in the soil and take in water and minerals from the soil. They carry the water and minerals upward to the stem and transport dissolved food downward from the stem. In addition, the roots of some plants are specialized for food storage. Usually, the root system underground is as large as the system of stems and branches above ground. The roots spread out, covering a large area. In many plants, they grow no deeper than one meter into the soil.

The first structure to emerge from a sprouting seed is the **primary root.** See Figure 18–7. As the plant grows and matures, new roots form from within the tissues of the primary root. These new branches of the primary root are called **secondary roots.** As roots grow, the direction of their growth is affected by obstructions,

Figure 18–7

Primary and Secondary Roots. Secondary roots branch from the tissues of the primary root. ▼

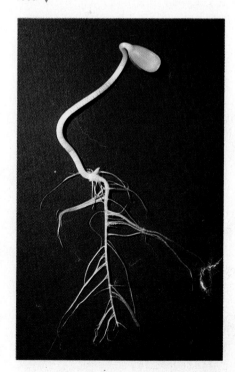

▲ **Figure 18–8**

Types of Root Systems. The taproot of the dandelion (left) grows rapidly and deeply into the soil. In the fibrous root system of grass (right), the numerous roots are all about the same size.

such as rocks, or other roots, in the soil. Other factors, such as moisture and the chemical makeup of the soil, also influence growth. These factors cause roots to grow in irregular ways with frequent bends and kinks.

Figure 18–8 shows the two common types of root systems: taproots and fibrous roots. A *taproot* system develops when the primary root grows rapidly and remains the largest root in the root system. Taproot systems grow deep into the soil and become thick and fleshy. Oak trees, carrots, turnips, and dandelions have taproots. A *fibrous root* system is made up of numerous roots, many of which are nearly equal in size. This type of system develops when branching secondary roots are as large as or larger than the primary root. Corn and grasses have fibrous root systems. In some plants, taproots and fibrous roots are modified for food storage. The carrot, radish, and beet are storage taproots, while the sweet potato and tapioca are fibrous storage roots.

Less common than taproot and fibrous root systems are various types of *adventitious* root systems. See Figure 18–9. These roots do not come from the primary root or from one of its

Figure 18–9

Adventitious Roots. The prop roots of corn (left) help to brace the root. The climbing roots of ivy (right) grow from the stem and attach the plant to a solid support. ▶

branches. Instead, they grow from stems or leaves. *Prop roots* grow from the stem down into the soil. These roots help to brace the plant. *Climbing roots,* for example, grow out from the stem and fasten the growing plant to a solid support. The climbing roots of ivy allow the plant to grow on building walls. Corn plants are an example of plants that have prop roots. Some plants, such as Spanish moss, live attached to trees and develop *aerial roots* that absorb moisture directly from the air.

Root Growth

Although the branches of a root system may be many meters long, only a small region at the tip of a root grows. There may be thousands of these root tips gradually extending into the soil. Other parts of the roots may become thicker, but they do not become longer. A mark made on the surface of a root will be found in the same spot year after year.

If you look closely at a root tip through a microscope, you will see that it is made up of a number of different zones. As you can see in Figure 18–10, each zone contains cells at different stages of development.

Root Cap   The **root cap** is a thimble-shaped group of cells that form a protective covering for the delicate meristematic tissues of the root tip behind it. As the addition of cells behind the root tip pushes it through the soil, the outer cells of the root cap are crushed. The crushed cells release a fluid that helps the passage of the root tip through the soil. To replace the crushed cells, new root cap cells are continuously formed by the meristematic tissue.

Meristematic Zone   The **meristematic zone** is a region of actively dividing cells just behind the root cap. The cells of this region are small and thin-walled. All the other cells of the root are formed from these cells.

Elongation Zone   Behind the meristematic zone is the **elongation zone.** In this zone, the cells, which were produced earlier in the meristematic zone, enlarge, pushing the root tip forward.

Maturation Zone   Behind the elongation zone is the **maturation zone,** or root hair zone, where the cells differentiate. **Differentiation** (dif uh RHEN she ay shen) is the process during which unspecialized cells develop into specialized cells. In the root, as in the stem, cells develop into fully grown, functioning cells of various types, such as xylem, phloem, and parenchyma.

Root Structure and Function

A cross section through the maturation zone will show that the root is made up of several tissue layers. See Figure 18–11. The outer-most layer—the epidermis—is only one cell thick. The taking-in of water and minerals from the soil is the primary function of the epidermis. Many epidermal cells have hairlike extensions that are

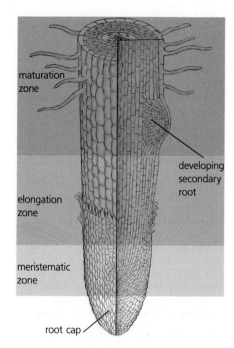

maturation zone

developing secondary root

elongation zone

meristematic zone

root cap

▲ **Figure 18–10**
Zones of the Root Tip. The meristematic zone is made of rapidly dividing, undifferentiated cells. In the elongation zone, the newly formed cells grow in length, forcing the root tip through the soil. In the maturation zone, the cells develop into specialized tissues.

Figure 18–11
Cross Section of Root Tip. The mature tissues of a root are seen in a cross section through the maturation zone. ▼

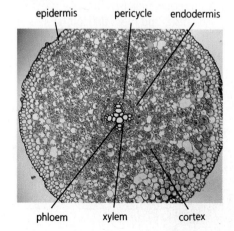

epidermis   pericycle   endodermis

phloem   xylem   cortex

Technology: Nitrogen-Fixing Corn

Plants need nitrogen to grow and carry out life processes. Although nitrogen gas is abundant in the atmosphere, plants cannot use it in that form. The nitrogen must be converted to ammonia or nitrate.

Plants in the pea family benefit from a relationship with nitrogen-fixing bacteria living in nodules on their roots. But, other crops, such as corn, have no such beneficial association. Farmers must apply fertilizers, which are expensive and environmentally damaging.

Now scientists are attempting to "engineer" nitrogen-fixing corn plants. First, they isolated genes from bacteria that control nitrogen-fixation. Then, they transferred the genes into strains of bacteria that they hope will live in corn roots. The next, and most difficult, step is to isolate genes that control nodule-formation in pea plants and transfer them into corn plants. The result, scientists hope, will be a symbiotic relationship between bacteria and corn plants—and increased crop yields.

■ *List some potential benefits and dangers of this nitrogen-fixing technology.*

called **root hairs.** These root hairs greatly increase the surface area for the absorption of water. They are present only in the small zone of maturation that lies behind the growing root tips. As the root tips grow, new root hairs are formed, and older ones die and fall off. It is in the region at the ends of the root branches that practically all water absorption occurs.

Just beneath the epidermis is the **cortex.** The parenchyma cells of the cortex store the plant's food, which is mainly starch. These cells also transport the water taken in by the root hairs to the conducting tissues in the center of the root. The innermost layer of the cortex is called the **endodermis** (en duh DER mis). The cells of this layer control the movement of water into the central cylinder.

The **vascular cylinder,** or central cylinder, is the core of the root. It is surrounded by a layer of parenchyma cells called the *pericycle* (PER uh sy kul), which is just inside the endodermis. All secondary roots grow from the pericycle layer. These roots push their way through the cortex and epidermis into the soil. Look again at Figure 18–11.

At the center of the vascular cylinder are the conducting tissues, xylem and phloem. The xylem carries water and minerals up the root to the stem and leaves. The phloem carries dissolved food, made in the leaves, throughout the plant. In the roots of woody plants, a vascular cambium develops between the xylem and phloem. The vascular cambium adds new xylem to its inside and new phloem to its outside.

Roots and Microorganisms

Plants often have bacteria or fungi living with their roots. Because this relationship helps at least one of the organisms, it is called a *symbiotic* relationship. In many cases, the symbiotic relationship is beneficial to both the plant and the organism.

Some plants, such as those in the pea family, have bacteria living in nodules on their roots. These bacteria convert nitrogen gas from the air in the soil into forms of nitrogen that the plant can use. In this symbiotic relationship, the plant benefits from the constant supply of usable nitrogen, and the bacteria benefit from an environment that offers plenty of food and water. Farmers may plow plants with nitrogen-fixing nodules into the ground in order to increase the nitrogen in their soil.

As you can see in Figure 18–12, many plants have fungi that grow on their roots. When a fungus grows in a symbiotic relationship with the roots of a plant, the resulting fungus root is called *mycorrhiza* (my kuh RY zuh) (plural, mycorrhizae). Some fungi grow meshlike coverings over the entire root surface, while others grow mostly within the root cortex. All mycorrhizal fungi have hairlike filaments that grow into the soil. These filaments act like a vast network of root hairs and provide the plant with water and nutrients that are absorbed from the soil. The fungi, in turn, seem to gain nutrients that are necessary for growth and development from the plant. Some plants with few or no root hairs at all are so dependent on the fungi living on their roots, that they cannot survive without them.

18-2 Section Review

1. What types of root systems are found in plants?
2. What happens in the maturation zone?
3. Where in the root are the xylem and phloem found?
4. What function do root hairs and mycorrhizae share?

Critical Thinking

5. If a permanent dye was injected into a cell in the apical meristem of a root, in what zone of the root would you expect to find the marker one week later? Six weeks later? (*Predicting*)

18-3 Stems and Leaves

Section Objectives:

- *Compare* the internal structures of herbaceous and woody stems.
- *Describe* the external structure of a woody dicot stem.
- *Make* and then *label* a drawing that shows the external structure of a leaf.
- *Describe* the internal structure of a typical leaf and relate it to its function.

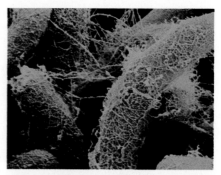

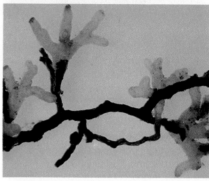

▲ **Figure 18–12**

Mycorrhizae. A scanning electron micrograph (top) reveals the meshlike structure of mycorrhizae. Mycorrhizae appear as swollen regions at the tips of the roots of an aspen tree (bottom).

Types of Stems

Like the roots of a plant, the stems of a plant also have several functions. Vascular tissue runs through the stem, transporting water, food, and minerals between the roots and the leaves. The stem also displays the plant's leaves to sunlight. Taller stems may hold leaves above other plants, thus increasing the leaves' exposure to sunlight. In addition, stems are adapted to different environments. Some underground stems, such as the white potato tuber, are specialized for food storage. The stem of the cactus is modified for water storage and photosynthesis. The stems of the strawberry plant run along the surface of the ground and sprout independent plants. This allows the plant to reproduce quickly.

Based on their stem structure, plants are grouped as herbaceous (her BAY shus) or woody. Herbaceous plants have soft, green, juicy stems that are called **herbaceous stems.** These plants usually live for one or two years. Corn and tomatoes are typical herbaceous

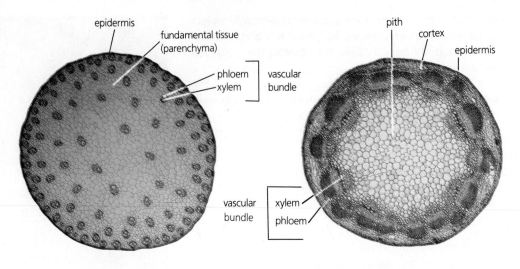

epidermis

fundamental tissue (parenchyma)

phloem

xylem

vascular bundle

Monocot Stem

pith

cortex

epidermis

vascular bundle

xylem

phloem

Dicot Stem

▲ **Figure 18–13**

Cross Sections of Herbaceous Monocot and Dicot Stems. The stem tissues of herbaceous monocots and dicots differ in organization. In cross section, the vascular bundles of a monocot are randomly scattered (left). In a dicot (right), the vascular bundles form a ring around the pith.

plants. Woody plants have **woody stems** that are made up of the thick, tough tissue that you know as wood. Plants with woody stems normally live for more than two years. Trees, such as oaks and maples, and shrubs, such as lilac and forsythia, have woody stems.

Herbaceous Stems—Internal Structure All the tissues of herbaceous plants develop from the cells produced by the apical meristems. Although the source of these tissues is the same for every herbaceous plant, the organization of the tissues depends on the type of plant. For example, the two groups of flowering plants, the *monocots* and *dicots,* each have a different type of stem structure. Refer to Figure 18–13 as you read about the stem structure of herbaceous monocots and dicots.

Corn is a typical herbaceous monocot. A protective epidermis encloses its soft, green stem. The epidermis is dotted with small openings, called **stomates** (STOH mayts). These openings allow an exchange of gases between the tissues inside the stem and the atmosphere.

Under the epidermis is a layer of chloroplast-containing cells, which are involved in photosynthesis. These cells include fiber cells that stiffen and support the stem. The interior of the corn stem is made of parenchyma cells. Bundles of vascular tissue are scattered throughout these cells. Each bundle, called a **vascular bundle,** contains xylem and phloem that are surrounded by supporting thick-walled cells. Because the stems of all herbaceous monocots have no cambium, they show little growth in diameter.

Typical herbaceous dicots include sunflowers, geraniums, buttercups, and alfalfa. In the herbaceous dicots, the stem is enclosed by a protective layer of epidermis. Inside the epidermis is the cortex, which is made up of collenchyma and parenchyma cells. These tissues provide support for the stem and serve for food storage. Inside the cortex is a ring of *vascular bundles.* Each bundle is made of an outer group of phloem cells, an inner group of xylem cells, and the vascular cambium, which is between the xylem and the phloem. The cambium may undergo a short period of cell division, adding a small amount of new xylem to its inside and a small amount of phloem to its outside. The central region of the stem is called the **pith.** Pith is made of parenchyma cells that store food.

Woody Stems—Internal Structure As you read earlier, the stems and roots of woody plants grow in thickness. This is the result of new tissues that are produced by vascular cambium throughout the plant's life. Almost all woody plants are dicots. Their stems are tough because of the large amounts of xylem that are added to the thickness of the stem. As shown in Figure 18–14, round layers of wood increase the thickness of the stem as xylem builds up on the inside of the vascular cambium. New phloem is also produced in round layers, but these are on the outside of the cambium. Unlike the xylem, the phloem produced by the vascular cambium does not build up. Instead, its older, outer layers break off as new phloem is produced.

Figure 18–14
Cross Section of a Woody Dicot Stem. The cell division activity of the vascular cambium produces xylem to its inside and phloem to its outside. The xylem accumulates as annual growth rings. The phloem, and the cork that develops within it, continuously peels off as it is being replaced. ▼

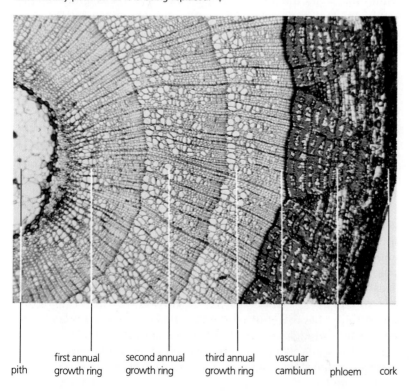

| pith | first annual growth ring | second annual growth ring | third annual growth ring | vascular cambium | phloem | cork |

Biology and You

Q: What are the health benefits of a high-fiber diet?

A: Recently, a great deal of attention has been paid to the health benefits of fiber, the nondigestible material found in plant cell walls. Fiber helps your digestive system function by providing bulk needed to move wastes through the colon. Vegetables, fruits, whole-grain breads, and cereals are rich in fiber.

Some studies show that a fiber-rich diet plays an important role in preventing colon cancer, gallstones, appendicitis, hemorrhoids, and colon infections. By strengthening your intestinal muscles and absorbing water, fiber may allow solid wastes to pass more quickly through the colon, giving only minimal exposure to infectious bacteria and cancer-causing agents.

For adults, 25 to 35 grams of fiber a day is recommended. Too much fiber may aggravate digestive conditions and prevent your body from absorbing essential minerals. A sensible approach to daily intake of fiber is to eat a normal diet that includes fresh fruits and vegetables, whole-grain breads, and cereals.

■ *Plan a day's menu that includes fiber-rich foods at each meal. Then, ask some friends if they would choose to eat the foods on your list.*

▲ **Figure 18–15**
Annual Rings. Each year's growth is visible as an annual ring in the cross section because of differences in spring and summer wood.

Figure 18–16
External Structure of Dormant Woody Dicot Stem. Woody stems produce a terminal bud at the end of each growing season. A longitudinal section through a terminal bud shows the bud scales surrounding the apical meristem and embryonic leaves. In spring, the bud scales fall off and the bud may develop into a new stem, leaves or flowers. ▼

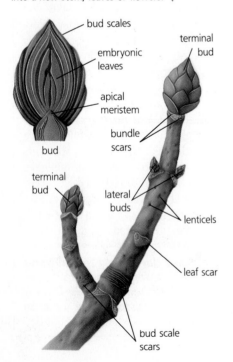

The growth of new xylem during each growing season results in the formation of *annual rings,* shown in Figure 18–15. The age of a woody dicot stem may be found by counting these rings. Each annual ring shows one year of growth. In some woody dicot stems, the cells of the xylem formed in the spring (known as *spring wood*) are larger and lighter in color than those formed in the summer (known as *summer wood*).

The width of the annual rings may vary according to climate that existed during the growing season. Favorable conditions produce wide growth rings. Scientists know by counting the annual rings that some trees, like the giant sequoias of California, live for thousands of years. These trees provide a historical record of changes in climate.

In young woody dicots, the center of the stem is filled with pith, and there is a cortex layer inside the epidermis. In older woody stems, the cells of the pith die, and the cortex is replaced by phloem from the vascular cambium. The living xylem cells, which conduct water, lie next to the cambium. This light-colored xylem is called *sapwood.* The thickness of the sapwood remains fairly constant from year to year. This is because old sapwood is converted to *heartwood* as new sapwood is produced by the cambium. Heartwood is the older, inner, dark-colored region of xylem. Since this layer is always being added to, the area occupied by heartwood increases over time.

The outermost layer of a woody stem is the bark, a protective tissue. On young stems, the bark may be thin, but older stems and trunks have bark that is much thicker. Bark is made of phloem, cork cambium, and cork cells. The cork cells are made by the cork cambium. The inner, younger part of the bark is alive, while the outer, older part is dead tissue. Bark is made as the stem grows in diameter. As the stem size gets larger, and the older outer bark cracks and peels off, new bark takes its place.

Woody Stems—External Structure

Figure 18–16 shows the external features of a dormant twig. A dormant twig is one that has lost its leaves for the winter. At the tip of the twig is the **terminal bud.** The terminal bud is made up of apical meristem, enclosed by overlapping protective scales, called *bud scales.* The bud scales are produced at the end of the previous growing season. When growth begins again in the spring, the apical meristem begins active cell division and forms new stem tissues and leaves. At this time, the bud scales fall off, leaving scars on the twig, called *bud scale scars.* These scars mark the point at which the season's growth began. The length of stem between two successive sets of bud scale scars is one year's growth.

Another feature of the dormant twig is the *leaf scar. Leaf scars* are formed when leaves drop off the stem in autumn. The scars mark the points where leaves from other growing seasons were fastened to the stem. A layer of protective tissue forms at the scar to protect the tissues inside the stem. Within the leaf scars are small dots called *vascular bundle scars.* These are the points at which vascular bundles containing xylem and phloem passed from the stem into the leaf.

Above each leaf scar is a **lateral,** or *axillary,* **bud.** Lateral buds are found just above the point where a leaf is or was attached to the stem. These buds may develop into new branches, or they may remain small and dormant. The points along the stem where leaves and lateral buds form are called *nodes.* The space between two nodes is called an *internode.* Along the surface of the twig, there are small raised openings called lenticels. **Lenticels** (LENT uh sels) are holes that pass through the cork tissue. They allow the exchange of oxygen and carbon dioxide between the atmosphere and the internal tissues.

Types of Leaves

Leaves are specialized to capture light for photosynthesis. The broad, flat structure of most leaves exposes a large surface area to the sun. In addition, the arrangement of leaves around the stem of the plant maximizes their exposure to whatever sunlight is available. The shape of the blade, the arrangement of the leaves, and the pattern of the veins make up some of the characteristics of each plant species.

Often, the environment in which a plant lives determines the type of leaf it has. For example, some plants are adapted to life in dry climates. The cactus plant is so highly specialized for life in the desert that its leaves have been reduced to spines. The stem is used for both photosynthesis and water storage, while the spines protect the stem.

A typical leaf has a thin, flat blade, and a stalk, or **petiole** (PET ee ohl). The petiole joins the leaf to the stem, as shown in Figure 18–17. A **simple leaf** has only one blade and one petiole. In a **compound leaf,** the blade is divided into several parts, or *leaflets,* that are attached to a petiole. The leaves of some plants, such as corn, lilies, and irises, do not have petioles. Instead, the leaf blades are fastened directly to the stem. A network of veins runs through the leaf. The veins contain the vascular tissues—xylem and phloem—of the leaf.

Figure 18–17

Simple and Compound Leaves. Leaves with one undivided blade are called simple leaves (left). Leaves with blades made of several divisions are called compound leaves (middle, and right). ▼

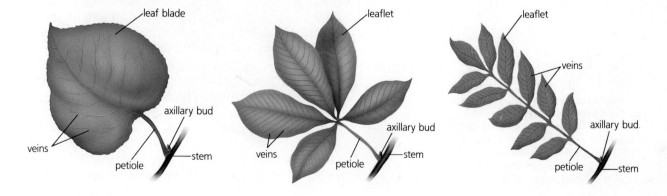

Internal Structure of the Leaf

No matter how they differ in their external appearance, all leaves are made of three types of tissues. These are protective, fundamental, and vascular tissue. Figure 18–18 shows a cross section of a typical leaf.

Cuticle and Epidermis The outermost layer of both the upper and lower leaf surfaces is the clear, waxy cuticle. This layer protects the inner tissues and slows down water loss from the leaf. Beneath the cuticle is the epidermis, which also protects the inner tissues. The epidermal layer, like other epidermal layers, is only one cell thick. The cells are flattened and fit together like the pieces of a jigsaw puzzle. Most of the cells of the epidermis are clear because they have little or no pigment. This allows light to reach the photosynthetic tissues below.

Like the epidermis of the stem, the leaf epidermis has many stomates. Usually, there are many more of these openings on the lower surface of the leaf than on the upper surface. The stomates allow the exchange of carbon dioxide and oxygen between the tissues inside the leaf and the environment. Water vapor also passes out of the leaf through the stomates. The stomates are not open all the time. Instead, they open and close according to the needs of the leaf. Each stomate is surrounded by a pair of specialized epidermal cells called **guard cells.** The kidney-shaped guard cells regulate the opening and closing of the stomates. The way this is done is described in Chapter 19.

Mesophyll Between the upper and lower layers of epidermis is a layer of photosynthetic tissue called **mesophyll** (MEZ uh fil). In some plants, the mesophyll contains two types of thin-walled cells. The upper portion of the mesophyll is called **palisade** (pal uh SAYD)

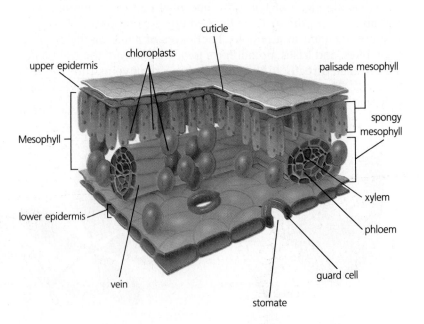

Figure 18–18

Internal Structure of a Leaf. A leaf is made up of different tissue types. Most of the photosynthesis takes place in the mesophyll. Water is carried to the mesophyll and food is carried away through vascular bundles, which are contained within veins. The epidermis protects the inner tissues. ▶

mesophyll. It is one or two cells thick. This layer is made of tall, tightly packed cells filled with chloroplasts. Below the palisade layer is the **spongy mesophyll.** This layer is made of irregularly shaped cells with large air spaces between them. The stomate openings of the lower epidermis are next to the intercellular air spaces of the spongy mesophyll. The cells of the spongy mesophyll have fewer chloroplasts than the cells the palisade layer.

Veins   Within the mesophyll layer is a network of veins. The veins contain the vascular tissues. The vein network is so fine that no mesophyll cell is far from a vein. The xylem and phloem of the leaf veins are continuous with the xylem and phloem of the stem and roots. The arrangement of veins in a leaf is called its **venation** (ven AY shun). There are distinct differences between the vein patterns of monocot and dicot leaves. In the leaves of monocots, the main veins usually run parallel to one another along the length of the leaf. In dicots, the veins form a network of branches, as seen in Figure 18–19.

Evolution of Plants

Plants first appeared about 440 million years ago. These early plants evolved in water. Water provides an environment that supports the plant and surrounds the plant with nutrients. In order for plants to survive on land, certain challenges had to be overcome. Stems, leaves, and roots helped plants adapt to life on land. Stems provided support, which enabled plants to hold their leaves up toward the sun. Roots anchored plants in place and absorbed water and nutrients from the soil. Once the water and nutrients were absorbed, an internal transport system was needed to carry them to the leaves where photosynthesis took place.

The first true land plants were the tracheophytes. Tracheophytes contain the internal transport system—vascular tissue–needed to transport the water and nutrients throughout the plant. The presence of vascular tissue allowed the tracheophytes to grow larger and to live in a wider range of habitats than the bryophytes, or nonvascular plants.

18-3 **Section Review**

1. What tissue produces growth in stem and root thickness?
2. What layer slows down water loss from a leaf?
3. Where does photosynthesis occur in the leaf?
4. Why are tracheophytes able to grow larger than bryophytes?

Critical Thinking

5. Compare a simple and a compound leaf. (*Comparing*)

Figure 18–19

Venation. Monocot plants have parallel venation (top). Dicot plants have netted venation (bottom). ▼

Laboratory
Investigation

Plant Tissues and Their Functions

A plant, like an animal, must transport water, minerals, and nutrients through its body. It must also transport the products of photosynthesis—such as sugars—to all parts of its body. In this investigation, you will examine tissues and organs that transport water through a plant.

Problem

What water-transport tissues can you **observe** in certain types of vegetables?

Materials (per group)

- Petri dish with radish seedlings
- hand lens
- whole carrot
- scalpel or single-edged razor blade
- round slice of carrot
- lettuce leaf
- microscope slide
- coverslip
- medicine dropper
- distilled water
- dissecting needle
- compound microscope
- forceps

Procedure

1. Using a hand lens, examine the radish seedlings in the Petri dish. Sketch and label one seedling.

2. Obtain a whole carrot and use the scalpel to cut it in half lengthwise. Make a second cut along the length of one of the carrot halves so that you have a very thin long slice.
   CAUTION: *Be careful when using sharp instruments.*

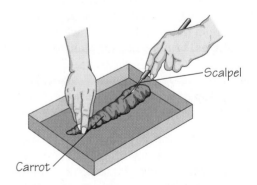

3. Hold the thin slice up to the light and examine it. Sketch and label this lengthwise section.

4. Using the hand lens, observe the carrot slice. Sketch and label what you observe.

5. Force the inner core out of the carrot slice by pushing it firmly. Examine the surface of the core.

6. Obtain a lettuce leaf that has had its lower surface soaking in distilled water. Bend the leaf so that it breaks and peels away the lower surface.

7. With the forceps, peel off a small piece of the leaf tissue. Put this piece of tissue on a microscope slide. Using a medicine dropper, add a drop of water to the slide. With a dissecting needle, slowly lower one edge of the coverslip and then the other onto the lettuce leaf.

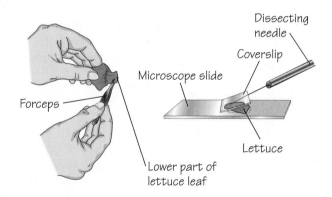

8. Observe the leaf tissue under the low-power objective of the microscope. Then switch to the high-power objective. Look for jigsaw-puzzle-shaped cells and pairs of rounded cells.

Observations

1. Describe the outer surface of the radish seedling root. What structures did you observe? Did the entire surface of the root have the same appearance?

2. What was the shape of the inner core of the carrot?

3. Can you find extensions growing from the surface of the core of the carrot? What are they?

4. What did you observe on the lettuce leaf between the two rounded cells in each pair?

Analysis and Conclusions

1. Are there root hairs at the tip of the radish root? Explain your answer.

2. What kind of tissue is found in the center of the carrot root? What is its function?

3. What kind of tissue makes up the thick, outer part of the carrot? What is its function?

4. What kind of tissue did you peel from the lettuce?

5. What are the rounded cells? What is their function?

Extensions

Design an experiment to determine the presence of starch and sugar in the plant tissues you observed. You can obtain indicators for starch and sugar from your teacher.

Chapter 18 Review

Study Outline

18-1 Plant Tissues

▶ Plants are made of tissues that form plant organs, which are the roots, stem, leaves, and reproductive structures.

▶ Meristematic tissues consist of rapidly dividing cells. Protective tissues form the outer layers on certain parts of plants. Vascular tissues carry nutrients and water. Ground tissues produce and store food and support the plant.

18-2 Roots

▶ Roots anchor the plant and absorb water and minerals from the soil. The two common root systems are taproots and fibrous roots.

▶ A root tip consists of a root cap, a meristematic zone, an elongation zone, and a maturation zone.

▶ The mature tissues of the root are the epidermis, the cortex, including the endodermis, and the vascular cylinder.

▶ Symbiotic relationships often exist between plant roots and bacteria or fungi.

18-3 Stems and Leaves

▶ Stems transport and store water and nutrients and support leaves and reproductive structures. Plants are herbaceous or woody, depending on stem structure.

▶ Herbaceous stems are soft and green. Monocots, which are nearly all herbaceous, have vascular bundles scattered throughout the stem. Herbaceous dicot stems have vascular bundles arranged in a ring. Woody dicot stems are thick and hard, containing successive layers of xylem produced by the vascular cambium.

▶ A typical leaf consists of a stalk, or petiole, and a thin, flat blade with a network of veins. Leaves are the major sites of photosynthesis in plants.

▶ The leaf epidermis is covered by the cuticle, which is a clear, waxy layer. In the epidermis, openings called stomates allow the exchange of gases between leaf tissues and the environment.

Chapter Assessment

Multiple Choice

Choose the letter of the answer that best completes each statement or answers the question.

1. In plants, the main organs of photosynthesis are the (a) roots. (b) leaves. (c) stems. (d) petioles.

2. The function of a plant's ground tissue is to (a) support and carry out photosynthesis. (b) protect the plant. (c) conduct fluids through the plant. (d) prevent water evaporation.

3. Plants take in almost all of their water and nutrients through structures called (a) guard cells. (b) osmosis. (c) vascular cylinders. (d) root hairs.

4. Most of the wood in a tree is made up of (a) cork cambium cells. (b) xylem tissue. (c) phloem tissue. (d) bark cells.

5. Phloem differs from xylem in that it (a) mainly transports food. (b) comprises the sap wood. (c) is not usually found in leaves. (d) transports water to roots.

6. All of the following are leaf structures except (a) lenticels. (b) stomates. (c) petiole. (d) epidermis.

7. Which of the following structures stores food in plants? (a) cambium (b) cortex (c) epidermis (d) xylem

8. Which of the following plants has a herbaceous stem? (a) lilac (b) forsythia (c) corn (d) oak

9. Which of the following tissues protects woody dicots? (a) bark (b) cortex (c) endodermis (d) pericycle

10. The climbing roots of ivy are (a) adventitious roots. (b) prop roots. (c) fibrous roots. (d) tap roots.

Content Review

Answer each of the following in complete sentences.

11. Describe the epidermis and state its main function.

12. Describe the kinds of cells that form vascular tissue.

13. List the different zones of the root tip, and describe the cellular activity in each zone.

14. What are the primary functions of the root? How is its structure suited to its functions?

15. What structure produces the cells that account for growth in the length of a stem?

16. Compare monocot stems with dicot stems.

17. What are lenticels? What is their function?

18. Describe the two main types of leaves.

19. Describe the structure of a leaf viewed in cross section.

20. Explain how leaves exchange gases with the environment.

Graphic Organizing

For information on graphic organizers, see Appendix G at the back of this text.

21. **Concept Map** Copy the incomplete concept map below onto a separate sheet of paper. Add the following concepts: *epidermis, cork, cambium, phloem, apical meristems, xylem.* Include other appropriate concepts of your own choosing. Be sure to add linking words between concepts.

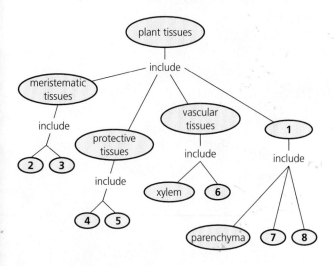

Critical Thinking and Problem Solving

Discuss each of the following in a brief paragraph.

22. **Predicting** What would happen to a plant if its leaves were coated with petroleum jelly? What would happen if just the stem were coated?

23. **Comparing** Compare the arrangement of mature tissues in the youngest region of a tree stem, just behind the growing tip, with that in a region where the stem has increased in width.

24. **Relating** Why is gas exchange with the environment essential for plants?

25. **Predicting** Root cells absorb water by osmosis. In view of this, how would a high salt concentration in the soil affect a plant's ability to grow?

26. **Classifying** You are given a leaf and a cross-section of the stem from the same plant. What features of these plants would you use to classify and identify the plant?

27. **Hypothesizing** Botanists claim that roots grow in a crooked, erratic pattern because of obstacles in the soil, such as rocks or other roots. Design a controlled experiment to test this hypothesis.

28. **Calculating** A botanist wanted to determine the average total surface area of the root hairs of mature bean plants. She estimated the surface area of a typical root hair to be 0.50 cm². The number of root hairs on the roots of five bean plants she recorded are shown in the table below. Calculate the total surface area of the root hairs for each plant and the average total surface area for the five plants.

Plant Number	Number of Root Hairs
1	1900
2	1700
3	1800
4	2000
5	1400

Discovery
Learning Activity

Where Did the Drops Come From?

1. Working in a group, obtain a potted plant from your teacher.

2. Place a plastic sandwich bag completely around one of the plant's leaves and secure it to the stem with tape.

3. Place the plant in an area where the leaf will receive direct sunlight for several hours. Write a prediction about whether leaves release anything into the atmosphere.

4. After 2 to 4 hours, examine the plant and see if your prediction was accurate.

Plant Function

19-1 Transport

Section Objectives:

- *Explain* how plants regulate water loss.
- *Explain* how water travels upward throughout a plant.
- *Summarize* the mechanism of food transport in plants.

Transpiration

Plants, similar to other organisms, must carry out the basic life processes. This chapter focuses on some of these processes. It describes how plants transport water and food and discusses the mechanisms that regulate their development

Plants that live on land must be adapted to supply water to all their tissues. Much of the water that plants take up, however, is lost to the atmosphere by evaporation. The evaporation of water vapor from plant surfaces is called **transpiration** (tranz puh RAY shun). Most transpiration takes place through the stomates. As you may recall from Chapter 18, stomates are the pores in the epidermis of leaves. Through the stomates, leaves exchange carbon dioxide and oxygen

▲ **Figure 19–1**

Plants and Water. Plants need water and other raw materials to carry out their life processes.

◀ Field of sunflowers.

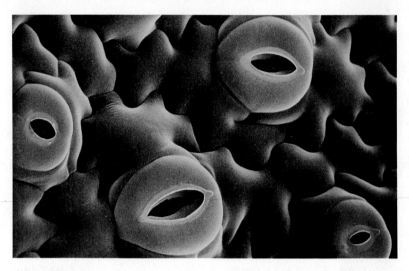

▲ **Figure 19–2**

Stomates. The stomates of a tobacco leaf are open in the light when the plant has enough water. (Magnification 660 X)

with the atmosphere during photosynthesis. See Figure 19–2. For these gases to diffuse through the cell membranes, plant cell surfaces must be kept moist by water supplied from the roots. This water continually evaporates into the spaces between the leaf cells. When the stomates are open, water vapor passes out through them and into the atmosphere. Rates of transpiration can be enormous. For example, a large tree may lose as much as 720 liters of water in a 12-hour day.

Regulation of Transpiration Rate   The rate of transpiration, that is, the amount of water lost from leaves in a given amount of time, is regulated by the size of the opening of the stomates. Stomates are usually closed when there is too little water available to a plant, when the temperature is low, or when there is little light. Stomates generally open in light if a plant has enough water.

The opening and closing of each stomate are controlled by the pair of guard cells that surrounds it. The guard cells are sausage-shaped, with thick walls along their inside edge and thin walls along their outside edge. The stomates open or close as the guard cells gain or lose water. When the guard cells become swollen with water, or *turgid* (TER jid), the uneven thicknesses of their walls cause them to bow outward, as shown in Figure 19–3. The opening created between the two cells is the stomate. When the guard cells lose water, they become less turgid, and the stomate closes. The stomates of most plants open during the day and close at night.

Guard cells gain and lose water by osmosis. For a review of osmosis, see Chapter 5. When guard cells build up their concentration of solutes by active transport, water from surrounding cells diffuses into the guard cells. This causes the guard cells to swell and, thus, the stomates to open. When guard cells release the solutes, water diffuses out from the guard cells and back into the neighboring tissues. As a result, the stomates close.

Figure 19–3

Stomates and Guard Cells. A stomate opens when the walls of the guard cells swell with water and bow outward. ▼

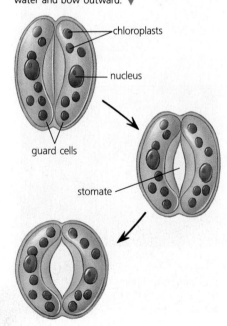

chloroplasts

nucleus

guard cells

stomate

Guard Cell Osmotic Control   The solute most important in changing the osmotic conditions of the guard cells is the potassium ion, K⁺. The concentration of potassium ions in the guard cells of open stomates is many times higher than the concentration in the guard cells of closed stomates. ATP is used to power an active transport system that pumps potassium ions into guard cells. Thus, ATP is required to keep the stomates open. During photosynthesis, the chloroplasts of the guard cells supply at least part of the ATP needed for this process. No ATP is needed for stomates to close. The active transport system simply stops, allowing potassium and other solutes to diffuse freely from the guard cells.

Although light is an important factor affecting stomate opening, carbon dioxide concentration *in the leaf* appears to be even more important. A low concentration of carbon dioxide causes stomates to open, even in complete darkness. A high concentration causes stomates to close, even in light. However, scientists do not know how these factors act to turn on or off the active transport system that controls guard cell solute concentrations.

Water Transport

The large amounts of water lost through transpiration must be replaced, or the leaves of the plant will wilt and die. Water in the soil is taken up by the roots and moved upward through the xylem of the roots, stems, and into the leaves.

In tall trees, water is supplied to leaves that may be more than 100 meters above the ground. See Figure 19–4. How water moves so high against the pull of gravity has long puzzled botanists. It cannot be due to active transport within the xylem, because the cells of the xylem that conduct water are not alive. Other processes, such as capillary action and root pressure, offer only a partial answer.

Capillary Action   The tendency of liquid to rise inside a narrow tube is called *capillary action.* The details of this process are discussed in Chapter 4. In plant roots and stems, the water-conducting cells of the xylem form a system of narrow, capillary-type tubes through which water moves. Because of the strong attraction between water and the cell walls that form these tubes, water rises in the xylem. However, capillary action can raise water in the xylem no more than several centimeters. Nevertheless, the forces of attraction between water and the walls of the water-conducting cells help to keep the columns of water intact.

Root Pressure   When the stem of a well-watered plant is cut off close to the soil, sap flows from the cut stem. If a glass tube is attached to the cut end of the stem, sap rises in the tube to a height of about one meter. The pressure that holds up the column of water is called **root pressure.** Root pressure is actually osmotic pressure caused by a buildup of solutes in the xylem of roots.

As you read in Chapter 5, osmosis is the diffusion of water across membranes from areas of high water concentration to areas of lower water concentration. In a root, the endodermis—the layer

Figure 19–4

Water Transport. Water must travel from the roots to the leaves of tall trees, such as this Jeffrey Pine in Yosemite National Park. ▼

▲ **Figure 19–5**

Guttation. In guttation, plants exude water as droplets along the edges of their leaves.

Figure 19–6

Transpiration Pull. Water is pulled up the xylem as water evaporates from leaves. ▼

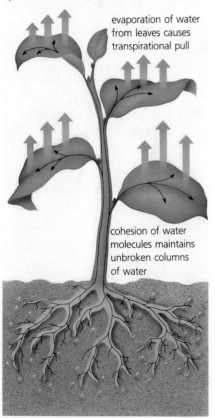

evaporation of water from leaves causes transpirational pull

cohesion of water molecules maintains unbroken columns of water

of cells that surrounds the root vascular cylinder—pumps solutes into the vascular cylinder by active transport. As a result, solute concentration increases in the root xylem, lowering the concentration of water there. Thus, water in the soil diffuses into the root xylem, causing a buildup of pressure. The pressure in the root xylem forces water upward through the xylem of the stem.

Root pressure does happen occasionally in some plants. When it does, a process known as guttation occurs. **Guttation** (gyoo TAY shun) is the formation of water droplets at the edges, or tips, of leaves as a result of root pressure. See Figure 19–5. Guttation usually occurs during the night and only in small plants growing under moist conditions. Because of the pressure buildup, water in the xylem of the leaf is forced out onto the surface of leaves in the form of droplets. These droplets usually can be seen early in the morning. They should not be confused with dew drops, which appear randomly on a leaf. Dew drops are the result of water vapor in the air condensing on cool leaf surfaces.

Even when root pressure occurs, it can cause water to rise no more than about one meter. Therefore, root pressure alone cannot account for the rise of water to the tops of trees. Nor can it cause water to move through a plant when it is growing with little water or when transpiration occurs. During transpiration, large volumes of water move through the roots, preventing solutes from building up in concentration.

Although root pressure is not the mechanism for water transport in plants, it does explain how water first enters the roots of plants when they are seedlings.

Transpiration Pull   Water in the xylem exists as thin, unbroken columns, stretching from the roots, through the stem, and into the leaves. Each water column is held together by strong attractive forces between the water molecules themselves (cohesion) and between the water molecules and the walls of the conducting cells (adhesion).

In roots, the water columns in the xylem are continuous with water that is present throughout the root tissue and in contact with films of water surrounding soil particles. Similarly, water in the leaf xylem is continuous with films of water surrounding all the leaf cells. This water also is continuous with water vapor in the leaf air spaces and atmosphere. See Figure 19–6.

During transpiration, water molecules evaporate from the surface of leaf cells into leaf air spaces and diffuse out through stomates. The lost water is replaced by water in contact with water at the end of a water column in the leaf xylem. When this happens, other water molecules in the column are drawn into the leaf tissue by the strong attractive forces between water molecules. Consequently, the loss of water by evaporation creates a pull or tension on the columns of water in the xylem. Water, therefore, is pulled up, not pushed up, through the xylem. This process, which is called **transpiration pull,** can account for the movement of water to the tops of the tallest trees.

Food Transport

Sugars produced in the leaves during photosynthesis are distributed to other cells in the plant where they are stored or used for energy. This movement of dissolved food through a plant is called **translocation** (tranz loh KAY shun). Translocation occurs only in the phloem. While materials flow through the xylem in only one direction—from the roots to the leaves—flow of materials through the phloem can occur in any direction.

As you may recall from Chapter 18, the conducting cells of the phloem are the sieve cells. The sieve cells are stacked end-to-end forming sieve tubes. Scientists have found that sieve cells in the leaves use active transport to build up high concentrations of sugars as they are made during photosynthesis. This causes water to move from the xylem by osmosis into the sieve tube. This results in a buildup of pressure within the sieve tubes. In other parts of the plant, sugars move from the sieve cells to the cells in which the sugars are used. As a result, water moves by osmosis out of the sieve cells into these areas, causing a drop in pressure. Thus, there is a pressure gradient—high pressure in the leaf phloem and lower pressure in the phloem in other parts of the plant. This gradient is what causes the liquid in the phloem to move. This explanation of translocation is called the **pressure-flow hypothesis.**

Figure 19–7

Pressure-Flow Hypothesis. Fluid in the phloem moves from areas of high pressure (where sugar concentration is highest—the leaves) to areas of lower pressure (where sugar concentration is lower—the roots, in this example). ▼

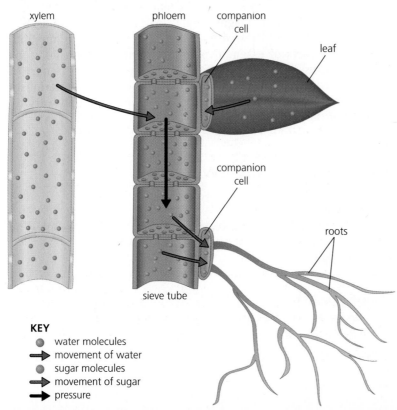

KEY
🔴 water molecules
➡️ movement of water
🔵 sugar molecules
⇨ movement of sugar
➡ pressure

Science, Technology and Society

Issue: Vanishing Habitats

Tropical rain forests grow in hot, wet regions near the equator in countries such as Brazil. They are the natural habitat for over half of the plant and animal species on this planet. Yet, these forests are disappearing at an alarming rate.

Some people contend that the destruction of the forests is unavoidable. Preservation of the environment should not be a priority when basic needs must be met. The people of tropical countries clear forests for timber, farmland, and cattle ranches. Timber, crops, and beef are major exports for poor, developing nations.

Other people argue that deforestation contributes to drought and mud slides. Some scientists warn that changes in the ecology of the rain forests may change temperature patterns and water cycles around the world. Those who oppose deforestation point out that many of the species being destroyed may be valuable to humankind. They argue that the rain forests must be saved.

■ *How can nations work together to save the tropical rain forests?*

▲ **Figure 19–8**
Nitrogen Deficiency. Compare the squash plants grown in nitrogen-deficient soil (left) with those grown in soil containing nitrogen (right).

Plant Mineral Nutrients

Plants are able to synthesize all the carbohydrates, proteins, and other organic compounds they need. To do so, however, they need inorganic raw materials. To make carbohydrates and fats, plants need water and carbon dioxide, which provide hydrogen, oxygen, and carbon. To make amino acids and proteins, they also need a source of nitrogen. Some plants get usable nitrogen compounds from bacteria that live in their roots. Most, however, must get nitrogen compounds from the soil. Besides nitrogen, plants must obtain a number of other inorganic substances, called minerals, from the soil. The minerals needed by plants include compounds of phosphorus, potassium, magnesium, iron, calcium, and sulfur. See Figure 19–8. Many of these are required for enzymes to function. Others form parts of essential plant substances. Magnesium, for example, forms part of the chlorophyll molecule. Iron is part of many electron carrier molecules. Plant growth can be seriously affected by a lack of any of these. Plant fertilizers supply varying amounts of the minerals that plants require.

19-1 Section Review

1. What is transpiration?
2. Why it is impossible for the water-conducting cells of xylem to carry on active transport?
3. What is guttation?
4. What is the transport of food through a plant called?

Critical Thinking

5. What beneficial effect do you think transpiration might have on the temperature of leaves? (*Predicting*)

19-2 Regulation of Plant Growth

Section Objectives:

- *Describe* the effects of auxins on different parts of the plant.
- *Explain* the difference between positive and negative tropisms.
- *List* the various types of plant hormones and describe the function of each.
- *Define* the terms *nastic movement* and *photoperiodism*.

A plant on a windowsill grows toward the sunlight. Plant roots grow toward gravity. What causes these specific growth patterns? Changes in the rate and direction of growth in plants are caused by changes in the levels of certain chemicals in response to environmental factors.

Plant Hormones

Chemical messengers, called hormones, regulate many plant functions. Most hormones are made in minute quantities by actively dividing tissues at the tips of roots and stems. Once produced, they are transported to various parts of the plant where they affect cell metabolism, cell division, and plant growth.

There are a number of different types of hormones in plants, but three of the most important kinds are auxins, gibberellins, and cytokinins. These hormones affect the growth of various plant tissues.

Auxins Hormones that affect the growth of plant tissues are called **auxins** (AWK sinz). Auxins may stimulate or slow growth, depending on the type of tissue and the amount of hormone. These hormones increase plant growth by stimulating cells to lengthen. In addition, they cause cells to differentiate. See Figure 19–9.

◄ **Figure 19–9**

Apical Dominance. The apical meristem on the left produces an auxin that inhibits the growth of lateral branches below it. If the apical meristem is snipped off, as with the plant on the right, the lateral branches grow, creating a bushy appearance.

▲ **Figure 19–10**
Effect of Gibberellins on Plant Growth.
Compare the height of these two-day old kidney bean seedlings. The taller seedlings on the right have been sprayed with gibberellins.

The most common auxin in nature is *indoleacetic* (in dohl uh SEE tik) *acid,* or IAA. IAA is produced in high concentrations in the terminal bud of plants. As the auxin diffuses down the stem, it prevents the growth of lateral buds. When a lateral bud on a stem is far enough away from the terminal bud on the same stem, the lateral bud will begin to grow. When this happens, it becomes the terminal bud of a branch. This explains why cutting off the terminal buds of house plants causes lateral buds to grow, and the plant to become bushier.

Auxins also affect the process of *abscission* (ab SIZH in)—the dropping off of leaves, flowers, or fruits from a plant. Synthetic auxins are sprayed on apple trees to prevent apples from dropping before they are fully ripe. Auxins are also used commercially to stimulate the production of roots on stem or leaf cuttings and to control weeds. Spraying weeds with synthetic auxins causes them to overgrow so much that they die.

Gibberellins   Hormones that affect plant growth and the development of fruits and seeds are called **gibberellins** (jib uh REL inz). Unlike auxins, gibberellins are distributed evenly throughout the plant tissues. Gibberellins have important effects on stem growth in plants. In fact, plant stems that are typically short can be made to grow by spraying them with gibberellins. See Figure 19–10. Commercially, these hormones are used to stimulate flowering and also to increase fruit size. Many commercial grapes are sprayed with gibberellins to increase cluster size.

Other Hormones   Another group of naturally occurring plant hormones is the **cytokinins** (syt uh KY ninz). Cytokinins stimulate cell division and growth during seed germination. They are thought to work together with auxins in stimulating cell differentiation.

A gas, **ethylene** (ETH uh leen), is another plant hormone. Ethylene, along with auxins, plays a role in abscission. It also stimulates the ripening of many fruits. As bananas ripen, the dark specks you see on their "skin" are concentrated areas of ethylene. In fact, clusters of green bananas are ripened at the supermarket by exposing them to low concentrations of ethylene.

The hormone **abscisic** (ab SIZ ik) **acid** increases in concentration as the days become shorter in the fall, and temperatures decrease. Abscisic acid is associated with the shedding of leaves and the seasonal slowing down of plant activities.

Auxins and Tropisms

The growth of a plant in a specific direction in response to a stimulus is called a **tropism** (TROH piz um). Plant growth or movement toward a stimulus is called a *positive tropism,* while movement away from a stimulus is called a *negative tropism.* The kinds of stimuli that plants grow toward or away from include light (phototropism), gravity (geotropism), touch (thigmotropism), and water (hydrotropism). The stem of a plant that is growing toward

Phototropism. No matter which direction this plant is turned, it will always grow toward the sunlight.

the light is an example of positive **phototropism** (foh tuh TROH piz um). See Figure 19–11. Roots, unlike stems, show negative phototropism—they grow away from the light source.

Roots generally show positive **geotropism** (jee uh TROH piz um). They grow down into the ground in the direction of the force of gravity. Stems, on the other hand, show negative geotropism. They grow up away from the force of gravity.

When the tendrils of a grapevine wind themselves around the stem of another plant, they are showing **thigmotropism** (thig muh TROH piz um), growth in response to touch. **Hydrotropism** (hy droh TROH piz um) is observed in plants such as willow trees in which roots grow toward water.

The growth responses seen in tropisms are thought to be caused by uneven distribution of auxins in the affected plant parts. In the positive phototropism of stems, for example, the concentration of auxins becomes higher on the shaded side of the stem than on the lighted side. Thus, the cells on the shaded side grow faster than the cells on the lighted side. The uneven rates of growth on opposite sides of the stem result in a bending toward the side of less rapid growth. In this case, the stem bends toward the light.

Nastic Movements

A plant movement that is in response to a stimulus but independent of the direction of the stimulus is called a **nastic** (NAS tik) **movement.** Some nastic movements are reversible and do not involve growth. For instance, the leaves of the prayer plant are spread out flat during the day but become vertical at night. Many other kinds of plants show similar movements of their leaves and flower parts over a 24-hour period.

▲ **Figure 19–12**
Nastic Movement. The leaves of the oxalis plant are open during the day (left) but closed at night (right).

Most nastic movements involve changes in the internal pressure, or turgor pressure, of specific cells. For instance, if you touch the leaflets of the sensitive plant, they will instantly collapse. They collapse because of changes in osmotic pressure. When the leaflets are touched, the concentration of ions in the cells at the base of each leaflet drops rapidly, causing water to flow out of the cells by osmosis. When this happens, the cells lose their turgor, and the leaflets drop.

The rapid movement of the leaves of the Venus flytrap is another example of a nastic movement. When the trigger hairs on a leaf are touched, cells on the upper surface of the leaf along the midline rapidly lose solute. As a result, water moves out of the cells, the cells collapse, and pressure from the other leaf cells causes the leaves to snap shut. In this way, the plant traps insects. After a while, the water pressure in the cells is restored and the leaves reopen.

Photoperiodism

Light affects plant growth and development in ways that are unrelated to its role in photosynthesis. For instance, the flowering of many plants is in response to changes in the length of day over the course of the year. The response of a plant to changes in the length of day or night is called **photoperiodism** (foh toh PIR ee uh diz em).

In many types of plants, flowering and other processes, such as leaf abscission, are controlled photoperiodically. At first, it was thought that the length of the light period was what caused flowering. Plants that flowered during short days were called *short-day plants*. Those that flowered during long days were called *long-day plants*. However, scientists later discovered that it is the length of uninterrupted darkness that causes flowering. Short-day

▲ **Figure 19–13**
Short-Day and Long-Day Plants. The poppy (left) is a long-day plant, and the morning glory (right) is a short-day plant.

plants, therefore, are better described as *long-night plants*. They require long periods of darkness in order to flower. Similarly, long-day plants are more appropriately called *short-night plants*. They flower when there are short periods of darkness. Nevertheless, the terms short-day plant and long-day plant continue to be used.

Some short-day plants are morning glory, forsythia, tulip, chrysanthemum, aster, and goldenrod. These plants flower in the early spring, late summer, or fall when the days are short and the nights are long. Long-day (short-night) plants include clover, potato, beet, poppy, and gladiolus. Long-day plants usually bloom in the summer. Plants whose flowering is unaffected by the lengths of light and dark are called *day-neutral plants*. Tomato, cucumber, dandelion, string bean, and corn are examples of day-neutral plants. Day-neutral plants have a long flowering season.

The effects of photoperiodism on flowering and on other processes are the result of changes that take place in a pigment called *phytochrome* (FY tuh krohm). This pigment, which is found in low concentration in plant cells, has a dramatic effect on plant growth and development. Although the details are not known, changes that take place in the phytochrome molecule during the dark period bring about metabolic changes in certain plant tissues. These changes may affect the production or release of certain hormones or may affect plant cells at other levels of metabolism.

19-2 Section Review

1. Define the term *positive phototropism*.
2. List three plant hormones.
3. What causes the leaflets of the sensitive plant to collapse when they are touched?
4. What is the term for the response of a plant to the changing duration of light and darkness?

Critical Thinking

5. How is a nastic movement different from a tropism? (*Comparing and Contrasting*)

MiniLab

Skill: Predicting

Growing My Way?

Procedure

1. Obtain six corn seeds that have been soaked overnight. Arrange the seeds across the bottom of a Petri dish with their pointed ends facing the same direction. Lay clear plastic tape across the seeds and attach the ends of the tape to the sides of the dish.

2. Cover the seeds with six layers of moistened paper towels trimmed to fit inside the dish. Be sure there is no water collecting in the dish. Cover and tape the dish shut.

3. Stand the dish on its edge in some modeling clay with the pointed ends of the seeds pointing downward. Place the upright dish in a dark place for about two days.

4. When the roots are about 2 cm long, remove the cover of the Petri dish and the moistened paper. Using a single-edge blade and a ruler, trim the last 2 mm from the root tips of three seedlings. Record the length of all the roots. Replace the moistened paper and tape the lid back on.

5. Rotate the dish so that the roots are pointing upward, replace it in the clay, and return the dish to a dark spot. Predict what will happen.

Problem

How can you **predict** the effect of various factors on root growth?

Analyze and Conclude

1. Did all the roots grow during the second part of the experiment? If not, explain why or why not.

2. In which direction did the roots grow?

3. Was your prediction correct? If not, what information would have been helpful?

A Transportation Problem for Plants

Problem

Plants always have been a major source of medicine for people. In fact, early plant reference books were often guides to the medicinal plants of a particular area. Even today, about one-fourth of all prescription drugs contain at least one ingredient that is plant derived.

Although pharmaceutical companies synthetically can make many of these medicines, the search for new medicinal plants continues. In one plant-collecting program, researchers at pharmaceutical companies have been working with botanists in an effort to collect plant samples that will lead to the discovery of new medicines. To date, more than 25 000 samples have been collected.

Unfortunately, this program is not without its problems. Botanists have discovered that when these exotic plants are transported from places such as the Central African Republic, Ghana, Madagascar, and Tanzania to the United States, the plants are exposed to changing temperatures, light intensities, and varying levels of humidity during their trip. Therefore, it is necessary to develop some type of shipping container that will maintain the plants' natural environment and allow them to arrive at their destination in a healthy condition.

Task

You are a member of a team of botanists that has been asked by a large pharmaceutical company to develop a shipping container that will transport plants safely from their collection site in Tanzania to New York where they will be cultivated and screened for possible medicinal compounds.

In order to do this task, you must complete each of the following:

1. Based on your knowledge of plants, design and make a detailed scale drawing of a shipping container that will transport four plants from Tanzania to New York. Use the scale 5 mm = 1 cm. Each plant is approximately 10 cm long from the tip of its topmost stem to the tip of its roots and each is 0.5 cm in diameter. The volume of the container should not exceed 5 000 cm^3.

2. Determine the types of materials that you would use in the construction of your team's shipping container.

3. Research and then record in your journal the type of environment that the plants from Tanzania need in order to grow.

4. Keep a well organized and clearly written journal in which you record your team's ideas, drawings, experiments, data, and any other related information.

Solution

Prepare a multimedia presentation for the researchers at the pharmaceutical company describing your team's approach to the problem, the sources of information used, conditions to be considered, the design itself, and what was learned during the project. A multimedia presentation includes the use of visuals (drawings, photographs, charts, graphs, or even video clips) to support your oral and written report. Include in your presentation a list of the materials needed and what your team would change if they were able to do the project again.

Laboratory
Investigation

Vascular Plant Tissues

The vascular system is the system of tubes that carries water and minerals through-out a plant. The vascular system is made up of two types of tissues—xylem and phloem. In this investigation, you will discover the role of the xylem and phloem.

Problem

Can you **predict** the role of a vascular system in a plant?

Materials (per group)

▶ celery stalk

▶ blue food coloring

▶ metric ruler

▶ clear plastic container

▶ scalpel

▶ microscope

Procedure

1. Fill the plastic container halfway with water. Add several drops of blue food coloring to make the solution a deep shade of blue.

2. Using the scalpel, cut off about 1 cm of the base of the celery stalk. **CAUTION:** *Be careful when using a scalpel—it is very sharp.*

3. Place the celery into the blue-colored solution, being sure the freshly cut base is in the solution.

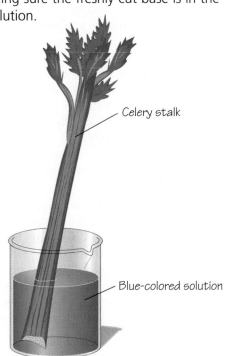

Celery stalk

Blue-colored solution

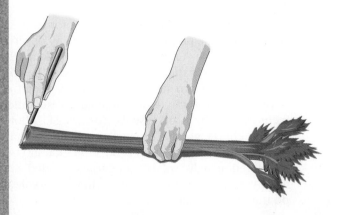

4. Construct a data table similar to the one shown.

5. After 5 minutes, measure the height in millimeters of the food coloring in the celery. Record your measurement.

6. Measure the height of the food coloring in the celery after 10, 15, and 20 minutes. Record each of your measurements.

7. What do you predict will happen to the food coloring in the celery after 24 hours? Write your prediction on a sheet of paper.

8. After 24 hours, measure the height of the food coloring in the celery.

9. Using the scalpel, cut off a thin slice about 2 to 3 mm from the base of the celery stalk. **CAUTION:** *Be careful when using a scalpel—it is very sharp.*

10. Observe the cross section of the celery under a microscope. Identify the xylem and make an illustration of what you see.

Observations

Data Table	
Time	**Height (in millimeters)**
5 minutes	
10 minutes	
15 minutes	
20 minutes	
24 hours	

1. What happens to the food coloring in the celery stalk?

2. What tissue is responsible for transporting the food coloring?

3. Does the vascular system of the celery stalk extend throughout its entire length? How do you know?

4. Does the movement of the liquid occur quickly or slowly? Support your answer using your data.

Analysis and Conclusions

1. What was your prediction? Was it correct?

2. What adaptation to life on land does this activity illustrate?

3. Why is a plant's vascular system important?

Extensions

Design your own experiment to determine what would happen if you placed a white carnation in a red-colored solution. Would the carnation change color? Perform your experiment to find out.

Chapter **19** Review

Study Outline

19-1 Transport

▶ Transpiration is the loss of water by evaporation from plant surfaces. It takes place mainly through the stomates.

▶ The opening and closing of stomates by guard cells controls the rate of transpiration. Guard cells change shape as they gain or lose water due to changes in their solute concentration.

▶ The loss of water from leaves results in a "pull" on the continuous columns of water that run through the xylem of the roots, stems, and leaves. This transpiration pull accounts for the movement of water from roots to leaves.

▶ The movement of dissolved food through a plant is called translocation.

▶ Plants need nitrogen and other minerals from the soil to carry out their normal metabolic activities.

19-2 Regulation of Plant Growth

▶ Growth responses toward or away from stimuli are known as tropisms. Tropisms can be stimulated by light, gravity, touch, and water.

▶ Auxins, gibberellins, cytokinins, ethylene, and abscisic acid are some of the known plant hormones. They regulate many aspects of plant growth and development.

▶ Nastic movements are usually reversible movements of plant parts that always occur in the same direction, regardless of the direction of the stimulus. They result from changes in the turgor pressure of certain cells.

▶ In many plants, flowering, leaf abscission, and other developmental events occur in response to the changing lengths of day and night. Such responses, which involve the plant pigment phytochrome, are examples of photoperiodism.

Chapter Assessment

Multiple Choice

Choose the letter of the answer that best completes each statement or answers the question.

1. The movement of dissolved food through a plant is called (a) translocation. (b) transpiration. (c) geotropism. (d) guttation.

2. The process that can account for the movement of water to the tops of tall trees is (a) tropism. (b) transpiration pull. (c) pressure-flow hypothesis. (d) translocation.

3. The loss of leaves in the fall is influenced by (a) geotropism. (b) nastic movements. (c) abscisic acid. (d) auxins.

4. Plant growth toward or away from a stimulus is caused by uneven distribution of (a) ethylene. (b) cytokinins. (c) gibberellins. (d) auxins.

5. The loss of water by evaporation from plant surfaces is known as (a) photoperiodism. (b) transpiration. (c) tropism. (d) root pressure.

6. Pressure caused by a buildup of solutes in root xylem is called (a) root pressure. (b) hydrotropism. (c) translocation. (d) guttation.

7. Hormones that affect stem growth and fruit and seed development are called (a) abscisic acids. (b) gibberellins. (c) auxins. (d) cytokinins.

8. The bending of a stem toward light is a growth response called (a) thigmotropism. (b) photoperiodism. (c) phototropism. (d) transpiration.

9. The formation of water droplets at the edges and tips of leaves is called (a) geotropism. (b) guttation. (c) thigmotropism. (d) transpiration.

10. Which of the following is not a plant hormone? (a) ethylene (b) auxins (c) potasium (d) gibberellins

Content Review

Answer each of the following in complete sentences.

11. What role does potassium play in guard cell movements?

12. Describe transpiration pull.

13. Explain why the columns of water in the xylem do not break apart during transpiration.

14. Explain how the pressure-flow hypothesis accounts for translocation.

15. How do auxins affect plant tissues?

16. What processes are affected by gibberellins?

17. What is the effect of cytokinins and auxins working together within a plant?

18. Explain the difference between a negative and a positive tropism.

19. What causes most nastic movements?

20. What is photoperiodism?

Graphic Organizing

For information on graphic organizers, see Appendix G at the back of this text.

21. **Line Graph** Construct a line graph based on the information in the table, which shows the hourly rate of transpiration in a plant over a 16-hour period. Plot time on the x-axis and transpiration rate on the y-axis. At what times are the rates highest? Lowest? How do you account for this?

Time	Transportation Rate (g/h)	Time	Transportation Rate (g/h)
8 AM	190	5 PM	220
9	200	6	213
10	209	7	208
11	215	8	190
12 Noon	221	9	120
1 PM	227	10	100
2	233	11	98
3	230	12	90
4	227 •		

Critical Thinking and Problem Solving

Discuss each of the following in a brief paragraph.

22. **Relating** Explain how each of the following features of many desert plants minimizes transpirational water loss: (a) thick, leathery leaves, (b) thickened cuticle, (c) leaves that drop off during dry season, (d) few stomates per unit of leaf surface area.

23. **Relating** How might it benefit a plant to have its terminal bud grow for a period of time before any lateral buds grow?

24. **Predicting** A substance that binds potassium ions (K^+) was dissolved in the water supplied to a plant. What effect, if any, do you think this substance would have on the plant's leaves and ultimately on the whole plant?

25. **Measuring** How would you measure the rate of transpiration of a potted plant?

26. **Experimenting** An experiment to determine how plants are induced to flower photoperiodically is shown in the illustration. Identify the control and propose a hypothesis to explain the results.

Long-day lighting conditions

Long-day lighting conditions

Leaf in light box under short-day conditions

Short-day plant

Short-day plant

Performance-Based Assessment

Chemicals From Plants

Background

Chemicals produced by plants were once thought to be waste products. Today, scientists know that this is not the case. Of the nearly 50 000 chemical compounds produced by plants, many give plants their nutritional value and distinctive odors and flavors. Some plants are used to flavor ice cream or beverages. Other plants produce chemicals that have pharmaceutical value and can be used to prevent or cure disease.

Scientific studies have also found that chemicals play an important role in protecting plants from plant-eating animals and insect pests. In essence, these substances are the plant's way of waging "chemical warfare" against attack by insects and other pests. A wild yam from Central America, for example, produces a chemical that resembles insect hormones. This hormone-like substance blocks the normal growth and development of plant-eating insects. Scientists think this substance if it could be produced in sufficient quantities, has the potential to act as a safe and effective pesticide. The substance, which decomposes in several days, could replace long-lasting, polluting chemical pesticides. Unfortunately, the wild yam is difficult to cultivate using normal agricultural methods, and it is also becoming rare in its natural habitat.

Problem

You are a member of a team of botanists assigned to search the rain forests of Costa Rica for a plant related to the yam that might produce the same insect-killing substance.

Task

Choose one of the following tasks.

1. Your team returns to camp with the field illustrations and four plant specimens—labeled W, X, Y, and Z—for chemical testing. Use the field illustrations and the dichotomous key to determine if the plants are related to the yam. (The purpose of a dichotomous key is to identify plants or plant groups.) Based on the dichotomous key, which specimen—W, X, Y, or Z—belongs to the same family as the wild yam?

   Obtain the extracts from the wild yam and the four plant specimens (W, X, Y, Z). Test the extracts from each plant by placing two drops of extract from each specimen (wild yam, W, X, Y, Z) into separate well plates. Test for the presence of the hormone-like substance in each extract with a small amount of the test substance (T). Record your results. Based on the results of your tests, which extract—W, X, Y, or Z—contains the same substance as the wild yam? Did the results of your chemical tests confirm your results with the dichotomous key? Which plant is most closely related to the wild yam?

2. The director of the National Institutes of Health has asked your team to make a presentation and submit a written report to a group of United Nations representatives on the importance of naturally occurring plant chemicals to humans. The object is to convince each government to set aside a portion of the forest in their countries

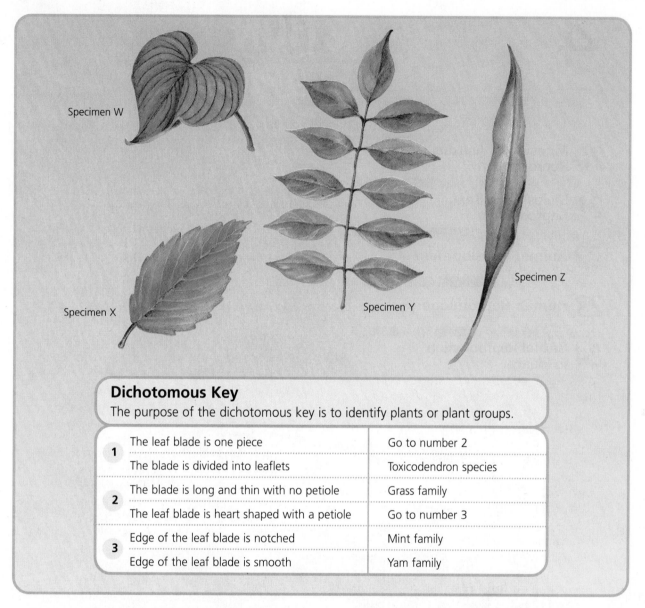

Specimen W

Specimen X

Specimen Y

Specimen Z

Dichotomous Key

The purpose of the dichotomous key is to identify plants or plant groups.

1	The leaf blade is one piece	Go to number 2
	The blade is divided into leaflets	Toxicodendron species
2	The blade is long and thin with no petiole	Grass family
	The leaf blade is heart shaped with a petiole	Go to number 3
3	Edge of the leaf blade is notched	Mint family
	Edge of the leaf blade is smooth	Yam family

as a natural preserve for research on plant chemicals. Include suggestions on how the United States can preserve its remaining stands of natural forest.

Your report and presentation should address the following issues:

- How are the natural chemical substances an adaptation for the plant's survival?
- What are the economic and environmental implications of exploiting plant chemicals?

- How can such naturally occurring chemicals be used for the benefit of humans?

Research your local library or the Internet for additional information. Include charts, graphs, illustrations, or photographs as appropriate. The presentation may be either an oral presentation with a written report or a videotaped presentation with a written report.

A brown bear with her cub.

Discovery Learning Activity

Mealworm Metamorphosis

1. Sprinkle several grains of uncooked rice in a large glass jar. Then fill the jar one-third full with bran cereal.

2. Place a potato slice on top of the bran and add 20 mealworms to the jar.

3. Cover the top of the jar with cheesecloth and secure it in place with a rubber band.

4. With a hand lens, observe the mealworms each day for four weeks. Keep a daily log of your observations. If you see any new stages in the mealworms' development, be sure to sketch them.

Discovery Learning Activity

Pinched Paramecia

1. Obtain a paramecium culture from your teacher and prepare a wet-mount slide of some paramecia.

2. Observe the paramecia under the low-power objective of a microscope, looking for paramecia that are pinched in at the middle or resemble double cells. Switch to the high-power objective and sketch a pinched paramecium. What life process do you think is occurring in the pinched paramecium?

Mitosis and Asexual Reproduction

Guide for Reading

Previewing the Chapter

Many amateur gardeners look forward to a crop of red, ripe strawberries every summer. They know that they can produce thick beds of strawberries by carefully allowing a few plants to spread their shoots, or runners, in every direction. Like other plants, such as African violets and spider plants, strawberries reproduce asexually through a process called vegetative propagation. How do the various types of asexual reproduction differ? What is the role of mitosis in asexual reproduction?

Key Words

asexual reproduction, binary fission, budding, cell cycle, chromosome, cytokinesis, mitosis, sexual reproduction, spore

Key Concepts

- **Summarize** the process of mitosis.
- **Compare** the various types of asexual reproduction.
- **Observe** the various phases of mitosis in a plant cell. (Laboratory Investigation)

20-1 Mitosis

Section Objectives:

- *Name* and briefly describe the two types of reproduction and the two basic processes involved in cell division.
- *Explain* what happens in interphase and in the stages of mitosis.
- *Compare* mitosis and cytokinesis in plant and animal cells.
- *Describe* the role of cyclin in the cell cycle.

Cell Division

All cells arise from other cells. In most cases, new cells are formed when one cell enlarges and divides into two cells. These two cells then enlarge and divide in two, and so on. Each round of growth and cell division is called a **cell cycle.** In unicellular organisms, cell division results in the creation of another individual of that species. In some multicellular organisms, cell division may be a method of reproduction if the new cells separate from the parent and form a complete, independent individual. In most multicellular organisms, however, cell division does not result in the creation of a new organism.

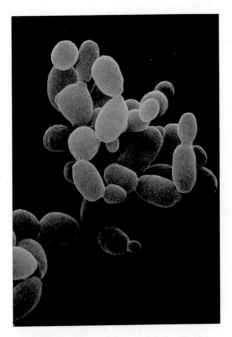

▲ **Figure 20–1**

Budding. Yeast is a one-celled organism that reproduces either by cell fission or by budding.

◀ Strawberry plants reproduce quickly by means of runners—horizontal stems.

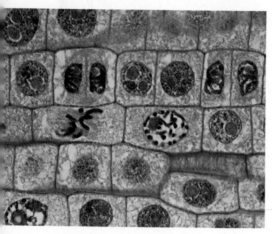

▲ Figure 20–2

Onion Cells Undergoing Mitosis. Stained onion root tip cells in various stages of mitosis as seen under a light microscope. (Magnification 700 X)

When a cell with a distinct nucleus divides, two processes take place. In one process, the nucleus divides to form two nuclei. This process is called **mitosis** (my TOH sis). During mitosis, the hereditary material in the parent cell duplicates and then divides into two identical sets. In the second process, called **cytokinesis** (sy toh kih NEE sis), the cytoplasm divides into two parts. Each part contains one of the newly formed nuclei, with one complete set of hereditary material, and about half of the other contents of the parent cell. Cytokinesis may take place at the same time as mitosis or after mitosis.

The first section of this chapter discusses mitosis and cytokinesis. The second section discusses *asexual reproduction*. **Asexual reproduction,** which is one of two forms of reproduction, involves only one parent. No special reproductive cells or organs are used to produce the new organism. Instead, asexual reproduction is accomplished by the processes of mitosis and cytokinesis. The new organism is simply a separated part of the parent organism. **Sexual reproduction**—the other form of reproduction—involves special reproductive cells. Usually, these reproductive cells are produced by two separate parent organisms. The details of sexual reproduction are discussed in Chapter 21. Some organisms reproduce only asexually, others reproduce only sexually, and still others reproduce by both methods.

Changes in the Nucleus

As you learned in Chapter 5, the nucleus is the control center of almost all cells. If the nucleus and the hereditary material in it are removed, the cell dies. The nucleus also plays a major role in cell division.

Before mitosis begins, a series of changes takes place in the nucleus and results in the duplication of the hereditary material. When the nucleus divides, each new nucleus, called a daughter nucleus, receives a complete copy of this material.

DNA (deoxyribonucleic acid), the hereditary material of the cell, is found in the cell's nucleus. The information needed to make the parts of each cell is stored in the DNA. The DNA also has information that determines how the organism is made up and works as a whole. This information must be passed on to all cells produced.

In nondividing cells, nuclear DNA exists in a mass of thin, twisted threads called **chromatin** (KROH muh tin). Chromatin is made up of DNA wound around small groups of proteins called **histones** (HIS tones). In cells undergoing mitosis, the threadlike chromatin shortens and thickens into the rodlike structures called **chromosomes** (KROH muh sohmz). See Figure 20–3.

Each type of organism has a specific number of chromosomes in its body cells. For example, humans have 46 chromosomes, wheat has 42, potatoes have 48, crayfish have 20, and fruit flies have 8. Look again at Figure 20–3. The number of chromosomes in the

Figure 20–3

Human Chromosomes. All human body cells have 46 chromosomes. The chromosomes shown in this light micrograph are from the cell of a human male. ▼

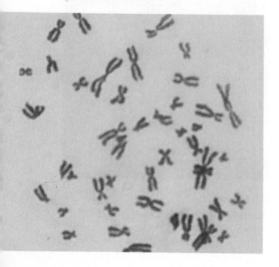

Interphase and Mitotic Cell Division in Animal Cells

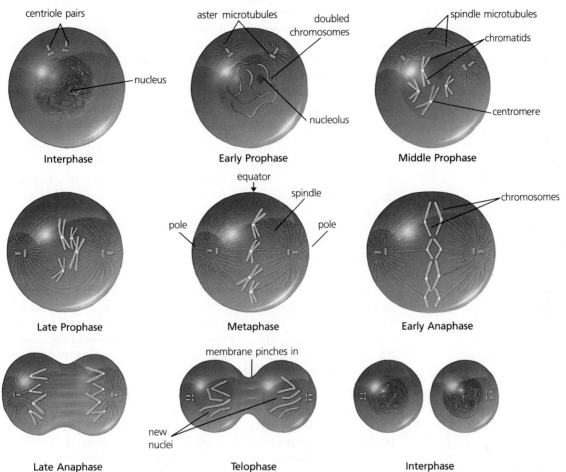

▲ **Figure 20–4**
Interphase and Mitotic Cell Division in Animal Cells.

body cells of an organism is constant. Because each chromosome has only part of the total hereditary information, each cell must have a complete set of chromosomes to work correctly.

Interphase and Mitosis in Animal Cells

Once begun, mitosis is a continuous process. However, it is easier to understand if it is divided into stages, or phases. These stages are known as prophase, metaphase, anaphase, and telophase. There is no sharp break between these stages. Each merges into the next. When a cell is between mitotic cycles, it is in the **interphase** (IN ter fayz) stage. Figure 20–4 shows interphase and the major events of each stage of mitosis in animal cells.

Interphase   Although interphase is also called the resting stage, the cell is never really at rest. Interphase lasts from the end of one cell division to the beginning of the next. During interphase, the cell grows in size, and more nucleic acids, proteins, and cellular organelles are produced. At some point before mitosis begins, each chromosome makes a copy of itself, or *replicates* (REP luh kayts), and becomes a doubled chromosome.

During interphase, the nucleus of the cell is contained within the nuclear membrane, and one or more nucleoli are present. The chromosomes cannot be seen with a microscope at this time. Instead, the DNA appears as a tangled, threadlike mass of chromatin. Near the nucleus are the **centrioles,** two tiny, cylindrical bodies that lie at right angles to each other. The centrioles also replicate during interphase and form two pairs.

Prophase During **prophase** (PROH fayz), the doubled chromosomes become visible as long threads that coil and contract into thick rods. Each strand of doubled chromosomes is called a **chromatid** (KROH muh tid). The chromatids are connected at a region called the **centromere** (SEN truh meer). See Figure 20–5b.

At the beginning of prophase, the two pairs of centrioles move toward the opposite ends, or *poles,* of the cell. Microtubules extend from the centrioles to form star-shaped structures called **asters.** Other microtubules go from pole to pole. These microtubules form a football-shaped structure called the **spindle.** Some of the microtubules become fastened to the centromeres of the chromosomes. As prophase goes on, the doubled chromosomes begin to move toward the *equator,* which is the place midway between the poles. See Figure 20–5b. By the end of prophase, the nuclear membrane and the nucleolus have disappeared.

Metaphase During **metaphase** (MET uh fayz), the centromeres of the doubled chromosomes are lined up on the equator. See Figure 20–5c. At the end of metaphase, the centromeres divide, and the two chromatids of each chromosome become separate chromosomes. In other words, each doubled chromosome gives rise to two single-stranded, identical chromosomes.

Anaphase In **anaphase** (AN uh fayz), the duplicate chromosomes move to opposite poles. See Figure 20–5d. The microtubules of the spindle help in this movement. As a result, one complete set of chromosomes goes to one pole while the other identical set goes to the other pole.

Telophase When the chromosomes reach the poles, **telophase** (TEL uh fayz) begins. During telophase, the chromosomes uncoil, get longer, and slowly take on the threadlike appearance of chromatin. See Figure 20–5e. The spindle and asters disappear. A nuclear membrane forms around each daughter nucleus, and the nucleoli reappear. This ends the nuclear division of an animal cell.

Cytokinesis in Animal Cells

Cytokinesis often begins during late anaphase and finishes during telophase. In animal cells, the division of the cytoplasm comes about by a pinching-in of the cell membrane. The pinching-in takes place in the middle of the cell and results in the formation of two daughter cells of about the same size. Each daughter cell receives one of the newly-formed nuclei and about half of the organelles from the parent cell.

Mitosis and Cytokinesis in Plant Cells

Cell division in plants can be seen fairly easily in developing seeds and in the growing regions of roots and stems. The main events of nuclear division are the same in plants as in animals. See Figure 20–6. However, plant cell division differs from animal cell division in two ways. First, because plant cells do not have centrioles, asters do not form. However, a spindle does form, and the chromosomes

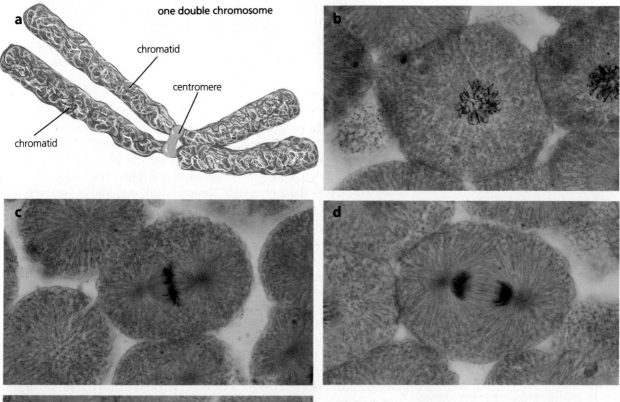

one double chromosome

a

chromatid

centromere

chromatid

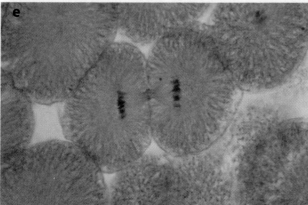

◀ **Figure 20–5**
The Stages of Mitosis. Following the duplication of chromosomes, which occurs during interphase, mitosis takes place. (a) Early in prophase, the double chromosomes become visible. Each chromosome is made up of two chromatids that are connected at the centromere. (b) Later in prophase, the double chromosomes become more distinct and begin to move toward the equator of the cell. In addition, the nuclear membrane slowly disintegrates. (c) In metaphase, the double chromosomes line up at the equator of the cell. At the end of metaphase, the centromeres divide. (d) During anaphase, the chromatids of each double chromosome move to opposite poles of the cell. (e) In the last stage of mitosis, telophase, the nuclear membrane reappears. At this point, the cell body divides into two daughter cells. (Magnification 625 X)

Figure 20–6

Interphase and Mitotic Cell Division in Plant Cells. ▶

Interphase and Mitotic Cell Division in Plant Cells

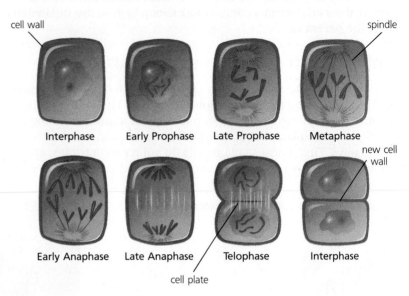

cell wall

spindle

Interphase Early Prophase Late Prophase Metaphase

new cell wall

Early Anaphase Late Anaphase Telophase Interphase

cell plate

move in the same way as in animal cells. Second, the rigid cell walls of plant cells do not pinch in during telophase. Instead, a structure called the **cell plate** forms across the middle of a cell. See Figure 20–7. The cell plate grows outward and joins the old cell wall, which divides the cell in half. New cell wall material is secreted on each side of the cell plate.

Time Span of Mitotic Cell Division

The time needed for a cell to pass through all the stages of mitosis varies from one type of organism to another and from one type of tissue to another. In general, interphase is long compared with the stages of mitotic cell division. For example, a human cell in tissue culture takes about 1 hour to divide and then remains in interphase for 16 to 20 hours.

Mitosis takes place most often in cells that are least specialized. Most cells in a developing embryo divide rapidly. However, as the embryo matures, the cells become specialized, and the rate of mitosis decreases. In adults, cells divide frequently only in certain tissues. Some cells, such as cambium and root tip cells in plants and bone marrow and skin epithelial cells in animals, divide rapidly. Specialized cells, such as xylem, nerve, and muscle cells, seldom or never divide once they are formed.

Figure 20–7

Cytokinesis in Plant Cells. In plant cells, such as this onion root tip, the cytoplasm is divided in half by the formation of a cell plate. ▼

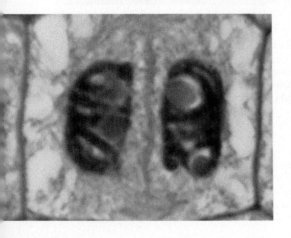

Control of the Cell Cycle

Cell growth and division in a large organism are carefully regulated. This means that something must control whether a cell is allowed to divide, or whether it can enter the next phase of the cell cycle. For years biologists wondered what that something might be. At long last, it seems as though they have the answer.

Nearly 20 years ago, scientists were trying to find out if there was a signal that caused the egg cell of a frog to begin dividing after it was fertilized by a sperm cell. They discovered that the dividing cell contained a protein that, if injected into a nondividing egg cell, would cause a spindle to form. To their surprise, they discovered that the amount of this protein in the cell rose and fell in timing with the cell cycle.

Scientists called this protein **cyclin** because the amount of this protein changed in time with the cell cycle. Cyclins regulate the timing of the cell cycle in all eukaryotic cells that have been studied. It turns out that there are many different cyclins, some of which regulate different phases of the cell cycle. For example, there is an S-phase cyclin that starts the process of DNA replication, and an M-phase cyclin that regulates the entry of the cell into mitosis.

As a cell goes through the cell cycle, cyclin is made at a fairly constant rate, and gradually builds up inside the cell. When the cyclin level reaches a critical point, it triggers the cell to enter mitosis. Once the cell has entered mitosis, it destroys nearly all of its cyclin. This means that the cell must start to make cyclin again before it can enter mitosis a second time. The time it takes for a cell to make more cyclin determines how long it will take the cell to move through the cell cycle.

MiniLab

Skill: Modeling

Oh Yarn—It's Mitosis!

Procedure

1. Obtain 60 cm of yarn, 100 cm of string, and scissors.

Problem

How can you **create a model** of mitosis?

2. Cut four pieces of yarn in 3-cm lengths, four pieces in 5-cm lengths, and four pieces in 7-cm lengths.

3. Cut two 25-cm lengths of string. Then cut the rest as needed.

4. Using the yarn and string, illustrate the processes of interphase and mitosis. Begin with six pieces of yarn—two of each length.

Analyze and Conclude

1. What do the pieces of yarn represent?

2. What do the pieces of string represent?

3. Does the process of mitosis in step 4 above change depending on whether you illustrate a plant cell or an animal cell?

Unlike normal cells, cancer cells do not respond to the usual signals that keep cells from growing uncontrollably. Cancer cells divide excessively in an uncontrolled fashion. Very often, the reason cancer cells don't respond to the signals is because of a defect in cell cycle regulation. Cyclin, and the proteins that interact with it, have turned out to be the master proteins in regulating the cell cycle. There is much excitement in the scientific community because biologists are hoping that an understanding of the cell cycle may lead to a cure for cancer.

20-1 Section Review

1. Name the two basic types of reproduction.
2. Identify the two processes involved in cell division.
3. List the stages of mitosis.
4. In what two ways does division in plant cells differ from division in animal cells?

Critical Thinking

5. Compare and contrast asexual and sexual reproduction. (*Comparing and Contrasting*)

20-2 Asexual Reproduction

Section Objectives:

- *Describe* the processes of binary fission, budding, and spore formation.
- *Explain* regeneration, and name three types of animals in which regeneration can be a form of asexual reproduction.
- *Describe* the various types of natural and artificial vegetative reproduction.

Producing Identical Offspring

Unicellular organisms, many simple animals, and many plants reproduce asexually, at least during one part of their life cycles. In asexual reproduction in multicellular organisms, the offspring develop from undifferentiated, unspecialized cells of the parent organism.

Because asexual reproduction takes place only by mitotic cell division, each offspring has exactly the same hereditary information as its parent. The offspring show little variation. That is, they are all nearly identical to each other and to the parent. Thus, asexual reproduction results in the same characteristics within a species from one generation to the next.

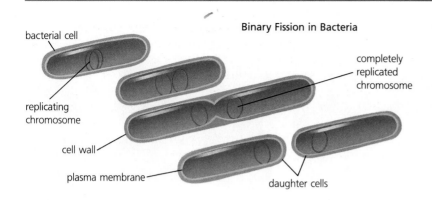

Binary Fission in Bacteria

bacterial cell

replicating chromosome

cell wall

plasma membrane

completely replicated chromosome

daughter cells

◄ **Figure 20–8**
Binary Fission in Bacteria. When bacteria reproduce by binary fission, the chromosome replicates, and a wall divides the cell into two approximately equal parts.

Asexual reproduction is usually rapid and often results in the production of large numbers of offspring. There are several methods of asexual reproduction, including binary fission, budding, spore formation, regeneration, and vegetative reproduction.

Binary Fission

In **binary fission** (BY nehr ee FISH un), the simplest form of asexual reproduction, the parent organism divides into two parts that are about equal. Each of the daughter cells becomes a separate individual and grows to normal size. No parent is left in this method of reproduction because the parent has become two individuals. Binary fission is the usual method of reproduction among one-celled organisms, including bacteria, protozoa, and many algae. When binary fission occurs in cells that have a distinct nucleus, the nucleus divides by mitosis.

Fission in Bacteria   Bacteria lack an organized nucleus. The hereditary material is in the form of a single circular chromosome. Before cell division, the chromosome attaches to the plasma membrane and then replicates. A cell wall forms between the chromosome and its copy. The wall divides the cell into two daughter cells, each containing one chromosome. See Figure 20–8. Each daughter cell grows to normal size before it too divides. Sometimes, the daughter cells do not separate from each other and thus form chains of bacteria. Under favorable conditions, some bacteria can divide every 20 minutes.

Fission in Protozoa   When an ameba reaches full size, it becomes round, and the nucleus undergoes mitosis. After nuclear division, the cytoplasm in the middle of the cell pinches in, or constricts, producing two daughter cells. See Figure 20–9. The two resulting cells are both smaller than the original parent cell, but they soon grow to full size.

The paramecium has two nuclei, a *micronucleus* (my kroh NOO klee us) and a *macronucleus* (mak roh NOO klee us). The small micronucleus controls the reproductive functions of the cell. During binary fission, the micronucleus divides by mitosis. The macronucleus divides by a modified form of mitosis. One of each kind of

Binary Fission in the Ameba

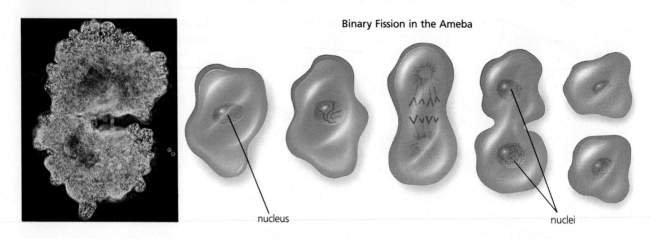

nucleus

nuclei

▲ **Figure 20–9**
Binary Fission in Ameba. Binary fission in ameba involves division of the nucleus by mitosis, followed by division of the cytoplasm into two approximately equal parts.

nucleus goes to each daughter cell. The oral groove and gullet also replicate, and two new contractile vacuoles appear. Thus, before separation takes place, the parts needed for two complete organisms are present. Division of the cytoplasm takes place when the middle of the cell pinches in. The paramecium can also reproduce sexually.

Budding

Budding is a type of asexual reproduction in which the parent organism divides into two unequal parts. New individuals develop as small outgrowths, or buds, on the outer surface of the parent organism. The buds may break off and live independently, or they may remain attached, forming a colony. Budding differs from binary fission in that the parent and offspring are not the same size. Budding takes place in yeast and hydra, as well as in sponges and some worms.

Budding in Yeast   When a yeast cell reaches a certain size, the nucleus moves toward the side of the cell. An enzyme softens the cell wall near the nucleus so that it bulges outward, forming a small knoblike structure called a *bud*. See Figure 20–10. The nucleus then undergoes mitosis, producing two daughter nuclei. One daughter nucleus moves into the bud, while the other remains in the parent cell. A cell wall forms between the parent cell and the bud. The bud may remain fastened to the parent, or they may separate. In either case, the bud is an independent cell that can increase in size and finally produce its own buds. Yeast can also reproduce sexually.

Budding in Yeast

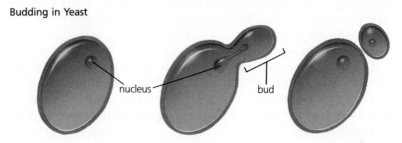

nucleus

bud

Figure 20–10
Budding in Yeast. In budding, the cytoplasm divides into unequal parts. ▶

Budding in Hydra. The bud begins as a small mound of cells on the side of the parent. The cells divide, producing a complete hydra, which eventually separates from the parent.

Budding in Hydra   Budding in hydra is different from budding in yeast. Hydras are made of several kinds of cells. As budding begins, undifferentiated cells on the side of the parent undergo several mitotic divisions, producing a small mound of cells. These cells go on dividing, and in a few days, a small, complete hydra with a mouth and tentacles is formed. See Figure 20–11. The bud finally separates from the parent. Hydras can also reproduce sexually.

Spore Formation

Spores are single, specialized cells that are produced by certain organisms. When released from the parent organism, spores germinate and grow to form new individuals. The term *spore* can refer to a large number of different single-celled structures. Although spores differ greatly in appearance, structure, and origin, all work as single units of reproduction. Each spore has the usual parts of a cell. Often, a spore is surrounded by a special thick, hard outer wall. Sometimes, however, spores lack these walls and have flagella.

Spores can be formed sexually or asexually. (Sexually formed spores are discussed in Chapters 24 and 31.) Asexually formed spores are a common method of reproduction in many simple organisms, such as fungi, algae, and protozoa. These spores are the products of mitotic cell division. Large numbers of them are generally produced during division. They are formed within, and released from, a single cell structure that is the remains of the original parent cell from which the spores came.

Spore Formation in Bread Mold   Bread mold, which is a fungus, can often be seen growing as a dark, cottony mass on bread and other foods. The spores are produced by mitotic cell division in spore cases on specialized stalks that grow upward from the surface. Thousands of black spores develop within each spore case. When fully grown, the walls of the spore case break down, and the tiny, light spores are carried away by air currents. When a spore lands in an environment where there is warmth, food, and moisture, it germinates and grows to form a new mass of mold. Bread molds also reproduce sexually, as described in Chapter 31.

Figure 20–12
Regeneration. The planarian, like many simple animals, can regenerate lost parts. ▶

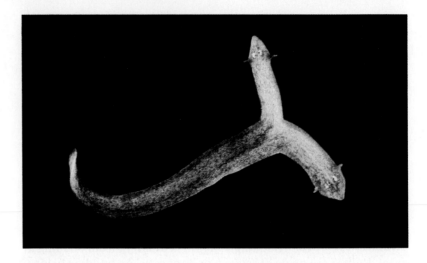

Regeneration

Regeneration (rih jen uh RAY shun) is the ability of an organism to regrow lost body parts. See Figure 20–12. Relatively simple animals, such as the hydra, planarian, starfish, and earthworm, can regenerate lost parts. If a hydra is cut in half, each half will regenerate into a new individual. A planarian can be cut into several pieces, each of which will grow into a complete worm.

Starfish feed on oysters. Workers gathering oysters used to try to destroy the starfish they caught by chopping them into pieces and tossing the pieces back into the water. However, each part of a starfish can regenerate into a whole new organism as long as it contains a piece of the central disk. Thus, the workers were really helping the starfish to multiply rather than destroying them.

The power of regeneration decreases as animals become more complex. A crab can regrow a lost claw but cannot regenerate a whole animal from small pieces. Mammals can repair damaged tissue but cannot regenerate a leg or even a toe. Although simple organisms have great powers of regeneration, they do not usually reproduce in this manner.

Vegetative Reproduction

Although most plants reproduce sexually by means of seeds, asexual reproduction involving roots, stems, and leaves is also common. Roots, stems, and leaves are called *vegetative* (VEJ uh tay tiv) structures. They normally play a part in the nutrition and growth of plants. When they give rise to a new plant, the process is called **vegetative reproduction,** or *vegetative propagation*.

In vegetative reproduction, undifferentiated cells, such as cambium and epidermal cells, divide mitotically and then differentiate to produce an independent plant. The new plant has the same hereditary characteristics as its parent. Vegetative reproduction takes place naturally, but it can be brought about artificially.

Natural Vegetative Reproduction Vegetative propagation takes place naturally in several different ways. See Figure 20–13.

Some plants, such as tulips, onions, and lilies reproduce by bulbs. A **bulb** is a short underground stem surrounded by thick, fleshy leaves that contain stored food. As the plant grows, small new bulbs sprout from the old one. Each of the new bulbs can give rise to a new plant. Other plants, such as gladioli, crocuses, and water chestnuts grow from corms (kormz). A **corm** is like a bulb, but it does not contain fleshy leaves. Rather, corms are short, stout underground stems that contain stored food.

A tuber (TOO ber) is another means of natural vegetative propagation. A **tuber** is an enlarged part of an underground stem that contains stored food. White potatoes are tubers. Along the surface of a tuber are indentations called "eyes." These eyes are tiny buds. When a farmer plants white potatoes, the tuber is cut into pieces, each piece having at least one "eye." Each eye grows into a

◀ **Figure 20–13**
Natural Vegetative Propagation. When a plant reproduces asexually, complete plants can develop from specialized structures other than the seeds, such as bulbs, corms, tubers, runners, or rhizomes. Shown here are: (a) silverweed runners; (b) an iris rhizone and a potato tuber; and (c) daffadil and saffron crocus corms.

shoot that grows upward through the soil surface and also produces roots. The young shoot uses the stored food of the tuber until it can carry on photosynthesis.

Strawberry plants and many kinds of grasses that reproduce quickly use runners. A **runner,** or *stolon* (STOH lun), is a stem that grows sideways and has buds. It usually grows along the surface of the ground. Where buds from a runner touch the soil, new independent plants develop.

Finally, a few plants, such as ferns, irises, cattails, and water lilies, reproduce by rhizomes (RY zohms). A **rhizome** is a stem that grows sideways underground. It is usually thick and fleshy and contains stored food. Along the rhizome are enlarged portions called *nodes.* Buds produced at nodes on the upper surface of the rhizome give rise to leaf-bearing branches. The lower surface of the rhizome produces roots.

Artificial Vegetative Reproduction Farmers and gardeners have developed several methods of artificial vegetative reproduction. See Figure 20–14. These techniques allow them to grow plants with desirable traits.

A **cutting** is any vegetative part of a plant—stem, leaf, or root—used to produce a new individual. In a *stem cutting,* a branch, or slip, is cut from a plant and placed in water or moist sand. Usually the bottom of the cutting is dipped into hormones to stimulate root growth. When roots develop, the cutting becomes an independent plant and is transplanted to soil. Geraniums, roses, ivy, and grapevines are propagated in this manner.

In a *leaf cutting,* a leaf or part of a leaf is placed in water or moist soil. After a while, a new plant develops from certain cells in the leaf. African violets, snake plants, and begonias are often propagated by leaf cuttings.

Under natural conditions, the leaves of kalanchoe give rise to tiny plants along their edges. These plantlets have tiny leaves,

Figure 20–14

Artificial Vegatative Propagation. (A) Many important ornamental plant species are propagated by means of leaf or stem cuttings. Here, a begonia leaf has been placed in soil to root. (B) Grafting makes it possible to combine the best qualities of different plant species or varieties into a single plant. ▼

stems, and sometimes roots. When they fall from the parent plant, they take root and go on growing in the soil. They can be separated and used to produce new plants.

The sweet potato is an enlarged root containing stored food. Farmers place it in moist sand or soil until it sprouts several new plants. Then the sprouts are removed and planted.

In **layering,** a stem is bent over so that part of it is covered with soil. After the covered part forms roots, the new plant may be cut from the parent plant. Layering is used to reproduce such plants as raspberries, roses, and honeysuckle. It also takes place naturally.

In **grafting,** a stem or bud is removed from one plant and joined permanently to the stem of a closely related plant. The part of this combination providing the roots is called the *stock;* the added piece is called the *scion* (SY en). The cambium layers (growing regions) of the scion and stock must be in close contact. Usually they are held together by tape and coated with wax to protect the growing tissue from water loss and disease. After a time the cambiums of the two pieces form new xylem and phloem, which grow together and connect the scion and stock. The stock supports and nourishes the scion. However, the scion keeps its own characteristics. For example, although scions of McIntosh apples can be grafted onto stock of any kind of apple tree, the scions will produce only McIntosh apples. Grafting is used to propagate roses, peach trees, plum trees, grapevines, and various seedless fruits, including navel oranges, grapes, and grapefruits.

▲ **Figure 20–15**
A Seedless Navel Orange.

Advantages of Artificial Vegetative Propagation   Plants grown from seeds do not always show the same characteristics as the parent plant. Vegetative propagation, however, produces new plants exactly like the parent. There is little variation because all offspring have the same hereditary makeup as the parent. Furthermore, the development of a plant by vegetative propagation is often faster than development from seed. In the development of an improved plant variety, stem cuttings or grafts made onto mature plants will produce fruit in much less time than it takes for small plants to bear fruit. Plants bearing *seedless fruit* can be grown only by vegetative propagation. See Figure 20–15. Grafting also can be used to obtain higher yields of fruits or nuts.

20-2 Section Review

1. How is binary fission different from budding?
2. Name an organism that reproduces by means of spores.
3. What is regeneration?
4. Give examples of natural and artificial vegetative reproduction.

Critical Thinking

5. Why would a farmer use artificial vegetative propagation instead of sexual reproduction by means of seeds? (*Identifying Reasons*)

Laboratory
Investigation

Mitosis

The tip of a root is a good place to look for cells that are in the process of dividing because roots grow at the tip. In this investigation, you will prepare slides from garlic root tips. If your preparation is a good one, you may be able to find all the phases of mitosis.

Problem

How many phases of mitosis can you **observe** in a plant cell?

Materials (per group)

- forceps
- garlic root tips
- 2 watch glasses or Petri dish covers
- 50% hydrochloric acid-50% ethyl alcohol solution (HCl-EtOH)
- Carnoy's fixative
- microscope slide
- scalpel
- medicine dropper
- aceto-orcein stain
- coverslip
- paper towel
- compound microscope

Procedure

1. Using the forceps, obtain a garlic root tip from your instructor. Place the root tip in a watch glass.

2. Carefully pour HCl-EtOH over the root tip so that the entire tip is immersed in the solution. **CAUTION:** *If the solution touches your skin, wash the area immediately with running water.* Soak the root tip in the solution for 5 to 6 minutes.

3. Using the forceps, transfer the root tip to the second watch glass. Pour Carnoy's fixative over the root tip. Leave the root tip in the fixative for 3 minutes.

4. Using the forceps, transfer the tip to a microscope slide.

5. Holding the root tips with the forceps, use the scalpel to cut off 2 cm from the root tip. **CAUTION:** *Be careful when using sharp instruments.* Discard the rest of the root tip.

6. Use the medicine dropper to add just enough aceto-orcein stain to cover the remaining tip. **CAUTION:** *Aceto-orcein will stain skin and clothing.* Leave the root tip in the stain for 5 minutes.

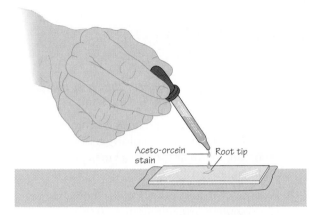

Aceto-orcein stain / Root tip

7. Place a clean coverslip over the root tip. Place a folded paper towel on a flat surface and fold the paper towel over the slide. Gently press down on the paper towel with your thumb to absorb the excess liquid.

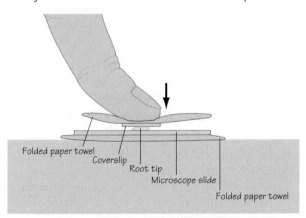

Folded paper towel
Coverslip
Root tip
Microscope slide
Folded paper towel

8. Place the slide under low power on your microscope. Focus the microscope. Then scan the slide until you find some stained cells.

9. Switch the microscope to high power and locate as many phases of mitosis as you can.

Observations

1. Sketch any cells that are in a phase of mitosis.

2. Label the sketch with the name of the appropriate phase. ·

Analysis and Conclusions

1. How do the cells that are in a phase of mitosis differ from cells that are not dividing?

2. What was the purpose of the hydrochloric acid-ethyl alcohol solution? (*Hint:* Consider how plant cells are held together.)

3. Did the aceto-orcein stain one part of the cell more so than any other? If so, which one?

4. In which phase of mitosis were most of the cells you observed? Why do you think this is so?

Extensions

Which phase of mitosis do you think takes the longest? Design an experiment that tests your hypothesis.

Chapter 20 Review

Study Outline

20-1 Mitosis

▶ New cells arise from existing cells by division of the original cell into two cells. Cell division consists of two processes: mitosis and cytokinesis.

▶ The nucleus contains the hereditary material. In cells undergoing mitosis, the hereditary material is found in the chromosomes.

▶ There are four stages of mitosis. They are prophase, metaphase, anaphase, and telophase.

▶ The period of time from the beginning of one cell division to the beginning of the next is called the cell cycle.

▶ The basic stages of mitotic division are the same in plant and animal cells. However, cytoplasmic division in plant cells differs from that in animal cells, since the dividing plant cells form cell plates and do not form asters.

20-2 Asexual Reproduction

▶ Asexual reproduction involves mitotic cell division of only one parent. The simplest form of asexual reproduction is binary fission, in which the parent divides into two daughter cells of approximately equal size.

▶ In budding, the parent organism divides into two individuals of unequal size. The new individual is smaller than the parent and grows to full size after separation from the parent.

▶ Regeneration is the ability to regrow lost body parts and is not usually a method of reproduction.

▶ Most plants reproduce sexually, but asexual reproduction involving roots, stems, and leaves is also common.

▶ Vegetative reproduction occurs naturally with bulbs, corms, tubers, runners, and rhizomes. It can also be accomplished artificially with cuttings, layering, and grafting.

Chapter Assessment

Multiple Choice

Choose the letter of the answer that best completes each statement or answers the question.

1. During which phase of mitosis do chromosomes line up across the middle of the cell?
(a) prophase (b) anaphase (c) metaphase
(d) telophase

2. A phase of mitosis during which duplicated chromosomes separate from each other is
(a) prophase. (b) anaphase. (c) metaphase.
(d) telophase.

3. The centromere is (a) connected to the cell plate. (b) part of the flagellum. (c) part of a chromosome. (d) part of a centriole.

4. The timing of the cell cycle is regulated by
(a) cyclins. (b) centromeres. (c) centrioles.
(d) chromatids.

5. Many unicellular organisms reproduce by the process of (a) binary fission. (b) regeneration.
(c) ovulation. (d) nondisjunction.

6. Which method of reproduction is carried on by both yeast and hydra? (a) budding (b) binary fission (c) sporulation (d) multiple fission

7. Regeneration is more often a characteristic of
(a) unicellular rather than multicellular organisms.
(b) animals rather than plants. (c) simple rather than complex organisms. (d) complex rather than simple organisms.

8. By which process do multicellular plants reproduce asexually? (a) binary fission (b) meiosis
(c) fertilization (d) vegetative propagation

9. Which is a form of vegetative propagation?
(a) grafting (b) pollination (c) conjugation
(d) sporulation

10. Fruit growers often propagate their plants by asexual means because the resulting offspring
(a) develops faster than it would from a seed.
(b) bears larger fruit than the parent. (c) shows no environmental variation. (d) shows genetic variation from the parent.

Content Review

Answer each of the following in complete sentences.

11. Compare mitosis with cytokinesis.

12. Using an animal cell with four chromosomes as an example, draw the four stages of mitosis and briefly describe each stage.

13. Contrast cytokinesis in plant cells with that in animal cells.

14. Why might an increase in size trigger mitotic cell division in unicellular organisms?

15. How does cancer affect mitotic division?

16. Describe binary fission in bacteria.

17. Compare bud formation in yeast and in hydra.

18. How are asexually formed spores produced?

19. Why does cutting individual starfish into pieces increase the population of starfish?

20. What are cyclins?

Graphic Organizing

For information on graphic organizers, see Appendix G at the back of this text.

21. **Circle Graph** Using the data in the table below, construct a circle graph of a cell cycle for a cell that completes a cycle in 24 hours. The cell cycle is made up of interphase (which is divided into three phases: G_1—the presynthesis period; S—the period when DNA replicates; and G_2—the postsynthesis period) and mitosis. Use the graph to explain why most of the cells in a population are in interphase at any given time.

Stage	Time Length
Interphase:	
G_1	10 hours
S	9 hours
G_2	4 hours
Mitosis (M)	1 hour

22. **Word Map** Construct a word map for the term *vegetative reproduction.*

Critical Thinking and Problem Solving

Discuss each of the following in a brief paragraph.

23. **Inferring** Cancer, which is the uncontrolled division of cells, is sometimes treated with radiation or drugs that attack rapidly growing cells. Explain why this type of treatment may harm the patient.

24. **Predicting** In some animal cells, certain cell structures divide prior to anaphase. Among these structures are the chromosomes, the centrioles, and the centromeres. What would be the effect on the daughter cells if each of these structures did not divide?

25. **Predicting** Nerve cells and muscle cells seldom divide after they are formed. What effect does this have on the human body in the event of injury to these cells?

26. **Relating** In what ways might the process of regeneration be useful to humans?

27. **Drawing conclusions** An investigation was carried out to determine if the movement of the spindle microtubules during mitosis depends on adenosine triphosphate (ATP). Cells that were about to divide were placed in a solution containing radioactive ATP, in which the last phosphate group was radioactively labeled. After 24 hours at 25°C, the cells were examined, and radioactive phosphate was found on the spindle microtubules. What conclusion could be drawn from this experiment? Is there a control? How might you improve the design of the experiment? What further steps might be performed?

28. **Experimenting** Design an experiment to investigate the effect of caffeine on mitosis. *Hint:* The process of mitosis can be easily observed in the onion root tip.

29. **Calculating** Some bacteria can divide every 20 minutes. Starting with one such bacterium, how many would be present after 4, 8, and 12 hours?

Discovery
Learning Activity

Flower Power

1. Working in a group, obtain several different flowers from your teacher.

2. With a hand lens, examine the sepals (leaflike structures that enclose a flower when it is a bud) and petals (colorful leaflike structures) for one flower. Remove these structures and look for a sticky or feathery stigma (female part of flower) and the powdery pollen that covers the stamens (male parts of the flower).

3. Place a stamen under the low-power objective of a microscope and look for pollen grains. Make a sketch of what you see. Look for the swollen part of the pistil, called the ovary. With a single-edged razor, make a lengthwise cut through the ovary. **CAUTION:** *Be careful when using a sharp instrument.* Describe the structures that you see inside the ovary. What do you think these structures are?

4. Repeat steps 2 and 3 with the remaining flowers.

Meiosis and Sexual Reproduction

Previewing the Chapter

A young foal warily views the world from under its mother's protective shadow. Although the foal resembles its mother, it also has its own characteristics, distinct from those of either parent. How does the process of sexual reproduction increase genetic variety among organisms, including humans? What is meiosis and how does this process produce reproductive cells, or gametes? How do gametes function in sexual reproduction in animals?

Key Words

conjugation, fertilization, gamete, meiosis, oogenesis, spermatogenesis, zygote

Key Concepts

- **Summarize** the process of meiosis
- **Describe** the role of gametes in sexual reproduction
- **Organize** human chromosomes into homologous pairs. (Laboratory Investigation)

21-1 Meiosis

Section Objectives:

- *Explain* the importance of meiosis.
- *Define* the terms *gamete, zygote, diploid,* and *haploid*.
- *Describe* the stages of meiosis.

Another Kind of Cell Division

As you may recall from Chapter 20, asexual reproduction involves only one parent cell. When reproduction occurs asexually, the parent cell divides to produce offspring with the same genetic makeup as the parent cell. Sexual reproduction, on the other hand, requires two different parent cells from two separate organisms or from two sexually different parts of a single organism. Sexual reproduction produces offspring that are genetically different from either parent.

In simple organisms, sexual reproduction involves a transfer of genetic material from one organism to another. In more complex organisms, two special sex cells—called **gametes** (GAM eets)—are needed. Usually, there are two kinds of gametes, one male and one female. A new offspring results when the male and the female

▲ **Figure 21–1**

Sexual Reproduction. The sperm and the egg each contain half the hereditary information needed to create a new organism.

◄ Mare and her foal.

gametes fuse, or join together. The fusion of the nuclei of the male and the female gametes is called **fertilization.** The single cell formed from this fusion is known as a **zygote** (ZY goht).

Gametes are formed by **meiosis** (my OH sis), a kind of cell division that results in gametes with half the number of chromosomes as the parent cell. Because of meiosis, each gamete has half of the regular number of chromosomes. The process of fertilization restores the regular number of chromosomes to the zygote.

Diploid and Haploid Chromosome Numbers

Somatic (soh MAH tic) **cells,** or body cells, are all the cells of an organism except for the specialized cells that play a part in sexual reproduction. Every species of organism has a certain number of chromosomes in its body cells. For example, human somatic cells typically have 46 chromosomes. The body cells of bull frogs have 26 chromosomes. Fruit fly body cells have 8 chromosomes.

The chromosomes of most organisms can be grouped into pairs of similar chromosomes. For example, in humans, the 46 chromosomes in body cells can be arranged into 23 pairs. The chromosomes that make up each pair are called **homologous** (hoh MAL uh guhs) **chromosomes.** See Figure 21–2. Homologous chro-

Figure 21–2

Human Chromosomes. The chromosomes of cells undergoing mitosis were stained and photographed. The photographs were then cut apart and assembled into pairs of homologous chromosomes. The set of chromosomes to the left were from a male. The pair labeled X and Y are the sex chromosomes. The set of chromosomes to the right were from a female cell and have a pair of X chromosomes. Chromosomes in the male are the same size as those in the female; they look smaller here because they are magnified less than the female's chromosomes. ▼

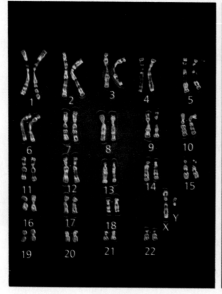
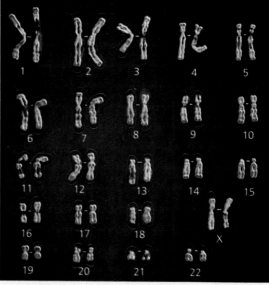

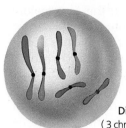

Diploid (2n) Cell
(3 chromosome pairs)

Haploid (n) Cell
(3 chromosomes)

◀   **Figure 21–3**
Diploid and Haploid Cells. The haploid cell contains only one chromosome from each pair of homologous chromosomes. The diploid cell contains both chromosomes from each pair of homologous chromosomes.

mosomes are similar in size and shape, and they have similar genetic content. (In some organisms, including humans, one pair of chromosomes, the sex chromosomes, are not homologous in one of the sexes.) Those cells that have all the homologous chromosomes that are characteristic of the species are referred to as **diploid** (DIP loyd), or 2n.

Unlike the body cells, gametes do not contain pairs of homologous chromosomes. Instead, they have only one chromosome from each pair. As a result, they have only half the diploid number of chromosomes. For example, human gametes contain 23 chromosomes—one from each of the 23 pairs of chromosomes in body cells. Cells that have only one chromosome from each pair are said to be **haploid** (HAP loyd), or *monoploid* (MAHN uh ployd). Haploid cells contain n chromosomes, rather than the 2n of diploid cells. See Figure 21–3.

If gametes were diploid cells, the number of chromosomes per cell would double with each generation. The doubling would take place when two gametes were united at the time of fertilization. Because of the process of meiosis, the doubling of the chromosome number does not take place. Meiosis, which produces gametes in animals and spores in plants and in some fungi, ensures that the gametes receive only half the number of chromosomes that are present in the parent cells.

Stages of Meiosis

Meiosis, which is also known as *reduction division,* takes place in special cells. At the start of meiosis, these cells have the diploid number of chromosomes. In meiosis, each cell divides twice. The chromosomes, however, replicate only once. This replication takes place before the first division. In the second division, no replication of the chromosomes takes place. As a result of the two meiotic divisions, each original cell produces four cells, which are known as *daughter cells.* Each of these cells contains the haploid number of chromosomes.

Both the first and second meiotic divisions can be divided into stages similar to the stages of mitosis. Thus, both divisions show a prophase, metaphase, anaphase, and telophase stage. The events of the first and second meiotic divisions are shown in Figure 21–4 using an animal cell as an example.

Prophase I   At the beginning of prophase in the first meiotic division, each chromosome has already replicated, producing two chromatids, as in mitosis. However, the pairs of chromatids do not move independently to the equator. Instead, each pair of chromatids lines up with its homologous pair, and they become fastened at their centromeres. This pairing process is called **synapsis** (suh NAP sis), and each group of four chromatids is called a **tetrad.** The strands of the tetrad sometimes twist about each other, and at this point, they may exchange segments. The exchange of segments between chromatids during synapsis is called *crossing-over.*

While these chromosomal changes are taking place, the nuclear membrane disappears and the spindle fibers form. As prophase I ends, the homologous chromosome pairs, each made up of four chromatids, move toward the equator of the cell.

Metaphase I   In metaphase in the first meiotic division, the centromeres of the tetrads line up on the equator. The tetrads are fastened to the spindle microtubules at their centromeres.

Anaphase I   During anaphase in the first meiotic division, the homologous chromosomes of each tetrad separate from each other and move to opposite ends of the cell. This process of separation is called **disjunction** (dis JUNK shun). The cluster of chromosomes around each pole is haploid—there are half as many chromosomes as in the original cell. However, each chromosome is double-stranded.

Telophase I   Telophase marks the end of the first meiotic division. The cytoplasm divides, forming two daughter cells. Each of the newly formed daughter cells has half the number of the parent cell's chromosomes, but each chromosome is already in replicated form.

Sometimes at the end of telophase I, nuclear membranes form and a short interphase follows. However, in most cases, the cells immediately begin the second division. No further replication of the chromosomes takes place, but the remainder of the division is exactly like mitosis.

Prophase II   During prophase II, each of the daughter cells forms a spindle, and the double-stranded chromosomes move toward the middle of the spindle.

Metaphase II   During metaphase II, the chromosomes become fastened to spindle microtubules at their centromeres, and the centromeres of the chromosomes line up on the equator. Each chromosome still consists of two strands, or chromatids.

Anaphase II   During anaphase II, the centromeres divide, and the two chromatids separate, each becoming a single-stranded chromosome. The two chromosomes then move toward the opposite ends of the spindle.

Telophase II   During telophase II, both daughter cells divide, forming four haploid cells. In each cell, chromosomes return to their interphase state, and the nuclear membrane forms again.

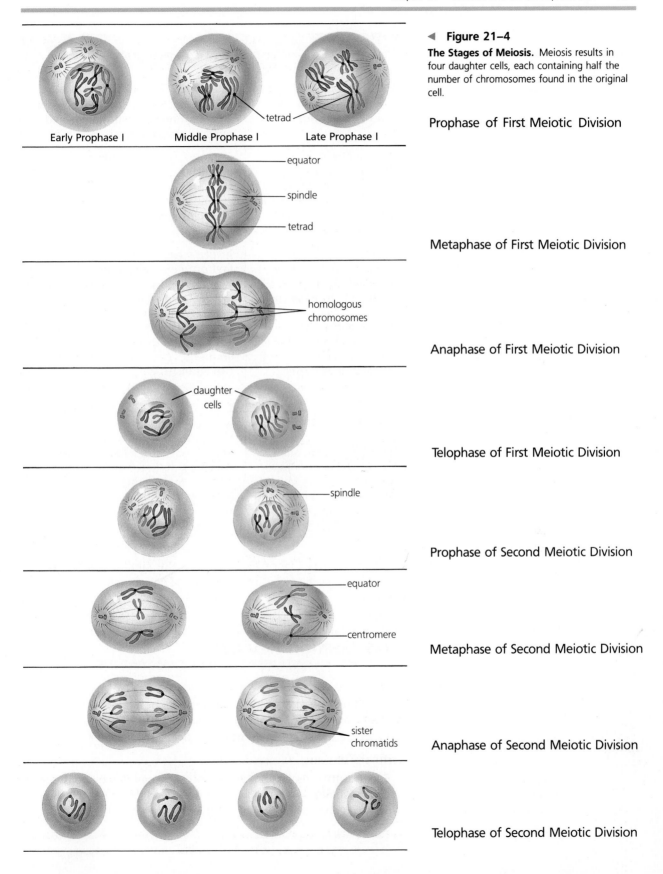

◀ **Figure 21–4**

The Stages of Meiosis. Meiosis results in four daughter cells, each containing half the number of chromosomes found in the original cell.

Early Prophase I   Middle Prophase I   Late Prophase I

tetrad

Prophase of First Meiotic Division

equator

spindle

tetrad

Metaphase of First Meiotic Division

homologous chromosomes

Anaphase of First Meiotic Division

daughter cells

Telophase of First Meiotic Division

spindle

Prophase of Second Meiotic Division

equator

centromere

Metaphase of Second Meiotic Division

sister chromatids

Anaphase of Second Meiotic Division

Telophase of Second Meiotic Division

Figure 21–5

Comparison of Mitosis and Meiosis. Both mitosis and meiosis result in the production of new cells. Mitosis produces two diploid cells from one diploid cell. Meiosis produces four haploid cells from one diploid cell. ▶

Comparison of Mitosis and Meiosis	
Mitosis	**Meiosis**
Occurs in growth and asexual reproduction	Occurs in production of gametes in animals, and spores in plants and in some simple organisms
Homologous chromosomes not paired up during prophase. There is no exchange of parts between homologous chromosomes.	Homologous chromosomes paired up during prophase of first division. While paired, there may be an exchange of parts between homologous chromosomes.
Involves one cell division. In the course of division, the double-stranded chromosomes line up at cell equator, centromeres divide, and one chromatid of each chromosome goes to each daughter cell.	Involves two cell divisions. During first division, pairs of homologous two-stranded chromosomes line up at equator. The members of each pair separate, and one two-stranded chromosome of each pair goes to each daughter cell. During second division, centromeres of two-stranded chromosomes divide, and chromatids separate, one going to each daughter cell.
As a result of mitosis, each daughter cell receives the same number of chromosomes as the original cell. Mitosis maintains the chromosome number.	As a result of meiosis, each daughter cell receives only one member of each pair of homologous chromosomes. It therefore has only one-half the number of chromosomes in the original cell. Meiosis reduces the chromosome number by one-half.

The chart in Figure 21–5 outlines the similarities and differences between the two different kinds of cell division, mitosis and meiosis.

21-1 Section Review

1. What is meiosis?
2. Which cells of an animal are diploid and which are haploid?
3. How many pairs of chromosomes are found in human body cells?
4. What are the products of meiosis in animals? In plants?

Critical Thinking

5. Suppose that disjunction did not occur in one homologous pair of chromosomes during anaphase I. How would this affect the chromosome number in the daughter cells? (*Predicting*)

Drugs—Do They Affect Development?

Problem

Caffeine is a stimulant drug found in colas, coffee, tea, candies, chocolate, and some over-the-counter and prescription drugs. When caffeine is consumed in large amounts, it can cause restlessness, nervousness, and insomnia. In pregnant women, caffeine not only crosses the placenta and affects the fetus, but it also acts as a diuretic, dehydrating the mother's body of precious water.

Alcohol consumption during pregnancy can cause the physical and mental defects that are associated with fetal alcohol syndrome (FAS). The birth defects can include mental retardation, growth deficiences, central nervous system dysfunction, and behavioral problems.

Because scientific experiments cannot be performed on humans, the effects of these substances will be observed in the external development of brine shrimp eggs. Brine shrimp, or *Artemia,* are small crustaceans found in salt lakes.

Task

You are a member of a team of scientists and have been asked by the Food and Drug Administration to investigate the effects that certain substances have on animal development.

In order to perform this task, you must complete each of the following:

1. Design an experiment to test the effect of alcohol or caffeine on the hatching and development of brine shrimp eggs.

2. Research how to grow and maintain brine shrimp.

3. Use a design brief that includes the hypothesis, materials, procedure, data, observations, and conclusions regarding your experiment. Be sure to include a control.

4. Perform the experiment quantitatively. In other words, determine the following: concentration of salt water you will use, the number of eggs you will use, the method of counting the eggs, preparation of the alcohol or caffeine samples, concentrations of the substance you will test, and calculation of the concentrations of the substance.

5. Demonstrate support of your conclusions in a clear and concise format using your data.

6. Use the scientific term LD (Lethal Dose) to determine the percentage of eggs that did not hatch (for example, LD 50 = 50% lethal dose).

7. Design a spread sheet or some type of data-collection format to indicate any of the quantitative data collected (for example, number of brine shrimp that hatched).

8. Research the effect(s) the substance you are testing has on reproduction and development of brine shrimp.

9. Keep a journal that contains your team's experiment, materials needed, observations, data, results, and any other related information.

Solution

Prepare a presentation of your experimental design and results to the Food and Drug Administration. Include in your presentation the title, hypothesis, a description of your research, materials, procedures followed, observations, charts, graphs, initial interpretations, and conclusions. In addition, provide the following: concentration levels of the substance that was tested and their effects on hatching of the eggs and a description of the relationship between the effects of the substance and the concentrations of the substance. Report the concentration at which no eggs hatched. Based on your research, describe when there is an LD 50 and an LD 25. What general statement can you make about the experiment based on your research? What sources of error could be present in your experiment? Describe how you could improve your experiment.

21-2 Sexual Reproduction in Simple Organisms

Section Objectives:

- *State* the advantages of sexual reproduction.
- *Define* the term *conjugation*.
- *Explain* the importance of mating types.
- *Describe* the process of conjugation in bacteria, spirogyra, and paramecium.

Advantages of Sexual Reproduction

All living things give rise to new members of their own kind by means of either asexual or sexual reproduction or both. As you read in Chapter 20, in asexual reproduction, each new individual receives a set of chromosomes that is exactly like its parent's chromosomes. This means that no inherited differences, or variations, are likely to occur. As long as the environment of the organisms remains the same, variations are not necessary for the survival of the species. If, however, the environment changes and the organisms are unable to adapt to the change, they are likely to die out.

In sexual reproduction, the offspring are not identical to either parent. Instead, they show new combinations of characteristics. Thus, in any species in which sexual reproduction takes place, the members of the species will show differences in structure and/or function. Increasing the amount of variation in members of a species increases the possibility that some individuals of that species will be better able than others to survive both short-term and long-term changes in the environment. The better-adapted individuals are more likely to survive environmental changes and to pass on the helpful variations to their offspring. Variations may also allow certain individuals in a population to move into new environments. Sexual reproduction helps to ensure the survival of the species by making a population more varied.

Conjugation and Mating Types

The simplest type of sexual reproduction takes place in protists and other simple organisms. Although these organisms usually reproduce asexually, some also reproduce sexually. In these organisms, sexual reproduction restores the organism's ability to grow and reproduce. If sexual reproduction is prevented in some species, the species may die out. Sexual reproduction also allows a recombination of hereditary material, which introduces variation within the species.

Among simple organisms that reproduce sexually, there are no distinct sexes. That is, all members of a single species look almost exactly the same. Although no male or female cells can be

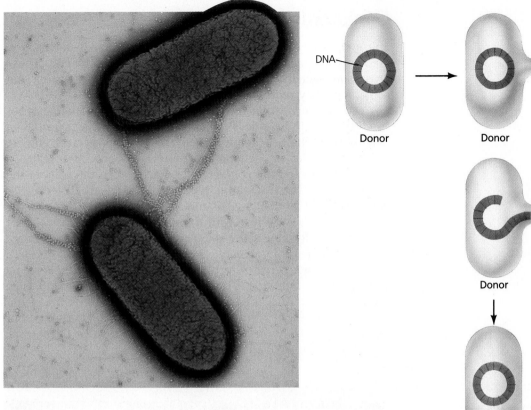

DNA

Donor

Donor   Recipient

Donor   Recipient

Donor is   Recipient
the same

Recipient
has part of
donor's DNA

distinguished, there are usually two different *mating types* or *strains*. These are commonly called plus (+) and minus (−). It appears that there are biochemical and chromosomal differences between different mating types.

The type of sexual process most commonly found among simple organisms is called **conjugation** (kahn juh GAY shun). In conjugation, a bridge of cytoplasm forms between two cells, and an exchange or transfer of nuclear material takes place through the bridge. Conjugation takes place only between two cells of different mating types.

Conjugation in Bacteria

Among certain species of bacteria, one mating type, called a *donor,* is able to give a copy of all or part of its DNA to another mating type, called a *recipient.* This is done by means of the process of conjugation.

During conjugation in bacteria, the donor bacterium extends a long, thin tube toward one or more of the recipients. See Figure 21–6. The tube has a sticky end that fastens onto the recipient. A copy of the donor's circle-shaped DNA slowly pushes through the tube toward the recipient. The amount of DNA that enters the recipient depends on the length of time that conjugation lasts. Usually, conjugation stops before a copy of all the donor's DNA has entered the recipient.

▲ **Figure 21–6**

Conjugation in Bacteria. This transmission electron micrograph (left) shows conjugation between two bacteria. (Magnification 23 220 X) During conjugation (right), DNA is transferred from the donor to the recipient through a fine tube.

Conjugation in Spirogyra

Spirogyra is a type of green alga that has threadlike filaments. The filaments are made of haploid cells fastened end to end. These organisms usually reproduce asexually by binary fission, but sometimes they reproduce sexually by conjugation.

During conjugation, two filaments of opposite mating types come to lie side by side. Projections are formed on the sides of neighboring cells. See Figure 21–7. These projections meet, and the walls where the projections meet break down. This creates a passageway, called the *conjugation tube,* between the cells of the two filaments. The two mating types of spirogyra are called *active* and *passive.* The contents of the active cells flow through the conjugation tube and fuse with the nucleus and cytoplasm of the passive cells, forming zygotes. Since the cells of the filaments are haploid, the newly formed zygotes are diploid.

Each zygote secretes a thick, protective wall and becomes a **zygospore** (ZY guh spor). The original filaments decay, releasing the zygospores. After a period of rest, and when favorable conditions return, each zygospore undergoes meiosis forming four haploid cells. Only one cell survives, and it divides by mitosis, giving rise to a new haploid filament.

Figure 21–7

Conjugation in Spirogyra. A photomicrograph of two spirogyra filaments (right) shows the connecting conjugation tubes. (Magnification 156 X) During conjugation in spirogyra (bottom), genetic material flows from the active cell into the passive cell. When the nuclei of the two cells fuse, a diploid zygospore is formed. ▶

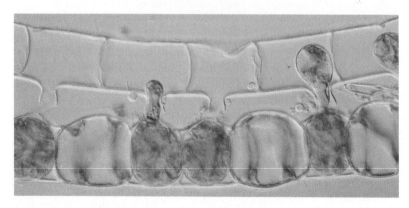

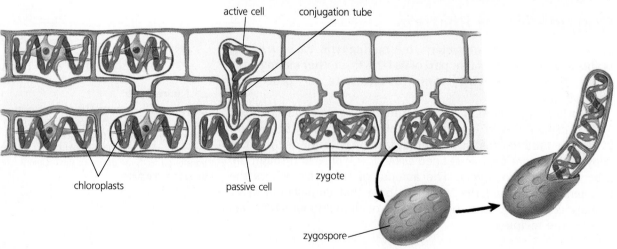

active cell

conjugation tube

chloroplasts

passive cell

zygote

zygospore

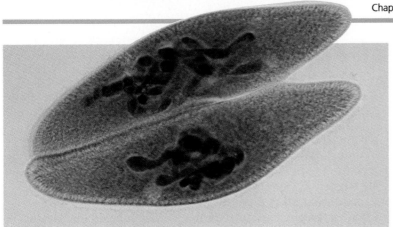

◄   **Figure 21–8**
Conjugation in Paramecia. Although paramecia reproduce asexually, they also reproduce by conjugation.

Conjugation in Paramecia

Paramecia usually reproduce asexually by binary fission. From time to time, however, they reproduce by conjugation. Conjugation takes place between two different mating types—plus and minus. In some species, the exchange of hereditary material must take place from time to time by conjugation in order for the cells to reproduce asexually. If it does not take place, the cell stops dividing and dies.

During conjugation, two paramecia—one plus, the other minus—stick together at their oral grooves. See Figure 21–8. A protoplasmic bridge forms between them. A complex series of changes takes place in the nuclei of each. Paramecia and other ciliates have two types of nuclei—macronuclei and micronuclei. Each cell may contain more than one of each type of nucleus. During conjugation, the macronucleus disappears. The micronucleus divides by meiosis. Only two of the resulting haploid micronuclei do not disappear. One of the two haploid micronuclei from each paramecium moves across the protoplasmic bridge into the opposite cell where it fuses with the remaining haploid micronucleus of that cell. Both cells now contain a diploid micronucleus. The conjugating paramecia now separate and the new micronuclei undergo several mitotic divisions. These divisions result in the formation of new macronuclei and micronuclei. Both organisms then divide twice without nuclear division. Eight new organisms are produced.

21-2 Section Review

1. Why is sexual reproduction important to the survival of a species?
2. What are mating types?
3. What type of sexual reproduction is found among protists?

Critical Thinking

4. How is conjugation in bacteria and spirogyra similar? How does it differ? (*Comparing and Contrasting*)

21-3 Sexual Reproduction in Animals

Section Objectives:

- *Define* the following terms: *gonad, ovary, ovum, testis, sperm, hermaphrodite, gametogenesis,* and *parthenogenesis.*
- *Describe* the processes of oogenesis and spermatogenesis and the structures of a sperm and an egg.
- *Explain* what takes place during fertilization.
- *Contrast* the processes of external fertilization and internal fertilization in animals.

Reproductive Systems

Sexual reproduction in animals usually involves two sexes—male and female. In many animals, the sex of an individual can be identified by physical appearance. Even in animals in which there is little or no difference in appearance between the sexes, there are internal differences. The gametes of animals develop in specialized organs called **gonads** (GOH nadz). The female gonads are called **ovaries** (OH vuh reez). The ovaries produce the female gametes, which are called *egg cells,* or **ova** (OH vuh) (singular, *ovum*). The male gonads are called **testes** (TES teez). The testes (singular, *testis*) produce male gametes, which are called **sperm cells.** Egg cells are commonly referred to as eggs, and sperm cells are referred to as sperm (either singular or plural). In addition to the gonads, most animals have other organs that are needed for reproduction. These organs together with the gonads form the reproductive system.

Figure 21–9

Earthworms Mating. Earthworms are hermaphroditic. Each earthworm has both testes and ovaries. ▼

Separation of Sexes and Hermaphroditism

In most animals, the sexes are separate. That is, each individual has either testes or ovaries and is either male or female. In some animals, however, the sexes are not separate. Instead, each individual has both testes and ovaries. These organisms are called **hermaphrodites** (her MAF ruh dyts). *Hermaphroditism* (her MAF ruh dit iz um) is usually found among animals that move slowly or those that are attached to a surface. Examples include earthworms, snails, and hydras.

Even though hermaphroditic organisms can produce both eggs and sperm, self-fertilization is rare. Instead, these organisms exchange sperm with another individual of the same species. For example, during the mating of earthworms, two individuals lie parallel to each other. See Figure 21–9. Each earthworm transfers sperm to the *sperm receptacle* of its partner. After they have separated, each worm uses the stored sperm from the partner to fertilize its own eggs.

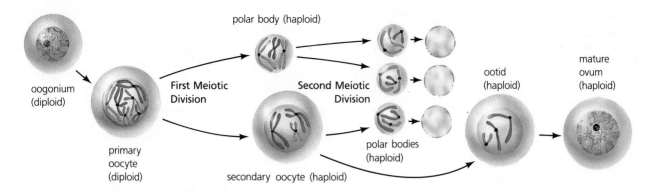

oogonium
(diploid)

primary
oocyte
(diploid)

First Meiotic
Division

polar body (haploid)

Second Meiotic
Division

secondary oocyte (haploid)

polar bodies
(haploid)

ootid
(haploid)

mature
ovum
(haploid)

▲   **Figure 21–10**

Oogenesis. A single functional egg cell is produced by meiotic division of a primary oocyte. The oocyte is diploid; the egg cell is haploid.

Gametogenesis: Meiosis in Females and Males

The process by which gametes develop in the gonads is called **gametogenesis** (guh meet uh JEN uh sis). More specifically, the formation of eggs in the ovaries is called **oogenesis** (oh uh JEN uh sis), while the formation of sperm in the testes is called **spermatogenesis** (sper mat uh JEN uh sis). Although the same basic processes are involved in the production of both eggs and sperm, there are some differences.

Oogenesis   Oogenesis is the production of eggs in the ovary. The major steps in oogenesis are shown in Figure 21–10. Eggs develop in the ovary from immature cells called *oogonia* (oh uh GOH nee uh) (singular, *oogonium*). In many animals, the oogonium is surrounded by a *follicle,* a small spherical sac of cells within which the mature egg develops. Oogonia contain the diploid number of chromosomes. During the early development of the female organism, the oogonia divide many times by mitosis to form a supply of oogonia. In human females, the production of oogonia stops at birth. Thus, each human female is born with all the oogonia she will ever have. Before birth and by the third month of development of a human female, oogonia within the baby's ovaries begin to develop into cells called *primary oocytes* (OH uh syts). By birth, the primary oocytes are in prophase in the first meiotic division. At this point, meiosis stops until the female reaches sexual maturity. Then, about once a month in most women, one of these primary oocytes finishes meiosis and develops into a functional egg.

When the first meiotic division takes place in the primary oocyte, the cytoplasm of the cell divides unequally. One of the daughter cells is large and receives most of the cytoplasm. This cell is called the *secondary oocyte.* The other daughter cell is small and is called the first *polar body.* Each of these daughter cells has the haploid number of chromosomes.

During the second meiotic division, the secondary oocyte divides unequally into a large cell called an **ootid** (OH uh tid) and another polar body. The first polar body may also divide into two polar bodies. The ootid grows into a mature egg, having the haploid chromosome number. The polar bodies break apart and die.

Figure 21–11

Spermatogenesis. Four functional sperm cells are produced by meiotic division of a primary spermatocyte. ▶

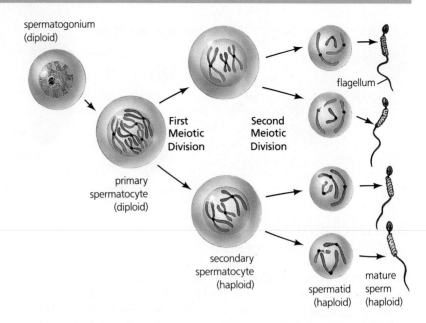

spermatogonium
(diploid)

First
Meiotic
Division

Second
Meiotic
Division

flagellum

primary
spermatocyte
(diploid)

secondary
spermatocyte
(haploid)

spermatid
(haploid)

mature
sperm
(haploid)

Spermatogenesis   Spermatogenesis is the production of sperm in the testes. The major steps in spermatogenesis are shown in Figure 21–11.

Within the testes, the sperm develop from immature sex cells called **spermatogonia** (sper mat uh GOH nee uh). Throughout childhood, these spermatogonia (singular, *spermatogonium*) divide mitotically many times to produce additional spermatogonia. The spermatogonia contain the diploid number of chromosomes. In humans, after a male matures sexually, there is a continual development of some spermatogonia into functional sperm. Other spermatogonia go on dividing mitotically, producing more spermatogonia. Thus, while the number of human eggs is limited in each female, the number of sperm is not limited in males.

In the course of development, a spermatogonium increases in size to become a *primary spermatocyte* (sper MAT uh syt). The primary spermatocyte undergoes the first meiotic division, forming two cells of equal size. These are *secondary spermatocytes*. Each secondary spermatocyte then undergoes the second meiotic division, forming four *spermatids* (SPER muh tids), all of equal size. The spermatids contain the haploid number of chromosomes. Without any further division, each one of the spermatids develops into a mature sperm with a flagellum. The flagellum is a long, thin tail that helps sperm swim. Thus, each primary spermatocyte gives rise to four haploid sperm.

Comparison of Egg and Sperm

Female gametes of animal species are different in structure and appearance from male gametes. Usually eggs are round and unable to move by themselves. They contain a nucleus and often have stored food in the form of yolk. The egg is usually larger than the sperm of the same species. The size of the egg is different from one

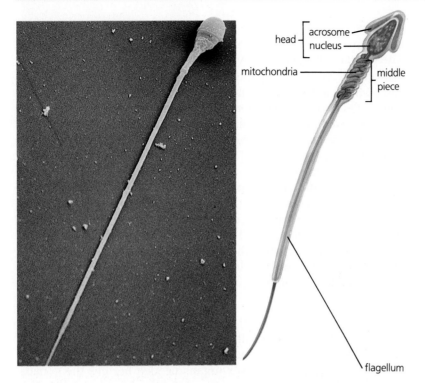

head — acrosome
nucleus

mitochondria

middle piece

flagellum

◀   **Figure 21–12**
Structure of a Human Sperm Cell. The sperm is specialized for swimming toward and penetrating the egg. The overall length of the sperm is about 0.05 millimeters, half the length of a human egg. The human sperm shown in this scanning electron micrograph is magnified about 2000 X.

species to another and depends on the amount of yolk stored in it. Yolk is used as food for the developing animal. For example, the yellow center of a chicken egg is the egg cell. It contains a great deal of yolk because the developing chicken receives no other nourishment while in the egg. The eggs of humans and other mammals are usually microscopic and contain no yolk because the developing animal gets nourishment from the mother. The human egg is about 0.1 millimeter in diameter.

Most sperm cells are microscopic. A typical sperm is made up of a head, a middle piece, and a flagellum. See Figure 21–12. The head is made up of the nucleus, which contains the chromosomes, and an *acrosome* (AK ruh sohm). The acrosome contains enzymes that help the sperm penetrate the egg. The middle piece is packed with mitochondria, which give the sperm energy so that it can move. The long, whiplike flagellum enables the sperm to swim through liquids.

Fertilization and Zygote Formation

The joining of the haploid sperm cell with the haploid egg cell produces a diploid zygote. Fertilization restores the species number of chromosomes.

Eggs cannot move by themselves. Sperm, on the other hand, are specialized for fast movement. When sperm are released by the male, their flagella beat rapidly, pushing them along in all directions. When a sperm comes in contact with an egg, the acrosome releases enzymes that dissolve an opening through the protective membranes of the egg. This allows the nucleus in the head of the sperm to enter the egg, while the rest of the sperm remains outside. The sperm cell nucleus moves through the cytoplasm toward the egg cell nucleus. The haploid sperm nucleus joins with the haploid egg nucleus to form a diploid zygote, which thus has $2n$ chromosomes. Because only the sperm nucleus enters the egg, all cytoplasmic DNA, such as DNA in mitochondria, comes from the egg.

A *fertilization membrane* forms around the egg after a sperm enters it. See Figure 21–13. This membrane stops other sperm from entering the egg and also serves as a protective covering.

For fertilization to take place, there must be a fluid medium so that the sperm can swim to the egg. Also, because sperm and eggs live for only a short period of time, the male and female gametes must be released together. There are two basic ways in which the gametes are brought together. One is **external fertilization,** in which the gametes fuse outside the body of the female. The other is **internal fertilization,** in which the gametes fuse inside the body of the female.

External Fertilization In external fertilization, the eggs are fertilized in the environment outside the body of the female. This type of fertilization takes place only in animals that breed in water. In these animals, the only sex organs needed besides the gonads are the ducts that carry the gametes from the gonads to the water. Fertilization takes place directly in the water after each parent releases its gametes. The sperm swim through the water to the eggs. Although there is no problem about moist surroundings for fertilization, there are many hazards in the environment. The sperm

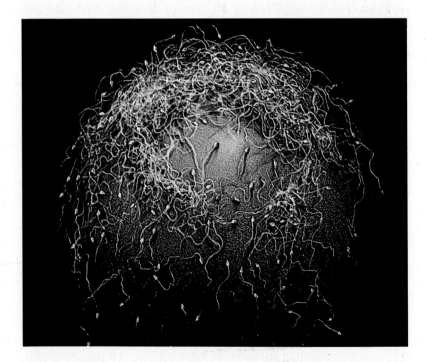

Figure 21–13

Fertilized Human Egg Surrounded by Sperm. Once a sperm has penetrated the egg, other sperm are prevented from entering by formation of a fertilization membrane around the egg. ▶

◀   **Figure 21–14**

Amplexus. Amplexus ensures that male and female frogs release their gametes into the water at the same time. This increases the probability that some of the eggs will be fertilized.

and eggs may not meet, the eggs or developing offspring may be eaten by other animals, they may die because of changes in the temperature and/or the amount of oxygen in the water, and so on. To overcome the hazards of external fertilization, large numbers of eggs and sperm are released. External fertilization takes place in almost all aquatic invertebrates, most fish (but not sharks), and many amphibians.

To improve the chances of eggs and sperm meeting, gametes are not released at random during external fertilization. There are many hormonally controlled behavior patterns that make certain that sperm and eggs are released at about the same time and place. In some fish, the female lays thousands of eggs, and the male swims over them releasing sperm. This process is known as *spawning*.

Spawning takes place with salmon, for example. Salmon hatch in freshwater streams. The young fish then travel downstream to the ocean where they mature. When the salmon are ready to spawn, they return to the freshwater stream where they were hatched. This behavior ensures that the males and females are in the same place and in the right environment for spawning.

In frogs, when a female is full of eggs and ready to mate, she goes to a male. The male embraces the female with his front legs in a process called *amplexus*. See Figure 21–14. This stimulates the female to release her eggs, and at the same time, the male releases his sperm. Because they are in close contact and the gametes are released at the same time, the sperm reach many of the eggs. Amplexus brings about the release of gametes at the same time and place.

Internal Fertilization   Fertilization within the body of the female is called internal fertilization. This kind of fertilization is found most often in animals that reproduce on land. It is also found in some aquatic animals, such as sharks and lobsters. Internal fertilization requires a specialized sex organ to carry the sperm from the body of the male into the body of the female. After the sperm are placed within the female's body, they travel to the eggs and fertilize them. The moist tissues of the female provide the watery environment needed for the sperm to swim to the egg. After fertilization, either the zygote is enclosed in a protective shell and released by the female, or it remains and develops within a special part of the female's body.

Internal fertilization does away with the scattering of gametes and the dangers of the outside environment. Fewer eggs are needed because they are well protected, and the chances of fertilization are much greater than they are when outside the body in water. However, even with internal fertilization, large numbers (often in the millions) of sperm are released by the male into the body of the female. Because the sperm store little food, they live only a short time. Therefore, even within the female's body, the sperm can fertilize the egg for only a brief period of time. Also, the egg can be penetrated by the sperm for only a brief time. In humans, the egg can be fertilized for only about 24 hours.

In animals with internal fertilization, many of the specialized adaptations involved in reproduction are concerned with the timing of the release of sperm and eggs. Because the gametes live only for a short time, mating must take place within certain time periods for fertilization to take place. Many of the reproductive adaptations are controlled by hormones. Reproductive adaptations include such things as singing, the display of special feathers, color patches on the skin, and the release of chemicals called *pheromones* (FER uh mohnz), which have distinctive odors. These adaptations stimulate the mating response and trigger the release of eggs and sperm.

In many insects and in bats, the problem of timing is solved in an interesting way. After mating, the sperm are stored in specialized structures in the female and then used to fertilize the eggs at some later time. In the queen honeybee, for example, enough sperm are stored from one mating to fertilize the hundreds of thousands of eggs she lays during her lifetime. In bats, mating takes place in the fall, and the sperm are stored until the following spring, when fertilization takes place. It is not known how the sperm remain alive for such long periods.

Parthenogenesis

The development of an unfertilized egg into an adult animal without fusion with sperm is called **parthenogenesis** (par thuh noh JEN uh sis). In nature, it takes place in many insects, including bees, wasps, aphids (plant lice), and certain ants, and in rotifers and other microscopic animals. For example, in bees, the queen bee mates

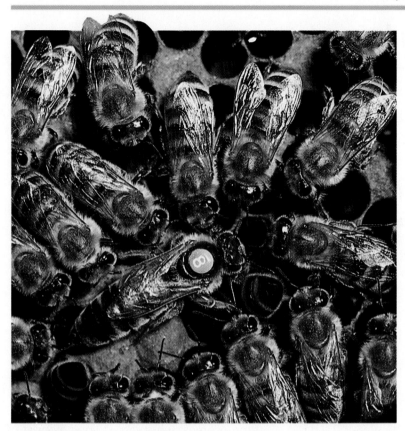

Beehive with Drones, Workers, and Queen. The queen honeybee, seen at the center of this photograph, lays both fertilized and unfertilized eggs. Fertilized eggs produce females, and unfertilized eggs produce males.

only once. She can then produce either unfertilized eggs or fertilized eggs. The unfertilized eggs become male drones while the fertilized eggs become female workers or queens. See Figure 21–15. Female aphids reproduce by parthenogenesis during the spring and summer. In the fall, the eggs produce both males and females. These insects mate, and the females produce fertilized eggs that hatch in the spring.

21-3 Section Review

1. Where do the gametes of animals develop?
2. How many mature sperm are produced from each primary spermatocyte? How many mature egg cells are produced from each primary oocyte?
3. Name one animal in which external fertilization occurs and one animal in which internal fertilization occurs.
4. What is parthenogenesis?

Critical Thinking

5. List three differences between oogenesis and spermatogenesis. (*Comparing and Contrasting*)

Laboratory Investigation

Preparing a Human Karyotype

A karyotype is a representation of individual chromosomes that have been cut out from a photograph and arranged in homologous (similar in structure) pairs. (See the photographs on the opposite page.) In this investigation, you will use photographic images of the chromosomes from a human cell to prepare a human karyotype.

Problem

How can you **organize** the chromosomes of a human cell into homologous pairs?

Materials (per student)

- ▶ photograph of a human cell nucleus in metaphase of mitosis
- ▶ scissors
- ▶ glue or transparent tape
- ▶ paper
- ▶ envelope

Procedure

1. Examine a copy of a photograph of the nucleus of a human cell in metaphase. The chromosomes, which are stained, consist of two chromatids joined together at a single point, the centromere. Chromosomes that have a central centromere appear roughly in the shape of the letter X, with the centromere at the center of the X.

2. Cut out each chromosome from the photograph. Work carefully to make sure that you do not lose any chromosomes. Store the chromosomes in an envelope.

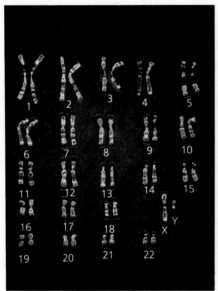
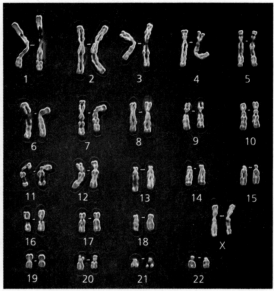

3. To prepare a karyotype, arrange the chromosomes in pairs according to size. Then, try to match them according to the position of the centromere. If banding is evident on the chromosomes, use this feature as another means of matching homologous chromosomes.

4. If possible, determine the sex of the person whose chromosomes are pictured. If the person is female, each chromosome will have a matching partner. If the person is male, a pair will consist of a large chromosome, the X chromosome, and a much smaller chromosome, the Y chromosome.

5. Line up the pairs of homologous chromosomes in order of decreasing size; then glue or tape them to a sheet of paper.

Observations

1. For each of the following, list the numbers that are present in your karyotype: (a) chromosomes, (b) centromeres, (c) pairs of homologous chromosomes, (d) chromatids.

2. How many chromosomes have a centromere at one end? How many have a centromere at the center?

Analysis and Conclusions

1. Are the chromosomes of the karyotype from the cell of a female or a male?

2. For any pair of homologous chromosomes, what is the origin of each member of the pair?

3. What is the relationship between sexual reproduction and having two chromosomes of each type?

Extensions

Many plants and some animals developed by hybridizers have triploid (3n) or tetraploid (4n) numbers. Observe karyotypes of the cells of these species and compare them with the one you made of a human cell.

Chapter *21* Review

Study Outline

21-1 Meiosis

▶ Sexual reproduction involves hereditary material from two parents. The offspring are genetically different from each parent.

▶ Complex organisms have sex cells, or gametes, that join during fertilization to form a zygote.

▶ Every species has a characteristic number of chromosomes in its somatic cells. In humans, the characteristic chromosome number is 46, which is known as the diploid number (*2n*).

▶ Gametes, which are formed by meiosis, are haploid cells containing *n* chromosomes, or half the diploid number. In meiosis, the chromosomes replicate once, and each cell divides twice. Meiosis results in the formation of four haploid cells.

21-2 Sexual Reproduction in Simple Organisms

▶ Sexual reproduction increases the amount of variation in a species, thus increasing the chance that some individuals will be better adapted to survive changes in the environment.

▶ Most simple organisms reproduce by the process of conjugation.

▶ In animals, ovaries of the female produce eggs. Testes of the male produce sperm.

▶ Eggs develop by the process of oogenesis. Diploid oogonia in the ovary undergo meiosis to form mature haploid eggs. In humans, oogonia production stops at birth, limiting the number of eggs.

▶ Sperm develop by the process of spermatogenesis. Diploid spermatogonia in the testes undergo meiosis to form mature haploid sperm. Sperm development in males is continuous, and therefore the number of sperm is not limited.

▶ External fertilization occurs only in animals that breed in water. Internal fertilization usually occurs in animals that breed on land. It also occurs in cartilagenous fishes and some bony fishes. A sex organ transports the sperm from the male's body into the female's body.

Chapter Assessment

Multiple Choice

Choose the letter of the answer that best completes each statement or answers the question.

1. During meiosis, homologous chromosomes pair together to form structures called (a) chromatids. (b) gametes. (c) tetrads. (d) centromeres.

2. What are the end products of meiosis? (a) two diploid cells (b) two haploid cells (c) four diploid cells (d) four haploid cells

3. Crossing-over is the exchange of genetic information between (a) reproductive cells. (b) diploid cells. (c) any two chromosomes. (d) chromatids.

4. Most bacteria reproduce by (a) conjugation. (b) binary fission. (c) budding. (d) sporulation.

5. The process of meiosis is most closely associated with (a) vegetative propagation. (b) sexual reproduction. (c) binary fission. (d) fission.

6. In the second meiotic division, the chromosome number is (a) halved. (b) doubled. (c) equalized. (d) not changed.

7. An organism that can successfully reproduce without meiosis is a(n) (a) ameba. (b) dog. (c) grasshopper. (d) earthworm.

8. Chromosomes do not normally appear in pairs in (a) somatic cells. (b) fertilized eggs. (c) gametes. (d) zygotes.

9. At metaphase of the first meiotic division, the chromosomes are attached to the spindle fibers as (a) single chromatid strands. (b) double chromatids. (c) a tetrad of four chromatids. (d) nonhomologous pairs.

10. Two cells that have a chromosome number different from that of their single parent cell are normally produced during the process of (a) meiosis. (b) mitosis. (c) fertilization. (d) conjugation.

Content Review

Answer each of the following in complete sentences.

11. Explain how meiosis differs from mitosis.

12. How do diploid cells differ from haploid cells?

13. Describe the process of crossing-over.

14. In sexual reproduction, why are the offspring different from the parents?

15. Describe conjugation in simple organisms.

16. Describe conjugation in paramecia.

17. What are the functions of ovaries and testes?

18. Explain how mating and fertilization take place in the earthworm.

19. Why do organisms in which external fertilization occurs produce large numbers of gametes?

20. What adaptations in animals make internal fertilization possible?

Graphic Organizing

For information on graphic organizers, see Appendix G at the back of this text.

21. Flow Chart Construct a flow chart showing the stages of meiosis. In each box, indicate the number of chromosomes present at that stage in an organism with a diploid number of 8. Also indicate whether the chromosomes would be single-stranded or double-stranded at each stage.

Critical Thinking and Problem Solving

Discuss each of the following in a brief paragraph.

22. Comparing Explain the similarities and differences between the first meiotic division and mitosis and between the second meiotic division and mitosis.

23. Predicting What might happen if one member of a pair of homologous chromosomes did not separate during anaphase I?

24. Relating Hermaphroditic organisms produce both sperm and eggs, but self-fertilization is rare. What is the advantage of mating for these organisms?

25. Comparing How does the structure of a sperm cell differ from that of an egg cell? How are their structures suited to their respective functions?

26. Hypothesizing Develop a hypothesis to explain why during oogenesis the meiotic divisions produce cells of unequal size—the secondary oocytes and the polar bodies.

27. Interpreting An investigation was conducted to determine the effect of temperature on the number of eggs produced by goldfish and the number of eggs that hatched. Using the data in the following table, calculate the percentage of eggs that hatched at each temperature. Interpret the data and draw some conclusions regarding the optimum temperature range for egg production and hatching. At what temperature do egg production and hatching decrease most drastically?

Temp. (°C)	Number of Eggs Produced	Number of Eggs Hatched
10°C	234	79
15°C	411	158
20°C	549	221
25°C	374	119
30°C	80	14

28. Experimenting Several beekeepers observe that more male drone bees hatch on some days than on others. To investigate which factors might influence the hatching rate of the bees, they select the following variables to be tested: (a) atmospheric temperature, (b) relative humidity, (c) amount of food (pollen) available in the surrounding area, and (d) number of bees living in the hive. Each of the variables is to be studied for its effect on the hatching rate. For each variable, suggest a controlled experiment in which it would be tested.

Discovery
Learning Activity

Observing a Chicken Egg

1. Working with a partner, obtain a hard-boiled egg from your teacher. Carefully crack and peel off the eggshell.

2. Examine the eggshell with a hand lens. Note the structure of the shell and any membranes attached to it. Make a sketch of what you see.

3. Lay the shell on a paper plate. With a knife, cut it in half length-wise and examine its parts. **CAUTION:** *Be careful when using a knife.* Make a sketch and write a description of what you see.

Animal Development

······················· *Guide for Reading* ·······················

Previewing the Chapter

Tiny bundles of fluffy feathers, these hooded merganser ducklings stick close to their parent on their first excursion outside the nest. After months of development inside an egg, each duckling emerged equipped to face the outside world. What happens during embryonic development? How do external and internal development differ? What structural adaptations allow bird and reptile eggs to develop externally on land?

Key Words

amnion, blastula, cleavage, differentiation, ectoderm, embryo, endoderm, gastrulation, mesoderm, placenta

Key Concepts

- **Compare** internal and external development.
- **Describe** the importance of the shelled egg.
- **Observe** embryonic development in frogs. (Laboratory Investigation)

22-1 Development

Section Objectives:

- *Define* the terms *development, embryo,* and *differentiation.*
- *Describe* the events of cleavage and embryonic development through the gastrula stage.
- *Name* the three germ layers and *list* a few of the tissues and organs formed from each.
- *Describe* the process of embryonic induction and explain how this process controls development.

Embryonic Development

In animals, as in plants, fertilization of an egg to form a zygote is only the first step in a complex series of events. It is this series of events that finally gives rise to a full-grown organism. These events, which are the subject of this chapter, are called development. In the following sections, you will learn about the changes the zygote undergoes as it develops.

In the early stages of development, the organism is called an **embryo** (EM bree oh). The study of the development of embryos is called *embryology.* Although embryos develop in many different ways, the basic processes are always the same in animals. These processes of development include cleavage, growth, and differentiation.

▲ **Figure 22–1**
A Red-Eyed Leaf Frog. This red-eyed leaf frog is fully developed.

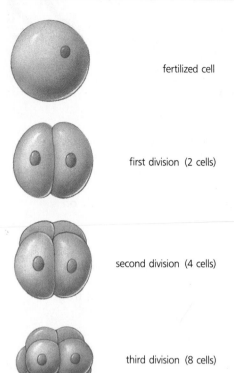

fertilized cell

first division (2 cells)

second division (4 cells)

third division (8 cells)

▲ **Figure 22–2**
Early Stages of Cleavage. Although the number of cells doubles at each division during cleavage, no growth occurs.

Cleavage

After fertilization, the zygote begins a series of cell divisions known as **cleavage** (KLEE vidj). During cleavage, the fertilized egg divides by mitosis into two cells. Each of these cells divides again, producing four cells. These four produce eight, and so on. See Figure 22–2.

During cleavage, the cells do not grow. Each division decreases cell size. Since the eggs of a species are usually larger than the average cell of the adult organism, cleavage changes a single, large fertilized egg into many small cells. Cleavage goes on until the cells of the developing embryo have been reduced to the size of the cells of the adult organism.

The early divisions of cleavage result in a solid ball of cells. At this stage, the embryo is called a **morula** (MOR yuh luh). As the cells continue to divide, they are rearranged to form a hollow sphere. Usually, the layer of cells in the sphere is only one cell thick. The inside of the sphere is filled with fluid. At this stage, the embryo is called a **blastula** (BLAS chuh luh), and the fluid-filled inside of the sphere is called the **blastocoel** (BLAS tuh seel).

Although these are the usual steps in cleavage, the arrangement of cells in the developing embryo depends on the amount and distribution of yolk in the egg. Some eggs, such as those of humans, have little yolk. In these eggs, cleavage results in a blastula in which all the cells are nearly equal in size. However, other eggs, such as those of amphibians, bony fish, birds, and reptiles, have a large amount of yolk at one end of the egg cell. Because yolk tends to slow down cell division, cleavage takes place mostly or only at the pole without yolk.

In frog eggs, the large amount of yolk found at one pole slows down cleavage at that pole. This slowdown results in a blastula that has larger cells at the yolk-filled, or *vegetal,* pole. More numerous, smaller cells form at the yolkless, or *animal,* pole, as shown in Figure 22–3. The blastocoel is formed only within the region of the animal pole.

In the chicken egg, the nucleus and cytoplasm are concentrated in the *germinal disk,* a platelike area on the surface of the ball of yolk. Only the cells of the germinal disk undergo cleavage. The blastocoel is formed when these cells separate from the yolk, leaving a space between the yolk and the cells. The developing chick uses the yolk for food and finally fills completely the space within the egg.

Gastrulation

As the blastula develops, it reaches a point at which the cells begin to grow before dividing. At this point, mitotic division continues, but it is also accompanied by growth. At the same time, various movements of the cells take place. These movements will set the shape of the embryo.

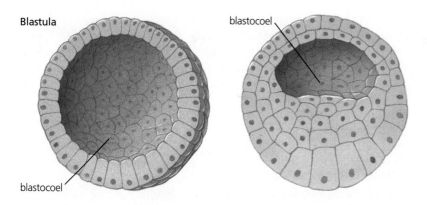

Blastula

blastocoel

blastocoel

◀ **Figure 22–3**

Blastula. When the developing embryo is a hollow sphere with a fluid-filled interior, it is called a blastula (left). The blastula of a frog egg has larger cells at the yolk-filled pole (right).

When the blastula reaches several hundred cells, **gastrulation** (gas truh LAY shun) takes place. The cells on one side of the blastula move inward and form a two-layered embryo called the **gastrula** (GAS truh luh). See Figure 22–4 (left). The opening created is called the **blastopore** (BLAS tuh por). It later becomes one of the openings to the digestive system in the adult organism.

The outer layer of cells in the gastrula is called the **ectoderm.** The inner layer is called the **endoderm.** The cavity within the gastrula is called the **primitive gut.** It later becomes the digestive system. Finally, the primitive gut cavity breaks through the end of the developing embryo opposite the blastopore, forming the second opening of the digestive system. After the endoderm and ectoderm are established, a third cell layer, the **mesoderm** (MEZ uh derm), forms between them. See Figure 22–4 (right).

In the frog, the yolk-containing cells of the vegetal pole do not take part in gastrulation. The blastopore forms next to the mass of yolk cells. Cells from the animal pole move downward and through the blastopore at the edge of the yolk mass.

In the chicken, the cells of the blastula separate into an outer and inner layer. The outer layer becomes the ectoderm, and the inner layer becomes the endoderm. The space between the two layers is the blastocoel. The cells of the outer layer roll inward to make the third cell layer, the mesoderm.

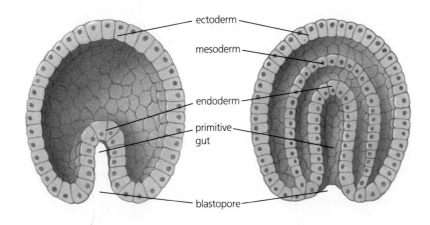

ectoderm

mesoderm

endoderm

primitive gut

blastopore

◀ **Figure 22–4**

Gastrulation. In gastrulation, a second cell layer is formed when the cells of one side of the embryo push inward (left), forming an indentation. Then, the mesoderm (right) forms between the ectoderm and the endoderm.

Development of Organs and Organ Systems from the Germ Layers		
Ectoderm	**Mesoderm**	**Endoderm**
nervous system, including brain, spinal cord, nerves lining of mouth, nostrils, and anus epidermis of skin, sweat glands, hair, nails	bones and muscles blood and blood vessels reproductive and excretory systems inner layer (dermis) of skin	lining of digestive tract lining of trachea, bronchi, and lungs liver, pancreas thyroid, parathyroid, thymus urinary bladder

▲ **Figure 22–5**

Development of Organs and Organ Systems from the Germ Layers. Each cell layer forms specific tissues during later development.

The three cell layers—ectoderm, mesoderm, and endoderm—are called the **germ layers,** because they give rise to all the tissues and organs of multicellular animals. Figure 22–5 shows some of the organs and systems that arise from each layer.

Growth and Differentiation

As the gastrula develops, the number of cells continues to increase. Since the cells now grow before dividing, the embryo begins to increase in size. Cell growth alone, however, would produce only a formless mass of cells. The cells of the embryo must be arranged into specific structures, and within these structures, the cells must be specialized to carry out particular functions. Although the cells of the gastrula are organized into distinct layers, they look very much alike. The changing of unspecialized embryonic cells into the specialized cells, tissues, and organs that make up the organism is called **differentiation.**

The first signs of differentiation are found on the upper surface of the gastrula. Here, the ectoderm cells divide, forming a *neural plate* that has two raised edges, called *neural folds.* See Figure 22–6a. The neural folds slowly come together over the center of the neural plate, forming a *neural tube,* as you can see in Figure 22–6b. In the later stages of development, the neural tube forms the brain and spinal cord.

Figure 22–6

Formation of the Neural Tube. The brain and spinal cord form the neural tube. ▶

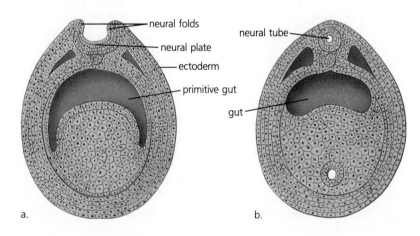

a.   b.

Role of the Nucleus and Cytoplasm

Within the nucleus of the fertilized egg is the hereditary material. This contains all the information needed for development. The information is encoded within the chemical structure of DNA in the chromosomes. DNA controls the chemical processes of the cell and determines which proteins are made by the cell. Because the cells of the embryo divide by mitosis, each cell has in it the same chromosomes and DNA as the original fertilized egg cell.

If DNA controls cellular activities and all cells of an organism have the same DNA, how are the many kinds of cells in the organism made? Scientists have discovered that different sections of the DNA in a cell can be turned off or on. This results in the formation of different types of cells. Thus, in muscle cells, for example, the part of the DNA that controls the making of muscle cell proteins is turned on, while the part of the DNA that controls the making of nerve cell proteins is not turned on. If this were not the case, differentiation would not take place, and all the cells of an embryo would be the same. However, little is known at this time about how the activity of DNA in different cells is controlled.

Experiments with frogs have shown that a nucleus from a fully differentiated cell contains a complete copy of the hereditary information. In 1962, the English biologist J. G. Gurden surgically replaced the haploid nuclei of unfertilized frog's eggs with diploid nuclei from the intestinal cells of tadpoles. Some of the eggs that received the intestinal nuclei became normal frogs. This means that some of the DNA that was switched off in the intestinal cell nucleus was turned on when the nucleus was placed in the egg cell. From this and other research, it appears that an interaction between the DNA and certain things in the cytoplasm controls development. As a result of the interaction, parts of the hereditary material are switched on and off, and this in turn determines the direction of cellular differentiation.

Other experimental evidence shows that differentiation begins early in development. For example, if the cells of a four-celled frog embryo are carefully separated, each cell will develop into a normal tadpole. If, however, the cells of an older embryo are separated, the cells do not develop correctly and die. In the older embryo, the cells have begun to differentiate and can no longer produce a whole, normal organism.

Role of Neighboring Cells

As an embryo grows, there must be coordination and communication between its tissues. By the late blastula or early gastrula stage, the way in which groups of cells will develop has been determined. Cells in certain regions develop along certain lines. For example, there is a particular place in the frog gastrula that normally develops into an eye. If this tissue is removed from the embryo and placed in a special nutrient solution, it develops into an irregular mass of cells. On the other hand, if it is transplanted into any other

part of another frog embryo, it will develop into a recognizable eye, even though it does not work like an eye. Not all the tissues in the extra, nonfunctioning eye develop from the transplanted tissue. Instead, the transplanted tissue causes some of the surrounding tissue, which would not usually make up part of the eye, to develop into eye structures. A tissue, then, can affect the differentiation of neighboring tissues.

Certain parts of the developing embryo act as *organizers* and influence the development of neighboring cells. The process by which the organizers cause, or induce, other structures to differentiate is called **embryonic induction.** Scientists do not yet know what brings about embryonic induction. Some chemical substances can cause induction. Cell contact probably is also important. It may be that as development goes on, organizers, in some way and at certain times, influence which parts of a cell's hereditary material become active. In doing this, the organizers determine the course of differentiation of those cells.

22-1 Section Review

1. What is cleavage?
2. Name the three germ layers in the gastrula.
3. Define the term *differentiation*.
4. What are embryo organizers?

Critical Thinking

5. Which germ layer do you think gives rise to the human heart? Explain your conclusion. *(Reasoning by Analogy)*

22-2 External and Internal Development

Section Objectives:

- *Compare* and *contrast* external development in water and internal development on land.
- *Describe* the adaptations of reptiles, birds, nonplacental animals, and placental mammals for reproduction on land.

Embryonic development may take place either outside or inside the mother's body, depending on the type of organism that is developing. Regardless of where the development takes place, the embryo has certain needs that must be met for survival. These include nourishment, proper temperature, oxygen, protection, and a means of getting rid of wastes.

External Development in Water

In most aquatic animals, fertilization and development take place outside the mother's body in the water. Nourishment for these embryos comes from the yolk stored in the egg. The young usually develop under proper environmental conditions because mating and fertilization take place at the right times of the year. Oxygen from the surrounding water diffuses into the embryo, and wastes diffuse from the embryo into the water.

In most aquatic animals, there is little or no care of the young by the parents. Some fish, however, do provide a certain amount of care for the developing young. For example, the male stickleback guards the nest and fans the embryos with water currents to provide oxygen. Some fish are "mouthbreeders." That is, the fertilized eggs are held in one parent's mouth until they hatch. In general, the survival of species that develop in water depends on the production and fertilization of large numbers of eggs. Many of the eggs are eaten or destroyed in other ways, and only a small part of the original number survive from each mating.

External Development on Land

Fertilization inside the mother's body followed by development outside her body takes place in birds and most reptiles, as well as in a few mammals. In these animals, the fertilized egg, which contains a large amount of yolk, is enclosed in a protective shell. The shelled egg is moist inside, which provides the embryo with a self-contained watery environment. The shell is almost waterproof, but is porous enough to allow oxygen from the air to diffuse into the egg and carbon dioxide from the embryo to diffuse out. The number of embryos that survive to hatching is greater for animals whose eggs have a shell than for those whose eggs lack a shell. In fact, animals that lay eggs with a shell produce fewer eggs than animals that lay eggs without a shell. Both the hard shell of the bird egg and the tough, leathery shell of the reptile egg provide protection for the

▲ **Figure 22–7**
Male Stickleback. This male stickleback fans a nest containing eggs in order to provide the embryos with oxygen.

◀ **Figure 22–8**
Eggs. The hard shells of the black redstart bird eggs (left) and the leathery shell of the green snake eggs (right) protect the embryos from harm.

Figure 22–9

Internal Structure of the Chicken Egg. The shell protects the embryo from drying out, nourishes it, and allows it to develop outside of water. ▶

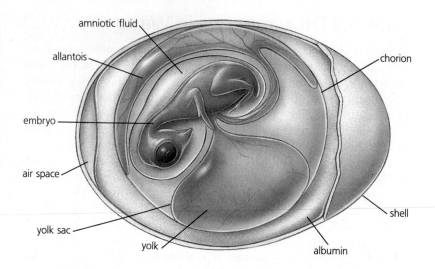

amniotic fluid

allantois

chorion

embryo

air space

shell

yolk sac

yolk

albumin

embryo. Reptiles, however, usually leave their eggs whereas bird eggs and young birds are carefully tended by the parents. Thus, the percentage of reptile eggs that survive is less than the percentage of bird eggs that survive. Knowing this, it is not surprising that reptiles lay many more eggs than birds.

Internal Structure of the Chicken Egg   As the chicken embryo develops, it forms four membranes that lie outside the embryo itself but inside the shell. These are the **extraembryonic membranes** shown in Figure 22–9. The extraembryonic membranes perform a number of important functions.

The outermost membrane, or the **chorion** (KOR ee ahn), lines the inside of the shell and surrounds the embryo and the other three membranes. The chorion aids in the exchange of gases between the embryo and the environment.

A second membrane, the **allantois** (uh LAN tuh wis), is a saclike structure that grows out of the digestive tract of the embryo. It is through the blood vessels of the allantois that the exchange of oxygen and carbon dioxide takes place. The metabolic wastes of the embryo also collect in the allantois.

The third membrane is a fluid-filled sac, known as the **amnion** (AM nee ahn), that surrounds the embryo. The amniotic fluid within the sac provides a watery environment for the embryo and acts as a cushion to protect it from shocks.

The fourth, and final, extraembryonic membrane is the **yolk sac,** which surrounds the yolk. The yolk sac is the source of food for the embryo. Blood vessels in the yolk sac carry the food to the developing embryo.

The shell-covered egg with its extraembryonic membranes is an important adaptation that allows bird embryos to develop on land. When the young bird hatches, the extraembryonic membranes are gotten rid of along with the shell. The eggs of reptiles have similar features. Figure 22–10 shows various stages of development in the chicken.

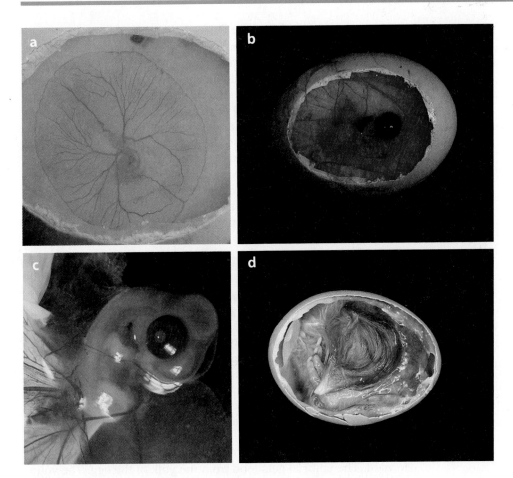

▲ **Figure 22–10**
Stages of Development of a Chicken. (a) Three days. (b) Seven days. (c) Fourteen days. (d) Nineteen days.

Internal Development

In some sharks and in some reptiles, such as garter snakes, fertilization and development take place inside the body. However, in these animals, the young do not receive food directly from the mother. Instead, the source of their food is yolk, which is stored in the egg. By the time the yolk is used up, the embryos have reached a stage of development at which they can take care of themselves, and they are born.

Among mammals, fertilization takes place inside the mother's body, and the embryos typically develop within a structure called the *womb* (woom), or **uterus** (YOO tuh rus), inside the body. They are born in an undeveloped condition and, for a period, feed on milk produced by the mother's mammary glands. The young are well protected during development and after birth, and a high percentage of them survive to adulthood. Thus, as might be expected in animals in which the young develop internally, relatively few eggs are produced.

Placental Mammals

Most mammals, including humans, are *placental* (pluh SENT ul) *mammals.* In these mammals, the blood vessels of the embryo's circulatory system are in close contact with the mother's circulatory system. See Figure 23–6. This contact takes place in a specialized structure called the **placenta** (pluh SENT uh), which is in the wall of the uterus.

In the placenta, nutrients and oxygen diffuse from the mother's blood into the embryo's blood. In turn, carbon dioxide and other wastes diffuse from the embryo's blood into the mother's blood. However, there is no direct connection between the two circulatory systems. The embryo is attached to the placenta by a structure called the **umbilical** (um BIL ih kul) **cord.** This structure contains blood vessels that connect the embryo's circulatory system to capillaries in the placenta.

Nonplacental Mammals

There are two types of *nonplacental mammals*—mammals in which no placenta forms during development of the embryo. These types are the *egg-laying mammals,* of which there are only two living species, and the *pouched mammals.*

The spiny anteater and duckbill platypus are egg-laying mammals. The embryo of the platypus is inside a leathery egg, which looks like the egg of a reptile. Unlike the eggs of other mammals, the eggs of the platypus contain a large amount of yolk. The female lays the eggs in a nest. When the young hatch out of the eggs, the female gathers them against her body. The young animals then feed on milk from the mother's mammary glands.

In the pouched mammals, or *marsupials,* some internal development of the embryo takes place in the uterus, but no placenta is formed. The embryo gets food from the yolk of the egg. The young animal is born in a very immature condition. It crawls into a pouch

Figure 22–11

A Duckbill Platypus. The duckbill platypus lays several eggs at a time. After the young hatch, they feed by licking milk from the mother's fur around the mammary glands. ▶

▲ **Figure 22–12**
A Western Grey Kangaroo. Young kangaroos complete development within the mother's pouch.

on the outside of the mother's body and attaches itself to a mammary gland. Development is completed in the pouch. Most marsupials are found in Australia. While the kangaroo is the most familiar example, the opossum, which is found in the Western Hemisphere, is also a marsupial.

22-2 Section Review

1. Where may embryonic development occur?
2. Name two groups of animals that have internal fertilization and external development.
3. What are the two types of mammals?

Critical Thinking

4. What would happen to a chicken embryo if the chorion were impermeable? *(Relating Parts and Wholes)*

Laboratory
Investigation

Embryo Development in the Frog

In order to study embryo development, fertilized frog eggs are often used. Frog eggs incubate in water, and the transparent egg case permits direct observation of the embryo inside. In this investigation, you will observe development in the embryos of the frog.

Problem

What processes take place during embryo development in animals? **Observe** the developing embryos of frogs to answer the question.

Materials (per group)

- fertilized frog eggs
- culture dish
- spoon
- plastic wrap
- thermometer
- stereomicroscope

Procedure

1. Pour about 1 mL of water that has stood overnight at room temperature into a small culture dish. With a spoon, transfer a few frog eggs from the main culture dish to the small culture dish.

2. Using the stereomicroscope, study the eggs. A fertilized egg will show a dark area on the uppermost part of the egg. Refer to the drawings below to identify the approximate stages of development of the embryos. Because the eggs were fertilized before you received them, the earliest stages of development have already occurred.

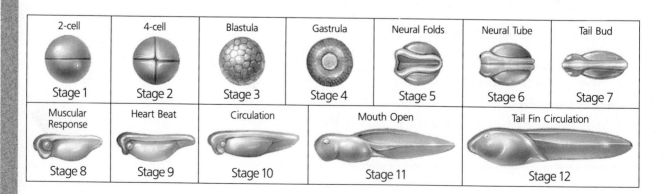

2-cell	4-cell	Blastula	Gastrula	Neural Folds	Neural Tube	Tail Bud
Stage 1	Stage 2	Stage 3	Stage 4	Stage 5	Stage 6	Stage 7

Muscular Response	Heart Beat	Circulation	Mouth Open	Tail Fin Circulation
Stage 8	Stage 9	Stage 10	Stage 11	Stage 12

3. In a data table similar to the one shown, record the date and time. Measure and record the temperature of the culture water. Include a sketch of the embryo.

4. When you have completed your observations, store the eggs in an area that is not exposed to direct sunlight or to temperature extremes.

5. Observe the embryos every day for at least one week. Each day record date, time, temperature, and observations and sketch the embryo in the data table. After one week, tadpoles may have developed. If you continue your observations, feed the tadpoles according to your teacher's instructions.

Observations

Describe the major changes that occur in the early stages of embryonic development.

Analysis and Conclusions

1. After how many days did gastrulation begin?

2. At what stage does differentiation become evident?

3. How does the embryo obtain oxygen before its gills develop?

4. How do you think development would be affected if the eggs were incubated at a lower temperature?

5. How does the embryo develop to the tadpole stage without ingesting food?

6. How do you think frog embryos could be used to help determine if a drug taken by a pregnant woman will harm her developing child?

Extensions

Observe prepared slides of the early development of sea urchins, starfishes, or chickens. Compare their development to the early development of the frog.

Data Table					
Date	Time	Stage	Temp. (°C)	Notes	Sketch

Chapter 22 Review

Study Outline

22-1 Embryonic Development

▶ Development is a complex series of events by which a single cell becomes an adult, multicellular organism. Development of all animal embryos includes cleavage, growth, and differentiation.

▶ Cleavage results in the formation of a blastula—a single layer of cells surrounding a fluid-filled cavity called the blastocoel.

▶ At the end of the blastula stage, gastrulation occurs, leading to the formation of a two-layered embryo called the gastrula.

▶ The three cell layers of the gastrula—ectoderm, mesoderm, and endoderm—make up the germ layers.

▶ Differentiation is controlled by the DNA of the chromosomes, parts of which are switched on and off by substances in the cytoplasm.

22-2 External and Internal Development

▶ In most aquatic animals, fertilization and development are external. The eggs do not have shells.

▶ Birds, reptiles, and a few mammals produce eggs with shells that develop externally. The egg with its shell provides protection and nourishment for the externally developing embryo.

▶ Development and fertilization are internal in mammals. In placental mammals, exchange of substances between the mother and developing young occurs in the placenta. The umbilical cord connects the embryo to the placenta.

▶ After the young of egg-laying mammals have hatched, they feed on milk produced by the mother's mammary glands. The young of pouched mammals undergo a period of internal development. Once this period has ended, the young finish their development in the mother's external pouch.

Chapter Assessment

Multiple Choice

Choose the letter of the answer that best completes each statement or answers the question.

1. The human embryo receives food and oxygen from the mother through the (a) extraembryonic membranes. (b) placenta. (c) primitive gut. (d) yolk sac.

2. After fertilization, the zygote begins a series of cell divisions known as (a) gastrulation. (b) embryonic induction. (c) cleavage. (d) differentiation.

3. The inner layer of cells in the gastrula is called the (a) ectoderm. (b) endoderm. (c) blastopore. (d) mesoderm.

4. The fluid-filled sac surrounding the chicken embryo is called the (a) yolk sac. (b) allantois. (c) germ layers. (d) amnion.

5. The cavity within the gastrula that eventually becomes the digestive system is called the (a) uterus. (b) mesoderm. (c) primitive gut. (d) blastocoel.

6. Unspecialized embryonic cells become specialized cells, tissues, and organs through the process of (a) cleavage. (b) embryonic induction. (c) allantois. (d) differentiation.

7. In placental mammals, the embryo is attached to the placenta by the (a) umbilical cord. (b) uterus. (c) allantois. (d) amnion.

8. The fertilized eggs of most mammals normally develop in the (a) ovary. (b) placenta. (c) uterus. (d) umbilical cord.

9. In animals that have external development, fertilization (a) does not occur. (b) is always internal. (c) is sometimes internal. (d) is never internal.

10. The metabolic waste products of a developing chick embryo collect in the (a) allantois. (b) chorion. (c) amnion. (d) yolk sac.

Content Review

Answer each of the following in complete sentences.

11. Describe the process of gastrulation.

12. Why does embryo size increase during gastrulation but not during cleavage?

13. Describe the location of each of the three germ layers in the gastrula.

14. How do the many different kinds of cells in an organism arise from the same DNA?

15. How do eggs that develop in water obtain nourishment and oxygen?

16. What are the advantages of an egg with a shell for external development on land?

17. Why do fish produce more eggs than birds do?

18. Diagram a bird's egg containing a developing embryo. Label and describe the function of each part.

19. Compare fertilization and development in mammals with that in birds.

20. What are the functions of the placenta?

Graphic Organizing

For information on graphic organizers, see Appendix G at the back of this text.

21. **Scale** Construct a scale for the gestation periods of various mammals using the information in the table below. Note that some gestation periods are given in days, some in months.

Mammal	Gestation Period
antelope	9 months
beaver	3 months
deer	7 months
dog	60 days
elephant	21 months
hog	114 days
horse	11 months
lion	108 days
rat	22 days
sheep	5 months
sperm whale	16 months
zebra	11 months

Critical Thinking and Problem Solving

Discuss each of the following in a brief paragraph.

22. **Comparing** Discuss the similarities and differences in fertilization, egg structure, and egg-laying patterns of frogs, reptiles, and birds.

23. **Sequencing** Arrange the factors that affect differentiation in order from most to least important.

24. **Predicting** What might happen to the embryo in a chicken egg if the amnion were not present?

25. **Drawing conclusions** Imagine that you have found two birds' nests—one on the ground, with two large speckled eggs in it, and one in a tree, with five small white eggs in it. Draw four conclusions about the two bird species and support each conclusion.

26. **Calculating** In experiment A, a laser was used to randomly destroy half the cytoplasm in 100 fertilized frog eggs. The frog eggs were then observed. Some eggs survived and developed normally. Others survived but did not develop normally. In experiment B, a similar technique was used on another 100 fertilized frog eggs. However, a special region of the cytoplasm was not destroyed in any of the embryos. The results of both experiments are given in the table below. For each experiment, calculate the percentage of eggs that survived, the percentage of surviving embryos that developed normally, and the percentage of surviving embryos that did not develop normally. What best accounts for the difference in the number of embryos that did not develop normally? Design a control for the experiments.

	Experiment A	Experiment B
number of eggs that survived	63	54
number of embryos that developed normally	15	54
number of embryos that did not develop normally	48	0

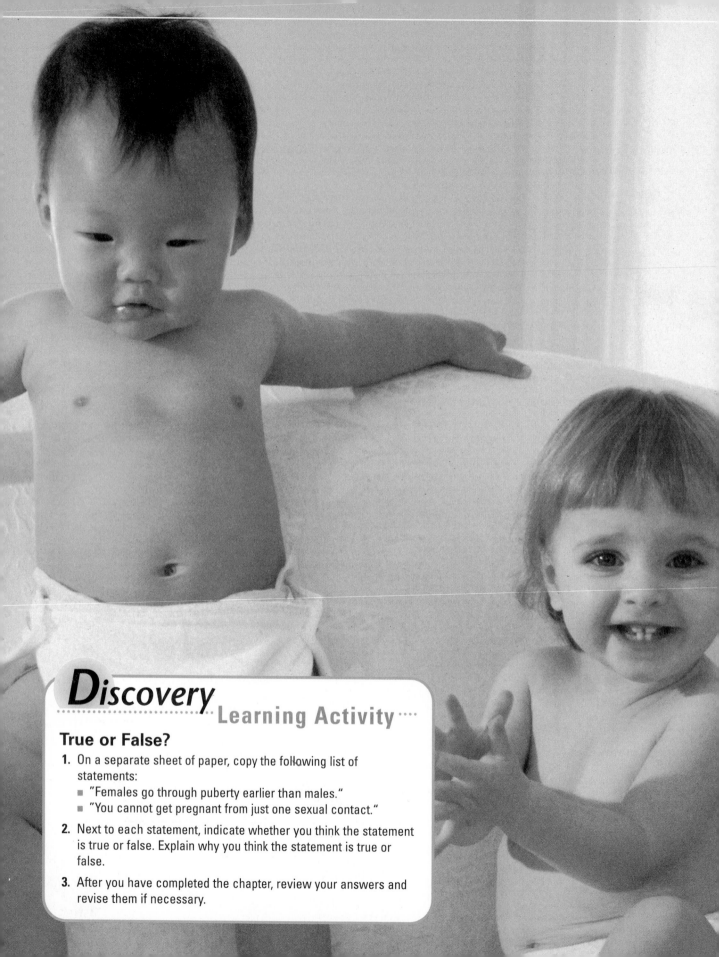

Discovery Learning Activity

True or False?

1. On a separate sheet of paper, copy the following list of statements:
   - "Females go through puberty earlier than males."
   - "You cannot get pregnant from just one sexual contact."

2. Next to each statement, indicate whether you think the statement is true or false. Explain why you think the statement is true or false.

3. After you have completed the chapter, review your answers and revise them if necessary.

Human Reproduction

Chapter 23

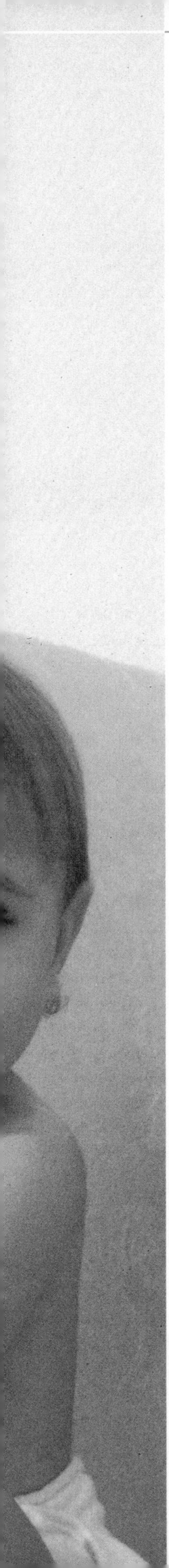

Guide for Reading

Previewing the Chapter

Before they were born, each of these beautiful babies spent about nine months developing inside its mother's body. Changes took place in the mother's body that allowed it to nourish the growing fetus. The fetus itself resulted from the union of a sperm cell from the father and an egg cell from the mother. How and where are human sperm and eggs produced? How is the human fetus nourished before birth? What role do hormones play in human reproduction?

Key Words

amniotic fluid, fetus, implantation, menstrual cycle, ovary, placenta, secondary sex characteristic, testis, umbilical cord

Key Concepts

- **Describe** the process of sperm development.
- **List** the four stages of the menstrual cycle.
- **Observe** the microscopic structures of reproductive organs and gametes. (Laboratory Investigation)

23-1 Human Reproductive Systems

Section Objectives:

- *Describe* the functions of the male and female reproductive systems.
- *Name* the hormones involved in the development of male and female secondary sex characteristics.
- *Explain* the role of hormones during the menstrual cycle.

Inheritance

You have inherited many of your physical characteristics and personality traits from your parents and, through time, from your grandparents and great-grandparents. In order to understand human reproduction, you first need to know how the male and female reproductive systems work.

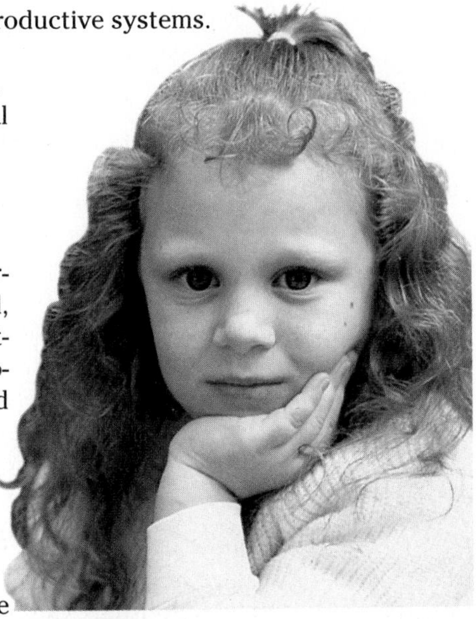

▲ **Figure 23–1**
Inherited Traits. Hair and eye color, as well as many other traits, are inherited from parents.

The Male Reproductive System

The male gonads are the **testes.** The testes make sperm, which are the male gametes, and the hormone *testosterone.* Testosterone causes the development of the **secondary sex characteristics** in the male. These characteristics are physical traits that usually

◀ These babies developed from the joining of an egg and a sperm.

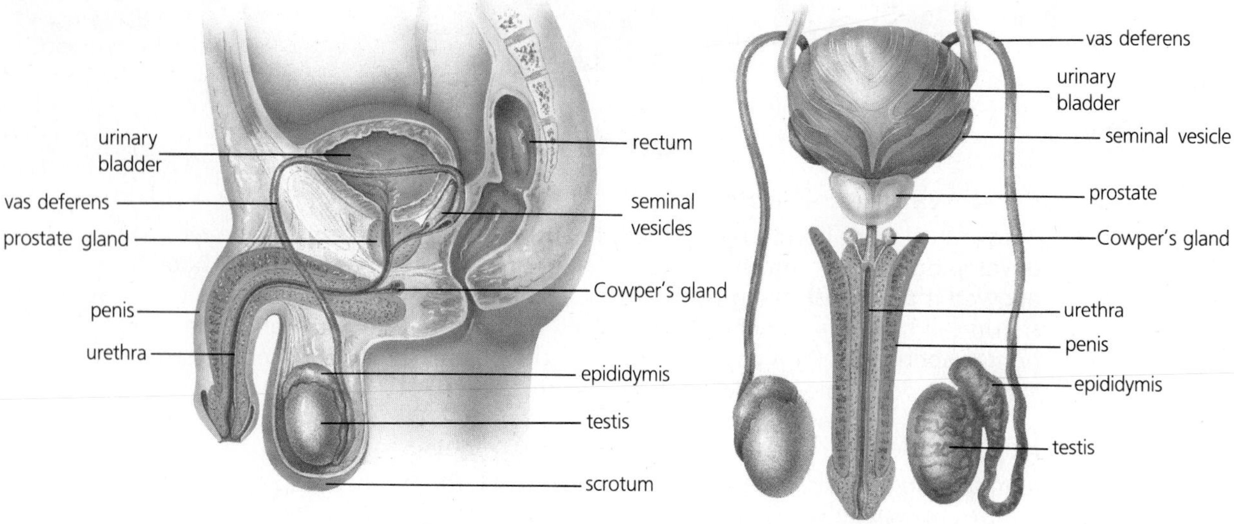

Figure 23–2 ▲

Reproductive System of Human Male. In the male, the testes produce sperm cells and the sex hormone testosterone. Fluid produced by the seminal vesicles, prostate gland, and Cowper's glands mix with sperm to form semen.

appear during adolescence but are not directly involved in reproduction. The secondary sex characteristics of men include body hair, muscle development, and a deep voice.

The male reproductive system is shown in Figure 23–2. A pair of testes hangs outside the body wall in a sac of skin called the **scrotum.** The scrotum keeps the testes at a temperature slightly lower than the rest of the body. This is necessary for the production and storage of sperm. If the testes become too warm, muscles in the scrotum relax, allowing the testes to fall away from the body. If the testes become too cool, the scrotal muscles pull them closer to the body.

The testes actually form inside the body during development and move down into the scrotum only in the last month before birth. Sometimes, one or both testes do not pass into the scrotum. Testes that stay within the body cannot make sperm because the temperature is too high. In some cases, however, they can be moved surgically or with hormone treatment.

Each testis is made up of small, coiled tubes called the *seminiferous* (sem uh NIF uh rus) *tubules.* There are 300 to 600 tubules in each testis. Immature sperm are made in the seminiferous tubules. From there, the immature sperm pass to the **epididymis** (ep uh DID uh mis), a storage area on the upper rear part of each testis. In the epididymis, the sperm mature, which takes about 18 hours. They leave the epididymis through the **vas deferens** (vas DEF uh renz), a tube that leads upward from each testis into the lower part of the abdomen.

The two vas deferens empty into the **urethra,** the passageway for the excretion of urine. In mammals, it is also the passageway through which sperm leave the body. In the human male, the urethra passes through the penis to the outside of the body. As sperm enter the urethra, the *seminal vesicles, Cowper's glands,* and the *prostate* (PRAHS tayt) *gland* all secrete fluids into the urethra. These fluids nourish the sperm and protect them from the acidity of

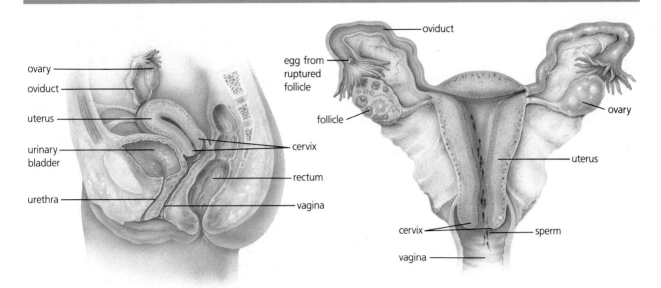

the female reproductive tract. The mixture of sperm and fluids is called **semen** (SEE men). Involuntary muscular contractions force the semen through the urethra and out of the body in a process called **ejaculation** (ih jak yuh LAY shun). For a short time before, during, and after ejaculation, reflex actions keep the outlet of the urinary bladder closed. This prevents urine from entering the urethra and mixing with the semen.

The Female Reproductive System

The female gonads are the **ovaries.** The ovaries make eggs, which are the female gametes. The ovaries also secrete the female sex hormone *estrogen.* Estrogen causes the development of female secondary sex characteristics and plays a large role in the menstrual cycle, which you will study later in this section. Female secondary sex characteristics include breasts, a broadened pelvis, and the distribution of body fat.

The female reproductive system is shown in Figure 23–3. There are two ovaries. These are found in the lower part of the abdomen. They are about four centimeters long and two centimeters wide. Each ovary contains about 200 000 tiny egg sacs called **follicles.** In each follicle, there is an immature egg. These immature eggs are present at the time of birth. During the life of a female, no more than 500 eggs mature.

When an egg matures, its follicle moves to the surface of the ovary. The follicle then breaks, releasing the egg as shown in Figure 23–3. This process is called **ovulation** (ahv yuh LAY shun). An egg can be fertilized for about 24 hours after ovulation.

Near each ovary, but not connected to it, is an **oviduct** (OH vuh duhkt), or *Fallopian* (fuh LOH pee un) *tube.* The oviduct is a tube with a funnel-like opening. Cilia lining the oviduct create a current that draws the released egg into the tube. The oviduct is where the egg may be fertilized if any sperm are present.

▲ **Figure 23–3**

Reproductive System of Human Female. In the female, the ovaries produce the female sex hormones estrogen and progesterone. Eggs mature in the follicles in the ovaries. When a follicle breaks, the egg is released and drawn into the oviduct, where fertilization may occur.

From the oviduct, the egg passes into the **uterus** (YOOT uh rus), a thick-walled, muscular, pear-shaped organ. If the egg has been fertilized, it finishes its development in the uterus, attached to the uterine wall. The narrow neck of the uterus is called the **cervix** (SER viks). The cervix opens into the **vagina** (vuh JY nuh), or *birth canal,* which leads to the outside of the body. At birth, the baby leaves the mother's body through this passageway.

In the early stages of the human female embryo, the vagina joins the urethra, as does the vas deferens in the male. During later development, however, a second opening is formed for the vagina. Thus, unlike the male, in the mature human female, the urinary and reproductive tracts are completely separate.

The Menstrual Cycle

Characteristics of the Menstrual Cycle

In the human female, a mature egg develops and leaves one of the ovaries about every 28 days. At this time, the wall of the uterus has thickened with a rich supply of blood vessels and is prepared to accept a fertilized egg for development. If the egg is not fertilized, the built-up portion of the uterine wall breaks down and along with the unfertilized egg, passes from the body. Then another egg matures, and the buildup of the uterine wall begins again. This cycle is known as the **menstrual** (MEN struhl) **cycle,** shown in Figure 23–4. The changes that take place involve the interaction of hormones made by the hypothalamus, pituitary gland, and ovary.

The menstrual cycle begins at puberty, which usually takes place in human females sometime between the ages of 10 and 14. The cycle stops during the time when a woman is pregnant. It stops permanently sometime in middle age, usually between the ages of 45 and 50. The permanent stopping of the menstrual cycle is called *menopause* (MEN uh pawz).

Figure 23–4

The Menstrual Cycle. During the menstrual cycle, the lining of the uterus thickens in preparation for a fertilized egg. The cycle is controlled by four interacting hormones and repeats itself about every 28 days. ▶

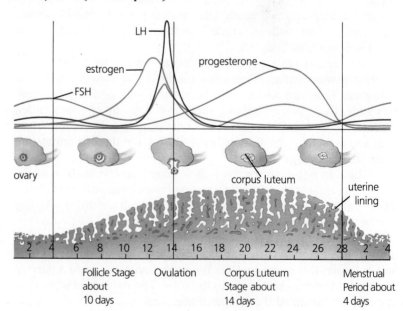

Stages of the Menstrual Cycle   The female human menstrual cycle can be divided into four distinct stages, of which menstruation is the final stage.

The first stage is the follicle stage. The pituitary gland secretes follicle-stimulating hormone (FSH), which you read about in Chapter 16. FSH causes several follicles in the ovary to begin developing. Usually, only one follicle matures. As the follicle develops, it secretes estrogen. The estrogen stimulates the uterine lining to thicken with mucus and a rich supply of blood vessels. These changes in the lining prepare the uterus for a possible pregnancy. This stage lasts 10 to 14 days.

The second stage is called ovulation. A high level of estrogen in the blood causes the pituitary to decrease the secretion of FSH and begin the secretion of luteinizing hormone (LH). When the concentration of LH in the blood reaches a certain level, ovulation takes

MiniLab

Skill: Interpreting

Changing Hormone Levels

Problem

What can you learn about hormone levels during pregnancy by **interpreting** data on a line graph?

Procedure

1. Study the line graph below that illustrates the changing levels of hormones during pregnancy.

2. Write down some generalizations you can make from the graph.

Analyze and Conclude

1. Which hormone is most abundant at 30 days?

2. Which hormones are increasing at 120 days? Which is decreasing?

3. What happens to the levels of these three hormones at the end of the pregnancy?

4. Based on what you know about the roles of these hormones, what might determine the "birth" day?

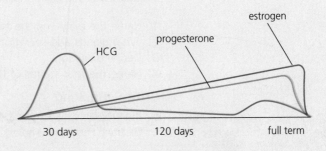

place. That is, at that point, the follicle breaks, releasing a mature egg. Ovulation usually takes place in about the middle of the menstrual cycle.

The third stage is the corpus luteum stage. After ovulation, LH causes the broken follicle to fill with cells, forming a yellow body called the **corpus luteum** (KOR pus LOOT ee um). The corpus luteum begins to secrete the hormone progesterone, which brings about the continued growth of the uterine lining. Because of its part in maintaining the uterine wall, progesterone is often called the hormone of pregnancy. It also stops the development of new follicles in the ovary by inhibiting the release of FSH. The corpus luteum stage lasts 10 to 14 days.

Menstruation is the fourth stage. If fertilization does not happen, secretion of LH decreases, and the corpus luteum breaks down. This causes a decrease in the level of progesterone. With a drop in the progesterone level, the thickened lining of the uterus is no longer maintained, and it breaks down. The extra layers of the lining, the unfertilized egg, and a small amount of blood pass out of the body through the vagina. This is called **menstruation** (men strou WA shun). It lasts from about three to five days. While menstruation is taking place, the amount of estrogen in the blood is dropping. The pituitary increases its output of FSH, and a new follicle starts to mature.

Humans and other primates are the only mammals that have a menstrual cycle. Other mammals have an *estrous cycle.* This cycle is marked by periodic changes in the female's sex organs and in the desire to mate, but there is little or no bleeding at the end of the cycle. Mammals such as foxes, coyotes, and wolves have one estrous cycle each year, whereas cats and dogs have two.

For most of the estrous cycle, the female is not fertile and will not mate. Mating takes place only when the female is fertile—when the uterus and associated structures increase in size in preparation for pregnancy. Ovulation takes place spontaneously during the fertile period, or after mating, depending on the species. During fertile periods, the female is said to be "in heat." If fertilization does not happen, the sex organs go back to their normal state.

23-1 Section Review

1. Name the male and the female gonads.
2. What glands add secretions to the sperm?
3. Define ovulation.
4. Name the four stages of the menstrual cycle.

Critical Thinking

5. If a woman's fallopian tubes are blocked, how is her body affected? *(Relating Parts and Wholes)*

23-2 Fertilization, Implantation, and Development

Section Objectives:

- *Summarize* the processes of fertilization and implantation in humans.
- *Explain* the roles of the placenta and umbilical cord in pregnancy.
- *Define* the following terms: *amniotic fluid, gestation period, labor, fraternal twins,* and *identical twins.*

The primary function of human reproductive systems is to create new individuals. This occurs in a process that begins with fertilization and ends with the birth of a baby.

Fertilization

In human mating, or sexual intercourse, hundreds of millions of sperm are ejaculated into the vagina. The sperm then pass through the cervix, up through the uterus, and into the oviducts. If an egg is passing down one of the oviducts at this time, fertilization—the fusion of a sperm and an egg nucleus—may take place. The egg secretes a chemical that attracts the sperm. One of the sperm breaks through the membranes surrounding the egg, and the sperm cell nucleus enters the cytoplasm of the egg cell. When this happens, the membranes around the egg change, stopping other sperm from entering the egg. The sperm nucleus fuses with the egg nucleus, resulting in the diploid cell called the zygote.

If a woman's Fallopian tubes are blocked or she cannot ovulate, a technique called **in vitro** (VEE troh) **fertilization** may be tried. In vitro fertilization is fertilization in a glass laboratory dish. An egg taken from the woman or from an anonymous donor is fertilized by sperm contributed by the woman's husband or, if the husband is infertile, an anonymous donor. Two days after fertilization, the zygote is placed in the woman's uterus, where it may become implanted and continue to develop.

Implantation and Development

After fertilization, the zygote undergoes cleavage and develops into a blastula as it moves down the oviduct toward the uterus. About 5 to 10 days after fertilization, the embryo enters the uterus. Within the uterus, the outer layer of cells of the embryo secretes enzymes that digest part of the thick lining of the uterus, and the embryo attaches itself at this spot.

The fastening of the embryo to the wall of the uterus is called **implantation** (im plan TAY shun). Implantation marks the beginning of **pregnancy,** the period during which the baby develops in the uterus. Sometimes, the embryo implants somewhere other than the uterus, such as in the oviduct or out in the abdomen. This is

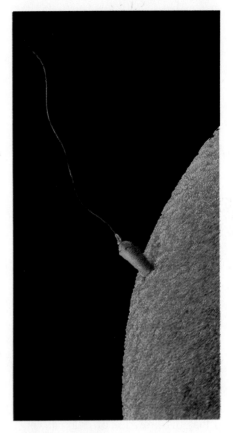

▲ **Figure 23–5**
Human Sperm Fertilizing an Egg. Fertilization occurs when a sperm unites with an egg.

Can You Explain This?

A young wife gave birth to her firstborn, a baby boy. At first, the baby appeared normal. Soon, however, a nurse noticed the newborn was showing signs of drug withdrawal. The baby had not been given any drugs since its birth.

The distraught mother was confused. She knew that her blood did not mix with the blood of the developing baby during her pregnancy. She had therefore assumed that the presence of drugs in her system would not affect her baby.

■ *Suggest an explanation for how this baby developed an addiction to drugs.*

called an *ectopic* (ek TAHP ik) *pregnancy*. Ectopic pregnancies usually end in the death of the embryo and sometimes cause severe bleeding inside the mother.

After implantation, the embryo undergoes gastrulation. The three germ layers are formed, and all the tissues and organs of the body develop from these layers by growth and differentiation. The developing human is called an *embryo* from the time of fertilization up until about eight weeks. After this time, the embryo is usually called a **fetus** (FEET us).

Extraembryonic Membranes

The human embryo develops the same extraembryonic membranes as birds and reptiles. However, these membranes play different parts in the development of humans.

In humans, the outer cell layer of the blastula becomes the **chorion**—the outermost of the extraembryonic membranes. As seen in Figure 23–6, the chorion completely surrounds the embryo and the other membranes. Small fingerlike projections called *chorionic* (kor ee AHN ik) *villi* form on the outer surface of the

Figure 23–6

Nourishment of the Fetus. Nutrients and oxygen diffuse from the mother's blood into fetal capillaries in the chorionic villi. Wastes from fetal blood diffuse into the mother's blood. Materials are transported to and from the fetus through blood vessels in the umbilical cord. There is no direct connection between the circulatory systems of the fetus and the mother. ▼

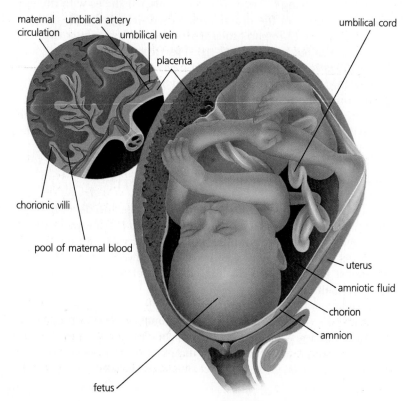

chorion and extend into the uterine lining. The chorionic villi and the uterine lining together form a temporary organ called the **placenta.**

The placenta allows the exchange of nutrients and wastes between the embryo and the mother. It also secretes a hormone that stops the menstrual cycle during pregnancy by preventing the breakdown of the corpus luteum. The corpus luteum goes on secreting high levels of progesterone, which, in turn, maintains the thickened wall of the uterus. The high progesterone level also prevents the development of new follicles in the ovaries. Thus, neither ovulation nor menstruation takes place during pregnancy.

In the human, the yolk sac and the allantois develop into the **umbilical cord.** This ropelike structure connects the developing fetus to the placenta.

The amnion is the innermost of the membranes. It completely surrounds the fetus within the chorion, like a balloon within a balloon. The amnion is filled with **amniotic fluid,** which protects the fetus, giving it a stable environment and absorbing shocks.

Nourishment of the Embryo From the time of fertilization until implantation in the uterus, food stored in the egg nourishes the embryo. Soon after implantation, the embryo begins receiving food and oxygen from the mother's body through the placenta.

Fetal blood carrying wastes flows to the placenta through arteries in the umbilical cord. These arteries branch again and again, finally forming capillaries in the chorionic villi. The villi are surrounded by the mother's blood, which has been forced by arteriole blood pressure out of her blood vessels into spaces around the villi. Nutrients and oxygen in the blood of the mother diffuse into the fetus's blood in the chorionic villi. Wastes diffuse from the fetal blood into the mother's blood. However, the blood of the fetus and that of the mother do not mix. The enriched fetal blood then travels back to the fetus through veins in the umbilical cord. The waste materials are excreted by the mother. Thus, the placenta allows the fetus to make use of the mother's organ systems while its own are developing.

The placenta acts as a barrier that protects the fetus from some harmful substances in the mother's blood. However, many dangerous substances can pass through the placenta from the mother's blood to the fetus's blood. Viruses, such as German measles and AIDS, as well as nicotine, alcohol, and many drugs, can pass through the placenta and harm the fetus. It is the responsibility of the mother to avoid such harmful substances.

Birth

The length of pregnancy is called the **gestation** (jes TAY shun) period. The human gestation period is a little over 9 months. The gestation periods for other placental mammals are different. For example, the gestation period for a mouse is only 20 days. For an elephant, it is about 21 months.

Biology and You

Q: My aunt is pregnant and refuses to drink any alcohol. How would alcohol affect an unborn child?

A: Your aunt is taking every precaution to ensure a healthy baby. Women who drink while pregnant risk giving birth to children with irreversible physical, mental, and behavioral problems. When a pregnant woman drinks, the alcohol passes from her bloodstream into the baby's. If a mother drinks enough to get drunk, the baby also gets drunk. The unborn infant has a difficult time ridding its undeveloped body of the alcohol.

Alcohol in a baby's bloodstream can lead to Fetal Alcohol Syndrome, or FAS. Infants with FAS may suffer from such birth defects as low birth weight, malformed facial features, and heart defects. Later, they may experience delayed growth, mental retardation, or coordination difficulties.

There is only one sure way to prevent FAS and that is to refuse all alcoholic beverages while pregnant. Nobody knows exactly how much alcohol causes birth defects, so pregnant women should avoid alcohol completely.

Research and write a report on how either tobacco or drug use during pregnancy affects unborn babies.

When the human fetus is ready to be born, the uterine muscles begin slow, rhythmic contractions. This is called **labor.** At this time, the opening of the cervix begins to get larger. Its diameter must go from 1 or 2 centimeters to 11 or 12 centimeters before the baby can pass out of the uterus and into the birth canal. When the opening of the cervix has gotten large enough, the contractions force the baby, head first, from the uterus into the vagina and out of the mother's body. During labor, the amniotic membrane bursts, releasing the amniotic fluid. This fluid eases the passage of the baby through the birth canal.

When the baby passes out of the mother's body, the umbilical cord still connects it to the placenta. The umbilical cord is then tied and cut, leaving a scar on the baby called the *navel.* Shortly after the birth of the baby, additional uterine contractions expel the placenta and amnion, which are known as the *afterbirth.*

During pregnancy, progesterone and estrogen prepare the breasts for nursing. After birth, the pituitary hormone prolactin causes the mammary glands in the breasts to secrete milk.

While most pregnancies take place without difficulty, problems can occur. Delivery of a fetus before it is ready to be born is *premature birth.* Because premature babies are not fully developed, they are placed in an *incubator,* a special chamber designed to protect the baby until it is more developed. See Figure 23–7. Sometimes delivery through the cervix and vagina is not possible or is not safe for mother and baby. In these circumstances, the doctor will make an incision into the abdomen and uterus and deliver the baby by *cesarian section.*

Figure 23–7

A Premature Baby. Premature births most often occur during the last three months of pregnancy. This premature baby rests safely within an incubator. ▼

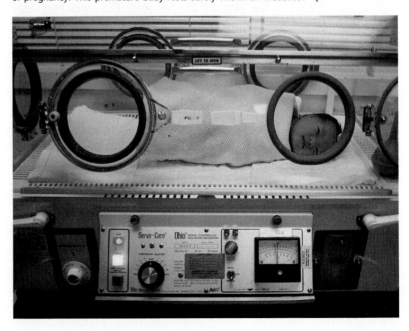

◀ **Figure 23–8**
Identical Twins. Identical twins develop from one fertilized egg and inherit identical traits.

Multiple Births

Once in a while, two eggs mature at the same time and pass into the oviduct during the same cycle. Each egg then may be fertilized by a different sperm. Both embryos may become implanted in the uterus and develop separately. Because the two embryos have received different hereditary material, they develop into people with different characteristics. Two people born from the same pregnancy are called *twins.* When they have developed from different eggs, they are **fraternal twins.** Fraternal twins may be of opposite sex and are no more alike than any two children of the same parents.

In other cases, a single fertilized egg divides into two embryos at a very early stage of development. The two individuals that then develop have the same hereditary makeup and are physically very much alike. Two individuals that develop from the same egg are called **identical twins.** Identical twins are always of the same sex.

Twins are the most common type of multiple birth. However, in rare cases, three or more embryos may form during the same pregnancy. Such multiple births may be fraternal, identical, or a combination of both types.

23-2 Section Review

1. In which part of the female reproductive system does fertilization generally occur?
2. What organ provides food and oxygen for the developing embryo?
3. Name the extraembryonic membranes that surround a fetus.
4. Define the term gestation.

Critical Thinking

5. Compare fraternal and identical twins. How are they alike? How are they different? *(Comparing and Contrasting)*

Laboratory
Investigation

Reproductive Organs and Gametes

The egg and sperm are microscopic structures that can best be observed in slides that have been professionally sectioned, stained, and preserved. In this investigation, you will examine some prepared slides of human reproductive organs and gametes.

Problem

What can you **observe** in the microscopic structure of reproductive organs and gametes?

Materials (per group)

- compound microscope
- prepared slides of the following:
  human testis
  human ovary
  human sperm

Procedure

1. Obtain a prepared slide of the cross section of a human testis. Using the low-power objective of the microscope, examine the slide and draw what you see. Find an area that has well-defined circular structures. These are the seminiferous tubules.

2. Switch to the high-power objective on the microscope. Select one seminiferous tubule and draw the structures inside it.

3. Locate and identify the cells at various stages of development. The cells located just inside the walls of the tubule are the cells in which meiosis begins. The cells closest to the center of the tubule are at later stages of meiosis, and the cells closest to the center of the tubule are the sperm.

4. Obtain a prepared slide of human sperm. Using the low-power objective of the microscope, examine the slide. Locate one sperm and then switch the microscope to high power. Draw what you observe.

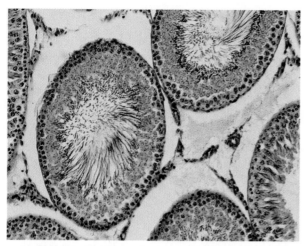

Cross-section of human testes. (Magnification 40 X)

5. Obtain a prepared slide of a human ovary and observe it under the low-power objective of the microscope. Locate a large cell that has a distinct nucleus surrounded by a lightly stained area of cytoplasm. This is an egg.

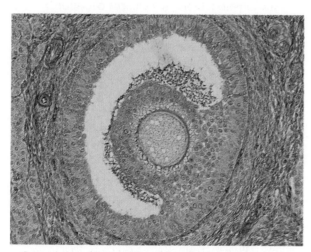

Cross-section of human ovary. (Magnification 50 X)

6. Find the largest follicle, a fluid-filled cavity that surrounds an egg. Switch the microscope to high power and draw what you observe. Try to locate the fluid-filled space, the egg itself, the egg's nucleus, and the layers of follicle cells surrounding the egg.

Observations

1. How many enlarged follicles with mature eggs did you observe in the cross section of the ovary?

2. How many mature sperm did you observe in the seminiferous tubule?

Analysis and Conclusions

1. How much of the testis did you see?

2. Explain how a human testis is able to produce millions of sperm each day.

3. How does the volume of cytoplasm in the egg compare with the volume of cytoplasm in the sperm?

4. Which structures were easiest to identify? Which were the hardest?

Extensions

Compare prepared slides of the reproductive organs of other mammals with slides of the same organs in humans.

Chapter 23 Review

Study Outline

23-1 Human Reproductive Systems

▶ The male gonads, the testes, produce sperm and secrete testosterone, which causes the development of male secondary sex characteristics.

▶ The female gonads, the ovaries, produce eggs and secrete estrogen, which causes the development of female secondary sex characteristics.

▶ The menstrual cycle is a hormone-controlled monthly cycle in the human female. It is divided into four stages—the follicle stage, ovulation, the corpus luteum stage, and menstruation.

23-2 Fertilization, Implantation, and Development

▶ After the egg is fertilized, it undergoes cleavage and forms a blastula as it passes down the oviduct into the uterus. Then the embryo attaches itself to the uterine wall in a process called implantation.

▶ Following implantation, the embryo forms three germ layers, which develop into all of the tissues and organs of the body. The embryo also forms extraembryonic membranes, parts of which extend into the uterine lining to form the placenta.

▶ Nutrients and oxygen from the mother's blood diffuse across the placenta into the fetus's blood. Wastes diffuse from the fetus's blood into the mother's blood.

▶ When two eggs are fertilized, the result is fraternal twins. Identical twins result when one fertilized egg divides into two embryos.

Chapter Assessment

Multiple Choice

Choose the letter of the answer that best completes each statement or answers the question.

1. Fertilization generally takes place in the
   (a) ovary. (b) vagina. (c) uterus. (d) oviduct.

2. Testosterone controls the development of (a) secondary sex characteristics. (b) secondary sex characteristics and sperm. (c) sperm. (d) eggs.

3. During the follicle stage, cell and tissue growth in the uterus is stimulated by (a) progesterone. (b) estrogen. (c) FSH. (d) LH.

4. As the embryo develops, the placenta supplies it with (a) metabolic wastes. (b) nutrients and blood. (c) blood and oxygen. (d) nutrients and oxygen.

5. At ovulation, (a) an egg is released from a follicle sac. (b) the egg is fertilized. (c) the egg enters the uterus. (d) secondary sex characteristics appear.

6. Progesterone (a) stimulates the development of follicles. (b) maintains the growth of the uterine lining. (c) stimulates development of the uterine lining. (d) stimulates secretion of LH.

7. The technique of uniting sperm with an egg in a glass laboratory dish is an example of (a) in vitro fertilization. (b) internal fertilization. (c) gametogenesis. (d) artificial ovulation.

8. The pathway of sperm leaving the male reproductive system is (a) vas deferens, urethra, epididymis. (b) epididymis, vas deferens, urethra. (c) epididymis, seminiferous tubules, urethra. (d) seminiferous tubules, urethra, vas deferens.

9. The rhythmic contractions that force a baby from its mother's body during birth is called (a) afterbirth. (b) gestation. (c) labor. (d) puberty.

10. If a human female produces two healthy eggs during her monthly cycle and both are fertilized, the result will be the development of (a) one zygote and the crowding out of the other. (b) fraternal twins. (c) identical twins. (d) Siamese twins.

Content Review

Answer each of the following in complete sentences.

11. What are the functions of the testes?

12. What are the functions of the seminal vesicles, Cowper's glands, and the prostate gland?

13. Trace the path of sperm from the testes until it leaves the body.

14. What are the functions of the ovaries?

15. Trace the path of an unfertilized egg from a follicle until it leaves the body.

16. In what ways does the estrous cycle differ from the menstrual cycle?

17. How do hormones regulate the menstrual cycle?

18. Trace the development of a zygote from fertilization through implantation.

19. How does the embryo obtain nutrients and get rid of wastes?

20. How and why do fraternal twins differ from identical twins?

Graphic Organizing

For information on graphic organizers, see Appendix G at the back of this text.

21. **Bar Graph** Mortality rates are reliable indicators of a nation's health. The infant mortality rate (IMR) is the number of deaths of children under one year of age per 1000 live births. Using the data table below, construct a bar graph of infant mortality rates for the countries listed. Graph the data for the two years given in two separate colors. According to your graph, which three countries have experienced the greatest drop in infant mortality rates?

Country	Infant Mortality Rate	
	1979	1989
Canada	14.0	7.9
Finland	12.0	5.8
France	11.0	7.6
Ireland	16.0	7.4
United Kingdom	14.0	9.0
United States	14.0	9.9
West Germany	16.0	9.3

Critical Thinking and Problem Solving

Discuss each of the following in a brief paragraph.

22. **Relating** Some scientists believe semen and amniotic fluid are adaptations by organisms to life on land. What reasons can you give to support this?

23. **Predicting** How would failure of the corpus luteum to develop affect the rest of a menstrual cycle?

24. **Inferring** Sperm can survive for about 24 hours in the female body, yet they survive much longer in the male testes. Explain why.

25. **Inferring** What could prevent the embryo from implanting in the uterus? Could it survive and develop anyway?

26. **Interpreting** Researchers conducted an investigation to determine the effect of secondhand cigarette smoke on pregnant women. A group of 1366 nonsmoking women participated in the study. The researchers divided the group into women whose husbands smoked and those whose husbands did not smoke. Data were gathered on the average weight of their babies at birth and on the number of miscarriages. Using the data presented in the table below, calculate the percentage of miscarriages for each group. Next, calculate the percentage difference in average birth weight between the two groups. What conclusions can you draw about the effects of secondhand smoke on pregnant women?

Effects of Secondhand Smoke on Pregnant Women		
	Wife Nonsmoker/ Husband Nonsmoker	Wife Nonsmoker/ Husband Smoker
Number of couples	837	529
Number of miscarriages	92	93
Average weight of baby at birth	3.2 kg	2.9 kg

Sexual Reproduction in Plants

························ **Guide** *for* **Reading** ························

Previewing the Chapter

These fuzzy young plants growing through the leaf cover on the forest floor are called fiddlehead ferns. They are known as "fiddleheads" because their curved structure resembles the scroll of a violin's head. Throughout the spring and summer months, the young fiddleheads will develop into mature fern plants, ready to begin the cycle again. How do plant life cycles differ from animal life cycles. What is the difference between a seed and a spore?

Key Words

alternation of generations, cotyledon, ovule, pistil, pollen grain, pollination, seed, stamen

Key Concepts

- **Compare** plant and animal life cycles.
- **Distinguish** between a seed and a spore.
- **Observe** a pea pod to relate the structures of a fruit to its function. (Laboratory Investigation)

24-1 Life Cycles of Nonseed Plants

Section Objectives:

- *Define* the terms *sporophyte* and *gametophyte*.
- *Describe* alternation of generations.
- *Compare* the life cycles of green algae, mosses, and ferns.

Nonseed Plants

Sexual reproduction in plants involves two processes—meiosis and fertilization. Plant groups differ in when, where, and how in their life cycles these events occur.

The major land plant groups are the mosses, ferns, and seed plants. The seed plants, include the **gymnosperms** (JIM noh spermz) and the **angiosperms** (AN jee oh spermz). Most gymnosperms are cone-bearing plants, such as the conifers. Their seeds develop on the surface of the cone scales. In contrast, the angiosperms have seeds that develop within protective structures.

In mosses and ferns, water is necessary for sexual reproduction. In these plants, the sperm have flagella, and water is needed for the sperm to swim to the egg. Gymnosperms and angiosperms, on the other hand, have adaptations for fertilization that do not require standing water. Thus, seed plants can thrive and reproduce sexually on land under conditions that make sexual reproduction in mosses and ferns impossible.

▲ **Figure 24–1**

A Seed Plant. The major land plant groups include the mosses, ferns, and seed plants. This common milkweed is a seed plant.

Alternation of Generations

The life cycle of a plant switches back and forth, or alternates, between two different plant forms. One form is always haploid and produces gametes. The other form is diploid and produces spores. This alternating between haploid and diploid plant forms is called **alternation of generations.** Figure 24–2 shows alternation between the haploid and diploid generations.

The gamete-producing plant is called the **gametophyte** (guh MEET uh fyt). All the cells of the gametophyte are haploid (*n*). The spore-producing plant is called the **sporophyte** (SPOR uh fyt). All the cells of the sporophyte are diploid (*2n*). During the growth of the sporophyte, some of the cells undergo *meiosis* and form haploid spores. When the spores are released from the sporophyte, they grow by mitosis into haploid, multicellular gametophytes. Some cells differentiate to form haploid gametes. When two gametes combine during fertilization, a diploid zygote is created. The zygote develops into a young sporophyte—the embryo. Through mitosis, the young sporophyte grows into a multicellular, mature sporophyte, and the life cycle begins again.

Usually one generation is more obvious than the other. This generation is said to be the *dominant generation*. The plant of the dominant generation is larger and lives longer than the plant of the other generation. In all plants, except the mosses, the diploid sporophyte is the obvious, dominant generation.

Life Cycle of Algae

Most botanists believe that plants are related to green algae. They believe this because green algae and plants share certain features, such as similar chlorophylls, the storage of food as starch, and cell walls made of cellulose. In fact, in some species of green algae there even is alternation of generations.

Figure 24–2
Alternation of Generations in Plants. In plants, there is a haploid, gamete-producing generation (the gametophyte) and a diploid spore-producing generation (the sporophyte). The gametophyte and sporophyte are not two stages in the life of an individual plant but rather two individual plants of the same species. ▶

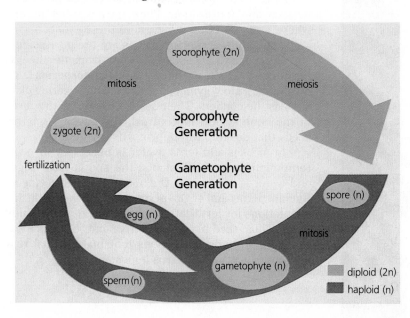

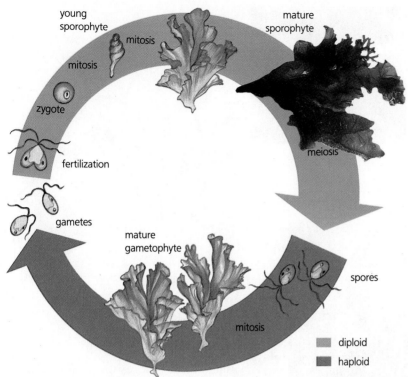

young
sporophyte

mitosis

mitosis

zygote

fertilization

gametes

mature
gametophyte

mature
sporophyte

meiosis

spores

mitosis

mitosis

diploid
haploid

◀ **Figure 24–3**
Life Cycle of *Ulva*. In sea lettuce, or *Ulva*, the haploid gametophyte and diploid sporophyte generations resemble each other closely.

Figure 24–3 illustrates the life cycle of a green alga, the sea lettuce *Ulva*. In this alga, alternation of generations happens. The diploid sporophyte of *Ulva* is a multicellular structure that looks similar to a lettuce leaf. Some of the cells of the sporophyte undergo meiosis to produce haploid spores. These spores use their flagella to swim away from the sporophyte. Eventually, the spores lose their flagella and become attached to rocks. They then develop into multicellular, leaflike gametophytes that are identical in form to the sporophytes. Certain cells of the gametophyte produce haploid gametes by mitosis. These gametes fuse to form a zygote, which develops into a multicellular, leaflike sporophyte, thus completing the life cycle.

Life Cycle of Mosses

The **mosses** are among the most primitive of plants. Mosses have structures similar in function to the roots, stems, and leaves of higher plants, but they are much simpler. The stemlike structure is usually only several centimeters high. It is surrounded by small, leaflike structures that are only one cell thick. Anchoring the plant are rootlike structures called **rhizoids.** Unlike roots, the rhizoids do not conduct water. Mosses do not have the specialized conducting tissues of higher plants, which makes the transport of materials somewhat inefficient. Because transport is inefficient, mosses are small and need a moist environment for growth and reproduction. Therefore, they are found on the damp floors of forests, on shaded rocks, and in swamps.

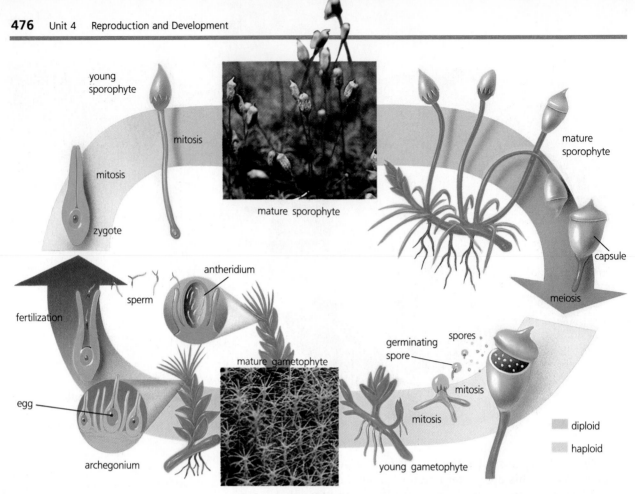

▲ **Figure 24–4**
Life Cycle of Mosses. In mosses, the haploid, or gametophyte, generation is dominant.

The gametophyte generation is dominant. The haploid gametophyte generation is what you would recognize as the moss plant. The sporophyte grows on the gametophyte and cannot live by itself. Figure 24–4 illustrates the life cycle of mosses.

In some mosses, there are separate male and female gametophytes. In the male gametophyte, the reproductive organ is called the **antheridium** (an thuh RID ee um). Within the antheridium, sperm are produced. In the female, the reproductive structure is called the **archegonium** (ar kuh GOH nee um). A single egg develops within each archegonium. When sperm are released from an antheridium, they swim through films of water to an egg in an archegonium of the female plant.

Fertilization produces a diploid zygote that grows into a sporophyte. The sporophyte grows out of the archegonium. It is a single leafless stalk that remains attached to the gametophyte and depends on it for nourishment. At the tip of the mature sporophyte, a *capsule* develops. Within the capsule, haploid spores are produced. These spores are released into the air. When they germinate, they form new haploid gametophytes, completing the life cycle.

Life Cycle of Ferns

As you can see in Figure 24–5, in **ferns,** the dominant generation is the sporophyte. The diploid sporophyte has an underground stem, called a *rhizome*, which grows just beneath the surface of

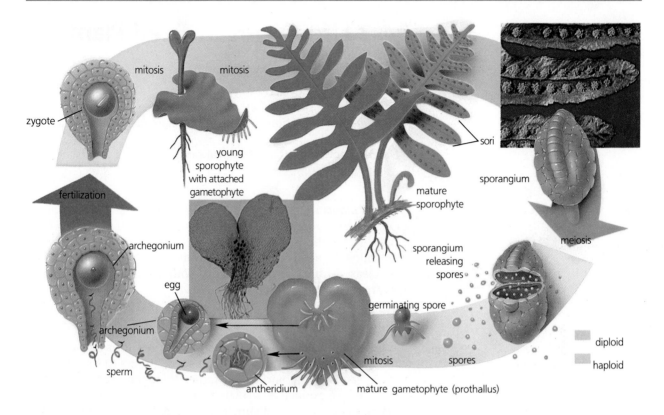

▲ **Figure 24–5**
Life Cycle of Ferns. In ferns, the diploid, or sporophyte, generation is dominant.

the soil. On the lower surface of the rhizome, true roots anchor the plant and absorb water and minerals. Large leaves, called *fronds*, grow from the upper surface of the rhizome.

On the underside of some fronds are rows of small dots called *sori* (SOR eye). Within the sori, meiosis results in haploid spores, which are eventually released into the air and scattered by the wind. A germinating spore forms a small, heart-shaped gameto-phyte, called a *prothallus* (proh THAL us). A prothallus has both antheridia and archegonia in which gametes develop. The sperm released from the antheridia can fertilize an egg in an archegonium on the same gametophyte, or they can swim to and fertilize eggs in a nearby gametophyte. The fertilized egg then grows into a mature sporophyte, the fern plant.

24-1 **Section Review**

1. In plants, which generations produce gametes?
2. Name the female reproductive structure of the moss.
3. Which is the dominant generation in ferns?
4. What is the gametophyte of a fern called?

Critical Thinking

5. Compare and contrast the antheridium and the archegonium of a moss. (*Comparing and Contrasting*)

24-2 Life Cycles of Seed Plants

Section Objectives:

- *Describe* the life cycle of a gymnosperm.
- *Draw* a flower and label all of its parts.
- *Describe* the formation of male and female gametes in flowering plants.
- *Describe* pollination and fertilization in flowering plants.

The *seed plants* are the most abundant of the plants. A **seed** is made up of the embryo, or young sporophyte, of the plant and its food supply. The embryo and its food are enclosed within a protective layer called the **seed coat.** The seed coat protects the embryo when it is released from the parent plant. Within the seed, the embryo has a ready supply of food for its growth.

The Life Cycle of Gymnosperms

The gymnosperms are seed plants that do not form flowers. The name gymnosperm, meaning "naked seed," refers to the development of seeds at the surface of, rather than enclosed within, the tissues of a reproductive structure. In most gymnosperms, called *conifers,* such as pine and spruce, seeds are borne on the scales of the reproductive structures known as cones.

Development of Gametes   Figure 24–7 shows the life cycle of a gymnosperm. In these plants, the sporophyte generation is dominant. In many of the gymnosperms, the leaves are in the form of needles, and the reproductive organs are located on cones. Pine trees and other gymnosperms produce two types of cones. The male cone is called the *pollen cone.* The larger female cone is the *seed cone.* A single tree usually produces both pollen and seed cones. Spore-producing structures are found on the *scales* of cones. These scales are actually modified leaves or branches.

In a pollen cone, there are two spore cases, or *sporangia* (spaw RAN jee uh), on the underside of each scale. In each sporangium, many haploid spores are formed by meiosis. Within its spore wall, each haploid spore undergoes mitosis twice. The result is an immature, male gametophyte, called a **pollen grain.** Two of its four cells die, leaving a *tube cell* and a *generative cell.*

In the seed cone, two sporangia are found on the upper surface of each scale. Meiosis within each sporangium produces four haploid spores, three of which die. The remaining spore divides many times by mitosis forming a female gametophyte. The female gametophyte, sporangium, and associated structures make up an **ovule** (OHV yool). Each female gametophyte forms two or three archegonia, and within each of these, an egg cell develops.

Pollination   The transfer of pollen grains to the vicinity of the female gametophyte is called **pollination** (pahl uh NAY shun). All

Figure 24–6

A Gymnosperm. Conifers dominate many temperate forests and may grow in particularly harsh environments. This lone pine grows at 7000 feet above sea level in Yosemite National Park. ▼

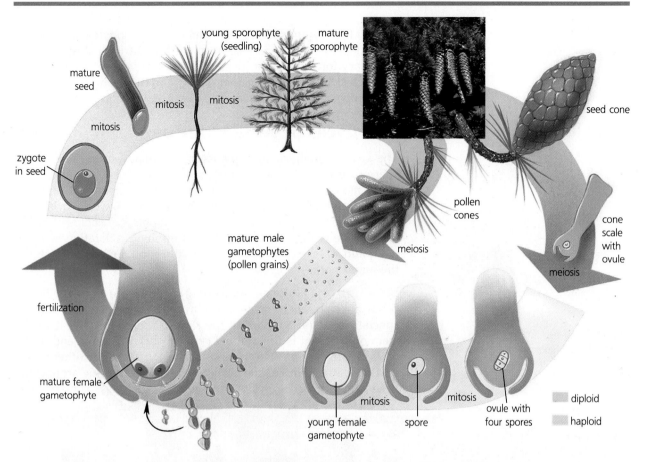

seed plants have pollination as part of their reproduction cycle. In the gymnosperms, pollination occurs when the sporangia of mature pollen cones burst, releasing millions of pollen grains into the wind. Many of the pollen grains land on the cone scales of seed cones. Some land near a small opening on an ovule, which is known as the **micropyle** (MY kruh pyl). Although the ovule is pollinated, fertilization does not take place for more than a year. During this time, the pollen grain and the female gametophyte develop into mature male and female gametophytes.

As a pollen grain matures, its tube cell grows through the micropyle and into the ovule, forming the **pollen tube.** The pollen tube serves as a bridge between the pollen grain and the egg. At the same time, the generative cell of the pollen grain divides by mitosis to form two sperm cells. Meanwhile, in the female gametophyte, a single egg cell matures within each archegonium.

Fertilization When the pollen tube finally reaches the female gametophyte, growth stops. At this point, the tube cell nucleus degenerates, and two sperm pass from the tube into an archegonium. One of the sperm dies, and the other fuses with the egg. The resulting zygote develops into the plant embryo. The ovule, which now contains the plant embryo, develops into a seed. Eventually, the seed is released from the cone. Under favorable conditions, the seed will germinate, growing into a new sporophyte.

▲ **Figure 24–7**

Life Cycle of Gymnosperms. In most gymnosperms, the spore-bearing organs are in the form of cones and the leaves are in the form of narrow leaves called needles.

In the gymnosperms, the small gametophytes are totally dependent on the parent sporophyte for nutrition. Water is not necessary for fertilization because wind carries the male gametophyte close to the female gametophyte, and the sperm travels to the egg through the pollen tube.

Life Cycle of Angiosperms

The second group of seed plants is the angiosperms. The angiosperms, or flowering plants, are the most successful and abundant of the modern-day plants. In contrast to gymnosperms, the reproductive structures of the angiosperms are found within structures called flowers, and the seeds, while developing, are enclosed within a fruit. Like the gymnosperms, the sporophyte generation is dominant, and water is not needed for fertilization. Figure 24–8 shows the angiosperm life cycle.

Structure of a Flower   As you can see in Figure 24–9, the flower of an angiosperm is made up of rings of modified leaves on a specialized stem. Supporting the flower and connecting it to the stem of the plant is the **pedicel** (PED uh sel). The large end of the pedicel is the **receptacle** (ruh SEP tuh kul) to which the other flower parts are attached. Leaflike structures that form a ring around the base of the flower are called the **sepals** (SEEP ulz). They enclose

Figure 24–8

Life Cycle of Angiosperms. In angiosperms, the reproductive structures are found within the flowers. Seeds are enclosed within a fruit. ▼

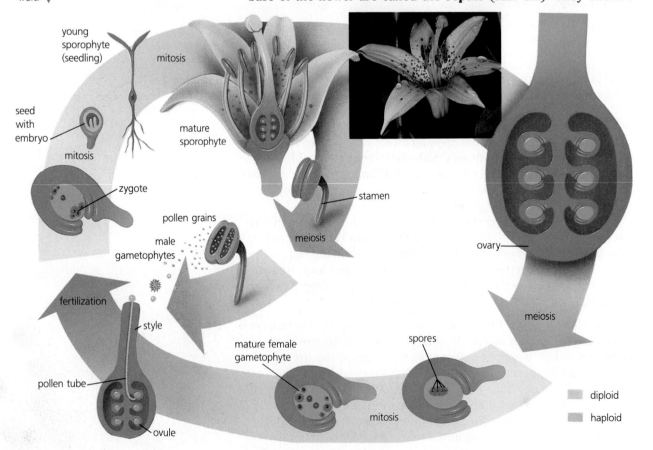

and protect the flower bud before it blossoms. The sepals may be small and green, or they may be large and brightly colored. The complete circle of sepals is called the **calyx** (KAY liks). Above the sepals are the **petals.** In some flowers, the petals are white; in others they are brightly colored. The complete circle of petals forms the **corolla** (kuh ROHL uh). The petals surround the reproductive organs of the flower.

The reproductive organs are in the center of the flower. These include the stamens and the pistil. The **stamens** (STAY menz) are usually called the male reproductive organs. They are located inside the corolla. A stamen is often made up of two parts—a stalklike **filament** and a saclike structure called the **anther** (AN ther) at the tip of the filament. Pollen grains are produced within the anthers. A flower may contain one or more stamens.

The **pistil** (PIS tul) is usually called the female reproductive organ of the angiosperms. It is located in the center of the flower. The pistil is made up of three parts. The top of the pistil is the **stigma** (STIG muh), which is an enlarged area that receives the pollen. Supporting the stigma is the **style.** At the base of the pistil is the expanded **ovary,** which contains the ovules. The ovary develops into the **fruit.** The ovules develop into seeds. A flower may have one or many pistils.

Stamens and pistils are the *essential organs* of the flower. The corolla and calyx are *accessory organs.* Some flowers contain stamens, pistil, corolla, and calyx, while others are missing one or more of these structures. *Pistillate* (PIS tuh layt) *flowers* contain pistils but not stamens, and *staminate* (STAM uh nayt) *flowers* contain stamens but no pistils. Plants that have only pistillate flowers are considered female plants, while those that have only staminate flowers are considered male plants. Some plants contain both pistillate and staminate flowers.

Development of Gametes   Haploid spores are produced by meiosis within the anthers of the stamens. See Figure 24–10. The spores undergo mitosis once, developing into pollen grains. These

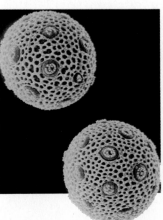

▲ **Figure 24–9**

Structure of a Flower. In a flower, the pistil is the female reproductive organ, and the stamen is the male reproductive organ.

Figure 24–10

The Stamen. The highly sculptured walls of two pollen grains are shown in the left photograph (Magnification 1400 X). In the right photo, the internal structure of a pollen grain is revealed. Note the two nuclei. (Magnification 4860 X).

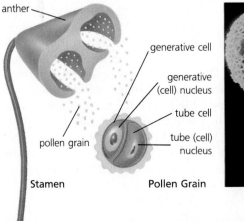

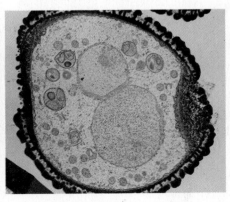

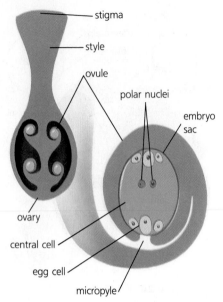

▲ **Figure 24–11**

The Pistil. After fertilization, the ovary develops into a fruit and each ovule develops into a seed.

Figure 24–12

Honeybee Gathering Nectar. As this honeybee gathers nectar at a crocus, pollen grains stick to its back. The next flower the bee visits will receive pollen from this flower. ▼

pollen grains are the young, male gametophytes. Two haploid cells are found within the thick, protective wall of each pollen grain. Like the pollen grain cells of the gymnosperms, one of the cells in the pollen grain is the tube cell, while the other is the generative cell. Once the pollen grains mature, the anther bursts, exposing the pollen to the air.

Every ovule within the ovary of the pistil has a micropyle. Every ovule also is attached to the wall of the ovary by a short stalk. In each ovule, meiosis of a single cell results in four haploid spores. Three of these spores die, and the remaining spore undergoes mitosis three times. The resulting female gametophyte, called an **embryo sac,** has only seven cells but eight haploid nuclei. See Figure 24–11. Two of the nuclei are found within a large central cell in the embryo sac. These are called the **polar nuclei.** The egg cell, which is near the micropyle, is surrounded by two cells. Three other cells are at the other end of the embryo sac.

Pollination In angiosperms, pollination is the transfer of pollen from an anther to a stigma. In some plants, pollen grains either fall or are transferred from an anther to a stigma on the same plant. This is known as *self-pollination.* When the pollen grains fall onto the stigma, the anthers usually are located above the stigmas. The transfer of pollen from the anthers of one plant to the stigma of another is called *cross-pollination. Artificial pollination* occurs when pollen is intentionally transferred by humans from one plant to another. Artificial pollination is used in plant breeding to produce plants with specific characteristics.

Cross-pollination may occur by wind, by animals or by water. This type of pollination is not as random as it seems. Flowers and flower parts are adapted for specific types of pollination. Flowers pollinated by animals are usually showy and/or give off an aroma to attract pollinators. These flowers often produce a sugary liquid, known as **nectar,** that pollinators use as food. As you can see in Figure 24–12, when pollinators gather nectar, the heavy pollen sticks easily to their bodies. Wind-pollinated flowers are not showy and produce no nectar or aroma. They do produce large amounts of light, loose pollen that is easily carried off by the wind. The stigmas of wind-pollinated flowers are expanded and feathery to help catch the wind-borne pollen.

Fertilization When a pollen grain reaches the stigma of a flower, it germinates. The protective coat of the pollen grain breaks open. As shown in Figure 24–13, a pollen tube grows down through the stigma and style and into the ovary. It then enters the ovule through the micropyle. The tube cell nucleus and the generative cell nucleus pass from the pollen grain down the pollen tube. As the generative nucleus moves down the pollen tube, it divides to form two haploid sperm nuclei. The two sperm nuclei enter the embryo sac. One fertilizes the egg cell to form a diploid zygote that develops into the sporophyte embryo. The other fuses with the two polar nuclei of the central cell to form a triploid (*3n*) *endosperm*

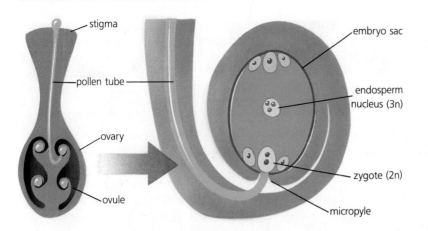

Figure 24–13

Fertilization in a Flower. When a pollen grain lands on a stigma and germinates, a pollen tube grows from the pollen grain down through the style of the pistil to an ovule. The generative nucleus divides into two sperm nuclei. The tube nucleus directs the growth of the pollen tube. The sperm nuclei enter the ovule through the micropyle. One sperm nucleus fuses with the egg cell nucleus to form a diploid zygote. The other sperm nucleus fuses with the two polar nuclei, forming a triploid (3n) cell that develops into endosperm tissue.

nucleus. Because one sperm fertilizes the egg and the other fertilizes the two polar nuclei, the process is called **double fertilization.** Double fertilization is a unique characteristic of flowering plants. Following fertilization, the endosperm nucleus divides by mitosis to form the **endosperm.** Endosperm is the tissue that stores food for the developing plant embryo.

24-2 Section Review

1. List three examples of gymnosperms.
2. What is a pollen grain?
3. Name the female reproductive organ of the angiosperm.
4. What serves as a bridge between the pollen grain and the egg?

Critical Thinking

5. Classify the following as either wind-pollinated or animal-pollinated plants: pine tree, carnation, rose, ragweed, African violet, orchid, grass, lily, cactus. (*Classifying*)

24-3 Fruits and Seeds

Section Objectives:

- *Explain* the differences between monocots and dicots.
- *Describe* the formation of fruits and seeds in flowering plants.
- *Draw* the structure of a seed and explain the functions of the cotyledon, epicotyl, and hypocotyl.
- *Describe* several mechanisms for seed dispersal.

After fertilization, each ovule develops into a seed, and the ovary develops into a fruit. In angiosperms, the seeds are always found within the fruit, which protects them. The parts of the flower not involved in the formation of the fruit wither and die. The ovary grows larger, and its wall thickens. The wall of the ripened ovary may be hard or soft, dry or fleshy, and it may be made up of several

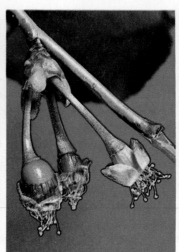

▲ **Figure 24–14**
Stages in the Development of a Cherry Fruit. In angiosperms, the fruit develops from the ovary.

Figure 24–15

Types of Fruits. A strawberry (top) is an aggregate fruit; a pineapple (center) is a multiple fruit; a grapefruit (bottom) is a simple fruit. ▼

separate layers. Figure 24–14 shows the development of a fruit from a fertilized ovary. If a flower has not been pollinated, a fruit usually does not form, and the flower withers and falls away.

Types of Fruits

There are thousands of different types of fruits. Many are rich in sugars, minerals, and vitamins. In fact, some of the foods we call vegetables are actually fruits. For example, many people think of the tomato as a vegetable, but it is, in fact, a fruit. Walnuts, pea pods, corn, and squash are all fruits.

Fruits are classified according to their origin. A fruit that develops from a single ovary is called a *simple fruit*. See Figure 24–15. Cherries and tomatoes are examples of simple fruits. When several ovaries are found within one flower, an *aggregate fruit* forms. Raspberries and strawberries are aggregate fruits. In some plants, such as the pineapple, the simple fruits of many separate flowers fuse together to form a *multiple fruit*.

Structure of the Seed

The seed, or ripened ovule, is made up of the seed coat, the embryo, and endosperm. The tough, protective seed coat develops from the wall of the ovule. On the outside of the seed coat is a scar called the *hilum* (HY lum), which marks where the ovule was attached to the ovary. The embryo develops by mitosis from the fertilized egg. The endosperm, which is a food storage tissue, develops by mitosis from the endosperm nucleus. The nutrients stored in the endosperm cells come from the parent plant.

All angiosperm embryos have at least one seed leaf, or **cotyledon** (kaht uh LEED un). In some plants, the endosperm is the only source of nourishment for the developing seedling. In other plants, however, the nutrients are stored in the cotyledons. The seeds of one group of angiosperms have only one cotyledon, and the plants that grow from these seeds are called **monocots.** Other angiosperms have two cotyledons and are called **dicots**. You can also recognize monocots and dicots by a number of other features, which are summarized in Figure 24–16. For example, in monocots, flower petals occur in groups of three, while in dicots, petals occur in groups of four or five.

In addition to one or two cotyledons, the plant embryo has three parts: the epicotyl, hypocotyl, and radicle. The part of the embryo above the point of attachment of the cotyledons is called the **epicotyl** (EP uh kaht ul). It usually gives rise to the terminal bud, leaves, and upper part of the stem of the young plant. The **hypocotyl** (HY puh kaht ul) is the part of the embryo below the point of attachment of the cotyledons but above the radicle. The **radicle** (RAD uh kul) is the lowermost part of the embryo, the embryonic root. In some plants, the stem forms entirely from the epicotyl, and the roots are formed from the hypocotyl and radicle. In other plants, the hypocotyl gives rise to the lower part of the stem, while the radicle gives rise to the roots.

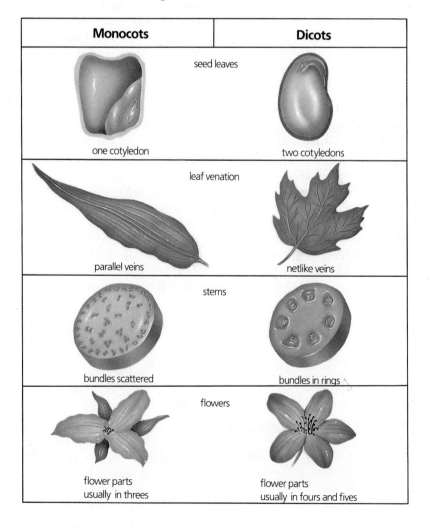

Monocots	Dicots
seed leaves	
one cotyledon	two cotyledons
leaf venation	
parallel veins	netlike veins
stems	
bundles scattered	bundles in rings
flowers	
flower parts usually in threes	flower parts usually in fours and fives

◀ **Figure 24–16**
Comparison of Monocots and Dicots.

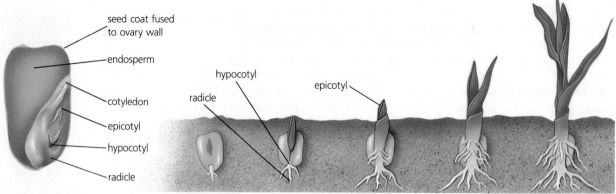

▲ **Figure 24–17**
Development of a Corn Seedling.

In a developing corn seedling, for example, the epicotyl gives rise to the stem and leaves, while the hypocotyl and radicle give rise to the roots. Figure 24–17 shows the development of a corn plant. Each kernel of corn is a single-seeded fruit. The embryo is partially surrounded by endosperm. The cotyledon stores food.

In the bean seed, which is a dicot, two large cotyledons make up most of the embryo. See Figure 24–18. In the mature bean seed, there is no endosperm, and nutrients are stored only in the cotyledons. In the developing bean seedling, the epicotyl gives rise to the terminal bud, the leaves, and the upper part of the stem. The hypocotyl gives rise to the lower part of the stem, and the radicle gives rise to the roots.

Seed Dispersal

The scattering, or dispersal, of seeds from the parent plant is important to the survival of the species. Plants that grow too close together must compete for water, minerals, and sunlight. Therefore, adaptations for seed dispersal help plants to survive. In some plants, pressure develops within the drying fruit. When the fruit bursts, seeds are released with enough force to scatter them over a large area. The snapdragon shows this type of dispersal. Many seeds and single-seeded fruits, such as those of milkweed, maple, and dandelion, are extremely light. These types of seeds can be carried great distances by the wind. Others, such as the coconut, float and are carried by water. Some seeds or fruits, such as those of

Figure 24–18
Development of a Bean Seedling. ▼

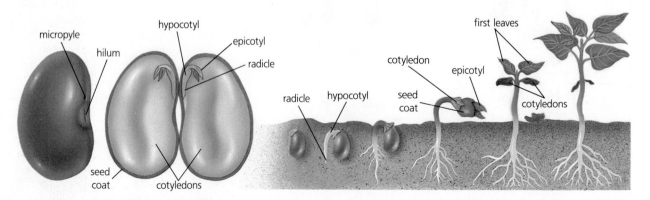

sandbur and wild carrot, have burs or hooks. When an animal brushes against them, they become attached to the fur of the animal, and they are carried away from the parent plant. Sweet, fleshy fruits are often eaten by birds and mammals. The seeds, which are usually indigestible, are later deposited elsewhere along with other digestive wastes.

Seed Dormancy

For a seed to begin to sprout, or germinate, it needs water, oxygen, and the proper temperature. Some seeds also require light. Many seeds go through a resting period before they begin to grow. During this time, growth is slowed, or stops altogether, and the seed is said to be in a state of **dormancy** (DOR mun see). The dormant seed will not sprout even if conditions are favorable. The length of the dormant period varies with the type of plant. Even within a single species, individual seeds show different lengths of dormancy. Some seeds may begin to grow after one year, some after two or three years, and so on. This characteristic is useful for the survival of the species, because not all the seeds will be killed by unusually harsh conditions during a given year.

There are several ways in which dormancy is brought about. In some species, dormancy occurs because the seed coat does not allow water and/or oxygen to reach the embryo. In others, the seed coat is so strong that the embryo cannot break through it. In still others, the embryo must undergo further development before growth can occur. Sometimes, chemical inhibitors that are present prevent germination. When dormancy is caused by the toughness of the seed coat, it lasts until the seed coat decays or is broken down enough for germination to occur. With immature embryos and chemical inhibitors, a certain amount of time must pass either for the embryo to mature or for the chemicals to break down.

In many species native to areas that have cold winters, seed dormancy is broken by a combination of exposure to low temperatures and moisture. Such a system makes sure that germination will happen only after the harsh conditions of winter have passed. Thus, the seeds will germinate in the spring, and the seedlings will have the whole growing season in which to complete their development.

24-3 Section Review

1. What kind of fruit develops from a single ovary?
2. What is a plant that has seeds with two cotyledons called?
3. What three parts of the embryo form the stem and roots?
4. How are the seeds of a dandelion dispersed?

Critical Thinking

5. What general characteristic would you expect the seed coat of a seed from a sweet, fleshy fruit to have? (*Predicting*)

Biology and You

Q: Every spring, I have sneezing fits because of hay fever. What causes hay fever?

A: Sneezing fits, itching eyes, runny nose, wheezing, all are symptoms of hay fever. Hay fever is an allergic response to pollen grains. During certain seasons, trees, flowers, shrubs, and grasses release pollen. If you are allergic to pollen, your body responds with the symptoms of hay fever.

People develop allergies because their bodies react to some substance. In the case of hay fever, your immune system releases antibodies to fight the invading pollen grains. As part of this response, certain immune cells release histamine, which causes sneezing, wheezing, and itching.

Having hay fever is like being allergic to the air you breathe. It is almost impossible to avoid breathing in pollen. Staying indoors can help. Also, you can avoid woods and fields where the pollen count is highest. A doctor may recommend antihistamines or decongestants to relieve symptoms. Serious cases of hay fever may require allergy shots.

■ *Interview some people who have hay fever. Questions should include: "When do you get it?" "What are the symptoms?" and "What do you do for relief?"*

Laboratory
Investigation

Structure of a Pea Pod

After pollination occurs, the ovary of a fruit matures into a fruit containing seeds. A pea pod meets this description, even though it usually is not thought of as a fruit. Peas and their pods usually are consumed before they mature and dry, so people rarely see their natural development. Similar to other fruits, the pea pod develops from a flower, and parts of the flower can still be identified after pollination. In this investigation, you will observe the features of the pea pod that are flower remnants and study how seeds form.

Problem

What are the parts of a fruit that are important to its reproduction? **Observe** a pea pod to help you answer this question.

Materials (per group)

- pea pod (or string bean or lima bean pod)
- soaked pea
- hand lens
- scalpel or razor blade
- dissecting needle

Procedure

1. With a hand lens, examine the external appearance of the pea pod. Record your observations.

2. Find the stalk that attaches the pod to the plant. Locate the sepals, which are the remaining parts from the base of the flower. Record the number of sepals.

3. At the opposite end of the pod, find the remains of the style.

4. Carefully open the pod along the curved edge using the razor blade or scalpel. **CAUTION:** *Be very careful when using a sharp instrument.*

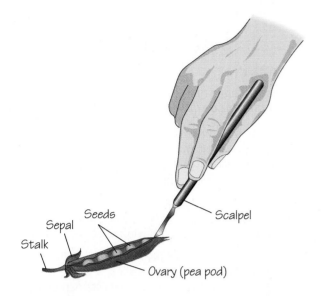

Sepal
Seeds
Stalk
Scalpel
Ovary (pea pod)

5. Count the number of peas in the pod and note their characteristics. Record the number of peas as well as your observations of their appearance.

6. Notice the fibers to which the peas are attached by a short stalk. Record the number of fibers you see.

7. Obtain a soaked pea and examine it. Locate the scar that shows where the pea was attached to the pod.

8. Using the dissecting needle, carefully remove the seed coat from the pea.

9. Separate the cotyledons. Use a hand lens to observe the embryo plant.

Observations

1. Describe the external appearance of the pea pod.

2. How many sepals does the pea pod have?

3. Are all the pea seeds attached to the same side of the pod?

4. Are all the peas alike?

5. Draw a sketch of the embryo plant of the soaked pea and label its parts.

Analysis and Conclusions

1. Based on your observations of the number of sepals and cotyledons present, classify the pea as a monocot or a dicot.

2. How do you explain any differences among the peas?

3. What is the function of the stalk that attaches the pea to the pod?

4. What reproductive structure does the pod represent?

5. Based on the color of the pea pod, can you identify one of the processes it carries out?

Extensions

Examine a tomato, a squash, and a pepper. Are these fruits? Give evidence to support your answer. For the plants that are fruits, count the seeds and make sketches of what you see.

Chapter 24 Review ....

Study Outline

24-1 Life Cycles of Nonseed Plants

▶ The life cycle of plants alternates between a multi-cellular diploid generation, the sporophyte, and a multicellular haploid generation, the gametophyte.

▶ Sporophytes produce haploid spores by meiosis. The spores develop into haploid gametophytes, which produce haploid gametes. Fused gametes develop into diploid sporophytes.

▶ In mosses, the gametophyte is the dominant generation. In ferns, the sporophyte generation is dominant. In mosses and ferns, water is required for fertilization.

24-2 Life Cycles of Seed Plants

▶ In seed plants, the gymnosperms and angiosperms, the sporophyte is dominant, and water is not required for fertilization.

▶ Fertilization in gymnosperms occurs when the pollen tube grows into the female gametophyte within an ovule and releases a sperm that fuses with an egg to form a zygote. The ovule develops into a seed.

▶ In the flowers of angiosperms, stamens produce spores that develop into male gametophytes, or pollen grains. Pistils produce spores that develop into female gametophytes inside ovules.

▶ Pollination in angiosperms may be by wind, animals, or water. Fertilization in angiosperms occurs when the pollen tube reaches the female gametophyte and releases two sperm nuclei. One fuses with the egg, forming the zygote, and the other fuses with the two polar nuclei, forming the endosperm nucleus. The endosperm nucleus develops into the endosperm.

24-3 Fruits and Seeds

▶ The ovules of a flower develop into seeds, and the ovary, which encloses the seeds, develops into the fruit.

▶ An angiosperm seed has a seed coat, embryo, and endosperm. The embryo consists of an epicotyl, cotyledon, hypocotyl, and radicle.

Chapter Assessment

Multiple Choice

Choose the letter of the answer that best completes each statement or answers the question.

1. Green algae are related to plants because they (a) live on land. (b) are protists. (c) have reproductive cycles that are similar to those of plants. (d) are multicellular organisms.

2. Moss sperm and eggs form a zygote that grows into a (a) capsule. (b) gametophyte. (c) zoospore. (d) sporophyte.

3. The male and female reproductive structures of a flower are the (a) corolla and calyx. (b) receptacle and cotyledon. (c) stamen and pistil. (d) sepals and petals.

4. In flowering plants, pollen formation occurs in the (a) filament. (b) anther. (c) ovule. (d) pistil.

5. Where does germination of pollen grains normally occur? (a) on the anther (b) on the stigma (c) in the ovary (d) in the ovule

6. Self-pollination can be prevented by removing the flower's (a) anthers. (b) petals. (c) sepals. (d) epicotyls.

7. Sperm nuclei must travel from the stigma of a flower to the ovule that it enters through the (a) oviduct. (b) micropyle. (c) stomate. (d) pollen tube.

8. Which of the following occurs during pollination of a flowering plant? (a) fertilization (b) cleavage of the zygote (c) formation of an endosperm nucleus (d) transfer of pollen from an anther to a stigma

9. A fruit develops from the (a) ovary and associated parts. (b) cotyledons. (c) endosperm nucleus. (d) receptacle.

10. Which three conditions are necessary for most plant seeds to germinate? (a) light, proper temperature, fertile soil (b) oxygen, carbon dioxide, proper temperature (c) fertile soil, oxygen, light (d) water, proper temperature, oxygen

Content Review

Answer each of the following in complete sentences.

11. Explain alternation of generations.

12. What is unique about the life cycle of *Ulva*?

13. Compare the gametophytes and sporophytes of mosses and ferns.

14. Describe the life cycle of gymnosperms.

15. What is the difference between a pistillate and a staminate flower?

16. Explain what is meant by self-pollination and cross-pollination.

17. Describe double fertilization in flowering plants.

18. How is reproduction in seed plants adapted for life on land?

19. Name and explain the function of the three basic parts of an angiosperm seed.

20. Draw and label the parts of a plant embryo. Into which mature plant part(s) does each develop?

Graphic Organizing

For information on graphic organizers, see Appendix G at the back of this text.

21. **Concept Map** Copy the unfinished concept map onto a separate sheet of paper. Add the following concepts where they best fit: anther, corolla, ovary, sepals, stamens, stigma, and style.

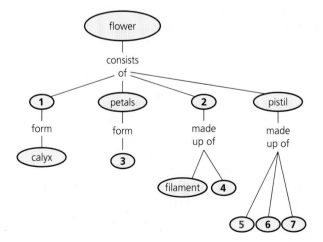

Critical Thinking and Problem Solving

Discuss each of the following in a brief paragraph.

22. **Relating** What part of the angiosperm female gametophyte (embryo sac) probably represents an archegonium?

23. **Comparing** How are the gametes produced by a gametophyte different from the gametes produced by an animal?

24. **Drawing conclusions** Explain why the cells of the endosperm could not undergo meiosis to produce haploid gametes.

25. **Classifying** Suppose you found a small, multicellular, green organism growing on the forest floor. How could you determine whether it is a gametophyte or a sporophyte?

26. **Drawing conclusions** You observe that all the flowers on a garden plant lack anthers. On another plant of the same species, you observe that all the flowers have anthers. What conclusion can you make about the plants' method of sexual reproduction? Does this method offer any advantages?

27. **Inferring** The seeds of maple trees are attached to long, thin, fibrous structures that act as wings. Why would seeds with wings be advantageous to maple trees?

Performance-Based Assessment

Hazardous Substances and Birth Defects

Background

Throughout the world, chemicals have come to play an important role in industry, agriculture, and the lives of every person. Over 70 000 different chemicals are used each day and each year about 1000 new compounds are synthesized. The United States disposes of 270 million tons of hazardous and toxic substances each year. Hazardous and toxic substances are chemicals that can affect human health and the environment.

Despite the threat posed by toxic substances, few people were aware of them until two tragedies occurred. In the 1960s, doctors in Europe were greatly alarmed by the huge increase in a rare birth abnormality in which children were born without arms or legs but with their hands and feet attached directly to the body. Physicians discovered that 40% of women who had taken thalidomide, a tranquilizer, during the first three months of pregnancy delivered babies with this condition. The sale of thalidomide was blocked in the United States because its safety in pregnant animals could not be proven.

In the late 1970s, the threat of a leaking hazardous waste site made news when the residents of Love Canal, a New York State community, began to notice a high incidence of cancers, miscarriages, and birth defects. Persistent efforts by concerned citizens forced a government investigation. The investigation revealed that the groundwater, basements, sewers, yards, and gardens of Love Canal were all seriously contaminated by toxic substances because the community had been built on top of a toxic waste dump.

After the Love Canal incident, many communities across the country learned that they too were at risk from improperly maintained hazardous and toxic waste dumps. In response to these findings, the federal government passed a law in 1980, commonly called the Superfund Law, for cleaning up hazardous waste sites. The Environmental Protection Agency (EPA) manages the Superfund. If a site poses potential harm to human or environmental health, the EPA can use Superfund money to remove hazardous substances, incinerate the contaminated soil or debris, and take measures to protect the public health. Unfortunately, it is estimated that there are over 30 000 potential sites that need to be cleaned up at an estimated cost of $30 billion to $500 billion.

Humans and other living things are more sensitive to environmental influences during the early stages of fetal development than they are at any other time in their lives. The table shown on the next page lists some known teratogens—substances that cause birth defects. These substances can cross the placenta and cause serious or fatal birth defects. Fetal vulnerability to teratogens depends on the stage of development at the time of exposure. The most sensitive period is the time of tissue and organ formation, a period lasting from about the 18th day after conception to approximately the 60th day. During this time, interference with development can result in structural defects. During the first week after conception, exposure to a teratogen would be fatal to the developing embryo. Exposure to teratogens after the eighth week can cause blindness or mental retardation.

Data Table: Some Known Teratogens

Teratogen	Effects
Drugs and Chemicals	
Thalidomide	Serious birth defects
DES (diethylstilbestrol)	Vaginal cancer in young women; genital abnormalities in men
Alcohol	Mental retardation, growth deficiencies, facial irregularities
Anesthesia	Miscarriages, structural deformities
Dilantin	Heart defects, cleft palate, hare lip
Valproic acid	Mental retardation, small brain
Actane	Cardiovascular abnormalities, deformed ear, small brain
Cigarette smoke	Low birth weight, miscarriage, stillbirth
Methyl mercury	Mental retardation, sensory and motor problems
Pathogens	
Rubella (German measles)	Heart defects, deafness, cataracts
Syphilis	Mental retardation, small brain
Herpes simplex (type 2)	Mental retardation, small brain
Ionizing Radiation	
X-rays, gamma rays	Nervous system disorders, small brain, eye problems, mental retardation

Problem

You have been invited to be a guest on a television talk show as part of a panel discussion on hazardous substances and birth defects. Choose one member of your class to serve as host, and two or three others to act as part of the panel. The rest of the class will represent the audience.

Task

Choose one of the following tasks.

1. The producer of the show has given you a list of questions that you will be asked to address.

   - Should every new chemical and product be tested as a possible teratogen?
   - How are new products tested for their potential to cause birth defects?
   - Are procedures for testing the safety of new drugs and chemicals thorough enough?
   - What are some ethical issues involved in product testing?
   - What is the purpose of a risk/benefit analysis? Do the benefits of certain products outweigh their risks?
   - Are the government's hazardous waste cleanup efforts succeeding?

2. With your fellow panel members, prepare a position paper in which you take a stand on each of the questions and defend your position. Reference materials, including Internet sources, should be listed in the bibliography. Your panel will be asked to reply to questions from the host as well as from members of the audience.

A colorful array of parakeets.

Discovery Learning Activity

Nature or Nurture?

1. Working in a group, brainstorm for a list of 15 human traits. Record these traits on a separate sheet of paper.

2. Next to each trait on your list, indicate whether you think it is inherited or influenced by the environment. Provide support for your choice.

3. Share your list with other groups. Create a class list. Revisit the list after you have completed this unit and revise it if necessary.

Mendelian Genetics

················· **Guide** *for Reading* ·················

Previewing the Chapter

A family of cheetahs relaxes on a quiet afternoon. Each cheetah surveys the horizon with the same confident, watchful gaze. Look closely and family resemblances become clear. Compare the shape of their heads and the pattern of black markings. Family members often look alike, but why? How are traits passed from parents to offspring? What laws govern how traits are inherited?

Key Words

allele, dominant, gene, genotype, heterozygous, homozygous, phenotype, recessive

Key Concepts

- **Identify** the basic principles of heredity.
- **State** the law of probability.
- **Observe** the differences among fingerprints of several people. (Laboratory Investigation)

25-1 Mendel's Principles of Heredity

Section Objectives:

- *Describe* the experimental procedures that were used by Gregor Mendel.
- *State* and *give* an example of Mendel's law of dominance and his law of segregation.
- *Explain* Mendel's law of segregation in terms of chromosomes and meiosis.

The Study of Heredity

In sexual reproduction, the new individual develops from a single cell—the zygote—which was formed by the union of two gametes, one contributed by each parent. The chromosomes of each gamete bring hereditary material to the new cell. This hereditary material controls the development and characteristics of the embryo, as well as determining the features of the adult organism. Because the hereditary material comes from two different parents, the offspring is similar to both parents in some ways but differs from both parents in other ways. The offspring has all the common characteristics of its species, but it also has its own distinct, individual characteristics that make it different from all other members of the species.

▲ **Figure 25–1**

Parent and Offspring. The white coloring of polar bears is hereditary. All offspring inherit traits from their parents.

◄ A family of cheetahs on the plains of Kenya.

Figure 25–2

Sugar Pea Flowers. The pea plant was the experimental subject in the first scientific study of heredity. ▶

Genetics (juh NET iks) is the branch of biology that studies the ways in which hereditary information is passed on from parents to offspring. The first scientific study of heredity was carried out by Gregor Mendel (MEN dul) in the 1800s, before much was known about either chromosomes or cell division.

Mendel's Experiments

Gregor Mendel was a monk who was interested in mathematics and science. Mendel lived in a monastery in the town of Brünn in what is now Czechoslovakia. For a while, he taught science at the local high school. From 1857 to 1865, Mendel investigated the inheritance of certain traits in pea plants grown in the monastery garden. After many experiments, Mendel arrived at some basic principles of heredity that are still accepted today.

Pea plants were a good choice for Mendel's investigations. They are easy to grow, and they mature quickly. Different plants show sharply contrasting traits. For example, some are tall; some are short. Some have green pods; some have yellow pods. Each pair of traits is easily seen. In addition, the structure of the pea flower and its natural method of pollination make it easy to use in controlled experiments. Pea flowers normally self-pollinate because the stigma and anthers are enclosed by the petals, as you can see in Figure 25–2. This reduces cross-pollination in nature. By removing the stamens before they ripened, Mendel could prevent self-pollination and cross-pollinate the flower by dusting pollen from another plant onto the stigma. If he wanted certain plants to self-pollinate in the normal way, he left them alone.

Mendel kept careful records of what he did to each generation of plants. He collected the seeds from each experimental cross, and then he planted them in a definite place so that he could see the

Figure 25–3

Seven Traits Studied by Mendel. Mendel used pea plants to study seven pairs of contrasting traits. ▼

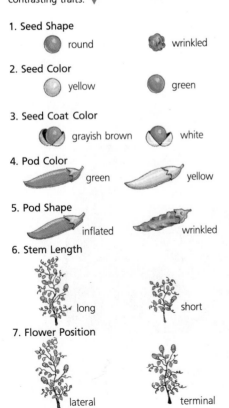

1. Seed Shape
   round   wrinkled

2. Seed Color
   yellow   green

3. Seed Coat Color
   grayish brown   white

4. Pod Color
   green   yellow

5. Pod Shape
   inflated   wrinkled

6. Stem Length
   long   short

7. Flower Position
   lateral   terminal

results. Mendel made a careful count of each type of offspring, and he used mathematics to understand the results. It was this use of mathematics that allowed him to draw the important conclusions that he did.

Mendel wrote a paper about his discoveries. It was published in the journal of his local scientific society and sent to other scientific organizations and libraries. Other scientists, however, do not seem to have understood its importance at the time. Mendel died in 1884, without receiving recognition for his discoveries. In 1900, however, three European scientists, all working separately, reached the same conclusions about heredity that Mendel had. Before they published their works, they read through the past scientific literature and found Mendel's papers. They gave him credit for his discoveries, and Mendel finally received the recognition he deserved.

The Law of Dominance

Mendel noticed that pea plants have certain traits that come in two forms. For example, plants are either tall or short, seeds are either yellow or green, and so on. In his experiments, Mendel studied seven pairs of contrasting traits. See Figure 25–3.

Mendel discovered that some plants "bred true" for a certain trait. For example, when short plants were allowed to self-pollinate through several generations, the offspring were always short. Mendel considered these plants to be pure for shortness. In his experiments, Mendel always started with plants that he knew were pure for the trait in which he was interested.

Mendel then wanted to find out what would happen if he cross-pollinated pure plants with contrasting traits. To do this, he stopped self-pollination by removing the stamens from a plant that was pure for one trait. He pollinated that plant with pollen from a plant that was pure for the contrasting trait. For example, he pollinated short plants with pollen from tall ones, and he pollinated tall plants with pollen from short ones. In these experiments, the pure plants made up the **parent, or P, generation.** Mendel collected the seeds produced by this cross-pollination, planted them, and allowed them to grow. Mendel found that all the offspring of this cross were tall. See Figure 25–4. That is, the short trait seemed to have disappeared in the **first filial, or F₁, generation.** The same kinds of results were obtained for all seven of the pairs of contrasting traits that Mendel investigated. The offspring of crosses between pure parents showing contrasting traits are called **hybrids.** In Mendel's experiments, the hybrids showed only one of the contrasting traits and not the other.

Mendel wanted to know if the trait of shortness had been lost forever as a result of the cross. To answer this question, he allowed the hybrid plants of the F₁ generation to self-pollinate. See Figure 25–5. When their seeds were planted and grown, about three-fourths of the offspring were tall and about one-fourth were short. The offspring of the self-pollinated hybrids made up the **F₂ (second**

Figure 25–4
A Cross of Pure Tall and Pure Short Pea Plants. All offspring in the first filial (F₁) generation are tall. ▼

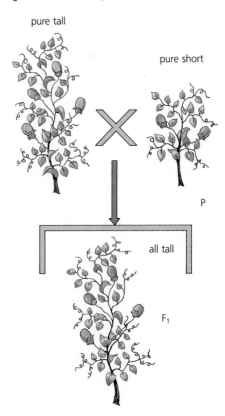

pure tall

pure short

P

all tall

F₁

Figure 25–5

A Cross of the Hybrid Plants of the F₁ Generation. In a cross of the F₁ generation, about three-fourths of the second filial (F₂) generation are tall, and one-fourth are short. ▶

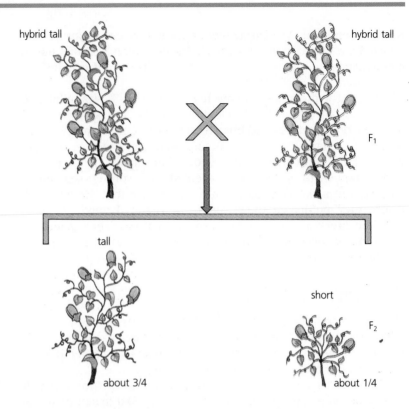

hybrid tall

hybrid tall

F₁

tall

short

F₂

about 3/4

about 1/4

filial) **generation.** The appearance of short plants in the F₂ generation showed that the factor that determined shortness was still present in the F₁ generation.

Mendel described the traits that were expressed in the F₁ generation as **dominant** and the traits that were hidden in the F₁ generation as **recessive.** He concluded that *when an organism is hybrid for a pair of contrasting traits, only the dominant trait can be seen in the hybrid.* This is called the **law of dominance.**

The Law of Segregation

Mendel tried to explain why the recessive trait disappeared in one generation and appeared again in the next generation. He hypothesized that each trait in an individual was controlled by a pair of "factors." (Remember that in Mendel's time, the role of chromosomes and genes in heredity was not known.) Mendel also hypothesized that a factor could be one of two kinds. There was, for example, a factor for tallness and another factor for shortness. The factors in a pair could be alike or different. In a cross, the offspring received one factor from each parent. Thus, in a cross between a tall plant and a short plant, the offspring received both kinds of factors. However, only the dominant factor was expressed. The recessive factor was hidden.

Because the factor for shortness was still present in these tall plants, it was possible for the factor to show itself in the later generations. This would happen when fertilization brought two shortness factors together in the same seed. The idea that *factors that occur in pairs are separated from each other during gamete formation and recombined at fertilization is called Mendel's* **law of segregation.**

The Gene-Chromosome Theory

The importance of Mendel's work may have been overlooked in the mid-1800s because little was known about chromosomes, mitosis, and meiosis. When Mendel's research was rediscovered in 1900, however, much more had been learned about cells. Chromosomes had been stained and observed in cells, and the processes of mitosis and meiosis had been described in detail.

The idea that Mendel's "factors" might be carried by homologous chromosomes was suggested first in 1903 by an American graduate student, W. S. Sutton. Sutton was studying the formation of sperm in the grasshopper. He observed the pairs of homologous chromosomes in diploid cells and the separation of the homologous chromosomes during spermatogenesis. He realized that the chromosomes that separated during meiosis were the same as the chromosomes that had united during the fertilization process that had originally produced the animal. After reviewing Mendel's work, Sutton began to think that the factors of Mendel's theory were carried on the chromosomes. Figure 25–6 shows how Sutton's chromosome theory would apply to a Mendelian cross of two tall hybrid plants.

As you can see in Figure 25–6, the separation of homologous chromosome pairs during meiosis and their recombination during fertilization would account for the separation and recombination of the Mendelian factors.

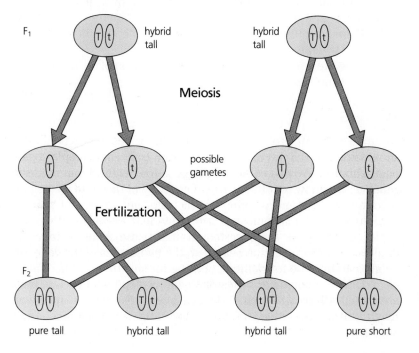

◄ **Figure 25–6**

The Gene-Chromosome Theory. T represents the factor for tallness and t the factor for shortness. Each factor is on a homologous chromosome. When the pairs of homologous chromosomes separate during gamete formation, they form two kinds of gametes: one with T, and the other with t. During fertilization, the chromosomes recombine.

Following the publication of Sutton's paper, titled "The Chromosomes in Heredity," in 1903, many experiments showed that this hypothesis was correct. At that time, the term **gene** was used in place of Mendel's "factor." Research showed not only that chromosomes carry genes but also that the genes are in a definite order along each chromosome. This work led to the modern gene-chromosome theory of heredity, which is discussed in detail in Chapter 26.

25-1 Section Review

1. Why are pea plants a good choice for genetic experiments?
2. What is a hybrid, and what is a dominant trait?
3. State Mendel's law of segregation.
4. What idea did Sutton propose?

Critical Thinking

5. What assumptions did Mendel make when he simply left plants alone that he wanted to self-pollinate? (*Identifying Assumptions*)

25-2 Fundamentals of Genetics

Section Objectives:

- *Define* the terms *alleles, homozygous, heterozygous, genotype,* and *phenotype.*
- *State* the law of probability, and explain how it applies to Mendel's experimental results.
- *Use* Punnett squares to work out the possible results of various types of genetic crosses.
- *Describe* the procedure for a test cross, and explain the significance of the results.

Alleles

To agree with Mendel's findings, each body cell of an organism should have two copies of the gene for each trait. For example, a pea plant should have two copies of the gene for height. From modern genetics, we know that this is true. One copy of the gene for height is found at the same position on each chromosome of a pair of homologous chromosomes. In an individual organism, the two copies of the gene for a certain trait may be alike or may be different. For example, in a pea plant, the two copies of the gene for height can both be for tallness, both be for shortness, or be one of each. Different copies or forms of a gene controlling a certain trait are called **alleles** (uh LEELZ). In pea plants, the gene controlling height exists as either an allele for tallness or an allele for shortness.

If the alleles for a certain trait in an organism are the same, the organism is said to be **homozygous** (hoh muh ZY gus) for that trait. For example, a pea plant that is homozygous for tallness would have two copies of the gene for tallness. If the alleles are different, the organism is said to be **heterozygous** (het uh roh ZY gous). Therefore, a pea plant that is heterozygous for tallness has one gene for tallness and one for shortness. Homozygous means *pure*. Heterozygous means *hybrid*.

Genotypes and Phenotypes

When writing about alleles, a capital letter is used for the allele for a dominant trait. For example, the allele for tallness is represented by the symbol T. A lowercase letter is used for the contrasting recessive allele. Therefore, the allele for shortness is represented by the symbol t.

A pure tall pea plant has two alleles for tallness. Its genetic makeup is represented as TT. The genetic makeup of a pure short plant is tt, while that of a hybrid is Tt. The genetic makeup of an organism is called its **genotype** (JEE nuh typ). The physical trait that an organism develops as the result of its genotype is called its **phenotype** (FEE nuh typ). It is possible for two different individuals to have the same phenotype but different genotypes. A pure tall plant and a hybrid tall plant have the same phenotype (both are tall), but they have different genotypes (TT for the pure plant and Tt for the hybrid). See Figure 25–7. An organism that shows a recessive trait is always homozygous for that trait. Thus, a short pea plant will have two copies of the gene for shortness (tt).

Probability in Genetics

Mendel's experiments involved hundreds of plants. He arrived at the laws of dominance and segregation by counting many, many offspring. To explain the *numerical* results of Mendel's experiments, you must understand the laws of chance. For example, if you toss a penny, you know that the chance of its turning up heads is 1 out of 2, or ½. If you toss the coin 100 times, you expect to get about 50 heads and 50 tails. That is, you expect to get about 1 head for every 1 tail. This can be expressed as a ratio of 1:1, or 1 head: 1 tail. In any real trial, the ratio of heads to tails is rarely exactly 1:1. In a short trial, say, 4 tosses, you might even get all heads or all tails. However, if you made a large number of tosses, 1000 or more for example, you would expect the ratio of heads to tails to be quite close to 1:1. Experiments have shown that the larger the number of trials, the closer the ratio comes to the expected value. This assumes, of course, that there is nothing special about the coin or the way in which it is tossed that would make one side *more likely* to turn up than the other.

Consider another example—the rolling of dice (singular, die). When a die is rolled, each face is as likely as any other to turn up. If you roll the die 600 times, you would expect to get about 100 of each face: 100 1's, 100 2's, 100 3's, and so on.

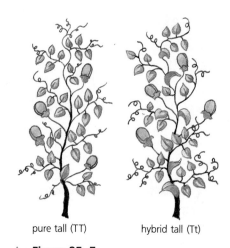

pure tall (TT)   hybrid tall (Tt)

▲ **Figure 25–7**

Phenotype and Genotype. Although both of these pea plants have the same phenotype (tall), they have different genotypes (TT or Tt).

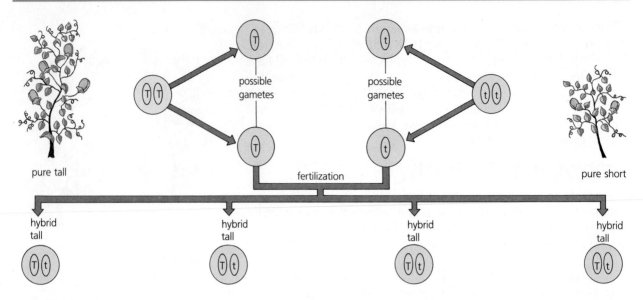

pure tall   possible gametes   possible gametes   pure short

fertilization

hybrid tall   hybrid tall   hybrid tall   hybrid tall

▲ **Figure 25–8**
Genetic Explanation of the Formation of Hybrids.

These are examples of the basic **law of probability,** or chance: If there are several possible events that might happen, and no one of them is more likely to happen than any other, then they will all happen in equal numbers over a large number of trials. This law allows you to predict the results of breeding experiments like those of Mendel. However, these predictions apply only when large numbers of individuals are involved.

The Punnett Square

Consider how alleles separate during meiosis and then recombine during fertilization, when a pure tall pea plant is crossed with a pure short plant. The body cells of the tall plant have two alleles for tallness. Their genotype is TT. When gametes form in this plant, each gamete receives one T allele. The genetic makeup of each gamete can be shown by the single letter T. See Figure 25–8. The cells of the short plant have two alleles for the recessive trait of shortness. Their genotype is tt, and the genotype of the gametes is t. Since each parent plant is homozygous, its gametes all contain the same allele.

Suppose that we transfer pollen from the tall plant to the pistil of a short plant. Each sperm cell nucleus will be carrying one T allele. The egg cell in each ovule of the short plant will contain one t allele. When fertilization takes place, the zygotes will receive one T allele and one t allele, and their genotype will be Tt. The plants that grow from these zygotes will be hybrid tall.

A diagram called a **Punnett square** is a helpful way to show the results of any cross. The Punnett square for the cross we have just discussed is shown in Figure 25–9. In this diagram, the alleles of the possible male gametes are written at the heads of the columns of boxes. The alleles of the possible female gametes are written at the sides of the rows of boxes. (The positions of the male and

Figure 25–9

Punnett Square for Cross of Pure Dominant (Tall) with Pure Recessive (Short). ▼

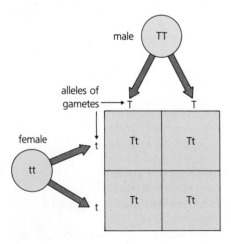

male   TT

alleles of gametes ⟶ T   T

female

tt

	T	T
t	Tt	Tt
t	Tt	Tt

female gametes can be interchanged.) Each box contains the genotype of the zygote that forms when the allele at the top of the column and the allele at the left of the row are brought together at fertilization.

In this case, there is only one combination of alleles. All the zygotes are alike. The results are 100% hybrid tall (Tt).

The Punnett Square for a Hybrid Cross

A Punnett square is even more useful for a more complicated case in which hybrid tall plants either self-pollinate or are cross-pollinated. The genotype of the tall hybrids is Tt. Because they contain two different alleles for plant height, they produce two types of gametes—one type with T and the other with t. Since the T and t alleles are present in equal numbers, the two types of gametes

MiniLab

Skill: Classifying

You and Your Genes

Problem

How can you **classify** the genotypes and phenotypes for six traits that you display?

Procedure

1. Classify your phenotype as either dominant or recessive for each of the traits described below.

   a. The presence of freckles is dominant. The absence of freckles is recessive.

   b. Free ear lobes are dominant. Ear lobes that are attached directly to the side of the head are recessive.

   c. Individuals having curly hair have at least one dominant allele. People having straight hair have the recessive allele.

   d. Individuals who have hair on the middle joints of their fingers have at least one dominant allele. Those who have two recessive alleles do not have hair on those joints.

   e. A widow's peak is a hairline that forms a downward point in the middle of the forehead. This is caused by a dominant allele. A smooth hairline is the recessive trait.

   f. Long eyelashes are the dominant trait. Short eyelashes are recessive.

2. Poll the class to find out how many students display each phenotype.

Analyze and Conclude

1. For which traits do you have the dominant phenotype? For which traits do you have the recessive phenotype?

2. For which traits can you determine your genotype? Explain your answer.

3. Is the dominant form of a trait necessarily more common than the recessive form? Explain your answer.

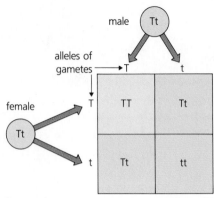

Expected Phenotypes
3/4 tall
1/4 short

Expected Genotypes
1/4 TT
1/2 Tt
1/4 tt

▲ **Figure 25–10**

Punnett Square for Crossing Two Hybrids. Of the offspring produced, about one-fourth should be pure tall (TT), one-half hybrid tall (Tt), and one-fourth short (tt).

Can You Explain This?

Father ● Bb

sperm Ⓑ   ⓑ

eggs

Mother Ⓑ | BB | Bb

Bb ⓑ | Bb | bb

A brown-eyed couple, both heterozygous for eye color (Bb), have three brown-eyed children and are expecting a fourth child. The mother insists that the child she is carrying will have blue eyes. She draws a Punnett square (see above) to back up her belief.

■ *Do you agree with the mother? What do you think are the chances of the fourth child having blue eyes? Explain.*

are produced in equal numbers. This is true for both male and female gametes, and it is an important fact for the discussion that follows.

The Punnett square for the fertilizations that take place between these gametes is shown in Figure 25–10. Each letter at the head of a column stands for one type of male gamete that is formed. Each letter at the left of a row stands for one type of female gamete. Remember that these types of gametes are produced in equal numbers.

Each box in the diagram stands for a possible union of a male gamete with a female gamete. Since the types of gametes are present in equal numbers, each combination is just as likely to happen as any other. The law of probability tells us that each of the four zygotes is equally likely to appear if there is a large number of pollinations and fertilizations.

The Punnett square shows the four possible combinations. Given a large number of fertilizations, all four combinations should happen in about equal numbers. Among a large number of offspring, you would expect about ¼ to be TT (pure tall), about ½ (¼ + ¼) to be Tt (hybrid tall), and ¼ to be tt (pure short). Therefore, the genotype offspring expected ratio would be 1:2:1. In terms of the way they appear, or phenotype, about ¾ would be tall and ¼ would be short. Thus, the expected phenotype ratio of the offspring of this cross would be about 3:1 (3 tall to 1 short).

You can see that the law of probability, combined with a Punnett square, allows you to explain the results that Mendel got with his experimental crosses.

The Test Cross

As you now know, it is not possible to tell from appearance alone whether an individual showing a dominant trait is pure for the trait (homozygous) or hybrid (heterozygous). Breeders often need to know the genotypes of plants and animals. A test cross can be used to find out.

In a **test cross,** an individual of unknown genotype is mated with an individual showing the contrasting recessive trait. The genotype of the individual showing the recessive trait must be homozygous. The genotype of the individual with the unknown genotype may be homozygous or heterozygous. The test cross will show which is the case.

To understand how the test cross works, suppose a breeder wants to know whether a tall pea plant is homozygous (TT) or heterozygous (Tt). The plant with the unknown genotype is crossed, by artificial pollination, with a short plant, which must be homozygous (tt). The Punnett squares in Figure 25–11 show the results of the two possible cases.

You can see that if the test plant is pure tall (TT), all offspring of the cross will be tall. If the test plant is heterozygous tall, half the offspring, on the average, will be short. That is, the test cross shows that the recessive allele is present in the tall parent being tested. The advantage of this method is that you do not need to test and count large numbers of phenotypes. One short offspring shows that the test plant carries one recessive allele. Thus, by crossing an individual of unknown genotype with a homozygous recessive individual and looking at the offspring, it is possible to determine whether the test individual is homozygous or heterozygous.

25-2 Section Review

1. Define the terms *allele, genotype,* and *phenotype.*
2. Why is it important to use a large number of fertilizations and offspring when studying Mendelian genetics?
3. What is a Punnett square used for?
4. How can you tell whether an organism showing a dominant trait is pure or hybrid?

Critical Thinking

5. According to the law of probability, if a coin is tossed and comes up heads 10 times in a row, what are the chances of heads coming up on toss number 11? (*Predicting*)

25-3 Other Concepts in Genetics

Section Objectives:

- *Explain* Mendel's law of independent assortment in terms of genes and meiosis.
- *Use* Punnett squares to predict the phenotype ratios in a dihybrid cross.
- *Describe* incomplete dominance, codominance, and multiple alleles and give examples of each.

The Law of Independent Assortment

The hybrid cross discussed in the last section is called a **monohybrid cross** because only one pair of contrasting traits is being studied. Mendel first experimented only with monohybrid crosses. In experiments on tallness and shortness, for example, he did not record the other traits of the plants. After a time, however, Mendel decided to follow two pairs of contrasting traits at the same time. From the experiments he did before, he knew that yellow color (Y) was dominant over green color (y) in pea seeds and that round seed shape (R) was dominant over wrinkled seeds (r). Using this information, Mendel made crosses in which he kept track of both seed color and seed shape.

   As he had done before, he started with plants that were pure, or homozygous, for these traits. For one parent, he used plants that were pure for both dominant traits. They produced yellow, round

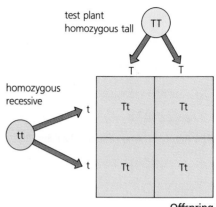

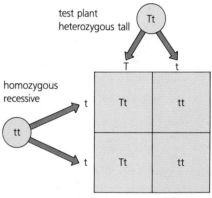

▲   **Figure 25–11**

A Test Cross. An individual showing a dominant trait is crossed with an individual showing the contrasting recessive trait. If any offspring show the recessive trait, the test individual must be hybrid.

yellow-round seeds = 315

yellow-wrinkled seeds = 101

green-round seeds = 108

green-wrinkled seeds = 32

▲ **Figure 25–12**
The Results of One of Mendel's Dihybrid Crosses.

seeds. The other parent plants were pure for both recessive traits. They produced green, wrinkled seeds. He artificially pollinated one type of plant with pollen from the other type and then observed the seeds that were produced. The results were as expected. All the seeds of the F_1 generation showed only the two dominant traits. That is, they were yellow and smooth. No green or wrinkled seeds appeared.

The next step was to plant the hybrid seeds and let the plants that grew from them self-pollinate. This would produce the F_2 generation of seeds. As expected, recessive traits appeared again in some of these seeds. Many seeds still showed both dominant traits. Some, however, were yellow and wrinkled (dominant-recessive), some were green and smooth (recessive-dominant), and a few were green and wrinkled (recessive-recessive). A breeding experiment like this one, involving two different traits, is called a **dihybrid cross.**

The data from one of Mendel's dihybrid crosses are given in Figure 25–12. Each trait considered by itself is close to the 3:1 ratio expected in a monohybrid cross. There are 416 yellow seeds and 140 green seeds. The ratio of 416 to 140 is 2.97:1, which is close to the expected 3:1 ratio. There are 423 round seeds and 133 wrinkled seeds. This ratio is 3.18:1, which is also close to 3:1. Note that there is about the same number of yellow, wrinkled seeds (dominant of one trait, recessive of the other) as green, smooth seeds (recessive of one trait, dominant of the other).

From data of this kind, Mendel concluded that different traits were inherited independently of one another. This principle is known as the **law of independent assortment.** In modern terms, this means that during meiosis, *genes for different traits are separated and distributed to gametes independently of one another.* See Figure 25–13. Today, we know that this is not always true. The reasons why are discussed in Chapter 26.

Figure 25–13

Independent Assortment. The alignment of homologous chromosomes during metaphase I of meiosis determines the combination of chromosomes in gametes. ▼

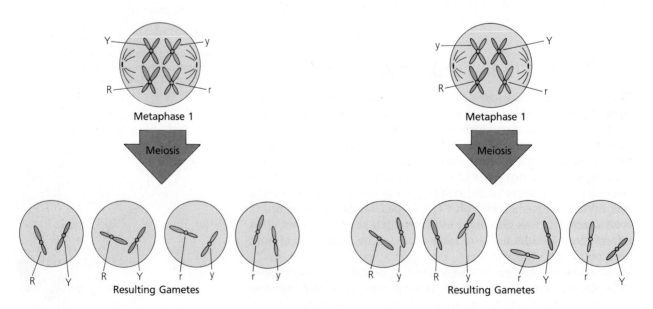

Metaphase 1

Meiosis

Resulting Gametes

Metaphase 1

Meiosis

Resulting Gametes

Phenotype Ratios in a Dihybrid Cross

With a Punnett square, you can predict the phenotype and geno-type ratios expected in a dihybrid cross. First, make the diagram for the cross between the pure dominant for both traits and the pure recessive for both traits. See Figure 25–14. Note that spaces are provided for four gametes from each parent. According to the law of independent assortment, four different but equally probable combi-nations of two alleles, one from each of the two genes involved, can end up in the same gamete. In this case, all four possible allele combinations in the gametes have the same genotype, but they are the result of four different pairings. In the second cross, this point will be important.

As you might expect, the phenotypes of the offspring in the F_1 generation are 100 percent dominant for both traits (yellow and smooth). The genotype is 100 percent hybrid for both traits (YyRr).

Now consider the Punnett square for a cross between the F_1 dihybrids. This time, the four possible gametes will be different: YR, Yr, yR, and yr. By the law of probability, there should be equal numbers of the four types of gametes. The zygotes produced by this cross are shown in Figure 25–15.

Again, by the law of probability, all 16 of the possible zygotes will be present in equal numbers. The Punnett square shows ratios of the types of offspring produced when large numbers are in-volved. The phenotypes are as follows:

- 9 yellow-round (dominant-dominant)
- 3 yellow-wrinkled (dominant-recessive)
- 3 green-round (recessive-dominant)
- 1 green-wrinkled (recessive-recessive)

This phenotype ratio of 9:3:3:1 is the ratio that is seen in dihybrid crosses when the numbers of offspring are large enough. Note that each trait considered by itself has the expected 3:1 phenotype ratio. There are 12 yellow seeds to 4 green. There are 12 round seeds to 4 wrinkled.

Incomplete Dominance

While many genes follow the patterns outlined by Mendel's laws, many do not. For example, in some organisms, both alleles contrib-ute to the phenotype of a heterozygous individual to produce a trait that is not exactly like either parent. This is known as **incomplete dominance.** For example, the inheritance of flower color in the Japanese four-o'clock plant does not follow the pattern of domi-nance. A cross between a plant with red flowers and one with white flowers produces offspring with pink flowers. See Figure 25–16. Note that genotypes for incomplete dominance can be written using the capital initial letter of each allele, since both alleles influence phenotype. In this case, red is represented by R and white by W. Individuals with red or white flowers are always homozygous (RR or WW). Individuals with a heterozygous genotype (RW) have an

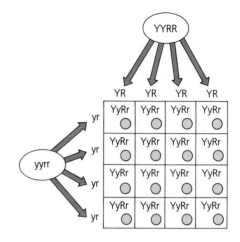

Phenotype   Genotype
100%   100%
yellow and round   hybrid for both traits

▲ **Figure 25–14**
Cross of Parents Pure for Two Contrasting Traits. All offspring are hybrid dominant for both traits.

Figure 25–15
Predicting the Results of a Dihybrid Cross. The phenotype ratios agree fairly well with Mendel's experimental results. ▼

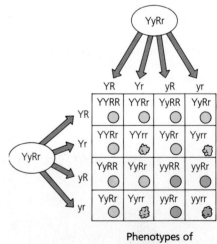

Phenotypes of
Offspring
9 yellow-round
3 yellow-wrinkled
3 green-round
1 green-wrinkled

Figure 25–16

Incomplete Dominance. The hybrids of the F₁ generation (left) show a trait different from both pure traits. When these hybrids are crossed (right), one-fourth of the offspring are pure dominant, one-fourth pure recessive, and one-half hybrid intermediate. ▶

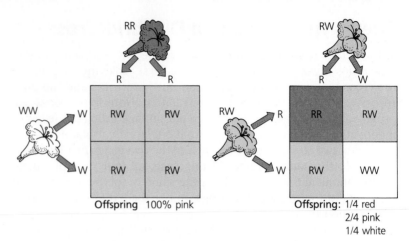

intermediate color. When two pink hybrid four-o'clocks are crossed, a 1:2:1 ratio of red to pink to white flowers is produced in the F₂ generation.

There is also a variety of chicken, called Andalusian, in which a cross between pure black and pure white chickens produces offspring that appear blue. When the blue chickens are crossed, the F₂ generation has a 1:2:1 ratio of black to blue to white chickens. When there is incomplete dominance, the F₁ generation has a phenotype different from that of either of the parents. Also, when there is incomplete dominance, the F₂ generation shows a phenotype ratio of 1:2:1 rather than the 3:1 ratio seen in normal Mendelian inheritance.

Codominance

In **codominance,** two dominant alleles are expressed at the same time. This is different from incomplete dominance, in which neither allele is completely dominant or completely hidden. One example of codominance is the roan coat in some cattle. A cross between homozygous red shorthorn cattle and homozygous white shorthorn cattle results in heterozygous offspring with a roan coat. The roan coat consists of a mixture of all red hairs and all white hairs. See Figure 25–17. Because each hair is either all red or all white, the condition shows codominance.

Capital letters with superscripts are often used to represent genotypes in codominance. For example, the symbol

Figure 25–17

Roan Coat. White hairs and red hairs in the coat of this strawberry roan horse show the full expression of each dominant allele in different hairs. ▼

C^R can represent the allele for red coat in shorthorn cattle, and the symbol C^W can represent the allele for white coat. The genotype for homozygous red coat is then symbolized as $C^R C^R$, and the genotype for homozygous white coat is $C^W C^W$. The heterozygous animal with a roan coat has a genotype of $C^R C^W$.

Codominance also occurs in human heredity. The inheritance of AB blood type is an example of codominance found in humans. Blood type inheritance is discussed in the next section.

Multiple Alleles

For some traits, there are more than two alleles in the species. They are referred to as **multiple alleles.** Although a single individual cannot have more than two alleles for each trait, different individuals can have different pairs of alleles when multiple alleles exist in a population.

The alleles for human blood type are an example of multiple alleles for a trait. The ABO blood group system is described in Chapter 10. The existence of multiple alleles explains why there are four different blood types. There are three alleles that control blood type. These alleles are called A, B, and O. O is recessive. A and B are both dominant over O, but neither one is dominant over the other. When A and B are both present in the genotype of an individual, they are codominant; that is, both alleles are expressed in the individual.

The usual way to write alleles in a multiple allele system is to use the capital letter I to show a dominant allele and the lowercase i to show a recessive allele. A superscript letter then stands for each particular dominant allele. Thus, I^A stands for the dominant allele A. I^B stands for the dominant allele B. Finally, i is understood to stand for the recessive allele O.

Since there are three alleles, there are six possible genotypes: $I^A I^A$, $I^A I^B$, $I^A i$, $I^B I^B$, $I^B i$, and ii. Figure 25–18 shows the blood types and their associated genotypes.

Rh blood factors are another example of multiple alleles in human genetics. See Chapter 10.

ABO Blood Group System

Genotype	Blood Type
$I^A I^A$ or $I^A i$	A
$I^B I^B$ or $I^B i$	B
$I^A I^B$	AB
ii	O

▲ **Figure 25–18**

Multiple Alleles in the ABO Blood Group System. I^A and I^B are each dominant over i but not over each other. When both dominant alleles are present, the blood type is AB. Type O blood is produced only when neither dominant allele is present (genotype ii).

25-3 Section Review

1. State the law of independent assortment in modern terms.
2. What phenotype ratios would you expect as the result of a dihybrid cross?
3. Give one example each of incomplete dominance and codominance.
4. Name a trait that is controlled by multiple alleles.

Critical Thinking

5. Compare and contrast incomplete dominance and codominance. (*Comparing and Contrasting*)

Laboratory
Investigation

The Genetics of Fingerprints

Fingerprints are often used to solve mysteries and crimes. Although there are similar patterns in fingerprints, no two are alike. In this investigation, you will identify what makes fingerprints unique.

Problem

Observe how fingerprints can be used to identify a person.

Materials (per group)

- ink pad
- 2 index cards
- hand lens

Procedure

1. Obtain an ink pad, two index cards, and a hand lens.

2. On an index card like the one shown below, write your name, the word "left" in the space next to "Hand," and the numbers 1 to 5.

Your Name _____

Hand _____

1	2	3	4	5

Arch

Loop

Whorl

3. On the second index card, include the same information except write the word "right" instead of "left."

4. Carefully roll the tip of one finger from left to right on the ink pad.

5. Roll the inked fingertip on the index card in the spot numbered 1. Lift your finger straight up after making the print to avoid smudging the print.

6. Repeat steps 4 and 5 until all fingertips of both hands appear in order on the index card.

Observations

1. For each fingerprint, determine whether you have an arch, a loop, or a whorl, and record it under the prints.

2. Fingerprints are formed before birth. The genotype LL forms a whorl, Ll forms a loop, and ll forms an arch pattern. For each fingerprint, record your genotype for each finger.

3. For each fingerprint, draw an imaginary line from the center of your pattern to the triradius. The triradius is the triangular area formed by intersecting ridges. Count the number of ridges for each fingertip and record the number under your prints.

Analysis and Conclusions

1. Study each of your fingerprints and describe any patterns you notice.

2. Compare your fingerprints with those of others in the class and describe the results.

3. How can fingerprints be used to identify a person? Explain your answer.

Extensions

Gather the relevant class data to determine whether there is a difference in ridge count between males and females.

Chapter 25 Review

Study Outline

25-1 Mendel's Principles of Heredity

▶ Genetics is the branch of biology that studies the ways in which hereditary information is passed on from parents to offspring.

▶ From studies of heredity in pea plants, Gregor Mendel developed the laws of dominance, segregation, and independent assortment.

▶ According to Mendel's law of dominance, when an organism is hybrid for a pair of contrasting traits, only the dominant trait can be seen in the hybrid.

▶ Mendel's law of segregation states that factors (genes) occur in pairs, are separated from each other during gamete formation, and are recombined at fertilization.

▶ In the early 1900s, it was shown that Mendel's "factors" were genes carried on homologous chromosomes. This discovery led to the modern gene-chromosome theory of heredity.

25-2 Fundamentals of Genetics

▶ Alleles are the different forms of a gene controlling a certain trait. An individual may be homozygous with two identical alleles or heterozygous with two different alleles for the same trait.

▶ The genetic makeup of an individual is called the genotype. The physical trait that an organism develops as a result of its genotype is called its phenotype.

25-3 Other Concepts in Genetics

▶ The law of independent assortment states that, during meiosis, genes for different traits are separated and distributed to gametes independently of one another.

▶ Incomplete dominance occurs when both alleles contribute to the phenotype of a heterozygous individual to produce a trait that is not exactly like that of either parent.

▶ In codominance, two dominant alleles are expressed at the same time.

▶ Some traits are controlled by multiple alleles, where there are more than two alleles in a species.

Chapter Assessment

Multiple Choice

Choose the letter of the answer that best completes each statement or answers the question.

1. An individual possesses two identical genes for a certain trait. For this trait, the individual is said to be (a) dominant. (b) hybrid. (c) homozygous. (d) heterozygous.

2. The outward appearance of a particular trait in an organism is referred to as a(n) (a) genotype. (b) phenotype. (c) allele. (d) chromosome.

3. The phenotype of a pea plant can be most easily determined by (a) looking at it. (b) crossing it with a recessive plant. (c) crossing it with a similar plant. (d) looking at the parents.

4. Mendel was able to formulate the law of segregation from his experiments with pea plants when he had (a) produced hybrids. (b) produced mutations. (c) recorded F_1 results. (d) counted F_2 types.

5. A pair of black (B) mice produce some offspring that are black and some that are white (b). The genotypes of the parents are most probably (a) BB and bb. (b) BB and Bb. (c) Bb and Bb. (d) bb and bb.

6. Two individuals heterozygous for a given trait are mated. In the resulting offspring, the ratio of the dominant phenotype to the recessive phenotype for this trait is expected to be (a) 1:1. (b) 2:1. (c) 3:1. (d) 4:1.

7. In Dalmatian dogs, the desired type is white with small black spots. Assume that the mating of two dogs, each with small black spots, results in some offspring with solid white coats, some offspring with large black spots, and some with small black spots. What is the probable genotype of the Dalmatians with small black spots? (a) homozygous dominant (b) homozygous recessive (c) heterozygous (d) sex-linked recessive

8. In guinea pigs, rough hair is dominant over straight hair. If heterozygotes are crossed, the largest number of any one genotype of offspring would probably be (a) homozygous straight hair. (b) homozygous rough hair. (c) heterozygous rough hair. (d) intermediate between rough hair and straight hair.

9. The coat of roan cattle is found to be a mixture of red hairs and white hairs. This is an example of (a) recombination. (b) codominance. (c) independent assortment. (d) segregation.

10. When one of two traits can be inherited without the other, the genes for these two traits are said to be (a) dominant. (b) recessive. (c) blended. (d) independent.

Content Review

Answer each of the following in complete sentences.

11. What is meant by the F_1 generation?

12. Give an example of Mendel's law of dominance.

13. How did Sutton's chromosome theory help explain Mendel's law of segregation?

14. What is the difference between a homozygous and a heterozygous individual?

15. Explain how two organisms can have the same phenotypes but different genotypes.

16. State the law of probability, and tell why it is important in the study of genetics.

17. How can Mendel's law of independent assortment be explained in terms of genes and meiosis?

18. When there is incomplete dominance in an organism, what phenotypic ratio would you expect to find in the F_1 generation? What ratio would you expect in the F_2 generation (when two hybrids are crossed)?

19. Explain how incomplete dominance and codominance differ.

20. When multiple alleles for a trait exist in a species, how many alleles can be present in the species as a whole? How many alleles for the trait can be present in one individual member of the species?

Graphic Organizing

For information on graphic organizers, see Appendix G at the back of this text.

21. **Circle Graph** Construct two circle graphs: (a) one showing the relative number of different phenotypes expected from a dihybrid cross, and (b) one showing Mendel's actual results (see Figure 25–12). How do Mendel's results compare with the expected results?

Critical Thinking and Problem Solving

Discuss each of the following in a brief paragraph.

22. **Drawing conclusions** Based on your knowledge of Mendel's law of segregation, explain why the shortness trait in pea plants disappeared and reappeared from generation to generation.

23. **Relating** A mother and father are each heterozygous for curly hair, with a genotype of Cc. (C is the dominant gene for curly hair.) The couple has four children, all of whom have the recessive straight hair (genotype cc). You might expect that three of the children would have the dominant curly hair and only one the recessive straight hair. Why did the actual phenotype ratios in this family differ from the expected ratios?

24. **Inferring** Why do scientists require that plants and animals used in research be "genetically pure," that is, that they breed true for as many characteristics as possible?

25. **Calculating** If two pea plants hybrid for a single trait produce 60 pea plants, about how many of the 60 F_2 pea plants would you expect to show the recessive trait?

26. **Relating** If a child with blood type O has a mother with blood type A and a father with blood type B, what are the parent's genotypes for blood type?

27. **Hypothesizing** What are the blood types that could appear in the children of parents who have the genotypes $I^A i$ and $I^B i$?

515

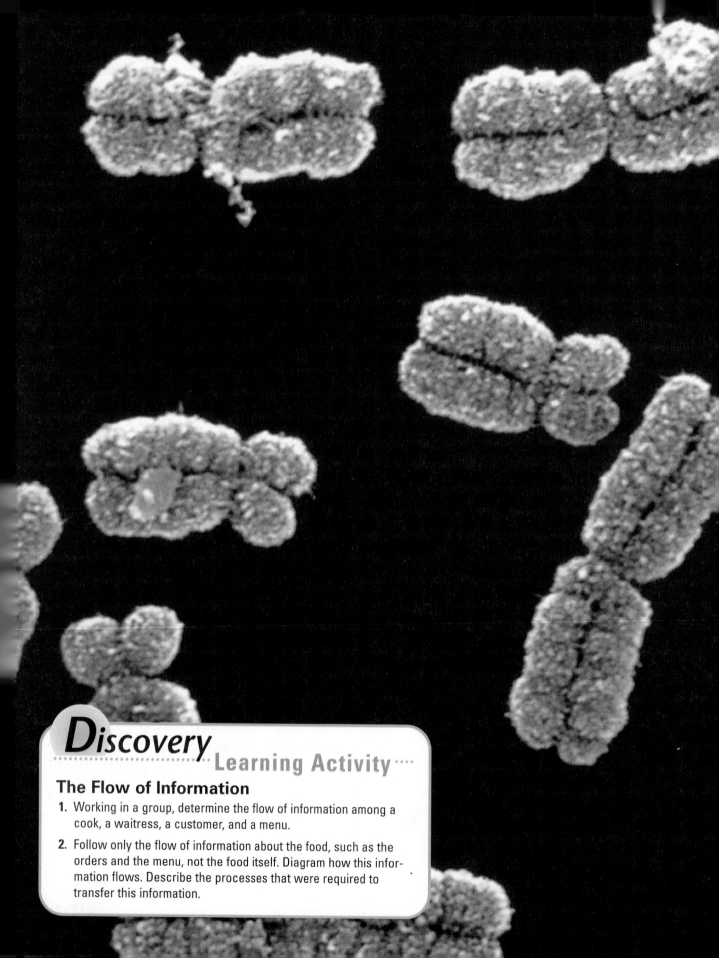

Discovery Learning Activity

The Flow of Information

1. Working in a group, determine the flow of information among a cook, a waitress, a customer, and a menu.

2. Follow only the flow of information about the food, such as the orders and the menu, not the food itself. Diagram how this information flows. Describe the processes that were required to transfer this information.

Modern Genetics

················· **Guide** *for* **Reading** ·················

Previewing the Chapter

Human chromosomes seem to float like puffy pink clouds in this highly magnified image. They are so small that scientists use powerful scanning electron microscopes to study them. Yet these chromosomes determine a person's appearance, makeup, and traits—as well as how these traits are passed on to offspring. What evidence helped confirm that genes are found on chromosomes? What is DNA, and how was the composition, structure, and function of DNA determined?

Key Words

autosome, crossing over, nucleotide, operon, sex chromosome, sex-linked trait, translation, transcription

Key Concepts

- **Describe** the structure of DNA.
- **Describe** the roles of DNA and RNA in protein synthesis.
- **Observe** the DNA from wheat germ. (Laboratory Investigation)

26-1 Chromosomal Inheritance

Section Objectives:

- *Explain* why *Drosophila* is a good experimental animal for genetics experiments.
- *State* the role of the X and Y chromosomes in determining sex.
- *Define* the terms *linkage group* and *crossing-over.*
- *Describe* multiple-gene inheritance.

T. H. Morgan and *Drosophila*

In the early 1900s, Thomas Hunt Morgan, an American geneticist, offered the first evidence that genes are parts of chromosomes. For his work, Morgan won a Nobel Prize in 1933. One reason for Morgan's success-ful research was his choice of the fruit fly, *Drosophila* (droh SAHF uh luh), as his experimental animal.

The fruit fly, which is often found around ripening fruits, is a useful organism for genetic experiments. It is so tiny that large numbers can be kept in a small space. It is easy to raise, and it produces hundreds of offspring. It also has a reproductive cycle of about 14 days. This allows a geneticist to study many genera-tions of flies in a short time. Another advantage to studying *Drosophila* is that it has only four pairs of chromosomes.

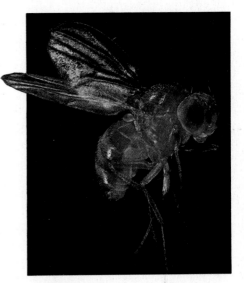

▲ **Figure 26–1**
Drosophila. Morgan used the fruit fly, *Drosophila,* as his subject for genetic experiments.

◀ Human chromosomes; as seen through a scanning electron microscope.

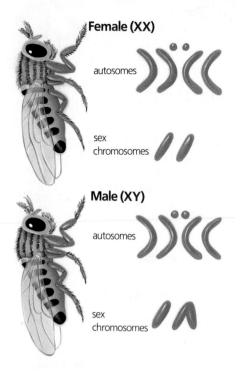

▲ **Figure 26–2**

***Drosophila* Sex Chromosomes.** A normal female *Drosophila* has two X chromosomes. A normal male has one X chromosome and one Y chromosome.

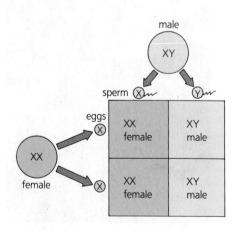

▲ **Figure 26–3**

Sex Determination in *Drosophila*. In *Drosophila*, as in humans, the male gamete can carry an X or a Y chromosome. For this reason, the male gamete determines the sex of the offspring.

Sex Determination and Chromosomes

Around 1890, scientists observed that chromosomes in cells from males and females were identical except for one pair. Scientists suspected that these different chromosomes determined the sex of the organism. This hypothesis now has been well confirmed. The two unmatched chromosomes are known as the **sex chromosomes;** the other homologous chromosomes are called **autosomes** (AW tuh sohmz). The discovery of sex chromosomes was important in the study of genetics because it linked an inherited trait (male or female) to a particular pair of chromosomes.

In the female *Drosophila,* the two sex chromosomes look the same. See Figure 26–2. Both are rod-shaped chromosomes, known as the **X chromosomes.** Male *Drosophila,* on the other hand, have one X chromosome and one hook-shaped chromosome, called the **Y chromosome.**

The sex of *Drosophila* is determined at fertilization. All the female gametes, or eggs, contain one X chromosome. They do because each egg cell receives one X chromosome during meiosis. The male gametes, or sperm, contain either one X chromosome or one Y chromosome. When a sperm containing a Y chromosome joins with a female gamete, the zygote will have one X and one Y chromosome. This zygote will develop into a male (XY). When a sperm containing an X chromosome joins with a female gamete, the zygote will be female (XX). Thus, the sex of the fruit fly is determined by the kind of sperm that fertilizes an egg cell. See Figure 26–3.

The sex of an organism is determined in a similar way in humans and other mammals. Not all animals, however, have the same system of sex chromosomes. In birds, butterflies, and some fish, the male has the two identical sex chromosomes, and the female has two different sex chromosomes. In these animals, the female produces two different types of gametes. The egg of the female determines the sex of the offspring for these animals.

Sex-Linked Traits

Morgan looked at thousands of fruit flies to find interesting traits to study. As you saw in Figure 26–1, the normal eye color of *Drosophila* is bright red. One day, Morgan discovered a white-eyed male fly. Since he had never seen this trait before, he decided to study it. His first step was to mate the white-eyed male with a normal red-eyed female. All offspring of this mating showed red eyes. Morgan concluded that the allele for white eyes is recessive.

If his cross obeyed the rules of Mendelian genetics, all the red-eyed flies of the F_1 generation would be heterozygous for eye color. If R represents the dominant allele for red eyes, and r the recessive allele for white eyes, the genotype of the F_1 generation should be Rr. To test this, Morgan mated males and females of the F_1 generation. The F_2 generation had the expected ratio of red eyes to white. About three-fourths of the flies had red eyes, and about one-fourth had white eyes. However, there was one peculiarity in

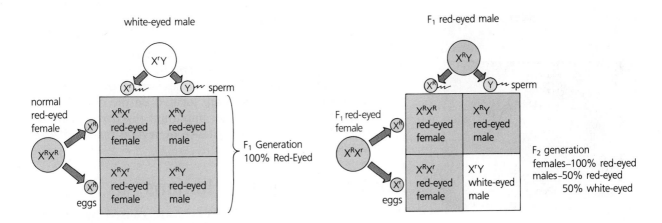

▲ **Figure 26–4**

Inheritance of the White-Eye Trait in *Drosophila*. The allele for white eyes is recessive and is carried only on the X chromosome. A white-eyed male (left) is crossed with a homozygous red-eyed female. Since all the offspring inherit the dominant red-eye allele from the female parent, all have red eyes. However, the females are heterozygous for eye color. A red-eyed male (right) is crossed with a heterozygous red-eyed female. Since all the female offspring receive the dominant allele from the male parent, they are all red eyed. However, the male offspring do not receive a gene for eye color from the male parent, only from the female parent. Half the males receive the recessive allele and are white eyed. While all the females are red eyed, half are carriers of the recessive allele. What are the genotypes of a male and female *Drosophila* that could result in a white-eyed female?

the results—all the white-eyed flies were male. All the females were red-eyed. For this reason, the inheritance of eye color seemed to be related to the sex of the offspring.

To learn more, Morgan performed a test cross. He mated the original white-eyed male with a red-eyed female from the F_1 generation. This time one-half the females had white eyes, and one-half had red. The males were also divided half white and half red.

Morgan knew that the Y chromosome is shorter than the X chromosome. He reasoned that some of the genes found on the X chromosome might be missing from the Y chromosome. It was possible, he reasoned, that the allele for eye color was carried on the X chromosome of the fruit fly, but the Y chromosome did not have a corresponding allele. If this were true, a male fly would show the recessive allele. To have white eyes, a female fly would have to have the recessive allele on both of her X chromosomes.

By means of Punnett squares, you can see that Morgan's hypothesis explains the results of the crosses he made. See Figure 26–4. In these diagrams, X^R represents an X chromosome carrying the dominant allele for red eyes. X^r indicates an X chromosome with the recessive allele for white eyes. Y stands for a Y chromosome with no gene for eye color.

Once a white-eyed female had been obtained, it was possible to make another test cross. Morgan crossed a white-eyed female with a red-eyed male. All the female offspring were red-eyed; all the males were white-eyed. You may want to draw a Punnett square that will explain this result.

A trait that is controlled by a gene found on the sex chromosome is called a **sex-linked trait.** The chance of showing the trait is affected by the sex of the individual. Most sex-linked traits are determined by genes found on the X chromosome but not on the Y chromosome. Morgan's discovery of sex-linked traits supported Sutton's hypothesis that genes are located on the chromosomes. (See Chapter 25). It was also an important discovery in its own right, since it explains the inheritance of several human diseases and disorders.

Sex-Linked Traits in Humans

Many human conditions and diseases are caused by abnormal recessive alleles of certain genes. The normal allele lets the body perform some function that the abnormal allele does not. The term *defective allele* is often used to refer to the abnormal alleles that cause genetic diseases. Several defective alleles in human genetics are sex-linked. Among the human diseases caused by defective sex-linked alleles are hemophilia, a disorder of the blood-clotting system, and muscular dystrophy, which results in the gradual destruction of muscle cells. A form of night blindness and color blindness are less serious sex-linked hereditary disorders.

Color blindness is a condition in which the individual cannot perceive certain colors, usually red and green. This condition is more common in males than in females. Few females suffer from red-green color blindness, although they may be *carriers* for it. Carriers have the allele for color blindness on one X chromosome. Females are not affected by the defective recessive allele because they have a normal dominant allele on the other X chromosome.

Every male receives an X chromosome from his mother and a Y chromosome from his father. If the mother is a carrier for color blindness, there is a 50 percent chance that any son she has will receive the defective allele. See Figure 26–5. Since the Y chromosome has no gene for color vision, when a son inherits the defective allele from his mother, the allele is expressed, and the son will be color blind. A female, on the other hand, receives an X from her mother and an X from her father. A daughter is a carrier only if she has a defective allele from her mother and a normal allele from her father or a normal allele from her mother and a defective allele from her father.

Since a father contributes only a Y chromosome to his sons, a color-blind father cannot transmit the allele to his sons. He will, however, transmit this defective allele to all his daughters. If the mother is a carrier of the defective allele, there is a 50 percent chance that a daughter will inherit the defective allele from her mother as well as from her father. Thus, on the average, half the daughters will be color blind. The other half will be carriers. Half the sons will be color blind also, but this result has nothing to do with the father's genotype. If both parents are color blind, all their offspring will be color blind because neither parent is carrying a normal dominant allele.

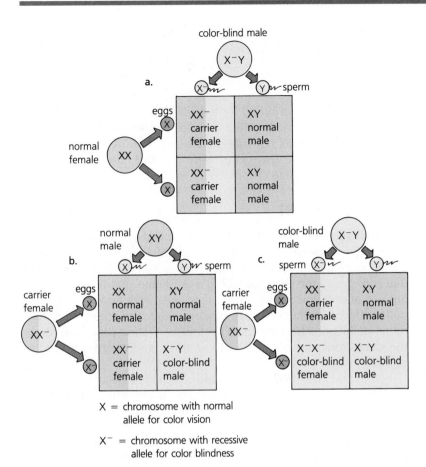

Inheritance of Color Blindness in Humans. (A and B) The allele for color blindness cannot be transmitted from father to son. It can be transmitted only through the female to later generations. (C) For a female to be color blind, she must inherit defective alleles from both parents, a relatively rare event.

X = chromosome with normal
allele for color vision

X⁻ = chromosome with recessive
allele for color blindness

Gene Linkage

Every organism has thousands of genes. Every organism also has a certain small number of chromosomes in each body cell. Therefore, many genes must be present on each chromosome. Genes on the same chromosome are said to be *linked*. All of the genes that are on the same chromosome make up a **linkage group.** *Drosophila,* with four pairs of chromosomes, has four linkage groups. Humans, with 23 pairs of chromosomes, have 23 linkage groups.

If genes are linked on the same chromosome, they cannot be distributed independently during meiosis. Therefore, linked genes do not obey Mendel's law of independent assortment, which was discussed in Chapter 25. Mendel arrived at the law of independent assortment only because the dihybrid traits he studied happened to be controlled by genes on different pairs of chromosomes.

One of the first examples of *gene linkage* was found by R. C. Punnett and William Bateson at Cambridge University in England. They were studying the inheritance of flower color in pea plants. Purple flowers were dominant; red flowers were recessive. Long pollen grains were dominant. Round pollen grains were recessive. Plants pure for both dominant traits were crossed with plants pure for both recessive traits. The expected phenotype of 100 percent dominant for both traits in the F_1 generation did occur. However, when the dihybrids were crossed, they did not show the expected 9:3:3:1 phenotype ratios in the F_2 generation. The results were closer to the 3:1 ratio from a single hybrid cross. The two dominant traits seemed to stay together, as did the two recessive traits. That is, they were not distributed independently.

T. H. Morgan had gotten similar results from *Drosophila*. Certain traits seemed to be inherited together. Morgan thought this was further evidence that genes were parts of chromosomes and that genes on the same chromosome were inherited together.

Crossing-Over

One difficulty with the hypothesis of linked genes was that the linkage did not seem to be perfect. In a small number of offspring in the F_2 generation, the linked genes separated. In the Punnett-Bateson study, for example, there were some plants with purple flowers and round pollen, and some with red flowers and long pollen. But the numbers were nowhere near the expected 9:3:3:1 ratios of Mendelian genetics. The unusual ratios remained about the same from one experiment to another, and they were hard to explain.

Morgan concluded that the ratios occurred because pieces of homologous chromosomes were exchanged sometimes during meiosis. The exchange happened before the chromosomes separated to go to different gametes. He called this exchange process **crossing-over.** See Figure 26–6. Scientists now know that crossing-over occurs during synapsis of the first meiotic division, when the four chromatids of each homologous chromosome pair are in close contact.

Because of crossing-over, the chromosomes that go into the gametes have new gene linkages. They are not identical to the chromosomes in the parent cells. Thus, crossing-over is an important source of variations, or genetic differences, in offspring.

Morgan reasoned that genes that are far apart on the same chromosome would become separated by crossing-over more often than genes that are close together. By studying the offspring ratios of dihybrid crosses for many different pairs of linked genes, Morgan was able to figure out how close or how far apart each particular pair was. In this way, Morgan was able to make gene maps of the chromosomes in *Drosophila*. Each gene map showed the order of genes on the chromosome. The order was based on how often the genes became separated by crossing-over.

Figure 26–6

Crossing-Over. During synapsis in meiosis, segments of homologous chromatids may be interchanged. If the exchanged segments carry different alleles for certain traits, new gene combinations result. ▼

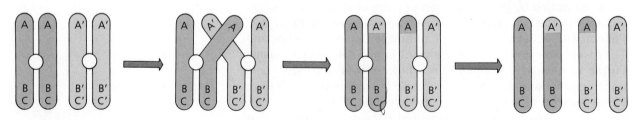

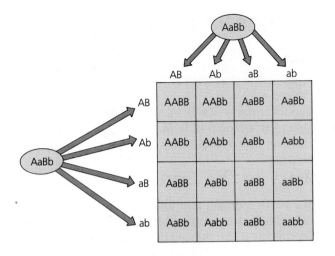

Multiple-Gene Inheritance. In multiple-gene inheritance, when there are two genes controlling a trait, there are nine different possible genotypes. There is a range of phenotypes between the pure dominant and the pure recessive extremes.

Multiple-Gene Inheritance

Many traits in both plants and animals do not appear in two contrasting forms. For example, humans are not just either tall or short. Instead, human height varies from very short to very tall. Traits that vary between two extremes are not controlled by the alleles of a single gene, but by the alleles of two or more different genes. When two or more independent genes affect one characteristic, it is called **multiple-gene,** or *polygenic,* **inheritance.**

The simplest example of multiple-gene inheritance would involve two genes, each with its own pair of alleles. For example, the length of the ears in corn is controlled by two genes. Suppose the genes for length are Aa and Bb. With these two genes, there can be four possible gametes and nine different genotypes. See Figure 26–7. Suppose that the greater the number of capital letters in the genotype, the longer the corn ear. Then, the longest corn ears would have the genotype AABB. The shortest corn ears would have the genotype aabb. All other genotypes would show ear sizes between these two extremes.

26-1 Section Review

1. Which sex chromosomes characterize female and male *Drosophila?*
2. Name a sex-linked trait in humans.
3. In what process are pieces of homologous chromosomes exchanged during meiosis?
4. Give an example of a human trait controlled by multiple genes.

Critical Thinking

5. Why might a geneticist use fruit flies to study how genes function? Why might a scientist choose *not* to use fruit flies? (*Identifying Reasons*)

26-2 The Genetic Material

Section Objectives:

- *Describe* the experiments that showed that DNA is the genetic material.
- *List* the three chemical parts of a DNA nucleotide.
- *Explain* the Watson-Crick model of DNA.
- *Describe* how DNA replicates in a living cell.

The Chemistry of the Gene

From the work of Sutton, Morgan, and many other researchers, it was known by 1950 that chromosomes carry hereditary information. It was also certain that the information is present in distinct units, called genes, arranged along the chromosomes like beads on a string. Still, no one knew what a gene was or how it worked. Without that knowledge, heredity and genetics could not be truly understood. This understanding came in the 1950s, when the chemical nature of the gene was discovered. The first clues to the chemical nature of the hereditary material were uncovered much earlier, however.

In 1869, Friedrich Miescher, a Swiss biochemist, isolated a material from the nuclei of fish sperm. He called the material *nuclein* (NOO klee un). Other scientists showed that nuclein was made of carbon, hydrogen, oxygen, and nitrogen. It was also rich in phosphorus. When nuclein was shown to be acidic, its name was changed to *nucleic acid.* Later research found two kinds of nucleic acid—deoxyribonucleic acid, or DNA, and ribonucleic acid, or RNA. DNA occurs mainly in the nuclei of cells. RNA is found mainly in the cytoplasm.

In the 1920s, scientists found that chromosomes contained DNA. It was already known that chromosomes contained proteins. While the chemical structure of proteins was well understood, the structure of DNA was completely unknown. Although a few scientists suggested that DNA was the hereditary material, most scientists believed that only proteins were complex enough to carry genetic information.

Protein vs. Nucleic Acids

It did not become clear until the 1950s that the hereditary material of the chromosomes was DNA. To understand how this came about, you need to understand the experiments performed by Frederick Griffith and several other researchers.

Griffith's Experiments In 1928, Frederick Griffith, an English bacteriologist, was trying to find a vaccine against pneumonia. Pneumonia is a disease caused by a kind of bacteria called *pneumococcus* (noo muh KAHK us). Griffith knew that there are two types of pneumococcus. See Figure 26–8. One type, called Type S, is surrounded by an outer covering called a *capsule.* Type S bacteria

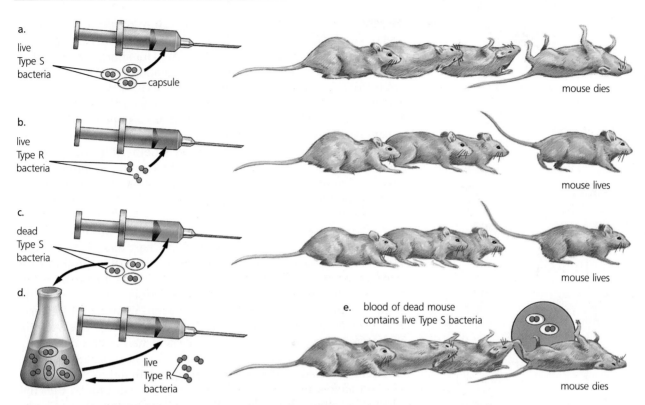

a. live Type S bacteria — capsule

mouse dies

b. live Type R bacteria

mouse lives

c. dead Type S bacteria

mouse lives

d.

live Type R bacteria

e. blood of dead mouse contains live Type S bacteria

mouse dies

cause a severe case of pneumonia. The other type, called Type R, is not surrounded by a capsule. Type R bacteria do not cause pneumonia. If mice are injected with Type S bacteria, they develop pneumonia and die. Mice injected with Type R bacteria show no ill effects.

Dead Type S bacteria do not cause pneumonia when injected into mice. In Griffith's key experiment, he mixed dead Type S bacteria with live Type R. When he injected the mixture into mice, the mice developed pneumonia and died. Furthermore, the tissues of the dead mice showed living Type S bacteria.

Remember that neither dead Type S nor live Type R bacteria alone cause pneumonia. When brought together, however, they do cause pneumonia and living Type S bacteria appear. Griffith concluded that some factor from dead Type S bacteria could change, or transform, Type R bacteria into Type S. The changed bacteria were able to make capsules and to cause pneumonia in mice.

Avery, MacLeod, and McCarty In 1944, Oswald Avery, Colin MacLeod, and Maclyn McCarty of the Rockefeller Institute in New York identified the transforming material in Griffith's experiment as DNA. In other words, DNA produced the new inherited traits in Type R bacteria. Although this was strong evidence that DNA is the genetic substance, many scientists remained unconvinced. They still thought that protein must carry the hereditary information. The conclusive evidence supporting DNA was obtained by Alfred Hershey and Martha Chase in 1952.

▲ **Figure 26–8**

Griffith's Experiment. (A) Live Type S bacteria will kill the mouse. (B) Live Type R bacteria are harmless. (C) Dead Type S bacteria are harmless. (D) Dead Type S bacteria are mixed with live Type R bacteria. (E) The mixture kills the mouse, and live Type S are present in the mouse's tissues. Griffith concluded that the Type R bacteria had been transformed into Type S bacteria.

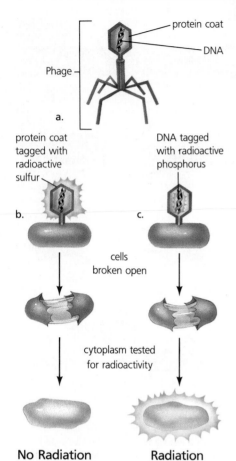

▲ **Figure 26–9**

The Hershey-Chase Experiment. (A) Structure of one type of bacteriophage. (B) Bacteria infected by phages with protein coats are tagged with radioactive sulfur. The cell contents do not become radioactive. (C) Bacteria infected by phages with DNA are tagged with radioactive phosphorus. The cell contents become radioactive. Hershey and Chase concluded that a phage infects a bacterial cell by injecting its DNA into the bacterium. The protein coat remains outside.

Hershey and Chase   Alfred Hershey and Martha Chase made use of viruses called bacteriophages to resolve the DNA *vs.* protein argument. A *bacteriophage,* or *phage* (FAYJ) for short, is a virus that infects bacteria. This kind of virus is made of a DNA core surrounded by a protein coat. See Figure 26–9. A phage invades a bacterium and makes hundreds of new phage particles once inside the bacterial cell. The bacterial cell then breaks open, and the new phage particles are let go. These can attack other bacterial cells. Hershey and Chase wanted to discover whether the whole phage entered the bacterium or whether just the DNA or the protein coat entered. In hopes of answering this question, they tagged the protein and the DNA of the phage particle with different radioactive elements.

DNA contains phosphorus but no sulfur. Virus protein contains sulfur but no phosphorus. Hershey and Chase tagged the phage DNA with radioactive phosphorus. They tagged the protein coat with radioactive sulfur. One group of bacteria was then exposed to phages with radioactive DNA. Another group was exposed to phages with radioactive protein. After large numbers of bacteria had become infected with phages, the cytoplasm of the bacteria was tested for radioactivity. The cells that had been infected by phages with radioactive DNA showed a great deal of radioactivity. The cells that had been infected by phages with radioactive protein showed almost no radioactivity. This experiment proved that the phage DNA enters the cells, while the phage protein stays outside when phages infect bacteria.

If phage DNA alone can cause bacteria to make more phages, it must be the DNA that carries the genetic instructions for making phages. This experiment established DNA as the genetic material. The problem then became that of finding what DNA is made of and how it works.

Composition of DNA

The first step in analyzing an unknown organic compound is to find out the chemical groups that form it. In the 1920s, P. A. Levene, a biochemist, carried out a chemical analysis of DNA. Levene found that the DNA molecule is made up of the following chemical groups: the 5-carbon sugar **deoxyribose** (dee ahk see RY bohs); a phosphate group; and four kinds of nitrogen-containing (nitrogenous) bases. Two of the four bases, known as **adenine** and **guanine,** are a kind of compound called a *purine* (PYOOR een). The other two, **cytosine** and **thymine,** are compounds called *pyrimidines* (pih RIM uh deenz).

Levene found that there was one phosphate group and one nitrogen-containing base for each sugar unit. He therefore concluded that the basic unit of DNA is a sugar, a phosphate, and one of the four nitrogen-containing bases. He called this unit a **nucleotide** (NOO klee uh tyd). Since there are four different bases, there are four different kinds of nucleotides. Many, many nucleotides make up a single DNA molecule.

Structure of DNA

After the chemical makeup of DNA was known, the second step was to work out the structure of the DNA molecule. This was done in 1953 by James Watson, an American biochemist, and Francis Crick, an English physicist, working together in Cambridge, England. To develop their model of DNA, Watson and Crick used everything that was known about DNA. An important piece of information transmitted by Maurice Wilkins came from Rosalind Franklin of Oxford University in England. She had made X-ray studies of DNA crystals. These X-ray photographs showed that the repeating units in the crystal are arranged in the form of a **helix** (HEE liks). A helix is the shape of a coiled spring.

After trying many different arrangements, Watson and Crick arrived at a model DNA molecule in which there are two chains of sugar-phosphate groups running parallel to each other. Pairs of bases link the chains together like the rungs of a ladder. See Figure 26–10. Twisting or coiling the ladder forms the helix of the molecule. Thus, the DNA molecule is a *double helix.*

Watson and Crick found that their model could work only if the pairs of bases that made each rung of the ladder were an adenine unit connected to a thymine or a guanine connected to a cytosine. This model agreed with all the data for the DNA molecule. For example, it explained why the amount of adenine in DNA is always the same as the amount of thymine. It explained why the amount of guanine is always the same as the amount of cytosine. It also explained how, since the order of bases along the chain could vary, the order could be a code for genetic information.

In the double-helix model, the order of bases along one strand determines the matching bases on the other strand. That is, every adenine (A) must be joined to thymine (T), and every guanine (G) must be joined to cytosine (C). No other pairings are possible. Suppose, for example, that the order of bases along one strand is AGGTTAC. The matching order along the second strand must be TCCAATG. The two strands are said to be *complementary.* Each strand is the complement of the other according to the A-T and G-C base pairing rule. The double-helix model of DNA was a great breakthrough in the science of genetics. Watson, Crick, and Wilkins received the Nobel Prize for this work in 1962. Had she lived, Franklin would also have been a recipient.

Replication of DNA

The double-helix model also explains how an exact copy of each chromosome is made during cell division. The base pairs that form each rung of the model are held together by a weak *hydrogen bond.* Before copying begins, these bonds break, and the two strands of the DNA molecule come apart. This exposes the bases along each strand. The bases of free nucleotides in the nucleus of the cell can then fasten onto the complementary bases on each exposed strand. When the nucleotides join together, they make a complete comple-

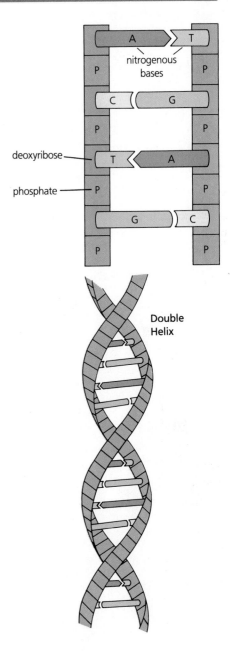

▲ **Figure 26–10**
Watson-Crick Model of DNA.

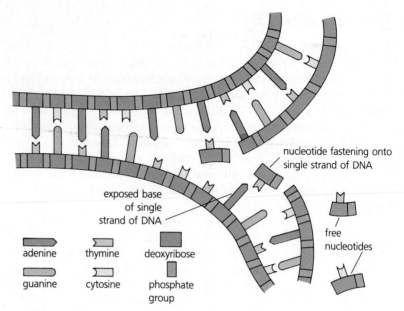

adenine

thymine

deoxyribose

guanine

cytosine

phosphate group

nucleotide fastening onto single strand of DNA

exposed base of single strand of DNA

free nucleotides

▲ **Figure 26–11**

DNA Replication. DNA replication results in the formation of two double-stranded molecules exactly like the original DNA molecule.

mentary strand exactly like the old one. In this way, two double-stranded molecules of DNA exactly like the original molecule are made. See Figure 26–11. Each double-stranded molecule contains one old strand and one new strand of DNA.

Where does replication start and end along the DNA molecule? Through experiments, scientists determined that replication does not begin at one end and continue to the other. Instead, replication begins at the same time at many points along the molecule. Enzymes then link the small segments of DNA into one long strand. In this way, a DNA molecule replicates much more rapidly than if there were only one starting point.

26-2 **Section Review**

1. What type of particles did Hershey and Chase use to show that DNA is the genetic material?
2. Which three chemical groups make up a nucleotide?
3. What is the shape of a DNA molecule?
4. How are the base pairs in a DNA molecule held together?

Critical Thinking

5. Suppose that a strand of DNA were to have the following base sequence: TGGCAATCTG. What would be the base sequence along the complementary strand? (*Ordering*)

26-3 Gene Expression

Section Objectives:

■ *Describe* the one gene-one polypeptide hypothesis.
■ *Explain* how the order of nucleotides in DNA codes for different amino acids and how this code is transcribed into RNA.
■ *Compare* the structures and functions of mRNA, tRNA, and rRNA.
■ *Describe* how a polypeptide is assembled.

Genes and Enzymes

The idea that hereditary material controls the synthesis of enzymes was suggested in the early 1900s. Sir Archibald Garrod, an English physician, studied certain diseases that he called "inborn errors of metabolism." He hypothesized that these diseases are caused by the body's inability to make a certain enzyme. He also hypothesized that this inability was inherited. Garrod published his ideas in 1909, but they were ignored at the time. It was not until the 1930s and 1940s that scientists realized their importance.

The best evidence that genes control the production of enzymes came from the experiments of George Beadle and Edward Tatum, two American scientists, in 1941. In their experiments, Beadle and Tatum used the red bread mold *Neurospora crassa*. From the results of their experiments, Beadle and Tatum were able to conclude that each gene produces its effects by controlling the synthesis of a single enzyme. This is known as the *one gene-one enzyme hypothesis*.

One Gene-One Polypeptide Hypothesis

It is now known that genes control the synthesis of all proteins. Some proteins are enzymes. Some are hormones. Some form the structures of the cell.

As you may recall, proteins are made of polypeptides—long chains of amino acids (see Chapter 4). Some proteins consist of two or more polypeptides linked and twisted around each other. Hemoglobin, for example, is a protein made of two different polypeptide chains.

It was found that the synthesis of each polypeptide is controlled by a different gene. Because of this fact, the one gene-one enzyme hypothesis was changed to the **one gene-one polypeptide hypothesis.** According to this hypothesis, each gene directs the synthesis of a particular polypeptide chain.

The DNA Code

To direct the synthesis of a polypeptide, a gene must be able to direct the order in which amino acids are put together. It was not clear from the Watson-Crick model of DNA how this could be done.

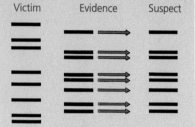
Among the ideas put forward was the idea that the order of bases along the DNA strands is a code that specifies the order of the amino acids.

There are 20 amino acids in the proteins of humans and most other organisms. Therefore, there must be at least 20 different code "words" to specify these amino acids. As you have read, there are 4 different bases in DNA: adenine (A), guanine (G), cytosine (C), and thymine (T). Using a 2-letter code, only 16 different 2-letter code sequences can be made from 4 bases: AA, AT, AG, AC, TT, TA, TG, TC, and so forth. This is not enough, so the code "words" must be at least 3 bases long. From 4 bases, 64 different 3-base sequences can be made—more than are needed. Research has shown that the code for specifying an amino acid is made of 3-base "words." Most amino acids are specified by more than one code "word."

Today, scientists know that a gene is made of many nucleotides. The order of the bases of three adjacent nucleotides is the code that specifies a particular amino acid to be added to a polypeptide chain. The code also contains "punctuation"—code "words" that tell where a polypeptide begins and ends. In most cases, these points are also the beginning and end of a gene.

RNA and Protein Synthesis

In cells with nuclei, the genes are found within the nucleus. Yet, protein synthesis takes place outside the nucleus. How, then, does DNA direct the synthesis of proteins? DNA does this with the help of RNA, or ribonucleic acid. The chemical makeup of RNA is similar to the chemical makeup of DNA, with two differences. In RNA, the 5-carbon sugar is ribose, and the nitrogen-containing base **uracil** (U) takes the place of thymine. Thus, the four bases found in RNA are adenine, guanine, cytosine, and uracil. The structure of RNA is also a little different. Unlike DNA, which is double-stranded, RNA is made of only a single strand of nucleotides.

Messenger RNA

The first step in directing protein synthesis is to copy the DNA code for a polypeptide into a molecule of RNA. To copy the code, the DNA strands separate for a short time and serve as a pattern, or *template,* for RNA. See Figure 26–12. Complementary RNA nucleotides take their places along the exposed strands by matching up complementary bases. When the assembled RNA sequence reaches the DNA "stop" code, it leaves the DNA strand. The RNA strand is now a separate molecule that carries the complete message for a single polypeptide in complementary form. That is, each A of the DNA is represented by a U in the RNA, each T by an A, each G by a C, and each C by a G. A strand of RNA that copies a genetic message from DNA in this way is called **messenger RNA,** or mRNA. The copying of a genetic message into a molecule of mRNA is called **transcription.** Each group of three bases on the mRNA that specifies an amino acid is called a **codon** (KOH dahn).

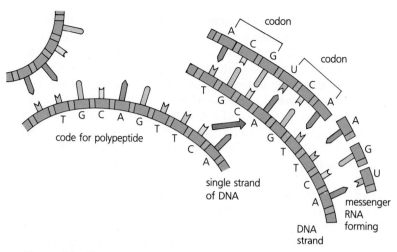

▲ **Figure 26–12**

Transcription of a Gene. The code for each polypeptide is copied from one of the DNA strands into a strand of messenger RNA. The copying process is similar to DNA replication, except that uracil replaces thymine as a complement for adenine.

Transfer RNA

Messenger RNA is only one of three kinds of RNA that are found in the cell. A second kind is called **transfer RNA,** or tRNA. While mRNA may have thousands of nucleotides along its length, tRNA has only about 80. The molecule of tRNA has an odd shape, as shown in Figure 26–13. At one end there is a short tail. A particular amino acid can become attached to this tail.

Each tRNA molecule will pick up only one kind of amino acid. There are 20 different forms of tRNA, one for each of the 20 different amino acids. At the other end of the tRNA molecule, there is a loop of exposed nucleotides. In this loop, there is a sequence of 3 bases, called an **anticodon,** that are complements of an mRNA codon. The codon that this anticodon matches is one that specifies the amino acid that each tRNA carries. Thus, tRNA is a device for bringing a certain amino acid to a certain place specified by mRNA.

Ribosomal RNA

Ribosomal RNA, or rRNA, is formed in the nucleoli of the cell. A ribosome consists of protein and rRNA. The ribosomal protein is made in the cytoplasm and then travels into the nucleus. In the nucleoli, the protein and the rRNA join together to form complete ribosomes. The ribosome is where a polypeptide is assembled during protein synthesis.

Assembly of a Polypeptide

The synthesis of the three kinds of RNA, as well as the assembly of ribosomes, occurs in the cell nucleus. The RNA and complete ribosomes migrate separately through the nuclear pores to the

Figure 26–13

Transfer RNA. The mRNA codon that matches the anticodon of the tRNA calls for the particular amino acid that is attached to the tail end of the tRNA. ▼

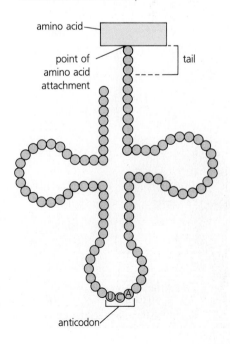

cytoplasm. Within the cytoplasm, there is contained a supply of all the amino acids that are needed to make the cell's proteins. Figure 26-14 lists all codons and the amino acids each codes for. This is called the genetic code. Within the cytoplasm polypeptides are assembled according to the instructions carried by mRNA.

In the cytoplasm, amino acid molecules become attached to their specific varieties of tRNA. See Figure 26-15. Ribosomes become attached to different places along each strand of mRNA. Where a ribosome is attached to mRNA, a molecule of tRNA with the right anticodon temporarily joins with the corresponding codon on the mRNA. The amino acid brought into position by the tRNA joins the last amino acid in the chain and separates from tRNA. The ribosome then moves along to the next codon. A new tRNA takes its place on the mRNA strand, and its amino acid joins the polypeptide chain. As the ribosome moves along, the tRNA that has delivered its amino acid is released. It is now free to pick up another amino acid and deliver it to the right place for assembly into the chain. Amino

Figure 26-14

The Genetic Code. Most of the amino acids are specified by more than one codon. For example, GCU, GCC, GCA, and GCG all code for the amino acid alanine. ▼

The Genetic Code					
First Base in Codon	**Second Base in Codon**				**Third Base in Codon**
	U	**C**	**A**	**G**	
U	phenylalanine	serine	tyrosine	cysteine	U
	phenylalanine	serine	tyrosine	cysteine	C
	leucine	serine	stop	stop	A
	leucine	serine	stop	tryptophan	G
C	leucine	proline	histidine	arginine	U
	leucine	proline	histidine	arginine	C
	leucine	proline	glutamine	arginine	A
	leucine	proline	glutamine	arginine	G
A	isoleucine	threonine	asparagine	serine	U
	isoleucine	threonine	asparagine	serine	C
	isoleucine (start);	threonine	lysine	arginine	A
	methionine	threonine	lysine	arginine	G
G	valine	alanine	aspartate	glycine	U
	valine	alanine	aspartate	glycine	C
	valine	alanine	glutamate	glycine	A
	valine	alanine	glutamate	glycine	G

An mRNA codon consists of three nucleotides. For example ACU codes threonine. The first letter, A, is read in the first column; the second letter C, from the second letter column; and the third letter, U, from the third letter column. Most amino acids are specified by more than one codon.

Math, Science, and Technology
$A = \pi r^2$
$V = l \times w \times h$

A Fruit-Fly Folly

Problem

Over the span of 90 years, numerous mutations in fruit flies have been discovered. But it was not until recently that geneticists came upon a new miniature strain of fruit fly that is approximately one third the size of the normal fruit fly. Unfortunately, the geneticists were having a great deal of difficulty culturing the miniature fruit fly. In each culture vial, only two to four adults remained alive, while numerous fruit flies lie dead on the surface of the food at the bottom of the vial. One graduate student hypothesizes that the miniature fruit flies cannot pull themselves free of the food media once they start feeding as adults.

Task

You are one of three high-school students working in a genetics lab for the summer that have been asked by the lab director to design and construct a plastic-net walkway inside the culture vials. The setup would permit the miniature fruit flies to feed without walking on the food and getting stuck.

In order to perform this task, you must complete the following:

1. Calculate the surface area of the base of the vial and the volume of the vial. See the diagram for the vial's dimensions. Use the following formulas for the calculations: $A = \pi r^2$, $V = \pi r^2 h$.

2. Calculate the perimeter of the plastic net that will be used for your design of fly walkways. Keep in mind that the walkway should not come into contact with the wall of the vial.

3. Design a scale drawing of the walkway for miniature-fruit-fly culture vials.

4. Using the materials provided, construct a walkway for the miniature fruit flies that is 8 cm high.

5. Perform several tests to determine the usefulness of the walkway using live fruit flies.

6. Keep a journal in which you record your team's ideas, drawings, experiments, data, and any other information relating to your design.

7. Prepare a presentation for the geneticists at the lab describing your team's approach to the problem, including the sources of information used in the design. Be sure to include your constructed design and the results of your tests.

Solution

Working as a team, share and discuss ideas concerning the design and construction of the walkway. Develop several designs and models. Carry out some preliminary studies exploring all possible variables using live fruit flies. How would you modify the walkway if a smaller fruit-fly mutation were discovered? Suggest modifications for other pieces of equipment used in culturing the miniature fruit flies. Be sure to include the details of your design; the completed construction of the walkway; the assumptions made by the team; supporting information used in the design and construction; and the descriptions and drawings for the team's solution to the problem.

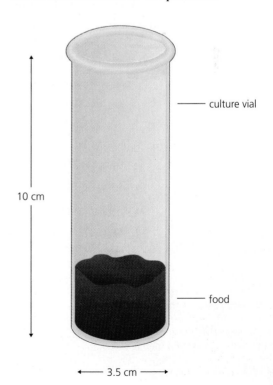

culture vial

10 cm

food

← 3.5 cm →

Figure 26–15

Protein Synthesis. As a ribosome moves into position at a codon of a messenger RNA, a transfer RNA with the complementary anticodon temporarily bonds to the codon. The tRNA adds its amino acid to the polypeptide chain, then detaches and moves away. ▶

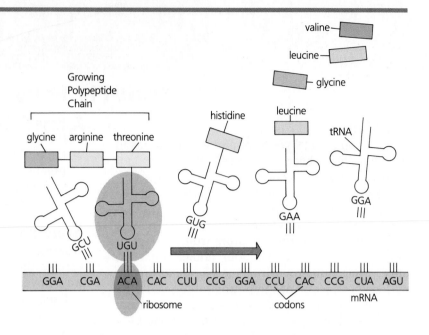

acids are added to the growing polypeptide chain until the ribosome reaches a "stop" codon. The polypeptide is then let go, and it forms itself into a complete protein molecule.

Every step in the process of translating the genetic message into a polypeptide chain is helped by a specific enzyme. There are enzymes that attach amino acids to tRNA. There are enzymes that attach tRNA to mRNA. There are enzymes that join the amino acids to the polypeptide chain. There are also enzymes in the nucleus that open the DNA molecule for transcription, and others that help in the assembly of RNA. All of these enzymes must be specified by genes.

The process by which the information coded in RNA is used for the assembly of a particular amino acid sequence is known as **translation.** Figure 26–16 shows how a genetic message is first

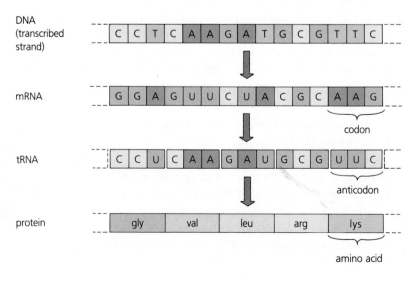

Figure 26–16

From DNA to Proteins. In transcription, the genetic code of DNA is copied into a molecule of mRNA. In translation, the information coded in mRNA is used to assemble a specific amino acid sequence, forming a polypeptide. This is done with the help of tRNA. ▶

transcribed from DNA to RNA and then translated into a polypeptide. By this remarkable system, all the cell's proteins are synthesized in the cytoplasm, while the chromosomes carrying the hereditary instructions for this synthesis remain in the nucleus.

26-3 Section Review

1. Which hypothesis states that each gene directs the synthesis of a particular chain of a protein?
2. How is information encoded in a gene?
3. What is the process by which genetic messages are copied into an RNA molecule?
4. Where in the cell are proteins made?

Critical Thinking

5. Suppose that, instead of the correct sequence AGC, an error occurred that changed the sequence to ATC. What would happen upon transcription? What would happen upon translation? (*Predicting*)

26-4 Control of Gene Expression

Section Objectives:

- *Explain* how gene expression is regulated in prokaryotes and in eukaryotes.
- *Compare* the operon of prokaryotes with the genes and control sections of DNA in eukaryotes.
- *Describe* homeotic genes and oncogenes.

Every cell in an organism has the complete set of genes characteristic of that organism. But, even though all the cells of an organism have the same genes, different cells perform different functions and produce different proteins. Why is a particular set of genes activated in one cell, while a different set is activated in another cell of the same organism? One of the major questions that biologists are trying to answer is what determines which proteins are produced in a given cell.

Gene Expression in Bacteria

In the early 1960s, three French biologists, François Jacob, Jacques Monod, and André Lwoff, discovered how the transcription of certain genes is controlled in the bacterium *E. coli*. They were awarded a Nobel Prize in 1965 for their work. Jacob, Monod, and Lwoff studied the production of the three enzymes the bacteria use to digest lactose, a sugar. They found that the enzymes are produced by the bacteria only when they are needed. That is, the bacteria produce the lactose-digesting enzymes when lactose is

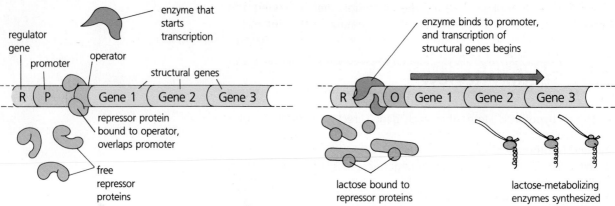

a. Lactose Absent—System "Off"

b. Lactose Present—System "On"

▲ **Figure 26–17**

Synthesis of Lactose-Digesting Enzymes in Bacteria. (A) When lactose is not present, repressor proteins bind to the operator of the operon. Because the repressor protein is much larger than the operator gene, it overlaps the promoter gene as well. The enzyme that starts transcription of the structural genes cannot bind to the promoter. No lactose-digesting enzymes are produced.

(B) When lactose is present, the lactose binds to the repressor protein. This means that the lactose-repressor complex cannot bind to the operator. Therefore, the enzyme that starts transcription is able to bind to the promoter, which means that lactose-digesting enzymes are produced.

present and other sources of energy are not available. Thus, enzyme production is turned on and off, depending on the needs of the cell.

Jacob, Monod, and Lwoff determined that production of the lactose-digesting enzymes is controlled by a cluster of genes. The amino acid sequences of the enzymes are determined by three structural genes. A *structural gene* is a DNA segment that codes for the production of a particular polypeptide.

The investigators found that the activity of the structural genes is controlled by an *operator gene,* a sequence of nucleotides found next to the structural genes. The structural genes cannot be transcribed unless the operator gene is in an active state. We can think of the operator as being switched "on" to cause transcription or switched "off" to prevent transcription. See Figure 26–17.

The activity of the operator is controlled by a protein called a *repressor protein.* The repressor protein is the product of another gene, called a *regulator gene.* When the repressor protein binds to the operator gene, transcription of the structural genes cannot start. The repressor protein is always present in the cell, and it is normally bound to the operator gene so that the operator is off. When lactose binds to the repressor protein, the protein changes shape. This makes it unable to bind to the operator gene. Therefore, when lactose is present, the operator gene is turned on. Then, transcription of the structural genes proceeds, and lactose-digesting enzymes are produced.

There is another control gene, called a *promoter,* that also plays a role in gene expression in bacteria. The promoter attracts and binds the enzyme that starts transcription. If the enzyme cannot bind to the promoter, transcription of the structural genes will not start. The promoter and the operator control the copying of a cluster of structural genes. In prokaryotes, such as bacteria, the promoter, the operator, and their associated structural genes are called an **operon** (OP er on).

Gene Expression in Higher Organisms

Scientists first thought that the control of gene expression in higher organisms (eukaryotes) would be similar to that in prokaryotes. However, this is not so for several reasons. In the first place, eukaryote genes relating to a certain function are not clustered together. Related genes are far apart from one another on a chromosome. Sometimes, they are on different chromosomes entirely. To further complicate matters, each eukaryote gene is split into parts, called *exons,* that are not next to each other. An **exon** is a segment of DNA that codes for amino acids that will become part of a protein. In between the exons, there are sections of DNA, called *introns.* An **intron** is a segment of DNA that does not code for amino acids of a protein.

When a gene is transcribed, both the introns and exons are made into RNA. The introns are then "edited out." To do this, enzymes cut out the intron RNA and then join, or splice, together the exon RNA pieces. Before this happens, two other strings of RNA nucleotides, one called a cap and the other a tail, are added to the ends of the RNA. See Figure 26–18. Because the enzymes can cut and splice the RNA in different ways, different proteins can be made from the same DNA segment.

Changes in the amount of coiling or in the shape of the DNA also affect the expression of genes in eukaryotes. A change in

Figure 26–18

mRNA Synthesis in Eukaryotes. Both the exons and introns are transcribed, producing one long RNA molecule. More nucleotides are added to the ends of the RNA. Enzymes then cut out the RNA introns and splice together the exons to form the completed messenger RNA. ▼

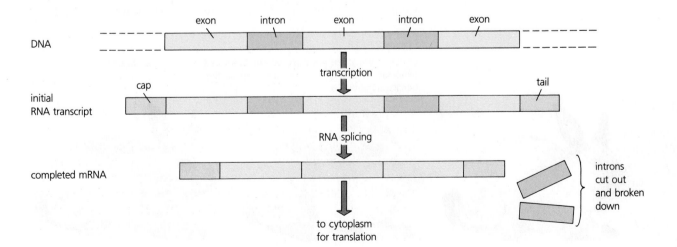

coiling or shape determines which parts of the DNA are accessible to enzymes and other proteins and to RNA. In turn, this accessibility influences the process of transcription. As you may recall from the discussion in Chapter 20, chromatin is made up of DNA wound around groups of proteins called histones. It is now thought that histones control the coiling and uncoiling of DNA in chromatin. Tightly packed DNA is not transcribed. Loosely packed DNA is transcribed. Finally, in some eukaryotes, certain chemical groups can attach to sections of DNA, changing its shape and reducing transcription.

Like the DNA of prokaryotes, the DNA of eukaryotes has sections that control the copying of genes. The control sections are not part of the gene itself. Instead, they are found elsewhere in the DNA. For example, eukaryotes have promoters that attract and bind the enzyme that starts the copying process. Another section of DNA, called the **enhancer,** controls the access of the enzyme to the promoter. Unlike the case in prokaryotes, in eukaryotes, control sections, such as enhancers, are usually far away from the genes they affect.

Gene Expression and the Environment

Some environmental factors also can switch genes on and off. You have already read about bacteria producing an enzyme when a certain sugar is present. In green plants, some development genes are switched on and off by light. Changes in temperature cause changes in the expression of the genes governing fur color in the Himalayan rabbit.

The Himalayan rabbit has white fur over most of its body, with black fur on the ear, nose, feet, and tail. See Figure 26–19. This pattern is produced by differences in temperature in certain parts of the body. A gene controls the production of black pigment. Black pigment is deposited in the fur over parts of the body in which the temperature falls below 33°C. This can be shown by placing an ice pack on a shaved area on the back of a Himalayan rabbit. Where the ice pack has lowered the temperature, the new growth of fur will be

Figure 26–19

Effect of Body Temperature on Fur Color of the Himalayan Rabbit. Cold temperatures turn on the gene that controls the production of black pigment in the Himalayan rabbit. ▼

black. Genes carry the basic information for all traits, but the phenotypes of organisms often can be changed by environmental factors that switch genes on and off.

In some reptiles, the incubation temperature of the eggs determines the sex of the offspring. In painted turtles, for example, high incubation temperatures tend to produce females, while low incubation temperatures produce mostly males.

Gene Expression in Development

During the development of an organism, different genes must be active at different times in its life cycle. The question of how genes are switched on and off during development has been studied thoroughly in the fruit fly *Drosophila*. Within the embryo of the fruit fly, scientists have discovered a group of genes, called **homeotic** (ho mee OH tik) **genes.** These genes control the key events in the development of a fruit fly. Homeotic genes switch other genes on and off. They do this by coding for homeotic proteins. It is thought that the homeotic proteins bind certain parts of the DNA and thus control the process of transcription. Similar sequences of DNA, known as *homeoboxes,* have also been found in many other animals, including humans.

Oncogenes and Cancer

Understanding the expression of genes may someday lead to a cure for cancer. **Oncogenes** (ON koh genes) are genes that cause some kinds of cancer. Oncogenes are present in most human cells, but usually they are switched off, or they are expressed in a way that does not cause cancer. When oncogenes are switched on, or when they begin to operate in an abnormal way, they lead to the uncontrolled growth of cells that we call cancer. If scientists can find a way to switch the oncogenes off, they may be able to develop a cure for many cancers.

26-4 Section Review

1. What is the term for the promoter, the operator, and the associated structural genes in prokaryotes?
2. What are the pieces of a split gene called in eukaryotes?
3. In what organism were homeotic genes first identified?
4. What environmental factor determines whether or not a Himalayan rabbit has black fur?

Critical Thinking

5. List some enviromental hazards that might cause oncogenes to be switched on. (*Identifying Causes*)

Laboratory
Investigation

Extracting DNA

DNA is stored in the nucleus of every eukaryotic cell. In this investigation, you will perform a DNA extraction—a procedure that removes the DNA from cells. You will extract the DNA from wheat germ, the fat-rich part of the seed of the wheat plant. A similar procedure, however, could extract the DNA from many different organisms.

Problem

How can you **observe** DNA?

Materials (per group)

- 200-mL plastic cup
- distilled water
- 1.5 g raw wheat germ
- hot plate
- 1000-mL beaker
- thermometer
- liquid dishwashing detergent
- 3 g meat tenderizer
- baking soda solution
- ice
- 10-mL graduated cylinder
- 10 mL alcohol solution
- glass stirring rod
- tongs

Procedure

1. Mix 100 mL of distilled water and the wheat germ in the 200-mL plastic cup.

2. Place the plastic cup in a water bath, as shown in the diagram.

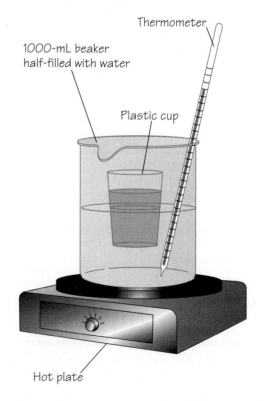

Thermometer

1000-mL beaker half-filled with water

Plastic cup

Hot plate

3. Heat the water bath to 50°C. As you perform steps 4 through 6 of the Procedure, adjust the hot plate as necessary to maintain the water temperature near 50°C. DNA will denature, or lose its structure, at temperatures above 60°C.

4. Add 5 mL of liquid dishwashing detergent to the plastic cup. Liquid dishwashing detergent breaks apart cell membranes.

5. Add the meat tenderizer to the plastic cup.

6. Add 10 mL of the baking soda solution to the plastic cup. Stir the mixture, then wait 10 minutes.

7. Turn off the hot plate. Using the tongs, transfer the plastic cup to a container of ice. Keep the plastic cup in the ice for at least 15 minutes.

8. Using the 10-mL graduated cylinder, slowly add the alcohol solution to the plastic cup. The alcohol solution should form a second layer on top of the wheat germ solution.

9. The DNA of the wheat germ precipitates at the interface of the two layers. Place the tip of the glass stirring rod at the interface and twist it to spool the DNA.

Observations
Describe the DNA you produced.

Analysis and Conclusions
1. What is the role of DNA in the cell?

2. Explain the purpose of adding liquid dishwashing detergent in step 4.

3. Can you directly observe the double-helix structure in the DNA sample you produced? Explain your answer.

4. Explain why a procedure similar to the one in this investigation could be used to extract DNA from the cells of other organisms.

Extensions
Following a similar procedure, extract DNA from onion cells or other plant cells.

Chapter 26 Review

Study Outline

26-1 Chromosomal Inheritance

▶ Thomas Hunt Morgan provided the first evidence that genes are parts of chromosomes.

▶ The sex chromosomes determine the sex of an individual.

▶ A sex-linked trait is a trait controlled by a gene located on a sex chromosome. Hemophilia, color blindness, and Duchenne muscular dystrophy, are caused by recessive alleles carried on the X chromosome.

▶ Genes located on the same chromosome cannot be distributed independently during meiosis because the genes are linked together. Linked genes may be separated by crossing-over of chromosomes during synapsis.

▶ When two or more genes affect an inherited characteristic, it is known as multiple-gene inheritance.

26-2 The Genetic Material

▶ James Watson and Francis Crick discovered the structure of the DNA molecule. Their model of DNA shows the molecule as a double helix.

▶ DNA replicates by separating at the nitrogen bases and then attaching new complementary bases to the exposed bases to form a new strand of DNA.

26-3 Gene Expression

▶ The DNA code for each of the 20 amino acids consists of three nitrogen bases. The genetic message from DNA is transcribed into messenger RNA. Each group of three nitrogen bases on mRNA, called a codon, specifies an amino acid.

▶ In the cytoplasm, each transfer RNA carries a specific amino acid and becomes temporarily joined by its anticodon to the condon of mRNA. A series of tRNAs carry amino acids that are assembled into a chain to form the polypeptide.

▶ The process by which the information coded in RNA is used for the assembly of a certain amino acid sequence is known as translation.

26-4 Control of Gene Expression

▶ The expression of certain genes in prokaryotes involves an operon, an operator gene, a regulator gene, and a promoter gene.

▶ Gene expression in eukaryotes involves genes that are far apart on a chromosome, or else are on entirely different chromosomes, and are split into introns and exons. During transcription, the introns are edited out and the exons are translated into polypeptides.

▶ Oncogenes, or genes that cause some types of cancer, are present in most human cells, but they are usually switched off or expressed in a way that does not cause cancer.

Chapter Assessment

Multiple Choice

Choose the letter of the answer that best completes each statement or answers the question.

1. Sex-linked genes (a) are located on the sex chromosomes. (b) control the production of the sex hormones. (c) can be found on autosomes. (d) are expressed only in males.

2. What is the probability that the sons of a colorblind man and a normal (homozygous) woman will be colorblind? (a) 0% (b) 25% (c) 50% (d) 75%

3. The gene for hemophilia is located on the X chromosome. If a hemophiliac man marries a normal woman, (a) all their sons will be hemophiliacs. (b) all their daughters will be hemophiliacs. (c) half their sons will be carriers. (d) all their daughters will be carriers.

4. During crossing-over, genes (a) are exchanged between adjacent cells. (b) are exchanged between homologous chromosomes. (c) switch locations on the same chromosome. (d) do not separate during meiosis.

5. Which statement about ribosomal RNA is not correct? (a) It is formed in the nucleus. (b) It is the site of protein synthesis. (c) With protein, it forms ribosomes. (d) It is involved in the process of transcription.

6. Thomas Hunt Morgan's experimental organism was the (a) bacteriophage. (b) fruit fly. (c) mosquito. (d) mouse.

7 Transcription is the process by which (a) DNA molecules are duplicated. (b) RNA molecules are transferred to polypeptides. (c) DNA serves as a template for RNA. (d) ribosomal RNA escapes from the nucleus.

8. How many different codons can be made from four different bases that are arranged into three-base sequences or words? (a) 4 (b) 12 (c) 24 (d) 64

9. Phenotype variation in the Himalayan rabbit is due to (a) polyploidy. (b) multiple-gene inheritance. (c) interaction of genes and environment. (d) sex-linked traits.

10. Replication is the process by which (a) DNA molecules are duplicated. (b) RNA molecules are duplicated. (c) DNA serves as a template for RNA. (d) proteins are synthesized.

Content Review

Answer each of the following in complete sentences.

11. Why are *Drosophila* chosen for use in genetic experiments?

12. Explain why hemophilia and color blindness occur much more often in men than in women.

13. How does crossing-over influence gene linkage?

14. What is a gene map and how is it constructed?

15. How did Hershey and Chase demonstrate that DNA carries hereditary information?

16. How does DNA replicate?

17. Compare the chemical composition and structure of RNA and DNA.

18. In what form is the hereditary information encoded in the DNA molecule?

19. How is the genetic message transcribed into mRNA?

20. What are the roles of mRNA, tRNA, and ribosomes in synthesizing a polypeptide?

21. What are the roles of introns and exons in gene expression of higher organisms?

Graphic Organizing

For information on graphic organizers, see Appendix G at the back of this text.

22. **Bar Graph** In multiple-gene inheritance, phenotypes vary from one extreme to another, with the phenotypes of most individuals falling between the two extremes. The chart below shows the number of plants of various heights in a sample of 64 plants of a certain species. Use the data to construct a bar graph showing the frequency of each phenotype. Plot the frequency of the phenotypes on the vertical axis and the height of the plants on the horizontal axis.

Height in cm	Number of Plants
10	1
11	6
12	15
13	20
14	15
15	6
16	1

23. **Compare/Contrast Matrix** Construct a matrix that compares and contrasts the characteristics of DNA and RNA.

Critical Thinking and Problem Solving

Discuss each of the following in a brief paragraph.

24. **Inferring** List some inheritance factors that may cause deviations from the Mendelian ratios that are expected.

25. **Drawing conclusions** How did Morgan come to the conclusion that chromosomes in *Drosophila* could be mapped?

26. **Relating** In humans, ear lobe appearance—free versus attached—is an inherited characteristic. What method could you use to determine whether the free-ear-lobe trait is dominant, recessive, or sex-linked?

27. **Relating** What is the probability that two parents with normal color vision will have color-blind sons and daughters if the mother's father is color blind?

Applied Genetics

Guide for Reading

Previewing the Chapter

An ordinary-looking sheep named Dolly stares placidly at the camera. But appearances are deceiving, because Dolly is no ordinary sheep. She is the end result of years of experiments on cloning—creating an organism that is genetically identical to another organism. Cloning is only one example of how genetics can be applied to bring about variations in organisms. What is the original source of all variations in organisms? How is genetic engineering used to produce desired traits in organisms?

Key Words

clone, genetic engineering, mutation, plasmid, recombinant DNA, restriction enzyme

Key Concepts

- **Describe** how selective breeding and mutations can produce new organisms.
- **Describe** some of the benefits of genetic engineering.
- **Design an experiment** to determine the effects of radiation on seeds. (Laboratory Investigation)

27-1 Mutations

Section Objectives:

- *List* some sources of genetic variation.
- *Distinguish* between gene mutations, chromosomal mutations, and jumping genes.
- *Describe* the kinds of chromosome and gene mutations.
- *Explain* the causes of mutations.

The Sources of Variation

As you have read, sexual reproduction brings about variation, or inherited differences, among offspring. The offspring of sexually reproducing organisms are genetically different from either parent. It is genetic variation that allows species to adapt to changing environments. It also allows breeders to develop new *strains* of plants and animals.

Most of the variation among individuals is the result of segregation and crossing over during meiosis and recombination during fertilization.

The differences in the genetic material of the members of a population can be traced back to mutations. A **mutation** (myoo TAY shun) is a sudden change in the structure or the amount of genetic

▲ **Figure 27–1**
Genetic Variation. Variation in genetic makeup is what makes people appear different from one another.

◀ Dolly: The first cloned sheep.

material. While most mutations are harmful to an organism, some have no effect, and others are beneficial. Beneficial mutations are the source of the variations that allow species to meet the needs of their environment.

Kinds of Mutations

Plant and animal breeders have known for a long time that new inherited traits, or mutations, may suddenly appear in a strain of plant or animal. The first individuals showing the new trait are called *mutants* (MYOOT unts). The Dutch botanist Hugo De Vries, one of the scientists who rediscovered Mendel's work, developed the concept of mutations. De Vries first observed mutations in a plant known as the evening primrose.

It is now known that there are two kinds of mutations. A **chromosomal mutation** is an abnormal change in the structure of all or part of a chromosome or in the number of chromosomes an organism has. The mutations De Vries saw in the evening primrose were chromosomal mutations. The other type of mutation is a gene mutation. A **gene mutation** is a change that affects a gene on a chromosome. The white-eyed male fruit fly that T. H. Morgan discovered was the result of a mutation of the gene for eye color.

For a mutation to be inherited in a sexually reproducing organism, it must be present in the DNA of a gamete. Thus, the mutation must occur in a gamete or in any cell from which a gamete develops. Mutations that occur in body cells normally cannot be inherited in sexual organisms, since body cells are not transmitted to offspring.

Causes of Mutations

Scientists have studied mutations that produce observable changes in traits in *Drosophila* and in other organisms. Each kind of mutation seems to occur naturally at a certain low rate in large populations. Although all the causes of natural mutation are not known, many may be the result of random errors in replication of the DNA.

When factors in the environment cause mutations, the factors are called **mutagens.** Hermann Muller, a student of T. H. Morgan, found that he could greatly increase the number of mutations in fruit flies by exposing them to X rays. Scientists now know that radiation, such as X rays and ultraviolet light, and chemicals, such as chloroform and mustard gas, are mutagens. Many mutations may be partly the result of mutagens that occur in the environment.

Chromosomal Mutations

Changes in Chromosome Structure
Permanent changes in chromosome structure sometimes take place during meiosis. The chromatids can become entangled and then their parts may be rearranged in several ways. These types of changes should not be

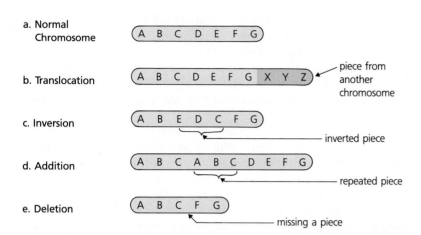

a. Normal Chromosome — A B C D E F G

b. Translocation — A B C D E F G X Y Z — piece from another chromosome

c. Inversion — A B E D C F G — inverted piece

d. Addition — A B C A B C D E F G — repeated piece

e. Deletion — A B C F G — missing a piece

◀ **Figure 27–2**
Changes in Chromosome Structure.

confused with crossing-over. **Translocation** is the transfer of a part of a chromosome to a nonhomologous chromosome. **Inversion** occurs when a piece of chromosome is rotated, which reverses the order of genes in the segment. **Addition** happens when a piece of a chromosome breaks off and attaches to a homologous chromosome. The homologous chromosome then has some gene repeated. **Deletion** occurs when a piece of a chromosome breaks off, resulting in the loss of some genes. See Figure 27–2.

Nondisjunction   The addition or loss of a whole chromosome is called **nondisjunction** (non dis JUNK shun). Nondisjunction takes place when chromosomes that normally separate during meiosis remain together. Nondisjunction causes several genetic disorders in humans.

Polyploidy   A condition in which cells have some multiple of the normal chromosome number is called **polyploidy** (PAHL ee ployd ee). Polyploidy occurs when chromosomes do not separate normally during mitosis or meiosis. This condition is commonly found in plant cells. For example, the number of chromosomes in some plant cells may be $3n$, $4n$, or even $5n$. Polyploid plants and their fruits are often larger than normal. Plant breeders sometimes use chemicals to develop polyploid plants. See Figure 27–3.

Gene Mutations

Genes specify the order of amino acids in a polypeptide chain for a specific protein. This information is coded into the sequence of bases along a DNA strand. Any change in this sequence is likely to change the message transcribed into mRNA. This is likely to change the structure of the protein that the cell makes. These types of changes are called *gene mutations*. Once a mutation occurs in a DNA molecule, it is copied in all the later replications of the DNA.

    A gene mutation that involves a single nucleotide—such as the substitution of one nucleotide for another—is called a **point mutation.** Such a substitution can change one of the amino acids for which the gene codes. However, when a nucleotide is added

Figure 27–3
Polyploidy. The plump strawberries in the top row are from polyploid plants. The smaller ones in the bottom row are from normal plants. ▼

▲ Figure 27–4

Mutation. The crossed bill on this robin is the result of a gene mutation.

or removed at some point, all the triplet codons beyond that point are changed. This is called a **frameshift mutation** because it shifts the "reading frame" of the genetic message.

In other cases, one base in a DNA nucleotide is substituted for another. This changes one mRNA codon and one amino acid in the protein. Changing one amino acid may result in a protein that does not function normally.

Most scientists believe that gene mutations occur from time to time randomly in all cells. Mutations in individual body cells usually are not important, since they are not likely to affect other cells or the functions of the organism as a whole. If a single cell loses the ability to make a certain protein, the cell may die, or it may obtain the protein from outside the cell. In either case, nothing noticeable happens. Mutations in sex cells, however, are important. If a mutation is present in a gamete at the time of fertilization, all the cells of the embryo and the adult organism will have the mutation.

Inherited gene mutations are usually recessive. Only about 1 in 100 gene mutations is dominant. Most gene mutations are harmful to the organism because the genes of a normal individual already meet the needs of the organism. See Figure 27–4. Any change is likely to result in a useless protein, or no protein at all, in place of one that is needed.

Jumping Genes

Genes that move or jump from chromosome to chromosome cause another kind of mutation. Although most genes stay in one place, a few are able to move to new locations on the chromosomes during replication. These mobile elements, or "jumping genes," were discovered by Barbara McClintock, an American geneticist. When a gene takes a new position in or near another gene during replication, it often causes an inactivation of that gene. Jumping genes are an important source of variation and are thought to exist in all species. McClintock was awarded the Nobel prize in 1983 for her discovery.

27-1 Section Review

1. What is the ultimate source of genetic differences in a population?
2. Give an example of a mutagen.
3. Name six kinds of chromosomal mutations.
4. What kind of mutation involves a change in one DNA nucleotide in a chromosome?

Critical Thinking

5. Which type of gene mutation would you expect to be more harmful to a protein—one where one nucleotide is removed or one where three nucleotides are removed? Explain. (*Ranking*)

27-2 Human Genetic Disorders

Section Objectives:

- *Explain* some of the difficulties that arise in studying human genetics.
- *List* some sex-linked disorders, recessive disorders, dominant disorders, and chromosomal disorders.
- *Describe* some techniques that are used in the diagnosis of some human genetic disorders.

Studying Human Heredity

Although a great deal is known about human genetics, heredity in humans cannot be studied in the same way it is studied in plants and other animals. The time between generations is too long, the number of offspring produced is too small, and no controlled experiments are possible.

Scientists have learned about certain genetic traits in humans by tracing the appearance of these traits in families over several generations. A **pedigree chart** is a diagram that shows the presence or absence of a particular trait in each member of each generation. Figure 27–5 shows a pedigree chart tracing the inheritance of color blindness in five generations of a family. The existence of female carriers of color blindness can be shown definitely only when the condition is found in a female's descendants.

Sex-Linked Disorders

As you may recall from Chapter 26, color blindness is a sex-linked condition in which an individual cannot perceive certain colors. Other more serious sex-linked disorders include *hemophilia* (hee muh FIL ee uh) and *Duchenne muscular dystrophy* (DIS truh fee).

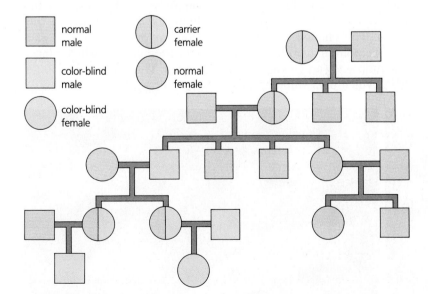

◀ **Figure 27–5**
A Pedigree Chart Tracing Color Blindness in a Family.

Hemophilia Hemophilia is a sex-linked disorder in which the blood is unable to clot because it lacks a certain blood-clotting protein. The recessive gene for hemophilia is carried on the X chromosome. Thus, most affected individuals are males. Females with one recessive gene are carriers but show no signs of illness.

Hemophilia is dangerous because the smallest cut or bruise can cause a person to bleed severely. Blood plasma transfusions and injections of the missing blood-clotting substance are used to treat hemophilia. Many hemophiliacs today live into adulthood.

Duchenne Muscular Dystrophy Another sex-linked inherited disorder is Duchenne muscular dystrophy. In this disorder, the muscle tissue of affected individuals begins to break down during childhood. A recessive gene carried on the X chromosome causes the disorder. Affected individuals have an inactive form of a protein that is required for normal muscle function. These individuals usually do not live beyond their teens.

Autosomal Genetic Disorders

There are a number of other human disorders that are caused by recessive defective alleles on autosomes. These alleles rarely cause signs of illness in people who are carriers because a dominant normal allele also is present. A few human disorders, however, are caused by dominant alleles.

Sickle-Cell Disease **Sickle-cell disease,** or sickle-cell anemia, is a recessive inherited disorder in which the red blood cells have an abnormal sickle shape. See Figure 27–6. The sickle shape causes the red blood cells to clump and to block small blood vessels. The oxygen-carrying capacity of these cells is decreased. A person with sickle-cell disease suffers from lack of oxygen in the blood and experiences pain and weakness.

The disease is caused by the change of one base in the gene that controls the production of one polypeptide chain in the hemoglobin molecule. There are about 300 amino acids in this chain. The change changes the codon for one amino acid at a specific point in the chain. The normal codon is GAA, which places glutamic acid (an amino acid) in the chain. The abnormal codon is GUA, which puts valine in place of glutamic acid.

Figure 27–6

Sickle and Normal Red Blood Cells. The normal red blood cells (left) are round and thinner in the center than near the edge. The sickle cells (right) are elongated and crescent-shaped. ▼

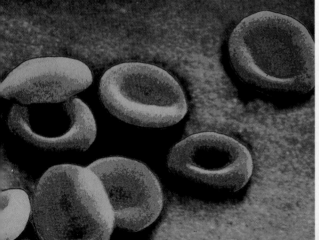

Sickle-cell disease exists mainly in people who can trace their ancestry to regions of Africa where malaria is found. Carriers of the trait—those with one normal and one sickle-cell allele—are more resistant to malaria than people without the defective allele. Because it offers some protection from malaria, this allele is more common than expected in African populations. Carriers of the trait usually are not troubled by symptoms of sickle-cell disease.

Screening for sickle-cell disease is done through examination of the red blood cells. Most people with sickle-cell disease do not live past childhood. With medical treatment, some individuals are able to live to early adulthood. As yet, there is no cure for the disease.

Phenylketonuria   PKU, which is short for *phenylketonuria* (fen ul kee tah NYOOR ee uh), is a recessive inherited disorder in which the enzyme that breaks down phenylalanine (an amino acid) is missing. Because of the missing enzyme, phenylalanine breaks down into chemicals that can damage the brain and cause mental retardation. In the past, it was not possible to diagnose PKU until brain damage had occurred. Now, however, PKU can be diagnosed at birth by a simple test of the infant's urine. This is done routinely in most hospitals. Brain damage can be avoided by a special diet low in phenylalanine.

Tay-Sachs Disease   Similar to PKU, *Tay-Sachs disease* is an incurable inherited disorder that damages the brain. The disease results from the lack of a specific enzyme for the breakdown of lipids in the brain. Without the enzyme, the lipids build up in the brain cells and destroy them. Tay-Sachs is a rare disease, found most often among Jewish families of Eastern European decent. The allele for the disease is recessive, and signs of illness occur only in the homozygous condition. Tay-Sachs disease appears before the age of one, and death occurs within several years.

Cystic Fibrosis   The most common fatal genetic disease in the United States is *cystic fibrosis* (SIS tik fy BROH sis). It is found among people of European ancestry. This disorder is caused by a recessive allele on chromosome 7. In children with two recessive alleles, some glands produce a thick mucus that clogs and damages the lungs. As the disease progresses, it becomes increasingly difficult for the person to breathe. New treatments using genetically engineered viruses have been tested. It is hoped that the promising results of these studies will help researchers find a cure in the near future.

Huntington Disease   *Huntington disease* is an example of an inherited disorder that is caused by a dominant allele. Every person who has the allele develops Huntington disease. Any child born to a parent with Huntington disease has a 50% chance of inheriting the allele and thus developing the disease.

Huntington disease is fatal, although symptoms usually do not appear until the person is in his or her thirties. The disease causes a progressive breakdown of the brain cells, leading to death.

Science, Technology and Society

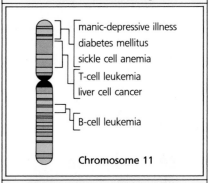

manic-depressive illness
diabetes mellitus
sickle cell anemia
T-cell leukemia
liver cell cancer
B-cell leukemia

Chromosome 11

Issue: Genetic Screening

Thousands of diseases can be linked to genetic factors. This means that people with a certain genetic makeup have a greater probability of contracting such illnesses. New developments in genetic engineering, however, make it possible to test people to determine their susceptibility.

Critics of genetic screening tests warn about the danger of genetic discrimination. Employers might use the data in evaluating candidates for jobs. Insurance companies might base decisions about insurance coverage on the tests. Critics argue that, like race or creed, genetic makeup should not be a factor in such decisions.

People who favor testing argue that determining susceptibility is valuable to both employer and job candidate. Individuals may be susceptible to job-related disorders. For example, a person who may develop genetic emphysema of the lung might not be an appropriate candidate for a job in which fumes are inhaled.

■ ***Should genetic screening tests be allowed? Why or why not?***

▲ **Figure 27–7**
Down Syndrome. This young girl (right) with Down syndrome has a karyotype (left) that shows three number 21 chromosomes.

Chromosomal Disorders

Nondisjunction causes several inherited disorders in humans. **Down syndrome** is a disorder that results from an extra copy of chromosome number 21. See Figure 27–7. Thus, a person with Down syndrome has three number 21 chromosomes in each cell. This causes mental retardation and physical abnormalities.

Nondisjunction can also occur in the sex chromosomes. One condition, called *Turner syndrome,* is caused by the presence of only one sex chromosome—an X—in the cells. It results in a female with underdeveloped sexual characteristics. In *Klinefelter syndrome,* each cell has two X chromosomes and one Y chromosome. This results in a male with underdeveloped sex organs.

Detecting Genetic Disorders

No treatment or cure is known for many inherited disorders. It is possible, however, for people who may be carriers of a genetic disorder to be tested and counseled before having children. Genetic counselors are people who give prospective parents an accurate idea about the risks of having a child with an inherited disorder. For some inherited disorders, there are tests that show whether or not the parents are carriers.

A person's genetic makeup may be examined by a process known as **karyotyping** (kar ee oh TYP ing). In karyotyping, a cell undergoing mitosis is photographed. The photograph is enlarged, and the photos of chromosomes are cut out and arranged in pairs. This is possible because chromosome pairs differ from each other in length, shape, and position of the centromere. The karyotype of the person then can be compared with a normal human karyotype (see Figure 21–2).

Karyotyping and a number of other techniques may be used by physicians to detect genetic disorders in a fetus. In a process called **amniocentesis** (am nee oh sen TEE sis), a long needle is inserted into the amniotic sac of a pregnant woman at about the sixteenth week of pregnancy. A small sample of amniotic fluid, which contains some cells shed by the fetus, is withdrawn. After four weeks, the fluid and the cells are examined for abnormalities. For example, they may be checked for the presence or lack of a certain enzyme. Tay-Sachs disease can be detected this way. The fetal cells may also be karyotyped to determine whether they contain any abnormal, missing, or extra chromosomes. The presence of an extra chromosome number 21 indicates that the fetus has Down syndrome. The karyotype also reveals the sex of the fetus.

Much of the same information obtained from amniocentesis may be obtained using a newer method, called **chorionic** (kor ee AHN ik) **villus sampling.** In this technique, a sample of the chorion,

MiniLab

Skill: Interpreting

Climbing a Family Tree

Problem

How can you **interpret** the data from a pedigree showing inheritance of a recessive trait in a family?

Procedure

1. Draw a pedigree for a family showing two parents and four children. Include the following in the pedigree:

   a. The two oldest children should be males and the two youngest children should be females.

   b. The second son has sickle-cell disease.

   c. The older son is married and has a daughter.

   d. The oldest daughter is married and has a normal daughter and a son who has sickle-cell disease.

2. Using this information and your knowledge about constructing pedigrees, fill in the pedigree. Record the genotypes for each member of the pedigree next to his or her symbol. Use N for a normal allele and n for the sickle-cell allele.

Analyze and Conclude

1. Can you determine the genotype for the people whose symbols are not shaded in? Explain your answer.

2. If the youngest daughter married, what would be the probability of her having a child with sickle-cell disease? Explain your answer.

3. Some diseases are carried as dominant genes. Marfan's syndrome is a disease caused by a dominant allele that causes extreme height and a weakened aorta in both sexes. Explain how a pedigree for a family with Marfan's syndrome would differ from the pedigree for a recessive disease.

Figure 27–8

Ultrasound. Ultrasound may reveal genetic defects or problems in the fetus, some of which can be treated during or after birth. ▶

a part of the placenta, is removed for examination. The cells of the chorion are genetically identical to those of the fetus. Chorionic villus sampling may be done much earlier than amniocentesis.

To determine the size and position of a developing fetus, a procedure using high-frequency sound waves, known as **ultra-sound,** may be used. The sound waves are reflected off the fetus to produce an image of the developing fetus. See Figure 27–8. By studying this image, doctors can detect abnormalities in bone, muscle, and heart formation. They may also confirm the presence of more than one fetus.

Another technique, called **fetoscopy** (fee TAH skuh pee), allows direct observation of the fetus and tissues. A needle-thin tube containing a viewing scope and a special light is inserted into the uterus. The fetus can be observed through this instrument, known as an endoscope. By inserting special tools through the endoscope, blood and cell samples may be taken for analysis.

27-2 Section Review

1. What type of mutation causes sickle-cell disease?
2. Give one example of a recessive disorder, a dominant disorder, and a chromosomal disorder.
3. Name the process in which a photograph of chromosomes is cut apart and the chromosomes are arranged into pairs.
4. What is the technique by which a small sample of amniotic fluid is removed from a pregnant woman?

Critical Thinking

5. To diagnose some genetic disorders, such as Huntington disease, family members must submit blood samples. Suppose that one member of a family wanted to know if he or she had the disease. Do you think that other family members should be required to provide blood samples against their will? (*Making Ethical Judgments*)

27-3 Genetic Engineering

Section Objectives:

- *Describe* the methods used by plant and animal breeders to improve their crops and animals.
- *Explain* how organisms can be cloned.
- *List* some ways in which genetic engineering has been used to benefit people.

Breeding Methods

People have always tried to improve their crops and domestic animals. They have tried to increase yields, upgrade quality, and expand growing and breeding areas. Today, a knowledge of genetics is used to produce organisms with desirable traits. A breeder can choose from several methods.

Selection   The process of choosing organisms with the most desirable traits for mating is called **selection.** A dairy farmer, for example, might select and mate only the cows that are the most hardy and that give the most milk. The breeder hopes to change the population by building up desired characteristics. After mating occurs, the breeder selects only the offspring with the desired traits for further mating.

Inbreeding   The mating of closely related individuals to obtain desired characteristics is called **inbreeding.** The degree of closeness can vary. The closest possible hereditary relationship is self-pollination by plants. In organisms that require cross-fertilization, the closest relationship would be brother-sister, mother-son, and father-daughter. Inbreeding is used to produce domestic animals, such as fowl, sheep, cattle, and swine, and pets, such as purebred cats and dogs. See Figure 27–9.

◀ **Figure 27–9**
Cross-Eyed Siamese Cat. Inbreeding may result in undesirable effects, such as the crossed eyes in this Siamese cat.

Inbreeding decreases variation in a population and thus tends to increase the number of homozygous genes. Continued inbreeding and selection eventually produce a line of animals that breeds nearly pure. At the same time, however, inbreeding can result in unwanted effects. Harmful recessive alleles may be brought together by inbreeding and be expressed. Problems in many dog breeds, including deformities in the joints and progressive blindness in German shepherds and golden retrievers, have resulted from repeated inbreeding.

Hybridization When individuals who are not closely related are mated to introduce new, beneficial alleles into the population, it is called **hybridization.** Hybrids, the individuals produced by such crosses, are often hardier than either of the parents. This is called *hybrid vigor.* The mule, the offspring of a male donkey and a female horse, is one example of hybridization. The mule is superior to its parents in physical endurance, strength, and resistance to disease. Mules, however, are usually sterile.

Mutations Naturally occurring mutations are used by plant and animal breeders to improve their stock. Many fruits, such as the navel orange and seedless grape, originated as natural mutations. Once discovered, a plant mutation may be reproduced by vegetative propagation. This avoids the segregation of traits that would occur in sexual reproduction.

Sometimes, mutations take place during meiosis. When a whole set of chromosomes fails to separate during meiosis, gametes with extra sets of chromosomes are produced. Organisms with three or more sets of chromosomes are called polyploids. This type of mutation is fairly common among plants. More than half of the known species of flowering plants are polyploids. Polyploid plants are hardier, bigger, and more productive than normal

Figure 27–10 ▶
Polyploid Daylilies

plants. Look back at Figure 27–3 on page 547 to see the difference between polyploid and normal strawberries.

A mutant polyploid plant cannot produce offspring by mating with a plant with only one set of chromosomes. Thus, polyploid plants usually form separate species or produce offspring by mating with plants with similar numbers of chromosomes.

Methods of Genetic Engineering

Understanding the gene has led to the remarkable development of methods for changing a cell's DNA. Biologists can cut, separate, and splice together DNA sequences in any order. This process allows biologists to engineer a set of genetic changes directly into an organism's DNA. This form of DNA manipulation is known as **genetic engineering.**

Genetic engineering is a multi-step process. The first step is to cut the DNA containing the desired gene away from the genes surrounding it. The second step is finding a way to combine that gene with a piece of DNA from the recipient organism; that is, the organism that will receive the DNA. The third step is to insert the combined DNA into the new organism. Finally, you would need to be able to read the sequences of nucleotide bases in the gene in order to analyze the genes that you are manipulating.

Isolating a Gene   As you just read, isolating the pieces of DNA that contain a desired gene is the first step in any genetic engineering procedure. Genes can be cut at specific DNA sequences by

MiniLab

Skill: Modeling

So Many Restrictions!

Procedure

1. Write a 100-character sequence of the letters A, C, G, and T in a random order.

2. Copy the sequence onto each of three different strips of paper.

3. Use a different colored pencil or paper to identify each copy.

4. Cut the strips to model the action of three restriction enzymes. You may use the restriction enzymes presented in the textbook, or use restriction enzymes of your own design. Use a different strip for each enzyme.

Problem

How can you **model** the action of restriction enzymes?

Analyze and Conclude

1. Which restriction enzyme produced the most pieces?

2. Which restriction enzyme produced the fewest pieces? The fewest pieces?

3. Why do biologists use more than one restriction enzyme to cut DNA?

proteins known as **restriction enzymes.** Restriction enzymes make it possible to cut DNA into fragments that can then be isolated, separated, and analyzed.

Molecular biologists have identified over 100 restriction enzymes. Each restriction enzyme cuts only a specific sequence of nucleotides, and it cuts the sequence in a very specific way. For three examples, the enzyme *EcoR1* cuts the sequence CTTAAG between the A and G. The enzyme *Bam1* cuts the sequence CCTAGG between the two G's. And the enzyme *Hae3* cuts the sequence CCGG right down the middle, between the C and G. Because restriction enzymes are so specific, researchers can readily piece together the DNA fragments that the enzymes create.

Making Recombinant DNA   DNA fragments cannot function all by themselves. They must become part of the genetic material of living cells before the genes they contain can be activated. In the second step of genetic engineering, DNA fragments are incorporated into part of the recipient cell's genetic material.

For example, DNA fragments may be combined with bacterial DNA so that they can later be inserted into a bacterial cell. Bacteria often contain small ring-shaped segments of DNA known as **plasmids.** These plasmids can be removed from bacterial cells and cut with the same restriction enzyme used to produce the DNA fragments. The cuts made by the restriction enzyme produce matching "sticky ends" on the DNA fragments and the cut plasmids. These sticky ends are the sites at which a DNA fragment and a plasmid can be joined end to end, thereby forming a new plasmid that contains a piece of foreign DNA. See Figure 27–12. This new DNA is also known as **recombinant DNA,** because DNA from two sources have been recombined to produce it.

DNA Insertion   In the first two steps of genetic engineering, DNA fragments containing the desired gene are obtained and then inserted into DNA that has been removed from the recipient cell, thereby producing recombinant DNA. But how is this DNA inserted back into living cells?

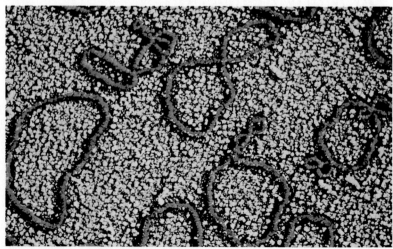

Figure 27–11 ▶

Plasmids. Bacterial plasmids appear as blue rings in this false-color image from an electron microscope. Biologists use plasmids as vehicles for introducing DNA to bacterial cells.

One of the easiest methods is to transfer the DNA into bacterial cells. To transfer DNA into bacteria, plasmids are first obtained from bacterial cells. This is done by crushing the bacteria and sorting out the plasmids. The plasmids then are placed in a solution containing the foreign DNA. A restriction enzyme is used to break open the plasmid. The foreign DNA attaches itself to the open end of the plasmid and closes the ring. DNA ligase, an enzyme, splices the new gene into the open plasmid cleaved by the restriction enzyme. Once this is done, the plasmid includes the foreign gene.

These bacteria can then be isolated and grown into large colonies that contain the recombinant DNA. This technique is called *cloning*. A **clone** is a large number of cells grown from a single cell. Organisms that reproduce asexually produce clones because each offspring receives an exact copy of the parent's genes. A great deal of research is now directed toward the production of clones of organisms that normally reproduce sexually.

DNA Sequencing   The final step in genetic engineering is to sequence a piece of DNA, or to read the sequence of DNA bases. Only one of the two strands of the DNA double helix is used in the process of DNA sequencing. However, many copies of this one strand are needed. These multiple copies can be produced through the process of DNA cloning.

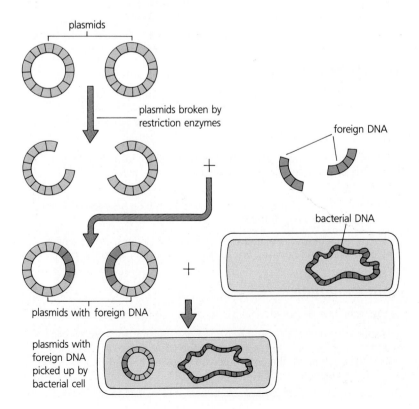

◀ **Figure 27–12**

Using Plasmids to Transfer Foreign DNA to Bacterial Cells. By introducing foreign genes into a plasmid, genetic engineers can change the genetic makeup of a cell, so that the transplanted genes are expressed.

Figure 27–13

The Effect of Growth Hormones on Pigs.

These pigs are genetically identical. The larger one has been fattened by the addition of growth hormones to its diet. ▼

Recombinant DNA technology has advanced rapidly in the past few years. Techniques now exist for cutting and splicing DNA molecules, for inserting DNA into cells of a wide variety of organisms, and for controlling foreign genes moved from one species into another. Organisms that contain such foreign genes are said to be transgenic.

Applying Genetic Engineering

Genetic engineering provides a way of producing large amounts of previously rare substances. For example, *interferon* (int ur FIR on) is a protein that helps the body fight off viruses. Genetic engineers have inserted the human gene for interferon into bacteria. Bacteria with the human gene for interferon are then able to make the protein. When the bacteria are cloned, large amounts of interferon are produced and can be collected. Other valuable substances made in this way include human insulin, used in the treatment of diabetes, and the clotting substance that is needed to treat people with hemophilia.

Perhaps the greatest promise of genetic engineering is gene replacement, correcting genetic defects by transferring normal genes into cells that lack them. The replacement of defective genes is called **gene therapy.** Gene therapy has been used in humans for various genetic defects.

MiniLab

Skill: Modeling

Changing Directions

Problem

How can you **model** the creation of recombinant DNA?

Procedure

1. On one side of a strip of paper, print simple directions describing how to get from your home to your school. Include all necessary information, but be as brief as possible.

2. On a second strip of paper, print simple directions describing how to get from your home to the nearest movie theater.

3. Using only scissors, adhesive tape, and the two sets of directions, create a new set of directions describing how you would get from your school to the movie theater.

Analyze and Conclude

1. Describe the technique you used in Step 3 to create the new set of directions.

2. DNA molecules carry directions—in the form of genes—that code for certain traits. Scientists are now able to cut and rearrange DNA molecules, creating recombinant DNA. Compare the procedure you followed in this MiniLab to the process of creating recombinant DNA.

Farmers also have been helped by genetic engineering. For example, genetic engineers have inserted genes into plants to make the plants resistant to disease, insects, and weed-killing substances. About 50 species of genetically engineered plants are currently being tested for their resistance to bacteria and viruses. In addition, growth-promoting hormones, produced by genetic engineering, are used to increase the amount of milk produced by cows and to fatten farm animals.

The Human Genome

The technology of genetic engineering has now turned toward the heredity of humans. It is estimated that the human genome consists of over 100 000 genes, each with at least 10 000 nucleotide pairs. A **genome** is all the genes possessed by an organism. In one of the largest research efforts ever undertaken, scientists involved in the *Human Genome Project* are attempting to decode all of the genes of human heredity. Results from this project have already identified a host of genes associated with genetic disorders. It has also provided clues to the genetic basis of cancer and heart disease.

Ethics and Human Genetics

An important new set of ethical issues has been raised by the rapid advances in human genetics. Should researchers carry out experiments that permanently change human DNA? Should genetic engineering only be used to cure certain disorders? Or should it be used to make people taller, stronger, or more disease resistant? How should we decide which genes should be transplanted, altered, or redesigned? Who should determine whether experiments with genetic engineering should be done?

What is the proper way to use genetic information? Does anyone own genetic information? Do individuals have the right to keep genetic information to themselves? As we move into the next century, these are just a few of the issues that need to be addressed.

27-3 Section Review

1. List three methods used by breeders to improve the yield and quality of their plant and animal products.
2. What is a group of organisms with exactly the same genes called?
3. Describe two applications of genetic engineering. Use specific examples.
4. Name the small circle-shaped DNA that is used to insert foreign pieces of DNA into bacteria.

Critical Thinking

5. What do breeding methods and recombinant DNA methods have in common? How do they differ? (*Comparing and Contrasting*)

Laboratory
Investigation

Designing an Experiment

The Effects of Radiation on Seeds

Mutations occur naturally in all organisms. However, an organism's mutation rate increases when it is exposed to certain chemicals or types of radiation. In this investigation, you will design an experiment to observe the effects of X-ray exposure on seeds.

Problem

Do irradiated seeds grow differently from nonirradiated seeds? **Design an experiment** to answer the question.

Suggested Materials

- irradiated seeds and nonirradiated seeds from the same organism
- 2 petri dishes
- paper towels
- pots with soil
- glass-marking pencil

Suggested Procedure

1. Design an experiment to determine whether irradiated seeds grow differently from non-irradiated seeds. Include two test groups in your experiment, with one test group as a control. Make sure that the test groups are treated identically.

2. To grow the seeds, follow any special directions on the seeds' packages. Otherwise, line a petri dish with a paper towel, place the seeds in the petri dishes and cover the seeds with water, as shown in the diagram.

3. Use the glass-marking pencil to label each petri dish. Every petri dish that your class uses in this experiment should have a unique label. Store the petri dishes in a location designated by your teacher.

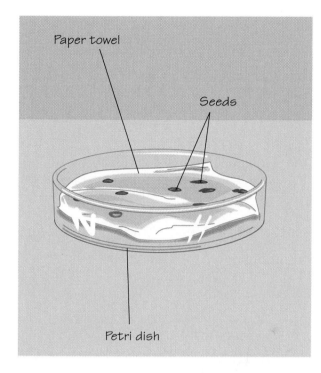

Paper towel

Seeds

Petri dish

Observations

Day	Nonirradiated Seeds	Irradiated Seeds
1		
2		
3		
4		

Data Table

1. Describe the roots produced by the seeds. In what ways are they similar? In what ways are they different?

2. Describe any leaves that the young plants produced. In what ways are the leaves similar in the two groups? In what ways are they different?

3. Note any other similarities or differences among the plants that the seeds produced.

4. Observe the growth of the seeds over the course of two weeks. Record your observations in a data table similar to the one shown. Add water to the petri dishes as necessary to keep the seeds moist.

5. After two weeks, carefully transfer five young plants in each test group from the petri dishes to pots containing soil.

6. Label the pots and place them in sunlight or under a fluorescent lamp. Water the plants regularly. Observe their growth for the next few weeks. Record your observations in the data table.

Analysis and Conclusions

1. Compare how the irradiated seeds and non-irradiated seeds grew into plants.

2. Did the irradiated seeds contain mutant DNA? How certain can you be of your answer? Explain.

3. How could you best determine whether a seed contains mutant DNA?

4. Formulate a hypothesis to explain the results of your experiment. Could a different hypothesis also explain the results? Discuss this possibility.

Extensions

Repeat your experiment with irradiated and non-irradiated seeds of other plants.

Chapter **27** Review ....

Study Outline

27-1 Mutations

▶ In sexually reproducing species, most genetic variation results from segregation and crossing-over during meiosis and from recombination during fertilization. The differences in genetic material among members of a population can be traced to new inherited traits called mutations.

▶ Chromosomal mutations involve permanent changes in chromosome structure, such as translocation, inversion, addition, and deletion; or changes in chromosome number, such as nondisjunction and polyploidy.

▶ Gene mutations result from a change in the sequence of bases in a DNA molecule, which ultimately alters the structure of a protein the cell synthesizes.

27-2 Human Genetic Disorders

▶ Sex-linked disorders, such as color blindness, hemophilia, and Duchenne muscular dystrophy, are caused by recessive genes located on the X chromosome.

▶ Autosomal genetic disorders include sickle-cell disease, phenylketonuria, Tay-Sachs disease, cystic fibrosis, and Huntington disease.

▶ Chromosomal disorders resulting from nondisjunction include Down syndrome, Turner syndrome, and Klinefelter syndrome.

▶ Genetic disorders can be detected by karyotyping, amniocentesis, or chorionic villus sampling.

27-3 Genetic Engineering

▶ People can improve crops and domestic animal stock by using breeding methods that include selection, inbreeding, hybridization, and naturally occurring mutations.

▶ Through genetic engineering, biologists can cut, separate, and splice together DNA sequences in any order. This process allows biologists to insert new genes directly into an organism's DNA.

▶ Genetic engineering is a multi-step process. It includes isolating the pieces of DNA that contain the desired gene; combining that gene with a piece of DNA from another organism; inserting the combined DNA into the new organism; and sequencing the gene in order to analyze it.

▶ The goal of the Human Genome Project is to identify the complete nucleotide sequences of human DNA. It is hoped that this information will help in the treatment of genetic disorders.

Chapter Assessment

Multiple Choice

Choose the letter of the answer that best completes each statement or answers the question.

1. A common practice used by breeders to maintain a desired trait in dogs is (a) selection. (b) hybridization. (c) regeneration. (d) vegetative propagation.

2. Which procedure can be performed during fetal development to detect Down syndrome? (a) genetic counseling (b) amniocentesis (c) urine analysis (d) cloning

3. A genetic disorder in which the blood does not clot properly is (a) PKU. (b) hemophilia. (c) Huntington disease. (d) Tay-Sachs disease.

4. People who are resistant to malaria often are heterozygous for (a) sickle-cell disease. (b) PKU. (c) Turner syndrome. (d) color blindness.

5. A human DNA segment was inserted into a bacterial cell and became incorporated into the bacterial DNA. This technique is an example of (a) genetic engineering. (b) cloning. (c) polyploidy. (d) selection.

6. Which breeding method results in the production of offspring with the same genetic makeup as its parents? (a) cross-pollination (b) vegetative propagation (c) inbreeding (d) hybridization

7. Traits that are controlled by genes found on an X chromosome are said to be (a) autosomal dominant. (b) codominant. (c) autosomal recessive. (d) sex-linked.

8. Polyploidy is an example of a (a) chromosomal mutation. (b) gene mutation. (c) point mutation. (d) frameshift mutation.

9. To cut DNA at specific sequences, biologists use (a) restriction enzymes. (b) RNA. (c) plasmids. (d) recombinant DNA.

10. What is the name of DNA that is recombined from two different sources? (a) mutant DNA (b) plasmid DNA (c) restriction DNA (d) recombinant DNA

Content Review

Answer each of the following in complete sentences.

11. What is the difference between a gene mutation and a chromosomal mutation?

12. Explain what happens in nondisjunction.

13. What types of changes in DNA can result in a point mutation?

14. How do sex-linked genetic disorders differ from autosomal disorders? Give an example of a human sex-linked disorder.

15. Name three autosomal genetic disorders of humans and describe the effects of each.

16. Describe the techniques of karyotyping, amniocentesis, and chorionic villus sampling.

17. Distinguish between selection, inbreeding, and hybridization.

18. What is a clone?

19. How do genetic engineers use plasmids?

20. Describe the four steps that usually take place in genetic engineering.

Graphic Organizing

For information on graphic organizers, see Appendix G at the back of this text.

21. **Concept Map** Construct a concept map for the following term: *genetic disorder*. Include both autosomal disorders and sex-linked disorders. Be sure to include linking words between concepts.

Critical Thinking and Problem Solving

Discuss each of the following in a brief paragraph.

22. **Inferring** Why do the majority of scientists assume that mutations are the ultimate sources of variation?

23. **Predicting** Predict what would happen during meiosis if a plant had three sets of chromosomes (3n) rather than the normal diploid number.

24. **Hypothesizing** Populations usually remain stable or change very slowly over a long period. The chart below shows data from a population genetics survey of a certain species of insect. Develop a hypothesis to account for the changes in the frequencies of the alleles. Note that the environment has remained stable for the past 50 years.

Year	Frequency of Allele B	Frequency of Allele b
1940	0.99	0.01
1950	0.95	0.05
1960	0.98	0.02
1970	0.96	0.04
1980	0.10	0.90
1990	0.08	0.92

25. **Drawing conclusions** The occurrence of Down syndrome in the population is recorded in the table below. Graph the data. Draw a conclusion about the relationship between the incidence of Down syndrome and the mother's age.

Age of Mother	Occurrence of Down Syndrome per 1000 Births
25	.8
30	1.0
35	3.0
40	10.0
45	30.0
50	80.0

Performance-Based Assessment

Genetics and Public Health

Background

The first antibiotic, penicillin, was discovered by Alexander Fleming in 1928. Since then, many other antibiotics have been discovered. Today, more than 100 antibiotics are available to doctors in the fight against bacterial diseases. It was once thought that antibiotics would eliminate bacterial diseases. What happened was quite different, however. Over the years, some bacteria have become resistant to antibiotics. Many of these antibiotic-resistant bacteria (ARB) eventually evolved into multiple antibiotic-resistant bacteria (MARB). In other words, some bacteria are resistant to many different antibiotics.

What are the causes of bacterial resistance to antibiotics? One possible answer appears to be related to so-called "jumping genes." Jumping genes, or transposons, were discovered by the Nobel Prize-winning American geneticist Barbara McClintock. Jumping genes are genes that can move from one chromosome to another chromosome during replication. In bacteria, genes are found on small circular segments of DNA called plasmids. Apparently, when certain jumping genes move to locations on specific plasmids, the bacteria develop a resistance to antibiotics. Several combinations of these jumping genes have been discovered that give resistance to such widely used antibiotics as streptomycin, tetracycline, and ampicillin. When composite, or "multiple," jumping genes are located on the same plasmid, multiple antibiotic resistance can result.

At present, few bacteria are resistant to all antibiotics. But many bacteria are resistant to all but a few antibiotics. What might happen if harmful bacteria became resistant to all existing antibiotics?

How Bacteria Become Antibiotic Resistant

Part One: One bacterium in a colony becomes antibiotic resistant by spontaneous mutation.

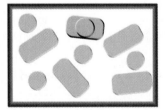

Part Two: A person takes a prescribed antibiotic. Most bacteria will be killed by the antibiotic. Those bacteria that are resistant to the particular antibiotic survive.

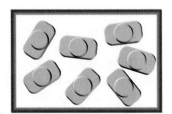

Part Three: The bacteria that survive multiply. Soon there is a whole colony of bacteria that are antibiotic resistant.

Problem

You are a member of a team of three bacteriologists assigned by the National Institutes of Health to investigate the occurrence of antibiotic-resistant bacteria and multiple antibiotic-resistant bacteria.

Task

Choose one of the following tasks.

1. Answer the following questions based on your Internet and/or library research and the diagrams. Record this information in a journal.

    ■ What are some possible mechanisms of antibiotic resistance?

    ■ What types of genetic mutations are involved in antibiotic resistance?

    ■ How does a particular strain of bacteria become antibiotic resistant?

    ■ How do antibiotic-resistant bacteria share their resistance with other bacteria in order to produce multiple antibiotic-resistant bacteria?

    ■ Through what mechanism is it possible for harmless antibiotic-resistant bacteria to pass on their drug resistance to harmful bacteria?

    ■ How has widespread and inappropriate use of antibiotics by people helped in the spread of antibiotic-resistant bacteria? What is the solution to this problem?

    ■ What can researchers do to preserve the effectiveness of antibiotics that are currently available?

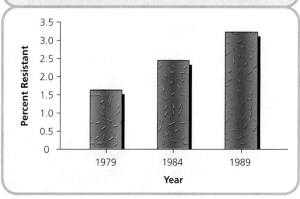

Increase in Antibiotic-Resistant Bacteria

■ How can drug companies develop new antibiotics?

■ Why are antibiotic-resistant bacteria and multiple antibiotic-resistant bacteria particularly prevalent, and dangerous, in hospitals and daycare centers?

■ Based on the information in the bar graph, predict what the entry for 1999 will look like.

2. Prepare a written report based on library and Internet research suggesting some solutions to the problems of antibiotic-resistant bacteria. Your report will be submitted to Congress by the National Institutes of Health. Be sure to include photographs, diagrams, charts, graphs, or other illustrations to support your conclusions. As part of your report, examine how the spread of antibiotic-resistant bacteria could have a real impact on your life and the lives of your family members.

Marine Iguanas with Sally Lightfoot crabs

Discovery
Learning Activity

Eyewitness to Evolution

1. From your teacher, obtain a photograph of a type of athletic shoe worn by people today. On a separate sheet of paper, describe the characteristics of the shoe.

2. Can you remember the first pair of athletic shoes you owned? How are they different from the ones people wear today? Have you ever seen photographs of athletic shoes that were worn by people 20 years ago? Forty years ago? How are these shoes different from the ones worn by people today?

Discovery
Learning Activity

Comparing Structures

1. Examine the wings of the different types of animals provided by your teacher.

2. Compare the wing structures and functions in all of the animals. Based on their wing structure, which animals do you think are more closely related? Make sure you explain the criteria that you used to determine those relationships.

Evidence of Evolution

······················· *Guide for Reading* ·······················

Previewing the Chapter

Millions of years ago, a fish swam in the shallow seas covering an area that is now Wyoming. When the fish died, it sank to the sea floor and was covered by sediments. Fast forward to the twentieth century—paleontologists (scientists who study ancient things) uncover the petrified remains of the fish. What can these remains tell scientists about the history of life on earth? How do clues found in the earth provide evidence for the evolution of living things? What were the origins of life on earth?

Key Words

absolute dating, evolution, fossil, geologic time scale, heterotroph hypothesis, relative dating

Key Concepts

- **Explain** how fossils provide evidence of evolution.
- **Discuss** the various hypotheses of the origins of life.
- **Sequence** the main events in the history of the earth. (Laboratory Investigation)

28-1 Evidence From the Past

Section Objectives:

- *Describe* at least five processes by which fossils may be formed.
- *Explain* how sedimentary rocks are formed and why fossils are often found in these rocks.
- *Define* the terms *relative dating* and *absolute dating*.

Evolution

Evolution is the central and unifying theme of biology. In its most general sense, the term *evolution* means a gradual change over time. Since its formation about 4.5 billion years ago, the earth itself has changed continuously. This slow change is known as **geologic evolution.** Many species also have changed since they first appeared on the earth. This process is known as **organic evolution.** How did life begin and how has it evolved into the species living today? In this chapter, you will learn about the scientific evidence for organic evolution and the theories of how life began on earth.

Fossils

The study of fossils provides the strongest evidence of organic evolution. A **fossil** is any trace or remains of an organism that has been preserved by natural processes. By studying fossils, scientists can compare the remains of ancient organisms with organisms living today to see whether or not organic evolution has occurred.

▲ **Figure 28–1**

A Living Fossil. This coelacanth represents a group of lobe-finned fishes that had been thought to be extinct.

◀ Fossil of a fish from the Miocene epoch.

▲ **Figure 28–2**

A Fly Fossil Preserved in Amber. This fly became trapped in sticky resin. The resin hardened into amber, preserving the insect.

When an organism dies, it usually decays without leaving any remains. Special circumstances are required for a fossil to form. In the majority of fossils, the soft tissues of the organism have decayed, and only the hard parts, such as bones or shells, have been preserved. In some fossils, however, an entire organism has been preserved with almost no decay.

Fossils in Amber and Ice   The soft tissues of animals usually decay because of the activities of bacteria and fungi. In some circumstances, such as anaerobic conditions or extreme cold, decay does not occur, and entire organisms are preserved.

As you can see in Figure 28–2, entire insect remains can be preserved in amber. *Amber* is a hard, yellow, transparent material formed by the hardening of resin, a sticky substance produced by trees. Insects often become trapped and embedded in the resin, which then hardens into amber.

In the cold Arctic regions, entire animal remains have been preserved in ice for thousands of years. The remains of several specimens—including a woolly mammoth and a furry rhinoceros—have been found with flesh, skin, and hair.

Fossil Bones and Petrifaction   Under some conditions, the hard, mineral parts of animals, such as shells, bones, and teeth, can be preserved for millions of years. Dinosaur bones, some more than 100 million years old, have been found all over the world. Usually only teeth, parts of the skeleton, or skull fragments are preserved. It is uncommon to find a complete fossil skeleton.

Many animal skeletons have been preserved in pools of tar in which the animals were trapped. The La Brea tar pits in Los Angeles, California, contain thousands of fossils. Although most of

Figure 28–3

The Iceman. In September of 1991, the remains of the "Iceman" were excavated from some melting glacial ice on a mountain. The body, which had been preserved in the ice, was estimated to be about 5000 years old. ▶

these animals lived less than 25 000 years ago, they include many extinct species, such as the saber-toothed tiger and the woolly mammoth.

In some cases, a dead organism lies in a body of water that contains a high mineral content. Gradually, the original substances of the organism dissolve and are replaced by minerals from the water. In this process, which is called **petrifaction** (peh truh FAK shun), the remains of the organism are turned to stone. Whole trees, estimated to be 200 million years old, have been preserved as stone fossils in the Petrified Forest in Arizona. See Figure 28–4. Many fossil bones actually are petrified replicas of the original bones.

Molds, Casts, and Imprints   By far the greatest number of fossils form on the bottoms of lakes and seas. A dead organism slowly sinks into the sandy or muddy bottom of a lake or ocean. As additional particles of sand or mud accumulate on the bottom, the organism becomes buried. The sand or mud later hardens into rock. Meanwhile, the remains of the organism decay, but its shape is preserved in the rock as a hollow form called a **mold.** Sometimes, a mold becomes filled with minerals, which in turn harden to form rock. The hardened minerals form a **cast,** or a copy of the external form of the original organism.

Impressions made in mud, such as animal footprints, may remain when the mud hardens into rock. The impression is called an **imprint.** Among the largest known imprints are the dinosaur footprints shown in Figure 28–5. Many imprints also have been left by thin structures, such as leaves.

Calculating the Age of Fossils

Most fossils have been found in a kind of rock that is called **sedimentary** (sed uh MEN tuhr ee) **rock.** Most sedimentary rocks form on the bottoms of shallow seas or on ocean bottoms near the shorelines of continents. As a river flows over land, it wears away, or erodes, fine particles of rock. These particles are called *sediments.* When the river waters enter the sea, the sediments slowly settle to the bottom. Gradually, sediments build up on the sea bottom. Various chemical processes, combined with the pressure exerted by the weight of the sediments, slowly harden the material into rock.

Figure 28–5
Dinosaur Footprints. The size of a dinosaur can be estimated relative to the size of its imprints. ▼

Figure 28–6

Deposition of Sediments. Streams flowing into a body of water carry fine rock particles called sediments. These sediments settle to the bottom and may gradually build up to a great thickness. The bodies of dead organisms that settle to the bottom may become fossils embedded in the sediments. The oldest fossils will be in the lowest layers, the youngest in the upper layers. ▶

living fish

ocean

stream

sediment

newest fossil

oldest fossil

The formation of sedimentary rock may continue for millions of years at any location. Because the size and mineral composition of the sediments will change from time to time, sedimentary rock acquires a layered structure. The oldest layers, those laid down first, are at the bottom. The youngest, or most recent, are at the top. The layers in between are arranged in a time sequence from older to younger. See Figure 28–6.

MiniLab

Skill: Relating

When Can Half a Clock Tell Time?

Problem

How does half-life **relate** to the amount of original element that remains?

Procedure

1. Place a round piece of filter paper in front of you. Label the center of the paper C-14 (carbon-14). At the top of the paper (the 12 o'clock position), write 0 years. At the 6 o'clock position, write 5730 years (the half-life of C-14). At the 9 o'clock position, write 11460 years.

2. Fold the filter paper in half down the middle, from top to bottom.

3. Repeat steps 1 and 2, using U-238 (half-life 4.5 billion years) and K-40 (half-life 1.3 billion years).

Analyze and Conclude

1. If the unfolded filter represents 12 g, what mass remains after folding the paper in half? After folding the paper in half again?

2. How many years does folding the paper in half represent? What is this time period called?

Relative Dating Over millions of years, the shifting of the earth's crust has raised some regions that once were under the seas. This shifting has caused some sedimentary layers to be exposed on the side of mountains or plateaus. Sometimes, a river has cut its way through the layers of sedimentary rock. The Grand Canyon, shown in Figure 28–7, is an example of this. If the exposed sedimentary layers have not been greatly disturbed by the motions of the earth's crust, they remain in their original sequence. The oldest are at the bottom, and the youngest are at the top. If these sedimentary layers contain fossils, scientists use the layers to determine when certain organisms existed in relation to others. Any method of determining the order in which events occurred is called **relative dating.** Fossils in the lower layers represent organisms that lived at an earlier time than the fossils in upper layers. This history of life is usually called the **fossil record.**

Absolute Dating Relative dating does not give the actual age of a rock or a fossil in years. Any method that determines how long ago an event occurred is called **absolute dating.** Many methods of absolute dating have been tried, but most scientists consider radioactive dating the most accurate and reliable method.

The technique of **radioactive dating** is based on the knowledge that certain elements have unstable isotopes. As you read in Chapter 3, the nuclei of these unstable isotopes tend to break down, or decay, changing to different isotopes. During this process, called *radioactive decay,* energy is given off in the form of radiation.

The rate at which a radioactive isotope decays is fixed and unchangeable. The time required for half the atoms of an isotope to decay is called the *half-life* of that isotope. For example, the half-life of carbon-14, which occurs naturally in all organisms, is 5730 years. If a fossil contains carbon-14 and was formed 5730 years ago, only half the original amount of carbon-14 would be left in the fossil today. The other half would have changed to carbon-14's decay product, nitrogen-14. See Figure 28–8. By comparing the ratio of carbon-14 to nitrogen-14, scientists can calculate a fossil's age. This method does not work for fossils older than about 50 000 years because most of the carbon-14 has decayed.

Other isotopes, such as uranium-238 or potassium-40, can be used to date older fossils or rocks in which fossils are embedded. Only *igneous* (IG nee us) rocks—formed when molten material in the crust cooled and hardened—can be dated using radioactive

▲ **Figure 28–7**
Sedimentary Rock. The layers of this rock formation in the Grand Canyon were formed from sediments deposited under water. Shifts in the earth's crust then raised the rock layers without disturbing their order. Each layer is older than those above it.

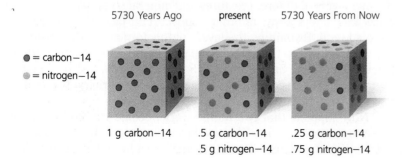

5730 Years Ago   present   5730 Years From Now

● = carbon–14
● = nitrogen–14

1 g carbon–14   .5 g carbon–14   .25 g carbon–14
.5 g nitrogen–14   .75 g nitrogen–14

◀ **Figure 28–8**
Half-Life of Carbon-14. The half-life of carbon-14 is 5730 years.

dating methods. These methods do not work with sedimentary rocks because they give the age of the sediments, which existed long before becoming rocks. However, the absolute age of sedimentary rocks can be estimated by the age of igneous rocks that formed above, below, or within them. In this way, scientists can determine the age of fossils found in sedimentary layers.

28-1 Section Review

1. What is a fossil?
2. Name six types of fossils.
3. In what kind of rock are most fossils found?
4. What is the fossil record?

Critical Thinking

5. If you could search for fossils under the ocean floor, where would you look? (*Predicting*)

28-2 Interpreting the Fossil Record

Section Objectives:

- *Define* the terms *correlation* and *index fossil.*
- *Explain* what is meant by the geologic time scale.
- *State* two important conclusions that can be drawn from the fossil record regarding the course of changes in living things over geologic time.
- *Explain* the importance of extinctions.

Fossils supply many clues about the organisms from which they were formed. By examining fossils and the fossil record, scientists have been able to piece together a history of life.

Correlation

Suppose a geologist finds a cliff made of sedimentary rock with five distinct layers of different textures and mineral compositions. Then, a few kilometers away, another exposed cliff face of sedimentary rock is found. Examining the layers of this formation, the geologist notices that the top three layers are exactly the same as the bottom three layers of the first formation. See Figure 28–9. It is reasonable for the geologist to conclude that the layers were originally continuous and were deposited at the same time.

Now suppose that two more layers become visible below the three in the second cliff. The two layers must have been deposited before the other three. Therefore, they must be older. In fact, they

Figure 28–9

Correlation of Separate Rock Formations. Layers C, D, and E on the left have the same composition and thickness as layers C, D, and E on the right. Comparable layers on the left and the right were probably laid down at the same time. Layers F and G on the right are therefore older than layers A and B on the left. ▼

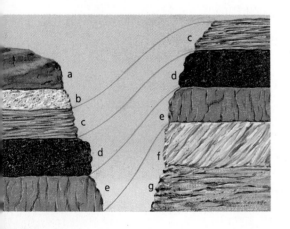

must be older than the bottom three layers of the first cliff. By this process of matching, or **correlation,** scientists can show that certain rock layers in one place are older than certain rock layers in another place. It also follows that the fossils in the older layers are older than fossils in the younger layers.

Correlation of sedimentary rock allows scientists to establish the relative dating of rocks and fossils in different places. Correlation by the comparison of rock layers can produce a fairly extended relative dating of the rocks and fossils in a region. But, the method cannot be used where there are no nearby rocks that are similar. Furthermore, scientists cannot provide a correlation between rocks in a particular region and rocks in another section of the continent or another part of the world.

A study of fossils from many regions has shown that certain types of organisms seem to have appeared, flourished for a time over wide regions of the earth, and then disappeared. Rock layers that have fossils of these organisms must have been formed when

MiniLab

Skill: Modeling

Making Model Fossils

Problem

How can you **create a model** of different kinds of fossils?

Procedure

1. Coat a small object, such as a shell, leaf, or nut, with a thin layer of petroleum jelly.

2. Pour a plaster of Paris mixture into a large paper cup. When the plaster just begins to harden, press the object into its surface.

3. After the plaster hardens, carefully remove the specimen.

4. Cover the fossil imprint and the plaster just around it with petroleum jelly. Pour fresh plaster into the cup until it overflows slightly.

5. Tap the cup on the table to force the air bubbles out of the plaster. When the plaster has hardened completely, carefully lift out the fossil duplicate.

6. With your teacher's permission, repeat the procedure with another small object that interests you. You may try a feather, a chicken bone, or a small toy or game piece.

Analyze and Conclude

1. Describe the fossils.

2. How are the fossils alike? How are they different?

3. Which fossil is the mold? Which is the cast? How do you know?

4. From the results of this MiniLab and your knowledge of how fossils are formed, do you expect that all objects fossilize equally well? Explain your answer.

Figure 28–10

Trilobite Fossils. These two fossilized trilobites were found in Morocco. Trilobites were distant relatives of insects. ▶

these organisms were in existence. Using the fossils, it becomes possible to match the relative ages of sedimentary rocks in different parts of the world. Fossils that permit the relative dating of rocks within a narrow time span are called **index fossils.** *Trilobites* are good examples of index fossils. See Figure 28–10. Some species of these shelled marine animals only lived between 500 and 600 million years ago. Scientists know, therefore, that sedimentary rock layers containing trilobite fossils must be between 500 and 600 million years old. Index fossils have enabled scientists to find a continuous fossil sequence from the time of the first fossils up to the recent past.

Through a correlation of absolute and relative dating of rocks, geologists have been able to construct a timetable of the earth's history. This timetable is known as the **geologic time scale.** In this time scale, the earth's history is divided into several major divisions called *eras.* Each era is further subdivided into *periods* and *epochs.* Figure 28–11 shows the main subdivisions of the geologic time scale, along with a brief summary of the various types of organisms that appeared, flourished, or disappeared during each time interval.

Patterns of Evolution

When the entire fossil record is studied, some important patterns can readily be seen. One obvious pattern is that the earliest organisms were all relatively simple. As time passed, organisms slowly became more and more complex. As you read in Chapter 5, eukaryotic cells came into existence after the simpler prokaryotic cells. Similarly, multicellular organisms appeared after single-celled organisms, and terrestrial plants and animals arrived later than aquatic species.

Scientists also have observed that the move from simpler species to more complex ones seems to have occurred over thousands or millions of years. Changes in the structure of the horse, for example, have been traced from the first appearance of a horselike mammal through various stages to what is now known as

Figure 28–11 The Geologic Time Scale. ▶

The Geologic Time Scale

Era	Period (or Epoch)			Millions of Years Ago	Plant Life	Animal Life
Cenozoic	Age of Humans	Quaternary	Recent epoch		herbs dominant	modern humans and modern animals
			Pleistocene epoch	.01	trees decrease; herbs increase	early humans; large mammals become extinct
	Age of Mammals	Tertiary Period	Pliocene epoch	2.5	grasses increase; herbs appear	mammals abundant; earliest humans appear
			Miocene epoch	12	forests decrease; grasses develop	mammals increase; prehumans appear
			Oligocene epoch	26	worldwide tropical forests	modern mammals appear
			Eocene epoch	37	angiosperms increase	early mammals at peak
			Paleocene epoch	53	modern angiosperms appear	early placental mammals appear; modern birds
Mesozoic	Age of Reptiles	Cretaceous period		65	conifers decrease; flowering plants increase	large reptiles (dinosaurs) at peak, then disappear; small marsupials; toothed birds; modern fishes
		Jurassic period		136	conifers, cycads dominant; flowering plants appear	large reptiles spread; first birds; modern sharks and bony fishes; many bivalves
		Triassic period		190	conifers increase; cycads appear	reptiles increase, first mammals; bony fishes
Paleozoic	Age of Amphibians	Permian period		225	seed ferns disappear	amphibians decline; reptiles increase; modern insects
		Carboniferous period		280	tropical coal forests; seed ferns, conifers	amphibians dominant; reptiles appear; rise of insects
	Age of Fishes	Devonian period		345	first forests; horsetails, ferns	early fishes spread; amphibians appear; many mollusks, crabs
	Age of Invertebrates	Silurian period		395	first land plants	scorpions and spiders (first air-breathers on land)
		Ordovician period		430	algae dominant	first vertebrates; worms; some mollusks and echinoderms
		Cambrian period		500	algae, fungi; first plant spores	most invertebrate phyla; trilobites dominant
Precambrian				570	probably bacteria, fungi	a few fossils; sponge spicules; soft-bodied invertebrates
				?		

Figure 28–12

Evolution of the Horse. The fossil record provides information on the changes in the structure of the horse over time. During its evolution the horse has increased in size and the number of toes has decreased from four to just one. ▶

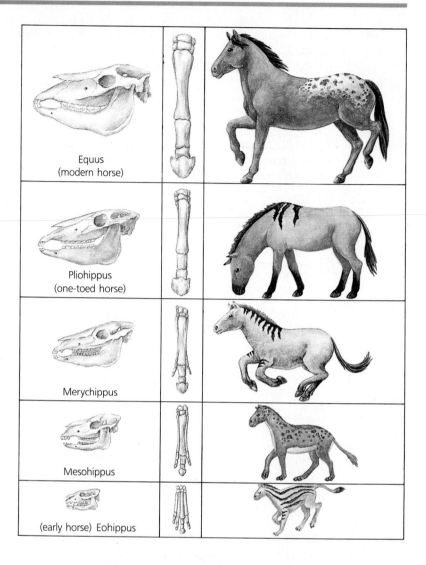

Equus
(modern horse)

Pliohippus
(one-toed horse)

Merychippus

Mesohippus

(early horse) Eohippus

a horse. See Figure 28–12. These changes occur over millions of years in the species, not in any one individual. Other sequences of this kind in the fossil record indicate that later species developed from earlier ones through a series of gradual changes passed on from generation to generation. There are also many interruptions in the fossil record. Species that have not been found in the fossil record are called missing links, or *transitional forms*. Because unusual conditions are needed to form a fossil, it is not surprising that there are gaps in the fossil record. As you have read, most often, the remains of organisms simply decay without leaving behind any traces. Despite its incompleteness, the fossil record is still considered the strongest evidence of organic evolution.

A study of the fossil record also reveals that many fossils come from species no longer living today. In fact, it has been estimated that, of all the species that ever lived, less than 1 percent exist today. When the last individual of a species has died, the species is said to be **extinct.**

The fossil record shows that on several occasions many species became extinct at the same time. The best known example of this is the extinction of the dinosaurs at the end of the Cretaceous period, 65 million years ago. Many other species of plants and animals also became extinct at this time. Some scientists think that the earth may have been struck by a small asteroid or comet, while others believe the extinctions were caused by severe volcanic activity. Whatever the cause, mass extinctions have played a major role in the course of evolution.

28-2 Section Review

1. Where is it not possible to use correlation?
2. What are index fossils?
3. What are the four eras of the geologic time scale?
4. State two patterns of evolution that can be seen in the fossil record.

Critical Thinking

5. Why would the fossil of an organism that lived only in one location be a poor index fossil? (*Reasoning Conditionally*)

28-3 Evidence from Living Organisms

Section Objectives:

- *Distinguish* among homologous, analogous, and vestigial structures.
- *Explain* how similarities in anatomy and embryological development are evidence for evolution.
- *Describe* how similarities in biochemistry show an evolutionary relationship between different species.

The classification system you read about in Chapter 7 is based on similarities and differences in anatomy, embryological development, and biochemistry. The remarkable similarity between some species has led scientists to conclude that similar species have evolved from a common ancestor. In many cases, the fossil remains of these common ancestors have been found. Comparing these remains with living organisms has added to the evidence for organic evolution.

Anatomical Similarities

Comparative anatomy is the study of structural similarities and differences among living things. The presence of certain types of similarities offers evidence for the evolutionary relationships between species.

Science, Technology and Society

Technology: Computer-Simulated Plant Evolution

From fossil evidence, biologists know that early plants looked quite different from plants today. They have developed hypotheses to explain why the plants changed. Now, with the help of a desktop computer, they can "recreate" these hypotheses.

Some scientists hypothesize plants evolved to become more efficient at gathering light. Using the computer, scientists simulate an environment in which three plant species compete against each other. The computer "creates" these plants by varying the pattern of their branches (see photo). Then, it calculates the amount of sunlight that might reach their leaves.

The species with the lowest score is eliminated, and the remaining species disperse spores. Some spores undergo mutations. These new plants enter into the competition. The game is repeated over many generations. The winners are the species that survive to the end.

So far, the computer's simulated pattern of evolution has been consistent with the pattern found in the fossil record.

- ■ *How might learning about the evolutionary history of plants benefit science?*

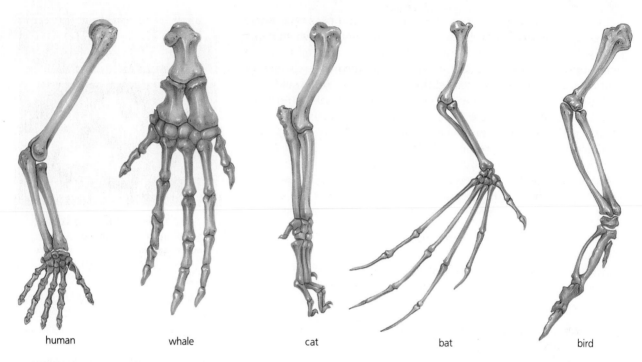

human   whale   cat   bat   bird

▲ **Figure 28–13**

Homologous Structures. Although these limbs function in different ways, they appear to have evolved from the same ancestral structure.

Figure 28–13 shows the structure of the arm and hand of a human, the flipper of a whale, the limb of a cat, the wing of a bat, and the wing of a bird. These structures are quite different in appearance because they are adapted to perform different functions. The human hand is adapted for grasping, and the whale's flipper is adapted for swimming. The wings of bats and birds are both adapted for flying. Even with these different functions, internally the structures of these organs are surprisingly similar. They all have the same number of bones arranged in a similar way. During embryological development of the animal, these structures develop in similar ways. Parts of different organisms that have similar structures and similar embryological development, but have different forms and functions, are called **homologous structures.** Homologous structures are regarded as evidence that some species evolved from a common ancestor.

The human, whale, cat, and bat are all mammals and share the characteristics of mammals. You could expect to find homologous structures among them. On the other hand, there are animals that have similar organs with similar functions but are entirely different kinds of organisms. For example, although birds and insects both have wings, they are different in structure and development. When you examine the internal structure of a bird's wing and an insect's wing, you find no similarity at all. Structures that have similar external forms and functions but different internal structures are called **analogous structures.** If birds and insects have evolved along different pathways, the fact that they have analogous structures, not homologous ones, is understandable. Analogous structures among different animals are regarded as evidence for evolution along different lines.

Another type of evidence for evolutionary relationships is the presence of **vestigial** (ves TIHJ ee ul) **structures** in modern animals. These structures are remnants of structures that were functional in an ancestral form. In modern organisms, vestigial structures are reduced in size and serve little or no function. In the human body, there are more than 100 vestigial structures, including the coccyx, or "tailbone," the appendix, the wisdom teeth, and the muscles that move the nose and ears. The human coccyx is an evolutionary remnant of an ancestral, reptilian tail, and the appendix is the remnant of a large digestive sac. Both whales and pythons have vestigial hind leg bones embedded in the flesh of the body wall. Apparently, whales and snakes evolved from four-legged ancestors.

Embryological Similarities

Comparison of the embryological development of different species can provide additional evidence of evolutionary relationships. Embryos of closely related species show similar patterns of development. Figure 28–14 illustrates various stages in the development of four different vertebrates. In these vertebrates, there are

Figure 28–14
Patterns of Development of Four Vertebrate Embryos. Similarities in the early stages of embryonic development suggest a common ancestor for these vertebrates. ▼

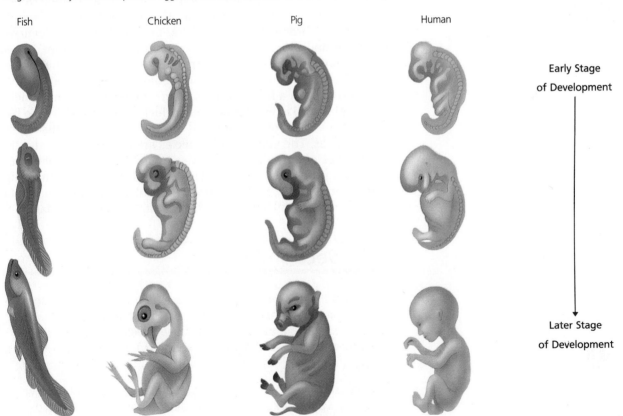

Fish   Chicken   Pig   Human

Early Stage
of Development

Later Stage
of Development

many similarities during the early stages of embryological development. For example, all of the embryos have gill slits, two-chambered hearts, and tails. These similarities support the idea that these four organisms have a common evolutionary origin. As development continues, the embryos begin to resemble the adults of their own species. The more closely related the animals, the longer they continue to resemble one another as they develop.

Molecular Similarities

Recent advances in molecular biology have provided evidence for the evolutionary relatedness of all organisms. The development of techniques to read the amino acid sequence of proteins and the DNA code "letter by letter" has enabled biologists to confirm evolutionary relationships. The more closely related the species are to one another, the greater the biochemical similarities. Because all DNA is descended from the DNA carried by the earliest life forms, the DNA of all organisms shares a common genetic code. And, because the genes of living organisms descended from the genes of common ancestors, many genes in many different organisms strongly resemble one another. These similar genes direct the synthesis of similar proteins.

One such protein is cytochrome c, a protein molecule that organisms need for cellular respiration. Virtually every organism uses cytochrome c; however, each species' cytochrome c differs slightly from the cytochrome c of other species. The differences among cytochrome c were produced by mutations that occurred after the ancestors of living species diverged. Therefore, if two species shared common ancestors until fairly recently, their genes and proteins are likely to be more similar. The data show that cytochrome c in a human differs from a monkey by 1 amino acid, from a pig by 10 amino acids, from a chicken by 13, and from a fish by 21. The results of DNA analysis are similar to the results of protein analysis. The more closely species are related, the greater the percentage of nucleotide sequences their DNA have in common.

Both protein and DNA analyses provide strong evidence supporting evolution. They confirm, in an objective fashion, evolutionary relationships indicated by anatomical and fossil data.

28-3 Section Review

1. Discuss the evidence, other than the evidence supported by the fossil record, that supports the theory of organic evolution.
2. Define homologous structures and analogous structures.
3. What molecular similarities are revealed by cytochrome c?

Critical Thinking

4. Look at Figure 28–14. Why is the evolutionary relationship between humans and chickens closer than the evolutionary relationship between humans and fishes? (*Comparing and Contrasting*)

28-4 The Origins of Life—Early Hypotheses

Section Objectives:

- *Describe* the evidence for spontaneous generation.
- *Explain* how Redi used controlled experiments to disprove the widely accepted hypothesis of the spontaneous generation of maggots.
- *Explain* how Spallanzani's and then Pasteur's experiments finally disproved the hypothesis of the spontaneous generation of microorganisms.

For thousands of years, people believed that living organisms could arise spontaneously, or naturally, in a few days or weeks from nonliving matter. This idea is called **spontaneous generation,** or *abiogenesis* (ay by oh JEN uh sis). Belief in spontaneous generation was based on common observations and intuition. The ancient Egyptians, seeing frogs and snakes coming out of the mud of the Nile River, concluded that these animals were formed from the mud. The Greek philosopher Aristotle reasoned that an "active principle" was responsible for life. This active principle was thought to be present in mud. Some other popular beliefs were that fleas and lice arose from sweat, mice from garbage, and flies from decaying meat.

Early Experiments

In the early 1600s, a Belgian physician named Jan Baptista van Helmont performed an experiment that seemed to support the idea of spontaneous generation. He placed wheat grains in a sweaty shirt. After 21 days, the wheat was gone, and mice were present. Van Helmont reasoned that human sweat was the active principle that changed wheat grains into mice. Even though this was an uncontrolled experiment, his experimental "proof" gained wide acceptance among the scientists of his time.

Then, in the mid-1600s, the Italian physician Francesco Redi struck the first blow against the popular idea of spontaneous generation. It was well known that whenever meat was left exposed to the air, maggots soon appeared on it. Most people were convinced that the maggots developed by spontaneous generation from the decaying meat.

Redi decided to test this idea scientifically. He began by placing many different kinds of meat in open containers. Maggots soon appeared on the meat. See Figure 28–15a. He watched the maggots consume the decaying meat, and he continued to observe them even after the meat was gone. He discovered that the maggots formed pupas, which then developed into flies of various kinds. Redi apparently was the first person to see that maggots developed into flies.

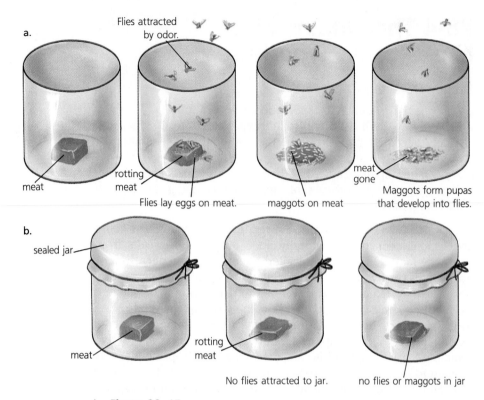

a.

Flies attracted by odor.

meat

rotting meat

Flies lay eggs on meat.

maggots on meat

meat gone

Maggots form pupas that develop into flies.

b.

sealed jar

meat

rotting meat

No flies attracted to jar.

no flies or maggots in jar

▲ **Figure 28–15**

Redi's First Experiment. This experiment showed that meat had to be exposed to the environment to develop maggots.

Redi hypothesized that the maggots developed from eggs laid on the meat by the flies. To test his hypothesis, he placed some pieces of meat in open jars, and he placed other pieces of the same meat in tightly sealed jars. Redi observed that flies entered the open jars and that maggots appeared on the meat. He further observed that no maggots appeared on the meat in the closed jars. See Figure 28–15b.

This experiment proved only that the meat had to be exposed to open air in order to develop maggots. It did not prove that the flies were the source of the maggots. Many scientists of the time claimed that fresh air was necessary for spontaneous generation. By sealing the jars, they argued, Redi had prevented the needed air from reaching the meat.

In order to answer this objection and convince the doubters, Redi performed another set of experiments. In these experiments the containers were covered by fine gauze, as shown in Figure 28–16. The gauze allowed the free circulation of air into the containers but kept the flies out of the containers. Redi observed that the flies attempted to reach the meat by landing on the gauze. The flies also deposited eggs on the gauze, which soon developed into maggots. Still, no maggots appeared inside the jars. Redi had proven conclusively that maggots did not arise spontaneously from decaying meat.

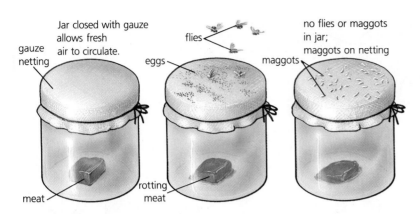

gauze netting

Jar closed with gauze allows fresh air to circulate.

eggs

flies

maggots

no flies or maggots in jar; maggots on netting

meat

rotting meat

◄ **Figure 28–16**
Redi's Second Experiment. Redi's second experiment showed that maggots arise in decaying meat from eggs laid by flies.

Spontaneous Generation of Microorganisms

At about the same time that Redi was performing his experiments, Anton van Leeuwenhoek (LAY ven huke) invented the microscope and made the startling discovery of microorganisms in a drop of water. Soon, it was found that when hay or soil was placed in sterile water, millions of microorganisms appeared within a few hours. Some thought this was a clear-cut case of spontaneous generation! The controversy flared up again and rages for the next 200 years.

In 1745, John Needham, an English scientist, performed some experiments that reinforced the belief in the spontaneous generation of microorganisms. He boiled flasks of chicken, lamb, and corn broth for a few minutes to kill any microorganisms in them. Then, he sealed the flasks. After several days he opened and examined the flasks and found them full of microorganisms. He repeated the experiment several times and always obtained the same results. Needham and other biologists concluded that the microorganisms developed by spontaneous generation.

About 20 years after Needham did his work, Lorenzo Spallanzani, an Italian scientist, challenged Needham's conclusions. Like Needham, Spallanzani set up flasks of chicken, lamb, and corn broth. However, he boiled the contents of the flasks for a much longer time. No living organisms appeared in the flasks.

Spallanzani claimed that Needham found organisms in his heated flasks because he had not heated them long enough to kill all the organisms originally present. Needham argued that Spallanzani had heated his flasks so long that he had destroyed the "vital principle" in the air that was needed to bring about the generation of new organisms. The debate remained unsettled for almost another 100 years.

Disproving Spontaneous Generation

In 1860, the French chemist Louis Pasteur set out to disprove the theory of spontaneous generation. Pasteur thought that microorganisms and their spores were present in the air and that they became active and reproduced when they entered the nutrient

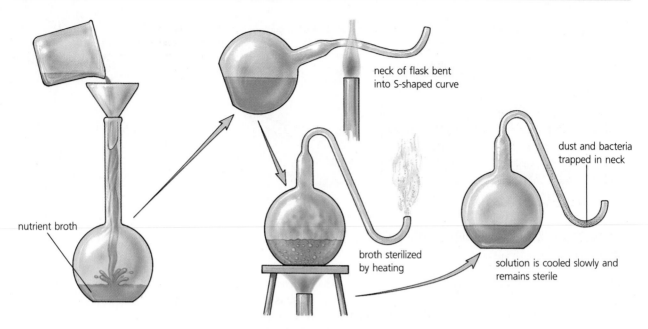

nutrient broth

neck of flask bent into S-shaped curve

dust and bacteria trapped in neck

broth sterilized by heating

solution is cooled slowly and remains sterile

▲ **Figure 28–17**

Pasteur's Experiment. This experiment showed that microorganisms that developed in a nutrient broth came from spores and microorganisms in the air.

broth. He hypothesized that the presence of air alone could not produce microorganisms in the broth. To test this hypothesis, Pasteur filled flasks with nutrient broth. He then heated the necks of the flasks and drew them out into a long S shape, leaving the ends open. See Figure 28–17. The contents of the flasks were then sterilized by boiling. Fresh air could reach the broth, but microorganisms and their spores were trapped in the long necks of the flasks. As long as the flasks were not disturbed, the contents remained sterile. Microorganisms grew in the flasks only when the flasks were tipped and some of the broth ran into the neck and became contaminated. Pasteur's experiment finally put an end to the idea of spontaneous generation.

28-4 **Section Review**

1. What is spontaneous generation?
2. What did van Leeuwenhoek discover?
3. Why did Pasteur alter the shape of his flasks in his experiments with spontaneous generation?

Critical Thinking

4. What assumption did Redi make in his first experiment that forced him to conduct his second experiment? (*Identifying Assumptions*)

28-5 The Origins of Life—Modern Hypothesis

Section Objectives:

- *Define* the term *biogenesis*.
- *Describe* the conditions thought to have existed on the primitive earth according to the heterotroph hypothesis.
- *Describe* any experiments that would appear to support the heterotroph hypothesis.

Today, as you read in Chapter 5, most scientists believe in **biogenesis,** the theory that living organisms originate only from other living organisms. But, this theory has one problem: How did the first living things originate on earth? In this section, you will learn about the conditions under which life may have originated on earth.

The Heterotroph Hypothesis

The most widely accepted hypothesis of the origin of life is called the **heterotroph hypothesis.** This hypothesis was formulated by a small group of scientists in the 1920s and 1930s. The scientist most often credited with development of the heterotroph hypothesis was the Russian biochemist A. I. Oparin.

Primitive Conditions on the Earth   Oparin's heterotroph hypothesis assumes that physical and chemical conditions on the earth billions of years ago were very different from those today. See Figure 28–18. For example, the earth's atmosphere now consists almost entirely of nitrogen (N_2) and oxygen (O_2), with a small amount of carbon dioxide (CO_2). Chemists and geologists have evidence showing that the earth's primitive atmosphere consisted of

Figure 28–18

Early Conditions on the Earth Compared with Modern Conditions. On the primitive earth, the composition of the atmosphere was different from the modern atmosphere. In addition, the temperature was higher, and there were more sources of energy for producing chemical change. ▼

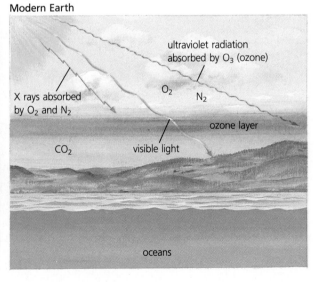

Primitive Earth

lightning
ultraviolet radiation
visible light
H_2
H_2O
CH_4
X-rays
NH_3
oceans

Modern Earth

ultraviolet radiation absorbed by O_3 (ozone)
X rays absorbed by O_2 and N_2
O_2
N_2
ozone layer
CO_2
visible light
oceans

hydrogen (H_2), water vapor (H_2O), ammonia (NH_3), and methane (CH_4). There also is evidence that early temperatures were much higher on the early earth than they are at present. The oceans, when they first formed, were probably not much below the boiling point of water. The oceans of this period have been described as a "hot, thin soup," in which chemical reactions were likely to occur more rapidly than in the cooler waters of the modern earth.

Natural Synthesis of Organic Compounds Under the primitive conditions just described, simple compounds in the atmosphere and in the oceans could have reacted to form more complex organic compounds. The synthesis of organic compounds from inorganic raw materials requires energy. Many sources of energy are thought to have been present on the primitive earth. There was heat given off by the earth itself; radiation from the decay of radioactive elements in the earth's crust; electrical energy from lightning; and ultraviolet light, visible light, and X rays from the sun. Under these conditions, there would have been enough energy available for the breakdown and formation of chemical bonds. The first nucleotides, amino acids, and sugars could have been formed during this period. There have been experimental results that support this hypothesis.

In 1953, Stanley Miller, working with Harold Urey at the University of Chicago, designed an experiment simulating the conditions of the primitive earth. The specially designed experimental apparatus contained four gases—hydrogen, water vapor, ammonia, and methane. See Figure 28–19. Boiling water in the apparatus forced these gases to circulate past sparking electrodes.

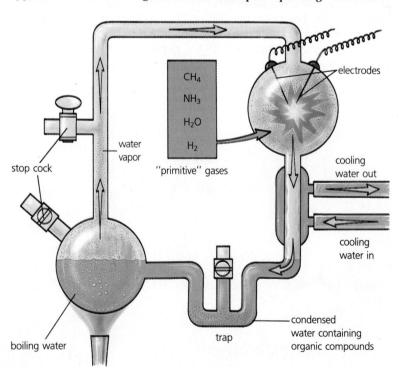

Figure 28–19

Miller's Experiment Simulating Early Conditions on the Earth. A mixture of gases thought to resemble the primitive atmosphere was continuously passed through an electric spark. Water in the apparatus dissolved the new substances produced. After a time, the solution was found to contain many organic compounds. ▶

Miller ran the experiment for a week. At the end of that time, he analyzed the contents of the apparatus and found that it contained urea, various amino acids, hydrogen cyanide, lactic acid, and acetic acid. His experiment clearly demonstrated that organic substances, including amino acids, could have been produced in nature under the conditions assumed for the primitive earth.

The work of an American biochemist, Sidney Fox, showed that, given a supply of amino acids, proteins could also be formed by nonbiological processes. Fox heated a mixture of amino acids at temperatures above 100°C for different lengths of time. Analysis of the resulting compounds revealed the presence of proteins.

Aggregates of Organic Compounds

The heterotroph hypothesis puts forth the idea that protein complexes could develop into nonliving structures that have some of the characteristics of life. Oparin thought that proteinlike substances in the prehistoric oceans may have formed aggregates, or clusters, of large molecules. See Figure 28–20. He called such

Figure 28–20

The Heterotroph Hypotheses. (a) In the early stages, coacervates absorbed organic nutrients from the physical environment. They obtained energy by anaerobic respiration, or fermentation. This released carbon dioxide into the atmosphere. (b) In later stages, autotrophs capable of producing nutrients by photosynthesis appeared. This added oxygen to the atmosphere and led to the development of aerobic respiration. ▼

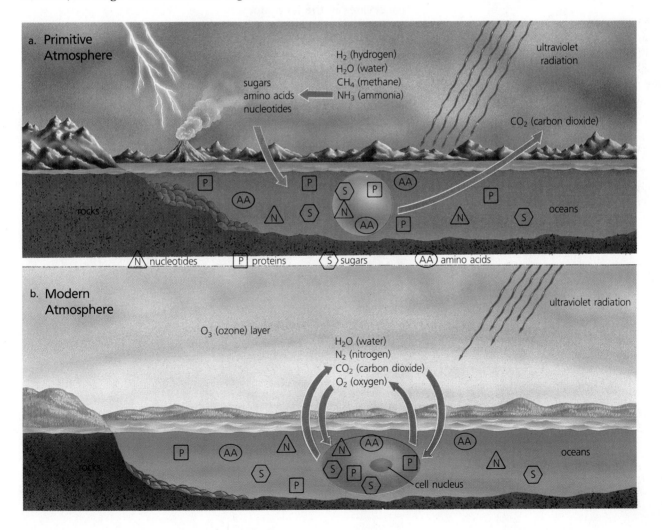

aggregates **coacervates** (koh AS er vayts). According to his hypothesis, these complex structures were surrounded by a "shell" of water molecules, which formed a sort of bounding membrane. The development of a limiting membrane would make it easier for the internal contents of the structure to be chemically different from the external environment. It would also keep various types of molecules in closer contact so that chemical reactions could occur more readily. Coacervates have been formed in laboratories from proteins and other organic molecules.

Oparin believed that within the coacervates, numerous chemical reactions occurred. As coacervates became more complex, they may have developed biochemical systems with the capacity to release energy from various organic nutrients, which were absorbed from the environment. By absorbing material from the environment, coacervates could grow in size. Eventually, they would split in half, and each half would again grow. Such structures would be primitive living things. Oparin called these structures *heterotrophs* because they obtained nutrients from the environment. However, no one yet has been able to produce self-replicating coacervates in the laboratory.

Recently, Graham Cairns-Smith at Glasgow University proposed that the first so-called organisms were inorganic crystals of clay. See Figure 28–21. These materials, which are produced by the weathering of hard rocks, would have been abundant on the early earth. Like all crystals, clay minerals self-assemble in specific patterns that are determined by the materials that compose them. Thus, these early organisms could have carried information.

Occasionally, errors may have occurred during the assembly process, resulting in new, "mutated" forms. Some scientists believe that those forms with favorable properties served as templates for organic molecules. Eventually, these more specialized organic

Figure 28–21
Structure of Clay Crystals. ▶

compounds completely replaced the clay crystals. Currently, scientists are experimenting with clay crystals in order to test this new hypothesis.

Respiration and Photosynthesis

Since the atmosphere of the primitive earth contained no free oxygen, it is thought that the first organisms carried on some form of anaerobic respiration to produce energy. This process would release carbon dioxide into the oceans and atmosphere. As the number of heterotrophs increased, the supply of available nutrients in the environment would decrease. Thus, competitions would arise between existing heterotrophs. Any organism with biochemical machinery that enabled it to use different or more complex nutrients than most other heterotrophs would have a distinct advantage. In this way, organisms containing more and more complex biochemical systems could gradually develop.

Eventually, organisms would develop that could use light energy directly for the synthesis of ATP. These would be the first photosynthetic organisms. In these organisms, the use of light energy for the synthesis of ATP would become coupled with reactions in which carbon dioxide and water were used in the synthesis of carbohydrates. These photosynthetic autotrophs would change the environment further by adding oxygen to the atmosphere.

The presence of oxygen led to the development of organisms with the capacity to carry on aerobic respiration. As you have read in Chapter 6, aerobic respiration is much more efficient than anaerobic respiration, so aerobic organisms became dominant.

The activities of living organisms eventually changed the earth's environment completely. Oxygen produced by organisms blocked the sun's X rays. Ozone (O_3), formed from the oxygen, blocked the intense ultraviolet light. Thus, the high-energy conditions that had originally led to the development of life were destroyed.

28-5 Section Review

1. What is biogenesis?
2. What is the name of Oparin's hypothesis of the origin of life?
3. Name the components of the atmosphere thought to have been present on the primitive earth.
4. List the sources of energy thought to have been present on the primitive earth.

Critical Thinking

5. What assumption was made in the Miller and Urey experiment? (*Identifying Assumptions*)

Laboratory Investigation

Constructing a Geologic Time Line

In order to develop a true perspective of the vast spans of earth's history during which different forms existed, it helps to construct a time line. In this investigation, you will construct a time line representing the earth's history and identify the main events of the beginnings of life on earth.

Problem

How can you **sequence** some of the main events in the history of life on earth?

Materials (per group)

- meterstick
- 5 m adding-machine paper
- colored markers
- photographs and artwork of different life forms
- index cards
- transparent tape

Procedure

1. For your geologic time line, use a scale in which 1 mm = 1 million years, or 1 m = 1 billion years.

2. Mark the adding-machine paper strip at appropriate intervals, such as every 25 million years, from the beginning of the earth to the present.

3. Using the table provided, identify and label the major geologic eras, periods, and epochs on the geologic time scale according to their relative lengths.

4. Decorate the geologic time scale using the paper strip and the art and photographs of the life forms. Write brief descriptions of the life forms on the index cards. Art, photographs, and descriptions should be affixed to the times during which the first fossils of a particular group were formed.

Major Events in the History of Life on Earth	
Event	**Millions of Years Ago**
Modern humans appear	0.1
Earliest humans appear	2.5–12
Modern mammals appear	26–37
Modern angiosperms appear	53–65
Dinosaurs at their peak	65–136
First birds appear	136–190
Tropical coal forests appear	280–345
Rise of insects	280–345
Amphibians appear	345–395
First land plants	395–430
First vertebrates appear	430–500

Observations

1. How long did it take for the first life forms to leave fossils?

2. When in earth's history did land plants first appear?

3. During which period were dinosaurs at their peak?

Analysis and Conclusions

1. Where on the time line do most life forms exist?

2. What percentage of your time line accounts for the Precambrian era?

3. Assume that humans have been around for about 250 000 years. What percentage of your time line accounts for the history of modern humans?

Extensions

Design an experiment that equates one year with the mass of one penny. What would be the mass, in grams, of all the pennies that represent the age of the earth? In kilograms?

Chapter 28 Review

Study Outline

28-1 Evidence From the Past

▶ The study of fossils provides the strongest evidence for organic evolution.

▶ In most fossils, only the hard parts of organisms are preserved. Sometimes, entire organisms may be fossilized in amber or ice.

▶ Relative dating determines the order in which events occurred. Absolute dating determines how long ago events occurred.

28-2 Interpreting the Fossil Record

▶ The process of correlation involves matching similar layers of rock formations to show the relative ages of rock layers and fossils.

▶ Index fossils are fossils of organisms that lived for a well-defined period of time over wide regions of the earth.

▶ Patterns in the fossil record show that organisms have evolved over thousands or millions of years.

28-3 Evidence From Living Organisms

▶ Certain types of anatomical similarities, such as homologous, analogous, or vestigial structures, provide evidence of evolutionary relationships between species.

▶ Embryological similarities, and similarities in DNA and protein, provide additional evidence of evolutionary relationships.

28-4 The Origins of Life—Early Hypotheses

▶ According to the theory of spontaneous generation, living organisms could arise naturally in a short time from nonliving matter.

▶ Redi's and Spallanzani's experiments demonstrated that organisms do not arise spontaneously. Pasteur's experiments with microorganisms conclusively disproved the theory of spontaneous generation.

28-5 The Origins of Life—Modern Hypotheses

▶ According to the heterotroph hypothesis, the conditions of the primitive earth produced organic substances that gave rise to heterotrophic organisms.

▶ Miller's experiment showed that organic substances could have been produced naturally under the conditions of the primitive earth.

▶ The presence of oxygen led to the development of organisms with the ability to carry on aerobic respiration.

Chapter Assessment

Multiple Choice

Choose the letter of the answer that best completes each statement or answers the question.

1. An impression, such as a footprint, left in mud is called a(n) (a) cast. (b) petrifaction. (c) mold. (d) imprint.

2. The determination of how long ago an event occurred is called (a) relative dating. (b) absolute dating. (c) correlation. (d) petrifaction.

3. The slow change of the earth itself is called (a) geologic evolution. (b) spontaneous generation. (c) biogenesis. (d) organic evolution.

4. The process whereby the original substances of an organism are replaced by minerals from water is called (a) geologic evolution. (b) biogenesis. (c) correlation. (d) petrifaction.

5. The timetable of the earth's history is known as the (a) fossil record. (b) correlation. (c) geologic time scale. (d) imprint.

6. The human hand and the wing of a bird are examples of (a) vestigial structures. (b) analogous structures. (c) index fossils. (d) homologous structures.

7. Louis Pasteur disproved the theory of (a) spontaneous generation. (b) coacervates. (c) biogenesis. (d) correlation.

8. Vestigial structures in organisms (a) look the same. (b) perform the same function. (c) serve little or no apparent function. (d) develop from the same embryonic tissues.

9. Most fossils have been found in (a) sedimentary rock. (b) ice. (c) amber. (d) tar pits.

10. Earth's primitive atmosphere consisted of all of the following, except (a) methane. (b) ammonia. (c) oxygen. (d) hydrogen.

Content Review

Answer each of the following in complete sentences.

11. Explain how fossils help scientists understand organic evolution.

12. What is the relationship between a mold and a cast?

13. How does relative dating differ from absolute dating?

14. How do homologous structures differ from analogous structures?

15. What could you conclude from information that cats and dogs have more homologous structures than do cats and bats?

16. How do patterns of embryological development provide evidence of evolutionary relationships?

17. Did Redi conclusively disprove the theory of spontaneous generation? Explain your answer, and identify what Redi showed in his experiments.

18. Describe Pasteur's experiment with flasks of nutrient broth. Explain why his experiment finally put an end to the idea of spontaneous generation.

19. According to the heterotroph hypothesis, what were the chemical and physical conditions characterizing primitive earth?

20. How were organic compounds synthesized under the primitive conditions of early earth?

Graphic Organizing

For information on graphic organizers, see Appendix G at the back of this text.

21. **Scale** Construct a scale of the Paleozoic era. Use the geologic time scale on page 579 as a reference. Plot "millions of years ago" on the scale and label the periods.

Critical Thinking and Problem Solving

Discuss each of the following in a brief paragraph.

22. **Drawing conclusions** How do biologists use the fact that fossils exist to support the theory of evolution?

23. **Relating** Why do scientists regard the presence of homologous structures as evidence about evolutionary relationships among organisms?

24. **Drawing conclusions** What would serve as an appropriate index fossil for the age of amphibians? For the Cambrian period? For the Cretaceous period? (Refer to the geologic time scale on page 579.)

25. **Predicting** What was the probable effect of the development of photosynthetic autotrophs on anaerobic organisms? What effect did this development have on the evolution of aerobic land animals?

26. **Formulating hypotheses** On a fossil-hunting expedition, a biologist finds at a vertical depth of 135 m on an exposed rock face the fossil skeleton of an adult bird that had a wing span of 48 cm. On the same rock face, but at a depth of only 40 m, the biologist finds a fossil skeleton of another adult bird, similar in appearance to the first one except for its wing span, which is only 22 cm. Based on these data, propose a hypothesis as to the relationship of the two birds. Describe the evidence for the hypothesis and the best way to test it.

27. **Calculating** A scientist studying a fossil determines that it contains only one-eighth the amount of carbon-14 that was originally present in it. The half-life of carbon-14 is 5730 years. Approximately how old is the fossil?

Discovery Learning Activity

Who Lives Where?

1. Examine the photographs of animals and environments provided by your teacher.

2. Match each animal with its environment. What characteristics of the animal helped you to determine the type of environment it would live in?

The Modern Theory of Evolution

Guide for Reading

Previewing the Chapter

A horned frog on a leaf in the forests of Borneo is almost indistinguishable from its surroundings. Species survive or die out depending on how effective their adaptations are for survival. All living things struggle for existence. They compete for food, for territory, for the chance to reproduce. Some species—such as the horned frog—blend into their environment, others stand out. What causes the changes that help species survive? What is the modern theory of evolution? What role does natural selection play in the evolution of species?

Key Words

adaptation, gene pool, genetic equilibrium, natural selection, population, speciation, variation

Key Concepts

- **Compare** early theories of evolution with the modern theory of evolution.
- **Describe** the role of natural selection in the evolution of species.
- **Formulate a hypothesis** to explain drug resistance in bacteria. (Laboratory Investigation)

29-1 Early Theories of Evolution

Section Objectives:

- *Outline* Lamarck's theory of evolution and describe Weissman's experiment on mice.
- *Explain* the principle of natural selection.
- *List* the six main points of Darwin's theory of evolution.
- *Distinguish* between gradualism and the theory of punctuated equilibrium.

In the previous chapter, you read about some of the scientific evidence for organic evolution. But, the evidence for evolution does not explain how or why it occurs. This chapter deals with the different theories about how evolutionary change occurs.

Lamarck's Theory of Evolution

One of the first theories of evolution was presented by the French biologist Jean Baptiste de Lamarck in 1809. From his studies of animals, Lamarck became convinced that species were not constant. Instead, he believed that they changed, that new species evolved from preexisting species.

▲ **Figure 29–1**

Evolution of Species. The theory of evolution accounts for how this Alaskan walrus and all other species have arisen.

◀ Notice how the coloring of this horned frog allows it to blend in with a leaf.

▲ **Figure 29–2**

Lamarck's Theory of Evolution. (a) Early giraffes had short necks. (b) When low-growing plants became scarce, giraffes stretched their necks to reach food. (c) The giraffes with stretched necks passed on their long-neck trait to their offspring.

He thought that these evolutionary changes in animals were caused by their need to adapt to changes in the environment.

According to Lamarck's theory, evolution involved two principles. He called his first principle *the law of use and disuse.* According to this principle, the more an animal uses a particular part of its body, the stronger and better developed that part becomes. At the same time, the less a part is used, the weaker and less developed it becomes. An athlete, for example, develops the strength of certain muscles by constant use. Muscles that are not used tend to become smaller and weaker. The second part of Lamarck's theory was *the inheritance of acquired characteristics.* Lamarck assumed that the characteristics an organism developed through use and disuse could be passed on to its offspring.

Using his theory, Lamarck offered the following explanation for the long neck of the giraffe. See Figure 29–2. The ancestors of modern giraffes had short necks and fed on grasses and shrubs close to the ground. As the supply of food near the ground decreased, the giraffes had to stretch their necks to reach leaves farther from the ground. Their necks became longer from stretching, and this trait was passed on to their offspring. In the course of generations, the giraffe's neck became longer and longer, thus giving rise to the modern giraffe.

Modern genetics has shown that traits are passed from one generation to the next by genes in an individual's gametes. As far as we can tell, however, these genes are not affected by an individual's life experiences or activities. Although there have been many experiments looking for evidence of such an effect, all have failed. The most well known of these experiments was performed in the 1870s by the German biologist August Weismann. Weismann cut the tails off mice for 22 generations. In each generation, the mice were born with tails of normal length. The acquired characteristic of shortened tails was not inherited.

Darwin's Observations

The name most closely connected with the theory of evolution is that of Charles Darwin. Darwin was the son of a well-to-do physician. At his father's urging, Darwin began to study medicine, but he did not enjoy the subject and gave it up. He then began to prepare for a career as a minister, but his real interest was in nature study—in observing the natural environment and collecting specimens.

In 1831, the British naval vessel HMS *Beagle* was about to set out on a scientific expedition to chart the coastline of South America and some of the islands of the Pacific Ocean. The expedition also planned to collect specimens of wildlife from the lesser-known regions of this part of the world. Darwin applied for the position of ship's naturalist and was accepted. He was 22 years old when he sailed from England on a voyage that was expected to take 2 years but actually lasted 5 years.

During those years, Darwin collected hundreds of specimens and made detailed observations of the regions through which he traveled. He left the ship several times to make inland journeys, rejoining the *Beagle* later. Darwin had plenty of time for thinking about what he saw. He also read the first volume of *The Principles of Geology* by Charles Lyell, which had been published shortly before Darwin left England. Lyell proposed that the earth was very old, that it had been slowly changing for millions of years, and that it was still changing. His ideas led Darwin to think that perhaps living things also changed slowly over long periods of time.

On his trip, Darwin made several types of observations that supported his idea. He noticed that there was a gradual change in each species as he traveled down the coast of South America. For example, the ostrichlike rheas that live in the latitudes around Buenos Aires are different from those found at the tip of South America. Darwin also observed fossils that were different from the living animals he saw in the same region. At the same time, the fossils had many similarities that suggested they might be related to modern forms.

The most significant of Darwin's observations were those he made on the Galapagos Islands, which lie about 1000 kilometers from the coast of Ecuador in the Pacific Ocean. He found many different species of finches living on these islands. The birds were alike, yet each species was slightly different from those on the next island or in another part of the same island. See Figure 29–3.

Darwin made similar observations about many plants, insects, and other organisms. While species on the Galapagos Islands resembled species on the mainland, they were always different in certain characteristics. See Figure 29–4. Darwin came to believe that these organisms originally had reached the islands from the mainland. Because of their isolation on the islands, the species had opportunities to develop special adaptations to each different region.

Darwin returned to England in 1836 convinced that species evolve. Although he had recorded many observations that supported such a hypothesis, he could offer no explanation of how evolution occurred. Because he could not, he did not publish his ideas at once. Instead, he continued to collect and organize his data and to search for a reasonable theory of how evolution occurs.

Darwin's Theory of Evolution

Shortly after he returned to England, Darwin read *An Essay on the Principle of Population* by Thomas Malthus. This essay greatly influenced Darwin's thinking and became the basis for his theory of evolution. Malthus, a minister, mathematician, and economist, was concerned about the social problems of an increasing human population. Malthus reasoned that the human population tends to increase geometrically (2, 4, 8, 16, . . .). For example, if each pair of parents produced four children, the new generation would have 4

▲ **Figure 29–3**
Darwin's Finches. Two of the finch species native to the Galapagos Islands are shown above.

Figure 29–4
Species Unique to the Galapagos Islands. The blue-footed booby (top) and the land iguana (bottom) are two species unique to the Galapagos Islands. ▼

individuals to replace the two that had produced them. The next generation would have 8, the next 16, and so on. On the other hand, food production could increase only arithmetically (1, 2, 3, 4, . . .) by gradually increasing the amount of land under cultivation. According to this reasoning, the food supply could not keep up with the increase in population. Therefore, to keep a balance between the need for food and the supply of food, millions of individuals had to die by disease, starvation, or war.

Darwin realized that all organisms face the same danger of overpopulation. He was also familiar with the competition and struggle for existence that occurs in nature. In 1838, the idea came to him that organisms with favorable variations would be better able to survive and to reproduce than organisms with unfavorable variations. He called this process **natural selection,** because nature "selects" the survivors. The result of natural selection would be evolution.

Darwin now had an explanation for how evolution occurred. Although many of his friends urged him to publish a book on the subject, Darwin would not be rushed. He insisted on building a strong case for his theory first. Then, in 1858, Darwin received an essay written by Alfred Russel Wallace, an English naturalist working in Indonesia. Wallace had arrived at the same conclusions as Darwin. Not knowing that Darwin had been thinking along the same lines, Wallace had sent the paper to Darwin for his opinion.

Darwin and Wallace agreed that Wallace's essay should be published along with a summary of Darwin's theory. A year later, in 1859, Darwin published his book under the title, *On the Origin of Species by Means of Natural Selection.* Darwin's book was fully supported by examples. His theory of evolution was eventually accepted by most of the leading scientists of his time.

The six main points of Darwin's theory are summarized below.

Overproduction   Most species produce far more offspring than are needed to maintain the population. Species populations remain more or less constant because only a small fraction of offspring live long enough to reproduce.

Competition   Since living space and food are limited, offspring in each generation must compete among themselves and with other species for the necessities of life. Only a small fraction can possibly survive long enough to reproduce.

Variation   The characteristics of the individuals in any species are not exactly alike. They may differ in the exact size or shape of a body, in strength or running speed, in resistance to a particular disease, and so on. These differences are called **variations.** Some variations may not be important. Others may affect the individual's ability to get food, to escape enemies, or to find a mate. These are of vital importance.

Adaptations   Because of variations, some individuals will be better adapted to survive and reproduce than others. In the competition for existence, the individuals that have favorable

Can You Explain This?

Several species of orchid emit a fragrance that is similar to the odor of female insects. Male insects are fooled by the scent and attempt to mate with the orchid's flowers. When the male lands on a flower, it makes contact with the orchid's pollen. Unsuccessful in its mating attempt, the insect flies off in search of a more appropriate mate, carrying the pollen to another orchid flower.

■ *Suggest an explanation for how this ability to deceive insects developed in orchids.*

adaptations to their environment will have a greater chance of living long enough to reproduce. An **adaptation** is any kind of inherited trait that improves an organism's chances of survival and reproduction in a given environment.

Natural Selection   In effect, the environment selects plants and animals with optimal traits to be the parents of the next generation. Individuals with variations that make them better adapted to their environment survive and reproduce in greater numbers than those without such adaptations. Experience has shown that the offspring of better adapted individuals usually inherit these favorable variations.

Speciation   Over many generations, favorable adaptations gradually accumulate in the species and unfavorable ones disappear. Eventually, the accumulated changes become so great that the net result is a new species. The formation of new species is called **speciation** (spee shee AY shun).

Applying Darwin's Theory

Figure 29–5 shows how Darwin's theory would account for the evolution of the modern giraffe. The original giraffe population had short necks and ate grass. However, unlike Lamarck's theory, Darwin's theory assumes some giraffes had longer necks than others. Those with longer necks could eat the lower leaves of trees as well as grass. In times when grass was scarce, the longer-necked animals could obtain more food than the others and, therefore, would be more likely to survive and reproduce. Their offspring would inherit the favorable variation of a longer neck. The longer the neck of a giraffe, the higher it could reach for leaves on the trees and the greater its chances for survival. As a result of natural selection, giraffe necks were slightly longer on the average in each succeeding generation. The modern long-necked animal is the result of this gradual process of evolution.

Overall, Darwin's theory of natural selection gives a satisfactory explanation of evolution. However, there are weaknesses in his theory. For one thing, it does not explain how variations originate and are passed on to the next generation. Also, it does not distinguish between variations caused by hereditary differences and variations caused by the environment, which are not inherited. For example, a plant growing in poor soil may be smaller than a plant of the same species growing in rich, fertile soil. Here, the differences in height are caused by the environment and cannot be inherited.

The Rate of Evolution

At present, scientists do not agree on the rate at which evolution or species formation occurs. According to Darwin's theory, new species arise through the gradual accumulation of small variations. In other words, evolution occurs slowly and continuously over

▲ **Figure 29–5**
Darwin's Theory of Natural Selection. (a) Adult giraffes' necks varied in length. (b) When the environment changed, only the long-necked giraffes could reach food. (c) The short-necked giraffes died, leaving only the long-necked giraffes to reproduce.

Figure 29–6

Gradualism and Punctuated Equilibrium. The gradualism model (left) sees evolution as proceeding more or less steadily through time. The punctuated equilibrium model (right) views evolution as being concentrated in short periods of time (dotted lines) followed by long periods of little or no change. Note that both models result in the same number of species. ▶

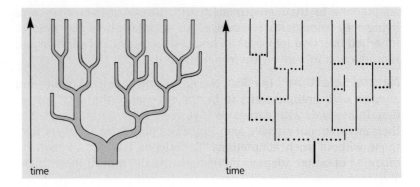

thousands and millions of years. This model is called **gradualism.** The gradualists believe that transitional forms, or links, between species are missing from the fossil record because they were less common. Thus, few of them were preserved.

Steven J. Gould and Niles Eldredge have proposed a different view of evolutionary change, which is known as **punctuated equilibrium.** According to their view, a species remains in equilibrium, or stays the same, for extended periods of time. This view is supported by the fossil record, which shows that each species seems to remain the same for thousands or millions of years. Then, in a relatively short period of time (a few hundred or a few thousand years) according to the fossil record, equilibrium is interrupted by the appearance of a new species. In other words, the long period of equilibrium is interrupted, or punctuated, by a short period of rapid evolution.

The supporters of punctuated equilibrium argue that transitional forms between species are missing because evolution occurs rapidly over a relatively brief period on the geologic time scale. Although the fossil record seems to support this new theory, the mechanisms that could produce new species in such a short interval are unknown. Figure 29–6 compares the Darwinian gradualistic model with the punctuated equilibrium model of evolution.

29-1 Section Review

1. Name the two principles involved in Lamarck's theory of evolution.
2. What is natural selection?
3. List the six main points of Darwin's theory of evolution.
4. Explain how the fossil record supports the theory of punctuated equilibrium.

Critical Thinking

5. Darwin observed similarities and differences between species on the Galapagos Islands and species on the mainland. Why were both similarities and differences necessary for Darwin's conclusion that evolution occurs? (*Reasoning Conditionally*)

29-2 Genetics and Evolution

Section Objectives:

- *Define* the term *population genetics* and explain evolution in terms of allele frequencies.
- *Describe* De Vries' contribution to Darwin's theory of evolution.
- *List* the causes of variation in a species according to modern genetic theory.
- *State* the Hardy-Weinberg law and list the conditions under which this law holds true.

In Darwin's time, little was known about heredity and genetics. However, modern biologists have combined Darwin's basic theory with the findings of genetics and population biology to form the **modern theory of evolution.** According to this theory, evolution happens to populations, not to individuals. Indeed, evolution is now defined as a change in the allele frequency within a population over time. Even with this new definition, however, individuals, not populations, are the units of natural selection.

Population Genetics

The modern theory of evolution stresses the importance of populations. See Figure 29–7. A **population** is a group of organisms of the same species living together in a given region and capable of interbreeding. According to the modern theory of evolution, *individuals* do not evolve. Their genetic makeup remains the same throughout their lives. However, *populations* do evolve. A population is made up of many individuals, each with its own unique assortment of alleles. As these individuals reproduce and die, the genetic makeup of the population as a whole may change. As its genetic makeup changes from generation to generation, the population evolves. The study of the changes in the genetic makeup of populations is called **population genetics.**

Each individual of a population has a set of alleles that is not exactly the same as the set of any other individual. Still, these individuals do have many of the same alleles. In a population as a whole, there are a certain number of alleles of each kind. Some alleles may be more common than others. For example, every individual in a population may have the alleles for producing a particular enzyme. The *frequencies* of these alleles in the population is 100 percent. On the other hand, only 1 in 100 individuals may have a mutant allele. Its frequency in the population is then 1/100, or 1 percent.

The total of all the alleles present in a population is called the **gene pool.** At any given time, each allele occurs in the population's gene pool with a certain frequency. This frequency may be any-

Figure 29–7

A Population of Penguins. According to the modern theory of evolution, it is a population that evolves over time, not individuals. ▼

▲ **Figure 29–8**

Mutations. De Vries formulated his theory of mutation after observing generations of evening primroses.

where from 100 percent to 1 per 10 000 or 1 per 1 000 000. As time goes on, the allele frequencies found in the gene pool may change as the result of natural selection. According to the modern theory, **evolution** is the gradual change of the allele frequencies found in a population.

Genetic Sources of Variation

The Dutch botanist Hugo De Vries introduced the concept of mutation at the beginning of this century. As you read in Chapter 26, De Vries based his theory of mutation on research that he conducted over several years with the evening primrose. See Figure 29–8. In the course of his research, De Vries observed that occasionally a plant appeared with a totally new structure or form. This plant would then breed true in later generations. De Vries considered these sudden changes in the hereditary material to be mutations.

De Vries added the idea of mutation to Darwin's theory of evolution. This overcame the question of how new traits could arise, one of the major weaknesses of Darwin's theory. De Vries claimed that the important changes leading to new species occurred as sudden, large changes in heredity that resulted from mutation. According to De Vries, a giraffe with a longer-than-normal neck would have been produced by a mutation. Because the long-necked giraffe and its offspring had an advantage over giraffes with necks of normal length, they survived and multiplied in greater numbers. Eventually, only the long-necked variety was left.

Mutations are not the only source of genetic variation. Recombination, as a result of sexual reproduction and the migration of individuals between populations, also contributes to variation.

Mutations   While gene mutations are a major source of variation in the modern theory of evolution, the mutation of any particular gene is a rare event. Out of 10 000 gametes, only one may have a mutated gene. The mutation rate for that gene is said to be 1 per 10 000. On the other hand, each gamete has thousands of genes. Among those thousands of genes, it is very likely that at least one of them has mutated. Thus, a few mutations are likely to be present in every zygote.

Most mutations are recessive. As a result, the mutant trait is usually hidden by the normal, dominant trait. Because of the low frequency of gene mutations, it is rare for mutant alleles to be brought together in the homozygous state. When this does happen, the effect may be harmful or helpful to the individual. However, if environmental conditions change, a harmful mutant allele may suddenly become useful to the species. Natural selection will then tend to gradually increase the frequency of this allele in the population.

Chromosomal mutations, which were described in Chapter 26, are another source of variation in a population. Although these mutations do not produce new genes, they do result in new combinations of genes in an organism. Since most physical traits are controlled by several genes, new gene combinations can give rise to new traits in a later generation.

Genetic Recombination   The formation of new combinations of alleles during sexual reproduction is called **genetic recombination.** Recombination can occur when two gametes undergo fusion to form a zygote. It is crossing-over and independent assortment that bring about recombination during meiosis. Crossing-over involves the exchange of segments between homologous chromosomes. When crossing-over occurs, it results in new allele combinations. Independent assortment provides that alleles on non-homologous chromosomes are randomly grouped, which also results in allele recombination.

Migration   Another source of variation may result from migration into or out of a population. As individuals move into a population, they may bring in genes not already present. When individuals leave a population, they may remove some genes from the population. Migration tends to have its greatest effect on variations in small populations.

Genetic Drift   Another factor that affects small populations is known as genetic drift. **Genetic drift** is a change in the gene pool of a small population that is brought about by chance. In small populations, there is a *chance* that a few individuals have certain alleles that the rest of the population does not have. If these individuals do not mate successfully, the alleles will be lost to the gene pool. For example, imagine that the population of an endangered plant species consists of 80 plants. Suppose that only three plants in this population have a certain allele. If these three plants are killed in a storm before they reproduce, the gene pool is reduced.

Genetic drift usually is harmful to the population because it decreases the variations in the gene pool. In a large population, genetic drift is less likely to occur because there are so many individuals. Therefore, it is unlikely that only a few individuals have an allele that no other individuals possess.

The Hardy-Weinberg Law

In Chapter 25, you read about Mendel's experiments with hybrid pea plants. In these experiments, there were two alleles for each trait that he studied. For example, the allele T produced tall plants, and the allele t produced short plants. The frequencies of T and t in the hybrid plants were equal: 50 percent T and 50 percent t. When the hybrids reproduced, the offspring had a genotype ratio of 1:2:1 and a phenotype ratio of 3:1, but the allele frequencies in the offspring remained the same—50:50. You can check this statement for yourself by counting the T and t alleles in the Punnett square shown in Figure 25–10.

Science, Technology and Society

Issue: Endangered Species

The snow leopard, northern spotted owl, and African elephant are only a few of many species facing a common threat: extinction. Today, the chief causes of extinction are human activities such as poaching (hunting illegally), and destroying natural habitats for industrial or agricultural use. The present extinction rate is over 1000 times higher than in prehistoric times, and it is increasing rapidly.

Environmentalists argue that governments must pass laws to control human activities that result in extinction. All organisms have a right to exist, and many species have potential value as sources of medicine and knowledge.

Other people argue that human needs are more important. Many people depend on the farmland for their food. Others make a living by logging or through other uses of the land. Moreover, competition for survival among species, including humans, is a natural process. Because it is, governments should not interfere.

■ *Should steps be taken to protect endangered species? Why or why not?*

The condition in which allele frequencies do not change from one generation to the next is called **genetic equilibrium.** To maintain genetic equilibrium, it is not necessary for two alleles in a population to have the same frequency. One may be much more common than the other. Suppose, for example, that there are two alleles for eye color in a certain species. One allele produces white eyes; the other, red eyes. We do not need to worry about dominance or about the eye color of a hybrid. Let us just assume that the allele for white eyes is more common than the allele for red eyes. We will say that 90 percent of the alleles are for white eyes, and 10 percent are for red. As these organisms mate and reproduce, what will happen to the allele frequencies for eye color as generation follows generation? While it might seem logical that the white-eye allele will eventually replace the red-eye allele, in fact, the allele frequency does not change.

In 1908, G. H. Hardy, an English mathematician, and W. H. Weinberg, a German physician, considered this question and came to the same conclusion independently. They showed that segregation and recombination of genes in sexual reproduction could not change allele frequencies by itself. If the frequency of allele p was 90 percent, and the frequency of allele q was 10 percent, random mating would always produce a new generation with the same ratio of 90 percent p and 10 percent q. Their conclusion that sexual reproduction alone does not affect genetic equilibrium is called the **Hardy-Weinberg law.** See Figure 29–9.

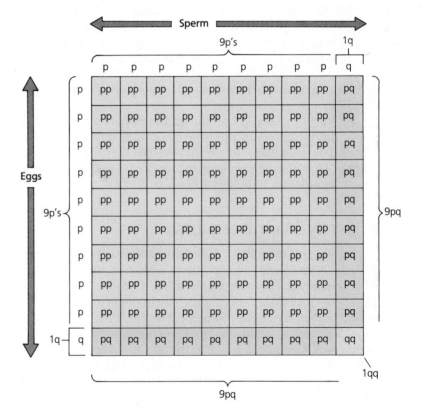

Figure 29–9

Illustrating the Hardy-Weinberg Law. Assume that the frequency of an allele p in a population is 90 percent and that of allele q is 10 percent. Then, out of every 10 sperm cells produced by the population, 9 will carry the p allele and 1 will carry q. The Punnett square shows the results of random fertilizations between these sperm and eggs. Of every 100 gametes formed, 81 are pp, 18 are pq, and 1 is qq. The total number of p's and q's in these 100 gametes is:

$$81 \text{ pp} = 162 \text{ p's}$$
$$18 \text{ pq} = 18 \text{ p's and } 18 \text{ q's}$$
$$\underline{1 \text{ qq} = 2 \text{ q's}}$$
$$\text{Totals: } 180 \text{ p's and } 20 \text{ q's}$$

We see that the ratio of p to q in the offspring generation is 180 to 20, or 9 to 1. This is the same as the ratio in the parent generation. ▶

For the Hardy-Weinberg law to hold true, four conditions must be met.

- The population must be large. In a small population, alleles of low frequency may be lost, or the frequency may change due to genetic drift.

- Individuals must not migrate into or out of the population. Any individuals that do so may change the allele frequencies of the population.

- Mutations must not occur because mutations obviously change the frequencies of the population.

- Reproduction must be completely random. This means that every individual, whatever its genetic makeup, should have an equal chance of producing offspring.

While the first two of these conditions can exist in nature, the last two conditions almost never exist. Populations can be large enough, and migration can be practically zero under certain circumstances. Mutations, however, are always occurring at fixed rates, thus changing allele frequencies. Furthermore, reproduction is not random. Individuals with helpful adaptations are more likely to reproduce because of natural selection. This also results in a change in the allele frequencies.

You may wonder about the usefulness of a law that does not apply to any situation in the real world. The Hardy-Weinberg law is important because it allows us to discover whether or not evolution is occurring in a population. The law tells us that under certain conditions, allele frequencies will remain constant and there will be no evolution. The fact that allele frequencies in a population change tells us that there are external factors causing them to change. In other words, the failure of the Hardy-Weinberg law is a sign that evolution is occurring. The extent of the variation from the Hardy-Weinberg prediction is a measure of how rapid the evolutionary change is.

29-2 Section Review

1. Name the sources of variation within a species according to the modern theory of evolution.
2. What is a population?
3. Define the term *gene pool.*
4. List the conditions that must exist for the Hardy-Weinberg law to hold true.

Critical Thinking

5. If mutations occur, then the allele frequencies in a population will change. In a population you are studying, the allele frequencies have changed. Does this prove that mutations have occured? Why or why not? (*Reasoning Conditionally*)

▲ **Figure 29–10**

Adaptations. The dormouse, like many mammals, hibernates in winter. During hibernation, the animal's metabolic rate and body temperature decrease. This adaptation allows the animal to survive long cold periods when food is scarce.

Figure 29–11

Camouflage. The sundial flounder is camouflaged against the sandy ocean floor. ▼

29-3 Adaptations and Natural Selection

Section Objectives:

- *Explain* the term *adaptation* and name some different kinds of adaptations.
- *Define* the terms *camouflage, warning coloration,* and *mimicry.*
- *Distinguish* among *directional selection, stabilizing selection,* and *disruptive selection.*

Under what conditions will a species evolve? By focusing on allele frequencies, the Hardy-Weinberg law allows scientists to understand the mechanisms of natural selection. In this section, we will look at how natural selection determines which adaptations are favorable for survival.

Types of Adaptations

As you read earlier, an adaptation is any kind of inherited trait that improves the chances of survival and reproduction for an organism. The environment is the selecting force that chooses the best and most useful inherited variations. For example, in a population of plants, there may be a genetic variation in the amount of waxy cutin covering the leaves of the plants. Some plants may be heavily covered with this protective layer, while other plants are only thinly covered. Because cutin protects the plant from drying out, plants with a thick cutin layer will be better able to survive and to produce seeds if the climate becomes very dry. In this case, the cutin is an adaptation that has been "selected" by the environment. After many generations, alleles for this adaptation will accumulate in the gene pool. Eventually, only plants with a heavy cutin layer will remain in the population.

Structural adaptations are adaptations that involve the body of the organism. The wings of birds and insects, for example, are structural adaptations for flight. The fins of fish and the webbed feet of ducks are structural adaptations for swimming. *Physiological adaptations* involve the metabolism of organisms. The protein web made by spiders and the poison venom made by snakes are examples of physiological adaptations. Still other adaptations involve particular behavior patterns. Of course, many adaptations are combinations of various types of adaptations. For example, the mating behavior and migration of birds, the spawning of fishes, and the hibernation of animals involve several types of adaptations. See Figure 29-10.

Many adaptations provide protection. In **camouflage,** the organism blends into the environment, as shown in Figure 29-11. Flounders can become practically invisible against a variety of backgrounds. Fawns are hard to see among the shadows in their usual environment. In **warning coloration,** the colors of the animal

▲ **Figure 29–12**
Mimicry and Warning Coloration. The inedible monarch butterfly (left) warns away potential predators with its bright colors. The edible viceroy butterfly (right) is avoided by predators because it so closely resembles the monarch in color and markings.

actually make it easier to see. This is an advantage for certain insects that birds and other enemies find unpleasant to eat. If a young bird happens to eat one of these insects, it quickly learns to avoid that species in the future. The brightly colored monarch butterfly, which is shown in Figure 29–12, is an example of this kind of warning coloration. In **mimicry,** one organism is protected from its enemies by its resemblance to another species. Birds can eat the viceroy butterfly without suffering unpleasant effects, but they tend to avoid it because it looks like the monarch butterfly. In contrast to mimicry, camouflage helps an organism avoid its enemies by making it difficult to see. As Figure 29–13 shows, shape and structure, as well as coloration, can contribute to an organism's camouflage.

◀ **Figure 29–13**
Camouflage. The lichen katydid is hidden from predators because it resembles the lichen on which it feeds.

Types of Natural Selection

According to the modern theory of evolution, natural selection disturbs genetic equilibrium. As a result, the allele frequencies in the population will change. In this way, natural selection determines which adaptations are favorable for a species. There are three main types of natural selection.

Directional Selection   One type of natural selection, in which an extreme phenotype becomes a favorable adaptation, is called **directional selection.** This type of selection usually operates when the environment changes or when species migrate. The new environmental conditions favor the extreme phenotype, causing the population to evolve.

The evolution of long-necked giraffes is an example of directional selection. The red graph in Figure 29–14a shows the continuous variation of neck length in a giraffe population at some time in the past. Most of the giraffes in this population had intermediate neck lengths, although some had short necks and some had long necks. Several alleles for short and long necks probably were present, with low frequencies, in the population. A change in the environment may have given the individuals with the alleles for longer necks a favorable adaptation. In later generations, their offspring made up a larger fraction of the population. Therefore, the

Figure 29–14

Types of Selection. Directional selection favors a relatively rare phenotype. Stabilizing selection favors average phenotypes and acts against extreme phenotypes. Disruptive selection favors two extreme phenotypes and acts against the average phenotype. ▼

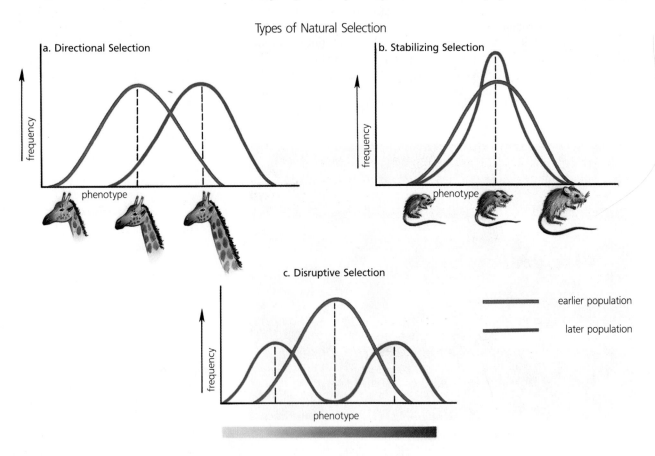

Types of Natural Selection

a. Directional Selection

b. Stabilizing Selection

c. Disruptive Selection

earlier population

later population

alleles they carried for long necks would be present at a greater frequency, and the population would have longer necks, on average. This is shown by the blue curve. Notice that the blue curve looks like the red curve, but it is shifted to the right. Thus, directional selection selects in the direction of an extreme phenotype.

Stabilizing Selection   Sometimes, the average phenotype may be a favorable adaptation, and extreme phenotypes are unfavorable. This is called **stabilizing selection.** For example, mice that are too small may not be strong enough to burrow underground in cold weather, while mice that are too large may use too much energy in keeping warm. If the climate becomes colder, fewer large and small mice will survive to reproduce. See Figure 29–14b. Notice that the average size of the population, shown by the dashed line, is the same in the two populations. However, the blue curve representing the population after the climate change is narrower because there is less variation in the population. This is because the frequencies of some alleles carried by the extreme phenotypes have decreased.

Stabilizing selection operates most of the time in most populations. This type of selection limits evolution by keeping allele frequencies relatively constant. In this way, populations of organisms, such as sharks and ferns, have remained stable for millions of years.

Disruptive Selection   A third, rare type of natural selection is called disruptive selection. In **disruptive selection,** two opposite phenotypes are favorable adaptations, while the average phenotypes are unfavorable. As you can see in Figure 29–14c, this creates two subpopulations. For example, a species of crab might show a continuous variation in color from light tan to dark brown. If the environment changed to include both sandy beaches and brown mud, both extremes of coloration could be favorable camouflage against predators. In time, alleles carried by the extreme phenotypes would increase in frequency, resulting in the evolution of two subpopulations. If these populations could not mate with each other, they would be considered two new species.

Can You Explain This?

Several centuries ago, a ship carrying emigrant families was blown off course and wrecked on a deserted tropical island. All of the people were very light skinned. After many years under the tropical sun, however, everyone became dark skinned.

■ *What color skin would babies born to the children of these couples have? What color skin would babies in the fifth generation have? Explain your answers.*

29-3 Section Review

1. Define the term *adaptation.*
2. Name two different types of adaptations and give an example of each.
3. What are the three main types of natural selection?
4. Which type of natural selection tends to prevent evolution?

Critical Thinking

5. How is mimicry of the environment different from camouflage? How is it similar? (*Comparing and Contrasting*)

29-4 Speciation

Section Objectives:

- *Define* the terms *range* and *speciation.*
- *Describe* the processes of isolation and adaptive radiation.
- *Distinguish* between convergent evolution and coevolution.

Under certain circumstances, one species can evolve into two or more species. This formation of new species is called **speciation** (spee shee AY shun).

Speciation and Geographic Separation

Each species is found in a particular region of the earth. This region is called the species' **range.** The characteristics of a species are often different in different parts of its range. Differences in environmental conditions have exerted different selective pressures, leading to different adaptive characteristics. The leopard frog, *Rana pipiens,* for example, has a wide range that extends over most of North America. Across this range, the frogs differ in body size, patterns of coloration, and the temperatures at which their embryos will develop. The species actually consists of separate populations with different gene pools. However, adjacent populations can mate and produce normal offspring. These separate populations are therefore called subspecies, or varieties, of the same species.

The frogs at opposite ends of the range show the greatest differences in characteristics and in gene pools. In fact, frogs from widely separated regions cannot mate successfully. They are still considered to be the same species because there is continuous interbreeding among adjacent subspecies. If, however, a population varies so much from its neighbors that it loses the ability to interbreed, a new species has developed.

Types of Speciation

Isolation   One of the most important factors involved in speciation is isolation. *Isolation* refers to anything that prevents two groups within a species from interbreeding. Isolating a group of organisms separates its gene pool from the gene pool of the rest of the species. Through mutation, genetic recombination, and natural selection, a different gene pool will evolve in each group.

It is generally believed that speciation is a two-step process that first involves geographic isolation, followed by reproductive isolation. **Geographic isolation** occurs when a population is divided by a natural barrier, such as a mountain, desert, river or other body of water, or a landslide caused by an earthquake. See Figure 29–15. As a result, the gene pool of each group becomes isolated, and the two can no longer intermix. Over a period of time, each group will become adapted to its particular environment. When the differences between the isolated groups become great enough, they will no longer be able to interbreed, even if they could get together. The loss of the ability to interbreed by two isolated groups is called **reproductive isolation.**

Reproductive isolation can be produced by several mechanisms. Differences may arise in courtship behavior, times of mating, or the structure of the sex organs. Such changes make it unlikely that mating will occur. Other changes affect events after mating and involve the inability of sperm to fertilize eggs, the death of the embryo early in development, or the development of offspring that are sterile. According to most biologists, if two groups of organisms cannot interbreed successfully, they can be considered different species.

The Kaibab squirrel and Abert squirrel are thought to be cases of speciation by geographic and reproductive isolation. The Kaibab squirrel inhabits the north side of the Grand Canyon, and the Abert squirrel inhabits the south side. It is believed that these two squirrels evolved from a common ancestor. The Grand Canyon, acting as a geographical barrier, divided the ancestral population, which once occupied the entire area. After a long period of geographical isolation, the Kaibab and Abert squirrels evolved. The two squirrels are similar in appearance but are different species because they cannot interbreed.

Polyploidy   Speciation can occur suddenly when abnormal meiosis or mitosis results in polyploidy. As you read in Chapter 25, polyploids are organisms, usually plants, that contain more than the usual number of chromosome sets. When the offspring can interbreed only among themselves, they are considered a new species.

Adaptive Radiation   The process by which a species evolves into a number of different species, each occupying a new environment, is called **adaptive radiation.** This spreading, or radiation, of the organisms into different environments is accompanied by adaptations.

For example, a single ancestral species may have migrated—radiated—into several different environments. If the descendants have few predators and little competition for food, they will be successful. Then, through isolation, genetic variation, and natural selection, they will evolve a variety of adaptations to their new environments. After many generations, they will have evolved into several new species, each having certain adaptive traits. However, their common ancestry is indicated by the traits they share in common.

Darwin's finches are an example of adaptive radiation. In this case, an ancestral type of finch probably arrived in the Galapagos Islands and then radiated into a variety of habitats and ways of life. The initial radiation involved living on the ground and living in trees. Further radiation occurred on the basis of food. Some finches live on the ground and feed on seeds of varying size. Some live in forests and feed on insects in trees. Others feed mainly on cactus or

▲ **Figure 29–15**
Speciation through Geographic Isolation. The spring-dwelling salamander (top) and the cave-dwelling salamander (bottom) can no longer interbreed. These two species are believed to share a common ancestor. The population was divided when one group took up residence in a cave. The differing selective pressures of the two environments resulted in the divergence of the species over time.

▲ **Figure 29–16**
Convergent Evolution. The koala bear is a marsupial that looks very much like a bear.

berries. One species lives in low bushes and feeds on insects. Without competition from other birds, the finches slowly radiated into and adapted to the various types of environment that were present.

Convergent Evolution

As a result of geographic isolation, organisms that are not closely related may develop similar adaptations and come to resemble each other. Natural selection that causes unrelated species to resemble one another is called **convergent evolution.** Convergent evolution produces analogous structures, which you read about in Chapter 28. Bird wings and insect wings are good examples of analogous structures that result from convergent evolution.

Another example of convergent evolution is the similarity between marsupials and their placental counterparts. The marsupial mouse looks much like a placental mouse. There is also a marsupial that resembles a wolf (the Tasmanian wolf) and one that resembles a bear (the koala), which is shown in Figure 29–16. These resemblances are only "skin deep." They evolved because of similar needs in similar environments, leading to the natural selection of analogous structural adaptations.

Coevolution

Two or more species also can evolve in response to each other through cooperative or competitive adaptations. This is called **coevolution.** One example of coevolution is the relationship between flowers and their pollinators. For example, some species of flowers have developed adaptations to attract bees. Bees are active during the day, attracted by bright colors and sweet or minty odors, and usually land on a petal before feeding. Flowers adapted to bees have a sweet or minty odor and are open in the daytime. They have a petal for the bee to land on and are usually bright blue or yellow, because bees cannot see red light. In comparison, bats, which are active at night, feed on the nectar of flowers that are open at night and easily visible in the dark. Coevolution reduces competition between species and benefits both species.

29-4 Section Review

1. What is speciation? Name the two steps involved in speciation.
2. What is adaptive radiation?
3. Give an example of convergent evolution.
4. Define the term *coevolution.*

Critical Thinking

5. What possible outcomes are likely if a species migrates into an area with many predators? Explain your answer. (*Predicting*)

Math, Science, and Technology

Antibiotics vs. Bacteria

Problem

For nearly 50 years, penicillin and the more than 100 other antibiotics have provided doctors with the primary weapons that were needed to fight the battle against bacterial diseases. Some members of the medical profession became so convinced that the war against bacterial diseases was won that they freely prescribed antibiotics. Patients also misused antibiotics by not completely finishing the entire medication as prescribed. Hospitals, too, relaxed their practice of infection control. And pharmaceutical companies stopped searching for and developing new drugs to fight bacterial diseases.

As a result of all of these factors, bacteria that were resistant to penicillin (antibiotic-resistant bacteria, or ARB) began to emerge in the 1940s. Soon, bacteria that were resistant to other antibiotics—such as streptomycin, tetracycline, erythromycin, and ampicillin—appeared. Since then, some of the ARB evolved into multiple antibiotic-resistant bacteria (MARB). MARB are those bacteria that have developed a resistance to more than one antibiotic.

The resistance of bacteria to the antibiotics that once controlled them illustrates natural selection. The outbreak of MARB is not solely due to natural selection, however. The widespread and inappropriate use of antibiotics by people has helped in its development.

Task

You are a member of a team of microbiologists that has been asked by a pharmaceutical company to trace the development of the resistance of an antibiotic called salmonycin to *Salmonella,* the bacteria that causes food poisoning.

In order to perform this task, you must complete the following:

1. Using the data table, calculate the percentage of the total population of *Salmonella* bacteria that are susceptible and resistant to salmonycin for each year during a 10-year period. Construct a table that contains these percentages.

2. Design and produce a pamphlet that will inform health professionals how to administer antibiotics properly.

3. Research antibiotic-resistant bacteria and multiple antibiotic-resistant bacteria on the Internet and in the library to find out what is being done to fight them.

4. Keep a journal of all the information and data you have collected during your research.

5. Apply your knowledge of evolution to the emergence of antibiotic-resistant bacteria.

Year	Number of Bacteria Susceptible to Salmonycin	Number of Bacteria Resistant to Salmonycin
1	999 999	1
2	896 407	37
3	901 363	590
4	889 242	3611
5	870 011	15 423
6	869 692	195 687
7	627 916	380 184
8	243 020	569 882
9	7438	867 103
10	512	987 833

Solution

Explain the progression of the number of susceptible and resistant strains of *Salmonella* to salmonycin changes over a 10-year period. Include graphs in the presentation of your data. What part did natural selection and human intervention play in the emergence of antibiotic-resistant bacteria?

29-5 Observed Natural Selection

Section Objectives:

- *Discuss* industrial melanism and the information gained from the study of the peppered moth in England.
- *Describe* how populations of antibiotic-resistant bacteria and DDT-resistant insects have arisen.

Natural selection may take many thousands of years to produce a change in a population. However, in recent years some excellent examples of natural selection have given scientists an opportunity to study evolution in action. One of these illustrates a kind of adaptation called industrial melanism. **Industrial melanism** is the term used for the development of dark-colored organisms in a population exposed to industrial air pollution.

Industrial Melanism

The peppered moth, *Biston betularia,* is found in wooded areas in England. Before the 1850s, most peppered moths were light in color. Black-colored moths that have a pigment called *melanin* occurred, but they were very rare. During the years from 1850 to 1900, England became heavily industrialized. Where there was a great deal of industry, heavy smoke darkened the tree trunks and killed the light lichens that were growing on them. By the 1890s in these regions, 99 percent of the peppered moths were black in color, while the light-colored variety was rare. In the cleaner, nonindustrial areas of southern England, the light-colored moth continued to predominate. See Figure 29–17.

A hypothesis for the change from light-colored to dark-colored moths can be found in natural selection. The light and dark color of the moth is genetically controlled. The dark color is a mutation that

Figure 29–17

Industrial Melanism. On the light tree (left), the lighter colored peppered moth is better camouflaged. On the dark tree (right), the darker moth is better camouflaged. ▼

occurs at a constant low frequency. During daylight, peppered moths rest on tree trunks. Before England became industrialized, the light-colored moths blended in well with the lichens that covered the tree bark. As a result of this camouflage, birds that feed upon the peppered moth could not easily find the light-colored moths. Dark-colored moths were easily seen and eaten by hungry birds. This situation gave the light-colored moths an obvious reproductive advantage. When the fumes and soot killed the lichens and blackened the trees, however, the light-colored moths were easy to see against the dark background of the tree trunks and became easy prey for birds. Now, the dark-colored moths had a distinct advantage. The blackened trees offered them good camouflage, as shown in Figure 29–17. Through natural selection, more dark moths survived and reproduced than light-colored moths. During the years from 1850 to 1900, a period of 50 generations for peppered moths, the dark-colored moths became the more frequent color in the population.

In the 1950s, H. B. D. Kettlewell and Niko Tinbergen performed controlled experiments that attempted to test the above hypothesis. Light- and dark-colored peppered moths were released in a polluted industrial area and in an unpolluted nonindustrial area. In the polluted area, where the trees were blackened with soot, Kettlewell and Tinbergen recorded more light-colored moths eaten than dark-colored moths. In the unpolluted area, birds ate more dark-colored moths than light-colored moths.

This research on the color change in peppered moths shows that a species can change gradually from one form to another over a period of time. Two details of the evolutionary process are clearly illustrated. One is the presence of variability in the population. Alleles for light color and dark color are in the gene pool. The other is the effect of the changing environment in selecting one color trait over another. The trait that makes the moth best adapted to the environment is preserved.

In the United States, the insects around many major cities are darker in color than the ones in the unpolluted countryside. Interestingly, since the 1950s, air pollution control in England has resulted in an increase in the number of light-colored peppered moths.

Bacterial Resistance to Antibiotics

Antibiotics usually kill bacteria. However, once the use of antibiotics became common, resistant strains of bacteria began to appear. Antibiotics were no longer effective in killing those strains.

Scientists wanted to know how this resistance developed. One possibility was that exposure to an antibiotic caused certain bacterial cells to develop resistance to it. This would be similar to the immunity an individual acquires to a disease organism after recovery from the disease. Another possibility was that in a large population of bacteria, there are always a few individuals with

Biology and You

Q: Can resistance to antibiotics spread from one bacterium to another? If so, will antibiotics soon be useless?

A: Nonresistant bacteria become resistant to antibiotics in many ways. Sometimes rings of DNA, called plasmids, carry antibiotic-resistance genes. Plasmids travel among bacterial cells. When a nonresistant cell acquires a plasmid, it may become resistant to antibiotics. Often resistance is coded for by "jumping genes," which move from chromosome to chromosome. Spontaneous mutation during replication and recombination can also lead to resistance.

During medical treatment, an antibiotic will kill off nonresistant organisms. Resistant strains, however, will survive. Because bacteria reproduce quickly, resistant strains can rapidly spread. This rise in resistant organisms causes antibiotics such as penicillin or streptomycin to be ineffective. One way to reduce this problem is to minimize the use of antibiotics. Another way is to give two unrelated antibiotics at the same time, assuming that resistance to both is unlikely.

■ *Survey five people to find out how many have taken antibiotics in the past three months. Do they know the type taken?*

Figure 29–18

The Lederberg Experiment. (a) Individual bacteria are spread out over an agar culture medium. (b) Each cell multiplies to form a colony of cells that are genetically alike. (c) A few cells from each colony are picked up by a velveteen cloth attached to a block. (d) The cells are transferred to an agar medium containing an antibiotic. (e) Most of the transferred cells do not multiply (dotted circles). One colony does form (solid color). Because of the way the cells were transferred, the original colony in dish 1 that they came from is known. All cells in that colony are found to be resistant to the antibiotic. ▶

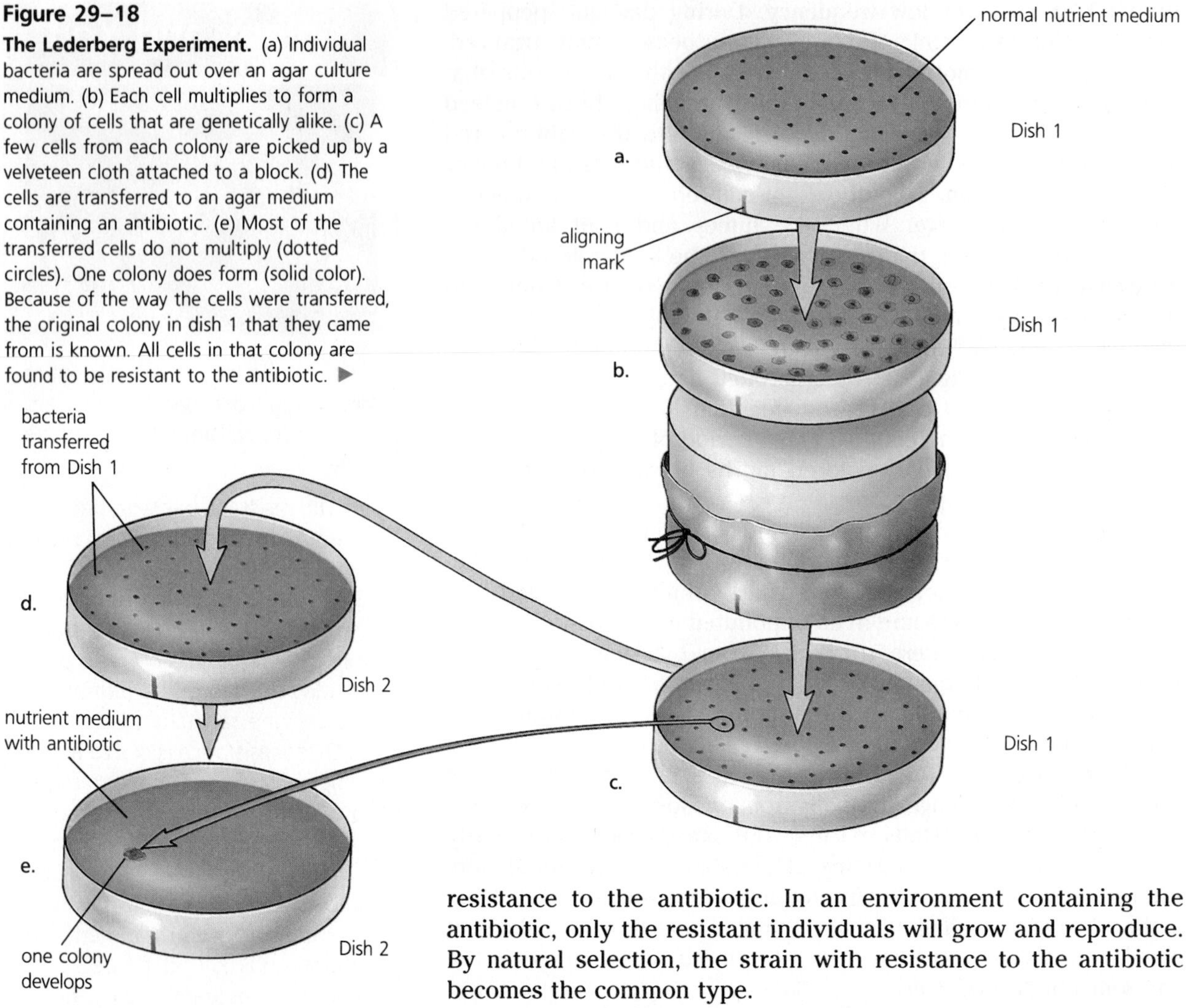

normal nutrient medium

Dish 1

a.

aligning mark

Dish 1

b.

bacteria transferred from Dish 1

d.

Dish 2

nutrient medium with antibiotic

e.

one colony develops

Dish 2

Dish 1

c.

resistance to the antibiotic. In an environment containing the antibiotic, only the resistant individuals will grow and reproduce. By natural selection, the strain with resistance to the antibiotic becomes the common type.

In the early 1950s, Esther and Joshua Lederberg carried out a series of experiments that showed that the second explanation, natural selection, was the correct one. The Lederbergs worked with the common intestinal bacterium *Escherichia coli,* which is normally killed by the antibiotic streptomycin. The first step of their experiment was to spread a culture of the bacteria very thinly on an agar nutrient medium in a petri dish. See Figure 29–18. This technique, which is called streaking, had the effect of separating the culture into individual bacteria. Each bacterial cell then multiplied on the agar, forming a distinct colony. In each colony, all the cells were genetically alike since they had developed from a single original cell.

The Lederbergs then looked for cells resistant to streptomycin. Since it would have taken too much time to investigate each colony separately, they used a velveteen cloth to pick up bacteria from all the colonies at once. The cloth was then touched to a second agar plate that contained streptomycin, thus transferring bacteria from all the colonies to the agar. Usually, none of the transferred bacteria formed a colony; they could not survive and multiply in the streptomycin environment. Occasionally, however, a colony did grow on the streptomycin plate. When this happened, the Lederbergs could identify the original colony the transferred cells had come from. They could because the velveteen cloth placed the bacteria in the same relative positions on the new agar as the colonies from which they were picked up. It was then a simple matter to test the original colony for streptomycin resistance.

When this test was carried out, it was found that all cells in the original colony were resistant. Remember that these cells had never been exposed to streptomycin. Their resistance was a genetic trait that they already possessed.

The Lederbergs concluded that a few bacteria with resistance to streptomycin had been in the original population. When no antibiotic was present in their environment, these cells had no advantage or disadvantage. However, when the environment was changed to include the antibiotic, the resistant cells had a survival advantage and multiplied, while the normal type died out. The population became 100 percent streptomycin-resistant.

This experiment showed that the change in the environment had not caused the resistance to develop. It had acted only as a selector for organisms that already had the gene for resistance to streptomycin.

Insect Resistance to DDT

When DDT was first introduced, it was an effective killer of insects, including mosquitos. Apparently, however, a small proportion of insects in various insect populations possessed a natural resistance to DDT. When the DDT-sensitive members of a population were killed by spraying, the DDT-resistant insects survived and passed on their natural DDT-resistance to their offspring. Eventually, many insect populations were completely resistant to DDT.

The DDT did *not* create the resistance of the insects. Rather, the DDT acted as the environmental agent for the selection of the resistant strains.

29-5 Section Review

1. What is industrial melanism?
2. Which moths were eaten more easily by birds in industrial areas?
3. Who discovered how antibiotic-resistant bacteria develop?

Critical Thinking

4. Explain why air pollution control in England since the 1950s has led to a greater number of light-colored moths. (*Identifying Causes*)

Laboratory
Investigation

Mutations in Bacteria

The environment of bacteria that live in the human body undergoes a significant change when antibiotics, such as penicillin or streptomycin, are used. Although most bacteria are killed by an antibiotic, some may survive because they are genetically resistant to the drug. These resistant forms can be thought of as mutants.

Problem

How do antibiotics affect the growth of bacteria? **Formulate a hypothesis** to answer this question.

Materials (per group)

- culture of bacteria
- sterile swabs
- sterile nutrient agar plate
- glass-marking pencil
- antibiotic filter paper discs
- forceps
- transparent tape
- metric ruler

Procedure

1. **CAUTION:** *Before and after working with bacteria, you must wash your hands and working surfaces with soap and water and disinfectant.* Carefully turn the sterile nutrient agar plate over and place it on your table. Do not open the plate.

2. With a glass-marking pencil, draw two lines at right angles to each other so that the plate is divided into four equal areas, or quadrants. Label the quadrants from 1 to 4.

3. Remove the covering from the sterile swab. Carefully dip the swab in the culture of bacteria. **CAUTION:** *Be careful when working with bacterial cultures.*

4. Remove the cover of a nutrient agar plate and rub the bacteria-containing swab over the entire surface of the agar. Follow the directions of your teacher as to how to dispose of the swab.

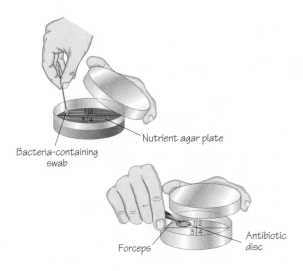

Bacteria-containing swab

Nutrient agar plate

Forceps

Antibiotic disc

5. With clean forceps, place the antibiotic discs on the nutrient agar, making certain that each disc is placed in the center of a numbered quadrant.

6. Cover the plate and tape the plate closed.

7. Using the glass-marking pencil, write your initials on the bottom of the plate.

8. Place the plate upside down in the area designated by your teacher.

9. After 24 hours, observe the growth of bacteria around each disc. Record your observations.

10. Using a metric ruler, measure in millimeters the diameter of the zone of no bacterial growth, or the zone of inhibition, that surrounds each of the antibiotic discs. Construct a data table and record the diameters of the zones of inhibition.

11. Carefully observe the zones of inhibition. Do you see a hazy secondary zone of bacterial growth? Record your observations in your data table.

Observations

How is the growth of bacteria affected by the antibiotic discs?

Analysis and Conclusions

1. What factor represents the selection pressure in this experiment?

2. Many of the infectious bacteria—such as *Staphylococcus*—have evolved a resistance to antibiotics. How has this occurred? What is the selection pressure? The adaptation?

3. Do the results of your experiment support your hypothesis?

Extensions

Design an experiment to test the drug resistance of the bacteria from the zone of inhibition. How many generations are needed to produce a strain that is very resistant to the antibiotic?

Chapter 29 Review

Study Outline

29-1 Early Theories of Evolution

▶ Lamarck's theory of evolution was based on the law of use and disuse and the inheritance of acquired characteristics.

▶ The six main points of Darwin's theory involve the concepts of overproduction, competition, variation, adaptation, natural selection, and speciation.

29-2 Genetics and Evolution

▶ The modern theory of evolution proposes that evolution is the change in allele frequency within a population over time.

▶ Genetic variation occurs as a result of gene mutations, genetic recombination, migration, and genetic drift.

▶ The Hardy-Weinberg law states that the frequency of alleles within a population remains constant if the population is large, reproduction is random, there are no mutations, and there is no migration.

29-3 Adaptations and Natural Selection

▶ Adaptations are inherited traits that improve an organism's chance of survival and reproduction in a given environment.

▶ There are three main types of natural selection: directional selection, stabilizing selection, and disruptive selection.

29-4 Speciation

▶ Speciation can take place by means of geographic and reproductive isolation, polyploidy, or adaptive radiation.

▶ Convergent evolution results in increased resemblance between unrelated species. Coevolution occurs when two or more species evolve in response to each other.

29-5 Observed Natural Selection

▶ Studies of industrial melanism in the peppered moth show that natural selection can act in favor of certain adaptations over short periods of time.

▶ Resistance of bacteria to antibiotics and of insects to DDT arises from genes that are already present in the population of bacteria or insects.

Chapter Assessment

Multiple Choice

Choose the letter of the answer that best completes each statement or answers the question.

1. In his theory of evolution, Lamarck assumed that (a) useful characteristics that are acquired are inherited. (b) the diversity of organisms depends upon genetic mutations. (c) variations are produced by gene recombinations. (d) new organisms arise as a result of common ancestry.

2. Darwin's theory of evolution is based on the concept of (a) use and disuse. (b) mutations. (c) natural selection. (d) hybridization.

3. If a species of insect lacks the variations needed to adapt to a changing environment, it will most likely (a) acquire them through evolution. (b) become extinct. (c) evolve into a lower form. (d) evolve into a higher form.

4. The special characteristics that make an organism particularly well suited to its environment are known as (a) abiotic factors. (b) aggregates. (c) biotic factors. (d) adaptations.

5. Which theory of evolutionary change suggests that species have long periods of stability interrupted by geologically brief periods of significant change during which new species are formed? (a) gradualism (b) geographic isolation (c) punctuated equilibrium (d) reproductive isolation

6. Pigeons of the same species inhabiting a city park represent a (a) population. (b) biome. (c) food chain. (d) food web.

7. Natural selection acting on a normal distribution of phenotypes in which the fittest individuals correspond to the center of the graph is called (a) disruptive selection. (b) directional selection. (c) stabilizing selection. (d) artificial selection.

8. For speciation to take place, a population must evolve enough genetic changes so that (a) breeding cannot occur between the emerging groups. (b) all offspring share the same gene pool. (c) offspring are genetically different from their parents. (d) the emerging groups can interbreed.

9. New species usually form only when populations (a) are isolated. (b) have similar gene pools. (c) have genetic drift. (d) are small and scattered.

10. The evolution of similar adaptations in unrelated species is called (a) adaptive radiation. (b) convergent evolution. (c) natural selection. (d) coevolution.

Content Review

Answer each of the following in complete sentences.

11. Describe Lamarck's theory of evolution.

12. Describe Darwin's theory of evolution by natural selection.

13. Explain how gradualism and punctuated equilibrium differ.

14. How did De Vries explain the appearance of new traits within a species?

15. Why is genetic drift less likely to affect large populations than small ones?

16. In what way is the Hardy-Weinberg law useful?

17. What is the difference between camouflage and warning coloration?

18. When are two groups of organisms considered two different species?

19. Explain why Darwin's finches may be said to represent an example of adaptive radiation.

20. What general conclusions were drawn from studies of the peppered moth in England?

Graphic Organizing

For information on graphic organizers, see Appendix G at the back of this text.

21. **Line Graph** Construct a line graph, using the data in the chart. The data represent the number of trilobite fossils of various lengths found at two different depths of sedimentary rock. In constructing your graph, plot the number of fossils on the vertical axis and the length of the fossil on the horizontal axis. Then, refer to Figure 29–14 to decide which type of natural selection the trilobites underwent as they evolved.

Length of Fossil (cm)	Number of Fossils (Lower Depth)	Number of Fossils (Higher Depth)
3.0	0	0
3.5	0	4
4.0	2	12
4.5	5	18
5.0	12	23
5.5	18	24
6.0	22	23
6.5	24	19
7.0	22	11
7.5	19	6
8.0	13	2
8.5	4	0
9.0	0	0

Critical Thinking and Problem Solving

Discuss each of the following in a brief paragraph.

22. **Comparing** Using the evolution of the modern giraffe as an example, compare Darwin's theory with Lamarck's theory of evolution.

23. **Predicting** If Lamarck's theory of evolution were correct, what characteristic might you expect in the offspring of two cats whose food was always placed at the top of a tall, smooth, wooden post?

Performance-Based Assessment

The Collapse of Biodiversity

Background

Biologists have identified more than 1.5 million species of living things. This incredible variety, or diversity, of life is called biodiversity. Biodiversity refers to the number of different types of organisms or species that live on earth. This great diversity of life is the result of millions of years of evolution. Since life first appeared on earth, species of organisms have arisen, existed for a time, and then become extinct, that is, died out. Extinction is a natural process. It is part of the normal process of evolution and change. As one group of organisms became extinct, others evolved.

Natural disasters and major environmental changes, such as volcanic eruptions or changes in climate, also cause extinctions. Sometimes mass extinctions occurred on a global scale. The most familiar example of mass extinction is the demise of the dinosaurs 65 million years ago.

Today, conditions on earth are significantly different from any previous period in the earth's history. The major difference is directly linked to the human population explosion and the development of technology. In the past 100 years, humans have changed the face of the globe at an unprecedented rate. These changes have occurred many times faster than the normal process of evolution. Consequently, a large number of species have been unable to adapt and have become extinct. Scientists estimate that the total number of species being lost each year is approaching 50 000. It has been estimated that humans will have caused 1 million species to become extinct by the year 2000.

The single greatest threat to biodiversity is the destruction of habitat. As the human population has grown, the amount of land used for agriculture, logging, mining, cities, and roads has steadily increased. This development has destroyed habitats that animals and plants need in order to survive.

A second cause of extinction is excessive harvesting or hunting. Elephants are killed for their tusks; rhinos are killed for their horns; whales are hunted for their oil; and cacti are collected for their unusual appearance. Sometimes, one species is depleted during the harvesting of another. For example, porpoises, sea turtles, and sea birds are often trapped in commercial fishing nets. Overfishing has depleted many of the world's fisheries. Many of these species are endangered because their depleted population is in danger of extinction.

A third cause of extinction is the introduction into an environment of non-native species. When humans bring non-native

animals or plants into an environment, the native species may not have evolved appropriate defenses, and the introduced species edge out the native ones.

Another cause of extinction is predator control. Ranchers in the western United States kill coyotes and wolves because they sometimes prey on cattle, sheep, and deer. As human population has grown, these predators have been pushed into smaller and smaller areas.

Finally, as pollution has grown to be a global problem, many environments have been seriously damaged. The burning of fossil fuels causes acid rain, which is seriously endangering trees, fish, aquatic plants, insects, and many other organisms around the world. Water pollution is a major threat to many species. Raw sewage and toxic chemicals dumped into rivers, lakes, and streams poison birds, fish, plants, and other forms of life. Oil spills in aquatic environments have threatened entire populations of fish, aquatic birds, and animals. When farmers use herbicides and pesticides to get rid of undesirable species, such as weeds and insects, the poisons often harm more than just the undesirable species. These powerful chemicals can also kill many desirable plants and animals, including beneficial insects, fish, birds, and certain mammals. For example, before DDT was banned in the United States, the high levels found in pelicans, falcons, eagles, and many other birds caused eggshell thinning and endangered the survival of these species. Unfortunately, DDT and other dangerous pesticides are still used in many countries.

Often, many species are endangered because of a combination of factors. For example, some salmon species are in trouble because they are over-fished, are sensitive to acid rain and other water pollutants, and cannot migrate upstream because dams block their way. Bald eagles are endangered because of pesticides, loss of habitat, and poisoning from lead shot.

Problem

You are a volunteer guide at a natural history museum. You have been asked to help sixth-grade students understand the concept of biodiversity.

Task

Choose one of the following tasks.

1. Produce a pamphlet about biodiversity in which you discuss the following questions:

   - Why is biodiversity important?
   - What can be done to preserve biodiversity?
   - Can biodiversity really be saved?
   - What can individuals do to preserve biodiversity?

   Your pamphlet may concentrate on a specific region. Include tables and graphs as appropriate. To get the most up-to-date information, do your research on the Internet.

2. Design a board game with easy-to-follow directions. The focus or subject of the game must be based on the loss of biodiversity, its consequences, and what is being done to preserve species. Provide the board and whatever else you need, such as dice, spinners, timers, play pieces, cards, play money, and so forth. The game may involve elimination, acquisition, strategy, luck, or a combination of these elements. Make sure the goal of the game is clearly stated. It must have some elements of originality, but may be based in part on existing board games. The game should be designed to be played by three or more students. Once you have designed your game, try it out with your classmates.

Four-eyed butterfly fish

Discovery
Learning Activity

Order Out of Disorder

1. Obtain a variety of objects from your classroom, such as pens, pencils, books, chalk, stapler, scissors, microscope, hand lens, and so on.

2. Working with a partner, look for common characteristics that can be used to sort the objects into two or three large groups. Make a list of these groups on a sheet of paper.

3. Then sort the large groups into smaller groups. List these groups on the sheet of paper. Continue sorting the objects this way until you cannot make any more groups.

4. On a large sheet of paper, make a chart of your classification system without revealing the characteristics used to classify the objects. Compare your classification system with the other groups. Were you able to identify the characteristics other groups used to classify their objects?

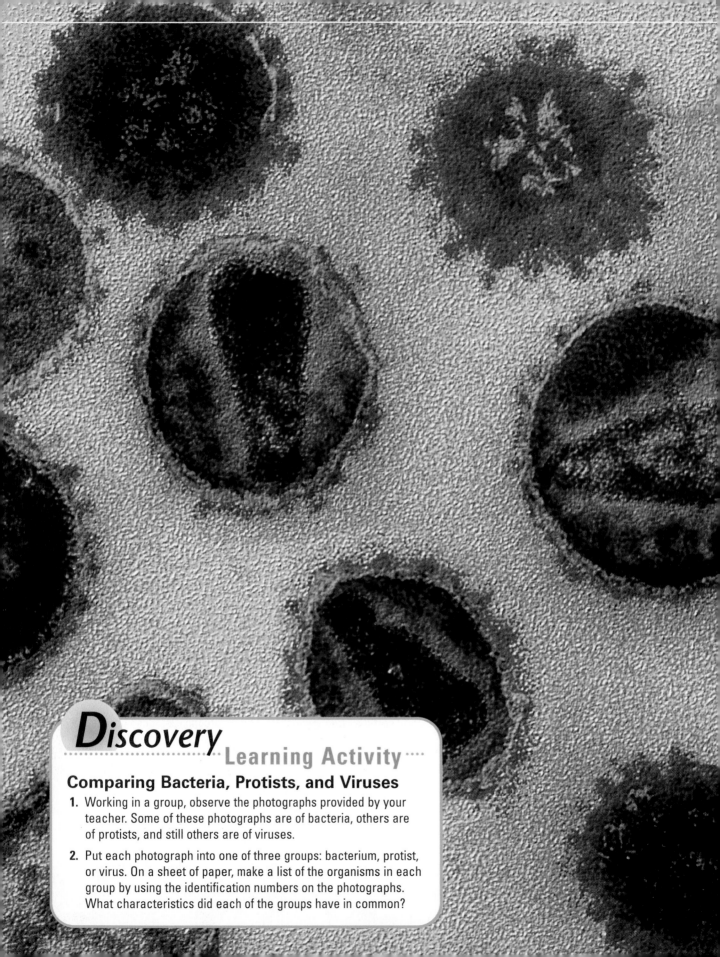

Discovery Learning Activity

Comparing Bacteria, Protists, and Viruses

1. Working in a group, observe the photographs provided by your teacher. Some of these photographs are of bacteria, others are of protists, and still others are of viruses.

2. Put each photograph into one of three groups: bacterium, protist, or virus. On a sheet of paper, make a list of the organisms in each group by using the identification numbers on the photographs. What characteristics did each of the groups have in common?

Bacteria, Protists, and Viruses

.... **Guide** *for Reading* ....

Previewing the Chapter

These colorful particles are anything but harmless. The transmission electron microscope image depicts the human immunodeficiency virus (HIV), the virus that causes AIDS. Viruses, such as HIV, are somewhere on the borderline between living and nonliving. Protists, while living, are neither plants nor animals. And bacteria are the most numerous living things on earth. What are the characteristics of bacteria? How do animal-like and plantlike protists differ? Why is it difficult to classify viruses as living or nonliving?

Key Words

Archaebacteria, Eubacteria, germ theory of disease, pathogen, protist, virus

Key Concepts

- **Describe** the main characteristics of bacteria.
- **Distinguish** between the different groups of protists.
- **Describe** the general characteristics of viruses.
- **Design an experiment** to observe the effects of tobacco mosaic virus on healthy tobacco plants. (Laboratory Investigation)

30-1 The Bacteria

Section Objectives:

- *Describe* the structure, shapes, and functions of bacterial cells.
- *Describe* the metabolic needs of bacterial cells.
- *Distinguish* between the two kingdoms of bacteria.
- *Compare* the harmful and beneficial aspects of bacteria.

Characteristics of Bacteria

Bacteria is the common name for members of the kingdom **Archaebacteria** (ahr kee bak TEER ee uh) and the kingdom **Eubacteria** (yoo bak TEER ee uh). Although some bacteria cause infections, the vast majority are beneficial. As you will learn, bacteria are important for health, for industry, and even for the air we breathe. Some bacteria can cure, as well as cause, disease.

Bacteria are found almost everywhere—in both fresh and salt water, in soil, in the air, and in plants and animals. In humans, they cover the skin and the linings of the nose and mouth. They are especially numerous in the digestive tract. Bacterial cells are much smaller than eukaryotic cells. In fact, they are the smallest known living cells and can only be seen with the aid of a microscope.

▲ **Figure 30–1**

Disease-causing Bacteria. These rod-shaped bacteria caused the bubonic plague, which killed about one-fourth of the European population in the fourteenth century.

◄ Human immunodeficiency viruses (HIV).

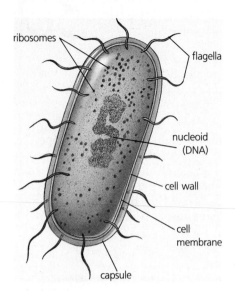

ribosomes

flagella

nucleoid (DNA)

cell wall

cell membrane

capsule

▲ **Figure 30–2**

Structure of a Prokaryote. Many types of bacteria are surrounded by a slimy capsule, in addition to a cell wall.

Cellular Structure The main structural feature that distinguishes bacterial cells from the cells of organisms in the other kingdoms is the absence of a distinct, membrane-bound nucleus. Cells that lack a true nucleus are called *prokaryotic cells.* Therefore, all bacteria are prokaryotes. In contrast, cells that have a membrane-bound nucleus are called *eukaryotic cells.*

As you can see in Figure 30–2, most prokaryotes are surrounded by a protective cell wall. Prokaryotic cell walls, however, have a different structure and chemical composition than plant cell walls. Instead of cellulose, prokaryotic cell walls contain a complex polysaccharide not found in eukaryotic cells. Many prokaryotes also secrete a slimy material that forms a capsule around the outside of the cell wall. The capsule provides additional protection for the cell. For example, many of the bacteria that cause diseases in animals are surrounded by capsules. A capsule prevents the animal's white blood cells and antibodies from destroying the bacterium.

Just inside the cell wall is the cell membrane, which surrounds the cytoplasm. In contrast to eukaryotes, prokaryotes lack organelles, such as mitochondria, endoplasmic reticulum, and chloroplasts, in their cytoplasm. Most of the enzymatic reactions that occur in eukaryotic cells, however, also occur in prokaryotes. Many of these reactions take place on the inner surface of the cell membrane. In bacteria that use oxygen, for example, the reactions of cellular respiration occur on the fingerlike folds of the cell membrane. In bacteria that carry out photosynthesis, membranes containing the photosynthetic pigments fill the cytoplasm.

Small ribosomes are scattered throughout the cytoplasm of prokaryotes. Although prokaryotes lack a true nucleus, they do contain a single, circular chromosome that is found in an area of the cell called the *nucleoid.* This area, which is usually in the center of the cell, contains the hereditary material, DNA. Some bacteria also have *plasmids,* which are smaller circular segments of DNA.

Many bacteria are able to form specialized structures, called **endospores,** within their cytoplasm. Endospores form when conditions for bacterial growth are unfavorable. They consist of a tough protective coat surrounding the nuclear material and a small amount of cytoplasm. In this dormant state, bacteria can survive for years and withstand extreme conditions, such as freezing, boiling, or extremely dry environments. Once conditions become favorable, the endospore again becomes an active, growing bacterial cell. The formation of endospores is an adaptive mechanism for survival. Some disease-causing bacteria can form endospores.

Shape Bacteria can be divided into three major groups according to shape. These shapes are shown in Figure 30–3. A spherical cell is called a **coccus** (KOK us), a rod-shaped cell is called a **bacillus** (buh SIL us), and a spiral or coiled cell is called a **spirillum** (spur IL um). Although many bacteria are single celled, some form colonies in the shape of chains or clumps. For example, cocci are found as single cells (*monococci*), in pairs (*diplococci*), in chains (*streptococci*), and in grapelike clusters (*staphylococci*). Bacilli are also found as single cells, in pairs (*diplobacilli*), or in chains (*streptobacilli*). Spirilla exist only as single cells. Each of the photographs in Figure 30–3 show bacteria as single cells.

Motility   Many bacteria are capable of movement. Some move with the aid of *flagella*. However, unlike flagella in eukaryotes, in prokaryotes, flagella do not contain microtubules. Instead, the flagella are strands of protein twisted around one another like the strands of a rope. Other bacteria move by gliding on a slimy substance, which they secrete.

Metabolic Needs   Prokaryotes can be described according to the substances they need to live and grow. All prokaryotes require an energy source and a food source. Most bacteria are *aerobic*— they require free oxygen to carry out cellular respiration. Bacteria that cannot live without oxygen are called *obligate aerobes*. Some bacteria, called *facultative anaerobes,* can live in either the presence or absence of oxygen. They obtain energy either by aerobic respiration when oxygen is present or by fermentation when oxygen is absent. Still other bacteria cannot live at all in the presence of oxygen. These are called *obligate anaerobes*. These bacteria obtain energy only by fermentation. Through fermentation, different groups of bacteria produce a wide variety of organic compounds. Besides ethyl alcohol and lactic acid, bacterial fermentation can produce acetic acid, acetone, butyl alcohol, glycol, butyric acid, propionic acid, and methane, the main component of natural gas.

Depending on its source of food, a bacterium is either *heterotrophic* or *autotrophic*. Most bacteria are heterotrophic—they must obtain ready-made food from the environment. Heterotrophic bacteria are either **saprobes** or **parasites.** Saprobes feed on the remains of dead plants and animals and ordinarily do not cause disease. They release digestive enzymes into the organic matter. The enzymes break down the large food molecules into smaller molecules, which are absorbed by the bacterial cells. Parasites live on or in living organisms, absorbing nutrients directly from their host's body. Parasites can cause disease.

Some types of bacteria are autotrophic—that is, they can synthesize the food they require from inorganic substances. Autotrophic bacteria are either *photosynthetic* or *chemosynthetic*. Like plants, many photosynthetic bacteria convert carbon dioxide and water to organic matter and oxygen. Other kinds of bacteria carry out different forms of photosynthesis. For example, some forms can use hydrogen sulfide instead of water.

Only certain groups of bacteria can perform *chemosynthesis*. Like photosynthetic bacteria, these groups synthesize food from carbon dioxide. Unlike photosynthetic forms, they do not use light as a source of energy. Instead, these bacteria use energy from the

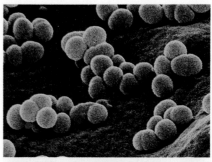
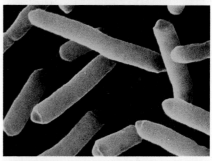
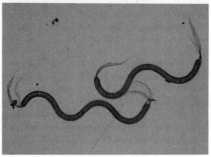

▲ **Figure 30–3**

Shapes of Bacteria. The spherical cocci (top) occur singly, in pairs, in chains, or in clumps. Shown here are clumps of *Micrococcus*. (Magnification 122 000 X). The rod-shaped bacilli (middle) most often appear as single cells but may form chains. This micrograph shows a number of solitary *Enterobacteria*. Spirilla may be S-shaped, like the *Spirillum volutans* shown in this micrograph (bottom), or corkscrew-shaped. (Magnification 700 X)

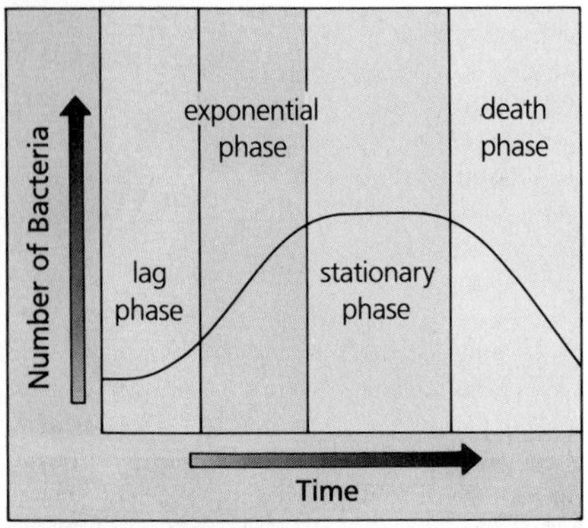

▲ **Figure 30–4**
Growth Curve of a Bacterial Culture.

breakdown of inorganic substances, such as compounds of nitrogen and sulfur, to synthesize food. Both bacterial photosynthesis and chemosynthesis are very important because they cycle the elements and compounds that all living things need.

Reproduction All bacteria reproduce asexually. Thus, they do not divide by mitosis but by the process of *binary fission*. As you read in Chapter 20, in binary fission the parent cell divides into two identical daughter cells. Some bacteria can reproduce very rapidly. For example, under ideal conditions of food, temperature, and space, some species can divide every 15 to 20 minutes. At this rate, one bacterial cell could produce millions of offspring in just a few days! However, factors such as heat, cold, or lack of food inhibit the rate of reproduction and prevent such rapid growth.

Figure 30–4 shows a typical growth curve for a culture of bacterial cells. (A *culture* is the laboratory growth of a group of bacteria on artificial food material.) It shows the number of bacteria in the culture plotted against time. The growth curve can be divided into four phases. In the *lag phase,* the bacteria are adjusting to their new environment, and growth is slow. In the *exponential phase,* the bacteria are dividing rapidly. In the *stationary phase,* the reproductive rate equals the death rate. In the *death phase,* the bacteria are dying off faster than they are reproducing.

Although bacteria do not reproduce sexually, some species are capable of sharing or exchanging genetic material. This genetic exchange is known as *genetic recombination.* The three methods by which bacteria can exchange DNA are *conjugation, transformation,* and *transduction.* As you learned in Chapter 21, in conjugation one bacterial cell can donate some of its DNA to another cell of the same species. This transfer occurs through a thin, temporary bridge between the two cells. The bacterium receiving the DNA can incorporate it into its own DNA. The DNA exchanged in conjugation may be in the form of plasmids. Some of these plasmids allow bacteria to become resistant to antibiotic drugs. Other plasmids may help bacteria to adapt to stressful environments or to make new nutrients.

Some bacterial cells release DNA when they die and break apart. This DNA can be taken up by other bacterial cells, which can then form new, genetically different cells. This process is called transformation. Transformation occurs in *pneumococcus* bacteria, which you read about in Chapter 27. The type R (rough) bacterial cells were transformed by DNA from dead type S (smooth) bacteria. These bacteria cause pneumonia.

In transduction, DNA is transferred from one bacterium to another by means of viruses. The viruses pick up small amounts of DNA from host bacteria. When they infect other bacterial cells, the new host bacteria can receive and incorporate the DNA into their own.

Recombinant DNA techniques use all three processes to transfer DNA from one organism to another and change the genetic makeup of cells. The technology that uses these techniques, *genetic engineering,* is discussed more fully in Chapter 27.

Types of Bacteria

The bacteria are divided into two kingdoms: the Archaebacteria and the Eubacteria. Each kingdom consists of several groups.

Archaebacteria Most members of the kingdom Archaebacteria live in environments that other organisms could not tolerate. Scientists believe that Archaebacteria are among the earliest organisms to inhabit the earth. The name *archaebacteria* is derived from the Greek *archaio,* which means "ancient." The habitats of these primitive bacteria are too harsh for most forms of life today, but they resemble the environments on earth billions of years ago when life was first evolving.

Biologists once classified the Archaebacteria and Eubacteria in the same kingdom. However, although the Archaebacteria are prokaryotes, they are unlike the Eubacteria in many ways. Archaebacteria lack an important carbohydrate found in the cell walls of nearly all eubacteria. They also have different types of lipids in their cell membranes, different types of ribosomes, and some very different gene sequences.

There are three different groups of Archaebacteria. One group includes methane-producing bacteria that break down organic matter and produce methane gas as a by-product. They inhabit the intestinal tracts of animals, including humans, and are also found at the bottom of marshes, swamps, and sewage treatment plants. A second group includes "salt-loving" bacteria that live in extremely salty environments such as the Dead Sea and the Great Salt Lake in Utah. The third group includes bacteria that inhabit hot, acidic environments, such as the hot springs of Yellowstone National Park, where the temperature may reach 80° to 90°C. Figure 30–5 shows some examples of Archaebacterial environments.

Eubacteria The Eubacteria make up the larger of the two prokaryote kingdoms. Although most Eubacteria are heterotrophic, some are autotrophic. These autotrophs are either phototrophs (photosynthetic) or chemotrophs (chemosynthetic). The main difference between them is that photosynthetic bacteria use light energy to synthesize food, whereas chemosynthetic bacteria use energy from chemical reactions.

The blue-green bacteria, or cyanobacteria (sy an oh bak TIR ee ah), are a major group of photosynthetic eubacteria. Similar to plants, these bacteria carry out photosynthesis. However, they do not have the chloroplasts of plant cells. Instead, their photosynthetic pigments are located on folded membranes in the cytoplasm. Cyanobacteria contain chlorophyll *a,* as well as a blue pigment, phycocyanin. Their blue-green color comes from these two pigments. Some species have additional pigments that change the color of these bacteria to yellow, brown, and even red. Figure 30–6 shows the structure of cyanobacterial cells.

Although most cyanobacteria are found in fresh water, others live in salt water, in soil, and on rocks. The Red Sea owes its name to the occasional appearance of huge numbers of red-colored

▲ **Figure 30–5**
Environments Inhabited by Archaebacteria. Although the Great Salt Lake in Utah (top) is too salty to be hospitable to most forms of life, it is well populated by "salt-loving" archaebacteria. Another type of archaebacteria live in the hot, acidic environment of the Hot Springs (bottom) in Yellowstone National Park in Wyoming.

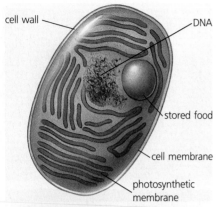

cell wall
DNA
stored food
cell membrane
photosynthetic membrane

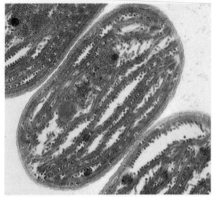

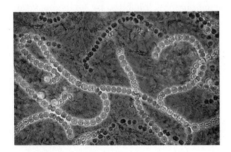

▲ **Figure 30–6**

Cyanobacteria. The structure of a typical cyanobacterial cell, shown at top, includes a series of folded membranes where photosynthesis occurs. *Spirulina* (middle) is a species of cyanobacteria sometimes grown commercially as a source of protein. (Magnification 21 600 X) Shown at bottom are filaments of *Nostoc*, a species of nitrogen-fixing cyanobacteria extremely useful in enriching the soil. (Magnification 256 X)

species of these bacteria. Ponds or lakes that contain a rich supply of organic matter often develop large populations, or *blooms*, of cyanobacteria. Because they thrive in polluted water, their appearance indicates the presence of organic pollutants.

Another group of eubacteria, called prochlorobacteria, also includes photosynthetic bacteria. These bacteria contain chlorophyll *a* and *b*. The presence of these pigments makes the prochlorobacteria more similar to the chloroplasts of green plants than to cyanobacteria. For this reason, prochlorobacteria are sometimes called Prochlorophyta.

Some cyanobacteria capture nitrogen from the air and incorporate (or "fix") it into organic compounds, such as nitrates, nitrites, and ammonia-related compounds. This process, called *nitrogen fixation,* occurs in specialized cells known as *heterocysts.* Nitrogen fixation plays an important role in fertilizing certain crops. The *nitrogen-fixing bacteria* include the cyanobacteria and a few other kinds. Some kinds of nitrogen-fixing bacteria may live on the roots of plants such as beans and alfalfa, thus providing the plants with a source of nitrogen and reducing the need for artificial fertilizers in nitrogen-poor soils.

Another group of photosynthetic eubacteria includes the green-sulfur bacteria and the purple bacteria. These have a form of chlorophyll that differs from the chlorophyll of plants. They are anaerobes and carry out photosynthesis without producing oxygen and without using water as a starting material. These organisms may be colored pink, green, or nearly black. They inhabit the muddy sediments of ponds and seas.

The largest group of heterotrophic eubacteria are called Schizophyta (skiz AH fuh tuh). Although there are several types of these bacteria, a universal method of classifying them is the Gram test, a staining method developed by the Danish physician Hans Christian Gram. The test divides bacteria into two classes, depending on their reaction to the Gram stain. Gram-positive bacteria retain a stain called *crystal violet* and appear purple under a microscope. Gram-negative bacteria do not retain this stain, and they appear light pink under a microscope. Figure 30–7 shows gram-positive and gram-negative bacteria as they appear under a microscope.

The chemical nature of the cell walls determines whether bacteria are gram-positive or gram-negative. Because of the differences in their cell walls, gram-positive bacteria can be harmed by antibiotics, such as *penicillin.* The cell walls of gram-negative bacteria are not harmed as easily. Thus, infections caused by gram-negative bacteria are more difficult to treat with antibiotics.

The heterotrophic eubacteria live everywhere—in soil, air, food, and water. Some inhabit other living organisms, and others decompose dead organic matter. They include both aerobic and anaerobic forms. Many of them cause human diseases, such as *bacterial pneumonia, diphtheria,* and *tetanus.*

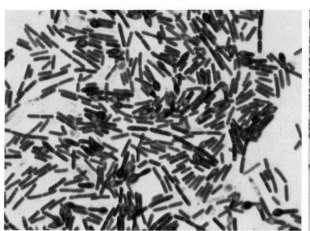

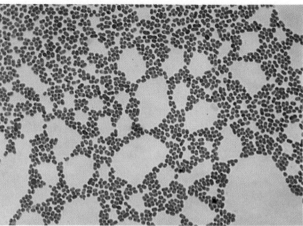

▲ **Figure 30–7**

Gram Stain. The Gram test classifies bacteria into two groups based on differences in their cell walls. When stained, gram-positive bacteria appear purple, as with *Clostridium botulinum* cells (left. (Magnification 1400 X) Gram-negative bacteria appear pink. These *Acinetobacter* cells (right) are gram-negative. (Magnification 2750 X)

Importance of Bacteria

Bacteria and Disease   Harmful bacteria—those capable of causing infections in animals or plants—are called **pathogens.** To cause disease in humans, pathogens must enter the body, overcome the body's immune defenses, and multiply.

Discovery of Bacterial Pathogens   The idea that bacteria can cause disease, known as the **germ theory of disease,** was developed by the French scientist Louis Pasteur in the mid-1880s. Since then, we have learned that bacteria harm the body in three ways. First, the bacteria can become so numerous that they interfere with the functioning of normal cells. Second, they can destroy body cells and tissues. Third, they can produce poisons, or toxins, that kill cells or interfere with their functioning. The third mechanism is the usual cause of harm.

Anthrax, a disease of sheep, cattle, horses, and sometimes humans, was the first disease ever proven to be caused by bacteria. In 1876, the bacterium that causes anthrax was isolated and identified by the German physician Robert Koch. Koch also identified the cause of the disease *tuberculosis* in 1882. Based on the methods he used to identify these bacteria as agents of disease, Koch developed a set of rules to determine whether a specific bacterium is the cause of a specific disease. His rules are:

   1. The suspected disease-causing organism should always be found in animals with the disease.

   2. The organism must be isolated from the diseased animal and grown in a pure culture. (A pure culture is one containing only one kind of bacterium.)

   3. When organisms taken from the pure culture are injected into a healthy animal, they must cause the disease.

   4. The organism must be isolated from the experimentally infected animal and grown in pure culture again, and it should be identified as the same organism isolated in step 2.

These rules, which are known as **Koch's postulates,** were developed in the late 1880s and are still used today. They have helped to identify the causes of many bacterial diseases, such as those listed in Figure 30–8.

Pasteur also performed several experiments related to anthrax, and in 1881, he produced a vaccine to prevent this infection. He exposed the anthrax bacteria to temperatures that were high enough to weaken them but not to kill them. He then injected the weakened bacteria into sheep that were healthy. The sheep became slightly ill and then recovered. Later, when the same sheep were injected with unheated bacteria, they did not develop the disease. Pasteur had succeeded in creating a vaccine to prevent this infection. He demonstrated his discovery by performing a series of similar experiments that were viewed by scientists, journalists, and public officials.

How important was the discovery of bacteria as agents of disease? Consider some of the bacterial diseases—leprosy, cholera, botulism, tuberculosis, and diphtheria—that have devastated human populations throughout history. Perhaps the worst killer of all time is the bubonic plague, a disease known in its day as the "Black Death." Along with related plagues, the bubonic plague swept through Europe throughout the 1300s. Within 100 years, the European population had shrunk by at least 50%. Today, we know that the root of this destruction was *Yersinia pestis,* a species of bacteria.

MiniLab

Skill: Observing

Not Exactly Bean Soup

Procedure

1. Obtain a small amount of bacterial culture prepared by your teacher.

2. Place a drop of the culture on a microscope slide and observe under high power using a low light setting.

3. Look for bacterial cells of different shapes and for bacteria that are moving.

4. Record your observations.

Problem

How can you **observe** some characteristics of bacterial cells through a microscope?

Analyze and Conclude

1. What is the appearance of the bacterial culture? Does it have an odor? How can you account for the odor and appearance?

2. What cell shapes did you observe?

3. Are any of the cells moving?

Controlling Bacterial Disease   Until this century, bacterial diseases were common causes of death. Around 1900, the work of Pasteur, Koch, and other scientists became known to public health workers in the United States and other developed countries. Knowledge about the germ theory of disease brought about a revolution in hygiene and sanitation. This revolution led to the prevention of many common, serious infections and increased life expectancy dramatically.

A major advance occurred with the development of the first antibiotic, penicillin. An antibiotic is a substance that prevents bacteria from growing. Some antibiotics act by disrupting the formation of bacterial cell walls at the time of cell division. Others interfere with the formation of substances needed by bacterial cells, such as proteins. *Tetracyclines,* which are effective against a wide range of both gram-positive and gram-negative bacteria, act in this manner.

Penicillin was discovered in 1928 by Sir Alexander Fleming, a Scottish bacteriologist. Fleming was growing a culture of bacteria when he noticed that a mold had contaminated the culture and that no bacteria were growing near the mold. The mold was a species of the genus *Penicillium.* The bacteria-inhibiting substance that was secreted by this mold was later to be named penicillin. Although physicians still routinely use penicillin to treat a wide variety of bacterial infections, many other antibiotics are now available.

Diseases Caused by Bacteria	
Disease	**Bacterium**
	Cocci
boils, carbuncles	*Staphylococcus aureus*
gonorrhea	*Neisseria gonorrhoeae*
meningitis	*Neisseria meningitidis*
pneumonia	*Diplococcus pneumoniae*
scarlet fever	*Streptococcus pyogenes*
strep throat	*Streptococcus pyogenes*
	Bacilli
anthrax	*Bacillus anthracis*
botulism	*Clostridium botulinum*
diphtheria	*Corynebacterium diphtheriae*
plague	*Yersinia pestis*
tetanus	*Clostridium tetani*
typhoid fever	*Salmonella typhi*
	Spirilla
cholera	*Vibrio comma*
syphilis	*Treponema pallidum*

◀ **Figure 30–8**
Diseases Caused by Bacteria.

Methods of Preserving Food		
Method	**Food Preserved**	**Why Effective**
freezing	meat, vegetables, desserts	stops growth and reproduction of bacteria
refrigeration	meat, eggs, butter, milk	slows growth and reproduction of bacteria
pasteurization (heating to moderate temperature followed by rapid cooling)	milk, egg products, apple juice, and other beverages	almost all the bacteria are killed by the heat. Cooling slows the growth of remaining bacteria.
drying	meats, grains, flour, starch, fruits, sugar, powdered milk, powdered eggs	removes moisture required by bacteria for growth
canning	vegetables, fruits, meats	high temperature kills all bacteria; sealed container prevents entrance of new bacteria
Preservatives: salt sugar lactic acid (from fermentation) vinegar	meats fruits cucumbers (pickles) and cabbage (sauerkraut) vegetables	high concentrations of sugar and salt osmotically dehydrate bacteria; acid conditions prevent bacterial growth

▲ **Figure 30–9**
Methods of Preserving Food

Bacterial infections can be spread in many ways. Some bacteria are carried through the air on droplets spread by coughing and sneezing. Others are spread by contaminated drinking water. Some are spread by direct contact, such as by shaking hands. *Sexually transmitted diseases* are spread by sexual contact. Still other diseases, such as *Lyme disease* or *typhus,* are spread by insect bites. Bacteria in food are a common cause of illness. The action of bacterial decomposers causes food to spoil and become harmful to eat. For example, *Clostridium botulinum* is an obligate anaerobe, obtaining its energy by fermentation. This organism produces toxins that cause *botulism,* the most dangerous of all types of food poisoning. *Clostridium botulinum* grows in canned foods that have not been heated sufficiently during canning. Even before the germ theory of disease was developed, people were preventing food spoilage by the methods listed in Figure 30–9. All these methods deprive bacteria of some condition they need for growth, such as nutrients, moisture, correct temperature, or oxygen.

Biologic Importance of Bacteria Bacteria play an important role in health as well as in disease. They are normal inhabitants of the human body, and most of them are harmless. Some give off substances that discourage the growth of harmful species. Others help to decompose food wastes in the intestines. Bacteria in the large intestine produce certain vitamins needed by the body. Bacteria cure disease by producing some of the most useful

◀ **Figure 30–10**

Cheese-Making. The production of cheese depends on certain lactic acid producing bacteria that cause milk products to solidify. This woman is coating wheels of cheese with a protective layer of plastic.

antibiotics, such as *streptomycin* and *erythromycin*. Scientists use bacterial cells to study cellular metabolism and molecular biology. The techniques of genetic engineering are based on experiments with the DNA of bacterial cells. Many medically important substances have already been made using genetically engineered bacteria. These include antibiotic drugs and vaccines, hormones such as insulin, and chemicals that fight cancer cells.

The role of bacteria in the environment is equally important. Bacteria are *decomposers*. They break down the tissues of dead animals and plants into organic substances, returning these substances to the environment where other living organisms depend on them for existence. Without bacterial decomposers, these basic substances—oxygen, carbon, nitrogen, phosphorus, and sulfur—would soon be depleted. Thus, bacteria are primarily recyclers, and without them life on earth would die out.

Bacteria are also important in industry and agriculture. They are used in the production of yogurt, buttermilk, cheeses, and vinegar. Chemical companies use bacteria to produce butanol, acetone, and fuels such as methane. Some bacterial species are used as natural pesticides to save crops from insects. Economically important crops, including alfalfa, clover, soybeans, and other beans depend on nitrogen-fixing bacteria for their growth.

30-1 Section Review

1. What are the three shapes of bacterial cells?
2. What are bacteria that cannot live without a supply of oxygen called?
3. Identify the two kingdoms of bacteria.
4. Name the drug discovered by Sir Alexander Fleming.

Critical Thinking

5. Why are bacteria in the human body considered both harmful and beneficial? (*Identifying Reasons*)

30-2 The Protists

Section Objectives:

- *Identify* the three major groups of protists.
- *Compare* the major characteristics of the four types of animal-like protists.
- *Identify* the six main groups of plantlike protists and their distinguishing characteristics.
- *Describe* the general features of the three types of funguslike protists.

The first eukaryotes were probably single-celled organisms much like many modern-day protists. Scientists estimate that the *protists* first evolved about 2 billion years after the bacteria were established. Because most protists require oxygen, it is thought that the earliest protists could not have evolved until the cyanobacteria had been producing oxygen for billions of years.

The kingdom **Protista** contains many species and a great variety of organisms. As eukaryotes, the protists have a membrane-bound nucleus and many different cytoplasmic organelles. They show amazing diversity in cell organization, in methods of reproduction, in metabolic needs, and in habitats. In fact, the members of this kingdom are sometimes defined on the basis of not belonging in any of the other four kingdoms.

Although most protists are unicellular, some are multicellular organisms and may be quite large. Some protists are heterotrophic; others are autotrophic. Reproduction may be sexual or asexual. Their habitats are both aquatic and terrestrial. Because they are so diverse, the members of the kingdom Protista are difficult to classify. They are divided into three main groups: the animal-like, plantlike, and funguslike protists.

Animal-like Protists

The animal-like protists are single-celled or colonial organisms called **protozoa.** They live in fresh and salt water, in the soil, and in the bodies of other organisms. All protozoa are heterotrophic. Some absorb nutrients through their cell membranes, whereas others engulf larger particles of food. The life processes of two common protozoa, ameba and paramecium, are discussed in Unit 2. Most protozoa are motile and are divided into phyla based on their means of locomotion. The major phyla are listed in Figure 30–11.

Sarcodines   The *sarcodines* move and capture prey by means of pseudopods, or "false feet." Members of this group belong to the phylum **Sarcodina** (sar kuh DY nuh). The sarcodines are found in both fresh and salt water and in the bodies of animals, where a few cause disease. Reproduction is both asexual and sexual.

The best known of the sarcodines are the amebas. Amebas are unicellular organisms that continually change shape. As explained in Chapter 13, amebas move by means of pseudopods in a type of locomotion known as ameboid movement. They also make use of

Major Divisions of Animal-Like Protists, or Protozoa	
Phylum	**Identifying Characteristics**
Sarcodina (sarcodines) Ameba	move and engulf food by extending pseudopods, which are extensions of the cell surfaces.
Ciliophora (ciliates) Paramecium	use cilia to move and feed.
Zoomastigina (zooflagellates) Trypanosoma	move by means of flagella.
Sporozoa (sporozoans) Plasmodium	nonmotile; mostly parasitic; have complex life cycles.

◀ **Figure 30–11**

Major Divisions of Animal-like Protists, or Protozoa.

pseudopods to surround and engulf food particles. Amebas reproduce asexually by binary fission. They are commonly found in freshwater ponds, lakes, and streams.

Amebas can be parasitic. For example, *amebic dysentery* is a disease caused by a parasitic species of ameba common in tropical areas. It lives in the human large intestine and feeds on the intestinal walls, causing bleeding. Such amebas can sometimes form cysts, which are ameba cells surrounded by a protective capsule. The disease is spread when these cysts pass out of the body with digestive wastes that enter fresh water or soil. A person becomes infected by drinking contaminated water or eating contaminated food.

Some sarcodines are surrounded by protective shells. Among these are the *radiolarians* (rayd ee oh LEHR ee unz) and the *forams*, shown in Figure 30–12. The radiolarians have glassy, silicon-

Figure 30–12

Radiolarians and Forams. A radiolarian (left) is a sarcodine with a delicate shell made of silica. (Magnification 4200 X) A foram (right) has a multichambered shell. The calcium carbonate shells of forams have left an excellent fossil record. ▼

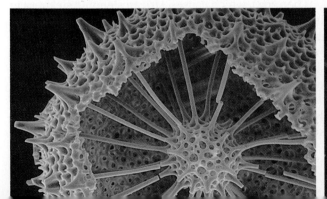

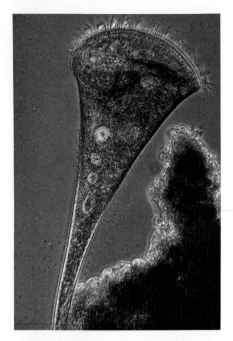

▲ **Figure 30–13**

A Stentor. Ciliates vary in form and in the pattern of cilia. The stentor is trumpet-shaped with cilia arranged in clumps.

Figure 30–14

Zooflagellates. The zooflagellate *Trypanosoma gambiense* causes African sleeping sickness. ▼

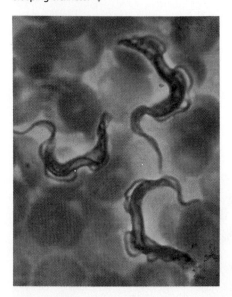

containing shells and long, thin pseudopods. The forams live in many-chambered, snail-like shells containing calcium. Thin projections of cytoplasm protrude through openings in the foram's shell.

Both radiolarians and forams are abundant in the oceans. When these organisms die, their shells drop into the mud of the ocean bottom. In some places, the buildup of tremendous numbers of foram shells has formed huge chalk deposits. The white cliffs of Dover on the English coast were formed in this way. Radiolarian shells make up much of the bottom ooze on some parts of the oceans, and they are also an important part of certain silicon-containing rocks.

Ciliates The *ciliates,* members of the phylum **Ciliophora** (sil ee AHF ur uh), are complex protozoa that live in both fresh and salt water. Ciliates are surrounded by hairlike projections, or cilia. In some species, the cilia are arranged in rows or tufts. In others, such as the stentor, the cilia form clumps. The beating of the cilia moves the organism through the water and propels food and water into its oral groove. The paramecium, a freshwater ciliate, is the most frequently studied member of this phylum.

The intake and digestion of food by the paramecium are described in Chapter 8. Food particles are enclosed and digested in food vacuoles. Some ciliates also have contractile vacuoles, which collect and excrete excess water from the cell.

Unlike amebas, which change shape, ciliates have a rigid outer covering called a **pellicle** that maintains their shape. Beneath the pellicle, some have *trichocysts* (TRIK uh sists), barbed structures that are discharged for defense or to aid in capturing prey.

Asexual reproduction in ciliates is by binary fission. Some also reproduce sexually by the process of conjugation. Both methods of reproduction are explained in Unit 4. Ciliates differ from other protozoa in having two kinds of nuclei, a macronucleus and a micronucleus. The large macronucleus controls cellular metabolism and divides during binary fission. The micronucleus is not necessary for life but is exchanged during conjugation.

Zooflagellates The *zooflagellates* (zoh uh FLAJ uh luhts), of the phylum **Zoomastigina** (zo uh mass tuh JINE uh) move by beating long, whiplike flagella. Some have only one flagellum; others have many. Most are unicellular. Although some zooflagellates are free-living in fresh water, most live in the bodies of animals or the tissues of plants. Zooflagellates reproduce both asexually and sexually.

Among the zooflagellates is *Trypanosoma gambiense* (try pan uh SOHM uh GAM bee enz), which causes African sleeping sickness in humans. This parasite multiplies in the blood where it releases toxins. Symptoms of the disease include weakness, sleepiness, and fever. If left untreated, the victim eventually dies. *Trypanosoma* lives in the blood of domestic and wild animals of Africa. It is spread between animals and humans by the bite of the tsetse fly.

Another zooflagellate is *Trichonympha* (trik uh NIM fuh), which lives in the digestive tract of the termite. Termites do not have the

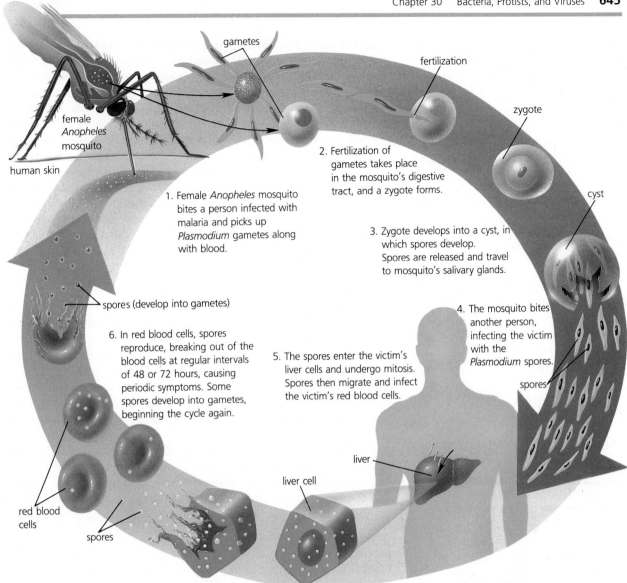

gametes

fertilization

zygote

female *Anopheles* mosquito

human skin

cyst

1. Female *Anopheles* mosquito bites a person infected with malaria and picks up *Plasmodium* gametes along with blood.

2. Fertilization of gametes takes place in the mosquito's digestive tract, and a zygote forms.

3. Zygote develops into a cyst, in which spores develop. Spores are released and travel to mosquito's salivary glands.

spores (develop into gametes)

6. In red blood cells, spores reproduce, breaking out of the blood cells at regular intervals of 48 or 72 hours, causing periodic symptoms. Some spores develop into gametes, beginning the cycle again.

5. The spores enter the victim's liver cells and undergo mitosis. Spores then migrate and infect the victim's red blood cells.

4. The mosquito bites another person, infecting the victim with the *Plasmodium* spores.

spores

liver

red blood cells

liver cell

spores

▲ **Figure 30–15**
Major Life Stages of the Malarial Parasite, *Plasmodium.*

enzymes necessary to break down wood, but *Trichonympha* does. The zooflagellate breaks down the wood eaten by the termite, and both organisms absorb and use the nutrients.

Sporozoans Members of the phylum **Sporozoa** (spor uh ZOE uh) are nonmotile and parasitic. They obtain nutrients from the bodies of their hosts. The members of this phylum, called sporozoans, cause disease in animals, including humans. Sporozoans get their name from the fact that they produce spores during the asexual phase of reproduction. These spores permit the spread of the parasites. The life cycles of sporozoans are complex and involve growth and reproduction in more than one kind of host.

The best known sporozoans are members of the genus *Plasmodium* (plaz MOHD ee um), a parasite that causes malaria in humans. The parasite is transmitted to humans by the bite of the female *Anopheles* (uh NAHF uh leez) mosquito. Figure 30–15 traces the life cycle of *Plasmodium* through the different stages of its reproduction within the human host and the mosquito. Sexual reproduction takes place in the digestive tract of the mosquito, and the asexual phase takes place within the liver and bloodstream of the human host.

At one stage of the life cycle of *Plasmodium,* the spores invade the red blood cells of the human host, multiply there, then break out and invade new cells. The destruction of the red blood cells releases toxic cell wastes into the bloodstream. These waste products cause fever, chills, and other symptoms of malaria.

Malaria is a serious, sometimes fatal, disease. Although it can be treated with drugs, one method of prevention is to eliminate the *Anopheles* mosquito. In spite of the widespread use of pesticides in many countries, millions of people are still infected with malaria, especially in tropical areas.

Plantlike Protists

The plantlike protists, commonly called **algae,** resemble plants in that they are all photosynthetic. Like the protozoa, algae are very diverse. Some are tiny, single-celled organisms with flagella. Others are large, multicellular organisms known as seaweeds.

Like plants, algae have chloroplasts, which contain the photosynthetic pigment chlorophyll. Although all algae have chlorophyll *a*, different groups of algae may have other types of chlorophyll, such as *b* or *c*. Some also have other pigments that give them distinctive colors. Their methods of reproduction vary. They inhabit fresh water, salt water, and moist environments on land. Based on their structure, photosynthetic pigments, and cell wall and food storage substances, algae are divided into six groups.

Euglenoids   The *euglenoids* (yoo GLEE noyds) belong to the phylum **Euglenophyta** (yoo gleen AH fuh tuh). These single-celled protists have both plantlike and animal-like characteristics. Like plants, they contain chloroplasts and photosynthetic pigments. However, they do not have cell walls. Like some of the protozoa, euglenoids move by means of flagella. Owing to their pellicles, or flexible protein coverings, they are able to change shape easily as they move. Euglenoids are unusual in that some forms are autotrophic, whereas others are heterotrophic. For these reasons the classification of euglenoids has been controversial, and some biologists still consider them protozoa. Figure 30–16 shows the cellular structure and microscopic appearance of a typical euglenoid, the *euglena,* an organism common in pond water.

The euglena is a single-celled organism having two flagella. The cell has a large, central nucleus and numerous chloroplasts, which contain chlorophylls *a* and *b*, as well as other pigments. The chlorophylls give euglenas their grass-green color. Euglenas are primarily photosynthetic. When light is available, they carry on photosynthesis. However, in the absence of light, they live as heterotrophs, absorbing dissolved nutrients from the environment. Food is stored as a nonstarch carbohydrate in a structure within each chloroplast called a *pyrenoid* (py REE noyd).

Figure 30–16

Euglena. The protist *Euglena* (top) has chloroplasts and carries on photosynthesis. This euglena (bottom) is magnified 560 times. ▼

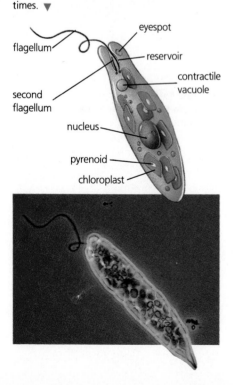

eyespot

flagellum

reservoir

contractile vacuole

second flagellum

nucleus

pyrenoid

chloroplast

Major Divisions of Plantlike Protists

Phylum	Photosynthetic Pigments	Cell Wall Components	Identifying Characteristics
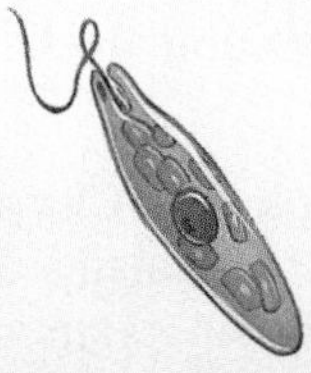 **Euglenophyta** (Euglenoids)	chlorophylls *a* and *c*, other pigments	no cell wall, flexible protein pellicle	when grown in dark, *Euglena's* chloroplasts disappear and it becomes heterotrophic; chloroplasts reappear upon exposure to light.
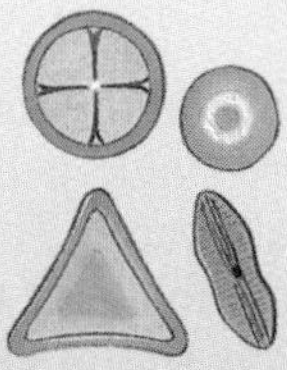 **Chrysophyta** (Golden algae)	chlorophylls *a* and *c*, other pigments	cellulose, some with silica	diatoms have glasslike, ornate shells in two halves
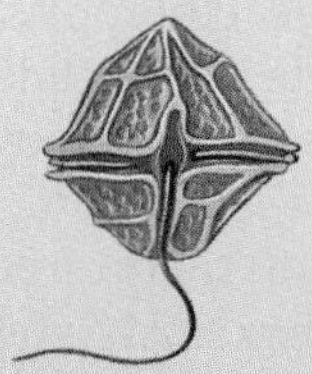 **Dinoflagellata** (Dinoflagellates)	chlorophylls *a* and *c*, other pigments	cellulose and silica	cell walls composed of armorlike plates; some forms are bioluminescent; colorful blooms form red tides.
 **Chlorophyta** (Green algae)	chlorophylls *a* and *b*, other pigments	cellulose and other substances	unicellular, colonial, and multicellular forms, such as the filamentous *Spirogyra*
 **Phaeophyta** (Brown algae)	chlorophylls *a* and *c*, other pigments	cellulose	are multicellular, varying in size from microscopic to more than 50 meters in length; include many common seaweeds
 **Rhodophyta** (Red algae)	chlorophyll *a*, other pigments	cellulose and other substances	most are multicellular; many form a hard crust of calcium carbonate; include many common seaweeds

▲ **Figure 30–17   Major Divisions of Plantlike Protists.**

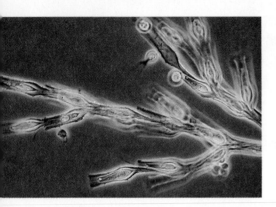

▲ **Figure 30–18**
Golden Algae. The colonial golden alga *Dinoloryon* forms branching colonies in its freshwater habitat.

Euglenas have one large flagellum that is used in movement and one short flagellum that is inactive. The bases of the flagella are within an inpocketing called the *reservoir.* Next to the reservoir is a contractile vacuole, which excretes excess water from the cell into the reservoir. Near the reservoir is the red-orange eyespot, or *stigma,* which is sensitive to light. The stigma enables the euglena to detect light intensity and direction and to position itself for maximum photosynthesis.

Golden Algae The golden algae belong to the phylum **Chrysophyta** (kris AH fuh tuh). They are mostly unicellular organisms that get their color from large amounts of yellow-brown pigments. Members of this phylum store food as oils or as a starchlike carbohydrate. Some may be flagellated and live in colonies in fresh water.

Of the approximately 10 000 species of golden algae, the most numerous are the **diatoms** (DY uh tahmz). Diatoms are single-celled or colonial organisms that live in both fresh and salt water. Their cell walls are glasslike shells made of silica, with tiny holes for the exchange of gases and other substances. These rigid shells form two halves that fit together like the top and bottom of a pillbox. Each diatom contains a nucleus and one or more chloroplasts. Although diatoms lack flagella, they are capable of a gliding movement. They usually reproduce asexually, but sexual reproduction does occur.

Because of the intricate geometric shapes of their ornate shells, diatoms are quite beautiful. They are tremendously abundant in the oceans, where they serve as food for fish and other aquatic animals. When diatoms die, their shells sink to the ocean floor. In some places, the shells have accumulated in layers hundreds of meters thick, forming rocklike deposits known as *diatomaceous* (dy uh tuh MAY shus) *earth.* Some of these deposits, formed millions of years ago, are now on land. Diatomaceous earth is mined and used in metal polishes, toothpaste, insulation, and filters.

Figure 30–19

Saltwater Diatoms. Diatoms are elaborate, single-celled organisms with glasslike cell walls. ▶

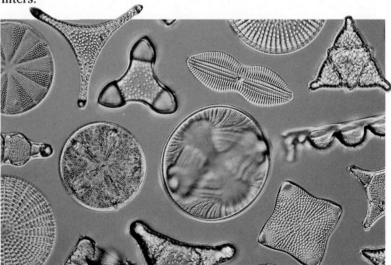

Dinoflagellates   The *dinoflagellates* (dy noh FLAJ uh layts), phylum **Dinoflagellata** (dy noh flag uh LAH tuh), are single-celled algae found mainly in the oceans. Some of them are photosynthetic, storing food as oil or starch. Others lack chloroplasts and are heterotrophic. The photosynthetic dinoflagellates, along with diatoms, serve as the major source of food for many aquatic animals. Reproduction is asexual.

The cell walls of dinoflagellates consist of numerous armorlike plates made up of cellulose and silica. Each organism has two flagella, one running in a beltlike groove around the middle, the other extending from one end. The actions of the flagella cause dinoflagellates to twirl or roll in the water.

In addition to chlorophyll, some of the photosynthetic dinoflagellates contain red and yellow pigments. Sometimes called "fire algae," these organisms vary in color from yellow-green to brown to red. Some of the red ones produce powerful toxins. Blooms (population explosions) of red dinoflagellates in warm, shallow waters cause the water to appear red, a condition called "*red tide.*" Shellfish living in areas of red tides should not be eaten because they contain toxins that cause illness in humans. Toxins in the water also kill many fish.

Many dinoflagellates have the property of *bioluminescence*—the ability to produce light. When present in large numbers, and if disturbed, these organisms may cause the ocean to sparkle or glow at night.

Green Algae   The *green algae,* phylum **Chlorophyta** (klor AH fuh tuh), are found in salt and fresh water and in moist places on land. This group has unicellular, colonial, and multicellular forms. Most green algae have a cell wall composed of cellulose, and most contain chlorophylls *a* and *b* in chloroplasts. Some green algae have flagella, which are used in movement.

Chlamydomonas (klam id uh MOH nus), shown in Figure 30–21, is a typical unicellular, freshwater green alga. It has two flagella of equal length, which are used in locomotion. There is one chloroplast and a pyrenoid for starch synthesis. There are two contractile vacuoles near the bases of the flagella. Like other green algae, *Chlamydomonas* has a cell wall made up of cellulose.

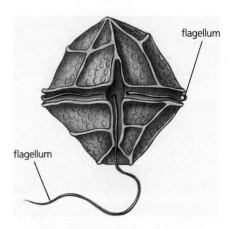

▲ **Figure 30–20**
Structure of a Dinoflagellate. Each dinoflagellate has a pair of flagella for locomotion.

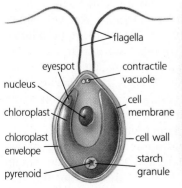

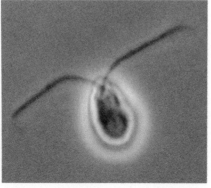

◄ **Figure 30–21**
Structure of *Chlamydomonas.* The unicellular green alga *Chlamydomonas* has two flagella at its anterior end that beat in opposite directions, allowing it to swim rapidly.

▲ **Figure 30–22**

Sargassum. *Sargassum* (top) is a type of brown algae that forms floating masses over wide areas of the Sargasso Sea. Blending into their surroundings, mollusk eggs and a crab are well adapted to life on this strand of sargassum (bottom).

Reproduction is usually asexual. Multicellular green algae include filamentous forms, such as spirogyra and other, more complex, forms.

Brown Algae The *brown algae,* phylum **Phaeophyta** (fee AH fuh tuh), include many of the common seaweeds. Members of this group are all multicellular and range in size from microscopic to more than 50 meters in length. They are found usually in cold ocean waters. The brown algae contain chlorophyll, which functions in photosynthesis, and other pigments that give them their brown color. Brown algae have cellulose in their cell walls and store food in the form of a polysaccharide or as oil. Their life cycles show an alternation of generations.

Some brown algae that live along the shoreline have rootlike structures that anchor them to rocks. Others found on the ocean surface have gas-filled structures that function as floats. The surface of the Sargasso Sea, an area stretching across the Atlantic Ocean from the West Indies to the coast of Africa, is densely covered with several types of floating brown algae that belong to the genus *Sargassum.*

Red Algae The *red algae,* phylum **Rhodophyta** (roh DAH fuh tuh), like the brown algae, include many common seaweeds. Red algae are found in warmer waters and at greater depths than brown algae. They usually are attached to rocks or other surfaces. Although most red algae are multicellular, they are not as large as the largest brown algae. The chloroplasts of red algae contain chlorophyll and several other pigments. Many red algae are reddish in color, but others are black, green, yellow, or purple. Red algae have complex life cycles, including an alternation of generations.

The cell walls of the red algae contain cellulose and other substances, including *agar,* which has various industrial uses. It is used as a thickener in foods such as ice cream and as a medium for growing bacteria and fungi in laboratories. *Carrageenan* (kar uh GEE nun), another product of red algae, is used to prevent separation in food mixtures. It is used, for example, in chocolate milk to prevent the milk and the chocolate from separating.

Funguslike Protists

The funguslike protists are similar to the fungi in some ways—namely in appearance and method of nutrition. You will study members of the kingdom Fungi in Chapter 31. *Fungi* are nonphotosynthetic organisms such as yeasts, molds, and mushrooms. The funguslike protists also have some stages in their life cycle that are similar to those of protozoa. For these reasons, their classification has not always been clear-cut. However, most scientists now agree that these organisms are different from fungi in many significant ways, and they classify them in the kingdom Protista.

All funguslike protists are heterotrophic. Most are decomposers (saprobes) that feed on dead and decaying matter in cool, damp environments. A few are parasites. There are three major phyla of funguslike protists, as listed in Figure 30–23.

Major Divisions of Funguslike Protists	
Phylum	**Identifying Characteristics**
Myxomycota (acellular slime molds)	single-celled organisms with many nuclei; feeding stage characterized by ameboid plasmodium.
Acrasiomycota (cellular slime molds)	feeding stage characterized by individual ameboid cells, which group together to form pseudoplasmodium when food is scarce.
Oomycota (water molds and downy mildews)	finely branched, single-celled filaments resemble fungi; water molds are saprobes or parasites; downy mildews are plant parasites.

◄ **Figure 30–23**
Major Divisions of Funguslike Protists.

Acellular Slime Molds   Acellular slime molds, also called *plasmodial slime molds,* are members of the phylum **Myxomycota** (mix uh my KHAT uh). They are single-celled organisms that contain many nuclei.

In the most commonly observed stage of their life cycle, acellular slime molds resemble giant amebas, or slimy masses, as shown in Figure 30–24. This feeding stage is called the *plasmodium.* The plasmodium is ameboid and feeds by engulfing bits of organic matter as it creeps along the forest floor. When conditions for growth become unfavorable, the plasmodium stops moving and develops stalked, spore-producing structures called *fruiting bodies.* Within the fruiting bodies, haploid spores are produced by meiosis. The spores are eventually released and, if they land in a moist, suitable environment, germinate to form flagellated gametes. Two

Figure 30–24
Life Cycle of an Acellular Slime Mold. ▼

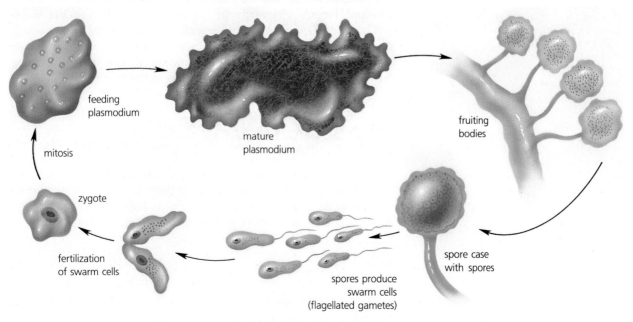

feeding
plasmodium

mature
plasmodium

fruiting
bodies

mitosis

zygote

fertilization
of swarm cells

spores produce
swarm cells
(flagellated gametes)

spore case
with spores

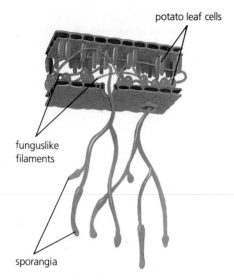

potato leaf cells

funguslike filaments

sporangia

▲ **Figure 30–25**

Growth of a Downy Mildew on a Potato Leaf. The growth of downy mildew on potato plants causes potato blight. As the parasite grows, it destroys the photosynthetic tissue of the leaf.

gametes join to form a diploid zygote, which undergoes mitosis and becomes a feeding plasmodium. Thus sexual reproduction occurs in the acellular slime molds.

Cellular Slime Molds Slime molds of the phylum **Acrasiomycota** (uh krayz ee oh my KAHT uh) are called cellular slime molds. They live in fresh water, in damp soil, or on decaying vegetation, such as rotting logs. In the feeding stage of their life cycle, the cellular slime molds move about as individual ameboid cells and feed on decaying matter. When food becomes scarce, the individual cells group together to form a mass of cells called a *pseudoplasmodium*. The pseudoplasmodium may migrate for a while. Then it forms fruiting bodies, which produce haploid spores. In favorable conditions, individual, haploid, ameboid cells emerge from the spores, and the feeding stage begins again.

The life cycle of cellular slime molds is less complex than that of the acellular types. Reproduction is asexual, and there is no diploid stage in their life cycle. The other major difference is that, unlike the unicellular feeding plasmodium, the pseudoplasmodium consists of many individual, membrane-bound cells.

Water Molds and Downy Mildews The water molds and downy mildews are members of the phylum **Oomycota** (oh uh my KAHT uh). These protists, consisting of finely branched, single-celled filaments, look like fungi and also have a funguslike method of nutrition. However, they differ from fungi in the content of their cell walls, their sexual mode of reproduction, and the dominance of the diploid stage in their complex life cycle.

Most water molds are saprobes that live on dead organisms in fresh water. Their filaments form cottony masses. Other water molds are parasites that live on the gills of fish. The downy mildews are parasites that live on plants. One species of downy mildew attacked French vineyards in the 1870s, threatening the wine-making industry. Another species caused late potato blight, which destroyed the potato crops of Ireland from 1845 to 1847. The resulting famine caused over 1 million deaths and the mass migration of nearly half the population of the country.

30-2 Section Review

1. What is the common name for the plantlike protists?
2. Name the substance that gives some protists their glassy cell walls.
3. Are the animal-like protists autotrophic or heterotrophic?
4. What is an acellular slime mold called during its feeding stage?

Critical Thinking

5. What is the main criterion for classifying animal-like protists? Compare this feature in the four types of animal-like protists. (*Comparing and Contrasting*)

30-3 The Viruses

Section Objectives:

- *Describe* the basic structure of a virus.
- *Identify* the criteria that scientists use to classify viruses.
- *Explain* how viruses enter host cells, replicate, and release new viruses.
- *Describe* the body's defenses against viral infection.

Viruses are tiny particles unlike any other living organisms. In fact, scientists do not consider viruses to be living. They are described as somewhere between living cells and nonliving things. Although viruses contain genetic material, they lack all other cell structures necessary for metabolism, reproduction, and growth. A virus consists of genetic material—DNA or RNA—wrapped in a protein coat. Since viruses are not cells, they are not included as members of any of the five kingdoms.

A virus particle cannot reproduce, or *replicate,* unless it is inside a living host cell. Therefore, viruses survive by attacking a living cell, using the cell's machinery to reproduce. This parasitic invasion of plant and animal cells leads to a wide variety of diseases. In humans, viruses cause many infectious diseases that range from the common cold to rabies and acquired immune deficiency syndrome (AIDS).

Size and Structure

The word *virus* is from the Latin word for poison. It originally referred to any poisonous substance. Later, it was used to refer to specific agents of disease.

Viruses are much smaller than cells and were not actually seen until the electron microscope was invented. Scientists knew about viruses about 100 years ago when they began looking for something smaller than bacteria that could cause disease. At that time an epidemic of a disease of tobacco plants, tobacco mosaic disease, occurred in the Soviet Union. In this disease, the tobacco leaves develop a "mosaic" of light- and dark-green patches. Although they could not see the viruses through their microscopes, scientists knew that some "invisible" pathogen was causing the disease. They deduced that the pathogen was not a bacterium, because it would not grow in laboratory cultures, and it could not be killed by alcohol, which is fatal to bacteria. In 1892, the Russian biologist Dmitri Iwanowski discovered the virus that caused tobacco mosaic disease. Martinus Beijerinck, a Dutch scientist, continued experimenting on the disease and was the first to use the term *virus* to describe the pathogen. However, it was not until 1935 that the tobacco mosaic virus was chemically isolated by Wendell Stanley, an American biochemist. Since then, our knowledge about viruses and their ability to cause disease has increased greatly. Through the use of the electron microscope and other scientific advances, many viruses have been isolated and identified.

Figure 30–26

Tobacco Mosaic Virus. These tobacco leaves (top) show the patchwork coloring of a tobacco mosaic virus infection. The rod-shaped virus particles are seen in this scanning electron micrograph (bottom). ▼

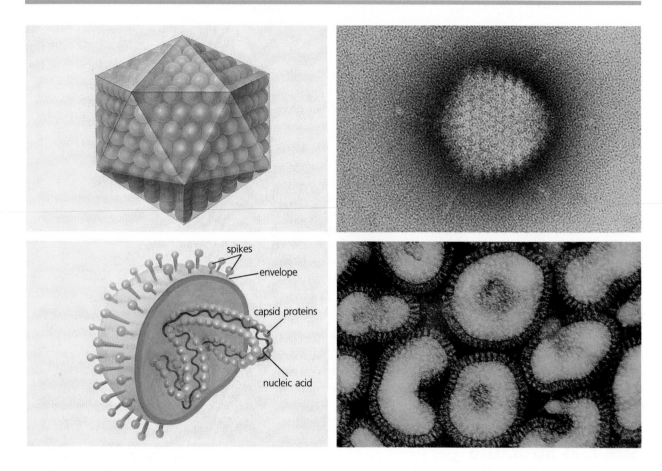

▲ **Figure 30–27**

Viral Shapes and Sizes. At upper left is a diagram of a polyhedron. At upper right is an electron micrograph of the polyhedral-shaped advenovirus. (Magnification 78 500 X) A diagram of an enveloped helical virus is at lower left. An electron micrograph of influenza viruses is at lower right. (Magnification 76 500 X)

Depending on the cells they infect, viruses are frequently classified as plant, animal, or bacterial viruses. Thus, some viruses infect the leaf cells of plants; others infect cells of the human respiratory or digestive tracts. There are many subcategories of each type of virus.

Viruses consist of a nucleic acid core of RNA or DNA surrounded by a protein coat called a **capsid.** In addition to the capsid, some viruses are enclosed in a membrane called an *envelope,* which consists of a portion of the cell membrane or nuclear membrane from the host cell and some viral proteins. The flu virus, for example, has an envelope with protein spikes that enable it to adhere to a host cell.

Viruses vary in their structure and shape. Some are rod-shaped, such as the tobacco mosaic virus. The herpes virus is polyhedral, or many-sided. Still others may be helical, such as the mumps virus. Some examples of different viral shapes and structures are shown in Figure 30–27.

As minute as the typical virus is, there are even smaller and simpler disease-causing viral particles. Scientists have recently isolated *viroids* and *prions.* Viroids, which infect plants, are very short pieces of RNA having no surrounding capsids. Prions, which cause slow, progressive diseases in animals, contain proteins but lack nucleic acid.

Genetic Makeup

Viruses may have either RNA or DNA as their genetic material, but not both. The nucleic acid strands may be single or double, depending on the virus. DNA viruses and RNA viruses have different effects on host cells. Within the host cell, a DNA virus produces RNA, which directs the production of viral proteins. Or the viral DNA may combine with the DNA of a host cell, which then produces new viruses.

RNA viruses work in a different way. Once inside the host cell, an RNA virus may direct the production of proteins by the host cell. Sometimes, the viral RNA may make DNA with the aid of an enzyme called *reverse transcriptase*. That DNA produces new RNA, which, in turn, synthesizes proteins that produce new viruses. Such an RNA virus is called a **retrovirus.** The AIDS infection is caused by a retrovirus.

Reproduction

Bacteriophages, or "*phages*" for short, are viruses that attack bacterial cells. They have a complex structure, consisting of a head and tail portion with long fibers projecting from the tail. Phages are a particularly well-studied group of viruses because their host cells, bacteria, can be easily and quickly grown in laboratory cultures. The following steps show how a phage attacks a bacterial cell, uses it to reproduce, and then destroys it. This is known as the **lytic cycle:**

   1. Many phages consist of a tadpole-shaped outer protein coat that transports its nucleic acid by means of a tail. When the phage finds the right host bacterium, it attaches its fibrous tail to the cell and uses an enzyme to eat a hole in the cell wall. The cell wall of a

Figure 30–28
Structure of a Bacteriophage. ▼

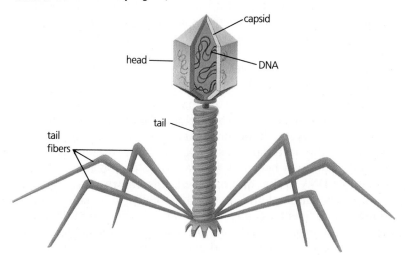

capsid

head — DNA

tail

tail fibers

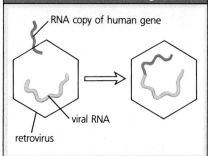

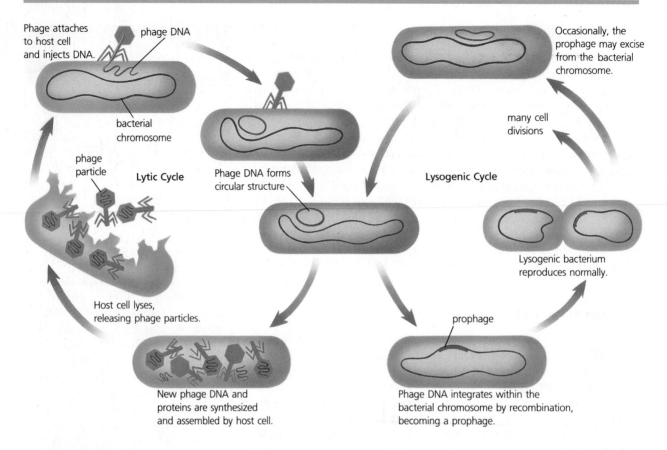

Phage attaches to host cell and injects DNA.

phage DNA

bacterial chromosome

phage particle

Lytic Cycle

Phage DNA forms circular structure

Host cell lyses, releasing phage particles.

New phage DNA and proteins are synthesized and assembled by host cell.

Occasionally, the prophage may excise from the bacterial chromosome.

many cell divisions

Lysogenic Cycle

Lysogenic bacterium reproduces normally.

prophage

Phage DNA integrates within the bacterial chromosome by recombination, becoming a prophage.

▲ **Figure 30–29**

The Lysogenic and Lytic Cycles of a Bacteriophage. Both the lysogenic and lytic cycles begin when the phage injects its DNA into a host cell. In the lytic cycle, the cell is forced to produce new phages. In the lysogenic cycle, the phage's nucleic acid merges with the host's DNA. When the host cell divides, the phage DNA divides with it, thereby producing more cells with viral DNA.

host cell has an area on its surface called a receptor. That area fits together with the capsid shape of a specific virus. For this reason, viruses usually infect only one kind of host cell.

2. The phage then injects its nucleic acid into the host bacterial cell. In some viral infections, the capsid remains outside the host cell. In others, the entire virus enters the cell. Once inside the host cell, the viral RNA or DNA takes over the cell's reproductive machinery. The cell is forced to produce viral nucleic acids and proteins, which are then put together in an assembly-line fashion.

3. Eventually the cell becomes so laden with the new whole viral particles that its wall bursts, or *lyses,* scattering a new generation of viruses that can infect other bacteria. The lytic cycle can be very fast. A whole new generation of phages can be produced in as little as 20 minutes, given optimum conditions.

Sometimes a phage and bacterial cell can coexist for a time without the destruction of the bacterium. This process is known as the **lysogenic cycle.** It occurs when the phage's nucleic acid merges with the bacterial cell's DNA, and the new combination is transmitted through bacterial generations. Once such a virus has attached its DNA to that of a host cell, it is known as a *prophage.* This process can be lethal to the host cell if it is subjected to sudden environmental changes, such as exposure to radiation or chemicals. Changes can activate the phage's nucleic acid, causing production of viral particles and destruction of the host cell. The lysogenic and lytic cycles are compared in Figure 30–29.

As you learned in Chapter 27, viruses sometimes carry DNA from one bacterial cell to another in a process called transduction. This results in the creation of bacterial types that are genetically different.

Viruses and Disease

Viral infections are spread in the same ways as bacterial infections. Viral diseases vary in their severity. If the harm to host cells is slight, the resulting infection is barely noticeable. If the host cells are damaged by the viral attack, a disease with more severe symptoms results. Thus, viruses can damage or destroy cells in their effort to reproduce in specific tissues and organs. Most of us recover completely from colds and the flu, which mainly affect the respiratory tract. The polio virus attacks nerve cells in the brain and spinal cord. As nerve cells cannot be replaced, the infectious spread of the virus through these cells can cause permanent paralysis or death. Other diseases caused by viruses include smallpox, chicken pox, measles, mumps, and AIDS.

Figure 30–30
Viruses that Cause Human Diseases. ▼

Examples of Viruses that Cause Human Disease		
Viral Group	**Nucleic Acid**	**Disease**
papovaviruses	DNA	warts
adenoviruses	DNA	respiratory infections
herpesviruses	DNA	herpes chickenpox shingles infectious mononucleosis Burkitt's lymphoma (a cancer)
poxviruses	DNA	smallpox wartlike skin lesions
picornaviruses	RNA	polio common cold gastrointestinal infections
myxoviruses	RNA	influenza measles mumps
retroviruses	RNA	tumors leukemia AIDS
rhabdoviruses	RNA	rabies
togaviruses	RNA	rubella (German measles)

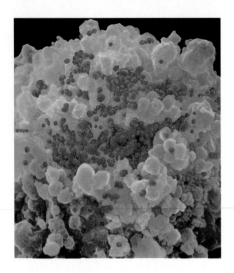

▲   **Figure 30–31**

HIV. This color-enhanced scanning electron micrograph shows a helper T cell (green) that has been infected with HIV (red).

The virus that causes AIDS, which is called the human immunodeficiency virus, or HIV, was identified by scientists working independently in France and in the United States in 1984. HIV attacks cells of the immune system called helper T cells. As a result of this damage, the immune response is seriously weakened. Because the immune systems of people with AIDS are so weakened, diseases and infections that would normally be prevented by a healthy immune system spread rapidly. People do not die from HIV infection, rather they die from complications of the diseases and infections that their bodies cannot fight. The dramatic, devastating effects of AIDS on the immune system are described in Chapter 10.

It is estimated that as many as 1 million people may be infected with HIV, but do not yet show symptoms of the disease and may be unaware that they are infected. Presently, there is no cure for AIDS, but scientists are actively studying the disease in laboratories around the world. Progress has been made in developing some promising drugs that may treat the disease and prolong the lives of people infected with HIV.

Viruses have also been implicated in the production of certain cancerous tumors by causing cells to multiply abnormally. Such viruses, known as tumor viruses, may carry genes that cause cancer, or **oncogenes.** They may also stimulate oncogenes already present in the host cell. Tumor viruses alter the genetic makeup of cells by incorporating their nucleic acid with the host cell's DNA. DNA tumor viruses are examples of viruses that direct the constant production of viral DNA and proteins in host cells. This causes rapid cell division and growth. The host cell does not produce new viruses, as it does in other viral infections. Therefore, the host cells are not destroyed but continuously grow and divide.

The human body can protect itself against viruses through its own immune system. Viruses stimulate a response from the immune system of the infected host. This response is the basis for vaccination, in which a weakened or dead virus is used to stimulate production of antiviral substances.

The first vaccine, against smallpox, was developed by Edward Jenner in 1798. In developing this vaccine, Jenner used material from the sores of people infected with cowpox, a disease similar to but milder than smallpox. The cowpox virus was so closely related to the smallpox virus that vaccination with it brought about immunity to smallpox infection. (The word *vaccination* is from the Latin *vacca,* which means "cow.") Smallpox was once one of the most feared diseases in human history, spreading in epidemics to many parts of the world. Now, the use of the smallpox vaccine has completely eliminated the disease.

In 1884, Louis Pasteur developed the first rabies vaccine. He soon used it as a preventive treatment in a nine-year-old who had been bitten by a rabid dog. Rabies is a serious, often fatal, disease that is transmitted to humans by the bite of infected animals, such as dogs and raccoons. In much the same way that he had earlier produced his anthrax vaccine, Pasteur developed weakened forms of the rabies virus. He used the weakened rabies virus in a series of increasingly strong injections. He found that this treatment could prevent rabies in a person exposed to the virus, if administered soon after a bite occurred.

In 1954, Dr. Jonas Salk developed the first polio vaccine, called the Salk vaccine. Salk took active polio viruses and killed them with a poison, formaldehyde. When injected as a vaccine, the killed viruses caused the production of polio antibodies that protected the person from polio. Around this time the United States was in the midst of a polio epidemic. In 1952, there were 57 000 reported cases of polio. Widespread use of the Salk vaccine resulted in a radical drop in the incidence of polio, and by 1957 the United States was free of the epidemic.

In the early 1960s, Dr. Albert Sabin developed a different type of polio vaccine. He treated polio viruses to weaken but not kill them. When fluid containing the weakened viruses is swallowed (in a flavored drink), the person will build antibodies against polio. Today the Sabin vaccine is routinely administered, as it induces a longer-lasting immunity than the Salk vaccine. In parts of the world where widespread vaccination against polio is not enforced, however, the disease still exists. Today, vaccines are available to prevent a wide variety of viral infections, including measles, mumps, and rubella (German measles).

Another natural defense against viruses is *interferon.* Interferon is a protein produced by a virus-infected cell that inhibits virus reproduction. Because human interferon is effective against many kinds of viruses, physicians have been trying to use it to treat viral infections. However, cells produce only minute quantities of interferon, making it impractical to extract. Synthetically produced interferon has only limited use because it can have toxic side effects in humans.

Although vaccines can prevent some viral infections, there is no cure for them once they occur. Antibiotics are not effective against viruses. A few drugs have been developed that can slow viral replication. However, immunity is still the most effective defense against viral diseases.

30-3 **Section Review**

1. The basic structure of viruses includes which two parts?

2. What is another name for bacterial viruses?

3. Which cycle of viral replication involves the disruption of host cell walls?

4. Dr. Jonas Salk developed the first vaccine for which viral infection?

Critical Thinking

5. Why are antibiotics not useful in treating the common cold? (*Identifying Reasons*)

Biology and You

Q: There are plenty of antibiotics to fight bacterial infections, yet no drugs to treat viral infections such as the common cold. Why not?

A: Viral diseases are difficult to treat because a virus becomes an integral part of the body cell it infects. Once a virus invades a cell, any drug that damages the virus affects the host cell as well. Because bacteria exist as independent cells, antibiotics kill bacteria without damaging body cells.

Some viral diseases are prevented by vaccines. A vaccine for the common cold is impractical, however, since over 200 cold viruses exist. Instead, other methods are being developed.

Doctors are experimenting with a nasal spray that contains interferon, an antiviral agent produced by body cells under viral attack. In experiments, families used the spray whenever a member showed signs of a cold. The spray prevented colds from being passed on, especially colds caused by rhinoviruses, the leading cause of colds. However, more studies need to be done before interferon nasal spray is approved for the public.

Write a one-page story from the perspective of a virus. Describe how you invade and destroy a cell.

Laboratory
Investigation

Designing an Experiment

Observing the Effects of the Tobacco Mosaic Virus

The tobacco mosaic virus (TMV) discovered in the 1890s still commonly infects field-grown tobacco today. Even though the virus cannot be seen, the symptoms caused by the virus can be easily observed. In this investigation, you will make an extract of TMV and then place it on the leaves of some healthy tobacco plants. The presence of spots on the healthy plants indicates that they have been infected with TMV.

Problem

What effect does the tobacco mosaic virus have on healthy tobacco plants? **Design an experiment** to answer this question.

Suggested Materials (per group)

- 2 young tobacco plants in pots with soil
- tobacco sample
- spatula
- carborundum powder
- dibasic potassium phosphate solution
- small beakers
- mortar and pestle
- cotton swabs
- small cards

Procedure

1. Formulate a hypothesis that you want to test.

2. Divide the dibasic potassium phosphate solution between two beakers. **CAUTION:** *Be careful when using this solution.* Dip a cotton swab into one of the beakers to moisten it.

3. With a spatula, sprinkle the swab with a small amount of carborundum powder. Gently stroke some of the leaves of one plant with the swab. The carborundum is an abrasive and will make microscopic scratches on the surface of the leaf. Try not to rub too hard or you will destroy the leaf entirely.

4. Place the tobacco sample into a mortar, slowly add the dibasic potassium phosphate solution from the other beaker to the sample, and grind the mixture with the pestle.

Allow the solid particles to settle. The extract contains the virus. Dampen a cotton swab with a small amount of the liquid in the mortar. Repeat step 3 using the second tobacco plant.

5. Plan to observe the plants for a two-week period. Make sure that the plants get sufficient water and light during that time. You may want to indicate on a small card which plant was swabbed with the virus extract and which one was not. Discard the cotton swabs, as directed by your teacher, and wash all equipment used with soap and water. Be sure to wash your hands with soap and water too.

Observations

1. What changes did your group see in each plant in the first five days? Over the next five days?

2. Did your group notice whether any changes were confined to one spot, or did they spread throughout the entire plant?

Analysis and Conclusions

1. What was your group's hypothesis for this investigation?

2. Did the result of the experiment support your hypothesis? Can you think of other hypotheses that the results also support?

3. What was the purpose of the plant that was not swabbed with the virus extract? Why was it prepared first?

4. What is the relationship between the treatment of the leaves with carborundum powder and what happens when you scrape a knee or an elbow in a fall?

5. Many plant growers do not allow any tobacco products near plants in their greenhouses. What reason can you give for this?

Extensions

Design and conduct an experiment to observe the effects of tobacco mosaic virus on tomato plants.

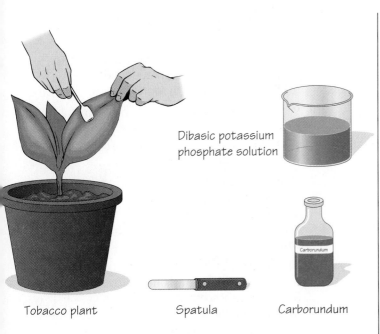

Dibasic potassium phosphate solution

Carborundum

Tobacco plant   Spatula   Carborundum

Applying Material to Leaves

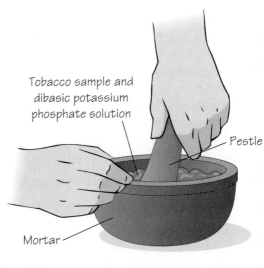

Tobacco sample and dibasic potassium phosphate solution

Pestle

Mortar

Grinding Mixture

Chapter **30** Review

Study Outline

30-1 The Bacteria

▶ Bacteria are the simplest, most numerous organisms on earth. Although some bacteria are harmful and cause diseases, most are beneficial. Because they lack a distinct membrane-bound nucleus, bacteria are classified as prokaryotes.

▶ Bacteria may be grouped according to shape: the spherical coccus, the rod-shaped bacillus, and the spiral-shaped spirillum. Some bacteria form colonies.

▶ All bacteria reproduce asexually. Some are capable of exchanging genetic material by conjugation, transformation, or transduction.

▶ Bacteria are divided into two separate kingdoms—the Archaebacteria and the Eubacteria.

▶ Pathogens are heterotrophic bacteria that are disease causing. Much of our understanding of bacterial pathogens can be attributed to the work of Pasteur and Koch. Koch's postulates are a set of rules to determine if a specific bacterium causes a specific disease.

30-2 The Protists

▶ The kingdom Protista contains many varied species, and is divided into animal-like, plantlike, and funguslike protists. All protists are composed of eukaryotic cells with a nucleus and cytoplasmic organelles.

▶ The animal-like protists, called protozoa, are divided into four phyla—Sarcodina, Ciliophora, Zoomastigina, and Sporozoa—based on their method of locomotion.

▶ The plantlike protists, or algae, are photosynthetic and are divided into six groups.

▶ Many funguslike protists are decomposers; a few are parasites.

30-3 The Viruses

▶ Viruses are tiny particles that consist of genetic material wrapped in a protein coat. Viruses lack all cell structures necessary for metabolism, reproduction, and growth.

▶ Viruses vary in shape and may contain either DNA or RNA. DNA and RNA viruses have different effects on the host cell.

▶ Viral infections are spread in the same ways as bacterial infections. Once inside a living cell, the virus replicates, destroying the host cell. Viral diseases include colds, flu, polio, measles, mumps, and AIDS.

Chapter Assessment

Multiple Choice

Choose the letter of the answer that best completes each statement or answers the question.

1. Which protist causes malaria? (a) Plasmodium. (b) Euglena. (c) Paramecium. (d) Ameba.

2. Organisms that have cells without nuclei are known as (a) prokaryotes. (b) eukaryotes. (c) fungi. (d) protists.

3. The type of asexual reproduction that takes place when a bacterium replicates its chromosome and divides in half is called (a) spore formation. (b) binary fission. (c) conjugation. (d) meiosis.

4. A virus that infects bacteria is called a (a) provirus. (b) bacillus. (c) bacteriophage. (d) spirillum.

5. Organisms in the phylum Zoomastigina move through water using (a) pseudopods. (b) flagella. (c) cilia. (d) spores.

6. Which of the following protists does not contain chlorophyll, a green pigment also found in plants? (a) euglenas (b) dinoflagellates (c) diatoms (d) water molds

7. How are cilia and flagella similar? (a) Both are hairlike structures used for movement. (b) Both are reproductive structures. (c) Meiosis occurs in both structures. (d) Digestion occurs in both structures.

8. An organism that makes its own food without the direct need for any light energy is known as a (a) chemosynthetic heterotroph. (b) chemosynthetic autotroph. (c) photosynthetic heterotroph. (d) photosynthetic autotroph.

9. Organisms that need a constant supply of oxygen in order to live are called (a) obligate anaerobes. (b) facultative anaerobes. (c) chemosynthetic autotrophs. (d) obligate aerobes.

10. In any lysogenic infection, the viral DNA (a) is inserted into the host DNA. (b) destroys the host DNA. (c) replicates repeatedly. (d) is destroyed by the host DNA.

Content Review

Answer each of the following in complete sentences.

11. Compare prokaryotic and eukaryotic cells.

12. Summarize both heterotrophic and autotrophic nutrition in bacteria.

13. How do bacteria exchange genetic material?

14. What are Koch's postulates?

15. Briefly describe the life cycle of the malarial parasite, *Plasmodium.*

16. How do euglenoids resemble plant and animal cells?

17. Describe the structure and life cycle of acellular slime molds.

18. How do viruses use a host cell?

19. Explain how phages attack bacterial cells.

20. How does the human body combat viral infections?

Graphic Organizing

For information on graphic organizers, see Appendix G at the back of this text.

21. **Scale** Draw a scale that shows the relative sizes of the following organisms and cells, from smallest to largest: the bacterium *E. coli,* .000001 m; ameba, .0001 m; certain human nerve cells, 1 meter; the marine alga *Acetabularia,* between .01 and .1 m; flu virus, .0000001 m; human red blood cell, .00001 m.

Critical Thinking and Problem Solving

Discuss each of the following in a brief paragraph.

22. **Comparing** Compare how viruses and bacteria affect an organism after they infect it.

23. **Drawing conclusions** Two scientists recently presented opposing views on whether viruses are living. What reasons might they give to support both views?

24. **Predicting** What might happen in a forest ecosystem if all the bacteria suddenly died?

25. **Inferring** From your knowledge of the *Plasmodium's* life cycle, suggest possible plans to eliminate malaria.

26. **Hypothesizing** A veterinarian suspects that a new disease of house cats is caused by a specific type of bacterium. Describe a set of procedures for proving this hypothesis.

27. **Interpreting** In an experiment on bacterial growth, equal amounts of methane-producing bacteria and water were placed in each of four test tubes. One of four sugars (A, B, C, or D) was added to each test tube in equal concentrations. The volume of methane gas (CH_4) liberated from each culture was measured and the data plotted on the graph shown below. What does the graph indicate about the effect of each sugar solution on the growth of the bacteria?

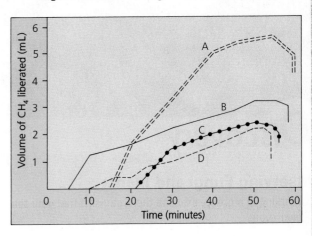

663

Discovery Learning Activity

Observing Fungi and Plants

1. Working in a group, examine the organisms that your teacher has given you.

2. Make a drawing of each organism and identify any structures that you can. In which type of environment do you think each organism lives? Which organisms are considered plants? Explain your answer.

Fungi and Plants

31-1 Fungi

Section Objectives:

- *Describe* the general characteristics of fungi.
- *State* the distinguishing characteristics of each phylum, and name two or three of its members.
- *Compare* fungi and lichens.

The fungi, kingdom Fungi, include yeasts, molds, mushrooms, and rusts and smuts. **Fungi** are non-green organisms that absorb the nutrients they need from the environment. Most fungi are saprobic. They obtain nutrients from the remains of dead plants and animals. To do this, they secrete digestive enzymes onto the food and absorb the digested nutrients. The fungi, along with the bacteria, play a key role in breaking down dead organisms and releasing the substances these organisms contain. Some fungi are parasitic. They obtain nutrients from the organisms on which they live.

General Characteristics

Fungi vary in size. Some are microscopic; others weigh several kilograms. The bodies of most fungi consist of threadlike filaments called **hyphae** (HY fee) (singular, hypha). As the hyphae grow, they branch, forming a tangled mass called a **mycelium** (my

▲ **Figure 31–1**

A Fungus. This red mushroom is a member of the kingdom Fungi. There are about 100 000 named species of fungi.

◀ A bright red mushroom pokes through a lush carpet of moss.

SEE lee um) (plural, mycelia). In some fungi, the cytoplasm in the hyphae is not divided by cell walls. The continuous cytoplasm contains several nuclei. In other fungi, the hyphae are divided by incomplete *septa,* or cross walls. In these fungi, the hyphae are partly divided into compartments, but the cytoplasm is still continuous. Each compartment may contain more than one nucleus. Unlike the cell walls of green plants, the cell walls of most fungi are composed of chitin, not cellulose.

Fungi reproduce both asexually and sexually by means of spores. There are over 80 000 species of fungi. Most of these are grouped into three phyla, based more or less on their pattern of sexual reproduction. These are the conjugation fungi, the sac fungi, and the club fungi. A fourth phylum, called the *imperfect fungi,* includes thousands of fungi that cannot be classified because their pattern of sexual reproduction is unknown.

The Conjugation Fungi

The *conjugation fungi,* phylum **Zygomycota** (zy goh my KOH tuh), produce a special type of thick-walled spore that develops from a zygote during sexual reproduction. These fungi produce another type of spore asexually. Most conjugation fungi are saprobes, but some are parasites on plants, insects, or other fungi. The hyphae of the conjugation fungi lack cross walls, but cross walls do form during the production of gametes and spores. The common bread mold, *Rhizopus,* is a typical member of this group.

Rhizopus grows on the surface of bread and fruit as a cottonlike mass of filaments. See Figure 31–2. The whitish or grayish mycelium consists of several kinds of hyphae. Rootlike hyphae, called **rhizoids,** anchor the fungus, secrete digestive enzymes, and absorb nutrients. Other hyphae, called **stolons,** grow in a network over the surface of the food. The stolons give rise to still another type of

Figure 31–2

Life Cycle of Bread Mold. The bread mold, *Rhizopus,* reproduces sexually by conjugation of different strains of hyphae. *Rhizopus* also reproduces asexually by releasing spores from sporangia. ▼

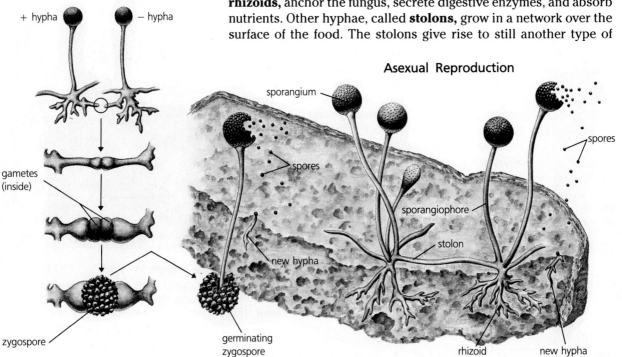

Sexual Reproduction

+ hypha   − hypha

gametes (inside)

zygospore

germinating zygospore

Asexual Reproduction

sporangium

spores

spores

sporangiophore

stolon

new hypha

rhizoid   new hypha

hyphae that grow upward from the surface of the food. These are reproductive hyphae, called *sporangiophores*. At the tip of each sporangiophore, a round spore case, or sporangium, develops. The black dots you see in common bread mold are sporangia. Many spores form within each sporangium. At maturity, when the cases open, the spores are released. Those that land in favorable environments germinate, form new hyphae, and eventually form new mycelia.

Usually, bread mold reproduces asexually by spore formation. Under certain conditions, however, bread mold reproduces sexually by conjugation. The pattern of conjugation is similar to the pattern found in spirogyra, an alga.

Conjugation occurs when hyphae of different strains touch. Once contact has occurred, the tips of both hyphae enlarge, and cross walls form behind the tips. These partitioned-off ends are now gamete-producing structures. The two strains of bread mold are called *plus* and *minus*. One tip contains several plus nuclei, while the other contains several minus nuclei. At the point of contact, the end walls of the two touching hyphae break up, and the nuclei of opposite strains fuse to form a number of diploid nuclei. A hard wall develops around the nuclei and cytoplasm, producing a thick-walled zygospore that can resist harsh environmental conditions. When conditions are favorable, the zygospore germinates. All but one diploid nucleus degenerates. The remaining nucleus undergoes meiosis. Meiosis produces four nuclei, three of which degenerate. The remaining haploid nucleus gives rise to a sporangiophore, which then produces spores asexually.

The Sac Fungi

The *sac fungi*, phylum **Ascomycota** (as koh my KOH tuh), are the largest group of fungi. They include cup fungi, powdery mildews, morels, truffles, blue and green molds, and yeasts.

Sac fungi produce two kinds of spores, each of which can give rise to new organisms under the proper conditions. Spores produced as a result of sexual reproduction are called *ascospores*. Usually eight, but occasionally four, ascospores develop inside a saclike **ascus** (plural, asci), which serves as a sporangium. Spores produced asexually are called *conidia*. Conidia are formed in chains at the tips of specialized reproductive hyphae.

Except for the yeasts, which are unicellular, the sac fungi are multicellular. Cross walls divide hyphae of multicellular sac fungi. Holes in the cross walls permit cytoplasm and nuclei to move from one compartment of the hypha to the next. Each compartment has one to several nuclei.

Most cup fungi are saprobic and grow on dead organic matter. Some cup fungi are shown in Figure 31–3. The visible portion of the fungus is the cup-shaped *fruiting body*, which contains the spore-bearing sacs, or asci. Beneath the surface of the soil is a large mycelium made up of many hyphae.

The unicellular yeasts are not typical of the Ascomycota. Yeasts reproduce by budding and by spore formation (see Chapter

▲ Figure 31–3

Sac Fungi. Cup fungi, a type of sac fungi, grow on decaying matter. Each cup-shaped fruiting body is lined with spore-bearing sacs, or asci.

Figure 31–4

Hunting for Truffles. Truffles, a sac fungus highly prized by cooks, must be rooted out of the ground by pigs or dogs trained specifically for this purpose. **▼**

20). In spore formation, the yeast cell itself acts as an ascus. Yeasts are economically important because they are used in the manufacture of bread, alcohol, and alcoholic beverages.

Some Ascomycota cause plant disease, including Dutch elm disease, chestnut blight, and ergot. Ergot is a disease of wheat and rye, which is caused by a parasitic species of Ascomycota. Ergot poisoning results from eating flour made from infected plants. Modern methods of flour production have eliminated this problem.

Truffles and morels are edible ascomycetes that are considered great delicacies. Truffles grow several centimeters below the surface of the soil. They are spherical, brown fruiting bodies that range from about one to seven centimeters in diameter. In France, where truffles have been used in cooking for hundreds of years, pigs and dogs are trained to locate them by their odor. Morels, which are also known as sponge or honeycomb fungi, are common in many areas of the United States. The stalk and distinctive cap are the fruiting body. The asci are located within the folds of the cap.

The Club Fungi

The *club fungi,* phylum **Basidiomycota** (buh sid ee uh my KOH tuh), include most of the large fungi seen in fields and woods. Mushrooms, toadstools, bracket fungi, puffballs, and various parasites, such as rusts and smuts, are club fungi.

In the club fungi, sexual reproduction involves the production of spores called *basidiospores.* These spores are formed in an enlarged, club-shaped reproductive structure, the *basidium,* at the end of a specialized hypha. Some club fungi also produce spores asexually. Incomplete cross walls divide the hyphae of the Basidiomycota. The cells of the hyphae may have one or two nuclei.

The most familiar of the club fungi are the mushrooms. The mushroom is actually a fruiting body, the spore-producing part of the fungus. The main part of the mycelium grows beneath the surface of the ground. This part lives on the remains of plant and animal matter. The mycelium may live for years, slowly growing underground. Only when growing conditions are favorable do mushrooms grow up above the surface.

As shown in Figure 31–5, a mushroom consists of a stalk and a *cap.* Mushrooms begin to develop as small knobs on the underground mycelium. As the cap pushes up through the soil, it is kept closed and protected by a thin membrane that connects the edges of the cap to the stalk. Once the mushroom is above ground, the membrane breaks, and the cap expands. The part of the membrane that remains attached to the stalk is called the *annulus.*

The undersurface of the cap contains many *gills* that radiate out from the center of the stalk like wheel spokes. Each gill is made of many hyphae that are pressed closely together. On the sides of the gills are the basidia, each bearing four basidiospores. One mushroom can produce over 1 billion spores.

Many types of mushrooms are edible, but others are extremely poisonous. It takes an expert to distinguish between edible and

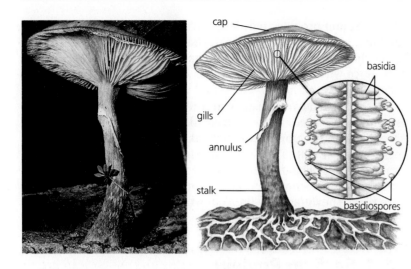

poisonous mushrooms. Never eat mushrooms that you find growing in the wild.

Rusts are club fungi that produce rust-colored spores during one phase of their life cycle. Rusts are parasites on wheat, barley, oats, and other crop plants. Each year they cause millions of dollars worth of damage to these crops. Smuts are similar to rusts. Their name refers to the black and dusty-looking mass of spores that they form within the tissues of the host plant. Smuts attack corn, wheat, oats, barley, and rye.

The Imperfect Fungi

The *imperfect fungi,* phylum **Deuteromycota** (do tur oh my KOH tah), include all fungi that are not known to have a sexual reproductive phase. This may be because the sexual phase does not occur or because it simply has not yet been observed. Because there are no known sexual stages, these fungi are difficult to classify. Therefore, they have been grouped together as "imperfect." If a fungus classified as imperfect is found to have sexual structures, it is reassigned to the appropriate phylum.

Many species of imperfect fungi are beneficial to humans. For instance, the fungus *Penicillium* produces the antibiotic penicillin. Penicillin cures a variety of bacterial diseases, including pneumonia, scarlet fever, and rheumatic fever. Other species of *Penicillium* give flavor to Roquefort and Camembert cheeses. A few imperfect fungi are harmful to humans. Some, for example, cause ringworm and athlete's foot. Others release spores that cause respiratory infections or allergic responses when inhaled.

Lichens

A **lichen** (LY ken) is made up of two organisms—an alga or a blue-green bacterium and a fungus—living together. The algal or bacterial cells are embedded in the mycelium of the fungus. The fungus is usually a sac fungus. Through photosynthesis, the alga or

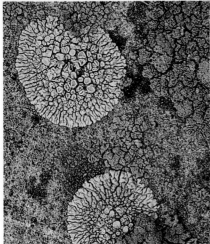

▲ **Figure 31–6**
Lichens. A lichen is made up of both a fungus and an alga. The lichens shown above are crustlike.

the bacterium provides nutrients for the fungus. At the same time, the fungus provides the alga or the bacterium with water, essential elements, and protection from intense light and dryness. Lichens reproduce when fragments break off, blow away, and start growing independently.

Some lichens are crustlike and resemble spots of paint. Some are flat but curled at the edges like leaves. Finally, some are shrublike and have branches. Lichens grow on the bark of trees, on rocks, and on soil. They can exist for months without water. In Arctic regions, lichens serve as food for caribou, musk ox, and other animals. Lichens are usually the first organisms to grow on bare rock. They gradually break down the rock, thus beginning the process of soil formation.

31-1 Section Review

1. What form of nutrition do all fungi have in common?
2. List the four major phyla in the kingdom Fungi.
3. What two organisms make up lichens?

Critical Thinking

4. Suppose that mushrooms appeared repeatedly in only one small part of your yard. What does this indicate about the soil in that area? (*Identifying Causes*)

31-2 Plants

Section Objectives:

- *Discuss* the evolutionary relationship thought to exist between green algae and plants.
- *Name* three kinds of bryophytes.
- *Distinguish* between nonvascular and vascular plants.
- *Describe* the various types of spore-dispersing and seed plants.

The kingdom Plantae is made up of organisms that most people refer to as plants. These include mosses, ferns, conifers, and flowering plants. Plants are multicellular, photosynthetic organisms that are adapted primarily for life on land. Many scientists believe plants have evolved from earlier, algal-like ancestors. Although all plants grow and reproduce on land, they have adapted to many different land environments. Some plants, like the mosses and their relatives, grow and reproduce only in wet or moist environments. Other plants are adapted for living in deserts, the driest of environments. In the following sections, you will read about the structural adaptations that allow plants to live in different environments.

General Characteristics of Plants

The plants, with their complex structural organization, are thought to have evolved from simpler algal-like ancestors. The green algae, which may be unicellular, colonial, or multicellular, are the most similar to plants. For the most part, green algae and plants have the same kinds of chlorophyll, the same food-storage polysaccharide (starch), and the same polysaccharides (cellulose) in their cell walls. These similarities suggest that plants and green algae share a common evolutionary ancestry.

Plants are divided into two groups—the *bryophytes* (BRY uh fyts) and the *tracheophytes* (TRAK ee uh fyts). The bryophytes include mosses, liverworts, and hornworts. These plants do not have conducting, or vascular, tissues. They are short plants and usually grow in areas that have a good supply of water. The tracheophytes include horsetails, ferns, gymnosperms, and flowering plants. Members of this group have well-developed vascular tissues for transport.

Life on land presents a number of problems that do not exist for organisms that live in water. The most immediate problems are obtaining and conserving water. All plants must be able to obtain water, transport it to all their cells, and control its evaporation from their tissues. Plants also need supporting tissues to stand upright against the force of gravity. Many of them need special reproductive mechanisms that enable the sperm to reach the egg without swimming through water.

Nonvascular Plants—The Bryophytes

The division **Bryophyta** (bry AH fuh tuh) includes *mosses, liverworts,* and *hornworts.* These are nonvascular land plants. That is, they have no specialized conducting tissues. The transport of materials through the plant takes place by diffusion, which is slow and inefficient. For this reason, the bryophytes must live where water is plentiful. They are found on forest floors, on damp rocks, in swamps and bogs, and near streams. Without xylem, bryophytes have little in the way of supporting tissues. Most are short, ranging from one to five centimeters in height.

In many bryophytes, some branch filaments of the young plant grow downward and enter the soil, where they function as roots. These rhizoids anchor the plant and absorb minerals and water. Other branches grow upward, forming stemlike shoots and leaves. Since, however, the cells in the rhizoids, shoots, and leaves are all similar, these structures are not true organs.

In the bryophyte life cycle, the haploid gametophyte is the dominant generation. The diploid sporophyte generation is small, short-lived, and dependent on the gametophyte for its nutrition. The life cycle of mosses is shown in Figure 24–4. In mosses and other bryophytes, the sperm must swim to the egg through water. Thus, these plants still display their ancestral origins.

Figure 31–7
Bryophytes. The mosses are the largest class of bryophytes and are found almost everywhere on earth. Like all bryophytes, mosses have no specialized conducting tissues and must live where water is abundant. ▼

General Characteristics of Vascular Plants

The *vascular plants,* division **Tracheophyta** (tray kee AH fuh tuh), are a diverse group that includes most modern-day plants. Whisk ferns, club mosses, and horsetails, as well as the ferns, conifers, and flowering plants, are vascular plants. In the sporophyte generation, all tracheophytes contain the vascular tissues xylem and phloem. In the tracheophytes, the sporophyte generation is dominant and the gametophyte is small and short-lived.

The vascular plants are divided into two groups—the spore-dispersing plants and the seed plants.

Vascular Spore-Dispersing Plants

The spore-dispersing vascular plants include the whisk ferns, club mosses, horsetails, and ferns. Fertilization in these ancient plants requires water.

The Whisk Ferns   The **whisk ferns** are the oldest known vascular plants. Fossil evidence indicates that this group was widespread about 400 million years ago, but there are only a few modern living species. These species, which live only in warm climates, are found from South Carolina to Florida. They are not really ferns. They do not have either true leaves or true roots. The plant body of the sporophyte consists of an underground stem anchored by rhizoids, which absorb water and minerals. Above ground, the stems are green and carry on photosynthesis. As the stems grow, they split into two branches, so that the ends of the stems are Y-shaped. Sporangia form at the tips of some branches. Within the sporangia, haploid spores are produced by meiosis. When the spores are released, some germinate, giving rise to small gametophytes that bear both male and female reproductive organs. These are the antheridia and archegonia, which are explained in Chapter 24, section 24–1. After fertilization occurs, the zygote develops into a new sporophyte.

The Club Mosses   The **club mosses** were one of the dominant forms of plant life during the Carboniferous, or coal-forming, period of the earth about 300 million years ago. There are only a few remaining small genera of club mosses. Some of the prehistoric forms were as large as trees and made up entire forests. Living club mosses are mostly small, reaching about 20 centimeters in height. A few tropical species may reach heights of 90 centimeters and look like bushes.

Club moss sporophytes have true roots, stems, and leaves. Like the whisk ferns, the stems branch so that the ends are Y-shaped. At the tips of some branches, groups of spore-producing structures form. Spores released from them give rise to gametophytes, which bear the reproductive organs. Fertilization results in a zygote that develops into the sporophyte.

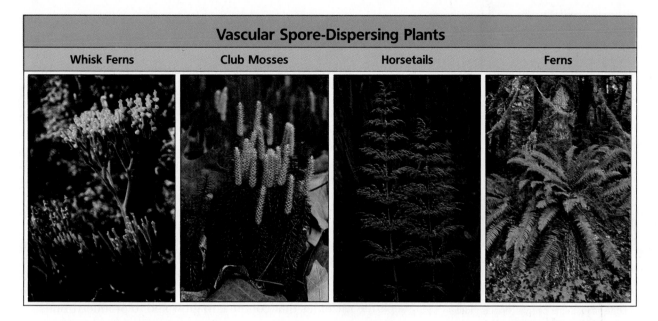

Vascular Spore-Dispersing Plants

Whisk Ferns	Club Mosses	Horsetails	Ferns

Some club mosses are evergreens and are used for holiday decorations. Ground pine and ground cedar are club mosses found in forests in the United States. One species from Mexico is known as the "resurrection plant." When dry, this club moss curls into a gray ball. When water is added, however, the moss opens, forming an attractive green plant.

The Horsetails   The **horsetails** include only about 20 living species of plants. They represent the remains of a group of plants that also flourished during the Carboniferous period. Some ancient horsetails were the size of trees. Over thousands of years, the remains of these and other plants of the Carboniferous period were eventually transformed into coal. Modern horsetails are usually less than one meter in height.

Horsetails are common in shaded woods and around streams, swamps, and ponds. The sporophytes have true roots and leaves. The stems are green and hollow. The leaves grow only at specific points along the stem, forming "collars" of leaves. Cone-shaped, spore-producing structures form at the ends of some stems. Haploid spores, produced by meiosis, are released and give rise to small gametophytes, which bear the reproductive organs. Following fertilization, the zygote gives rise to the sporophyte.

The stems of horsetails contain crystals of silicon. Early settlers often used horsetails for scouring pots and pans, which is why they are also known as *scouring rushes*.

The Ferns   Like the club mosses and horsetails, the **ferns** were most abundant during the Carboniferous period. There are now about 9000 living species of ferns. They are particularly abundant in tropical rain forests, but they are also found in cooler climates. Some tropical tree ferns have a woody, unbranched trunk and may reach heights of more than 15 meters. These ferns may have leaves

▲   **Figure 31–8**
Vascular Spore-Dispersing Plants. There are four groups of vascular spore-dispersing plants alive today. These plants require water for fertilization. The sporophyte generation is always dominant in the life cycle of these plants.

▲ **Figure 31–9**

Ferns. When the fronds of ferns first emerge from the soil, they are curled into the form of a fiddlehead. Some people consider fiddleheads a delicacy in the spring.

4 meters long. The ferns of cooler climates are much smaller. They have horizontal stems, called *rhizomes,* that grow just beneath the surface of the soil. Hairlike roots grow from the rhizomes deeper into the soil. The only visible parts of these ferns are the leaves, or fronds, that grow up from the rhizome. When the leaves first emerge from the soil, they are coiled in a bud called a *fiddlehead.* The fiddlehead gradually uncoils and develops into a mature frond. The fronds usually are divided into tiny leaflets that give them a feathery appearance.

The internal structure of ferns is similar to that of seed plants. Ferns contain xylem and phloem. Their roots have a root cap and show the growth zones found in the roots of higher plants. Because fern stems have no cambium, they show little or no growth in diameter.

Sexual reproduction in ferns is discussed in Chapter 24. In asexual reproduction, the rhizome grows through the soil. As it grows, it branches and produces new fronds at the tip of each branch. Over time, older portions of the rhizome die, leaving behind separate rhizomes that continue to grow and to produce fronds.

Vascular Seed Plants

The seed plants have become the dominant and most successful group of plants. There are more than 250 000 species, that range in size from the giant redwood tree to the tiny duckweed, a water plant with leaves only a few millimeters wide. As you can see in Figure

MiniLab

Skill: Relating

Cones and More Cones

Procedure

Problem

How do the various structures found on male and female pine cones **relate** to their function?

1. Examine a pollen cone. Dust some of the pollen grains on a microscope slide, prepare a wet-mount slide, and observe through the low-power objective of a microscope. Sketch a pollen grain.

2. Look at a seed cone. Observe the scales and note their arrangement. Gently shake the cone. Observe what happens.

3. Remove one of the scales and examine its base. Even if the seeds have been shed, an impression of the seed still remains.

Analyze and Conclude

1. How is the structure of the pollen grain related to its function?

2. How is the structure of a seed related to its function?

3. What function do the scales of a seed cone serve?

Vascular Seed Plants

Gymnosperms			Angiosperms	
Conifers	Cycads	Ginkgoes	Dicots	Monocots

▲ **Figure 31–10**

Vascular Seed Plants. Seed plants are the most successful of land plants. They include the gymnosperms and the angiosperms. In gymnosperms, the seeds are exposed, but in angiosperms, the seeds are enclosed within fruits.

31–10, there are two major groups of seed plants—the gymnosperms and the angiosperms. The **gymnosperms** are a diverse group in which the seeds are exposed. That is, they are not contained within a specialized organ. The **angiosperms** are the flowering plants, and their seeds are enclosed within fruits. In both groups, the seed is surrounded by a protective seed coat and contains stored food that nourishes the young seedling until it can function independently. In these plants, water is not needed for fertilization.

The Gymnosperms The gymnosperms are nonflowering seed plants that usually bear their seeds on the upper surface of scales that form a cone-shaped structure. The gymnosperms have true roots, stems, and leaves. The stems contain cambium, which causes the stem diameter to grow. The gymnosperm plant is the sporophyte generation. The life cycle of gymnosperms is discussed in Chapter 24.

Fossil evidence shows the presence of gymnosperms as early as 350 million years ago. By about 250 million years ago, they were the dominant form of plant life. There are now about 700 living

◀ **Figure 31–11**

Gymnosperms. Gymnosperm cones, like these hemlock, pine, and spruce cones, vary in size and structure.

▲ **Figure 31–12**
Redwood Tree. Some redwood trees are more than 3000 years old.

species of gymnosperms. The conifers are the most important group of gymnosperms. Two other gymnosperm groups are the cycads and the ginkgoes.

The **conifers,** or evergreens, are the best known of the gymnosperms. Members of this group are cone-bearing plants with leaves in the form of needles. In most conifers, the leaves remain green throughout the year. The conifers include pine, spruce, fir, hemlock, redwood, sequoia, cedar, and cypress trees. These trees show wide geographic distribution. In colder regions, they are the dominant trees of the forest. At high altitudes, pine and spruce are most abundant.

Sequoias and redwoods include some of the oldest-living and largest trees in the world. Some are between 3000 and 4000 years old and are more than 90 meters tall. Pine, spruce, and fir trees are widely used as holiday trees, and they and other conifers are used for lumber.

The **cycads** (SY kuds) look like palm trees except that they have cones. Members of this group are slow-growing and may live to be more than 1000 years old. Several species may reach heights of 15 meters. In some, the ovules are the size of large eggs and the cones weigh as much as 45 kilograms. Cycads grow in tropical and semitropical regions. The only cycad found in the United States is *Zamia,* which is found in Florida.

Maidenhair trees, or **ginkgoes,** are the only living representatives of a once numerous group. This species has survived because the trees have been cultivated as ornamental and shade trees. Few survive in the wild. Ginkgo trees, which may reach heights of more than 30 meters, are very hardy. They can survive with limited water and in the presence of air pollution.

The Angiosperms   The angiosperms, the flowering plants, are the most successful of all living plants. This group includes about 250 000 species, many of which are used for food. Flowering plants are found in all types of climates and environments. Some live in the desert where there is almost no water, and others live completely underwater.

In the angiosperms, the flower serves a reproductive function. It contains the structures that produce spores by meiosis. The angiosperm plant is the sporophyte, while the gametophytes are reduced to only a few cells. Fertilization is followed by the development of a seed, which is enclosed in a fruit. The life cycle of angiosperms is discussed in Chapter 24.

The angiosperms are divided into two major groups—the *dicots* and the *monocots.* The seeds of dicots contain two seed leaves, or cotyledons, whereas the seeds of monocots have only one. The monocots include the grasses, palms, lilies, sedges, irises, orchids, and various aquatic plants. The dicots are much more numerous than monocots. Figure 31–13 lists some of the major families of dicots and monocots and representative members of each.

Major Families of Dicots and Monocots

	Family	Representative Species
Dicots	**magnolia**	magnolia and tulip trees
	rose	rose, hawthorn, flowering quince, flowering almond, apple, pear, strawberry, blackberry, raspberry, apricot, cherry, peach, plum
	beech	beech, oak, chestnut trees
	parsley	parsley, carrot, celery, parsnip, dill, caraway, fennel, poison hemlock, anise
	mustard	mustard, cabbage, broccoli, kale, cauliflower, brussels sprout, turnip, horseradish, rutabaga
	heath	heath, heather, rhododendron, mountain laurel, blueberry, huckleberry, cranberry, wintergreen
	pea	pea, soybean, lima bean, peanut, clover, alfalfa, wisteria, sweet pea, black locust, rosewood
	composite	sunflower, dandelion, aster, dahlia, marigold, zinnia, lettuce, artichoke, endive
	nightshade	potato, tomato, tobacco, eggplant, red pepper, petunia
	mallow	hollyhock, okra, cotton
	mint	spearmint, peppermint, lavender, rosemary, thyme, sage
Monocots	**lily**	tiger lily, easter lily, lily of the valley, day lily, onion, leek, chive, garlic, asparagus, tulip, crocus
	grass	rice, wheat, corn, rye, barley, oats, sugar cane, bamboo, buffalo grass, Kentucky bluegrass
	palm	coconut palm, date palm

▲ **Figure 31–13**
Major Families of Dicots and Monocots.

31-2 Section Review

1. From what group of algae did plants probably arise?
2. Name three kinds of bryophytes.
3. Name two tissues that are common to all vascular plants.
4. What are four spore-dispersing tracheophytes?

Critical Thinking

5. What reasons do biologists have for believing that plants and green algae probably have evolved from the same common ancestors? (*Identifying Reasons*)

Laboratory
Investigation

Comparing a Mold and a Mushroom

Fungi are classified according to their methods of reproduction. In this investigation, you will observe a bread mold, a zygomycete, and a mushroom, a basidiomycete, and compare the basic structure of each.

Problem

Compare a mold and a mushroom.

Materials (per group)

▶ bread

▶ petri dish

▶ 2 medicine droppers

▶ 2 microscope slides

▶ dissecting needle

▶ 2 coverslips

▶ microscope

▶ iodine solution

▶ paper towel

▶ mushroom

▶ forceps

Procedure

1. Moisten a piece of bread with tap water. Place the moistened bread in the bottom of a Petri dish.

2. Allow the petri dish to remain uncovered for 30 minutes. After 30 minutes, put the cover on the Petri dish.

3. Place the petri dish in a warm, dark place where it will remain undisturbed for one to two weeks. Examine the bread daily for mold.

4. After the bread becomes moldy, use a medicine dropper to place a drop of water in the center of a microscope slide.

5. With the dissecting needle, separate a small piece of the mold from the bread. **CAUTION:** *Be careful when using a dissecting needle.* Add the mold to the water on the microscope slide and cover with a coverslip.

6. Locate some hyphae with the low-power objective of the microscope. Then switch to the high-power objective and use the fine adjustment to locate some hyphae. Notice their color.

7. With the other medicine dropper, place a drop of iodine solution at one edge of the coverslip. Hold a piece of paper towel at the opposite edge of the coverslip to draw the iodine solution across the coverslip.

8. Examine the hyphae again under the low and high powers of the microscope. Observe the shape and arrangement of the hyphae. Notice the sporangia, or bulb-shaped structures, at the ends of some of the hyphae. Make a labeled diagram of the structures of the mold.

9. Place a drop of water in the center of the second microscope slide.

10. Break the stalk off the mushroom slightly below the place where the stalk meets the cap. Insert the dissecting needle just under the surface of the stalk and carefully remove a small flap of the stalk.

11. With the forceps, peel off a thin layer of mushroom that runs parallel to the stalk. This layer contains the secondary mycelia (mass of hyphae).

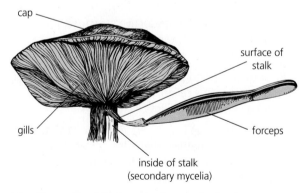

cap

surface of stalk

gills

forceps

inside of stalk
(secondary mycelia)

12. Place the thin layer of mycelia in the water on the microscope slide. Flatten the layer before covering it with a coverslip.

13. Repeat steps 6 to 8 using the mass of hyphae of the mushroom.

Observations

1. How many different kinds of mold do you see growing on the bread?

2. What is the color of the hyphae in the bread mold? In the mushroom stalk?

3. Describe the shape and arrangement of the structures of the mold and the mushroom.

Analysis and Conclusions

1. Explain why the bread was exposed to the air.

2. Why was the bread allowed to remain undisturbed in a warm, dark place for several weeks?

3. What was the purpose of examining the unstained mold and mushroom structures under the microscope?

4. How are a mold and a mushroom similar? How are they different?

Extensions

Using a similar procedure, grow mold on an orange or other piece of fruit. Compare the mold that grows on the fruit to the bread mold and the mushroom.

Chapter **31** Review

Study Outline

31-1 Fungi

▶ The kingdom Fungi includes yeasts, molds, mushrooms, rusts, and smuts. All are nongreen and absorb nutrients from the environment. Most are saprobic; some are parasitic.

▶ Fungi are made up of a tangled mass of hyphae that form a mycelium. In most fungi, the cell walls are composed of chitin.

▶ Fungi are classified according to their method of sexual reproduction. They are divided into four phyla—conjugation fungi, sac fungi, club fungi, and imperfect fungi. All but the imperfect fungi reproduce both sexually and asexually by means of spores.

▶ Lichens are made up of an alga or a cyanobacterium and a fungus living together in symbiotic association.

31-2 Plants

▶ The kingdom Plantae includes mosses, ferns, conifers, and flowering plants. Plants are multicellular, photosynthetic organisms.

▶ The simplest plants, the bryophytes, include the mosses, liverworts, and hornworts. Bryophytes are short plants and must live in a moist area because they do not have vascular tissue.

▶ Tracheophytes contain the vascular tissues xylem and phloem. Tracheophytes are divided into two groups—the spore-dispersing plants and the seed plants.

▶ The spore-dispersing plants include the whisk ferns, club mosses, horsetails, and ferns. The seed plants include gymnosperms and angiosperms.

▶ Gymnosperms are plants that bear their seeds exposed on the scales of a cone. The gymnosperms include conifers, cycads, and ginkgoes.

▶ Angiosperms are flowering plants that have seeds enclosed within fruits. The angiosperms are divided into two major groups—the dicots and the monocots.

Chapter Assessment

Multiple Choice

Choose the letter of the answer that best completes each statement or answers the question.

1. The tangled mass that makes up the body of a fungus is the (a) hypha. (b) rhizoid. (c) mycelium. (d) stolon.

2. Fungi are organisms that do not (a) capture other organisms for food. (b) grow on their food source. (c) digest food outside their bodies. (d) absorb food through their cell walls.

3. The Basidiomycota are also known as (a) sac fungi. (b) club fungi. (c) imperfect fungi. (d) conjugation fungi.

4. An ascus is a (a) reproductive structure of a basidiomycete. (b) tough sac that contains spores. (c) mycelium specialized for absorbing nutrients. (d) mycelium specialized for absorbing water.

5. Which of the following are vascular plants? (a) ferns (b) mosses (c) liverworts (d) hornworts

6. Gymnosperms are plants that bear their seeds on the surfaces of (a) leaves. (b) flowers. (c) stems. (d) scales.

7. The specialized reproductive structure of an angiosperm is the (a) flower. (b) egg. (c) pollen. (d) cone.

8. Spruce, fir, and pine trees belong to the class of gymnosperms called (a) cycads. (b) conifers. (c) ginkgoes. (d) dicots.

9. Because of the lack of water in the desert, the only plants that live there are (a) seed plants. (b) ferns. (c) mosses and liverworts. (d) club mosses and horsetails.

10. The bryophytes have evolved life cycles that enable them to (a) survive in fresh water. (b) survive on land. (c) produce seeds. (d) produce flowers.

Content Review

Answer each of the following in complete sentences.

11. Describe the general structure of fungi.

12. How are sac fungi different from club fungi?

13. Describe the structure of a mushroom.

14. How are imperfect fungi different from other types of fungi?

15. What important role do lichens play in nature?

16. Why are green algae considered the evolutionary ancestors of plants?

17. What problems does life on land pose for plants?

18. What are the characteristics of bryophytes? What are the characteristics of tracheophytes?

19. Compare the production of seeds in gymnosperms and angiosperms.

20. Classify the following angiosperms as either monocots or dicots: Easter lily, cotton, magnolia, eggplant, onion, corn, tomato, coconut palm, oak, Kentucky bluegrass, rose, peppermint.

Graphic Organizing

For information on graphic organizers, see Appendix G at the back of this text.

21. Concept Map Copy the incomplete concept map onto a separate sheet of paper. Fill in the missing information. Add any other concepts you feel are important.

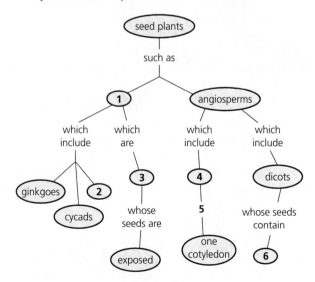

Critical Thinking and Problem Solving

Discuss each of the following in a brief paragraph.

22. Comparing Explain how obtaining nutrients is similar and how it differs in bryophytes and tracheophytes.

23. Predicting What might happen to bryophytes if they were grown in a dry environment? Explain.

24. Classifying Suppose that, while walking in the forest, you find three different kinds of fungi. Using a hand lens, you observe the spore-producing bodies of each specimen. The first fungus has a spore case at the end of a single upward-growing hyphae. The second has spores developing inside a saclike structure. The third has spores developing in a club-shaped structure. To which phylum of the kingdom Fungi does each specimen belong?

25. Comparing Conifers, cycads, grasses, and roses belong to four different plant groups. What characteristics do all of these plants share? How are conifers similar to cycads? How are grasses similar to roses? What characteristics are unique to each of these plants?

26. Experimenting Your friend claims that mold grows more rapidly in the daytime as a function of light. Design an experiment to test the validity of that claim. Use bread as a medium for the mold.

27. Calculating A mushroom examined under a microscope had five spores in the high-power field. Further examination would reveal that there are about 250 high-power fields on one side of one gill of this mushroom, which has 100 gills in its cap. Approximately how many spores are there on this mushroom?

Discovery Learning Activity

Observing Invertebrates

1. Working in a group, obtain the following animals from your teacher: a cnidarian, a flatworm, a nematode, a mollusk, and an annelid.

2. Observe these organisms for a few minutes using a hand lens. How does each animal move? Make labeled drawings of what you see.

Invertebrates—Sponges to Mollusks

Guide for Reading

Previewing the Chapter

A brightly colored crinoid emerges from an equally colorful soft coral. Although both of these organisms may look like plants, they are actually animals. Specifically, they are invertebrates—animals without backbones. Less exotic invertebrates include leeches, tapeworms, flukes, earthworms, and jellyfish. How are sponges different from jellyfish and corals? How are flatworms, roundworms, and segmented worms different from one another? What are the characteristics of mollusks?

Key Words

cnidarian, flatworm, invertebrate, mollusk, roundworm, segmented worm, sponge

Key Concepts

- **Compare** sponges and cnidarians.
- **Describe** the general characteristics of flatworms, roundworms, segmented worms, and mollusks.
- **Design an experiment** to determine how a hydra and a planarian respond to stimuli. (Laboratory Investigation)

32-1 The Animal Kingdom

Section Objectives:

- *Describe* the basic characteristics of animals.
- *Explain* how vertebrates and invertebrates differ.
- *Distinguish* between radial and bilateral symmetry.

Basic Characteristics of Animals

The animal kingdom, kingdom **Animalia,** is the largest of the six kingdoms. Animals are multicellular organisms that must obtain food from their environment. Most have nervous and muscular systems that allow them to move. Most animals reproduce sexually. Some of the simpler forms also reproduce asexually. In some animals, the young are different from the adult. In these cases, the young forms are known as **larvae** (LAR vee). The larvae undergo a series of developmental changes that produce the adult form.

Zoologists, scientists who study animals, divide the animal kingdom into about 30 phyla. The nine largest phyla contain the majority of species. It is these phyla that you will study. In this chapter and the next one, you will learn about those animals without backbones—the **invertebrates.** The following two chapters will deal with the **vertebrates,** animals with backbones.

▲ **Figure 32–1**

Invertebrates. These larvae of the sphinx moth are but one example of the many types of invertebrates that exist.

◀ A crinoid and some soft coral.

Symmetry

The bodies of most animals show *symmetry* (SIM uh tree). This means the body can be cut into two halves that have matching shapes. A few organisms, including amebas and most sponges, are *asymmetrical* (ay suh MEH trih kul). These organisms cannot be cut into two matching halves.

There are different kinds of symmetry. **Spherical symmetry** is found in a few protists. These organisms are in the shape of a sphere. As you can see in Figure 32–2, any cut passing through the center of the sphere divides the organism into matching halves.

In **radial** (RAY dee ul) **symmetry,** there is a central line, or axis, that runs the length of the animal from top to bottom or from front to rear. Any cross section at right angles to the central axis will show repeating structures arranged around the center like spokes in a wheel. See Figure 32–2. Cross sections at different levels are not alike, but any lengthwise cut down the center divides the animal into matching halves. The hydra shows radial symmetry. One end of the animal has a mouth and tentacles. The other end is closed and rounded. Any lengthwise cut down the center divides the hydra into matching halves, like the halves of a vase. Most animals showing radial symmetry either drift with the water currents or are *sessile,* living attached to a stationary object.

In **bilateral** (by LAT uh rul) **symmetry,** the organism varies from top to bottom and from front to back. See Figure 32–3. The human body shows bilateral symmetry. In this type of symmetry, there is only one way to divide the body into two symmetrical halves. Each half is a mirror image of the other. Bilaterally symmetrical animals have fixed right and left sides. There are special terms that describe positions other than right and left on bilaterally symmetrical animals. **Dorsal** (DOR sul) refers to the upper side or the back of the animal; **ventral** (VEN trul) is the lower, or belly, side of the animal. The front, or head, end of the animal is **anterior,** while the rear, or tail, end is **posterior.**

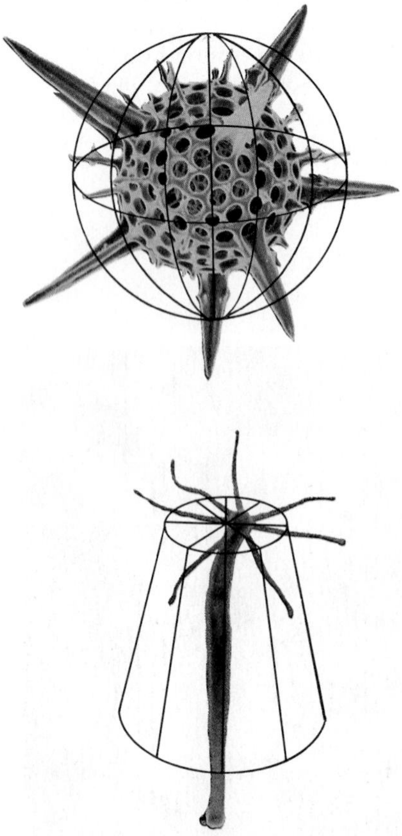

Figure 32–2

▲ **Figure 32–2**

Spherical and Radial Symmetry. A radiolarian skeleton (top) displays spherical symmetry. Any cut passing through its center divides it into equal parts. The hydra (bottom) displays radial symmetry. It can be divided into equal halves along many lengthwise planes.

Figure 32–3

Bilateral Symmetry. In bilateral symmetry, there is only one way to cut an organism into two equal parts. ▼

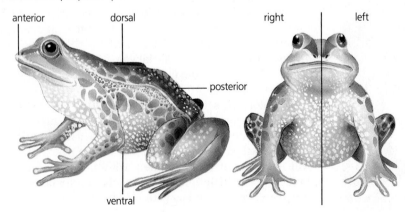

anterior   dorsal   right   left

posterior

ventral

32-1 **Section Review**

1. How do larvae compare with adult forms?
2. List the three kinds of body symmetry.
3. Give four characteristics that most animals have.

Critical Thinking

4. What type of symmetry is exhibited by the following objects: a basketball, a football, a baseball bat, a fork, and a pair of eyeglasses? (*Classifying*)

32-2 Sponges and Cnidarians

Section Objectives:

- *Describe* the structure of sponges and cnidarians.
- *Explain* how the following life processes are carried out in sponges and cnidarians: nutrition, excretion, respiration, and reproduction.
- *Describe* the two body forms found among cnidarians and name a cnidarian showing each body form.
- *Describe* the life cycle of *Aurelia*.

General Characteristics of Sponges

The *sponges,* phylum **Porifera** (puh RIF uh ruh), are the simplest multicellular animals. *Porifera* means "pore bearing." Sponges are pierced by many **pores,** or holes, through which water moves continuously. All sponges are aquatic. Most are marine, which means they live in salt water. A few live in fresh water. Although the larvae are free-swimming, adult sponges are *sessile.* They usually live attached to shells or rocks on the ocean floor. There are some sponges that are found in colonies. Some colonies look like plants with individuals branching from a common stem. Other sponges live singly.

Sponges vary widely in size and shape. Most sponges are asymmetrical. Some are the size of a pearl, while others may be the size of a bathtub. Simple sponges are shaped like hollow, upright cylinders or vases. More complex sponges have folds in the body walls. Still other types of sponges have complex systems of canals and chambers within the body walls. Many sponges are gray or black, but others are bright red, yellow, orange, or blue, as you can see in Figure 32-4.

In the past, some types of sponges were used for household cleaning and as bath sponges. Today, however, most commercial sponges are artificially made.

Figure 32–4

Sponges. Sponges are the simplest multicellular animals. There are about 10 000 species of sponges. ▼

Structure and Life Functions of Sponges

Sponges have a simple level of organization. Although their cells show specialization and are present in layers, they do not form true tissues. As Figure 32–5 illustrates, the sponge body is composed of three layers. The outer layer, which consists of thin, flat, epidermal cells, is pierced by numerous pores. These pores allow water, dissolved oxygen, and food particles (microscopic plants and animals) to enter the sponge. The inner layer contains specialized cells called **collar cells.** These cells have a collar of cytoplasm that extends from the cell into the central cavity. Extending through the collar of each cell is a flagellum.

Between the outer and inner cell layers is a middle layer of jellylike material that contains wandering *amebocytes,* amebalike cells. Embedded in the jellylike material of many sponges are small skeletal structures called **spicules** (SPIK yoolz), which are secreted by some of the amebocytes. Spicules provide support and give shape to the sponge. Sponges are classified according to the chemical makeup of their spicules. One group of sponges has spicules composed of calcium compounds; another group has spicules composed of silica. The third group has a network of tough, flexible fibers made of a protein-containing substance called **spongin.**

The pores of the sponge allow water to enter the body of the sponge. Water is drawn into the sponge and circulated in the central cavity by the beating of the flagella of the collar cells. From the central cavity, water passes out of the sponge through the **osculum** (AHS kyoo lum). The osculum is a large opening at the top, or unattached end, of the sponge.

As water passes through the sponge, food particles are captured, ingested, and digested by the collar cells. The amebocytes of the middle layer pick up partly digested food from the collar cells. The amebocytes finish digesting the food and then carry the nutrients to other parts of the sponge.

Wastes diffuse out of the cells into the central cavity of the sponge and leave with the water through the osculum. Gases (oxygen and carbon dioxide) are exchanged by diffusion between the cells and the water. Although sponges have no specialized nerve or muscle cells, some of the cells surrounding the pores respond to harmful substances in the water by closing the pores.

Sponges can reproduce sexually or asexually. In sexual reproduction, some collar cells change into gametes. Both male and female gametes are formed in the same sponge, but self-fertilization does not occur. Mature sperm leave the sponge through the osculum and are drawn into other sponges through their pores. The eggs are found in the jellylike middle layer. After fertilization, the zygote begins cleavage. Eventually, the embryo develops into a free-swimming larva. The larva passes through the inner cell layer and leaves the mother sponge through the osculum. After a time, the larva becomes attached to the ocean floor and develops into an adult sponge.

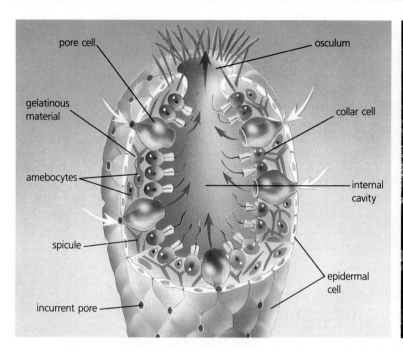

Asexual reproduction usually occurs by budding. Groups of cells on the parent sponge divide to form buds. The buds eventually break off and grow into new individuals. When conditions that are unfavorable for budding or sexual reproduction arise, some fresh-water sponges form asexual reproductive structures that are called **gemmules** (JEM yoolz). The gemmule is a group of cells that are enclosed by a tough outer covering. When environmental conditions become favorable, each gemmule develops into a new sponge. Sponges also have a remarkable capacity for regeneration. They can be cut up into many small pieces, and each piece will grow into a new sponge.

▲ **Figure 32–5**

Structure of a Sponge. Sponges filter food from water pumped through the pores of their body. Water passes out of the osculum, the opening at the unattached end of the sponge.

General Characteristics of Cnidarians

Hydras, jellyfishes, corals, and sea anemones (uh NEM uh neez) belong to the phylum **Cnidaria** (nigh DAIR ee ah) with over 10 000 living species. *Cnidarians* show a more complex level of organization than the sponges. Cnidarians are aquatic. Hydras live in fresh water, but most other cnidarians are marine. There are two general body forms found among the cnidarians. These are shown in Figure 32–6. The **polyp** (PAHL ip) form is usually sessile and has a cylindrical body with a mouth and tentacles at the upper free end. Corals, sea anemones, and hydras are some examples of polyps. The other form, the **medusa** (muh DOO suh), is shaped like an upside-down bowl, with the mouth and tentacles facing downward. The medusa is usually free-swimming. Jellyfishes show the medusa body form. Although the two body forms look different, they possess the same basic structure—a hollow sac with a single opening, the mouth, surrounded by tentacles. Most adult cnidarians show radial symmetry.

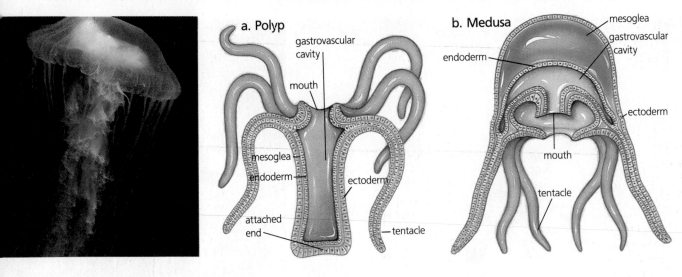

▲ **Figure 32–6**

Body Forms of Cnidarians. The sea nettle (left) is a common jellyfish found along the Atlantic coast. Cnidarians have two body forms, the polyp form (middle), which is usually sessile, and the medusa form (right), which is free-swimming.

Structure and Life Functions of Cnidarians

The cnidarians show a tissue level of organization. There are two cell layers, the endoderm (inner layer) and the ectoderm (outer layer). These are separated by a jellylike material, composed largely of protein, called the **mesoglea** (mez uh GLEE uh). The ectoderm cells contain contractile fibers. When these fibers contract, the animal moves. However, for the medusas, which are free-swimming, the strength of these contractions is not great enough to overcome the movement of the water. Thus, medusas drift with currents in the water.

Specialized stinging cells called **cnidoblasts** (NYED uh blasts) are characteristic of cnidarians. They are used for defense and for capturing food. Within the cnidoblasts are **nematocysts** (NEM uh tuh sists), which are small, fluid-filled capsules containing a coiled thread. When a cnidoblast on a tentacle is stimulated by pressure, the nematocyst is discharged. The thread uncoils and entangles the prey. Some nematocysts contain poison, which is injected into the prey and paralyzes it. Once the prey is captured, the tentacles of the cnidarian stuff it into the mouth. The structure and function of cnidoblasts in the hydra are discussed in Chapter 8.

The internal body cavity of cnidarians is known as the **gastrovascular cavity.** The single opening serves as both a mouth and an anus. Extracellular digestion takes place in the cavity. Enzymes secreted into the cavity by some of the cells of the endoderm begin the process of extracellular digestion. When the food is partially digested, it is engulfed by the endoderm cells, where digestion is completed within food vacuoles. Thus, digestion is both extracellular and intracellular.

No respiratory or excretory system is found in cnidarians. Oxygen is obtained and wastes are excreted by diffusion. The first true nerve cells are found in the cnidarians. The nerve cells form

Corals. Corals are small polyps that grow in colonies. Unlike hydras, they are surrounded by a hard skeleton.

a *nerve net,* which sends impulses in all directions. These animals do not have brains, but the movement of the tentacles shows coordination.

Corals   Many of the structures and life functions of polyps are described in the sections on the hydra in Unit 2. *Corals* (KOR ulz) are small polyps that grow in colonies. See Figure 32–7. Corals are surrounded by a hard, calcium-containing skeleton, which they secrete. In warm, shallow parts of the ocean, islands and large coral reefs are formed by massive colonies of corals. These reefs are among the most productive areas in the world. Coral reefs provide shelter to a great number of different species of invertebrates and fish. In fact, some coral reefs in the Caribbean sea are home to more than 300 species of fish.

Aurelia   *Aurelia* (or EEL yuh) is a common jellyfish. Its life cycle includes both medusa and polyp forms, as shown in Figure 32–8. The jellylike body of the medusa is the form frequently seen on beaches. Protective tentacles hang from the edge of the umbrella-like body. The sexes are separate in *Aurelia,* but the male and female look alike. Sperm from the male medusa are released into the surrounding water. Some sperm cells enter the gastrovascular cavity of a female medusa, where fertilization occurs. Early development occurs while the zygote is attached to the female. The zygote develops into a small, oval-shaped, ciliated larva called a **planula** (PLAN yuh luh). The planula is free-swimming for some time. It then becomes attached by one end to a rock or some other structure on the ocean floor. At this point, the larva develops a mouth and tentacles at the unattached end and becomes a polyp. The polyp grows until it can reproduce asexually by budding to form medusas. During the fall and winter, a series of horizontal divisions make the polyp look like a stack of saucers. One by one, the saucer-shaped structures break off from the top and grow into full-sized medusas.

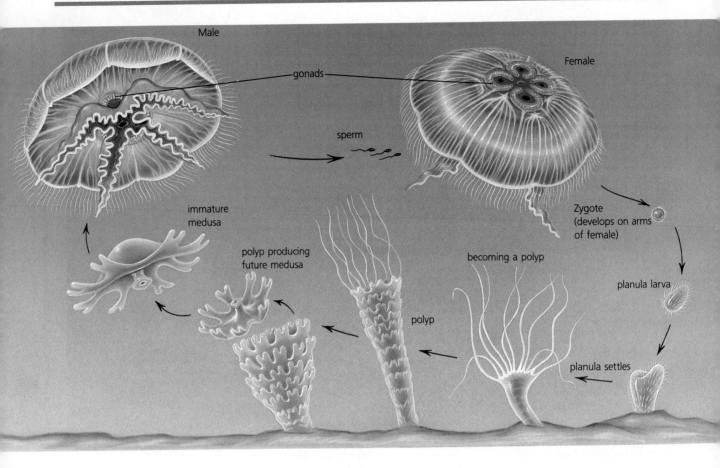

Male

gonads

Female

sperm

immature
medusa

polyp producing
future medusa

becoming a polyp

Zygote
(develops on arms
of female)

planula larva

polyp

planula settles

▲ **Figure 32–8**

Life Cycle of *Aurelia*. The life cycle of *Aurelia* shows an alternation of the polyp and medusa body forms.

The alternation of the medusa form with the polyp form is characteristic of some cnidarians. The medusa stage reproduces sexually by the production of eggs and sperm. It gives rise to the polyp stage. The polyp stage reproduces asexually by budding and gives rise to the medusa stage.

32-2 Section Review

1. How does water enter the body of a sponge?
2. What structures provide support to the sponge?
3. Name four cnidarians.
4. Name the two body forms found in the cnidarians.

Critical Thinking

5. Do you think a sponge could survive without amebocytes? Explain. (*Relating Parts and Wholes*)

32-3 Flatworms and Roundworms

Section Objectives:

- *Name* the phylum to which flatworms belong and list a representative animal from each of the three classes of flatworms.
- *Describe* the structure and life cycle of planaria, blood flukes, and tapeworms.
- *Describe* the general characteristics and structure of roundworms.
- *Explain* the life cycles of the following roundworms and how they affect humans: trichina, filaria, pinworm, and hookworm.

General Characteristics of Flatworms

The *flatworms,* phylum **Platyhelminthes** (plat ee hel MIN theez), are the simplest animals showing bilateral symmetry. The flatworms are also the simplest invertebrate group showing definite head and tail regions. These animals are called flatworms because their bodies are flattened. There are three major groups of flatworms: free-living flatworms, such as planaria (pluh NEHR ee uh); parasitic flukes; and parasitic tapeworms. Many parasitic flukes and tapeworms have life cycles with more than one host. Usually, the first host is an invertebrate, while the final host is a vertebrate. Free-living flatworms are usually aquatic and are found in both fresh and salt water.

Structure and Life Functions of Flatworms

The body of the flatworm has three distinct tissue layers—ectoderm, mesoderm, and endoderm. These tissues are organized into organs and organ systems. Thus, the flatworms are also the simplest animals with mesodermic layers and organ-system levels of organization.

Planaria   *Planaria,* class **Turbellaria** (ter buh LEHR ee uh), are examples of typical flatworms. Planaria are found in freshwater streams and ponds, where they cling to the bottoms of leaves, rocks, and logs. These animals are gray, brown, or black in color and about 5 to 25 millimeters in length. As you can see in Figure 32–9, the triangular head contains a pair of *eyespots.* Although the eyespots cannot actually detect images, they are sensitive to light, which these animals avoid.

   Planaria can move about freely. A piece of liver placed in a stream will be covered with them in a few hours. Moving planaria appear to be gliding over a surface because the underside of the body is covered with microscopic cilia that move the animal. Muscles enable them to change their shape or direction.

Figure 32–9
External Structure of a Planarian. The planarian is a common freshwater flatworm. ▼

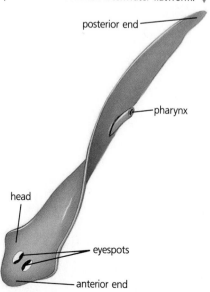

posterior end

pharynx

head

eyespots

anterior end

Figure 32–10

Internal Structure of a Planarian. Flame cells move excess water and liquid wastes into and along the planarian's excretory canal. The nervous system is ladderlike, with two main nerves connected by shorter nerves that run the length of the body. The digestive system consists of a mouth, pharynx, and a highly branched intestine. ▶

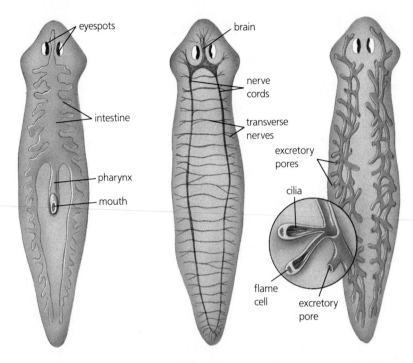

The planarian has a digestive system made up of a mouth, a pharynx, and a highly branched intestine, as shown in Figure 32–10. The muscular **pharynx** is a tube that can be extended through the mouth opening for eating. The mouth is located at the midline on the underside of the body. Planaria feed on living or dead small animals. The pharynx can suck small bits of food into the digestive cavity. Most digestion takes place within food vacuoles in the cells lining the intestine. Digested food diffuses to all cells of the body. Indigestible materials are expelled through the pharynx and mouth.

Planaria have no skeletal, circulatory, or respiratory system. Oxygen and carbon dioxide diffuse into and out of individual cells. A series of tubules that run the length of the body make up the excretory system of planaria. Side branches of the tubules have cells called *flame cells.* These cells remove excess water and liquid wastes from the body and pass them into ducts. The contents of the ducts pass out of the worm through small *excretory pores* on the dorsal surface.

The nervous system includes a small brain beneath the eyespots. From the brain, two nerve cords run the length of the body along either side. Connecting transverse nerves make the nervous system look like a ladder. This ladderlike nervous system enables the planarian to respond to stimuli in a coordinated manner.

Planaria have well-developed reproductive systems. They are *hermaphroditic,* which means that each individual has both ovaries and testes. However, self-fertilization does not occur. Instead, two planaria mate and exchange sperm. Fertilization is internal, and the fertilized eggs are shed in capsules. In a few weeks, the eggs hatch into tiny worms, which grow into adults. The planarian can

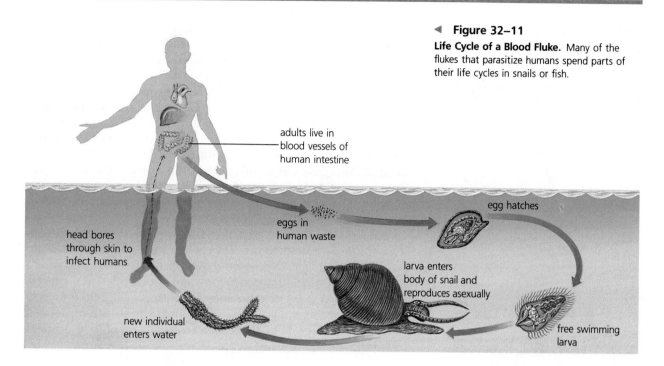

Figure 32–11
Life Cycle of a Blood Fluke. Many of the flukes that parasitize humans spend parts of their life cycles in snails or fish.

adults live in
blood vessels of
human intestine

egg hatches

eggs in
human waste

head bores
through skin to
infect humans

larva enters
body of snail and
reproduces asexually

new individual
enters water

free swimming
larva

regenerate an entire animal from a fairly small segment. It can also reproduce asexually by fission, separating its tail end from its head end. Each half regenerates the missing structures.

Flukes   *Flukes* are parasitic flatworms of the class **Trematoda** (trem uh TOHD uh). The body of the fluke is covered with a thick cuticle that protects the parasite from the enzymes of its host once it has entered the host's body. Suckers allow the fluke to attach itself to the tissues of its host. Because the food obtained from the host has already been broken down, flukes do not need well-developed digestive systems.

The blood fluke is a typical fluke. In humans, this parasite causes a disease called *schistosomiasis* (shis tuh soh MY uh sis). The adult fluke is about one centimeter long and lives in the blood vessels of the human intestine. See Figure 32–11. Here, it lays thousands of eggs that pass out of the body with digestive wastes. If the eggs land in water, they hatch into free-swimming larvae. They then enter the bodies of snails, where they reproduce asexually. The new individuals leave the snails and infect streams, rice paddies, and irrigation ditches. Upon contact with humans, the flukes bore through the skin and start their reproductive cycle again. The blood fluke causes loss of blood, diarrhea, and severe pain.

Tapeworms   *Tapeworms* are parasitic flatworms of the class **Cestoda** (ses TOHD uh). The beef tapeworm, which can infect humans, is a long, ribbonlike flatworm. Adults may be from four to nine meters in length. These worms have excretory and nervous systems and highly developed reproductive systems. They lack mouths and digestive systems. Tapeworms live as parasites in the

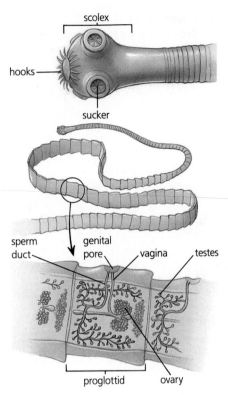

▲ **Figure 32–12**
Structure of a Tapeworm. The sucker and hooks on the tapeworm's scolex are adaptations for attachment.

intestine and absorb digested food through their skin. The suckers on the knoblike head, or *scolex* (SKOH leks), hold the tapeworm in place. Some tapeworms, such as the pork tapeworm, have hooks as well as suckers. See Figure 32–12.

Below the head and neck are square body segments called **proglottids** (proh GLAHT idz). These segments are produced continuously by budding from the neck region. The proglottids are reproductive structures that produce both sperm and eggs. Periodically, the end segments, filled with over 100 000 fertilized eggs, break off and pass out of the host in the feces. If cattle eat food contaminated with eggs, the eggs develop into larvae in the intestine. The larvae burrow into blood vessels and are carried to the muscle, where they form a dormant capsule.

Humans can become infected when they eat undercooked beef. The capsule surrounding the larva is digested, which releases the small tapeworm. The tapeworm then attaches itself to the wall of the human intestine. Proglottids form and are excreted in the feces. When cattle eat grain or grass infected with proglottids, the cycle begins again. Human tapeworms cause illness by absorbing needed nutrients. They may actually obstruct the passage of food through the intestine.

General Characteristics of Roundworms

The phylum **Nematoda** (nem uh TOHD uh) consists of slender, bilaterally symmetrical *nematodes* (NEM uh tohdz), or *roundworms*. Roundworms have elongated, cylindrical bodies that are tapered at both ends and covered with a tough cuticle. Roundworms range in length from less than one millimeter to more than one meter. Many roundworms are free-living, while others are parasitic. The free-living forms are found in fresh water, salt water, and in soil anywhere from the polar regions to the tropics. They feed on algae, plant sap, and decaying organic matter. Parasitic roundworms live on or in most kinds of plants and animals. The actual number of roundworms present in the environment is tremendous. It has been estimated that 1 million or more roundworms are present in one shovel load of garden soil.

Structure and Life Functions of Roundworms

Roundworms, unlike flatworms, have two openings to their tubular digestive system. Food is taken in through the mouth at the anterior end, and undigested material passes out through the *anus* at the posterior end. Roundworms are the simplest of the animals having complete digestive systems with two openings and a tube-within-a-tube body plan.

Roundworms have no circulatory or respiratory system. They do have a simple excretory system as well as a nervous system. Well-developed muscles located in the body wall allow them to move in a characteristic whiplike fashion.

Roundworms also have well-developed reproductive systems. The sexes are separate, and fertilization occurs within the body of the female. In free-living forms, the fertilized eggs, which are surrounded by a thick shell, are deposited in soil. The newly hatched young resemble the adults.

Most roundworms are parasites, and the diseases caused by them are widespread. Many of those diseases can be controlled by good personal hygiene, proper sanitation, and thorough cooking of food. Some drugs are also useful in controlling these parasites. Trichina, filaria, pinworm, and hookworm are parasitic roundworms that infect humans.

Trichina   The roundworm that causes *trichinosis* (trik uh NOH sis) in humans is called *trichina* (trih KY nuh). Adult trichina worms live in the intestines of hogs. When these worms reproduce, the resulting larvae invade the muscles of the hog. They grow to about one millimeter in length, then curl up, and become enclosed in hard cysts. When pork that has not been cooked well enough to kill the organisms is eaten by a human, digestive enzymes release the larvae from the cysts. The larvae develop into adults in the human intestines and reproduce sexually. The new larvae move through the blood vessels and muscles just as the larvae did in hogs. The movement of the worms through muscle causes intense pain and can cause permanent damage to the muscle. Trichinosis can be prevented easily by cooking pork thoroughly. Hogs become infected when they are fed infected scraps of uncooked meat. Because of better sanitary procedures used today for raising hogs, trichinosis is no longer very common.

Filaria   *Filaria* (fuh LEHR ee uh) cause a disease known as *elephantiasis* (el uh fun TY uh sis). These roundworms are carried by a species of mosquito found in tropical and subtropical regions. Filaria worms are spread to humans by the bite of an infected mosquito. Once in the human body, they invade the lymphatic system. There, they block lymph vessels and cause fluid to accumulate and tissues to swell. The area of the body in which they lodge often becomes abnormally large, damaging the tissues involved. Within the lymph tissues, the worms reproduce sexually and reproduce larvae that enter the bloodstream. A mosquito becomes infected when it bites an infected person. The larvae mature within the mosquito, and the cycle begins again with the bite of the infected mosquito.

Pinworms   One of the more common parasitic roundworms often found in children is the *pinworm*. Tiny adult pinworms live in the large intestine. The female worms deposit their eggs in the anal region. The presence of the eggs causes itching. When the child scratches, some eggs get on the fingers. Children reinfect themselves when they put their unclean fingers in their mouths. Pinworms live only a few weeks. Thus, if reinfection can be prevented by cleanliness, the pinworms disappear within a short time.

Hookworm The *hookworm* is a roundworm that infects people in warm climates who walk barefoot on contaminated soil. The hookworm lives in the small intestine, and its eggs leave the body in the feces. When sewage disposal is inadequate, the eggs hatch into larvae on the ground. If people then come into contact with them, the larvae bore through the skin. Once in the body, they are carried to the lungs by the circulatory system. They bore through the lungs, are coughed up, swallowed, and pass again to the small intestine. There, they suck blood from the intestinal wall. Symptoms of hookworm infection include anemia and lack of energy.

32-3 Section Review

1. What type of symmetry do flatworms have?
2. List the three major groups of flatworms.
3. Where are roundworms found?
4. List some parasitic roundworms that infect humans.

Critical Thinking

5. List two similarities and two differences between roundworms and flatworms. (*Comparing and Contrasting*)

32-4 Segmented Worms and Mollusks

Section Objectives:

- *Describe* the general characteristics and structure of segmented worms and mollusks and give representative examples of classes of these phyla.
- *Compare* and *contrast* the structure of the marine worm *Nereis* with the structure of the earthworm.
- *Describe* respiration, nutrition, circulation, excretion, and reproduction in clams.
- *Explain* some of the ways in which gastropods and cephalopods differ from bivalves.

General Characteristics of Segmented Worms

The most familiar worms are those of the phylum **Annelida** (uh NEL uh duh), the *segmented worms*. This phylum includes the earthworm, class **Oligochaeta** (ahl ig oh KEET uh), and the leech, class **Hirudinea** (hir yuh DIN ee uh). The most striking characteristic of the segmented worms, which are also called the *annelids* (AN uh lidz), is the division of the body into separate sections, or segments. Segmented worms are found in both salt and fresh water and on land. Most of these worms are free-living, but a few of them are parasites. Segmented worms can range in length from less than one millimeter to more than two meters.

Structure and Life Functions of Segmented Worms

Segmented worms are bilaterally symmetrical. Their bodies are divided, externally and internally, into segments. These worms are the simplest of the invertebrates that have a closed circulatory system. Like more complex animals, segmented worms have a tube-within-a-tube body plan. The digestive tract, which is lined with endoderm, is the inner tube. It is open at both ends—mouth and anus. The body wall, which is covered with ectoderm, makes up the outer tube. A fluid-filled body cavity is found between the two tubes. This cavity is called a **coelom** (SEE lum) and is lined with mesoderm, as shown in Figure 32–13. The segmented worms are the simplest of the animals that have true coeloms.

Nereis   In most ways, the marine sandworm *Nereis* (NEHR ee is), class **Polychaeta** (pahl ee KEET uh), is similar to the earthworm, which was described in Unit 2. However, there are a few important differences between these two animals.

Nereis lives at tide level, in the intertidal zone. It emerges at night and crawls along the sand or swims in the shallow sea. During the day, it stays in a temporary burrow in mud or sand with its head poking out. Green in color, *Nereis* is composed of about 200 similar segments. The first two segments form a distinct head. The first segment, which is called the *prostomium* (proh STOH mee um), has two short tentacles, two pairs of small eyes, and two other appendages called *palps*. The second segment, which is called the *peristomium* (pehr uh STOH mee um), surrounds the mouth. It has four pairs of tentacles. The structures found on the first two segments serve for finding food and for protection. Except for the first, second, and last segments, a pair of paddlelike extensions called **parapodia** (par uh POHD ee uh) is found on each segment. Parapodia are used for swimming and for creeping over the sand. Parapodia also aid in respiration by providing a surface for gas exchange. Bristlelike *setae* are located on the parapodia. See Figure 32–14.

Nereis eats small animals, which it captures by extending its pharynx out through its mouth. The pharynx has a pair of hard, pointed jaws that grasp the food. As the jaws are pulled back into the mouth, the food is swallowed. The food passes into the esophagus and then to the intestine, where it is digested. Undigested food is eliminated through the anus on the last segment.

Circulation, excretion, and respiration in *Nereis* are basically the same as in the earthworm. The nervous system is also similar.

In *Nereis,* sexes are separate. During the mating season, eggs and sperm develop in the coelom. Eventually, they pass out through the excretory organs (nephridia) or break through the body surface into the sea. Fertilization is external, and the zygote

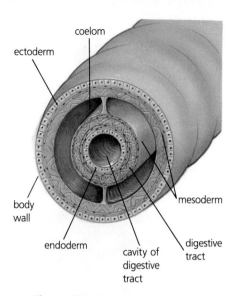

▲ **Figure 32–13**

The Coelom. The coelom is a fluid-filled cavity found between the inner and outer body tubes of annelids and more complex animals.

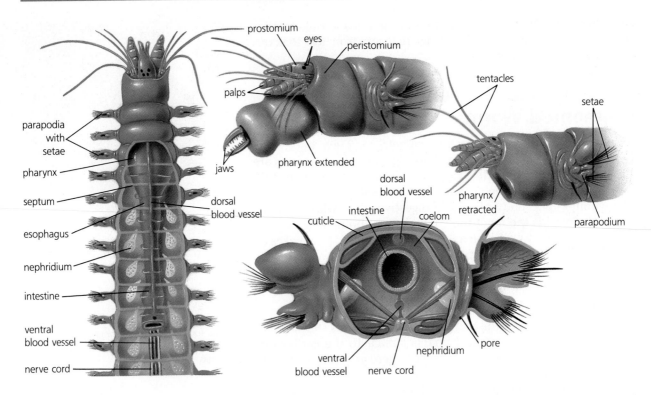

▲ **Figure 32–14**
Structure of the Marine Sandworm *Nereis*.

Figure 32–15

A Trochophore Larva. The life cycle of many mollusks includes the free-swimming, ciliated trocophore larva. ▼

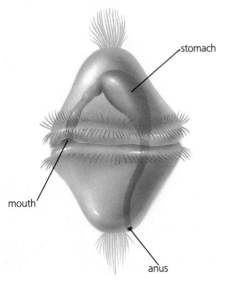

develops into a free-swimming, ciliated **trochophore** (TROH kuh for) **larva,** as shown in Figure 32–15. As the larva develops, the mouth and segments with parapodia appear. Eventually, the young worm settles to the ocean bottom and begins the adult stage of life.

Leeches   *Leeches* are mostly freshwater animals that are parasites of vertebrates. Some are found in moist soil. Most live on the blood of their prey. Segmentation is not easily noticed in leeches. Leeches have suckers at both their anterior and posterior ends. In feeding, the leech attaches itself to its host with its hind sucker. It then attaches the anterior sucker, which contains the mouth and three small jaws. The jaws break through the host's skin. The saliva of the leech contains an enzyme that prevents the host's blood from clotting while it is being sucked up. The leech can ingest many times its own body weight of blood in one feeding. When the leech is full, it drops off the host and remains inactive for long periods. During these periods the blood, which has been stored in the digestive tract, is gradually digested. Leeches are hermaphrodites, but cross fertilization takes place when two leeches exchange sperm. The fertilized eggs develop in water or soil.

General Characteristics of Mollusks

The *mollusks,* phylum **Mollusca** (mahl US kuh) are a highly successful animal group. They are the second largest animal phylum, after the arthropods. Oysters, clams, snails, squids, and octopuses are familiar mollusks. Mollusks are found in salt water, in fresh water, and on land. Members of this group vary greatly in size and shape. See Figure 32–16. Mollusks range from tiny snails 1 millimeter long to giant squids, which can reach 16 meters in length and weigh 2 tons. The giant clam of the South Pacific Ocean can be 1.5 meters long and weigh 250 kilograms.

Many types of mollusks are used by humans for food. Among them are oysters, clams, scallops, mussels, snails, squids, and octopuses. Pearls from oysters are used in jewelry, and mollusk shell is used in buttons and decorative objects. On the other hand, some snails and slugs feed on crops and are highly destructive.

There are three major classes of mollusks: the *bivalves,* class **Bivalvia** (by VALV ee uh), include mollusks with two-part shells, such as clams, oysters, and mussels. The *gastropods* (GAS truh pahdz), class **Gastropoda** (ga STRAHP uh duh), include mollusks with a single shell, such as snails. And the *cephalopods* (SEF uh luh pahdz), class **Cephalopoda** (sef uh LAHP uh duh), include mollusks with little or no shell, such as squids and octopuses. Many marine mollusks have a trochophore larva similar to the trochophore larva of marine segmented worms. This is thought to indicate an evolutionary relationship between the two groups.

▲ **Figure 32–16**

A Mollusk. The nudibranch, or sea slug, has lost its shell during evolution.

Structure and Life Functions of Mollusks

Although adult mollusks vary widely in appearance, they share a number of common characteristics. They are bilaterally symmetrical, and they are composed of three tissue layers. They also have a coelom. All mollusks have a soft body that houses all the organ systems—the digestive system, heart, nervous system, reproductive system, and so on. The foot, mantle, shell, and radula are structures found only in mollusks.

The large, ventral muscular **foot** functions in movement. In clams, the foot is used to burrow or plow through wet sand or mud. The snail uses its foot to creep over rocks or plants. The foot of the squid and octopus is divided into tentacles and covered with suckers. The tentacles are used for seizing and holding prey.

The **mantle** is a fold of skin that surrounds the body organs. In the squid and octopus, the muscular mantle is used for movement. In mollusks with shells, the mantle is a glandular tissue that secretes part of the shell.

Figure 32–17

Oyster with Pearl. The finest natural pearls are produced by the pearl oysters, but pearls are formed in most bivalves, including freshwater clams. ▼

The **radula** (RAD joo luh) is a rasping, tonguelike organ found in all mollusks except bivalves. The radula has many rows of teeth and can extend out of the mouth to scrape food from an object and bring it into the digestive system. Some snails use the radula to drill holes in the shells of other mollusks. They then suck out the soft body of the mollusk for food.

The Bivalves   Bivalves, such as clams, scallops, oysters, and mussels, have a shell made up of two parts. The smooth, shiny, innermost layer of the shell, which is just outside the mantle, is called *mother-of-pearl.* See Figure 32–17. In some bivalves, pearls are produced when an irritant, such as sand, gets between the mantle and the shell. The mantle walls off the irritant by secreting mother-of-pearl around it. Eventually, a pearl is formed.

Figure 32–18
Structure of a Clam. ▶

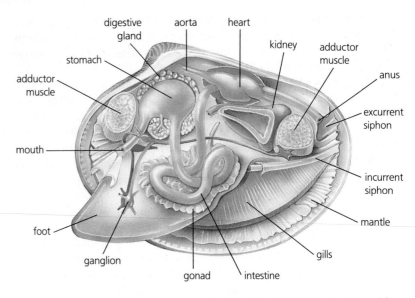

The two halves of the clam's shell can be held firmly closed by two strong *adductor* muscles. See Figure 32–18. When the muscles relax, an elastic hinge keeps the shell open. Usually, the shells are partly open with two tubes extending into the water. One tube, the *incurrent siphon* (SY fun), carries water containing food particles into the mantle cavity. The water is kept in motion by the beating of cilia on the gills. As the water moves over the gills, the exchange of respiratory gases occurs between the blood in the gills and the water. Food particles in the water are trapped by mucus on the gills. The water then flows out of the mantle cavity through the *excurrent siphon.*

Food particles stuck in the mucus on the gills are transported by the cilia into the mouth and then into the rest of the digestive system. Animals that feed by filtering water through their bodies are called *filter feeders.* They feed on organic particles and dead and decaying microscopic organisms in the water.

The clam has an open circulatory system that is made up of a heart and vessels. When the blood reaches the body tissues, it flows out of the vessels and into the body spaces, or *sinuses,* where it bathes the body tissues. From the sinuses, the blood flows into vessels that carry it to the gills. After the exchange of respiratory gases, the blood flows back to the heart.

The clam has a pair of kidneys that remove organic wastes from the blood and empty them into the water through the excurrent siphon. The nervous system consists of three pairs of ganglia connected by nerves to the foot and body organs. Sensory cells enable the clam to respond to chemical changes in the water, to touch, and to light.

In clams, the sexes are separate. Sperm leave the male through the excurrent siphon. They then enter the female through the incurrent siphon. The eggs are held on the gills, where they are fertilized. The young bivalves pass through one or more distinct larval stages before reaching the adult form.

Figure 32–19

A Gastropod. The garden snail, like most gastropods, has a coiled shell. Other gastropods may have cone-shaped shells, and some have no shells at all. ▼

The Gastropods   Snails, whelks, abalones (ab uh LOH neez), conches (KAHN chez), and slugs make up the largest group of mollusks, the gastropods. Most gastropods have a single shell, which is often coiled. A few, such as the slug, lack a shell. Some are aquatic; others are terrestrial.

The common garden snail has a head with tentacles, eyes, and a mouth, as shown in Figure 32–19. The head is connected to the foot. The shell is on top of the foot. For protection in times of danger, all the soft parts of the body can be drawn into the shell. Land snails have simple lungs rather than gills, which are found in aquatic snails. Air is drawn into the mantle cavity, and gas exchange occurs through the mantle.

Land snails usually travel at night when the air is moist. They slide along on a layer of mucus secreted by the foot. To keep from drying out during the day, the snail withdraws into its shell and seals the opening with mucus. The land snail feeds by rubbing its radula against plant material. As the pieces of plant are shredded, they are taken into the mouth.

The Cephalopods   The most advanced mollusks, the cephalopods, include squids, octopuses, and cuttlefish. All cephalopods are marine predators. See Figure 32–20. These animals do not look like other mollusks. The most obvious difference is that most cephalopods have either no shell (the octopus) or a small, internal shell (the squid and cuttlefish). Only a few, such as the nautilus, are enclosed in a shell.

In cephalopods, the mouth is surrounded by tentacles. The tentacles are used to gather food and to manipulate objects. The streamlined bodies of cephalopods permit rapid swimming. Cephalopods swim by expelling a jet of water from their mantle cavity. They have a well-developed nervous system with a large brain. In structure, the eye of the octopus is similar to the eyes of vertebrates, and it works in the same way. In times of danger, some cephalopods, such as squids and octopuses, discharge an inky fluid. This creates a "smoke screen," which distracts the enemy and allows the animal to escape.

▲ **Figure 32–20**

A Cephalopod. Octopuses live on the sea floor where they search for crabs and other food. These animals are believed to be one of the most intelligent of the invertebrates.

32-4 Section Review

1. What is the most striking characteristic that is found in the segmented worms?
2. Where are segmented worms found?
3. Name an organism from each of the three major classes of mollusks.
4. Where are mollusks found?

Critical Thinking

5. Why do taxonomists believe that segmented worms and mollusks are closely related? (*Identifying Reasons*)

Laboratory
Investigation

Designing an Experiment

Observing a Hydra and a Planarian

Like all living things, hydras and planarians respond to stimuli, or changes in their environment. In hydras and planarians, these responses depend on a nervous system. The hydra's nervous system consists of a nerve net, whereas the planarian's nervous system has a small brain, two eyespots, and two main nerve cords. In this investigation, you will observe a hydra and a planarian and see how they respond to different stimuli.

Problem

How do a hydra and a planarian respond to different stimuli? **Design an experiment** to answer this question.

Suggested Materials

- hydra culture
- planarian culture
- medicine droppers
- culture dishes
- colored brine shrimp
- compound microscope
- toothpicks
- stereomicroscope
- blunt metal probe
- coverslips
- petroleum jelly
- depression slides
- dilute acid solution

Suggested Procedure

1. Using a medicine dropper, transfer a hydra to a small culture dish half filled with water.

2. Observe the hydra under the stereomicroscope. Sketch and label its structures.

3. Add a few brine shrimp to the culture dish. Use the stereomicroscope to observe how the hydra reacts to brine shrimp.

4. To observe the hydra under the compound microscope, prepare a "hanging drop." First, use a toothpick to dab a small amount of petroleum jelly on the corners of the upper side of a coverslip.

5. Use a medicine dropper to transfer the hydra to the middle of the coverslip. Hold a depression slide over the coverslip, depression side down, and lower it onto the coverslip, as shown in the illustration. Turn the slide over so the coverslip faces up.

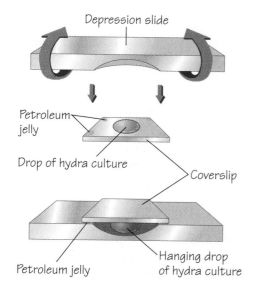

Depression slide

Petroleum jelly

Drop of hydra culture

Coverslip

Petroleum jelly

Hanging drop of hydra culture

6. Using the low-power objective of a compound microscope, observe the hydra and brine shrimp. Record your observations. When you have finished, return the hydra to your teacher.

7. Using a similar procedure, design an experiment to determine how a hydra responds to the following stimuli:
   • light touch from a toothpick
   • dilute acid solution

8. Using steps 1 to 3, design an experiment to determine how a planarian responds to the following stimuli:
   • light touch from a metal probe
   • brine shrimp

9. Write your hypotheses. With your teacher's approval, carry out the experiments you designed. Record your observations.

Observations

1. Draw and label the parts of the hydra and the planarian.

2. Describe the hydra's responses to brine shrimp, touch, and the dilute acid solution.

3. Describe the planarian's responses to touch and the brine shrimp.

Analysis and Conclusions

1. Did the hydra detect the shrimp at a distance or by physical contact?

2. What reaction did the hydra have to touch? To the dilute acid solution? Why might such reactions be useful?

3. Based on your observations, how does the planarian respond to brine shrimp? What can you infer about the structures in the planarian that are involved in this response?

Extensions

Design an experiment to determine how hydras and planarians react to changes in temperature.

Chapter 32 Review ....

Study Outline

32-1 The Animal Kingdom

▶ Members of the kingdom Animalia are multicellular organisms that must obtain food from their environment.

▶ The animal kingdom is divided into two major groups—vertebrates and invertebrates.

▶ Animals may exhibit spherical, radial, or bilateral body symmetry. Some animals are asymmetrical.

32-2 Sponges and Cnidarians

▶ The sponges are the simplest multicellular animals. The sponge body consists of three layers. The outer layer is pierced by pores through which water containing food and oxygen flows. The spicules of the sponge are embedded in the middle layer. Inner layer cells are specialized for feeding and digestion.

▶ Sponges can reproduce sexually or asexually.

▶ Cnidarians include hydras, jellyfish, and corals. They are radially symmetrical and have cells that are organized into tissues.

▶ Cnidarians have two general body forms: the polyp and the medusa.

32-3 Flatworms and Roundworms

▶ The flatworms include planaria, flukes, and tapeworms. They are the simplest animals showing bilateral symmetry and definite head and tail regions. Flatworms' tissues are organized into organs and systems.

▶ Roundworms include trichina, filaria, pinworms, and hookworms. They are the simplest animals having a digestive system with two openings.

▶ Although roundworms lack circulatory and respiratory systems, they do have simple excretory and nervous systems and well-developed reproductive systems.

32-4 Segmented Worms and Mollusks

▶ The segmented worms include the earthworm, the *Nereis,* and the leech. They have bodies that are divided into segments.

▶ Segmented worms have a tube-within-a-tube body plan, coelom, and a closed circulatory system.

▶ The mollusks include bivalves, gastropods, and cephalopods. They are bilaterally symmetrical and have three distinct tissue layers.

▶ Mollusks have a muscular foot for movement, a soft body that houses all the organ systems, and a mantle.

Chapter Assessment

Multiple Choice

Choose the letter of the answer that best completes each statement or answers the question.

1. Multicellular organisms pierced by many holes through which water flows are part of the phylum (a) Nematoda. (b) Porifera. (c) Cnidaria. (d) Mollusca.

2. The tonguelike organ found in most mollusks is called the (a) parapodia. (b) foot. (c) radula. (d) gemmule.

3. Specialized cells characteristic of the phylum Cnidaria are (a) cnidoblasts. (b) trocophore larvae. (c) coeloms. (d) gemmules.

4. The lower or belly side of an animal is referred to as (a) dorsal. (b) ventral. (c) posterior. (d) anterior.

5. A mollusk with a shell consisting of two parts is considered a member of the class (a) Cephalopoda. (b) Annelida. (c) Bivalvia. (d) Gastropoda.

6. The earthworm belongs to the phylum (a) Nematoda. (b) Cnidaria. (c) Platyhelminthes. (d) Annelida.

7. Because it can be divided into equal halves in only one way, the human body is said to show (a) spherical symmetry. (b) bilateral symmetry. (c) parapodia. (d) radial symmetry.

8. The sessile body form of the cnidarian is called a (a) polyp. (b) medusa. (c) planula. (d) trocophore larva.

9. Flatworms are the simplest animals to have (a) radial symmetry. (b) a mouth and anus. (c) bilateral symmetry. (d) a respiratory tract.

10. The cavity found between the inner and outer body tubes of annelids and more complex animals is called a (a) segment. (b) coelom. (c) nephridium. (d) mesoderm.

Content Review

Answer each of the following in complete sentences.

11. Compare radial and bilateral symmetry and give an example of an organism that shows each.

12. Briefly describe nutrition, gas exchange, and excretion in a sponge.

13. Compare sexual and asexual reproduction in sponges.

14. How do gemmules contribute to the biological success of sponges?

15. What function do cnidoblasts serve?

16. Explain how feeding and digestion occur in planarians.

17. What distinguishes the roundworm's body plan from that of the flatworm?

18. Identify two characteristics that annelids and nematodes have in common.

19. Describe the structure and function of the foot, mantle, and radula of mollusks.

20. What type of circulatory system does the clam have? How does blood flow through the clam?

Graphic Organizing

For information on graphic organizers, see Appendix G at the back of this text.

21. **Compare/Contrast Matrix** Construct a compare/contrast matrix to compare flatworms, roundworms, and segmented worms. Use the following characteristics in your comparison: body plan, digestive system (number of openings), circulatory system (presence and type of), separateness of sexes, mode of life (parasitic or free-living).

Critical Thinking and Problem Solving

Discuss each of the following in a brief paragraph.

22. **Predicting** What would happen to a land snail if its foot stopped producing mucus?

23. **Comparing** Compare the parasitism of leeches and flukes.

24. **Predicting** Predict what would happen if a small piece of hard plastic were placed between the mantle and the shell of an oyster.

25. **Inferring** A team of geologists examining hills in Michigan find a thick bed of fossilized coral about 400 million years old. What assumptions can they make about the environment of this area 400 million years ago?

26. **Interpreting** A scientist is interested in studying the effects of chemical fertilizers and pesticides on the earthworm population. She chooses two nearly identical fields for her study. One field is treated with chemicals to grow the crop, whereas in the second field the crop is grown without the use of fertilizers or pesticides. She randomly selects five sites in each field. By using a gentle electric shocking device to force the earthworms to the surface, she counts the earthworms per unit area at each site. Using the data displayed in the table below, calculate the average number of earthworms in one square meter of each field. Interpret the data and then draw a conclusion. What is the control? How could the design of this experiment be improved?

Treated Field		Untreated Field	
Sites	Worms/m²	Sites	Worms/m²
1	7	A	9
2	2	B	6
3	3	C	8
4	4	D	5
5	4	E	7

Discovery
Learning Activity

Identifying Arthropods in Soil

1. In the area designated by your teacher, mark a 0.5 m² area on the ground.

2. With a small shovel, dig up the soil in this area to a depth of 8–10 cm. Examine the soil for living arthropods (insects) and molted exoskeletons. Using forceps, place the insects along with some soil in a container. Mark the container with the date, place where the contents were collected, and your name.

3. Using a hand lens, closely examine the insects in the container. Do not remove any insects from the container. Use field guides to identify the insects and find out the types of food they eat. After completing the activity, return the insects in the containers to your teacher.

Invertebrates— Arthropods and Echinoderms

Guide for Reading

Previewing the Chapter

A galaxy of brightly colored starfish rests in a tide pool along the Oregon coast. Starfish are not really fish, they are invertebrates called echinoderms. This chapter deals with the echinoderms and another group of invertebrates, the arthropods. Arthropods include insects, crabs, crayfish, and spiders. In what ways are insects both helpful and harmful to humans? How are echinoderms closely related to vertebrates?

Key Words

arachnid, arthropod, crustacean, echinoderm, metamorphosis

Key Concepts

- **List** the characteristics of insects.
- **Explain** the relationship between echinoderms and vertebrates.
- **Design an experiment** to determine the foods that fruit fly larvae prefer. (Laboratory Investigation)

33-1 Arthropods: Crustaceans

Section Objectives:

- *Describe* the general characteristics of arthropods.
- *Describe* the general characteristics of crustaceans.
- *Explain* the major life processes in the crayfish.

The phylum **Arthropoda** (ar THRAHP uh duh) ranges from flies, bees, mosquitoes, butterflies, spiders, and ants to crabs, lobsters, and shrimp. Of all animal groups, *arthropods* are the most biologically successful and the most abundant. There are about 400 000 known species of plants and about 250 000 known species of animals other than arthropods. But, there are more than 1 million known species of arthropods. Arthropods are found in all regions of the earth and are of the greatest importance to human beings.

The phylum Arthropoda is divided into five classes. These are the crustaceans, centipedes, millipedes, arachnids, and insects. The characteristics of each class will be described separately later in the chapter.

▲ **Figure 33–1.**
A Crustacean. This shrimp is just one of the 1 million known species of arthropods.

◀ Starfish can be found in a variety of colors.

General Characteristics of Arthropods

In many ways, arthropods are the most advanced invertebrates. They are bilaterally symmetrical and have a small coelom.

Although the phylum consists of a large number of unlike species, all arthropods share certain common features.

Arthropods have jointed legs. The legs are made of several pieces that are connected at hinged joints. These joints are controlled by opposing sets of muscles. Different arrangements of hinged joints allow such different functions as crawling, swimming, hopping, jumping, flying, grabbing, digging, and biting.

*Arthropods have exoskeletons composed of protein and **chitin*** (KYT un), *a carbohydrate.* The tough, lightweight exoskeleton protects soft body parts. The exoskeleton is also waterproof and prevents water loss, allowing many arthropods to live on land. Because the exoskeleton cannot grow, young arthropods periodically must undergo a process called **molting.** See Figure 33–2. During molting, the exoskeleton is shed and replaced by a new, larger one. Growth takes place before the new exoskeleton hardens. Until the new exoskeleton hardens, the young animal is unable to move or defend itself. Therefore, many arthropods hide until their new exoskeleton has hardened.

Like annelids, arthropods are segmented. However, the body segments are usually modified and fused to form specific body regions. In most arthropods, there is a head, **thorax** (THOR aks), and **abdomen.** The head, which is always composed of six segments, is well developed. It contains a mouth that is specialized for chewing or sucking. The thorax is the middle region of the arthropod, and the abdomen is the posterior region. The number of segments in the thorax and abdomen changes from one group of arthropods to another.

Figure 33–2
A Tarantula Molting. All arthropods molt their exoskeletons periodically. This red-kneed Mexican tarantula has just crawled out of its old exoskeleton. ▼

Arthropods have well-developed nervous systems. There is a distinct brain and a ventral nerve cord located beneath the digestive system. There are a variety of sense organs, including eyes, organs of hearing, sensory cells sensitive to touch, and antennae that are sensitive to touch and chemicals.

Arthropods have an open circulatory system. There is a dorsal tubular heart located above the digestive system. Arteries carry blood away from the heart to the body spaces, where it bathes the tissues directly. The blood eventually reenters the heart through openings in its sides.

General Characteristics of Crustaceans

The class **Crustacea** (krus TAY shuh), the *crustaceans,* includes lobsters, crayfish, crabs, shrimp, waterfleas, sow bugs, barnacles, and many others. Most crustaceans are marine, but some live in fresh water. A few, such as the sow bug, live on land in moist places. Crustaceans vary in size from tiny water fleas to huge crabs with leg spans of 3.5 meters. Microscopic crustaceans are the main source of food for many larger marine animals. All crustaceans have two pairs of antennae on the head.

Figure 33–3

Crustaceans. Representative crustaceans include: (A) Southeast Asian land crab, (B) scarlet reef lobster, (C) blood red shrimp, (D) sow bug, (E) goose barnacles, and (F) waterflea. ▼

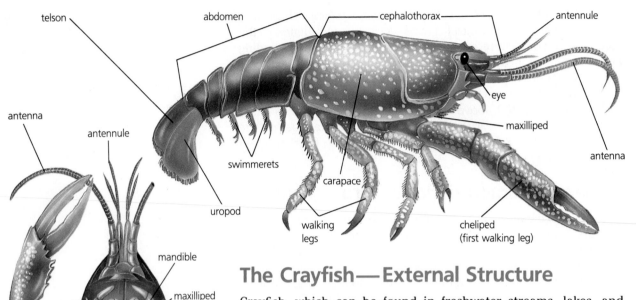

▲ **Figure 33–4**
External Structure of the Crayfish. A ventral view of the crayfish head (bottom) shows the maxilla, mandibles, and maxillipeds. The crayfish has two body sections (top right), the cephalothorax and the abdomen.

The Crayfish—External Structure

Crayfish, which can be found in freshwater streams, lakes, and swamps, are typical crustaceans. They are covered by an exoskeleton hardened with lime. At the joints, where bending occurs, the exoskeleton is softer, thinner, and folded. The crayfish body has two main regions, shown in Figure 33–4. At the anterior end, the segments of the head and thorax are fused to form the **cephalothorax** (sef uh luh THOR aks). The part of the exoskeleton that protects and covers the dorsal and side surfaces of the cephalothorax is called the *carapace* (KAR uh pays). The seven segments behind the cephalothorax form the abdomen. The paddle-shaped last segment of the abdomen is called the *telson.*

The paired appendages of the crayfish have specific functions. Starting at the front, the first pair of appendages are the *antennules* (an TEN yoolz), which function in touch, taste, and balance. Next come the *antennae* (an TEN ee), which are also used for touching and tasting. The **mandibles** (MAN duh bulz), or jaws, crush food by moving from side to side. Two pairs of *maxillae* (mak SIL ee) handle food. Three pairs of *maxillipeds* (mak SIL uh pedz) function in touch and taste and also handle food. The large first legs are called *chelipeds* (KIHL uh pedz). Their grasping claws are used for defense and to catch food. Behind the chelipeds are four pairs of walking legs. On the abdomen are *swimmerets* (swim uh RETS), which are used in swimming. In females, the swimmerets are used to carry the developing eggs. The last pair of appendages are the broad *uropods* (YUR uh pahdz). The uropods, along with the telson, form a fan-shaped tail that is used for backward movement. When the crayfish senses danger, the powerful abdominal muscles whip the tail forward under the abdomen causing the animal to shoot backward.

If a crayfish injures an appendage, it can shed the injured limb at a joint. This process of self-amputation prevents blood loss. Gradually, with each molt, the lost appendage grows back. Regeneration in crayfish is limited to the appendages and eyes.

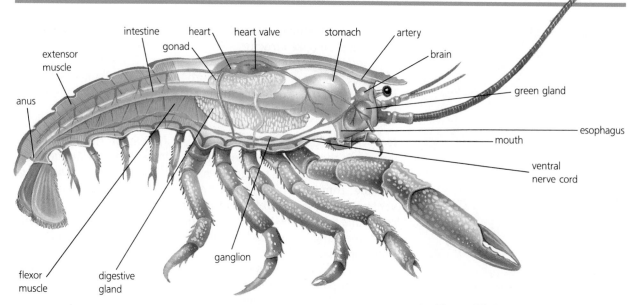

extensor muscle · intestine · gonad · heart · heart valve · stomach · artery · brain · anus · green gland · esophagus · mouth · ventral nerve cord · flexor muscle · digestive gland · ganglion

The Crayfish—Internal Structure and Life Functions

Nutrition   The crayfish feeds on dead animals or living animals that it catches with its chelipeds. The food is crushed by the mandibles and passed to the mouth by the maxillae and maxillipeds. The mouth leads into a short esophagus. From there, food passes into the stomach, where it is chewed up by chitinous teeth. The finely ground food particles are digested by enzymes, then passed into the digestive glands and absorbed into the blood. Undigested material passes through the intestine and out the *anus.*

Excretion   The excretory organs of the crayfish are called the *green glands.* They are located in the head region. The green glands remove wastes from the blood. These wastes are then excreted from the body through an opening near the base of the antennae.

Circulation and Respiration.   The open circulatory system consists of a dorsal heart surrounded by a cavity called the *pericardial* (pehr uh KARD ee ul) *sinus.* Blood in the pericardial sinus enters the heart through three pairs of valves. When the heart contracts, the valves close, and blood is pumped out through arteries to all parts of the body. There are no capillaries or veins. The arteries open into spaces, or sinuses, among the body tissues. There, the blood bathes the cells directly. Oxygen and nutrients from the blood diffuse into the cells, and carbon dioxide and wastes from the cells diffuse into the blood. Eventually, the blood collects in the *sternal* (STERN ul) *sinus,* where it is channeled to the gills. In the gills, it picks up oxygen, gets rid of carbon dioxide, and returns to the pericardial sinus. Dissolved in the plasma of the colorless blood is **hemocyanin** (hee moh SY uh nin), a copper-containing respiratory pigment that aids in the transport of oxygen. Hemocyanin is blue when oxygenated.

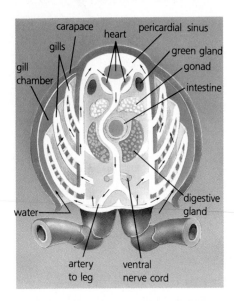

carapace
heart
pericardial sinus
gills
carapace
green gland
gill chamber
gonad
intestine
water
digestive gland
artery to leg
ventral nerve cord

▲ **Figure 33–6**

Crayfish Gills. Gas exchange in the crayfish is through the gills, which are located in gill chambers on either side of the thorax. As water flows over the gills, oxygen diffuses into the blood, and carbon dioxide diffuses out.

Figure 33–7

Female Crayfish Carrying Newly Hatched Young. The newly hatched crayfish young remain attached to the mother's swimmerets for several weeks. ▼

The **gills,** where the exchange of respiratory gases occurs, are delicate, plumelike structures. They are located in *gill chambers* on each side of the thorax. The gill chambers are protected by the carapace. Water is kept flowing through the gill chambers by the movement of the second maxillae. Figure 33–6 is a cross section of the thorax, showing the gills in the gill chamber.

Nervous Regulation   The nervous system of the crayfish is similar to the annelids' system. The brain, which is in the head, is connected by nerves to the eyes, antennules, and antennae. Extending from the brain, two nerves circle the esophagus and join ventrally to form a double, ventral nerve cord. As the ventral nerve cord runs toward the rear, it enlarges into ganglia in each segment. From the ganglia, nerves branch to the appendages, muscles, and other organs.

The sensory organs of the crayfish are well developed. They include a pair of *compound eyes* located at the ends of movable stalks. Each eye contains about 2000 visual units. Each unit contains a lens system. Unlike the human eye, the eye of a crayfish cannot focus at different distances. While this type of eye is sensitive to movement and offers a wide angle of vision, it produces only a crude image.

The crayfish has two kinds of small sensory hairs that are found on the appendages and other parts of the body. One type of hair is sensitive to touch. The other is sensitive to chemicals and provides information similar to the human senses of taste and smell.

The sense organs of equilibrium, or balance, are found in sacs that are called *statocysts* (STAT uh sists).These sacs are located at the bases of the antennules. Each statocyst contains sensory hairs and grains of sand. When the crayfish moves, the sand grains move, which stimulates some of the sensory hairs. From the stimulated hairs, impulses pass to the brain of the crayfish. The brain interprets the information and initiates impulses that allow the crayfish to adjust its position and to maintain its equilibrium. Each time the animal molts, the sand grains are shed along with the exoskeleton. New sand grains are picked up when the new exoskeleton forms.

Reproduction   In crayfish, sexes are separate. Mating takes place in the fall. The male uses his first pair of swimmerets to transfer sperm from his body to the *seminal* (SEM in ul) *receptacle* of the female. The sperm are stored in the receptacle until spring. During the spring, the female lays several hundred eggs that have been fertilized by the stored sperm. The eggs are attached to the female's swimmerets. The waving of the swimmerets back and forth keeps the embryos well supplied with oxygen for development. After five to six weeks, the eggs hatch, but as you can see in Figure 33–7, the young crayfish remain attached to the mother for several more weeks. During this time, the young crayfish begin to molt. Crayfish live for three to five years.

33-1 Section Review

1. Name the five major classes of the arthropod phylum.
2. What characteristic do all crustaceans have in common?
3. What are the two main body regions of the crayfish?
4. Hemocyanin functions in what important life process in the crayfish?

Critical Thinking

5. How is the ability to amputate and regenerate injured appendages a survival advantage for the crayfish? (*Judging Usefulness*)

33-2 Arthropods: Centipedes to Arachnids

Section Objectives:

- *Describe* the general physical characteristics of both centipedes and millipedes.
- *Name* four members of the arachnids and describe their general characteristics.

General Characteristics of Centipedes

Centipedes, or "hundred-leggers," belong to the class **Chilopoda** (ky LAHP uh duh). Some centipedes have more than 150 pairs of legs, but 30 to 35 pairs are most common in centipedes. A centipede has a distinct head made up of six segments. The head is followed by a long, wormlike, slightly flattened body made up of many similar segments. Centipedes live on land in dark, damp places, such as under logs or stones.

In the centipedes, all body segments, except the one behind the head and the last two, have one pair of legs. The head has one pair of antennae and various mouthparts. Centipedes feed mainly on insects. The centipede bites its victim with *poison claws,* which are on the first body segment. Small centipedes are harmless to humans. The common house centipede is about 2.5 centimeters long. At night, it searches for food, eating cockroaches, bedbugs, and other insects.

General Characteristics of Millipedes

Millipedes, or "thousand-leggers," belong to the class **Diplopoda** (dih PLAHP uh duh). They do not have 1000 legs, but they may have more than 300 pairs. Like a centipede, a millipede has a distinct head and a long, wormlike body made of many segments. Except for the last two segments, millipedes have two pairs of legs per segment. The head has a pair of antennae and various mouthparts. Unlike centipedes, millipedes do not have poison claws. Millipedes

Figure 33–8

A Centipede and a Millipede. The centipede (top) has one pair of legs per segment, while the millipede (bottom) has two pairs of legs per segment. ▼

also move more slowly than centipedes. They feed mainly on decaying plant material. When they are disturbed, millipedes usually roll themselves into a ball. Many have "stink" glands that give off an unpleasant odor.

General Characteristics of Arachnids

Arachnids, members of the class **Arachnida** (uh RAK nih duh), include spiders, scorpions, ticks, mites, and daddy longlegs. Some arachnids are dangerous to humans and other animals. Mites and ticks live as temporary parasites on the skin of many animals, including humans, dogs, chickens, and cattle. Mites often cause terrible itching. Ticks are carriers of several diseases, including Lyme disease, Rocky Mountain spotted fever, and Texas cattle fever. Scorpions sting with their tail. While the sting is painful, it is usually not fatal to humans.

Spiders are usually harmless. In fact, they are often helpful because they feed on insects. The poisonous spiders of the United States are the black widow and the brown recluse. Spiders rarely bite unless they are disturbed.

Structure and Life Functions of Arachnids

Most arachnids live on land, and many resemble insects. The body of an arachnid is made up of a cephalothorax and an abdomen. Arachnids do not have either antennae or chewing jaws. They have six pairs of jointed appendages, all on the cephalothorax. The first pair of appendages are the fang-like **cheliceras** (kuh LIS uh res), which are used to pierce the prey. The body fluids of the prey are then drawn into the spider's mouth by the action of the *sucking stomach.* Usually, poison glands associated with the cheliceras inject a poison that paralyzes the prey. The second pair of appendages, the **pedipalps** (PED uh palps), is sensitive both to chemicals and to touch. The pedipalps also hold food and are used

Figure 33–9

Arachnids. Arachnids are an extremely successful group containing more than 60 000 species. Some common arachnids include, from top: the scorpion, the spider, the tick, the mite and the daddy longlegs (lower right). ▼

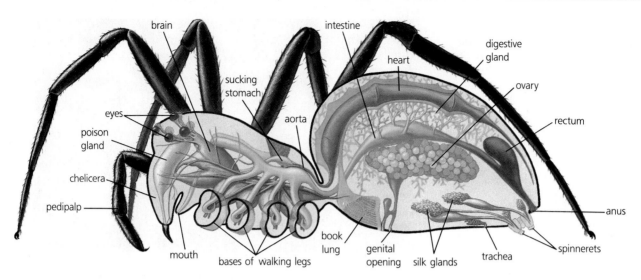

by the male in reproduction. The next appendages are four pairs of walking legs. You can tell arachnids from insects because insects have three pairs of walking legs.

The respiratory organs of the arachnids are called **book lungs.** Located in chambers on the underside of the abdomen, book lungs are a series of leaflike plates containing blood vessels. Air, drawn into the chambers through slits in the abdomen, circulates between the plates. Gas exchange occurs between the blood in the plates and the air in the chamber. Oxygen and carbon dioxide are transported in the blood between the body cells and the book lungs. Although some insectlike air tubes, or *tracheae,* are present, they play only a minor role in respiration.

In spiders and some other arachnids, the pedipalps of the male are modified for sperm transfer. Following elaborate courtship behavior, the male uses the pedipalps to place the sperm in the seminal receptacle of the female. In spiders, as the female lays the eggs, they are fertilized by the stored sperm, and wrapped in a cocoon. In some species, the female carries the cocoons until the young hatch. An example of this is shown in Figure 33–11. In other species, the eggs in cocoons are deposited on the ground. In still other types of arachnids, sperm are not transferred into the body of the female by the male. Instead, the sperm are enclosed in a case and deposited on the ground. The female then takes up the case into a special body opening.

In spiders and one other small group of arachnids, there are three pairs of **spinnerets** (spin uh RETS) at the end of the abdomen. Spinnerets are used to spin silk produced by silk glands within the abdomen. As the fluid protein is squeezed out of the spinnerets, it hardens into a thread. Spiders use these threads for many purposes. Some use them to construct webs in which they capture prey. Threads are also used to line nests and to make cocoons for the fertilized eggs. Spiders also use threads as a way of raising or lowering themselves from trees and other objects to escape from danger.

▲ **Figure 33–10**
Structure of an Arachnid. The body of an arachnid is divided into a cephalothorax and an abdomen, and there are four pairs of walking legs. Arachnids are predators, and the sucking stomach is used to draw in the body fluids of prey. The book lungs are specialized structures for gas exchange. Spiders, and some other arachnids, have spinnerets used to spin silk for webs and other purposes.

Figure 33–11

Female Wolf Spider. The newly hatched young covering this female wolf spider have emerged from the white cocoon attached to her abdomen. ▶

33-2 Section Review

1. How many pairs of legs per body segment do centipedes have? Millipedes?
2. Name three members of the class Arachnida.
3. What do spiders eat?

Critical Thinking

4. How are centipedes and spiders similar? How do they differ? (*Comparing and Contrasting*)

33-3 Arthropods: Insects

Section Objectives:

- *List* several reasons for the success of insects as land animals.
- *Describe* the external structure of the grasshopper.
- *Describe* reproduction and metamorphosis in insects.
- *Name* two members of each of the six major insect orders.

General Characteristics of Insects

Biologically, *insects,* class **Insecta** (in SEK tuh), are the most successful class of arthropods. There are more than 900 000 known species. Nearly all insects are land animals, although a few live in fresh water and a few in salt water. Insects range in size from tiny beetles 0.25 millimeters long to some large tropical moths with a wingspan of 30 centimeters. Most insects, however, are less than 2.5 centimeters long.

There are several reasons for the remarkable success of insects. The most important of these are listed below.

■ Insects are the only invertebrates capable of flying. The ability to fly allows them to travel over great distances in search of food. It also allows them to escape from enemies and to spread into new environments.

■ Among the insects, there is tremendous variation in how they are adapted for feeding and reproduction. These adaptations allow insects to exist in all types of environments and to obtain nourishment from many sources.

■ Insects have a high rate of reproduction and a short life cycle. A single female can lay hundreds or even thousands of eggs at a time. These eggs develop rapidly and may produce millions of offspring during a year. This increases the ability of insects to adapt.

■ Insects are small, which means that they do not need large areas in which to live.

All insects have three separate body regions—the head, thorax, and abdomen. On the head is one pair of antennae, several mouthparts, and in most insects, compound eyes. On the thorax are three pairs of walking legs. In flying insects, the wings are also located on the thorax. The abdomen has as many as 11 segments, with no leglike appendages.

Figure 33–12

Variation Among Insects. Insects are well-adapted for life in a wide variety of environments. This diverse class includes, clockwise from top left: the American cockroach, the bumble bee, the diving beetle, and treehoppers. ▼

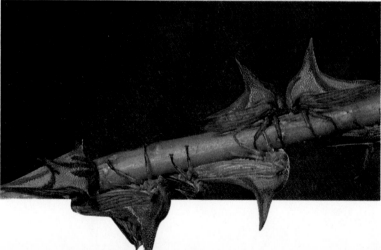

Variations Among Insects

While the grasshopper, which is discussed later in this chapter, shows the general characteristics of the insect class, many insects have other, highly specialized structures. These specialized structures allow them to feed on a particular plant or animal or to live in a particular environment.

Mouthparts   The structure of an insect's mouthparts reflects the way in which it obtains food. There are two basic types of mouthparts. Some insects, such as grasshoppers, have chewing mouthparts. Others, such as bees, having sucking mouthparts, which are usually in the form of a tube. Some insects have needlelike projections that enable them to pierce the tissues of animals and plants and suck their juices. In butterflies, the coiled siphoning tube uncoils to suck nectar from flowers. Houseflies have sponging and lapping mouthparts.

Body Form   Insects vary greatly in body form. Cockroaches have flattened bodies that are suited for living in cracks and crevices. Beetles have thick, plump bodies. Damsel flies and walking sticks have long slender bodies. Moths are covered with hairs that may serve to protect them from cool evening temperatures. The hairs or bristles on bees help in the collection of pollen.

Legs   The legs of insects show many types of modifications. For example, water bugs and some beetles have paddle-shaped legs that are used in swimming. The walking legs of honeybees are modified for the collection of pollen. The forelegs of the praying mantis are modified for grasping prey.

Reproduction and Development in Insects

All insects reproduce sexually. Eggs are produced in the ovaries of the female, and sperm are produced in the testes of the male. In a few insects, eggs hatch directly into miniature adults. The young molt several times, growing larger each time molting occurs. In most species, however, insects undergo a series of distinct changes as they develop from eggs to adults. This series of changes is called **metamorphosis** (met uh MOR fuh sis), and it is controlled by hormones.

Incomplete Metamorphosis   The eggs of some insects, such as grasshoppers, crickets, and cockroaches, undergo **incomplete metamorphosis.** In this type of development, the eggs hatch into **nymphs.** The nymph resembles the adult, but lacks certain adult features. As you can see in Figure 33–13, the grasshopper nymph looks like the adult, but it lacks wings and reproductive structures. Nymphs molt several times. With each molt, they become larger and more like the adult. In incomplete metamorphosis, the three stages of development are the egg, nymph, and adult.

Figure 33–13

An Immature Grasshopper. The grasshopper nymph lacks the wings and reproductive structures of the adult. ▼

MiniLab

Skill: Designing an Experiment

Flying to the Light

Suggested Procedure

1. Obtain a light source and a culture tube containing fruit flies.

2. Position the culture tube at different distances in front of the light source.

3. Observe the behavior of the fruit flies at each position.

4. Formulate a hypothesis and design an experiment to find the farthest distance at which the light affects the behavior of the fruit flies. Check with your teacher before beginning the experiment.

Problem

How does a fly react to light?
Design an experiment to answer this question.

Analyze and Conclude

1. What conclusion can you draw from your results?

2. Explain how the data you collected supports your conclusion.

3. What other variables might have affected your experiment? Explain your answer.

4. Design an experiment to determine how the color of light affects the behavior of fruit flies.

Complete Metamorphosis   The eggs of most insects undergo **complete metamorphosis.** Moths, butterflies, beetles, bees, and flies are among the insects that undergo complete metamorphosis. The eggs of these insects hatch into segmented larvae. These larvae are known as *caterpillars, maggots* (MAG uts), or *grubs*. During this stage, the larva eats and grows. After several molts, it passes into a resting stage called the **pupa** (PYOO puh). The pupa is surrounded either by a cocoon or by a case made from its outer covering. During the pupal stage, the tissues are reorganized into the adult form. When the changes are complete, the case or cocoon splits open, and the adult emerges. In complete metamorphosis, the four stages of development are the egg, larva, pupa, and adult.

The development of the cecropia (sih KROH pee uh) moth is typical of insects that undergo complete metamorphosis. It includes the egg, larva, pupa, and adult stages. Figure 33–14 shows the development of the cecropia moth through the four stages of metamorphosis. The stages of metamorphosis are controlled by the interaction of three hormones. These hormones are brain hormone, molting hormone, and juvenile hormone.

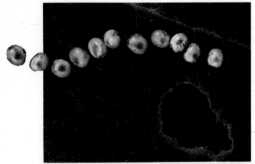

▲ **Figure 33–14**
Development of the Cecropia Moth. The developmental stages of the Cecropia moth include, from top to bottom, eggs, larva, pupa, and adult.

The egg hatches into the larva, in this case a caterpillar. As the caterpillar eats and grows, cells in the brain secrete a hormone that stimulates production of a molting hormone. The molting hormone, produced by an endocrine gland in the thorax, stimulates molting of the exoskeleton. The transformation of the larva into more mature forms is inhibited by a hormone called the juvenile hormone. Juvenile hormone is produced by endocrine glands, which are near the brain. As long as the juvenile hormone is secreted, the larva can molt, but it will not change into the next stage, known as the pupa. At the end of the larval period, the secretion of juvenile hormone decreases. At the time of the next molt, the larva forms a pupa. During the pupal stage, the insect appears inactive, but great changes in body form are occurring. At the end of pupation, the adult moth emerges.

A recent approach to insect control involves the use of substances similar to juvenile hormone. These substances prevent the metamorphosis of larvae into adults, which prevents the insects from reproducing.

Classification of Insects

The branch of biology that deals with the study of insects is called **entomology** (ent uh MAHL uh jee). Scientists who study insects are called *entomologists.* Entomologists divide the class Insecta into 27 orders. Of these 27, only 6 are of major importance. The 6 major orders are the **Hymenoptera** (hy muh NAHP tuh ruh), **Orthoptera** (or THAHP tuh ruh), **Coleoptera** (kohl ee AHP tuh ruh), **Lepidoptera** (lep uh DAHP tuh ruh), **Diptera** (DIP tuh ruh), and **Hemiptera** (heh MIP tuh ruh). Figure 33–16 on page 722 shows the basic characteristics of these and other insect orders.

The Grasshopper—A Representative Insect

Like all insects, the body of the grasshopper is divided into three sections—the *head, thorax,* and *abdomen.* The head is made up of six fused segments. Two large compound eyes, similar to those of the crayfish, are located on the sides of the head. See Figure 33–15. In addition, the grasshopper has three simple eyes located between the compound eyes. The simple eyes do not form images. They are only sensitive to light and dark. On the front of the head is a pair of jointed antennae. The antennae are sensitive to smell and touch.

The mouthparts used in chewing are located outside the mouth. These structures are adapted for eating leafy vegetation. The upper lip and the lower lip hold the food. The mandibles are lined with rough-edged chitinous teeth. In biting off and chewing food, the mandibles move from side to side. Behind the mandibles are the maxillae, which hold the food and pass it to the mandibles. Sensory palps on both the maxillae and the lower lip feel and taste the food. Beneath the lower lip is a tonguelike organ.

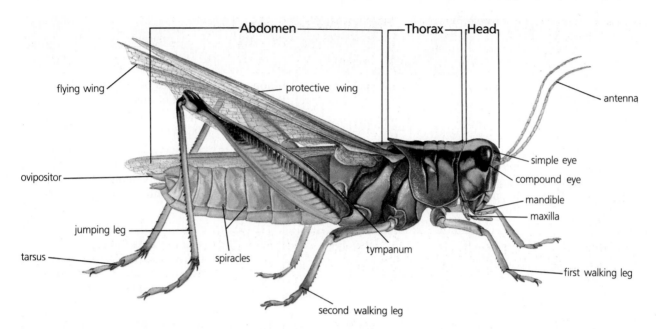

Abdomen — Thorax — Head

flying wing

protective wing

antenna

ovipositor

simple eye

compound eye

mandible

maxilla

jumping leg

tarsus

spiracles

tympanum

first walking leg

second walking leg

▲ **Figure 33–15**

External Structure of the Grasshopper. The grasshopper body is divided into three sections—the head, the thorax, and the abdomen.

The thorax is composed of three segments. Each segment bears a pair of legs. Each leg has five segments. The last segment is called the *tarsus,* or foot. On the tarsus are pads that enable the grasshopper to cling to smooth surfaces and claws that enable it to climb rough surfaces. The first two pairs of legs are for walking. The third pair of legs is larger than the first two pairs, and it is modified for jumping.

Attached to the last two segments of the grasshopper's thorax are two pairs of wings. The outer pair, known as the fore wings, is hard and serves as a protective covering for the inner pair of wings, called the hind wings. The hind wings, which are flexible, are used in flight. When the hind wings are not in use, they are folded like fans. The thin membranes of the hind wings contain veins that serve to strengthen them.

The abdomen is made up of 10 segments. Along the lower sides of the abdomen and thorax are 10 pairs of **spiracles,** or openings into air tubes. On either side of the first abdominal segments are the *tympana* (TIM puh nuh), the organs of hearing. Each tympanum consists of an oval, flat membrane that vibrates when it is hit by sound waves.

The last segment of the abdomen is modified for reproduction. When grasshoppers mate, the male transfers sperm into the body of the female. The sperm are stored in the seminal receptacle of the female. When the eggs leave the ovary of the female, they enter the oviduct, where fertilization occurs. They then pass out of the body of the female. On the end of the abdomen of the female is a hard, four-pointed organ called the **ovipositor** (OH vee pahz it er). It is used to dig holes in the ground in which the eggs are deposited. The eggs are laid in the fall but do not hatch until spring. For more information about the structure of the grasshopper, see Unit 2.

Classification of Insects

Order	Examples	Mouthparts	Wings	Characteristics/Habitat
Anopleura 	sucking lice	sucking	none	parasites of mammals; suck blood of hosts, including humans. Their bites are irritating, and they spread disease.
Coleoptera 	beetles (diving, bark, carpet, and Japanese beetles, fireflies, ladybirds, june bugs)	chewing	usually 2 pair	largest insect order; found in all habitats. Many feed on plants and are serious pests.
Collembola 	springtails	chewing	none	small insects found in leaf litter, on rotting logs, on beaches, and on surface of pond water. Some species are jumpers.
Diptera 	flies (houseflies, black flies, mosquitos, midges, gnats, horseflies)	sucking	1 pair	found in various habitats; some feed on plants; others are parasites; others feed on insects. Many types are pests. Some damage plants; some transmit animal diseases.
Ephemeroptera 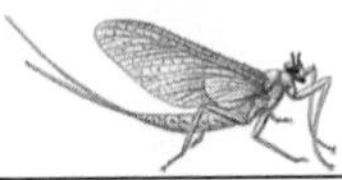	mayflies	vestigial	2 pairs	found in and around ponds and streams. Adults live only a day or so and do not eat.
Hemiptera 	bugs (water striders, bedbugs, assassin bugs, stinkbugs)	sucking	none or 2 pairs	most terrestrial; some aquatic; few parasitic. Some eat plants, others, insects.
Homoptera 	cicadas, aphids, leafhoppers, spittlebugs, plant hoppers, whiteflies, lac insects	sucking	none or 2 pairs	feed on plants. Many cause serious damage, and some transmit diseases. Lac insects are the source of lac, from which shellac is made.
Hymenoptera 	bees, wasps, ants, sawflies	bee: sucking; wasps, ants, and sawflies: chewing	none	large order whose members live mainly on vegetation, particularly flowers, in various habitats. Some are parasites of other insects. Ants and some wasps and bees are social insects, living in colonies divided into several castes, each serving a function. Honeybees are important pollinators of many types of plants.

▲ **Figure 33–16.   Classification of Insects.**

Classification of Insects (continued)

Order	Examples	Mouthparts	Wings	Characteristics/Habitat
Isoptera	termites	chewing	none or 2 pairs	small social insects that feed mainly on wood. Termites damage or destroy buildings and objects made of wood.
Lepidoptera	butterflies and moths	sucking, coiled sucking tube	usually 2 pairs	found on vegetation. The larvae of this group are caterpillars, which feed on plants and often do serious damage. Adults commonly feed on plant nectar and may serve to pollinate the plants they visit. Salivary glands of larvae produce silk used to make coccoon. Silk is produced by silkworm moth larvae.
Mallophaga	chewing lice	chewing	none	parasites of birds and mammals (but not humans).
Odonata	dragonflies, damselflies	chewing	2 pairs	found around water; feed on mosquitos and other insects.
Orthoptera	cockroaches, crickets, grasshoppers, katydids, walking sticks, praying mantis	chewing	usually 2 pairs	large insects found on ground or on low vegetation. Many make noise by rubbing body parts together. Many feed on plants and can do great damage. Cockroaches are pests in buildings.
Siphonaptera	fleas	sucking	none	small parasites on birds and mammals. Fleas are pests, attacking domestic animals and humans. A few types of fleas transmit disease, including bubonic plague.
Thysanura	silverfish, bristletails	chewing	none	small insects. Bristletails found in leaf litter, under logs, etc. Silverfish found in cool, damp places, often pests in buildings.

Economic Importance of Insects

Insects are so widespread and so numerous that they affect almost every part of daily life in some way. Each year, insects cause billions of dollars of damage to crops. Insects spread many plant diseases, such as Dutch elm disease and corn smut. They also transmit animal diseases: mosquitoes carry malaria, yellow fever, and elephantiasis; houseflies carry dysentery and typhoid fever; tsetse (SEET see) flies carry African sleeping sickness; lice carry typhus; and fleas carry plague. Insects also destroy property: termites destroy wood; moths and carpet beetles damage clothing, fabrics, furs, and carpets; silverfish destroy paper; and weevils, cockroaches, and ants ruin food.

Insects also serve some valuable functions. Some insects are necessary for the pollination of important crops. For example, bees pollinate the flowers of apple and pear trees, clover, and berries. They also produce honey. Lac, which is used to make shellac, comes from from lac insects, and silk from silkworm moths.

Some insects destroy other insects that are harmful to humans and property. Ladybird beetles eat scale insects, which injure orange and lemon crops. The praying mantis eats almost any insect it can catch. Wasps, by laying their eggs in caterpillars, eventually kill them. Aquatic bugs eat mosquito larvae. Insects also serve as a source of food for birds, frogs, and fish. Finally, some insects act as scavengers, eating dead plant and animal remains.

Scientists are still searching for ways of controlling harmful insects without harming other insects or animals. Chemical insecticides poison environments, kill harmful and helpful insects, and endanger other animals, including humans. Furthermore, in time, insect populations become resistant to chemicals.

Many scientists believe that biological methods of insect control are safer than chemical insecticides. Biological controls include: sterilizing males and releasing them; developing resistant plants; introducing specific predators and parasites that destroy only harmful insects; and using insect sex attractants, called pheromones, to lure insects into traps.

33-3 Section Review

1. List three reasons for the biological success of insects.
2. What are the stages of complete metamorphosis?
3. List the six major orders of insects.
4. What are two useful products obtained from insects?

Critical Thinking

5. An animal is discovered that has an exoskeleton, sucking mouthparts, head fused with thorax, abdomen, no wings, and four pairs of walking legs. Could you classify the animal as an insect? Why or why not? (*Reasoning Categorically*)

33-4 Echinoderms

Section Objectives:

- *Name* four echinoderms and describe the general characteristics of these organisms.
- *Explain* why echinoderms are considered to be more closely related to the vertebrates than other invertebrate phyla.
- *Describe* the structure and life functions of the starfish.

General Characteristics of Echinoderms

The phylum **Echinodermata** (ih ky nuh der MAH tuh) includes starfish (sea stars), sea urchins, sea cucumbers, and sand dollars. These animals are all marine and live mainly on the ocean floor. Some stay in the same place but most move around. The larvae are bilaterally symmetrical, but the adults are radially symmetrical. *Echinoderms* have a well-developed coelom.

Almost all echinoderms have an internal skeleton that serves as support and protection for the animal. The skeleton consists of hard, calcified plates that are embedded in the body wall. Spiny projections on the plates stick out through the skin. These projections give echinoderms their spiny-skinned appearance.

In all the invertebrates that you have studied so far, the first opening of the digestive system formed in the embryo is the mouth, which is formed from the blastopore (see Chapter 22, section

Figure 33–17

Echinoderms. All echinoderms are marine organisms. Common echinoderms include: (A) the sea urchin, (B) the starfish, (C) the sand dollar, and (D) the sea cucumber. ▼

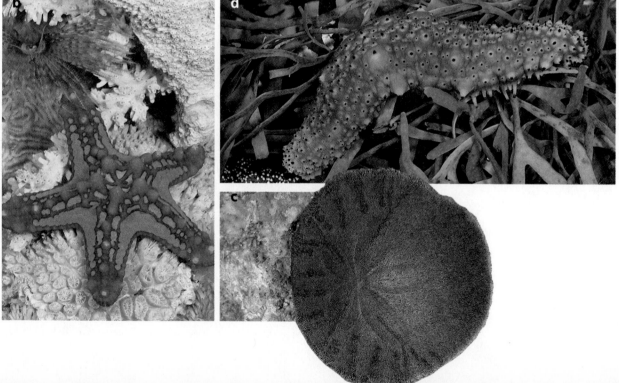

22–1). The opening for the anus later develops opposite the mouth. In the echinoderms, however, the pattern of development is just the opposite. The blastopore becomes the anus, and the mouth forms at a later stage opposite the anus. This pattern of development is characteristic of vertebrates. It may show, therefore, a possible evolutionary relationship between echinoderms and more complex animals.

The starfish is representative of the phylum, so it can be used to study the structure and life functions of echinoderms. Because it is an echinoderm and not a fish, some people prefer to call it a *sea star.*

Structure and Life Functions of the Starfish

The body of the starfish consists of a central disk from which the arms, or rays, radiate. Most starfish have 5 arms, but some have as many as 20.

Locomotion and food getting in starfish involve a system called the **water-vascular system.** This system is found only in echinoderms. See Figure 33–18. On the dorsal surface of the starfish is an opening called the *sieve plate.* Sea water enters through the sieve plate and enters a system of **canals,** which run into each arm. Connected to the canals in the arms are many small, tubular structures called **tube feet.** Each tube foot has a bulblike structure at one end and a sucker at its tip. The bulbs are within the body of

Figure 33–18

Structure of the Starfish. The water-vascular system is a network of water-filled canals that serves in locomotion and food-getting. Connected to the canals are tube feet, which allow the starfish to crawl along the ocean floor. ▼

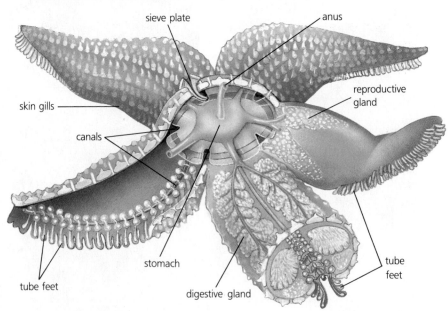

the starfish, but the tube feet extend from the ventral, or bottom, surface of the arms. When the bulb contracts, water is forced into the tube foot, causing it to elongate. When the tube foot touches a surface, its sucker holds fast. As the tube foot contracts, or shortens, water is forced back into the bulb, and the starfish is pulled forward. Movement of the animal requires the coordinated action of hundreds of tube feet.

Starfish feed on clams and oysters. They use their water-vascular system to pry open their prey. In feeding, the starfish wraps its arms around both sides of the mollusk, attaches tube feet to each shell, and pulls. Eventually, the mollusk tires, and its shell opens slightly. The stomach of the starfish is then extended out through the mouth, and inserted into the small opening between the mollusk's shell. (The starfish can insert part of its stomach into an opening as small as 0.1 millimeter.) Enzymes secreted by the stomach partly digest the soft body of the mollusk. The food is then taken into the stomach, and the stomach is pulled back into the starfish. Food passes from the stomach into the digestive glands in the arms, where digestion is completed.

Respiration in the starfish occurs by the diffusion of gases across the skin gills and tube feet. *Skin gills* are small, fingerlike structures that extend out from the body surface. They are filled with coelomic fluid. Many materials are distributed by the fluid in the coelom. This fluid bathes the body organs and supplies them with nutrients and oxygen and removes wastes. Excretion takes place by diffusion through the body surface.

Sexes are separate in the starfish. The gametes are shed through openings in the central disk into the water, where fertilization will take place. The fertilized egg develops into a bilaterally symmetrical, free-swimming larva. After several weeks of growth, the larva attaches itself to a solid surface and develops into a small starfish.

Starfish have an amazing ability to regenerate missing parts. An entire new body can grow from as little as a single arm and a tiny part of the central disk.

▲ **Figure 33–19**
Starfish Feeding on a Mussel. Starfish eat many types of shellfish. This starfish has attached its tube feet to the shell of a mussel and is prying it open.

33-4 Section Review

1. Name four echinoderms.
2. Where are echinoderms found?
3. What system of locomotion and food getting is found only in starfish and other echinoderms?

Critical Thinking

4. In a developing sand dollar, which develops first — the mouth or the anus? Explain. (*Reasoning Conditionally*)

Laboratory
Investigation

Designing an Experiment

Feeding Fly Larvae

Fruit fly larvae are particularly fond of yeast and other microorganisms present in overripe, fermenting fruit. In this investigation, you will determine which foods fruit fly larvae prefer.

Problem

Which foods do fruit fly larvae prefer? **Design an experiment** to answer this question.

Suggested Materials (per group)

- drawing paper
- pencil
- drawing compass
- metric ruler
- various foods
- fruit fly larvae

Suggested Procedure

1. Using a compass, draw a circle with a diameter of 10 cm on a sheet of paper. You may also want to use the pencil and ruler to draw more lines at any time during the investigation.

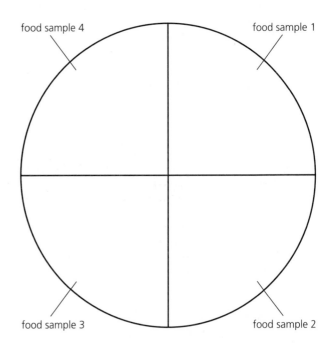

food sample 4

food sample 1

food sample 3

food sample 2

2. Working with a partner, choose four different food samples you will test to find which one the fruit fly larvae prefer. You might try cooked oatmeal, canned pumpkin, or pieces of crushed ripe fruit.

3. Decide how to arrange the food and larvae on the paper circle. Remember to include a control setup and to verify your experiment by repeating it.

4. Discuss with your partner what behaviors you will look for during each test.

5. Check with your teacher before carrying out the experiment. Make sure you keep a record of your procedure and observations at each step.

Observations

1. Prepare a data table to record the types of food and the reactions of the fruit fly larvae.

2. Describe the behavior of the larvae during each part of your experiment.

Analysis and Conclusions

1. Which of the four foods did the fruit fly larvae prefer? What evidence in your data table supports your conclusion?

2. How do you think fruit fly larvae sense food?

3. What sources of error could be present in your experiment?

4. How would you improve your experiment if you were to do it again?

5. Examine the laboratory investigations done by other pairs of students. What did you learn that gave you ideas about how you might change your own investigation?

Extensions

Design an experiment to study how various other arthropods respond to various foods.

Chapter **33** Review

Study Outline

33-1 Arthropods: Crustaceans

▶ Arthropods have jointed legs, a chitinous exoskeleton, and a segmented body. They have a well-developed ventral nervous system with specialized sensory receptors and an open circulatory system.

▶ Class Crustacea is characterized by two pairs of antennae on the head, and several pairs of appendages.

33-2 Arthropods: Centipedes to Arachnids

▶ Centipedes have a flattened, segmented body with one pair of legs on most segments.

▶ Millipedes have a rounded, segmented body with two pairs of legs on most segments.

▶ Class Arachnida includes spiders, scorpions, ticks, mites, and daddy longlegs. The arachnid body is divided into a cephalothorax and an abdomen. Attached to the cephalothorax are a pair of cheliceras, a pair of pedipalps, and four pairs of legs.

33-3 Arthropods: Insects

▶ Insects have three distinct body sections—head, thorax, and abdomen. The head contains a pair of antennae, mouthparts, and compound eyes. Attached to the thorax are three pairs of legs. Some insects have wings attached to the thorax.

▶ Most insects undergo distinct changes, or metamorphosis, as they develop from eggs to adults. Metamorphosis may be complete or incomplete.

33-4 Echinoderms

▶ Echinoderms have an internal skeleton, spiny skin, and a water-vascular system. The water-vascular system is used for locomotion, feeding, and gas exchange.

Chapter Assessment

Multiple Choice

Choose the letter of the answer that best completes each statement or answers the question.

1. Arthropods have tough exoskeletons made mostly of a (a) lipid. (b) phosphate. (c) carbohydrate. (d) wax.

2. In molting, an arthropod sheds its entire exoskeleton and manufactures a new one that (a) allows the arthropod's body to grow. (b) is harder than the first one. (c) is softer than the first one. (d) coordinates interacting hormones.

3. Specialized mouth parts in crustaceans are called (a) arachnids. (b) pedipalps. (c) chelicerae. (d) mandibles.

4. The process by which an insect develops from an egg to a nymph to an adult is called (a) evolution. (b) incomplete metamorphosis. (c) complete metamorphosis. (d) recycling.

5. How many pairs of walking legs do all insects have? (a) one (b) two (c) three (d) four

6. In a crayfish, the abdomen contains the (a) sensory hairs. (b) mandibles. (c) swimmerets. (d) chelipeds.

7. What body symmetry do echinoderms have? (a) lateral symmetry (b) vertical symmetry (c) radial symmetry (d) spherical symmetry

8. An example of an echinoderm is a (an) (a) earthworm. (b) starfish. (c) snail. (d) octopus.

9. In echinoderms, the water-vascular system is involved with each of the following except (a) response to environment. (b) respiration. (c) movement. (d) internal transport.

10. The group of arthropods that use book lungs for respiration includes the (a) insects. (b) spiders. (c) crabs. (d) millipedes.

Content Review

Answer each of the following in complete sentences.

11. Why is molting necessary in the arthropod life cycle?

12. What external feature does the crayfish have that explains why it is classified as a crustacean?

13. Describe the circulatory system of the crayfish.

14. Compare the body structure of the centipede with that of the millipede.

15. Describe the respiratory process of the spider.

16. What common arthropod characteristics are shared by spiders, crustaceans, and insects?

17. Describe the stages of incomplete metamorphosis.

18. How are the reproductive processes of the crayfish, spider, and grasshopper similar?

19. Why are echinoderms thought to be closely related to vertebrates?

20. Describe the structure of the water-vascular system of the starfish.

Graphic Organizing

For information on graphic organizers, see Appendix G at the back of this text.

21. **Concept Map** Copy the incomplete concept map onto a separate sheet of paper and fill in the missing information. Add any additional concepts you think are important.

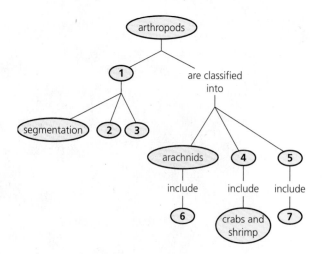

Critical Thinking and Problem Solving

Discuss each of the following in a brief paragraph.

22. **Predicting** What would happen if a spider's silk glands and spinnerets were removed?

23. **Comparing** How are complete metamorphosis and incomplete metamorphosis similar? How are they different?

24. **Inferring** What could keep an insect larva from developing into a mature form?

25. **Hypothesizing** Suppose you found a clamshell on the beach that was only slightly open, and the clam inside was gone. What would you think was the probable cause of the clam's "disappearance"? What evidence would you look for to support your hypothesis? What evidence might you find that would not support your hypothesis?

26. **Classifying** A student was given a fossilized extinct animal called a trilobite to study. How might the student determine if the trilobite was an arthropod or an echinoderm? What problems might be encountered in trying to classify the animal?

27. **Classifying** A scientist has discovered two fossil animals. Both fossils reveal an exoskeleton and jointed legs. One fossil seems to have a cephalothorax, abdomen, and four pairs of legs. The other seems to have a head, thorax, abdomen, and three pairs of legs. Into what phylum and class should each be classified?

28. **Hypothesizing** Propose a hypothesis to explain why starfish are more numerous on rocks and coral reefs than on sandy areas. After doing this, design an experiment to test the hypothesis.

Discovery
Learning Activity

Maintaining an Aquarium

1. Working in a group, observe the behavior of the freshwater fishes such as guppies or tetras for 15 minutes each day for three days. Record your observations. What structures do all fishes have in common? Did you observe any unusual behavior? If so, describe the behavior.

2. Make sure that the fishes are fed as needed and that the aquarium is properly maintained.

Vertebrates— Fishes to Reptiles

Guide for Reading

Previewing the Chapter

On a rain-soaked heliconia flower in the tropical rain forest, red-eye treefrogs keep a watchful eye out for predators. A safe environment is essential for the frogs to survive. Yet, survival depends on many factors. This chapter covers the unique features and functions of a wide variety of animals—from saltwater fishes to versatile amphibians to land-dwelling reptiles. What are the similarities and differences among fishes, amphibians, and reptiles? Why do scientists think that amphibians evolved from primitive fishes?

Key Words

amphibian, chordate, ectothermic, endothermic, fish, reptile, vertebrate

Key Concepts

- **List** some of the characteristics of chordates.
- **Compare** fishes, amphibians, and reptiles.
- **Design an experiment** to show how a chameleon changes color in response to its environment. (Laboratory Investigation)

34-1 The Chordates

Section Objectives:

- *List* the three basic characteristics that are present in all chordates.
- *Describe* the structure and life functions of the tunicates and the lancelets.
- *List* the basic characteristics of the vertebrates.

General Characteristics of Chordates

The *chordates,* phylum **Chordata** (kor DAH tah), are divided into three subphyla. The largest of these are *vertebrates,* subphylum **Vertebrata** (vert uh BRAH tah). The other two chordate subphyla are the *urochordates,* subphylum **Urochordata** (yur uh kor DAH tah), and the *cephalochordates,* subphylum **Cephalochordata** (SEF uh loh kor dah tah). The urochordates are also called the *tunicates.* The cephalochordates are commonly called *lancelets.* All the members of these two subphyla live in marine environments, do not have backbones, and are considered to be more primitive than vertebrates.

At some time in their lives, all chordates show the following three characteristics. These characteristics distinguish them from all other animals.

▲ **Figure 34–1**
A Vertebrate. This snake belongs to the largest chordate subphylum, Vertebrata.

◀ Red-eye treefrogs on a heliconia flower.

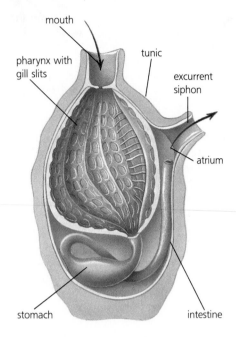

▲ **Figure 34–2**

Internal Structure of a Tunicate. Water passes through the gill slits into the atrium and out of the body through the excurrent siphon. Adult tunicates have gills but lack the hollow nerve cord and the notochord typical of chordates.

Figure 34–3

Blue-and-Gold Adult Tunicates. Tunicates are marine dwellers and grow singly or as colonies on the ocean floor. ▼

■ Chordates have a dorsal, hollow **nerve cord.**

■ Chordates have a flexible, rodlike, internal supporting structure called a **notochord** (NOHT uh kord).

■ Chordates have paired **gill slits** in the throat region, which are used in respiration.

In land-dwelling chordates, the gill slits are seen only in the embryo. In certain other chordates, such as the fishes, the gill slits function in respiration throughout life. The notochord, which is dorsal to the digestive tract, is found in the embryos of all chordates. In the tunicates, the notochord is the only supporting structure. In most vertebrates, it is replaced early in embryonic development by cartilage or bone. The cartilage or bone forms a supporting backbone, or spinal column.

The Tunicates and Lancelets

The tunicates are soft-bodied animals, found only in marine, or saltwater, environments. Adult tunicates are sessile animals that obtain food and oxygen from water that flows through their bodies. See Figure 34–2. Water enters the mouth and then passes into the pharynx. There, it flows through the gill slits in the walls of the pharynx, where gas exchange occurs. The water then passes into a chamber called the atrium and out of the body through the excurrent siphons. The gill slits also trap food particles, which then pass into the digestive system.

Adult tunicates lack a dorsal, hollow nerve cord and notochord. Larval tunicates, unlike adults, have all three chordate characteristics. They are motile and resemble tadpoles. Eventually, the larvae settle to the ocean floor, develop into adults, and lose the three chordate characteristics.

The lancelets are small marine animals. The most common member of this group is *amphioxus* (am fee AHK sus). Lancelets usually live buried in the sand with only their anterior end exposed. Adult lancelets show the three characteristic chordate structures. See Figure 34–4. As in the tunicates, water enters the body through the mouth and passes into the pharynx. From the pharynx, water passes through the gill slits, where gas exchange occurs. Food particles do not pass through the gill slits. Instead, the particles enter the digestive system directly. Water leaves the body through the atrial pore.

The Vertebrates

The vertebrates are the most numerous and complex of the chordates. The basic characteristic distinguishing vertebrates from other chordates is a spinal column made up of vertebrae. The spinal column, or backbone, is the basis for an internal supporting skeleton and allows flexibility and movement. In adult vertebrates, the spinal column surrounds or replaces the notochord.

◀   **Figure 34–5**
A River Lamprey. The lamprey attaches itself to other fish with its suckerlike mouth. It then bores a hole in the fish with its teeth and feeds on its blood.

Lampreys   *Lampreys* are found in both fresh and salt water. Most are parasites. They obtain their food by attaching their round, suckerlike mouths to the bodies of other fishes. See Figure 34–5. Once attached, the lamprey uses the teeth on its tongue to gnaw a hole in the body of its victim. The lamprey then sucks the blood and body fluids of the fish.

Lampreys shed their eggs, or *spawn,* in freshwater streams. The eggs are fertilized by the male and hatch into larvae about one centimeter long. The larvae live in the mud of the streams until they mature, which takes three to seven years. The adult lives only one or two years. However, adult lampreys can do serious damage to fish populations.

Hagfishes   *Hagfishes* are found only in salt water. They feed on dead fishes, worms, or other small invertebrates that live on the ocean floor. Hagfishes are also called "slime eels" because their skin glands release large amounts of mucus if they are disturbed. Unlike the lampreys discussed above, hagfishes do not have a larval stage of development.

The Cartilaginous Fishes

The *cartilaginous* (kart ul AJ uh nus) *fishes,* class **Chondrichthyes** (kahn DRIK thee eez), include sharks, rays, and skates. Almost all members of this group are marine. They range in size from small skates less than 1 meter in length to whale sharks 15 meters long. Manta rays may be 6 meters across and weigh as much as 1200 kilograms. In members of this group, the skeleton is made entirely of cartilage, and traces of the notochord are present in the adult. Unlike the jawless fishes, the cartilaginous fishes have movable upper and lower jaws that are equipped with several rows of sharp teeth. These biting jaws enable the cartilaginous fishes to eat a wide variety of food. Like all fishes, members of this class have two-chambered hearts.

Figure 34–6

A Blue-Spotted Stingray. The stingray has a sharp poisonous spine at the base of its tail, which it uses as a weapon. ▶

Skates and Rays   *Skates* and *rays* have flattened, winglike bodies with whiplike tails. They live on the ocean floor and feed on worms, mollusks, and crustaceans. As you can see in Figure 34–6, stingrays have poison stingers in their tails, which they use for defense. Electric rays can produce a large electric charge, which they use to stun their prey.

Sharks   *Sharks* are streamlined fishes that swim by moving their trunks and powerful tails from side to side. See Figure 34–7. Swimming forces water through the mouth, over the gills, and out through five to seven pairs of gill slits. The shark obtains the oxygen it needs from this flow of water. If a shark is caught in a net, for example, where it cannot move, it will die from lack of oxygen.

Unlike most fishes, fertilization is internal in the shark. In some species of sharks, the embryos develop within the body of the mother and are born live. In others, the eggs are covered with a leathery coat before they are released from the body of the female.

The shark's sense organs, particularly those for smell and vibration, are well developed. The shark uses its **lateral lines**—lines that extend along each side of the body—to sense vibration. The shark can smell when water enters the nostrils and passes through the *olfactory sacs*. These sacs are sensitive to various chemicals and can detect the presence of food.

Figure 34–7

Sharks. Sharks are well-adapted for predatory life. They are fast swimmers with well-developed sense organs, and powerful jaws. The jaws of the shark are lined with many sharp, triangular teeth that are replaced by other rows of teeth when lost. ▼

Most sharks are meat eaters and active hunters. However, the two largest sharks, the basking shark and the whale shark, are filter feeders. That is, they obtain food by straining microorganisms from the water.

The skin of the shark is covered with embedded, toothlike *placoid* (PLAH koyd) *scales,* which make the skin so tough that it can be used as sandpaper. Unlike the scales of bony fishes, the scales of the shark do not overlap one another.

The Bony Fishes

The *bony fishes,* class **Osteichthyes** (ahs tee IK thee eez), are the largest class of vertebrates. Most of the members of this group have bony skeletons, paired fins, and protective, overlapping scales. They are found in both fresh and salt water all over the earth. Bony fishes vary greatly in size, ranging from the Philippine goby, which is 10 millimeters long, to the swordfish, which may be more than 4 meters long.

Bony fishes differ in structure from the moray eel, which looks much like a snake, to the seahorse. See Figure 34–8. Most, however, are streamlined animals, like the perch. Their fins, which are made of skin webbing, are usually supported by bone or cartilage ribs. Most bony fishes swim by side-to-side movements of the body and tail. The fins aid in maintaining balance and in controlling the direction of movement.

Many adaptations for protection are found among the bony fishes. The pufferfish, for example, is covered with sharp spines. In

Figure 34–8

Bony Fishes. Although most fish resemble the perch in form, the moray eel (left) and the sea horse (right) are fishes too. ▼

▲ **Figure 34–9**
A **Spiny Pufferfish.** The spines of this pufferfish stand out in response to a threat.

times of danger, it inflates itself with air or water so that its spines stand out. See Figure 34–9. A flying fish has a pair of winglike pectoral fins. To escape its enemies, it leaps out of the water and glides through the air for distances of 100 meters or more. The large South American electric eel can stun or kill its enemies with a strong electric charge.

Bony fishes have a complex nervous system. Ten pairs of cranial nerves extend from the brain, and spinal nerves radiate from the spinal cord. Bony fishes usually have a pair of well-developed eyes, two nostrils, and lateral lines, like those on the shark, on each side of the body. The nostrils are used only for smelling, not for breathing.

There are usually four pairs of gills. These lie on each side of the body under a protective bony flap called the *gill cover,* or **operculum** (oh PER ka lum). Water moves in through the mouth, passes over the gills, and then flows out of the body. The movement of muscles in the mouth and gill covers maintains the flow of water over the gills. A bony fish has a two-chambered heart, consisting of an atrium and a ventricle. Blood travels from the heart to the gills, where oxygen is picked up and carbon dioxide is released. The blood is then distributed through blood vessels to all parts of the body before it returns to the heart.

Most of the body of the fish is muscle. As shown in Figure 34–11, along the ventral side is a small space containing the digestive, excretory, and reproductive organs. The digestive system includes the mouth, pharynx, esophagus, stomach, intestine, liver, gallbladder, pancreas, and anus. The gills are located on the sides of the pharynx. Attached to the short intestine are three tubular structures that are called *pyloric caeca* (SEE kuh). These structures

Figure 34–10
Perch. Most of the fish familiar to us, such as the perch, belong to the class Osteichthyes. ▼

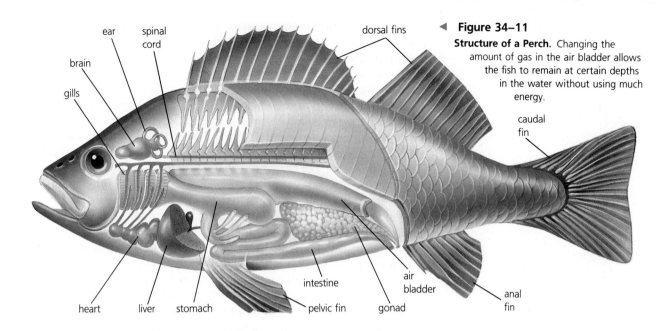

◀ **Figure 34–11**
Structure of a Perch. Changing the amount of gas in the air bladder allows the fish to remain at certain depths in the water without using much energy.

Labels: ear, spinal cord, brain, gills, dorsal fins, caudal fin, heart, liver, stomach, pelvic fin, intestine, gonad, air bladder, anal fin

MiniLab

Skill: Designing an Experiment

A Fishy Story

Suggested Procedure

1. Fill a large beaker about halfway with water from an aquarium. Use a net to move one fish from the aquarium to the beaker. Let the fish adjust to its new environment for at least 5 minutes.

2. Observe how the fish moves. Look at its fins and general body shape.

3. Using a clock with a second hand, count how many times the fish opens its mouth per minute. Observe any movement of the gill covers (operculum) during the same time period. Record your data. Return the fish to the aquarium.

4. Using a similar procedure, design an experiment to determine what effect the presence of another fish has on the first fish's breathing rate.

5. Write out your hypothesis and, with your teacher's approval, carry out your experiment.

Problem

What factors affect the breathing rate of a fish? **Design an experiment** to answer this question.

Analyze and Conclude

1. How many times did the fish open its mouth per minute?

2. Did you observe any coordinated movement of the gill covers with the opening and closing of the mouth?

3. What effect did the presence of another fish have on the first fish? Give evidence to support your answer.

aid in the absorption of digested materials. Two kidneys filter some nitrogenous wastes from the blood. These wastes, which are in the form of urea, pass through the ureters to the urinary opening and into the water. The gills, however, excrete most of the nitrogenous wastes in the form of ammonia.

All fishes are slightly heavier than water. In order to keep from sinking, they must have some type of flotation device, or they must keep swimming to maintain their level in the water. Most bony fishes have a gas-filled sac called the **swim bladder,** or *air bladder,* in the upper part of their body cavities. The swim bladder acts as a float. That is, it regulates the buoyancy of the fish. By increasing or decreasing the amount of gas in the swim bladder, the fish is able to change the density of its body. The ability to change density allows the fish to remain suspended in the water at any depth. In lungfishes, which are air-breathing fishes, the swim bladder serves as a lung.

As in vertebrates in general, the sexes are separate in bony fishes. The male has testes, and the female has ovaries. Fertilization and development are usually external. The female deposits eggs in the water, and the male then discharges *milt,* a sperm-containing fluid, over the eggs.

34-2 Section Review

1. Describe the feeding habits of lampreys. What are the feeding habits of hagfishes?
2. List the general characteristics of the cartilaginous fishes.
3. What is the function of the olfactory sacs in the shark?
4. List the general characteristics of the bony fishes. What structures aid in maintaining balance and in controlling the direction of movement in bony fishes?

Critical Thinking

5. Which of the following marine animals are bony fishes: perch, skates, moray eels, manta rays, lampreys, sharks, and sea horses? Explain your answer. (*Classifying*)

34-3 The Amphibians

Section Objectives:

- *List* the major characteristics of amphibians and name three members of this class.
- *Describe* the structure and life functions of the frog, including the circulatory and respiratory systems.
- *Describe* metamorphosis in the frog.

General Characteristics of Amphibians

The *amphibians,* class **Amphibia** (am FIB ee uh), include frogs, toads, salamanders, and newts. Some amphibians live their entire adult lives on land. Others are found only in or around water. In either case, for most amphibians, reproduction and development must take place in water or in a moist place. It is thought that amphibians evolved from primitive, air-breathing fishes. Most scientists believe that amphibians were the very first land-dwelling vertebrates.

In addition to their need for water for reproduction, amphibians share the following characteristics.

- The skin is generally thin and contains mucus-secreting glands.

- There are two pairs of limbs, which are used for walking, jumping, and/or swimming.

- There is a pair of nostrils connected to the mouth cavity.

- The heart has three chambers—two atria and one ventricle.

- The young usually show a distinct larval form and gradually develop adult characteristics.

There are two major groups of amphibians: the tailed amphibians, such as salamanders, and the tailless amphibians, such as frogs. A third, minor group consists of small, tropical, wormlike animals that burrow in moist soil.

Salamanders   The tailed amphibians include salamanders and newts. (Newts are actually a type of salamander.) These animals have long bodies, long tails, and two pairs of short limbs. See Figure 34–12. Most salamanders range from 8 to 20 centimeters in length. However, the Japanese giant salamander, which is the largest living amphibian, may reach a length of 1.5 meters. Salamanders eat fishes, snails, insects, worms, and other salamanders. Some are entirely aquatic, while others live under rocks or logs or in other moist places. They are active only at night. Freshwater salamanders retain their gills, which are used for breathing. The mudpuppy is a well-known salamander that lives in the streams and lakes of the eastern United States. Both the mudpuppy and the *axolotl* (AK suh lot ul), which is a salamander found in the Rocky Mountains and Mexico, are actually larval forms that can reproduce sexually. See Figure 34–13.

Frogs and Toads   The tailless amphibians include frogs and toads. As adults, they have short, squat bodies and lack tails. Their large, powerful hind legs are well suited for jumping.

Toads have dry, rough, warty skins. They can live on land far away from water. Toads burrow or take shelter during the day and come out to feed at night when it is cooler and more humid. Some toads live in the desert, but like most amphibians, they need water for reproduction. During the winter, toads hibernate by burrowing into the ground. During hibernation, life processes slow down, and an animal becomes inactive. See Figure 34–14.

▲   **Figure 34–12**
A Blue-Spotted Salamander. Salamanders live in most northern temperate and tropical regions throughout the world, but most are found in North America.

Figure 34–13
An Axolotl. While most salamanders change form as they develop into adults, the axolotl and the mudpuppy remain in the larval form throughout life. ▼

Figure 34–14

A Texas Toad. Unlike frogs, toads can live far away from water. ▶

Frogs have thin, moist skins that are loosely attached to their bodies. They generally live near ponds, streams, swamps, or other bodies of water. During the winter, they hibernate in the mud at the bottom of pools and streams. Frogs and toads eat insects and worms. The larval forms, called **tadpoles,** eat aquatic plants.

Frogs and toads have many enemies, including snakes, birds, and turtles. Among their protective adaptations are their coloring, which provides good camouflage, and their ability to leap. They often dive underwater to escape their enemies. Glands in their skin produce secretions that are unpleasant tasting or poisonous to their enemies.

Structure and Life Functions of the Frog

The organ systems of the frog are similar to those of most other vertebrates, including humans. For this reason, they are often studied in detail in biology courses.

External Features of the Frog The frog has a short, broad body with two short forelimbs and two long, muscular hind limbs. See Figure 34–15. The hands have four fingers and are not webbed, while the feet have five webbed toes and are adapted for jumping and swimming. The upper surface of the frog is yellow-green to green-brown in color, and the underside is whitish. This coloring allows the animal to blend in to its surroundings. The skin can change color to some extent to further hide the animal.

Two large, movable eyes protrude from the head. They permit vision in all directions. Each eye is protected by three eyelids—the upper eyelid, the lower eyelid, and the **nictitating** (NIK tuh tayt ing) **membrane.** The nictitating membrane is transparent, which allows the frog to see underwater. Behind each eye is a round eardrum called the **tympanic membrane,** which picks up sound waves from air or water. Two nostrils on the tip of the head enable the frog to breathe air while the rest of the body is floating underwater.

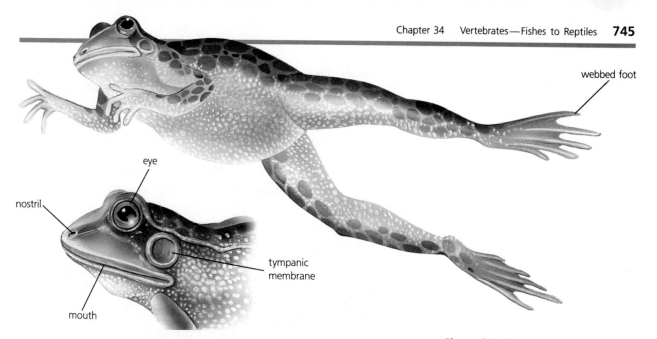

▲ **Figure 34–15**
External Structure of the Frog.

The Digestive System   The mouth of the frog is large. The sticky tongue is attached to the front end of the lower jaw. The frog can flip out its tongue rapidly to catch insects in flight. The food sticks to the tongue, which is then pulled back into the mouth. Teeth along the edge of the upper jaw and on the roof of the mouth aid in gripping the food. From the mouth, the food is forced down the opening of the esophagus in the back of the throat.

Food passes down the esophagus into the stomach, where digestion begins. See Figure 34–16. The partially digested food

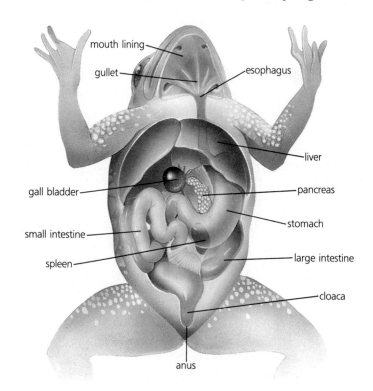

◀ **Figure 34–16**
Digestive System of the Frog.

then passes through the pyloric valve into the small intestine. The pancreas and liver secrete digestive juices that pass through ducts into the small intestine. Most digestion and absorption of food takes place in the small intestine. Undigested food passes from the small intestine into the large intestine and then into the **cloaca** (kloh AY kuh). The cloaca empties through the anal opening. The cloaca serves as a passageway for urine, eggs, and sperm.

The Circulatory System   The frog has a three-chambered heart made up of two thin-walled atria and one muscular ventricle, as shown in Figure 34–17. Blood leaving the ventricle enters a large blood vessel that branches immediately into two arteries. Each of these arteries divides into many smaller arteries and then into capillaries. Blood from the capillaries is returned to the heart through the veins. Blood from the lungs is carried to the left atrium by the right and left pulmonary veins. This blood is oxygenated only when the frog is breathing air with its lungs. Blood from all the other parts of the body is returned through three large veins into a thin-walled sac. Blood from the sac enters the right atrium. Both the right and left atria empty blood into the ventricle. Thus, blood pumped out by the ventricle is a mixture of oxygenated blood from the left atrium and deoxygenated blood from the right atrium.

The Respiratory System   The respiratory system of the adult frog includes the lungs, the lining of the mouth, and the skin. These structures have thin, moist surfaces and blood vessels.

The frog uses its lungs to meet most of its oxygen requirements. The two lungs are elastic sacs with thin walls. Air is forced

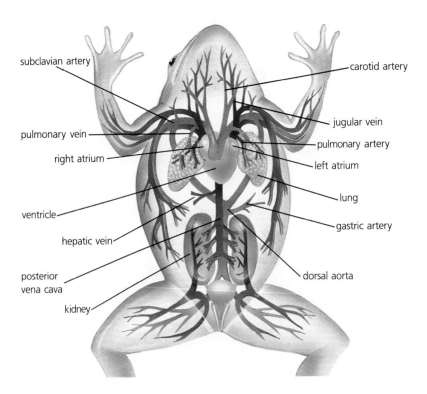

Figure 34–17
Circulatory System of the Frog. ▶

into the lungs by the pumping action of muscles in the floor of the mouth. The floor of the mouth is lowered, and air is drawn into the closed mouth through the nostrils. Then, the nostrils are closed, the floor of the mouth is raised, and air is forced from the mouth, through the glottis, and into the lungs. The exchange of oxygen and carbon dioxide occurs in the capillaries of the lungs.

The thin roof of the mouth also serves as a respiratory surface. The thin, moist skin of the frog can serve as a respiratory surface either in air or in water. This is especially important when the frog remains underwater for long periods of time. When the frog hibernates during winter, its body metabolism is reduced, and skin respiration alone meets the oxygen needs of the animal.

The Nervous System   Like humans, frogs have a central nervous system and a peripheral nervous system. See Figure 34–18. The brain and the spinal cord make up the central nervous system. Ten pairs of cranial nerves connect the brain to parts of the head and abdomen. The spinal cord, encased in vertebrae, is connected to parts of the body by 10 pairs of spinal nerves. The cranial and spinal nerves make up the peripheral nervous system.

The frog's brain is made up of the olfactory lobes, the optic lobes, the cerebrum, the cerebellum, and the medulla. The function of olfactory lobes is smell, and the function of optic lobes is vision. The cerebrum interprets sensory information and controls voluntary muscle action. The cerebellum coordinates movement. The medulla, which connects the brain to the spinal cord, controls many involuntary muscle actions.

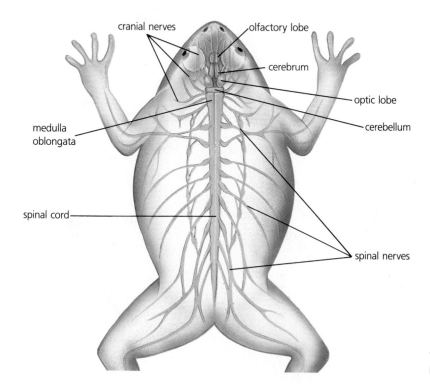

◀ **Figure 34–18**
Nervous System of the Frog.

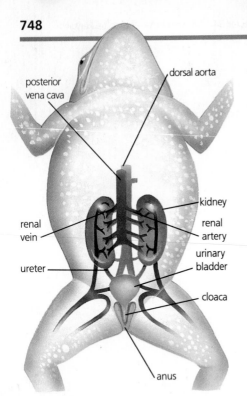

▲ **Figure 34–19**
Excretory System of the Frog.

The sense organs of the frog include eyes, tympanic membranes for hearing, inner ears for balance, taste buds on the tongue, odor-sensitive nerve endings in the nasal passages, and sensory nerve endings in the skin.

The Excretory System   Although most of the carbon dioxide produced by the frog is excreted through the skin, other metabolic wastes are excreted by the kidneys. The kidneys are located in the back of the body cavity on either side of the spine. See Figure 34–19. Wastes filtered from the blood form urine. Urine from each kidney is carried by the ureters to the bladder for temporary storage. From the bladder, the urine passes into the cloaca and out of the body.

The Reproductive System   In the female, the ovaries are located along the back, above the kidneys, as shown in Figure 34–20a. Large numbers of eggs, produced by the ovaries, enter the oviducts, which are coiled tubes. There, the eggs are surrounded by a jellylike substance secreted by the walls of the oviducts. At the base of the oviducts are sacs in which the eggs are stored until they are released from the body through the cloaca.

In the male, the testes are small, yellowish, bean-shaped organs located just above the kidneys. See Figure 34–20b. Sperm

Figure 34–20
Reproductive System of the Frog. In male and female frogs, the reproductive organs are ventral to the kidneys. ▼

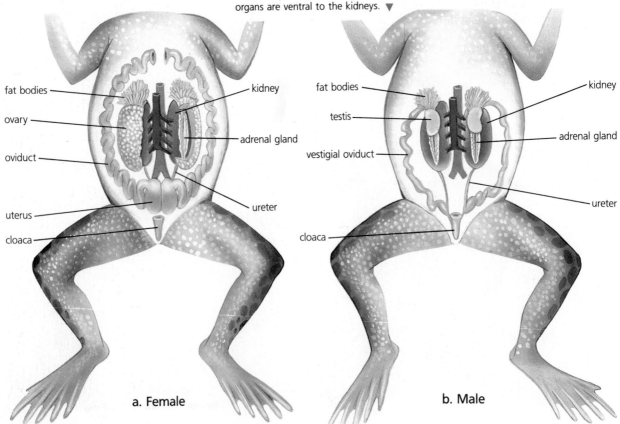

a. Female

b. Male

produced in the testes then pass to the kidneys through microscopic tubules. From the kidneys, the sperm are carried by the ureters to the cloaca. During mating, the sperm are discharged from the male through the cloaca.

Fertilization and Development   Fertilization in frogs is external. During mating, the male clasps the female with his short front legs. This is known as *amplexus* (am PLEK us) (see page 433). As the eggs leave the body of the female, the male releases sperm over them, so that many are fertilized.

After six to nine days, the eggs hatch into tadpoles. See Figure 34–21. They are fishlike, with no legs, a long tail, and gills. The tadpole has a two-chambered heart. Metamorphosis of the tadpole into the adult frog involves the development of legs, the absorption of the tail, the disappearance of gills, and the development of lungs and a three-chambered heart, as well as still other changes. The leopard frog completes metamorphosis in about three months, while bullfrogs take two or three years to complete the process.

Figure 34–21

Development of the Frog. (a) A mass of eggs. (b) Newly hatched tadpoles. (c) Tadpole with limbs. (d) Adult frog. ▼

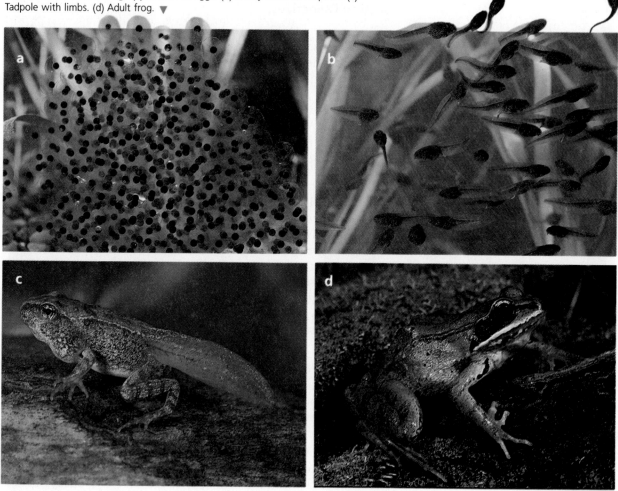

34-3 Section Review

1. Name the two main groups of amphibians and give an example of each.
2. What is the function of the nictitating membrane in the frog?
3. What is the tympanic membrane?
4. Name the respiratory surfaces of the frog.

Critical Thinking

5. An ecologist studying a local frog species observed that the population declined in years with droughts in the spring but was not affected by droughts at other times of the year. How would you explain this observation? (*Identifying Causes*)

34-4 The Reptiles

Section Objectives:

- *Explain* why reptiles are better adapted to life on land than amphibians.
- *List* the general characteristics of reptiles.
- *Compare* and *contrast* the external structures of crocodiles and turtles.
- *Describe* the major characteristics of lizards and snakes.

General Characteristics of Reptiles

The *reptiles,* class **Reptilia** (rep TIL ee uh), include crocodiles, alligators, turtles, tortoises, lizards, and snakes. Reptiles are well adapted for life on land. Unlike amphibians, they do not require water for reproduction. Fertilization is internal. The fertilized egg is enclosed in a thick, leathery, waterproof shell that protects it from drying out (see page 447). Unlike amphibians, reptiles do not have gills at any stage in their life cycle, and they do not undergo metamorphosis. As you can see in Figure 34–22, when reptiles hatch from eggs, they look like miniature adults.

In addition to their shelled eggs, reptiles share a number of other characteristics.

- The skin of reptiles is dry and covered with scales. This waterproof covering protects them from excessive water loss and from predators.

- Except for snakes, reptiles have two pairs of legs. Most reptiles have five clawed toes on each leg. The legs are adapted for climbing, running, or paddling.

- In most reptiles, there is a three-chambered heart consisting of two atria and one partly divided ventricle. The partial separation of the ventricle lessens the mixing of oxygenated and deoxygenated

◄ **Figure 34–22**
Newly Hatched Wood Turtle. The newly hatched wood turtle, like all reptile young, looks like a miniature adult.

blood in the heart. This in turn increases the amount of oxygen carried to the body cells. Crocodiles and alligators have four-chambered hearts.

■ Reptiles have well-developed lungs that are protected by a rib cage.

■ Nitrogenous wastes are excreted mainly as uric acid, so that the urine of many reptiles is a semisolid paste. This is an excellent adaptation for conserving water.

From the fossil record, it appears that reptiles were once a highly successful group. Prehistoric reptiles were a diverse group that included the dinosaurs. There were swimming reptiles, flying reptiles, reptiles that walked on four legs, and reptiles that walked on two legs. Today, however, there are only four orders of living reptiles. One of these orders has only one member, the *tuatara,* which is a lizardlike animal found only in New Zealand. This primitive reptile, shown in Figure 34–23, has an extra eyelike structure on the top of its head.

◄ **Figure 34–23**
A Tuatara. The tuatara is the only living member of the order Rhynchocephalia, a group that has characteristics more primitive than those of the lizards.

Figure 34–24

Alligators. The American alligator is found in the rivers, bayous, and swamps of the southeastern United States. ▶

Crocodiles and Alligators

Crocodiles and alligators are the largest living reptiles. They range in length from 2.5 meters to more than 7 meters. They are found in lakes, swamps, and rivers in tropical regions all over the world. Both alligators and crocodiles have long snouts, powerful jaws with large teeth, and long, muscular tails. See Figure 34–24. The tails are used in swimming. These two types of reptiles look very much alike, but their teeth are arranged differently. Furthermore, the American alligator has a much broader snout than the American crocodile. In both alligators and crocodiles, there are nostrils at the tip of the snout. This allows the animals to lie in water, with only the tip of the snout and the eyes above the surface.

Alligators and crocodiles feed on animals that they capture with their massive, toothed jaws. Crocodiles are more vicious and aggressive than alligators. They will attack large animals, including humans, cattle, and deer. It is the less aggressive alligator that is most commonly found in the southeastern United States. Alligator hides are used for leather goods. Overkilling brought some species close to extinction, but protective laws have allowed the populations to increase again.

Turtles

Turtles are found on land and in both fresh and salt water. Land-dwelling turtles are sometimes called tortoises. As you can see in Figure 34–25, the body of a turtle is enclosed in protective shells. The upper shell is called the *carapace,* and the lower shell is called the *plastron.* For defense, the legs, tail, neck, and head of some turtles can be pulled completely inside the shell. Turtles feed on plants and small animals. They have no teeth, but they grab and tear their food with the hard, sharp edges of their beaks.

Land-dwelling turtles are slow moving. Their short legs have claws that are used in digging. Sea turtles have paddle-shaped legs

that are used in swimming. All turtles, including ocean-dwelling turtles, lay their eggs on land in holes that they have dug with their hind legs.

Some species of marine turtles reach lengths of 2 meters and weights of more than 500 kilograms. Some land turtles have reached weights of more than 180 kilograms. Turtles may live to be more than 100 years old.

▲ **Figure 34–25**

Turtles. The turtle is unique in having a protective shell around its body. If threatened, the turtle will pull its legs, tail, neck and head into its shell.

Lizards and Snakes

Lizards and snakes belong to the same order, but there are many differences between them. Most lizards are four-legged, while snakes have no legs. Lizards have movable eyelids and external ear openings, while snakes have immovable eyelids and no external ear openings. In both lizards and snakes, the skin is covered with scales. Both animals shed their skins periodically. Unlike the scales of the lizard, which are almost uniform in size, the scales of the snake vary in size. While scales on the back and sides of a snake are small, on the belly of the snake, there is a single row of large scales. These scales act as cleats to give the snake traction as it moves across the terrain.

Lizards   Lizards are an extremely diverse group. They are found in deserts, in forests, and in water. Smaller lizards feed on insects, worms, spiders, and snails. Larger ones may also eat eggs, small birds, other lizards, and small mammals. A few lizards feed on plants. Many lizards can shed their tails if seized by an enemy. The tail wiggles, distracting the other animal, and the lizard escapes. A new tail is regenerated in a short time.

The gecko is a small lizard that has sticky toe pads. These pads allow it to walk on vertical surfaces and upside down. It catches insects with a flick of its long, sticky tongue. The American chameleon, the anole, has a remarkable ability to change color and blend in with its surroundings. See Figure 34–26. The Gila monster is a highly colored lizard found in the deserts of the southwestern United States. Its bite is poisonous but rarely fatal to humans. The largest lizard is the Komodo dragon of Indonesia. It weighs over 100

▲ **Figure 34–26**

Lizards. The Komodo dragon (right) is the largest of the lizards. Some species of Anoles (top) have the ability to change color, generally from green to brown. The gecko (bottom) is the most primitive of all lizards.

Figure 34–27

Internal Structure of a Snake. A snake's skeleton is made of a skull and many vertebrae and ribs. Most of the snake's internal organs are long and thin. ▼

kilograms and may be 3 meters long. The Malaysian flying lizard has skin extensions on its sides that enable it to glide from tree to tree.

Snakes Although snakes are feared by many people, only about 200 of the 2500 known species are poisonous. Snakes are actually more helpful than harmful because they kill large numbers of rodents.

Snakes are found on the ground, in trees, and in both fresh and salt water. They are most abundant in tropical areas. The body of a snake consists of the head, trunk, and tail. See Figure 34–27. The trunk contains the body cavity with elongated internal organs. The digestive tract is a straight tube running from the mouth to the anus. The tail is the portion of the body following the anus. The skeleton has a large number of vertebrae and ribs.

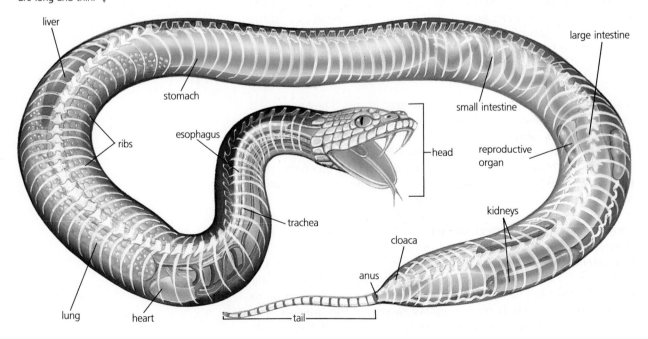

Snakes have special sense organs that are used in hunting for food. The forked tongue of the snake picks up odor-bearing particles. The particles are identified by the *Jacobson's organs* located in the roof of the mouth. Snakes are deaf to airborne sounds, but there are sense organs within the skull that respond to vibrations in the ground. Some snakes are known as *pit vipers.* These snakes have heat-detecting pit organs on their heads, between the nostrils and the eyes. With these organs, pit vipers can accurately track and strike warm-blooded prey, even at night or in deep burrows.

Snakes feed on mice, rats, frogs, toads, insects, fish, and other small animals, depending on where they live. Some snakes swallow their prey alive, while others kill their prey before they swallow it. Large snakes, such as pythons, boas, and king snakes, coil their bodies around their victims and crush or strangle them to death. Some snakes poison their victims.

Snakes can swallow animals that are much larger than they are because the structure of the jaw allows the mouth to open wide. Furthermore, the ribs are unattached at one end, which allows the body cavity to expand. Swallowing is a slow process. The teeth point backward so that the prey cannot pop out of the mouth, and the windpipe is projected forward so that breathing is not blocked. After one large meal, a snake is able to go for weeks or months without eating.

Poisonous snakes have a pair of specialized teeth called *fangs,* shown in Figure 34–28. The fangs are connected to salivary glands, which produce a poison, or venom. Some venoms are *neurotoxins,* or poisons that attack nervous tissues. They can paralyze muscles and affect the action of the heart and lungs. Other venoms, called *hemotoxins,* break down red blood cells and blood vessels. When a snake bites, the fangs carry the venom into the victim. Some snakes have hollow fangs that act like hypodermic needles, injecting the venom. In others, the fangs are grooved, and the venom passes into the victim by capillary action. The poisonous snakes of the United States include rattlesnakes, water moccasins, copperheads, and coral snakes. The best known and most common snake is the garter snake, which is harmless.

▲ **Figure 34–28**

Fangs of a Diamondback Rattlesnake. The rattlesnake, which is most common in the southwestern United States and western Mexico; injects toxin into its victims through hollow fangs. When its jaws are closed, the fangs are folded back against the roof of its mouth.

34-4 Section Review

1. Name four members of the class Reptilia.
2. What are the upper and lower shell of the turtle called?
3. Name the poisonous snakes of the United States.
4. What heat-sensing organs are used by some snakes to detect prey?

Critical Thinking

5. Name two characteristics of reptiles that are important adaptations for life in arid climates. (*Judging Usefulness*)

*L*aboratory
Investigation

Designing an Experiment

Adaptation for Survival

American chameleons, or anoles, are native to the southeastern United States, where they can be seen on fences, trees, and wooden buildings. In this investigation, you will explore an unusual adaptation of chameleons—their ability to change color rapidly.

Problem

How can you **design an experiment** to determine how chameleons change color with their environment?

Suggested Materials (per group)

- American chameleon
- 20-gallon terrarium
- screen terrarium lid
- sand or gravel
- dried branches
- rocks
- moistened sponge, with a surface area of about 4 cm × 4 cm
- mealworms or other small live insects
- heat source
- thermometer
- colored pencils
- colored paper
- light source
- watch or clock

Suggested Procedure

1. To create housing for the chameleon, construct a screen top that fits tightly over the 20-gallon terrarium. Cover the bottom of the terrarium with sand or gravel. Add rocks and small branches to create an environment in which the chameleon can climb and hide. Suspend the moistened sponge from the screen to maintain proper humidity.

2. Place the thermometer inside the terrarium. If necessary, use a heat source to maintain the temperature between 22°C and 27°C.

3. Obtain a chameleon from your teacher. **CAUTION:** *Follow your teacher's instructions for handling chameleons. Be especially careful not to grab a chameleon by the tail. This could trigger a response in which the tail falls off.* Place the chameleon in the terrarium. Cover the terrarium with the screen top.

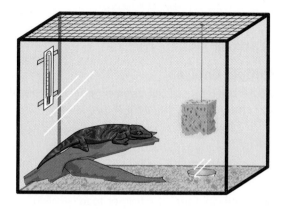

4. Feed live insects to the chameleon three to four times a week. **CAUTION:** *Always wash your hands after handling live animals.*

5. Observe the chameleon twice a day. Note its coloration and behavior. Use colored pencils to sketch the chameleon's appearance.

6. Design an experiment to test the effect of an environmental factor on color changes in chameleons. Choose one of these variables to investigate:
  • background color
  • light intensity
  • temperature (within 22°C to 27°C)
  Your experiment should test only one variable and should test the chameleon's long-term and short-term response to its environment. Your experiment should not involve handling the chameleon and should not harm the chameleon in any way.

7. With your teacher's approval, perform the experiment you designed.

Observations

1. Describe any color changes you observed in the chameleon.

2. If there was a color change, was it the same on all parts of the chameleon's body?

3. How much time did it take for you to notice a change? For the change to be complete?

Analysis and Conclusions

1. Did the chameleon change color in response to the environmental factor you investigated? Explain.

2. How quickly was the chameleon able to change color? For how long was the chameleon able to maintain a new color?

3. How does the chameleon's ability to change color help it to survive?

4. Formulate a hypothesis to explain how a chameleon is able to change color. How might you test this hypothesis?

Extensions

Research other animals that are able to change color rapidly. Do these animals use similar mechanisms to change color?

Chapter 34 Review

Study Outline

34-1 The Chordates

▶ All chordates have, at some stage in their life, a dorsal, hollow nerve cord, a notochord, and paired gill slits.

▶ Tunicates are soft-bodied marine animals that use gill slits for respiration and feeding. Lancelets are small marine animals with completely separate respiratory and digestive systems.

▶ Vertebrates have a spinal column consisting of vertebrae. They include fishes, amphibians, reptiles, birds, and mammals.

34-2 The Fishes

▶ Jawless fishes include lampreys and hagfishes. They have cartilage skeletons and a notochord that is present throughout life.

▶ Cartilaginous fishes include sharks, rays, and skates. They have cartilage skeletons, and movable upper and lower jaws with teeth.

▶ Bony fishes have bony skeletons, paired fins, and overlapping scales.

34-3 The Amphibians

▶ The amphibians have thin skin with mucus-secreting glands, two pairs of limbs, a pair of nostrils, and a three-chambered heart. They need water for reproduction, and they have a distinct larval form. Development generally involves metamorphosis.

▶ Tailed amphibians have long bodies and two pairs of short limbs. Tailless amphibians have short, squat bodies and powerful hind legs.

34-4 The Reptiles

▶ Reptiles do not require water for reproduction. Fertilization is internal. They do not have gills at any stage, and they do not undergo metamorphosis.

▶ Reptiles have eggs with shells, dry, scaly skin, a three- or four-chambered heart, and well-developed lungs. Except for snakes, reptiles have two pairs of legs. Nitrogenous waste is excreted mainly as uric acid.

Chapter Assessment

Multiple Choice

Choose the letter of the answer that best completes each statement or answers the question.

1. Animals whose body temperature remains fairly constant regardless of the temperature of the environment are (a) Reptilia. (b) endothermic. (c) Amphibia. (d) ectothermic.

2. The larval form of a frog or toad is called a (a) notochord. (b) cloaca. (c) tadpole. (d) reptile.

3. Animals with an enlarged brain and a spinal column made up of vertebrae that enclose the nerve cord belong to the subphylum called (a) Urochordata. (b) Vertebrata. (c) Chordata. (d) Cephalochordata.

4. The gas-filled sac that regulates buoyancy in most bony fishes is called the (a) lateral line. (b) tympanic membrane. (c) operculum. (d) swim bladder.

5. Chordates that may live on land but that need water for reproduction and development belong to the class (a) Reptilia. (b) Osteichthyes. (c) Cephalaspidomorphi. (d) Amphibia.

6. All chordates at some time in their lives have a dorsal, hollow (a) nerve cord. (b) swim bladder. (c) notochord. (d) cloaca.

7. In frogs, the structure located behind the ear that picks up sound waves is known as the (a) nictitating membrane. (b) lateral line. (c) tympanic membrane. (d) operculum.

8. The largest group of vertebrates is the (a) cartilaginous fishes. (b) bony fishes. (c) amphibians. (d) reptiles.

9. Nictitating membranes cover and protect a frog's (a) eyes. (b) lungs. (c) gills. (d) kidneys.

10. Reptiles excrete nitrogenous wastes in the form of (a) carbon dioxide. (b) venom. (c) uric acid. (d) ammonia.

Content Review

Answer each of the following in complete sentences.

11. Why are tunicates classified as chordates?

12. Describe the general characteristics of vertebrates.

13. What is the adaptational advantage of being warm-blooded?

14. Describe the general characteristics of the jawless fishes.

15. What is the advantage to the cartilaginous fishes of having movable upper and lower jaws?

16. Describe the respiratory system of the bony fishes.

17. Describe the characteristics of amphibians.

18. How is respiration in frogs suited to life both in the water and on land?

19. Describe the characteristics of reptiles.

20. What special adaptations of snakes enable them to swallow large prey?

Graphic Organizing

For information on graphic organizers, see Appendix G at the back of this text.

21. Concept Map Construct a concept map showing the basic characteristics of the phylum Chordata and its three subphyla. Include the following concepts: urochordates, vertebrates, dorsal hollow nerve cord, soft-bodied, tunicates, spinal column, cephalochordates, lancelets, brain, red blood cells, gas exchange, gill slits, heart, notochord. Include other appropriate concepts of your own choosing. Be sure to use linking words between concepts.

Critical Thinking and Problem Solving

Discuss each of the following in a brief paragraph.

22. Classifying Why have biologists classified tunicates as chordates rather than as members of the phylum Porifera? (See Chapter 32.)

23. Comparing In what ways is an adult whale shark similar to an adult flounder? In what ways are the two different?

24. Comparing Compare and contrast the ways in which snakes and frogs are adapted for life on land. Consider such features as their water needs, reproduction, respiration, and excretion.

25. Inferring Reptiles generally inhabit warm climates as opposed to cold regions. Suggest the probable cause for this geographic distribution.

26. Interpreting Pacific sardine fishing is done off the coast of Washington, Oregon, and California. In 1916, there were 4 boats catching sardines, whereas by 1936 there were 137 boats. Because of World War II, only 67 boats were available for fishing from 1939 to 1944. After World War II, the fishing fleet increased to over 100 boats. The graph below illustrates the Pacific sardine catch from 1916 to 1961. Interpret the graph in terms of the change in quantity of sardines caught over the years. Develop a hypothesis as to what caused the great reduction of the total catch after 1944.

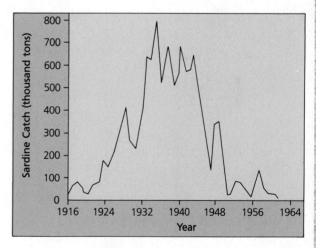

27. Experimenting If large tadpoles are placed in a tank with smaller tadpoles, the smaller ones may stop feeding and die, even though food is plentiful. Design an experiment to determine if the agent inhibiting them from eating is a chemical given off by the larger tadpoles.

Discovery Learning Activity

Mammal Adaptations

1. Examine the photographs of the different kinds of mammals in their environment. What adaptation allows the mammal to live in its environment?

2. Working in groups, make a list of characteristics that would fit all or most of the mammals that you have seen.

Vertebrates— Birds and Mammals

Guide for Reading

Previewing the Chapter

The long, elegant neck of the flamingo allows the bird to use its downward curving beak as a sieve to filter food from the water. The flamingo's specialized beak is only one of the characteristics that help flamingos survive in their environment. What are some general characteritics of birds? What is the evolutionary relationship between reptiles, birds, and mammals? What are the major groups of placental mammals?

Key Words

bird, Cro-Magnon, gizzard, mammal, marsupial, monotreme, Neanderthal, placental mammal

Key Concepts

- **Describe** the general characteristics of birds and mammals.
- **Discuss** fossil evidence of human origins.
- **Predict** the relatedness of several species from their amino acid sequences. (Laboratory Investigation)

35-1 Birds

Section Objectives:

- *List* the general characteristics of birds.
- *Describe* the structure and functions of feathers.
- *Describe* the internal body systems of birds.

General Characteristics of Birds

Birds, class **Aves** (AY veez), are found in almost all types of environments. Feathers distinguish birds from all other animals. Birds are thought to have evolved from reptiles, and the feathers are thought to be modified scales. Figure 35–1 shows the fossil bird *Archaeopteryx.* Many scientists believe it represents an evolutionary link between reptiles and birds. Contemporary birds do have reptilelike scales on their legs and feet.

Birds also share a number of other characteristics.

- The body is usually spindle-shaped and divided into a head, neck, trunk, and tail.
- There are two pairs of limbs. The forelimbs are wings, which, in most birds, are used for flying. The hind limbs are legs that are adapted for perching, walking or swimming, or prey-catching, depending on the type of bird.
- The bones are strong and light, and many bones are filled with air spaces.
- The circulatory system is well developed and includes a four-chambered heart.

▲ **Figure 35–1**

Archaeopteryx. The fossil bird *Archaeopteryx* lived about 150 million years ago. It had some features of both reptiles and birds.

◀ A closeup of the downward curving beak of a greater flamingo.

▲ **Figure 35–2**

Adaptation in Bird Beaks and Feet. Examples of variation in bird beaks and feet include, from left to right, the Swainson's hawk, the mallard duck, the yellow-bellied sapsucker, and the ostrich.

■ The respiratory system is highly efficient and consists of lungs connected to air sacs.

■ The mouth is in the form of a horn-covered beak or bill. There are no teeth.

■ The excretory system does not include a urinary bladder.

■ Fertilization is internal. The large, shell-covered eggs are incubated by the parents, and at hatching, the young are cared for by the parents.

■ Birds are warm-blooded. Compared to many vertebrates, their body temperature is quite high.

The beaks and feet of birds show adaptations for different ways of life. The pelican uses its long, sharp beak for catching fish. The cardinal uses its strong beak to crack open seeds. The hooked beak of the hawk allows it to tear its food. The woodpecker uses its beak to bore into trees and extract insects. A duck scoops and strains its food from mud with its beak. The ostrich and other ground-dwelling birds have sturdy feet and toes that enable them to run. Ducks and geese have webbed feet that are useful in swimming. The position of the toes and the presence of sharp claws permit woodpeckers to cling to the sides of trees. Grasping feet with sharp claws or talons are characteristic of falcons, hawks, and perching birds. In these birds, the tendons of the feet are so arranged that the weight of the body forces the toes to grasp the branch when the bird lands on it. This arrangement allows perching birds to sleep without falling off their perches.

Feathers

Feathers are lightweight and flexible, yet incredibly tough. They provide a body covering that protects the skin from wear, supports the bird in flight, and provides insulation from the weather. Feathers grow from follicles in the skin. As the feather grows in the follicle, pigments are deposited in the epidermal cells making up the feather. The color pattern of the feathers is typical of the species. In many species, the male and female have different coloring. Usually, the male is brighter than the female. The difference in coloring between sexes plays a role in the mating behavior of birds.

Figure 35–3 shows a typical feather. The flat area, the *vane,* is supported by a central shaft. The hollow part of the shaft that is attached to the skin follicle is called the *quill.* Each vane consists of many, closely spaced **barbs.** The barbs spread out diagonally from the shaft. Each barb has many **barbules.** The barbules of one barb overlap the barbules of the barb next to it. The barbs are held together by tiny hooks on the barbules themselves. When neighboring barbs become separated, the bird can zip them together with its beak.

Feathers grow only on certain parts of the skin. When fully grown, feathers are not living structures. Usually in the late summer, molting occurs. The feathers are shed and replaced by new feathers. Molting is usually a slow process. No part of the body is ever completely without feathers.

There are several different types of feathers. Elongated *contour feathers* are shown in Figure 35–3. They cover, insulate, and protect the body. Contour feathers that extend beyond the body are called *flight feathers.* Those on the wings support the bird in flight, while those on the tail serve as a rudder for steering. *Down feathers* have short shafts with long barbs. They are soft because the barbules lack hooks. In ducks, geese, and other water birds, down feathers are present beneath the contour feathers. Down feathers provide insulation by trapping air, which helps to save body heat. The winter coats of many birds include down feathers.

An oil gland near the base of the tail in birds helps to make the feathers waterproof. Birds use their beaks to take oil from the gland and spread it over the feathers.

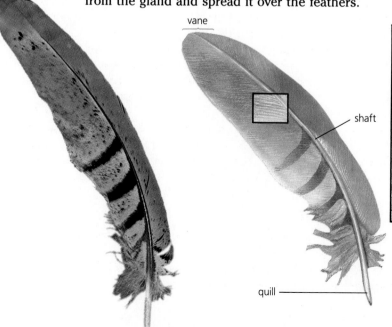

vane

shaft

quill

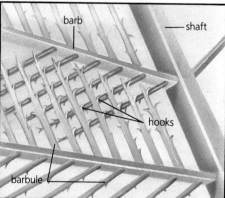

barb

shaft

hooks

barbule

◀ **Figure 35–3**

Structure of a Feather. Elongated contour feathers cover, insulate, and protect the body. Each feather is made up of barbs with overlapping barbules.

Internal Structure of Birds

Respiratory and Circulatory Systems The bird's unusual and highly efficient respiratory system can provide the large amount of oxygen needed for flight. Pouching out from the small lungs are **air sacs.** These are shown in Figure 35–4. The sacs occupy space between the internal organs and even run into the spaces in the larger bones. Air enters the respiratory system through the nostrils and passes down the *trachea,* which divides into two *bronchi.* The bird's *syrinx,* or song box, is located at the point at which the bronchi divide. One bronchus enters each lung. The bronchi pass through the lungs to the posterior air sacs. Thus, oxygen-rich air coming into the respiratory system passes through the lungs to the posterior air sacs without any exchange of respiratory gases. A system of small air tubes leads from the posterior air sacs into the lungs. The air tubes subdivide many times and make close contact with blood capillaries in the lungs. Oxygen-rich air from the posterior sacs is forced through the fine air tubes in the lungs, and gas exchange occurs with the blood. The air, now oxygen-poor, enters the anterior air sacs. From these sacs, it passes back up the trachea and out of the body. The one-way flow of air through the lungs for gas exchange increases the efficiency of the system.

The bird's circulatory system is similar to that of humans. There is a four-chambered heart and a complete separation of oxygenated and deoxygenated blood. Also like humans, birds generate and regulate their body heat internally. In other words, they are endothermic.

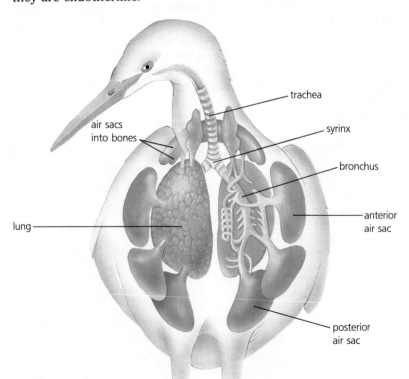

Figure 35–4

The Respiratory System of the Bird. The highly efficient respiratory system of the bird provides it with the large amounts of oxygen needed for flight. Air sacs increase the amount of air inhaled by the bird, and help to make the bird lighter. ▶

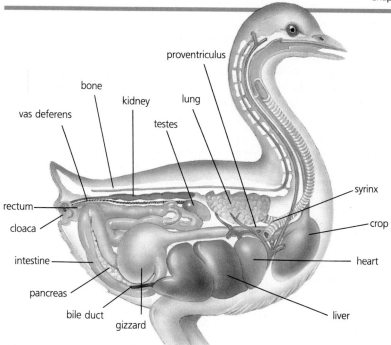

Digestive System Because of their high rates of metabolism and the energy needed for flight, birds eat large amounts of food. They feed on seeds, fruits, insects, worms, and in some cases, small reptiles and mammals. Some small birds take in an amount of food equal to 30 percent of their body weight each day.

Food is taken into the mouth, mixed with saliva, and passed down the esophagus to the *crop,* where it is stored and softened. From the crop, it passes into the first portion of the stomach, the *proventriculus* (proh ven TRIK yuh lus), where it is partially digested by gastric juice. It then passes to the **gizzard,** the second part of the stomach. The gizzard is a thick-walled, muscular organ that may contain small stones that have been swallowed by the bird. In the gizzard, the food is ground up and thoroughly mixed with the gastric juices. Next, the food moves into the intestine, where digestion is completed and nutrients are absorbed into the bloodstream. Undigested food enters the short rectum and leaves the body through the *cloaca.* The genital ducts and the ureters from the kidneys also open into the cloaca.

Excretory System Nitrogenous wastes, in the form of uric acid, are removed from the blood by the kidneys. Since there is no urinary bladder, these wastes pass through the ureters to the cloaca. They combine with the fecal matter in the cloaca to form a whitish, semisolid material.

Nervous System The brain of the bird is fairly large. The cerebellum, which is involved in muscle coordination, is well developed and allows the bird to perform precise movements in flight. In most birds, the senses of smell and taste are poorly developed, but the senses of sight, hearing, and balance are highly developed.

Reproductive System There are no external sex organs in birds. During mating, the sperm are transferred from the male to the female by contact of the cloacas. After fertilization in the female's reproductive tract, a protective shell is deposited around each egg. The female deposits her eggs in a nest, and they are incubated until hatching.

35-1 Section Review

1. Name the single characteristic that distinguishes birds from all other animals.
2. List three different types of feathers.
3. What unique structures are found in the lungs of birds?

Critical Thinking

4. How is the absence of a urinary bladder an adaptation for flight? *(Judging Usefulness)*

35-2 Mammals

Section Objectives:

■ *List* the major characteristics of mammals.
■ *Name* the three different kinds of mammals.
■ *List* the major orders of placental mammals and name some members of each.

General Characteristics of Mammals

The *mammals,* class **Mammalia** (muh MAYL ee uh), include many familiar animals—cats, dogs, bats, monkeys, horses, cows, deer, whales, and humans. Members of this group are found all over the earth in both cold and warm climates. Most are land dwelling, but a few, such as the whale, porpoise, and seal, are found in the oceans. Mammals range in size from the tiny pygmy shrew, which is less than 5 centimeters long and weighs less than 5 grams, to the giant blue whale, which may be 30 meters long and weighs more than 100 000 kilograms.

It is thought that mammals evolved from a group of reptiles that had some mammal-like characteristics. Two characteristics distinguish mammals from all other vertebrates. Mammals nourish their young with milk produced by mammary glands. The body covering of mammals is hair. The amount of hair varies. In whales and porpoises, just a few whiskers are found around the mouth of the animal. In many other mammals, the hair is in the form of a thick coat of fur that covers the body.

Mammals also share several other characteristics. Like birds, they are warm-blooded and have a four-chambered heart. An internal muscular wall, the *diaphragm,* separates the chest cavity from the abdominal cavity. The cerebrum of the brain is more highly developed than in any other group. Mammals are, therefore, the most intelligent of the animals.

Mammals have highly differentiated teeth. The structure and arrangement of the teeth vary from group to group, depending on feeding habits. There are four types of teeth: **incisors** (in SYZ erz), which are for cutting; **canines** (KAY nynz), which are for tearing; and **premolars** (pree MOHL erz) and **molars,** which are for grinding. These are shown in Figure 35–6.

Except for a few egg-laying mammals, all mammals give birth to living young. The number of offspring produced at each birth is fewer than in most other animals. However, because the young are cared for by the parents, they have a better chance of survival.

There are three different kinds of mammals—the **monotremes,** the **marsupials,** and the **placental mammals** (see Chapter 22). The monotremes are egg-laying mammals. They are the most primitive and reptilelike of the mammals. The duckbill platypus and spiny anteater of Australia are the only living monotremes. The marsupials are pouched mammals, such as the kangaroo, opossum, and koala. Marsupials are born at an immature stage and complete their development in their mother's pouch. Marsupials were once more common and widespread than they are today. Except in Australia, wherever placental mammals arose, marsupials eventually died out. Placental mammals are the largest and most successful group of mammals. In the placental mammals, the developing young remain within the uterus of the female until embryonic development is complete. The young are born in a stage of development more advanced than that in the marsupials.

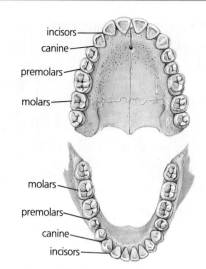

▲ **Figure 35–6**

The Teeth of Mammals. Mammals have differentiated teeth, including incisors, canines, premolars, and molars.

◀ **Figure 35–7**

Marsupials. Opossums are marsupials found in North America.

▲ **Figure 35–8**
Insect-Eating Mammals. These water shrews are feeding on grasshoppers.

Figure 35–9
Rodents and Lagomorphs. Rodents, such as this beaver (top), use their chisel-like incisor teeth to gnaw. The snowshoe hare (bottom), a lagomorph, has powerful hind legs for hopping. ▼

Kinds of Placental Mammals

There are about 15 different orders of placental mammals. Members of these groups range from tiny bats to enormous whales. The major orders of placental mammals are discussed below.

Insect-Eating Mammals Moles, hedgehogs, and shrews are insect-eating mammals, members of the order **Insectivora** (in sek TIV uh ruh). *Insectivores* (in SEK tuh vors) are usually small, mouselike animals. Many live underground. They feed on ants, grubs, beetles, and other insects.

Rodents Mice, rats, beavers, porcupines, squirrels, hamsters, and guinea pigs are all members of the order **Rodentia** (roh DENCH ee uh), the largest order of placental mammals. Their sharp, chisel-like incisor teeth are used for gnawing. These teeth grow throughout the animal's life to replace the ends that wear away. Rodents reproduce rapidly. Some are serious pests, destroying food and carrying disease.

Lagomorphs Rabbits and hares are members of the order **Lagomorpha** (lag uh MOR fuh). Like rodents, they are gnawing animals that feed on plants. Both rabbits and hares have long ears and fluffy tails. Newborn rabbits cannot see or move, and they have no fur. Newborn hares, on the other hand, are covered with fur and become active within a few hours. Both rabbits and hares move by hopping, using their powerful hind legs. They are among the fastest-moving mammals.

Flying Mammals Bats, members of the order **Chiroptera** (ky RAHP tuh ruh), are the only mammals capable of real flight. The wing of a bat consists of four long fingers covered by a membrane of skin. The first finger is used for grasping, as are the small hind legs. At rest, bats hang upside down by their hind legs. Bats are active at night.

While the most common bats feed on insects, some feed on fruit, pollen, or small animals. The vampire bat, which is found in Central and South America, preys mainly on cattle. To obtain blood,

Figure 35–10
Flying Mammals. Bats are the only true flying mammals. ▼

the bat bites off a small piece of skin and then laps up the blood. The total amount of blood lost is small, and the wound itself usually is not serious. However, bat bites can spread diseases.

Bats use a sonarlike system of *echolocation* to find their way around in the dark and to locate their prey. They produce high-frequency sound waves that bounce off any object the waves strike, producing an echo that the bat can hear. The distance to the object is determined by the time between when the sound was made and the echo returns.

Mammals Without Teeth   Anteaters, armadillos, and sloths belong to the order **Edentata** (ee den TAH tuh). These animals have either very small teeth or no teeth at all. Members of this order are found mainly in Central and South America. Anteaters and sloths are covered by long hair, while armadillos are covered by hard plates. Sloths spend much of their time hanging on trees. They feed on leaves and young shoots. Anteaters and armadillos primarily eat ants, termites, and other insects. Both of these animals have long claws and long tongues. They use their claws to break open anthills and termite mounds and their tongues to lick up the insects.

Mammals with Trunks   The order **Proboscidea** (proh buh SID ee uh) includes only African and Asiatic elephants. The muscular trunk of the elephant is formed from a greatly elongated upper lip and nose. The trunk is used to bring food to the mouth. The huge ivory tusks of the elephant are actually greatly enlarged upper incisor teeth. Elephants feed on plants. They are the largest living land animals. To maintain their huge bodies, elephants must feed for as long as 18 hours a day.

Hoofed Mammals   Mammals with feet in the form of hooves are called *ungulates* (UNG yoo lets). The ungulates are divided into two orders according to the number of toes on the hoof. Those with an even number of toes on the hoof belong to the order **Artiodactyla** (art ee uh DAK tuh luh). This order includes pigs, deer, antelopes, sheep, cattle, giraffes, and camels. Ungulates with an odd number of toes belong to the order **Perissodactyla** (puh ris uh DAK tuh luh). This order includes horses, rhinoceroses, and tapirs.

▲ **Figure 35–11**
Mammals Without Teeth. Anteaters use their tongue to gather ants and termites.

Figure 35–12
Mammals with Trunks. Elephants are the only mammals with trunks. ▼

◄ **Figure 35–13**
Hoofed Mammals. The hoofed animals, or ungulates, include goats (left) and zebras (right).

All ungulates are plant eaters (herbivores) and tend to feed in herds. Their flattened teeth can crush and grind tough plant material. Some ungulates, such as cattle, sheep, camels, and deer, are *ruminants* (ROO muh nents). Their stomachs have four chambers. When grazing, they store large amounts of food in a chamber of the stomach called the **rumen** (ROO men). Later, they bring the food back up into their mouths and chew it thoroughly before swallowing it for a second time.

Meat-Eating Mammals The order **Carnivora** (kar NIV uh ruh) includes cats, dogs, bears, skunks, and other mammals that eat meat. Some meat eaters (carnivores), such as the bear, eat plant material as well as meat. Most carnivores are strong and fast moving and have sharp claws. Their powerful jaws and large teeth are specialized for seizing, cutting, and tearing meat. They have a well-developed sense of smell. Carnivores are generally intelligent, and much of their hunting behavior is learned.

Aquatic Mammals Walruses, sea lions, and seals are meat-eating, aquatic mammals that belong to the order **Pinnipedia** (pin uh PEED ee uh). They feed mainly on fish. Their limbs are modified as flippers, and their body shape is adapted for swimming.

Whales, dolphins, and porpoises are members of the order **Cetacea** (see TAYSH ee uh). These animals are well adapted to life in the ocean. Although they are air breathers, they can remain underwater for long periods of time by holding their breath. As you can see in Figure 35–15, the forelimbs of cetaceans also are modified as flippers. There are no hind limbs. Cetaceans swim by moving their powerful tails up and down through the water. Like other mammals, cetaceans give birth to live young, which are fed on milk from the mammary glands.

Porpoises, dolphins, and some whales have teeth and feed on fish. The largest whales, however, feed on plankton, the small organisms that float in the oceans. Plankton is strained from the water by a series of horny plates called *baleen*. Blue whales, which feed on plankton, are the largest animals that have ever lived.

Manatees and dugongs belong to the small order **Sirenia** (sie REEN ee ah). They are plant eaters. Like cetaceans, they lack hind limbs and have flattened tails to help them move through the water.

▲ **Figure 35–14**
Meat-Eating Mammals. The grizzly bear is one of many meat-eating mammals, or carnivores.

Figure 35–15
Aquatic Mammals. Aquatic mammals belong to one of three orders. Examples include, from left to right, the sea lion, a member of the order Pinnipedia, the Beluga whale, a Cetacean, and the manatee, which belongs to the order Sirenia. ▼

◀ **Figure 35–16**
A Primate. An orangutan has hands with opposable thumbs.

Primates   Humans, apes, and monkeys are members of the order **Primates** (pry MAYT eez). All *primates* (PRY mayts) have well-developed grasping hands that allow them to handle and manipulate objects. Their fingers and toes have flat nails instead of claws. Humans, apes, and monkeys have **opposable thumbs.** An opposable thumb can be positioned opposite to the other fingers, making it possible to grasp objects in one hand.

Except for humans, gorillas, and baboons, which live on the ground, most primates live in trees. Primates eat both plant material and meat. Primates are the most intelligent of the mammals. Their brains are large and complex, and their sense of sight is well developed.

35-2 Section Review

1. What two characteristics can be used to distinguish mammals from other vertebrates?
2. Name the three different kinds of mammals.
3. What is the largest order of placental mammals?
4. To what order do whales, dolphins, and porpoises belong?

Critical Thinking

5. Why do scientists classify egg-laying *monotremes,* such as the duckbill platypus, as mammals? (*Identifying Reasons*)

Winging It

Problem

To this day, the origin of bird flight remains a mystery. Did the first birds take off from the ground or glide from trees? Scientists have yet to come to an agreement regarding this controversy.

Except for wings and feathers, *Archaeopteryx*, which lived about 150 million years ago, basically had the same structural features as a running, two-legged theropod dinosaur. *Archaeopteryx*, the earliest bird, had claws on its wings that might have been used for climbing. Unlike modern birds, *Archaeopteryx* did not have a breastbone, fused bones, or hollow bones. It probably flew or glided clumsily and may have had to take off from higher places such as trees and cliffs.

Fossils from the Cretaceous period indicate the presence of birds that had many of the features found in modern birds, such as beaks and flaps of feathers on the wings. The latter gave birds their maneuverability and enabled them to fly at slower speeds. Then about 65 million years ago, birds began to resemble modern birds.

Task

You are a member of a team of museum scientists that has been asked by the Audubon Society to set up an exhibit on various topics about birds. You specifically have been asked to set up the section on gliding birds.

In order to perform this task, you must complete each of the following:

1. Research the topic of bird flight on the Internet and in the library to discover how the gliding birds move in flight.

2. Using the diagram, construct a glider that will model a gliding bird's flight.

3. Launch the glider and measure how far it travels. Make modifications in structure and calculate the change in wing surface area for each model tested (Area=1/2 hb).Continue testing and recording data in a table. Describe how the changes that were made in your design affected the flight duration and distance.

4. Keep a journal of all the flight data and the information collected during your research.

5. Show the relationship between modern birds and their ancestors' adaptations to flight in different types of environments.

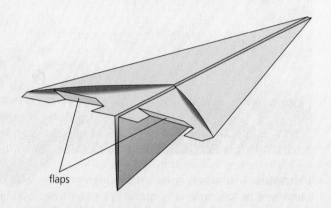

flaps

Solution

Find a large, open area in which to launch the model glider. Perform all launches at chin height, being careful not to hit anyone. Using a stopwatch, determine the glider's duration aloft, or length of time it stays in the air. Measure and record the straight-line distance from the launch point to the landing point. For accuracy, aim for a target, such as a chair, placed four meters from the launch point. Measure and record the distance the glider lands from target. Perform a total of five launches for each of three flap positions: both flaps up, both flaps down, and one flap up and the other down. Based on your results, draw conclusions as to why some launches traveled farther distances than others.

As a member of the team, include the design of your glider and the data you collected in your exhibit. Add any other information that will show visitors that the Audubon Society conducts research on ornithology, or the study of birds.

35-3 Human Origins

Section Objectives:

- *List* the characteristics that distinguish humans from other primates.
- *Describe* the characteristics of *Australopithecus, Homo habilis,* and *Homo erectus.*
- *Compare* and *contrast* Neanderthals, Cro-Magnons, and modern humans.

Identifying Human Fossils

The branch of science that attempts to trace the development of the human species is called **anthropology** (an thruh PAHL uh jee). Anthropology deals with human physical, social, and cultural development. It also deals with the study of the origin of humans. Few areas of scientific research have produced more confusion and disagreement than the interpretation of the human fossil record. This record is fragmentary. Often, it consists of a few teeth or scattered pieces of bone. Occasionally, a complete jawbone, skull, pelvis, or thigh bone is found. Putting these bone fragments together to form a complete picture of an organism is like doing a jigsaw puzzle when all the pieces are the same color, many pieces are missing, and you do not know what the finished puzzle is supposed to look like. Dating the fossils is difficult. Their ages must be inferred from the age of the rocks in which they are found. Accurate measurements by absolute dating methods are not always possible.

Humans, apes, and monkeys are all primates that are structurally similar in many ways. However, there are several characteristics that distinguish humans from other primates.

The size and shape of the skull are different from other primates. The human brain is much larger than that of other primates. To hold the brain, the human skull is larger than that of other primates and has a unique shape. The cranium, or brain case, is higher and more rounded than that of other primates. Humans also have relatively flat, vertical foreheads, while other primates have sloping foreheads with bony eyebrow ridges. See Figure 35–17.

Figure 35–17

Comparison of Human and Gorilla Skulls and Jaws. The gorilla's brain capacity is about 450 cm³ while that of the human is about 1450 cm³. ▼

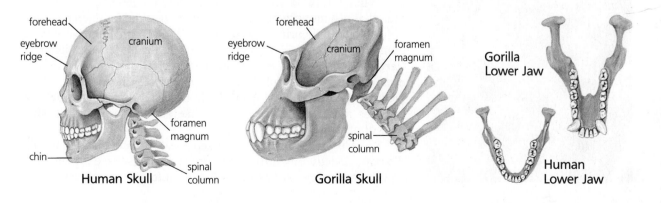

Human Skull

Gorilla Skull

Gorilla Lower Jaw

Human Lower Jaw

The jaws and teeth are different from other primates. Primates other than humans generally have heavy, rectangularly shaped jawbones. The jawbones of humans are lighter and typically U-shaped in front. Also, humans have distinct chins, while the other primates are chinless. Human teeth are generally smaller than those of other primates.

The pelvis and foramen magnum are different. Another unique characteristic of humans is their ability to walk on two legs in an upright position. This is called **bipedal locomotion.** With the exception of birds and kangaroos, most other animals walk on four legs. There are several structural adaptations connected with bipedal locomotion. The pelvis is adapted for upright posture. The back of the pelvis is thick and strong and serves as a site of attachment for the long muscles of the legs. The bowl shape of the pelvis helps to support the internal organs. The S-shaped spinal column places the center of gravity over the pelvis and legs.

The **foramen magnum** (fuh RAY men MAG num) is the opening in the skull where the spinal cord enters. In humans, this opening is under the skull. Its location allows the head to be balanced on top of the spinal column. In other primates, the foramen magnum is toward the back of the skull. This position means that the skull is held forward and tends to face downward. In fossils, the location of the foramen magnum determines whether or not a primate had bipedal locomotion.

Modern humans, and humanlike fossils that exhibited bipedal locomotion, are called *hominids.* The only hominids alive today are humans.

Fossil Evidence of Human Origins

From the fossil record, it is thought that apes began to evolve around 30 million years ago. Based on fossil and biochemical evidence, most scientists believe that humans and apes evolved along different paths from a common ancestor.

Australopithecus   In 1924, workers in a limestone quarry in South Africa found some skulls embedded in the rock. Most of the skulls were those of monkeys, but one skull showed some human characteristics. It looked like the skull of a child about five years old. While the brain size was greater than an ape's, it was smaller than that of a modern human. The position of the foramen magnum indicated that the primate was bipedal. Finally, the teeth were more humanlike than apelike, as can be seen in Figure 35–18. Raymond Dart, a famous anthropologist, named the new species *Australopithecus africanus* (aus truh luh PITH uh kus af ruh KAN us), which means "ape of southern Africa." He believed that **Australopithecus** was more humanlike than apelike and represented an early type of hominid.

In 1936, Dr. Robert Broom discovered the remains of an adult *Australopithecus.* Since then, hundreds of such fossils have been found, and the genus has been divided into several species.

Figure 35–18

Skull of *Australopithecus africanus.* Features of *Australopithecus* indicate a closer link to humans than to apes. ▼

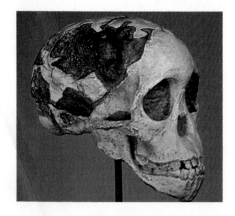

It is believed that *Australopithecus africanus* (also called *A. africanus*) lived between 3 million and 2 million years ago. Members of this group were about 1 meter tall and weighed about 25 kilograms. They could stand and walk upright. In proportion to body size, their brain size was somewhat larger than that of a gorilla.

In 1938, Robert Broom found a fossil of a species that was similar to *A. africanus* but larger and more muscular. He named this massively built but related species *Australopithecus robustus* (roh BUS tus). *A. robustus* was a little over 1.5 meters in height and weighed about 65 kilograms. The jaw of *A. robustus* was heavier than that of *A. africanus*, and the teeth were larger. Extensive pitting in the molars of *A. robustus* suggested that they fed on vegetation containing sand. The teeth of *A. africanus* do not show this pitting, and it is thought, therefore, that they were meat eaters.

A. robustus lived between 2.2 and 1.4 million years ago. Most experts believe that this hominid became extinct and was not an ancestor of modern humans.

In 1974, Donald Johanson and Maurice Taieb discovered the bones of a small female *Australopithecus*. Johanson called her Lucy. Although she had an ape-sized brain and jaw, the pelvis clearly showed she was bipedal. Then, in 1975, they found the fossilized bones of a group of adults and children, apparently all killed at the same time, possibly by a flash flood. All these prehuman fossils are between 3.8 and 2.8 million years old and were named *Australopithecus afarensis*.

At the present time, scientists cannot agree on how many species of *Australopithecus* there were or whether or not they were the ancestors of human beings. Although scientists disagree on these issues, they do agree that bipedal locomotion apparently evolved before an increased brain size.

Homo Habilis Since 1959, fossils found in East Africa by Louis and Mary Leakey and their son Richard indicate that other hominids lived at the same time as *Australopithecus*. Compared to *Australopithecus*, these hominids had more humanlike teeth and

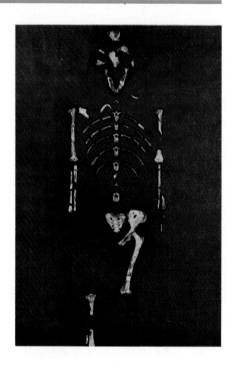

▲ **Figure 35–19**

Australopithecus afarensis. Lucy, a small female *A. afarensis*, lived about 3.6 million years ago.

◄ **Figure 35–20**

The Leakeys. The fossil discoveries made by anthropologists Louis and Mary Leakey (left) and by their son, Richard (right), have been central to our understanding of human evolution.

Figure 35–21

Hand and Skull of *Homo habilis*. The hand shows that *H. habilis* had good manual dexterity. ▶

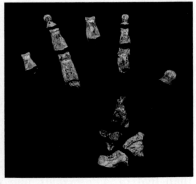

larger brains. Found with these fossils were pebbles chipped to form sharp-edged tools. Because they were toolmakers, these fossils have been classified as *Homo,* the same genus as modern humans. They have been named *Homo habilis* (HOH moh HAB uh lus), which means "handy man." A hand and skull of *H. habilis* is shown in Figure 35–21. *Homo habilis* is thought to have lived between 2.2 and 1.6 million years ago.

Homo Erectus   The first remains showing truly human characteristics appear in the fossil record about 1.5 million years ago. These hominids, thought to be descendants of *Homo habilis,* are classified as *Homo erectus* (uh REK tus). See Figure 35–22. Fossil bones, tools, and living sites of *H. erectus* have been found in Asia, Africa, and Europe. *H. erectus* was the first user of fire. Members of this species lived in groups. Their brain size, although larger than that of *H. habilis,* was significantly smaller than that of modern humans. It is thought that *H. erectus* survived until 350 000 to 250 000 years ago and that they gave rise to the earliest members of the species ***Homo sapiens*** (SAY pee inz), the species of modern humans.

Neanderthals   The **Neanderthals** (nee AN der thals) were an early type of *Homo sapiens.* They are classified as *H. sapiens neanderthalensis.* The Neanderthals first appeared about 130 000 years ago. Their fossils have been found throughout Europe, Africa, and Southeast Asia. These humans were only about 1.5 meters tall but powerfully built. Their faces had heavy, bony eyebrow ridges. According to skull measurements, their brain size was as large as or slightly larger than that of modern humans, but it was shaped differently.

Neanderthals lived in family groups in caves or in simple shelters built of rocks. They used fire and produced a variety of stone tools. It appears that some of these tools were used to scrape hides, which were then used to make clothing. Tools were also used

▲ **Figure 35–22**

Early People. These artist's representations show, clockwise from upper right, *Homo erectus*, Neanderthal, and Cro-Magnon figures.

to kill large animals, such as mammoths and woolly rhinoceroses, which were trapped in pits lined with wooden spikes. Fossil evidence indicates that the Neanderthals buried their dead, sometimes with weapons and food.

Cro-Magnons   About 35 000 years ago, the Neanderthals disappeared from the fossil record and were replaced by the **Cro-Magnons** (kroh MAG nuns). Fossil remains of Cro-Magnons have been found in Europe, Asia, Africa, and Australia. Scientists do not know what happened to the Neanderthals. They may have been killed off by the more advanced Cro-Magnons, or possibly the two groups interbred, and the Neanderthals lost their identity.

The skeletons of Cro-Magnons were like those of modern humans, and their brain size was about the same. They lived not only in caves but also in dwellings built of rock, wood, and hides. They made finely chipped stone and bone tools, including axes, knives, awls, chisels, and scrapers. They also made fishhooks, needles, and spear points. They wore clothing sewn from animal skins. On the walls of caves in France are paintings by Cro-Magnons

Figure 35–23
A Cro-Magnon Cave Painting. ▶

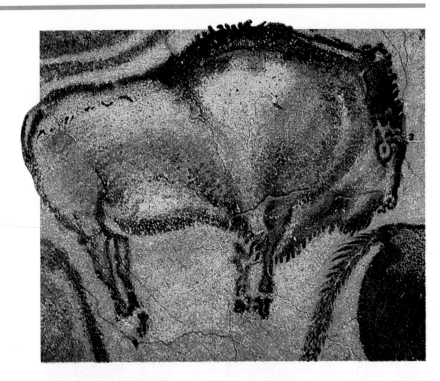

of the animals they hunted. These drawings may have had some spiritual significance. The Cro-Magnons seem to have had a ritual for burying their dead. Often, the body was covered with dye and buried with food and personal articles.

Until the Cro-Magnons, most of the evolutionary changes in the human species apparently were physical changes, such as brain volume. See Figure 35–24. From the Cro-Magnons on, however, changes are thought to have been mainly behavioral and cultural rather than physical. It is believed that the Cro-Magnons migrated to various parts of the world. The different groups gave rise to the three primary human races—Negroid (black), Oriental (yellow), and Caucasoid (white).

Interpreting the Fossil Evidence

Because fossil evidence is limited, the ancestry of humans is still vague. Often, there are large gaps in the fossil record. Therefore, as new fossils are discovered and interpreted, the human evolutionary sequence is revised. Figure 35–25 shows two possible patterns of human evolution that have been proposed by different scientists.

Recent studies by molecular geneticists indicate that as different species evolve from a common ancestor, their DNA sequences change at a fairly constant rate. By comparing the DNA sequences of particular genes in related species whose ages are already known from fossil evidence, the rates of change in the DNA can be assessed. This can be done indirectly by comparing changes in the amino acid sequences of similar proteins. This measurement can serve as a genetic, or *molecular,* clock. It has been shown that there are fewer differences in similar proteins between closely related

Figure 35–24
Brain Volume Increase During Hominid Evolution. The brain size of *Australopithecus* was about three times smaller than that of the earliest *Homo sapiens.* ▼

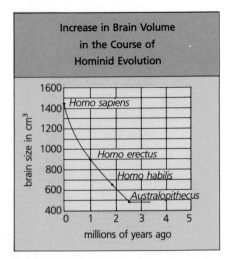

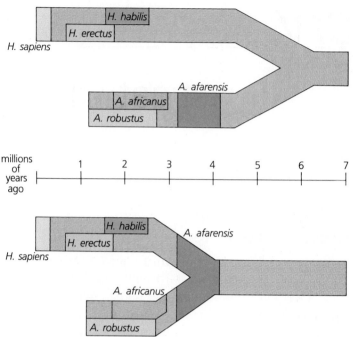

◀ **Figure 35–25**
Two Hypotheses for Human Evolution. The scheme on the top has been proposed by Richard Leakey; the scheme on the bottom has been proposed by Donald Johanson. Gray areas represent gaps for which there is no fossil information.

species than between distantly related species. Thus, the number of base differences in the DNA of related species can be used as a measure of the time at which the species diverged from a common ancestor.

Evidence based on the molecular clock indicates that the split between humans and apes occurred about 5 or 6 million years ago. Fossil evidence suggests that the split occurred between 12 million and 6 million years ago. However, since so few humanlike fossils have been discovered from this period, much about our evolutionary past is not yet known.

35-3 **Section Review**

1. What is bipedal locomotion?
2. List the names of three species of *Australopithecus*.
3. Which human ancestors or prehumans probably used tools?
4. Which human ancestors are classified as *Homo sapiens?*

Critical Thinking

5. A scientist analyzed the DNA sequence of a single gene in three closely related species. She determined that there were fewer sequence differences between species *X* and *Y* than between either species *Y* and *Z* or species *X* and *Z*. From this, the scientist concluded that species *X* and *Y* were more closely related. What assumption(s) does this conclusion rest on? (*Identifying Assumptions*)

Laboratory

Investigation

Comparing Amino Acid Sequences in Vertebrates

Natural selection and evolution would predict that species which diverged from one another relatively recently in the history of life on earth will share more genetic similarities than species that diverged from one another earlier. Because proteins are programmed by genes, a comparison of the amino acid sequence of their proteins would indicate the relatedness among species. In this investigation, you will compare the amino acid sequences of the same protein in several vertebrates.

Problem

How can you **predict** the degree to which various species are related from the amino acid sequences in their proteins?

Materials

Data table of amino acid sequences of the protein cytochrome-c

Procedure

1. Use the amino acid sequences to calculate the percentage difference between a rhesus monkey and a rattlesnake. To calculate the percentage difference between two species, determine the number of amino acids that differ between the two species, then divide that number by the total number of amino acids in the sequence. (The sequences provided have 60 amino acids.)

2. Make an approximate prediction regarding the percentage difference of the cytochrome-c amino acid sequences of a human and a chimpanzee. Record this information in a data table.

Amino Acid Sequences in Cytochrome-C

Human	GDVEKGKKIFIMKCSQCHTVEKGGKHKTGPNLHGLFGRKTGQAPGYSYTAANKNKGIIWG
Chimpanzee	GDVEKGKKIFIMKCSQCHTVEKGGKHKTGPNLHGLFGRKTGQAPGYSYTAANKNKGIIWG
Rhesus monkey	GDVEKGKKIFIMKCSQCHTVEKGGKHKTGPNLHGLFGRKTGQAPGYSYTAANKNKGITWG
Horse	GDVEKGKKIFVQKCAQCHTVEKGGKHKTGPNLHGLFGRKTGQAPGFTYTDANKNKGITWK
Donkey	GDVEKGKKIFVQKCAQCHTVEKGGKHKTGPNLHGLFGRKTGQAPGFSYTDANKNKGITWK
Chicken	GDIEKGKKIFVQKCSQCHTVEKGGKHKTGPNLHGLFGRKTGQAEGFSYTDANKNKGITWG
Turkey	GDIEKGKKIFVQKCSQCHTVEKGGKHKTGPNLHGLFGRKTGQAEGFSYTDANKNKGITWG
Rattlesnake	GDVEKGKKIFTMKCSQCHTVEKGGKHKTGPNLHGLFGRKTGQAVGYSYTAANKNKGITWG

The letters represent the amino acids as shown:

G = glycine, A = alanine, V = valine, L = leucine, I = isoleucine, M = methionine, F = phenylalanine, W = tryptophan, P = proline, S = serine, T = threonine, C = cysteine, Y = tyrosine, N = asparagine, Q = glutamine, D = aspartic acid, E = glutamic acid, K = lysine, R = arginine, H = histidine

3. To test your prediction, repeat step 1 for a human and a chimpanzee.

4. Repeat steps 1 to 3 using the amino acid sequences of a horse and a donkey.

5. Repeat steps 1 to 3 using the amino acid sequences of a chicken and a turkey.

6. Repeat steps 1 to 3 using the amino acid sequences of a chimpanzee and a rhesus monkey.

7. Repeat steps 1 to 3 using the amino acid sequences of birds, rattlesnakes, and mammals.

Observations

1. How different are humans and chimps in the first 60 amino acids of the cytochrome-c sequence?

2. What pattern of relatedness did you observe from the percentage differences among various vertebrates?

Analysis and Conclusions

1. Which vertebrates share the most recent common ancestors? Which share more distant common ancestors?

2. Would you be able to draw a "family tree" of the organisms named, showing when they diverged from one another? Would such a family tree be very accurate?

3. Some positions on the amino acid sequence are the same for all cytochrome-c molecules shown. Why might this be so?

4. As a rule, what general conclusion can you draw regarding how closely related species are and how their cytochrome-c amino acid sequences compare?

Extensions

Research data on the gene sequences of various proteins in vertebrates. Use this data to construct a family tree of related organisms.

Chapter 35 Review

Study Outline

35-1 Birds

▶ Similarities between birds and reptiles suggests an evolutionary link between the two groups.

▶ Feathers provide a protective body covering for birds, support them in flight, and insulate them from the weather.

▶ Birds are warm-blooded and have a four-chambered heart. Their respiratory, circulatory, and digestive systems provide the large amounts of oxygen and energy needed for flight.

35-2 Mammals

▶ Mammals nourish their young with milk produced by mammary glands. The body covering of mammals is hair. They are warm-blooded and have a four-chambered heart.

▶ Monotremes are egg-laying mammals. Marsupials are pouched mammals. In placental mammals, the developing young are retained in the mother's uterus until development is complete.

35-3 Human Origins

▶ Unique characteristics of humans include the size and shape of the skull, jaws and teeth different from those of other primates, and the ability to walk on two legs in an upright position.

▶ The earliest prehuman primate group for which we have fossil evidence is *Australopithecus.* Other hominids include *Homo habilis, Homo erectus,* Neanderthals, and Cro-Magnons.

▶ The fossil evidence of human ancestry is limited. Different interpretations of human evolution have been proposed by scientists.

Chapter Assessment

Multiple Choice

Choose the letter of the answer that best completes each statement or answers the question.

1. Birds are thought to have evolved from
(a) amphibians. (b) reptiles. (c) small mammals.
(d) duck-billed platypuses.

2. The crop of a bird is used to (a) grind food into small particles. (b) store and soften food. (c) store air and pass it to its lungs. (d) filter wastes from the blood.

3. How many chambers are in a bird's heart?
(a) two (b) three (c) four (d) six

4. Birds are less dense than other vertebrates mainly due to the presence of (a) feathers. (b) light breast muscles. (c) air space in their bones. (d) beaks and claws.

5. Because mammals regulate body heat and temperature, they are called (a) endoderms. (b) ectotherms. (c) endoblasts. (d) endotherms.

6. Into which three main groups are mammals classified? (a) primates, carnivores, and herbivores (b) monotremes, marsupials, and placental mammals (c) insectivores, carnivores, and herbivores (d) aquatic, land, and flying mammals

7. The most primitive mammals are (a) marsupials. (b) primates. (c) monotremes. (d) placentals.

8. Members of which order of mammals navigate using a sophisticated echolocation system? (a) Dermoptera (b) Chiroptera (c) Insectivora (d) Lagomorpha

9. To which order do Indian and African elephants belong? (a) Perissodactyla (b) Cetacea (c) Sirenia (d) Proboscidea

10. Compared to a reptile, a bird's body temperature is (a) higher and more constant. (b) lower and more constant. (c) higher and more variable. (d) lower and more variable.

Content Review

Answer each of the following in complete sentences.

11. What are the general characteristics of birds?

12. Explain how birds are adapted for flight.

13. Trace the path of air through the respiratory system of the bird.

14. Describe the structure and function of the digestive system in birds.

15. List four types of mammal teeth and describe their functions.

16. How do monotremes, marsupials, and placentals differ?

17. How does reproduction in birds differ from reproduction in placentals?

18. What makes primates well adapted to life in trees?

19. Why is *Homo erectus* considered closer to humans than *Homo habilis* is?

20. Why do scientists disagree about how humans evolved?

Graphic Organizing

For information on graphic organizers, see Appendix G at the back of this text.

21. **Scale** The average brain volume of chimpanzees is about 395 cm³; that of gorillas is about 450 cm³. Using this information and the data for *Australopithecus, Homo habilis, H. erectus,* and *H. sapiens* shown in Figure 35–24, construct a scale from smallest brain volume to largest, placing each of these primates on the scale. Start the scale at 300 cm³ and end it at 1500 cm³. How does the difference in brain volume between gorillas and *Australopithecus* compare with that between *Australopithecus* and *Homo habilis?*

Critical Thinking and Problem Solving

Discuss each of the following in a brief paragraph.

22. **Classifying** Since bats are capable of true flight, why are they not classified as birds?

23. **Relating** What assumptions have been made by anthropologists about the intelligence of early hominids?

24. **Relating** Why are the placentals the most successful group of mammals?

25. **Inferring** Figure 35–22 shows an artist's representations of *Homo erectus,* Neanderthal, and Cro-Magnon people. What would you need to know in order to determine whether these drawings are reliable?

26. **Interpreting** An investigation was conducted to determine whether latitude affects brood size (number of young produced per mating season) in robins. Using the data in the table below, calculate the average value for each group. Interpret the data and draw a conclusion about robin brood sizes. What further experiments could be done both in the field and in the laboratory to study brood size?

Brood	Number of Young Robins		
	Group A 22°N Latitude	**Group B 42°N Latitude**	**Group C 62°N Latitude**
1	3	4	5
2	2	3	7
3	3	5	6
4	4	4	6
5	3	5	7
6	4	5	5
7	3	4	7
8	5	6	6
9	3	5	7
10	3	5	6
11	2	4	6
12	3	4	7

Discovery Learning Activity

Dog Behavior

1. Working in a group, brainstorm for a list of 20 behaviors that are common to dogs.

2. Classify each behavior as inborn (being present at birth) or learned as the dog grows and matures. Have a member of your group read aloud to the class all behaviors classified as inborn. Discuss any disagreements.

Behavior

36-1 The Nature of Behavior

Section Objectives:

- *Distinguish* between a behavioral response and a physiological response.
- *Explain* how organisms coordinate behavior.

Stimuli and Behavior

An organism's environment is always changing. These changes may involve one or more external factors, including heat, light, carbon dioxide, oxygen, moisture, and the activities of other organisms. Environmental changes also may involve internal factors, such as thirst or hunger. Any change in the external or internal environment is called a **stimulus** (plural, stimuli).

In a living organism, metabolic processes work best when *homeostasis,* or a stable internal environment, is maintained. Living things maintain homeostasis by physiological or behavioral responses to stimuli. When a hungry dog smells food, it salivates. The smell of food is a stimulus. Secreting saliva is a physiological response. The dog may then actively hunt for food or whine to its owner. Such responses are behavioral. All of these responses help the dog to digest food and restore homeostasis. As another example, a person sweats when hot. If this

▲ **Figure 36–1**

Courtship Behavior. The male frigate bird has a bright red, inflatable throat sac used for courtship display.

◀ Two female baboons caring for an infant.

▲ **Figure 36–2**
Perception of Light. Evening primrose as it is seen by a human (top). Evening primrose as it is seen by a honeybee (bottom). Honeybees are able to see ultraviolet light, whereas humans are not. Thus, the same flower is perceived differently by different species.

response does not cool the body, the person may remove outer clothing. Sweating is a physiological response. Removing outer clothing is a form of behavior. **Behavior** is the series of activities performed by an organism in response to stimuli. Although stimuli may bring about physiological responses, such as sweating, these responses usually are not classified as behavior.

Each species has its own pattern of behavior. In flight, a robin usually does not respond to the sight of a rabbit. A hawk, however, may respond by capturing and eating the rabbit.

Behavior aids in the survival of the individual and the species. When a rabbit sees an attacking hawk, it runs first in one direction, and then abruptly changes direction. This behavior may confuse the attacker and allow the rabbit to escape.

Perceiving and Responding to Stimuli

Organisms are exposed to countless environmental stimuli involving sound, light, chemicals, movement, and many other factors. But, one organism may not perceive something that another perceives. The honeybee, for example, can see ultraviolet light, but humans cannot. See Figure 36–2. Because of its form of vision, the bee can distinguish between white light with ultraviolet light and white light without ultraviolet light. Therefore, a bee's "white" and a human's "white" are different.

Many organisms, especially bats, have a keen sense of hearing. Bats feed on moths and other night-flying insects. A bat uses echolocation by bouncing high-pitched sounds off objects. The bat is able to detect the echoes and determine whether an object is an obstacle or moving prey. Having processed this information, the bat responds by directing its flight toward the insect or around the obstacle. Some moths are able to hear the bat sounds. They respond by trying to avoid the bat. See Figure 36–3.

Figure 36–3
Significant Stimulus. A bat responds to a small object that moves, but not to a stationary object. Here, a horseshoe bat pursues a moth in flight. ▶

▲ **Figure 36–4**

Cheetah Chasing Prey. The behavior of an organism is dependent on its body structure.

Another type of environmental factor that can be perceived differently by different organisms involves the sense of smell and chemicals. The female gypsy moth, for example, releases a chemical sex attractant. Male gypsy moths are able to detect minute quantities of this chemical from great distances. In comparison, humans have a poor sense of smell.

Because there are so many stimuli in the environment, an organism must respond only to signs or "messages" that are significant to it. A frog flicks outs its tongue to catch small, dark objects that move. It does not respond to stationary objects. A spider in its web responds only to web vibrations caused by a trapped insect and not to web movements caused by wind. Responding only to particular messages is important when quick action is necessary to capture food or to avoid danger. Each message triggers a specific behavior pattern that is unique to the species involved.

Coordinating Behavior

The behavior of an organism depends on its form and structure. As you can see in Figure 36–4, the cheetah's body structure permits it to run swiftly to catch prey. The robin escapes predators by flying away. Humans and other organisms respond in ways that are suited to their bodies.

Behavior is affected by all the body systems. The nervous system, endocrine system, muscles, and skeleton influence an organism's responses. The more complex an organism's nervous system and structure are, the more complex its behavior is. A frog's behavior, for example, is more complex than a grasshopper's. The behavior of a chimpanzee is more complex than that of a frog. Human behavior is the most complex of all.

▲ **Figure 36–5**

Canada Geese in Flight. Some behavioral activities, such as flying in a "V" formation, occur at the population level.

The Nervous System   All multicellular animals, except the sponge, have nervous systems. The nervous system coordinates complex behavior. The simplest nervous systems occur in the coelenterates, which include the hydra, jellyfish, and sea anemone. The members of this group have nervous systems consisting of cells that form a *nerve net* (see Chapter 14). A nerve net produces little or no coordination of activity. In the sea anemone, if a tentacle touches a small piece of food, only that tentacle bends toward the mouth. If the prey is large and struggling, the stimulus spreads over the nerve net, and other tentacles join in the response.

The flatworm exhibits more complex behavior. A flatworm moves by the beating of cilia on its lower body surface and by the rippling and crawling motions of its body. Crawling requires a brain that can act as a center for the coordination of muscles. The flatworm's nervous system includes enlarged ganglia that form a centralized, simple brain. If these ganglia are removed, the crawling activity stops. In higher animals, the brain is more complex. In all animals with brains, the brain coordinates complicated behavioral sequences.

Heredity   The development of an organism's body structure, nervous system, and behavior patterns depends on its heredity. DNA carries a "blueprint" for the development of body form and structure. Within this so-called blueprint is a "program" for behavior that uses body form and structure for continued survival. For example, within a spider's DNA are instructions for building the kind of web that its species constructs.

Behavior occurs in groups as well as in individual organisms. An example of group behavior is the flight of geese in a "V" formation, as shown in Figure 36–5. Instructions for this pattern of flight are coded in the DNA of each individual goose. A complex sequence of events links the DNA codes of individuals to their behavior as a group.

As you read earlier, behavior also depends on the ability to perceive and interpret stimuli. Sense organs receive information about environmental conditions. Heredity determines the types of stimuli that can be perceived, how they are interpreted, and the responses that can occur. Heredity also determines the coordinated patterns of muscular movement that form the resulting behavior sequence.

Cycles of Behavior

Although the behavior of an individual organism may vary over time, certain behaviors may be repeated at particular time periods. For example, some activities may occur only at certain times each day. Field mice are active at night and quiet during the day. Morning-glory flowers open during the day and close at night. Hawks hunt by day and owls by night. The activities of these organisms seem to be influenced by a *rhythm,* or cycle, of approximately 24 hours.

Early investigations into biological rhythms were conducted with fiddler crabs. These animals usually become darkly colored during the day and pale at night. To study biological rhythms, some crabs were placed in rooms with complete darkness and constant temperature and humidity. Even in these conditions, a regular cycle of color changes continued. This demonstrated that the cycle involved a physiological process.

Physiological and behavioral cycles occurring over a period of about 24 hours are called **circadian** (sur KAY dee un) **rhythms.** This term comes from the Latin words *circa* (about) and *dies* (day). Circadian rhythms are so regular that sometimes they are said to be controlled by an internal "biological clock." A biological clock, however, usually runs a little faster or slower than a normal clock. It must be adjusted constantly by an external stimulus such as daylight. Suppose, for example, that the inborn cycle of an insect is 25 hours. Each day, the insect's biological clock will adjust by one hour to keep it in phase with the normal day-night cycle. But, if the insect is kept under daylight conditions for a long period, its biological clock will not be adjusted each day. Thus, it gradually becomes out of phase with the actual day-night cycle. If the insect were kept under daylight conditions for 10 days, on day 10, its clock would be 10 hours out of phase with the normal daily cycle.

A similar disruption of a daily cycle is experienced by someone who flies from San Francisco to London. Upon arrival, the person is still oriented to the daily cycle in San Francisco. Most people in London are sleeping when this person is awake, hungry, and ready to work. This phenomenon is commonly called jet lag. In a few days, the individual's biological clock will be reset to London time and the traveler's activities will coincide with the London pattern.

Some animal phenomena follow monthly or even yearly cycles. The menstrual cycle is an example of a monthly cycle in humans.

Biology and You

Q: Are some people born shy? Can you overcome shyness?

A: Have you ever been alone at a party because you were too shy to speak to people? One study has reported that as many as 80 percent of all Americans say they were shy at one time. Shyness can be frustrating and damaging to your social life and your self-esteem.

What causes shyness? Some research shows a link between shyness and genetic makeup. If this is the case, you may be born with a hereditary trait for shyness. This does not mean that you will always be shy. The research shows that people can overcome shyness given the right environment and support. Other research suggests that shyness is not inherited. Instead, it is learned by children in response to their surroundings.

To overcome shyness, one doctor suggests imagining how you might act if you were more outgoing. Another approach is to practice ways of striking up conversations. Whatever the cause, shyness can be overcome.

Write a two paragraph story from the perspective of a shy teenager at a party or some other new social situation.

Another monthly cycle involves the grunion, a small fish that lives along the Pacific coast. Each year from April to June, this fish lays its eggs in the wet sand of the beach during the three or four days of the highest monthly tides. Yearly cycles occur in animals such as the ground squirrel, which hibernates during the colder months of each year. Experiments with ground squirrels kept under constant environmental conditions showed that the animals entered hibernation without environmental stimuli. This indicates that they, too, are influenced by biological clocks.

36-1 Section Review

1. Define the term *behavior*. How does behavior aid an individual or species?
2. List some environmental factors that are important in behavior.
3. What is the role of heredity in behavior?
4. What are circadian rhythms?

Critical Thinking

5. Classify each of the following as a stimulus or a behavior: hunger, a sneeze, running from a predator, thirst, pain, a noise, scratching an itch, a baseball thrown at you, being tickled. (*Classifying*)

36-2 Innate Behavior

Section Objectives:

- *Describe* some innate behavior patterns in plants and protists.
- *Explain* the mechanism and importance of reflexes.
- *Explain* the concept of instinct and give several examples of instincts.
- *Describe* several factors that can influence instinctive behavior.

Innate Behavior in Plants and Protists

Any form of behavior that has not been learned is **innate behavior,** or inborn behavior. Most innate behavior aids survival and reproduction. Innate behavior results from impulse pathways built into the nervous system. Instructions for the impulse pathways are carried in the DNA of the individual. These instructions are all the same for a given species. They are passed from parent to offspring as an inherited trait. An organism cannot "choose" to perform an innate behavior—it occurs automatically.

Innate behavior is found in most organisms. In simple organisms, such as the paramecium, sea anemone, and flatworm, all behavior is almost entirely innate. In more complex animals, only part of the behavior is innate. The remainder is learned behavior, which you will learn about in Section 36-3.

Plants also have inborn responses to stimuli. In plants, as you read in Chapter 19, growth toward or away from stimuli is called a *tropism*. This growth may involve the roots, stems, or leaves. Environmental factors, such as light, gravity, water, heat, and chemicals, act as stimuli for a tropism. Like the sponge, plants do not have a nervous system. Tropisms are controlled by hormones and may take hours or even days to occur.

Some plants exhibit rapid responses. Leaves of the sensitive plant, a type of mimosa, quickly fold and droop after they are touched. The leaves of the Venus flytrap rapidly close when sensitive hairs on its surface are touched. See Figure 17–12. These types of rapid responses in plants are not controlled by hormones. They are brought about by changes in turgor pressure in certain cells.

One characteristic of cells is their sensitivity to stimuli. The ameba and the paramecium do not have a nervous system, but they are able to respond to environmental changes. When a paramecium bumps into an obstacle, it stops. Then, it reverses its ciliary beating and backs away before turning and going forward again. If the paramecium hits the same obstacle, it repeats the back-up and turn. Eventually, it avoids the obstacle.

The ameba avoids intense light in a similar fashion, as you can see in Figure 36–6. It can, however, pursue a food particle until it has engulfed it. If the ameba loses actual contact with the food, it can still sense the location of the food by chemical stimuli.

Any movement by a simple animal or a protist toward or away from a particular stimulus is called a **taxis.** For example, the movement of an ameba away from a strong light is a *negative* taxis. An ameba moving toward food is an example of *positive* taxis.

Figure 36–6

Taxis in Protists. When a paramecium encounters an obstacle (left), it backs away (1⟶2) and then goes forward (3⟶4). If it is still blocked, it repeats the process (4⟶5, 6⟶7) until it avoids the obstacle. An ameba avoids strong light by moving away from the stimulus (middle). It pursues food by moving toward the stimulus (right). ▼

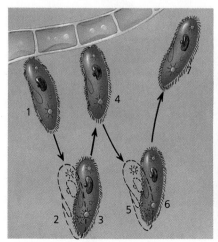
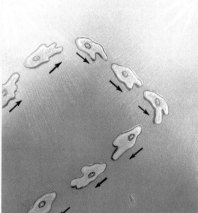
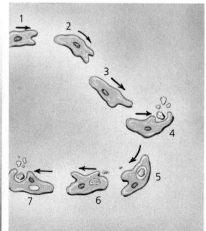

Reflexes

As an animal develops, its neurons develop connections that form a system. For the most part, once the system is formed, neurons do not change their connections with other nerves. As you read in Chapter 15, these fixed pathways in the nervous system are the basis for a type of innate behavior called the **reflex.** A reflex involves a *receptor* (sense organ) that detects stimuli and an *effector* (muscle or gland) that produces a reaction. Nerve cells connecting the receptor and effector through the spine or lower brain complete the nerve pathway, which is called the *reflex arc.* A reflex arc always produces the same response.

Reflex actions are simple, quick, and automatic because they do not require control by the upper brain. You can respond to a stimulus faster if you do not have to process information in your brain and decide what to do. If you touch a hot object, a reflex response causes you to pull back your hand quickly, before you are consciously aware of the pain. Thus, reflexes help an organism to avoid injury by allowing it to react quickly to environmental changes.

Reflexes occur in all animals with a nervous system. A flatworm subjected to electric shock automatically contracts. If a frog's toe is pinched, the leg is always drawn away. If you rub the hind area of a dog's back, it responds by scratching. In complex animals, reflexes account for only a small portion of behavior. In simple animals, reflexes account for a great part of the total behavior.

Sometimes, reflex arcs are linked to produce a complicated series of reflex actions. The behavior of the praying mantis is an example. When a fly or other insect appears in the mantis's field of vision, the mantis turns its head to face the insect. This is the first reflex. Then, the mantis orients its body in the same direction as the head—the second reflex. If the fly is close enough, the mantis instantly strikes, grasping the fly with its front legs. The strike—the third reflex—takes only a fraction of a second. See Figure 36–7.

Figure 36–7

Series of Reflex Actions. When a praying mantis sees a fly, a three-step series of reflex actions occurs. First, the mantis's head turns toward the insect (left). Next, its body orients in line with its head (middle). Finally, the mantis strikes, capturing the fly with its front legs (right). ▼

The stimulus triggering the turning of the mantis's head is the sight of the fly. The subsequent stimulation of receptors in the neck of the mantis results in the turning of the body. The strike follows the stimulus of aligning the head and body. Thus, this series of reflex actions depends on a succession of particular stimuli.

Instincts

Some animal behavior patterns involve a complicated set of unlearned activities that occur in response to a stimulus or series of stimuli. Such a complex, inherited behavior sequence is called an **instinct.** One example of instinctive behavior is nest building in birds. While instincts are quite complicated, they do not have to be learned and are performed automatically. However, an organism performing an instinctive behavior can be consciously aware of what it is doing. In contrast, a taxis and a reflex are simpler behaviors that are performed unconsciously.

Instincts usually are associated with either individual survival or species survival. They often involve activities related to feeding, defense, or reproduction. Instincts provide an animal with ready-made "answers" to its problems of survival because no time is required to learn a response. This is especially important for an animal with a short life span.

Instincts are found primarily in vertebrates and complex invertebrates. Each species displays its own characteristic instinctive behaviors, which are performed by all members of the species. The migration of salmon up the same river in which they were hatched, the communication "dances" of bees, the migration patterns of geese, and the construction of a hanging nest by the Baltimore oriole are instincts unique to those organisms.

Instincts in Invertebrates   Behavior is almost entirely instinctive in most invertebrates. A spider's construction of its intricate web, for example, is an instinct. In fact, the structure of its web can identify a spider as easily as its anatomy. There are four basic types of webs. Within each type, every species exhibits its own unique pattern of construction.

Some spiders perform courtship rituals before mating. A male jumping spider may perform a certain "sidestep" dance in front of his mate. An orb-weaving male spider may "strum" on the strands of a female's web before approaching her. Although these ritualistic acts seem complicated, they are instinctive and appear to communicate the male's intent to mate. Usually, such behavior prevents the male from being eaten by the female.

As you have read, the life cycle of an insect occurs in several stages. Each stage has its own set of instincts. For example, the june beetle larva shuns light. However, adult june beetles are attracted to light, often scraping loudly against the screens of lighted windows.

In insects and spiders, certain complex acts are performed only once, but correctly, without experience. Without being taught, the caterpillar of the gypsy moth climbs upward when hungry. Just

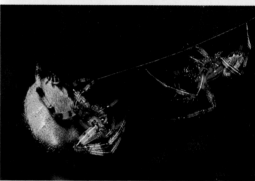

▲ **Figure 36–8**

Instinct. Among spiders, web construction and mating rituals are instinctive. Most orb web spiders (top) weave their web in a single night. Before mating, there is usually a courtship ritual. These two garden spiders (bottom) are about to mate.

1. Egg-laden female appears with head up.

2. Male swims in "zigzag dance."

3. Female swims, with head up, toward male.

4. Male swims toward nest.

5. Female follows male.

6. Male points to nest.

7. Female enters nest.

8. Male "trembles" and nudges female.

9. Female lays eggs in nest.

10. Female leaves nest.

11. Male enters nest and fertilizes eggs.

▲ **Figure 36–9**

Mating Behavior of the Three-Spined Stickleback. The ordered sequence of behavior depends on hormones and is triggered by sight.

before it enters the pupa stage, it spins a particular type of cocoon in a series of steps performed only once in its life. If a female spider builds a silken egg case but misses the opening when laying her eggs, she still completes and guards the empty case.

Instincts in Vertebrates All vertebrates exhibit instinctive behavior. Fishes, like birds, act instinctively when they build their nests. The male sunfish scoops out a shallow, saucerlike nest in the bottom sediments of a pond or lake. He removes all the pebbles, leaving a layer of sand. After the female lays her eggs in the nest and they are fertilized, the eggs adhere to the sand. Only the male cares for the eggs. He fans the eggs with his tail and drives away predators until the eggs hatch.

In an instinct, one activity may trigger the next. That is, each activity in a behavior sequence may depend on the previous activity. For example, the reproductive behavior of the three-spined stickleback, a fish, is composed of a sequence of ordered stimuli and responses. After establishing a territory (discussed in Section 36–4), the male builds a nest. If an egg-laden female enters his territory, the male performs a "zigzag" courtship dance. The female responds by swimming toward the male. The male then swims toward the nest, and the female follows him. The male points to the entrance to the nest with his head. This act stimulates the female to enter the nest. Her presence in the nest stimulates the male to "tremble" and nudge her at the base of the tail. His trembling and nudging stimulate her to lay eggs. The female leaves the nest, and the male enters and fertilizes the eggs. See Figure 36–9.

Besides nest building, birds exhibit other types of behavior that are primarily instinctive. Many species of birds make an annual round trip, called a **migration,** between their winter feeding grounds in the south and their spring breeding grounds in the north. Every year, these birds follow the same route, sometimes flying thousands of miles in each direction. The golden plover, for example, flies more than 8000 miles each year from its Arctic breeding grounds to southeastern South America and back again. Many other animals, such as the humpback whale and the monarch butterfly, migrate each year.

What prompts these animals to migrate at the same time every year, and how do they know where they are going? They may respond to environmental changes that tell them to start. Research has shown that many migratory birds navigate by using the angles of the sun or stars above the horizon. Certain pigeons and other birds may use the earth's magnetic field to orient themselves.

Hormonal Control of Instincts

Many physiological stimuli, which are related to an organism's metabolism, can trigger instincts. Often, the animal responds to these stimuli with instinctive behavior that tends to restore homeostasis. For example, a lack of food upsets an animal's homeostasis.

This physiological stimulus results in a sensation of hunger. The animal then responds with feeding behavior. Another example is the sensation of thirst, which is triggered by the blood's composition. This physiological stimulus triggers drinking behavior. Once homeostasis is restored, the instinctive behavior ceases.

Reproductive, or sex, hormones are the physiological stimuli that lead to courtship, mating, and care of young. These hormones may act directly on specific organs, such as gonads, causing them to produce eggs or sperm. See Chapter 21. These changes, along with a high level of reproductive hormones, prepare the individual for reproduction. Under these conditions, sight of a mate usually stimulates courtship behavior, which ultimately results in mating.

In some animals, once mating occurs, reproductive behavior stops. In other animals, however, care of the eggs or young is stimulated by the presence of reproductive hormones and the presence of offspring. For example, the hormone *prolactin* influences parental feeding in doves. Doves feed their young "pigeon milk," a thick, white substance produced in the bird's crop. The "milk" is composed of sloughed epithelial cells lining the crop.

Hormones may also influence behavior by acting on the central nervous system. Female canaries, unlike males, usually do not sing. But, if a pellet of male sex hormone (testosterone) is placed under the skin of a female, she will sing a typical canary song until all the hormone is metabolized.

Experiments with thirsty goats have shown that the brain, as well as hormones, is involved in some instincts. When a goat is thirsty, the lack of water in its blood stimulates cells in the hypothalamus. The *hypothalamus* is a portion of the brain to which the *pituitary gland* is attached. A message from the hypothalamus is passed into the pituitary gland, which secretes a hormone. The hormone causes the blood to absorb more water from the filtrate passing through the tubules of the nephrons in the kidneys. (Refer to Chapter 12.) While this physiological means of saving water goes on, the goat looks for water to drink.

The hypothalamus and the pituitary may also control reproductive behavior and parental care of offspring. The hypothalamus or pituitary can be triggered by information from the internal or external environment. For example, in many birds and mammals that reproduce seasonally, increasing daylight stimulates the hypothalamus. In turn, the hypothalamus stimulates the pituitary gland to produce sex hormones. Warmer temperatures also may begin the seasonal production of sex hormones in vertebrates.

Sometimes, a visual stimulus can trigger the hypothalamus. For example, if a female ring dove sees a male, the visual image stimulates cells in her hypothalamus, which activates her pituitary gland. Hormones from the pituitary gland cause the growth of the ovaries and secretion of the female hormone estrogen. The female then lays eggs. Normally, the hormone level of a female ring dove that does not see a male remains low. A female, however, can lay eggs without seeing a male if she is given an injection of hormones.

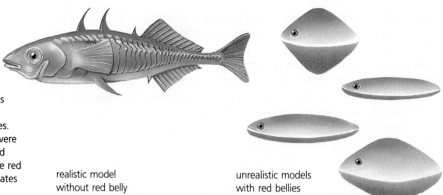

Figure 36–10

Models of Male Sticklebacks.
Experiments found that male sticklebacks attack models of fish with red bellies more often than those without red bellies. Even when the models with red bellies were unrealistically shaped, they were attacked more often. Scientists concluded that the red color of a male stickleback's belly stimulates aggressive behavior in another male. ▶

realistic model
without red belly

unrealistic models
with red bellies

Once internal conditions have been altered by hormones, the animal responds to external stimuli that do not ordinarily affect it. Specific environmental stimuli can then start various forms of reproductive behavior. For example, after hormones have caused the male three-spined stickleback to establish a territory and build a nest, he guards his territory against the intrusion of other males. When other males approach, he becomes aggressive and drives them away. During the mating period, the belly of a male becomes red. It is the red color on the belly of another male that stimulates the aggressive behavior. See Figure 36–10.

36-2 Section Review

1. Define the term *innate behavior.*
2. What is a taxis?
3. What is the chief advantage of instincts?
4. List three instincts that are controlled by hormones.

Critical Thinking

5. How are instincts similar to reflexes? How are they different? (*Comparing and Contrasting*)

36-3 Learned Behavior

Section Objectives:

- *Distinguish* between learned behavior and innate behavior and between classical conditioning and operant conditioning.
- *Explain* habituation and habit formation, and give examples of each.
- *Describe* the process of imprinting and explain its significance.
- *Explain* the concept of insight and relate it to learning.

Experience and Learning

Behavior that changes as a result of experience is called **learned behavior.** Experiences are "stored" in the brain as memory and can be recalled. In learning, a recalled experience is used to help modify behavior in a new situation. Unlike innate behavior, learning permits an animal to choose responses that are appropriate to the stimuli in any new situation. As a result of learning, an animal can adapt to change.

While innate behavior is controlled by genes, learned behavior is controlled only indirectly by genes. Heredity determines the type and complexity of the nervous system, which controls the ability to learn. Animals with more complex nervous systems exhibit a greater capacity to learn. Animals with long life spans and long periods of parental care exhibit mostly learned behavior as adults. In some animals, parents actually teach their offspring certain behaviors. Lions, for example, teach their offspring how to hunt.

Learning has several forms. The simplest type of learning is called **habituation.** In this type of learning, an animal learns to ignore repeated "unimportant" stimuli. Squirrels in a park become accustomed to people and will come quite close to them. Crows learn to ignore a harmless scarecrow in a field.

Humans and other animals can learn to perform many complex activities with little or no thought. A **habit** is a series of actions that is learned first and then becomes automatic through repetition. Dressing, writing, talking, tying shoelaces, typing, and dancing are habits. All habits are performed slowly at first, with concentration and often with difficulty. The habit is learned through repetition until it becomes automatic and requires little or no conscious effort. As the habit continues to develop, the actions become easier and faster to perform and more accurate.

Brushing your teeth is an example of a good habit. The benefits of brushing are best realized if the habit is maintained regularly. A bad habit, such as smoking, is dangerous to your health because its ill effects are repeated again and again. It can be difficult to break a bad habit, just as it can be hard to develop a good habit.

Conditioning

A simple type of learning that changes behavior through forming new associations is called **conditioning.** One type, called *classical conditioning,* was first studied by the Russian physiologist Ivan Pavlov (1849–1936). In classical conditioning, a new stimulus is paired with the stimulus and response of a simple reflex action. The new stimulus, which does not normally cause the reflex response, becomes associated with the response by a process of reinforcement or reward. As a result, the new stimulus can be substituted for the original one.

Dogs normally salivate when they smell or see food. Secretion of saliva is the reflex response. In studies carried out by Pavlov, a bell was rung (new stimulus) every time dogs were given food (old

Stimulus: sight and smell of food

Response: salivation

Stimulus: sight and smell of food and ringing of bell

Response: salivation

Stimulus: after many pairings of food and bell, ringing of bell only

Response: salivation

▲ **Figure 36–11**

Classical Conditioning. Classical conditioning involves the association of a new stimulus with a response. A hungry dog salivates at the sight or smell of food. Pavlov exposed a dog to a ringing bell whenever the dog received food. Eventually, ringing of the bell alone caused the dog to salivate.

stimulus). The association of the new stimulus (bell) with the reflex response (salivation) was reinforced by presenting food immediately after ringing the bell. After a while, the dogs salivated upon hearing the bell without the presence of food. See Figure 36–11.

In Pavlov's experiment, the food was the *unconditioned stimulus*. The ringing bell was the *conditioned stimulus*. Salivation became a *conditioned response*. House pets often become conditioned in a similar manner. Pet owners know that the sound of the refrigerator door or can opener can cause their pets to be quite attentive and to salivate.

Operant conditioning is a type of conditioning in which animals learn to "operate" or do something by associating the action with a reward. The animals may learn to push a lever, open a door, respond to a command, or perform other kinds of actions. In this case, the conditioned response is a behavior that produces the reward. An animal first must be *motivated* to seek the reward by performing the activity. The motivation is usually hunger.

B. F. Skinner, a psychologist, constructed a special cage with a food-release mechanism to study operant conditioning. A rat placed in the cage eventually learns that pressing a bar releases a pellet of food. At first, the rat explores its cage. This leads to a period of trial and error before the rat accidentally performs the correct act—pressing the bar. Food is the reward for pressing the bar. By rewarding the rat for pressing the bar, the rat is more likely to repeat the act. The rat learns to associate the action of pressing the bar with the reward of food. Because of the initial period of exploration, operant conditioning is also called *trial-and-error learning*.

Trainers teach animals to perform tricks by rewarding them for desired behavior and punishing them for undesired behavior. To the animal, the absence of an expected reward is the same as a punishment. Some sea mammals, such as porpoises, sea lions, and whales, will perform tricks at a trainer's command when rewarded with a fish. Hunger is the motivation for doing the trick. During training, the animal is given a fish only after the trick is performed correctly. A poor performance results in no reward.

Imprinting

In 1935 Konrad Lorenz, an Austrian biologist, discovered a simple type of learning that occurs in young animals of certain species. He found that newly hatched ducks, geese, and chickens follow and form a strong attachment to the first moving object they see. If the moving object makes sound, it is more likely to be followed. Forming an attachment to an object or environment soon after hatching or birth is called **imprinting.** This form of learning is rapid and cannot be reversed.

Imprinting in birds occurs several hours after hatching. The young bird will follow the object even over obstacles. Ordinarily, the first object a young bird sees is its mother. Imprinting on the mother bird helps the young bird survive. This behavior creates a bond between the mother bird and her young. It also helps the young birds recognize others of their kind, which is important for mating later in life. See Figure 36–12.

If eggs are hatched under experimental conditions in an incubator, the young birds may imprint on a foreign object, such as a person, a mechanical object, or a dog. The young birds will follow the object when it moves around. Once the period of imprinting has passed, about 36 hours after hatching, the young birds cannot imprint on another object. For example, mature mallard ducks that imprinted on a "decoy" mother duck will court and attempt to mate with the decoy. At maturity, geese and other birds that imprinted on foster parents of another species try to mate with members of the foster species.

Although imprinting was first described in birds, it is now known to occur in other animals. Animals whose young can walk shortly after birth, such as buffalo, deer, sheep, and goats, are capable of imprinting. Puppies that have human contact during their sixth and seventh weeks are easily trained to be good pets. However, if puppies have no human contact until after their fourteenth week, they rarely make friendly pets. Scientists speculate that imprinting plays an important part in the ability of migrating salmon to return to the stream in which they were hatched.

Figure 36–12

Imprinting. Imprinting is a rapid, irreversible form of learning. These young swans are imprinted on their mother (left). Here, young geese have imprinted on Konrad Lorenz, the first living creature they saw (right). ▼

Figure 36–13

Insight. Insight is the ability to plan a solution to an unfamiliar problem. Here, chimpanzees use insight to get bananas suspended from the ceiling. ▶

a. b. c.

Insight

Insight is the ability to "create" a solution to an unfamiliar problem without a period of trial and error. The animal surveys a new situation and uses the memory of past learning and experiences to "plan" a reasoned response. Insight is found only in complex vertebrates.

In one of the best-known studies of insight, a hungry chimpanzee is released in a room with boxes scattered on the floor and a bunch of bananas hanging from the ceiling out of reach. The chimp finds that it cannot reach the bananas. Eventually, it piles the boxes up and then climbs them to reach the bananas. Reasoning has resulted in the correct response to a new situation. Chimpanzees and monkeys are often successful at solving problems. Most other animals, including dogs, fail at first.

The ability to reason is most highly developed in humans. At first, young children solve problems by trial and error and by imitation. This helps them master such motor skills as tying shoes. As children mature and learn, they begin to use insight to solve problems. Insight is enhanced by the ability to exchange ideas through speech and written symbols. These skills allow each person to use someone else's experiences to solve problems—an ability that is unique in the animal kingdom.

36-3 Section Review

1. List three types of learned behavior.
2. Which animals exhibit a greater capacity to learn?
3. How does a habit become automatic?
4. What are some benefits of imprinting?

Critical Thinking

5. The day after hatching, a young goose was seen following an adult duck. When the goose matures, will it try to mate with a duck or a goose? Explain. (*Reasoning Conditionally*)

36-4 Social Behavior

Section Objectives:

- *Describe* several forms of helpful and hostile social behavior.
- *Describe* three types of signals used by animals and give an example of each type.
- *Explain* the function of territoriality and the role of communication in maintaining territories.
- *Explain* the organization of a honeybee society and describe how these bees communicate with one another.

Helpful Behavior

Animals often encounter other animals in their environment. Interactions occur between individuals of the same species and between animals of different species. Many environmental factors bring animals together in a group. A street light is a stimulus that attracts a variety of insects. The rich African grassland draws grazing animals such as the zebra, wildebeest, and antelope to feed side by side. A water hole may be a gathering place for many species. These groups of mixed animal species, called *aggregations,* are not social. They are together merely by chance.

Animals belonging to the same species exhibit **social behavior,** which consists of both helpful and hostile interactions. Helpful social behavior includes mating behavior, family interactions, and activities by larger groups. Mating behavior brings a female and a male together, and results in the fertilization of eggs. This form of social behavior may involve courtship as well as actual mating. *Courtship* is a form of communication that signals a readiness to mate and prevents conflict.

Family interactions involve helpful relationships between parents and young. The interactions between members of a family are the basis for the providing of food, shelter, and defense for the young. The interactions usually require certain stimuli. Birds incubate their eggs and later feed their chicks. A gull incubates the eggs only when they are visible and when certain hormones are produced in the parent.

◀ **Figure 36–14**
Courtship Display. This male prairie chicken displays its colorful feathers to attract females for mating.

The needs of the young are often satisfied when their behavior stimulates other forms of behavior among family members. Many birds will not feed their young unless the chicks "communicate" in a form of behavior called *begging.* Begging is usually done by opening the mouth widely. This stimulates the parent to place food in the chick's mouth. Initially, the young are stimulated to beg when the parent's head appears over the edge of the nest or by the jolt of the adult landing on the nest. Sea gull chicks peck at a red spot on the parent's beak when begging. See Figure 36–15. The parent then regurgitates food, picks some up, and presents it to the chick.

Helpful behavior also occurs within larger groups such as herds of animals, schools of fish, and flocks of birds. Individuals can cooperate in groups as long as they can communicate with one another. Information is passed between members of a group by sound signals, visual signals, and chemical signals.

Species that live in groups often depend on the group for survival. A group of animals is more alert than a single individual. When one member senses danger, it communicates it to the whole group. The group then tries to escape the danger. Groups also offer various forms of protection against attack by predators. Male musk oxen form a protective ring around the young and females. Some animals attack in groups as a form of defense. Small birds will attack crows and hawks in groups—a behavior called *mobbing.* Hunting in groups is practiced by wolves, lions, and wild dogs.

Conflict and Dominance Hierarchies

Close association among animals of the same species can result in conflict instead of cooperation. When resources are limited, individuals of a species must compete for food, water, space, and mates. Many animals resolve this competition by aggressive behavior. *Aggression* is threatening or fighting another animal to force it away from something it possesses or is trying to obtain.

There are numerous forms of aggression. Animals may bite, butt, kick, or claw one another. However, aggressive behavior among members of a species seldom causes serious injury or death. See Figure 36–16. More often, "symbolic" threatening behavior results in a "winner." Such displays are instinctive and clearly understood by other species members. In threat displays, animals assume aggressive postures and show the contrasting or brightly colored parts of their bodies. Robins display their red breasts. Fish display colored body parts or puff themselves up.

When actual fights occur, they are mostly symbolic and cause little injury to the rivals. Poisonous male snakes wind themselves together during a bout, and each attempts to butt the other's head with its own. The snake that becomes fatigued first retreats from the fight. Although the snakes have fangs, they never bite each other. Rival male bighorn sheep butt their heads together, resulting in spectacular fights. The sounds of their butting heads can be heard for a long distance.

The animal that loses a fight may simply run away. In some cases, it signals defeat by a *subordination ritual.* A wolf or dog

Figure 36–15

Begging Behavior. A herring gull chick begs for food by pecking at a red spot on its parent's beak. ▼

▲ **Figure 36–16**
Aggressive Behavior. These two male elephants will fight until it is clear which one is dominant. They will not fight to the death

signals submission by presenting its neck to the winner. This display stops further aggression by the victor. Its position of superiority has been established. The animal that wins a fight achieves *dominance,* or better access to contested resources, such as food, water, space, and mates.

In some animals that live in organized groups, or *societies,* fighting establishes a **dominance hierarchy,** or ranking, within the group. Individuals with a high rank have first choice of necessities. In duck and chicken societies, a *pecking order* is established by pecking action. Those birds with the highest standing have uncontested access to food, water, and the roost. Pecking order reduces tension in the group because there is less fighting over who gets what first. Due to their lower position in the group, subordinates must wait their turn to drink or eat. If no food is left, the subordinates go without nourishment. For members of the lowest rank, survival is most difficult.

In baboons, dominance hierarchy is more complicated than a sequence of individuals with decreasing dominance. A group of baboons, called a *troop,* is governed by a clique of dominant males. Any member of the ruling clique that is challenged by an outsider is supported by the other members of the governing group. This helps keep the troop stable by preventing frequent changes in the hierarchy. The clique of dominant males protects the troop against attack by predators.

Communication

Communication plays an important role in both helpful and hostile social behavior. The male and female of many animal species are brought together by signals. The signals sent out by both sexes include visual signals, sound signals, and chemical secretions.

a.   b.   c.

▲ **Figure 36–17**

Courtship Display. To attract a mate, a male mallard duck displays his brightly colored feathers. Normal swimming (left). "Head up, tail up" display (middle). "Down up" display (right).

Visual signals are common among fish and birds. These signals include movement and posture as well as displays of certain body parts. The zigzag dance of the male stickleback causes the female to approach him and be led to the nest. The male mallard duck courts the female by displaying his brightly colored plumage. See Figure 36–17. The female identifies herself with a signal. She may beg food from the male, which will act as a signal to him not to attack her as he would a male during the reproductive period. Other examples of visual signals during aggression were given in the previous section.

Sound signals are important among insects, frogs, birds, whales, and many other animals. The male *Aedes* mosquito is attracted to the sounds produced by the wings of the female while in flight. Male crickets attract females with sound signals made by rubbing their wings together. Male toads and frogs have characteristic songs that attract the females to the pond or bog. Male birds such as the robin, meadowlark, wood thrush, and vireo produce distinctive high-pitched songs as a signal to the female. Humpback whales can communicate across distances greater than 10 kilometers by using underwater songs. Biologists are still investigating the function of these songs.

Chemical secretions are used by many animals as signals. Such secretions are called **pheromones** (FEHR uh mohnz). These chemicals influence the behavior of other members of the same species. Pheromones can act as sex attractants. The female silkworm moth releases a pheromone so strong that it attracts males from a distance as great as three kilometers. Gypsy moths, cockroaches, and many other insects produce pheromones that act as sex attractants.

Territoriality

A **territory** is an area defended by an individual against intrusion by other members of the same species. Claiming or defending a territory is another aspect of social behavior. Territorial behavior usually takes place during the breeding season and is often limited to males. Maintaining a territory gives an animal the space needed to acquire food, court a mate, and raise a family.

To defend its territory, an individual may spend long periods of time in a conspicuous place. The animal may also "announce" ownership with certain forms of communication. In some birds, such as thrushes, a male will choose an unoccupied area and then sing loudly and vigorously to stake his claim. The loud singing warns away other males but attracts females. A singing duel between competing males often can resolve a boundary dispute. Usually, the loudest-singing male gains the largest territory.

Some mammals use pheromones to mark territory. Deer have pheromone-secreting glands in their hooves. As you can see in Figure 36–18, male antelopes have similar glands close to their eyes. The civet, a cat, has pheromone-secreting glands around its anus. Dogs and wolves mark their "turf" with urine.

Primates vary in their territorial behavior. Although chimpanzee and gorilla troops live on a large range, they show no defense of territory. Different troops may intermingle without causing disturbances. The tree-living howler monkey of Central America displays strong group territoriality. A troop consists of several dozen monkeys. They defend the boundaries of their territory by sessions of howling, which discourages intrusion by other troops. See Figure 36–19. The rhesus, a monkey found in southern Asia, is also territorial and will drive off intruders with active threat displays and, if necessary, ferocious attacks.

Territoriality has several advantages. Due to territories, groups or individuals are evenly distributed throughout the available area. This enables an animal species to use the resources in the environment efficiently. Dividing an area into territories tends to reduce conflict between members of a species. In some cases, especially in birds, position of a territory helps attract a mate.

▲ **Figure 36–18**

Pheromones. A male antelope claims his territory by marking twigs with a secretion produced by a gland near his eye.

◀ **Figure 36–19**

Territoriality. Red howler monkeys defend their territory as a group. Their loud howling scares away other monkey troops.

Honeybee Societies

Insect societies are found among termites, ants, and bees in addition to other insects. In an insect society, every effort is directed toward the survival of the entire group. The activities of most insect societies are centered around one female, the *queen.* The queen may live for five years or more. During that time, her only responsibility is to reproduce. All members of the group are offspring of the queen.

A honeybee society involves a complex organization and division of labor. See Figure 36–20. The queen is usually the only reproductive female. She is the focus of hive activity. The colony continues as a group as long as she is healthy and functioning. A queen mates only once with each of several *drones,* or male bees, during a "nuptial" flight. The drones develop from unfertilized eggs and live for only a short time after mating with the queen bee. From the single mating flight, the queen stores enough sperm to fertilize the thousands of eggs she will lay for the colony. Most of these eggs will hatch into sterile females called *worker bees.* These worker bees carry on the essential activities that maintain the hive, including producing honey, feeding larvae, and protecting the hive. See Figure 36–21.

Chemical signals are one form of bee communication. Even the status of the queen's health is passed to members of the hive by means of a chemical signal. This signal originates from the queen as a secretion. It is first passed to workers attending her and then to others in the hive. Chemical signals help maintain the organization of the hive.

Workers at the hive entrance fan hive odor outward, which guides foraging workers home. After a worker locates a food source, it uses visual and other signals to communicate the location of the

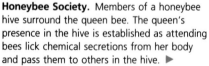

Figure 36–20

Honeybee Society. Members of a honeybee hive surround the queen bee. The queen's presence in the hive is established as attending bees lick chemical secretions from her body and pass them to others in the hive. ▶

queen

drone

worker

◀ **Figure 36–21**
Types of Bees. The three types of bees that live in a hive are the queen, the worker, and the drone.

MiniLab

Skill: Observing

How Sweet It Is

Procedure

1. Locate an active anthill outdoors. Observe the ants' activity. Put a spoonful of honey on the ground about 1 m away from it. **CAUTION:** *Do not touch the ants.*

2. Place a sheet of paper between the honey and the anthill, and observe the ants. Some ants, called scouts, will find the honey and establish a chemical trail directly back to the anthill for other ants to follow.

3. When ants are traveling back and forth on the trail regularly, quickly turn the paper one-quarter turn so the old trail on the paper now crosses the most direct route to and from the honey. Again, observe the ants.

Problem

What can you **observe** about the way in which ants communicate with one another?

Analyze and Conclude

1. How did the ants react when you turned the paper?

2. How did the ants' movements change over time?

3. What questions do you have about ants' behavior? How could you investigate answers to these questions?

food to other workers in the hive. The work of Karl von Frisch, a German scientist, helped explain this form of communication between honeybees. In his experiments, he placed sheets of paper smeared with honey near a hive. Eventually the bees discovered the honey. Von Frisch noticed that when one bee discovered the honey, others would come in a short time. Somehow the other bees were informed by the first bee.

Von Frisch set up a hive with glass sides so he could observe the scout bees returning from a new food supply. A bee that landed at the new food supply was marked with a little paint to help identify her. Upon returning to the hive, the bee fed several other workers. Then she performed a "dance" on the inner wall of the honeycomb. Other workers near her became excited and followed with antennae held close to her. One by one, the other workers left the dancer and in a short time appeared at the location of the food. The dance pattern, called the *round dance* by von Frisch, consists of circling first in one direction and then in the other direction. See Figure 36–22. The round dance is repeated many times. This dance seems to inform other workers that food is nearby, while the bee passes on the scent of the flower to the workers.

To determine if the round dance told other workers the direction of the food, von Frisch placed four dishes of sugar water

Figure 36–22

Bee Communication. The round dance informs the bees of a hive that food is nearby (left). The waggle dance indicates the direction and distance of the food from the hive (right). ▼

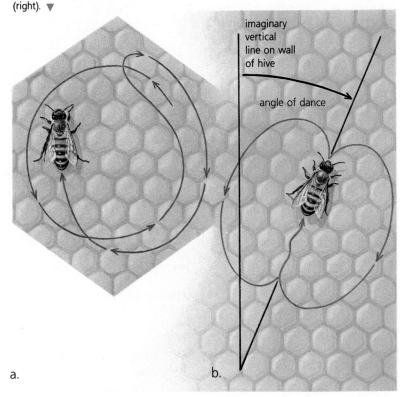

imaginary
vertical
line on wall
of hive

angle of dance

a.

b.

scented with honey 10 meters from the hive—one dish north, one south, one east, and one west. Although von Frisch observed that a worker might find only one sample, he also noticed that equal numbers of bees appeared at each dish. He concluded that the round dance did not communicate direction. Other experiments were performed, which showed that the dance did not communicate distance. The round dance, then, seems only to tell the bees that food is nearby.

Von Frisch set up another experiment. He used two dishes of sugar water scented with lavender oil. He placed one dish at 10 meters from the hive and the other at 300 meters from the hive. The foraging bees that discovered the dish at 10 meters returned to the hive and danced the round dance. Workers returning from the dish 300 meters away performed a different dance. Von Frisch called this dance the *waggle dance.* In this dance, the bee runs along the wall of the hive in a straight line for a short distance while wagging her abdomen from side to side. She then circles back, runs forward again, circles in the opposite direction, and runs forward again. This "figure eight" motion is repeated several times. See Figure 36–22b. The distance of the food is communicated by the number of straight runs and the number of waggles given in a 15-second time period. As distance increases, the number of straight runs decreases while the number of waggles increases. The waggle dance appears to be used to communicate food distances greater than 50 meters.

The direction of the food source is indicated by the direction of the waggle dance on the honeycomb wall. If the food is located in the direction of the sun, the dancer travels vertically up the wall of the honeycomb on the straight run. If the food is in a direction away from the sun, the dance is directed down the honeycomb wall. If the food is located at some angle between the line from the hive to the sun, the straight run is oriented at the same angle relative to a vertical line. Bees are thus able to translate information concerning the distance and direction of food into the speed and angle of a dance.

36-4 **Section Review**

1. Define the term *social behavior.*
2. What is a dominance hierarchy?
3. What signals bring together the male and female of a species during courtship?
4. What are two insects that form complex societies?

Critical Thinking

5. What are some advantages of "symbolic" threatening behavior? (*Judging Usefulness*)

Laboratory
Investigation

Learning by Trial and Error

Learned behavior is behavior that develops as a result of experience. Of all the ways humans learn, trial and error is one of the most time-consuming. In this investigation, you will participate in trial-and-error learning and observe the effect of practice on the time it takes to reach a solution.

Problem

Observe the relationship between practice and the time it takes to solve a problem by trial and error.

Materials (per group)

- ▶ envelopes containing puzzles 1 and 2
- ▶ watch with second hand
- ▶ graph paper

Procedure

1. Obtain the envelopes containing puzzles 1 and 2 from your teacher. Make a data table similar to the one shown. Take the envelope marked puzzle 1. Your partner should have the watch. When your partner tells you to begin, remove the pieces and arrange them so they form a perfect square while your partner times you. In the data table, record the time it took to complete the puzzle. Mix the pieces and return them to the envelope.

2. Repeat step 1 and record your results in the data table. Wait two minutes. Repeat step 1 again, and again record your results in the data table. Return the puzzle pieces to the envelope.

3. Take the envelope marked puzzle 2. On your partner's signal, remove the pieces and arrange them so that they form the letter T while your partner times you. Record the time it took to complete the puzzle in your data table. Return the puzzle pieces to the envelope.

4. Repeat step 3 two more times, following the procedure outlined in steps 1 and 2.

5. Switch roles with your partner and repeat steps 1 to 4.

6. Using the format shown, make bar graphs that show the time it took to complete each puzzle in each trial.

Observations

Data Table		
Time to Complete Task (minutes)		
Trial	**Puzzle 1**	**Puzzle 2**
1		
2		
3		

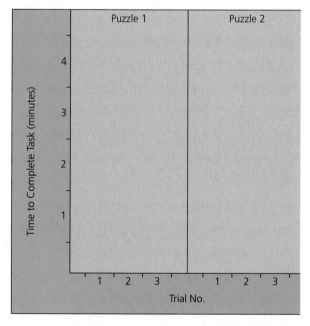

How did the time to complete the puzzles differ between the first trial and second trial? Between the second trial and third trial?

Analysis and Conclusions

1. How did practice affect the amount of time it took you to complete each puzzle?

2. What was the purpose of waiting two minutes between trials?

3. How did the time to complete the task vary from puzzle 1 to puzzle 2? Can you explain why?

4. What factor favors the possibility that the second-round partner will solve the puzzles faster than the first-round partner? How could you design the experiment to eliminate this factor?

5. How does each instance of solving a puzzle affect how you go about solving the puzzle in a subsequent trial?

Extensions

Design an experiment to test the effects of practice and mental rehearsals on other tasks, such as improving athletic skills.

Chapter 36 Review

Study Outline

36-1 The Nature of Behavior

▶ Behavior is a series of activities performed by organisms in response to stimuli.

▶ Living things respond only to pertinent stimuli with a behavior pattern unique to the species involved. The unique behavior depends on the organism's form and structure and on information coded in the DNA.

36-2 Innate Behavior

▶ Innate behaviors, such as reflexes and instincts, aid in survival and reproduction. In some simple organisms, behavior is entirely innate.

▶ Reflexes are simple, quick, and automatic. They result from fixed pathways in the nervous system.

▶ Instincts are complex innate behavior sequences associated with individual or species survival.

36-3 Learned Behavior

▶ Learned behavior changes as a result of experience. The experiences are stored in the memory and recalled at a later time, helping the animal to adapt to change.

▶ Habituation, conditioning, and imprinting are simple forms of learned behavior. Insight is a more complex learned behavior.

36-4 Social Behavior

▶ Social behavior consists of interactions among animals of the same species. The interactions may include courtship, mating behavior, family interactions, and large-group interactions.

▶ In a large group, conflict can result in a ranking of the group's members. This ranking is called a dominance hierarchy.

▶ A member of a species may claim a territory to provide it with food and a place to raise a family. The individual will defend the territory against intrusion by others of the same species.

▶ Ants, termites, and bees live in insect societies. Honeybee societies are highly organized.

Chapter Assessment

Multiple Choice

Choose the letter of the answer that best completes each statement or answers the question.

1. A form of behavior in which animals learn to ignore repeated unimportant stimuli is called (a) habit. (b) conditioning. (c) habituation. (d) imprinting.

2. A type of instinct in which a bird makes an annual round trip is called (a) migration. (b) reflex. (c) taxis. (d) conditioning.

3. A female gypsy moth may attract a mate with (a) habit. (b) conditioning. (c) a pheromone. (d) a circadian rhythm.

4. A form of behavior that changes as a result of experience is a(n) (a) response. (b) instinct. (c) social behavior. (d) learned behavior.

5. A form of behavior inherited by offspring is called (a) innate behavior. (b) imprinting (c) conditioning. (d) insight.

6. By moving toward or away from a stimulus, a protist exhibits a form of behavior known as (a) taxis. (b) migration. (c) reflex. (d) conditioning.

7. Baby geese follow the first large object they encounter during a critical period in their development. This phenomenon is an example of (a) insight learning. (b) imprinting. (c) habituation. (d) operant conditioning.

8. Many animals use pheromones as (a) chemical signals. (b) sound signals. (c) visual signals. (d) temperature signals.

9. A bee communicates the location of a food source to other bees in its hive by (a) rubbing antennae. (b) the round dance. (c) pheromones. (d) the waggle dance.

10. Circadian rhythms (a) are monthly cycles. (b) are controlled by a biological clock. (c) are never found in humans. (d) cause unpredictable behavior.

Content Review

Answer each of the following in complete sentences.

11. Why do organisms respond only to specific stimuli?

12. Describe the functions of the receptor and the effector in producing a reflex.

13. Describe the relationships among a single reflex, a series of reflexes such as those exhibited by a praying mantis capturing food, and an instinct.

14. Explain the difference between innate behavior and learned behavior.

15. What is a conditioned response?

16. How does insight differ from instinct?

17. Describe the types of helpful social behavior.

18. What is the advantage of a dominance hierarchy as a type of social organization?

19. In what ways is the establishment of territories a useful form of social behavior?

20. Describe the social organization of a beehive.

Graphic Organizing

For information on graphic organizers, see Appendix G at the back of this text.

21. **Concept Map** Construct a concept map of learned behavior using the following concepts: learned behavior, conditioning, insight, imprinting, habit, habituation, classical conditioning, and operant conditioning. Select 10 additional concepts to add to the map that help explain the different types of learned behavior. As you link the concepts, do not forget the lines and linking words.

Critical Thinking and Problem Solving

Discuss each of the following in a brief paragraph.

22. **Drawing conclusions** The migration of birds and the nest building of fishes are inherited behavior patterns known as instincts. From these examples, make a general statement about why some behaviors are passed on from generation to generation.

23. **Comparing** How are genetically determined behaviors different from more complex learned behaviors?

24. **Inferring** Some biologists think that lower vertebrates such as fishes are capable of learning. What assumptions must these biologists have made?

25. **Experimenting** Biologists have evidence that the chicks of herring gulls beg food from their parents by pecking at a red spot on the beaks of the adult birds. Design a controlled experiment to determine whether chicks peck only a red spot.

26. **Interpreting** The ability of an animal to learn can be tested in a maze. A maze consists of a route with several choices. The choices are like forks in a road. By choosing the correct turn at each fork, the animal will complete the maze. In a learning experiment, two groups of rats—a control group and a test group—were tested daily for 14 days. The test group received a reward of food upon completing the maze. The control group received no food. The errors, or wrong turns, for each group were counted, and the averages were graphed, as shown below. From this data, what can you conclude about learning and the use of rewards?

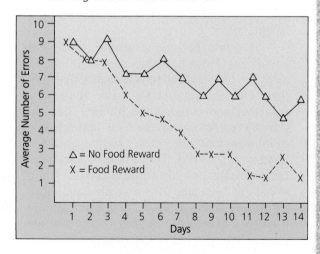

Performance-Based Assessment

The Role of Zoos and Aquariums

Background

The first zoos and aquariums existed mainly to provide entertainment. Their philosophy of "more is better" led to as large a collection as possible of exotic animals, even if each species was represented by just one or two individuals. When animals died, replacements were obtained from the wild. Once at the zoo, the animals were kept in small dark cages that had heavy bars and were poorly ventilated. Little attention was paid to the animals' needs for companionship, surroundings, stimuli, and the opportunity to pursue normal behavior.

Most modern zoos and aquariums no longer see their primary role as providing entertainment. Instead they see their role as "arks" for the world's vanishing wildlife. In order to focus on the conservation of endangered species, modern zoos and aquariums have made changes in three major areas: naturalistic exhibits, captive breeding, and public education.

As funds become available, zoos and aquariums are renovating their exhibits to meet the physical and psychological needs of their animals. And at the same time they entertain and educate the public. They do this by exhibiting animals in natural surroundings that are similar to the animals' habitat in the wild. These naturalistic habitats give animals more stimulation than traditional exhibits. Since the animals have more to do and more privacy, they often pursue their normal behavior patterns. To encourage normal behavior and social organization, natural family groups are housed together.

Many zoos and aquariums maintain active breeding programs for a variety of endangered species. To avoid inbreeding, the International Species Inventory System (ISIS), a computerized information system for zoo animals, was developed to track and coordinate the preservation and crossbreeding of captive animal species. It contains biological information—such as gender, age, parentage, place of birth, and cause of death—for the animals in most of the large zoos of the world. This information allows zoos to keep records, to analyze the genetic status of zoo populations, and to coordinate and cooperate in breeding programs

The American Association of Zoological Parks and Aquariums has developed another program called the Species Survival Plans that, using ISIS data, helps zoos and aquariums breed animals to ensure maximum genetic diversity in the total captive population. Their aim is not only to save threatened and endangered species, but also to reintroduce animals into their native habitats. They have been successful with the Arabian oryx, black-footed ferret, American bald eagle, and California condor. They have plans for many other species. Finally, some species are not

put on public display because the zoo or aquarium is concentrating on breeding them.

Zoos and aquariums often use nontraditional methods to enhance their breeding efforts. For example, artificial insemination increases the chance of reproduction among hard-to-breed species. It also can overcome the logistical problems of transporting and breeding large animals, such as rhinos. More importantly, this technology can be used to fertilize eggs with sperm obtained from animals in the wild. This enables zoos and aquariums to rejuvenate the genetic variability of their captive population without taking animals from their natural habitat.

Modern zoos and aquariums have done an excellent job of blending their breeding programs with education and entertainment. The emphasis on entertaining and educating the public is essential because public understanding and support is vital for these organizations to achieve their goals. In addition, public support is critical if we are going to save endangered species.

Problem

You are a biologist and have been asked by the local zoological society to compare the behavior of one animal in the wild with that animal's behavior in a zoo or aquarium.

Task

Choose one of the following tasks.

1. Because funds are limited, you have been asked to base your observations of the animal in the wild on videos. You can borrow a video from the library or record a nature program from a public television station or cable channel. Do research about the species you are studying in the library and on the Internet. Then watch the video and carefully observe the behavior of the animal in the wild. Next, go to a zoo or aquarium and observe the behavior of the animal in captivity. Take good notes or use a camcorder to record your observations. Keep all the information that you collected in a journal. If you used a camcorder, include the tape along with your journal.

2. Prepare and make a five-minute oral presentation followed by a three-minute question-and-answer session. You are anticipating the following questions being asked:

   ■ How has captivity changed the behavior of the animal?

   ■ What are the consequences of inbreeding to a population that biologists want to reintroduce into the wild?

   ■ How effective are the breeding programs of zoos and aquariums?

   ■ Why are captive breeding programs not enough to stop the extinction of many animals?

   ■ What kind of breeding program is in place at your local zoo or aquarium?

   ■ Should zoos and aquariums be given support from the federal government for their education and breeding programs?

3. Based on your research and observations of the zoo or aquarium, design and construct a scale model of a natural habitat for the animal you have chosen using appropriate materials. Present your model to the zoological society.

Leaf-cutter ants taking leaves to their nest.

Discovery Learning Activity

Making a Mini-Habitat

1. As a group, collect living and nonliving things from the outdoors to set up a mini-habitat. Make sure that the organisms and materials that you collect all come from the same immediate area. **CAUTION:** *Be careful when handling all living organisms (animals and plants).*

2. Place a layer of pebbles in the bottom of a small aquarium, a clear-plastic shoe box, or a gallon jar turned on its side. If you use a jar, tape two pencils to it to keep the jar from rolling. Mix damp soil, peat moss, and sand in 2:1:1 proportions. Spread the mixture over the pebbles in a layer 5–7 cm deep.

3. Add the living and nonliving things that you collected from outdoors. Cover the container's opening with screening, and secure it with an elastic band or tape. Place the mini-habitat in an area that will get natural light but not long periods of direct sunlight. As needed, add water by misting.

4. Observe the mini-habitat for a week or two. When observations are complete, return the living things to their original location.

Discovery Learning Activity

Observing a Food Chain

1. Plant a bean seedling in each of two large glass jars labeled A and B. Put about 20 aphids in each jar.

2. Add several ladybugs to jar B.

3. Cover both jars with a piece of screening and place them in a sunny location. Water the plants as needed.

4. Observe the jars every day for a week, and note the number of aphids and the condition of each plant.

Organization in the Biosphere

Chapter **37**

.... *Guide for Reading* ....

Previewing the Chapter

It is morning in the tropical rain forest. Birds call, insects hum, and raindrops splash onto broad, shiny leaves. In the midst of the lush vegetation, orchids are found growing on a tree. You can see why humans value orchids for their beauty. But orchids have other uses as well. The seed pod of one type of orchid is used to make vanilla. Parts of orchid plants are also used to make folk medicines, beverages, and foods. How are the orchids, trees, and all the other living and nonliving parts of the rain forest connected? How do living and nonliving things interact to permit life on our planet? How are materials cycled between living things and the environment?

Key Words

carbon cycle, climax community, ecology, ecosystem, food chain, food web, nitrogen cycle, oxygen cycle, population, succession

Key Concepts

• **Define** ecology.
• **Describe** how materials are cycled between living things and the environment.
• **Describe** the processes of ecological succession.
• **Analyze** the feeding relationship between organisms from two terrestrial communities. (Laboratory Investigation)

37-1 The Environment

Section Objectives:

■ *List* seven important abiotic factors in the environment.
■ *Describe* how light, temperature, and precipitation vary with position on the earth's surface.
■ *Describe* the process of soil formation and the different soil layers.

The Biosphere

The portion of the earth in which all living things exist is known as the **biosphere.** Compared to the diameter of the earth, the biosphere is a thin zone. It is about 20 kilometers in thickness, extending from the ocean floor to the highest point in the atmosphere where life is found. The biosphere includes portions of the *lithosphere* (the solid part of the earth's surface), the *hydrosphere* (the water on and under the earth's surface as well as the water vapor of the air), and the *atmosphere* (the mass of air surrounding the earth).

▲ **Figure 37–1**

Environmental Adaptatations. In order to survive in a desert environment, these plants have had to adapt to conditions of little water and large changes in temperature.

◀ Orchids growing on a tree in South America.

819

The Physical Environment

All types of organisms have adaptations that allow them to survive in a particular environment. They may show adaptations for getting food and for reproduction, as well as for avoiding predators. Living things are affected by physical factors in their environment, such as the availability of water, changes in temperature, the amount of light present in the environment, and the composition of the soil. The physical environment is also affected by the organisms that live in it. For example, some organisms help to break rock into soil. The growth of plants contributes to the filling in of ponds. Finally, organisms are affected by other organisms living in the same area. Plants compete for growing space with other plants, animals eat plants or other animals, and microorganisms decompose the remains of larger organisms, returning nutrients to the soil.

The branch of biology that deals with the interactions among organisms and their environment is called **ecology** (ih KAHL uh jee). In studying the interaction between organisms and their environment, both the living and nonliving factors must be considered. The living, or **biotic** (by AHT ik), factors include all the living organisms in the environment and their effects, both direct and indirect, on other living things. The nonliving, or **abiotic** (ay by AHT ik), factors include water, oxygen, light, temperature, soil, and inorganic and organic nutrients.

Abiotic factors determine what types of organisms can survive in a particular environment. For example, in deserts there is little water available, and the temperature can change daily from very hot to cold. Only plants that are adapted to these conditions, such as sagebrush and cactus, can survive. Other types of plants, such as corn, oak trees, and orchids, grow in other environments with different abiotic conditions to which they are adapted.

Light

The energy for almost all living things on earth comes directly or indirectly from sunlight. The amount of sunlight striking a given area of the earth's surface changes with the latitude of the area. *Latitude* is the distance north or south of the equator. Both the *intensity*, or strength, of sunlight and the *duration,* or length, of daylight vary with latitude. The intensity and duration of sunlight affect the growth and flowering of plants. Some plants require high light intensity; others require low light intensity.

Light conditions also vary in aquatic environments. Light is absorbed as it passes through water. Thus, the amount of light present decreases with increasing depth. The layer of water through which light penetrates is called the *photic* (FOH tik) *zone.* About 80% of the earth's photosynthesis takes place in this zone. Below the photic zone is the *aphotic* (ay FOH tik) *zone,* where there is no light. Except for a few chemotrophs, organisms in the aphotic zone are heterotrophs that derive their energy from organisms that drift or migrate down from the photic zone.

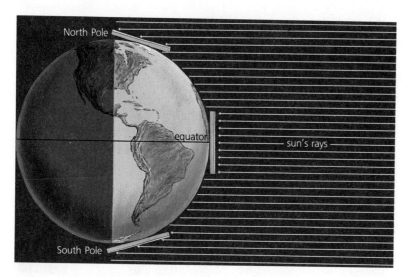

Intensity of Sunlight at Different Latitudes. In this diagram, each ray represents the same amount of light. Note that near the equator a larger amount of surface is struck by more rays than is struck near the poles.

Temperature

Temperature patterns on the earth's surface vary with latitude and with altitude. *Altitude* is the vertical distance above sea level. The temperature pattern of a region may be affected by the presence of a nearby major geographic feature, such as a mountain or an ocean. As the altitude rises, the temperature falls. Thus, the tops of mountains may be snow-covered even in warm regions.

The warmest average temperatures on the earth's surface are around the equator. Traveling north or south of the equator, the average temperatures drop. The North and South Poles are the coldest regions on earth.

Water

The release of water from the atmosphere as rain, snow, dew, and fog is called *precipitation*. The annual amount of precipitation varies from one region to another on the earth's surface. Annual precipitation patterns are related to latitude and to altitude. They are also influenced by local features, such as mountains and large bodies of water. Areas around the equator are hot and humid with heavy rainfall throughout the year. Because of the pattern of airflow over the earth's surface, most deserts are found around latitudes 30° north and 30° south of the equator. In these regions, there is a brief rainy season and almost no rain at all during the rest of the year. Still further north and south of the equator are *temperate* regions with hot summers and cold winters. Rainfall is fairly abundant in these regions. The polar regions are cold, and precipitation is in the form of snow.

Soil and Minerals

Soil consists of inorganic and organic materials. The inorganic material is mostly rock particles broken off from larger rocks by the action of water and wind—a process known as *weathering*.

Figure 37–3

Three Stages in the Development of Soil.
The forces of weathering and the action of
certain small organisms gradually break down
bedrock into fine particles. The products and
remains of organisms add organic matter to
the rock particles, forming soil. ▶

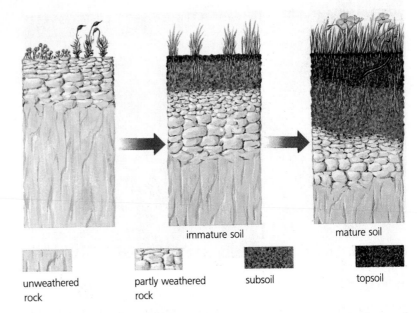

immature soil

mature soil

unweathered
rock

partly weathered
rock

subsoil

topsoil

Alternate freezing and thawing of water helps to crack the rock
and break off pieces. Soluble minerals in the rock dissolve in
water, breaking down the rock still further. Lichens and other
organisms also help to break down rock. When these organisms
die, their remains are mixed with the rock particles, thus adding
organic matter to the developing soil. Plants may take root in the
soil. When they die, their remains add more organic matter to the
soil.

The minerals present in soil depend partly on the type of rock
from which the soil was formed and partly on the types of organisms living in the soil. The amount of precipitation determines the
extent to which minerals will be retained in, or washed out of, the
soil.

As soil development slowly proceeds, three distinct layers
form. See Figure 37–3. The uppermost layer, which is called *topsoil,*
includes organic matter and various living organisms. Plant "litter," such as fallen leaves and twigs, overlies the topsoil and gradually blends into it. The dark, rich organic matter in the topsoil is
called *humus* (HYOO mus). Humus is formed from the decay of
dead plants and animals. The living organisms found in the topsoil
include plant roots, earthworms, insects, and many other animals
and protists. The organisms of decay—bacteria and fungi—are
also found in this layer.

Beneath the topsoil is a layer of *subsoil* made of rock particles
mixed with organic compounds, including mineral nutrients.
Water-soluble materials from the topsoil are carried downward
into the subsoil by the downward movement of water. The bot-
tommost layer of the soil is made of bits of rock broken off from
the parent bedrock below.

There are many types of soils. They are classified according to
their organic content, mineral composition, pH, and size of the
rock particles.

37-1 Section Review

1. What is ecology?
2. List some common abiotic environmental factors.
3. What are some geographic features that influence temperature?
4. Which environmental factors cause the weathering of rock during soil formation?

Critical Thinking

5. Compare and contrast topsoil with subsoil. (*Comparing and Contrasting*)

37-2 The Living Environment

Section Objectives:

- *Explain* the terms *population, community,* and *ecosystem.*
- *List* and describe the different types of symbiotic relationships.
- *Describe* the feeding relationships in an ecosystem.
- *Explain* the flow of energy in an ecosystem using the concepts of pyramids of energy and biomass.

Organization in the Living Environment

In studying organisms in nature, ecologists often look at a particular group of organisms in a particular natural setting. The simplest grouping of organisms in nature is a **population.** A population includes all individuals of a single species that live within a certain area. All the black oak trees in a forest make up a population. All the bullfrogs in a pond make up a population. Populations can also be considered as parts of larger groups. All the populations of different organisms within a given area make up a **community.** For example, all the frogs, fishes, algae, plants, and other living things in and around a pond make up a pond community.

An **ecosystem** includes a community and its physical environment. In an ecosystem, both the biotic and abiotic factors are included. There is an ongoing exchange of materials between the nonliving and living parts of an ecosystem. All the ecosystems of the earth are linked to one another. Organisms move from one ecosystem to another. Water and other inorganic substances pass from one ecosystem to another. Also, organic compounds, with their stored energy, are transferred between ecosystems.

Population Dynamics

A population will change size depending on how many organisms are added to it and how many organisms are removed from it. Populations grow when resources are not limited. Growth occurs when the number of new individuals added to a population (births) exceeds the number of individuals who leave the population (deaths). Because birth rates are usually higher than death rates, populations will grow unless something stops them. A population remains the same size when the number of births is equal to the number of deaths. If the number of deaths exceeds the number of births, the population declines.

Under ideal environmental conditions, without limitations of resources or space, a population will increase. At first, the rate of growth is slow. Then the growth becomes rapid. As long as conditions remain ideal, rapid growth will continue. Environmental limiting factors, such as nutrients, water, disease, competition, or predation, can act on a population and prevent further growth. This will cause the population growth to slow and eventually enter a state of equilibrium. This is called the **carrying capacity** of a particular environment for a particular species. Carrying capacity is the maximum population that can be supported by resources in the environment.

▲ **Figure 37–4**

Herbivores. Giraffes are just one of many kinds of herbivores that inhabit the African tropical grasslands.

Autotrophs and Heterotrophs

An ecosystem includes all kinds of organisms—microorganisms, plants, and animals. Autotrophs are organisms that can make their own food using carbon dioxide. Most autotrophs carry on photosynthesis. A few, however, carry on chemosynthesis. Directly or indirectly, autotrophs provide the food for heterotrophs—those organisms that cannot synthesize their own food.

Heterotrophs are divided into several groups according to what they eat and how they obtain their food. Heterotrophs include herbivores, carnivores, omnivores, and decomposers. Herbivores (HER buh vorz) are animals that feed only on plants. Rabbits, cattle, horses, sheep, and deer are herbivores. Carnivores (KAR nuh vorz) are animals that feed on other animals. Some carnivores are predators, and some are scavengers. Predators, such as lions, hawks, and wolves, attack and kill their prey and feed on their bodies. Scavengers feed on dead animals they find. Vultures and hyenas are scavengers. Omnivores (AHM nih vorz) are animals that feed on both plants and animals. Humans and bears are omnivores. Decomposers are organisms that obtain nutrients by breaking down the remains of dead plants and animals. Many bacteria and fungi function as decomposers.

Symbiotic Relationships

Symbiotic relationships are relationships in which two different organisms live in close association with each other to the benefit of at least one of them. There are three types of symbiotic relationships: mutualism, commensalism, and parasitism.

In **mutualism** (MYOOCH uh wuh liz um), both organisms benefit from their association. For example, termites have cellulose-digesting microorganisms living in their digestive tracts. Without these microorganisms, termites could not get nutrients from the wood they eat. In turn, the termites provide the microorganisms with food and a place to live.

Lichens consist of algal or blue-green bacterial and fungal cells. Both types of cells benefit from this association. It allows them to live in environments in which neither could survive alone. Through photosynthesis, the algae or blue-green bacteria produce food for themselves and for the fungi. The fungi provide moisture and the structural framework and attachment sites in which the algae or bacteria grow.

Peas, clover, and alfalfa are *legumes*. Legumes have nodules on their roots in which certain bacteria grow. The bacteria convert nitrogen gas from the air in the soil into forms usable by the plants. In this relationship, the plants are supplied with the nitrogen compounds they need, while the bacteria are given an environment in which they can grow and reproduce. Legumes are part of the nitrogen cycle described in section 37–3.

In **commensalism** (kuh MEN suh liz um), one organism benefits from a symbiotic relationship, and the other is not affected. For example, pilotfish are small fish that live with sharks. They eat the scraps left over from the shark's feeding. Thus, the shark provides the pilotfish with food. As far as is known, the pilotfish neither helps nor hurts the shark. Barnacles may attach themselves to the large body surface of a whale. Barnacles are sessile and rely on water currents to bring them food. The movements of the whale provide them with a constantly changing environment and food supply. The whale is not affected by the presence of the barnacles.

In **parasitism** (PAR uh suh tiz um), one organism benefits from a symbiotic relationship, and the other is harmed. The organism that benefits is called the *parasite,* while the organism that is harmed is the *host*. Some parasites cause only slight damage to their hosts, while others kill the host. Tapeworms, for example, are parasites that live in the digestive tracts of various animals. There,

▲ **Figure 37–5**

Mutualism. These termites have microorganisms within their intestines that allow the termites to obtain nutrients. The microorganisms benefit from the presence of food and a place to live.

◀ **Figure 37–6**

Commensalism. The pilotfish around this shark eat leftover scraps from the shark's feeding. The shark is neither helped nor harmed by the presence of the pilotfish.

they are provided with nutrients and an environment in which to grow and reproduce. However, the host is harmed by the presence of the tapeworms. The loss of nutrients and tissue damage caused by the worm can cause serious illness. There are also parasitic plants that grow on other plants. Two examples of plant parasites are mistletoe and Indian pipe.

Symbiotic relationships, particularly those involving mutualism or commensalism, are not always permanent. Also, it is not always possible to say whether an organism is helped or harmed by such a relationship. For example, in many environments the algal cells of a lichen can survive well without the fungal cells. The fungal cells, on the other hand, may not be able to survive alone.

Competition in Ecosystems

Each type of organism within an ecosystem has a particular part of the environment in which it lives. This is its **habitat.** For example, the habitat of a slime mold is the damp floor of a forest. Because of the complex interactions that occur within an ecosystem, each species also plays a particular role in an ecosystem. The role of a species in an ecosystem is its **niche.** An organism's habitat is part of its niche, but only part. Also included are how, when, and where it obtains nutrients, its reproductive behavior, and its direct and indirect effects on the environment and on other species within the ecosystem.

In a balanced ecosystem, each species occupies its own niche. It occupies a particular territory (its habitat) and obtains nutrients in a particular way. Competition arises when the niches of two species overlap. The greater the overlap—the more requirements the two species have in common—the more intense the competition. Competition between two different species is called **interspecific competition.** As the resources being competed for become

Figure 37–7

Habitat of a Slime Mold. This white slime mold has grown around a small twig on the forest floor. Slime molds are found in cool, shady, moist places in the woods. ▶

Math, Science, and Technology

A New Arrival in the Ecosystem

Problem

In the past, natural barriers such as mountains, deserts, and oceans kept populations separate. Today, efficient modes of transportation bridge natural barriers, carrying living things from one part of the world to another. For example, the zebra mussel—a pest in the Great Lakes and Hudson River—was introduced to this country on cargo ships from Eastern Europe. The introduction of foreign organisms into nonnative habitats is continuing to be a problem.

Biologists wish to study one of these organisms and the effect it has on an ecosystem. The organism to be studied is a mouse that originated from Southeast Asia and was carried to North America in a cargo of bamboo. A field study is necessary to determine if natural predators will feed upon the Asian mice, preventing them from overwhelming the native populations. The mice will be captured, "banded" with descriptive labels from the National Wildlife Service, and then released.

Task

You are asked to be a member of a team of ecologists assigned to develop and test a "live" trap for the National Wildlife Service. Ecologists often use live traps to sample mice and other rodent populations because these devices capture animals in their natural habitat unharmed. The trap will be used to sample the population of Asian mice to determine their success in exploiting the new environment and their impact on native populations.

In order to perform this task, you must complete each of the following:

1. Research on the Internet or in the library the design and construction of a "live" trap.

2. Design and make a scale drawing of a live animal trap that will house an adult mouse. Adult mice range in size from seven to nine centimeters in length and have a diameter of approximately three centimeters. A veterinarian suggests that an animal should have 20 times its body volume of living space in order to be treated humanely. Calculate the approximate volume of a mouse, using the formula: Volume = $\pi r^2 h$. Then, calculate the dimensions, surface area, and volume of the trap. Use the following formulas: Area = Length $\times$ Width, and Volume = Length $\times$ Width $\times$ Height

3. Explore all the possible variables by carrying out preliminary studies, such as testing the mechanism that closes the trap for effectiveness, and selecting easy-to-handle construction materials.

4. Construct the trap using the scale drawing as a guide. Keep a journal of the decisions made in formulating the design, in gathering the materials, and in the construction and testing of the trap.

Solution

As a team, prepare a presentation describing your group's approach to the problem. Include sources of information used in the design and construction of the trap. The presentation should include: the details of the design and photographs of the completed trap, the assumptions made by the team, and any other supporting information.

more scarce, the competition becomes more intense. Eventually, one of the species is eliminated from the ecosystem, leaving the more successful species to occupy the niche.

Competition also occurs between members of the same species. This is called **intraspecific competition.** The intensity of the competition between members of the same species is affected by population density and the availability of resources. If conditions become harsh, those individuals with the most helpful adaptations will survive. The less-well-adapted individuals will not.

Producers, Consumers, and Decomposers

In all but a few small ecosystems, the autotrophs are plants and other photosynthetic organisms. They trap energy from sunlight and use it for the synthesis of sugars and starch. These substances can be changed to other organic compounds that are needed by the plant, or they can be broken down for energy. Heterotrophs can only use the chemical energy stored in organic compounds for their life processes. These organic nutrients must be obtained from the bodies of other organisms—either plants or animals. Because autotrophs are the only organisms in an ecosystem that can produce organic compounds (food) from inorganic compounds, they are called **producers.** Since heterotrophs must obtain nutrients from other organisms, they are called **consumers.**

Saprobes play an important role in an ecosystem. They function as *organisms of decay,* or **decomposers.** They break down the remains of dead plants and animals, releasing substances that can be reused by other members of the ecosystem. In this way, many important substances are recycled in an ecosystem.

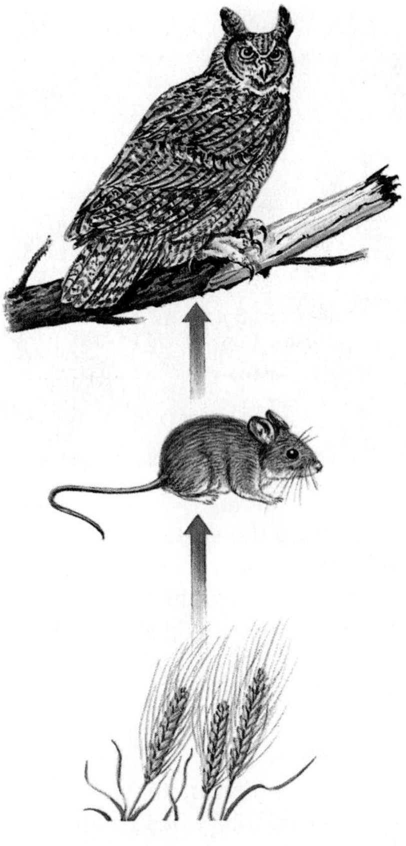

Food Chains and Food Webs

Within an ecosystem, there is a pathway of energy flow that always begins with the producers. Energy stored in organic nutrients synthesized by the producers is transferred to consumers when the plants are eaten. Herbivores are the primary consumers, or *first-order consumers.* The carnivores that feed on the plant-eating animals are secondary consumers, or *second-order consumers.* For example, mice feed on plants and are first-level consumers. The snake that eats the mice is a second-level consumer, while the hawk that eats the snake is a third-level consumer. Since many consumers have a varied diet, they may be second-, third-, or higher-level consumers, depending on their prey. Each of these feeding relationships forms a **food chain,** a series of organisms through which food energy is passed. A simple food chain is shown in Figure 37–8.

Feeding relationships in an ecosystem are never just simple food chains. There are many types of organisms at each feeding level, and there are always many food chains in an ecosystem. These food chains are connected at different points, forming a **food web**. One of these is shown in Figure 37–9.

▲ **Figure 37–8**

A Simple Food Chain. The grass is a producer, the field mouse is a first-order consumer, and the owl is a second-order consumer. The arrows show the flow of energy in the food chain.

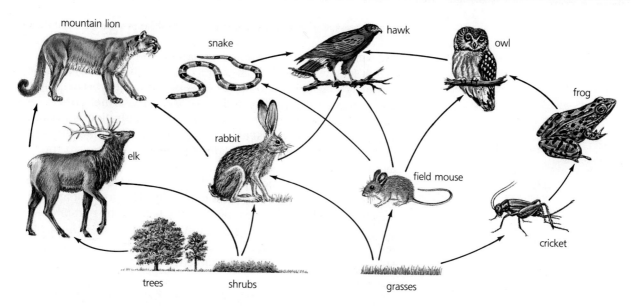

mountain lion

snake

hawk

owl

frog

elk

rabbit

field mouse

cricket

trees

shrubs

grasses

At every level in an ecosystem, there are organisms that act as decomposers. The decomposers make use of the wastes and remains of all organisms in the system. They use the energy they find in these materials for their own metabolism. At the same time, they break down organic compounds into inorganic compounds and make substances available for reuse. The decomposers are the final consumers in every food chain and food web.

▲ **Figure 37–9**
A Simple Food Web. Usually, each organism is part of several different food chains.

MiniLab

Skill: Classifying

Life in Your Neighborhood

Procedure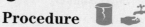

Problem

How can you **classify** the organisms in your area?

1. Choose an area around your school or around your home. Make a list of the different kinds of organisms—such as plants, insects, animals, and people—that you see.

2. Classify each organism as either a primary producer or a consumer.

3. Further classify each consumer as a carnivore or herbivore.

Analyze and Conclude

1. What organisms did you classify as primary producers? Consumers?

2. Did you observe any herbivores? What were they?

3. Did you observe any carnivores? If so, what were they?

4. What do you think would happen if all the primary producers in the area died out?

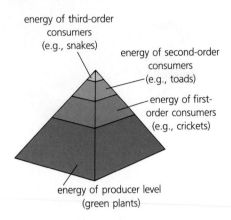

energy of third-order
consumers
(e.g., snakes)

energy of second-order
consumers
(e.g., toads)

energy of first-
order consumers
(e.g., crickets)

energy of producer level
(green plants)

▲ **Figure 37–10**

The Pyramid of Energy in an Ecosystem. At each level in an ecosystem, the energy available is only about 10 percent of the energy at the level below it.

Pyramids of Energy and Biomass

The amount of energy available in a food web decreases with each higher feeding level. This happens because only a small fraction of the energy taken in as food becomes stored as new tissue. Much of the food eaten is not digested and absorbed. Furthermore, a large part of the energy in the food is used for respiration and maintenance. This energy is lost as heat. As a result, only about 10 percent of the energy taken in at any feeding level is passed to the next feeding level.

The amount of energy available in an ecosystem is commonly shown in the form of a **pyramid of energy.** The greatest amount of energy is present in the producers—the base of the pyramid—and the least energy is present at the top of the pyramid—the highest-level consumers. Because the amount of available energy decreases so steeply, there are usually no more than four or five feeding levels in an ecosystem.

Figure 37–10 is an example of a pyramid of energy. In a field, green plants are the producers, trapping the sun's energy for photosynthesis. For every 1000 calories of energy absorbed by the plants, only 100 are stored. Thus, 100 calories are available to a first-order consumer, such as a cricket, that feeds on the plants as they grow. As a second-order consumer, a toad that eats the cricket receives only 10 of the original 100 calories consumed by the cricket. At the top of the energy pyramid, a snake that eats the toad receives only 1 calorie of the 10 calories received by the toad. This amount is only 0.001 percent of the energy originally absorbed by the plants at the base of the pyramid.

Since the total amount of energy available decreases with each higher feeding level, the total mass of living organisms that can be supported at each level decreases, too. This relationship can also be represented by a pyramid. The relationship, known as the **pyramid of biomass,** shows the relative mass of the organisms—the *biomass*—at each feeding level. The greatest amount of biomass is in the lowest level, the producers. The least is found in the highest level of consumers.

37-2 Section Review

1. What is a population?
2. List three types of symbiotic relationships.
3. Which kind of organisms are always found at the base of a food chain?
4. Which level of an energy pyramid contains the most energy?

Critical Thinking

5. Can two species occupy the same habitat? Can they occupy the same niche? Explain. (*Reasoning Conditionally*)

37-3 Cycles of Materials

Section Objectives:

- *Describe* each of the following biogeochemical cycles: the nitrogen cycle, the carbon and oxygen cycles, and the water cycle.

In all ecosystems, materials recycle between living things and the environment. Organisms incorporate certain substances from the environment into their bodies. When these organisms die, their bodies are broken down by decomposers, and the substances returned to the environment. If these substances were not returned to the environment, their supply would eventually become exhausted. The cycles of materials between living things and the environment are called *biogeochemical cycles*. Nitrogen, carbon, oxygen, and water are among the substances involved in such cycles.

The Nitrogen Cycle

Nitrogen is an important element in living things. It is a basic component of amino acids, which form proteins, and of nucleotides, which form nucleic acids. Nitrogen gas (N_2) makes up almost 80 percent of the earth's atmosphere. However, most organisms cannot use N_2 directly. They must use nitrogen compounds. Most plants can use nitrogen only in two inorganic forms, ammonia (NH_3) and nitrate (NO_3^-). Usually, nitrate is the major source of nitrogen for plants. From nitrate and ammonia, plants can make proteins and nucleic acids. Animals lack this ability. They can use nitrogen only in an organic form. Thus, animals must ingest plants or other animals to meet their nitrogen needs.

Nitrogen in the wastes and in the remains of organisms must be made available to living plants for reuse. This is accomplished through the activity of decomposers that break down the complex organic compounds in plant and animal remains. During decomposition, most of the nitrogen in organic compounds is released as ammonia. Some of this may be taken up directly by plants, but most is converted by **nitrifying bacteria** to nitrite (NO_2^-) and finally to nitrate. The nitrate then is available for uptake again by plants.

Not all nitrate in the soil and in water remains as nitrate until taken up by plants. **Denitrifying bacteria** get energy for their life processes by converting nitrite and nitrate to nitrogen gas (N_2). This form of nitrogen, which is released into the atmosphere, cannot be used by plants and animals. However, nitrogen gas can be changed to a form available to plants. A few kinds of bacteria, including blue-green bacteria, convert nitrogen gas directly to ammonia through a process called **nitrogen fixation.** Some of these **nitrogen fixers** are free-living. The ammonia they produce is used to synthesize their own nitrogen-containing compounds. Other nitrogen-fixers are symbiotic. They fix nitrogen only when living in close association with a host plant. Figure 37–11 shows the

Figure 37–11

Root Nodules of a Legume. The nodules on this legume root contain nitrogen-fixing bacteria that provide the plant with usable forms of nitrogen. ▼

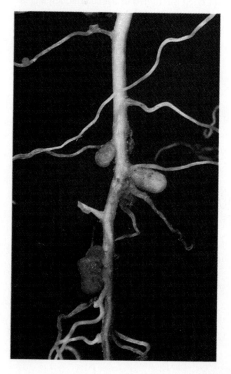

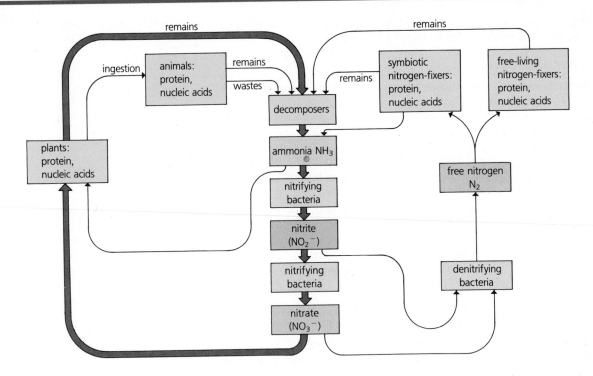

▲ **Figure 37–12**

The Nitrogen Cycle. The nitrogen cycle is a complex pathway by which nitrogen moves through an ecosystem. Most nitrogen enters living organisms through nitrogen-fixing bacteria that oxidize it to nitrites and nitrates. Nitrogen is returned to the soil through animal waste products and the decay of organisms.

bacteria-containing nodules on the roots of one of the legume plants. In these symbiotic associations, the nitrogen fixers utilize the ammonia themselves. They also supply some ammonia directly to the host plant. When the nitrogen fixers die, their nitrogen is recycled through decomposition.

Figure 37–12 shows the various pathways of the nitrogen cycle. The nitrogen cycle keeps the level of usable nitrogen in the soil fairly constant. The nitrogen cycle also occurs in lakes, streams, and oceans. Most of the nitrogen being cycled remains in compound form. Only a small fraction is cycled through the atmosphere.

The Carbon and Oxygen Cycles

Carbon, in the form of carbon dioxide, makes up about 0.03 percent of the atmosphere. Carbon dioxide is also found dissolved in the waters of the earth. In the course of photosynthesis, carbon dioxide from the atmosphere is incorporated into organic compounds, a process known as *carbon fixation*. Some of these organic compounds are broken down during cellular respiration by photosynthetic organisms. This releases carbon dioxide into the atmosphere. If the plants or other photosynthetic organisms are eaten by animals, the carbon compounds pass through a food web. At each level, some are broken down by cellular respiration, releasing carbon dioxide into the atmosphere. Finally, the remains of dead plants and animals and animal wastes are broken down by decomposers, which also releases carbon dioxide.

In the **carbon cycle,** carbon dioxide is removed from the atmosphere by photosynthesis, and it is returned to the atmosphere by cellular respiration. The carbon cycle is shown in Figure 37-13. These two processes are normally in balance, maintaining a relatively constant level of carbon dioxide in the atmosphere. However, the burning of fossil fuels (oil, coal, and natural gas) also releases carbon dioxide. Because of the increasing use of these fuels, there has been a gradual increase in the carbon dioxide content of the atmosphere since the mid-1800s. The long-term effects of this change are not known. However, some scientists think that it will result in an increase in temperature on the earth's surface. This would occur because the atmospheric carbon dioxide absorbs heat from the earth that would otherwise be radiated away into space. This phenomenon is known as the "greenhouse effect."

Oxygen makes up about 20 percent of the earth's atmosphere. During photosynthesis, water molecules are split into hydrogen and oxygen. The hydrogen is used in the formation of carbohydrates, and the oxygen is released into the atmosphere. Animals, plants, and many protists use oxygen in cellular respiration and release carbon dioxide. Thus, in the **oxygen cycle,** oxygen is released into the atmosphere by the process of photosynthesis and removed from the atmosphere by cellular respiration.

Figure 37-13
The Oxygen and Carbon Cycles. The cycling of carbon and oxygen in an ecosystem results from photosynthesis and respiration. ▼

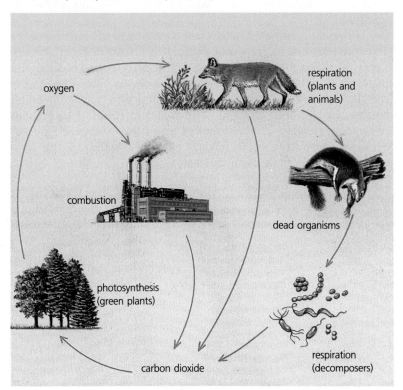

Science, Technology and Society

Issue: Greenhouse Effect

For years, scientists have been worried about the greenhouse effect. Many human activities, especially the burning of fossil fuels, release carbon dioxide into the air. Carbon dioxide traps the sun's heat, which is reflected back to the earth. This is causing the average temperature of the earth to rise gradually.

Some scientists fear that global warming may lead to drought and famine. As the earth warms, the melting of icecaps may cause floods in major coastal cities. If we do not prevent the greenhouse effect soon, they claim, it will be too late. Thus, they want to look for solutions and explore alternatives to fossil fuels now.

Other scientists claim that the greenhouse effect may have been blown out of proportion. Scientific data is somewhat contradictory and does not explain all the factors affecting climate. They argue that global warming is a gradual process and no quick decisions should be made. Time and money should be spent on research now and not on taking action.

■ *Should we take immediate action against the greenhouse effect? Why or why not?*

Figure 37–14

The Water Cycle. Water from the earth's surface enters the atmosphere in the form of water vapor through the processes of evaporation and transpiration. It returns to the surface through condensation and precipitation. ▶

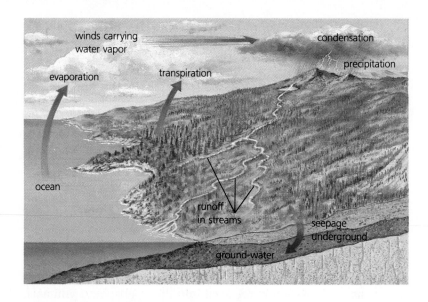

The Water Cycle

The cycling of water on the earth is almost entirely a physical process. Wherever water is exposed to the air, it evaporates—escapes into the air in the form of water vapor. Plants contribute to this loss of water to the air by the process of transpiration. However, there is a limit to the amount of water vapor the air can hold. Through various physical processes, excess water vapor condenses to form clouds and falls back to the earth's surface as precipitation.

This cycling of water between the surface of the earth and the atmosphere is called the **water cycle.** It is shown in Figure 37–14. Unlike the other cycles we have examined, no chemical changes are involved. Nor do any truly biological processes enter into it. It is true that some water is broken down chemically to hydrogen and oxygen during photosynthesis. This water is restored by cellular respiration. However, the amount of water involved in the photosynthesis-respiration cycle is only a small fraction of the total amount that passes through the water cycle.

37-3 Section Review

1. Name three biogeochemical cycles.
2. What kind of organisms return soil nitrogen to the atmosphere?
3. What carbon compound is released as the result of burning fossil fuels?

Critical Thinking

4. List two similarities between the nitrogen cycle and the carbon cycle. (*Comparing and Contrasting*)

37-4 Maintenance and Change in Ecosystems

Section Objectives:

- *Describe* the conditions necessary for a stable, self-sustaining ecosystem.
- *Explain* the terms ecological succession, dominant species, climax community, primary succession, and secondary succession.
- *Compare* succession on land, which leads to development of a forest community, with succession in lakes and ponds.

Maintenance in an Ecosystem

For an ecosystem to be stable and self-sustaining, certain conditions must exist. First, there must be a constant source of energy. For almost all ecosystems on earth, the source of energy is light from the sun. Only a few ecosystems are based on chemosynthesis. In these ecosystems, the producers derive energy for the synthesis of organic compounds from chemical reactions involving various inorganic compounds. Second, there must be organisms within the ecosystem that can use incoming energy (light) for the synthesis of organic compounds. This role is filled by green plants and algae, which are the producers of the ecosystem. Third, there must be a cycle of materials between living organisms in the ecosystem and the environment. The producers incorporate inorganic compounds from the environment into organic compounds, which may then pass through a food chain or food web. Eventually, however, the decomposers break down the remains of dead organisms, releasing the inorganic substances back into the environment for reuse.

Ecological Succession

Although ecosystems appear stable, they do undergo change. Change occurs because the living organisms present in the ecosystem alter the environment. Some of the changes tend to make the environment more suitable for new types of organisms and less suitable for the existing organisms. Thus, the original organisms in an ecosystem are slowly replaced by other types. A new community replaces the original community in the ecosystem. Over time, this community is gradually replaced by still another community. The process by which an existing community is slowly replaced by another community is called **ecological succession.** In land environments, ecological succession usually depends upon the types of plants that are present at any given time. Plants determine the type of community that develops because plants are the producers. The types of animals that can survive in the community depend, directly or indirectly, on the types of plants.

During each stage of ecological succession, only a few species have a great effect on the environment and on other members of the

Early Plant Forms

Intermediate Forms

Climax Forest
maples

beeches

oaks

pines

shrubs and grasses

ferns

lichens and mosses

soil and humus

rock

▲ **Figure 37–15**
Stages of Primary Succession. The sequence of stages is shown from left to right. In an actual succession, only one stage is present at any given time.

community. These species are called the **dominant species.** The conditions imposed on the environment by the dominant species determine the types of other species that can survive in each successive community.

Succession of one community by another goes on until a mature, stable community develops. Such a community is called a **climax community.** In an ecosystem with a climax community, the conditions continue to be suitable for all the members of the community. The climax community remains until it is upset by a catastrophic event, such as a fire, flood, or volcanic eruption. After the destruction of a climax community, succession begins again and continues until a new climax community develops. Such catastrophic events are not necessarily bad. For example, some conifer species require a fire in order to release their seeds.

When succession occurs in an area that has no existing life, for example, on a bare rock, it is called **primary succession.** Succession that occurs in an area in which an existing community has been partially destroyed and its balance upset is called **secondary succession.**

Succession on Land Primary succession occurs on land in areas that are nearly lifeless. The process is shown in Figure 37–15. Such conditions exist on rocky cliffs, sand dunes, newly formed volcanic islands, and newly exposed land areas. Primary succession is a slow process because it must begin with the formation of soil.

Soil forms slowly over thousands of years. By the process of weathering, large rocks are gradually broken into smaller and smaller pieces. Eventually, some of the rock is broken down into small particles. The first organisms to inhabit an area are called *pioneer organisms.* These organisms include bacteria, fungi, and lichens. They break down the rock still further and add organic matter to the developing soil. Lichens are adapted to exposed conditions. They become attached to irregularities in the surface of the rock by rootlike rhizoids. They secrete acids that dissolve the rock. Some lichens die, and their remains are added to the soil. Mosses appear in areas where a little soil has accumulated. The mosses may shade the lichens, causing them to die and thus adding more organic material to the still primitive soil.

Eventually, grasses and annual plants grow in the areas where organic material has accumulated. When these plants die, the soil becomes richer. Small shrubs begin to grow, and their roots break rocks apart. The shrubs may shade the grasses, killing them. Tree seedlings may take root. The trees eventually shade out the shrubs. The seedlings that grew among the shrubs may have required a fair

MiniLab

Skill: Observing

Successful Succession?

Problem

How can you **observe** ecological succession and a climax community?

Procedure

1. Obtain a clean jar with a cover and place a handful of dried plant material into the jar.

2. Fill the jar with boiled pond water or sterile spring water. Determine the initial pH of the water with pH paper.

3. Cover the jar and place it in an area that receives indirect light.

4. Examine the jar every day for the next few days. Test and record the pH each day.

5. When the jar appears cloudy, prepare microscopic slides of water from various levels of the jar. Use a pipette to collect the samples.

6. View the slides under the low-power objective of a microscope and record your observations.

Analyze and Conclude

1. Why did you use boiled or sterile water?

2. Where did the organisms you saw come from?

3. Did the pH of the water change?

4. Was ecological succession occurring? Give evidence to support your answer.

5. Did your community reach a stable, or climax, condition?

amount of sunlight. Thus, when they become mature trees, there may not be enough sun on the forest floor for seedlings of the same type to survive. However, seedlings of other trees may grow well in the shade. In this way, one community of trees will be succeeded by another community with different trees. After thousands of years, a climax community will develop. Climax communities are usually described in terms of their dominant plant forms.

The dominant plants of a climax community are determined by the physical factors of the environment. Where there is adequate rainfall and suitable soil, the climax community is likely to be a forest. If there is not enough water for a forest, the climax community can consist of grasses or some other type of plant.

Animal life changes with the plant communities. For example, as a succession proceeds toward a forest community, animals that live among grasses and shrubs will be replaced by animals that live on the forest floor and at varying levels in the trees.

Secondary succession occurs in areas in which the climax community has been destroyed. For example, a forest may be cut down in order to clear the land for farming. If, after being farmed for awhile, the land is left untended, a new succession will begin. Eventually, it, too, will end in another forest climax community. In secondary succession, the area already has existing soil. Since the sequence does not begin with soil formation, the process is faster than primary succession. A climax community may become reestablished after a few hundreds of years, rather than the thousands originally needed for the primary succession. After the forest fires in 1988, the process of succession has begun to occur in Yellowstone National Park.

Succession in Lakes and Ponds Lakes and ponds may also pass through stages of ecological succession, eventually developing into a forest climax community as shown in Figure 37–17. The

Figure 37–16

Secondary Succession. In 1988, forest fires swept through Yellowstone National Park in Wyoming, destroying much of the vegetation. As seen in this recent photo, the process of secondary succession has already begun. ▶

a

b

c

d

process begins when sediment, fallen leaves, and other debris gradually accumulate on the lake bottom, decreasing its depth. Around the edges of the lake, sphagnum moss and many of the rooted plants, such as cattails, reeds, and rushes, grow out into the shallower water. They gradually extend the banks inward, decreasing the size of the lake. As the lake fills in, it becomes rich in nutrients that can support a large population of organisms. The increased number of plants and animals contribute organic material to the sediment, which hastens the filling-in process. As succession continues, the lake becomes a marsh. Still later, the marsh fills in, forming dry land. Land communities replace aquatic forms. Over time, the filled area becomes part of the surrounding community.

▲ **Figure 37–17**

Ecological Succession in a Pond. A pond may gradually change to dry land that supports a forest community.

37-4 Section Review

1. By what process do ecosystems change?

2. What is any group of organisms that is the first to inhabit an area?

3. How does secondary succession differ from primary succession?

Critical Thinking

4. A fire has wiped out an old maple forest near your home. Predict the dominant plants that will inhabit the area 400 years after the fire. (*Predicting*)

Laboratory
Investigation

Analyzing Feeding Relationships Among Organisms

Within a community, organisms interact in many ways. Tracing the flow of energy within a community can help you understand how the organisms interact. In this investigation, you will construct and compare food webs for two different communities.

Problem

How does the energy flow through a community affect the community's complexity and stability? **Analyze** the feeding relationships among the organisms from two terrestrial communities.

Materials (per group)

- 2 large sheets of unlined paper
- plain notebook paper
- pen or pencil
- several colored markers
- transparent tape or glue

Procedure

1. On the next page, you will find a chart that contains two lists of organisms. One list includes organisms from a hickory/oak forest community in a temperate deciduous forest. The other list is from a cultivated cornfield community.

2. Carefully read the lists and identify as many feeding relationships as you can. In many cases, one species may be linked to several others—either as a food or as a feeder.

3. Write the names of the organisms from the first community on a sheet of notebook paper. Cut the names out and place them on one of the large sheets of paper. *Note:* Do not attach them to the sheet yet.

4. Discuss with your partner how the organisms should be arranged. Keep in mind that the names have to be connected to one another to indicate feeding links.

5. When you have decided on the arrangement, attach the names of the organisms to the large sheet with tape or glue.

Organisms in Deciduous Forest and Cornfield Communities

Organisms	Hickory/Oak Forest Community	Cultivated Cornfield Community
Plant species	White oak, black oak, tulip tree, white pine, birch, big tooth aspen, dogwood, sassafras, viburnum	Corn
Animal species	Invertebrates, such as beetle, ant, sow bug, earthworm, snail, termite, moth, centipede, and spider; birds, such as cardinal, warbler, chickadee, woodpecker, flycatcher, and owl; other animals, such as raccoon, squirrel, chipmunk, black bear, opossum, wood mouse, vole, deer, and black racer (snake)	Raccoon, corn snake, woodchuck, field mouse, deer; invertebrates, such as corn borer, grasshopper, cricket, earthworm, butterfly, moth, and fly; birds, such as sparrow, meadowlark, crow, and hawk
Fungi and bacteria	Various fungi and bacteria	Various fungi and bacteria

6. Use the markers to construct food chains by drawing arrows from the food source to the feeder. Use different-colored markers to indicate different food chains. Make your food web as complex as possible.

7. Repeat steps 3 through 6 for the second list of organisms.

Observations

1. Compare your webs to those created by other groups.

2. Which community—the hickory/oak forest or the cornfield—is more complex?

Analysis and Conclusions

1. Are the food webs for the hickory/oak forest community the same for different groups? If not, how are they different?

2. Are the food webs for the cornfield community the same for different groups? If not, how are they different?

3. Which community has the greater variety of primary producers? The greater number of trophic levels?

4. Suppose a parasite destroyed most of the oak trees in the forest community and the corn plants in the cultivated field. How would each community be affected?

Extensions

Choose one animal species from each of the two communities and assume that it has become extinct. Predict the effect the loss of each animal would have on its community. Which community will be less affected by the loss? Why?

Chapter 37 Review ....

Study Outline

37-1 The Environment

▸ Ecology deals with the interactions among organisms and between organisms and their environment. The environment consists of biotic factors and abiotic factors.

▸ Abiotic factors include light, temperature, water, soil, and minerals. They determine the kinds of organisms that can survive in an environment.

37-2 The Living Environment

▸ Living things in the environment are divided into populations that include individuals of a certain species within a given area. All the populations in a given area make up a community.

▸ Autotrophs are organisms that synthesize their own nutrients. Heterotrophs, which feed on other organisms, include herbivores, omnivores, and carnivores.

▸ A food chain flows from producers to consumers and finally to decomposers. Interconnections between food chains form a food web.

▸ The amount of energy in an ecosystem is greatest at the producer level and decreases with each higher feeding level of the food web.

37-3 Cycles of Materials

▸ In all ecosystems there exist biogeochemical cycles, which are exchanges of materials between organisms and their environment.

▸ Biogeochemical cycles include the nitrogen cycle, the carbon cycle, the oxygen cycle, and the water cycle.

37-4 Maintenance and Change in Ecosystems

▸ Ecosystems remain stable and self-sustaining if there are a constant source of energy, the presence of autotrophs, and the cycling of materials between living organisms and the environment.

▸ Ecosystems undergo change called ecological succession in which an existing community is replaced by another community. The final stage of succession is called the climax community.

Chapter Assessment

Multiple Choice

Choose the letter of the answer that best completes each statement or answers the question.

1. Ecology is the study of the (a) habitats of living things. (b) role of the nonliving parts of the environment. (c) interaction among organisms and their environment. (d) comparison of the size of living things on earth.

2. Organisms that eat other organisms in order to obtain energy and nutrients are called (a) autotrophs. (b) heterotrophs. (c) parasites. (d) decomposers.

3. Energy flows through an ecosystem from the sun to (a) producers, then consumers. (b) consumers, then producers. (c) primary consumers. (d) heterotrophs.

4. Sunlight, rain, and soil acidity are (a) biotic factors. (b) habitats. (c) niches. (d) abiotic factors.

5. The role of a species in its ecosystem is its (a) microclimate. (b) habitat. (c) niche. (d) competition.

6. Consumers and decomposers are classified as (a) autotrophs. (b) heterotrophs. (c) omnivores. (d) carnivores.

7. When food chains are connected at various points, they form (a) pyramids of energy. (b) pyramids of biomass. (c) food webs. (d) niches.

8. Evaporation, condensation, and precipitation are processes that are involved in the (a) carbon cycle. (b) water cycle. (c) nitrogen cycle. (d) oxygen cycle.

9. The process by which an existing community is slowly replaced by another community is known as (a) climate change. (b) climax community. (c) evolution. (d) ecological succession.

10. In a food chain involving green plants, insects, birds, and mammals, the original source of energy is (a) chlorophyll. (b) glucose and oxygen. (c) water and carbon dioxide. (d) sunlight.

Content Review

Answer each of the following in complete sentences.

11. What is an ecosystem?

12. Compare a predator with a scavenger, and give examples of each.

13. What are the kinds of symbiotic relationships? Give one example of each.

14. How does a niche differ from a habitat?

15. Summarize the parts of a simple food chain.

16. Outline the nitrogen cycle.

17. How is the carbon cycle related to the oxygen cycle?

18. Under what conditions does an ecosystem tend to be stable and self-sustaining?

19. Describe the stages of primary succession both on land and in a pond.

20. What is secondary succession?

Graphic Organizing

For information on graphic organizers, see Appendix G at the back of this text.

21. Flow Chart Referring to the pyramid of energy shown on page 830, construct a flow chart to show the order of the feeding levels. Begin with the level that contains the greatest amount of energy, and end with the one that contains the least. As you move up the pyramid of energy, only 10 percent of the energy taken in at any feeding level is passed on to the next. Assume the producers supply 2697 calories. Use a calculator to compute the amounts of energy in the three feeding levels.

Critical Thinking and Problem Solving

Discuss each of the following in a brief paragraph.

22. Predicting Suppose the intensity of sunlight was drastically reduced for several months by smoke and ash from an erupting volcano such as Mt. St. Helens. Predict how each of the following members of nearby ecosystems would be affected: sweet grass, rabbits, and hawks.

23. Relating All consumers, either directly or indirectly, depend on producers for their food. Humans are consumers. Therefore, humans depend on producers for their food. Is this a valid argument? Explain your answer.

24. Interpreting An ecologist samples a shrubby meadow to determine the populations of certain key organisms. Data from the investigation are recorded in the table shown below. On a piece of graph paper, construct a pyramid showing the numbers of organisms at each feeding level for each of the three months. What is the relationship between population size and time of the year? How could you explain this relationship?

Type of Organism	Number of Organisms		
	May	**July**	**September**
grasshoppers	100	500	150
birds	25	100	10
shrubs and grass	700	2000	600
spiders	75	200	50

25. Hypothesizing The graph below shows changes in two populations—the snowshoe hare, a large relative of the rabbit, and the lynx, a small wildcat. Analyze the graph and develop a hypothesis to explain the changes in the two populations.

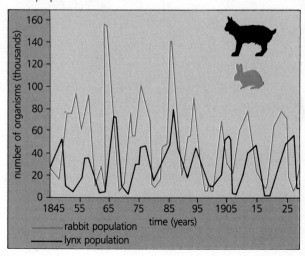

843

Biomes of the Earth

Guide for Reading

Previewing the Chapter

Wetlands provide rich habitats for an enormous diversity of plants and animals. Many endangered species, including birds, fishes, and amphibians, rely on wetlands for food and shelter. Wetlands represent just one of the earth's many biomes—large geographic regions with specific climates and particular types of plant and animal communities. What are the earth's major terrestrial and aquatic biomes? What problems do organisms encounter in adapting to conditions in specific terrestrial or aquatic biomes?

Key Words

biome, desert, grassland, taiga, temperate deciduous forest, tropical rain forest, tundra

Key Concepts

- **Describe** the different terrestrial biomes.
- **Compare** saltwater and freshwater biomes.
- **Compare** the water-holding capacity and porosity of various types of soil. (Laboratory Investigation)

38-1 Terrestrial Biomes

Section Objectives:

- *List* the major terrestrial biomes of the earth and specify the location of each.
- *Describe* the climatic factors that characterize each of the terrestrial biomes.
- *Name* the dominant plant and animal types of each biome.

The climate and other physical conditions of an area determine the type of climax community that can develop in that area. Areas that are similar in climate and other physical conditions develop similar types of climax communities. A **biome** (BY ohm) is a large geographical region that has a particular type of climax community. In the case of a land, or terrestrial, biome, the climax community is defined by the dominant type of plant life found there. For example, one biome may consist of climax communities of grasses. Another biome may contain evergreen trees. The species may vary from one part of a biome to another, but the general type of plant life, or vegetation, is the same throughout the biome. The major terrestrial biomes are the tundra, taiga, deciduous forest, grassland, desert, and tropical rain forest. In the sections that follow, you will read more about these major biomes and learn about their vegetation and inhabitants.

▲ **Figure 38–1**

A Mountain Environment. The physical conditions of this environment determine the types of organisms that thrive there.

◄ Papyrus growing in a freshwater biome—a wetland.

The term *biome* is also applied to communities that develop in aquatic environments. Ecologists refer to freshwater biomes, or communities of organisms inhabiting lakes and streams, and to saltwater, or marine, biomes.

The Tundra

The **tundra** (TUN druh) is a region that lies south of the ice caps of the Arctic and extends across North America, Europe, and Siberia. In the Southern Hemisphere, the areas that would be tundra are oceans. The tundra is characterized by a low average temperature and a short growing season of about 60 days. During the long, cold winters, the ground is completely frozen. During the short summer, only the topmost layer of soil thaws. The layers beneath this layer remain frozen. These layers are called **permafrost** (PER muh frost). The average precipitation in the tundra is only about 10 to 12 centimeters a year. However, because of the low rate of evaporation, the region is wet with bogs (see page 857) and ponds during the warm season.

Vegetation in the tundra is limited to lichens, mosses, grasses, sedges, and shrubs. There are almost no trees because of the short growing season and the permafrost. The vegetation that does grow

Figure 38–2

The Tundra. Caribou live in large herds that migrate across the Alaskan tundra. Many other large grazing animals and carnivores live in the tundra. ▼

in the tundra supports a limited number of animal species. Animals found in the tundra include reindeer, musk oxen, caribou, wolves, Arctic hares, Arctic foxes, lemmings, snowy owls, and ptarmigans, which are a type of bird.

During the warm season, a great number of flies and mosquitos appear in the region. Various types of birds, including sandpipers, ducks, and geese, migrate to the tundra during this season. Here, these migratory birds can nest and breed in safety, because of the relative absence of their usual predators. During their breeding season, the birds feed on the growing vegetation and the abundant supply of insects.

The Taiga

Moving south across the tundra, the vegetation slowly changes. Groups of stunted trees begin to appear in sheltered places. Farther south, the trees become larger and closer together, at last giving way to evergreen forests. This belt of evergreen forest, which extends across North America, Europe, and Asia, is the **taiga** (TY guh). The taiga has cold winters during which the ground is covered by deep snow. However, the growing season is longer than that of the tundra—about 120 days. The summer days are warmer than in the tundra, and the ground thaws completely. Precipitation is greater than in the tundra, averaging between 50 and 100 centimeters a year. As in the tundra, there are many ponds and bogs. Pines, firs, and spruce are the dominant vegetation, although some deciduous trees, which shed their leaves, are also present. These include willows and birches. There are also shrubs and herbaceous plants.

Figure 38–4

A Temperate Deciduous Forest. Temperate deciduous forest covers much of the eastern United States. In the summer, the broad-leaved deciduous trees shade the forest floor. In the spring, many species of herbs and other low-growing plants cover the forest floor before the trees develop leaves. ▶

Animals of the taiga include moose, wolves, bears, lynx, deer, elks, wolverines, martens, snowshoe hares, porcupines, and various rodents, birds, and insects.

The Temperate Deciduous Forest

The areas south of the taiga have varying amounts of rainfall, so there is no single type of biome that can be said to stretch across these latitudes. In eastern North America and Europe, these areas are regions of **temperate deciduous forest.** In temperate deciduous forest biomes the summers are usually hot and humid, and the winters are cold. Rainfall averages between 75 and 150 centimeters a year.

The species present in deciduous forests vary with the local amount of rainfall. Common trees of deciduous forests include oak, maple, hickory, beech, chestnut, and birch. Smaller trees and shrubs are also present, as well as herbaceous plants, ferns, and mosses.

Animals of the deciduous forest include wolves, gray foxes, bobcats, deer, raccoons, squirrels, and chipmunks, as well as a wide variety of birds and insects.

Grasslands

Grasslands, or prairies, are found in the interiors of North America, Asia, South America, and Africa. They occur in both temperate and tropical climates where rainfall ranges from 25 to 75 centimeters a year. This quantity of rainfall cannot support a deciduous forest, and grasses become the dominant form of vegetation. See Figure 38–5. The soil of the grasslands is often deep and rich, and these areas have become the most productive farmlands of the earth.

▲ **Figure 38–5**

Grasslands. The natural vegetation of the grasslands includes many species of grass and wildflowers. Grasshoppers are a common sight.

The natural vegetation of the grasslands includes many species of grasses and wild flowers. In wetter areas, near rivers, the vegetation may be dense and include various shrubs.

Animals of the North American grasslands include coyotes, badgers (carnivorous, burrowing mammals), rattlesnakes, prairie dogs, jackrabbits, and ground squirrels. In the past, great herds of bison and pronghorn antelope were common. Now, most have been replaced by domesticated cattle and sheep. In Africa, the grasslands are populated by zebras, giraffes, gazelles, and other large grazing animals. Predators, such as lions, that feed on the grazers are also present. There are fewer types of birds in the grasslands than in the deciduous forest. In the North American grasslands, there are meadowlarks, ringnecked pheasants, prairie chickens, hawks, and owls. There are many insects, but the grasshopper populations, in particular, may be huge.

Deserts

Deserts occur in regions that are too dry to support grasses. The soil is sandy and poor. Rainfall is usually less than 25 centimeters in one year. In North America, there is a desert extending from Mexico, north to the eastern part of Washington. Huge areas of desert are also found in South America, Africa, Asia, and Australia. Temperatures in the desert vary widely in the course of a day. While the day is hot, the temperature may drop as much as 30° C at night. Some deserts have almost no vegetation at all, while others have a variety of plants.

▲ **Figure 38–6**

Fennec Fox in African Desert. The fennec is a small desert fox found in the North African desert. Most small animals avoid the harsh conditions of the desert by living in burrows and feeding at night.

Desert plants have special adaptations for the conservation of water and for the completion of their reproductive cycles. Most have widespread, shallow roots that allow them to absorb the maximum amount of water when it is available. Many desert plants, such as cacti, store water in their tissues. Many live only a short time. They sprout, flower, and produce seeds during brief rainy periods, which may last only a few days. Cactus, yucca, mesquite, sagebrush, and creosote bush are characteristic plants of the North American deserts.

Like desert plants, desert animals have a wide variety of adaptations for survival in the harsh environment. Most are active at night and spend the hot days in burrows in the ground or hidden in any available shade. Many desert rodents can survive with little drinking water. They get by on the water produced by cellular metabolism and the water present in the plants they eat. The fennec, a small desert fox, spends its days in a burrow, coming out only at night to feed on birds and other small animals. Its long ears provide a surface area for getting rid of excess body heat. Also found in the desert are snakes, lizards, spiders, and insects.

Tropical Rain Forests

Tropical rain forests are found in areas around the equator. In these regions, the climate is uniform throughout the year. There is a constant supply of rainfall, which may total between 200 and 400 centimeters a year. Rain occurs nearly every day, and the humidity is high. Temperatures remain constant at about 25° C throughout the year. Tropical rain forests contain an enormous variety of plants and animals. At present, the habitats of these animals are disappearing at an alarming rate as the rain forests are destroyed. (See page 379.)

Figure 38–7

Tropical Rain Forests. Tropical rain forests contain more plant and animal species than any other biome. The green forest of huge trees supports a wide variety of plants and animals in its branches, high above the forest floor. ▶

Within a tropical rain forest, the tree cover is so dense that little light reaches the ground, as you can see in Figure 38–7. The treetops form a canopy about 50 meters high. Below the canopy are shorter trees that can grow in the shade. The trees of the rain forest have shallow root systems that allow them to absorb nutrients from the thin layer of wet soil. Many have braces, or buttresses, that extend from the trunks to the ground. Like prop roots, these buttresses help to keep the tree standing upright.

Organic materials decay quickly in this warm, humid environment. Minerals released by decomposition are rapidly taken up again by the plants. Materials not absorbed by the plants are washed away by the frequent rains. Little organic matter is stored in the soil. Most of the nutrients in a topical rain forest are found within organisms. Because of the poor soil, a cleared tropical rain forest makes poor farm land. It cannot support crops for more than one or two years.

Among the 100 or more different species of trees found in a rain forest, there are many with large, broad leaves. In addition to trees, there are thick vines, called *lianas*, that are attached to the tree trunks and grow up through the treetops. The roots of these vines are in the ground. There are also many *epiphytes* (EP uh fyts).

▲ **Figure 38–8**

Epiphytes. Epiphytes grow on the branches of other plants. Bromeliads are epiphytes with leaves at their bases that absorb water.

MiniLab

Skill: Predicting

Do Leaves Have Waxy Skin?

Procedure

1. Obtain three paper towels and dampen them with water so they are wet but not dripping.

2. Cut two pieces of waxed paper the same size as a towel and sandwich one wet towel between the two pieces of waxed paper. Fasten the corners with paper clips and place this setup flat on a tray.

3. Roll up the two remaining towels. Place one roll on the tray uncovered and the other covered with a length of waxed paper. Secure the edges with paper clips.

4. Place the tray in direct sunlight. Predict which paper towel setup will lose the least amount of water.

Problem

Can you **predict** how leaves control the amount of water loss to the environment?

Analyze and Conclude

1. How did the towels differ after 24 hours?

2. Which of the setups conserved water best?

3. Was your prediction correct? Explain your answer.

4. Explain how the leaves of desert plants conserve water.

▲ **Figure 38–9**
Animals of the Rain Forest. Rainbow lorikeets are among the many animals that live in the trees of the rain forest.

Epiphytes are plants that grow on other plants but are not parasites. Various orchids, cacti, and ferns are epiphytes. The roots of some epiphytes absorb moisture from the air. Others have leaves that form cups at their bases. Water-absorbing structures pick up the moisture trapped in the leaves. Plants that are tolerant of almost complete shade cover the floors of tropical rain forests.

A wide variety of animal species inhabit tropical rain forests. Many of them have adaptations that allow them to live at a particular level in the trees. Monkeys, bats, squirrels, and parrots and other birds feed on fruits and nuts in the treetops. Flying squirrels leap from one tree to another. Snakes and lizards live in the branches of the trees. Rodents, tapirs, antelope, deer, and other large animals live on the forest floor. Spiders and insects are present at all levels. There are also ants, termites, bees, butterflies, and moths.

Effects of Altitude on Climax Vegetation

With the exceptions of the tundra and the taiga, the terrestrial biomes of the earth are distributed in irregular belts around the earth, more or less in sequence according to latitude. Their distribution is shown in Figure 38–10. Because increasing altitude usually produces climatic effects similar to increasing latitude,

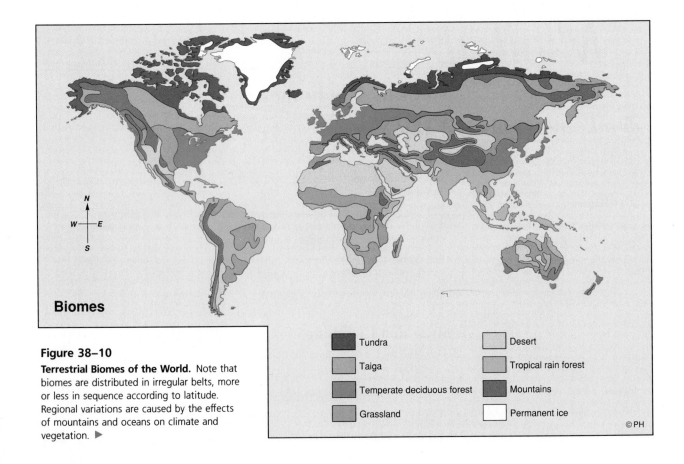

Biomes

Figure 38–10

Terrestrial Biomes of the World. Note that biomes are distributed in irregular belts, more or less in sequence according to latitude. Regional variations are caused by the effects of mountains and oceans on climate and vegetation. ▶

	Tundra		Desert
	Taiga		Tropical rain forest
	Temperate deciduous forest		Mountains
	Grassland		Permanent ice

©PH

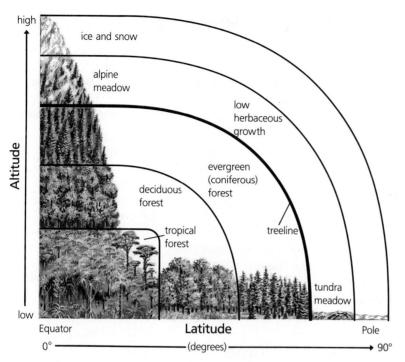

▲ **Figure 38–11**

Effects of Altitude on Climax Vegetation. The climactic effects of altitude and latitude roughly correspond. For example, note that plant life near the top of a mountain resembles that of a tundra.

mountainous regions are often left out of the biome classifications. The sides of mountains may show a succession of plant communities that change with increasing altitude. These communities will have many characteristics in common with those of specific biomes. For example, the climatic conditions and types of plant life near the top of a mountain may resemble those of the tundra. Lower down, evergreen forests that are characteristic of the taiga will appear. This relationship between higher altitude and higher latitude is shown in Figure 38–11.

38-1 **Section Review**

1. Define the term *biome*.
2. What vegetation characterizes the taiga?
3. In what kinds of climate do grasslands usually develop?
4. List three types of plants common to tropical rain forests.

Critical Thinking

5. Order the terrestrial biomes from least rainfall received to most rainfall received. (*Ordering*)

38-2 Aquatic Biomes

Section Objectives:

- *Compare* the physical factors in aquatic biomes with those in terrestrial biomes.
- *Describe* marine and freshwater biomes, and *name* some representative organisms of each.

The problems of life in aquatic biomes are different from the problems in terrestrial biomes. For one thing, in aquatic biomes, water is always present. However, in fresh water, organisms must excrete excess water, and in salt water, excess salt may be excreted by organisms. Temperature changes in the course of a year are much less in aquatic environments than they are on land. Temperatures in the oceans show the least change, while those in lakes and ponds show more change. Other physical factors that affect living things in aquatic biomes are the amounts of oxygen and carbon dioxide dissolved in the water, the availability of organic and inorganic nutrients, and light intensity.

The Marine Biome

Since all the oceans of the earth are interconnected, they are said to form a single marine, or saltwater, biome. Conditions and life forms vary from one region of the marine biome to another but without the clearcut differences of the terrestrial biomes.

Characteristics of the Marine Biome
The marine biome covers more than 70 percent of the earth's surface. Because of the heat capacity of water, the oceans absorb solar heat energy during warm seasons and hold it during cold seasons. As a result, ocean temperatures remain fairly stable. The oceans also have a stabilizing effect on average temperatures of land areas. Temperatures on the earth would vary much more than they do if the oceans did not exist. The aquatic environment of the oceans is stable in other respects, too. In any given region, the supply of nutrients and the concentration of dissolved salts remain relatively constant although they may vary from region to region.

Although environmental conditions tend to remain constant in any particular region of the marine biome, they can vary from region to region within the biome. The salt content in particular varies from one place to another. It is lower where large rivers bring fresh water into the ocean, and it is higher where atmospheric temperatures cause rapid evaporation. In general, salt concentrations in the ocean are similar to those in living cells. Marine organisms, therefore, do not usually have the problem of water balance that freshwater organisms have.

Although temperatures remain fairly constant in any given part of the marine biome, there is a variation with latitude. Ocean temperatures vary from near 0° C in the polar regions to 32° C near the equator.

Figure 38–12

Tropical Ocean Reef. This Australian coral reef, like all tropical ocean reefs, supports a wide variety of marine life forms. At deeper depths, conditions are not as favorable for life, and far fewer marine species are found. ▼

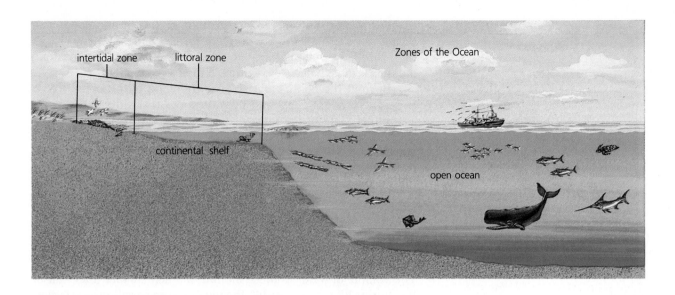

intertidal zone   littoral zone

Zones of the Ocean

continental shelf

open ocean

▲ **Figure 38–13**
Zones of the Ocean. Oceans are divided into
several zones, according to depth of the water.

Organisms of the Oceans   The marine biome supports a great variety of life forms. Some marine organisms are sessile and live attached to the ocean floor or to other fixed surfaces. Sessile organisms include sponges, sea anemones, corals, and barnacles. Organisms that live on the ocean floor are called **benthos.** Starfish, which are sometimes called seastars, clams, worms, snails, and crabs are benthic organisms. Small organisms that float near the surface and are carried by ocean currents are called **plankton.** Planktonic organisms include protozoa and algae, tiny crustaceans called copepods, the larvae of various animals, small jellyfish, and worms. Photosynthetic planktonic organisms, called **phytoplankton,** are the major producers of the oceans. Nonphotosynthetic planktonic protists and planktonic animals are called **zooplankton.** Both phytoplankton and zooplankton make up the lowest level of the complex marine food web. Many types of animals, from small worms to whales, feed on plankton. Free-swimming organisms that live in the oceans are called **nekton.** Nektonic organisms include squid, fishes, turtles, seals, and whales.

Zones of the Oceans   As you can see in Figure 38–13, the oceans are divided on the basis of depth into several zones. The **intertidal zone** is the area along the shoreline that is covered by water at high tide and uncovered at low tide. Various types of seaweeds—red and brown algae—are abundant in this zone. On sandy beaches, clams, crabs, sand fleas, and worms live in the sand. Many types of birds live along the shore, including gulls, terns, and sandpipers. On rocky coasts, algae, barnacles, mussels, and starfish cling to the rocks.

Beyond the intertidal zone is the **littoral zone,** which includes the shallow waters above the continental shelf. The gently sloping continental shelf extends out from the edge of the continent for about 300 kilometers. This zone contains nutrients carried into the oceans by rivers and streams. Because the water is shallow, light reaches all the way to the ocean floor in the littoral zone. The littoral zone contains many different forms of life. In many places there are large populations of algae, as well as fishes, oysters, mussels, crabs, barnacles, worms, and sea cucumbers.

Beyond the continental shelf is the zone of the open ocean. Here, the water is deep, and light does not reach the ocean floor. The upper layer of the open ocean is filled with plankton. In this zone, there are also large animals, including sharks, porpoises, squids, and whales. Below the zone of photosynthesis, the organisms are heterotrophs. They feed on organic matter that drifts downward from the photosynthetic zone above.

Freshwater Biomes

Freshwater biomes can be divided into two types—running water (streams) and standing water (lakes, ponds, swamps, and bogs). The volume of water in these biomes is much smaller than that of the marine biome. As a result, the temperature variations are larger. Organisms living in fresh water must be able to adapt to greater seasonal variations than those living in the ocean. They also have the problem of maintaining water balance. In a freshwater environment, water enters living cells by osmosis, as explained in Chapter 5, Section 5–3. Freshwater organisms usually need a mechanism for removing excess water by active transport. The contractile vacuoles of the ameba and paramecium are examples of such mechanisms.

Acid rain is an increasingly serious problem in freshwater biomes. (See Chapter 3.)

Streams   In fast-moving streams, the bottom is made of rocks and gravel. Most organisms are found in calmer, shallow areas near the banks of the stream. Here, algae grow on rocks, and there are many insects and insect larvae. Fish and microscopic floating algae are found both in running water and in the calmer pools. Where streams are slow moving, muddy sediment accumulates on the bottom. Many animals, including aquatic insects and their larvae, worms, snails, and crayfish, live in the bottom mud. Raccoons, birds, and other animals that live along the banks catch fish and other animals from the stream.

Lakes and Ponds   Lakes and ponds are bodies of standing water. Usually, lakes are larger than ponds and so deep that light does not reach the bottom in all parts. Ponds are usually shallow enough for light to reach the bottom throughout.

Around the shores of a lake is a zone of shallow water in which light reaches the bottom. In this zone, cattails, bulrushes, and other plants grow above the surface of the lake. These plants have roots in the lake bottom. In deeper water, out from the shore, there are floating plants, such as water lilies, which are also rooted in the bottom. Many types of animals are found in the bottom in the shallow water zone. There are insect larvae, crayfish, worms, hydra, clams, and snails. Free-swimming animals include diving beetles, mosquito larvae, giant water bugs, fish, frogs, salamanders, turtles,

Figure 38–14

Streams. These racoon kittens live along the stream and fish for food from its banks. ▼

◀ **Figure 38–15**
Lakes and Ponds. Floating plants, such as water lilies, often are seen on the surface of a pond.

and snakes. On the surface, there may be water striders, water boatmen, and whirligig beetles. Life in ponds is much the same as life in the shallow waters of lakes.

In the deep, open waters of the lake where light does not reach the bottom, the main producers are microscopic algae (phytoplankton) that float near the surface. Zooplankton is also present. These microscopic, heterotrophic organisms are the primary consumers in a complex food web. The planktonic organisms are eaten by small fish, which, in turn, are eaten by larger fish, and so on.

Swamps and Bogs   Swamps are low, wetland areas in which the vegetation includes shrubs and trees. Fresh and saltwater swamps and marshes are often called *wetlands*. Some of these regions, especially those in coastal areas, are threatened by development. Many types of plants and animals are found in wetlands. Wetlands are also important nesting sites for water birds.

Bogs are shallow bodies of water that contain sphagnum moss. The moss and other factors create an acid environment in which the rate of decay is slowed. This reduces the cycling of nitrogen through the ecosystem. Several plants common in bogs are insectivorous. These include pitcher plants and sundews.

Figure 38–16
Swamps and Bogs. Insectivorous plants, such as these pitcher plants, thrive in the shallow water of bogs. ▼

38-2 Section Review

1. Name the two basic kinds of aquatic biomes.
2. How do plankton move from one place to another in the ocean?
3. What are the two basic types of freshwater biomes?

Critical Thinking

4. Predict what would happen to a marine animal placed in freshwater. (*Predicting*)

Laboratory
Investigation

Physical Properties of Soil

Terrestrial biomes have a climax community that is defined by the dominant type of plant life. The types of plants that can grow in an area are often determined by the type of soil found in that area. In this investigation, you will measure two physical properties of soil—water-holding capacity and porosity (pore space).

Problem

How does the water-holding capacity and porosity of various types of soil **compare?**

Materials

- topsoil
- sand
- clay soil
- local soil sample
- stereomicroscope
- 4 funnels
- 4 ring stands
- 4 iron rings
- filter paper
- 4 250-mL beakers
- 4 100-mL graduated cylinders
- 4 25-mL graduated cylinders
- glass-marking pencil
- stirring rod

Procedure

1. Examine each of the four different soil samples under a stereomicroscope. Observe the size and shape of the particles. Draw a diagram of what you observe.

2. Using a ring stand and an iron ring, set up a funnel with filter paper above a 250-mL beaker, as shown in the diagram. Use the glass-marking pencil to label the beaker, topsoil.

3. Place 25 mL of topsoil into the funnel.

4. Repeat steps 2 and 3 for the other three soil samples, labelling the beaker with the type of soil.

5. Note the time. Then pour exactly 100 mL of water into each funnel. After 10 minutes, measure the amount of water in each beaker and record the values in a data table similar to the one shown.

6. Calculate the water-holding capacity (the amount of water retained by each sample) by subtracting the volume of water in each beaker from 100 mL. Record these values.

7. Add sand to a 25-mL graduated cylinder. Gently tap the cylinder with a pencil for 30 seconds to pack the sand. Add more sand to make the final packed volume 25 mL. Repeat this procedure for each soil sample.

8. Pour 50 mL of water into a 100-mL graduated cylinder, and add the packed sand. Stir the mixture with a stirring rod and wait five minutes.

9. Measure, and then record, the final volume of the soil-water mixture. Repeat this for each sample.

10. Calculate the porosity of each sample by subtracting the volume of the soil-water mixture from 75 mL (the combined volume of the soil and water before mixing). Record these values in your data table.

Observations

Data Table

Soil Sample	A Volume of Water in Beaker After 10 Minutes	B Water-Holding Capacity (100 mL – mL from Column A)	C Volume of Soil-Water Mixture	D Porosity (75 mL – mL from Column C)
Topsoil				
Sand				
Clay soil				
Local-soil sample				

Analysis and Conclusions

1. Which type of soil has the largest water-holding capacity? Which has the smallest?

2. How does your local soil sample compare with sand with respect to the two properties? How does it compare with clay?

3. Based on your observations, how do soil particle size and shape affect water-holding capacity and porosity?

4. How do you think water-holding capacity and pore space are related?

5. What would you predict to be the water-holding capacity of a soil made up of primarily small, jagged-edged particles?

Extensions

Design an experiment to see which of the four soil samples is best suited for growing plants. Be sure to include a control in your experiment.

Chapter 38 Review

Study Outline

38-1 Terrestrial Biomes

▶ A biome is a large geographical region determined by climate and other physical conditions. Biomes are divided into two major types—terrestrial and aquatic.

▶ The major terrestrial biomes are tundra, taiga, temperate deciduous forest, grassland, desert, and tropical rain forest.

▶ The tundra is characterized by a low average temperature with a short growing season, permafrost, and low rainfall.

▶ The taiga is characterized by cold winters, warm summers, and a higher rainfall and longer growing season than the tundra.

▶ The temperate deciduous forest has cold winters, hot, humid summers, and abundant rainfall.

▶ Grasslands occur where rainfall will not support a temperate deciduous forest.

▶ In deserts, rainfall is slight. The days can be very hot and the nights extremely cold.

▶ In tropical rain forests, the climate is uniform, with abundant daily rainfall.

▶ Increasing altitude produces climatic effects similar to those produced by increasing latitude.

38-2 Aquatic Biomes

▶ There are two types of aquatic biomes—marine and freshwater.

▶ The marine biome includes all the oceans of the world. The marine environment remains largely constant, although the temperature varies from the polar regions to the equator.

▶ Freshwater biomes are divided into two types— running water, and standing water. Running water includes streams and rivers. Lakes and ponds are bodies of standing water, as are swamps and bogs.

Chapter Assessment

Multiple Choice

Choose the letter of the answer that best completes each statement or answers the question.

1. Small floating organisms that are the major producers in the ocean are (a) benthos. (b) phytoplankton. (c) nekton. (d) lichens.

2. Permafrost is found in which biome? (a) tundra (b) taiga (c) deciduous forest (d) grassland

3. The area of shallow water above the continental shelf is called the (a) intertidal zone. (b) shoreline. (c) littoral zone. (d) open ocean.

4. Squid, fishes, turtles, and whales are examples of (a) benthic organisms. (b) nektonic organisms. (c) plankton. (d) zooplankton.

5. Climate conditions and types of plant life near the top of a mountain resemble those of the (a) tundra. (b) deciduous forest. (c) tropical rain forest. (d) taiga.

6. A climax forest in which leaves are shed in the fall is found in the (a) taiga. (b) desert. (c) temperate deciduous forest. (d) grassland.

7. Sparse rainfall and extreme daily temperatures occur in the (a) taiga. (b) desert. (c) tropical rain forest. (d) temperate deciduous forest.

8. A warm, uniform climate and daily rainfall occur in the (a) grassland. (b) desert. (c) tropical rain forest. (d) taiga.

9. A climax forest of pine, fir, and spruce trees, inhabited by snowshoe hare, lynx, bear, wolves, and moose, is a (a) tundra. (b) temperate deciduous forest. (c) desert. (d) taiga.

10. The biome with rich, deep soil but no trees is a (a) grassland. (b) tropical rain forest. (c) temperate deciduous forest. (d) taiga.

Content Review

Answer each of the following in complete sentences.

11. What physical factors are unique to the tundra?

12. Describe the physical characteristics of the taiga.

13. Much of the eastern United States is in the temperate deciduous forest biome. Why does this biome not extend farther west?

14. What characteristics of grasslands make these regions good farmland?

15. How are desert plants and animals adapted to desert conditions?

16. Why is the soil of the tropical rain forest poor?

17. How does altitude affect climax vegetation?

18. List examples of benthos, plankton, and nekton.

19. Why are temperature variations larger in fresh water than in the marine biome?

20. How do the vegetation and animal life of streams compare with those of lakes and ponds?

Graphic Organizing

For information on graphic organizers, see Appendix G at the back of this text.

21. **Bar Graph** Using the rainfall information in your textbook, construct a bar graph of annual rainfall for the terrestrial biomes. Since rainfall is given as ranges, indicate both the low and high figures on the bar for each biome.

Critical Thinking and Problem Solving

Discuss each of the following in a brief paragraph.

22. **Comparing** How do you think conditions for marine algae that live in the intertidal zone differ from those for marine algae in the littoral zone? How are they alike?

23. **Problem solving** Successive biology classes studied a water bird population for four years. Their data showed a sharp decrease in the water bird population. List as many possible causes as you can for this decrease.

    Upon investigation, it was discovered that a local wetland area had been filled in to build a shopping mall five years before. Might the shopping mall be the cause of the decrease in the water bird population? Explain.

24. **Inferring** Why would bats be good pollinators in the desert biome?

25. **Classifying** Indicate the suitability of each terrestrial biome for (a) growing crops, (b) building new cities, and (c) maintaining wildlife preserves.

26. **Interpreting** An ecologist studied the climate on a mountain range in Central America. She divided the region into four zones based on elevation, with Zone 1 at the lowest elevation and Zone 4 at the highest. She assigned a student to collect temperature and precipitation data in each zone. The student's data are recorded in the table. Do you think the data are correct or incorrect? Why?

			Month			
			May	June	July	August
Z	1	T	22	24	25	23
		P	1.5	2	3	6
O	2	T	28	30	31	30
		P	10	8	10	8
N	3	T	19	19	20	18
		P	0.5	1	1	2
E	4	T	31	32	33	33
		P	28	29	32	31

T = Temperature, °C   P = Precipitation, cm

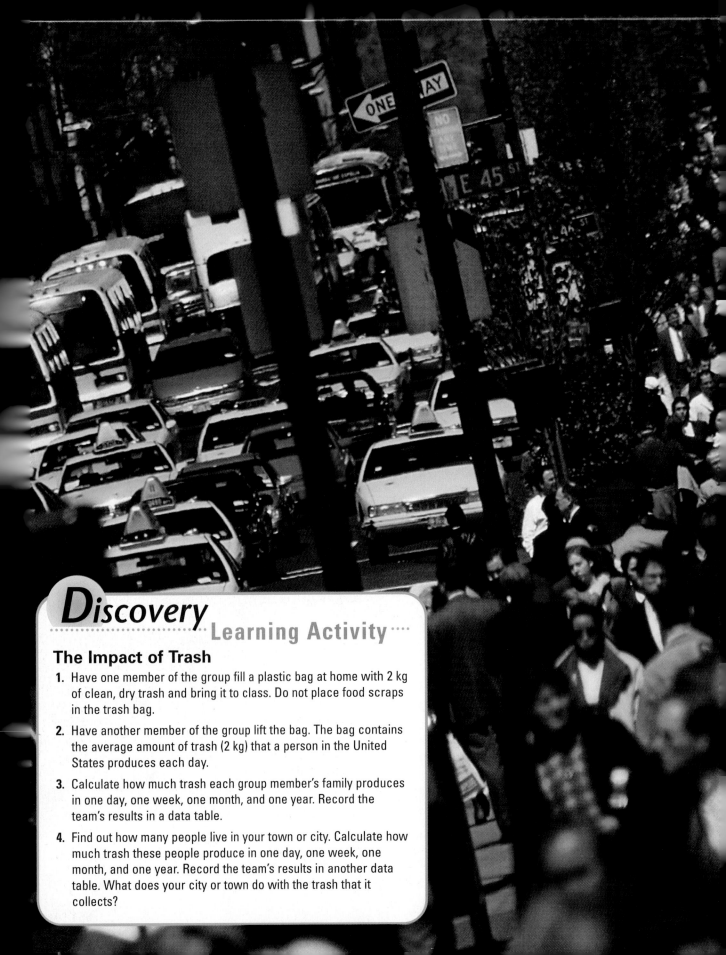

Discovery *Learning Activity*

The Impact of Trash

1. Have one member of the group fill a plastic bag at home with 2 kg of clean, dry trash and bring it to class. Do not place food scraps in the trash bag.

2. Have another member of the group lift the bag. The bag contains the average amount of trash (2 kg) that a person in the United States produces each day.

3. Calculate how much trash each group member's family produces in one day, one week, one month, and one year. Record the team's results in a data table.

4. Find out how many people live in your town or city. Calculate how much trash these people produce in one day, one week, one month, and one year. Record the team's results in another data table. What does your city or town do with the trash that it collects?

Human Ecology

.... *Guide for Reading* ....

Previewing the Chapter

A hectic city street illustrates one of the results of human population growth. People have dramatically altered the delicate biosphere on which all living things depend. How do human activities—in cities, on farms, or in factories—threaten various ecosystems? How are concerned people working to rescue endangered species and to restore the environment?

Key Words

biodegradable, erosion, nonrenewable resource, pollution, recycling, renewable resource, urbanization

Key Concepts

• **Describe** the impact of human activities on ecosystems.
• **Describe** how environmental damage can be repaired and how the health of the environment can be maintained.
• **Construct a model** compost column and **predict** the suitability of various materials for composting. (Laboratory Investigation)

39-1 Causes of Environmental Damage

Section Objectives:

- *Discuss* the importance of human population control in improving the quality of human life.
- *Describe* the problems that can arise from the movement of populations to the cities and from the importation of organisms into new environments.
- *Describe* how poor farming practices and the use of pesticides have damaged the environment.
- *List* the major types of pollution and describe the ways in which they damage the environment and/or human health.

Human Ecology

In the past, most people did not worry about the effects of human activities on the environment. Forests were cut down, rivers were dammed, and soil erosion was not prevented. Wastes from mines and other industries were dumped on the land, into waterways, and into the air. Within the past 30 years or so, however, more and more people have come to realize that the environment cannot be used thoughtlessly any longer. Human activities have damaged the environment, and the damage may be dangerous and permanent. In response to this awareness, many agencies are now devoted to restoring the environment. Rivers that had been so polluted that

▲ **Figure 39–1**

Environmental Damage. Although forests may be replanted, poor tree-cutting practices can damage the forest ecosystem.

◀ A crowded city street in New York City.

▲ **Figure 39–2**

Lake Erie. Several years ago, pollution seriously threatened fish and other life in Lake Erie. Recent cleanup efforts have been effective.

they contained no fish have now been cleaned up. Lake Erie, for example, is one lake that has been saved. In some cities where the air was dangerously polluted, it is now somewhat cleaner.

Human ecology deals with the relationship between humans and their environment. In this chapter, we will discuss some of the important aspects of this relationship.

Human Population Growth

Many of today's most serious environmental problems are related to the growth in the human population in recent decades. In 1850, the population of the earth was estimated to be about 1 billion. Within 80 years, by about 1930, the population had doubled, reaching 2 billion. It doubled again, reaching 4 billion by the mid-1970s. In 1995, there were about 5.7 billion people in the world. As you may have noticed, the time needed for the doubling of the world's population has become shorter. It is estimated that by the year 2000, the human population may reach 6.2 billion.

As in other natural populations, if the human population continues to grow indefinitely, it will eventually reach a point at which the environment cannot support it any longer. A lack of food, water, space, or some other basic necessity acts as a limiting factor for every population. A **limiting factor** is some factor, such as a lack of food, that halts any further growth in a population. The size of a population that can be supported by the environment is called the **carrying capacity** of the environment. At some point in the future, human population growth must stop because the earth will reach its carrying capacity and will not be able to support any more humans.

A population remains the same size if the birth rate and death rate are equal and no changes result from migration. In this century, the death rate in the developed countries has declined sharply because of improvements in medical care, food production, and sanitation. In many of these countries, however, there has also been a decline in the birth rate. This has led to a stable, but older, population. In a few countries, the birth rate has dropped below the death rate, resulting in a shrinking population. In developing countries, the birth rate remains high. At the same time, the death rate in many of these countries has dropped because of improved living conditions. Thus, the continued high birth rate is causing a rapid growth in the populations. Unfortunately, food production in these countries is not increasing as fast as the population. Any failure in crop production in these countries can result in malnutrition and starvation.

Directly or indirectly, the problem of human population growth affects everyone. If food becomes the limiting factor in human population growth, then starvation will become the major means of population control in many parts of the world. One way to avoid this situation is to reduce the birth rate to a level that maintains the population at its present size. This level is called the level of *reproductive replacement*. At this level, the number of births equals the number of deaths over a period of time.

Population control, alone, however, will not guarantee adequate supplies of needed materials. If the developed nations of the world reduced their levels of wasteful consumption, more resources would be available for use by developing countries. The careful use of conservation measures in farming, lumbering, mining, and water use could ensure an increase in the production of food. Conservation measures could also ensure constant levels of other needed materials. The use of fertilizers and irrigation, as well as the development of crops with higher yields, could increase the food supply. New sources of food could be developed—from the oceans, for example. Most ecologists feel, however, that no matter what steps are taken, the food supply will eventually become inadequate if the current rate of population growth continues.

Disruption of Existing Ecosystems

Population increases and technological advances have resulted in the careless destruction or disruption of many ecosystems. As the population has increased, patterns of land use have changed. There has been a shift from rural (farming) areas to cities. The movement of the population to cities, or **urbanization,** has resulted in the destruction of productive farmland. As the cities have grown, farms have been turned into housing developments and shopping centers. The growth of cities has also destroyed or endangered other ecosystems, such as wetlands, which previously had been untouched. These changes have destroyed the natural habitats of many species of plants and animals.

Biology and You

Q: Why do children in photos of famine-stricken areas have large bellies? They don't look like they are starving.

A: Although these children have swollen bellies, they are starving. Their bellies swell from a buildup of gas. Malnutrition disturbs the bacteria that live in the intestines. The bacteria grow out of control and produce large amounts of gas, causing the belly to bulge.

The body needs nutrients and fuel to function. When a person does not get enough of these, he or she is malnourished. In famine-stricken areas, diets often are lacking in calories, in protein, or in both. Children usually are the first to be affected by malnutrition because their bodies need extra calories and protein during the growing phases of childhood.

Malnutrition occurs all over the world and is a serious public-health problem. Some long-term effects of severe malnutrition are irreversible. Brain damage and stunted growth are common. With enough food and care, a starving child will regain weight, but some physical problems may remain.

 Write a letter to your local newspaper outlining what you think should be done to end world hunger.

Figure 39–3

Destruction of Wetlands. Wetlands, like many other ecosystems, are easily destroyed by careless development. ▶

In a balanced ecosystem, the number of organisms at each level in a food chain is controlled by the number of organisms at the next higher feeding level. For example, the number of insects in a region is controlled by the number of organisms that feed on them. When an organism is removed from its ecosystem and introduced into a new ecosystem, there may be no predators to control its numbers. This has happened in a number of cases in which insects and other organisms have accidentally or intentionally been introduced into new environments. The Japanese beetle, the fungus that causes Dutch elm disease, and the gypsy moth were all imported into North America. With few natural enemies, they have spread, doing great damage to plants.

Poor Farming Practices

Overfarming and Overgrazing

In a natural ecosystem, dead plants cover the ground. They decompose and form rich humus that is added to the soil. In farmland, the crops are harvested each year, and most of the plant parts are removed from the fields. When these plant parts are removed, the nutrients these plants have absorbed from the soil are also removed. If these nutrients are not returned, the soil becomes less fertile, and crop yield drops. In the past when this happened, the fields were abandoned. When fields are left without a cover of vegetation, heavy rains or winds can carry away the topsoil. The removal of soil by wind and water is called **erosion.** Wind action blows the soil away, occasionally causing dust storms. The dust bowls of the 1930s in Oklahoma and other states were caused by overfarming and wind action. After rainstorms, water running over the surface of the land carries soil into nearby streams. Eventually the land becomes useless for cultivation.

Figure 39–4

Soil Erosion. Without a protective covering of vegetation, topsoil is easily washed or blown away. Strong winds result in dust storms such as the one in this Texas desert. ▼

In many areas, overgrazing by herds of cattle and sheep has left former grasslands without a cover of vegetation. In these areas, too, the end result of thoughtless farming practices has been the loss of topsoil.

Misuse of Pesticides   Pesticides, used indiscriminately, have contaminated the air and water in many places. They have also disrupted food chains by killing organisms that are not pests. After years of use, some widely used pesticides have been found to be dangerous. DDT, for example, was used for many years before it was found to be highly poisonous to many animals, including humans. DDT sprayed on plants was washed off by rainwater and carried into streams and rivers. Eventually it entered the oceans, where it was taken up by the plankton. DDT is not readily broken down. Eventually it became concentrated in the bodies of the higher-level consumers. Following the path of DDT through the ecosystem well illustrates the interconnected nature of the world's ecosystems. DDT has been found in the bodies of polar bears, in the ice of the Antarctic, and even in the fatty tissues of humans.

Frequently, the organisms the pesticides were intended to kill become resistant to them. As you read in Chapter 29, this type of resistance is an inherited trait, which makes the pests even more difficult to control.

Pollution

Adding anything to the environment or affecting the environment in a way that makes it less fit for living things is called **pollution.** Pollution of the environment takes many forms and has increased with population growth and industrial development. One example of pollution is **noise pollution,** loud sounds that can cause hearing loss. Other examples are sewage and industrial wastes dumped into streams and rivers. Gaseous wastes from cars and trucks, the burning of fuels, and industrial gases have polluted the air. The land has been polluted by tremendous quantities of solid wastes generated by industry and by the population in general. Some of those industrial wastes are highly toxic.

Water Pollution   Industrialized countries use enormous quantities of water each day. The most recent data indicate that 693 liters (183 gallons) of water per person are consumed every day in the United States. Much of the available water, however, is polluted. There are six major sources of water pollution: organic wastes, inorganic chemicals, disease-causing microorganisms, changes in water temperature, oil spills, and radioactive wastes.

Many *organic wastes* are materials from plants and animals. Usually, these materials are **biodegradable** (by oh duh GRAYD uh bul). That is, they can be broken down by bacteria and other decay organisms into simpler substances. Sewage and wastes from canning, brewing, meat packing, and paper mills are major sources of organic materials in waterways. If organic wastes are added in small quantities, bacteria and other decay organisms break them down,

Figure 39–5

Noise Pollution. Construction sites are just one of many sources of noise pollution in urban areas. ▼

Science, Technology and Society

Technology: Biodegradable Plastics

Plastic waste makes up almost one-third of this country's garbage. It threatens to clog landfills and litter beaches. Plastics, unlike many wastes, do not degrade quickly in a landfill. But, chemists may have the answer to the problem: plastics that decay in sunlight and soil.

Plastics normally take 200 years to break down. They do not degrade quickly because they are composed of polymers, long chains of repeating molecules linked together. These chains are so tightly bound that they cannot be penetrated by decay organisms.

For chemists, the challenge was to find a way to weaken the chains without robbing the plastic of its strength. They achieved this by inserting cornstarch, a polymer that microorganisms can penetrate, into the plastic polymer. The organisms eat the cornstarch, breaking apart the molecule chains. Although these biodegradable plastics are expensive to produce, several states have laws requiring that the plastic yokes that hold six-packs together be made of them.

■ *Do you think states should require the use of biodegradable plastics? Why or why not?*

keeping the water clean. However, the breakdown of these materials uses oxygen from the water. If sewage and other organic materials are discharged into the water in large quantities, the oxygen content of the water is seriously reduced. The lack of oxygen kills off fish and other aquatic organisms.

Some organic wastes are plant nutrients. When large amounts of these substances are present, they stimulate the growth of algae and aquatic plants. In lakes, the presence of nutrients can speed up the process of succession. As the organisms die, material is added to the lake bottom, which reduces its depth. Growth around the shores further reduces the size of the lake. This accelerated aging process is called **eutrophication** (yoo truh fuh KAY shun).

When nutrients cause an explosive growth in the algae populations, only the topmost layer of algae receives enough light and oxygen for survival. The lower layers die. When they decay, the oxygen content of the lake is reduced, which kills various other forms of aquatic life.

Various pesticides, fertilizers, and detergents, as well as other synthetic organic chemicals, are poisonous to aquatic life. At the same time, these fertilizers and detergents contain plant nutrients. The net effect is to upset the natural balance of an ecosystem and possibly to destroy it.

Inorganic chemicals are dumped into waterways by mining and other industrial processes. Some of these wastes contain metals, particularly mercury and lead, that are poisonous to humans and other animals.

When dumped into waterways, mercury, lead, and some pesticides are picked up first by small aquatic plants and algae. These in turn are eaten by first-level consumers. Because these consumers eat large amounts of plants and algae, the toxic substances build up in their bodies. In the food web, larger second-level consumers eat many first-level consumers. The toxic substances then build up in higher concentrations in the bodies of the second-level consumers. As the food chain proceeds, each higher level of consumers accumulates larger quantities of poisonous substances. This process is called **biological magnification.** The animals at the end of the food chain, where the concentrations are highest, are most harmed by the pesticide or chemicals. In some cases, this has been humans. People in Japan who rely heavily on fish in their diet have suffered mercury poisoning from mercury that had been dumped into the ocean. Through biological magnification, the mercury accumulated in high concentrations in the bodies of large food fish.

Disease-causing microorganisms may enter the water from untreated sewage and wastes. Sewage contamination can be detected by testing for the bacterium *Escherichia coli*. These organisms, as well as other infectious bacteria and viruses, live in the intestines of warm-blooded animals and are found in their wastes.

Changes in the water temperature in streams and rivers can kill the fish and other organisms living there. This type of pollution, called **thermal pollution,** occurs when water is taken from a stream and used for cooling industrial equipment. The cold stream water is

▲ **Figure 39–6**
Oil Spill. In 1989, the Exxon Valdez oil tanker spilled about 240 000 barrels of oil off the coast of Alaska. This photograph shows seals coated by oil from the spill. The long-term effects of the spill on the ecosystem will only become apparent over time.

run through pipes next to pipes containing hot water. Heat is transferred from the hot water to the cold water, and the stream water, now heated, is returned to the waterway. In addition to the direct effects it has on living organisms, the warmed stream water holds less oxygen than the cold water. Nuclear power plants, in particular, require great amounts of water for cooling.

Other forms of water pollution involve oil spills. Oil is toxic to all forms of aquatic life and even kills many types of bacteria. Water birds die when they ingest the oil in trying to clean it off their feathers. The Valdez oil spill in Alaska was the worst of these oil spills to date.

Radioactive wastes are produced by nuclear reactors, mining, and the processing of radioactive materials. Exposure to relatively small amounts of radioactivity can be harmful.

Air Pollution   Industrialized countries with large urban populations and many cars face serious air pollution problems. In the United States alone, more than 200 million metric tons of pollutants are released into the atmosphere each year.

Some pollutants are **aerosols.** Aerosols have tiny solid particles or liquid droplets that remain suspended in air. Dust and smoke are aerosols. There are also artificial aerosols such as hair spray. Aerosol particles scatter sunlight, reducing the amount of light reaching the earth's surface, and thus lowering the surface temperature.

Some pollutants are gases that mix with the air. Sulfur dioxide (SO_2) is a pollutant produced by the burning of coal and oil that contain sulfur. In the atmosphere, sulfur dioxide may react chemically to form sulfuric acid, a harsh irritant to the respiratory system.

▲ **Figure 39–7**
Acid Rain. This statue in Rome has been destroyed by acid rain.

Sulfuric acid dissolved in rainwater is a major component of acid rain. Acid rain can gradually destroy stone buildings and other structures. It can also lower the pH of lakes and ponds, killing many of the organisms they contain or affecting their ability to reproduce.

Hydrogen sulfide (H_2S) is a pollutant produced by several industrial processes, including the refining of oil and the manufacture of paper pulp. This gas, which has an odor similar to rotten eggs, is a nuisance in low concentrations but can be poisonous in high concentrations.

Carbon monoxide (CO) is produced by the burning of gasoline, coal, and oil. It combines easily with the hemoglobin of the red blood cells and reduces the hemoglobin's capacity to carry oxygen. In low concentrations, carbon monoxide can cause drowsiness and slow reaction times. In high concentrations, it causes death.

Nitrogen oxide (NO) and nitrogen dioxide (NO_2) are produced by the burning of gasoline, oil, and natural gas. When nitrogen dioxide is exposed to sunlight, it turns a dirty brownish color, darkening the air. Reactions in the atmosphere between nitrogen oxide, oxygen, and ultraviolet light produce ozone (O_3), which is a pollutant at lower levels. However, the ozone layer is a necessary part of the upper atmosphere. This layer protects us from damaging ultraviolet radiation. As you may already know, exposure to ultraviolet radiation may cause skin cancer.

Pollutants released into the atmosphere have caused the ozone layer to become thinner. The ozone layer prevents much of the potentially dangerous ultraviolet radiation from reaching the earth. Decreased ozone protection increases your risk of skin cancer, cataracts, and immune-system damage. In addition, it causes crop damage and a decrease in marine algae productivity.

These damaging pollutants are categorized as chlorofluorocarbons (CFCs). CFCs, such as Freon—which is used in air conditioners and refrigerators—combine with the ozone and destroy it. International agreements have been introduced banning the production and the use of CFCs in refrigerators, air conditioners, and in manufacturing.

Hydrocarbons, which are compounds of hydrogen and carbon, are produced by the burning of gasoline, coal, oil, natural gas, and wood. Several related compounds, such as formaldehyde and acetaldehyde, irritate the eyes, nose, and throat, but most are not dangerous at existing levels. However, when hydrocarbons react with nitrogen oxides in the presence of sunlight, they form a dirty-brown haze called smog. Smog, which is a combination of smoke and fog, is harmful to living things.

Usually, the air layer closest to the earth's surface is the warmest layer, and the air temperature drops with increasing altitude. Under these conditions, the less dense, warmer air rises,

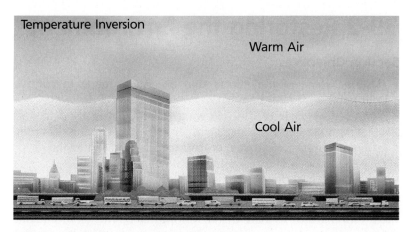

Temperature Inversion

Warm Air

Cool Air

Temperature Inversion. In a temperature inversion, a layer of cool air becomes trapped beneath a layer of warm air.

carrying pollutants away from the earth's surface. In a **temperature inversion,** however, a layer of cooler, denser air becomes trapped below a layer of warmer air, as shown in Figure 39–8. The warm air acts as a lid, preventing the upward movement of air from the earth's surface. Pollutants accumulate in the cool layer. The condition lasts until the air masses move away.

Land Pollution   As cities have grown, land pollution has become a growing problem. Even small cities produce many tons of solid waste, or refuse, every day. Two ways of disposing of refuse are sanitary landfills and incineration (burning).

A *sanitary landfill* is a large area where the refuse is dumped into a trench. A liner is used to prevent seepage into the water supply. The refuse is compacted and covered over with dirt. However, as cities have grown, it has become increasingly difficult to find land for this purpose.

Burning refuse in large furnaces, or incinerators, is another method of disposal. However, incinerators must be equipped with pollution control devices, or they release large quantities of pollutants into the air. After burning, the ashes must still be disposed of in sanitary landfills. Some cities are using the steam produced by the burning of refuse to generate electricity.

39-1 **Section Review**

1. What is human ecology?
2. Define the term *carrying capacity.*
3. What problem may arise when an organism is imported into a new environment?
4. List some of the major sources of water pollution.

Critical Thinking

5. Rank the major types of pollution from the most difficult to clean up or control to the least difficult.   *(Ranking)*

Science, Technology and Society

Issue: Nuclear Wastes

Tons of radioactive waste from nuclear power plants sit in temporary storage facilities. Finding a suitable permanent site is difficult. Much of the waste will remain dangerous to humans and the environment for thousands of years.

Many people fear the storage of nuclear waste near their homes. Studies have shown that exposure to radiation can cause cancer and birth defects. What if the waste leaks from the storage site? How can wastes be transported to the site safely? Would catastrophes, such as earthquakes, cause radioactive substances to leak into groundwater? These people argue that the safety of waste sites cannot be guaranteed.

Others claim that building a permanent facility would create jobs and bring money into a community. The location of the site would be determined by years of scientific research. Such a facility would be constructed under strict guidelines to ensure safety. Besides, they argue, temporary storage sites are more dangerous than permanent sites would be.

■ **What should be done about the storage of nuclear wastes?**

39-2 Restoring the Environment

Section Objectives:

■ *Describe* some of the efforts that are being made to control pollution.
■ *Explain* how each of the following techniques is used in soil conservation: cover crops, strip cropping, terracing, contour farming, windbreaks, dams, crop rotations, and fertilizers.
■ *Discuss* methods of forest and wildlife conservation.
■ *Describe* several biological methods of pest control.

Many countries have introduced programs to improve the lives of their citizens and to halt the deterioration of the environment. Some programs are aimed at family planning to slow the rate of population growth. Other programs deal with disease control and sanitation. In terms of the environment itself, there are national and international programs aimed at pollution control, conservation of natural resources, and preservation of existing species. Various methods of maintaining and restoring the environment are discussed in the following sections.

Controlling Pollution

In some countries where much of the air pollution is caused by exhaust from automobiles, the introduction of emission controls and the use of unleaded gasoline have reduced pollution. Waste gases from industrial processes are treated in many different ways to remove the most serious pollutants before the gases are released into the atmosphere. Some areas are now banning the use of aerosol sprays to help protect the atmosphere.

Sewage treatment plants that use bacteria to break down sewage before it is released into waterways have greatly reduced water pollution. Where these plants have been built, the waterways are much cleaner. However, many additional plants are needed. Although some of the most toxic industrial wastes are no longer dumped into waterways, others are still pouring into lakes, streams, and rivers. The dumping of wastes into the oceans by coastal nations, combined with wastes carried into the oceans by rivers, threatens the future productivity of the oceans.

Some efforts are being made to reclaim land that has been strip-mined. Other efforts are being made to control the dumping of wastes on land. In many areas, there are now special sites reserved for the disposal of toxic wastes. Because these wastes remain toxic for long periods of time, there is always a problem with leakage and the contamination of surrounding areas. The disposal of radioactive wastes from nuclear reactors is proving to be an especially difficult problem. These wastes must be stored so that the radioactivity is safely absorbed by surrounding materials and cannot leak into the environment for the thousands of years during which the wastes remain radioactive.

Conserving Natural Resources

Natural resources are materials in the environment that are used by humans either for their life processes or for cultural activities. There are two types of natural resources—renewable and nonrenewable. **Renewable natural resources** include air, water, soil, sunlight, and living things. Natural events replace these resources as they are used. However, careless human activities can disrupt the natural events that replace renewable resources. **Nonrenewable natural resources** are resources that can be taken from the earth only once. Coal, oil, natural gas, metals, and minerals are nonrenewable natural resources. The conservation of both types of resources is essential.

Some products made from nonrenewable resources can be reprocessed and used again for their original purpose. This process is called **recycling.** Newspapers, glass bottles, metal and tin cans, as well as many kinds of plastic, can be recycled. Most states have enacted laws requiring the recycling of many of these materials.

Conserving Soil   Although soil is a renewable resource, the process of soil formation is very slow. It may take thousands of years to yield a few centimeters of topsoil. Therefore, it is important to prevent the loss of soil through erosion and the loss of nutrients. There are a number of techniques used in soil conservation.

To prevent soil erosion, some farmers use cover crops. **Cover crops** are crops planted to cover a whole field. These crops have fibrous roots that form a dense mat in the soil. This mat prevents

Figure 39–9
Recycling. Each of these products was made from recycled plastic. ▼

Figure 39–10
Some Soil Conservation Practices. ▶

strip cropping

terracing

contour plowing

windbreak

soil erosion. Commonly used cover crops include clover, alfalfa, oats, and wheat. Crops that are planted in rows, such as corn, beans, and cabbage, do not prevent erosion of the exposed soil between the rows of plants.

When row crops are planted, strip cropping may be used to protect the soil. **Strip cropping** is a conservation practice in which cover crops are planted between strips of row crops. Thus, no exposed soil is left open to erosion.

Terracing is used on the sides of hills. Flat areas, or terraces, are dug in the hillside, providing areas for planting. Each terrace has a boundary made up of an earth bank held in place by plants and rocks. Terracing prevents surface water from running directly down the hill, carrying the soil with it.

On uneven landscapes, **contour farming** may help to prevent erosion. In contour farming, rows are plowed across slopes, following the contour of the land. The mounds formed by the plow and the plants prevent water from running straight down the slopes.

Windbreaks are used to prevent wind erosion. Windbreaks usually consist of rows of trees. Poplar trees are commonly used for this purpose.

In areas that are already eroded, **dams** are often built to slow down the running of water and to reduce or to prevent further erosion. Dams are also a major means of water conservation. Large amounts of water collect behind the dam. This collected water can be used for drinking, irrigation, and recreation, as well as for the generation of electricity.

Since each plant has its own mineral requirements, planting the same crops every year can remove valuable nutrients from the soil. **Crop rotation** involves growing different crops in succeeding years. Planting different crops prevents the reduction of soil nutrients, which is known as *soil depletion*. Legumes, such as clover, are rotated along with other crops to restore nitrates to the depleted soil.

Fertilizers also are used to replace essential soil materials removed by crops. Both natural fertilizers, such as manure, and commercial chemical fertilizers are widely used.

Conserving Forests   Forests, which supply a wide variety of materials for human use, are another renewable natural resource. In addition to furnishing wood, trees are used for the production of paper, charcoal, turpentine, and rayon. Forest soils hold large quantities of water, and the trees and undergrowth of the forest prevent soil erosion. However, like soil, the replacement of forests is a slow process, and poor tree-cutting practices can cause permanent damage to the forest ecosystem.

As populations have grown, the need both for cleared land and for forest products has increased. As a result, in many parts of the world, especially the tropics, the amount of forest land is shrinking. In an attempt to raise productivity and ensure future supplies, a variety of conservation practices are being applied to remaining forests.

Sustained-yield tree farming involves cutting down trees in only certain areas of a forest. This leaves surrounding areas untouched. In *block cutting*, square areas of forest are cut. Reseeding of the cut section takes place naturally by seeds coming from the surrounding forest. In *strip cutting*, strips of trees are cut between strips of untouched forest. In *selective harvesting*, certain trees are marked and cut, leaving the others undisturbed to grow and mature.

To replace trees lost in cutting, **reforestation** programs plant seeds or seedlings of a particular type in cut areas. The seeds or seedlings planted are usually fast-growing, disease-resistant types

◀ **Figure 39–11**

Reforestation. In the tropics, forests are being cleared at an increasing pace for agriculture and cattle farming. In Brazil, as in many other areas of the world, efforts are being made to replant these deforested areas.

Endangered Species		
	Number of Species	
	Extinct Since 1600	**Endangered Today**
amphibians	1	46
reptiles	20	191
birds	109	634
mammals	73	458

▲ **Figure 39–12**

Endangered Species. By the end of this century, thousands of species may have become extinct. Examples of endangered species include the cheetah, the leatherback sea turtle, the golden coqui frog, and the California condor.

that will produce a good quality of lumber. In all forestry programs, undesirable, diseased, or dead trees are removed to allow space for growth of good timber.

Conserving Wildlife The growth of cities and suburbs has led to the destruction of the natural habitats of many types of plants and animals. Furthermore, hunting has brought about the extinction of a few species and the near-extinction of many others. The passenger pigeon was a bird that was found in large numbers in North America until the mid-1800s. A prime target of bird hunters, the huge flocks were killed off, and the last known passenger pigeon died in the early 1900s. Many other species of birds, as well as whales and other animals, are now in danger of becoming extinct. Among them are the golden coqui frog of Puerto Rico, the leatherback sea turtle, the California condor, and the cheetah. Figure 39–12 shows the numbers of species of amphibians, reptiles, birds, and mammals that are in danger of extinction today. Compare these figures with the numbers that have become extinct since 1600. Sadly, the rate of extinctions is rising. Several plant species have also become extinct, and others are endangered.

Concern over the possible extinction of various species of animals and plants has resulted in wildlife conservation practices that are being carried out in many areas. Hunting and fishing laws now restrict the sex, size, and number of prey that can be taken and limit the hunting season. In many areas, game and bird preserves, where no hunting is allowed, have been established.

In some areas, game fish are being bred in fish hatcheries. These fish are used to restock heavily fished lakes and streams. This keeps the populations at a reasonable level but also allows recreational fishing.

Finally, restricting the use of pesticides and herbicides has limited the number of accidental deaths caused by these chemicals.

Legal protection for endangered species has made it possible for some species that were near extinction to begin to show a population increase. This is true of the bison, egret, and whooping crane. Other endangered species are still decreasing in numbers.

Controlling Pests Biologically

Although chemical pesticides have helped to control insect damage to agricultural crops, they have also created some serious ecological problems. As you have read, many chemical pesticides are not readily broken down in nature, so they build up in the environment, harming plants and animals. In response to this problem, scientists have developed some chemical pesticides that break down within a few days to harmless substances. These pesticides will not build up. On the other hand, they have to be applied more frequently, which makes them more expensive and difficult to use.

As an alternative to chemical pesticides, various biological methods of pest control have been discovered. These methods are more specific than the chemical pesticides and have much less of an effect on the environment in general.

In some areas, natural enemies have been imported to control certain pests. For example, ladybugs have been used to control aphids, and a wasp that preys on the alfalfa weevil has been used to control that insect pest. In introducing one organism to control the population of another organism, it is important to know whether or not there is any way to control the population of the introduced organism.

Sometimes, various insect larvae, including gypsy moth caterpillars and mosquito larvae, can be controlled when they are infected with a particular type of bacterium. Viruses have been used against worms that attack vegetable crops.

Crop rotation, which helps to prevent soil depletion, also helps to control pests. Planting different crops in succeeding years removes the favored food source of a pest organism and thereby decreases the pest population.

Figure 39–13

Biological Control of Insects. Several methods of insect biological control have been developed. Scientists continue to experiment with new ways to control insect damage to agricultural crops. ▶

Scientists have also developed ways to use insecticides without contaminating the environment. **Pheromones** (FEHR uh mohnz) are a type of animal secretion that serves as a sex attractant between members of a species. Scientists have developed pheromones that are used to lure insects into traps where they are exposed to contact poisons. Although the insects are killed, the environment is not polluted.

Another method of insect control involves the release of sterile males into the population. The males, which have been sterilized by exposure to radiation, mate with the females but no offspring result.

Key to the Future

Pollution is a pressing societal issue, one that directly affects the future survival of all the earth's living organisms. Yet, although there are various technologies to stop pollution, it is difficult to devise an overall plan to deal with environmental problems. Any solution usually requires social and cultural changes that are not easily brought about. The views and attitudes of any society are based on the values important to the society. For this reason, environmental problems cannot be left only to the scientist. Every member of every community should be involved in these decisions.

Some people are already trying to preserve and improve the environment voluntarily, but many more people need to become involved in these efforts. Unfortunately, some people show little concern about their surroundings, and continue their destructive habits, while other people do not have enough information to make the correct choices.

The actions of individuals are only a small part of the problem. It is people in groups—in towns, cities, and industries—who produce the greatest effects on the environment. Often, industries will not voluntarily reduce their polluting activities because the costs are high, a factor which reduces profits. Some cities and states that have industries are hesitant to set strict pollution standards for fear of placing heavy financial burdens on the companies. If costs become too high, the industry may move out of the community, resulting in unemployment and lower tax revenues. Also, the major causes of pollution are not limited to industries. Cities themselves often degrade the environment with inefficient sewage plants and poorly managed landfills. The reasons are the same—cost factors. Efficient operation increases cost, which in turn affects taxes, and this touches all members of the community. Yet, well-informed individuals know that failure to stop pollution will also endanger the community in the long run.

One method of controlling pollution is through legislation. At present there are many laws regulating pollution in the United States and Canada. However, laws that regulate water pollution, air pollution, landfills, heat, and noise often do not prevent pollution. Some states are now proposing new economic incentives in the form of lower taxes to industries that reduce pollution.

Perhaps the most promising way to influence people is by educating them. In successful environmental education, individuals obtain the essential facts, identify the relevant values, analyze the effects of different values in decision-making processes, and predict the consequences of various choices. Once people realize that certain consequences are unacceptable, they may recognize that individual and collective behavior must be changed. People must learn to "think globally." Countries need to work together to solve many interrelated environmental problems.

Well-informed citizens know that the problem of pollution *must* be solved if the earth is to remain a safe, stable place for future inhabitants. They understand that informed voters in a democratic society can bring out an enlightened government. A government supported by its people could enforce strong laws that are based on an understanding of earth's delicately balanced biosphere. With such insight, the life-sustaining conditions of our earth could be preserved for all the living organisms that will follow us.

39-2 Section Review

1. What are the two major types of natural resources?
2. List three methods of soil conservation.
3. Name two conservation practices being used to protect forests.
4. How are pheromones used to control insects biologically?

Critical Thinking

5. Compare renewable and nonrenewable resources.   (*Comparing and Contrasting*)

Laboratory Investigation

Constructing a Model Compost Column

With the growing waste disposal problem, there is a great deal of interest in composting as a valuable way of reducing the amount of waste to be disposed and converting it into a useful product. Composting is a process by which biodegradable matter is decomposed by microorganisms such as bacteria and fungi. In this investigation, you will see how essential nutrients are recycled and make the soil more fertile.

Problem

Construct a model compost column and **classify** various materials according to their suitability for composting.

Materials (per group)

- 2 2-liter plastic bottles
- knife
- scissors
- porous cloth
- transparent tape
- balance
- rubber band
- materials for composting
- water
- microscope slide
- microscope
- rubber gloves
- plastic trash bags

Procedure

1. Prepare a list of materials—both biodegradable and nonbiodegradable—to be composted. Show your list to your teacher for approval.

2. Predict which material will decompose the fastest, the next fastest, and so on.

3. Record your predictions in a data table.

4. Remove the labels from the bottles. Using the knife, make the first cut and then use scissors to cut the bottles as indicated in the diagram. **CAUTION:** *Be careful when using a knife.* Make windows in the bottle tops as shown, taping strips of porous cloth over them to allow air to circulate.

5. Cover the mouth of the longer bottle top with a piece of porous cloth. Secure this with a rubber band. In this way, liquid can percolate through the bottom of the compost column.

6. Invert the bottle top into the bottle base and tape them together securely with transparent tape. See the diagram.

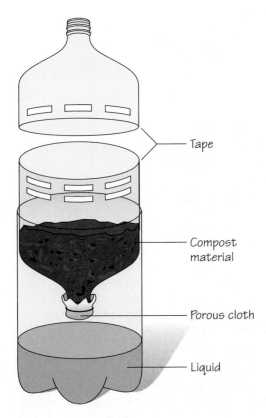

Tape

Compost material

Porous cloth

Liquid

7. Determine and record the mass of the materials to be composted using a balance. Use enough material to fill approximately half of the inverted bottle section of the column.

8. Add approximately 250 mL of water to the material in the column. Then tape the remaining bottle top to the top of the column.

9. Place the column in an area that will provide the best environment for decomposition.

10. Examine the compost column every week for at least four weeks, and observe and record any changes.

11. During each observation, carefully loosen the tape from the bottom of the column to remove any liquid that has accumulated in the bottom section of the column.

12. Examine several drops of the liquid under the low-power objective of a microscope. Record your observations.

13. After four weeks, spread out a plastic trash bag on your table. Carefully empty the contents of the column onto the plastic bag.

14. Wearing rubber gloves, examine the compost and record your observations.

15. Record the mass of the compost material.

Observations

1. Describe the changes you observed in your compost column.

2. Which material appears to decompose the fastest? The slowest?

3. What changes did you observe in the water samples from week to week?

4. How did the mass of the compost material compare to its initial mass?

Analysis and Conclusions

1. How do your results compare with your predictions? What factors might explain any differences?

2. Calculate the percentage change in the mass of the compost material. How can you account for this difference?

3. Did the location of the compost column affect the results of the experiment in any way? You may consult with your classmates.

4. What can you conclude regarding the benefits of composting as one option for waste disposal?

Extensions

Design an experiment using a variety of materials and investigate their suitability for composting.

Chapter 39 Review

Study Outline

39-1 Causes of Environmental Damage

▶ There is a growing awareness that humans have damaged the environment. It can no longer be used thoughtlessly.

▶ The rapidly growing human population places a strain on the earth's resources.

▶ Movement of human population to growing cities has resulted in loss of farmland and ecosystems important to many plants and animals.

▶ Overfarmed and overgrazed land has been lost by erosion.

▶ Pollution has increased with human population growth and industrial development. The release of industrial wastes and sewage into streams and rivers causes water pollution. Gaseous wastes from fossil fuels, cars, and industries pollute the air. Solid wastes from many sources result in land pollution.

39-2 Restoring the Environment

▶ Efforts are being made to control pollution by sewage treatment, emission controls, and sanitary disposal of solid wastes. Some natural resources can be conserved by recycling.

▶ Many techniques are used to conserve soil. Various farming practices can be used to prevent soil erosion by water and wind. Crop rotation and fertilizers can be used to prevent soil depletion.

▶ Because the natural habitats of many plants and animals are being destroyed, many species are endangered. Some have already become extinct. The use of conservation practices is helping to save some species.

Chapter Assessment

Multiple Choice

Choose the letter of the answer that best completes each statement or answers the question.

1. The size of a population that can be supported by the environment is called the (a) limiting factor. (b) population density. (c) reproductive replacement. (d) carrying capacity.

2. Which does not contribute to human population growth? (a) a shorter life span (b) a high birth rate (c) a low adult death rate (d) a low infant death rate

3. If a substance can be broken down by bacteria and other decay organisms it is said to be (a) recyclable. (b) biodegradable. (c) non-biodegradable. (d) magnified.

4. The accumulation of toxic metals and chemicals in the food chain is known as (a) recycling. (b) biodegradation. (c) biological magnification. (d) extinction.

5. Due to an increase in nutrients in a pond, algae grew so quickly that they covered the surface of the water and killed off other forms of life. This is an example of (a) biological magnification. (b) eutrophication. (c) thermal pollution. (d) sanitary landfill.

6. Two methods of soil conservation that inhibit erosion are (a) strip cropping and crop rotation. (b) crop rotation and fertilization. (c) fertilization and terracing. (d) terracing and contour farming.

7. When a garden became infested with a large population of aphids, ladybird beetles were introduced into the community as predators of the aphids. The resultant decrease in the aphid population was due to (a) biological control. (b) parthenogenesis. (c) vegetative propagation. (d) chemosynthesis.

8. Thermal pollution of river water usually is caused by (a) acid rain. (b) smog. (c) temperature inversion. (d) industrial use.

9. Which is a renewable resource? (a) coal (b) water (c) natural gas (d) oil

10. The pollutant most responsible for acid rain is (a) ozone. (b) sulfur dioxide. (c) carbon dioxide. (d) lead.

Content Review

Answer each of the following in complete sentences.

11. What could happen if human population growth continues at the present rate?

12. How has the shift of populations from rural to urban areas affected the environment?

13. Describe some of the problems that can arise from the use of chemical pesticides.

14. Describe the harmful effects of organic wastes as water pollutants.

15. Name the major air pollutants, and describe how each is harmful.

16. Explain the difference between renewable and nonrenewable natural resources, and give examples.

17. Describe five farming techniques used to prevent soil erosion.

18. Although soil and forests are renewable natural resources, it is important that they be conserved. Why?

19. List five wildlife conservation practices.

20. What are some of the advantages of biological pest control over chemical pesticides?

Graphic Organizing

For information on graphic organizers, see Appendix G at the back of this text.

21. Concept Map Construct a concept map that shows the major types of water pollution. Include at least 10 concepts. Be sure to include linking words between related concepts.

Critical Thinking and Problem Solving

Discuss each of the following in a brief paragraph.

22. Hypothesizing Suppose a pond suddenly becomes overgrown with algae and plants. Suggest some possible causes for the growth. What questions would you ask to determine the most probable cause for the sudden algae growth?

23. Comparing Discuss farming methods that destroy resources and other farming methods that could conserve resources.

24. Experimenting Your friend notices cracks in the tires of his car. A chemistry teacher tells you that ozone, an air pollutant, can cause tires to deteriorate. Design a controlled experiment to test the validity of that statement.

25. Calculating The human population 2000 years ago was approximately 250 million people. By 1850, the population had reached 1 billion. It had doubled by 1930. Presently, the population exceeds 5 billion people and is increasing at a rate of about 1.5 million people per week. Calculate the projected population for each of the next five years. Assume that the population in 1999 was 6.012 billion.

26. Interpreting Carrying capacity affects the size of all natural populations living in an area. The graph below shows the relationship between the carrying capacity of an island and the number of deer living on it over a 45-year period. How would you explain the decline in carrying capacity around 1925?

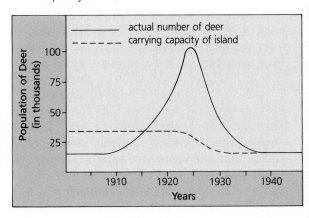

Performance-Based Assessment

Deep-Ocean Ecosystem

Background

A team of scientists using a research submarine descended to 2600 meters below the surface of the Pacific Ocean to explore a deep oceanic ridge. During the dive, species were discovered that were previously unknown to science. They were living in complete darkness near hydrothermal vents, or hot springs, on the ocean bottom. The populations of organisms—consisting of tube worms, large white clams, and mussels—formed dense clusters around the vents. Roaming freely among these sessile organisms were fish, vent crabs, filter-feeding crabs, and other invertebrates. The environment near the vents was found to be rich in hydrogen sulfide, a condition known to exist in hot springs on land.

Most ecosystems in the deep ocean must depend for food on organic material from organisms in the photic zone above. How then can such dense populations survive in this community without autotrophs? To answer this question, studies were done on bacteria isolated from the vent water. They indicated that the bacteria were chemosynthetic, using inorganic hydrogen sulfide from the vents as a source of energy.

It was found that the large tube worms had no digestive system. Anatomically, each worm was a closed sac, with internal organs but no passages to the outside. Further studies indicated that a large internal space in the worms was filled with vast numbers of chemosynthetic bacteria. Tube worms have an organ called a plume that normally catches food and absorbs oxygen from the surrounding water. But in this case the plume absorbs oxygen and the fuel needed by the bacteria—hydrogen sulfide and carbon dioxide. The worms' hemoglobin has a special adaptation for carrying oxygen and hydrogen sulfide at the same time.

The clams and the mussels also harbor chemosynthetic bacteria on the surface of their gills. The tube worms, clams, and mussels all depend on the bacteria for nutrition. In turn, they supply the bacteria with essential chemicals from the environment and a suitable place to live.

The vent crabs have no nutritional relationship with the chemosynthetic bacteria, and have been observed feeding directly on other organisms.

Data Table: A Population Study

Hydrothermal Vents	1	2	3	4	1	2	3	4
Dive	Tube Worms				Vent Crabs			
1	10	7	19	14	3	2	6	4
2	15	12	24	19	4	3	7	5
3	25	22	34	29	4	3	7	4
4	28	25	37	32	10	9	16	13
5	24	20	31	26	15	12	20	19
6	20	14	26	20	28	31	30	27
7	7	5	12	8	27	22	28	23
8	14	11	16	12	2	3	4	2

Problem

You are a member of a team of three ecologists assigned to study deep-ocean ecosystems.

Task

Choose one of the following tasks.

1. As a team, you must answer the following questions.

   - What is the role of the vent bacteria in the deep-ocean ecosystem?
   - What might be a probable path for hydrogen sulfide from the hydrothermal vent into the tube worms?
   - How do tube worms acquire nutrients?
   - What is the relationship between the tube worms, the bacteria, and the crabs?
   - What are the most important abiotic factors in the vent ecosystem? How do these factors influence each population of organisms making up the vent community?
   - Does studying the hydrothermal vent ecosystem have applications to other parts of the biosphere?

During several dives, one of the research biologists noticed changes in the tube worm populations. A population study was started to investigate the causes of the changes. The data table lists observations made on a series of eight dives. Using these data, calculate the average number of tube worms and vent crabs. Construct a graph illustrating the average number of tube worms in relation to the average number of vent crabs. Then construct a model of a food web based on the hydrothermal vent ecosystem.

2. As a team, prepare a scientific paper for presentation to the board of directors of the Duke University Marine Institute supporting deep-ocean research. Include the results of your analysis of the hydrothermal vent ecosystem as part of your presentation, with supporting visuals, predictions concerning population fluctuations, and environmental factors.

3. As a team, prepare an article on deep-ocean ecosystems for a popular children's science magazine. Make sure that your article is appropriate for an audience of fifth- or sixth-grade students and that it is visually appealing.

Appendix A: Care and Use of the Microscope

One of the biologist's most important tools is the microscope. Microscopes allow biologists to study structures so small they cannot be seen with the unaided eye. The type of microscope used in most biology classrooms is the compound microscope.

coarse adjustment: moves body tube

fine adjustment: moves body tube

arm: supports body tube

clip: holds slide

base: supports microscope

ocular (eyepiece): contains lens

body tube: separates ocular from the nosepiece

nosepiece: hold objectives

high-power objective: contains lens

low-power objective: contains lens

stage: supports slide

diaphragm: controls amount of light

mirror

Learning the Parts of a Microscope

Figure 1 shows the parts of the compound microscope. You should become familiar with all the parts and the function of each part. At the top of the microscope is the *ocular,* or *eyepiece, lens.* This is the part into which you look. Usually, the ocular lens has a magnifying power of 10X or less. A magnifying power of 10X means that the lens makes an object appear 10 times larger than it really is.

Beneath the ocular is the *body tube.* At the bottom of the body tube is a revolving *nosepiece* containing two more lenses. These are called the objective lenses. The shorter objective lens is the *low-power objective,* which usually has a magnification of 10X. The longer objective is the *high-power*

objective, and it usually has a magnification of about 40X. The magnification of each objective lens will be marked on it. Powers of magnification may vary.

When you are observing specimens with the microscope, you should know how much they are being magnified. To compute the total magnification, multiply the magnifying power of the ocular lens (10X) by the magnifying power of the objective lens (either 10X or about 40X). For example, if you are looking at an object with the low-power objective, the magnification would be 10 times 10, which equals 100X. Thus the object would appear to be 100 times larger than its natural size.

Preparing the Microscope for Use

To prepare a microscope for use, follow these steps:

1. Remove the microscope from its storage case by grasping the arm of the microscope with one hand and placing your other hand under the base. Carry the microscope upright to your lab table.
2. Gently set the microscope down on its base on the lab table. Position it so that the ocular and the arm are toward you. Make sure that the base of the microscope rests evenly on the table and that the front edge of the base is at least 10 centimeters from the edge of the table.
3. Clean the ocular and the objective lenses with a piece of lens paper. Touch the lenses only with lens paper; anything else may damage them.
4. Use the coarse adjustment knob to raise the body tube to its highest point above the stage. Then, turn the revolving nosepiece until the low-power

objective clicks into place. When in place, the objective lens should be directly above the opening in the stage.

5. Look through the ocular with both eyes open. Switch on the illuminator lamp or turn the mirror until you see an evenly lit field of white light. If the field of light is too dark or too light, open or close the diaphragm. CAUTION: If your microscope has a mirror, never use direct sunlight as a light source. It can injure your eyes.

Observing a Prepared Slide

To observe a prepared slide, follow these steps:

1. Place a prepared slide on the stage so that the stage clips hold down the left and right sides of the slide and the specimen is on top. Move the slide so that the specimen is centered beneath the low-power objective.

2. Looking at the side of the microscope, slowly lower the low-power objective with the coarse adjustment knob until it is just above, but not touching, the slide. CAUTION: Do not let the low-power objective touch the slide, as it may damage the objective or break the slide.

3. With both eyes open, look through the ocular. Move the slide back and forth with your fingers until the specimen is centered. If the specimen looks out of focus, turn the coarse adjustment knob slowly to raise the body tube. When the specimen comes into view, stop turning. For fine focusing, use the fine adjustment knob. Always look through the eyepiece as you adjust the focus.

4. If necessary, adjust the diaphragm to increase or decrease the amount of light.

5. To view the specimen with the high-power objective (40 X), lift your head away from the ocular and revolve the nosepiece until the high-power objective clicks into place. (Do *not* look through the ocular while switching from low to high power.) Then look through the ocular and use the fine adjustment knob to bring the specimen into focus. CAUTION: Do not let the high-power objective touch the slide.

6. After using the microscope, clean the lenses with lens paper. If necessary, also clean the stage.

Preparing a Wet Mount

To make a wet mount, follow these steps:

1. Obtain from your teacher a clean microscope slide and a clean coverslip.

2. Place the specimen in the middle of the microscope slide. Make sure the specimen is thin enough for light to pass through it.

3. With an eyedropper, place a drop of water on the specimen.

4. Hold the coverslip by its thin edges between your index finger and your thumb, and lower it at a 45° angle into the drop of water. After the water spreads along one edge of the coverslip, slowly lower it until it lies flat on top of the slide. This is called a wet mount. If air bubbles are trapped beneath the coverslip, lift it up and lower it again, or tap it gently with the eraser end of a pencil.

5. Remove any excess water with a piece of paper towel. If the specimen starts to dry out, add another drop of water at one edge of the coverslip.

6. To view the wet mount, follow the same steps as for viewing a prepared slide.

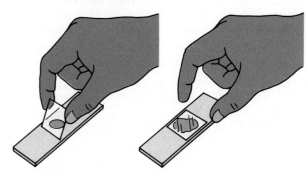

Staining a Specimen

To stain a microscope specimen, follow these steps:

1. Obtain from your teacher a clean microscope slide and a clean coverslip.

2. Place the specimen in the middle of the slide.

3. With an eyedropper, place one drop of water on the specimen.

4. Holding the coverslip by its thin edges, lower it at a 45° angle into the water on the slide. Continue lowering it gently until it lies flat on the slide.

5. Using the eyedropper again, add a drop of stain along one edge of the coverslip. Touch a small piece of paper towel to the opposite edge so as to draw the stain under the coverslip. Stains are used to make the structures of a specimen easier to see.

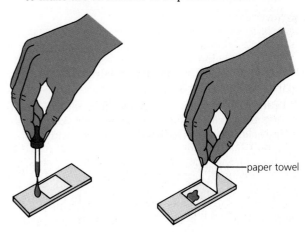

paper towel

Appendix B: Safety in the Laboratory

Laboratory work is an important part of your biology class. The work, however, may require you to handle strong chemicals, sharp instruments, hot materials, or expensive equipment. To prevent accidents, you need to act with care and observe all safety rules at all times.

Dress Code

1. Many materials in the laboratory can cause eye injury. To protect yourself from injury, wear safety goggles whenever you are working with chemicals, burners, or any substance that might get into your eyes. Never wear contact lenses in the laboratory.

2. Wear a laboratory apron whenever you are working with any chemicals or heated substances.

3. Tie back long hair to keep it away from any chemicals, burners, or any other laboratory equipment.

4. Remove or tie back any article of clothing or jewelry that could hang down and touch chemicals and flames.

General Safety Rules

1. Read all directions for an experiment several times. Then follow the directions exactly as they are written. If you are in doubt about any part of the experiment, ask your teacher for assistance.

2. Never perform investigations that are not authorized by your teacher. Obtain permission before "experimenting" on your own.

3. Never handle any equipment unless you have specific permission.

4. Take extreme care not to spill any material in the laboratory. If spills occur, ask your teacher immediately about the proper cleanup procedure. Never simply pour chemicals or other substances into the sink or trash container.

5. Never eat in the laboratory.

First Aid

1. Report all accidents, no matter how minor, to your teacher immediately.

2. Learn what to do in case of specific accidents, such as getting acid in your eyes or on your skin. (Rinse any acids that may splash on your body with lots of water.)

3. Know the location of the first-aid kit. Your teacher should administer any required first aid due to injury. Or your teacher may send you to the school nurse or call a physician.

4. Know where and how to report an accident or fire. Find out the location of the fire extinguisher, phone, and fire alarm. Report any fires to your teacher at once.

Safety Symbols

You should recognize the following safety symbols and know what they mean. **In the event of an accident or unusual occurrence, remember to report it to your teacher immediately.**

Safety Clothing Wear a lab apron or lab coat whenever working with materials that could damage your skin or clothing. For some activities, you may also need protective gloves. Wear safety clothing at all times during a specified laboratory activity.

Safety Goggles Use safety goggles in any lab activity involving chemicals, flames, or the possibility of broken glassware. Wear goggles at all times during these activities. Place them over eyeglasses to protect the sides of the eyes.

Gloves Wear protective gloves to protect your hands from contact with corrosive substances, broken glass, or hot objects.

Heating Safety Be careful not to touch hot objects with your bare hands. Use either tongs or heat-proof gloves to pick up hot objects. Never heat a chemical you are not instructed to heat.

Fire Safety Tie hair back, roll up sleeves, and remove or secure any loose clothing, such as ties, scarves, or jackets, that may get too close to a flame. Never reach across a flame. Keep all flammable items away from the area of a flame or from an electrical source of appliance. Follow your teacher's instructions on how to light a burner safely. Turn burners completely off when you have finished with them. When heating a test tube, point the open end away from yourself and others. Do not heat liquid in a closed container. Never leave a lighted burner unattended.

Corrosive Substance Avoid letting any corrosive substance, such as a strong acid or base, touch your skin, eyes, or clothing. Wear protective clothing and goggles. Do not inhale vapors. Never touch, smell, or taste chemicals in the laboratory. Be careful when working with acids or bases. Pour such chemicals over the sink, not your work area. When diluting an acid, pour the acid into water. Never pour water into the acid. Dispose of all hazardous chemicals in a toxic-waste-disposal container.

Breakage Handle breakable equipment, such as glassware, carefully. Do not use cracked, chipped, scored, or badly scratched glassware. Never force glass tubing into a rubber stopper. A turning motion and lubricant will be helpful when inserting glass tubing into rubber stoppers or rubber tubing. Do not plunge hot glassware into cold water or let empty glassware get too hot. Never leave any glassware unattended while it is being heated. Place hot glassware on an insulated surface. Remember that glass may remain hot for quite a while after it has been removed from a heat source, even though it may not look hot; handle it with caution. If glassware breaks, notify your teacher immediately.

Dangerous Vapors Use a fume hood when directed to do so by your teacher. When testing an odor, use a wafting motion of your hand to direct the vapor toward your nose. Never directly inhale laboratory vapors. If you begin to get a headache or feel dizzy or weak, leave the room or open a window to get fresh air.

Explosion Danger Avoid the danger of explosion by studying laboratory instructions and following them exactly. Never look into the top of a container that is being heated. Do not bring any substance into contact with a flame unless instructed to do so. When heating a substance, point the mouth of the test tube away from yourself and others.

Poison Do not let a poisonous substance come into contact with your skin, do not swallow any of the substance, and do not breathe any of its vapors. If you accidentally come into contact with a poison, notify your teacher immediately.

Electrical shock Avoid electrical shock by reading laboratory instructions carefully and following them exactly. Disconnect all electrical equipment when not in use. Do not use any electrical equipment around water or when the equipment is wet.

Disposal When an experiment is completed, clean up your work area and return all equipment to its proper place. Dispose of all potentially hazardous materials as directed by your teacher. Do not place hazardous materials in the wastebasket or wash them down the sink.

Hygiene Always wash your hands after completing a laboratory investigation. Never touch your face or eyes during a laboratory investigation.

Animal Safety Treat all animals in as humane a way as possible. Follow your teacher's directions when handling animals. Handle animals gently to avoid producing undue excitement or trauma. Avoid subjecting animals to stressful conditions, such as exhausting exercise or painful stimuli. Wash your hands thoroughly after handling animals or their cages.

Sharp-Instrument Safety Handle any sharp instrument—such as scalpels or razor blades—with extreme care. Direct sharp-edged instruments away from yourself and others. Cut in a direction away from yourself and others. Notify your teacher immediately if you cut yourself when in the laboratory.

Appendix C: Humane Treatment of Animals

Some of the most exciting parts of a biology course are those that deal with living animals. Some classrooms have a permanent collection of living animals. Others use living animals only occasionally as part of laboratory activities. It is the moral and ethical responsibility of the teacher and students to give adequate care to all living animals and to treat them humanely. In all your dealings with living animals, you should show a respect for life.

To insure humane treatment of animals in the laboratory or classroom, follow these steps:

1. Be sure that a proper environment can be created and maintained for an animal before it is brought into the classroom. Research the animal's needs and make sure you can meet them.
2. In general, avoid bringing wild animals into the classroom. Most wild animals cannot adapt to a classroom or laboratory setting. Exceptions are small animals, such as earthworms, spiders, insects, fish, and some amphibians. Do not collect any animals that are members of an endangered species. Do not collect animals that are sick or dying. Handle wild animals as infrequently as possible. After a period of observation, return the animals to their natural habitats.
3. Obtain healthy animals from pet stores or biological supply houses.
4. Make sure you know how to treat each kind of animal. Get directions from your teacher before handling a live animal. You need to know how to handle an animal properly in order to prevent injury to it and to yourself. Do not make loud noises, tap on the animals' cages or containers, or otherwise disturb or frighten the animals.
5. Keep records of who is feeding the animals and how much and how often they are fed. Make sure that the animals' nutritional needs are met but not exceeded.
6. Make sure that the areas in which the animals are housed are cleaned regularly.
7. Arrange for the animals to be cared for when school is not in session, such as during weekends and vacations.
8. Do not cause any animal pain or injury. Experiments with live animals should have humane objectives and be closely supervised by the teacher. Follow your teacher's instructions carefully.
9. **Discuss your attitudes and feelings about dissection of preserved animals with your teacher. If you are strongly opposed to dissecting animals, alternatives are available to you. Your textbook and lab manual present these alternatives. Some of them are: (1) computer simulations, (2) anatomical models and charts, (3) laser discs, (4) films, (5) filmstrips, (6) transparencies, (7) videotapes, and (8) books.**

Appendix D: Careers in Biology

Biology offers a wide range of different careers in which a variety of interests may be pursued. Some jobs in biology-related fields require only on-the-job training, while others require up to eight years of college and post-college education. Below is a list of some biology-related careers along with a brief description of each and the address of organizations providing more information. Further information can be found in the *Occupational Outlook Handbook* published by the U.S. Department of Labor. Your school guidance counselor may also be able to provide you with information.

Careers Requiring a High School Diploma or a Two-Year Degree

Animal lab assistants care for animals treated by veterinarians or used in biomedical research. They feed the animals, maintain records on them, collect specimens, perform laboratory procedures, and sometimes assist in breeding and medical procedures. WHERE TO WRITE: American Veterinary Medical Association, 1931 N. Meacham Road, Suite 100, Schaumburg, IL 60173. ON THE INTERNET at www.avma.org.

Biomedical engineer technicians install, operate, repair, and maintain electronic biomedical equipment used in the diagnosis and treatment of diseases. They also teach health workers how to operate the instruments. WHERE TO WRITE: Biomedical Engineering Society, P.O. Box 2399, Culver City, CA 90231. ON THE INTERNET at www.mecca.org/ BME/BMES/society/bmeshm.html

Biophotographers provide the photographs that illustrate magazines, books, articles, and teaching materials in the biomedical sciences. Their work may range from photographing bacteria under a microscope to photographing whales in the ocean. WHERE TO WRITE: Professional Photographers of America, 57 Forsyth Street NW, Suite 1600, Atlanta, GA 30303. ON THE INTERNET at www.ppa-world.org.

Dental technicians construct a variety of dental appliances, such as dentures, bridges, crowns, and inlays, based on a dentist's prescriptions. WHERE TO WRITE: American Dental Association, 211 E. Chicago Avenue, Chicago, IL 60611. ON THE INTERNET at www.ada.org.

Emergency medical technicians are trained to deal with medical emergencies. Arriving at the scene of an emergency in an ambulance, they treat patients in shock, perform cardiopulmonary resuscitation, control bleeding, and administer other emergency care until the patient can be given hospital care. WHERE TO WRITE: National Association of Emergency Medical Technicians, 102 W. Leake Street, Clinton, MS 39056-4252. ON THE INTERNET at www.naemt.org.

Fish culturists supervise the day-to-day operations of fish hatcheries, under the direction of fish biologists. They monitor the breeding, development, feeding, and health of the fish, and oversee the crews that maintain hatchery equipment. WHERE TO WRITE: American Fisheries Society, 5410 Grosvenor Lane, Suite 110, Bethesda, MD 20814-2199. ON THE INTERNET at www.esd.ornl.gov/societies/AFS.

Floral designers design, create, and often sell ornamental flower arrangements. They help customers choose the appropriate flowers for a particular occasion, and some grow the plants and flowers they use. WHERE TO WRITE: American Society for Horticultural Science, 600 Cameron Street, Alexandria, VA 22314. ON THE INTERNET at www.ashs.org.

Histological technicians cut, stain, and mount body tissues for microscopic examination by a pathologist. WHERE TO WRITE: National Society for Histotechnology, 4201 Northview Drive, Suite 502, Bowie, MD 20716-2604. ON THE INTERNET at www.nsh.org.

Medical assistants help physicians manage their offices efficiently. They function as receptionists or secretaries, prepare patients for examination, and perform simple laboratory tests. WHERE TO WRITE: American Association of Medical Assistants, 20 N. Wacker Drive #1575, Chicago, IL 60606-2903. ON THE INTERNET at www.aama-ntl.org.

Medical laboratory technicians conduct a wide range of routine and specialized laboratory tests to help physicians diagnose and treat disease. They prepare and analyze specimens of body fluids and tissues under the supervision of a laboratory supervisor. WHERE TO WRITE: American Medical Technologists, 710 Higgins Road, Park Ridge, IL 60068.

Museum technicians help museum curators and others prepare, construct, and maintain exhibits. They may also assist in preserving specimens and interpreting historical research. WHERE TO WRITE: American Association of Museums, Department 4002, Washington, DC 20042-4002. ON THE INTERNET at www.aam-us.org.

Careers Requiring a Bachelor's Degree

Dental hygienists provide preventive dental services by cleaning teeth, applying compounds that prevent decay, and instructing patients in proper oral hygiene. In addition, they may assist dentists by taking patient histories and preparing diagnostic aids. WHERE TO WRITE: American Dental Hygienists' Association, 444 N. Michigan Avenue, Suite 3400, Chicago, IL 60611. ON THE INTERNET at www.adha.org.

Foresters develop and manage forests for their many uses, from timber production to recreation. They plan and supervise the growth and harvesting of trees, and they protect forests from fires, floods, insects, and disease. WHERE TO WRITE: Society of American Foresters, 5400 Grosvenor Lane, Bethesda, MD 20814-2198. ON THE INTERNET at www.safnet.org.

Horticulturists cultivate orchards and garden plants. They breed, grow, and distribute flowers, fruits, vegetables, trees, and bushes. Using a knowledge of genetics, they develop new plants with such traits as high crop yield or physical beauty. WHERE TO WRITE: American Society for Horticultural Science, 600 Cameron Street, Alexandria, VA 22314. ON THE INTERNET at www.ashs.org.

Medical illustrators draw and diagram medical instruments, procedures, and anatomical structures for publications, film, television, medical supply companies, and exhibits. Artists must be acomplished in drawing, painting, and modeling techniques, and must be experienced in various forms of media. WHERE TO WRITE: Association of Medical Illustrators, 1819 Peachtree Street NE, Suite 620, Atlanta, GA 30309. ON THE INTERNET at www.medical-illustrators.org.

Pharmacists prepare and dispense medications prescribed by physicians and dentists. They must know the compositions and interactions of drugs to predict the effects of a particular medication. They also advise customers on medications and health aids. WHERE TO WRITE: American Pharmaceutical Association, P.O. Box 85080, Richmond, VA 23285-4008. ON THE INTERNET at www.aphanet.org.

Physician's assistants examine and treat patients under the guidance of a physician. They collect patient histories, perform examinations, give treatment, prescribe certain drugs, and counsel patients on health problems. WHERE TO WRITE: American Academy of Physican Assistants, 950 N. Washington Street, Alexandria, VA 22314-1552. ON THE INTERNET at www.aapa.org.

Registered nurses plan, administer, and supervise patient nursing care. They monitor and record patients' symptoms and progress and give medications ordered by physicians. They may also supervise nursing assistants and teach. WHERE TO WRITE: National League for Nursing, 350 Hudson Street, New York, NY 10014. ON THE INTERNET at www.nln.org.

Careers Requiring a Master's or Doctorate Degree (Ph.D.)

Biochemists study the chemistry of organisms to determine what compounds make up living things and how these compounds interact in processes such as metabolism, growth, and reproduction. Some study the effects of foods, drugs, and toxins, while others develop methods for diagnosing and treating disease. WHERE TO WRITE: American Society of Biological Chemists, 9650 Rockville Pike, Bethesda, MD 20814.

Dentists treat oral diseases and disorders such as tooth decay, gum disease, and crooked teeth. They may extract teeth, fill cavities, and provide dentures. WHERE TO WRITE: American Dental Association, 211 E. Chicago Avenue, Chicago, IL 60611. ON THE INTERNET at www.ada.org.

Geneticists study the process of inheritance and the structures and chemicals involved. Some geneticists do applied research and study genetic diseases and plant and animal breeding, while others do basic research and study biological processes at the molecular level. WHERE TO WRITE: Genetics Society of America, 9650 Rockville Pike, Bethesda, MD 20814. ON THE INTERNET at www.faseb.org/genetics/gsa/gsamenu.htm.

Pathologists are specialized physicians who interpret the nature of diseases and the changes they produce in the body. They examine tissues and body fluids to determine the levels of various biochemicals, the presence of certain types of cells and infectious organisms, and the status of the immune system. WHERE TO WRITE: American Medical Association, 515 N. State Street, Chicago, IL 60610. ON THE INTERNET at www.ama-assn.org.

Physicians are responsible for the overall health care of patients. They examine, diagnose, and treat patients, perform routine and emergency medical procedures, and advise patients on ways to stay healthy. WHERE TO WRITE: American Medical Association, 515 N. State Street, Chicago, IL 60610. ON THE INTERNET at www.ama-assn.org.

Veterinarians examine, diagnose, and treat animals with diseases and other medical conditions. They perform surgery and laboratory tests, and administer medications and immunizations. Some specialize in the care of small domestic animals, while others specialize in the care of farm or zoo animals and wildlife. WHERE TO WRITE: American Veterinary Medical Association, 1931 N. Meacham Road, Suite 100, Schaumburg, IL 60173. ON THE INTERNET at www.avma.org.

Appendix E: The SI System of Measurement

The abbreviation SI refers to the International Metric System (formally, Système Internationale d'Unités). This widely used system of measurement is conveniently based on units of 10. Tables of SI base units, their multiples and submultiples, and selected Metric/English conversions are presented below. Also included are notes on temperature and temperature conversions, and heat energy.

SI Base Units

To Measure	SI Base Unit Used	Common Multiples and Submultiples	Approximate Size
Length	meter (m)	meter = 1 m kilometer 1 km = 1000 m centimeter 1 cm = 0.01 m millimeter 1 mm = 0.001 m micron 1 μm = 10^{-6} m (micrometer) nanometer 1 nm = 10^{-9} m	1 m—height of a doorknob 1 km—length of 5 city blocks 1 cm—width of a paper clip 1 mm—thickness of a dime 1 μm—diameter of a bacterium 1 nm—length of an amino acid
Mass	gram (g)	gram = 1 g kilogram 1 kg = 1000 g milligram 1 mg = 0.001 g	1 g—mass of a paper clip 1 kg—mass of a pair of adult shoes 1 mg—mass of a grain of rice
Volume	liter (L)	liter = 1 L milliliter 1 mL = 0.001 L cubic centimeter 1 cm³ (also cc) ≈ 1 mL	1 L—capacity of a water pitcher 1 mL (1 cm³)—capacity of an eye dropper

Metric Prefixes

Prefix	Symbol	Meaning	Multiples and Submultiples
atto-	a-	quintillionth	10^{-18}
femto-	f-	quadrillionth	10^{-15}
pico-	p-	trillionth	10^{-12}
nano-	n-	billionth	10^{-9}
micro-	μ-	millionth	10^{-6}
milli-	m-	thousandth	10^{-3}
centi-	c-	hundredth	10^{-2}
deci-	d-	tenth	10^{-1}
deka-	dk-, da-	ten	10
hecto-	h-	hundred	10^{2}
kilo-	k-	thousand	10^{3}
mega-	M-	million	10^{6}
giga-	G-	billion	10^{9}
tera-	T-	trillion	10^{12}

Some Metric/English Conversions

To Obtain	Multiply	By
Feet	Meters	3.2808
Miles	Kilometers	0.6214
Ounces	Grams	0.0353
Pounds	Kilograms	2.2046
Liquid quarts	Liters	1.0567
Fluid ounces	Milliliters	0.0338
Meters	Feet	0.3048
Kilometers	Miles	1.6093
Grams	Ounces	28.3495
Kilograms	Pounds	0.4536
Liters	Liquid quarts	0.9463
Milliliters	Fluid ounces	29.5735

Temperature

The SI base unit for temperature is the kelvin (K). However, as a matter of convenience, the degree Celsius (°C) is more commonly used.

Some Sample Temperatures

Scale	Water Freezes	Water Boils	Range
K	273	373	100
°C	0	100	100
°F	32	212	180

Heat Energy

1 calorie (cal) = The amount of heat needed to raise the temperature of 1 g of water 1 °C (also called the small calorie or gram calorie)
1 cal = 4.2 joules

1 Calorie (Cal) = 1 kilocalorie, or 1000 cal (also called the large calorie or kilogram calorie)
1 Cal = 4184 joules

Temperature Conversion Formulas
°C = K − 273   K = °C + 273
°C = 5/9(°F − 32)   °F = (9/5)°C + 32
°F = 9/5(K − 273) + 32   K= 5/9 (°F − 32) + 273

Appendix F: Classification of Organisms

Kingdom Archaebacteria

Archaebacteria are prokaryotes that live in harsh environments that other organisms cannot tolerate. They are different from other prokaryotes by the chemical makeup of their cell membranes and the unique structure of their DNA. There are three groups of Archaebacteria.

Methanogenic Bacteria
These archaebacteria breakdown organic matter and produce methane gas. They are found in the intestinal tracts of animals and in marshes, swamps, and sewage treatment plants. **EXAMPLE:** *Methanobacterium*

Halophilic Bacteria
These salt-loving archaebacteria are found mainly in salt lakes. **EXAMPLE:** *Halococcus*

Thermoacidophilic Bacteria
These archaebacteria live in very hot, acidic environments. **EXAMPLE:** *Thermoplasma*

Kingdom Eubacteria

Eubacteria include all bacteria except the archaebacteria. Most eubacteria are heterotrophic; the rest—the autotrophic eubacteria—are either phototrophs or chemotrophs.

Anaerobic Phototrophic Bacteria
These bacteria carry out photosynthesis without using water as a starting material and without producing oxygen. This phylum includes green-sulfur bacteria and purple bacteria.

Cyanobacteria
Members of this phylum, the *blue-green bacteria,* carry out photosynthesis using chlorophyll *a* and the blue pigment phycocyanin. Cyanobacteria include both unicellular and colonial species; some perform nitrogen fixation. **EXAMPLE:** *Nostoc.*

Prochlorophyta
These bacteria carry out photosynthesis with both chlorophyll *a* and *b*. They live in association with certain marine animals. **EXAMPLE:** *Prochloron.*

Schizophyta
This is a diverse group of heterotrophic eubacteria that includes both saprobes and parasites, and both aerobic and anaerobic forms. Many cause diseases. **EXAMPLES:** *E. coli, Rickettsia, Streptococcus, Chlamydia, Mycoplasma, Treponema, Actinomyces.*

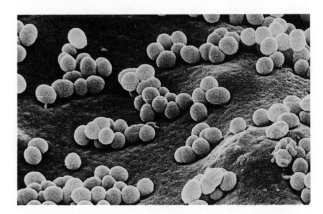

Kingdom Protista

Protists are unicellular, colonial, and multicellular organisms. The cells of protists are eukaryotic with a membrane-bound nucleus and other organelles. Protists may be animal-like, plantlike, or funguslike.

Phylum Sarcodina
The unicellular, animal-like *sarcodines* move and capture prey by means of pseudopods. They are found in both fresh water and salt water and in the bodies of animals. A few cause disease. Reproduction is both asexual and sexual. Of the sarcodines, amebas are surrounded only by a cell membrane, while radiolarians and forams have protective shells. **EXAMPLES:** *Ameba, Entamoeba, Globigerina, Pelomyxa.*

Phylum Ciliophora
Ciliates are complex, animal-like protists that move by means of cilia. Their cells contain a macronucleus and a micronucleus. They are found in both fresh water and salt water. Reproduction is both asexual and sexual. **EXAMPLES:** *Paramecium, Stentor, Tetrahymena, Vorticella.*

Phylum Zoomastigina The *zooflagellates* move by means of one or more flagella. Most are unicellular and live inside animals or plants. A few are free-living in fresh water. Reproduction is both asexual and sexual. **EXAMPLES:** *Trypanosoma, Trichonympha.*

Phylum Sporozoa The *sporozoans* are nonmotile, spore-producing protists. They are parasites with a complex life cycle that includes more than one kind of host. **EXAMPLES:** *Plasmodium, Toxoplasma.*

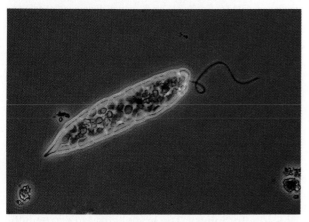

Phylum Euglenophyta The *euglenoids* are unicellular, photosynthetic protists. They do not have cell walls but have pellicles, or flexible protein coverings. They move by means of flagella and are found mainly in fresh water. Reproduction is asexual. **EXAMPLE:** *Euglena.*

Phylum Chrysophyta The *golden algae* are a diverse group of photosynthetic protists that contain yellow-brown pigments and store food as oils or starchlike carbohydrates. They are mostly unicellular; some are colonial. They are found in both fresh water and salt water. The most numerous kind, the diatoms, have shells made of silica. Reproduction is both asexual and sexual. **EXAMPLES:** *Botrydium, Chrysameba, Pinnularia.*

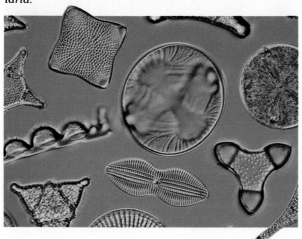

Phylum Dinoflagellata The *dinoflagellates* are unicellular algae with two flagella and armorlike cell walls containing cellulose and silica. Some are photosynthetic; others are heterotrophic. Most live in salt water. Reproduction is asexual. **EXAMPLES:** *Gonyaulax, Gymnodinium.*

Phylum Chlorophyta The *green algae* are unicellular, colonial, or multicellular protists. Some have flagella. Most contain chlorophylls *a* and *b* and cell walls made of cellulose. They are found in salt water and fresh water and in moist places on land. **EXAMPLES:** *Ulothrix, Chlamydomonas, Chlorella, Volvox, Spirogyra, Ulva.*

Phylum Phaeophyta The multicellular, photosynthetic *brown algae* include many common seaweeds found in ocean waters. The brown algae contain a brown photosynthetic pigment in addition to chlorophyll. They have cellulose in their cell walls and store food in the form of polysaccharides or oils. Their life cycles show alternation of generations. **EXAMPLES:** *Sargassum, Macrocystis, Fucus, Laminaria.*

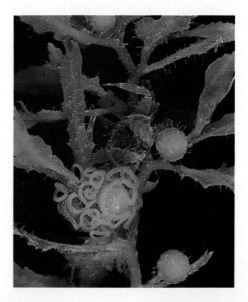

Phylum Rhodophyta The *red algae* are mostly multicellular, marine protists that include many common seaweeds. They contain chlorophyll as well as other pigments. They have complex life cycles, including alternation of generations. **EXAMPLES:** *Porphyra, Polysiphonia, Chondrus.*

Phylum Myxomycota *Acellular slime molds* are unicellular organisms with many nuclei. They are found on damp soil, on rotting logs, and in leaf litter. Reproduction is sexual. The life cycle includes an ameboid plasmodium and spore-producing fruiting bodies. **EXAMPLE:** *Physarum.*

Phylum Acrasiomycota The *cellular slime molds* are found in fresh water, on damp soil, or on decaying vegetation. Reproduction is asexual. The life cycle includes a pseudoplasmodium, or mass of many individual, membrane-bound cells. The pseudoplasmodium can form fruiting bodies that produce haploid spores. Their feeding stage consists of independent ameboid cells. **EXAMPLE:** *Dictyostelium.*

Phylum Oomycota *Water molds* and *downy mildews* consist of finely branched, single-celled filaments. Most water molds are saprobes that live in fresh water. Some are parasites of fish. Their cell walls contain cellulose, and they have a complex life cycle dominated by a diploid stage. The downy mildews are plant parasites. **EXAMPLE:** *Saprolegnia.*

Kingdom Fungi

Fungi are eukaryotic, heterotrophic organisms that absorb nutrients from their environment. A few are unicellular, but most are multicellular and are made up of masses of threadlike filaments, hyphae. In most, the cell walls are made up of chitin. Reproduction is either asexual or sexual by means of spores.

Phylum Zygomycota *Conjugation fungi* reproduce sexually by conjugation. The also reproduce asexually. Their hyphae lack cross walls. Most of these fungi are saprobes; some are parasites. **EXAMPLES:** *Rhizopus, Phycomyces.*

Phylum Ascomycota The *sac fungi* are the largest group of fungi. They reproduce sexually by ascospores, which develop inside the ascus, a saclike structure. They also reproduce asexually by conidia. Except for unicellular yeasts, sac fungi are multicellular with incomplete cross walls dividing the hyphae. This group includes cup fungi, yeasts, powdery mildews, truffles, morels, and blue and green molds. **EXAMPLES:** *Saccharomyces, Neurospora.*

Phylum Basidiomycota *Club fungi* have a clublike reproductive structure called a basidium. Club fungi

may reproduce either asexually, or sexually by basidiospores. Incomplete cross walls divide the hyphae of club fungi. This group includes mushrooms, bracket fungi, puffballs, rusts, and smuts. **EXAMPLES:** *Amanita, Lycoperdon, Phragmidium.*

Phylum Deuteromycota In the *Fungi Imperfecti,* the pattern of sexual reproduction is unknown. They can reproduce asexually by conidia, however. Many species are beneficial to humans. A few cause diseases, such as athlete's foot and candidiasis. **EXAMPLES:** *Trichophyton, Candida, Aspergillus, Penicillium.*

Kingdom Plantae

Plants are generally nonmotile, multicellular, photosynthetic organisms. Their cells contain plastids and are surrounded by cell walls. Chlorophylls and carotenoids are present in chloroplasts. Most plants have specialized tissues and organs. Reproduction may be asexual or sexual. Sexual reproduction in plants involves an alternation of generations with multicellular diploid (sporophyte) and multicellular haploid (gametophyte) stages.

Division Bryophyta The bryophytes are small multicellular plants that lack xylem and phloem, and do not have true leaves, stems, or roots. Bryophytes are found usually in moist areas, and water is needed for fertilization. The gametophyte generation is dominant; the sporophyte generation is reduced in size and is dependent on the gametophyte. Dispersal is by means of spores.

Class Musci In mosses, the gametophyte generation consists of small, erect plants that have tiny leaf-like structures arranged spirally around a stalk. **EXAMPLES:** *Sphagnum, Polytrichum.*

Class Hepaticae In liverworts, the gametophytes consist of flattened or leaflike structures. **EXAMPLES:** *Marchantia, Riccia.*

Class *Antherocerotae* In hornworts, the gameto-phyte is thalluslike; the sporophyte is cylindrical. **EXAMPLE:** *Anthoceros.*

Division Tracheophyta The vascular plants contain xylem and phloem and have true leaves, stems, and roots. The sporophyte generation is dominant, and the gametophyte generation is greatly reduced. Chlorophylls *a* and *b* are present, and food is stored as starch in plastids. Tracheophytes include most modern-day plants.

Subdivision Psilophyta In whisk ferns, the highly branched vascular stems lack true leaves and roots. Whisk ferns are rare plants that are found mainly in warm regions. **EXAMPLE:** *Psilotum.*

Subdivision Lycophyta Club mosses have small leaves arranged in a spiral. Spores are found at the tips of some branches in conelike strobili. **EXAMPLES:** *Lycopodium, Selaginella.*

Subdivision Sphenophyta Horsetails have small leaves arranged in whorls at specific points along the stems. Conelike strobili form at the ends of some stems. **EXAMPLE:** *Equisetum.*

Subdivision Pterophyta This group includes the ferns, gymnosperms, and angiosperms. These plants have relatively large expanded leaves or are derived from plants with leaves of that type.

Class *Filicineae* Ferns have fronds that grow up from horizontal underground stems. Sori are found on the backs of the leaflets of some fronds. The independent gametophyte generation consists of a small prothallus. The sperm are motile, and water is required for fertilization. **EXAMPLES:** *Polypodium, Dryopteris, Osmunda.*

Class *Gymnospermae* Gymnosperms are the plants that bear seeds not enclosed in a fruit. The tiny gametophytes grow on the dominant sporophyte. Sperm are enclosed in a pollen tube, so water is not needed for fertilization.

Subclass Coniferophyta Conifers, or evergreens, are cone-bearing trees with needlelike or scalelike leaves. **EXAMPLES:** pines *(Pinus)*, spruce *(Picea)*, hemlocks *(Tsuga)*, firs *(Abies)*, redwoods *(Sequoia).*

Subclass Cycadophyta Cycads are tropical, palmlike gymnosperms. **EXAMPLES:** *Cycas, Zamia.*

Subclass Ginkgophyta Ginkgo, or maidenhair, trees, have fan-shaped leaves. The only surviving species is *Ginkgo biloba.*

Class *Angiospermae* Angiosperms are flowering plants whose seeds are enclosed in an ovary that ripens into a fruit. The tiny gametophytes grow on the dominant sporophyte. Sperm are enclosed in a pollen tube so that water is not needed for fertilization.

Subclass Monocotyledonae Monocots have an embryo with a single cotyledon, leaves with parallel veins, flower parts in threes or sixes, and vascular bundles scattered throughout the stem tissue. They are primarily herbaceous plants. **EXAMPLES:** grasses, including rye *(Secale)*, corn *(Zea)*, and wheat *(Triticum);* lilies *(Lilium)*, tulips *(Tulipa);* orchids *(Orchis).*

Subclass Dicotyledonae Dicots have an embryo with two cotyledons, veins of leaves in the form of a network, flower parts in fours or fives, and vascular tissue organized in a concentric ring. They include both herbaceous and woody plants. **EXAMPLES:** oaks *(Quercus, Lithocarpus)*, maples *(Acer)*, magnolias *(Magnolia)*, cucumbers *(Cucumis)*, carrots *(Daucus)*, roses *(Rosa).*

Kingdom Animalia

Animals are multicellular, heterotrophic organisms with specialized tissues. Most are motile. Their cells are eukaryotic and lack cell walls. Reproduction is mainly sexual.

Phylum Porifera *Sponges* are sessile, aquatic animals; most are marine. Their asymmetrical bodies have two cell layers and are pierced by pores; they are stiffened by skeletal elements called spicules. Reproduction is both asexual and sexual. **EXAMPLES:** *Grantia, Scypha, Euplectella.*

Phylum Cnidaria In *cnidarians*, the radially symmetrical body is saclike and is made up of two cell layers. There are two body forms—the polyp and the medusa. The digestive cavity has a single opening surrounded by tentacles containing cnidoblasts—specialized stinging cells. Cnidarians are all aquatic; most are marine. Some cnidarians, such as corals, are colonial. Reproduction is sexual in the medusa stage and asexual in the polyp stage. **EXAMPLES:** hydra *(Hydra)*, jellyfish *(Aurelia, Obelia, Physalia)*, corals *(Gorgonia)*, sea anemones *(Actinia).*

Phylum Platyhelminthes The *flatworms* have flattened, bilaterally symmetrical bodies made up of three tissue layers. The digestive system has only one opening.

Class Turbellaria These are free-living flatworms with eyespots. **EXAMPLES:** *Planaria, Dugesia.*

Class Trematoda Flukes are parasitic flatworms, usually with suckers. **EXAMPLES:** *Schistosoma, Fasciola.*

Class Cestoda Tapeworms are parasitic flatworms without digestive systems. **EXAMPLE:** *Taenia.*

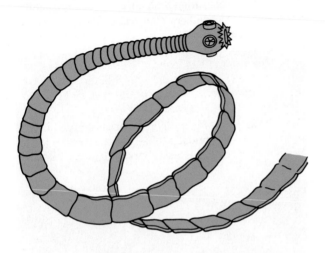

Phylum Nematoda Roundworms have long, cylindrical bodies; there is a digestive system with both a mouth and an anus. Most are parasitic. **EXAMPLES:** *Ascaris, Necatur, Trichinella.*

Phylum Annelida Segmented worms have a body made up of many similar segments. They have a well-developed coelom, a complete digestive tract, a closed circulatory system, and a ventral nervous system.

Class Polychaeta These include mostly marine worms. They have a well-developed head. **EXAMPLE:** *Nereis.*

Class Oligochaeta This class includes terrestrial and aquatic worms. Members of this group, including earthworms, have poorly developed heads. **EXAMPLES:** *Lumbricus, Tubifex.*

Class Hirudinea Leeches are parasitic annelids with suckers at one or both ends of the body. **EXAMPLE:** *Hirudo.*

Phylum Mollusca Mollusks have a soft, unsegmented body, often with a muscular foot, mantle, and radula. The digestive, circulatory, and nervous systems are well developed.

Class Bivalvia Bivalves include clams, oysters, mussels, and scallops. These mollusks have a two-part, hinged shell and no head or radula. **EXAMPLES:** *Mytilus, Pecten, Teredo.*

Class Gastropoda Gastropods include snails, slugs, and whelks. These mollusks have a head with tentacles; most have a spiral shell. **EXAMPLES:** *Limax, Helix, Busycon.*

Class Cephalopoda Cephalopods have a large head surrounded by arms, or tentacles. The octopus has no shell, the squid has an internal shell, and the nautilus has an external shell. The nervous system is particularly well-developed. **EXAMPLES:** octopus *(Octopus),* squid *(Loligo),* nautilus *(Nautilus).*

Phylum Arthropoda Arthropods have a segmented body with paired, jointed appendages and an exoskeleton composed of chitin.

Class Crustacea Crustaceans have two pairs of antennae. Most are aquatic and respiration is by gills. **EXAMPLES:** lobsters *(Homarus),* crabs *(Cancer),* crayfish *(Cambarus),* water fleas *(Cyclops, Daphnia).*

Class Chilopoda Centipedes have one pair of antennae, many body segments, and one pair of legs on most body segments. **EXAMPLE:** *Scolopendra.*

Class Diplopoda Millipedes have one pair of antennae, many body segments, and two pairs of legs on most body segments. **EXAMPLE:** *Glomeris.*

Class Arachnida Arachnids have no antennae, two body regions, four pairs of legs, and book lungs. **EXAMPLES:** spiders *(Argiope),* scorpions *(Chelifer).*

Class Insecta Insects have one pair of antennae, three body regions, three pairs of legs, and tracheal respiration; many have two pairs of wings. Group includes flies, ants, beetles, fleas, lice, bees, and roaches. (See pages 722–723 for a table of insect classification.)

Phylum Echinodermata Echinoderms have a water-vascular system, an internal skeleton, and a spiny skin. Adults are radially symmetrical. All are marine. **EXAMPLES:** starfish *(Asterias)*, sea urchins *(Arbacia)*, sea cucumbers *(Cucumaria)*, sand dollars *(Echinarachnius)*.

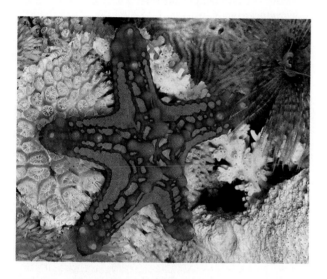

Phylum Chordata At some stage of development chordates have a notochord, paired gill slits, and a dorsal, hollow nerve cord.

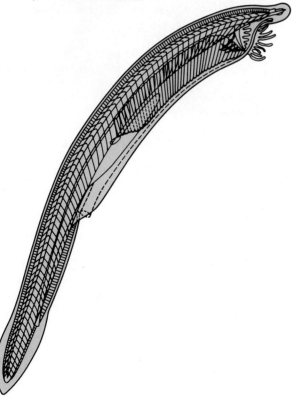

Subphylum Urochordata Adult tunicates are soft, saclike, sessile, marine animals. Larvae are free-swimming. **EXAMPLES:** *Ciona, Appendicularia.*

Subphylum Cephalochordata Lancelets are small, fishlike, marine animals. A notochord is present in adults. They have prominent gill slits. **EXAMPLE:** *Branchiostoma.*

Subphylum Vertebrata Vertebrates have an enlarged brain and a spinal column made up of vertebrae that enclose the dorsal nerve cord.

Class Cephalaspidomorphi The lampreys have skeletons made of cartilage, snakelike bodies, and no scales. They lack true jaws and retain their notochord throughout their life. **EXAMPLE:** *Petromyzon.*

Class Myxini The hagfishes, another type of jawless fish, are found only in salt water. They also have cartilaginous skeletons, snakelike bodies, and smooth skins without scales. **EXAMPLE:** *Myxine.*

Class Chondrichthyes The cartilaginous fishes have a skeleton composed of cartilage, movable jaws, scales, and fins. **EXAMPLES:** sharks *(Squalus)*, skates *(Raja)*.

Class Osteichthyes The bony fishes have a skeleton made of bone, movable jaws, overlapping scales, paired fins, and an air bladder. **EXAMPLES:** salmons and trouts *(Salmo)*, carps *(Cyprinus)*, perches *(Perca)*, codfish *(Gadus)*.

Class Amphibia Most amphibians have moist, smooth, scaleless skin and four limbs. Water is needed for reproduction. Aquatic larvae have gills and undergo metamorphosis. Adults are usually terrestrial and have lungs and a three-chambered heart. **EXAMPLES:** frogs *(Rana)*, toads *(Bufo)*, salamanders *(Necturus, Triturus)*.

Class Reptilia The reptiles have dry skin and a scale-covered body with four limbs (absent in snakes). Fertilization is internal. Their eggs have a leathery shell and protective membranes. Most reptiles live and reproduce on land. They have lungs and a three-chambered heart with a partially divided ventricle. **EXAMPLES:** turtles *(Chelydra, Terrapene)*, crocodiles *(Crocodylus)*, alligators *(Alligator)*, snakes *(Crotalus)*.

Class Aves Birds have feathers and their front limbs are wings. Their eggs have a hard shell. They have a four-chambered heart and are warm-blooded. **EXAMPLES:** robins and thrushes *(Turdus)*, chickens *(Gallus)*, ducks *(Anas)*, sparrows *(Passer, Melospiza)*, starlings *(Sturnus)*.

Class Mammalia Mammals nourish their young with milk produced by mammary glands. Their body covering is hair or fur. They have a four-chambered heart and are warm-blooded.

Subclass Prototheria Monotremes are egg-laying mammals. **EXAMPLES:** duckbill platypus *(Ornithorhynchus)*, spiny anteater *(Tachyglossus)*.

Subclass Metatheria Marsupials are pouched mammals, found mainly in Australia. **EXAMPLES:** kangaroos *(Macropus)*, opossums *(Didelphis)*, koalas *(Phascolarctos)*.

Subclass Eutheria The placental mammals include most living mammals. Developing embryos receive nourishment from the mother's circulatory system by means of a structure called the placenta.

Order Insectivora moles *(Scalopus)*, shrews*(Sorex)*

Order Rodentia rats *(Rattus)*, mice *(Mus)*, squirrels *(Sciurus)*

Order Lagomorpha rabbits *(Sylvilagus)*, hares *(Lepus)*

Order Chiroptera bats *(Myotis)*

Order Pinnipedia walruses *(Odobenus)*, sea lions *(Zalophus, Otaria)*, seals *(Arctocephalus, Callorhinus, Phoca)*

Order Cetacea whales *(Balaena)*, dolphins *(Delphinus)*, porpoises *(Phocaena)*

Order Sirenia manatees *(Trichechus)*, dugongs *(Dugong)*

Order Edentata anteaters *(Myrmecophaga)*, armadillos *(Dasypus)*

Order Proboscidea elephants *(Elephas, Loxodonta)*

Order Artiodactyla camels *(Camelus)*, sheep *(Ovis)*, pigs *(Sus)*, cattle *(Bos)*

Order Perissodactyla horses *(Equus)*, rhinoceroses *(Rhinoceros)*

Order Carnivora cats *(Felis)*, dogs *(Canis)*, bears *(Ursus)*, raccoons *(Procyon)*

Order Primates humans *(Homo)*, chimpanzees *(Pan)*, orangutans *(Pongo)*, monkeys *(Macacus)*

Appendix G: Graphic Organization

In your study of biology, you will learn many new facts to increase your understanding of the world around you. But, more than simply a collection of facts, the science of biology is a dynamic field in which, each day, scientists combine new information with prior knowledge to gain new insights into the living world.

How do scientists do this? They train themselves to step back from the individual facts and look at the "big picture." Have you ever seen an aerial view of a city at rush hour? If so, then you understand how useful the "big picture" can be in making sense of something complex and ever-changing.

One way to develop a "big picture" of each topic that you study is to organize information in a visual fashion, using what is known as a **graphic organizer.** Think of a graphic organizer as a visual representation of a topic that emphasizes relationships between concepts or data. A good graphic organizer can show at a glance key information and relationships that are not apparent in a verbal description. By constructing and using graphic organizers, you will improve your ability to understand, summarize, and interrelate biological information. Some graphic organizers that you may find useful in this course are explained below.

Flow Chart

A biological process or sequence of events can be depicted in a flow chart like the one below.

Problem: To start a car

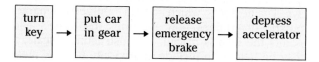

Flow charts can be used to outline the procedures of an experiment or to break down a complex process into its component steps.

Compare/Contrast Matrix

To compare and contrast two or more items, the graphic organizer shown in the next column can be used. Use this organizer to clarify differences between similar items and to analyze opposing viewpoints on a controversial issue.

Problem: How do compact disks compare with vinyl records?

Characteristic	Compact Disk	Record
cost	$15–$20	$10
sound quality	excellent	good
durability	excellent	fair
availability	good and improving	good, but decreasing

Word Map

When a new term is introduced, it may help to define it visually, in relation to other terms. This can be done in the following manner.

Problem: To define the term *bicycle*

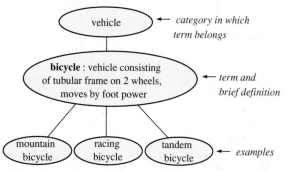

Notice that the term being defined is placed in an oval in the center of the map and a brief definition is given. The general category in which the term belongs is written above it, and specific examples are written below.

Depending on the term, a slightly different type of word map may be useful. In this type of word map, instead of including examples, components are listed in the third level of ovals, as shown below.

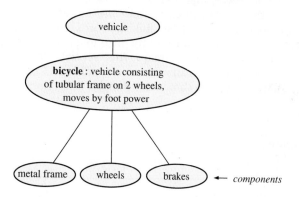

Word maps are useful for gaining a complete understanding of an unfamiliar term and for exploring how a term relates to both larger and smaller concepts.

Concept Map

A concept map is a useful graphic tool for organizing information on an entire topic. Concept maps emphasize relationships between the important concepts of a topic in a way that can be easily modified as you gather additional information.

A concept map is constructed by placing *concept words* (usually nouns) in ovals and connecting them with *linking words,* which are written along lines extending between the ovals. The most general concept word is placed in an oval at the top of the map, and the words become more specific as you move downward. This is shown in the concept map below.

Problem: To organize information on the topic of *mammals.*

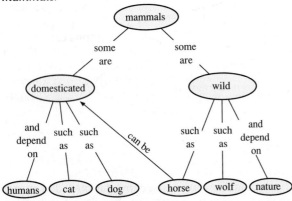

Note how the concept words flow from general to specific in the example above. Note also how each set of linking words describes the relationship between the two concept words it connects. If you follow any string of concept and linking words down the map, it reads like a sentence. There is one set of linking words, however, that does not follow the downward flow—the words *can be* between the concepts *horse* and *domesticated.* These linking words connect a concept from one branch of the map to a concept on another branch of the map. This special type of linking word is often known as a *cross-linkage.* Cross-linkages are used to show more complex interrelationships among concepts. Some cross-linkages are designated with arrows to show the direction of the connection.

To construct your own concept map, follow these guidelines.

1. List all the concepts to be mapped.
2. Pick out the main concept. Rank the remaining concepts from most general to most specific. Group together related concepts.
3. Arrange the concepts in a downward, branching structure. (It may be helpful to write each term on a separate index card and then arrange the cards in a branching structure.)
4. Link related concepts and choose appropriate linking words.
5. Look for places where cross-linkages can be drawn.

Concept maps are useful for summarizing or for clarifying information on a complex topic (such as some sections or chapters in your textbook). They are also helpful study aids that can be used to review a topic for an examination. In addition, concept maps may help you to organize your notes before you write a report.

Concept maps are dynamic tools. Once you have constructed one, you can alter it or add to it as you learn more about a particular topic. Furthermore, by linking individual concept maps together, you can begin to develop an overall picture of how broad topics are interrelated.

Scale

A scale can be used to put several items in a sequence with respect to a single characteristic, such as size or age. The degree to which an item exhibits the characteristic determines how far from the scale's end points the item is placed. In constructing a scale, it may be helpful to include appropriate units of measurement along the scale. For example, decibel units could be written along the scale shown below. A scale is useful for ordering items based on a specific characteristic or for showing a chronology of events, as in a timeline.

Problem: Order these everyday sounds from softest to loudest.

Line Graph

One way to depict a numerical relationship between two variables is with a line graph, as in the following example.

Problem: What is the relationship between plant size and light exposure?

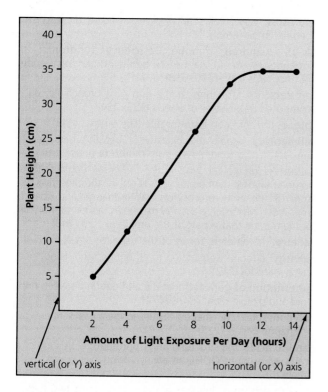

vertical (or Y) axis   horizontal (or X) axis

Line graphs can be used to depict data collected in experiments where one quantity changes in response either to time or to changes in another quantity. The data are plotted as individual points, which are then connected to form a continuous line.

Bar Graph

Bar graphs are useful for depicting data collected in a number of discrete but related categories. You can see at a glance how the categories compare with respect to the characteristic for which the data were collected. For each category, the data are plotted as a bar of a particular height, which is determined by a numerical scale along the vertical axis.

By presenting related sets of data side by side, a bar graph makes comparing data easy. This is shown in the following example.

Problem: How much precipitation fell in each summer month?

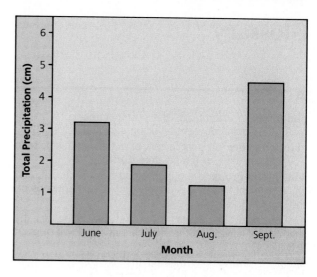

Circle Graph

In addition to bar graphs, circle graphs can also depict related sets of data in discrete categories. Unlike bar graphs, however, circle graphs can be used only when *all* of the categories that comprise a particular subject are represented. Circle graphs are sometimes called pie graphs because they resemble a pie cut into slices, as you can see in the example below.

Problem: How do I spend my time on a typical weekday?

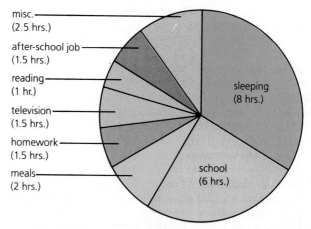

Circle graphs are useful for showing how something is divided into components, when each component has a numerical value that describes it. Each triangular section, or slice of the pie, represents one component. The size of each section is determined by its numerical value. Together, all of the sections should fill the circle completely.

Glossary

A

abdomen: in *arthropods,* the posterior region; in *mammals,* the region between the diaphragm and pelvis (709)

abiotic factors: physical factors of the environment, such as water, air, light, or temperature (820)

ABO blood group: a group of blood types (A, B, AB, and O), each identified by the presence of certain antigens on the surface of red blood cells (206)

abscisic acid: an organic compound that influences the shedding of leaves and the seasonal slowing down of plant activities (382)

absolute dating: any method that enables scientists to find out how long ago an event occurred (575)

absorption: the passage of materials across a cell membrane into the cell; the process by which usable materials are taken into an organism (155)

absorption spectrum: the different colors, or wavelengths, of light absorbed by each pigment in photosynthesis (341)

acetyl CoA: a compound produced during pyruvic acid breakdown by the combination of an acetyl group with coenzyme A (115)

acid: any compound that produces hydrogen ions in water solution (48)

Acrasiomycota: a protist phylum; cellular slime molds; life cycle includes a stage as separate ameboid cells and a stage as a pseudoplasmodium—an aggregate of cells (652)

active immunity: a type of acquired immunity in which the body produces its own antibodies to attack a particular antigen (205)

active site: the region on the surface of an enzyme where substrate molecules attach, thus enabling a reaction (69)

active transport: a process in which the movement of materials across a cell membrane requires the expenditure of cellular energy (96)

adaptation: any kind of inherited trait that improves the chances of survival and reproduction for an organism (603)

adaptive radiation: the process by which a species evolves into a number of different species, each occupying a new environment (615)

addition: the breaking-off of a segment of a chromosome and its attachment to the homologous chromosome (547)

adenine: a nitrogenous base found in DNA and RNA (526)

adhesion: the attraction between molecules of two different substances (59)

ADP (adenosine diphosphate): the lower-energy compound remaining after one phosphate group is removed from ATP (108)

adrenal glands: the endocrine glands that secrete hormones that help the body deal with stress (324)

aerobic respiration: respiration requiring the presence of free oxygen, in which glucose is completely oxidized to carbon dioxide and water (112)

aerosols: very small solid particles or liquid droplets suspended in air (869)

AIDS—Acquired Immune Deficiency Syndrome: an immune system disease; caused by the human immunodeficiency virus (HIV) (210, 658)

air sacs: the structures at the end of a bronchiole; each composed of a cluster of alveoli (223, 764)

algae: the common term for plantlike protists (646)

alimentary canal: the digestive tube; the passageway through which food moves from mouth to anus (158)

allantois (uh LAN tuh wis)**:** in *bird and reptile eggs,* a saclike extraembryonic membrane; grows out of the digestive system of the embryo; controls gas exchange and collects metabolic wastes; in *placental mammals,* an extraembryonic membrane that is part of the umbilical cord (448)

alleles: the different forms of the gene for a trait (502)

allergy: a rapid overreaction to an antigen that is not normally harmful (212)

alternation of generations: the alternation between haploid and diploid plant forms (474)

alveoli: small, cup-shaped cavities in the air sacs where gas exchange occurs (226)

amino acids: the structural unit of proteins; consisting of a carboxyl group (COOH), an amino group (NH_2), and a side chain (66)

amino group: a chemical group consisting of two hydrogen atoms and one nitrogen atom (NH_2), found in amino acids (66)

amniocentesis: a technique used to detect genetic disorders in a fetus; a long needle is used to draw out fluid from the amniotic sac in which the fetus lives (553)

amnion: in both shelled eggs and mammals, a fluid-filled extraembryonic sac that surrounds the embryo, provides a watery environment, and protects the embryo (448)

amniotic fluid: the fluid that fills the amnion (465)

Amphibia: a class of water- and land-dwelling vertebrates having moist, smooth skin and four limbs; need water for reproduction; amphibians (743)

anaerobic respiration: respiration in the absence of free oxygen, in which glucose is partially oxidized (112)

anal pore: the opening through which indigestible wastes are ejected from a paramecium (156)

analogous structures: structures found in different types of organisms that are similar in function or outward appearance but dissimilar in basic structure or embryological development (582)

anaphase: the stage of mitosis during which the daughter chromosomes move to opposite poles (400)

anemia: a condition in which a person has too few red blood cells or an insufficient amount of hemoglobin (197)

angiosperms: flowering plants (473, 675)

Animalia: one of the six kingdoms, composed of multicellular, usually motile, heterotrophic organisms; animals (135, 683)

Annelida: a phylum of animals with bodies made up of many similar segments; segmented worms (138, 696)

anterior: pertaining to the front, or head, end of a bilaterally symmetrical animal (684)

anther: the saclike structure of a stamen in which pollen grains are produced (481)

antheridium: the male gametophyte in mosses (476)

anthropology (an thruh PAHL uh jee): the branch of science that traces the development of the human species (773)

antibodies: proteins in the blood that bind to help destroy foreign substances in the body (196)

anticodon: a sequence of three bases of a tRNA molecule that pairs with the complementary three-nucleotide codon of an mRNA molecule during protein synthesis (531)

antigen (ANT uh jin): any substance that can cause an immune response (202)

anus: the opening of the digestive tube through which undigested materials are eliminated from the body (158)

aorta: the largest artery of the body (180)

appendicitis: inflammation of the appendix (165)

appendicular skeleton: the division of the human skeleton that includes the arms, legs, pectoral girdle, and pelvic girdle (260)

appendix: a small, fingerlike pouch found where the small intestine joins the large intestine (165)

Arachnida (uh RAK nih duh): a class of arthropods having no antennae, two body regions, four pairs of legs, and book lungs; includes spiders and scorpions; arachnids (714)

Archaebacteria (ahr kee bak TEER ee uh): one of the six kingdoms; made up of bacteria that live in environments that other organisms could not tolerate (134, 635)

archegonium: the female gametophyte in mosses (476)

arteries (AR tuh reez): blood vessels that carry blood away from the heart to the tissues and organs of the body (177)

Arthropoda: the phylum of animals having a segmented body with paired, jointed appendages and an exoskeleton; arthropods (138, 707)

Artiodactyla (art ee uh DAK tuh luh): an order of hoofed mammals having an even number of toes; includes camels and deer (769)

Ascomycota (as koh my KOH tuh): the largest phylum of fungi, both aquatic and terrestrial, which produce spores in asci; sac fungi (667)

ascus: serves as a sporangium; saclike (667)

asexual reproduction: reproduction with only one parent; offspring are identical to parent (7, 398)

asters: star-shaped structures formed during mitosis or meiosis in animal cells by fibers from the centrioles (400)

atomic number: the number of protons in the nucleus of an atom; the number that identifies an element (35)

atoms: the smallest particles of an element that have the properties of that element; consist of electrons, protons, and neutrons (34)

ATP (adenosine triphosphate): the compound in which energy released by cellular respiration is stored (109)

atria (AY tree uh): the two upper, thin-walled chambers of the heart; also called auricles (179)

auditory canal: the passage leading from the outer ear to the middle ear (302)

auditory nerve: the nerve that carries impulses from the inner ear to the brain during the process of hearing (304)

Australopithecus: a genus of fossil bipedal mammals found in southern Africa, showing more human than ape characteristics (774)

autoimmune disease: any disease in which the immune system of an individual fails to recognize certain of the body's cells as "self" and produces antibodies to combat them (212)

autonomic nervous system: a division of the peripheral nervous system consisting of motor fibers from the brain and spinal cord that serve the internal organs of the body; not under voluntary control (296)

autosomes: the chromosomes other than the sex chromosomes (518)

autotrophs: plants and other organisms that make their own food from inorganic substances (137, 150)

auxins: the hormones that affect the growth of all types of plant tissues (381)

Aves (AY veez): a class of warm-blooded vertebrates that have feathers, a four-chambered heart, front limbs as wings, and eggs with hard shells; birds (761)

A-V node (atrioventricular node): a small bundle of muscle cells at the base of the right atrium; triggers an impulse that causes contraction of the ventricles (181)

axial skeleton: the division of the human skeleton that includes the skull, vertebrae, ribs, and breastbone (260)

axon: a long, thin fiber that carries nerve impulses away from the cell body of a neuron (273)

B

bacillus: a rod-shaped bacterium (632)

bacteria (sing. bacterium): unicellular prokaryotic cells (133)

bacteriophages: viruses that attack bacterial cells (655)

ball-and-socket joints: a type of joint that permits movement in all directions (262)

barbs: thin, hairlike branches growing diagonally from the shaft of a feather (763)

barbules: threadlike branches of a feather made up of many tiny hooks, which provide support to adjacent barbs (763)

base: any compound that produces excess hydroxide ions when dissolved in water (48)

Basidiomycota (buh sid ee uh my KOH tuh): a phylum of terrestrial fungi that produce spores in a clublike structure called a basidium; club fungi (668)

B cells: a type of lymphocyte that is produced and matured in the bone marrow, then released into the circulatory and lymphatic systems (203)

behavior: the series of activities performed by an organism in response to stimuli (786)

benthos: organisms that live on the ocean floor (855)

bilateral symmetry: a type of symmetry in which there is only one longitudinal section that will divide the organism into two parts that are mirror images of each other (684)

bile: a fluid secretion of liver cells that aids in the breakdown of fats (164)

binary fission: the simplest form of asexual reproduction, in which a unicellular parent organism divides into two approximately equal cells (405)

binomial nomenclature: two-word system of identifying an organism (129)

biodegradable: organic wastes that can be broken down by bacteria and other organisms into simpler substances (867)

biogenesis: the theory that living organisms only originate from other living organisms (589)

biological magnification: the accumulation of substances in larger and larger quantities in the bodies of organisms at each higher level of a food chain (868)

biology: the study of living things (4)

biome: a large geographical region that has a particular type of climax community (845)

biosphere: the portion of the earth in which living things exist (819)

biotic factors: all the living organisms in an environment and their effect on other living things (820)

bipedal locomotion: walking upright on two legs (774)

Bivalvia: a major class of the phylum Mollusca; includes mollusks with two-part shells such as clams, oysters, and mussels (699)

blastocoel: the fluid-filled cavity in a blastula (442)

blastopore: the opening in a gastrula created by the gastrulation process; becomes an opening to the digestive system in the adult organism (443)

blastula: a stage of development in which the embryo consists of a single layer of cells surrounding a fluid-filled cavity (442)

bone: a type of connective tissue made up of living cells, connective tissue fibers, and inorganic compounds (259)

book lungs: respiratory organs of the arachnids, consisting of leaflike plates in which gas exchange occurs (715)

Bowman's capsule: a double-walled, cup-shaped structure surrounding the glomerulus (244)

brain: a group of specialized nerve cells that control and coordinate the activities of a nervous system (272)

brainstem: the pons, the medulla oblongata, and the midbrain (291)

bronchi: two cartilage-ringed tubes that branch off the trachea and enter the lungs (226)

bronchial tubes: the branches of the bronchi (226)

bronchioles: the finest branches of the bronchial tubes; each ends in an air sac (226)

Bryophyta: a phylum of land plants lacking specialized conducting tissues; these mosses, liverworts, and hornworts grow in moist areas; bryophytes (671)

budding: a type of asexual reproduction in which the parent organism divides into two unequal parts (406)

bulb: a short underground stem with thickened storage leaves; plants develop by vegetative reproduction (409)

C

calorie: the amount of heat that will raise the temperature of 1 g of water 1°C (151)

Calorie: unit used to measure the energy content of foods; equal to 1000 calories; also called a kilocalorie (151)

calyx: the complete circle of sepals in a flower (481)

cambium: in woody plants, a meristematic tissue (356)

camouflage: a protective adaptation that enables an organism to visually blend into the environment (610)

canals: in echinoderms, a system of channels connecting the sieve plate to the tube feet; part of the water vascular system (726)

canines: a type of tooth specialized for tearing food (767)

capillaries: microscopic blood vessels (176)

capillary action: the upward movement of a liquid in a tube of narrow diameter (59)

capsid: in viruses, the protein coat that surrounds the nucleic acid core of RNA or DNA (654)

carbohydrates: organic compounds of carbon, hydrogen, and oxygen in which the ratio of hydrogen to oxygen to carbon is 2:1:1 (60)

carbon cycle: the pathways by which carbon is circulated through the biosphere (833)

carboxyl group: the characteristic chemical group (COOH) of organic acids (62)

Carnivora: an order of flesh-eating mammals; includes cats, dogs, bears, and seals; carnivores (770)

carrying capacity: the maximum size of a population that can be supported by an environment (824)

cartilage: a type of flexible connective tissue (260)

cast: a type of fossil formed when a mold becomes filled with minerals and then hardens, producing a copy of the external features of an organism (573)

catalyst: a substance that increases the rate of a chemical reaction without being changed itself (68)

cell: the basic unit of structure and function in living things; the smallest units in living things that show the characteristics of life (78)

cell body: the part of a nerve cell that contains the nucleus; cyton (273)

cell cycle: the period of time from the beginning of one cell division to the next (397)

cell membrane: the structure that encloses the interior of a cell and controls the passage of materials into and out of the cell; plasma membrane (82)

cell plate: a structure formed during cytokinesis in a plant cell that divides the cell in half, forming part of the new cell walls of the daughter cells (402)

cellular respiration: the process by which the energy stored in food inside the cells is released (108)

cell wall: the rigid structure that encloses the cells of plants and various microorganisms; often composed of poly-saccharides (82)

central nervous system: the division of the nervous system that includes the brain and spinal cord (282)

centrifugation: a process in which materials of different densities are separated from each other by suspending them in a liquid (25)

centrioles: cylindrical organelles found near the nucleus in animal cells that are involved in mitosis (88, 400)

centromere: the region of attachment of two sister chromatids (400)

Cephalaspidomorphi (sef uh LASS peh duh morf ee)**:** the class of jawless fishes that includes the lampreys and hagfishes; the most primitive of all living vertebrates (736)

Cephalochordata (sef uh loh kor DAH tah)**:** a subphylum of chordates; small, fishlike, marine animals with a notochord present in adults; lancelets (733)

Cephalopoda: a major class of the phylum Mollusca; includes mollusks with little or no shell such as squids and octopuses (699)

cephalothorax (sef uh luh THOR aks)**:** the anterior portion of some arthropods, made up of the fused segments of the head and thorax (710)

cerebellum: a part of the human brain below the rear part of the cerebrum; coordinates voluntary movements (293)

cerebral cortex: the outer layer of the cerebrum; the gray matter of the brain (292)

cerebral hemispheres: the two halves of the cerebrum, which are partially separated by a deep groove (291)

cerebrum: the largest part of the human brain (291)

cervix: the narrow neck of the uterus (460)

Cestoda: the class of parasitic flatworms without digestive systems (693)

Cetacea (see TAYSH ee uh)**:** an order of nearly hairless marine mammals having paddlelike forelimbs; includes whales, dolphins, and porpoises; cetaceans (770)

cheliceras: in arachnids, a pair of fanglike appendages used to pierce prey; the first pair of appendages (714)

chemical bond: a force of attraction between atoms that holds them together in compounds (40)

chemical formula: a written representation of a compound in which a chemical symbol replaces each element (43)

chemical reaction: the process in which chemical bonds are broken and the atoms form new bonds, producing new substances (44)

chemiosmosis: process of ATP formation during aerobic respiration (116)

chemoautotrophs: the autotrophs that carry on chemosynthesis (340)

chemosynthesis: a form of autotrophic nutrition in which energy for synthesizing organic compounds is obtained from inorganic compounds rather than from light (349)

Chilopoda (ky LAHP uh duh)**:** a class of arthropods with one pair of antennae, many body segments, and one pair of legs on most body segments; centipedes (713)

Chiroptera (ky RAHP tuh ruh)**:** an order of mammals capable of real flight; bats (768)

chitin: the polysaccharide that makes up the exoskeleton of arthropods (254, 708)

chlorophylls: the major photosynthetic pigments of plants and algae (342)

Chlorophyta (klor AH fuh tuh)**:** a phylum of mainly aquatic plantlike protists; green algae (649)

chloroplasts: the plastids that contain chlorophyll; the sites of photosynthesis in eukaryotic cells (89, 343)

cholesterol: an essential compound found in most animal tissues; plays a role in the buildup of fatty deposits in arteries (63)

Chondrichthyes (kahn DRIK thee eez)**:** the cartilaginous fishes including sharks, rays, and skates (737)

Chordata: a phylum of animals having at some stage of development a notochord, paired gill slits, and a dorsal, hollow nerve chord; chordates (138, 733)

chorion: the membrane that surrounds the embryo and the other extraembryonic membranes in mammals, birds, and reptiles (448, 464)

chorionic villus sampling: a technique used by physicians to detect genetic disorders; a sample of the chorion, a part of the placenta, is removed for genetic analysis (553)

choroid coat: the darkly pigmented middle layer of the eye (300)

chromatid: one of the two strands of a doubled chromosome (400)

chromatin: the material of which chromosomes are composed (398)

chromatography: any technique that separates substances in a mixture on the basis of their chemical properties (26)

chromoplasts: the plastids that contain pigments other than chlorophyll (89)

chromosomal mutation: a change in chromosome structure, resulting in new gene combinations (546)

chromosomes: rodlike structures in cells that undergo division and that contain hereditary information of the organism (398)

Chrysophyta: a phylum of algaelike protists; chrysophytes are mostly unicellular and contain large amounts of yellow-brown pigment (648)

chyme: the thin, soupy liquid produced from food by the stomach (163)

cilia: short, hairlike organelles at the surface of a cell, with the capacity for movement (88, 255)

Ciliophora: a phylum containing the most complex protozoa, which have an abundance of hairlike cilia; ciliates (644)

circadian rhythms: the physiological or behavioral cycles that repeat approximately every 24 hours (798)

circulatory system: a system that links the cells of a complex organism with its environment (173)

class: a group of related orders (128)

cleavage: in a fertilized egg, the first series of cell divisions that occur without growth and continue until the cells of the embryo are reduced to the size of the cells of an adult organism (442)

climax community: a mature, stable community that is the final stage of ecological succession (836)

cloaca: in *reptiles, birds, amphibians,* and in many *fishes,* the cavity into which both the intestinal and genitourinary tracts empty; in some *vertebrates,* a cavity that serves as a duct for excretion, respiration, and reproduction (745)

clone: a group of genetically identical organisms produced by the division of a single cell (559)

closed circulatory system: a system in which the blood is always contained within tubes or vessels in the body (175)

clotting: the solidification of blood (199)

club mosses: small, spore-dispersing tracheophytes with true roots, stems, and leaves (672)

Cnidaria: a phylum of simple aquatic invertebrates that have a mouth, tentacles, and cnidoblasts; includes hydras, jellyfishes, and corals (138, 687)

cnidoblasts: the stinging cells found in cnidarians; used for defense and capturing food (688)

coacervates: according to the heterotroph hypothesis, an aggregate of large proteinlike molecules; thought to have developed into the first forms of life on the primitive earth (592)

coccus: a spherical bacterium (632)

cochlea: the organ of hearing, found in the inner ear, consisting of coiled, liquid-filled tubes (304)

codominance: a type of inheritance in which two dominant alleles are expressed at the same time without blending of traits (510)

codon: a group of three bases in an mRNA molecule that specifies a particular amino acid (530)

coelom: The fluid-filled body cavity between the body wall and the digestive tube in most multicellular animals (697)

coenzymes: the nonprotein, organic substances necessary to the functioning of particular enzymes (71)

coevolution: when two or more species can evolve through cooperative or competitive adaptations (616)

cohesion: the force of attraction between molecules of the same substance (58)

Coleoptera (kohl ee AHP tuh ruh)**:** the largest insect order, having front wings modified to form a horny covering for hind wings; beetles (720)

collagen: a fibrous structural protein that is a constituent of connective tissue (259)

collar cells: the flagellated cells found in the inner layer of a sponge (686)

colloidal dispersion: a mixture in which the solute particles are larger than molecules or ions, but are too small to settle out (47)

color blindness: a sex-linked trait in which an individual cannot perceive certain colors (520)

commensalism: a type of symbiotic relationship in which one organism benefits from the association and the other is not affected (825)

community: all the populations of different organisms within a given area (823)

complement system: a series of enzymes in blood that catalyze reactions that help destroy invading cells (204)

complete metamorphosis: the type of development in most insects; involves the stages of larva, pupa, and adult (719)

compound: substance made of two or more kinds of atoms combined in different proportions (34)

compound leaf: a leaf in which the blade is divided into several parts, or leaflets, that are attached to a petiole (367)

compound microscope: a microscope with two lenses (20)

concentration gradient: the difference in concentration between a region of greater concentration and one of lesser concentration (92)

conditioning: a simple form of learning in which behavior is changed through association (797)

cones: in the *retina of the eye,* the structures responsible for color vision (301); in *gymnosperms,* the seed-bearing or pollen-bearing structures (478)

conifers: subclass Coniferophyta of the gymnosperms; cone-bearing seed plants with needlelike or scalelike leaves (676)

conjugation: a form of sexual reproduction found in protists; individual organisms appear to be identical but are of different mating types (425)

connective tissue: a type of tissue that supports other body tissues and binds tissues and organs together (99)

consumers: the heterotrophs; the organisms that obtain nutrients from other organisms (828)

contour farming: a method of farming in which rows are plowed horizontally across slopes, following the contour of the land, and acting to reduce the flow of water down the slopes (874)

control: the setup in an experiment in which no factor was changed (15)

controlled experiment: an experiment set up in duplicate in which a single factor is changed in one setup but not the other (15)

convergent evolution: the evolution of outward similarities in organisms that are not closely related, because they have to meet similar problems in their habitats (616)

cork: a protective plant tissue that covers the surface of woody stems and roots (357)

cork cambium: the meristematic tissue that produces cork (356)

corm: a short, stout underground stem that contains stored food (409)

cornea: the transparent part of the sclera in the front of the eye through which light enters (300)

corolla: the complete circle of petals in a flower (481)

coronary circulation: the branch of the systemic circulation that supplies the heart muscle with blood (187)

corpus callosum: the bridgelike connection between the hemispheres of the brain (292)

corpus luteum: a progesterone-secreting yellow body in the ovary, formed when luteinizing hormone causes a ruptured follicle to fill with cells (462)

correlation: a process by which geologists determine the relative ages of rock layers and fossils in a local region (577)

cortex: the outer region or layer of a plant or animal organ or structure (362)

corticosteroids: a type of hormone produced by the adrenal cortex, synthesized from cholesterol (325)

cotyledon: a modified leaf of a seed plant embryo; often provides nourishment for the developing seedling (484)

covalent bond: a chemical bond that is formed by the sharing of electrons (40)

cover crops: crops planted over a whole field instead of in rows; used to prevent soil erosion (873)

cranial nerves: the nerves connected to the brain (295)

cranium: the upper part of the skull, which houses and protects the brain (260)

Cro-Magnons: a type of prehistoric human, considered to be the same as modern humans; replaced the Neanderthals about 35 000 years ago (777)

crop: in birds and many invertebrates, a thin-walled organ that temporarily stores food from the esophagus (158)

crop rotation: a method of farming in which different crops are grown on a field in successive years to prevent the reduction of soil nutrients (875)

crossing-over: the process in which pieces of homologous chromosomes are exchanged during synapsis in the first meiotic division (522)

Crustacea (krus TAY shuh)**:** a class of mostly aquatic arthropods having two pairs of antennae; includes lobsters, crabs, shrimp, and barnacles; crustaceans (710)

cuticle: the layer of cutin that covers plant epidermis (356)

cutting: any vegetative part of a plant used to produce a new plant by artificial vegetative reproduction (410)

cycads: subclass Cycadophyta of the gymnosperms; tropical plants resembling ferns or palm trees (676)

cyclin: protein that regulates the cell cycle (403)

cytokinesis: the division of the cytoplasm of the cell after mitosis or meiosis; the cell divides into two parts, each containing one of the newly formed nuclei and half of the other contents of the parent cell (398)

cytokinins: a type of plant hormone that stimulates cell division and growth (382)

cytoplasm: the watery material between the nucleus and the cell membrane of a cell (85)

cytosine: a nitrogenous base found in DNA and RNA (526)

D

dams: barriers built to hold back flowing water (874)

decomposers: organisms of decay (828)

dehydration synthesis: a type of reaction in which two molecules are bonded together by the removal of a water molecule (61)

deletion: a type of chromosomal alteration in which a portion of a chromosome and the genes it contains is lost (547)

dendrites: the short, branched parts of a neuron specialized for receiving nerve impulses and transmitting them to the cell bodies (273)

denitrifying bacteria: anaerobic bacteria that convert nitrates and nitrites to nitrogen gas, which is released into the atmosphere (831)

deoxyribose: a five-carbon sugar found in DNA (526)

dermis: the layer of skin beneath the epidermis, consisting of elastic connective tissue (247)

deserts: a type of biome in which there is too little rainfall to support trees or grasses; may show great variation in temperature between day and night (849)

Deuteromycota (do tur oh my KOH tuh)**:** the phylum that includes all fungi that are not known to have a sexual reproductive phase; *Penicillium* (669)

diabetes mellitus: a condition caused by an insufficient concentration of insulin in the blood (326)

diaphragm: the muscle that forms the floor of the chest cavity (225)

diastole: the period of relaxation of the heart (180)

diatomic molecule: a molecule formed when two atoms of the same element combine in a covalent bond, such as O_2 (40)

diatoms: members of the phylum Chrysophyta; unicellular, silica-shelled organisms found largely in salt water (648)

dicots: the plants whose seeds have two cotyledons (485)

differentiation: the series of changes that transforms unspecialized embryonic cells into the specialized cells, tissues, and organs that make up an adult organism (361, 444)

diffusion: the movement of molecules or particles from an area of greater concentration to an area of lesser concentration (92)

digestion: the breakdown of complex food materials into simpler forms that an organism can use (5, 155)

dihybrid cross: a genetic cross in which two pairs of contrasting traits are studied (508)

Dinoflagellata: a phylum of single-celled algae found mainly in the oceans (649)

dipeptide: the molecule formed when two amino acids are joined by a peptide bond (67)

diploid: having two sets of chromosomes, or all the homologous chromosomes that are characteristic of the species (419)

Diplopoda (dih PLAHP uh duh)**:** a class of arthropods with one pair of antennae, many body segments, and two pairs of legs on most body segments; millipedes (713)

Diptera (DIP tuh ruh): a widespread insect order having one pair of functional, membranous wings; includes flies (720)

directional selection: a type of natural selection in which an extreme phenotype becomes a favorable adaptation (612)

disaccharide: the molecule formed by the joining of two simple sugars (61)

disjunction: the separation of homologous chromosomes during anaphase I of meiosis (420)

disruptive selection: a rare type of natural selection in which two opposite phenotypes are favorable adaptations and the average phenotypes are unfavorable; creates two subpopulations (613)

DNA (deoxyribonucleic [dee AHK see ry boh noo klay ik] **acid):** the nucleic acid found in all the cells of an organism; the hereditary material passed on during reproduction (64)

dominance hierarchy: a ranking within a group of animals that is established through fighting or displays of aggression (803)

dominant: the inherited characteristic that appears in an organism (500)

dominant species: the species that exert the greatest effects on the environment and on other members of the community (836)

dormancy: a period during which growth and other metabolic activities stop or are severely reduced (487)

dorsal: pertaining to the upper side or the back of a bilaterally symmetrical animal (684)

double fertilization: in flowering plants, the fertilization of the egg and of the two polar nuclei to form the diploid zygote and the triploid endosperm nucleus, respectively (483)

Down syndrome: a disorder that results from an extra number 21 chromosome (552)

E

Echinodermata (ih ky nuh der MAH tuh): a phylum of marine animals having a water-vascular system, an internal skeleton, and a spiny skin; echinoderms (725)

ecological succession: the process by which an existing community is slowly replaced by another community (835)

ecology: the branch of biology that deals with the interactions among organisms and between organisms and their environment (820)

ecosystem: a community and the physical environment that it occupies (823)

ectoderm: the outer layer of cells in a simple animal or embryo; one of the germ layers of an animal embryo (443)

ectothermic (ek tuh THER mik): having a body temperature that varies with the temperature of the environment; cold-blooded (735)

Edentata (ee den TAH tuh): an order of mammals having only molars or no teeth at all; includes anteaters, sloths, and armadillos (769)

effector: a muscle or gland; responds to a stimulus (272)

ejaculation: a process by which involuntary muscular contractions force the semen through the urethra and out of the body (459)

electrons: negatively charged particles found in the spaces outside the nuclei of atoms; have much less mass than protons or neutrons (35)

electron transport chain: a series of oxidation-reduction reactions in which most of the energy produced from the breakdown of glucose is transferred to ATP (116)

electrophoresis (ih lek truh fuh REE sis): a technique for separating substances made up of particles that have an electrical charge (26)

elements: substances made entirely of one kind of atom (34)

elongation zone: in plants, a region behind the meristematic zone of the root, in which the cells produced in the meristematic zone grow longer (361)

embryo: a multicellular organism in the early stages of development (441)

embryonic induction: the process by which one group of cells (the organizer) induces another group of cells to differentiate (446)

embryo sac: the mature female gametophyte of a flowering plant (482)

endocrine glands: the ductless glands (314)

endocrine system: the system of the body that regulates overall metabolism, homeostasis, growth, and reproduction (314)

endocytosis: the process of transporting material into a cell by means of a vesicle (97)

endoderm: the inner layer of cells in a simple animal or embryo; one of the germ layers of an animal embryo (443)

endodermis: in plants, the innermost layer of the cortex of the root (362)

endoplasmic reticulum: a system of fluid-filled canals enclosed by membranes (85)

endoskeleton: a skeleton composed of bone and/or cartilage located within the body walls (254)

endosperm: the tissue that develops from the endosperm nucleus, often serving as a food supply for the plant embryo (483)

endospores: structures containing genetic material formed by bacteria and found in their cytoplasm when conditions for growth are unfavorable (632)

endosymbiosis: the condition in which one organism lives inside the cell of another to the benefit of both (89)

endothermic: having a body temperature that remains relatively constant regardless of the temperature of the environment; warm-blooded (735)

enhancer: a section of DNA that controls the access of an enzyme to a promoter (538)

entomology: the branch of biology that deals with the study of insects (720)

enzymes: protein catalysts that are necessary for most of the chemical reactions that occur in living cells (68)

epicotyl: the part of a plant embryo above the point of attachment of the cotyledons; gives rise to the terminal bud, leaves, and stem (485)

epidermis: in *plants,* a protective tissue that forms the outer layer of leaves, green stems, and roots (356); in *animals,* the outer layer of skin consisting of layers of tightly packed epithelial cells (246)

epididymis: a storage area for sperm on the upper, rear part of the testis (458)

epiglottis: a flap of tissue that covers the trachea during swallowing, so that food passes only into the esophagus (162)

epinephrine: a hormone produced by the adrenal medulla; a neurotransmitter produced by some nerve cells; adrenaline (324)

epithelial tissues: the tissues that cover body surfaces and line body cavities and organs (99)

erosion: the removal of soil by the action of wind and/or water (866)

esophagus: the tube that is the passageway for food from the mouth to the stomach (158)

estrogen: a hormone secreted by the ovaries that promotes development of female secondary sex characteristics and regulates the reproductive cycle (327)

ethylene: an organic compound that stimulates flowering in some plants and hastens the ripening of fruit (382)

Eubacteria (yoo bak TEER ee uh)**:** one of the six kingdoms; the larger of the two kingdoms of bacteria (134, 635–37)

Euglenophyta: a phylum of protists; euglenoids show both plantlike and animal-like characteristics (646)

eukaryotic cells: cells containing membrane-bound nuclei (79)

Eustachian tube: the tube extending between the middle ear and the throat that equalizes the pressure between the middle ear and the environment (303)

eutrophication: an accelerated aging process in a lake or pond, in which the body of water fills in with plant remains and is reduced in size (868)

evolution: the gradual change of allele frequencies found in a population (606)

excretion: the removal of waste substances from an organism (6, 237)

exhalation: the phase of breathing in which air is pushed out of the lungs (227)

exocrine glands: the glands that discharge their secretions into ducts (314)

exocytosis: movement of materials out of the cell by the reverse of endocytosis (97)

exon: a segment of DNA that codes for amino acids that will become part of a protein (537)

exoskeleton: a skeleton found on the outside of the body, enclosing the soft parts (254)

extensor: a muscle that extends a joint (264)

external fertilization: the process in which eggs are fertilized outside the body of the female (432)

extinct: the end of a species when the last individual of that species has died (580)

extraembryonic membrane: in shelled eggs of reptiles and birds, any one of four membranes outside the embryo but inside the shell (448)

F

F₂ (second filial) generation: the second generation produced in a breeding experiment (499)

facilitated diffusion: a process by which certain molecules diffuse quickly across a cell membrane (92)

family: a group of related genera (128)

farsighted: a vision condition that occurs because the eyeball is too short (301)

fatty acid: an organic molecule with two parts: a carbon chain, and one or more carboxyl groups (COOH); one of the end products of the digestion of fats (62)

feces: undigested and indigestible food material that is solidified in the large intestine and then eliminated (167)

fermentation: following glycolysis, the conversion of pyruvic acid to an end product with no further release of energy (113)

ferns: a type of spore-dispersing tracheophyte; Filicineae (476, 673)

fertilization: the fusion of the nuclei of the male and female gametes (418)

fertilizers: materials used to provide or replace soil nutrients (875)

fetoscopy: a technique that allows direct observation of the fetus and surrounding tissues (554)

fetus: the developing baby after about the second month of pregnancy (464)

fiber: indigestible materials, such as cellulose, found in the cell walls of fruits (153)

filament: the starlike part of a stamen that supports the anther (481)

first filial (F₁) generation: the first generation produced in a breeding experiment (499)

flagella: long, hairlike organelles at the surface of a cell, with the capacity for movement (256)

flexor: a muscle that bends a joint (264)

follicles: the structures in the ovaries in which the mature eggs develop (459)

food chain: a series of organisms through which food energy is passed (828)

food web: food chains that are interconnected at various points (828)

foot: a large, ventral, muscular structure that is used for locomotion in mollusks (699)

foramen magnum (fuh RAY men MAG num)**:** the opening in the skull where the spinal cord enters (774)

fossil: any trace or remains of an organism that has been preserved by natural processes (132, 571)

fossil record: the history of life as determined by the relative age of fossils (575)

frameshift mutation: gene mutation that involves the insertion or deletion of a nucleotide, thus changing the grouping of codons (548)

fraternal twins: two individuals formed when two eggs are fertilized at the same time; twins that are genetically different (467)

fruit: a structure that develops from the ovary and associated flower parts after fertilization; contains seeds (481)

Fungi: one of the six kingdoms; its members are saprobic or parasitic, mostly multicellular, and usually consist of filaments (135, 665)

G

gallbladder: the organ that stores bile produced by the liver (165)

gametes: the haploid cells that fuse with other haploid cells to form zygotes; the sperm cells or egg cells (417)

gametogenesis: the process by which gametes develop in the gonads (429)

gametophyte: a gamete-producing plant (474)

ganglion: a group of cell bodies and interneurons that switch, relay, and coordinate nerve impulses (282)

gas exchange: the process by which protist and animal cells get rid of excess carbon dioxide (219)

gastric juice: the digestive secretion of glands in the stomach, containing hydrochloric acid and pepsin (162)

Gastropoda: a major class of the phylum Mollusca; includes mollusks with a single shell, such as snails (699)

gastrovascular cavity: the internal body cavity of a cnidarian (157, 688)

gastrula: in animals, an early stage of embryonic development during which the second germ layer is formed (443)

gastrulation: the process in which the cells on one side of a blastula move inward to form the two-layered gastrula (443)

gemmules: asexual reproduction structures that form on some freshwater sponges (687)

gene: a distinct unit of hereditary material found in chromosomes; a sequence of nucleotides in DNA that codes for a particular tRNA, rRNA, or polypeptide (502)

gene mutation: a change in the sequence of the bases in a gene, which changes the structure of the polypeptide that the gene codes for (546)

gene pool: the total of all the alleles in a population (605)

gene therapy: the process of correcting genetic defects by transferring normal genes to cells that lack them (560)

genetic drift: a change in the gene pool of a small population that is brought about by chance (607)

genetic engineering: the process of producing altered DNA, usually by breaking a DNA molecule and inserting new genes (557)

genetic equilibrium: the condition in which allele frequencies do not change from one generation to the next (608)

genetic recombination: the formation of new combinations of alleles during sexual reproduction (607)

genetics: the branch of biology that studies the ways in which hereditary information is passed on from parents to offspring (498)

genome: all the genes possessed by an organism (561)

genotype: the genetic makeup of an individual (503)

genus: a group of closely related species (127)

geographic isolation: the first stage of speciation, in which a population of organisms is prevented from interbreeding with other populations of that species by a natural barrier (614)

geologic evolution: the process of continual change that the earth undergoes (571)

geologic time scale: a timetable of the earth's history constructed by geologists (578)

geotropism: the growth of a plant in response to the stimulus of gravity; roots of a plant generally grow down in the direction of the gravity force (383)

germ layers: the three embryonic cell layers—the ectoderm, mesoderm, and endoderm—that give rise to all tissues and organs of animals (444)

germ theory of disease: the idea that bacteria and other microorganisms can cause disease (637)

gestation: the length of pregnancy (465)

gibberellins: the hormones that affect plant growth as well as the development of fruits and seeds (382)

gills: in aquatic animals, thin layers of tissue, richly supplied with blood vessels, that are the respiratory organs (223, 712)

gill slits: a structure found in pairs in the throat region of all chordates during some part of their lives (734)

ginkgoes: subclass Ginkgophyta of the gymnosperms; the maidenhair trees with fan-shaped leaves—the only surviving species (676)

gizzard: in birds and many invertebrates, a thick-walled grinding organ that crushes food released from the crop (158, 765)

glands: organs made up of epithelial cells that specialize in the secretion of substances needed by the organism (314)

gliding joint: a joint that permits limited flexibility in all directions (262)

glomerulus (pl. **glomeruli**): a group of capillaries in the nephron of a kidney (244)

glucagon: a hormone secreted by the pancreas that increases the blood-glucose level (325)

glycolysis: the process of breaking down the glucose molecule into two three-carbon pyruvic acid molecules (112)

Golgi bodies: the organelles consisting of stacks of membranes forming flattened sacs in the cytoplasm, which serve as storage centers for proteins synthesized by cells (86)

gonads: in animals, the specialized organs in which gametes develop (326, 428)

gradualism: Darwin's theory of evolution, in which new species arise through gradual changes in their characteristics, and thus evolution occurs very slowly over millions of years (604)

grafting: a type of artificial vegetative propagation accomplished by permanently joining a part of one plant to another plant (411)

grana: stacks of thylakoids in plant chloroplasts (343)

grasslands: a type of biome in which there is not enough rainfall to support trees and the dominant form of vegetation is grasses; prairies (848)

ground tissues: the tissues involved in the production and storage of food and in the support of plants; parenchyma, collenchyma, and sclerenchyma (358)

growth: the process by which living organisms increase in size (6)

guanine: a nitrogenous base found in DNA and RNA (526)

guard cells: in leaves, pairs of specialized epidermal cells that regulate the opening and closing of the stomates (368)

gullet: in the paramecium, the part where food particles enter the cell (156)

guttation: the formation of water droplets at the edges, or tips, of leaves as a result of root pressure (378)

gymnosperms: a seed plant whose seeds are not enclosed within a fruit (473, 675)

H

habit: learned behavior that becomes automatic (797)

habitat: a particular part of the environment where an organism lives (826)

habituation: the simplest type of learning; the animal learns not to respond to repeated "unimportant" stimuli (797)

haploid: having only one chromosome from each pair of homologous chromosomes (419)

Hardy-Weinberg law: the principle that sexual reproduction alone does not affect allele frequencies in a population (608)

Haversian canal: a cavity in bone that contains the blood vessels and nerves that serve the osteocytes (259)

heart: the organ that pumps blood through the circulatory system (174)

helix: a shape like a coiled spring, used to describe the structure of DNA molecules (527)

Hemiptera (heh MIP tuh ruh)**:** a large order of insects—mostly terrestrial, some aquatic; bugs (720)

hemocyanin (hee moh SY uh nin)**:** a copper-containing respiratory pigment that aids in the transport of oxygen in some vertebrates (711)

hemoglobin: a substance that increases the amount of oxygen the blood can carry (175, 197)

hemophilia: a hereditary disease in which one or more of the clotting factors are missing from the blood (200)

hepatic-portal circulation: the branch of the systemic circulation that carries blood to the liver from the digestive tract (188)

herbaceous stems: plant stems that are soft, green, and juicy (363)

herbivores: animals that feed only on plants (824)

hermaphrodites: the individual organisms that possess both testes and ovaries (428)

heterotroph hypothesis: the hypothesis that the first organic compounds were formed by natural chemical processes on the primitive earth and that the first lifelike structures developed from coacervates and were heterotrophs (589)

heterotrophs: the organisms that cannot synthesize their own food and must obtain it ready-made (137, 150)

heterozygous: having two different alleles for a trait (503)

hinge joints: a type of joint that permits back-and-forth motion; e.g., at the elbow and knee (262)

Hirudinea: a major class of the phylum Annelida; includes the leeches (696)

histones: small groups of proteins around which DNA is wrapped to form chromatin (398)

HIV—human immunodeficiency virus: the virus that causes AIDS (210)

homeostasis: the condition of a stable internal environment in an organism (5)

homeotic genes: in fruit flies, the genes that control key events in the flies' development (539)

homologous chromosomes: a pair of chromosomes having the same size and shape and carrying alleles for the same traits (418)

homologous structures: structures found in different kinds of organisms that have the same basic arrangement of parts and a similar pattern of embryological development (582)

Homo sapiens: the species of modern humans (776)

homozygous: having two identical alleles for a trait (503)

hormones: the secretions of the endocrine glands (315)

horsetails: the spore-dispersing members of the tracheophytes, each having a hollow stem and a collar of small leaves (673)

human ecology: the study of the relationship between humans and their environment (864)

hybridization: mating of two organisms with dissimilar genetic characteristics (556)

hybrids: individuals that are heterozygous for particular traits; individuals produced by a cross between members of two closely related species (499)

hydrolysis: the process by which molecules are broken apart by the addition of water molecules (62)

hydrotropism: growth of plant roots toward water (383)

Hymenoptera (hy muh NAHP tuh ruh)**:** a large, varied order of colonial insects; includes bees, wasps, and ants (720)

hypersecretion: an excess of a hormone (319)

hypertonic solution: a solution whose concentration of solutes is higher than that of a cell placed in it (96)

hyphae (HY fee)**:** threadlike filaments, many of which make up the bodies of most fungi (665)

hypocotyl: the part of a plant embryo between the radicle and the point of attachment of the cotyledons (485)

hyposecretion: a deficiency of a hormone (319)

hypothalamus: the part of the brain located below the thalamus; controls body temperature, blood pressure, and emotions (291, 321)

hypothesis: a possible explanation for an observed set of facts (14)

hypotonic solution: a solution that contains a lower concentration of dissolved substances than that of a cell placed in it (95)

I

identical twins: two individuals formed when one fertilized egg divides at an early stage of development, producing two organisms with the same genetic makeup (467)

immovable joints: a type of joint in which the bones are fitted tightly together and cannot move (262)

immune response: the reaction of the immune system to the presence of foreign cells or molecules (202)

immunity: the ability of the body to resist a disease (202)

implantation: the fastening of the embryo to the wall of the uterus (463)

imprint: a type of fossil formed when an impression made in mud by a living thing is preserved when the mud is transformed into rock (573)

imprinting: in some animals, the forming of an attachment to an organism, object, or other environmental factor soon after hatching or birth (799)

impulses: messages carried by the nerve cells of a nervous system; regions of electrical and chemical changes that pass along the cell membrane of a neuron (272)

inbreeding: a breeding method in which closely related individuals are mated to retain or strengthen certain desirable traits (555)

incisors: a type of tooth specialized for cutting food (767)

incomplete dominance: a type of inheritance in which two contrasting alleles contribute to the individual a trait not exactly like either parent; blending inheritance (509)

incomplete metamorphosis: a type of development in some insects in which there is no larval stage (718)

index fossils: fossils that permit the relative dating of rocks within a narrow time span (578)

indicator: a substance that changes color when the pH goes above or below a certain value (50)

industrial melanism: the development of dark-colored organisms in a population exposed to industrial air pollution (618)

inferior vena cava: veins, some of the largest in the body, that return blood from the lower regions of the body into the right atrium of the heart (187)

inflammatory response: the result of a pathogen activating the second line of defense (201)

ingestion: the taking in of food from the environment (5)

inhalation: the phase of breathing in which air is drawn into the lungs (227)

innate behavior: behavior determined by heredity (790)

inorganic compounds: any type of compound that is not an organic compound; usually do not contain carbon (58)

Insecta: a class of arthropods having no antennae, three body regions, three pairs of legs, and tracheal respiration; insects (716)

Insectivora: an order of generally small, primitive mammals that feed mainly on insects; includes moles, shrews, and hedgehogs (768)

insight: the ability to create a solution to an unfamiliar problem without a period of trial and error (800)

instinct: a complex, inborn behavior pattern (793)

insulin: a hormone secreted by the pancreas that lowers blood glucose levels (315)

intercellular fluid: a fluid that helps move materials between the capillaries and the body cells (188)

interferon: a protein produced by body cells in response to an attack by viruses (202)

internal fertilization: the process in which eggs are fertilized inside the body of the female (433)

interneurons: the neurons that relay impulses from one neuron to another in the brain and spinal cord (274)

interphase: the stage of the cell reproductive cycle lasting from the end of one mitotic cycle to the beginning of the next (399)

interspecific competition: competition between members of two different species in an ecosystem (826)

intertidal zone: the area along the ocean shoreline that is covered by water at high tide and uncovered at low tide (855)

intestinal juice: a secretion of the cells of the walls of the small intestine, containing digestive enzymes (164)

intestine: the organ in which most digestion and the absorption of food occurs (158)

intraspecific competition: competition between members of the same species in an ecosystem (828)

intron: a segment of DNA that does not code for amino acids of a protein (537)

inversion: a type of chromosomal mutation in which a piece of chromosome is rotated, resulting in reversal of the order of the genes in that segment (547)

invertebrate: an animal without a backbone (683)

in vitro fertilization: the process of fertilization in a glass laboratory dish (463)

ion: an atom or group of atoms with an excess electrical charge (41)

ionic (i AHN ik) **bond:** the force of attraction between two ions in a chemical compound (42)

iris: the round, colored part of the eye formed from the choroid layer; controls the size of the pupil (300)

irritability: the capacity of a cell or organism to respond to stimuli (272)

islets of Langerhans: the endocrine portion of the pancreas, consisting of clusters of hormone-secreting cells (325)

isotonic solution: a solution that contains the same concentration of dissolved substances as does a living cell placed in it (95)

isotopes (I suh tohps): atoms that differ from other atoms of the same element by the number of neutrons in their nucleus (37)

J

joint: a point in the skeleton where bones meet (262)

K

karyotyping: a technique for examining the chromosome makeup of an individual (552)

kidneys: a pair of organs in vertebrates that excrete nitrogenous wastes and regulate the blood's chemical balance; produce urine (242)

kilocalorie: 1000 calories or 1 Calorie (151)

kingdom: a group of related phyla; the largest category in classification systems (128)

Koch's postulates: a set of rules to determine the specific bacterium causing a particular disease (638)

Krebs cycle: the series of chemical reactions that begins with the acetyl coenzyme A (CoA) formed from pyruvic acid (115)

L

labor: the slow, rhythmic contractions of the uterine muscles during childbirth (466)

lacteals: the small lymph vessels found in the center of a villus (164)

Lagomorpha (lag uh MOR fuh): an order of plant-eating mammals having short tails and two pairs of upper incisors, one behind the other; includes rabbits and hares (768)

large intestine: the final section of the digestive tract; reabsorbs water, absorbs vitamins, and eliminates undigested and indigestible material (165)

larva (pl. **larvae**): an early developmental stage of some animals after hatching; must undergo metamorphosis to reach the adult form (683)

larynx: the voice box; connects the pharynx with the trachea (225)

lateral bud: a bud in the upper angle where a leaf joins a stem; axillary bud (367)

lateral lines: lines that extend along each side of a shark to help sense vibration (738)

law of conservation of mass: the principle stating that mass can neither be created nor destroyed (44)

law of dominance: the principle of genetics stating that when organisms pure for contrasting traits are crossed, all their offspring will show the dominant trait (500)

law of independent assortment: the principle of genetics stating that different traits are inherited independently of one another (508)

law of probability: the principle stating that if there are several possible events that might happen, and no one of them is more likely to happen than any other, then they will happen in equal numbers over a large number of trials (504)

law of segregation: the genetic principle stating that the alleles of a gene occur in pairs and are separated from each other during meiosis and are recombined at fertilization (501)

layering: a type of artificial vegetative propagation, accomplished by covering part of a growing plant with soil (411)

learned behavior: behavior that develops as a result of experience (797)

leaves: the usually thin, flat outgrowths of stems; carry out photosynthesis (355)

lens: in the eye, the structure behind the iris that focuses light on the retina (300)

lenticels: the openings in cork tissues that allow the exchange of respiratory gases between the atmosphere and the plant tissues (367)

Lepidoptera (lep uh DAHP tuh ruh): an insect order having two pairs of broad, membranous wings; butterflies and moths; (720)

leucoplasts: the colorless plastids in which starch or other plant nutrients are stored (89)

leukocytes: the nucleated blood cells that protect the body from disease-causing organisms, such as bacteria and viruses; white blood cells (197)

lichen: an organism consisting of an alga or a blue-green bacterium and a fungus living together in symbiosis; they grow on soil, rocks, and tree trunks (669)

ligaments: the tough, fibrous bands of connective tissues that hold the bones together at movable joints (262)

light-dependent reactions: in photosynthesis, a series of reactions requiring light in which water or some other compound is oxidized and ATP and NADPH are produced (344)

light-independent reactions: the series of reactions in photosynthesis in which carbon fixation occurs and for which light is not required (344)

light microscope: any device that enables us to see small details in an object by enlarging the object (19)

light system: the mirror and diaphragm in a microscope (22)

limiting factor: a condition of the environment that limits the growth of a population, such as availability of food, water, space, or some other necessity (864)

linkage group: all the genes that are on the same chromosome (521)

lipids: the organic compounds other than carbohydrates, consisting of carbon, hydrogen, and oxygen; fats, oils, or waxes (62)

littoral zone: the area between the intertidal zone and the continental shelf; the water is relatively shallow, and light reaches the ocean floor (855)

liver: an organ that secretes bile and removes toxic substances from the blood (161)

lungs: in vertebrates, the organs specialized for the exchange of gases between the blood and the atmosphere (224)

lymph: intercellular fluid and proteins are called *lymph* once they are inside the lymphatic system (189)

lymphatic system: a system of vessels that return excess fluid and proteins from the intercellular spaces to the blood (188)

lymph nodes: lymphatic glands that play an important role in the body's defense against disease (189)

lymphocytes (LIM fuh syts)**:** a type of white blood cell that recognizes and destroys antigens present in the body tissue (197)

lysogenic cycle: the process that occurs when the phage's nucleic acid merges with the bacterial cell's DNA, and the new combination is transmitted through bacterial generations (656)

lysosomes: the small, saclike structures surrounded by single membranes and containing strong digestive or hydrolytic enzymes (86)

lytic cycle: the process in which a phage attacks a bacterial cell, uses it to reproduce, and then destroys it (655)

M

macrophages: giant white blood cells that can ingest large numbers of bacteria (201)

magnification: the ratio of the image size to the object size (19)

Malpighian tubules: the excretory organs of grasshoppers and other insects (240)

Mammalia: a class of warm-blooded vertebrates that have a four-chambered heart, are covered with hair or fur, and nourish their young with milk; mammals (766)

mandibles: the jaws of crustaceans that crush food by moving from side to side (710)

mantle: a fold of skin that surrounds the body organs in mollusks and contains glands that secrete the shell of shelled mollusks (699)

marrow: the soft tissue that fills the hollow spaces in bone (260)

marsupials: nonplacental mammals in which the fetus is born at a very immature stage and completes its development in a pouch on the mother's body (767)

mass number: the sum of the protons and neutrons in the nucleus of an atom (36)

maturation zone: the region behind the elongation zone of the root in which cells differentiate (361)

mechanical system: the structural parts of a microscope that hold the specimen and lenses and permit focusing of the image (20)

medulla oblongata: the part of the brain beneath the cerebellum and continuous with the spinal cord; controls involuntary activities (293)

medusa: the body form of free-swimming cnidarians (687)

meiosis: cell division in diploid cells that results in haploid cells; reduction division (418)

menstrual cycle: the hormone-controlled cycle in the human female, lasting about a month, in which an egg matures and is released from the ovary and the uterus prepares to receive it (460)

menstruation: the last stage of the menstrual cycle, marked by the shedding of some of the uterine lining, the unfertilized egg, and a small amount of blood through the vagina, which occurs about once a month in the human female (462)

meristematic tissues: plant tissues whose cells undergo, or are capable of, repeated cell division; meristems (356)

meristematic zone: a region of actively dividing cells just behind the root cap (361)

meristems: in plants, a region or tissue composed of cells that undergo or are capable of repeated cell division (356)

mesoderm: the germ layer between the endoderm and ectoderm (443)

mesoglea: the jellylike material, composed largely of protein, found between the ectoderm and endoderm layers of cnidarians (688)

mesophyll: a layer of photosynthetic tissue found between the epidermal layers of a leaf (368)

messenger RNA (mRNA): the type of RNA that carries the code for a polypeptide from DNA to the ribosomes where it is translated (530)

metabolism (muh TAB uh liz um)**:** all the chemical reactions occurring within the cells of an organism (7)

metamorphosis: the series of changes that certain types of organisms undergo as they develop from a larva or nymph to an adult (718)

metaphase: the stage of mitosis or meiosis during which the centromeres of the chromosomes are lined up at the equatorial plane (400)

microdissection (my kroh dis EK shun)**:** dissections using tiny instruments to perform operations on living cells (26)

microfilaments: long, threadlike strands found in the cytoplasm of some cells; involved in movement (87)

micropyle: a small opening in the ovule through which the pollen tube grows (479)

microtubules: the long, cylindrical organelles found in cilia and flagella (87)

migration: an annual round trip made by many species between their winter feeding grounds in the south and their spring breeding grounds in the north (794)

mimicry: a protective adaptation in which one species is protected from its enemies by its resemblance to another species (611)

minerals: chemical elements that organisms need for normal functioning (149)

mitochondrion (pl. **mitochondria**)**:** an oval membrane-enclosed organelle in which most of the reactions of cellular respiration occur (86)

mitosis: the process by which the nucleus of a cell divides, while maintaining the chromosome number (398)

mixture: a combination of substances that are physically mixed without forming new chemical bonds (45)

modern theory of evolution: a theory of evolution stating that populations evolve, rather than the individuals within populations (605)

molars: a type of tooth specialized for grinding food (767)

mold: a type of fossil formed when sediment, in which an organism is embedded, hardens, preserving the shape of the organism after its remains decompose (573)

molecule: an uncharged group of atoms held together by covalent bonds; the smallest particle that retains the properties of a covalent compound (39)

Mollusca: a phylum of invertebrates having soft, unsegmented bodies, often enclosed in a mantle; mollusks (698)

molting: in arthropods, shedding of the exoskeleton (709)

monocots: the flowering plants whose seeds have one cotyledon (485)

monohybrid cross: a genetic cross in which only one pair of contrasting traits is studied (507)

monosaccharides: the simplest type of carbohydrates; the simple sugars (60)

monotremes: egg-laying mammals; includes the duckbill platypus and spiny anteater (767)

morula (pl. **morulae**)**:** an early stage of animal development in which the embryo consists of a solid ball of cells formed by cleavage of the fertilized egg (442)

mosses: any of a class of bryophytes; small, simple, green plants that grow in moist environments; Musci (475)

multiple alleles: three or more different forms of a gene, each producing a different phenotype (511)

multiple-gene inheritance: the type of inheritance in which two or more pairs of genes affect the same characteristic; polygenic inheritance (523)

muscle tissues: the tissues consisting of cells that have the capacity to contract and exert a pull (100)

muscle tone: the state of partial contraction in which all muscles are kept (265)

mutagens: factors in the environment that cause mutations (546)

mutation: the appearance of a new allele on a chromosome (545)

mutualism: a symbiotic relationship in which both organisms benefit from their association (825)

mycelium: a tangled mass of grown-out hyphae (665)

myelin: layers of white, fatty substance produced by Schwann cells on some axons (273)

myofibrils: the small fibers that are arranged in a bundle making up the larger muscle fiber (263)

Myxini (mik SIH nee)**:** a class of vertebrates that lack paired fins, true jaws, and scales of other fishes, and in which the notochord persists throughout life (736)

Myxomycota: a phylum of protists with characteristics of both protozoa and fungi during their life cycles; slime molds (651)

N

nasal passages: the hollow spaces in the nose through which air flows from the nostril to the pharynx (225)

nastic movement: a plant movement that is in response to a stimulus but independent of the direction of the stimulus (383)

natural selection: the process whereby organisms with favorable variations survive and produce more offspring than less well-adapted organisms (602)

Neanderthals: an early type of *Homo sapiens* that first appeared about 100 000 years ago (776)

nearsighted: a vision condition that occurs because the eyeball is too long (301)

nectar: a sugary liquid produced by flowers (482)

negative feedback: chemical response to chemical regulation of glandular secretions that opposes the original change (316)

nekton: free-swimming marine organisms (855)

nematocysts: the capsules within cnidoblasts containing coiled, hollow threads that are discharged when the cnidoblasts are stimulated (688)

Nematoda: the phylum consisting of slender, bilaterally symmetrical roundworms (694)

nephridia: the organs of excretion in the earthworm and other annelids (238)

nephrons: the functional units of the kidney (243)

nerve cord: in chordates, a dorsal hollow structure (734)

nerve net: a type of nervous system found in the hydra; the nerve cells are formed into an irregular network through which coordinated movement can occur (282)

nerves: bundles of axons or dendrites that are bound together by connective tissues (274)

neuromuscular junctions: the junctions between motor neurons and muscle fibers (280)

neuron: a cell specialized for the transmission of impulses; a nerve cell (273)

neurotransmitters: a substance released from the synaptic knob into the synaptic cleft that initiates impulses in adjacent neurons (279)

neutralization: the reaction of an acid with a base to produce a neutral solution (49)

neutrons: particles in the nuclei of atoms that have no electrical charge; have roughly the same mass as protons (34)

niche: the role of a species in an ecosystem (826)

nictitating membrane: a transparent kind of eyelid present in many vertebrates, allowing them to see underwater (744)

nitrifying bacteria: bacteria that can convert ammonia to nitrite and nitrate (831)

nitrogen fixation: a process by which nitrogen-fixing organisms produce nitrogen compounds from the gaseous nitrogen of the atmosphere (831)

nitrogen fixers: bacteria and blue-green algae that can produce nitrogen compounds from the gaseous nitrogen of the atmosphere (831)

noise pollution: loud sounds that can cause hearing loss (867)

nomenclature: a system for naming things (129)

nondisjunction: the failure of homologous chromosomes to separate normally during meiosis, producing gametes or spores with one more or one less chromosome than normal (547)

nonrenewable natural resources: resources that can be used only once, such as coal, oil, and minerals, and cannot be replaced (873)

norepinephrine: an excitatory neurotransmitter; noradrenaline (324)

notochord: a flexible, rodlike, internal supporting structure found in all chordates during some part of their lives (734)

nuclear envelope: the membrane that surrounds the nucleus (84)

nucleic acids: compounds that contain phosphorous and nitrogen in addition to carbon, hydrogen, and oxygen; DNA or RNA (64)

nucleoli: dense, granular bodies that are found in the nucleus of cells and are a site of RNA production (85)

nucleotides: the base units of nucleic acids, each containing a sugar, a phosphate group, and one of four nitrogenous bases (64, 526)

nucleus: in a *eukaryotic cell,* a large, membrane-enclosed organelle that contains the cell's DNA; in an *atom,* containing protons and neutrons (34, 77)

nutrients (NOO tree unts)**:** the substances that an organism needs for energy, growth, repair, or maintenance (5, 149)

nutrition: the process by which organisms take in food and break it down so it can be used for metabolism (5, 149)

nymphs: the young of an insect, such as a grasshopper, hatched from an egg in incomplete metamorphosis; resembles the adult insect but lacks some of the adult features (718)

olfactory cells: receptors for smell located in the mucous membrane lining the upper nasal cavities (306)

Oligochaeta: a major class of the phylum Annelida; includes the earthworm (696)

oncogenes: any of various genes that, when activated, may cause normal cells to become cancerous (539, 658)

one gene-one polypeptide hypothesis: the hypothesis that every gene directs the synthesis of a particular polypeptide chain; originally called the one gene-one enzyme hypothesis (529)

oogenesis: the formation of eggs in the ovaries (429)

Oomycota (oh uh my KOH tuh)**:** a phylum of protists that look like fungi but differ from fungi in the content of their cell walls and in their mode of sexual reproduction; water molds (652)

ootid: the large, haploid daughter cell produced by the meiotic division of the secondary oocyte; matures into an egg (429)

open circulatory system: the blood flows directly into body tissues (176)

operculum: a protective flap that covers the gills of bony fishes; gill cover (740)

operon: in prokaryotes, such as bacteria, the promoter, the operator, and their associated structural genes (537)

opposable thumb: a thumb positioned opposite to the other fingers, making it possible to grasp objects; found in primates (771)

optical system: the lenses of a compound microscope (20)

optic nerve: the nerve that carries impulses from the receptors in the retina of the eye to the brain (300)

oral groove: the opening in the paramecium through which food is ingested (156)

order: a group of related families (128)

organ: a group of tissues that work together to perform a specific function (100)

organelles: the specialized structures in the cytoplasm of cells that carry out specific functions (82)

organic compounds: compounds that contain carbon and usually hydrogen; most occur naturally only in the bodies and products of organisms (57)

organic evolution: the process of continual change that occurs in species over time (571)

organism: a living thing (4)

organ system: a group of organs that work together to perform a specific function (101)

Orthoptera (or THAHP tuh ruh)**:** a large order of insects that exhibit incomplete metamorphosis, have biting mouthparts, and inhabit the ground or low vegetation; includes cockroaches and grasshoppers (720)

osculum: an opening at the unattached end of a sponge that serves as the excurrent opening (686)

osmosis: the diffusion of water across a semipermeable membrane from a region of high concentration of water to a region of low concentration of water (93)

osmotic pressure: the increase in pressure resulting from the flow of water in osmosis (94)

ossification: the process by which cartilage is replaced by bone in the skeletons of most vertebrates (260)

Osteichthyes (ahs tee IK thee eez)**:** a class of vertebrates having a bony skeleton, movable jaws, overlapping scales, paired fins, and an air bladder; bony fishes (739)

osteocytes: the bone-forming cells entrapped in small cavities within the bone substance (259)

ova (pl. **ovum**)**:** egg cells (428)

oval window: the membrane between the middle and inner ear, connected to the eardrum by three small bones (303)

ovary (pl. **ovaries**)**:** in *animals,* the female gonad, which produces egg cells; in *flowering plants,* the basal part of the pistil, which contains ovules and, later, seeds, and which develops into a fruit (428, 459, 481)

oviduct: a tube that carries the egg away from the ovary (459)

ovipositor: a hard, four-pointed organ that is used to dig holes in the ground in which eggs are deposited (721)

ovulation: the release of an egg from an ovary (459)

ovule: in seed plants, a structure within the ovary that contains a female gametophyte and that develops into a seed after fertilization (478)

oxidation: any chemical change in which an atom or a molecule loses electrons (110)

oxidation-reduction reaction: a reaction in which one substance is oxidized and another substance is reduced (110)

oxygen cycle: the pathways of oxygen in the bisophere (833)

P

palisade mesophyll: the upper portion of the mesophyll (368)

pancreas: an organ that is both an exocrine gland and an endocrine gland and that secretes digestive juice and the hormones insulin and glucagon (161)

pancreatic juice: the digestive secretion of the pancreas containing sodium bicarbonate, amylase, proteases, and lipases (164)

parapodia: paired, paddlelike extensions on each segment of some annelids; used for swimming and creeping (697)

parasites: a type of heterotroph which obtains nutrients from living organisms in or on which they live (633)

parasitism: a symbiotic relationship in which one organism benefits from the association and the other is harmed (825)

parasympathetic nervous system: the division of the autonomic nervous system that slows down the functioning of various body systems (296)

parathyroid glands: the four small glands embedded in back of the thyroid that secrete parathormone (323)

parent (P) generation: the starting generation in a breeding experiment (499)

parthenogenesis: the development of an unfertilized egg into an adult animal without fusion with sperm (434)

passive immunity: a type of immunity that is acquired when a person is given antibiotics, obtained from the blood of either another person or an animal, to attack a particular antigen (205)

passive transport: a process by which materials move across cell membranes without the expenditure of cellular energy (96)

pathogens: viruses, bacteria, and other microorganisms that cause disease (201, 637)

pedicel: the stalk that bears a single flower (480)

pedigree chart: a diagram that shows the presence or absence of a particular trait in each member of each generation (549)

pedipalps: in arachnids, the second pair of appendages; sensitive both to chemicals and to touch (714)

pellicle: a grooved, flexible, proteinaceous structure found inside the cell membrane of some protists (644)

pepsin: a protein-digesting enzyme in gastric juice (162)

peptide bond: the bond formed between two amino acids by dehydration synthesis (67)

pericardium: a tough membrane that covers and protects the heart (179)

periosteum: a tough membrane covering the outside of bones, except at joints (259)

peripheral nervous system: the division of the nervous system that includes all the neurons and nerve fibers outside the brain and spinal cord (282)

Perissodactyla (puh ris uh DAK tuh luh)**:** an order of hoofed mammals having an uneven number of toes on each foot; includes horses and rhinoceroses (769)

peristalsis: the alternate waves of contraction and relaxation in the walls of the alimentary canal (162)

permafrost: the lower layers in the tundra that remain frozen throughout the year (846)

petals: the usually showy flower structures located between the sepals and the stamens (481)

petiole: the structure that attaches the leaf to the stem of a plant (367)

petrifaction: the process by which the body of a dead organism is slowly replaced by dissolved minerals (573)

pH: a unit of measurement that indicates the concentration of hydrogen ions in a solution (50)

Phaeophyta (fee AH fuh tuh)**:** a plant phylum that includes multicellular seaweeds and kelps; brown algae (650)

phagocytosis: the process in which large particles or small organisms are ingested into a cell (97)

pharynx: the throat (158, 225, 692)

phase-contrast microscope: a form of compound microscope that allows the details within living specimens to be seen without straining (24)

phenotype: the physical traits that appear in an individual as a result of its genetic makeup (503)

pheromones: a type of animal secretion that serves as a means of communication between members of the same species (804, 878)

phloem: the tissue that conducts food and other dissolved materials throughout the body of a vascular plant (357)

photoautotrophs: organisms that use light energy to drive the reactions needed to make food; photosynthetic organisms (340)

photon: a particle of light (341)

photoperiodism: the response of a plant to the changing duration of light and darkness during the year (384)

photosynthesis: the process by which organic compounds are synthesized from inorganic carbon; i.e., CO_2, in the presence of light in most autotrophic organisms (340)

phototropism: the growth of a plant in response to the stimulus of light; the stem of a plant grows toward light or away from it (383)

phylogeny: the evolutionary history of a species or a group of organisms (130)

phylum: one of the largest or most inclusive groups within a kingdom (128)

phytoplankton: photosynthetic organisms that float near the surface of water (855)

pigment: a substance that absorbs only certain wavelengths of light; a substance that has color (341)

pineal gland: a pea-sized gland attached to the base of the brain that produces melatonin (328)

Pinnipedia (pin uh PEED ee uh): an order of aquatic mammals having flippers; seals and walruses (770)

pinocytosis: the process in which liquids or very small particles from the surrounding medium are taken into a cell by the formation of a vesicle (97)

pistil: the part of a flower that contains the ovules and through which pollen tubes grow (481)

pith: the center of a herbaceous dicot system, made up of parenchyma cells (365)

pituitary gland: the endocrine gland attached to the hypothalamus that controls the activities of many other endocrine glands in the body (320)

pivot joints: a type of joint that permits rotation from side to side as well as up-and-down movement (262)

placenta: in mammals, a temporary organ through which the fetus receives food and oxygen from the mother's body and gets rid of wastes (450, 465)

placental mammals: mammals in which a placenta forms during development of the embryo (767)

plankton: organisms that float in a body of water (855)

Plantae: one of the six kingdoms; members are mostly multicellular and photosynthetic; plants (135)

planula: the small, ciliated larva of many cnidarians (689)

plasma: the liquid part of blood (196)

plasmids: the small, circular segments of DNA that are found in bacteria and that stay separate from the bacterial chromosomes; used in genetic engineering (558)

plasmolysis: the shrinking of cytoplasm resulting from loss of water by osmosis in a cell placed in a hypertonic solution (96)

plastids: membrane-enclosed organelles found in the cells of some protists and almost all plants; includes chloroplasts, chromoplasts, and leucoplasts (89)

platelets: small, round or oval blood fragments that trigger the blood-clotting process (198)

Platyhelminthes: the simplest animals showing bilateral symmetry (691)

pleura: a two-layered membrane that encloses the human lung (225)

point mutation: a type of gene mutation in which only a single nucleotide in the gene has been changed (542)

polar molecule: a molecule with regions of partial negative and partial positive charges (58)

polar nuclei: the two nuclei found within the embryo sac (482)

pollen grain: the male gametophyte of seed plants (478)

pollen tube: the tubelike outgrowth of the pollen grain through which the sperm nuclei pass to the ovule (479)

pollination: the transfer of pollen from an anther to a stigma of a flower (478)

pollution: the addition of anything to the environment that makes it less fit for living things (867)

Polychaeta: a class that includes the marine sandworm *Nereis;* similar to the earthworm (697)

polymers: large molecules consisting of chains of repeating units (61)

polyp: the sessile body form of a cnidarian (687)

polypeptide: a chain of amino acids joined by peptide bonds (67)

polyploidy: a condition in which the cells have some multiple of the normal chromosome number (547)

polysaccharides: a long chain of repeating sugar units formed by joining simple sugars by dehydration synthesis (61)

pons: a part of the brain that serves as a relay system linking the spinal cord, medulla oblongata, cerebellum, and cerebrum (291)

population: the simplest grouping of organisms in nature (605, 823)

population genetics: the study of the changes in the genetic makeup of populations (605)

pores: the tiny openings found in plant leaves and animal skins through which fluids are absorbed or discharged (685)

Porifera: a phylum of the simplest multicellular animals; aquatic, immobile animals with an outer layer pierced by many pores; sponges (685)

positive feedback: feedback from chemical regulation of glandular secretions that reinforces the original change (317)

posterior: pertaining to the rear or tail end of a bilaterally symmetrical animal (684)

pregnancy: in mammals, the period during which the developing embryo is carried in the uterus (463)

premolars: a type of tooth specialized for grinding food (767)

pressure-flow hypothesis: an explanation for the movement of liquid in plant phloem from an area of high concentration to one of low concentration (379)

primary immune response: the body's initial response to an antigen; does not produce measurable amounts of antibodies (203)

primary root: the first structure to emerge from a sprouting seed (359)

primary succession: succession that occurs in an area that had no previously existing life (836)

Primates: an order of mammals having grasping hands and flexible feet, each with five digits; includes humans, apes, monkeys, and lemurs (771)

primitive gut: the cavity within the gastrula of an embryo that eventually forms the digestive tract (443)

Proboscidea (proh buh SID ee uh): an order of mammals having tusks and long, flexible, tubelike snouts; includes elephants (769)

producers: organisms, such as green plants, that produce organic compounds from inorganic compounds; the autotrophs (828)

products: the new substances produced by chemical reactions (44)

progesterone: a hormone secreted by the ovaries that helps to regulate the menstrual cycle and maintains the uterus during pregnancy (327)

proglottids: the segmentlike divisions of a tapeworm's body (694)

prokaryotic cells: cells lacking distinct membrane-bound structures; monerans; bacteria or blue-green algae (79)

prophase: the stage of mitosis or meiosis in which the chromosomes and spindle appear and the nuclear membrane disappears (400)

prostaglandins: local hormones that produce their effects on the cells in which they are synthesized, without entering the bloodstream (315)

proteins: organic compounds consisting of one or more chains of amino acids; contain nitrogen as well as carbon, hydrogen, and oxygen (66)

Protista: one of the six kingdoms; includes simple, mostly unicellular, eukaryotic organisms; protists (134, 642)

protons: positively charged particles found in the nuclei of all atoms; have roughly the same mass as neutrons (34)

protozoa (sing. **protozoan**): protists that are usually motile, e.g., amebas and paramecia (642)

pseudopods: in certain cells, the temporary projections of cell surfaces that enable cells to move and engulf particles (255)

pulmonary artery: the two-branched vessel that brings blood from the right ventricle of the heart to the lungs (180)

pulmonary circulation: this pathway in the body carries blood between the heart and the lungs (184)

pulse: the expansion and relaxation that can be felt in an artery each time the left ventricle of the heart contracts and relaxes (182)

punctuated equilibrium: a theory of evolution stating that a species remains the same for a long time and then evolves rapidly during a short time interval (604)

Punnett square: a diagram, used in genetics, to show the results of a cross (504)

pupa: the resting stage that larvae pass into after several molts (719)

pupil: the opening in the center of the iris of the eye, which allows light to enter the eye (300)

pyramid of biomass: the relative mass of organisms at each feeding level in an ecosystem (830)

pyramid of energy: the amount of available energy in an ecosystem (830)

R

radial symmetry: a type of symmetry in which any section through and parallel to the central axis of the organism divides it into similar halves (684)

radicle: the root portion of a seed embryo (485)

radioactive dating: a dating method based on the rate of disintegration of radioactive isotopes; used to determine the age of rocks and fossils (575)

radioactivity: the process in which the nucleus of an atom gives off radiation or charged particles; changes the atom to another isotope or a different element (38)

radioisotopes: radioactive isotopes (38)

radula: a rasping, tonguelike organ in mollusks (699)

range: the particular region of the earth where a species is found (614)

reactants: the substances that take part in chemical reactions (44)

receptacle: the expanded end of the pedicel, to which the flower parts are attached (480)

receptors: in a nervous system, the specialized structures sensitive to certain types of stimuli; sense organs (272)

recessive: the inherited characteristic often masked by the dominant characteristic and not seen in an organism (500)

recombinant DNA: DNA that has been altered by genetic engineering (558)

rectum: a structure in which undigested food (feces) is stored prior to elimination from the body (159)

recycling: the process of reusing materials rather than discarding them as waste (873)

red blood cells: red cells that carry oxygen and carbon dioxide; erythrocytes (196)

reduction: chemical reaction in which a substance gains an electron (110)

reflex: an involuntary, automatic response to a given stimulus, not involving the brain (297, 792)

reflex arc: the pathway over which the nerve impulses travel in a reflex (298)

reforestation: a program that plants seeds or seedlings to replace trees lost in cutting (875)

refractory period: the brief recovery period during which the cell membrane of a neuron cannot carry impulses (277)

regeneration: the ability of an organism to regrow lost body parts (408)

regulation: all the activities that help to maintain an organism's homeostatis (7)

relative dating: any method of determining the order in which events occurred (575)

releasing factors: hormones that are produced by the hypothalamus and that control the release of a hormone from the anterior pituitary (321)

renal arteries: the vessels that bring blood to the kidneys (244)

renal circulation: the branch of the systemic circulation that carries blood to and from the kidneys (188)

renal veins: the vessels through which blood flows from the kidneys (244)

renewable natural resources: a natural resource, such as air, water, soil, sunlight, and living organisms, that can be replaced by natural processes (873)

reproduction: the process by which living things produce new organisms of their own kind (7)

reproductive isolation: the loss of the ability to interbreed by two isolated groups (615)

Reptilia: a class of cold-blooded vertebrates with dry skin, scales, four limbs (except for snakes), lungs, and a three-chambered heart; fertilization of eggs is internal; reptiles (750)

resolution: the ability of a microscope to show two points that are close together as separate images (23)

respiration: the process of releasing energy in a complex series of chemical reactions (6)

respiratory pigments: colored substances in the blood of most multicellular animals which carry oxygen and carbon dioxide between the respiratory surface and the body cells (221)

respiratory surface: a moist surface through which the exchange of respiratory gases takes place (220)

restriction enzymes: the proteins used to cut DNA molecules at specific places so that scientists can isolate pieces with the desired genes (558)

retina: the innermost layer of the eye, on which an image is projected by the lens (300)

retrovirus: an RNA virus; a virus whose genetic material is RNA (655)

Rh factor: a group of antigens found on the surface of red blood cells (208)

rhizoids: rootlike hyphae that anchor a fungus, secrete digestive enzymes, and absorb nutrients (475, 666)

rhizome: a thick, horizontal stem containing stored food, which forms new plants by vegetative reproduction (410)

Rhodophyta (roh DAH fuh tuh)**:** a phylum of plants that includes unicellular organisms and multicellular seaweeds; red algae (650)

ribosomal RNA (rRNA): a type of RNA transcribed from DNA in the nucleolus and found in the ribosomes (532)

ribosomes: the organelles that are the sites of protein synthesis in cells (85)

RNA (ribonucleic [ry boh noo KLAY ik] **acid):** the nucleic acid that is transcribed from DNA (64)

Rodentia: the largest order of placental mammals, having sharp incisors for gnawing; includes rats, mice, and squirrels; rodents (768)

rods: structures in the retina of the eye responsible for black-and-white vision (301)

root cap: a thimble-shaped group of cells that form a protective covering for the root tip (361)

root hairs: hairlike extensions of root epidermal cells that increase the surface area for absorption (362)

root pressure: the osmotic pressure in the xylem of a root (377)

roots: the structures containing vascular tissues adapted for anchoring plants and absorbing water and dissolved substances (355)

rumen: in ruminants, the chamber of the stomach in which food is stored (770)

runner: a horizontal stem with long internodes that forms independent plants by vegetative reproduction; a stolon (410)

S

saliva: the secretion of the salivary glands (159)

salivary amylase: the enzyme in saliva that hydrolyzes starch into maltose; ptyalin (161)

salivary glands: the glands that secrete saliva into the mouth (159)

salt: an ionic compound produced by the neutralization reaction between an acid and a base (49)

S-A node (sinoatrial node): a small group of specialized muscle cells in the wall of the right atrium; stimulates contraction of the heart; pacemaker (181)

saprobes: the organisms that obtain nutrients by breaking down the remains of dead plants and animals (633)

Sarcodina: a phylum of protists that move and capture prey by using pseudopods; sarcodines (642)

saturated fats: fats formed from fatty acids in which all carbon-to-carbon bonds are single bonds (63)

scanning electron microscope: an electron microscope that uses an electron beam focused to a fine point and passed back and forth over the surface of the specimen (25)

Schwann cells: cells that surround some axons and form myelin (273)

scientific law: a statement that describes some aspect of a phenomenon that is always true (17)

scientific method: a universal approach to scientific problems, consisting of defining the problem, formulating a hypothesis, testing the hypothesis, and recording and reporting observations (13)

sclera: the tough, fibrous, white outer layer of the eye (299)

scrotum: a sac of skin outside the body wall in which the testes are located (458)

sebaceous glands: the glands in the skin that produce oily secretions (247)

secondary response: a rapid response by the immune system when it encounters the same antigen a second time in the body; produces high levels of antibodies within two days (203)

secondary roots: the roots that branch off from primary roots (359)

secondary sex characteristics: characteristics—such as body hair, muscle development, broadened pelvis, or voice depth—controlled by the male and female sex hormones, but not essential to the reproductive process (457)

secondary succession: succession that occurs in an area in which an existing community has been partially destroyed and its balance upset (836)

sedimentary rock: a type of rock formed from layers of particles that settled to the bottom of a body of water, often containing fossils (573)

seed: in seed plants, the structure formed from the ovule following fertilization; contains the plant embryo, stored nutrients, and a seed coat (478)

seed coat: a tough, protective covering around a seed that develops from the wall of the ovule (478)

selection: a technique in which only those animals and plants with the most desirable traits are chosen for breeding (555)

selectively permeable: a characteristic of a cell membrane that allows some substances to pass freely through the membrane, while others can pass through to a slight extent or not at all (84)

semen: the mixture of sperm and fluids released during ejaculation (459)

semicircular canals: a system of loop-shaped tubes in the inner ear that enable the body to maintain balance (304)

sensory neurons: nerve cells that carry impulses from receptors toward the spinal cord and brain (274)

sepals: the leaflike structures at the base of flowers (480)

setae: tiny bristles on the body segments of annelids, used in locomotion (257)

sex chromosomes: the two unmatched chromosomes that determine the sex of an individual; represented as X and Y (518)

sex-linked trait: a trait that is controlled by a gene found on one of the sex chromosomes (520)

sexual reproduction: a form of reproduction in which a new individual is produced by the union of the nuclei of two specialized sex cells, i.e., gametes, usually from two separate parent organisms (7, 398)

SI: the International System of Units; the metric system (17)

sickle-cell disease: a recessive inherited disorder of the blood in which the red blood cells have an abnormal sickle shape (550)

simple leaf: a leaf with only one blade and one petiole (367)

simple microscope: a hand lens (20)

Sirenia (sy REEN ee ah)**:** an order of large, vegetarian sea mammals; manatees and dugongs (770)

skeletal muscle: muscle that is attached to bone and is involved in locomotion and voluntary movement; striated muscle (263)

small intestine: the part of the digestive tract where most chemical digestion and almost all absorption occurs (164)

smooth muscle: muscle tissue made up of individual cells, not marked by striations, and not under voluntary control (265)

social behavior: animal behavior consisting of both helpful and hostile interactions (801)

sodium-potassium pump: an active transport mechanism that pumps sodium ions out of, and potassium ions into, a nerve cell; sodium pump (276)

solutes: substances that are dissolved in solvents (46)

solution: any homogeneous mixture (46)

solvent: the substance, usually a liquid, that makes up the bulk of a solution (46)

somatic cells: the body cells, as distinguished from the sex cells (418)

somatic nervous system: the division of the peripheral nervous system that contains sensory and motor neurons that connect the central nervous system to skeletal muscles, skin, and sense organs (296)

speciation: the formation of new species (603)

species: a group of organisms that are structurally similar and that pass these similarities on to their offspring (128)

spectrophotometry: a method of identifying and quantifying a substance by measuring the amount of light at different wavelengths that it absorbs (26)

spermatogenesis: the formation of sperm in the testes (429)

spermatogonia: diploid cells in the testes, from which sperm are formed through meiosis and differentiation (430)

sperm: the male gametes (428)

spherical symmetry: a type of symmetry in which any cut passing through the center of the organism divides it into matching halves (684)

sphincter: a ring of muscle that acts as a valve (162)

spicules: the small skeletal structures embedded in the middle layer of sponges that provide support and give shape to the organism (686)

spinal column: in vertebrates, the series of vertebrae connected by cartilage disks that surrounds and protects the spinal cord; the backbone (260)

spinal cord: the cord of nervous tissue in vertebrates that extends down from the brain, running through the vertebrae of the spinal column (294)

spinal nerves: the nerves connected to the spinal cord (295)

spindle: a structure formed by fibers during mitosis (400)

spinnerets: the organs in spiders and other small arachnids that are used to spin silk (715)

spiracles: several paired openings through which air enters and leaves the body of terrestrial arthropods (223, 721)

spirillum: a spiral or coiled bacterium (632)

spongin: protein-containing substance that makes up the fibers in the skeleton of some sponges (686)

spongy mesophyll: the lower portion of mesophyll in a leaf, consisting of irregularly shaped, chloroplast-filled cells separated by large air spaces (369)

spontaneous generation: the idea that living things regularly arise from nonliving matter; abiogenesis (585)

spores: the specialized reproductive cells that can give rise to new organisms (407)

sporophyte: a spore-producing plant (474)

Sporozoa: a phylum of protists composed of nonmotile, parasitic protozoans; sporozoans (645)

stabilizing selection: a type of natural selection in which the average phenotype may be a favorable adaptation, and the extreme phenotypes are unfavorable (613)

stamen: the organ of a flower that bears pollen grains (481)

starch: a polysaccharide that is the main food storage compound in plants (61)

stem: the leaf-bearing structure of vascular plants (355)

stereomicroscope: a microscope used in studying the external, or surface, structure of specimens; has low magnifying power, ranging from 6X to 50X, thus providing a three-dimensional image of the specimen (24)

stigma: in a *pistil,* the enlarged, sticky knob on top of a style that receives the pollen; in *protists,* an eyespot (481)

stimulus (pl. **stimuli**)**:** any factor that causes a receptor to trigger impulses in a nerve pathway, resulting in a change of activity (272, 785)

stolons: in fungi, hyphae that grow in a network over the surface of food (666)

stomach: the organ of the digestive tract in which food is temporarily stored and partially digested (159)

stomates: the openings in the epidermis of leaves that allow the exchange of respiratory gases between the internal tissues of the leaf and the atmosphere (364)

strip cropping: a conservation practice in which cover crops are planted between strips of row crops, leaving no soil open to erosion (874)

stroma: in plant chloroplasts, the regions between the grana (343)

structural formula: a kind of chemical formula that shows how atoms in a molecule are bonded to one another (43)

style: in flowers, the part of the pistil between the stigma and the ovary (481)

substrate: the substance that an enzyme acts upon (68)

superior vena cava: veins, some of the largest in the body, that return blood from the head, arms, and chest into the right atrium of the heart (187)

suspension: a mixture that separates when left still (46)

sustained-yield tree farming: a method of forest conservation in which trees are cut down in certain areas of a forest, leaving surrounding areas untouched (875)

sweat glands: a gland composed of a tiny coiled tube that opens to the surface of the skin and secretes perspiration (247)

swim bladder: in bony fishes, a gas-filled sac that regulates the buoyancy of the fish; air bladder (742)

symbiotic relationships: relationships in which two different organisms live in close association with each other to the benefit of at least one of them (824)

sympathetic nervous system: the division of the autonomic nervous system that generally accelerates body activities (296)

synapse: the region where nerve impulses pass from one neuron to another (274)

synapsis: the pairing of replicated homologous chromosomes during prophase I of meiosis (420)

synthesis: the chemical combining of simple substances to form more complex substances (6)

systemic circulation: a pathway that carries blood between the heart and the rest of the body, excluding the lungs (184)

systole: the period of contraction of the heart (180)

T

T cells: lymphocytes that are produced in the bone marrow and matured in the thymus gland and are then released into the circulatory and lymphatic systems (203)

tadpoles: larval form of frogs and toads (744)

taiga: a biome with cold winters and warm, moist summers; climax flora are evergreen vegetation (847)

taste buds: the taste receptors on the tongue (306)

taxis: any movement by a simple animal or a protist toward or away from a particular stimulus (791)

taxonomic key: a procedure that is a series of instructions biologists use to identify an organism (136)

taxonomy: the branch of biology that deals with the classification and naming of living things (125)

telophase: the stage of mitosis during which the chromosomes uncoil, the spindle and asters disappear, and the nuclear membrane reforms (400)

temperate deciduous forest: a biome in which the climax vegetation is deciduous trees; characterized by hot, humid summers and cold winters (848)

temperature inversion: a situation in which a layer of cooler, denser air becomes trapped below a layer of warmer air (871)

tendons: strong bands of connective tissues that attach skeletal muscle to bone (264)

terminal bud: the bud at the tip of a plant stem (366)

terracing: a method of altering land for cultivation, in which flat areas are cut into the sides of a hill to prevent soil erosion from water running over the surface (874)

territory: an area defended by an individual against intrusion by other members of the same species (804)

test cross: a genetic cross in which a test organism showing the dominant trait is crossed with one showing the recessive trait; used to determine whether the test organism is homozygous dominant or heterozygous (506)

testes: the male gonads, which produce sperm and secrete male sex hormones (428, 457)

testosterone: a male sex hormone secreted by the testes; stimulates development of the male reproductive system and promotes male secondary sex characteristics (327)

tetrad: the group of four chromatids formed in prophase I of meiosis (420)

thalamus: a relay center between various parts of the brain and the spinal cord (291)

theories: explanations based on facts that apply to a broad range of phenomena (17)

theory of evolution: theory of gradual change in species over time (130)

thermal pollution: a type of pollution in which warmed water, which has been used to cool industrial equipment, is returned to a stream or river; the change in water temperature kills fish and other organisms (868)

thigmotropism: growth of a plant in response to the stimulus of touch, as when tendrils of a grapevine wind themselves around the stem of another plant (383)

thorax: the head in most arthropods (709)

threshold: the minimum sensitivity level of a nerve cell; impulses below this level do not initiate responses (277)

thylakoids: the photosynthetic membranes in the chloroplast which are arranged in the shape of flattened sacs (343)

thymine: a nitrogenous base found in DNA (526)

thymus: a gland located in the upper part of the chest cavity that is involved in immunity (327)

thyroid gland: the endocrine gland located in front of the trachea; secretes thyroxine and calcitonin (322)

thyroxine: an iodine-containing hormone that is secreted by the thyroid and that regulates the rate of metabolism in the body (317)

tissue: in multicellular organisms, a group of cells that are similar and are organized into a functional unit; usually integrated with other tissues to form an organ (99)

tissue culture: a technique of maintaining living cells or tissues in a culture medium outside the body (26)

trachea: the tube through which air passes from the pharynx to the lungs (225)

tracheal tubes: a system of branching air tubes that carries air directly to all the cells of the body (222)

Tracheophyta: the phylum of vascular plants; contain the water-conducting and food-conducting tissues—xylem and phloem; tracheophytes (672)

transcription: the copying of a genetic message from a strand of DNA into a molecule of RNA (530)

transfer RNA (tRNA): the type of RNA that carries a particular amino acid to mRNA at the ribosome in protein synthesis (531)

translation: the process by which the information coded in RNA is used for the assembly of a particular amino acid sequence (534)

translocation: in *plants,* the movement of dissolved materials; in *genetics,* the transfer of a chromosome segment to a nonhomologous chromosome (379, 547)

transmission electron microscope: a microscope that uses electron beams rather than light and electromagnetic lenses rather than glass lenses (24)

transpiration: the evaporation of water vapor from plant surfaces (375)

transpirational pull: the chief process by which water moves through the xylem of a plant (378)

transport: the process by which substances move into or out of cells or are distributed within cells (5, 173)

Trematoda: a class of the phylum Platyhelminthes; the parasitic flatworms; flukes (693)

trochophore larva: a type of free-swimming, ciliated larva (698)

tropical rain forests: a biome found around the equator in which there is a constant supply of rainfall and the temperature remains at about 25°C throughout the year (850)

tropism: a growth response in a plant caused by a stimulus that comes primarily from one direction (382)

tube feet: in echinoderms, water-filled tubes, each ending in a suction disk; used in locomotion, feeding, and respiration (726)

tuber: an enlarged portion of an underground stem that can grow into a new plant by vegetative reproduction (409)

tundra: a region that lies south of the ice caps of the Arctic and extends across North America, Europe, and Siberia (846)

Turbellaria: the class of free-living flatworms with eyespots; *Planaria* (691)

tympanic membrane: a delicate membrane stretched across the inner end of the auditory canal of the ear; eardrum (303, 744)

typhlosole: a longitudinal fold in the intestinal wall of some animals, such as the earthworm, that increases the surface area of the intestine (158)

U

ultrasound: a procedure used to determine the size and position of a developing fetus; high-frequency sound waves are reflected off the fetus to produce an image that can be studied (554)

umbilical cord: in placental mammals, the structure that connects the fetus and the placenta (450, 465)

universal donors: individuals with type O blood (209)

universal recipients: individuals with type AB blood (209)

unsaturated fats: fatty acid molecules that have one or more double or triple carbon-to-carbon bonds (63)

urbanization: the transformation of a rural area to a city environment (865)

urea: a nitrogenous waste formed from ammonia and carbon dioxide (239)

ureter: a tube that carries urine from a kidney to the bladder (242)

urethra: the tube that carries urine from the bladder to the outside of the body (243, 458)

uric acid: a dry, nitrogenous waste product excreted by birds, reptiles, and insects (240)

urinary bladder: a saclike organ where urine is stored before being excreted (242)

urinary system: the system involved in the production and excretion of urine, including the kidneys, bladder, and associated tubes (242)

urine: an excretory liquid composed of water, urea, and salts (239)

Urochordata: a subphylum of chordates that are soft, saclike, sessile, marine animals; tunicates (733)

uterus: the thick, muscular, pear-shaped organ in the female mammal in which the embryo develops (449, 460)

V

vacuoles: a membrane-enclosed, fluid-filled cavity in a cell (88)

vagina: the structure leading from the uterus to the outside of the body in mammalian females; the birth canal (460)

valves: flaplike structures that allow blood to flow in only one direction—toward the heart (178)

variable: a single factor that is changed in a controlled experiment (15)

variations: the characteristics in individuals that differ from the typical characteristics of other individuals of the same species (602)

vascular bundle: a structure within a stem containing parallel strands of xylem and phloem; may also contain cambium (364)

vascular cambium: the meristematic layer of cells that causes growth in width of a stem or root (356)

vascular cylinder: the central core of the root, which contains xylem and phloem; central cylinder (362)

vascular tissues: the xylem and phloem of a plant; conducting tissues (357)

vas deferens: the tubes that carry sperm from each testis to the urethra (458)

vegetative reproduction: the process in which undifferentiated plant cells first divide mitotically and then differentiate to produce an independent plant; vegetative propagation (408)

veins: vessels that return blood from the body tissues to the heart (178)

venation: the arrangement of veins in a leaf (369)

ventral: pertaining to the lower or belly side of a bilaterally symmetrical animal (684)

ventricles: the two lower, thick-walled chambers of the heart (179)

vertebrae: the bones of the spinal column that surround and protect the spinal cord (260)

Vertebrata: the largest subphylum of chordates having an enlarged brain and a spinal column made up of vertebrae that enclose the dorsal nerve cord; vertebrates (733)

vertebrates: the animals with backbones, including mammals, fishes, birds, reptiles, and amphibians (683)

vestigial structures: nonfunctional structures in an organism that are a remnant of structures that were functional in some ancestral form of the organism (583)

villi (sing. **villus**): small, fingerlike projections of the lining of the small intestine (164)

viruses: extremely small particles of DNA and RNA surrounded by protein coats; capable of reproducing themselves inside living cells (653)

vitamins: organic molecules required in the diet in very small amounts; exist as coenzymes or are converted into coenzymes in the cell (150)

vocal cords: two pairs of membranes that are stretched across the interior of the larynx, and which, when air passes over them, can be controlled to make sounds (225)

W

warning coloration: a protective adaptation in which the bright colors of an organism make it easily recognized (610)

water cycle: the cycling of water between the surface of the earth and the atmosphere (834)

water-vascular system: a system found only in echinoderms, for locomotion and food getting (726)

whisk ferns: the oldest known vascular plants (672)

white blood cells: blood cells that fight infection (197)

windbreaks: rows of trees used to prevent wind erosion of the soil (874)

woody stems: a type of stem containing wood (364)

X

X chromosomes: one of the two types of sex chromosomes (518)

xylem: the tissue that conducts water and minerals from the roots upward through the plant and helps to support the plant (357)

Y

Y chromosomes: one of the two types of sex chromosomes (518)

yolk sac: in *shelled eggs,* the extraembryonic membrane that surrounds the yolk, containing blood vessels that transport food to the embryo (448); in *humans,* an extraembryonic membrane that forms part of the umbilical cord (465)

Z

Zoomastigina: the most primitive of the animal-like protists; most are unicellular (644)

zooplankton: small animals and nonphotosynthetic protists that float near the surface of water (855)

Zygomycota (zy goh my KOH tuh)**:** a phylum of terrestrial fungi that produces two types of spores, one for sexual reproduction and the other for asexual reproduction; conjugation fungi (666)

zygospore: a zygote covered by a thick, protective wall (426)

zygote: the diploid cell resulting from fusion of two gametes (418)

Index

A

abdomen, of arthropods, 708
abiogenesis (spontaneous generation), 585–88
abiotic factors: 820; light, 820; soil and minerals, 821–22; temperature, 821; water, 821
ABO blood group, 206, 208, 209
abscisic acid, 382
abscission, 382
absolute dating, 575
absorption, 155
absorption spectrum, 341, 343
accessory organs, of flowers, 481
accommodation, 300
acellular slime molds, 651–52
acetylcholine, 279, 297
acetyl CoA, 115
acid rain, 48, 49, 856
acids, 48–49
acquired characteristics, inheritance of, 600
acquired immune deficiency syndrome (AIDS), 210–12, 655, 657–58
Acrasiomycota, 652
acrosome, 431
ACTH (adrenocorticotropic hormone), 321
actin, 87, 263
active immunity, 205
active site, 69
active transport, 96–97
adaptation, 307, 602–03, 610–11
adaptive radiation, 615–16
addition, in chromosomes, 547
adductor muscles, 700
adenine, 65, 526, 527
adenosine, 108
adenosine diphosphate (*see* **ADP**)
adenosine triphosphate (*see* **ATP**)
ADH (antidiuretic hormone), 322
adhesion, 59
adipose tissue, 247
ADP (adenosine diphosphate), 109, 110; cellular respiration and, 112–13; electron acceptors and, 111; structure of, 109
adrenal cortex, 320, 325
adrenal glands, 324–25
adrenalin, 324
adrenal medulla, 324
adrenocorticotropic hormone (ACTH), 321
adventitious roots, 360–61
aerial roots, 361
aerobic respiration, 6, 112, 114–19
aerosols, 869
African sleeping sickness, 644

afterbirth, 466
agar, 650
aggregate fruit, 484
aggregations, 801
aggression, 802–03
Agnatha (jawless fishes), 736–37
AIDS (acquired immune deficiency syndrome), 210–12, 655, 657–58
air bladder, 742
air pollution, 869–71; controlling, 872
air sacs, 223, 764
albumin, 196
alcohol, 465
aldosterone, 320, 325
algae, 135; brown, 650; golden, 648; green, 649–50; life cycle of, 474–75; red, 650
alimentary canal, 158
allantois, 448
alleles, 502–03; defective, 520; multiple, 511
allergens, 212
allergies, 212, 487
alligators, 752
alpha cells, 325
alternation of generations, 474
altitude, of biomes, 821; effects of, on climax vegetation, 852–53
alveoli, 226–27
amber, 572
ameba, 137, 642–43; binary fission in, 405, 406; excretion in, 238; gas exchange in, 220, 221; innate behavior in, 791; locomotion in, 255; nutrition in, 155–56; regulation in, 281; transport in, 174
amebic dysentery, 643
amebocytes, 686
amino acids, 66, 242
amino group, 66
ammonia, 238, 242
amniocentesis, 553
amnion, 448, 465
amniotic fluid, 465
amphetamines, 280–81
Amphibia (amphibians), 742–49
amphioxus, 734
amplexus, 433, 749
amylase, 165, 166
anabolic steroids, 315, 327
anaerobic respiration, 6, 112–14
analogous structures, 582
anal pore, 156
anaphase: in meiosis, 420, 421; in mitosis, 400
anatomy, comparative, 581–83
androgens, 327
anemia, 197

Angiospermae (angiosperms), 473, 675, 676–77; life cycle of, 480–83
animal breeding, 555–56
animal cells; cytokinesis in, 400–401; interphase and mitosis in, 399–400
animal experimentation, 677
Animalia (animals), 133, 135, 683–84; basic characteristics of, 133, 683; endangered species of, 607, 876–77; symmetry in, 684
animal-like protists, 642–46
Annelida (segmented worms), 138, 696–98
annual rings, 366
annulus, 668
Anopheles mosquito, 645–46
Anopleura, 722
anteater, 769
antennae, 283, 710
antennules, 710
anterior, 684
anterior pituitary, 320, 321–22
anther, 481
antheridium, 476
anthrax, 637, 638
anthropology, 773
antibiotics, 636, 639, 641; bacterial resistance to, 619–21
antibodies, 196, 203–05, 206
anticoagulants, 199
anticodon, 532
antidiuretic hormone (ADH), 322
antigens, 202–03, 206
antihistamines, 212
anus, 158, 167
anvil, of ear, 303
aorta, 176, 180
aortic arches, 175, 176
aphotic zone, 820
appendicitis, 165
appendicular skeleton, 262
appendix, 165
aquatic biomes (*see* **biomes, aquatic**)
aquatic mammals, 770
aqueous humor, 300
Arachnida (arachnids), 714–15, 716
Archaebacteria, 133, 134, 631, 635
Archaeopteryx, 761
archegonium, 476
Aristotle, 127, 585
armadillo, 769
arteries, 177–78, 185
arterioles, 178
arthritis, 212
Arthropoda (arthropods), 138, 254, 707–09
artificial joints, 262

Acknowledgments

PHOTO CREDITS

KEY TO PHOTO SOURCE ABBREVIATIONS
Animals Animals: AA; Peter Arnold, Inc.: PA; Biological Photo Service: BPS; Bruce Coleman, Inc.: BC; Grant Heilman Photography: GH; Photo Researchers, Inc.: PR; Visuals Unlimited: VU.

KEY TO PHOTO POSITION ON TEXT PAGE
t=top, **m**=middle, **b**=bottom, **l**=left, **r**=right

Front Cover: Daniel J. Cox/Natural Selection Stock Photography, Inc.

Frontis: iv–xi, Corel Professional Photos CD-ROM™

UNIT 1: xvi–1, Jim Brandenburg/Minden Pictures, Inc.; **2,** David Crisp and the WFPC2 Science Team (Jet Propulsion Laboratory/California Institute of Technology)/NASA; **3,** NASA; **4,** ©Barry Dowsett/Science Photo Library/PR; **5,** K. Wothe/Natural Selection Stock Photography, Inc.; **6,** Frans Lanting/Minden Pictures, Inc.; **7 t.,** Larry Ulrich/DRK Photo; **b.,** ©CNRI/Science Photo Library/PR; **12,** ©Mark Moffett/Minden Pictures, Inc.; **13,** Bonnie Kamin/Comstock; **14 l.,** Kevin McCarthy/Offshoot Stock; **m.,** Runk/Schoenberger/GH; **r.,** ©Gould/DeAnza Graphics/PA; **15,** Nancy Sheehan; **16,** John Kennard; **18 l.,** Norman Tomalin/BC; **r.,** Kevin Galvin/BC; **20 t.,** Dr. E.R. Degginger; **b.,** Beth Ullman/Taurus Photos; **23 t.,** James Webb/BC; **b.l., b.r.,** Bruce Iverson; **24 t., m.,** ©Biophoto Assoc./PR; **b.l.,** ©Leonard Lessin/PA; **b.r.,** ©SIU School of Medicine/PA; **25,** ©Jeremy Burgess (SPL)/PR; **26,** Dr. E.R. Degginger; **27,** ©Ohio-Nuclear Corp. (SPL)/PR; **32,** Carr Clifton/Minden Pictures, Inc.; **33,** Skip Moody/M.L. Dembinsky; **34 t., b.,** Dr. E.R. Degginger; **38,** Julie Houck; **39,** Phototake; **43,** Dr. E.R. Degginger; **44,** Norman Tomalin/BC; **45,** Bruce Iverson; **47 l., r.,** Dr. E.R. Degginger; **48,** M.L. Miller/Picture Group; **49,** Mike Greenlar/Picture Group; **50,** Dr. E.R. Degginger; **51,** Bob & Clara Calhoun/BC; **56,** ©Dr. Dennis Kunkel/Phototake NYC; **57,** ©Mike Monamee/PR; **59,** Bruce Iverson; **64,** ©Blair Seitz/PR; **67,** Lawrence Livermore National Lab; **76,** ©Dr. Dennis Kunkel/Phototake NYC; **77,** Peter Parks/Oxford Scientific Films/AA; **78 t.,** W. Amos/BC; **b.,** Paul W. Johnson/BPS; **79 t.,** ©Lee D. Simon/PR; **r.,** ©Don W. Fawcett/PR; **83 t.,** ©Don W. Fawcett/PR; **b.,** ©Biophoto Assoc./PR; **84,** ©Don W. Fawcett/PR; **85,** Warren Rosenberg/BPS; **86,** M. Powell/VU; **87 t.,** K.G. Murti/Visuals Unlimited; **b.l.,** M. Schliwa/VU; **b.r.,** ©Gopal Murti/PR; **88 t.,** David M. Phillips/VU; **b.l.,** ©Don W. Fawcett/PR; **b.r.,** David M. Phillips/VU; **89,** GH; **97,** Don W. Fawcett/PR; **99,** Kim Taylor/BC; **101 t.l.,** Fred Hossler/VU; **t.r.,** Fred Hossler/VU; **b.,** Willis, G.W., Ochsner Med. Instit./BPS; **106,** ©1996 Scott R. Indermaur c/o Mira; **107,** ©Paulo Bonino/PR; **108,** John Kennard; **115,** M. Schliwa/VU; **118,** ©Deni McIntyre/PR; **124,** ©Hans Pfletschinger/PA; **125,** Alvis Upitis/The Image Bank; **126,** Corel Professional Photos CD-ROM™; **128 t.,** ©Tom McHugh/PR; **m.,** ©Stephen J. Krasemann/PA; **b.,** ©Tom McHugh/PR; **132 l.,** ©Tom McHugh/PR; **r.,** E.R. Degginger; **134 t.,** T.E. Adams/VU; **m.,** Henry C. Aldrich/VU; **b.,** ©Tom Branch/PR; **135 t.,** GH; **b.,** Kevin McCarthy/Offshoot Stock; **136,** Dr. E.R. Degginger; **137,** ©M.I. Walker/PR; **138 t.,** M. Abbey/VU; **m.,** Campbell, Richard, University of California, Irvine/BPS; **b.,** ©Hans Pfletschinger/PA; **139,** Gay Baumgarner/Photo Nats.

UNIT 2: 146–147, ©The Stock Market/ZEFA Germany; **148,** ©The Stock Market/Sanford/Agliolo 95; **149,** Maslowski Photo/VU; **153 l.,** U. S. Department of Agriculture; **r.,** ©Gary Buss/FPG International Corp.; **154,** Nancy Sheehan; **155,** Earth Images; **156 t.l., t.m., t.r.,** ©Michael Abbey/PR; **b.,** ©Eric V. Grave/PR; **157 l., m.l., m.r., r.,** Kim Taylor/BC; **159,** William J. Weber/VU; **162,** Jim Caccavo/Stock, Boston; **164,** David Phillips/VU; **165,** Jeffrey W. Myers/Stock, Boston; **167,** Charles Gupton/Tony Stone Images; **172,** Image Shop/Phototake NYC; **173,** Steve Allen/PA; **178,** from *Tissues and Organs;* **179,** John D. Cunningham/VU; **180,** Custom Medical Stock Photo; **181,** VU; **182,** ©Manfred Kage/PA; **187,** ©Hans Halberstadt/PR; **194,** ©Jean Claude Revy/Phototake NYC; **195,** David M. Phillips/VU; **196,** Martin Rotker/Taurus Photos; **197,** S.M. Phillips/VU; **198,** ©Omikron/PR; **200,** ©Bob Daemmrich; **203,** David Phillips/VU; **205,** ©Jeremy Burgess/PR; **206,** North Wind Picture Archives; **208,** Jonathan Nourok/PhotoEdit; **211,** Lennart Nilsson/Bonnier Alba; **212,** Custom Medical Stock Photo; **213,** ©A. Liepens/PR; **218,** Check Six,1994/PNI; **219,** Tom Ulrich/Tony Stone Images; **222,** Dr. E.R. Degginger; **223,** Vail Cart Tyler/Offshoot Stock; **225,** Michael Gabridge/VU; **226 l.,** ©The Stock Market/Chuck Savage 1996; **m.,** ©Manfred Kage/PA; **r.,** O. Auerbach/VU; **229,** American Cancer Society; **236,** Peter Lolacono/Natural Selection Stock Photography, Inc.; **237,** Paul Sutton/Duomo Photography, Inc.; **238, 245 t.,** ©Biophoto Assoc./PR; **b.,** ©Peter Arnold/PA; **247,** ©The Stock Market/Chuck Savage 1996; **248,** Stan Elams/VU; **252,** ©1994 The Stock Market; **253,** ©Fred McConnaughey/PR; **254 t.,** Owen Franken/Stock, Boston; **b.,** Kevin McCarthy/Offshoot Stock; **256 t.,** ©Kessel & Shih/PA; **b.,** ©Manfred Kage/PA; **258,** ©Stephen Dalton/PR; **259,** Lawrence

Migdale/Stock, Boston; **260,** ©Manfred Kage/PA; **264,** David Madison/BC; **265,** ©Manfred Kage/PA; **270,** Jeremy Woodhouse/DRK Photo; **271,** F. McConnaughey/BC; **274,** from *Tissues and Organs;* **288,** ©Oliver Meckes/Ottawa/PR; **289,** Michael George/BC; **292,** ©Dan McCoy/Rainbow; **301 t., b.,** Runk/Schoenberger/GH; **302,** ©Ralph Eagle/PR; **304,** John Coletti/Stock, Boston; **307,** from *Tissues and Organs;* **312,** ©1994, Jim Tuten/FPG International Corp.; **313,** ©Gregory Dimijian/PR; **315,** Bill Dobbins/Allsport; **322,** ©C. Edelmann, Petit Format/PR; **325,** Larry Lawfer/Offshoot Stock; **326,** Offshoot Stock; **327 t.,** ©Sylvain Legrand/PR; **b.,** ©Jean Marc Barey/PR; **328,** Kevin McCarthy/Offshoot Stock; **335,** Jeffry Myers/Stock, Boston/PNI.

UNIT 3: 336–337, ©Clyde H. Smith/PA; **338,** ©Werner H. Muller/PA; **339,** C.E. Jeffree/Oxford Scientific Films/PR; **340,** Corbis-Bettmann; **341,** Runk/Schoenberger/GH; **342,** John D. Cunningham/VU; **348 t.,** ©Plant-Economic/PA; **b.,** Norma J. Lang, Univ. of California/BPS; **349 l.,** E.R. Degginger/BC; **r.,** Bob Gossing/BC; **354,** BC; **355,** Russell Schleipman/Offshoot Stock; **357 t., b.,** John D. Cunningham/VU; **358 t.,** Randy Moore/VU; **t.l., m.l.,** Ed Reschke; **b.l.,** John D. Cunningham/VU; **359,** William E. Ferguson; **360 t.l.,** ©John Kaprielian/PR; **t.r.,** David Newman/VU; **b.l.,** David Newman/VU; **b.r.,** Dr. E.R. Degginger; **361,** Ed Reschke; **362,** Larry Lefever/GH; **363 t.,** Stanley L. Flegler/VU; **b.,** N.C. Schenck/VU; **364 l., r.,** Ed Reschke; **365 t.,** Nathan Benn/Stock, Boston; **b.,** John D. Cunningham/VU; **366,** ©W. Gilbert Grant/PR; **369 t.,** ©James Foote,1977/PR; **b.,** ©Ed Reschke/PA; **374,** Corel Professional Photos CD-ROM™; **375,** John Gerlach/VU; **376,** ©Jeremy Burgess/PR; **377,** ©Gilbert Grant/PR; **378,** Robert P. Carr/BC; **379,** Dr. E.R. Degginger; **380 l.,** GH; **r.,** David Newman/VU; **381 l.,** Runk/Schoenberger/GH; **r.,** Robert P. Comport/AA; **382,** Runk/Schoenberger/GH; **383,** GH; **384 l., r.,** John D. Cunningham/VU; **385 l.,** Richard D. Poe/VU; **r.,** ©Brock May/Photo Researchers, Inc.; **386,** ©Linda K. Moore/Rainbow; **387,** Corel Professional Photos CD-ROM™.

UNIT 4: 394–395, ©The Stock Market/Kennan Ward; **396,** D. Cavagnaro/DRK Photo; **397,** David M. Phillips/VU; **398 t.,** Ed Reschke; **b.,** Runk/Schoenberger/GH; **401 t.,** ©Ed Reschke/PA; **m.l., m.r., b.,** Ed Reschke; **402,** Ed Reschke; **403,** ©Blair Seitz/Photo Researchers, Inc.; **406,** ©Biophoto Assoc./PR; **407,** Kim Taylor/BC; **408,** T.E. Adams/VU; **409 t.,** Ed Reschke; **b.l., b.r.,** Runk/Schoenberger/GH; **410 l.,** Runk/Schoenberger/GH; **r.,** GH; **411,** N. Pecnik/VU; **416,** Alan & Sandy Carey/Natural Selection Stock Photography, Inc.; **417,** ©SPL/PR; **418 l.,** ©CNRI/PR; **425,** ©SPL/PR; **426,** ©M.I. Walker/PR; **427,** Ed Reschke; **428,** ©Hans Pfletschinger/PA; **431,** ©Manfred Kage/PA; **432,** ©Francis Leroy/PR; **433,** ©Zig Leszczynski/AA; **435,** ©Hans Pfletschinger/PA; **436,** Dr. E.R. Degginger; **437 l.,** ©CNRI/PR; **440,** ©The Stock Market/Jay Schlegel; **441,** ©Michael P.L. Fogden/AA; **447 t.,** Dwight Kuhn/BC; **b.l.,** ©Manfred Danegger/PA; **b.r.,** Kerry T. Givens/Tom Stack & Associates; **449 t.l., t.r., b.l., b.r.,** Kim Taylor/BC; **450,** ©Tom McHugh/PR; **451,** ©J. Cancalosi/PA; **456,** ©Gary Buss, 1995/FPG International Corp.; **457,** David Dempster/Offshoot Stock; **463,** ©Francis Leroy/PR; **464,** Leif Skoogfors/Woodfin Camp & Associates; **465,** ©Erika Stone/PR; **466 t.,** Tom McCarthy/The Picture Cube; **b.,** Herb Snitzer/Stock, Boston; **467,** Leffel, Heather A. & Hollie L./Woodfin Camp & Associates; **469 t.,** Ken Wagner/Phototake; **b.,** ©Ed Reschke/PA; **472,** Stephen G. Maka/DRK Photo; **473,** ©Robert Bornemann/PR; **475,** ©Wilson, D.P./ Hosking, Eric and David/PR; **476 t.,** ©Richard L. Carlton/PR; **b.,** John D. Cunningham/VU; **477 t.,** ©Biophoto Assoc./PR; **b.,** Stan Elems/VU; **478,** ©George Kleiman/PR; **479,** Brooking Tatum/VU; **480,** ©Pat Lynch/PR; **481 l.,** ©R. Litchfield/PR; **r.,** ©G.F. Leedale/PR; **482,** ©Stephen P. Parker/PR; **484 t.l., t.m.l, t.m.r,** Runk/Schoenberger/GH; **t.r.,** Larry Lefever/GH; **t.,** N. Pecnik/VU; **m.,** ©A.W. Ambler/PR; **b.,** ©John L. Pontier/AA; **487,** Dr. E.R. Degginger.

UNIT 5: 494–495, ©Coco McCoy/Rainbow; **496,** Shin Yoshino/Minden Pictures, Inc.; **497,** ©Leonard Lee Rue, III/PR; **498,** Jane Grushow/GH; **505,** Runk/Schoenberger/GH; **510 l., r.,** Larry Lefever/GH; **513,** FBI; **516,** ©Biophoto Associates/Science Source/PR; **517,** ©Darwin Dale/PR; **520,** John Running/Stock, Boston; **544,** AP/Wide World Photos; **545,** SuperStock; **547,** William E. Ferguson; **548,** Jim Brandenburg; **550 l., r.,** ©Bill Longcore/PR; **552 l.,** ©Leonard Lessin/PR;. **r.,** Cathlyn Melloan/Tony Stone Images; **553,** Julie Houck; **554,** Charles Gupton/Tony Stone Images; **555,** ©Richard Kolar/AA; **557 t.,** Dave Schaefer; **b.,** Runk/Schoenberger/GH; **558,** Bruce Hoertel; **558,** K.G. Murti; **560,** ARS-USDA.

UNIT 6: 568–569, Michio Hoshino/Minden Pictures, Inc.; **570,** ©The Stock Market/Bill Summer; **571,** Peter Scoones/Woodfin Camp & Associates; **572 t.,** Dr. E.R. Degginger; **b.,** ©Sygma; **573 t.,** ©Walter H. Hodge/PA; **b.,** Photo by R.T. Bird, Courtesy Department of Library Services American Museum of Natural History; **575,** Jeff Foott/Tom Stack & Associates; **577,** William E. Ferguson; **578,** John Cancalosi/Tom Stack & Associates; **581,** James Kilkelly; **592,** Walter D. Keller/University of Missouri; **594 t.,** John Cancalosi/Tom Stack & Associates; **b.,** Kevin Schafer/Tom Stack & Associates; **595,** Don & Pat Valenti/DRK Photo; **598,** Frans Lanting/Minden Pictures, Inc.; **599,** ©William W. Bacon, III/PR; **601 t.,** BC; **t.m.,** ©Miguel Castro/PR; **m.b.,** Keith Gunnar/BC; **b.,** ©Fred Bavendam/PA; **602,** ©J.A.L. Cooke/AA; **605,** Art Wolfe/Allstock; **606,** ©John Bova/PR; **607,** R.S. Virdee/GH; **610 t.,** Kim Taylor/

BC; **b.,** Runk/Schoenberger/GH; **611 t.l.,** ©George K. Bryce/AA; **t.r.,** ©Ralph Reinhold/AA; **b.,** Michael P.L. Fogden/BC; **613,** ©Jack Fields/PR; **615 t.,** Joe McDonald/BC; **b.,** E.J. Maruska/VU; **616,** J. Cancalosi/Tom Stack & Associates; **618 l.,** M.W.F. Tweedie/BC; **r.,** ©M.W.F. Tweedie/Photo Researchers, Inc.; **619,** Patrick L. Pfister/Stock, Boston; **626** © Al Grillo, 1995/Alaska Stock Images/PNI; **627** © Renne Lynn, 1994/AllStock/PNI.

UNIT 7: 628–629, ©Fred Bavendam/PA; **630,** ©Oliver Meckes/Gelderblom/PR; **631,** ©CNRI (SPL)/PR; **633 t.,** David M. Phillips/VU; **m.,** David M. Phillips/VU; **b.,** John D. Cunningham/VU; **635 t.,** John D. Cunningham/VU; **b.,**F.C.F. Earney/VU; **636 t.,** Paul W. Johnson/BPS; **b.,**©Sinclair Stammers/PR; **637 l.,** ©M. Abbey/PR; **r.,** Leon J. Le Beau/BPS; **638,** Corbis-Bettmann; **641,** John Colwell/GH; **643 l.,** ©Manfred Kage/PA; **r.,** ©Manfred Kage/PA; **644 t.,** ©Eric V. Grave/PR; **b.,** ©Eric V. Grave/PR; **646,** Paul W. Johnson/BPS; **648 t.,** J.R. Waaland, Univ. of Washington/BPS; **b.,** ©Manfred Kage/PA; **649,** Waaland, J.R., Univ. of Washington/BPS; **650 t.,** Heather Angel/Biofotos; **b.,** ©Robert C. Hermers/National Audobon Society/PR; **653 t.,** ©R. Knauft/PR; **b.,** ©Biology Media/PR; **654 t.,** ©M. Wurtz/PR; **b.,** K.G. Murti/VU; **658,** ©NIBSC/Science Photo Library/PR; **659,** ©Michael P. Gadomski/PR; **664,** ©Stephen J. Krasemann/PA; **665,** Rod Planck/Tom Stack & Associates; **667,** Joe Baraban; **668 t.,** Michael P.L. Fogden; **b.,** Adam Woolfit/Woodfin Camp & Associates; **669,** ©Terry G. Murphy/AA; **670 t.,** GH; **b.,** Doug Sokell/Tom Stack & Associates; **671, 673 t.,** Heather Angel/Biofotos; **m.l.,** Rod Planck/Tom Stack & Associates; **m.r.,** Heather Angel/Biofotos; **r.,** Brian Parker/Tom Stack & Associates; **674 t.,** John Shaw/Tom Stack & Associates; **b.,** Julie Houck; **675 t.l.,** Luis Castenada/The Image Bank; **t.m.l,** ©Ed Reschke/PA; **t.m.,** Dr. E.R. Degginger; **t.m.r,** ©E.R. Degginger/AA; **t.r.,** Heather Angel/Biofotos; **b.l.,** Dr. E.R. Degginger; **b.m.,** ©Michael P. Gadomski/PR; **b.r.,** Michael P. Gadomski; **676,** Thomas Kitchin/Tom Stack & Associates; **682,** ©Secret Sea Visons/PA; **683,** Runk/Schoenberger/GH; **684 t.,** ©Manfred Kage/PA; **b.,** Heather Angel/Biofotos; **685,** Runk/Schoenberger/GH; **687,** Carl Roessler/Tom Stack & Associates; **688,** Runk/Schoenberger/GH; **689 l.,** ©Bob Evans/PA; **r.,** Dave Fleetham/Tom Stack & Associates; **699 t.,** ©Tom McHugh/PR; **b.,** ©Breck P. Kent/AA; **700,** Milton Rand/Tom Stack & Associates; **701,** Jane Burton/BC; **706,** ©The Stock Market/Craig Tuttle; **707,** ©Zig Leszcynski/AA; **708 b.,** ©Raymond A. Mendez/AA; **708 t.,** ©E.R. Degginger/AA; **709 t.,** Dr. E.R. Degginger; **m.l.,** Dr. E.R. Degginger; **m.r.,** ©Gary Retherford/Photo Researchers, Inc.; **b.l.,** ©Breck P. Kent/AA; **b.m.,** Fred Bavendam/Allstock; **b.r.,** Dr. E.R. Degginger; **712,** ©Breck P. Kent/AA; **713 t.,** Dr. E.R. Degginger; **b.,** Michael P.L. Fogden/BC; **714 t.,** Dr. E.R. Degginger; **m.,** John Cancalosi/Tom Stack & Associates; **b.l.,** Jeff Foott/BC; **b.m.,** ©Sean Morris/AA; **b.r.,** Russ Lappa/The Picture Cube; **716,** ©G.C. Kelley/PR; **717 t.l.,** Runk/Schoenberger/GH; **t.r.,** Runk/Schoenberger/GH; **b.l.,** ©Richard Kolar/AA; **b.r.,** Dr. E.R. Degginger; **718,** ©Jack Wilburn/AA; **719,** William E. Ferguson; **720 t.,** Dr. E.R. Degginger; **t.m.,** Dr. E.R. Degginger; **b.m.,** ©Paul Metzger/PA; **b.,** Dr. E.R. Degginger/BC; **725 t.,** Dr. E.R. Degginger; **b.r.,** Brian Parker/Tom Stack & Associates; **m.r.,** ©E.R. Degginger/AA; **b.r.,** Dr. E.R. Degginger; **727,** Thomas Kitchin/Tom Stack & Associates; **729,** ©Oxford Scientific Films/AA; **732,** ©Michael Sewell/PA; **733,** ©James H. Carmichael/PR; **734,** F. Stuart Westmorland/PR; **737,** Heather Angel/Biofotos; **738 t.,** Dave Fleetham/Tom Stack & Associates; **b.l.,** Ron & Valerie Taylor/BC; **b.r.,** ©Norbert Wu/PA; **739 l.,** Ian Took/Biofotos; **r.,** ©Tom McHugh/Photo Researchers, Inc.; **740 t.,** ©W. Gregory Brown/AA; **b.,** ©Colin Milkins/AA; **741,** Dr. E.R. Degginger; **743 t.,** ©Zig Leszcynski/AA; **b.,** Michael P.L. Fogden/BC; **744,** ©Zig Leszcynski/AA; **749 t.l., t.r., b.l.,** ©Hans Pfletschinger/AA; **b.r.,** ©Zig Leszcynski/AA; **751 t.,** ©Zig Leszcynski/AA; **b.,** Heather Angel/Biofotos; **752,** ©Zig Leszcynski/AA; **753 l.,** ©Breck P. Kent/AA; ©Breck P. Kent/AA; **754 t.l.,** Dr. E.R. Degginger; **r.,** ©Tom McHugh/PR; **b.,** ©Zig Leszcynski/AA; **755 t.,** Dr. E.R. Degginger; **b.,** ©Tom McHugh/PR; **756 t.,** Runk/Schoenberger/GH; **b.,** D.J. Lyons/BC; **760,** ©John Cancalosi/PA; **761,** ©Breck P. Kent/AA; **762 l.** GH; **m.l.,** Mary Clay/Tom Stack & Associates; **m.r.** Thomas Kitchin/Tom Stack & Associates; **r.,** Laura Riley/BC; **763,** Heather Angel/Biofotos; **766,** ©The Stock Market/Richard Dunoff; **767,** E.R. Degginger/BC; **768 t.,** ©Stouffer Prod. Ltd./AA; **m.,** Jim Brandenburg; **b.l.,** Rod Planck/Tom Stack & Associates; **b.r.,** ©Stephen Dalton/PR; **769 t.,** ©Breck P. Kent/AA; **m.,** Gordon Langsbury/BC; **b.l.,** Mary Clay/Tom Stack & Associates; **b.r.,** Martin W. Grosnick/BC; **770 t.,** Dr. E.R. Degginger; **b.l.,** ©Alan G. Nelson/AA; **b.m.,** Dr. E.R. Degginger; **b.r.,** ©Harvey Barnett/PA; **771,** ©Adrienne T. Gibson/PA; **774,** Courtesy Department of Library Services American Museum of Natural History; **775 t.,** Cleveland Museum of Natural History; **b.l.,** Des & Jen Bartlett/BC; **b.r.,** Delta Willis/BC; **776 l.,** M. Crabtree/AAAS; **r.,** M. Crabtree/AAAS; **777 l.,** ©Tom McHugh/PR; **t.r.,** ©Tom McHugh/PR; **r.,** Robert Frerck/Odyssey/Field Museum of Natural History; **778,** Douglas Mazonowicz/Gallery of Prehistoric Art; **784,** ©David J. Cross/PA; **785,** John K. Nakata/Terraphotographics/BPS; **786 t., m.,** Heather Angel/Biofotos; **b.,** ©Stephen Dalton/AA; **787,** ©Y. Athus-Bertrand/PA; **788,** S. Nielsen/BC; **789,** Billy E. Barnes/Stock, Boston; **793 t.,** Dr. E.R. Degginger; **b.,** ©Hans Pfletschinger/PA; **799 l.,** Nina Leen/Life Picture Service; **.,** ©G. Ziesler/PA; **801,** ©C.W. Schwarz/AA; **802,** ©J.H. Robinson/AA; **803,** m Haagner/BC; **805,** Diana Rogers/BC; **806,** ©C. Allen Morgan/PA; **807,** Guravich/PR; **814, 815,** Corel Professional Photos CD-ROM™.

UNIT 8: 816–817, Mark W. Moffett/Minden Pictures, Inc.; **818,** ©The Stock Market/Viviane Holbrooke; **819,** Phil Degginger/BC; **824,** Dr. E.R. Degginger; **825 t.,** ©Norm Thomas/PR; **b.,** ©Carl Roessler/AA; **826,** ©Ken Brate/PR; **827,** Gregory Dimijian, M.D./PR; **829,** Leonard Lee Rue, III/BC; **831,** Dr. E.R. Degginger; **833,** ©Gerhard Gscheidle/PA; **837,** ©The Stock Market/Gabe Palmer; **838,** Joe McDonald/BC; **840,** Dr. E.R. Degginger; **844,** Frans Lanting/Minden Pictures, Inc.; **846,** ©David Muench; **847,** ©Johnny Johnson/AA; **847,** ©Charlie Ott/PR; **848,** ©Michael P. Gadomski/PR; **849 t.,** ©Jack Ryan/PR; **b.,** ©Breck P. Kent/AA; **850 t.,** ©Jeff Rotman/PA; **b.,** ©Gregory Dimijian/PR; **851 t.,** ©Patti Murray/AA; **b.,** Nancy Sheehan; **852,** John Cancalosi/Tom Stack & Associates; **854,** ©Carl Roessler/AA; **856,** Dr. E.R. Degginger; **857 t.,** Heather Angel/Biofotos; **857 b.,** Rod Planck/Tom Stack & Associates; **862,** ©1996, Richard Laird/FPG International Corp.; **863,** ©M.J. Balick/PA; **864,** Runk/Schoenberger/GH; **865,** Anthony Suau/Black Star; **866 t.,** Robin Jane Solvano/PR; **b.,** Jim Brandenberg/BC; **867,** Wendell Meltzer/PR; **868,** Franz Kraus/The Picture Cube; **869,** ©B. Nation/Sygma; **870,** Amanda Merullo/Stock, Boston; **872,** ©Will McIntyre/PR; **873,** Tony Freeman/PhotoEdit; **875,** ©Luiz Claudio Maurio/PA; **876 t.l.,** Kenneth W. Fink/BC; **t.r.,** ©Y. Arthus-Bertrand/PA; **b.l.,** ©Raymond Mendez/AA; **b.r.,** Emily Harsie/BC; **878 l.,** Mark Sherman/BC; **r.,** Stephenie Ferguson/William E. Ferguson; **884,** Corel Professional Photos CD-ROM™.

APPENDIX: 894, David M. Phillips/VU; **895 t.,** Paul W. Johnson/BPS; **m.,** ©Robert C. Hermes/National Audubon Society/PR; **b.,** ©Manfred Kage/PA; **896 l.,** Michael P.L. Fogden/BC; **r.,** Rod Planck/Tom Stack & Associates; **897,** ©Rod Planck/AA; **898,** ©Tom McHugh/PR; **899 t.,** Dr. E.R. Degginger; **b.,** Dave Fleetham/Tom Stack & Associates; **900,** Mary Clay/Tom Stack & Associates.

ILLUSTRATION CREDITS

Edmond S. Alexander/Alexander and Turner: 158, 190, 232, 257B, 308RT, 308RB, 329, 330L, 346T, 350, 518T, 698T, 698T, 698B, 658 TR.

Sally J. Bensusen/Visual Science Studio: 159, 175, 176, 222, 239, 240, 282B, 283, 715, 721, 807, 808.

Black Dot Group: 11, 21, 29, 53, 57, 72, 73, 81, 113, 114, 116, 117, 133, 141, 143, 144, 145, 207, 215, 217, 231, 249, 251, 263, 267, 269, 331, 318, 316, 329, 335, 344, 345, 346, 347, 373, 379, 389, 393, 423, 453, 461, 491, 492, 493, 533, 563, 566, 567, 595, 617, 626, 627, 679, 681, 728, 731, 772, 811, 814, 815, 827, 841, 859, 884, 885.

Kent Boughton: 228.

Carmella M. Clifford: 161, 227, 246, 262T, 278, 284BL, 284TR, 300, 302, 303, 305, 306T, 306B, 307, 370, 767, 773.

Barbara Cousins: 255, 318T, 391R.

Paul Foti/Boston Graphics Inc.: 886, 887, 894, 898, 899, 903.

Howard Friedman: 22, 72BL, 91, 93B, 94, 576, 589, 693, 820, 822, 827, 828, 829, 833, 834, 836, 839, 853, 855.

Andrew Grivas: 157, 174B, 221B, 282T, 356L, 356R, 357, 358, 361, 491, 604, 688, 690, 697, 791R.

Steven J. Harrison/Fine Line Studio: 150, 586, 587, 588, 590, 620.

Jackie Heda: 452B, 574BR, 574BL, 684L, 684BL, 684BR, 687, 700, 710, 711, 712, 726, 728, 735, 741, 745T, 745B, 746, 747, 748T, 748B, 754, 763, 764, 765, 794, 796.

Floyd E. Hosmer: 81, 92T, 92B 123, 179T, 189, 263B, 273, 274, 275, 276, 277, 287, 295, 298, 391L, 597, 625, 654, 655B, 678, 702.

Keith Kasnot: 83T, 83B, 84B, 85, 86, 87, 89, 160, 163, 185, 186, 188, 224, 241, 243, 244, 314, 368, 399, 401, 402, 405, 406T, 406B, 464, 575, 583, 652.

Elizabeth McClelland: 580, 666, 669, 722, 723, 792, 798, 800, 804, 805.

Robert Margulies / Margulies Medical Art: 84T, 93T, 95, 96, 156, 164, 174T, 221T, 256, 257T, 279, 281, 376, 426, 442, 443TL, 443TR, 443B 444, 448, 632, 636, 643, 646, 647, 649BL, 649TR, 655T, 691, 692, 694, 734, 791L.

Martucci Studio/Jerry Malone: 15TR, 35, 36, 37T, 37B, 39, 40, 41, 42, 43T, 43B, 44, 46,50, 54, 55, 58, 59, 60, 61T, 61B, 62T, 62B, 63T, 63B, 65, 66T, 66B, 69, 70T, 70B, 71, 80, 104, 105L, 109T, 109B, 118, 119, 127, 128, 131, 170, 171, 193L, 207, 242, 251, 269, 311R, 323T, 340, 341, 343, 353L, 498, 499, 500, 501, 503, 504T, 504B, 506T, 506B, 507, 508TL, 508B, 509TR, 509BR, 510, 518B, 519T, 519M, 519B, 521, 522, 523, 527, 528, 530, 531T, 531B, 533L, 534T, 534B, 536, 537, 540L, 543R, 547, 549, 551, 559, 565R, 608, 634, 663L, 731, 759L, 778, 779, 810R, 813, 830, 832, 843, 883.

Fran Milner: 178T, 178B, 179B, 181, 198, 199, 204, 260, 261, 262B, 265, 290B, 290L, 291L, 291R, 292, 293, 294, 296, 321, 322, 323B, 324, 419, 421, 425, 429, 430, 431, 458, 459, 460, 468L, 468R, 526, 582.

Sanderson Associates: 852, 873.

Lois Sloan: 475, 538, 574T, 600, 603, 861L, 874.

Gary Torrisi: 474, 525, 591, 871.

Cynthia Turner/Alexander and Turner: 102L, 102R, 120, 168L, 266, 366, 367, 378, 388, 436, 476, 477, 479, 480, 481T, 481B, 482, 483, 485, 486T, 486B, 533MR, 533TR, 612, 622L, 645, 651, 656, 660L, 840R.

Any photo or illustration acknowledgment inadvertently omitted will be amended upon notification.

Editorial Support: Lillian Duggan.

Production Support: Jim Wigdahl.